D0411131

PEARS ADVANCED
WORD-PUZZLER'S DICTIONARY

PEARS ADVANCED WORD-PUZZLER'S DICTIONARY

Compiled, Written and Edited by

PETER NEWBY

PELHAM BOOKS

London

First published in Great Britain by
Pelham Books Ltd
27 Wrights Lane
London W8 5TZ
1987

Typeset by MS Filmsetting Limited, Frome, Somerset
Printed by Billings and Sons Ltd, Worcester

Other word games such as HANGMAN and WORDS and non-word games such as NINE MEN'S MORRIS and REVERSI are traditional games marketed as commercial products sometimes with a different name. All other word games mentioned are not, as far as is known, commercial products.

British Library Cataloguing in Publication Data

Newby, Peter
Pears advanced word-puzzler's dictionary.
1. English language—Glossaries,
vocabularies, etc. 2. Word games
I. Title
793.73'2 GV1507.W8

ISBN 0–7207–1774–4

To my favourite word game opponents

CHARLES CLEWLOW	Code Breaking
IVY DIXON-BAIRD	Words
VALERIE GALE	Wordsworth
CHRISTINE HASPEL	Word for Word®
CHRISTINE KILROY	Countdown®
MARCUS MACLAINE	Pelham
LISA NEWBY	Hangman
DAVID NEWBY	Word Maker®
SYLVIA SYMS	Scrabble®
JULIE TITCHENER	Crossword
JANET WILKINSON	Call My Bluff
JOHN WILKINSON	French Crosswords
TOM WRIGHT	Pentery Web

and to my son resident in the USA
MAXWELL CAULFIELD
whom I challenge to any game played on a table –
except arm wrestling!

CONTENTS

Apart from the standard explanations of individual words, the dictionary also carries the following special subject entries, each usually containing a series of related words.

INTRODUCTION

Pears Advanced Word-Puzzler's Dictionary is concerned with the types of word which are of the greatest significance to the crossword solver and the word game player. The significant words and their value are outlined in the INDICATORY SECTION and the DICTIONARY SECTION is concerned with detailing them and explaining their individual meanings.

CROSSWORD SOLVERS

The most annoying problem is in having solved a clue only to discover that one's dictionary doesn't list such a word. Thus, *unusual words* are the major feature of this book. This applies not only to a complete word but also to a *word-syllable*, a small word used as part of a larger word in the answer to a cryptic clue.

Equally vexing is the *perfect anagram*, as it is difficult enough to cope with the fact that **evil, Levi, live, veil, vile, vlei** and **vlie** are perfect anagrams of each other, but when one has to deal with the thirty perfect anagrams of the word **nastier** it becomes a positive nightmare! A list of perfect anagrams is given in the INDICATORY SECTION and their meanings will be found in the ADVANCED DICTIONARY.

WORD GAME PLAYERS

Depending on the game being played, 2–letter, 3–letter, 6–letter and 7–letter words are of the greatest significance. The reasoning is explained in the INDICATORY SECTION. Every unusual word mentioned in this section is defined in the ADVANCED DICTIONARY.

THE GENERAL READER

As a high percentage of the words listed do not feature in any standard popular dictionary, you can consider this work as being the perfect supplement to your existing book and, if your present dictionary does not define words such as **aaber, aalii, Aani, abdat** or **aburabozo** then *Pears Advanced Word-Puzzler's Dictionary* demands a place next to it on your bookshelf.

THE INDICATORY SECTION

Pears Advanced Word-Puzzler's Dictionary is unique. It is the first ever indicatory dictionary. From the hundreds of thousands of words in the English language from Anglo-Saxon times to the present day, it isolates those which have the greatest potential for crosswords and word games and then, where necessary, explains their meanings.

For example, not every dictionary mentions the word **indicatory**. As an adjective with a sense of 'serving to indicate', it is simply a normal word for a crossword or a word game. Thus, at face value, it has no more worth than any other word. But, **indicatory** is the only perfect anagram of **dictionary** and this immediately increases its likelihood of appearing in a crossword and doubles the utility of its constituent letters for a word game. Therefore, this fact should be indicated and, as **indicatory** might not be explained in the particular standard dictionary possessed by the reader, it is defined in the *Advanced Dictionary* which forms the major part of this work.

In essence, the INDICATORY SECTION pinpoints such words and the DICTIONARY SECTION defines those which might not be known to the reader. The whole book, therefore, is a perfect supplement for any standard dictionary normally used for crosswords and word games.

Words for crosswords and word games are governed by two factors. The first factor is the number of letters in a word. The second factor is the arrangement of letters which make up the word. Strictly, nothing else matters. The fact that one has never encountered the word before or has no idea of the meaning does not affect the issue. Important, yes. Essential, no.

The crossword compiler doesn't start off with the words and then design a grid to fit. He or she first draws the grid, *then* produces the words. The words themselves are chosen with care but not for what they mean or for what clue can be devised for them. Whilst that is important and relevant, the vital factor is that the 'easy' letters coincide with the junctions. The first task is to fill the grid; the clever clue is very much a secondary aspect.

The same is equally true for a word game. The number of letters available for play is limited and the player who 'plays the percentages' will, almost invariably, defeat an opponent with an obsession to accumulate the letters of just one particular word. As will be explained later, the player with a knowledge of **andagrams** (see page 175) *without necessarily knowing their meanings* has the percentages in his or her favour and, other things being equal, wins every time.

Even a game such as hangman is governed by the same twin factors. Though one attempts to defeat the opponent by choosing an obscure word with a curious array of letters, the length of the word is known to begin with and the constituent letters of that word make it 'hard' or 'easy'. Neither player *needs* to know what the word means in order to play.

Anagrams, andagrams and 'hangman words' are, therefore, just three of the types of words which the INDICATORY SECTION discusses in greater detail in their own sub-sections but, first, a problem which besets many who enjoy word play. This is the phrasing peculiar to the cryptic crossword.

CROSSWORD ENGLISH

The essence of a cryptic clue is that it doesn't say what it appears to say. A typical clue carries two definitions of the same word within a framework of incorrect punctuation. One of these definitions is normally a synonym or similar simple statement of the answer, the other may be such as an anagram. An anagram is usually indicated by a word which implies that the *letters* of the word or words to which it refers are not in the correct sequence to correspond with the synonym. In effect this means that words such as about, around, change, deranged, disordered, disorderly, irregular, mad, malformed, odd, peculiar, queer, rearranged, reformed, strange or unusual simply mean anagram.

Thus, a clue for a 3–letter space which reads, *Act differently for the creature (3)* is readily understandable as *differently* indicating *act* as the anagram *for the creature.* **Cat** is the obvious answer.

The clue for cat could just as easily be written, *The animal found in the plastic attache case (3).* In this instance the compiler has used the ploy of a hidden word (*plastiC ATtache*) with *found* being used to indicate the second clue for *the animal.*

The ploys are many and various. *Spain's capital* is not Madrid but the letter S, the capital letter of Spain. Roman numerals are an equally popular source of an individual letter, 5 really means V, 10 is X, 50 is L and so on. *Cardinal* means a cardinal point of the compass and, therefore, stands for N, E, S or W. Individual letters expressed in this fashion are usually the additional element of an andagram (an anagram of a word or words *and* an additional letter which then becomes a new word). A typical andagram clue is, *The company act differently around the first of September (4).* Here the definition, as a simple statement, is *The company.* The andagram is *Act differently* (as before, cat) *around* the letter S which is *the first* (letter) *of September.* Thus, cat *around* S becomes **cast** which is *The company.*

Word play of this type is almost invariably used for the secondary or confirming definition. *March endlessly with us* meaning the masculine personal name, **Marcus**, would never be the complete clue in a good crossword. Equally consigned to a secondary role would be the example fully detailed at the *Advanced Dictionary's* definition of **polianite**.

Occasionally cryptic word play is so obvious that one fails to see it. *Man's laughter ought to be seen as a crime (12)* whilst having every appearance of being a quote from a feminist publication is, quite simply, **manslaughter**. This use of the possessive case is immediately apparent; not so obvious is the following, *Render crazy the princess's pamphlet (8).* At first glance *crazy* might suggest, as it often does, an anagram. But, there is no combination of eight letters logically placed to comply. Correctly punctuated, the clue should read, *Render crazy. The princess's pamphlet (8).* The confirming definition is Di's tract, the standard definition is **distract**.

Finally, two clues with anagrams which could prove especially frustrating. *Send some unusually covered with a bog plant (8). Send some* is the anagram, but the only solution likely to be confirmed by a standard dictionary is the word, **demoness**. That is obviously wrong, but this is where *Pears Advanced Word-Puzzler's Dictionary* makes its major contribution to word reference. Arrange the letters of *Send some* in their strict alphabetical order as DEEMNOSS. The following sub-section, ANAGRAMS, will now show that these eight letters give the choice of **demoness** or **enmossed** as perfect anagrams of each other. The *Advanced Dictionary* will confirm that **enmossed** is correct.

Perhaps you may consider that using the anagram list is 'cheating'. If so, try the following clue, bearing in mind that you are given a full explanation of the cryptic elements. *Compress strange great sin (8)*. The meaning is *compress*, the anagram is *great sin*. If you can't solve it, which would you think is the correct answer from a choice of 23, yes 23, perfect anagrams of the letters AEGINRST? And, AEGINRST is not the biggest possible selection. There is one 7–letter combination and no fewer than four 6–letter combinations which top even AEGINRST! The anagram list is not intended to solve *every* crossword anagram but is designed to eradicate the problem caused by a duplication of possibilities. It is also ideal for various word games, especially Pelham the anagram card game.

ANAGRAMS

Solving an anagram of five or fewer letters is relatively easy. But the mathematical permutations from six letters upwards, however, become increasingly horrendous, eventually reaching a point where they cease to be a source of pleasure especially where one solves an anagram only to discover it is wrong!

For practical purposes this section ends at the realistic upper limit of 10 letters. Knowing that the 22–letter scientific words **hydropneumopericardium** and **pneumohydropericardium** are perfect anagrams of each other is not really essential for a crossword solver and the only word game which could possibly use this pure trivia is Pentery Web.

The anagram list includes plural forms and verbal inflections except where every possible anagram of a particular combination of letters which includes an S merely consists of plural forms of words. However, where the shared plural is produced by the suffixes '–es' or '–ies' then it is given.

To solve the anagram, arrange the letters of the problem word or words in strict alphabetical order and consult the respective entries for 6–letter, 7–letter, 8–letter, 9–letter or 10–letter words according to the number of letters with which you are concerned. For example, if a cryptic clue begins, *Rat Les oddly*... the anagram is obviously produced from *Rat Les*. In alphabetical order of letters this becomes AELRST and the 6–letter listing gives you a choice of *36 complete words using these very letters!*

The list is in strict alphabetical order of constituent letters within each individual numerical grouping. (Note: The anagrams mirror the convention of crosswords and word games in ignoring accents. These, however, are correctly shown in the *Advanced Dictionary*.)

AAABLT
albata
atabal
balata
tabula

AAAKLS
alakas
Alaska

AABCRS
barcas
carabs
scarab

AABDER
Abdera
abrade

AABDOR
aboard
abroad

AABEGT
atabeg
tea bag

AABELR
alabre
arable
Arbela

AABHSW
bashaw
Wabash

AABIMN
Ambian
Bimana

AABINR
arabin
Bairan

AABINS
banias
Sabian
Sabina

AABINZ
banzai
Zabian

AABLTU
ablaut»

AABMNT
bantam
batman

AABORT
abator
rabato

AACCIL
Alcaic
cicala

AACEPR
earcap
Parcae

AACERT
acater
cerata

AACEST
acates
sea cat

AACETV
caveat
vacate

AACFIL
cafila
facial

AACFLU
facula
faucal

AACHKN
achkan
Kachan

AACHKP
chapka
pachak

AACHNS
ashcan
Sancha

AACHRT
Cathar
charta

AACHTT
attach
chatta

AACIMN
caiman
maniac

AACINR
arnica
carina
crania

AACIOT
atocia
coaita

AACLPS
calpas
pascal

AACLRS
carals
craals
lascar
rascal
sacral
scalar

AACLSU
casual
causal

AACMRT
ramcat
tarmac

AACNPT
captan
catnap

AADDEL
aadled
daedal

AADELS
aadles
aldeas
salade

AADEMN
anadem
maenad

AADEMT
amated
maated

AADENV
Adaven
Nevada
venada

AADERS
arased
areads

AADGNP
padang
pad nag

AADIMN
Damian
maidan

AADINO
Adonai
Adonia

AADINR
Adrian
radian

AADIST
ditaas
stadia

AADLNS
alands
sandal

AADMRS
damars
dramas
madras

AADNRS
nasard
Sandra

AAEGLN
alnage
Angela
anlage
galena
lagena

AAEGLR
alegar
laager

AAEGLT
algate
talage

AAEGMN
agname
manage

AAEGSV
agaves
avages
savage

AAEHNT
aneath
Anthea
Athena

AAEILM
amelia
lamiae

AAEILR
aerial
realia

AAEIRS
air-sea
araise
sea air

AAELLP
apalle
paella
pallae

AAELMP
Palmae
Pamela

AAELMT
malate
meatal
tamale

AAELNT
lanate
teanal

AAEMNR
Amen-Ra
Ramean

AAEMRT
ramate
retama

AAEMST
amates
sea-mat

AAENST
aneast
ansate

AAEPRS
Pareas
pasear

AAEPRT
patera
petara

AAERST
astare
reatas
searat

AAESTV
Avesta
savate

AAFFIR
affair
raffia

AAGGRT
ragtag
tagrag

AAGHNR
arghan
hangar

AAGILR
argali
garial

AAGINN
aaning
angina

AAGINR
Graina
nagari

AAGMRY
magyar
margay

AAGNOR
angora
Aragon
Onagra

AAGNRS
argans
sangar

AAHIPR
pariah
raphia

AAHISV
avahis
Shaiva

AAHJRS
Jashar
rajahs

AAHLLN
hallan
nallah

AAHLMM
hammal
mahmal

AAHLMS
almahs
halmas
hamals
shamal

AAHLRS
ashlar
lahars

AAHMRS
ashram
harams
marahs

AAHMSS
Massah»

shamas

AAHNPS
ashpan
hanaps

AAHNST
Sathan
thanas

AAHRSS
harass
hassar
shaars

AAHSSY
sashay
shayas

AAIKLM
kalmia
kamila

AAILMN
almain
animal
lamina
manila

AAILMS
alisma
lamias
salami

AAILNS
lianas
Salian
salina

AAILNT
antlia
Latian

AAILRT
Altair
atrial
lariat
latria

AAILSV
avails
saliva
salvia

AAIMNR
airman
Marian
marina

AAIMNS
amains
animas
manias
Samian

AAIMRT
amrita
tamari

AAIMTT
tatami
Tiamat

AAINPR
Parian
pirana

AAINPT
patina
taipan

AAINRU
anuria
Urania

AAIPRY
apiary
piraya

AAIRST
arista
riatas
tairas
tarsia
tiaras

AAKNSS
Asansk
Kansas
Kassan
Nassak

AAKNST
askant
tankas

AAKSSV
kavass»
vakass

AALLRV
larval
vallar

AALMNU
alumna
manual

AALMNY
Almany
layman

AALMPS
lampas
plasma

AALMSU
masula
maulas

AALNPT
planta
platan

AALNRT
antral
tarnal

AALNST
aslant
natals
santal

AALRST
altars
astral
talars
tarsal

AALRSV
arvals
larvas
lavras
varsal

AAMNTU
mantua
tamanu

AAMORS
aromas
Masora

AAMRTU
Ratuma
trauma

AANPRT
partan
tarpan
trapan

AANRTT
rattan
Tantra
tartan

AAPRST
atraps
satrap
Sparta

AARSST
assart
tassar

AARSTT
astart
attars
strata
Tatars

AARSTY
astray
satyra
tayras
yartas

ABBDEL
babled
dabble

ABBDER
barbed
dabber
drabbe
debarb
rabbed

ABBDET
tabbed
tebbad

ABBELM
balmbe
belamb
mabble

ABBELR
babler
barbel
barble
brable
rabble

ABBELS
babels
bables
labbes
slabbe

ABBELW
bawble
wabble

ABBERT
barbet
rabbet
tabber

ABBRSU
Barbus
bus bar

ABCDER
braced
becard
decarb

ABCEHR
brache
breach
Chebar
Rechab

ABCEIR
cabrie
caribe

ABCELM
becalm
clambe

ABCELS
cabels
cables
scable

ABCEMR
camber
cembra

ABCERS
braces
cabers
scrabe

ABCMOR
comarb
crambo

ABCMOT
combat
tombac

ABCNOR
carbon
corban

ABDDEI
abided
baddie

ABDDER
badder
barded
braded

ABDEEL
beadle
bealed
belead
delabe

ABDEES
debase
seabed

ABDEGR
badger
barged
garbed

ABDEHS
bashed
bedash

ABDEIL
bailed
belaid
deblai

ABDEIR
abider
airbed
baried
braide

ABDEIS
abides
biased

ABDEKR
barked
braked
bedark
debark

ABDELM
ambled
balmed
bedlam
beldam
blamed
lambed
mabled

ABDELO
albedo
doable

ABDELR
balder
bardel
bedral
blader
blared
rabled
rebald

ABDELS
blades
blased
bleads
dables
sabled

ABDELT
blated
dablet
tabled

ABDELU
bauled
belaud

ABDEMR
bramed
dambre
rambed

ABDEOR
boarde
boared

ABDERS
ardebs
beards
brased
breads
debars
serdab

ABDERY
brayed
red bay

ABDILR
bridal
ribald

ABDIRR
braird
Briard

ABDIRS
braids
disbar

ABDORS
abords
adsorb
boards
broads

ABEEGR
barege
bargee

ABEEKR
beaker
rebake

ABEELN
baleen
enable

ABEEMR
beamer
breame

ABEERT
beater
berate
rebate»

rebeat
re-beat

ABEGGR
bagger
beggar

ABEGLR
gabler
garble
grable

ABEGLU
beluga
blague

ABEGNR
banger
engarb
graben

ABEHRT
bather
bertha
breath

ABEHST
bathes
Shebat

ABEILL
Belial
labile
liable

ABEILM
embail
lambie

ABEILR
bailer
braile
librae
rebail

ABEILS
blaise
isabel

ABEILT
albeit
albite
libate

ABEINT
betani
binate

ABEIRS
baries
beiras
braise
erbias
rabies

ABEIRT
baiter
barite
Bartie
rebait
terbia

ABEIRZ
braize
zeriba

ABEKLY
bleaky
Kabyle

ABEKNR
banker
barken
branke

ABEKRS
bakers
barkes
basker
brakes
breaks

ABELMR
ambler
balmer
blamer
lamber
marble
ramble

ABELMS
ambels
ambles
balmes
belams
blames
mables
samble

ABELNU
nebula
unable

ABELOT
boatel
lobate
oblate

ABELRS
balers
blares
blaser
blears
rables

ABELRT
albert
balter
Bartle
labret
tabler

ABELRW
bawler
wabler
warble

ABELRY
barely
barley
bleary

ABELST
ablest
ablets
balest
balets
belast
Bestla
blates
bleats
stabel
stable
tabels
tables

ABELSU
suable
usable

ABELSY
basely
bayles»

belays
yables

ABELTT
balett
batlet
battel
battle
tablet

ABELWY
bawley
bye-law

ABEMRS
ambers
brames
breams
embars
samber
sambre

ABENRT
banter
Barnet

ABENRU
braune
unbare
unbear
urbane

ABENRY
barney
near-by

ABENST
abnets
absent
basnet
basten

ABEORT
boater
borate
rebato

ABEPST
bepats
bespat

ABEQSU
basque
quebas

ABERRT
barret
barter

ABERSS
basser
brases
brasse
sabers

ABERST
abrets
barest
barets
baster
baters
bestar
breast
tabers

ABERSU
abuser
bursae

ABERTT
batter
bratte
tabert
tabret
tarbet

ABESST
basest
basset
bastes
beasts
Sebats

ABESSU
abuses
sub-sea

ABETTU
battue
tubate

ABGGIT
baggit
gag-bit

ABGIKN
baking
inkbag

ABGILN
abling
baling

ABGINO
bagnio
gabion

ABHIMR
Brahmi
mihrab

ABHINS
ashbin
banish

ABHORT
athrob
Hobart

ABHOST
bathos
boshta

ABILNO
albino
Albion

ABILNS
ablins
balins
blains

ABILRS
brails
Brasil
libras

ABIMRS
bismar
imbars

ABINOT
bonita
obtain

ABINRY
binary
brainy

ABINSU
Anubis»

bunias
nubias
unbias

ABIOST
biotas
Tobias

ABJLMU
jambul
jumbal

ABLMRU
brumal
labrum
lumbar
umbral

ABLOST
bloats
oblast

ABLRSU
bursal
Labrus
lubras

ABLRWY
brawly
byrlaw

ABMNSU
busman
subman

ABMRSU
rumbas
sambur
umbras

ABNORY
barony
baryon

ABORTU
outbar
rubato
tabour

ABOSTU
abouts
Basuto
U-boats

ACCEIP
ice cap
ipecac

ACCEIT
accite
acetic

ACCILO
accoil
calico

ACCIRR
circar
ric-rac

ACCOSS
cascos
saccos

ACCOST
accost
coacts

ACDDEI
caddie
decadi
decaid
Eddaic

ACDDEL
caddel
caddle

ACDDEN
canded
danced

ACDEEL
Caldee
cealed
delace

ACDEEN
cadene
decane

ACDEGR
cadger
cradge
graced

ACDEHR
arched
chared
dearch
rached

ACDEHT
chated
detach
tached

ACDEHW
chawed
wached

ACDEIN
candie
cnidae
decani

ACDEKL
calked
lacked

ACDEKR
arcked
carked
craked
dacker
racked

ACDEKS
casked
sacked

ACDELL
Cadell
called

ACDELM
calmed
clamed
macled

ACDELN
candle
cendal
lanced

ACDELR
carled
clared
cradle
credal»

declar
reclad

ACDELS
clades
cleads
decals
scaled

ACDELT
clated
tacled
talced

ACDELU
caudle
cauled
cedula
Claude

ACDELV
calved
claved

ACDELW
cawdel
cawdle
clawed

ACDELY
clayed
lac dye

ACDEMP
camped
decamp

ACDENR
cedarn
craned
dancer
nacred
ranced

ACDENS
ascend
dances
decans

ACDENT
cadent
canted
decant

ACDEPR
carped
craped
redcap

ACDEPS
scaped
spaced

ACDERR
carder
carred

ACDERS
caders
cadres
cedars
crased
dacres
sacred
scared

ACDERT
carted
cedrat
crated
decart
Dectra
redact
traced

ACDERV
carved
craved

ACDESS
cassed
scades

ACDEST
cadets
casted
scated

ACDESW
cawsed
scawed

ACDETU
acuted
cauted

ACDIJU
Judaic»

Judica

ACDINO
Adonic
anodic

ACEEHT
eatche
Hecate
thecae

ACEELN
elance
enlace

ACEELR
alerce
cereal
cleare
relace

ACEEMR
amerce
careme
creame
raceme

ACEENR
careen
enrace
recane

ACEENS
encase
seance
Seneca

ACEENT
cetane
tenace

ACEEPR
preace
repace

ACEEPS
escape
espace
peaces

ACEERS
acrese
ceaser
crease»

searce

ACEERT
cerate
create
ecarte

ACEFIL
facile
fecial

ACEFIN
facine
fiance

ACEFIS
facies
scaife

ACEFSS
fasces
scafes

ACEGHR
charge
creagh

ACEGNU
cangue
uncage

ACEHIR
acheri
achier
Archie
chaire
eriach

ACEHLP
chapel
Lepcha
pleach

ACEHLR
larche
Rachel

ACEHLS
chales
chalse
chelas
laches
sealch

ACEHLT
chalet
thecal
Thecla

ACEHMS
chames
sachem
schema

ACEHNR
charne
chenar
enarch
enrach
rachen

ACEHNS
chanes
chanse
encash
hances
naches

ACEHOP
epocha
phocae

ACEHOR
chorea
Horace
ochrea
orache

ACEHPR
chaper
eparch
preach

ACEHPS
chapes
cheaps
Pasche
Pesach
spache
speach

ACEHRS
achers
arches
casher
chares
chaser
chears»
eschar
raches
recash
sarche
search

ACEHRT
archet
charte
charet
chater
chatre
hectar
ratche
tarche

ACEHST
chaste
chates
cheats
sachet
scathe
schate
steach
taches

ACEHSW
cashew
waches

ACEILM
limace
maleic
malice
Melica

ACEILN
ancile
inlace

ACEILP
epical
palice
plaice
plicae

ACEILR
carlie
Claire
eclair
lacier

ACEIMN
anemic»
cinema
iceman

ACEIMS
amices
camise

ACEIMT
acmite
micate

ACEINN
canine
neanic

ACEINR
cerain
craine

ACEINS
acsien
casein
eniacs
incase
snaice

ACEINT
actine
anetic

ACEIRR
Carrie
racier

ACEIRS
caries
cerias
craise
ericas

ACEISV
cavies
vesica

ACEITT
cattie
tietac

ACEKLR
calker
lacker
rackel
rackle

ACEKLT
lacket
tackle

ACEKNR
canker
reckan

ACEKRS
ackers
crakes
creaks
recask
resack
sacker
screak

ACEKRT
carket
racket
retack
tacker

ACEKRY
creaky
yacker

ACEKST
casket
sacket
tackes

ACELLR
arcell
caller
cellar
recall

ACELMR
calmer
camrel
Carmel
clamer
marcel
mercal

ACELMS
camels
calmes
clames
cleams
macles
mascle
mescal»
scamel

ACELNR
claner
lancer
rancel

ACELNS
ancles
cansel
clanes
cleans
lances

ACELNT
cantel
cantle
cental
lancet

ACELNU
cuneal
launce
unlace

ACELOR
coaler
oracle
recoal

ACELOT
Alecto
colate
locate

ACELOV
alcove
coeval

ACELPR
carpel
claper
parcel
placer

ACELPS
capels
caples
clapes
clapse
claspe
cleaps
places
plasce»
scalpe
scapel
scaple

ACELQU
calque
claque

ACELRS
arcels
carles
Clares
clears
recals
scaler
scarle
sclaer
sclera
scrale

ACELRT
carlet
cartel
cartle
claret
clarte
clater
lacert
rectal
tarcel

ACELRU
cauler
craule
raucle

ACELRV
calver
carvel
claver

ACELRW
cawler
crawle

ACELST
castle
clates
cleats
eclats
elacts
lacets
scalet
sclate»
tacles

ACELSU
caules
clause

ACELSV
calves
cavels
claves
Sclave

ACEMOS
cameos
cosmea

ACEMOT
comate
mateco

ACEMPR
camper
crampe

ACEMRS
crames
creams
macers
scream

ACENOR
cornea
encora

ACENPR
crapen
prance

ACENRS
caners
casern
cranes
cranse
crenas
nacres
rances
sarcen

ACENRT
canter
carnet
cranet
creant
Cretan»

nectar
recant
tanrec
trance

ACENRV
carven
cavern
craven

ACENRY
carney
crayne

ACENST
ascent
casten
enacts
secant
stance

ACENSU
causen
uncase
usance

ACENSV
canves
vances
vsance

ACENTU
Canute
uncate

ACEOPR
croape
Pecora

ACEOPT
capote
toecap

ACEORS
coarse
rosace

ACEORT
coater
recoat

ACEOTV
avocet
octave

ACEPRS
capers
Casper
carpes
crapes
escarp
pacers
parsec
recaps
scaper
scarpe
scrape
spacer

ACEPST
aspect
capets
epacts

ACEQSU
casque
sacque

ACERRS
carers
crares
racers
scarer
scarre

ACERRT
arrect
carret
carter
crater
recart
tracer

ACERRV
carver
craver

ACERRY
crayer
recray

ACERSS
caress
carses
casser
crases
crasse
sacres
scares»

scears
scraes
seracs

ACERST
arects
carets
cartes
caster
caters
crates
reacts
recast
rescat
sacret
scater
traces

ACERSU
acurse
carues
causer
cesura
saucer

ACERSY
cayers
crayes
creasy
scarey
scraye

ACERTU
acuter
cauter
curate

ACESTT
cattes
sceatt
stacte

ACESTU
acutes
cuesta

ACESUY
causey
cayuse

ACFIOS
fascio
fiasco

ACFLNO
falcon
flacon

ACFORT
factor
forcat

ACGINO
agonic
angico

ACGINR
arcing
caring
racing

ACGINT
acting
cating

ACGONS
congas
gascon
Scogan

ACHINR
chinar
inarch

ACHIPS
chaips
phasic
siphac

ACHIPT
haptic
pathic
phatic

ACHIRS
chairs
Charis
rachis

ACHIST
scaith
taisch

ACHKLY
chalky
hackly

ACHLNU
launch
nuchal
unlach

ACHLOR
choral
lorcha

ACHMOS
camsho
machos
mochas

ACHMSU
chaums
sumach

ACHNOR
anchor
archon
Charon
rancho

ACHNST
chants
snatch
stanch

ACHNTU
chaunt
nautch

ACHOPY
poachy
pochay

ACHRST
charts
scarth
starch

ACIILS
iliacs
sialic
silica

ACIKNP
ink cap
panick

ACILLS
lilacs
scilla

ACILNR
carlin
crinal

ACILNU
Lucina
uncial

ACILRT
clairt
rictal

ACILRU
uracil
Uralic

ACILSU
caulis
clusia

ACILSV
cavils
clavis
Slavic

ACIMNO
anomic
camion
conima
manioc
Monica

ACIMOT
atomic
matico

ACIMRS
cimars
craims
racism

ACINNT
tannic
tin can

ACINOS
casino
sonica

ACINOT
action
atonic
cation

ACINPS
panics
panisc

ACINST
antics
nastic
sancti

ACINTU
anicut
nautic

ACIOPT
atopic
copita

ACIOST
coatis
Scotia

ACIRST
artics
cairts
crista
racist
tsaric

ACIRTU
tauric
urtica

ACISTT
attics
static

ACKORT
rockat
tarock

ACKRST
sakret
strack
tracks

ACLLSU
callus
sulcal

ACLLSY
scally
Scylla

ACLMSU
caulms
lacmus
muscal

ACLOPU
copula
cupola

ACLORT
carlot
crotal

ACLOSY
acloys
Lycosa

ACLRSU
crauls
cursal
scraul

ACLRSW
crawls
scrawl

ACLSTU
clauts
scutal

ACMNOS
Macons
mascon
socman

ACMOST
comsat
mascot

ACMRSU
Marcus
sacrum
scarum

ACNNOT
cannot
canton

ACNOOR
corona
racoon

ACNORT
cantor»
carton
contra
craton

ACNOTU
Noctua
toucan

ACNSTU
cantus
Tuscan
unacts
uncast

ACORRT
carrot
trocar

ACORST
actors
castor
co-star
Croats
torcas

ACPSSU
scapus
scaups

ACPSTU
catsup
upcast

ACRSSU
Scarus
scaurs

ACRSTU
crusta
curats
turcas

ADDDEL
addled
daddle
ladded

ADDEER
deader
deared

ADDEEV
deaved
evaded

ADDEFN
fanded
feddan

ADDEGG
dagged
gadged

ADDEGR
gadder
graded

ADDEHS
dashed
shaded

ADDEIL
daidle
laddie

ADDEIM
diadem
maided

ADDEIN
dained
Dandie

ADDEIW
waddie
waided

ADDELN
dandle
ladden
landed

ADDELP
dapled
paddle

ADDELR
dalder
ladder
larded
raddle

ADDELS
addles
dasled
dedals
laddes
saddle
sladed

ADDELW
dawdle
waddle

ADDELY
deadly
ladyed

ADDEMN
damned
demand
madden
manded

ADDENR
addren
dander
darned
draned
nadder
naddre
narded
randed

ADDENS
dansed
dedans
sadden
sad end
sanded
snaded

ADDENW
dawned
wanded
wedand

ADDEOR
adored
deodar
roaded

ADDEOT
doated
toaded

ADDEPR
draped
padder
parded

ADDEPS
paddes
spaded

ADDERR
darred
radder

ADDERS
adders
addres
dreads
readds
sadder
sarded

ADDERT
darted
detard
drated
tarded
teddar
traded

ADDERW
Edward
wadder
warded

ADDERY
drayed
yadder
yarded

ADDMNO
dodman
odd-man

ADEEFR
deafer
feared

ADEEFT
defeat
feated

ADEEGL
eagled
gealed
gleade

ADEEGR
agreed
dragee
geared

ADEEHR
adhere»
header
Hedera

ADEEIR
dearie
rediae

ADEEKL
kealed
leaked

ADEELM
leamed
mealed

ADEELN
aneled
enlead
leaden
leaned
nealed

ADEELP
leaped
pealed

ADEELR
dealer
delare
ealdre
earled
leader
leared
ledare
relade
relead

ADEELS
alesed
aldees
leased
sealed

ADEELT
delate
deleat
elated
tealed
tele-ad

ADEELV
leaved
vealed

ADEEMN
amende
demane
demean
dename
meaned

ADEEMR
amered
dreame
meader
meared
rademe
reamed
remade
remead

ADEEMS
adeems
ameeds
amesed
deames
edemas
meades
meased
seamed

ADEEMT
meated
teamed

ADEENR
aernde
ardene
arende
deaner
denare
dreane
earned
endear
erande
neared

ADEENS
deanes
seaned

ADEENT
detane
neated

ADEENV
advene
envade
Evadne

ADEEPR
peared
pedera
reaped

ADEEPS
peased
pesade
seaped

ADEERR
dearer
reader
reared
reread

ADEERS
aredes
areeds
erased
reased
Red Sea
resade
seared

ADEERT
derate
redate
teared

ADEERV
evader
reaved
veared

ADEERW
drawee
weared

ADEEST
asteed
easted
seated
sedate
teades
teased

ADEESV
deaves
evades
veased

ADEFGN
fag-end»
fanged

ADEFIL
afield
defail
defial
failed
fideal

ADEFIN
fade in
fade-in
fained

ADEFIR
fadier
faired
fraide
Frieda
raifed

ADEFIT
daftie
faited

ADEFKL
defalk
falked
flaked

ADEFLO
afoled
feodal
foaled
loafed

ADEFLR
Alfred
fardel
fardle
farled
flared
rafled

ADEFLY
deafly
flayed

ADEFMR
defarm
farmed
framed

ADEFNR
fander
farden
farned

ADEFRS
faders
farsed
frased

ADEFRT
dafter
farted
frated
rafted

ADEFRY
defray
frayed

ADEGGL
daggle
lagged

ADEGGN
ganged
nagged

ADEGGR
dagger
ragged

ADEGGS
gadges
sagged

ADEGGT
gadget
tagged

ADEGHL
Gadhel
hagled

ADEGHN
hagden
hanged

ADEGLN
angled
dangle
gladen
lagend
langed

ADEGLR
argled
dargle
dragle
Gerald
glader
glared
larged

ADEGLS
glades
glased

ADEGMR
gramed
marged

ADEGNR
angred
danger
gander
garden
gnared
graned
negard
ranged

ADEGNT
ganted
tag end
tanged

ADEGOS
dagoes
dosage
seadog
sea dog
sea god
sogaed

ADEGOT
dogate
dotage
togaed

ADEGPR
graped
parged

ADEGRR
garred
Gerard
grader
regard

ADEGRS
degras
grades
grased

ADEGRT
grated
targed

ADEGRU
argued
guarde

ADEGST
degast
gasted
staged

ADEHIL
hailed
halide

ADEHLN
Handel
handle

ADEHLR
hareld
harled
herald

ADEHLS
delash
halsed
lashed
shaled

ADEHLT
daleth
halted
lathed

ADEHLW
hawled
whaled

ADEHMR
derham
harmed
rhamed

ADEHMS
mashed
shamed

ADEHNO
hoaned
head-on

ADEHNR
dherna
hander
harden

ADEHNS
ashend
handes
nashed
shaned

ADEHPS
hasped
phased
shaped

ADEHPT
heptad
pathed

ADEHRS
dasher
hardes
heards
rashed
red ash
shader
sharde
shared

ADEHRT
dearth
hatred
rathed
red hat
thread

ADEHSS
dashes
shades

ADEHST
deaths
'sdeath
tashed

ADEHSW
hawsed
shawed
washed

ADEIKR
daiker
darkie
raiked

ADEILM
mailed
medial

ADEILN
Aldine
alined
Daniel
Delian
denial
enlaid
inlead
lained
lead-in
nailed

ADEILP
aliped
elapid
laiped
paidle
pailed
Pleiad

ADEILR
daleir
dalier
derail
dialer
ieldra
laired
railed
redial
relaid

ADEILS
aisled
dalies
deasil
eliads
ideals
ladies
ladise
laides
laised
sailed
slaide
slaied

ADEILT
delait
detail
dilate
laited
tailed

ADEILW
Dewali
wailed

ADEIMM
demaim
maimed

ADEIMN
daimen
Damien
demain
inamed
maiden
mained
median
medina

ADEIMR
admire
arimde
arimed
raimed
remaid

ADEIMS
amides
medias
mid-sea

ADEINN
Andine
annied

ADEINR
dainer
derain
rained
randie

ADEINS
Adenis
asiden
enaids
naides
sained
sdaine

ADEINT
Danite
dantie
detain
naited
tained

ADEINV
invade
vained

ADEINW
dewani
wained

ADEIOT
iodate
Otidae

ADEIPR
depair
diaper
paired
pardie
raiped
repaid

ADEIRR
arider
arride
raider
raired

ADEIRS
aiders
draies
irades
raised
redias
resaid
saired

ADEIRT
airted
raited
taired
tirade

ADEISS
asides
dassie

ADEISU
adieus»
Suidae

ADEISV
advise
Davies
vaised
visaed

ADEITV
dative
vaited

ADEITW
dawtie
waited

ADEKLN
ankled
Kendal
lanked

ADEKLR
darkle
karled
larked

ADEKLS
lasked
skaled
slaked

ADEKLT
takled
talked

ADEKMR
demark
marked

ADEKMS
masked
smaked

ADEKNR
danker
darken
endark
knared
narked
ranked

ADEKNS
dankes
kneads»
sanked

ADEKRR
darker
karred

ADEKRS
dakers
rasked
sarked

ADEKRY
darkey
yarked

ADELLU
allude
aludel

ADELMM
lammed
malmed

ADELMP
ampled
lamped
mapled
palmed

ADELMR
dermal
larmed
marled
medlar

ADELMS
damsel
lameds
medals

ADELMT
malted
talmed

ADELNO
enodal
loaden
loaned

ADELNR
aldern
darnel
enlard
ladren»
lander
Randle
reland
Renald

ADELNS
elands
ladens
ladnes
landes
sandel
sandle
sendal

ADELNT
deltan
dental
lanted
natled
tandle

ADELNU
launde
unlade
unlead

ADELNW
lawnde
lawned
wandle

ADELOP
opaled
pedalo

ADELOR
loader
ordeal
reload
roaled

ADELOS
aldose
soaled

ADELPP
appled
dapple
lapped
palped

ADELPR
parled
pedlar

ADELPS
daples
lapsed
padles
pedals
pleads
slaped
spalde
spaled

ADELPT
patled
plated

ADELPU
pauled
uplead

ADELPW
dewlap
pawled
plawed

ADELRR
Darrel
larder

ADELRS
alders
arsled
dalers
eldars
laders
lardes
sardel
slared

ADELRT
altred
dartle
lardet
tardle
traled

ADELRU
alured
aulder
lauder

ADELRY
dearly
rayled

ADELSS
dasels
dasles
dassel
slades
sleads

ADELST
aldest
deltas
desalt
lasted
salted
satled
slated
staled

ADELSU
salued
sauled

ADELSV
salved
slaved
valsed

ADELSW
dwales
salewd
salwed
slawed
swaled
walsed
wealds

ADELSY
delays
deslay
slayed

ADEMMR
dammer
dramme
marmed
rammed

ADEMNO
daemon
modena
moaned
nomade

ADEMNR
damner»

mander
manred
randem
red man
remand

ADEMNS
amends
desman
mansed

ADEMNT
manted
tandem

ADEMNU
mauned
maunde
unmade

ADEMOP
apedom
pomade

ADEMOR
radome
roamed

ADEMPR
damper
ramped

ADEMRT
dreamt
marted

ADEMSS
desmas
massed

ADEMSU
amused
medusa

ADENNP
panned
pednan

ADENNT
dannet
tanned

ADENOT
anoted»

atoned
donate

ADENPP
append
napped

ADENPR
pander
repand

ADENPS
pansed
snaped
spaned

ADENPT
depant
panted
pedant
pentad

ADENPW
nawped
pawned

ADENRR
darner
errand
narder
narred
rander
redarn

ADENRS
danser
dearns
denars
dranes
dreans
ransed
redans
sander
sandre
snared

ADENRT
ardent
danter
endart
ranted
red ant
terand
traned»

treand

ADENRU
dauner
rauned
undear
unread

ADENRW
Andrew
Darwen
dawner
drawne
nawder
rawned
redawn
wander
warden
warned

ADENRY
denary
rayned

ADENSS
assden
sedans
sneads

ADENST
dantes
stande
staned

ADENTT
attend
tanted

ADENTU
tauned
undate

ADENTV
advent
vanted

ADENTW
tawned
wanted

ADEOPR
poared
roaped

ADEORR
adorer
roared
roader

ADEORS
adores
doreas
oreads
orsade
soared

ADEORT
doater
orated
roated
toader
troade

ADEORW
redowa
woader

ADEPPR
dapper
rapped

ADEPRR
draper
drepar
parred

ADEPRS
dapers
drapes
padres
parsed
prades
prased
preads
rasped
spader
spared
spread

ADEPRT
depart
drapet
padtre
parted
petard
prated
traped

ADEPRW
rawped
warped
wraped

ADEPSS
depass
passed
sepads
spades
spased

ADEPSW
pawsed
spawde
wasped

ADERRT
darter
dartre
redart
retard
tarred
trader

ADERRW
drawer
redraw
reward
warder
warred

ADERST
dartes
daster
daters
drates
stared
stread
tardes
trades
treads

ADERSW
sawder
seward
swared
sweard
waders
weards

ADERSY
drayes
raysed»

yardes
yeards

ADERTT
ratted
tarted
tetrad

ADESTT
stated
tasted

ADESTU
sauted
sudate

ADESTV
devast
staved
vasted

ADESTW
stawed
tawsed
wadset
wasted

ADESTY
dayset
stayed
steady
taysed

ADFLYY
dayfly
ladyfy

ADGILN
alding
daling
lading
ligand

ADGILO
algoid
dialog

ADGINR
Dargin
daring
gradin
nigard
rading

ADGORW
wardog
war god

ADGRSU
gradus
guards

ADHIJS
hadjis
jadish
jihads

ADHINS
Danish
sandhi

ADHPRU
hard up
purdah

ADILMY
diamyl
milady

ADILNR
aldrin
inlard

ADILNT
daltin
tindal

ADILNU
dualin
unlaid

ADILRS
drails
lairds
liards
lisard

ADILST
distal
ditals

ADIMNS
admins
disman

ADIMRS
disarm
marids

ADIMST
admits
amidst

ADINOR
Dorian
inroad
ordain

ADINOS
Adonis
danios
sodain

ADINOX
diaxon
dioxan

ADINRT
indart
tirand

ADINRW
Darwin
inward
wardin

ADINSW
diwans
windas

ADIORT
adroit
otarid

ADIPRS
rapids
sparid
spraid

ADIPSS
dipsas
spaids

ADIRRS
rairds
sirdar

ADISST
sadist
saidst
staids

ADISTV
davits
vista'd

ADJNOR
jardon
jordan

ADLMNO
almond
dolman

ADLNOR
Arnold
lardon
Roland
Ronald

ADLNOS
soland
soldan

ADMNOR
random
rodman

ADMNOS
damson
monads
nomads

ADMNOY
dynamo
Monday

ADNNOT
dannot
danton
donnat

ADNRST
drants
strand

ADNRTU
draunt
durant
tundra

ADPRUW
draw up
updraw
upward

ADPSSY
dypsas
spayds

AEEFRT
afreet
feater
terefa

AEEGLN
aengel
aengle
angele
eangel
engeal
gleane

AEEGLR
elrage
galere
leager
leagre
regale
regeal

AEEGLT
eaglet
gelate
legate
teagle
telega

AEEGMN
manege
menage

AEEGMT
gamete
metage

AEEGNR
enrage
gearne
genera
greane
neager
renage

AEEGNS
sagene
senega

AEEGNV
avenge»
geneva

AEEGRR
agrege
raggee
reggae

AEEGRS
agerse
agrees
eagers
eagres
grease

AEEGRV
greave
regave

AEEGST
egesta
etages

AEEHLR
healer
rehale

AEEHMR
hareem
hermae

AEEHNT
Athene
ethane
heaten

AEEHPS
heapes
spahee

AEEHRR
hearer
rehear

AEEHRT
aether
heater
hereat
reheat

AEEHSV
heaves
sheave

AEEILS
Elaeis
laesie

AEEIPR
epeira
pereia

AEEIRS
aeries
easier

AEEKLR
kealer
kelare
leaker

AEEKRP
parkee
repeak

AEELMR
almere
leamer
mealer
realme

AEELNP
alpeen
neaple

AEELNR
lanere
leaner
learne

AEELNS
aneles
enseal

AEELNT
elanet
lateen
teanel

AEELPR
leaper
pealer
repale
repeal

AEELPS
asleep
elapse»
please
sapele
speale

AEELRS
larees
leares
leears
leaser
resale
reseal
sealer

AEELRT
earlet
elater
realte
relate
retale
tealer
telare

AEELRV
laveer
leaver
revale
reveal
vealer

AEELSS
aleses
easels
easles
eassel
leases
seales

AEELST
elates
estale
leates
saltee
steale
stelae
teales
teasel
teasle

AEELSV
leaves
sleave
veales

AEELSW
aweels
weasel
weasle

AEELTV
velate
veleta

AEEMNR
enarme
meaner
remane
rename

AEEMNS
enemas
enseam
meanes

AEEMNT
enamet
entame

AEEMPR
ampere
empare

AEEMRS
amears
ameres
maseer
ramees
reames
reseam
seamer

AEEMSS
ameses
meases
seames
sesame

AEENNT
Etnean
neaten

AEENPS
peasen
sea pen

AEENRR
earner
nearer

AEENRS
enrase
ensear
ranees
Serena

AEENRT
entera
neater
renate
terane

AEENST
aneest
ensate
enseat
sateen
senate
steane

AEEPRR
reaper
repare

AEEPRS
Parsee
peares
pearse
prease
serape

AEEPRT
pearte
repeat
retape

AEEPST
etapes
peates
peseta

AEEPSY
payees
Yapese

AEERRS
earers
eraser
searer
serrae

AEERRT
re-rate
tearer»
terrae

AEERST
aretes
asteer
Astere
easter
Eastre
eaters
reates
reseat
saeter
seater
steare
teaser
Teresa

AEERSV
averse
eavers
reaves
resave
seaver
veares

AEERTT
teater
teatre

AEESTT
estate
tea set
testae

AEFGLN
fangel
fangle
flange

AEFHRT
father
freath
hafter
tharfe
thrafe

AEFILR
failer
ferial

AEFIMN
famine
infame

AEFINR
fainer
farine
fraine
infare
naifer

AEFIRS
faiers
faires
faries
fraise
safire
sea fir

AEFIST
faites
fiesta

AEFLOR
florae
loafer

AEFLRS
falser
farles
ferals
flares
flaser
flears
frales
freals
rafles
salfer

AEFLRT
falter
farlet
flater
lafter

AEFLRU
earful
ferula

AEFLST
falset
festal
flates
fleats

AEFLTY
fealty
featly

AEFMOR
femora
foamer

AEFMRR
farmer
framer

AEFNST
enfats
fasten
nefast
saften

AEFNSY
fansey
fansye
faynes

AEFRRT
farter
frater
rafter

AEFRST
afters
arfest
farset
fartes
faster
frates
freats
raftes
safter
strafe

AEFRTW
fawter
wafter

AEFSST
fasset
feasts
festas
safest
stafes

AEGGLR
gargle
lagger
raggle

AEGGNR
ganger»
grange
nagger

AEGGRS
aggers
eggars
ragges
sagger
seggar

AEGGRT
garget
tagger

AEGHLS
ghasel
hagles
sealgh

AEGHLT
glathe
haglet

AEGHNR
hanger
rehang

AEGILN
aleing
Ealing
genial
inegal
linage

AEGILR
gailer
graiel
graile
lairge
lea-rig

AEGILS
gailes
glaise
silage

AEGILT
aiglet
ligate
taigle

AEGILV
glaive
vagile

AEGIMN
enigma
gamine
igname

AEGIMR
gamier
maigre
mirage

AEGINR
aering
earing
gainer
graine
ingear
inrage
reagin
regain
regina

AEGINS
agnise
easing

AEGINT
eating
gianet
ingate
tangie
teaing

AEGIRS
agrise
graise
sagier

AEGIRT
aigret
gaiter
triage

AEGIRV
Argive
garvie
gravie
igrave
rivage

AEGLLN
engall
langle
leglan

AEGLLY
egally
galley

AEGLMN
gleman
legman
leg man
mangel
mangle

AEGLMY
gamely
gleamy
mygale

AEGLNO
engaol
galeon

AEGLNR
angler
garnel
glenar
langer
largen
Nergal
rangle
regnal

AEGLNS
angels
angles
englas
Galens
glanse
gleans
langes
sangle

AEGLNT
anglet
langet
tangel
tangle

AEGLNU
lagune
langue

AEGLOR
galore
gaoler

AEGLOT
galeot
legato

AEGLOV
lovage
volage

AEGLRR
larger
ragler

AEGLRS
argles
galers
glares
glaser
lagers
larges
regals

AEGLRT
raglet
tergal

AEGLRU
ragule
regula

AEGLRV
glaver
gravel

AEGLRY
argyle
gleary

AEGMMR
gammer
gramme

AEGMNR
engram
german
gramen
manger
ragmen

AEGMNS
magnes
manges

AEGMNT
agment»
magnet

AEGNNT
gannet
gnatte

AEGNOR
onager
orange

AEGNRR
garner
gnarre
graner
ranger
re-rang

AEGNRS
angers
angres
gnares
granes
ranges
rengas
resang
sangre
serang

AEGNRT
argent
garnet
garten
grante
graten

AEGNRW
gnawer
wanger

AEGNST
agents
agnets
ganets
gantes
geants
gnaste
stange
tanges

AEGORS
orages
sorage

AEGORT
garote
orgeat
toe rag

AEGPRS
gapers
gasper
grapes
grapse
graspe
pagers
parges
prages
sparge

AEGQSU
quages
squage

AEGRRT
garret
garter
grater

AEGRSS
gasser
grases

AEGRST
agrest
ergats
garest
garets
gaster
gestar
grates
Greats
stager
strage
targes

AEGRSU
argues
augers
sauger
usager

AEGRSV
Gervas
graves
vagers
varges

AEGRSW
grawes
sawger
Swerga
wagers

AEGRTT
gatter
target
traget
tregat

AEGRTU
argute
rugate
Tuareg

AEGSTY
gayest
stagey

AEHHRS
hasher
rehash

AEHHST
heaths
sheath

AEHILS
Elisha
hailes
hailse
sheila

AEHILT
halite
laithe

AEHINS
ashine
haines

AEHIRS
ashier
haires
shaire
sheria

AEHIST
Hestia
hiates
saithe

AEHJRS
hejras
Jasher

AEHKLS
halkes
shakle
shalke

AEHKNR
hanker
harken

AEHKNS
kanehs
shaken

AEHKRS
harkes
hearks
shaker
shreak

AEHKSY
ash key
shakey

AEHLMP
pelham
phleam

AEHLNS
halsen
hansel

AEHLNT
hantle
lathen

AEHLRS
ashler
halers
halser
harles
lasher
shaler

AEHLRT
halter
lather
rathel
thaler

AEHLRW
hawler
whaler

AEHLSS
halses
hassle
lashes
selhas
shales
sheals

AEHLST
athels
ethals
halest
haltes
haslet
hatels
lathes
leaths
Shelta
slathe

AEHLSW
hawles
shawle
washel
whales
wheals

AEHLSY
hayels
hayles
haysel

AEHLTY
eathly
hyetal

AEHMNT
anthem
hetman

AEHMNU
humane
Humean

AEHMOS
hamose
mahoes

AEHMRR
harmer»
reharm

AEHMRS
hamers
harems
masher
rhames
shamer

AEHMRT
marthe
mather

AEHMSS
mashes
shames

AEHMST
mathes
meaths
smeath

AEHNRS
harnes
harnse
hearns
hernas
rashen
sharen
sharne
shearn

AEHNRT
anther
nather
Tehran
thenar

AEHNST
Athens
hasten
nathes
snathe
sneath
thanes

AEHNSV
havens
Hesvan
shaven

AEHNSW
washen
whenas

AEHORS
ahorse
ashore
hoares
hoarse

AEHPRS
harpes
hepars
phares
phears
phrase
raphes
seraph
shaper
sharpe
Sherpa
shraep
shrape
sphaer
sphear

AEHPRT
teraph
threap

AEHPST
pathes
spathe

AEHRRS
harres
rasher
sharer

AEHRSS
rashes
shares
shears

AEHRST
earths
hartes
haster
haters
hearst
hearts
rathes
'sharte
'sheart
Theras

AEHRSV
havers»
shaver

AEHRSW
hawers
hawser
rewash
washer
whares

AEHRSY
ashery
hayers
hearsy
shayre

AEHRTT
hatter
threat

AEHRTW
thawer
wather
wrathe
wreath

AEHRTY
earthy
hearty

AEHSST
ashets
asseth
hastes
sheats

AEHSSW
hawses
washes

AEHSTW
swathe
wathes
weaths
wheats

AEIKRS
aikers
kaiser
raikes

AEIKRT
arkite
karite

AEILLM
maille
mallei
mallie

AEILLN
lienal
lineal

AEILMN
lamine
maline
menial

AEILMR
mailer
milrea
remail

AEILMS
mailes
maleis
malise
melias
mesail
mesial
samiel
Selima

AEILNP
alpine
neapil
Nepali
penial
pineal

AEILNR
aliner
enrail
lainer
lanier
larine
linear
nailer
renail

AEILNS
aliens
alines
aniles
elains
Elians
Elinas
inseal»
laines
lianes
nailes
saline
Selina
silane
snaile

AEILNT
atelin
entail
tenail

AEILNV
alevin
alvine
neavil
valine
venial

AEILNX
alexin
xenial

AEILPR
pailer
perial

AEILPS
espial
laipse
lapise
lipase
pailes
paleis
palise
plaise
spaile

AEILPT
aplite
pailet
plaite

AEILRR
railer
rerail

AEILRS
aisler
ariels
Israel
laires
lasier»
railes
resail
sailer
serail
serial
slaire

AEILRT
elitra
laiter
retail
retial
tailer

AEILSS
aisles
eassil
laisse
lassie
liases
sailes
slaies

AEILST
aislet
laites
staile
stelai
taisel

AEILSV
alives
lavies
silvae
valise
vlaies

AEILSX
Alexis
six ale

AEIMMN
ammine
immane

AEIMNR
airmen
arimen
maneir
marine
remain

AEIMNS
Amiens
amines»
animes
inseam
maines
mesian
semina

AEIMNT
etamin
inmate
inmeat
mantie
tamein
tamine

AEIMRT
armite
imaret
marite
matier
rimate

AEIMST
amites
ismate
maties
misate
miseat
samite
tamise

AEINNP
painen
pinnae

AEINNR
inaner
narine
ranine

AEINNS
annies
inanes
insane
sienna

AEINPR
aprine
arpine
enpair
napier
panier
parine
rapine

AEINPS
paines
pansie
pisane
snaipe

AEINPT
patine
pianet
pineta

AEINRS
arisen
arneis
arsine
enairs
inears
inrase
Naires
raines
raesin
sarnie

AEINRT
atrine
earnit
nerita
ranite
ratine
retain
retina
riante
tanier
tirane
traine

AEINRV
navier
navire
ravine
vainer

AEINSS
anises
sanies
sasine

AEINST
aneist
naites
sainte
santie
satine
staine»

stanie
tansie
tenias
tineas
tisane
tsaine

AEINSV
naives
navies
savine

AEINTU
auntie
Uniate

AEINTV
native
vinate

AEIPRR
pairer
rapier
repair
ripare

AEIPRS
aprise
aspier
aspire
iaspre
paries
parsie
perais
Persia
praise
raipes
spaier
spirea

AEIPRT
paiter
pirate
praite
pratie
pteria

AEIPRV
pavier
Vipera

AEIPST
apiest
pietas

AEIPSV
pavies
pavise

AEIRRS
airers
raiser
sairer
sierra

AEIRRT
arteir
artier
artire
raiter
ratier

AEIRRV
arrive
varier

AEIRSS
arises
raises
Sisera

AEIRST
aister
aistre
asteir
satire
staier
staire
steiar
stiera
striae
terais

AEIRTT
attire
ratite
tertia

AEIRVW
waiver
wavier

AEISST
ieasts
Saites
siesta
taises
tassie

AEITTW
tawtie
twaite
waitte

AEJPRS
japers
jasper

AEKLNR
lanker
rankle
relank

AEKLNS
ankles
slaken

AEKLNT
anklet
lanket
tankle

AEKLRS
lakers
larkes
slaker

AEKLRT
kartel
retalk
talker

AEKLST
lasket
skealt
sklate
stalke
takels
takles
talkes

AEKMRR
marker
remark

AEKMRS
makers
masker

AEKNRR
knarre
ranker

AEKNRS
ankers
knares
nakers
rakens
rankes
resank

AEKNST
entask
stanke
takens
tankes

AEKORS
arkose
oakers
resoak
soaker

AEKPRS
kapers
parkes
preaks
sparke

AEKQSU
quakes
squake
squeak

AEKRST
katers
kreats
rakets
skater
starke
strake
streak
takers
tasker
trakes

AELLMY
lamely
mellay

AELLRT
taller
tellar

AELLRU
allure
laurel

AELLRW
waller
wellar

AELLST
estall
sallet
stella

AELLTY
lately
lealty

AELLVY
valley
yevall

AELMMR
lammer
rammel

AELMNO
leamon
mealon
melano

AELMNS
Anselm
lamens
lemans
menals
mensal

AELMNT
lament
malten
mantel
mantle
mental

AELMNY
meanly
namely

AELMPR
ampler
lamper
palmer

AELMPS
amples
elamps
lampes
mapels»

maples
psalme
psealm
sample
spalme

AELMRS
almers
lamers
larmes
marles
realms
semlar

AELMRT
armlet
malter
marlet
martel
tramel
tremal

AELMRY
Aylmer
marley

AELMST
amlets
lamest
malets
metals
samlet

AELMSU
maules
Samuel
ulemas

AELMSY
measly
samely

AELNNR
lanner
rannel
rannle

AELNPR
parnel
planer
replan

AELNPS
Naples»

palens
panels
pensal
planes
slapen

AELNPT
pantel
pantle
planet
platen

AELNPU
unpale
uplean

AELNRS
laners
learns
narels
ransel
renals
snarle

AELNRT
altern
antler
entral
lanret
lanter
learnt
rantle
rental
ternal

AELNRU
neural
ulnare
unreal

AELNRV
nerval
vernal

AELNRY
anerly
nearly

AELNSV
elvans
navels
slaven
vanels
venals

AELNSY
enlays
nayles
sanely
snayle

AELNTT
latent
latten
nattle
talent

AELNTU
eluant
lunate

AELOPT
pelota
pot ale

AELORS
orales
roseal
solera

AELORT
elator
lorate

AELOST
osteal
solate

AELOSW
leasow
sea owl

AELPPR
lapper
perpal
rappel

AELPPT
lappet
tapple

AELPPU
leap up
papule
upleap

AELPRS
lapers
lapser»
lepras
paerls
palers
parles
parsel
pearls
preals
slaper
slepar

AELPRT
palter
plater
pratle

AELPRW
prawle
warple
wraple

AELPRY
parley
pearly
player
replay

AELPSS
lapses
plasse
saleps
sepals
slapes
spales
speals

AELPST
aslept
palest
palets
pastel
patels
patles
petals
plaste
plates
pleats
septal
spatel
spatle
splate
stapel
staple
talpes
tepals

AELPTT
patlet
pattel
pattle
T plate

AELQSU
equals
laques
lasque
quales
queals
quesal
squale
squeal

AELRSS
arless
arsles
lasers
rassle
salers
serals
slaers
slares
slears

AELRST
alerts
Alster
alters
altres
arslet
artels
astler
Astrel
Elstra
estlar
estral
laster
laters
ralest
rastel
rastle
ratels
ratles
relats
resalt
salter
slater
slatre
staler
starle
stelar»
strale
streal
Strela
talers
tarles
tarsel
tasler
telars
tersal
trales

AELRSU
alures
laures
saurel

AELRSV
lavers
ravels
salver
serval
slaver
velars
versal

AELRSW
larews
lawers
slawer
swaler
walers
warsle

AELRSY
layers
rayles
relays
re-lays
reslay
sayler
slayer

AELRTT
artlet
latter
rattel
rattle
tarlet
tatler

AELRTV
travel
valter
varlet

AELRTW
awlter
lawter
rewalt
Walter
wartle

AELRTY
elytra
layter
lyrate
raylet
realty
telary
trayle

AELRUV
valuer
valure

AELRYY
yarely
yearly

AELRZZ
lezzar
razzle

AELSSS
lasses
salses
sassle

AELSST
astels
estals
lasset
lastes
leasts
salets
saltes
satles
seatls
slates
sleats
stales
steals
tassel
teslas

AELSSV
salves
selvas
slaves»
valses

AELSSW
salwes
swales
sweals
walses
wassel

AELSTT
attles
latest
sattel
sattle
slatte
stealt
taslet
tastle
tatles

AELSTV
tavels
valets
vestal

AELSTW
stawle
swalte
walets
waltes
wastel
wastle
watles

AELSTY
astely
slatey
ylaste

AELSUV
avulse
values

AEMMNT
met man
nammet

AEMNOR
enamor
moaner
monera
normae

AEMNOT
maneto
Moneta
omenta
toname

AEMNRS
enarms
namers
ramsen
remans

AEMNRU
manure
murena

AEMNSS
manses
messan
samens

AEMNST
aments
mantes
stamen
tenasm

AEMNSY
yamens
yes-man

AEMNTU
unmate
untame
unteam

AEMORR
remora
roamer

AEMORS
ramose
sea orm

AEMORT
amoret
moater
morate

AEMOST
moates
osmate

AEMOSV
amoves
vamose

AEMPPR
mapper
pamper

AEMPRT
empart
tamper
tempra
trampe

AEMPRV
revamp
vamper

AEMQSU
masque
quames
squame

AEMRRT
marret
marter
martre

AEMRRW
rewarm
warmer

AEMRSS
masers
masser
Ramses
remass
smears

AEMRST
armets
martes
master
mastre
maters
remast
smaert
smarte
smeart
stream
tamers
trames

AEMRSU
amuser
maures
Mauser
saumer

AEMRSW
mawers
mawres
swarme
warmes

AEMRSY
maryes
smeary

AEMSSU
amuses
assume
Seamus

AEMSTT
mattes
tamest

AEMSTY
mayest
steamy

AEMSYZ
azymes
zymase

AENOPS
ensoap
paeons
peason

AENORS
reason
senora

AENORT
atoner
ornate

AENOST
anotes
astone
atones
oatens
seaton

AENPPR
napper
parpen

AENPPS
nappes
pasnep
snappe

AENPRS
aperns
arpens
aspern
paners
pranes
pranse
prasne
snaper
snarpe

AENPRT
arpent
enrapt
entrap
panter
parent
parten
praent
pterna
trepan

AENPRW
enwrap
pawner
prawne
repawn

AENPRY
napery
prayne

AENPSS
aspens
panses
passen
pesans
sneaps
spaens
spanes
speans

AENPST
enapts
napets»

patens
pentas
pesant
stapen

AENPSU
naupes
paunes
spaune

AENPSW
nawpes
pawens
pawnes
spawne

AENPSY
paynes
Spayne
yaspen

AENPTT
patent
patten
tapnet

AENPTU
peanut
untape

AENQSU
quanes
queans
squean

AENQTU
equant
quante

AENRRS
narres
serran
snarer

AENRRT
arrent
errant
ranter
Terran

AENRRW
rawner
rewarn
warner»

warren

AENRSS
Nasser
ranses
sarsen
snares
snears

AENRST
anters
antres
arents
arnest
arnets
astern
enstar
narest
naster
naters
natres
ranets
renats
santer
santre
sarten
sertan
snater
staner
starne
sterna
strane
tarnes
tranes
transe

AENRSW
answer
awners
resawn
swarne
warnes
wranes

AENRSY
raynes
renays
sarney
senary
yarens
yarnes
yearns

AENRTT
natter
ratten
tanter
terant

AENRTU
aunter
auntre
nateur
nature
tea urn

AENSST
assent
neasts
sanest
snaste
staens
stanes
steans

AENSTU
Austen
nasute
taunes
unseat

AENSTX
sextan
Texans

AENSTZ
stanze
zantes

AENSWY
sawney
swayne
waynes

AENTTU
attune
nutate
tauten

AEOPRT
portae
protea

AEOPTT
aptote
teapot

AEORST
oaters
orates
Ostrea
roates
roseat

AEOSTV
avoset
ovates

AEPPRS
appres
papers
pasper
sapper

AEPPRW
wapper
warppe
wrappe

AEPPRY
papery
prepay
yapper

AEPRRS
parers
parres
parser
rapers
rasper
sparer

AEPRRT
parret
parter
prater
rapter
repart
traper

AEPRRY
prayer
repray

AEPRSS
aspers
parses
passer
prases
raspes
repass»

respas
sarpes
spaers
spares
sparse
spears

AEPRST
aspert
partes
paster
pastre
paters
pearst
pearts
petars
prates
preast
raptes
repast
retaps
septar
sparte
sprate
spreat
sterap
strape
streap
tapers
tapres
tapser
trapes
trapse
trepas

AEPRSW
prawes
sparwe
warpes
wasper
wrapes

AEPRSY
aspyre
payers
prayes
prayse
repays
spayer
spayre
speary

AEPRTU
pautre»

uprate
uptear

AEPSSS
passes
spases

AEPSST
pastes
seapts
spates
speats
stapes
steaps

AEPSTT
aptest
pattes
tapets

AEPSTU
espaut
taupes

AEQRSU
quares
quears
sequar
square
squear

AEQRSV
qvares
sqvare

AEQRTU
quarte
quater
quatre

AEQSTU
squate
tasque

AEQSTW
qwaste
sqwate

AERRST
arrest
arrets
arters
astrer
raters
raster»

restar
starer
tarres
terras

AERRTT
ratter
tarter

AERSST
arests
assert
asters
astres
essart
reasts
saster
saters
stares
stears
straes
strase
streas
tarses
tessar

AERSSW
sawers
sewars
swares
swears
warses
wasser
wrases
wrasse

AERSTT
astert
aretts
atters
stater
strate
streat
taster
taters
tetras
traste
treats

AERSTU
auster
autres
estuar
sauter»

sautre
urates

AERSTV
averts
ravets
servat
starve
staver
strave
tavers
traves
vaster
vastre

AERSTW
awters
sawter
sawtre
strawe
tawers
trawes
waster
waters
wraste

AERSTX
astrex
extras
sextar
taxers

AERSTY
estray
reasty
restay
stayer

AERSUU
aureus
uraeus

AERSVW
swarve
swaver
warves
wavers

AERSWY
sawyer
swayer
sewary
wayers
wayres

AERTTW
tewart
trawet
watter

AERTTY
treaty
yatter

AERTWY
tawery
watery

AESSST
assets
tasses

AESSTT
assett
esstat
states
taests
tasset
tastes
teasts

AESTTU
astute
statue

AFGINR
faring
Grafin
rafing

AFHLSY
ash fly
flashy

AFHORS
shofar
shorfa

AFIKRS
fakirs
friska
Kafirs

AFIRST
afrits
fraist

AFLMRU
armful»

fulmar

AFLORS
floras
safrol

AFLOST
floats
flotas
fostal

AFLSTU
faults
flatus

AFNSTU
faunts
unfast

AFORSY
forays
forsay

AFORTU
far out
fautor
foutra

AGGILN
gingal
laggin

AGGIMN
gaming
gigman

AGGINN
ganing
naggin

AGGINP
gaping
paging

AGGINR
arging
garing
raging

AGGINT
gating
gigant

AGHINS
anighs
ashing
ghains
Hsiang

AGHINT
anight
a'thing
hating

AGHIRT
aright
graith

AGHNRT
Granth
thrang

AGIILN
ailing
nilgai

AGIJLN
jaling
jingal

AGIKMN
kaming
making

AGIKNR
arking
raking

AGIKNS
akings
asking
gaskin
kiangs
saking

AGIKNW
gwakin
kawing
waking

AGILMN
laming
lingam
malign
maling

AGILNN
laning
lingan
Ningal

AGILNP
laping
paling

AGILNS
algins
aligns
glasin
lasing
liangs
ligans
lingas
saling
signal

AGILNT
langit
lating
taling

AGILNU
lingua
nilgau

AGILNW
lawing
waling

AGILNY
ayling
gainly
laying

AGILOT
galiot
latigo

AGILRS
argils
glairs
grails
slairg

AGIMNR
arming
ingram
margin
maring
raming

AGIMNS
gamins
masing

AGIMNT
mating
taming

AGIMNW
awming
mawing

AGINNP
naping
paning

AGINNS
ingans
saning

AGINNU
auning
guanin
ungain

AGINNW
awning
nawing
waning

AGINOR
gainor
ignaro
ingoar
oaring
onagri
origan

AGINOS
ngaios
sagoin
Saigon

AGINOT
gitano
oating

AGINPR
grapin
paring
raping

AGINRR
arring»
raring

AGINRT
gratin
rating
taring
tringa

AGINRU
air gun
Ugrian

AGINRY
grainy
raying

AGINST
gainst
giants
gnaist
sating
signat
taings
tangis

AGINSU
Anguis
saguin

AGINSW
aswing
sawing
wigans

AGIRST
graits
gratis
striga

AGIRSV
vargis
virgas

AGKNRU
karung
kurgan

AGLLNO
gallon
gollan

AGLNOS
golans
logans»
slogan

AGLNRU
langur
lurgan

AGLNUU
ungual
ungula

AGLOTY
galyot
otalgy

AGLRSU
glaurs
guslar

AGLRUY
glaury
raguly

AGMORY
goramy
morgay

AGNORS
argons
groans
nagors
orangs
organs
sarong

AGNOST
Gaston
sontag
tangos
tongas

AGNPRS
prangs
sprang

AGNRST
grants
strang

AGNRTY
gantry
gyrant

AGRSSU
sargus»
sugars

AHIKRS
rakish
shikar
shikra

AHILPS
palish
phials

AHILST
laiths
lathis
latish
tahsil

AHIMPS
impash
mishap
pashim

AHIMRS
harims
ihrams
mahsir
marish
ramish

AHIMRT
Mithra
thairm

AHINRS
arshin
hairns
ranish
shairn

AHIORT
hariot
hot air

AHIPRS
parish
raphis

AHIRRS
arrish
Harris
shirra
sirrah

AHIRST
airths
hairst
hairts
Ishtar
raiths

AHISTT
staith
taiths

AHISTU
hiatus
hutias

AHLLMO
mollah
ollahm

AHLLOO
halloo
holloa

AHLMOS
omlahs
shalom

AHLNSU
uhlans
unlash

AHLOST
loaths
lotahs
shalot

AHLSTU
haulst
haults
shault

AHMSSU
mushas
samshu
shamus

AHNORS
harons
Sharon
shoran

AHNSTU
haunts
sunhat»
unhats

AHOPST
Pashto
pathos
potash

AHPNSU
unhaps
unhasp

AHRSSU
hussar
surahs

AHRSTW
swarth
thraws
warths
wraths

AIINRS
raisin
Sirian

AIKLPS
kalpis
palkis

AIKRST
kraits
straik
traiks

AILLPU
pillau
pilula

AILMNO
monial
oilman

AILMNS
lamins
manils
maslin
milans
minlas

AILMNU
alumni
lumina
unmail

AILMPR
impar
primal

AILMRT
mitral
ramtil

AILMSS
missal
salmis

AILMST
malist
Tamils

AILMSX
laxism
smilax

AILNNU
annuli
unnail

AILNPS
pinsal
plains
spinal

AILNPT
plaint
pliant
taplin

AILNRT
ratlin
trinal

AILNST
instal
Latins
Stalin

AILNSU
insula
inulas

AILNSY
inlays
snaily

AILNVS
anvils
silvan

AILORT
rialto
tailor

AILPRS
lispar
prials
spiral

AILPST
atslip
pastil
plaist
plaits
plasit
spital

AILPTU
tail-up
tipula
Tulipa

AILQSU
quails
squail

AILRST
liarts
strail
trails
trials

AILSTV
vistal
vitals

AIMMOS
Maoism
mimosa

AIMNNO
amnion
Minoan

AIMNRT
Antrim
martin

AIMNST
mantis
matins
stamin
tamins

AIMNSZ
Nazism
nizams

AIMOST
Maoist
Samiot
Taoism

AIMPRT
armpit
impart
partim

AIMPSS
impass
passim

AIMRST
amrits
mairts
Marist
mastri
Ramist
timars

AIMSSW
missaw
swamis

AINNOS
anions
nasion

AINNOT
anoint
nation

AINNPS
inspan
pinnas

AINORS
norias
onsair

AINORT
aroint
ration

AINPRS
nipars
prains
spinar»
sprain

AINPST
paints
patins
pintas
ptisan

AINPTY
painty
pyanit

AINQTU
quaint
quinta

AINRST
arnits
instar
santir
strain
tirans
trains

AINSST
naists
saints
satins
snaist
stains

AINSTT
sattin
staint
taints
tanist
titans

AINSTU
Austin
Uniats

AINSTY
naisty
sanity
satiny

AIOPST
patios
patois

AIORST
aorist
aristo»
ratios
satori
stiora

AIPRSS
Parsis
raspis

AIPRST
pairts
partis
pirats
rapist
sprait
tapirs

AIPRTT
rat pit
tar pit

AIPSST
pastis
Piasts
stipas

AIPSTT
pittas
tapist

AIPSTW
pitsaw
sawpit

AIQRSU
quairs
squair

AIRSST
sistra
sitars
stairs

AIRSTT
artist
sittar
strait
traist
traits

AISSST
assist
stasis

AKOORR
karroo
korora

AKOSTY
Ostyak
tokays

AKQRSU
quarks
squark

AKQSUW
quawks
squawk

AKRSTU
krauts
kurtas
tuskar

ALLMOS
mollas
slalom

ALLOOP
apollo
palolo

ALLOSW
allows
sallow

ALLQSU
qualls
squall

ALLSTY
lastly
saltly

ALMNOS
monals
salmon

ALMORS
molars
morals
morsal
romals
somlar

ALMORT
marlot»
mortal

ALMOST
almost
matlos
smalto

ALMTUU
mutual
umlaut

ALNOOS
alsoon
saloon
solano

ALNORT
latron
tornal

ALNRUY
lunary
uranyl

ALNSTU
launts
slaunt
sultan
unlast
unsalt

ALOPRS
parols
polars
sporal

ALOPRT
patrol
portal

ALOPST
ploats
postal

ALOQTU
loquat
quotal

ALORSS
rossal
solars

ALORSU
rosula»

soular

ALORSV
orvals
salvor

ALORTU
rotula
torula

ALORUV
ovular
valour

ALPRTY
paltry
partly

ALRSTU
lustra
trauls
ultras

ALSSTU
saltus
saults
tussal

AMNOOR
maroon
ramoon

AMNOPT
potman
tampon
topman

AMNORS
manors
marons
ramons
ramson
ransom
Romans

AMNORY
mornay
Romany

AMNOSS
masons
Samson

AMNOTU
amount
moutan
outman

AMNRTU
antrum
Truman

AMNTTU
mutant
tutman

AMORST
morats
stroam
stroma

AMORSU
amours
ramous

AMPRST
stramp
tramps

AMPSUW
mawpus
wampus

AMRSTU
struma
sumtar

AMRSTY
mastry
smarty

ANNOST
santon
sonant

ANNPSU
sannup
sun pan
unspan

ANNSTU
naunts
suntan

ANOPRS
aprons
parson

ANOPRT
parton
patron
tarpon

ANORST
arnots
orants
raston
rotans
Snotra
stroan
torans
troans
tronas

ANORTT
attorn
ratton
rottan

ANORTY
aroynt
notary
Troyan

ANRSTU
arnuts
naturs
santur
Saturn

ANRUWY
runway
unwary

ANSTTU
taunts
tutsan

AOPRRT
parrot
raptor

AOPRST
asport
pastor
portas
proats
sap rot
sproat
stroap

AORRST
rostra
sartor

AORRWY
arrowy
yarrow

AORSST
assort
roasts
rosats

AORSTT
ottars
stator
tarots
troats

AORSTX
storax
taxors

AOSSTT
assott
stoats
toasts

APRSTY
pastry
sparty

ARSSTU
russat
surats
sutras
tarsus
tussar

ARSTTU
astrut
Stuart
tuarts

ARSTWY
sawtyr
strawy
swarty
wastry

BBDEIL
dibble
libbed

BBDEIR
bribed
dibber
ribbed

BBDELU
bulbed
dubbel
dubble
lubbed

BBDEMO
bombed
mobbed

BBDEOR
dobber
robbed

BBEILR
Bibler
libber
ribble

BBEILT
biblet
libbet
tibble

BBEIRR
briber
ribber

BBELPY
pebbly
plebby

BBELRU
burbel
burble
lubber
rubbel
rubble

BBEMOR
bomber
mobber

BBERTU
rubbet
tubber

BCDEEK
becked»
bedeck

BCDEKU
beduck
bucked

BCEEKN
becken
nebeck

BCEEKR
becker
rebeck

BCEIKR
bicker
bricke

BCEMOR
comber
combre
recomb

BCEMRU
cumber
cumbre
recumb

BCIINO
bionic
niobic

BCISTU
cubist
cubits

BDDEIR
bidder
birded
brided

BDDELU
buddel
buddle
dubled

BDDEOR
bodder
broded

BDDERU
budder
redbud

BDEEET
beeted
debtee

BDEEIL
belied
debile
edible

BDEEKR
bederk
berked

BDEELL
bedell
belled

BDEELT
belted
deblet

BDEEST
bedets
bested

BDEGIL
begild
bilged

BDEGIR
begird
bridge

BDEGLU
bludge
bugled
bulged

BDEGNU
bedung
bunged

BDEGRU
budger
burged
red bug

BDEHOS
boshed
debosh

BDEIIR
birdie
bridie

BDEIKL
bilked
bliked

BDEILM
dimble
limbed

BDEILO
boiled
bolide

BDEILR
bilder
birled
bridle
dibler

BDEIMR
brimed
dimber

BDEINR
binder
brined
inbred
rebind

BDEIRS
biders
brides
brised
debris
rebids

BDEIRT
bedirt
brited
tribed

BDEIRU
burdie
buried
rubied

BDEIST
bed-sit
bidets
debits

BDEKNU
bunked
debunk

BDELMO
blomed
mobled

BDELMU
blumed
dumble

BDELNO
blonde
bolden
boldne
nobled

BDELNU
bundle
unbled

BDELOO
boodle
booled

BDELOR
belord
blored
bolder
bordel
brodel
dorbel

BDELOT
bolted
doblet

BDELOU
bouled
double

BDELOW
blowed
bowled

BDELRU
bruled
dubler
rubled

BDENOR
bonder
borden
bronde

BDENOW
bowden»

bowned

BDENRU
bruned
bunder
burden
burned
unbred

BDENSU
sunbed
unbeds

BDENTU
bunted
but-end

BDEOPR
bedrop
probed

BDEORR
border
broder
brodre

BDEORS
bordes
brodes
brosed
derobs
desorb
sorbed

BDEORT
betrod
debtor

BDEORW
bowder
browed

BDERSU
brused
burdes
surbed

BDERTU
bruted
burted

BDESTU
bedust
bestud»

busted
debuts

BDNOUY
unbody
ybound

BEEEMT
bemeet
bemete
beteem

BEEGRU
burgee
Gueber
Guebre

BEEHRT
berthe
brethe

BEEHST
behest
Thebes

BEEIMR
bemire
bireme

BEELMS
embles
semble

BEELRT
belter
treble

BEENOR
boreen
enrobe

BEERRW
brewer
rebrew

BEFFRU
buffer
rebuff

BEFLMU
beflum
fumble

BEGILR
gerbil
grible

BEGINS
begins
beings
besing
binges

BEGINU
beguin
bungie

BEGLNU
blunge
bungle

BEGLOT
boglet
goblet

BEGLRU
bugler
bulger
burgle

BEGLTU
buglet
bulget

BEGNSU
beguns
besung

BEGOOR
bog ore
goober

BEGORU
brogue
gouber

BEGRRU
Bruger
burger

BEHILT
blithe
thible

BEHORT
bother
brothe»

theorb

BEHSTU
bushet
Teshub

BEIJLR
jerbil
jirble

BEILLR
biller
brille

BEILMO
bemoil
emboil
mobile

BEILMR
limber
relimb

BEILOR
boiler
broile
reboil

BEILRR
birler
blirre

BEILRS
birles
birsle
brisle
libers

BEILRT
belirt
birtle
britle
riblet
trible

BEIMOS
biomes
obeism

BEIMRT
betrim
timber
timbre

BEIMRU
erbium
imbrue

BEINRS
brines
enribs
nebris

BEINRU
Brunei
burnie
rubine

BEIRRU
burrie
rubier

BEIRST
bestir
bister
bistre
biters
brites
tribes

BEIRSU
bruise
rubies

BEIRTT
bitter
bittre
tibert

BEKORS
bosker
brokes

BEKRSU
brukes
burkes
busker

BELLOU
boulle
lobule

BELMMU
bummle
mumble

BELMRU
lumber»

rumble
umbrel

BELOOS
lobose
sobole

BELORT
bolter
brotel
brotle
orblet
rebolt
roblet
torbel
torble
trobel
troble

BELORU
bloure
rouble

BELORW
blower
blowre
bowler
worble

BELOSU
blouse
boules
obelus

BELOSW
belows
blowes
blowse
bowels
elbows

BELRRU
blurre
burler
burrel

BELRSU
bluers
brules
brusle
lubers
rubels
rubles

BELRTU
bulter
burlet
butler
truble
turbel
turble

BELSTU
bluest
bluets
bustle
sublet
subtle

BEMORS
bromes
ombers
ombres
somber
sombre

BEMOSS
besoms
emboss

BENNTU
ben nut
unbent

BENORS
boners
bornes
resbon

BENORU
bourne
unrobe

BENORZ
bonzer
bronze

BENOSW
besnow
bownes

BENRRU
bruner
burner
reburn

BENRSU
brunes»
burnes
resnub

BENRTU
brunet
bunter
burnet

BEORRS
borers
resorb
robers

BEORST
besort
Osbert
sorbet
strobe

BEORSU
bourse
brouse

BEORSW
bowers
bowser
browes
browse

BEORWY
bowery
bowyer
owerby

BEOSSS
bosses
obsess

BEOSST
besots
betoss

BEOSTT
bottes
obtest

BEOSTW
bestow
bowets

BERRTU
burret
burter

BERSTU
bruste
brutes
burtes
buster
rebuts
sturbe
surbet
tubers

BGGIIN
biggin
gibing

BGILNO
boling
globin
goblin
lobing

BGINOR
boring
orbing
robing

BGINOS
bingos
obsign

BINOSS
bisons
bisson

BINOST
bionts
bonist

BIOOST
oboist
oobits

BIORST
bistro
orbits

BIOSTU
oubits
subito

BLSTUY
butyls
subtly

BMOORY
broomy
byroom

BMORSU
morbus
rumbos

BNOOTU
bouton
unboot

BNORSU
bourns
suborn

BNOSUW
sunbow
unbows

BORSTU
brouts
robust
turbos

CCDEIR
Cedric
Cerdic

CCEHIL
chicle
cliche

CCEHIO
choice
echoic

CCEILL
cilice
icicle

CCEILR
circle
cleric

CCEKOR
cocker
recock

CCEORS
escroc
soccer

CCERSU
cercus
cruces

CCHINO
chicon
Cochin

CCHLTU
clutch
cultch

CCIIRT
citric
critic

CCIMOS
comics
cosmic

CCORSU
crocus
succor

CDDEEU
deduce
deuced
educed

CDDELO
clodde
coddle

CDDELU
cuddle
dulced

CDDEOR
codder
corded
red cod

CDEEER
ceered
decree
recede

CDEEES
ceedes
secede

CDEEFT
defect
fected

CDEEIL
ceiled
cieled
decile
delice

CDEEIN
Edenic
incede

CDEEKR
decker
recked
redeck

CDEEMR
cremed
merced

CDEENO
encode
endoce

CDEENR
cerned
decern

CDEENT
decent
tenced

CDEEPR
creped
decerp
perced

CDEERS
ceders
cedres
credes
creeds
cresed
screed
screde
serced

CDEERT
decret
rected

CDEESS
cessed
scedes

CDEESU
deuces
educes
seduce

CDEETT
detect
tected

CDEHIM
chimed
miched

CDEHIN
chined
inched
niched

CDEHIR
chider
chired
dreich
driche
driech
herdic
rechid
riched

CDEHIS
chides
schide

CDEHOR
chored
ochred
roched

CDEIKN
dicken
nicked

CDEIKR
dicker
ricked

CDEILO
coiled
docile

CDEIMR
crimed
dermic

CDEINR
cinder
crined
rinced

CDEINW
Wendic
winced

CDEIOP
copied
epodic

CDEIRS
ciders
dicers
scried

CDEIRT
credit
direct
triced

CDEIST
cisted
edicts
scited

CDEKLO
cloked
locked

CDEKNO
conked
docken
nocked

CDEKOR
corked
docker
redock
rocked

CDEKRU
ducker
rucked

CDEKSU
duckes
sucked

CDEKTU
ducket
tucked

CDELNO
cloned
colden

CDELOO
cooled
locoed

CDELOW
clowde
clowed
cowled

CDELOY
cloyed
coyled

CDELPU
cluped
culped
cupled
pulced

CDELRU
curdle
curled

CDELTU
cluted
dulcet

CDEMOO
comedo
coomed

CDENOR
Cerdon
conder
corned
croned
recond

CDENSU
dunces
secund

CDEORR
corder
corred
record

CDEORS
coders
cordes»
corsed
decors
escrod
scored
scrode

CDEORW
crowde
crowed

CDEOST
costed
scoted

CDEOSU
coused
douces
escudo

CDERRU
cruder
curred

CDERSU
crudes
cursed

CDERSY
cyders
descry
scryde
scryed

CDERTU
decurt
ducter
ructed
truced

CDESSU
cussed
decuss

CDHIOR
droich
orchid
rhodic

CDIORS
Dorics
roscid

CDIPSU
cupids»
cuspid

CDLLOY
clodly
coldly

CDNOOR
condor
cordon

CEEFHL
fleche
fleech

CEEGIR
cierge
griece

CEEHLS
cheels
sleech

CEEHMS
meches
scheme
smeech

CEEHNT
chenet
thence

CEEHNW
chewen
whence

CEEHOR
cheero
choree
cohere
echoer
re-echo

CEEHPR
cheper
pecher
preche

CEEHPS
cheeps
peches
speech

CEEHRS
cheers»
creesh
reches

CEEHRW
chewer
rechew

CEEHRY
cheery
reechy

CEEHST
chetes
etches
teches

CEEHSW
chewes
eschew

CEEILR
ceiler
cieler

CEEINP
neipce
niepce
picene
piecen

CEEINT
entice
tenice

CEEINV
evince
Venice

CEEIPR
piecer
pierce
recipe

CEEIPS
espice
pieces
specie
spiece

CEEIRT
cerite
certie
receit
reciet»
recite
tierce

CEEKLR
clerke
lecker
reckle

CEEKLS
cleeks
seckel
seckle

CEELRS
cleers
cleres
creels
sclere

CEELRT
celter
tercel

CEELST
celest
cleets
cletes
elects
select

CEEMRS
creems
cremes
merces
screme

CEENRS
censer
cernes
creens
scerne
screen
secern

CEENRT
center
centre
certen
necter
recent
tenrec

CEEPRS
creeps»

crepes
perces
preces
screpe

CEEPRT
cepter
ceptre
recept

CEEPTX
except
expect

CEERSS
cesser
cresse
recess
screes
serces

CEERST
certes
creste
cretes
erects
resect
screte
secret
terces

CEERSU
Cereus
ceruse
cesure
cursee
recuse
rescue
secure

CEFHIT
fetich
fitche

CEFORS
corfes
forces
fresco

CEGILN
cingle
clinge

CEGINR
cering
cringe

CEGNOR
conger
congre
cronge

CEHILS
chesil
chiels
chiles
chisel
elchis
liches

CEHIMR
chimer
micher

CEHIMS
chimes
miches
smiche

CEHINR
enrich
incher
nicher
richen
rinche

CEHINS
chines
chinse
inches
niches
schine

CEHINV
chevin
chiven

CEHIOR
coheir
heroic

CEHIPR
ceriph
chirpe
cipher

CEHIRS
chiers
chires
riches

CEHIRT
chiter
cither
thrice

CEHIST
ethics
Sethic
theics
tische

CEHISV
chives
schive

CEHKOR
choker
hocker

CEHLOR
choler
orchel

CEHLPS
chelps
schlep

CEHNOS
chones
chosen

CEHOOS
choose
cohoes

CEHOPS
Cheops
epochs

CEHORS
chores
cosher
ochers
ochres
roches

CEHORT
hector
rochet»

rotche
tocher
troche

CEHOSW
chowse
owches

CEHPRU
cherup
churpe
pruche

CEHPRY
chypre
cypher

CEHSTU
chuets
chutes
cuthes
tusche

CEHSTY
chesty
cythes
scythe

CEIILS
ceilis
ilices

CEIIST
cities
scitie

CEIKLN
inckle
licken
nickel

CEIKLR
licker
re-lick
rickle

CEIKLT
Keltic
tickle

CEIKPR
picker
repick
ripeck

CEIKRS
crikes
ericks
ickers
scrike
sicker

CEIKRT
criket
ricket
ticker
tricke

CEILLO
collie
ocelli

CEILMS
climes
melics
miscel

CEILNT
client
lentic

CEILNU
leucin
nuclei

CEILOR
coiler
recoil

CEILPS
clipes
splice

CEILRS
criles
crisle
relics
slicer

CEILSV
clevis
clives

CEIMRU
cerium
uremic

CEINOR
coiner»

norice
orcein
orcine
recoin

CEINOS
conies
cosine
oscine

CEINOT
noetic
notice

CEINPR
pincer
prince

CEINPT
incept
pectin
peinct

CEINQU
cinque
quince

CEINRS
crines
rinces
scrine

CEINRT
cintre
cretin
crinet

CEINRU
ice run
nurice

CEINST
encist
incest
insect
nicest
scient

CEIOPT
picote
poetic

CEIORS
cories»

cosier
croise
scorie

CEIORT
erotic
tercio

CEIORW
cowier
cowrie

CEIOST
cotise
oecist

CEIPRS
cipers
cipres
cripes
Persic
precis
prices
scripe
spicer

CEIPSS
Pisces
spices

CEIRRS
cerris
criers
ricers
scrier

CEIRSS
cisers
crises
crisse
scries

CEIRST
certis
cister
citers
criste
steric
trices

CEIRSU
cruise
crusie
curies

CEIRSV
cervis
sciver
scrive

CEIRTU
cuiter
curiet
uretic

CEISST
citess
scites

CEISTU
cestui
cueist
cuties

CEKLOR
locker
relock

CEKLOS
clokes
lockes
slocke

CEKMOR
mocker
remock

CEKNOR
conker
reckon

CEKORR
corker
croker
recork
rocker

CEKORS
ockers
rockes
socker

CEKOST
socket
tockes

CEKQSU
quecks
squeck

CEKRSU
ruckes
sucker

CEKSTU
sucket
tuckes

CELLRU
culler
recull

CELMSU
clumes
clumse
muscle

CELNOR
cornel
cronel

CELNOS
clones
closen

CELNRU
cluner
lucern

CELOOR
cooler
recool

CELOOS
cloose
locoes

CELOOT
cloote
ocelot

CELORS
ceorls
closer
colers
cresol
escrol

CELORT
cloter
colter
lector

CELOST
clotes
closet

CELOSU
coleus
coules
oscule
scoule

CELOSW
clowes
clowse
cowles
scowle

CELPSU
clupes
culpes
cupels
cuples
pulces
sculpe

CELRTU
culter
curlet
cutler
reluct

CELTTU
cutlet
cuttle

CEMORR
cremor
Cromer

CEMRSU
crumes
scumer

CENOPR
crepon
poncer

CENOPU
pounce
uncope

CENORS
censor
cornes
crones»
norces
oncers
scorne
scrone

CENORT
conter
contre
cornet
cronet

CENORU
rounce
uncore

CENOVY
convey
covyne

CENRSY
crynes
scryne

CEOOTY
coyote
oocyte

CEOPRS
copers
corpes
corpse
cropes
scoper

CEOPRU
couper
croupe
recoup

CEORRS
corers
corser
crores
scorer

CEORSS
cessor
corses
cosers
cosser
croses
crosse
scores
scorse

CEORST
corset
Cortes
coster
coters
croste
crotes
escort
recost
scorte
scoter
sector

CEORSU
course
crouse
source

CEORSV
corves
covers
croves

CEORSW
cowers
crowes
escrow
scower
scowre
scrowe

CEORTU
couter
croute

CEORTV
corvet
covert
vector

CEOSST
cosset
costes
escots
estocs
scotes

CEOSSU
couses
cousse
scouse

CEOSTW
scowte»
stowce

CEPRSU
crupes
spruce

CERRSU
curers
curres
curser
recurs

CERRSY
cryers
scryer

CERRTU
curret
curter
ructer

CERSSU
cruses
curses
cusser
sucres

CERSTU
cruets
cruset
cruste
curets
curset
curste
curtes
Custer
cuters
eructs
rectus
recuts
truces

CESTTU
cutest
cuttes
tucets

CGGLOY
cloggy
coggly

CGIINT
citing
ticing

CGILNY
clingy
clying
glycin

CGIMNO
coming
gnomic

CGINRU
cruing
curing

CHIILT
litchi
lithic

CHIKRS
chirks
kirsch

CHIKST
kitsch
schtik
shtick
thicks

CHIMRS
chirms
chrism
smirch

CHINOP
chopin
phonic

CHINRU
unrich
urchin

CHINST
chints
snitch

CHIORS
choirs
ichors
orchis

CHIPSY
physic
scyphi

CHIPTY
pitchy
Pythic

CHIRST
chirts
Christ
criths
richts
strich

CHISTU
cu sith
schuit

CHLOOT
Clotho
coolth

CHOSTU
chouts
schout
scouth

CHOTUY
couthy
touchy

CIINOR
ironic
oniric

CIINRT
citrin
nitric

CIKNSU
suck-in
unsick

CILNOU
ulicon
uncoil

CILOTU
coutil
toluic

CIMOTY
comity
myotic

CIMPRS
crimps»
scrimp

CINORT
citron
cornit
cortin

CINOST
tocsin
tonics

CIORSU
crious
curios

CIPRST
cripts
script

CIPRSY
crispy
cypris

CIRSTU
citrus
cruits
rictus
rustic

CKRSTU
struck
trucks

CLNOSU
clonus
consul

CLOSTU
clouts
locust

CMPRSU
crumps
scrump

CNOOST
contos
nostoc
oncost

CNOOTY
coonty
tycoon

CNOSTU
counts
Tucson
uncost

CNRSTU
crunts
scrunt

COOPRS
croops
scroop

COPRSU
corpus
croups

CORRSU
cruors
cursor

COSSTU
costus
custos
scouts

CRSSUU
cursus
ruscus

CRSTUY
crusty
curtsy

DDDEIL
diddle
lidded

DDDEIR
didder
ridded

DDDEOR
dodder
rodded

DDDERU
dudder
rudded

DDEEEM
deemed
meeded

DDEEER
deered
reeded

DDEEES
deesed
seeded

DDEEFL
delfed
feddle

DDEEFN
defend
fended

DDEEGL
gelded
ledged

DDEEGR
dredge
greded

DDEEIN
deined
denied
indeed

DDEEIR
deider
deride
diedre

DDEEIT
dieted
edited

DDEELM
meddle
melded

DDEELP
peddle
pleded

DDEELR
ledder
leddre
reddle

DDEELU
delude
dueled»
eluded

DDEELW
dweled
welded

DDEENR
derned
redden
rended

DDEENT
dented
tended

DDEENU
denude
dudeen
Dundee
endued

DDEENW
wedden
wended

DDEEPR
dreped
pedder

DDEERR
Derdre
redder

DDEERV
derved
dreved
vedder

DDEERY
eddyre
yedder

DDEFNU
defund
funded
unfeed

DDEFOR
fodder
forded

DDEGIL
gilded
glided

DDEGIN
dindge
dinged
gnided
nidged

DDEGIR
dirged
girded
grided
ridged

DDEGIU
guided
iudged

DDEGLO
golded
lodged

DDEGLU
guddle
ludged

DDEGNU
dudgen
nudged

DDEGRU
drudge
rudged

DDEHIN
hidden
hinded

DDEHIS
dished
eddish

DDEIKN
dinked
kidden
kinded

DDEILN
dindle
niddle

DDEILO
dildoe
doiled

DDEILR
dirled
lidder
riddel
riddle

DDEILW
dwilde
widdle
wilded

DDEIMN
midden
minded

DDEIMS
desmid
dismed
middes

DDEINR
nidder
ridden
rinded

DDEINT
dinted
tinded

DDEINW
dwined
winded

DDEIOV
devoid
voided

DDEIPR
driped
prided

DDEIRT
dirted
drited
teddir
tidder

DDELOP
plodde
poddle

DDELOT
dolted
toddle

DDELPU
dupled
puddel
puddle

DDEMOO
doomed
mooded

DDEMOR
dromed
modder

DDENNO
donned
nodden

DDENOR
droned
nodder
rodden
ronded

DDENOS
sodden
sonded

DDENOW
downed
wodden
wonded

DDENRU
dunder
durned
rudden

DDEORS
dorsed
roddes
sodder

DDEORT
dorted
droted
todder

DDEORW
wodder
worded

DDERSU
dursed»
sudder
surded
udders

DEEEFR
feeder
feered
reefed

DEEEHT
heeted
teheed

DEEEJR
jeered
jereed

DEEEKL
keeled
leeked

DEEELN
leened
needle
neeled

DEEELR
eelder
eldere
leeder
leered
reeled

DEEELS
deeles
leedes
leesed
seeled

DEEELT
delete
leeted
teedle
teeled

DEEELV
devele
leveed

DEEEMR
deemer
dreeme
meeder
meered»
redeem
reemed
remede

DEEEMS
deemes
meedes
meesed
seemed

DEEENP
deepen
neeped
peened
penede

DEEENR
endeer
needer
neered
reeden

DEEENS
deenes
neesed

DEEENV
evened
vendee

DEEEPR
deeper
peered
reeped

DEEERR
deerer
reeder

DEEERS
reedes
reesed
reseed
seeder

DEEERT
reeted
teeder
teered

DEEERV
reeved
veered

DEEFIR
defier
Ferdie

DEEFLW
flewed
welfed

DEEFLX
deflex
flexed

DEEFNR
fender
ferned
freend

DEEFRS
defers
fersed

DEEGGL
gledge
legged

DEEGIN
deeing
deigne
dingee
inedge

DEEGLN
glened
legend
lenged

DEEGLR
gelder
ledger
redleg

DEEGLS
gledes
gleeds
ledges
sledge

DEEGMR
degerm
germed
merged

DEEGNR
denger»
gender
gendre
gerned
grened

DEEGNU
dengue
unedge

DEEGRS
edgers
gredes
greeds
gresed

DEEGST
gested
tedges

DEEHNR
enherd
herden

DEEHRS
heders
hersed
sheder

DEEIKR
keired
reiked

DEEILR
eilder
leired
relide
relied

DEEILS
diesel
ediles
elides
sedile
seiled

DEEILT
delite
elited
teiled

DEEILV
deevil
levied
veiled

DEEIMS
demies
demise
Medise

DEEIMT
itemed
medite

DEEINP
neiped
penide

DEEINR
denier
diener
neider
neired
nereid
reined
renied

DEEINS
deines
denies
Denise
neised
seined

DEEINT
detein
eident
endite

DEEINV
devine
endive
envied
veined

DEEIPR
peired
perdie

DEEIPS
espied
peised
seiped

DEEIRS
deries
desire
eiders
reised»
reside

DEEIRT
dieter
reedit
retied
teired
tiered

DEEIRV
derive
redive
reived
revied
rieved

DEEIRW
dewier
weired

DEEISS
dieses
seised

DEEIST
isteed
teised

DEEISV
devise
sieved
viseed

DEELMR
lermed
melder
merled
red elm

DEELMW
mewled
welmed

DEELMY
medley
yelmed

DEELNP
pendel
pendle
plened

DEELNR
eldern»

eldren
lender
lerned
relend

DEELNS
lendes
lensed
sendle

DEELNT
dentel
Lented
tendle

DEELPR
pedler
perled

DEELPS
pledes
plesed
sedlep
sleped
speled

DEELPT
pelted
pleted

DEELPY
deeply
pleyed
yelped

DEELRS
elders
red els

DEELRU
dueler
eluder

DEELRW
reweld
rewled
welder
werdle
wereld
werlde

DEELRY
dreely
yelder

DEELSS
lessed
sledes
sleeds

DEELST
eldest
lested
steeld
steled

DEELSW
dewles
dweles
slewed
swelde
sweled
weldes

DEELTT
ettled
letted

DEELTU
delute
eluted
teledu

DEELTW
dwelte
lewted
telwed
welted

DEEMNR
mender
red men
remend

DEEMNT
dement
mented

DEEMOT
demote
emoted

DEEMRS
mersed
smered

DEEMRU
demure
emured»

remued

DEEMSS
demess
messed

DEEMST
stemed
temsed

DEENOS
donees
enosed

DEENPR
prened
repend

DEENRR
derner
render
rendre

DEENRS
deners
denser
dreens
enders
rensed
resend
sender
sendre

DEENRT
denter
rented
retend
tender
tendre
terned
trende

DEENRU
enduer
endure
enured
undere

DEENRV
Denver
nerved
vender

DEENRW
rewden
rewend

DEENSS
denses
nessed
sensed

DEENST
dentes
desent
nested
sedent
sendet
sented
steden
teends
tensed

DEENSU
endues
ensued

DEENTT
detent
netted
tented

DEENTX
dentex
extend

DEENUV
vendue
venued

DEEOPS
depose
epodes
speedo

DEEPPR
depper
repped

DEEPRS
dreeps
drepes
espred
peders
predes
presed
speder»

spered
spreed
sprede

DEEPRU
depure
perdue
puered
pureed

DEEPST
pested
speted
steped

DEERRW
redrew
werred

DEERST
desert
dester
deters
rested
stered
teders

DEERSV
dreves
served
versed

DEERSW
ewders
reweds
swerde
weders
werdes
wersed

DEERTT
detter
retted

DEERTU
deruet
reuted
tedure

DEERTV
verdet
verted

DEERTW
dew-ret
trewed

DEESSS
desses
sessed

DEESSW
dewess
swedes

DEESTT
detest
dettes
tested

DEESTV
devest
vested

DEESTW
stewed
tweeds
wedset
wested

DEFFIR
differ
riffed

DEFFLU
duffel
duffle
luffed

DEFFRU
duffer
ruffed

DEFGIT
fidget
gifted

DEFGLO
Geldof
golfed

DEFGOR
forged
red fog

DEFILO
defoil»

foiled
folied

DEFILR
flired
rifled

DEFILT
flited
lifted
tifled

DEFINR
finder
friend
redfin
refind

DEFIST
fisted
sifted

DEFLNO
enfold
folden
fondle

DEFLOR
flored
folder
fordel
refold

DEFLOU
defoul
fouled

DEFLOW
deflow
flowed
fowled
wolfed

DEFLRU
fulder
furdel
furdle
furled

DEFLUX
deflux
fluxed

DEFMOR
deform
formed

DEFNOR
fonder
Fronde

DEFNRU
funder
refund
underf

DEFORT
forted
froted

DEFRRU
furder
furred

DEFRTU
dufter
turfed

DEGGIL
diggle
ligged

DEGGIN
edging
gnidge
nigged

DEGGIR
digger
girged
rigged

DEGGLO
dogleg
logged

DEGGOR
dogger
gorged
groged
rogged

DEGGRU
drugge
grudge
gurged
rugged

DEGHIN
heding
hinged

DEGIKN
deking
kinged

DEGILM
glimed
midleg
milged

DEGILN
deling
dingle
elding
engild
gilden
i-lengd
ingled
lindge
linged

DEGILO
Goidel
goldie

DEGILR
gilder
girdle
girled
glider
lidger
regild
ridgel

DEGILS
glides
glised

DEGIMN
deming
imengd
mengid
mingde
minged

DEGINN
ending
ginned
gniden

DEGINP
deping
pinged

DEGINR
dering
dinger
dreign
dringe
engird
erding
girned
grinde
reding
rigned
rindge
ringed

DEGINS
deigns
design
dinges
gnides
nidges
sdeign
seding
signed
sindge
singed
snidge

DEGINT
nidget
teding
tinged

DEGINW
dewing
weding
widgen
winged

DEGINY
dingey
dyeing

DEGIRR
girder
ridger

DEGIRS
dirges
girsed
grides»

grised
ridges

DEGIST
digest
gisted

DEGISU
guides
guised
iudges
usidge

DEGLNO
engold
golden
longed

DEGLNU
gulden
lunged
nudgel

DEGLOR
glored
golder
lodger

DEGLOS
glodes
glosed
lodges
slodge

DEGLOT
gloted
godlet

DEGLSU
ludges
sludge

DEGMRU
grumed
red gum

DEGMSU
degums
mudges
smudge

DEGNRU
dunger
durgen»

gerund
nudger

DEGNSU
nudges
snudge

DEGOOR
goorde
roodge
rooged

DEGOPR
groped
porged

DEGORR
droger
gorred

DEGORS
gorsed
grosed
sodger

DEGORU
drogue
gourde
rogued
rouged

DEGOST
godets
stodge

DEGRSU
grused
rudges
surged

DEGRTU
rudget
trudge

DEGSTU
degust
gusted

DEHILS
heilds
shield

DEHILT
hilted»

lithed

DEHIMR
dirhem
rhimed

DEHINO
hoiden
hoined
honied

DEHINS
inshed
shined

DEHIRS
disher
hersid
hiders
shider
shired

DEHISS
dishes
hissed

DEHISW
dewish
wished

DEHITW
whited
withed

DEHLOS
dholes
holdes
loshed
sholed

DEHLOW
howled
wholed

DEHLRU
hurdle
hurled

DEHMOT
method
mothed

DEHNOR
dehorn»

hondre
horned

DEHNOY
hoyden
hoyned

DEHNRU
hurden
hurned
unherd

DEHORS
dehors
hordes
horsed
reshod
Rhodes
shoder
shored

DEHORT
dehort
redhot

DEHOST
hosted
toshed

DEHOSW
howsed
showed

DEIINT
indite
tineid

DEIIRS
irides
irised

DEIKLN
denkli
inkled
kindel
kindle
linked

DEIKLS
delisk
kidels
silked
sliked

DEIKNR
dinker
dirken
drinke
rinked

DEIKNT
knited
tinked

DEIKNZ
zendik
zinked

DEIKRS
dikers
risked
skired

DEIKSW
swiked
wisked

DEILLT
lilted
tilled

DEILMN
limned
milden
Mindel

DEILMP
dimple
limped

DEILMR
midler
milder
mirled

DEILMS
misled
slimed
smiled

DEILMW
mildew
mwiled

DEILNN
dinnel
dinnle
linden»
linned

DEILNO
indole
Leonid
loined

DEILNR
linder
nirled

DEILNS
Densil
eldins
sindel
sindle

DEILNT
dentil
tindle

DEILNW
wilned
windle

DEILOP
diploe
dipole
peloid

DEILOR
droile
roiled

DEILOS
oldies
siloed
soiled
solide

DEILOT
dolite
idolet
toiled

DEILOV
olived
violed

DEILPR
lirped
pirled
plider
ripled

DEILPS
diples
dispel
lipsed
lisped
plides
plised
sliped
spilde
spiled

DEILPT
plited
tipled

DEILRS
idlers
reslid
ridels
slider
slidre

DEILRT
tirdel
tirled
tridel

DEILST
delits
destil
listed
slited
stiled
tildes

DEILSV
devils
slived

DEILTT
litted
tilted
titled

DEILWY
dewily
widely
wieldy

DEIMMN
dimmen
nimmed

DEIMMR
dimmer
immerd
rimmed

DEIMMS
Medism
simmed

DEIMNN
enmind
minned

DEIMNO
domine
monied

DEIMNP
impend
nimped

DEIMNR
minder
remind

DEIMOR
dormie
moider
moired

DEIMRS
dermis
dimers

DEIMRT
mitred
trimed

DEIMSS
deisms
demiss
dismes
missed

DEIMST
demist
demits
misted
smited
stimed

DEINNS
Dennis
sinned

DEINNT
dentin
indent
intend
tinned

DEINOP
opined
pioned

DEINOR
dinero
inrode
iorden
ironed
roined

DEINOS
donsie
Edison
noised
onside

DEINOT
ditone
intoed
tonied

DEINPR
pinder
prined

DEINPS
pendis
piends
pinsed
sniped
spined

DEINRS
diners
dreins
riends
rindes
rinsed
sinder
sindre
snider

DEINRT
dirten
dreint
rident
tinder»
trined

DEINRU
inured
ruined
urined

DEINRV
driven
vrined

DEINRW
rewind
winder
wrined

DEINST
destin
dintes
snited
teinds

DEINSU
indues
nudies
sinued
suiden
undies

DEINSV
devins
snived
vendis

DEINSW
dwines
widens
winsed

DEINTU
dunite
united
untied

DEIOPR
dopier
period

DEIOPS
episod
poised

DEIOPT
pioted»
podite

DEIORS
dories
dorise
soired

DEIORT
dotier
editor
rioted
triode

DEIORV
devoir
voider

DEIOST
todies
toised

DEIPPR
deppir
dipper
ripped

DEIPRS
dreips
dripes
prides
prised
redips
risped
spider
spired

DEIPRT
dipter
trepid
triped

DEIPSS
pissed
speids
spides

DEIRRS
derris
driers
reirds
riders
sirred

DEIRST
direst
disert
dister
diters
driest
drites
risted
stired
stride
stried
trised

DEIRSV
divers
drives

DEIRTU
reduit
ruited

DEIRTV
divert
trived
verdit

DEISST
deists
desist
sisted
tissed

DEISSU
disuse
issued

DEISTU
duties
suited

DEISTV
divest
divets
stived
Vedist

DEISTW
widest
wisted

DEITTW
dewitt
twited
witted

DEKLRU
kurled
lurked

DEKNRU
druken
Dunker
runked

DEKRUY
dukery
duyker

DEKSTU
skuted
tusked

DELLNU
dullen
nulled

DELLOR
doller
rolled

DELMNO
dolmen
lemond

DELMOR
medlor
molder
remold

DELMOS
models
seldom
slomed

DELMOU
module
mouled

DELMOY
melody
moyled

DELMPU
dumple
lumped
plumed

DELNOR
dronel»
rondel
rondle

DELNOU
louden
louned
nodule

DELNOW
lowned
new-old

DELNRU
lunder
lurden
lurned
nurled
rundel
rundle

DELNTU
duntle
lunted
unteld

DELOOP
looped
poodle
pooled

DELOOR
loored
rooled

DELOOS
deloos
loosed
oodles
soloed
soodle
sooled

DELOOT
looted
tooled

DELOPR
podler
polder
plored
proled

DELOPS
podels»
podles
sloped
spoled

DELOPU
louped
pouled

DELOPW
lowped
plowed
powled

DELOPY
deploy
ployed
podley

DELORS
dolers
dorsel
droles
loders
olders
resold
slored
solder
soreld

DELORT
retold
troled

DELORU
doleur
louder
lourde
loured
rouled

DELORW
red owl
rowled
weldor
wordle
worled

DELORY
royled
yodler

DELOSS
dossel
lossed»
soldes

DELOST
dotels
oldest
sloted
sodlet
stoled

DELOSU
loused
souled

DELOSW
dowels
dowles
lowsed
slowed
sowled

DELOTT
dottel
dottle
lotted

DELOTU
louted
outled
touled

DELPRU
drupel
purled

DELPSU
duples
pulsed
pusled
sulped
supled

DELSSU
dulses
dussel

DELSTU
lusted
sluted
tudels
tudles

DEMNOR
modern
modren»
morned
rodmen

DEMOOR
doomer
droome
mooder
moored
redoom
roomed

DEMORS
dromes
Morsed
smored

DEMORT
Dermot
morted
tromed

DEMOST
demots
modest

DEMOSU
dumose
moused
odeums
soumed

DEMRRU
murder
murdre
murred

DEMSTU
dumest
musted

DENNOT
ontend
tendon

DENNRU
dunner
runned
undern

DENOOS
nodose
noosed
odeons
soonde

DENOOW
wooden
woonde

DENOPR
Pernod
ponder
pondre
proned

DENORR
droner
ronder

DENORS
doners
drones
drosen
endors
orsden
rondes
snored
sonder
sondre
sorned

DENORT
dronet
norted
rodent

DENORU
enduro
undoer

DENORW
downer
drowen
drowne
owndER
wonder
worned

DENORY
royned
yonder

DENOSS
endoss
sondes

DENOST
Donets
Ostend»

stoned
tonsed

DENOSU
noused
undose

DENOSW
downes
endows
snowed
sownde
swoned
wondes

DENOUW
unowed
wounde

DENPRU
pruned
punder
pundre

DENPSU
punsed
send up
spuned
unsped
upends
upsend

DENPTU
pudent
pundet
punted

DENRSU
nursed
rudens
sunder
unders

DENRTU
deturn
dunter
nurted
retund
rudent
runted
tunder
turned

DENRTY
rynted
trendy

DENSTY
syndet
tyndes

DENSUW
sundew
wundes

DEOOPR
poored
rooped

DEOORV
overdo
rooved

DEOPRS
dopers
prosed
spored

DEOPRT
deport
ported
proted
redtop

DEOPRU
droupe
pouder
poudre
poured
rouped

DEOPRW
drowpe
powder
powred
prowde

DEOPSS
possed
spodes

DEOPST
depost
depots
despot
posted
stoped

DEOPSU
poused
pseudo
souped

DEORRS
dorser
orders

DEORRT
detort
dorter
droter
red rot
retrod

DEORRU
dourer
ordure

DEORRW
reword
worder
worred

DEORSS
dorses
dosser
rossed
sordes

DEORST
Dorset
doters
drotes
rosted
sordet
sorted
stored
strode
torsed
trodes

DEORSU
douser
drouse
roused
soured
uredos

DEORSW
dowser
drowse»

rowsed
sowred
sworde
wordes
worsed

DEORTT
detort
dotter
rotted
troted

DEORTU
derout
detour
douter
outred
redout
routed
toured

DEORTW
dew-rot
dowter
rowted
towred
trowed
worted

DEOSSU
douses
soused

DEOSSW
dowses
sowsed

DEOSTU
douset
douste
doutes
ousted
souted
toused

DEOSTW
dowset
stowed
towsed
wodset

DEPRRU
pruder
purred

DEPRSU
drupes
dupers
perdus
prudes
pursed
spured

DEPSTU
sputed
stuped

DERSSU
druses
duress
durses

DERSTU
deturs
durets
duster
redust
restud
rudest
rusted
strude

DGHINY
dinghy
hyding

DGIINN
dining
indign
niding

DGIINR
ingird
Ingrid
riding

DGINNO
noding
onding

DGINOP
doping
pongid

DGINOR
doring
roding

DGINOS
doings
dosing

DGINOW
dowing
Godwin

DGINRU
during
ungird

DGINSU
dingus
gundis
undigs

DGNOSU
sundog
sungod
ungods

DHIOST
dhotis
dotish

DHNOSU
hounds
unshod

DIIMOS
idioms
iodism

DIIOST
idiots
Idoist

DILMOU
dolium
idolum
moduli

DILOSS
dossil
sloids
solids

DIMOSU
modius
odiums
sodium

DINOPU
dupion
unipod

DINOSW
disown
indows

DINPTU
pundit
undipt

DINRST
strind
trinds

DINTUY
nudity
untidy

DIOOSU
iodous
odious

DIOPRT
torpid
tripod

DLLORY
drolly
lordly

DLMOSU
moulds
smould

DLNOSU
lounds
unsold

DMNOSU
mounds
osmund

DNORTU
rotund
untrod

DNRSTU
drunts
strund

EEEFLR
feeler»

refeel
releef

EEEGNR
en-gree
greene
neeger
reenge
regnee
renege

EEEHLR
heeler
reheel

EEEHST
seethe
tehees

EEEILR
eelier
Leerie

EEEKLR
keeler
releke

EEEKRS
kreese
reekes
reseek
seeker

EEELNR
elerne
elrene
leerne

EEELNS
neeles
seenle
Selene

EEELNV
eleven
enleve

EEELPR
leeper
leepre
lepere
peeler
repele

EEELRR
leerer
reeler

EEELRS
leeres
sleere

EEELRV
levere
revele

EEELSS
lessee
seeles

EEELST
eelets
eel set

EEELSV
leeves
levees
sleeve

EEEMRS
emeers
seemer

EEEMRT
meeter
remeet
teemer

EEEMSS
emeses
semees
semese

EEEMST
esteem
mestee
steeme
teemes

EEENRS
neeres
reseen
serene

EEENRT
entree
eterne
retene»

teener

EEENRV
enerve
evener
revene
veneer

EEENSS
Essene
neeses
seenes

EEENST
steene
teenes

EEENSZ
neezes
sneeze

EEEPRV
peever
preeve

EEERRT
reeter
retree

EEERRV
reever
revere
veerer

EEERSV
reeves
severe

EEERTT
teeter
terete
treete

EEESTT
settee
testee

EEESTV
steeve
vestee

EEFILN
enfile
feline

EEFILR
liefer
refile
relief

EEFINR
enfire
ferine
fineer
infere
neifer
refine

EEFIRS
feries
fersie
fieres

EEFLLR
feller
refell

EEFLRS
fleers
refels
selfer

EEFLRT
felter
refelt

EEFLRU
ferule
refuel

EEFRRT
ferret
ferter
refert

EEFRST
erfest
ferets
fertes
fester
freest
freets
refets

EEFRTT
fetter
frette

EEFRTU
feture
feuter
feutre
refute

EEFSTT
eftest
fettes

EEFSTW
fewest
fewtes
weftes

EEGGIR
eggier
greige
Reggie

EEGGLR
eggler
legger

EEGILN
eeling
elinge
iengle
ilenge
lignee

EEGIMR
emigre
regime

EEGINR
greine
ineger
ingere
niegre
reeing
reigne
reinge
riegne

EEGINS
genies
gesine
seeing

EEGINV
eveing
gineve

EEGIRS
regies
seiger
sieger

EEGIRV
grieve
regive

EEGLMN
glemen
mengel
mengle

EEGLMU
emulge
legume

EEGLNR
gernel
lenger

EEGLNS
Engels
engles
gleens
sengle

EEGLNU
englue
lungee
unglee

EEGNRT
gerent
greten
regent

EEGNRY
energy
greeny

EEGNST
genets
gentes

EEGRRT
gerret
gerter
regret

EEGRSS
egress
greses

EEGRST
egrets
gester
greest
greets
gretes
regest

EEGRSV
greves
verges

EEGRTT
getter
treget

EEHINR
herein
inhere

EEHIRS
heiers
heires
hereis
heries
sheire
sherie
shiere

EEHIRT
either
heriet
hetire

EEHLMT
helmet
methel

EEHLRT
helter
lether
rethel
therle

EEHLSV
helves
shelve

EEHLSW
hewels
shewel
Welshe
wheels

EEHMRS
Hermes
mesher

EEHMRT
hermet
themer
therme

EEHMST
meeths
methes
smeeth
smethe
themes

EEHNPS
phenes
sephen
sphene

EEHNRT
henter
nether
therne
threne

EEHNSS
neshes
sheens
sneesh

EEHPRS
herpes
Hesper
pheers
pheres
sherpe
sphere

EEHPRT
pether
threep
threpe

EEHRSS
ershes
sheers

EEHRST
Esther
ethers
hertes
Hester»
hestre
heters
sether
sherte
sheter
sthere
threes

EEHRSW
hewers
shewer
shewre
shrewe
wheres

EEHRSY
heresy
heyers
heyres

EEHRTT
hetter
tether

EEHSST
heests
sheets
shetes
theses

EEHSTW
thewes
wheest

EEILLS
eisell
Leslie

EEILNR
lierne
reline

EEILNS
enisle
ensile
nelies
seinel
seinle
senile
silene

EEILPT
pelite
pielet

EEILRS
relies
resile
selier

EEILRV
eviler
levier
liever
livere
relive
reveil
revile
rivele

EEILSS
eisels
eissel
esiles
seseli

EEILSV
levies
lieves
sevile
sleive
veiles

EEILSX
exiles
ilexes

EEIMNS
inseem
meines

EEIMNT
emetin
neemit

EEIMPR
empire
epimer

EEIMRS
merise
misere
remise

EEIMRT
emerit
ermite
mereit
merite»
metier
reemit
retime
tremie

EEIMSS
emesis
Messie
missee
semies

EEIMST
mesite
Semite

EEINPR
enripe
repine

EEINPS
penies
spinee

EEINRS
neires
nieres
nieser
reines
reinse
resine
seiner
serein
serine
sirene

EEINRT
entier
entire
intere
nerite
renite
retein
retine
treine
triene

EEINRV
enrive
envier
neiver
veiner
venire
Verein

EEINSS
neises
nieses
Nessie
seisen
senies

EEINST
entise
setine
tenise

EEINSV
envies
neives
nieves
Venise
veines

EEIPRS
espeir
espier
espire
peirse
peries
persie
preise
repise
speire
spiere

EEIRRT
etrier
reiter
reteir
retier
retire
terrie
tierer

EEIRRV
reiver
reveir
riever
rivere
verier
verrie

EEIRSS
eiress
reises
seiser
series

EEIRST
Eister
iester
reites
resite
reties
setier
steire
sterie
stiere
teiser

EEIRSV
reives
revies
revise
rieves
siever

EEIRVW
review
viewer

EEISST
teises
Tessie

EEISSV
essive
sieves

EEISTV
evites
stieve

EEJKRR
jerker
rejerk

EEKLRS
kreles
rekels
rekles

EEKLRT
kelter
kertel
kertle

EEKLST
kleets
skelet
skelte

EEKLSY
skeely
sleeky

EEKNRS
kernes
skreen
skrene

EEKPRU
Keuper
peruke

EEKQSU
queeks
squeek
squeke

EEKRST
sterke
streek
streke
tereks

EELLRS
ellers
resell
seller

EELLRT
retell
teller

EELMPT
pelmet
temple

EELMRT
melter
mertle
remelt
tremel
tremle

EELMST
metels
telesm

EELMTT
meltet
mettel
mettle

EELNNT
lennet
lenten
tennel
tennle

EELNPS
pensel
pleens
plenes
spleen
splene

EELNRS
lernes
renels

EELNRT
relent
trenle

EELNSS
elsens
lenses
lessen
nessel

EELNSV
nevels
snevel

EELPRS
lepers
lepres
perles
persel
persle
pleser
presle
repels
reples
sleper
speler
sperel

EELPRT
pelter
peltre
petrel
pleter

EELPRY
pleyer
yelper

EELPSS
pessel
pleses
sleeps
slepes
speels
speles

EELPST
pestel
pestle
pleets
pletes
spleet
steple

EELQSU
queels
queles
sequel
squeel
squele

EELRSS
lesser
sleers

EELRST
estler
Lester
letres
relets
restle
setler
streel
telers
treles
tresle

EELRSV
elvers
levers
revels
selver

EELRTT
ettler
letter

EELRTW
lewter
lewtre
welter
weltre

EELSSS
essels
lesses
sessle

EELSST
sleets
steels
steles
tessel

EELSSV
selves
vessel

EELSSW
sewels
slewse
sweels
wessel

EELSTT
ettles
lettes
settel
settle
tetels

EELSTV
elvets
levets
svelte

EELSTW
lewest
swelte
telwes
tewels
tweels
westle

EELSTY
sleety
steely

EELTVW
twelve
velwet
welvet

EEMMST
emmets
stemme
Temmes

EEMNSS
menses
mesnes
messen
semens

EEMNSU
enmuse
neumes
unseem

EEMNTU
menuet
unmeet

EEMORT
emoter
meteor
remote

EEMPRS
preems
premes
semper
sempre

EEMPRT
temper
tempre
trempe

EEMRRT
metrer
termer

EEMRSS
merses
messer
smeers
smeres

EEMRST
mester
meters
metres
restem
smerte
streem
streme
temser
termes

EEMRSU
emures»
remues
resume
reumes

EEMSST
messet
mestes
steems
stemes
temses
tmeses

EENNRT
rennet
tenner

EENNST
ennets
sennet
tennes

EENOPR
opener
perone
reopen
repone

EENORS
onrese
rosene
serone

EENPRS
nepers
preens
spener

EENPRT
penter
preent
prente
repent
terpen

EENPSS
pessen
spenes
spense

EENPSY
penyes
peynes
Speyne
yepsen»
yespen

EENQSU
queens
quenes
squene

EENRRT
renter
terren

EENRSS
senser
sneers

EENRST
enters
entres
Ernest
nertes
nester
renets
rentes
resent
sentre
serten
streen
strene
tenser
ternes

EENRSU
enures
ensuer
ensure

EENRSV
nerves
serven
Severn
snever

EENRSY
reneys
sneery

EENRTT
netter
retent
tenter

EENRTU
neuter
neutre»
retune
teneur
tenure
tureen
untree

EENRTV
revent
venter
ventre

EENRTX
extern
nexter

EENSSS
nesses
senses
sneses

EENSST
nesset
netest
sneest
steens
tenses

EENSTT
entest
netest
stente
tenets
tentes

EENSTU
neuest
tenues

EENSTV
envest
events
steven
ventes

EENSTY
steyne
teensy

EEOPST
poeste
postee
topees

EEORSS
Eroses
sorees

EEORST
Erotes
oestre
steore
stereo

EEPRRS
perres
sperre

EEPRSS
perses
preses
presse
serpes
speers
speres
sperse
sprees

EEPRST
erepts
peerts
pertes
pester
pestre
peters
petres
preest
preset
preste
pteres
repets
septer
septre
sperte
spreet
sprete

EEPRSU
persue
peruse
purees
rupees

EEPRSW
prewse
sperwe
spewer

EEPSSS
pesses
sepses

EEQRSU
queers
queres
resque
squere

EEQRSW
qweers
qweres
sqwere

EEQSTU
queest
queste

EERRST
erters
rester
sterre
terres
terser

EERRSV
revers
server
verser

EERRTT
retret
retter
terret
terter
tertre

EERRTV
revert
vreter

EERRVY
revery
verrey

EERSST
esters
estres
reests
resets
restes
serest
sertes»

sester
steers
steres
strees
terses

EERSSU
reuses
ureses

EERSSV
serves
severs
Sevres
verses
versse

EERSTT
retest
setter
street
strete
tester
teters
treets

EERSTU
retuse
steure
suerte
surete
Surete

EERSTV
everts
revest
revets
servet
stever
treves
verset
verste
vester

EERSTW
rewets
sewrte
sewter
stewer
strewe
sweert
tewers
tweers
werste»

wester

EERSTX
exerts
exsert
exters

EERSTY
eyster
reesty
steery
steyre
yester
yeters

EESSTT
sestet
settes
teests
testes
tsetse

EESTTU
suttee
tutees

EFFGIR
giffer
griffe

EFFIRS
eriffs
riffes
seriff

EFFLRU
luffer
ruffle

EFFRSU
ruffes
suffer

EFFRTU
ruffet
tuffer

EFGINR
fering
finger
fringe

EFGLNU
engulf»

flunge

EFHIRS
fisher
sherif
shrife

EFHLSY
fleshy
shelfy

EFHORT
forthe
fother
frothe

EFIKNR
erfkin
ferkin
knifer

EFILLR
filler
refill

EFILNO
enfoil
olefin

EFILNS
elfins
filsen
filsne
snifle

EFILNT
finlet
infelt

EFILNY
finely
lenify

EFILOR
foiler
folier

EFILOS
filose
folies

EFILRS
filers
fleirs»

fliers
flires
frisel
frisle
lifers
refils
rifels
rifles

EFILRT
filter
flirte
fliter
lifter
reflit
relift
trifle

EFILST
filets
fistle
flites
itself
stifle
tifles

EFINST
feints
festin
finest
infest

EFIORX
Fire Ox
foxier
orifex

EFIRRS
Ferris
friers

EFIRST
feirst
firste
fister
freist
freits
friste
refits
resift
rifest
sifter
strife

EFIRTT
fitter
titfer

EFIRTY
ferity
freity

EFLLOW
elf owl
fellow

EFLNTU
fluent
netful
unfelt

EFLORT
ferlot
floret
lofter
tolfre

EFLORU
fouler
furole

EFLORW
flower
fowler
reflow
wolfer

EFLOSU
flouse
foules

EFLOSW
flowes
flowse
fowels
fowles
wolfes

EFLRTU
fluter
furlet
lufter
turfel

EFMORR
former
morfer
reform

EFNOST
feston
fosten
soften
softne
stofne

EFNRTU
enturf
turfen

EFNSTU
funest
unfest

EFOORR
reroof
roofer

EFOORT
foetor
footer
refoot
tofore

EFOPRT
forpet
profet

EFORST
fetors
forest
forets
forset
forste
fortes
foster
fostre
froste
frotes
softer

EFOSTU
foetus
fouets

EFRRTU
returf
turfer

EFRSTU
festur
frutes
fuster»

stufer
turfes

EGGILN
gingle
liggen
niggle

EGGILR
ligger
riggle

EGGILT
giglet
ligget

EGGINR
gering
ginger
nigger

EGGLOR
logger
roggel
roggle

EGGLOT
goglet
logget
toggel
toggle

EGGLRU
gurgle
lugger
ruggle

EGGORT
gorget
togger

EGGRSU
gurges
rugges
sugger

EGGRTU
trugge
tugger

EGHHIT
eighth
height
thighe

EGHHSU
heughs
sheugh

EGHILN
heling
hengil
hingel
hingle

EGHINS
hinges
sheing

EGHINW
hewing
whinge

EGHLPU
Guelph
pleugh

EGHNOS
Goshen
Hogens

EGHNRU
hunger
rehung

EGIINT
ignite
tieing

EGIKLN
keling
kingle
leking

EGILLN
leglin
lingel
lingle

EGILLR
giller
grille

EGILMN
elming
leming
meling
mingel
mingle

EGILNN
ginnel
ginnle
lening

EGILNO
eloign
legion

EGILNP
leping
peling
pingle
pinleg

EGILNR
girnel
lering
linger
reling
ringel
ringle

EGILNS
elgins
elings
esling
Glenis
glinse
glisen
ingles
lesing
lignes
nigels
seling
singel
single
slinge

EGILNU
lueing
lungie

EGILNY
elying
eyling
leying

EGILNZ
zeling
zingel

EGILRS
girles»

girsle
Glires
grilse
grisel
grisle
ligers

EGILRT
gliter
regilt
riglet
trigle

EGILRU
gluier
guiler
ligure
uglier

EGILRZ
Grizel
grizle

EGILST
gilets
gleits
legist
legits
tigels

EGIMMR
gimmer
grimme
megrim

EGIMNR
erming
germin
megrin
mergin
mering
reming

EGIMNS
ingems
mesing
minges
seming

EGINNR
enring
erning
ginner
grinne»

rening
ringen

EGINNS
ensign
ginnes
nesing
sening

EGINNT
ginnet
tening

EGINOP
epigon
pigeon

EGINOR
eringo
groine
ignore
ingore
origen
region

EGINOS
gonies
soigne

EGINOT
ignote
toeing

EGINPP
Epping
peping
pigpen

EGINPR
gripen
pering
pinger
reping

EGINPS
genips
gipsen
pesing
pinges

EGINRR
erring
re-ring
ringer

EGINRS
girnes
greins
griens
grines
nigers
reigns
renigs
resign
re-sign
resing
rignes
ringes
sering
signer
singer

EGINRT
engirt
erting
ingert
tering
tinger

EGINRU
rueing
rugine

EGINRV
reving
vering
vigner

EGINRW
rewing
wering
winger
wringe

EGINSS
essign
gneiss
seings
sesing
singes

EGINST
engist
ginets
ingest
seting
signet
steing
stinge»

tesing
tinges

EGINSU
genius
sueing

EGINSW
sewing
swinge
wesing
wigens
winges

EGINTW
ewting
tewing
twinge
weting

EGIORS
orgies
origes

EGIOST
egoist
stogie

EGIPRS
gipser
gripes

EGIRRT
girter
griter
triger

EGIRST
gister
greist
greits
griest
griets
griste
grites
tegirs
tigers
tigres

EGIRSU
guiser
regius

EGIRSV
givers
grives
vergis
virges

EGLNOR
longer
relong

EGLNSU
gunsel
lunges
slunge

EGLNSY
Glenys
syngle

EGLNTU
englut
gluten
lugent
ungelt

EGLOPS
golpes
gospel

EGLORS
glores
gloser

EGLORT
gloter
grelot

EGLORV
glover
grovel

EGLOST
glotes
goslet

EGLRSU
gluers
gruels
grusle
Lugers

EGLRTU
gluter
gurlet

EGMNOR
germon
monger
morgen

EGMNOY
gemony
myogen

EGMNTU
Gnetum
nutmeg

EGNOOR
Oregon
orgone
oronge

EGNOOY
gooney
oogeny

EGNORT
getron
groten
tonger

EGNORY
eryngo
groyne

EGNOSS
gnoses
segnos
songes

EGNPRU
punger
repugn
repung

EGNPSU
punges
spunge
unpegs

EGNRTU
grunte
gunter
gurnet
urgent

EGOORV
groove»

overgo

EGOOST
gooste
gootes
stooge

EGOPRR
groper
porger

EGOPRS
gropes
porges
sporge

EGORRS
gorres
groser
rogers

EGORRW
grower
regrow

EGORSS
gorses
gorsse
groses
grosse
ogress
sogers

EGORST
ergots
gestor
goster
groset
groste
grotes
storge

EGORSU
grouse
orgues
rogues
rouges
rugose

EGORSY
gorsey
gyrose

EGPRRU
gruper
purger

EGPRSU
purges
spurge

EGRRSU
surger
urgers

EGSSTU
guests
gusset
gustes

EHHRST
herths
thresh

EHIIST
histie
Shiite

EHIKRS
hikers
shirke
shreik
shriek
shrike

EHILMU
helium
humile
humlie

EHILRS
elrish
erlish
hirsel
hirsle
lisher
relish
shirle

EHILRT
Hitler
lither
lithre
thirle
thrile

EHILST
hilest
hiltes
leiths
lithes
slithe

EHIMRT
hermit
mirthe
mither

EHIMST
meiths
theism
Themis
thimes

EHINOR
heroin
Hornie

EHINRS
hernis
hirens
renish
rheins
rhines
shiner
shrine

EHINRT
hinter
nither
thrine

EHINSS
shines
sneish

EHINST
sithen
snithe

EHINSW
newish
whines

EHIOPT
Ethiop
ophite

EHIPRS
hirpes»
perish
pheirs
reship
seriph

EHIRRS
errish
hirers

EHIRSS
hisser
rhesis
shiers
shires

EHIRST
hirste
Hister
rithes
shirte
sither
sithre
theirs
thirse

EHIRSV
hivers
shiver
shrive

EHIRSW
rewish
re-wish
rishew
wisher

EHIRTT
hitter
tither

EHIRTW
whiter
wither
writhe

EHISST
heists
shiest
shites
sieths
sithes
thesis

EHISTT
theist
tieths
tithes

EHISTW
swithe
tishew
wetish
whiste
whites
withes

EHITTW
tewhit
thwite
whitte

EHLNOP
holpen
phenol

EHLORT
herlot
thorle

EHLOSS
hosels
loshes
sholes

EHLOST
helots
holets
hostel
hostle
hotels
lothes
slothe
tholes

EHLOSU
houles
housel
housle
shoule

EHLOSV
hovels
sholve
shovel

EHLOSW
howles»
howsel
showel
showle
wholes

EHLOTW
howlet
thowel
thowle

EHLRSU
hurles
lusher
rushle

EHLRTU
hurlet
hurtel
hurtle
Luther

EHLSTU
hulets
hustle
sleuth

EHLSTW
lewths
slewth

EHLSTY
ethyls
lythes
shelty

EHMRSU
musher
rheums

EHMSTY
mythes
smythe
thymes

EHNORS
herons
horsen
rhones
shoren

EHNORT
hornet
northe
nother»
thoner
thorne
throne

EHNOSU
unhose
unshoe

EHNSTT
stenth
tenths

EHOPRT
pother
thorpe
thrope
trophe

EHORRS
horres
horser
shorer

EHORRT
horter
rethor
rhetor
rother

EHORST
hoster
hostre
others
shorte
throes
tosher

EHORSV
hovers
shover
shrove

EHORSW
howers
howres
shower
showre
shrowe
whores

EHORTT
hotter
tother

EHPRSU
pusher
uphers

EHPRSY
hypers
shyrpe
sphery

EHRRTU
hurter
ruther

EHRSSU
rhesus
rushes
russhe
ushers

EHRSTU
heurts
hurste
hurtes
reshut
rueths
rushet
ruthes
thurse

EHSSTU
shutes
tusseh

EHSSTY
shyest
sythes

EIILLN
liniel
nielli

EIILMS
milsie
simile

EIILNR
inlier
linier
nirlie

EIILNS
inisle
sileni

EIILRV
livier
virile

EIIMNT
imeint
intime

EIIMRR
mirier
rimier

EIINNT
intine
tinnie

EIINPR
pinier
pirnie

EIINPS
pinies
snipie
spinie

EIINPT
pinite
tiepin

EIINRT
inteir
intier
intire
tinier

EIINSS
niseis
seisin

EIINTV
invite
viniet
vinite

EIJNOR
joiner
rejoin

EIKLLR
killer
rekill

EIKLNR
Kilner»
linker
rinkle

EIKLNS
inkles
likens
linkes
silken
slinke

EIKLNW
welkin
winkle

EIKLRS
kirles
kreils
likers
rikels
skirle
skleir

EIKLRT
kilter
kirtel
kirtle

EIKLSY
kylies
skeily
ylikes

EIKMNS
mikens
misken

EIKMRS
kermis
krimes
mirkes
skirme
smirke

EIKNPR
perkin
pinker

EIKNPS
knipse
pekins
pinkes
spinke

EIKNRS
inkers
reinks
resink
sinker
skrine

EIKNRT
reknit
tinker

EIKNST
kenits
knites
nisket
stinke
tinkes

EIKPRS
pikers
preiks
prikes
spiker

EIKRSS
kersis
kisser
krises
rekiss
skiers
skires

EIKRST
kirset
kiters
skirte
steirk
streik
striek
stirke
strike
trikes

EIKRSV
kivers
skiver
vikers

EILLNO
lionel
niello

EILLNT
lentil»

lintel
lintle

EILLPT
liplet
pellit
pillet

EILLRS
reills
siller

EILLRT
retill
rillet
tiller
trille

EILLRW
rewill
willer

EILLST
listel
litles
stille
tilles

EILLTT
little
tillet

EILLVY
evilly
lively
vilely

EILMNN
enlimn
Millen

EILMNO
leimon
limone
moline
oilmen

EILMNR
limner
merlin
milner
remlin

EILMNS
limens
milnes
simnel

EILMNU
lumine
unlime

EILMOS
moiles
molies

EILMPR
limper
prelim
rimple

EILMPS
impels
simpel
simple

EILMRS
limers
merils
milers
rimels
smiler

EILMRT
mertil
milter
mirtel
mirtle
rimlet
trimle

EILMSS
missel
missle
slimes
smiles

EILMST
milets
miltes
mistel
mistle
smilet

EILMTT
meltit
mittle

EILNNT
linnet
tennil

EILNOS
eloins
esloin
insole
lesion
lionse
oleins
solein

EILNOT
entoil
lionet
Nilote

EILNPP
lippen
nipple

EILNPS
esplin
lipens
pensil
pleins
spinel
spline

EILNPT
niplet
pintel
pintle

EILNPU
line up
line-up
lupine
pinule
unpile
up-line

EILNRS
liners
nirles

EILNSS
elsins
lissen
silens

EILNST
enlist»

inlets
linets
lintes
listen
silent
slinte
snitel
snitle
tensil
tinsel

EILNSV
levins
livens
nevils
nivels
sliven
snivel
vilens

EILNSY
linsey
lysine

EILNTT
litten
nittle

EILNTU
luiten
lutein
lutine
untile

EILNTY
lenity
yetlin

EILNUV
unlive
unveil

EILOPS
pilose
polies
spoile

EILOPT
piolet
plotie
polite

EILORR
lorrie»

roiler

EILORS
elisor
eslior
loeris
lories
oilers
oriels
reoils
resoil
slorie
soiler

EILORT
loiter
toiler
triole

EILORV
lovier
oliver
violer

EILOST
isolet
stoile
toiles

EILOSV
olives
solive
violes
voiles

EILOTT
Lottie
toilet

EILOTV
olivet
violet

EILPPR
lipper
lippre
ripple

EILPPS
lippes
sipple

EILPPT
lippet»

tippel
tipple

EILPRS
lisper
perils
persil
pilers
pliers
priles

EILPRT
tipler
triple

EILPSS
lipses
lispes
pesils
pisles
plises
plisse
sleips
slipes
speils
spiels
spiles

EILPST
pistel
pistle
pitels
plites
spilte
spitel
spitle
splite
stepil
stipel
stiple
tiples

EILPSU
epulis
pileus
pulies

EILPTT
pittel
pittle
tiplet

EILPTU
plutei»

puteli

EILQRU
liquer
quiler

EILQSU
liques
quiles
quisle
squeil

EILRST
lister
listre
liters
litres
relist
ristle
steril
tilers
tirles
trelis
triels
triles

EILRSV
ervils
livers
livres
rivels
silver
sliver

EILRTT
litter
littre
tilter
titler

EILRVY
livery
livyer
verily

EILSST
islets
istles
lisste
listes
sistle
sliest
slites
steils»

stiels
stiles

EILSSV
slives
vessil

EILSTT
stilet
titles

EILSTV
levits
vilest
vilets

EILSTW
twiles
twisle
wiltes
wistle

EILSVW
swivel
swivle
wevils
wivels

EILSZZ
sizzle
zizels

EIMMRS
merism
Mermis
mimers
rimmes
rismme
simmer

EIMMRT
timmer
trimme

EIMNOR
merino
merion
monier

EIMNOS
eonism
monies
Simeon

EIMNPT
piment
pitmen

EIMNRT
minter
remint

EIMNRU
murein
murine
Nerium

EIMNSS
messin
missen

EIMNST
inmest
mintes
misten
nimest
smetin
smiten
tinesm

EIMNTU
minuet
minute
munite
mutine
untime

EIMNTY
enmity
ymeint

EIMORS
isomer
moires
rimose

EIMOST
moiste
moites
somite

EIMPRS
primes
simper

EIMPRT
impert
permit»

premit

EIMPRU
impure
umpire

EIMRRT
merrit
retrim
trimer

EIMRSS
misers
misser
remiss
rismes

EIMRST
ermits
merist
merits
mirets
mister
mistre
miters
mitres
Remist
remits
smiter
streim
strime
timers
timser
tremis
trimes

EIMRSV
verism
vermis

EIMSSS
misses
seisms

EIMSST
mestis
misset
mistes
smites
stimes
timses
tmesis

EINNPT
pinnet
tenpin

EINNRS
inners
renins
sinner

EINNRT
intern
rennit
rinnet
tinner

EINNST
sennit
sinnet
tennis
tinnes

EINNTT
intent
tinnet

EINOPR
opiner
orpine
pioner
poiner
proine
repoin

EINOPT
pointe
pontie

EINORR
ironer
Renoir
roiner

EINORS
noiser
nories
norise
nosier
rosine
senior
serion
snoire
soneri

EINORT
norite
orient
tonier

EINOSS
enosis
eosins
essoin
noesis
noises
nosies
ossein
sonsie

EINOST
ionets
Nesiot
notise
on-site
ostein
tonies

EINPRS
nipers
Pernis
piners
preins
prines
repins
ripens
sniper
sprein

EINPRT
nipter
pintre
prient
printe
pterin
terpin

EINPRU
punier
purine
unripe

EINPST
instep
nepits
pentis
ptisen
spinet

EINPSU
puisne
punise
supine

EINPSY
snipey
spiney

EINQSU
quines
quinse
sequin
sinque
squine

EINQTU
quinet
quinte

EINRRS
riners
rinser

EINRST
ernits
estrin
inrest
insert
inters
intres
nister
niters
nitres
re-tins
sinter
sniter
strein
strine
triens
trines
tserin

EINRSU
insure
inures
ruines
rusine
urines
ursine

EINRSV
nvreis
revins»

versin
viners
vrines

EINRSW
nwreis
winers
winser
wrines

EINRTT
nitter
tinter

EINRTU
triune
uniter
untire

EINRTV
invert
vinter
virent

EINRTW
twiner
winter

EINSST
insets
nisest
sients
snites
steins
stines
tsines

EINSTT
ettins
stinte
tintes

EINSTU
intuse
tenuis
unites
unties

EINSTV
invest
stevin
vinets
vitnes

EINSTW
stewin
twines
wisent
witnes

EINSTY
inyets
tinsey

EINSWY
sinewy
winsey

EIOPRR
priore
ropier

EIOPRT
epirot
periot
porite

EIOPSS
isopes
poises
posies
possie

EIOPST
espiot
poiets
poites
posite
postie
sopite

EIORSS
osiers
seisor
sories

EIORST
oister
oistre
oriest
ostrie
reiots
riotes
roites
sortie
storie
stroie
tiroes»
Tories
triose

EIORSV
vireos
virose

EIPPRS
pipers
sipper

EIPPRT
rippet
tipper
trippe

EIPPST
pipets
sippet
tippes

EIPRRS
priers
priser
ripers
sprier

EIPRSS
pisser
prises
respis
speirs
spiers
spires

EIPRST
esprit
peirts
perits
pierst
pierts
pister
preist
priest
priste
Pteris
repits
respit
ripest
septir
sitrep
sperit
spreit
sprite»
stiper
stipre
stirpe
stripe
tripes

EIPRSU
pursie
uprise

EIPRSW
swepir
swiper
wipers

EIPRTT
pitter
tripet

EIPRTY
pyrite
typier

EIPSSS
pisses
sepsis
speiss

EIPSST
pistes
speits
spiets
spiset
spites
steips
stieps
stipes

EIPSTT
petits
pittes
speitt
spitte
tipets

EIQRSU
quiers
quires
risque
squier
squire

EIQSTU
queist»
quiest
quiets
quiste
quites

EIRRST
stirre
tirers

EIRRTT
ritter
territ
triter

EIRSST
reists
resist
resits
sister
sistre
steirs
stiers
stires
stries
trises

EIRSSU
issuer
uresis

EIRSSW
swires
wisser

EIRSTT
rittes
sitter
sterit
titers
titres
treist
triste
trites

EIRSTU
resuit
ruites
rustie
sturie
suiter
surtie
urites

EIRSTV
rivets
servit
stiver
strive
trevis
tivers
trives
verist
vitres

EIRSTW
sweirt
trewis
tweirs
twires
witers
writes

EIRTTW
trewit
witter

EISSTT
testis
tistes

EISSTU
suites
tissue

EISSTX
exists
sexist

EJLORT
jolter
rejolt

EJNOST
jetons
jetson

EKLNOS
kelson
sloken

EKLOOR
looker
relook

EKNORW
knower
reknow»
wroken

EKOPRR
porker
proker

EKORRW
rework
worker

EKORST
stoker
storke
stroke
torkes
trokes

EKRRSY
skerry
skryer

EKRSTU
kuters
trukes
turkes
tusker

ELLNOR
enroll
ornell

ELLOPR
poller
prolle

ELLOPT
pollet
potell

ELLORR
re-roll
roller

ELLORS
lorels
orells
rolles
soller
sorell

ELLORT
toller
trolle

ELLOSS
losels
lossel
solles

ELLOST
tolles
tolsel

ELLOVY
lovely
volley

ELLPRU
puller
repull

ELLSTU
Tellus
tuells
tulles

ELMNOS
Lemnos
lemons
melons
molens
solemn

ELMNOT
loment
molten
tolmen

ELMNOY
lemony
myleon

ELMNPU
lumpen
plenum

ELMORS
molers
morels
morsel
romels
somler

ELMOSS
mossel
slomes

ELMOST
metols
molest
motels
smolet

ELMOSU
moules
mousel
mousle
oleums

ELMOSW
mowles
mowsle

ELMOSY
moyles
smoyle

ELMPRU
lumper
plumer
replum
rumple

ELMRTY
myrtel
myrtle
termly
tremyl
trymle

ELNNTU
nunlet
tunnel

ELNOOS
loones
loosen

ELNOPY
openly
poleyn

ELNORS
enrols
loners
norsel
snorle

ELNOSS
elsons
lesson»
nossel
solens

ELNOST
Solent
stolen
telson

ELNOSU
ensoul
noules
nousel
nousle
Olenus

ELNOSV
novels
sloven

ELNOSW
lownes
Nowels
nowles
nowsle

ELNPRU
prunel
punler

ELNRTU
lunter
runlet

ELNSSU
lessun
snules
unless

ELNTTU
lutten
nutlet

ELOOPR
looper
pooler
proole

ELOOPS
loopes
pooles
sloope
soople
spoole

ELOORS
loores
looser

ELOORT
looter
retool
rootle
tooler

ELOPPR
lopper
popler
propel

ELOPPS
loppes
peplos

ELOPPT
loppet
poplet
topple

ELOPRS
lopers
plores
polers
proles
sloper
splore

ELOPRT
petrol
poltre
torple
tropel
trople

ELOPRU
louper
proule

ELOPRW
plower
plowre
prowle
replow
worple

ELOPSS
Poless
slopes
sopels»
spoles

ELOPST
postel
postle
potels
spotel
spotle
stopel
stople

ELOPSU
loupes
poules
souple

ELOPSW
lowpes
pelows
plowes
powles
sowpel
sowple
spowle

ELOPSY
ployes
polyse
spoyle

ELOPTU
poulet
tupelo

ELORRS
lorres
rolers
sorrel

ELORSS
lessor
losers
rosels
rossel
rossle
slores
solers
sorels

ELORST
lerots
loters
ostler
rostel»
rostle
rotels
sorelt
sterol
strole
tolers
tolser
torsel
troles

ELORSU
loures
louser
roules
souler

ELORSV
lovers
solver

ELORSW
lowers
lowres
lowser
owlers
rowels
rowles
slower

ELORTT
eltrot
lotter
rottel
rottle
tolter
tortel
tortle

ELORTU
elutor
louter
outler
routle
tourel
troule

ELORTW
lowter
lowtre
rowlet
towler
trowel
wortle

ELORUV
louver
louvre
velour

ELORVY
lovery
overly
volery

ELORWY
lowery
owlery
Rowley

ELOSST
losset
slotes
stoles
tossel

ELOSSU
eusols
louses
ousels
slouse
soleus
soules

ELOSTU
solute
soulet
stoule
toules
tousle

ELOSTW
lowest
owlets
sowlet
stowle
towels
towles
towsel

ELOSTY
tolsey
tylose

ELOSUZ
ouzels
slouze

ELOSVW
vowels
wolves

ELPPRU
pulper
purpel
purple
repulp

ELPPSU
peplus
supple

ELPRRU
purler
purrel

ELPRSU
leprus
pulers
purles
sprule
supler

ELPRSY
plyers
spyler

ELPRTU
pulter
pultre
turple

ELPRTY
peltry
pertly

ELPSSU
pulses
pusels
pusles
pussel
pussle
spules
suples

ELPSTU
lets up
let ups
pultes
pustel
pustle

ELPUZZ
puzzel
puzzle

ELQSTU
quelts
squelt

ELRSTU
luster
lustre
luters
result
rustle
rutsel
sulter
sultre
sutler
truels
trules
trusel
turles
ulster

ELRSTY
lyster
styler
trelys
tryels
tylers
tyrles

ELRTTU
lutter
ruttle
turtle

ELSSTU
slutes
tussel
tussle

ELSSTY
slyest
styles

ELSTTY
stylet
tylets

EMMNNO
Memnon
mnemon

EMMNOT
moment
montem

EMMNTU
mentum
nummet

EMNORS
enorms
moners
morens
mornes
sermon

EMNORT
mentor
montre
tormen

EMNOST
montes
Ostmen

EMNRSU
Mensur
rumens

EMOORS
moores
morose
Romeos
roomes

EMOORT
mooter
remoot

EMOPRS
mopers
Merops
Mesrop
proems

EMOPRT
emport
trompe

EMORRT
morter
mortre
termor
tremor

EMORSS
morses
morsse
mosers
mosser
smores

EMORST
metros
mortes
moster
mostre
moters
motser
somter
steorm
storem
storme
strome
tromes

EMORSU
moures
mouser
soumer

EMOSSU
mouses
mousse
smouse

EMPPRU
pumper
repump

EMRSTU
estrum
muster
mustre
mu'ters
strume
stumer
sturme
sumter
trumes

EMSSTY
stymes
system

EMSTTU
musett
mutest

ENNORT
ronnet
tonner
tronne

ENNOST
nonest
nonets
sonnet
stonen
stonne
tenons
tenson
tonnes

ENNPTU
punnet
unpent

ENNRTU
runnet
tunner
unrent

ENNSTU
tunnes
unnest
unsent

ENOORS
noorse
nooser
roneos
seroon
snoore
sooner

ENOOSS
nooses
snoose

ENOOST
nootes
stoone

ENOOSZ
noozes
ozones
snooze

ENOPRS
perons
person
prones»
prosne
sporne

ENOPRU
peroun
unrope

ENOPST
pontes
posnet

ENOPTT
potent
topnet

ENORRS
snorer
sorner
sorren

ENORSS
norses
norsse
nosers
rosens
rossen
senors
sensor
serons
snores
sorens

ENORST
nestor
noters
rontes
rotnes
snoter
stoner
strone
tenors
tensor
toners
trones

ENORSU
souren
unsore

ENORSW
owners
resown
rowens
snowre»
sworen
worsen

ENORTT
rotten
tentor
torten

ENORTY
troyne
tyrone

ENOSST
nosets
onsets
seston
setons
stones
tesson
tonses
tossen

ENOSTT
ostent
snotte
teston

ENOTTU
tenuto
Teuton

ENPRST
prents
sprent

ENPRSU
prunes
spurne

ENRRSU
nurser
reruns

ENRRTU
return
turner

ENRSTU
enruts
Ernust
rusten
tuners
unrest
urnets

ENSSTU
sunset
unsets

EOOPRT
Pooter
troope

EOORRT
rooter
torero

EOORST
oostre
rooste
rootes
troose

EOPPRT
topper
troppe

EOPPRY
popery
pyrope

EOPPST
epopts
popets
soppet
toppes

EOPRRS
porers
porres
porser
prores
proser
repros
resorp
ropers
sporre

EOPRRT
porret
porter
proter
pretor
report
troper

EOPRRU
pourer
repour»

rouper

EOPRSS
opress
posers
proses
prosse
spores

EOPRST
porest
porets
portes
poster
poters
presto
proset
protes
repost
repots
respot
septor
sporte
sprote
stoper
strope
topers
tropes

EOPRSU
poseur
roupes
souper
uprose

EOPRSW
powers
powres
prowes
prowse

EOPRTU
pouret
pouter
troupe

EOPRTW
powter
prowte
trowpe

EOPSST
estops»

posset
ptoses
stoeps
stopes

EOPSSU
pouses
soupes
spouse

EOPSSY
posyes
pyoses
ysopes

EOPSTU
pouste
poutes
spoute
stoupe
toupes

EOPSTW
powtes
spowte
towpes

EOQRSU
quores
quorse
roques

EOQRTU
quetor
quoter
roquet
torque
troque

EORRRT
rorter
terror

EORRSS
rosers
rosser
sorres

EORRST
orrest
resort
re-sort»

retros
roster
roters
sorter
storer
storre
torres

EORRSU
rouser
sourer

EORRSW
rowers
worres
worser

EORRTT
retort
rotter
torret

EORRTU
retour
router
tourer

EORRTW
rowter
trower

EORSST
osters
retoss
rosets
rosset
rostes
sorest
sortes
stores
torses
tosers
tosser
trosse

EORSSU
rouses
serous
souser

EORSSW
rowses
serows
sowres»

worses
worsse
wrosse

EORSTT
otters
ottres
rottes
sotter
stoter
stotre
tortes
toters
totres
trotes

EORSTU
ouerts
ouster
outers
outres
rouets
routes
souter
stoure
touser
trouse

EORSTV
overts
stover
strove
troves
vostre
voters

EORSTW
owters
restow
rowets
rowste
rowtes
sowter
stower
stowre
towers
towres
towser
trowes
trowse
twoers
worste
wortes
wrotes

EORSTX
exorts
oxster
oxters

EORSTY
ostery
ostrey
ostrye
oyster
oystre
rosety
storey
storye
stroye
toyers
troyes
tyroes
yoters

EORSTZ
rozets
tozers
zoster

EORTTU
routte
touret
touter
troute

EORTTW
towret
trowet
trowte
wet rot

EOSSTW
stowes
stowse
towses

EOSTTU
outset
set out
stoute
toutes

EOSTTW
stowte
towtes

EPPRSU
supper»

uppers

EPRRSU
purres
purser
spurre

EPRRSY
pryers
pryser
spryer

EPRSST
prests
sperst
sperts
sprets
streps

EPRSTU
erupts
purest
purset
sprute
stupre
uprest

EPRSWY
swyper
wypers

ERRSTU
rustre
ruters
sturer
sturre
turres

ERRSTY
styrre
tryers

ERRTTU
rutter
turret

ERSSTU
estrus
russet
stuers
stures
surest
suster
suters»

tessur
tusser
tussre

ERSSTY
steyrs
styres
syrtes
tressy

ERSTTU
ruttes
sturte
truest
turets
utters

ERSTUU
suture
uterus

ERSTUV
stuver
turves
vestur

ERSTUY
rustye
surety
surtey
surtye

ERSTVY
styver
vestry

FFIQSU
quiffs
squiff

FGIILN
filing
lifing

FGILNU
fluing
fuling
ginful
ingulf
lufing

FGINRY
fringy
frying

FHIRST
firths
friths
shrift

FHORTY
forthy
frothy

FIOPRT
forpit
profit

FLNRUU
unfurl
urnful

FNOSTU
founts
futons
unsoft

GGILNO
loggin
loging
ogling

GGILNU
gluing
guling
luging
lunggi

GGILNY
glying
niggly

GGINNO
goning
nig-nog
noggin

GGINOR
goring
gringo
roging

GGINRU
ruging
urging

GHHOSU
houghs
shough

GHILST
lights
slight

GHINST
nights
snight
things

GHINTY
nighty
thingy

GHLOSU
ghouls
loughs
slough

GHOSTU
oughts
sought
toughs

GIIKNP
kiping
piking

GIIKNR
girkin
irking
riking

GIIKNS
siking
skiing

GIILMN
liming
miling

GIILNN
lignin
lining

GIILNR
liring
riglin
riling

GIILNT
liting
tiling

GIILNV
living
viling

GIINNP
niping
pining

GIINNS
ingins
insign
sining

GIINPR
piring
riping

GIINRS
rising
siring

GIINRV
Irving
riving
virgin
viring

GIKLNY
kingly
lyking

GILMNU
lignum
muling

GILNOO
logion
looing
ooling

GILNOP
loping
poling

GILNOR
gorlin
loring

GILNOS
goslin
losing
soling

GILNOT
lignot
lingot
loting
tiglon
toling

GILNOV
loving
voling

GILNOW
lowing
owling

GILNPU
gulpin
plug in
puling

GILNPY
plying
pyling

GILNRU
luring
ruling

GILNSU
lungis
sluing

GILNSY
Glynis
lyings
singly
slying

GILNTU
inglut
luting
ungilt

GILNTY
tingly
tyling

GIMNOR
moring
roming

GIMNRU
ingrum
muring

GINNOO
gonion
ooning

GINNOT
noting
toning

GINNOW
nowing
owning
woning

GINNTU
tuning
unting

GINOPR
orping
poring
proign
roping

GINOPS
posing
soping

GINOPT
opting
poting
toping

GINORS
girons
grison
groins
rosing
signor
soring

GINORT
girnot
roting
trigon

GINOSS
gnosis
ossing

GINOST
ingots
stingo
tigons
tosing

GINOSW
owings
sowing
wosing

GINOTU
outing
touing

GINOTW
owting
towing

GINOTY
toying
yoting

GINPRY
prying
pyring

GINPSY
pigsny
pyings
spying
syping

GINRRU
runrig
urring

GINRST
grints
string
trings

GINRSU
gruins
ruings
rusing
suring
unrigs

GINRTU
ruting
truing
ungirt

GINRTY
trying
tyring

GINSTY
stingy»
stying
tyings

GLNOTU
glotun
gluton
lutong

GNOPPU
oppugn
popgun

GNRSTU
grunts
strung

GOSTUY
gousty
guyots

HIIMSS
imshis
Shiism

HIINTW
inwith
within

HILOST
holist
lithos
thiols

HILOSW
lowish
owlish

HIMOPS
mopish
Ophism

HIMORS
morish
Romish

HINOST
Shinto
tonish

HINPSU
punish
unship

HIOPPS
hippos
popish
shippo

HIPPSU
hippus
uppish

HIRSTY
shirty
thyrsi

HLOSTU
hoults
shoult
tholus
thouls

HMOSTU
mouths
smouth

HMPTUY
humpty
tumphy

HMSTUY
mythus
thymus

HNOPSY
Hypnos
syphon

HNOPTY
phyton
python
Typhon

HNORTY
rhyton
thorny

HOPSSY
hysops
hyssop
sposhy

HOPSTU
Pushto
tophus
upshot

HORSTY
hostry
shorty

HORTWY
worthy
ywroht

IKLNSY
kylins
slinky

IKMNOR
mikron
morkin

IKNQSU
quinks
squink

IKQRSU
quirks
squirk

ILLQSU
quills
squill

ILMNSU
muslin
ulmins

ILNOST
Nilots
tonsil

ILNOTU
oilnut
ultion

ILNSTU
insult
lunist
sunlit
unslit

ILOPST
pilots
pistol
poltis
postil
spoilt

ILOPSU
pilous
poilus

ILOSTW
lowist
lowsit

ILQSTU
quilts
squilt

IMMNOS
monism
nomism
simmon

IMMSTU
mutism
summit

IMNOSS
misons
misson
simons

IMNOST
inmost
minots
monist
monits

IMNOSY
myosin
simony

IMOPRS
porism
primos

IMOPST
impost
impots

IMORST
Romist
stormi
timors

IMPRSU
primus
purims
purism

IMSSTU
mussit
mustis

INNOSU
unions
unison

INOOPT
option
potion

INOPRS
orpins
pinors
prions
prison

INOPST
instop
pintos
piston
pitons
points
posnit
postin
potins

INORTT
intort
triton

INPRST
prints
sprint

INQSTU
quints
squint

INQSUY
quinsy
squiny

INSTUW
unwist
unwits

IOPRST
prosit
tripos

IOPSST
posits»
possit
ptosis

IOQSTU
quoist
quoits

IORSST
roists
rosist
rosits

IORSTU
rousti
suitor

IOSSTT
stoits
tsotsi

IPRSST
prists
spirts
sprits
stirps
strips

IPRSTU
purist
spruit
tripus
uprist

IQRSTU
quirts
squirt

LLORST
stroll
trolls

LMOSTU
moults
smoult

LNOPTU
pluton
pulton

LOPPSY
polyps
sloppy

LOPRTY
portly
protyl

MMNOSU
musmon
summon

MMOOTT
motmot
tom-tom

MORSTU
stumor
tumors

NOOPRT
pronto
proton

NOOPSY
snoopy
spoony

NOORTU
notour
unroot

NOOSST
nostos
snoots
stoons

NOPSTU
unstop
untops

NORSTY
roynts
snorty

NPRSTU
prunts
sprunt

OOPRST
poorts
sproot
stroop
troops

OPRSTU
putors
sprout
stroup
stupor
troups

OPRSTW
sprowt
strowp
trowps

OPSSTU
possut
spouts
stoups

ORSTTU
strout
trouts
tutors

ORSTUY
rousty
stoury

AACIMR
Aramaic
cariama

AAACMRS
maracas
marasca
mascara

AAADIRT
dataria
Radiata

AAADMRS
armadas
madrasa

AAAMNRT
amarant
maranta

AAANRTT
tantara
tartana

AABCCER
baccare
Cabecar

AABCELP
capable
pacable

AABCERT
abreact
bearcat
cabaret

AABCORT
abactor
acrobat

AABDEGN
bandage
Dagbane

AABDELT
ablated
datable

AABDGMO
Dagomba
gambado

AABDNRS
bandars
sandbar

AABDRST
bastard
tabards

AABEGLR
Alberga
algebra

AABEGMR
bergama
megabar

AABEILT
Baalite
labiate

AABEIRS
air base
arabise

AABELLS
sabella
salable

AABELRT
Alberta
ratable

AABELST
ablates
astable

AABELTU
tableau
tabulae

AABERTT
rabatte
tabaret

AABHIRT
airbath
Bharati

AABILST
Baalist
balista

AABIMRS
Arabism»
Bairams

AABINST
abstain
Tsabian

AABLLST
ballast
ballats

AABLMSY
abysmal
balsamy

AABMNST
bantams
batsman

AACCLRU
accrual
caracul

AACDEIN
aidance
Canidae

AACDELN
candela
decanal

AACDERS
arcades
sea-card

AACDIRS
acarids
ascarid

AACDNRS
cadrans
canards

AACEGNR
carnage
cranage

AACEINR
acarine
narceia

AACEIRV
avarice
caviare

AACELMN
laceman
manacle

AACELMR
cameral
caramel
Carmela

AACELST
acetals
lactase

AACENRT
cateran
tar acne

AACENST
Anstace
catenas

AACERST
acaters
cat's ear
sacaret

AACFILS
cafilas
facials
fascial

AACHIMR
Amharic
machair

AACHKSW
hacksaw
kwachas

AACILNT
actinal
alicant

AACILPT
capital
placita

AACIMPR
Campari
picamar

AACINOR
Aaronic
conaria»
ocarina

AACINPT
capitan
captain

AACINRZ
czarian
czarina

AACIRSS
air sacs
ascaris

AACJKMN
jackman
manjack
man jack

AACLLNU
Calluna
lacunal

AACLMNT
calmant
clamant

AACLMSU
calamus
maculas

AACLNSU
Calanus
lacunas

AACLOST
catalos
coastal

AACLRVY
Calvary
cavalry

AACNPST
capstan
captans
catnaps

AACORST
ostraca
Tarasco

AACORTU
acatour»
autocar

AADDGNR
graddan
grandad

AADEGRY
drayage
yardage

AADEHRW
rawhead
warhead

AADEILR
Laridae
radiale

AADEILV
availed
vedalia

AADEINR
arained
araneid
Ranidae

AADEIPS
apaised
diapase

AADEIRT
radiate
tiaraed

AADELLP
apalled
padella

AADENNT
andante
Dantean

AADENSW
Sandawe
weasand

AADEPRT
adapter
aparted
readapt

AADEPSS
espadas»
passade

AADGMNR
dragman
grandam
grandma

AADHNRS
darshan
dharnas
Hansard

AADIINN
anidian
Indiana

AADILMR
admiral
amildar

AADLLNW
land law
lawland

AADMNOR
madrona
mandora
monarda
roadman

AADMNRY
drayman
yardman

AADMNSY
daysman
man-days

AADNRST
astrand
tarands
tar sand

AADOPSS
passado
posadas

AAEEGST
eatages
sage tea
seagate

AAEEMNT
emanate»

enemata
manatee

AAEFLPR
earflap
parafle

AAEGLLR
Algeria
lairage
regalia

AAEGLLR
glareal
Grallae

AAEGLLT
gallate
tallage

AAEGLNS
alnages
anlages
galenas
lagenas
lasagne

AAEGLST
agelast
algates
lastage

AAEGMNR
manager
marenga

AAEGMNT
gateman
magenta
magnate

AAEGMRT
Margate
regmata

AAEGNNT
tannage
tangena

AAEGNST
agnates
sea tang

AAEGRST
gastrea
teargas

AAEGSSU
assuage
sausage

AAEGSTW
sawgate
sawgeat
wastage

AAEGTWY
gateway
getaway

AAEHIRT
hetaira
Rhaetia

AAEILMN
Almaine
laminae
Limnaea

AAEILNT
ailante
antliae
Natalie

AAEILRV
availer
velaria

AAEIMNS
amnesia
anemias

AAEIMNT
amentia
animate

AAEINST
entasia
taenias

AAEIRST
aristae
asteria
atresia

AAEIRTT
arietta»

Ratitae

AAEKRSS
kaesars
karasse
keasars

AAEKRST
karates
sakaret

AAELMST
malates
maltase
tamales

AAELNPT
panatel
platane

AAELNRS
arsenal
lanares

AAELNRT
lanaret
lateran

AAELNST
sealant
teanals

AAELRST
Alaster
laaters
tar-seal

AAELSST
atlases
Salt Sea
sea salt

AAENPST
anapest
peasant

AAENRST
Antares
anearst

AAERSST
searats
sea star

AAERSSY
arayses
assayer
reassay

AAERSTT
Astarte
tsarate

AAGILNN
anginal
Anglian

AAGILNP
apaling
paginal

AAGILNV
availing
vaginal

AAGIMNS
gas main
magians
siamang

AAGIMNT
amating
maating

AAGINRS
arasing
sangria
sarangi

AAGMNRT
tangram
trangam

AAHINST
shaitan
tahinas

AAHLMMS
hammals
mahmals
mashlam

AAHPLST
asphalt
taplash

AAILMMS
Lamaism»

miasmal

AAILMNR
laminar
railman

AAILMRT
marital
martial

AAILNOP
Opalina
Pianola

AAILNOT
ailanto
Laotian

AAILNOV
novalia
valonia

AAILNRU
ulnaria
Uralian

AAILNSS
Nasalis
Salians
salinas

AAILNTV
Latvian
valiant

AAILPRT
partial
patrial

AAILSSV
salivas
salvias
vassail

AAIMNRT
Martian
Martina
tamarin

AAIMNST
manatis
stamina

AAINNRV
navarin
nirvana

AAINORZ
Arizona
Azorian
Zonaria

AAINPST
Antipas
patinas
taipans

AAINRST
antiars
artisan
tsarian
tsarina

AAINRSU
anurias
saurian

AAINRTZ
artizan
tzarian
tzarina

AAKLRSU
kursaal
rusalka

AALMPRY
palmary
palmyra

AALNPST
plantas
platans
saltpan

AALOPRS
oarlaps
parasol

AALRSTY
astylar
satyral

AAMNNOT
Manaton
Montana

AAMNPRT
mantrap
rampant

AAMNPSS
passman
sampans

AAMNRST
artsman
star man

AAMRSTU
sumatra
traumas

AANPRST
partans
Spartan
tarpans
trapans

AAOPSST
potassa
sapotas

AARRSWY
sawarry
warrays

ABBBDEL
babbled
blabbed

ABBBELR
babbler
blabber
brabble

ABBCELR
cabbler
clabber

ABBCELS
cabbles
scabble

ABBDELM
balmbed
mabbled

ABBDELR
brabled
dabbler»

drabble
rabbled

ABBDELS
dabbles
slabbed

ABBDELW
bawbled
wabbled

ABBDEST
stabbed
tebbads

ABBEGLR
gabbler
grabble

ABBELRS
bablers
barbels
barbles
brables
rabbles
slabber

ABBELRW
wabbler
wrabble

ABBELSU
basbleu
baubles

ABBELSW
bawbles
swabble
wabbles

ABBERST
barbets
rabbets
stabber
tabbers

ABBGILN
babling
labbing

ABBGINR
barbing
rabbing

ABBHOOS
baboosh
haboobs

ABCCEIR
acerbic
breccia

ABCCIOR
boracic
braccio

ABCDEKR
bracked
redback

ABCDERS
becards
decarbs
scrabed

ABCEERR
acerber
rebrace

ABCEHMR
becharm
brecham
chamber
chambre

ABCEHRT
brachet
Berchta

ABCEINS
cabines
scabine

ABCEIRS
ascribe
cabries
caribes
Caribes

ABCEKST
backets
backset
setback

ABCELLU
bullace
cue ball

ABCELMR
cambrel
clamber
cramble

ABCELMS
becalms
scamble

ABCELRU
burlace
curable

ABCELSS
cabless
scables

ABCKSTU
sackbut
subtack

ABCKSUW
bucksaw
sawbuck

ABDDEER
bearded
bedared
breaded

ABDDEIN
abidden
bandied

ABDDEOR
aborded
boarded
broaded
roadbed

ABDDERW
bedward
brawded

ABDEEKR
rebaked
redbeak

ABDEELM
beldame
bemedal
embaled

ABDEELR
bederal
bleared
rebaled

ABDEELT
beadlet
belated
bleated

ABDEEMR
ambered
breamed

ABDEEMS
bemased
embased

ABDEERS
bedares
debaser
sabered

ABDEERT
berated
betread
debater
rebated
taberde
tabered

ABDEEST
beasted
bestead
debates

ABDEGIR
abridge
brigade

ABDEGLR
belgard
garbled
grabled

ABDEGNO
bondage
dogbane

ABDEILN
Belinda
blained
nail bed

ABDEILP
bipedal
piebald

ABDEILR
bedrail
brailed
bridale
ridable

ABDEILS
blaised
disable

ABDEILT
daiblet
libated

ABDEINR
badiner
brained

ABDEINS
bandies
basined

ABDEIRS
abiders
airbeds
braides
braised
darbies
seabird

ABDEIRT
redbait
tribade

ABDEKRS
bedarks
brasked
debarks

ABDELMR
marbled
rambled

ABDELNR
blander
brandle

ABDELOT
bloated
lobated
oblated

ABDELRW
brawled
warbled

ABDELST
baldest
blasted
dablets
stabled

ABDENOR
bandore
boarden
broaden

ABDENRR
brander
Bernard

ABDENSU
sudane
subdean

ABDEORR
boarder
broader
reboard

ABDEOTU
abouted
boutade

ABDERSS
bardess
brassed
red bass
serdabs

ABDERST
brasted
dabster
red bats

ABDERSU
daubers
subedar

ABDGILN
balding
blading
dabling

ABDGINR
barding
brading
brigand

ABDGINW
bawding
windbag

ABDHRSU
burdash
rhabdus

ABDIRSU
ribauds
subarid

ABDNOSU
abounds
bausond

ABEEHNS
banshee
beenahs
has-been

ABEEHRT
breathe
herb tea

ABEEILS
bailees
besaile

ABEEKPS
bespake
bespeak

ABEELLR
labeler
relabel

ABEELMS
embales
emblase

ABEELNT
Beltane
entable
tenable

ABEELRT
bleater
retable

ABEELSU
sea blue
sueable

ABEEMRS
beamers
besmear
breames
embrase

ABEERRT
rebater
terebra

ABEGILN
bealing
Belgian
Bengali
gab-line

ABEGINY
abeying
gaybine

ABEGLMR
gambler
gambrel

ABEGRST
bargest
bargets

ABEHLRT
blather
halbert

ABEHLSU
ale bush
Beulahs

ABEHNOS
bone ash
hebonas

ABEILLR
air bell
Braille
liberal

ABEILMR
balmier
Mirabel
mirable
remblai

ABEILMT
bimetal
limbate
timbale

ABEILNS
aeblins
lesbian

ABEILRT
librate
triable

ABEILST
albites
bastile
bestail
bestial
blastie
libates
stabile

ABEINST
basinet
besaint
bestain
betanis

ABEINTT
tabinet
Tibetan

ABEIRRT
arbiter
rarebit

ABEIRRZ
bizarre
brazier

ABEIRSS
braises
brassie

ABEIRST
bairest
baiters
barites
rebaits
terbias

ABEIRTT
battier
biretta

ABELLOV
lovable
volable

ABELLRU
rubella
rulable

ABELMRR
marbler
rambler

ABELNTU
abluent
tunable

ABELORS
boreals
labrose
Rosabel

ABELRRW
brawler
warbler

ABELRSS
blasers
braless

ABELRST
alberts
balters
blaster
labrets
larbets
stabler
tablers

ABELRTT
Bartlet
battler
blatter
brattle

ABELSTT
baletts
batlets
battels
battles
stablet
tablets

ABELSTY
baetyls»

beastly

ABEMNOS
ambones
bemoans

ABEMNRY
byreman
myrbane

ABEMRSS
embrass
sambers
sambres

ABENORS
boranes
sea-born

ABENORT
baronet
reboant

ABENRSU
braunes
sun bear
unbares
unbears

ABENSTU
butanes
sun-beat
unbeast

ABEORST
boaster
boaters
borates
rebatos
sorbate

ABEORTT
abettor
taboret

ABERSSS
bassers
brasses

ABERSST
basters
bestars
brasset
breasts

ABERSSU
abusers
surbase

ABERSTU
arbutes
surbate

ABERSTW
bestraw
wabster
webstar

ABERSTY
betrays
barytes

ABFLOTY
boatfly
flyboat

ABGIKNR
barking
braking

ABGIKNS
bakings
basking
inkbags

ABGILMN
ambling
balming
blaming
lambing
mabling

ABGILNS
ablings
balings
blasing
sabling

ABGILNT
batling
blating
tabling

ABGIMNR
braming
rambing

ABGIMST
gambist»

gambits

ABGINOR
boaring
Grobian

ABGINRY
barying
braying

ABGINST
basting
batings

ABHKRSU
burkhas
kurbash

ABIILNS
aiblins
bilians

ABILOPR
bipolar
parboil

ABILRSU
burials
railbus

ABINOST
bastion
bonitas
obtains

ACCDESU
accused
succade

ACCEHIL
caliche
chalice

ACCEHNR
chancer
chancre

ACCEHOR
caroche
coacher

ACCEIKP
icepack
pack-ice

ACCEIMR
ceramic
racemic

ACCEINO
cocaine
oceanic

ACCEIST
accites
ascetic

ACCEKLR
cackler
clacker
crackle

ACCERRU
accruer
accurre

ACCERSU
accrues
accurse
accuser

ACCIIST
ascitic
sciatic

ACCILNO
conical
laconic

ACCISTU
cicutas
caustic

ACCKOSS
cassock
Cossack

ACCMOPT
accompt
compact

ACDDELS
caddels
caddles
scalded

ACDDESU
adduces
scauded

ACDEEFR
defacer
redface
refaced

ACDEEHL
Chaldee
Cheadle
leached

ACDEEHP
cheaped
depeach
peached

ACDEEHR
cheared
reached

ACDEELN
cleaned
elanced
enlaced

ACDEELP
cleaped
deplace

ACDEELR
Cedrela
cleared
creedal
declare
relaced

ACDEELS
Caldees
delaces
seed-lac

ACDEELT
cleated
decalet
eclated
elacted

ACDEEMR
amerced
creamed
racemed

ACDEENR
enraced
recaned

ACDEENS
cadenes
decanes
encased

ACDEENV
encaved
vendace

ACDEEPR
capered
preaced
repaced

ACDEERS
acresed
creased
decares
searced

ACDEERT
catered
cedrate
cerated
created
reacted

ACDEFRT
crafted
fracted

ACDEGLN
clanged
glanced

ACDEGNU
cangued
uncaged

ACDEHIN
chained
echidna

ACDEHIP
chaiped
edaphic

ACDEHKR
charked
dekarch

ACDEHMR
charmed
decharm»
marched

ACDEHNR
charned
endarch
ranched

ACDEHNT
chanted
natched

ACDEHOT
cathode
coathed

ACDEHRR
charred
red char

ACDEHRS
crashed
sarched

ACDEHRT
charted
chatred
ratched

ACDEHST
chasted
scathed

ACDEHTT
chatted
Datchet

ACDEILM
claimed
decimal
declaim
maliced
medical

ACDEILN
Iceland
inlaced

ACDEILR
claired
claried
decrial
radicel
radicle

ACDEILT
citadel
deltaic
dialect
edictal

ACDEINO
codeina
oceanid

ACDEINR
cairned
carnied
crained

ACDEINS
candies
incased

ACDEIRR
acrider
carried

ACDEIRS
craised
darices
radices
sidecar

ACDEIST
dacites
die-cast

ACDELNS
calends
candles
cendals

ACDELOT
colated
located

ACDELPS
clapsed
clasped
scalped
scapled

ACDELRS
cradles
scalder
scraled

ACDELSS
classed
declass

ACDELST
castled
sclated

ACDELSU
caudles
cedulas
claused

ACDEMPS
decamps
scamped

ACDENRT
cantred
centrad
Tancred
tranced

ACDENRU
durance
unraced

ACDENST
cadents
decants
descant
scanted
stanced

ACDEORT
cordate
redcoat

ACDEOST
coasted
scoated

ACDEPRS
redcaps
scarped
scraped

ACDERRS
carders
scarred

ACDERST
cedrates
decarts»
Dectras
redacts
scarted

ACDERSU
acursed
crusade
scaured

ACDERTT
detract
tracted

ACDHLOR
chordal
dorlach

ACDIIRS
cidaris
sciarid

ACDIIRT
triacid
triadic

ACDILOP
placoid
podalic

ACDIMNO
mandioc
monacid
monadic
nomadic

ACDIOPR
parodic
picador

ACDIORT
arctoid
carotid

ACDIOST
dacoits
Sotadic

ACDNORU
candour
caudron

ACEEFIN
faience
fiancee

ACEEHIT
hicatee
teachie

ACEEHLS
Chelsea
leaches

ACEEHNS
achenes
enchase

ACEEHPR
cheaper
peacher

ACEEHRT
cheater
hectare
rechate
recheat
reteach
teacher

ACEEHST
eatches
escheat
teaches

ACEEINR
Cairene
cinerea

ACEELNR
cleaner
reclean

ACEELNS
cleanse
elances
enlaces
enscale
scalene

ACEELNV
enclave
valence

ACEELPR
percale
replace

ACEELRR
clearer»

reclear

ACEELRS
alerces
cereals
cleares
relaces
rescale
sclerae

ACEEMNS
casemen
menaces

ACEEMRT
ceramet
cremate
meercat
mercate

ACEENRS
careens
caserne
enraces
recanes

ACEENRT
centare
crenate
reenact

ACEENRV
carvene
encarve

ACEEOST
acetose
coatees

ACEEPRS
caperes
escaper
percase
preaces
repaces

ACEERRS
careers
creaser
resarce

ACEERRT
caterer
recrate»

retrace
terrace

ACEERST
cerates
creates
ecartes
secreta

ACEERTX
exacter
excreta

ACEFINS
facines
fascine
fiances

ACEFIRS
farcies
fiacres

ACEFRRT
crafter
refract

ACEFRTU
facture
furcate

ACEGILL
ellagic
Gallice

ACEGILN
angelic
anglice
cealing
Galenic

ACEGILR
glacier
gracile

ACEGINS
ceasing
incages

ACEGNOR
acrogen
cornage

ACEGNOT
coagant»

cognate

ACEGORS
cargoes
corsage

ACEHILR
alriche
Charlie

ACEHINN
cain hen
enchain

ACEHINT
chantie
teach-in

ACEHIPT
aphetic
hepatic

ACEHIRS
acheris
Archies
cashier
chaires

ACEHIRT
Rhaetic
theriac

ACEHIST
achiest
taiches

ACEHKLS
hackels
hackles
shackel
shackle

ACEHLNR
charnel
larchen

ACEHLOR
cholera
chorale

ACEHLOS
oscheal
sea loch

ACEHLRS
Charles
larches
relasch

ACEHLRT
archlet
charlet
chartel
lachter
trachle

ACEHLST
chalets
latches
satchel

ACEHLTT
chattel
chattle
latchet

ACEHMNR
encharm
Marchen

ACEHMRR
charmer
chermar
marcher
remarch

ACEHMRS
charmes
marches
mesarch

ACEHMRT
matcher
rematch

ACEHNRS
charnes
chenars
rachens
ranches

ACEHNRT
chanter
rechant
tranche

ACEHNST
chasten
natches

ACEHNTU
uncheat
unteach

ACEHOLT
cholate
tachole

ACEHORS
choreas
oraches
roaches

ACEHPRT
chapter
patcher

ACEHPRY
eparchy
preachy

ACEHRRT
charret
charter
rechart

ACEHRST
archets
chartes
charets
chaters
chatres
hectars
ratches
starche

ACEHRTT
chatter
ratchet

ACEILLM
limacel
micella

ACEILMN
enclaim
melanic

ACEILMR
Almeric
claimer
Eric Lam
miracle»

reclaim

ACEILMS
limaces
malices

ACEILNP
capelin
capline
panicle
pelican

ACEILNR
carelin
carline
lancier

ACEILNS
inlaces
sanicle
scaleni

ACEILOR
calorie
cariole
Coralie
loricae

ACEILOT
aloetic
Coalite

ACEILPR
caliper
replica

ACEILPS
palices
plaices
special

ACEILRR
cerrial
clairer
Clarrie

ACEILRS
carlies
claries
eclairs
scalier

ACEILRT
article
recital

ACEILRV
caliver
calivre
clavier
varicle
velaric

ACEILST
elastic
laciest
latices
salicet

ACEILTT
lattice
tactile

ACEIMNS
amnesic
cinemas

ACEIMNT
emicant
nematic

ACEIMST
acmites
etacism
micates
sematic

ACEINOT
aconite
anoetic

ACEINPR
caprine
cinaper

ACEINPS
icepans
inscape
pincase

ACEINRS
arsenic
carines
carnies
cerains
cerasin
craines

ACEINRT
ceratin»

certain
crainte
creatin
crinate
nacrite

ACEINSS
caseins
cassine
incases

ACEINST
Anstice
caniest
cineast
Insecta

ACEINTT
nictate
tetanic

ACEIPPR
crappie
epicarp

ACEIPRS
epacris
icespar
scrapie
Serapic

ACEIPRT
paretic
picrate

ACEIPST
aseptic
spicate

ACEIQSU
caiques
caisque

ACEIRRS
carries
scarier

ACEIRSS
craises
crassie

ACEIRST
cristae
raciest
stearic

ACEIRSU
cauries
saucier
scaurie
uricase

ACEIRSV
varices
viscera

ACEIRTT
cattier
citrate

ACEISST
ascites
ectasis

ACEISTT
catties
statice
tietacs

ACEKLNS
lackens
slacken
snackle

ACEKLRS
calkers
lackers
rackles
slacker

ACEKLST
lackets
sacklet
tackles

ACEKRST
carkets
rackets
restack
retacks
stacker
tackers

ACEKSTT
stacket
tackets

ACELLOR
corella
ocellar

ACELLRS
arcells
callers
cellars
recalls
scleral

ACELLRU
cauller
cure-all

ACELMOU
caulome
leucoma

ACELMST
calmest
camlets

ACELNPS
enclasp
spancel

ACELNRS
lancers
rancels

ACELNRT
cantler
central

ACELNRU
lucarne
nuclear
unclear

ACELNST
cantels
cantles
centals
lancets
scantel
scantle

ACELNSU
censual
launces
unlaces
unscale

ACELORS
claroes
coalers
escolar
oracles
recoals
solacer

ACELOST
alecost
colates
lactose
locates
scatole
talcose

ACELOTY
acolyte
cotylae

ACELPRS
carpels
clapers
clasper
parcels
placers
reclasp
scalper

ACELPSU
capsule
lace-ups
specula

ACELRST
carlets
cartels
cartles
clarest
clarets
clartes
claters
crestal
lacerts
scalter
scaltre
scarlet
tarcels

ACELRSU
craules
scraule
secular

ACELRSW
crawles
scrawle

ACELSTU
cautels
sulcate

ACELSTY
acetyls
scytale

ACEMNOR
cremona
romance

ACEMOPR
compare
compear

ACEMPRS
campers
crampes
scamper

ACEMRSY
cramesy
screamy

ACENNOS
ancones
sonance

ACENNRS
canners
scanner

ACENNST
cannets
nascent

ACENORS
carnose
coarsen
corneas
encoras

ACENORT
cantore
enactor

ACENOST
costean
octanes

ACENPRS
prances
scrapen

ACENRSS
ancress
caserns
cranses
cressan
sarcens

ACENRST
canters
carnets
cranets
Cretans
nectars
recants
rescant
scanter
tanrecs
trances

ACENRTU
caunter
centaur
uncrate
untrace

ACENRTY
encraty
nectary

ACEOPST
capotes
scopate
toecaps

ACEORRS
coarser
corrase

ACEORRT
acroter
creator
reactor

ACEORST
coaster
coaters
recoast
recoats

ACEORSU
acerous
carouse

ACEPRRS
carpers
scarper
scraper

ACEPRST
carpets
precast
spectra

ACEPRSU
apercus
scauper

ACEPSTU
cuspate
teacups

ACEQSTU
acquest
casquet

ACERRSS
crasser
scarers
scarres

ACERSST
actress
casters
recasts
rescats
sacrets
scaters

ACERSSU
causers
cesuras
saucers
sucrase

ACERSTU
cauters
crustae
curates
turcase

ACESSTU
caestus
cuestas

ACESSTY
cytases
ecstasy

ACESTTU
acutest
scutate

ACFIMOR
aciform
Formica

ACFINRT
frantic
infarct
infract

ACGHINR
arching
chagrin
charing
raching

ACGHINS
achings
cashing
chasing

ACGHINT
chating
gnathic
taching

ACGHINW
chawing
chinwag
waching

ACGIKLN
calking
lacking

ACGIKNR
arcking
carking
craking
racking

ACGIKNS
cakings
casking
sacking

ACGILMN
calming
claming

ACGILNS
lacings
scaling

ACGILNT
catling
clating
tacling
talcing

ACGINNR
craning
rancing

ACGINOT
coating
cotinga

ACGINPR
carping
craping

ACGINPS
pacings
scaping
spacing

ACGINRS
arcings
carings
crasing
racings
sacring
scaring

ACGINRT
carting
crating
tracing

ACGINRV
carving
craving

ACGINSS
casings
cassing

ACGINST
actings»
casting
scating

ACGINTU
acuting
cauting

ACGIRST
gastric
tragics

ACHILRS
archils
carlish

ACHIMNO
manihoc
Mohican

ACHIMOS
chamiso
chamois

ACHIMST
mastich
tachism

ACHIORT
chariot
haricot

ACHIPST
haptics
spathic

ACHISTT
cattish
tachist

ACHLNTU
tulchan
unlatch

ACHLORS
chorals
lorchas
scholar

ACHMNOR
marchon
monarch
nomarch

ACHNRUY
raunchy
unchary

ACHNSTU
canthus
chaunts
staunch

ACHOPRY
charpoy
Corypha

ACIILSS
Liassic
silicas

ACIIMST
ismatic
itacism

ACIKNST
catkins
catskin

ACILNOR
clarion
Locrian

ACILNOS
Nicolas
oilcans

ACILNPS
caplins
inclasp

ACILOPT
Capitol
coalpit
optical
pit coal
topical

ACILOST
citolas
stoical

ACILOTV
volatic
voltaic

ACILPST
placits»
plastic

ACILPTY
clay pit
typical

ACILRST
Carlist
clairts

ACILRTU
curtail
trucial

ACIMNOR
Marconi
Minorca
Romanic

ACIMNOS
camions
conimas
maniocs
masonic

ACIMNRU
cranium
cumarin

ACIMOPT
potamic
Tampico

ACIMOST
atomics
masicot
maticos
somatic

ACIMPRT
crampit
ptarmic

ACIMSST
mastics
miscast

ACINNOT
actinon
cantion
contain

ACINNST
stannic»
tin cans

ACINOPT
caption
paction

ACINORT
anticor
carotin
Cortian
Cortina

ACINOSS
caisson
casinos
cassino

ACINOST
actions
atonics
cations
Scotian

ACINOTU
auction
caution

ACINRTU
curtain
turacin

ACINSTU
anicuts
nautics

ACIOPRT
apricot
parotic
patrico

ACIORSU
carious
curiosa

ACIRSST
cristas
racists
sacrist

ACIRSTU
Austric
urticas

ACKKOOR
cork oak
rock oak

ACKNSTU
unstack
untacks

ACKORRT
rock rat
rock tar
tarrock

ACLNORU
cornual
courlan

ACLOPRT
caltrop
proctal

ACLOPSU
copulas
cupolas
scopula

ACLORST
carlots
crotals
scrotal

ACLORSU
Carolus
oculars
oscular

ACLOSTU
locusta
talcous

ACLRSTU
crustal
curtals

ACNNOSY
canyons
sonancy

ACNOORT
cartoon
coranto

ACNOSTU
conatus»

toucans

ACNSSTU
Sanctus
Tuscans
uncasts

ACORSTT
cottars
scotart

ACORSTU
surcoat
turacos

ACOSTTU
outacts
outcast

ADDDEER
dreaded
readded

ADDDELS
daddles
saddled

ADDDELW
dawdled
waddled

ADDEEEM
adeemed
ameeded

ADDEELN
delenda
ladened

ADDEEMN
amended
deadmen
demaned
denamed

ADDEEMR
dearmed
dreamed
rademed

ADDEENR
dearned
dreaned

ADDEENV
advened
envaded

ADDEERT
derated
redated

ADDEEST
deadest
dead set
sedated
steaded

ADDEFLR
faddler
fardled

ADDEFRU
defraud
frauded

ADDEGHO
doghead
godhead

ADDEGLN
dangled
gladden

ADDEGLR
dragled
gladder

ADDEGNR
gradden
granded

ADDEHRS
shadder
sharded

ADDEILL
dallied
dialled

ADDEILP
paidled
plaided

ADDEILR
diedral
drailed

ADDEILS
daidles
dislade
laddies

ADDEINR
dandier
drained
randied

ADDEINS
dandies
sdained

ADDEINV
invaded
videnda

ADDEIRT
tardied
tiraded

ADDELPS
paddles
spaddle

ADDELRS
ladders
raddles
saddler

ADDELRW
dawdler
waddler

ADDELRY
dreadly
laddery

ADDELSS
laddess
saddles

ADDELSW
dawdles
swaddle
waddles

ADDENOT
donated
nodated

ADDENRU
daunder»

undared

ADDENTU
daunted
undated

ADDERST
addrest
detards
raddest
teddars

ADDERSW
swadder
swarded
wadders

ADDERSY
dryades
yadders

ADDMNOS
dodmans
oddsman

ADEEFLR
federal
fleared

ADEEFLT
deflate
fleated

ADEEFRT
draftee
freated

ADEEFST
deafest
defeats
feasted

ADEEGLN
angeled
gleaned

ADEEGLR
lagered
regaled

ADEEGLT
gelated
gleated
legated»

teagled

ADEEGNR
angered
derange
enraged
gearned
grandee
greaned
grenade
renaged

ADEEGNT
agented
negated

ADEEGOT
dogeate
goateed

ADEEGRS
dragees
greased

ADEEGRW
ragweed
wagered

ADEEHLR
hederal
rehaled

ADEEHLS
leashed
shealed

ADEEHRR
adherer
reheard

ADEEHRS
adheres
headers
hearsed
sheared

ADEEHRT
earthed
hearted
red-heat

ADEEILN
Adeline
aliened»

delaine

ADEEILS
aediles
deiseal

ADEEIRS
dearies
readies

ADEEISS
disease
seaside

ADEEKNR
kneader
nakered
rakened

ADEELMP
elamped
empaled

ADEELMT
medalet
metaled

ADEELNR
Leander
learned
red lane

ADEELNS
enleads
leadens
sandeel

ADEELNT
edental
latened

ADEELPR
pearled
pedaler
pleader
repaled

ADEELPS
delapse
elapsed
pleased
spealed

ADEELPT
petaled
pleated

ADEELOU
equaled
quealed

ADEELRT
alerted
altered
related
retaled
treadle

ADEELRV
lavered
raveled
revaled

ADEELRY
delayer
layered
relayed

ADEELST
delates
deleats
sleated
stealed
teasled
tele-ads

ADEELTV
valeted
velated

ADEEMNR
amender
enarmed
meander
reamend
remaned
renamed

ADEEMNS
amendes
demanes
demeans
denames
samened
seedman

ADEEMRR
dreamer
rearmed

ADEEMRS
dreames
meaders
rademes
remades
remeads
smeared

ADEENPS
sneaped
speaned

ADEENRS
deaners
denares
dreanes
endears
enrased
erandes
sneared

ADEENRY
deanery
renayed
yearned

ADEENST
densate
detanes
steaned

ADEEPRS
pearsed
pederas
preased
speared

ADEEPRT
padtree
predate
red tape
retaped
tapered

ADEEPRV
deprave
pervade
repaved

ADEERRS
readers
redsear
rereads

ADEERRT
re-rated
retrade
retread
treader

ADEERRV
averred
Everard

ADEERST
arested
dearest
derates
estrade
reasted
redates
sadtree
sedater
steared

ADEERSV
adverse
aversed
evaders
resaved

ADEERSW
drawees
resawed
sewared

ADEERTT
aretted
attered
treated

ADEERTV
averted
tavered

ADEERTW
dewater
tarweed
watered

ADEESTT
destate
detaste»

estated
teasted

ADEFGLN
fangled
flanged

ADEFILS
defails
defials
disleaf

ADEFINR
frained
fridean
infared

ADEFINS
fade-ins
fades in
fansied

ADEFINT
defiant
fainted

ADEFIST
dafties
fadiest

ADEFKLS
defalks
flasked

ADEFLNN
fenland
flanned

ADEFLTU
default
faulted

ADEFORY
feodary
foreday

ADEFRRT
drafter
redraft

ADEGGIU
gaudgie
guidage

ADEGGLR
draggle
gargled
raggled

ADEGGLS
daggles
slagged

ADEGGST
gadgets
stagged

ADEGHIN
anighed
heading

ADEGHIR
hag-ride
headrig

ADEGILN
aligned
dealing
leading

ADEGILR
draigle
gladier
glaired

ADEGILS
glaised
silaged

ADEGILT
lidgate
ligated
taigled

ADEGINR
angried
areding
dangeir
dangier
dearing
deraign
erading
gradine
grained
grandie
inraged
nigarde
reading

ADEGINV
deaving
evading

ADEGINW
weading
windage

ADEGIRS
agrised
graised

ADEGIRV
igraved
Rigveda

ADEGLNR
dangler
glander
gnarled
rangled

ADEGLNS
dangles
gladens
glandes
glansed
lagends
slanged

ADEGLNT
danglet
tangled

ADEGLRU
glaured
raguled

ADEGNOR
groaned
oranged
organed

ADEGNRR
gardner
gnarred
grander

ADEGNRS
dangers
ganders
gardens
negards
sangred

ADEGNRT
dragnet
granted

ADEGNST
gnasted
stanged
tag ends

ADEGORW
dowager
wordage

ADEGPRS
grapsed
grasped
spadger
sparged

ADEGRRU
duergar
guarder
regaurd
reguard

ADEGRSU
guardes
sugared

ADEHILS
halides
hailsed
shailed

ADEHINP
headpin
pinhead

ADEHINS
handies
inshade
shadine

ADEHIRR
hardier
harried

ADEHIRS
dashier
hardies
shadier
shaired

ADEHIST
haisted
tea dish

ADEHLNS
handles
handsel

ADEHLRS
drashel
harelds
heralds

ADEHLSS
hassled
slashed

ADEHMRS
derhams
marshed

ADEHNRS
dhernas
handers
hardens
harnsed

ADEHNSS
ashends
snashed

ADEHNST
handset
snathed

ADEHOPT
pot head
top head

ADEHPRS
phrased
sharped
shraped

ADEHPST
heptads
spathed

ADEHRST
dearths
hardest
hardset
hatreds
red hats»

threads
trashed

ADEHRTY
hydrate
thready

ADEIILR
deliria
irideal
lairdie

ADEIILS
aedilis
dailies
liaised
sedilia

ADEIIRS
dairies
diaries
diarise

ADEIKRS
daikers
darkies

ADEILLR
dallier
dialler
rallied

ADEILLS
dallies
disleal
laldies
sallied

ADEILMP
implead
pelamid

ADEILMS
medials
misdeal
mislead

ADEILNN
annelid
lindane

ADEILNS
aindles
Daniels»
denials
inleads
lead-ins
snailed

ADEILNU
aliunde
dualine
unideal

ADEILOS
deasoil
isolead

ADEILPR
lip read
pedrail
predial

ADEILPS
alipeds
elapids
lapides
lapised
paidles
palised
palsied
plaised
pleiads

ADEILPT
plaited
taliped

ADEILRR
lardier
larried

ADEILRS
daleirs
daliers
derails
dialers
redials
sideral

ADEILRT
dialter
trailed

ADEILSS
aidless
deasils
slaides

ADEILST
delaits
details
dilates
slaited
stailed

ADEILSU
audiles
deasiul

ADEILSW
Dewalis
swailed

ADEILSY
dialyse
eyliads

ADEIMMS
demaims
mismade

ADEIMNR
adermin
Amerind
marined

ADEIMNS
demains
maidens
medians
medinas
sideman

ADEIMNT
inmated
mediant

ADEIMRR
admirer
mardier
married
redimar

ADEIMRS
admires
misread
remaids
sedarim
sidearm

ADEIMST
ismated»
misdate

ADEINOS
adonise
anodise
Diasone
sodaine

ADEINOZ
adonize
anodize

ADEINPR
pardine
prained
rapined

ADEINPS
pansied
spained

ADEINPT
depaint
painted
patined

ADEINRR
drainer
randier

ADEINRS
inrased
randies
sandier
sardine

ADEINRT
atrined
dainter
dantier
detrain
tainder
tan ride
trade in
trained

ADEINRU
unaired
uranide

ADEINRV
invader
ravined

ADEINST
dainest
Danites
destain
details
instead
sainted
satined
stained

ADEINSW
dewanis
sea wind
swained

ADEIORS
Isadore
roadies
soredia

ADEIORV
avodire
avoider

ADEIOST
iodates
toadies

ADEIPPR
drappie
prepaid

ADEIPRR
drapier
paredri
parried
rapider

ADEIPRS
aspired
depairs
despair
diapers
draipse
pardies
praised
spaired

ADEIPRT
diptera
partied
pirated

ADEIRRT
tardier
tarried

ADEIRRV
arrived
varried

ADEIRST
aridest
asterid
astride
diaster
disrate
staider
staired
tardies
tirades

ADEIRSV
adviser
vardies

ADEISST
disseat
saidest

ADEISTV
datives
vistaed

ADEISTW
dawties
waisted

ADEKNST
dankest
stanked

ADEKRST
darkest
starked

ADELLRU
allured
udaller

ADELMOR
earldom
moraled

ADELMOS
damosel
sloamed

ADELNOR
ladrone
Leonard

ADELNPT
pantled
planted

ADELNRS
alderns
darnels
enlards
landers
relands
slander
snarled

ADELNRU
launder
laundre
lurdane
rundale

ADELNSS
andless
sandels
sandles
sendals

ADELNST
dentals
slanted
tandles

ADELNTU
lunated
unlated

ADELOPR
leopard
paroled
poadler

ADELOPS
deposal
pedalos
sloaped

ADELOPT
ploated
tadpole

ADELORS
loaders»

ordeals
reloads
sea lord

ADELORT
delator
leotard

ADELORU
roulade
Urodela

ADELOSS
aldoses
lassoed

ADELOTT
alotted
toadlet
totaled

ADELPPS
dapples
slapped

ADELPST
spatled
splated
stapled

ADELPSU
slauped
spauled
spaulde
upleads

ADELPSW
dewlaps
slawped

ADELPSY
splayed
yplasde

ADELPTT
pattled
platted

ADELRSS
aldress
rassled
sardels

ADELRST
dartles
lardets
rastled
slarted
slatred
tardles

ADELRTY
lyrated
trayled

ADELSTT
sattled
slatted

ADELSTU
auldest
saluted

ADEMMRS
dammers
drammes
smarmed

ADEMNNU
mundane
unnamed

ADEMNOS
daemons
masoned
monades
modenas
nomades

ADEMNRS
damners
manders
manreds
ramsden
randems
remands

ADEMNRU
duramen
manured
maunder
unarmed

ADEMNRY
draymen
yardmen

ADEMNSS
desmans
madness

ADEMNSU
maundes
medusan
sudamen

ADEMNTU
unmated
untamed

ADEMOSY
Samoyed
someday

ADEMPST
dampest
stamped

ADEMSSU
assumed
medusas

ADENNOY
annoyed
anodyne

ADENNST
standen
stanned

ADENOPR
aproned
operand
padrone
pandore

ADENORT
ornated
tornade

ADENOST
astoned
donates
onstead

ADENPPS
appends
snapped

ADENPRS
panders»
pransed

ADENRRS
darners
errands
randers
redarns
snarred

ADENRSS
sanders
sarsden

ADENRST
danters
endarts
restand
santred
stander
starned
straned
terands
transed
treands

ADENRSU
asunder
danseur
dauners
unreads

ADENRTU
auntred
daunter
natured
unrated
untread

ADENRTY
dentary
rent day

ADENSTU
saunted
unsated

ADENTTU
attuned
nutated
taunted

ADEOPRR
eardrop
padrero

ADEOPRT
adopter
proated
readopt

ADEORRS
adorers
drosera
roaders

ADEORST
doaters
roasted
toaders
torsade
troades

ADEORTT
rotated
troated

ADEORTU
outdare
read-out

ADEOSTT
stoated
toasted

ADEPRRS
drapers
drepars
sparred

ADEPRSS
adpress
spaders
sparsed
spreads

ADEPRST
departs
drapets
padtres
petards
sprated

ADEQRSU
quaders
squader
squared

ADERRST
darters»
dartres
redarts
retards
starred
traders

ADERSTT
started
tetrads

ADERSTV
adverts
starved

ADERSTW
steward
strawed
swarted
wrasted

ADERSTY
rest day
strayed

ADESSTU
sea dust
sudates

ADESTTW
swatted
wadsett

ADFILOR
Florida
forlaid

ADFOOPT
footpad
padfoot

ADFORRW
fordraw
forward
froward

ADGGGIN
dagging
gadging

ADGGILN
gadling
glading

ADGGINR
grading
niggard

ADGHINS
dashing
shading

ADGHONS
hagdons
sandhog

ADGIILN
dialing
gliadin
laiding

ADGIINW
gwiniad
waiding

ADGILNP
dapling
padling

ADGILNR
darling
larding
radling

ADGILNS
dalings
dasling
ladings
ligands
slading

ADGILNU
languid
lauding

ADGIMNN
damning
manding

ADGINNR
darning
draning
narding
randing

ADGINNS
andings
dansing»

sanding
snading

ADGINNW
dawning
wanding

ADGINOR
adoring
Gordian
gradino
idorgan
roading

ADGINOT
doating
toading

ADGINRS
darings
gradins
sarding

ADGINRT
darting
drating
tarding
trading

ADGINRW
drawing
warding

ADGINRY
draying
yarding

ADGNOOR
dragoon
gadroon

ADHILOY
holiday
hyaloid

ADHILSY
ladyish
shadily

ADHIMPS
dampish
phasmid

ADHIMRS
dirhams
Midrash

ADHMNOO
hoodman
manhood

ADIILMS
dismail
mislaid

ADIINPR
pindari
pridian

ADIINSU
indusia
suidian

ADIKNPS
kidnaps
skidpan

ADILMSY
diamyls
dismayl
ladyism

ADILNOR
nailrod
ordinal

ADILNSU
dualins
sundial
unlaids

ADILPRY
pyralid
rapidly

ADIMOST
diatoms
mastoid

ADIMSTU
dumaist
stadium

ADINNOP
dipnoan
Pandion

ADINOPR
padroni
poniard

ADINORS
Dorians
inroads
ordains
sadiron

ADINPST
pandits
sandpit

ADINRSU
Drusian
durians
sundari

ADINRSW
inwards
sinward
wardins

ADINSTT
Dantist
distant

ADIOPRT
dioptra
parotid

ADIORST
astroid
otarids

ADKORWY
daywork
workday

ADLNOSU
souldan
unloads

ADMNOOR
doorman
madrono

ADMNORS
randoms
rodsman

ADMNORT
dormant»
mordant

ADMORST
stardom
tsardom

ADMRSTU
durmast
mustard

ADNOORT
donator
adorant
tornado

ADNOSTT
dotants
stand-to

ADNPSTU
dustpan
stand up
upstand

ADNRSUW
sunward
undraws

AEEFHRT
feather
terefah

AEEFILR
filaree
leafier

AEEFIRS
faeries
freesia
sea fire

AEEFLLT
fellate
leaflet

AEEFLMS
almsfee
females

AEEFMNR
enframe
freeman

AEEFRST
afreets
feaster
sea fret

AEEGLMN
gleeman
melange

AEEGLNR
engrale
enlarge
general
gleaner

AEEGLNT
angelet
elegant

AEEGLRS
galeres
leagers
leagres
rageles
regales
regeals

AEEGLRU
leaguer
regulae

AEEGLSS
ageless
algeses
sea legs

AEEGMNS
emanges
maneges
menages

AEEGMSS
megasse
message

AEEGNRT
engreat
grantee
greaten
negater
reagent

AEEGNRV
avenger»
engrave

AEEGNST
enstage
negates
nestage

AEEGPRS
asperge
presage

AEEGRRS
agreges
greaser
raggees
reggaes

AEEGRRT
greater
rag tree
regrate

AEEGRST
ergates
restage

AEEGRSV
Gervase
greaves

AEEGSTT
gestate
tagetes

AEEHLRT
leather
tarheel

AEEHMRS
hareems
mahseer

AEEHNPT
heptane
phenate

AEEHNRT
earthen
enheart
hearten

AEEHNST
Asenath
ethanes»
heatens
sneathe

AEEHPRS
heapers
phearse
reshape
sphaere
spheare

AEEHPRT
preheat
threape

AEEHRRS
hearers
rehears
reshare
shearer

AEEHRST
aethers
heaters
reheats
Theresa

AEEHRTT
teather
theater
theatre
thereat
threate

AEEHRTW
weather
whereat
wreathe

AEEIKLP
apelike
pealike

AEEILMS
mealies
sea mile

AEEILNT
elatine
lineate

AEEILPT
epilate
pileate

AEEILRR
earlier
learier

AEEILRT
atelier
realtie
retaile

AEEILRV
leavier
Valerie
vealier

AEEIMNR
amerine
remanie

AEEIMNS
meanies
nemesia

AEEIMNT
etamine
matinee

AEEIMRS
seamier
seriema

AEEIMRT
emerita
emirate
meatier

AEEIMSS
misease
siamese

AEEINRT
neritae
retinae
trainee

AEEINTV
naivete
Venetia

AEEIRST
aeriest
ieaster
seriate

AEEIRTT
ariette
iterate

AEEITTV
aviette
evitate

AEEKNRS
Keresan
sneaker

AEEKPRS
parkees
repeaks
respeak
speaker

AEEKRST
retakes
sakeret

AEELMNP
empanel
emplane

AEELMNT
manteel
teleman

AEELMPR
empaler
emparle
empearl

AEELMPX
example
exempla

AEELMRT
lameter
remetal

AEELMST
Maltese
telesma

AEELNPS
alpeens
neaples
spelean

AEELNRR
learner»
relearn

AEELNRT
alterne
enteral
eternal
laneret
teleran

AEELNST
elanets
lateens
leanest
teanels

AEELNSV
enslave
leavens

AEELPRS
leapers
pealers
pleaser
relapse
repales
repeals
sleaper
slepare
spealer
spelare

AEELPRT
prelate
replate
repleat

AEELPTT
palette
peltate

AEELQSU
equales
queleas
sequela
squeale

AEELRRT
alterer
realter
relater

AEELRSS
earless
leasers»
resales
reseals
sealers

AEELRST
alteres
earlets
elaters
realest
realtes
relates
retales
saltere
streale
stealer
tealers
telares

AEELRSV
laveers
leavers
revales
reveals
several
vealers

AEELSSW
aweless
weasels
weasles

AEELSTT
Seattle
tsatlee

AEELSTU
eluates
setuale

AEEMMRT
ammeter
metamer

AEEMNST
enamets
entames
meanest
tenasme

AEEMOSW
awesome
waesome

AEEMPST
empaste
stampee

AEEMRSS
Rameses
seamers

AEEMRST
mastere
sea term
steamer
teamers

AEENNPT
pennate
pentane

AEENNRS
ensnare
rennase

AEENPST
penates
pesante

AEENPSY
Espayne
yeaspen

AEENRST
earnest
eastern
nearest
renates
steaner

AEENRTT
entreat
ratteen
ternate

AEENRTV
nervate
veteran

AEENSST
enseats
entases
sateens
senates
steanes

AEEORST
roseate
tea rose

AEEPPRR
paperer
prepare
repaper

AEEPRRT
repater
taperer

AEEPRSS
asperse
esparse
pareses
Parsees
pearses
praeses
preases
preasse
serapes

AEEPRST
asprete
pastree
peartes
repaste
repeats
retapes
streape

AEEPSTT
septate
spattee

AEERRST
rearest
re-rates
restare
serrate
tearers

AEERRSW
reswear
swearer
wearers

AEERRTT
retrate
retreat
treater

AEERRTW
rewater
waterer

AEERSST
easters
eastres
eatress
reseats
saeters
searest
seaters
tessera
teasers

AEERSSU
reseaus
seasure

AEERSSV
assever
asserve
averses
resaves
seavers

AEERSTT
estreat
restate
retaste
teaters
teatres

AEERSTU
austeer
austere
sauteer
sautere

AEERSTW
sawtere
sweater

AEFFRST
affrets
restaff
staffer

AEFGILN
fealing
finagle
leafing

AEFGINR
fearing
ingrafe

AEFGITU
ague fit
fatigue

AEFHRST
fathers
freaths
hafters
shafter
thrafes

AEFILMN
feminal
inflame

AEFILSS
falsies
filasse

AEFILST
festial
fetials

AEFIMNR
fireman
infamer

AEFINRS
fansier
infares

AEFINRT
fainter
fenitar
fire ant

AEFINST
fainest
naifest

AEFIRRS
farries
reifars

AEFIRST
afrites
fairest
fraiste

AEFLLNN
fannell
flannel

AEFLNRU
flaneur
funeral

AEFLORS
loafers
safrole

AEFLORT
floater
floreat
refloat

AEFLOSW
seafowl
sea wolf

AEFLRSU
earfuls
ferulas
fur seal
refusal

AEFLRTU
faulter
refutal
tearful

AEFLSST
falsest
falsets
festals

AEFMNOR
foramen
foreman

AEFMNRU
fraenum
unframe

AEFNSST
Fastens
fatness
saftens

AEFRSTW
fawters
fretsaw
wafters

AEGGILN
eagling
gealing
lignage

AEGGRSS
aggress
saggers
seggars

AEGGRST
gagster
gargets
stagger
taggers

AEGHINT
gahnite
heating

AEGHLST
haglets
shaglet

AEGHMNO
hogmane
Mohegan

AEGIKLN
kealing
leaking
linkage

AEGIKNS
askinge
seaking
sea king
sinkage

AEGILLS
gallies
gallise

AEGILMN
leaming
mealing

AEGILMR
gremial
lamiger

AEGILMS
gas-lime
milages

AEGILNN
Angelin
eanling
leaning
nealing

AEGILNP
apeling
leaping
pealing
pleaing

AEGILNR
aligner
earling
engrail
ingrale
inlarge
langier
learing
nargile
realign
reginal

AEGILNS
aleings
alesing
leasing
linages
salinge
sealing

AEGILNT
atingle
elating
gelatin
genital
langite
lingeat
tealing
Telinga

AEGILNV
leaving
vealing

AEGILNZ
leazing
zealing

AEGILRS
gailers
glasier
grailes»

lairges
seragli

AEGILSS
algesis
glaises
silages

AEGIMNR
amering
germain
germina
mangier
margine
mearing
reaming

AEGIMNS
amesing
enigmas
gamines
measing
seaming

AEGIMNT
meating
mintage
teaming
tegmina

AEGIMPR
epigram
primage

AEGIMRS
gisarme
maigres
mirages
simagre

AEGIMRT
migrate
ragtime

AEGIMST
gamiest
sigmate

AEGINNR
aginner
earning
engrain
Grainne
grannie»

nearing

AEGINNS
eanings
seaning

AEGINNT
anteing
antigen
gentian
neating

AEGINNU
anguine
guanine

AEGINNV
Angevin
neaving

AEGINOS
agonies
agonise

AEGINPR
grapien
pearing
reaping

AEGINPS
peasing
seaping
spaeing
Spaigne
spinage

AEGINRR
angrier
earring
grainer
granier
raigner
rangier
rearing

AEGINRS
angries
angrise
earings
erasing
gainers
graines
grainse
ingears»

inrages
reagins
reasing
regains
reginas
searing
seringa

AEGINRT
angrite
gairten
granite
Gretian
ingrate
ingreat
renigat
tangier
tearing

AEGINRV
igraven
ingrave
reaving
vearing
vinegar

AEGINST
easting
eatings
gainest
gnaiste
gnastie
ingates
ingesta
seating
stigean
tangies
teaings
teasing
tsigane

AEGIPPS
gaspipe
gas pipe
pipages

AEGIPRS
pargies
prisage
spairge

AEGIRSS
agrises
gassier

AEGIRST
agister
aigrets
gairest
gaiters
seagirt
stagier
strigae
tirages

AEGIRTV
virgate
vitrage

AEGISST
ageists
sagiest

AEGLLNO
allonge
galleon

AEGLLOT
galleot
tollage

AEGLLRS
laggers
slagger

AEGLLRY
allergy
gallery
largely
regally

AEGLLSU
seagull
sullage
ullages

AEGLNOT
angelot
tangelo

AEGLNPR
grapnel
prangle

AEGLNRS
anglers
garnels
glenars
largens»
rangles
sangler

AEGLNRT
tangler
trangle

AEGLNRW
wangler
wrangle

AEGLNSS
glassen
sangles

AEGLNSU
angelus
lagunes
langues

AEGLORT
gloater
legator

AEGLPRU
earplug
graupel

AEGLPSU
plagues
plusage

AEGLRSS
glasers
largess

AEGLRST
galstre
glaster
largest
raglets
stragel
stragle

AEGLRSV
glavers
gravels
verglas

AEGLRTU
gaulter
tegular
tragule

AEGLSSU
saulges
sea slug

AEGMNOT
magneto
megaton
montage

AEGMNRT
garment
margent
ragment

AEGMNTU
augment
mutagen

AEGNORS
nose rag
onagers
oranges

AEGNRRT
Gartner
granter
regrant

AEGNRST
argents
garnets
gartens
gnaster
strange

AEGOPRT
portage
potager

AEGOPST
Gestapo
postage
potages

AEGORST
garotes
orgeats
storage
toe rags

AEGORTU
outgear
outrage

AEGOSTW
stowage
towages

AEGPRRS
grapers
grasper
sparger

AEGRRUV
gravure
verruga

AEGRSSS
gassers
grasses

AEGRSSU
arguses
saugers
usagers

AEGRSTU
gauster
Tuaregs

AEGRSTV
gravest
gravets

AEGRSTY
grayest
gyrates
stagery

AEHILNR
hernial
inhaler

AEHILST
hailest
halites
heliast
laithes

AEHILTT
lithate
tile hat

AEHIMSS
mashies
Messiah

AEHIMST
atheism
athisme
Hamites
mathesi

AEHINPS
inphase
Phineas

AEHINRS
arshine
hernias
sharnie

AEHINRT
hairnet
inearth
Rhetian

AEHINST
sheitan
sthenia
thaines

AEHIPRS
harpies
parishe
phairse
pharise
sharpie

AEHIQSU
haiques
quashie

AEHIRST
hastier
sheriat

AEHIRSW
washier
wearish

AEHISST
ashiest
saithes

AEHISTT
atheist
staithe

AEHKNRS
hankers»
harkens
shanker

AEHLLRS
hallers
harsell

AEHLNST
hantles
lanshet

AEHLNSU
Hulsean
unleash
unhales
unheals
unshale

AEHLORT
loather
rathole

AEHLPRS
halpers
plasher
spheral

AEHLRSS
ashlers
halsers
lashers
shalers
slasher

AEHLRST
halters
harslet
hastler
lathers
rathels
shaltre
slahter
slather
thalers

AEHLRTY
earthly
hartely
heartly
lathery

AEHLSST
haslets
hatless

AEHMMRS
hammers
shammer

AEHMRSS
marshes
mashers
shamers
smasher

AEHMRST
hamster
marthes
mathers

AEHNOPT
phaeton
phonate

AEHNORS
hoarsen
senhora

AEHNPRS
harpens
sharpen

AEHNPSU
phaunes
unhaspe
unshape

AEHNRSS
harness
harnses
sharens
sharnes
shearns

AEHNRST
anthers
harnest
thenars

AEHNRTU
haunter
unearth
unheart
urethan

AEHNSST
hastens
snathes
sneaths»

thaness

AEHNSTU
hauntes
shea nut
uneaths

AEHOPST
tap shoe
teashop

AEHORST
asthore
earshot

AEHPRRS
harpers
phraser
sharper

AEHPRST
sparthe
spather
threaps

AEHRSST
hasters
hatress
hearsts
rashest
'shartes
'shearts
shaster

AEHRSSW
hawsers
swasher
washers

AEHRSTT
hatters
rathest
shatter
threats

AEHRSTV
harvest
thraves

AEHRSTW
swather
thawers
wathers
wrathes
wreaths

AEIILNT
intaile
liniate

AEIILSS
liaises
silesia

AEIIMNT
intimae
miniate

AEIINNS
asinine
insanie

AEIIRST
airiest
irisate

AEIKLMN
Malinke
manlike

AEIKLRT
ratlike
talkier

AEIKLST
lakiest
talkies

AEIKMNR
mankier
ramekin

AEIKNNR
Karenni
Rankine

AEIKNRT
Katrine
keratin

AEIKNSY
kyanise
yankies

AEIKRSS
kaisers
sea risk

AEILLPR
pallier»

prelial

AEILLRT
literal
tallier

AEILLSS
allises
sallies

AEILLST
tailles
tallies

AEILMNN
Lemnian
lineman
melanin

AEILMNP
impanel
maniple

AEILMNR
manlier
marline
mineral
railmen

AEILMNS
isleman
lamines
Malines
masline
menials
mislane
seminal

AEILMNT
ailment
aliment

AEILMPR
impaler
imparle
impearl
lempira
palmier

AEILMPS
impales
palmies

AEILMPT
implate
palmiet

AEILMRR
larmier
marlier

AEILMRS
mailers
milreas
realism
remails

AEILMRT
lamiter
latimer
maltier
marlite

AEILMSS
aimless
Melissa
mesails
samiels
seismal

AEILNNS
nainsel
naselin

AEILNOR
aileron
alerion
alienor

AEILNOT
elation
toenail

AEILNPR
pearlin
plainer
praline

AEILNPS
alpines
neapils
spaniel
splenia

AEILNPT
pantile
pentail
platine
talpine

AEILNRS
aliners
enrails
lainers
laniers
larines
linears
nailers
renails
reslain
saliner

AEILNRT
entrail
Latiner
latrine
ratline
reliant
retinal
trainel
trenail

AEILNRY
inlayer
nailery

AEILNST
atelins
eastlin
elastin
entails
nailset
salient
saltine
slainte
staniel
tenails

AEILNSU
insulae
inulase

AEILOPR
peloria
rape oil

AEILOPS
leipoas
opalise

AEILPRS
pailers
perials
pleasir»

spelair

AEILPRT
paltrie
plaiter
platier
replait

AEILPRV
prevail
viperal

AEILPSS
espials
lapises
lipases
palises
palsies
plaises
spailes

AEILPST
aplites
pailets
paliest
plaites
talipes

AEILQTU
liquate
tequila

AEILRRS
larries
railers
rerails

AEILRRT
retiral
retrial
trailer

AEILRSS
airless
aislers
resails
sailers
serails
serials

AEILRST
Alister
astiler
laiters»

realist
restial
retails
saltier
saltire
slaiter
slatier
tailers
tarlies
traisle
traleis

AEILRSV
revisal
vailers

AEILRTY
irately
reality
tearily

AEILSST
aislets
lasiest
stailes
taisels

AEILSSV
valises
vessail

AEIMMNS
ammines
mismean
misname

AEIMNOR
moraine
romaine

AEIMNPR
permain
Permian

AEIMNRR
mariner
rein arm

AEIMNRS
maneirs
marines
remains
seminar
sirname

AEIMNRT
minaret
raiment

AEIMNRV
Minerva
vermian

AEIMNSS
inseams
samisen

AEIMNST
etamins
inmates
inmeats
manties
Samnite
stamine
tameins
tamines

AEIMNSW
manwise
wiseman

AEIMNTY
amenity
anytime

AEIMOPR
emporia
pomeria

AEIMOST
atomise
osmiate
Samiote

AEIMPRS
impresa
sampier
sampire

AEIMPST
impaste
pastime

AEIMPSW
mapwise
pawmies

AEIMRRS
marries»
marseir
simarre

AEIMRST
Artemis
imarets
maestri
maister
maistre
marites
mastrie
misrate
semitar
smartie

AEIMSST
asteism
ismates
matiest
miseats
samites
tamises

AEIMSSV
massive
mavises

AEINNOT
enation
Etonian
Noetian

AEINNPT
pantein
pantine
piannet
pinnate

AEINNRS
insaner
insnare
rannies

AEINNRT
entrain
tannier
Tiernan
tiranne
trannie

AEINNST
ensaint
inanest
innates»
sinnate
tannies

AEINOPR
open air
pea iron

AEINOPS
epinaos
senopia

AEINPRS
arpines
enpairs
napiers
paniers
pansier
Persian
prasine
rapines
saprine
snapier

AEINPRT
painter
pertain
Petrina
pine tar
repaint

AEINPST
panties
pastine
patines
pianets
ptisane
sapient
spinate

AEINQTU
antique
quinate

AEINRRS
rainers
sierran
snarier

AEINRRT
rantier
retrain
terrain
trainer

AEINRST
anestri
antsier
asterin
earnits
eranist
estrain
inserta
nastier
neritas
ranites
ranties
rantise
ratines
resiant
Resinat
restain
retains
retinas
retsina
sarient
seriant
sertain
stainer
stanier
straine
starnie
stearin
taniers
tiranes
traines

AEINRSV
naviers
navires
ravines
Servian

AEINRTT
intrate
intreat
iterant
nattier
nitrate
tainter
tartine
tertian

AEINRTU
ruinate
taurine
uranite
urinate

AEINRTW
tawnier
tinware

AEINSST
entasis
nasties
satines
sestina
Staines
staines
tansies
tisanes

AEINSSV
savines
vinasse

AEINSTT
instate
satinet

AEINSTU
aunties
sinuate
Uniates

AEINSTV
naivest
natives
vainest

AEINSTW
tawnies
waniest

AEINSTZ
zaniest
zeatins

AEIORRR
arriero
roarier

AEIORST
osteria
otaries

AEIPPRS
apprise
sappier

AEIPPRT
periapt»
Rappite

AEIPRRS
aspirer
pairers
parries
praiser
rapiers
raspier
repairs
ripares

AEIPRSS
aspiers
aspires
paresis
parises
parsies
praises
raspies
raspise
Serapis
spireas

AEIPRST
paiters
parteis
parties
partise
pastier
piaster
piastre
pirates
praites
praties
spirate
tapiser
traipse

AEIPRSU
spuriae
upraise

AEIPRSV
parvise
paviers
paviser

AEIPRTT
partite
tear pit

AEIPSSV
passive»
pavises

AEIPSTT
patties
pistate
stipate
tapetis

AEIRRSS
arrises
raisers
sierras

AEIRRST
arteirs
artiers
artires
raiters
rastier
stairer
tarries
tarsier

AEIRRSV
arrives
variers
varries

AEIRRTT
retrait
rattier
tartier

AEIRSST
aisters
aistres
asteirs
sairest
satires
staires
tirasse

AEIRSTT
artiest
artiste
attires
iratest
ratiest
ratites
striate
tastier
tertias
traiste

AEIRSTV
taviers
vastier
veritas

AEIRSTW
waister
waiters
wariest
wastrie

AEIRTTT
attrite
tattier
titrate

AEJLOSU
jalouse
jealous

AEKKRSY
streaky
yakkers

AEKLNST
anklets
asklent
kantels
kantles
lankest
lankets
tankles

AEKLRST
kartels
retalks
stalker
talkers

AEKNPSU
sneak up
unspeak

AEKNRST
knaster
rankest
stanker
starken
tankers

AEKOTTU
outtake
take out

AEKPRRS
parkers
sparker

AELLMSY
mallays
mesally

AELLORV
all over
overall

AELLPST
pallets
spatell

AELLRST
restall
staller
stellar
tellars

AELLRTY
alertly
elytral

AELLSST
sallets
stellas
tassell

AELLSTT
tallest
tallets

AELLSTW
setwall
swallet
wallets

AELMMRS
lammers
rammels
slammer

AELMMST
malmest
stammel
tammels

AELMNOR
almoner
nemoral

AELMNOT
lomenta
omental
telamon

AELMPRS
lampers
palmers
sampler

AELMPRT
templar
trampel
trample

AELMRSS
armless
semlars

AELMRST
armlets
lamster
malster
malters
marlets
martels
stramel
tramels

AELNNRS
ensnarl
lanners
rannels
rannles

AELNNRT
lantern
lantren
lentran

AELNPRT
pantler
planter
replant

AELNPTY
aplenty
penalty

AELNRRS
snarler
snarrel

AELNRST
alterns
antlers
entrals
lanrets
lanters
rantles
rentals
reslant
saltern
santrel
slanter
starnel
sternal

AELNSSU
sensual
unseals

AELNSSY
nayless
snayles

AELNSTU
eluants
unleast

AELOORS
aerosal
roseola

AELOPRS
paroles
reposal

AELOPRT
ploater
prolate

AELOPST
apostle
pelotas
pot ales

AELORRT
realtor
relator

AELORSS
lassoer
oarless
serosal
soleras

AELORST
elators
oestral
ostreal

AELORTU
rotulae
torulae

AELPPRS
lappers
perpals
rappels
slapper
sparple

AELPPST
lappets
slappet
stapple
tapples

AELPPSU
appulse
leaps up
papules
upleaps

AELPRST
palters
pastler
persalt
plaster
plastre
platers
pratles
psalter
spalter
spartel
spartle
stapler

AELPRSU
perusal
pleuras
serpula

AELPRSY
parleys
parsley
players
replays
sparely
splayer

AELPRTT
partlet
platter
prattel
prattle

AELPRTY
peartly
prelaty
pterlya

AELPSSS
plasses
sapless

AELPSST
pastels
plastes
slapest
spatles
splates
stapels
staples

AELPSTT
patlets
pattels
pattles
peltast
spattle
T plates

AELPSTU
pulsate
puteals
spatule

AELRSSS
rassles
sassler

AELRSST
arslets
artless
astlers
estlars
lasters
rastels
rastles
resalts
salters
slaster
slaters
starles»

strales
streals
tarsels
taslers
tersals
trassel
tressal

AELRSSY
rayless
reslays
saylers
slayers

AELRSTT
artlets
latters
rattels
rattles
sattler
slatter
starlet
startle
tatlers
Telstar
tsarlet

AELRSTU
estrual
saluter
saulter

AELRSTV
travels
valters
varlets
vestral

AELRSTW
awlters
lawters
rewalts
sawlter
slawest
swalest
walters
warstel
warstle
wartles
wastrel
wrastle

AELRSTY
layters»

raylets
strayle
trayles

AELRTTT
tartlet
tattler
trattle

AELSSTT
sattels
sattles
slattes
stalest
taslets

AELSSTU
salutes
taluses

AELSTTY
stately
stylate

AEMNNOS
mannose
nameson

AEMNNRT
manrent
remnant
rent man

AEMNORS
enamors
moaners
oarsmen
Romanes

AEMNORU
enamour
neuroma

AEMNOTU
notaeum
outname

AEMNPST
enstamp
pasment
tapsmen

AEMNRST
artsmen»

martens
sarment
smarten
star men

AEMNRSU
manures
murenas
surname

AEMOOST
osteoma
Sao Tome

AEMORST
amorets
maestro
moaters
morates

AEMORSW
seaworm
womeras

AEMPRST
emparts
restamp
stamper
tampers
tempras
trampes

AEMQRSU
marques
masquer

AEMRRST
arsmert
marrets
marters
smarter

AEMRRSW
reswarm
rewarms
swarmer
warmers

AEMRSSU
amusers
assumer
Erasmus
masseur
Mausers»

saumers

AEMRSTT
matters
smatter

AEMRSTU
matures
strumae

AEMRSTY
mastery
mastrye
mayster
maystre
streamy

AENNQTU
quannet
tanquen

AENNRTY
tannery
tyranne

AENOOTZ
entozoa
tan ooze

AENOPRS
peronas
persona

AENOPRT
operant
patrone
pronate
protean

AENORST
Anteros
atoners
nor' east
ornates
senator
treason

AENOSTU
soutane
tan ouse

AENPPRS
nappers
parpens»

parsnep
snapper

AENPRST
arpents
entraps
panters
parents
partens
pastern
Spertan
trepans

AENPRSW
enwraps
pawners
prawnes
repawns
spawner

AENPRTT
pattern
reptant
trap net

AENPSST
aptness
patness
pesants

AENPSSY
synapse
yapness

AENPSTU
peanuts
pesaunt
untapes

AENRRST
arrents
errants
narrest
nerrast
ranters
Terrans

AENRSST
arnests
enstars
nasters
santers
santres
sarsnet»

snaters
staners
starnes
stranes
transes

AENRSSW
answers
rawness

AENRSTT
natters
rattens
restant
snatter
stentar
tanters

AENRSTU
aunters
auntres
nasuter
nateurs
natures
saunter
tea urns

AENRSTV
servant
starven
taverns
versant

AENRSTW
strawen
strawne
wanters

AENRSUW
unswear
unwares

AENRTTY
nattery
tyrante

AENSTTU
attunes
nutates
tautens
tetanus
unstate

AEOPRRT
praetor
prorate

AEOPRST
esparto
proteas
seaport

AEORSTT
Rosetta
rotates
stoater
toaster

AEPPRRT
pre-part
trapper

AEPPRSS
appress
sappers

AEPPRSU
paupers
upspear

AEPPRSW
swapper
wappers
warppes
wrappes

AEPPSTU
paste up
pupates

AEPRRSS
parsers
raspers
sparers
sparser

AEPRRST
parrets
parters
praters
rapters
reparts
sparret
trapers

AEPRRSY
prayers»

reprays
respray
sprayer

AEPRRTU
parture
rapture

AEPRSST
pasters
pastres
preasts
repasts
septars
sparest
spartes
sprates
spreats
strapes
streaps
tapsers
trapses

AEPRSTT
patters
spatter
tapster

AEPRSTU
Pasteur
pasture
pautres
psauter
uprates
upstare
uptears

AEQRSTU
quartes
T square

AERRSST
arrests
astrers
rasters
restars
starers
straser
tarress

AERRSSU
assurer
rasures

AERRSTT
ratters
restart
starter

AERRSTW
sawtrer
strawer

AERRSWY
sewarry
warreys

AERSSST
asserts
essarts
sasters
tessars
trasses

AERSSTT
asterts
starets
staters
strates
streats
tasters

AERSSTU
austers
Erastus
estuars

AERSTTT
stretta
tartest
tatters

AERSTTW
Stewart
swatter
tewarts
watters

AERSTTY
trayste
yatters

AESTTTU
statute
tautest

AFFGINR
ingraff»
raffing

AFFGINY
affying
yaffing

AFFINRU
funfair
ruffian

AFGIINR
fairing
ingraif
raifing

AFGILNO
afoling
foaling
loafing

AFGILNR
farling
flaring
rafling

AFGILNT
fatling
flating

AFGILNY
anglify
flaying

AFGIMNR
farming
framing

AFGINRS
farings
farsing
frasing
Grafins
rafings

AFGINRT
farting
frating
ingraft
rafting

AFGLLUY
fall guy
fugally

AFILLUV
fluvial
vialful

AFINSTU
faunist
fustian
infaust

AFLLOTU
fallout
outfall

AFMORST
farmost
formats

AFORRSY
forrays
forsary

AGGGINN
ganging
nagging

AGGILLN
galling
gingall

AGGILNN
angling
langing

AGGILNR
argling
glaring
larging

AGGILNS
gingals
glasing
laggins

AGGILNT
Lagting
tagling

AGGIMNR
graming
marging

AGGINNR
angring
gingran»
gnaring
graning
ranging

AGGINNT
ganting
tanging

AGGINPS
gapings
gasping
pagings

AGGINRS
gas ring
grasing
ragings
sirgang

AGGINRT
grating
targing

AGGINST
gasting
gatings
gigants
staging

AGHIILN
hauling
nilghau

AGHIKNS
hakings
shaking

AGHILNS
ashling
halings
halsing
langish
lashing
shaling

AGHILNT
Althing
halting
lathing
thingal

AGHILNW
hawling
whaling

AGHIMNR
harming
rhaming

AGHIMNS
mashing
shaming

AGHINNS
nashing
shaning

AGHINPS
hasping
phasing
shaping

AGHINRS
garnish
rashing
sharing

AGHINST
hasting
hatings
tashing

AGHINSW
hawsing
shawing
washing

AGIILNN
alining
laining
nailing

AGIILNP
laiping
pailing

AGIILNR
glairin
ingrail
lairing
railing

AGIILNS
ailings
gaislin
liasing
nilgais
sailing

AGIILNT
intagli
laiting
tailing

AGIINNR
ingrain
raining

AGIINNT
naiting
taining

AGIINPR
pairing
raiping

AGIINRS
airings
arising
raising
sairing

AGIINRT
airting
raiting
tairing

AGIINSV
vaising
visaing

AGIKLNR
karling
larking

AGIKLNS
lasking
skaling
slaking

AGIKLNT
takling
talking

AGIKMNS
kamings
makings
masking
smaking

AGIKNNR
narking
ranking

AGIKNNT
tangkin
tanking

AGIKNRS
rakings
rasking
sarking

AGIKNRT
karting
traking

AGIKNST
skating
staking
takings
tasking

AGILLNU
lingual
lingula

AGILLSU
ligulas
lugsail

AGILMMN
lamming
malming

AGILMNP
ampling
lamping
palming

AGILMNR
larming
marling

AGILMNT
malting
talming

AGILNNS
Lansing
lingans
linsang

AGILNNT
antling
lanting
natling
tanling

AGILNPP
appling
lapping
palping

AGILNPS
lapsing
palings
sapling
slaping
spaling

AGILNPT
patling
plating
tapling

AGILNPW
lapwing
pawling
plawing

AGILNRT
altring
ratling
traling

AGILNRY
angrily
nargily

AGILNSS
glassin
signals

AGILNST
anglist
langits
lasting
salting
satling
slating
staling
talings

AGILNSU
nilgaus
saluing
sauling

AGILNSV
salving
slaving
valsing

AGILNSW
lawings
salwing
slawing
swaling
walsing

AGILNSY
layings
slaying

AGILORS
girasol
glorias

AGILOST
galiots
latigos
saligot

AGIMMNR
marming
ramming

AGIMNNS
mansing
namings

AGIMNOR
moringa
roaming

AGIMNRT
marting
migrant

AGIMNRY
marying
myringa

AGIMNST
masting
tamings

AGINNOT
anoting
atoning

AGINNPS
napings
pansing
snaping
spaning

AGINNPW
nawping
pawning

AGINNRS
ransing
snaring

AGINNRT
ingrant
ranting
traning

AGINNST
antings
staning

AGINNSW
awnings
snawing
wanings

AGINNTU
tanguin
tauning

AGINNTW
tawning
wanting

AGINOPR
poaring
roaping

AGINORS
gainors
ignaros
ingoars
origans
signora
soaring

AGINORT
Grotian
orating
roating

AGINOST
agonist
gitanos
oasting

AGINPRS
parings»
parsing
prasing
rapings
rasping
sparing

AGINPRT
parting
prating
traping

AGINPRW
rawping
warping
wraping

AGINPSS
passing
spasing

AGINPSW
pawings
pawsing
wasping

AGINRST
gastrin
gratins
ratings
staring
tringas

AGINRSY
signary
syringa

AGINRTT
ratting
tarting

AGINRTW
ring taw
trawing
warting

AGINRWY
ringway
warying
wraying

AGINSSS
assigns
sassing

AGINSTT
stating
tasting

AGINSTV
staving
vasting

AGINSTW
stawing
tawings
tawsing
wasting

AGINSTY
staying
Stygian
taysing

AGIORST
agistor
orgiast

AGLNOSS
glossan
slogans

AGLNOST
alongst
langots

AGMNORU
morunga
organum

AGNORST
art song
rotangs

AHIKLST
khilats
silk hat

AHIKNRS
Krishna
rankish

AHIKNSS
Nashkis
snakish

AHILPPS
Lappish
shiplap

AHILSST
saltish
tahsils

AHILSTU
halitus
thulias

AHIMRST
Mithras
thairms

AHIPRST
harpist
thraips

AHIRSST
hairsts
tsarish

AHIRSTT
athirst
rattish
tartish

AHIRSTV
ravisht
travish

AHIRSTW
trishaw
wraiths

AHLLOSW
hallows
shallow

AHLLOTY
loathly
tally ho

AHMOOPS
oompahs
shampoo

AIILRTV
trivial
vitrail

AIIMNPT
impaint
timpani

AIIMNST
animist
intimas

AIIMRST
maistri
simitar

AIINRSS
raisins
Rissian
Sirians

AIINRTV
vitrain
Vitrina

AILLMOP
oil lamp
oil palm
palm oil

AILLPST
pastill
spatill

AILMNOS
malison
monials
Osmanli
Soliman
somnial

AILMPST
lampist
palmist

AILMRST
mistral
mitrals
ramtils

AILNNSU
unnails
unslain

AILNPTU
nuptial
patulin
unplait

AILNPTY
inaptly
ptyalin

AILNRSU
insular
urinals

AILNSTY
nastily
saintly

AILOPST
apostil
topsail

AILPRSU
parulis
uprisal

AILRSTU
rituals
trisula

AILRTUV
virtual
vitular

AIMMOSS
mimosas
Mosaism

AIMNNOS
amnions
mansion
Minoans
onanism

AIMNOPT
maintop
tampion
timpano

AIMNOTU
manitou
tinamou

AIMNRSU
Surinam
uranism

AIMNSTU
manitus
tsunami

AIMORST
amorist
Miastor

AIMRSST
Marists
Ramists
tsarism

AIMRSTU
atriums
Maurist

AINNOST
anoints
nations
onanist

AINNQTU
quinnat
quintan

AINOORT
Ontario
oration

AINOPRS
parison
soprani

AINOPTU
opuntia
utopian

AINORST
aroints
astrion
rations
traison

AINOSSU
sanious
suasion

AINPRST
inparts
partins
spirant
spraint

AINPRTU
puritan
uptrain

AINQSTU
asquint
quaints
quintas

AINRSTT
intrats
straint
transit

AINSSTU
Austins
issuant
sustain

AIOPRRT
airport
paritor

AIOPRST
airstop
parotis

AIORSUV
saviour
various

AIRSSTT
artists
sittars
straits
traists
tsarist

AIRSSTU
aurists
Tarsius

AKLOTUW
outwalk
walkout

AKMNRTU
trankum
Turkman

ALMSSUY
alyssum
asylums

AMNOPST
postman
tampons
topsman

AMNORST
matrons
transom

AMNORSY
masonry
mornays

AMORSST
matross
stroams

AMPRSUW
upswarm
warm ups
warms up

ANOOPRS
pronaos
soprano

ANOOPRT
patroon
pronota

ANOORTT
arnotto
rattoon

ANORSTU
rousant
santour

ANORSUU
anurous
uranous

ANPRSTU
suntrap
unstrap

AOPRRTY
parroty
portray

AORRSWY
sowarry
yarrows

AORSSUY
ossuary
suasory

APRSTTU
start up
upstart

BBCELOR
clobber
cobbler

BBDEILO
bilobed
lobbied

BBDEILR
dibbler
dribble
ribbled

BBDELRU
burbled
dubbler
rubbled

BBDELSU
dubbels
dubbles
slubbed

BBEGILR
glibber
gribble

BBEILNS
nibbles
snibble

BBEILST
libbets
stibble
tibbles

BBEIQSU
quibbes
squibbe

BBELRSU
burbels
burbles
lubbers
rubbels
rubbles
slubber

BBELSTU
stubble
tubbles

BBERSTU
stubber»
tubbers

BBGIINR
bribing
ribbing

BBGILNU
bulbing
lubbing

BBGIMNO
bombing
mobbing

BBGINOS
gibbons
sobbing

BBGINSU
gubbins
subbing

BBHIMOS
Hobbism
mobbish

BCDEKOR
bedrock
brocked

BCEIKNR
bickern
bricken

BCEILMR
climber
reclimb

BCEILOR
bricole
corbeil

BCEKLRU
bruckle
buckler

BCEKSTU
bestuck
buckets

BCELMRU
clumber
crumble

BCEMORS
combers
combres
recombs
scomber
scombre

BCEMRSU
cumbers
recumbs
scumber

BCILMPU
plumbic
upclimb

BDDEEIT
betided
debited

BDDELRU
bludder
buddler

BDEEILL
bellied
delible

BDEELOW
belowed
boweled
debowel
elbowed

BDEENOR
deboner
redbone

BDEEORS
bedsore
derobes
sobered

BDEERTT
bretted
Debrett

BDEGLNU
blunged
bungled

BDEILLR
brilled
ill-bred»

redbill

BDEILNR
blinder
brindle

BDEILRR
blirred
bridler

BDEILRS
bilders
birsled
bridles
brisled
diblers

BDEILRT
driblet
tribled

BDEILRU
builder
rebuild

BDEIMOR
bromide
embroid

BDEIORS
borides
disrobe

BDEIRST
bedirts
bestrid
bistred

BDEIRSU
bruised
burdies

BDEKOOR
brooked
red book

BDELLOR
bedroll
brolled

BDELMMU
bummled
mumbled

BDELMRU
drumble
lumbred
rumbled

BDELNRU
blunder
bundler

BDELORU
boulder
doubler

BDELORW
bowlder
low-bred
worbled

BDELOSU
bloused
doubles

BDELOTT
blotted
bottled

BDELOTU
boulted
doublet

BDELSSU
budless
bussled

BDELSTU
bustled
subtled

BDEMOOR
bedroom
boredom
broomed

BDEMSTU
dumbest
stumbed

BDENORU
bounder
bourned
rebound
unrobed

BDENSTU
but-ends
subtend

BDEORRU
bordure
bourder
brouder

BDEORSU
broused
obdures
rosebud

BDEORSW
bowders
browsed

BDEORTU
doubter
obtrude
outbred
redoubt

BDERSTU
brusted
bursted
sturbed

BDGELRU
bludger
burgled

BDGIINR
birding
briding

BEEEFIR
beefier
freebie

BEEGINR
beering
bigener

BEEHRST
berthes
sherbet

BEEHRSW
Hebrews
beshrew

BEELLRS
bellers
rebells

BEELRST
belters
blester
trebles

BEEMRSU
Burmese
embrues
emburse

BEEORSV
observe
obverse
verbose

BEERSTU
rebutes
tuberes

BEERSTW
bestrew
webster

BEGGLOR
boggler
broggle

BEGIINR
biering
bingier

BEGILNO
gobelin
gob-line
ignoble
inglobe

BEGILRS
bilgres
gerbils
gribles

BEGINSS
besings
bigness

BEGLNRU
blunger
bungler

BEGORSU
brogues
goubers
rose bug

BEHINOP
hipbone
hopbine

BEHLORT
blother
brothel

BEHLRSU
blusher
burhels

BEHLRTU
bluther
thruble

BEHOORT
boother
theorbo

BEHORST
boshter
bothers
brothes
theorbs

BEIKOOS
bookies
booksie

BEILLRS
billers
brilles

BEILLST
bestill
billets

BEILNOO
bone oil
obelion

BEILNSY
bylines
yeblins

BEILRSS
birsles
ribless

BEILRST
birtles
blister
bristle
britles
riblets
stibler
tribles

BEILRTT
blitter
brittle
triblet

BEIMORW
imbower
wombier

BEIMRSU
erbiums
imbrues
imburse

BEIMRTU
imbrute
terbium

BEINNOS
benison
bonnies

BEINOST
boniest
ebonist

BEINRSU
burnies
rubines
suberin

BEINRTU
tribune
turbine

BEIRRSU
brisure
bruiser
burries

BEIRSTU
brutise
bustier
rubiest

BELLOSU
boulles
lobules
soluble

BELMOOR
bloomer
rebloom

BELMPRU
plumber
replumb

BELMRSU
lumbers
rumbles
slumber
umbrels

BELMRTU
tumbler
tumbrel

BELMSTU
stumble
tumbles

BELNSTU
unbelts
unblest

BELORST
bolster
bolters
lobster
orblets
rebolts
roblets
stroble
trobels
trobles

BELORTT
blotter
bottler

BELORTU
blue rot
boulter
tourbel
troubel
trouble

BELOSTU
Boletus
boulets

BELRSTU
bluster
brustel
brustle
bulters
burlets
burstle
bustler
butlers
struble
subtler
trubles
turbels
turbles

BEMORST
bestorm
mobster
retombs

BENNORW
Bronwen
newborn

BENORST
Bretons
sorbent

BENRSTU
brunest
brunets
bunters
burnets
bursten
subrent

BEOORST
booster
reboots

BERRSTU
burrets
burster
burters

BFLLOWY
blowfly
flyblow

BGGILNU
bugling
bulging

BGIIKLN
bilking
bliking

BGIIMNR
briming
imbring

BGIINNR
brining
inbring

BGIINRT
briting
ringbit
tribing

BGILMNO
bloming
mobling

BGILNOR
gorblin
robling

BGILNOT
biltong
bolting

BGILNOW
blowing
bowling

BGILNRU
bruling
rubling

BGINOOR
bog iron
booring

BGINORS
borings
brosing
orbings
robings
sorbing

BGINOSS
bossing»
obsigns

BGINPRU
burping
upbring

BGINRTU
bruting
burting

BGINRUY
burying
rubying

BILORST
Bristol
trobils

BINORST
Britons
ribston

BMORSUU
brumous
umbrous

BNORTUU
burnout
outburn

BOPSSTU
bus stop
post bus

CCDEKOR
crocked
red cock

CCEEHKR
checker
recheck

CCEEHRS
creches
screech

CCEINOR
cornice
crocein
crocine

CCENNOT
concent
connect

CCHKOSY
cockshy
shy cock

CCIKLOY
cockily
colicky

CDDDELO
clodded
coddled

CDDDELU
cludded
cuddled

CDDEEER
decreed
receded

CDDEEIR
decider
decried

CDDEENO
encoded
endoced

CDDEESU
deduces
seduced

CDDELOR
clodder
coddler

CDDELOS
cloddes
coddles
scolded

CDDELRU
cludder
cruddle
curdled

CDDELSU
cuddles
scuddle

CDEEEHR
cheered
reeched

CDEEENR
creened
decener
decerne

CDEEEPR
creeped
deceper
preceed

CDEEERR
decreer
receder

CDEEERS
creesed
decrees
recedes
seceder

CDEEERT
decreet
decrete
erected

CDEEHOR
cohered
ochered

CDEEHPR
perched
preched

CDEEHST
chested
steched

CDEEILP
icelped
pedicel
pedicle

CDEEINR
cedrine
deciner

CDEEIPR
pierced
reciped

CDEEIRR
decrier
recried

CDEEIRS
decries
deicers

CDEEIRT
decreit
recited
tierced

CDEELRU
reclude
ulcered

CDEELSU
Culdees
seclude

CDEENOR
encoder
encored

CDEENOS
encodes
endoces
seconde

CDEENRS
decerns
scerned

CDEENRT
centred
credent

CDEENST
descent
scented

CDEEOST
cestode
escoted
tedesco

CDEERRU
recured
reducer

CDEERSS
cressed
screeds
scredes

CDEERSU
cerused»
decurse
recused
reduces
rescued
secured
seducer

CDEERTU
cutered
eructed

CDEFKOR
defrock
frocked

CDEHILO
cheloid
helcoid

CDEHILR
childer
chirled
eldrich
rechild

CDEHIRT
chirted
ditcher

CDEHNRU
chunder
churned

CDEHORT
torched
troched

CDEHORW
chowder
chowred
cowherd

CDEHOSU
choused
douches
hocused

CDEHOSW
chowsed
cowshed

CDEIINS
incised
indices

CDEIKLS
sickled
slicked

CDEIKNS
dickens
snicked

CDEIKRS
dickers
scriked

CDEILLO
codille
collide
collied

CDEILNU
include
nuclide

CDEILTU
ductile
dulcite

CDEIMOR
dormice
moriced

CDEINOR
croined
decinor

CDEINOT
ctenoid
deontic
noticed

CDEINRS
cinders
discern
rescind

CDEINSU
incudes
induces

CDEIOST
cestoid
cotised
decoits

CDEIPST
depicts»
discept

CDEIRRU
curdier
curried

CDEIRST
credits
cristed
directs

CDEKNOS
dockens
snocked

CDEKNRU
crunked
drucken

CDEKNSU
sun deck
undecks

CDEKRSU
duckers
red cusk

CDELMSU
clumsed
muscled

CDELOOR
cloored
colored
croodle
decolor

CDELORW
crowdle
crowled
redcowl

CDELOSU
dulcose
scouled

CDELOSW
clowdes
scowled

CDELRSU
curdles
scudler

CDENOPU
pounced
uncoped

CDENORS
conders
corsned
reconds
scorned

CDENORW
crowned
decrown

CDENOTU
counted
decount

CDEOOST
coosted
scooted

CDEOPRU
crouped
produce

CDEORSS
crossed
escrods
scorsed
scrodes

CDEORSU
coursed
croudes
croused
scouder
scoured
sourced

CDEORSW
crowdes
scowder

CDEORTU
courted
decourt
eductor

CDEOSSU
coussed
escudos

CDEOSTU
custode
doucets
scouted

CDEOSTW
dowcets
scowted
stowced

CDEPRTY
crypted
decrypt

CDERSTU
crudest
crusted
decurts
ducters

CDGILNO
codling
colding

CDGINNO
condign
conding

CDHIOOR
choroid
ochroid

CDINOTU
conduit
noctuid

CDIOSTY
cystoid
cytoids

CDNOORY
Corydon
Croydon

CEEERRT
erecter
re-erect

CEEERSV
creeves
screeve

CEEFHIT
fetiche»
fitchee

CEEFKLR
flecker
freckle

CEEFPRT
perfect
prefect

CEEGINR
ceering
ceringe
creeing
energic
generic

CEEGIRS
cierges
Grecise
grieces

CEEHILS
helices
lichees

CEEHINS
Chinese
sinches

CEEHIRT
etheric
heretic
techier

CEEHLRY
cheerly
lechery

CEEHLSY
lychees
sleechy

CEEHNST
chenets
enchest

CEEHORS
cheeros
chorees
coheres
echoers
rechose

CEEHRST
chester
etchers

CEEILNS
license
selenic
silence

CEEILRT
reticle
tiercel

CEEINPR
crepine
percine

CEEINRS
ceresin
cerines
sincere

CEEINRT
enteric
enticer

CEEINRV
cervine
revince

CEEINST
entices
neicest

CEEIPRR
crepier
piercer

CEEIPRS
perseic
piecers
pierces
precise
recipes
respice

CEEIPSS
espices
species
spieces

CEEIRST
cerites
certies»
receits
reciets
recites
resceit
tierces

CEEIRSV
cervise
screive
scrieve
service

CEELNRU
lucerne
unclere

CEELORS
creoles
reclose

CEELORT
elector
electro

CEELPRT
plectre
prelect

CEELRSU
celures
recluse

CEEMOPR
compeer
compere

CEEMRRY
mercery
remercy

CEENORS
encores
necrose

CEENRSS
censers
cressen
scernes
screens
secerns

CEENRST
centers
centres»

certens
necters
recents
rescent
scenter
tenrecs

CEEPPRT
percept
precept

CEEPRST
cepters
ceptres
recepts
respect
scepter
sceptre
specter
spectre

CEERRSU
recures
recurse
rescuer
securer

CEERRSW
recrews
screwer

CEERSST
cresset
crestes
resects
secrets

CEFFORS
coffers
scoffer

CEFIKLR
fickler
flicker

CEFINOR
coinfer
conifer
fir cone
inforce

CEFIRTY
certify
rectify

CEGHINT
etching
teching

CEGHIRS
chigres
screigh

CEGILNR
clering
cringle

CEGILNY
cleying
glycine

CEGIMNR
creming
mercing

CEGINOS
cognise
coignes

CEGINPR
creping
percing

CEGINRS
cerings
cresing
cringes
scringe
sercing

CEGKLOR
cork leg
grockle

CEGNORY
congery
cryogen

CEGORSU
scourge
scrouge

CEHIINT
ichnite
nitchie

CEHIKNT
kitchen
thicken

CEHIKRS
shicker
skreich
skriech

CEHILNO
choline
helicon

CEHILNT
linchet
tinchel

CEHILSS
chesils
chisels
chissel

CEHILST
eltchis
sleitch

CEHIMOR
Homeric
moriche

CEHINOP
chopine
phocine

CEHINOR
Cheiron
chorine

CEHINPR
nephric
phrenic
pincher

CEHINSS
chinsed
schines
sinched

CEHINST
chinste
ethnics
inchest
sthenic

CEHIORT
rotchie
theoric

CEHIOST
echoist
toisech

CEHIPRS
ceriphs
chirpes
ciphers
spheric

CEHIRST
chiters
cithers
estrich
richest

CEHIRTT
chitter
retitch
titcher

CEHISTW
chewits
witches

CEHKORS
chokers
hockers
shocker

CEHLORT
chortle
lochter

CEHNPRU
puncher
unperch

CEHOORS
chooser
soroche

CEHORST
hectors
rochets
rotches
tochers
torches
troches

CEHORSU
choreus
chouser

CEHORTU
retouch
toucher

CEIILPT
pelitic
tie clip

CEIINNO
coniine
inconie

CEIINRS
irenics
sericin
sirenic

CEIINRT
citrine
crinite
inciter
neritic

CEIINSS
iciness
incises

CEIINTZ
citizen
zincite

CEIIRST
eristic
riciest

CEIKLNR
clinker
crinkle

CEIKLNS
inckles
lickens
nickels
slicken

CEIKLPR
pickler
prickle

CEIKLRS
lickers
re-licks
rickles
sickler»
slicker

CEIKLRT
tickler
trickle

CEIKLST
stickle
tickles

CEIKNRS
nickers
snicker

CEIKORR
corkier
rockier

CEIKORT
corkite
Rockite

CEIKPST
pickets
skeptic

CEIKRRS
rickers
scriker

CEIKRST
crikets
rickets
sticker
tickers
trickes

CEIKSTW
swicket
wickets

CEILMOP
compile
polemic

CEILNOP
cinople
pinocle

CEILNOS
cineols
conseil
inclose

CEILNPS
pencils
splenic

CEILNTS
clients
lentisc
scintle
stencil

CEILNTU
cutline
linecut
tunicle

CEILPPR
clipper
cripple

CEILRSS
crissel
slicers

CEILSSU
Celsius
sluices

CEIMNOS
incomes
mesonic

CEIMNOT
entomic
Metonic
tonemic

CEIMRST
cretism
metrics

CEIMRSU
ceriums
murices

CEINOPR
cinoper
porcine

CEINOPT
entopic
nepotic

CEINORS
coiners»

crinose
cronies
norices
orceins
orcines
recoins
sericon

CEINORT
cointer
noticer
rection

CEINOSS
cession
cosines
Oscines

CEINOST
noetics
notices
section

CEINOTT
entotic
tonetic

CEINPRS
encrisp
pincers
princes

CEINPST
incepts
inspect
pectins
peincts

CEINQSU
cinques
quinces
squince

CEINRST
cintres
cistern
cretins
crinets

CEIOPRS
copiers
persico

CEIORRS
cirrose
correis
corries
croiser
crosier

CEIORSS
croises
scories

CEIORSU
couries
scourie

CEIORSV
corsive
voicers

CEIORSW
cowries
scowrie

CEIORTX
excitor
xerotic

CEIOSST
cosiest
cotises
oecists

CEIOSTT
cottise
Scottie

CEIOSTX
coexist
exotics

CEIPRRS
crisper
pricers

CEIPRTU
cuprite
picture

CEIPSST
cesspit
septics

CEIRRSU
cruiser»

curries
sucrier

CEIRSSU
cruises
crusies
cuisser

CEIRSTU
cuiters
curiets
icterus

CEIRSUV
cruives
cursive

CEISSTU
cestuis
cueists
ictuses

CEKLNOS
enlocks
slocken

CEKLRSU
ruckles
suckler

CEKMORS
mockers
remocks
smocker

CEKORST
restock
rockets
stocker

CELLOSU
locules
ocellus

CELLRSU
cruells
cullers
reculls
sculler

CELLRUY
cruelly
cullery

CELNOSU
counsel
unclose

CELNSUU
nucleus
nucules

CELOOST
coolest
ocelots

CELOPSU
close up
couples
opuscle
upclose

CELOPTU
couplet
octuple

CELORST
cloters
colters
corslet
costrel
crotels
lectors

CELORSU
closure
colures

CELORSW
cowlers
scowler

CELORTT
clotter
crottle

CELORTU
cloture
coulter

CELOSST
closest
closets

CELOSSW
clowses
cowless
scowles

CELPRSU
curpels
curples
scruple

CELRSTU
cluster
culters
curlets
custrel
cutlers
relucts

CELRTUY
cruelty
cutlery

CELSTTU
cutlets
cuttles
scuttle

CEMMRSU
cummers
scummer

CENNORS
conners
sconner

CENNOST
consent
nocents

CENNRSU
cunners
scunner

CENOORR
coroner
crooner

CENORRS
corners
scorner

CENORRW
crowner
recrown

CENORSS
censors
crossen
scornes»

scrones

CENORST
conster
constre
conters
contres
cornets
cronets
scontre

CENORSU
rounces
uncores
unscore

CENORTU
cornute
counter
recount
trounce

CENOSTU
contuse
econuts

CEOOPRS
coopers
scooper

CEOORST
cooters
scooter

CEOPRRS
coppers
scorper

CEOPRSS
corpses
process
scopers

CEOPRSU
coupers
croupes
recoups
scouper

CEOQRTU
croquet
rocquet

CEORRSS
corsers
crosser
recross
scorers
scorser

CEORRSU
courser
scourer

CEORSSS
cessors
cossers
crosses
scorses

CEORSST
corsets
costers
crosset
escorts
recosts
scortes
scoters
sectors

CEORSSU
courses
Croesus
crouses
scourse
sources
sucrose

CEORSTU
couters
croutes
rose-cut
scouter

CEPPRSU
cuppers
scupper

CEPRSSU
percuss
spruces

CERSTTU
curtest
cutters
scutter

CGHIIMN
chiming
miching

CGHIINN
chining
inching
niching

CGHIINR
chiring
riching

CGHIKNO
choking
hocking

CGHINOR
choring
ochring
roching

CGIINNR
crining
rincing

CGIKLNO
cloking
locking

CGIKNNO
conking
nocking

CGIKNOR
corking
rocking

CGIKNPU
kingcup
pucking

CGILNOO
cooling
locoing

CGILNOW
clowing
cowling

CGILNOY
cloying
coyling

CGILNPU
cluping
culping
cupling
pulcing

CGILNTU
cluting
cutling

CGINNOR
corning
croning

CGINNOS
conings
consign

CGINORS
corings
corsing
scoring

CGINOST
costing
gnostic
scoting

CGINRSU
curings
cursing

CGINRSY
cryings
scrying

CGINRTU
ructing
trucing

CHIKORS
chikors
corkish
rockish

CHIORST
chorist
ostrich

CIILOST
colitis
solicit

CIIMOST
mistico
somitic

CIKLNOS
inlocks
slockin

CIKNPSU
snick up
unpicks

CIKNSTU
tuck-ins
tucks in
unstick

CILNPSU
insculp
sculpin

CILOSTU
coutils
oculist

CIMMOST
commits
Comtism

CIMNOOR
moronic
omicron

CIMNORS
crimson
microns

CIMOPSY
copyism
miscopy

CIMOSST
cosmist
Scotism
sitcoms

CINORST
cistron
citrons
cornist
cornits
cortins

CINOSST
consist
tocsins

CINOSSU
cousins
Oniscus

CIOOPRT
portico
prootic

CIPRSSU
prussic
Scirpus

CKLOPTU
potluck
putlock

CKNSTUU
unstuck
untucks

CLMOSUU
lucumos
osculum

CLNOSTU
consult
uncolts

CMOOPST
compost
compots

CNOOPSU
coupons
soupcon

CNOORST
crotons
consort

CNOORTU
contour
cornuto
crouton

COOPSTU
cop-outs
octopus

DDDEILN
dindled
niddled

DDDEILR
diddler
driddle
riddled

DDDEILS
diddles
siddled

DDEEEGR
degreed
greeded

DDEEELT
deleted
teedled

DDEEEMR
dreemed
remeded

DDEEFII
deified
edified

DDEEGIN
dedeign
dedigne
deeding
deigned
inedged

DDEEHRS
shedder
sherded

DDEEIMS
demised
Medised
misdeed

DDEEINS
indeeds
neddies
sdeined

DDEEINT
endited
teinded

DDEEIRR
Deirdre
derider
reddier
redried
ridered

DDEEIRS
derides
desired
diedres
resided

DDEEIRV
derived
redived

DDEEIST
deidest
teddies

DDEELTU
deluted
tudeled

DDEENPS
depends
spended

DDEENRS
Dresden
reddens
sendred

DDEENRU
endured
rudened
undered

DDEEPRS
pedders
spreded

DDEEPRU
depured
perdued

DDEERST
reddest
tedders

DDEFLRU
fuddler
furdled

DDEGGRU
drugged
grudged

DDEGILN
dingled
lindged

DDEGILR
girdled
glidder
griddle

DDEGINR
dreding
redding

DDEGLSU
guddles
sludged

DDEGNSU
dudgens
snudged

DDEGORS
dodgers
gorsedd

DDEHIRS
hidders
reddish
shidder

DDEIIOS
iodides
iodised

DDEIIRT
dirtied
tiddier

DDEIIST
stiddie
tiddies

DDEILMR
middler
Mildred

DDEILNS
dindled
niddles
slidden»

sniddle

DDEILNW
dwindle
windled

DDEILRS
riddels
riddles
slidder

DDEILRT
tiddler
triddle

DDEILTU
diluted
Luddite

DDEILTY
lyddite
tiddley

DDEIORS
dorised
soddier

DDEIRRU
Derdriu
ruddier

DDEIRSW
swidder
widders

DDELMOO
moduled
moulded

DDELNOU
lounded
noduled

DDELNRU
dundrel
rundled

DDELOOR
doodler
drooled

DDELOOS
doodles
soodled

DDELPSU
puddels
puddles
spuddle

DDENNOR
dendron
donnerd

DDENOOW
wood-end
woonded

DDENOPS
despond
sponded

DDENORS
nodders
roddens
snodder
sondred

DDENORU
drouned
redound
rounded
underdo

DDENORW
drowned
wondred

DDENOSS
oddness
soddens

DDENSTU
studden
suddent

DDEOPRU
drouped
poudred

DDEOPRW
dewdrop
drowped

DDEORSS
drossed
sodders

DDEORSW
sworded
wodders

DEEEFRS
feeders
freesed

DEEEGNR
greened
reenged
reneged

DEEEGRS
degrees
greesed

DEEEGRT
deterge
greeted

DEEEHLW
wheedle
wheeled

DEEEHRS
heeders
sheered

DEEEHST
seethed
sheeted

DEEELNR
denerel
needler

DEEELPT
deplete
pleeted

DEEELRS
eelders
sleered

DEEELRV
levered
reveled

DEEELST
deletes
seedlet
sleeted
steeled»

teedles

DEEEMNS
demesne
seedmen

DEEEMRS
deemers
demerse
dreemes
emersed
redeems
remedes
smeered

DEEEMRT
Demeter
metered

DEEENPS
deepens
penedes
sneeped

DEEENRS
endeers
needers
serened
sneered

DEEENRT
entered
eterned
red eten

DEEENRV
enerved
revened

DEEEPRS
speeder
speered

DEEEPRT
erepted
deperte
depeter
petered

DEEEPST
deepest
speeted
steeped

DEEERST
deerest
deserte
deterse
reested
steered
teeders

DEEERSV
deserve
severed

DEEERSW
sewered
sweered
weeders

DEEERTV
everted
reveted

DEEFGIN
feeding
feigned

DEEFIIR
deifier
edifier

DEEFILR
defiler
fielder
fleired
refiled

DEEFINR
definer
enfired
nedfire
refined

DEEFIRR
ferried
fire-red
red fire
refired
refreid
refried

DEEFMOR
deforme
freedom

DEEGHIN
dinghee
heeding
neighed

DEEGILN
deeling
iengled
i-lenged
leeding

DEEGIMN
deeming
imengde
meeding

DEEGINN
endeign
engined
needing

DEEGINP
deeping
depinge

DEEGINR
deering
dreeing
energid
greined
ingered
ingrede
reeding
reigned
reinged
riegned

DEEGINS
deesing
deignes
dingees
inedges
sdeigne
seeding

DEEGIRT
greited
grieted
tigered

DEEGIRV
diverge
grieved

DEEGLNT
gentled
glented

DEEGLRS
gelders
ledgers
redlegs
sledger
slerged

DEEHIST
heisted
siethed

DEEILNS
enisled
ensiled
linseed
seindle

DEEILNY
dyeline
needily

DEEILOS
oilseed
seed oil

DEEILPS
pleised
sedelip
seedlip
speiled

DEEILRS
resiled
reslide

DEEILRV
deliver
livered
relived
reviled

DEEILSS
diesels
idlease

DEEILST
delites
isleted
steiled
til seed

DEEILSY
eyelids
seedily

DEEIMNS
desmine
sideman

DEEIMPR
demirep
empired
epiderm
impeder

DEEIMPS
impedes
semiped

DEEIMRS
misered
remeids
remised

DEEIMRT
demerit
dimeter
merited
mitered
retimed

DEEINNT
dentine
entined

DEEINPR
enriped
preined
repined
ripened

DEEINRS
deniers
desiner
dieners
nereids
reinsed
rendies
resined
sirened
sneired

DEEINRT
enditer
entired»
renited
retined

DEEINRW
rewiden
widener

DEEINST
denties
destine
deteins
endites
entised
steined

DEEINSV
devines
endives
vendise

DEEINSW
endwise
sinewed

DEEIORS
oreides
osiered

DEEIPRS
deprise
espired
peirsed
perdies
Perseid
predies
preised
preside
speired
spiered

DEEIPRV
deprive
vipered

DEEIPSS
despise
pedesis

DEEIRRS
derries
desirer
redries
resider
serried

DEEIRRT
retired
retried
tireder

DEEIRRV
deriver
redrive
rivered

DEEIRRW
rewired
weirder

DEEIRST
diester
dieters
rediest
reedits
reisted
resited
steired
stiered

DEEIRSU
residue
ureides

DEEIRSV
derives
deviser
diverse
redives
revised
sivered
visered

DEEIRTU
erudite
reduite

DEEISTW
dewiest
sweited

DEEKLRS
kelders
skelder
skerled

DEELMOR
modeler
remodel

DEELNPS
pendels
pendles
splened

DEELNRS
elderns
eldrens
lenders
relends
rendles
slender
snerled

DEELNST
dentels
nestled
slented
tendles

DEELORS
red sole
resoled
solered

DEELORV
lovered
reloved

DEELORW
lowered
roweled

DEELPRS
pedlers
presled
spelder

DEELRTW
lewtred
weltred

DEELSTW
lewdest
swelted

DEEMPRT
tempred
tremped

DEEMRST
smerted
stremed

DEEMRSU
demures
resumed

DEENNOR
enderon
enorned

DEENNST
dennets
stenned

DEENOPS
depones
spondee

DEENORT
erodent
tenored

DEENORW
endower
reendow

DEENOST
denotes
setoned

DEENPRS
repends
spender
sperned

DEENPRT
prented
pretend

DEENRRU
endurer
underer

DEENRSS
redness
resends
senders
sendres

DEENRST
denters
dernest
drentse
retends
sterned
strened»
tenders
tendres

DEENRSU
endures
end-user
ensured

DEENRTU
denture
entrude
retuned
untreed

DEENSST
densest
desents
stedens

DEENSTT
detents
stented

DEEOPRS
deposer
reposed

DEEOPSS
deposes
despose
speedos

DEEORRR
orderer
reorder

DEEORRS
rerdose
reredos
red rose
rose-red

DEEORRV
overred
redrove

DEEORST
oersted
roseted
teredos

DEEORTT
ottered
tetrode»
totered

DEEORTV
devoter
revoted

DEEORTW
dew-rote
towered

DEEPPST
deppest
stepped

DEEPRRS
drepers
sperred
spreder

DEEPRRU
perdure
repured

DEEPRSS
depress
pressed
speders
spersed
spreeds
spredes

DEEPRST
pestred
prested

DEEPRSU
depures
depurse
perdues
persued
perused

DEEPRTU
deputer
erupted
reputed

DEERRSS
dresser
redress

DEERRST
destrer
sterred

DEERSST
deserts
dessert
desters
tressed

DEERSTT
destert
detters
sterted

DEERSTW
dew-rets
strewed
wrested

DEFFLSU
duffels
duffles
sluffed

DEFFNOS
offends
send off

DEFGINR
ferding
fringed

DEFIILN
infidel
infield
infiled

DEFILOS
defoils
odslife

DEFILRT
flirted
trifled

DEFIRST
firsted
fristed

DEFLNOR
fondler
forlend

DEFLNRU
dernful
durned

DEFLORU
floured
foulder
fouldre

DEFLOSU
defouls
floused

DEFMORS
deforms
serfdom

DEFMPRU
frumped
rump-fed

DEFNORU
founder
refound

DEFORST
defrost
fostred
frosted

DEGGILN
gelding
gingled
niggled
ledging

DEGGINS
edgings
gnidges
sedging
snigged

DEGGINW
wedging
wind egg

DEGGLOR
doggrel
roggled

DEGGLOS
doglegs
slogged

DEGGRRU
drugger
grudger

DEGGRTU
drugget
trugged

DEGHILN
helding
hindleg

DEGHILT
delight
lighted

DEGHIRT
dighter
girthed
righted

DEGHOSU
doughes
soughed

DEGIINN
deining
indeign
indigen

DEGIINT
dieting
editing
ignited

DEGIKLO
doglike
godlike

DEGIKNS
dekings
desking

DEGILLN
delling
lingled

DEGILMN
melding
mingled

DEGILNN
ginnled
lending

DEGILNO
dogline
glenoid

DEGILNP
pingled
pleding

DEGILNR
derling
dringle
grindel
grindle
ringled

DEGILNS
dingles
eldings
engilds
gildens
glinsed
lindges
singled
slinged

DEGILNT
glinted
tingled

DEGILNU
dueling
eluding
indulge

DEGILNV
delving
devling

DEGILNW
dweling
welding

DEGILOR
gloried
godlier
goldier

DEGILRS
gilders
girdles
gliders
grisled
lidgers
ridgels

DEGINNR
derning
grinned»
rending

DEGINNS
densing
endings
sending

DEGINNT
denting
tending

DEGINOR
eroding
groined
ignored
ingored
negroid
redoing

DEGINOW
wendigo
widgeon

DEGINPR
dreping
preding

DEGINRR
derring
grinder
regrind

DEGINRS
dingers
dreigns
engirds
erdings
grindes
rindges
serding

DEGINRU
dungier
rugined

DEGINSS
designs
dessing
sdeigns
sindges
snidges

DEGINST
nidgets»
steding
stinged
tedings

DEGINSU
gundies
sueding

DEGINSW
dewings
swindge
swinged

DEGIRSS
digress
girssed
grissed

DEGLNPU
plunged
pungled

DEGLNSU
guldens
nudgels
slunged

DEGLORS
lodgers
slodger

DEGLOSS
glossed
godless
slodges

DEGLOST
godlets
goldest

DEGLRSU
gluders
sludger

DEGMRSU
red gums
smudger

DEGNORU
guerdon
undergo
ungored

DEGNRTU
grunted
trudgen

DEGOORS
dog rose
goordes
roodges

DEGOORV
grooved
overgod

DEGORSS
grossed
sodgers

DEGORSU
drogues
gourdes
groused

DEGORTU
droguet
grouted

DEHIKRS
shirked
shriked

DEHILRS
hilders
hirsled
shirled

DEHIMOR
heirdom
Homerid

DEHIMST
midseth
smithed

DEHINRS
hinders
shrined

DEHIRRU
dhurrie
hurried

DEHIRST
dithers
shirted

DEHIRSV
dervish
shrived

DEHISSW
Swedish
swished
whissed

DEHISTW
swithed
whisted

DEHITTW
thwited
whitted

DEHLOST
hostled
slothed

DEHLOSU
housled
shouled

DEHLRSU
hurdles
rushled
Sheldru
shurled

DEHLSSU
hussled
slushed

DEHNORT
northed
thonder
thondre
thorned
throned

DEHNOSU
houndes
unhosed
unshoed

DEHORST
dehorts
redhots
shorted

DEIILMT
delimit»
limited

DEIILOS
doilies
idolise

DEIIMPR
demirip
impired

DEIIMST
misdiet
mistide

DEIINOS
iodines
ionised

DEIINOT
edition
tenioid

DEIINRT
inditer
intired
nitride

DEIINRV
diviner
drive-in

DEIIORS
iodiser
Isidore

DEIIPRT
dirt pie
riptide
tiderip

DEIISTT
dietist
ditties
tidiest

DEIKLNR
drenkil
drinkel
drinkle
kindler

DEIKLNS
kindels
kindles»
slinked

DEIKNPS
knipsed
spinked

DEIKNRS
dirkens
drinkes
redskin

DEIKRST
skirted
striked

DEILLNW
indwell
windell

DEILLSU
illudes
ill-used
sullied

DEILMNU
lumined
unlimed

DEILMPR
dimpler
rimpled

DEILMPS
dimples
simpled

DEILMRT
mirtled
trimled

DEILMST
mildest
mistled
smilted

DEILNOS
indoles
lionsed
sondeli

DEILNPS
speldin
spindel
spindle»
splined

DEILNPU
lined up
unpiled

DEILNRS
linders
rindles
snirled

DEILNRT
tendril
trindel
trindle

DEILNST
dentils
slinted
tindles

DEILNSW
swindle
windles

DEILNTU
diluent
untiled

DEILNTW
indwelt
wintled

DEILOPS
despoil
diploes
dipoles
peloids
soliped
spoiled

DEILORS
droiles
soldier
solider

DEILPPR
dripple
rippled

DEILPPS
sippled
slipped

DEILRSS
ridless
sliders

DEILRST
listred
slirted
tirdels
tridels

DEILSST
destils
sistled

DEILSTT
slitted
stilted

DEIMMRT
midterm
trimmed

DEIMNOS
domines
misdone

DEIMNRU
murined
unmired
unrimed

DEIMNSS
dimness
missend

DEIMNTU
minuted
munited
mutined
untimed

DEIMOOR
moidore
moodier

DEIMORS
misdoer
moiders

DEIMOST
distome
modiste
moisted

DEIMPRU
dumpier
impured
umpired

DEIMPSU
dumpies
mud pies

DEINNOT
intoned
nointed

DEINNRU
dunnier
inurned

DEINNSU
dunnies
undines

DEINNSW
enwinds
swinden

DEINOPR
poinder
proined

DEINOPS
dispone
spinode
spondie

DEINORS
dineros
donsier
indorse
inrodes
iordens
ordines
rosined
sordine

DEINORU
dourine
oundier

DEINORV
drive on
on drive
vine rod

DEINORW
re-indow
windore

DEINOST
ditones
notised
stonied

DEINPST
dipnets
stipend

DEINPSU
punised
unipeds
unspied

DEINQSU
quinsed
squined

DEINRSU
insured
sundrie
surdine
undries

DEINRTU
intrude
turdine
untired
untride
untried

DEINSST
destins
disnest
dissent
snidest

DEINSTT
dentist
distent
stinted

DEINSTU
distune
dunites

DEINSTY
density
destiny

DEIOPRT
diopter
dioptre
peridot
proteid
torpide

DEIOPSS
dispose
episods

DEIOPST
deposit
dopiest
podites
posited
sopited
topside

DEIORRS
dorries
sorried

DEIORRW
rowdier
wordier
worried

DEIORSS
dorises
dossier

DEIORST
editors
roisted
rosited
sortied
steroid
storied
triodes

DEIORSV
devisor
devoirs
visored
voiders

DEIORSW
dowries
rowdies
weirdos
wordies

DEIORTT
Detroit
dottier

DEIORTU
doutier
etourdi
ioduret
outride
ride out

DEIOSTT
dotiest
stoited

DEIOSTU
outside
tedious

DEIPRSS
prissed
spiders

DEIPRST
dipters
spirted
sprited
striped

DEIPSSU
Pseudis
upsides

DEIQRSU
risqued
squired

DEIRRST
disterr
stirred
strider

DEIRSST
disrest
dissert
disters
strides

DEIRSSU
disuser
sudsier

DEIRSTU
dustier
reduits
rustied
studier
sturdie

DEIRSTV
diverst
diverts
strived
verdits

DEISSTU
studies
tissued

DEISTTW
dewitts
twisted

DEKLNRU
knurled
runkled

DELLOPR
prolled
redpoll

DELLORS
dollers
drosell

DELMORS
medlors
molders
remolds
smolder

DELMORU
moulder
remould

DELMOSU
modules
mousled

DELMOTU
modulet
moulted

DELMPSU
dumples
slumped

DELMRTY
myrtled
trymled

DELNOOS
noodles
snooled

DELNORS
dronels
rondels
rondles
snorled

DELNORU
lounder
roundel
roundle

DELNOSU
loudens
nodules
nousled

DELNPRU
plunder
pundler

DELNRSU
lunders
lurdens
nursled
rundles
snurled

DELNRTU
rundlet
trundle

DELOOPR
poodler
prooled

DELOOPS
poodles
slooped
soopled
spooled

DELOPRS
podlers
polders
slorped
splored

DELOPRT
droplet
torpled

DELORSS
dorsels
drossel
rodless
rossled
solders

DELORST
drolest
oldster
rostled
slorted
strodle
stroled

DELORSU
Lourdes
sloured

DELORTT
dottler
dottrel
rottled

DELORTU
routled
trouled

DELOSTT
dottels
dottles
slotted

DELOSTU
loudest
soluted
tousled

DELPRSU
drupels
slurped
spruled
spurled

DELRSTU
lustred
rustled
strudel

DELRTTU
ruttled
turtled

DEMNOOR
doormen
morendo

DEMNORS
moderns
rodsmen

DEMNOTU
demount
mounted

DEMORST
mostred
stormed
stromed

DEMRRSU
murders
smurred

DENNORT
donnert
tendron

DENNOST
stonned
tendons

DENNOTU
unnoted
untoned

DENNOUW
enwound
unowned

DENOOPS
snooped
spooned

DENOORS
noorsed
snoored

DENOOST
snooted
stooden
stooned

DENOOSW
swooned
woondes

DENOOTU
duotone
outdone

DENOPRS
Pernods
ponders
pondres
respond
sporned

DENOPRT
dropnet
portend
protend

DENOPRU
pounder
unroped

DENOPSU
spouned
unposed

DENORRU
rondure
rounder
unorder

DENORST
dronets
rodents
snorted
stroned

DENORSU
drousen
enduros
resound
sounder
undoers

DENORSW
downers
drowens
drowsen
drownes
snowred
wonders

DENORUW
rewound
wounder

DENOSTU
deutons
snouted

DENOSTW
set down
stownde

DENPRSU
punders
snurped
spurned

DENPRTU
prudent
prunted
uptrend

DENPSSU
sends up
send ups
suspend
upsends

DENRSSU
sunders
undress

DENRSTU
deturns
Dunster
dunters
retunds
snurted
tunders
undrest

DENSTTU
student
stunted

DEOOPRS
rose drop
spoored

DEOOPRT
torpedo
trooped

DEOPRST
deports
redtops
sported
stroped

DEOPSTU
outsped
spouted
stouped

DEORRSS
dorsers
drosser

DEORRST
dorters
rodster
storred

DEORRSU
ordures
sourdre

DEORRSW
drowser
rewords
sworder
worders

DEORSSS
dossers
drosses

DEORSST
sordets
trossed

DEORSTT
detorts
dotters
stotred

DEORSTU
derouts
destour
detours
dourest
douters
outreds
redouts
rousted
sourdet
stoured»

trousèd

DEORSTW
dew-rots
dowters
strowed
trowsed
worsted

DEORSTY
destroy
roysted
stroyed

DEORTTU
trouted
tutored

DEOSTTU
duettos
testudo

DEPRSTU
prudest
spruted
spurted
stupred

DEPRSUU
purdues
pursued
usurped

DERRSTU
red rust
rustred
sturred

DERSSTU
detruss
dusters
redusts
restuds
strudes
trussed

DERSTTU
sturted
trusted

DFGHIOS
dogfish
fish god

DGGIILN
gilding
gliding

DGGIINN
dinging
gniding
nidging

DGGIINR
dirging
girding
griding
ridging

DGGIINU
guiding
iudging

DGGILNO
godling
golding
lodging

DGHIILN
hidling
hilding

DGHIINS
dishing
hidings
shiding
shindig

DGHINTU
hindgut
undight

DGHIOPS
doghips
dogship
godship

DGIIKNN
dinking
kinding

DGIIMNS
disming
smidgin

DGIINNS
dinings
indigns»

sinding

DGIINNT
dinting
tinding

DGIINNW
dwining
winding

DGIINPR
driping
priding

DGIINRT
dirting
driting

DGIINTY
dignity
tidying

DGIKNOR
Dorking
king rod

DGIMNOO
dooming
mooding

DGINNOR
droning
ronding

DGINNOS
ondings
sonding

DGINOOR
dog iron
rooding

DGINORS
dorsing
rodings

DGINORT
dorting
droting

DGINOSU
dousing
guidons

DGINOSW
disgown
dowings
dowsing

DGINRSU
durings
dursing
surding
ungirds

DHIMORU
humidor
midhour
rhodium

DHINORS
dishorn
dronish

DHORSUY
hydrous
shroudy

DILORWY
rowdily
wordily

DILOSSU
dulosis
solidus

DIMOPSU
podiums
spodium

DINOORS
indoors
sordino

DINORSW
in words
Windsor

DINPSTU
pindust
pundits

DIOORST
disroot
toroids

DIOPRST
disport»

torpids
tripods

EEEFRRS
reefers
referse

EEEFRTV
evereft
feveret

EEEGILS
elegies
elegise

EEEGNRR
greener
regreen
reneger

EEEGRRT
greeter
regreet
regrete

EEEHNST
ethenes
sheeten

EEEHRST
rehetes
seether
sheeter

EEEILST
eeliest
steelie

EEEIRRT
retiree
teerier

EEEIRST
eeriest
steerie

EEEKLRS
keelers
rekeles
sleeker

EEELMNT
element
telemen

EEELMST
meteles
telesme
remeets
streeme
teemers

EEELNSV
elevens
enleves

EEELPRS
leepers
leepres
leperes
peelers
repeles
sleeper
slepere
speeler

EEELPRT
pletere
replete

EEELPSS
esplees
sleepes

EEELPST
pleetes
steeple

EEELRST
leerest
steeler

EEELRSV
releves
reveles
sleever

EEELSST
steeles
teleses

EEEMMSS
meseems
sememes

EEEMNSS
enseems
nemeses

EEEMRST
meerest
meeters»

EEENPRT
preteen
terpene

EEENPST
ensteep
steepen

EEENRRS
serener
sneerer

EEENRRT
enterer
reenter
terreen
terrene

EEENRST
enteres
entrees
estrene
eternes
neerest
retenes
teeners

EEENRSV
enerves
eveners
revenes
sevener
sneever
veneers

EEENRUV
revenue
unreeve

EEENSST
sneeste
steenes

EEENSTV
evenest
stevene

EEEPRST
estrepe
repetes»
steeper

EEEPRSW
sweeper
weepers

EEEQSUZ
queezes
squeeze

EEERRST
retrees
steerer

EEERRSV
reevers
reserve
reveres
reverse
severer
veerers

EEERSTT
reetest
streete
teeters
treetes

EEERSTV
Everest
revetes
steever

EEERSVW
servewe
weevers

EEFFORR
offerer
reoffer

EEFGILN
feeling
fleeing
leefing

EEFGINR
engrief
feering
feigner
feringe
freeing
reefing

EEFHLRS
flesher
herself

EEFHRRS
fresher
refresh

EEFIIRR
feirier
fierier

EEFILST
felsite
lefties
liefest

EEFINRR
fernier
refiner

EEFINRS
enfires
ferines
fineers
frenesi
frenise
frensie
neifers
refines

EEFIRRS
ferries
refires
refries

EEFIRRT
ferrite
fir tree

EEFIRTW
weftier
wet fire

EEFORRV
forever
frovere

EEFRRST
ferrest
ferrets
ferters

EEGGILN
gleeing
neglige

EEGHINR
heering
neigher
rehinge

EEGHIRW
reweigh
weigher

EEGIKLN
keeling
leeking

EEGIKNP
keeping
peeking

EEGIKNS
eekings
ekeings
seeking
skeeing

EEGILNN
leening
neeling

EEGILNR
girleen
ingrele
leering
reeling

EEGILNS
iengles
leesing
lignees
seeling

EEGILNT
gentile
leeting
teeling

EEGILST
elegist
elegits

EEGIMMR
gemmier»
immerge

EEGIMNR
meering
mereing
reeming
regimen

EEGIMNS
meesing
seeming

EEGIMNT
imenget
meeting
teeming

EEGIMRS
emigres
regimes
remiges

EEGINNP
neeping
peening

EEGINNR
enginer
ingener
neering
negrine

EEGINNS
engines
neesing

EEGINNU
genuine
ingenue

EEGINPR
peering
reeping

EEGINRS
greisen
inegers
ingeres
niegres
reesing
reignes
reinges
resigne
riegnes»
seering

EEGINRT
gentier
integer
reeting
treeing
reteign
treeing

EEGINRV
evering
ingreve
reeving
veering
vineger
vinegre

EEGINSS
genesis
gesines
seeings

EEGIOST
egotise
goeties

EEGLNST
gentles
lengest

EEGLRST
gelstre
leg-rest
reglets

EEGMNOS
emonges
genomes

EEGNORS
engores
negroes

EEGRRSU
resurge
reurges

EEGRSTT
gertest
getters
tregets

EEGRSTU
gesture
guester
guetres

EEHINRS
henries
inheres

EEHINRT
neither
therein

EEHINST
isehtne
teenish
theines

EEHIRRS
herries
rehires

EEHIRSS
heiress
herisse
sheires
sheries

EEHIRST
heister
shirtee

EEHLLRS
hellers
sheller

EEHLRST
helters
lethers
rethels
shelter
therles

EEHLRSV
helvers
shelver

EEHLSTT
shettle
shtetel
thestel

EEHNORW
Erewhon»
nowhere
whereon

EEHOPRT
hop tree
trophee

EEHORVW
however
whoever

EEHPRST
hepster
pethers
sperthe
threeps
threpes

EEIINRT
erinite
niterie

EEIKLST
kelties
sleekit

EEILLRV
eviller
reville

EEILLSS
eisells
sellies

EEILMPR
empaler
emparle
empearl

EEILMST
elmiest
limetes
metelis
smelite
telisme

EEILNNT
leinten
lenient

EEILNPS
peniles
penisle
pensile

EEILNPT
penlite
pentile

EEILNSS
enisles
ensiles
seniles
sensile
silenes

EEILNST
enstile
setline
tensile

EEILOPT
petiole
pilotee

EEILORT
oil tree
troelie

EEILORV
liverei
overlie
relievo

EEILPRS
replies
spieler

EEILPRT
peitrel
peltier
peltrie
perlite
reptile

EEILPST
epistel
epistle
pelites
pielets
septile
sleipet

EEILRRS
lerries
reliers
serreli

EEILRRV
liverer
reliver
reviler

EEILRSS
ireless
resiles

EEILRST
leister
liester
sterile
trelies

EEILRSV
leviers
relevis
relives
reveils
reviles
servile

EEILSSS
seselis
sessile

EEILSST
seliest
telesis
tieless

EEILSTV
evilest
levites
lievest
velites

EEIMNSS
inseems
Meissen
misseen
nemesis
siemens

EEIMNSW
misween
wisemen

EEIMPRR
premier
reprime

EEIMPRS
empires
emprise
epimers
imprese
premise
spireme

EEIMPST
empties
septime

EEIMRRT
meriter
miterer
trireme

EEIMRSS
merises
messier
messire
miseres
remises

EEIMRST
emerits
ermites
mereits
meriest
merites
metiers
reemits
retimes
tremies
triseme

EEIMSST
mesites
metisse
Semites

EEINNRV
enriven
innerve
nervine

EEINNST
entines
intense

EEINOPR
pereion
pioneer

EEINOSS
eosines
osseine

EEINPRR
repiner
ripener

EEINPRS
enripes
enspire
erepsin
pensier
repines

EEINPRT
Petrine
priente
terpine

EEINPST
pentise
pienets
septine

EEINPSV
pensive
vespine

EEINRRS
reinser
resiner

EEINRRT
reinter
rentier
terrien
terrine

EEINRST
entiers
entires
entries
interes
nerites
renites
reteins
retines
trenise
trienes

EEINRSV
enrives
enviers»
inverse
neivers
veiners
venires
Vereins
versine

EEINRSW
newsier
weiners
wieners

EEINRTT
nettier
tentier

EEINRTU
retinue
reunite
uterine

EEINSST
entises
niesest
sestine
setines

EEINSTX
extines
sextine
sixteen

EEIPQRU
perique
re-equip
repique

EEIPRRS
perries
reprise
respire

EEIPRSS
espiers
espires
peirses
Perseis
persies
preises
repises
speires

EEIPRST
esprite»

peirtes
piertes
respite
seipter
septier
sperite

EEIPRSU
previse
prieves

EEIQRTU
quieter
requite

EEIRRRT
retirer
terrier

EEIRRSS
serries
sirrees

EEIRRST
etriers
reiters
restier
reteirs
retiers
retires
retries
stirree
terries
tierers

EEIRRSV
reivers
reveirs
reversi
reviser

EEIRRTV
riveret
riveter

EEIRSST
Eisters
iesters
resites
setiers
steires
stieres
teisers
tessier

EEIRSTT
Trieste
ti trees

EEIRSTV
restive
Servite
veriest
verites

EEKLRST
kelters
kertels
kertles
kestrel
skelter

EELLMRS
merells
smeller

EELLORS
roselle
sollere

EELLPRS
pellers
respell
speller

EELLRSW
reswell
sweller
wellers

EELMPSS
empless
semples

EELMPST
pelmets
stempel
stemple
temples

EELMRST
melters
mertles
remelts
resmelt
smelter

EELMRSU
lemures»

relumes

EELMSTT
mettles
stemlet

EELNOSV
elevons
Slovene

EELNRST
nestler
relents

EELNSTY
enstyle
tensely

EELOPRS
elopers
leprose

EELORST
leetors
roselet
soleret

EELOTUV
evolute
velouet
veloute

EELPRSS
lepress
persels
plesers
presles
slepers
spelers

EELPRST
pelters
peltres
petrels
pleters
Prestel
spelter
speltre
spertle
spleter

EELPRSY
pleyers
sleepry»

yelpers

EELRSST
estlers
restles
setlers
slester
streels
tresles
tressel
tressle

EELRSTT
ettlers
letters
settler
sterlet
trestle

EELRSTW
lewters
lewtres
swelter
sweltre
welters
weltres
wrestle

EELRSTY
restyle
tersely

EEMMNOT
memento
momente

EEMNOST
temenos
tonemes

EEMNRST
rements
serment
stemner

EEMORRS
remorse
roemers

EEMORST
emoters
meteors
remotes
someter

EEMPRST
emprest
tempers

EEMPRSU
presume
supreme

EEMRRST
metrers
smerter
termers

EENNORT
enteron
tenoner

EENNSSU
unseens
unsense

EENOPRS
openers
perones
persone
reopens
repones
senoper

EENOPST
onestep
openest
pentose
posteen
poteens

EENORSS
senores
serones

EENORST
ensorte
enstore
estrone

EENOSTV
ventose
voteens

EENPRSS
enpress
pressen
spenser

EENPRST
penster
penters
prentes
present
repents
serpent

EENPRSY
pyrenes
syneper

EENRRST
nerrest
renters
restren
sterner
strener

EENRSST
entress
nesters
resents
sentres
sertens
streens
strenes
tensers

EENRSTT
netters
retents
stenter
sternet
testern
tenters

EENRSTY
styrene
yestern

EENSSST
nessets
setness
sneests

EENSTTY
steynte
teentsy

EEOPRTT
proette
treetop

EEOPSSU
espouse
poseuse

EEOPSTY
eyespot
peyotes

EEORSST
osseter
stereos

EEORSTV
estover
overset
revotes
vetoers

EEORSUV
oeuvres
overuse

EEPRRSS
presser
repress
sperres

EEPRRSU
peruser
repures

EEPRSSS
presses
sperses

EEPRSSU
Perseus
persues
peruses

EEPRSSW
spewers
sprewse

EEPRSTU
pertuse
reputes

EEQRSTU
quester
request

EERRSTT
retrets»

retters
sterter
terrets
terters
tertres

EERRSTU
retruse
ureters

EERRSTW
strewer
werrest
werrets
wrester

EERRTTU
reutter
utterer

EERSSST
sesster
sesters
tresses

EERSSTT
retests
setters
streets
stretes
testers
tersest

EERSSTW
sewster
sewters
stewers
strewes
werstes
westers

EERSSTX
exserts
sexters

EERSTTT
strette
tetters

EERSTTY
streety
yetters

EERSTUV
versute
vertues
vertuse
vesture

EFFINRS
niffers
sniffer

EFFIORX
firefox
foxfire

EFFLRSU
luffers
ruffles
sluffer

EFFLRTU
fretful
truffle

EFFRSTU
restuff
ruffest
ruffets
stuffer

EFFSTTU
stuffet
tuffest
tuffets

EFGHIRT
fighter
freight
refight

EFGILNR
ferling
flinger

EFGINNT
fenting
fingent

EFGINRS
fersing
fingers
fringes

EFHILMS
Flemish»
himself

EFHILPS
elfship
pelfish

EFHINST
fishnet
net fish

EFHIRSS
fishers
serfish
sherifs

EFIINST
finites
nifties

EFILNSS
finless
snifles

EFILOOS
floosie
foliose

EFILORT
loftier
trefoil

EFILRRT
flirter
reflirt
trifler

EFILRST
filters
flirtes
fliters
frislet
lifters
reflits
relifts
slifter
stifler
trifles

EFILRTT
flitter
triflet

EFILSST
fistles»
selfist
stifles

EFINSST
fitness
infests

EFIORST
foister
forties

EFIRSSU
fissure
fussier

EFIRSTU
fustier
surfeit

EFIRTTU
tuftier
turfite

EFLNOTT
fletton
fontlet

EFLORSU
foulers
furoles
ourself

EFLORTT
flotter
fortlet

EFLORVY
flyover
overfly

EFLORWY
flowery
ryewolf

EFLRSTU
fluster
fluters
furlets
lufters
restful

EFMOPRR
perform
preform

EFNOOST
eftsoon
festoon

EFNRSTU
funster
unfrets

EFOOPRT
foretop
poofter

EFORRSU
ferrous
furores

EGGILLN
gelling
gingell

EGGILNN
glening
lenging

EGGILNR
gingler
niggler

EGGILNS
gesling
gingles
leggins
niggles
sniggle

EGGILRW
wiggler
wriggle

EGGIMNR
germing
merging

EGGINNR
gerning
grening

EGGINRS
gingers
gresing
niggers
serging
snigger

EGGINRY
gingery
greying
niggery

EGGLMSU
muggles
smuggle

EGGLORS
loggers
slogger

EGGLRSU
gurgles
luggers
ruggles
slugger

EGGRSTU
stugger
trugges
tuggers

EGHHIST
eighths
heights
highest
high-set
thighes

EGHIINT
heiting
nightie

EGHIINV
heiving
inveigh

EGHIKNR
gherkin
herking

EGHILNS
English
helings
hengils
hingels
hingles
shingle

EGHILNT
enlight
lighten

EGHILRT
lighter
relight

EGHILST
lightes
sleight

EGHINOS
hoeings
shoeing

EGHINRT
enright
herting
righten
thinger

EGHINST
ensight
hesting
sheting
thinges

EGHINSW
hewings
shewing
whinges

EGHINTT
hetting
tighten

EGHNORU
enrough
roughen

EGHORTU
roughet
tougher

EGIIKNR
keiring
reiking

EGIILNN
lignine
neiling

EGIILNR
glirine
leiring
lingier

EGIILNT
eliting
lignite
teiling

EGIINNR
ginnier
neiring
reining

EGIINNS
insigne
neising
seining

EGIINPR
giniper
igripen
peiring

EGIINPS
peising
pigsnie
seiping

EGIINRT
igniter
teiring
tiering
tigrine

EGIINSV
sieving
vieings

EGIINUV
Iguvine
vieuing

EGIKLNR
erl king
kerling
lerking

EGIKLNS
kingles
lesking

EGIKNRY
key ring
yerking

EGILLNS
leglins»
lingels
lingles
selling

EGILLRS
gillers
grilles
Grisell

EGILLSU
gullies
ligules

EGILMNR
gremlin
lerming
merling
mingler
remling

EGILMNW
mewling
welming

EGILMPS
glimpse
megilps

EGILNNS
ginnels
ginnles
lensing

EGILNOS
eloigns
legions
lingoes
sloe gin

EGILNPR
perling
pingler
pringle

EGILNPS
leg spin
pingles
pinlegs
plesing
sleping
speling
spignel

EGILNPT
pelting
pleting

EGILNPY
pleying
yelping

EGILNRS
girnels
lerings
lingers
ringels
ringles
singler
slinger

EGILNRT
glinter
ringlet
tingler
treling
tringle

EGILNSS
glinses
glissen
lessing
singles
slinges

EGILNST
glisten
lesting
lingets
singlet
steling
stingle
tingles

EGILNSW
slewing
sweling
swingel
swingle

EGILNSY
eylings
sleying

EGILNTT
ettling
letting

EGILNTW
lewting
telwing
twingle
welting
winglet

EGILRSS
girsles
grilses
grisels
grisles
grissel
grissle

EGILRST
glister
glistre
gliters
gristel
gristle
riglets
trigles

EGILRZZ
grizzel
grizzle

EGILSTU
gluiest
ugliest

EGIMNNT
menting
mingent

EGIMNOS
emongis
misgone

EGIMNOT
emoting
mentigo
mignote

EGIMNPT
pigment
temping

EGIMNRS
germins
megrins
mergins
merings»
mersing
smering

EGIMNRT
metring
terming

EGIMNRU
emuring
remuing

EGIMNST
steming
temsing

EGINNRS
enrings
ginners
grinnes
rensing
ringens

EGINNRT
renting
ringent
ring net
terning

EGINNRY
ginnery
renying

EGINNSS
ensigns
nessing
sensing

EGINNST
ginnets
nesting
senting
tensing

EGINNSU
ensuing
gunnies
gunnise
ingenus

EGINNTT
netting
tenting
tingent

EGINOOS
goonies
isogone

EGINOPR
perigon
poreing
proigne
ropeing

EGINORR
groiner
ignorer

EGINORS
eringos
groines
ignores
ingores
origens
regions
signore
sorgien

EGINORT
genitor
Negrito
trigone

EGINOSW
ingowes
ownings
snowing
wigeons

EGINPRS
pingers
presign
presing
spinger
springe

EGINPSS
gipsens
pessing

EGINPST
pesting
speting
steping

EGINPSY
espying
pigsney»
speying

EGINRRS
errings
re-rings
ringers
serring

EGINRRT
grinter
terring

EGINRRW
werring
wringer

EGINRSS
ingress
resigns
re-signs
resings
signers
singers

EGINRST
engirts
ertings
ingerts
resting
stering
stinger
streing
stringe
tingers

EGINRSU
reusing
rueings
rugines
signeur
surgien

EGINRSV
serving
versing

EGINRSW
rewings
swinger
wersing
wingers
wringes

EGINRTT
gittern
retting

EGINRTU
reuting
trueing

EGINRTW
trewing
twinger

EGINSSS
essigns
sessing

EGINSTT
setting
testing

EGINSTV
vesting
vignets

EGINSTW
stewing
tewings
twinges
westing

EGIOPRS
porgies
serpigo

EGIORST
goistre
goiters
goitres
goriest

EGIRSST
gisters
greists
griests
gristes
striges
tigress

EGIRSTT
girtest
gitters
gritest

EGLNOST
englots
longest
songlet

EGLNOSU
lounges
slounge

EGLNOXY
loxygen
xylogen

EGLNPSU
plunges
splunge

EGLNRSU
lungers
slunger

EGLNSSU
gunless
gunsels
slunges

EGLORSS
glosers
glosser

EGLORST
gloters
strogel
strogle

EGLPRSU
replugs
splurge
spurgel

EGLRSTU
gurlets
strugle

EGLSTUU
gluteus
Telugus

EGMORSU
grumose
morgues

EGNOPRY
progeny»

pyrogen

EGNORRW
regrown
wronger

EGNORSS
engross
grossen

EGNRSTU
gruntes
gunster
gunters
gurnets
surgent

EGNRTTU
grutten
turgent

EGOPRRU
grouper
regroup

EGOPRSU
progues
spourge

EGORRSS
grosers
grosser

EGPRRSU
purgers
spurger

EHIKNRT
rethink
thinker

EHILNOT
neolith
Othniel

EHILOST
Elohist
eoliths
holiest
hostile

EHILRST
lithers
slither»

thirles
thrisle

EHILSST
slithes
thissel

EHILSTT
Lettish
listeth
lithest
shittle
thistel
thistle

EHIMNRU
inhumer
rhenium

EHIMORS
heroism
moreish

EHIMORT
moither
mothier

EHIMRST
hermits
mirthes
mithers
Rhemist
smither

EHINNRT
thinner
thrinne

EHINORS
herison
heroins
inshore

EHINOST
ethions
histone

EHINOSU
heinous
in-house

EHINRST
hinters
nithers»

renisht

EHINRTW
whitner
writhen

EHINSSS
shiness
snishes

EHINSTW
swithen
whitens

EHIOPST
ethiops
ophites
Peshito

EHIORRT
heritor
herriot

EHIORST
heriots
hoister
horiest
hostrie
rehoist
shortie

EHIORTU
outhire
routhie

EHIPPRS
hippers
shipper

EHIPRST
hipster
threips

EHIRRTW
wherrit
whirret
writher

EHIRSSW
swisher
wishers

EHIRSTW
swither»

whister
withers
writhes

EHIRTTW
whitret
whitter

EHISTTW
tewhits
thwites
wettish
whitest
whittes

EHLOOPT
pothole
top hole

EHLORST
holster
hostler

EHLRSSU
hussler
lushers
rushles

EHLRSTU
hurlets
hurtles
hustler

EHLSSTU
hustles
lushest
sleuths

EHMNOOR
hormone
moorhen

EHMORST
mothers
smother
thermos

EHNNORT
northen
thornen

EHNOORS
onshore
sorehon

EHNORRT
horrent
norther

EHNORST
hornets
northes
shorten
thornes
threnos
thrones

EHNOSST
honests
hotness

EHNRSTU
hunters
shunter
threnus

EHOORST
hooters
reshoot
shooter
soother

EHOPPRS
hoppers
shopper

EHOPRST
pothers
strophe
thorpes
thropes
trophes

EHOPRSU
Orpheus
uphroes

EHORRST
horters
rethors
rhetors
shorter

EHORSTU
shouter
souther

EHOSTUY
Southey»

youthes

EHRSSTU
hurstes
reshuts
rushets
thrusse
thurses
thursse

EHRSSTY
shyster
thyrses

EIILMRS
milreis
slimier

EIILMSS
missile
similes

EIILMST
elitism
limiest
limites

EIILNOS
elision
isoline
lionise

EIILNOV
olivine
violine

EIILNRT
lintier
nitrile

EIILNST
instile
liniest
linties

EIILOST
iolites
oiliest

EIILPPS
lippies
slippie

EIIMNRT
interim
mintier
termini

EIIMPRS
impires
pisimer
pismire
primsie

EIIMRST
meistri
miriest
mistier
mistrie
rimiest
trimsie

EIIMSTT
mitiest
mitties

EIINORS
ironies
ironise
noisier

EIINPRS
inspire
pirnies
snipier
spinier

EIINPST
pinites
piniest
tiepins

EIINRTT
nitrite
nittier

EIINRTV
inviter
vitrine

EIINRTW
twinier
write-in

EIINSTT
sitient
sittine»

tiniest

EIINSTV
invites
viniest
viniets
vinites

EIJNORT
jointer
rejoint

EIKLNPR
plinker
prinkle

EIKLNRS
Kilners
linkers
rinkles
slinker

EIKLNRT
tinkler
trinkle

EIKLNRW
winkler
wrinkle

EIKLNSS
inkless
kinless
silkens
slinkes

EIKLNST
lentisk
skinlet
skintle
Stenkil
tinkles

EIKLSTT
kittles
skittle

EIKMMRS
kimmers
skimmer

EIKMORS
irksome
smokier

EIKMRSS
kermiss
smirkes

EIKNNOS
kinones
Soninke

EIKNRST
reknits
stinker
tinkers

EIKNRTT
knitter
trinket

EIKPPRS
kippers
peskier
skipper

EIKRRST
skirret
skirter
striker

EIKRSTT
kirsett
skitter

EIKRSTU
turkeis
turkies
turkise

EILLMST
millets
mistell

EILLNPS
pinsell
spillen

EILLOSV
lovlies
villose

EILLPRS
pillers
spiller

EILLPSS
lipless»

spilles

EILLRST
retills
rillets
stiller
tillers
trellis
trilles

EILLRSW
reswill
rewills
swiller
willers

EILLSTW
willest
willets

EILMNRS
limners
merlins
milners
smerlin

EILMNSU
emulsin
lumines
unlimes

EILMORS
moilers
somlier

EILMPRS
limpers
prelims
rimples
simpler

EILMPRW
wimpler
wrimple

EILMPST
limpest
limpets

EILMRSS
rimless
smilers

EILMRST
mertils
milters
mirtels
mirtles
rimlets
smirtle
trimles

EILMRSY
milreys
miserly

EILMSSY
messily
milseys

EILMSTT
meltits
mittles
smittel
smittle

EILNOPS
epsilon
pinoles
sinople

EILNOPT
pointel
pontile
topinel
top line

EILNOSS
esloins
insoles
lesions
lioness
lionses

EILNOST
entoils
lionets
Nilotes
tonsile

EILNOTU
elution
line-out
outline

EILNOTW
towline»

two-line

EILNPSS
esplins
pensils
pinless
spinels
splines

EILNPST
niplets
pintels
pintles
plenist

EILNPSU
lines up
line-ups
lupines
pinules
spinule
unpiles
up-lines

EILNRST
linters
snirtle

EILNSST
enlists
listens
silents
snitels
snitles
stensil
tinsels

EILNSSU
insulse
silenus

EILNSTT
littens
nittles
slitten
snittle
tilsent

EILNSTU
luniest
luteins
lutines
untiles
utensil

EILNSTW
westlin
wintles

EILOOPR
loopier
poolier

EILOOST
oolites
ostiole
stoolie

EILOPRS
slopier
spoiler

EILOPRT
poitrel
politer

EILOPST
piolets
pistole
ploties
polites

EILOQRU
liquore
quoiler

EILORRS
lorries
roilers

EILORSS
elisors
esliors
eslisor
lorises
resoils
rissole
soilers

EILORST
estriol
loiters
toilers
trioles

EILORSU
louries
lousier
soilure

EILORSW
lowries
low-rise

EILORTT
tortile
triolet

EILOSTT
litotes
toilets

EILPPRS
lippers
lippres
ripples
slipper

EILPPRT
ripplet
tippler
tripple

EILPPSS
pipless
sipples

EILPPST
lippets
slippet
stipple
tippels
tipples

EILPRST
pistler
spilter
spirtle
tiplers
triples

EILPRTT
prittle
triplet

EILPSST
pistels
pistles
pitless
spitels
spitles
splites
stepils
stipels»
stiples
tipless

EILPSTT
pittles
spittel
spittle
tiplets

EILPSTU
putelis
stipule

EILRRSU
lurries
slurrie
surlier

EILRSST
listers
relists
ristles
slestir
slister

EILRSTT
litster
litters
littres
slitter
sterlit
stilter
testril
tilters
titlers

EILRSTU
lustier
ruliest
rutiles

EILRSVY
livyers
silvery
slivery

EILRTTT
tittler
trittle

EILRTTY
littery
tritely

EILSSTT
stilets
titless

EILSSTW
twisles
twissle
wistles

EILSTTW
sweltit
twistle

EILSTTY
stylite
testily

EIMMRST
misterm
stimmer
timmers
trimmes

EIMNOOS
Moonies
noisome

EIMNOOT
emotion
moonite

EIMNOPT
emption
pimento

EIMNORS
merinos
merions
mersion
moniers

EIMNOST
mestino
moisten

EIMNOSW
Owenism
winsome

EIMNRST
entrism
minters
minster
minstre»
remints

EIMNRTU
minuter
unmiter
unmitre

EIMNSSS
messins
missens
sensism

EIMNSST
inmests
mess tin
missent
mistens

EIMNSTU
minuets
minutes
mistune
munites
mutines
untimes

EIMOORR
moorier
roomier

EIMOPRS
imposer
impreso
promise

EIMOPST
mopiest
optimes

EIMORST
erotism
moister
mortise
stormie
trisome

EIMOSST
mitoses
moistes
somites

EIMPRRU
primeur
umpirer

EIMPRSS
impress
Persism
premise
simpers

EIMPRST
imperts
imprest
permits
premits

EIMPRSU
impures
rumpies
sumpier
umpires

EIMPRTU
imputer
tumpier

EIMPSTU
impetus
imputes

EIMRSST
merists
misters
mistres
Remists
smiters
timsers

EIMRSSU
misuser
surmise

EIMRSTY
mistery
mysteri
smytrie

EINNOPS
pension
spinone

EINNORT
intoner
ternion

EINNORU
reunion
Unioner

EINNOST
intones
Sonnite
tension

EINNOTT
nonetti
tontine

EINNPRS
pinners
spinner

EINNPST
pinnets
spinnet
tenpins

EINNRST
interns
rennits
rinnets
sin rent
tinners

EINNRSU
sunnier
unreins
unrisen

EINOPPR
poperin
propine

EINOPRS
opiners
orpines
pioners
poiners
prisone
proines
repoins
sinoper

EINOPRT
pointer
protein
pterion
repoint
tropine

EINOPST
pintoes
pointes»

ponties
sopient
stopine

EINORRS
ironers
norreis
roiners
snorier

EINORSS
noisers
norises
rosines
seniors
snoires
soneris
sonsier

EINORST
instore
norites
oestrin
orients
stonier
tersion
treison
triones

EINORSV
renvois
version

EINOSSS
essoins
osseins
session

EINOSST
Nesiots
nosiest
notises
osteins
sonties

EINOSTT
toniest
tonites

EINOSTW
Owenist
townies

EINOSUV
envious
niveous
veinous

EINPPRS
nippers
snipper

EINPRRT
printer
reprint

EINPRSS
pinsers
snipers
spreins

EINPRST
nipters
pintres
printes
pterins
spriten
terpins

EINPRSU
purines
uprisen

EINPSTU
puniest
punties

EINQSTU
inquest
quinets
quintes

EINQTUU
iunquet
unquiet
unquite

EINRRSU
insurer
ruiners

EINRSST
estrins
inrests
inserts
sinters
sniters»

streins
strines
tserins

EINRSSU
insures
sunrise

EINRSTT
entrist
nitters
snitter
stinter
tinters
tristen

EINRSTU
sturine
triunes
uniters

EINRSTV
inverts
sirvent
striven
vinters

EINRTTW
twinter
wren tit
written

EINRTUV
unrivet
venturi

EINSSTW
wisents
witness

EINSTTW
entwist
twin-set

EIOORST
rooties
sootier
toories

EIOPRRS
priores
prosier

EIOPRST
epirots
periost
periots
porites
poister
reposit
riposte
ropiest

EIOPSST
espiots
posites
posties
sepiost
seposit
sopites

EIOPSTU
piteous
poustie

EIORRSS
orrises
rosiers
rossier
sorries

EIORRST
rioters
roister
roriest
storier

EIORSST
oisters
oistres
ostries
rosiest
soriest
sorites
sorties
stories
tossier
trioses

EIORSTT
riotest
stoiter

EIORTTV
tortive
viretot

EIOSSTV
soviets
stovies

EIPPRST
rippets
strippe
tippers
trippes

EIPRSSS
pissers
prisses

EIPRSST
esprits
persist
pisters
preists
priests
pristes
respits
sitreps
sperits
spreits
spriest
sprites
stipers
stirpes
stripes

EIPRSSU
pursies
pussier
suspire
uprises

EIPRSTT
Petrist
pitters
spitter
tipster
tripets

EIPRSTY
pyrites
stripey

EIQRSTU
querist
quister
squiret
squirte

EIQRTTU
quitter
triquet

EIRSSSU
issuers
risuses

EIRSSTU
resuits
rusties
suiters
surties

EIRSSTV
servits
stivers
strives
treviss
trivess
verists

EIRSTTT
stretti
titters
tritest

EIRSTTW
retwist
switter
twister
witters

EIRSTUV
stuiver
virtues

EISSSTU
tissues
tussies

EJLORST
jolters
jostler
rejolts

EJOSTTU
outjest
outjets

EKNORST
stonker
storken

EKNORWY
New York
ywroken

EKOPRST
porkets
sproket

EKRSSTU
turkess
tuskers

ELLNOSW
swollen
Nowells

ELLOSTU
outsell
sellout

ELLPRSU
pullers
repulls
spuller

ELLPSUW
upswell
upwells

ELMOPSU
plumose
pumelos

ELMORSU
emulsor
musrole

ELMPRSU
lumpers
rumples
slumper

ELMSSSU
mussels
sumless

ELNOPSY
poleyns
synople

ELNORST
lentors
snortle

ELNOSSS
lessons
sonless

ELNOSSW
lowness
nowsels

ELNSTTU
luntest
nutlets

ELNSUZZ
nuzzles
snuzzle

ELOOPRS
loopers
poolers
prooles
spooler

ELOORTT
rootlet
tootler

ELOPPRS
loppers
poplers
propels
slopper

ELOPPST
loppets
poplets
stopple
topples

ELOPRSS
plessor
slopers
splores
sporles

ELOPRSU
leprous
loupers
pelorus
perlous
proules
sporule

ELOPRTT
plotter»
portlet

ELOPRTU
plouter
poulter

ELOPRTW
plowter
powlter
trowple

ELOPRVY
overply
plovery

ELOPSST
postels
postles
spotels
spotles
stopels
stoples
stopsel
topless

ELOPSTT
pottels
pottles
spottle

ELOPSTU
poulets
stouple
tupelos

ELOQSUY
quoyles
squoyle

ELORSTT
eltrots
lotters
rottels
rottles
settlor
slotter
tolters

ELORSTU
elutors
louters
outlers
routles
stroule»
troules

ELORSTW
lowters
rowlets
strowle
towlers
trowels
wortles

ELORTTT
tortlet
trotlet
trottle

ELOSSTU
lotuses
solutes
stoules
tousles

ELOSSTW
lowsest
slowest
stowles
towsels

ELOSSTY
systole
tolseys
tyloses

ELPPRSU
pulpers
purples
repulps
suppler

ELPRSSU
sprules
surples

ELPRSTU
pulters
spurtel
spurtle
turples

ELPSSTU
pultess
pustels
pustles

ELPSTUU
pluteus
pustule

ELRSSTU
lusters
lustres
results
rustles
rutsels
sulters
sultres
sutlers
trusels
trussel
trussle
ulsters

ELRSTTU
ruttles
suttler
turtles

ELSSSTU
tussels
tussles

EMMNOSU
mu-meson
musmone

EMNOOST
monetos
moonset

EMNOPST
postmen
topsmen

EMNORST
mentors
monster
monstre
montres

EMNORTU
monture
mounter
remount

EMNRSTU
munster
munters
sternum

EMOOSTY
myosote
toysome

EMOPRST
emports
postrem
sompter
trompes

EMORRST
morters
mortres
stormer
termors
tremors

EMORSSU
mousers
smouser
soumers

EMORSTU
mouters
oestrum

EMPRSTU
stumper
sumpter
trumpes

ENNORST
ronnets
stonern
tonners
tronnes

ENNORSU
neurons
non-user

ENNOSTU
neuston
unstone
untones

ENNPSTU
punnets
unspent

ENNRSTU
runnets
stunner
tunners

ENOOSST
soonest
stoones

ENOPRST
orpents
postern

ENOPRSY
prysone
pyoners
synoper
synopre

ENOPSST
posnets
possnet
stepson

ENORRST
snorter
troners

ENORSST
nestors
rotness
stoners
strones
tensors

ENORSSU
sourens
sun rose

ENORSTT
rottens
snotter
stentor
tentors

ENORSTU
tenours
tonsure
unstore

ENORSTW
nor' west
strowen

ENORSTY
stonery
troynes
tyrones

ENOSTTU
stouten
tenutos
Teutons

ENPRRSU
pruners
spurner

ENPRSTU
punster
punters
unprest

ENRRSTU
returns
snurter
turners
unstern

ENRRTUU
nurture
untruer

ENRSTTU
entrust
nutters
trusten
tunster

EOOPPRS
opposer
propose

EOOPRST
poorest
Pooters
stooper
troopes

EOOPRTV
overpot
overtop

EOORRST
rooster
rooters
toreros

EOORSST
oostres
roostes
soorest

EOPPRRS
propers
prosper

EOPPRSS
oppress
soppers

EOPPRST
prepost
stopper
toppers
troppes

EOPRRST
porrets
porters
pretors
proters
reports
resport
sporter
tropers

EOPRSST
portess
posters
prestos
prosets
reposts
respots
septors
sportes
sprotes
stopers
stropes

EOPRSTT
potters
protest
spotter

EOPRSTU
petrous
posture
pourets
pouters
proteus
septour
spouter
sproute
stroupe
troupes

EOPRSTW
powters
prowest
spowter
sprowte
strowpe
trowpes

EOPSSST
possest
possets

EOPSSTT
possett
spottes

EOPSTTU
outstep
toupets

EOPSTTW
stewpot
two-step

EOQRSTU
questor
quoters
roquets
torques
troques

EORRSST
resorts
re-sorts
rosters
sorters
storers
storres
trosser

EORRSTU
retours
rouster
routers
stourre
tourers
trouser

EORRSTW
rowters
strower

EORRSTY
royster»
storyer

EORRTTU
torture
trouter
tutorer

EORSSTU
estrous
oestrus
ousters
sourest
souters
stoures
strouse
tousers
trouses
tussore

EORSSTW
restows
sowters
stowers
stowres
towsers
worsest

EORSTTT
stotter
stretto
totters

EORSTTU
routtes
tetrous
touters
troutes

EORSTTW
swotter
towrets
trowets
trowtes
wet rots

EPPRSSU
press up
suppers

EPRRSUU
pursuer
usurper

EPRSTTU
putters
sputter

ERRSSTU
retruss
rustres
sturers
sturres
trusser

ERRSTTU
retrust
rutters
truster
turrets

ERSSSTU
russets
tessurs
trusses
tussers
tussres

ERSSTTU
sturtes
tutress

FFGIINR
griffin
riffing

FGIILNR
fliring
rifling

FGIILNT
fliting
lifting
tifling

FGIINST
fisting
sifting

FGIINZZ
fizzing
gin fizz

FGILNOW
flowing
fowling
wolfing

FGINORT
forting
froting

FHLRTUU
hurtful
ruthful

FIKLNOW
fowlkin
wolfkin

FILORST
firlots
florist

FLLOPTU
plotful
topfull

FNOORSU
sunroof
unroofs

GGGIINR
girging
rigging

GGGINOR
gorging
groging
rogging

GGGINRU
gurging
rugging

GGIILMN
gliming
milging

GGIILNN
ingling
linging

GGIILNR
girling
rigling

GGIINNR
girning
rigning
ringing

GGIINNS
signing
singing

GGIINRS
girsing
grising

GGIINRT
girting
ringgit

GGILNOS
glosing
gosling
loggins
logings
oglings

GGILNOU
glouing
Guignol

GGINOPR
groping
porging

GGINORS
gorings
gringos
grosing

GGINORU
roguing
rouging

GGINRSU
grusing
surging
urgings

GHIIKNT
king hit
kithing

GHIILNT
hilting
lithing

GHIINNT
in-thing
nithing

GHIINRS
hirings
shiring

GHIINST
histing
insight
shiting
sithing

GHIINTT
hitting
tithing

GHIINTW
whiting
withing

GHILNOS
holings
longish
loshing
shinlog
sholing

GHILNOW
howling
wholing

GHILNTY
lything
nightly

GHIMNOS
gnomish
homings
shoming

GHINOPS
ginshop
hopings

GHINORS
horsing
shoring

GHINOST
hit song
hosting
toshing

GHINOSW
howsing
showing

GHINOTT
hotting
tonight

GHINPSU
gunship
pushing

GHINRTU
hurting
ruthing
ungirth
unright

GHINSTU
husting
shuting
unsight

GHNOSTU
gunshot
noughts
shotgun

GIIKLNN
inkling
linking

GIIKLNS
likings
sliking

GIIKNNP
kingpin
pink gin
pinking

GIIKNNS
inkings
sinking

GIIKNNT
kniting
tinking

GIIKNPS
kipings
pigskin
spiking

GIIKNRS
girkins
griskin
irkings
rikings
risking
skiring

GIIKNSS
kissing
skiings

GIIKNSV
skiving
vikings

GIIKNSW
swiking
wikings
wisking

GIILLNT
lilting
tilling

GIILMNS
limings
milings
sliming
smiling

GIILNOR
ligroin
roiling

GIILNOS
oilings
siloing
soiling

GIILNOT
litigon
toiling

GIILNPR
lirping
pirling
ripling

GIILNPS
lipsing
lisping
pilings
plising
sliping
spiling

GIILNPT
pliting
tipling

GIILNST
listing
litings
sliting
stiling
tilings

GIILNSV
livings
sliving

GIILNTT
litting
tilting
titling
Tlingit

GIIMMNS
mimings
simming

GIIMNRT
mitring
triming

GIIMNST
misting
smiting
stiming
timings

GIINNNS
innings
sinning

GIINNOR
ironing
roining

GIINNPS
nipings
pinings
pinsing
sniping
spining

GIINNRU
inuring
ruining
urining

GIINNSW
inswing
winsing

GIINORS
origins
signior
soiring

GIINPPS
pipings
sipping

GIINPRS
prising
ripings
risping
spiring

GIINRST
risting
stiring
tirings
trising

GIINRTW
twiring
writing

GIINSST
sisting
sitings

GIINSTT
sitting
tisting

GIINTTW
twiting
witting

GIKLNRU
kurling
lurking

GIKNNOO
kongoni
nooking

GIKNSTU
skuting
tusking

GILMNPU
lumping
pluming

GILNNRU
lurning
nurling

GILNOOP
looping
pooling

GILNOOR
looring
rooling

GILNOOS
logions
loosing
soloing
sooling

GILNOOT
looting
tooling

GILNOPR
ploring
proling

GILNOPS
polings
sloping
spoling

GILNOPU
louping
pouling

GILNOPW
lowping
plowing
powling

GILNORS
gorlins
lorings
sloring

GILNORU
louring
rouling

GILNORW
rowling
worling

GILNOSS
losings
lossing

GILNOST
lignots
lingots
stoling
tiglons
tolings

GILNOSU
lousing
souling

GILNOSW
lowings
lowsing
owlings
slowing
sowling

GILNOTU
louting
touling
tung oil

GILNOVS
lovings
solving

GILNPSU
pulsing
pusling
sulping
supling

GILNSTU
ingluts
lusting
lutings
singult
sluting
ungilts

GIMNNRU
Murngin
murning

GIMNOOR
mooring
rooming

GIMNORS
Morsing
smoring

GIMNORT
morting
troming

GIMNOST
gnomist
motings

GIMNOSU
mousing
souming

GINNORS
snoring
sorning

GINNORW
ingrown
worning

GINNOST
notings
stoning
tonings

GINNOSW
snowing
swoning
wonings

GINNPSU
punsing
spuning

GINNRSU
nursing
urnings

GINNRTU
nurting
runting
turning

GINNSTU
gunnist
tunings

GINOOPR
pooring
rooping

GINOPRS
orpings
porings
prosing
proigns
ropings
sporing

GINOPRU
ingroup
pouring
rouping

GINOPSS
posings
possing

GINOPST
posting
potings
stoping
topings

GINOPSU
pousing
souping

GINORSS
grisons
ingross
rosings
rossing
signors

GINORST
girnots
rosting
rotings
sorting
storing
trigons

GINORSU
rousing
souring

GINORSW
rowings
rowsing
sowring»
worsing

GINORTT
rotting
torting

GINORTU
outgrin
outring
routing
touring

GINORTW
rowting
towring
trowing
worting
wroting

GINOSST
stingos
tosings
tossing

GINOSSW
sowings
sowsing

GINOSTT
sotting
totings

GINOSTU
ousting
outings
souting
tousing

GINOSTV
stoving
votings

GINOSTW
owtings
stowing
towings
towsing

GINPPSU
supping
uppings

GINPRSU
pursing»
spuring

GINPRSY
pryings
springy
sprying

GINPSSY
pyssing
spyings

GINPSTU
pignuts
sputing
stuping

GINRSTU
rusting
truings
ungirts

GINRSTY
stringy
styring
tryings

HIIKNPS
kinship
pinkish

HIMOPRS
Orphism
rompish

HIMSSTU
Humists
isthmus

HINOPSS
siphons
sonship

HIOTTUW
outwith
without

HOOPSTT
hotpots
potshot

HOOPSTU
Pushtoo
upshoot

IIORSTV
ivorist
visitor

IIPRSST
spirits
tripsis

IKLNOOS
look ins
looks in
skolion

IKLNPSU
links up
link ups
skulpin

IKNPSTU
sputnik
upknits

ILOOPST
poloist
topsoil

ILOSSTY
tossily
tylosis

IMMSSTU
mutisms
summist
summits

IMRSSTU
sistrum
trismus
truisms

INOOPST
options
positon
potions

INOORST
isotron
nitroso
torsion

INOPSSU
poussin
spinous

INOPSTU
sit-upon
spinout

INORSUU
ruinous
urinous

INPRSTU
turnips
unstrip

INRSTTU
intrust
untrist

INSSTUU
sunsuit
unsuits

IOPRSST
prosist
prosits

IOPRSTT
protist
tripots
tropist

KLOOOTU
lookout
outlook

KOORTUW
outwork
workout

LLOOPRT
rolltop
trollop

MMNOSSU
musmons
summons

MOOPSTT
tompots
topmost

NOOPRST
postron
protons

NOORSTU
unroost
unroots

NORTTUU
outturn
turnout

NRSSTUU
Sturnus
untruss

OOPRSTU
portous
uproots

OOPSTTU
outpost
outtops

AAACDINR
acaridan
Arcadian

AAAILRST
Alastair
salariat

AABCDKRW
backward
drawback

AABCELNR
balancer
barnacle

AABCERST
abreacts
bearcats
cabarets
cabresta

AABCFKLL
backfall
fallback

AABCIJNO
Bajocian
Jacobian

AABCILMS
balsamic
cabalism

AABCILST
basaltic
cabalist

AABDLORR
Labrador
larboard

AABDORWY
broadway
wayboard

AABEEKMT
bakemeat
makebate

AABEELLS
leasable
saleable

AABEELMN
amenable
nameable

AABEGOST
boatages
sabotage

AABEILLS
isabella
sailable

AABEILST
Baalites
labiates
satiable

AABEKNRS
bankeras
Branksea
Nebraska

AABELMST
blastema
lambaste

AABELPRS
parables
parsable
sparable

AABELRTY
betrayal
rateably

AABELSTT
statable
tastable

AABENRST
antbears
ratsbane

AABFLOTT
faltboat
flatboat

AABMORTU
marabout
tamboura

AACCERTU
accurate
carucate

AACCOSTT
staccato
stoccata
toccatas

AACDEGMR
card game
decagram

AACDELNR
calander
calandre
calendar
landrace

AACDELOS
case load
escalado

AACDGINR
arcading
cardigan

AACDILNU
Claudian
dulciana

AACDINRT
radicant
tridacna

AACEEMRT
camerate
macerate
racemate

AACEENRS
Canarese
Cesarean

AACEILLN
alliance
canaille

AACEILMN
analcime
calamine

AACEILNT
analcite
laitance

AACEILST
Castalie»
saliceta

AACEIMNR
American
Cinerama

AACEIMRS
macarise
mesaraic

AACEINRS
acarines
canaries
cesarian
narceias

AACEINRT
carinate
craniate

AACEIPTT
apatetic
capitate

AACELMRS
caramels
macerals

AACELNOR
Carolean
lecanora

AACELOST
alecoast
cataloes

AACELSTY
catalyse
scytalae
staylace

AACENRST
canaster
caterans

AACGILNN
Anglican
canaling

AACGIMNP
campaign
pangamic

AACHIMRS
archaism
charisma

AACHINRT
antiarch
canthari

AACILMNT
calamint
claimant

AACILNOR
Carolina
conarial

AACILNTT
Atlantic
tantalic

AACILSTT
cat's tail
cattails
statical

AACIMNOR
macaroni
marocain

AACINOPT
capitano
pacation

AACINORT
Croatian
raincoat

AACLLSUY
casually
causally

AACLPRSU
capsular
scapular

AACORTTU
actuator
autocrat

AADDNRST
sand dart»
standard

AADEELRW
aleeward
Delaware
Weardale

AADEENTT
antedate
Edentata

AADEFIRS
faradise
safaried

AADEGINR
areading
drainage
gardenia

AADEHILR
headrail
railhead

AADEILPT
lapidate
Talpidae

AADEIMNT
animated
diamante

AADEIMST
Adamites
adamsite
diastema

AADEINRS
araneids
arsadine

AADEIPRS
paradise
Sparidae

AADEIRST
dataries
radiates

AADELMNR
alderman
malander

AADELMNS
dalesman
leadsman

AADELMPT
date palm
palmated

AADGILMR
madrigal
mail drag

AADGILNO
diagonal
gonadial

AADGMNOR
dragoman
Garamond

AADGMNRS
dragmans
dragsman

AADIMNRY
dairyman
mainyard

AADQRSTU
quadrats
squadrat

AAEEHRTW
aweather
wheatear

AAEEILNT
alienate
Atelinae

AAEELNNR
annealer
lernaean

AAEELNPS
seaplane
spelaean

AAEENRST
arsenate
serenata

AAEEPPRR
appearer»
rapparee
reappear

AAEEPRST
asperate
separate

AAEERSTW
seawater
teawares

AAEFMRSW
frame saw
sawframe

AAEGILNR
Algerian
regalian

AAEGILNT
agential
alginate

AAEGILRS
gasalier
lairages
regalias

AAEGIMNT
agminate
enigmata

AAEGIMRT
gematria
maritage

AAEGINRS
anergias
angaries
arginase

AAEGINTV
navigate
vaginate

AAEGLNRS
alnagers
Sangreal

AAEGNRST
staragen
tanagers

AAEHIIRT
hetairai
hetairia

AAEHIMNT
anthemia
haematin

AAEHINRT
Atherina
Rhaetian

AAEHLPRS
harp seal
pearl ash

AAEHMNRS
shareman
shearman

AAEIKLLS
alkalies
alkalise

AAEILNSS
nasalise
Salesian
sea snail

AAEILNTT
antliate
Latinate

AAEILRSS
assailer
reassail
salaries

AAEILSTV
aestival
salivate

AAEIMNRT
animater
marinate

AAEINPRT
Patarine
Tarpeian

AAEINRST
antisera
artesian
artisane»
Asterina
Erastian
Raetians
ratanies
resinata
seatrain

AAEINRTT
attainer
reattain

AAEINSTT
astatine
sanitate
tanaiste

AAEIPRST
aspirate
parasite
septaria

AAEIRSTT
ariettas
aristate

AAELLPST
patellas
stapella

AAELNPRT
parental
paternal
prenatal

AAELNPST
platanes
pleasant

AAELNRTT
alterant
alternat

AAEMNPRS
Parmesan
spearman

AAEMNPRT
name part
parament

AAEMNRST
sarmenta
semantra

AAENPPRT
apparent
trappean

AAEPRTTW
tap water
water tap

AAERRTTW
tar water
water rat

AAERSTTU
saturate
tuateras

AAFLLPRT
falltrap
pratfall
trapfall

AAGILMNR
alarming
marginal

AAGIMNSS
amassing
gas mains
siamangs

AAGIRSTV
gravitas
stravaig

AAGNORRT
arrogant
tarragon

AAIILPRR
Prairial
riparial

AAILMNOR
manorial
morainal

AAILMNST
staminal
talisman

AAILMRST
alarmist
alastrim

AAILNNPT
plainant
plantain

AAILNNST
annalist
santalin

AAILNORT
notarial
rational

AAIMNNOR
Maronian
Romanian

AAIMNORT
animator
montaria
tamanoir

AAIMNSST
mantissa
satanism
staminas

AAINNRTU
nutarian
Turanian

AAINORRS
orarians
rosarian

AAINPRST
aspirant
partisan
Patarins

AAINRSTU
Austrian
Saturnia

ABBBGILN
babbling
blabbing

ABBCELRS
cabblers
clabbers
scabbler
scrabble

ABBDERST
drabbets
drabbest

ABBELORS
belabors
sorbable

ABBEORRS
absorber
reabsorb

ABBGILMN
balmbing
mabbling

ABBGILNR
brabling
rabbling

ABBGILNW
bawbling
wabbling

ABCDEGIR
birdcage
cagebird

ABCDEIRS
ascribed
carbides

ABCDEKLO
bale-dock
blockade

ABCDIILO
biocidal
diabolic

ABCDILLR
birdcall
callbird

ABCEFIKR
backfire
fireback

ABCEILLR
Claribel
cribella

ABCEILOR
albicore»
cabriole

ABCEINRS
brisance
carbines

ABCEKOOS
bookcase
casebook

ABCELMRS
cambrels
clambers
crambles
scambler
scramble

ABCGIKNR
bracking
king crab

ABCGILNS
cablings
scabling

ABCGINRS
bracings
scrabing

ABCJKOOT
bootjack
jackboot

ABDDEEKR
bedarked
debarked

ABDEEERV
beavered
bereaved

ABDEEGLR
belgarde
Belgrade

ABDEEILR
brideale
rebailed
rideable

ABDEEIRT
Abderite
ebriated
rebaited

ABDEEIST
beadiest
diabetes

ABDEEKMR
bedmaker
embarked

ABDEEKNR
barkened
bedarken

ABDEELMS
beldames
bemedals
emblased

ABDEELNT
bandelet
entabled

ABDEEMNS
beam-ends
bedesman

ABDEEPRS
bedrapes
bespread

ABDEERST
betreads
breasted
debaters

ABDEERTT
battered
drabette
rebatted

ABDEESST
basseted
besteads

ABDEFLNU
fundable
unfabled

ABDEGILN
blindage
delabing

ABDEGINR
bearding
bedaring»
breading

ABDEGINS
beadings
debasing

ABDEHOLT
bolthead
Theobald

ABDEILNR
bandlier
bilander

ABDEINRS
air bends
brandise

ABDELNST
bandlets
blandest

ABDEMRTU
drumbeat
umbrated

ABDENRTU
breadnut
turbaned

ABDEORRW
barrowed
wardrobe

ABDGINOR
abording
boarding
broading

ABEEENRT
rebeaten
tenebrae

ABEEILLV
leviable
liveable

ABEEILNS
Balinese
baseline

ABEEILSZ
seizable
sizeable

ABEELMMR
embalmer
emmarble

ABEELMSS
assemble
beamless
emblases

ABEELNOP
beanpole
openable

ABEELNST
Beltanes
enstable
tenables

ABEELOPR
operable
ropeable

ABEELRST
bleaters
restable
retables

ABEELSTT
seat belt
testable

ABEEMNTT
abetment
batement

ABEERRTY
betrayer
teaberry

ABEGIKNR
breaking
rebaking

ABEGILNR
blearing
rebaling

ABEGILNS
bealings
Belgians
Bengalis
gab-lines
singable

ABEGILNT
belating
bleating
tangible

ABEGIMNR
ambering
breaming

ABEGIMNS
beamings
embasing

ABEGINRS
bearings
sabering

ABEGINRT
berating
rebating
tabering

ABEGKORS
brokages
grosbeak

ABEGMNOY
bogeyman
moneybag

ABEIILST
albitise
sibilate

ABEIILTV
live bait
vitiable

ABEIKNRS
bearskin
inbreaks

ABEILLRY
beryllia
reliably

ABEILLST
bastille
listable

ABEILMNS
bailsmen
bimensal

ABEILMST
balmiest
bimetals
timbales

ABEILRST
blastier
librates

ABEILSST
baitless
bastiles
bestails
bestials
blasties
stabiles

ABEILSSU
issuable
suasible

ABEIMRTV
ambivert
verbatim

ABEINORS
baronies
sea robin

ABEINORT
baritone
obtainer
reobtain
taborine

ABEINOST
botanies
botanise
obeisant

ABEINRST
banister
barniest

ABEINRTU
braunite
urbanite

ABEINSST
basinets
bassinet
besaints
bestains

ABEIRRSS
brasiers
brassier

ABEIRRTT
birretta
brattier

ABEIRSTY
bestiary
sybarite

ABEKLNST
blankest
blankets

ABEKORTU
breakout
outbreak

ABELLNRU
Brunella
rubellan

ABELNOST
notables
stonable

ABELNRSS
barnless
bransels
bransles

ABELNSTU
abluents
unstable

ABELORST
bloaters
sortable
storable

ABELOSTW
bestowal
stowable
teabowls

ABELRSTU
baluster
rustable

ABELRTTU
burletta
rebuttal

ABELSSTT
stablest
stablets

ABEORTTU
obturate
tabouret

ABERSSTU
abstruse
surbates

ABGGILNR
garbling
grabling

ABGIILNS
blaising
saibling

ABGIINOR
aborigin
baignoir

ABGIKNRS
brakings
brasking

ABGILMNR
marbling
rambling

ABGILNOT
bloating
Bog Latin
oblating
obligant

ABGILNRW
brawling
warbling

ABGILNST
batlings
blasting
stabling
tablings

ABGIMOSU
bigamous
subimago

ABGINOST
boatings»

boasting
bostangi

ABHKOOOT
boathook
book oath

ABILNOTU
ablution
abutilon

ABILNRTU
tribunal
turbinal

ABILORST
orbitals
strobila

ABIOORST
arborist
rib roast

ACCDINOR
cancroid
draconic

ACCEHIKP
chickpea
peachick

ACCEHILM
alchemic
chemical

ACCEHNOR
charneco
encroach

ACCEILNS
calcines
scenical

ACCEISTT
cattiest
ecstatic

ACCENOST
coenacts
cosecant

ACCHIORT
thoracic
trochaic

ACCINOTY
canticoy
cyanotic

ACCIORST
acrostic
Socratic

ACDDEERT
cedrated
decarted
redacted

ACDDEINR
candider
riddance

ACDDEKLO
deadlock
deck-load

ACDDERSU
adducers
crusaded

ACDDGILN
caddling
cladding

ACDDHKOS
haddocks
shaddock

ACDEEFRS
defacers
frescade
redfaces

ACDEEHLS
Chaldees
cheadles
lachesed

ACDEEHNR
enarched
enrached
rachened

ACDEEHNS
encashed
enchased

ACDEEHRS
cashered»

dearches
recashed
rechased
searched

ACDEEHRT
chatered
rechated

ACDEEHST
detaches
sacheted

ACDEEIMT
decimate
medicate

ACDEEINV
deviance
vice-dean

ACDEEKRS
recasked
resacked
screaked

ACDEEKRT
racketed
retacked

ACDEELLR
cellared
recalled

ACDEELNR
calender
calendre
encradle

ACDEELNS
cleansed
enscaled

ACDEELPR
clapered
replaced

ACDEELRS
declares
red scale
rescaled

ACDEELRT
clareted»

clatered
decretal
treacled

ACDEELRV
calvered
clavered

ACDEEMRT
cremated
mercated

ACDEENOT
anecdote
toe dance

ACDEENRS
ascender
reascend

ACDEENRT
cantered
crenated
decanter
nectared
recanted

ACDEENRV
caverned
cravened
encarved

ACDEEORT
coatered
decorate
ocreated
recoated

ACDEERRT
arrected
cratered
recarted
recrated
retraced
terraced

ACDEHILR
Heraclid
heraldic

ACDEHINS
echidnas
inchased

ACDEHIRT
thridace
tracheid

ACDEHLNU
launched
unlached

ACDEHNOR
anchored
rondache

ACDEHNST
snatched
stanched

ACDEHNTU
chaunted
nautched

ACDEIINT
actinide
ctenidia
diactine
indicate

ACDEIITV
caitived
cavitied
vaticide

ACDEILLN
incalled
declinal

ACDEILRT
articled
lacertid

ACDEILRU
auricled
radicule

ACDEIMNO
comedian
daemonic
demoniac
mid-ocean

ACDEIMRT
dermatic
timecard

ACDEINOS
codeinas
diocesan
oceanids

ACDEINPT
pedantic
pentadic

ACDEINRT
crinated
dicentra

ACDEIRTT
citrated
tetracid
tetradic

ACDELNRY
calendry
dry-clean

ACDENRTU
cedar nut
uncrated
underact
untraced

ACDEORRS
corrades
corrased

ACDERSTU
traduces
turcased

ACDGHOTW
dogwatch
watchdog

ACDHINOR
hadronic
rhodanic

ACDHLNOR
chaldron
chondral

ACDIILTY
calidity
dialytic

ACDIINOT
actinoid»
diatonic

ACDILLOU
caudillo
lodicula

ACDIOPRS
picadors
sporadic

ACDMNORY
dormancy
mordancy

ACDOORST
ostracod
scordato

ACEEHIRT
aetheric
hetaeric

ACEEHMRS
cashmere
machrees
marchese

ACEEHPRS
cheapers
peachers
sea perch

ACEEHRRS
reachers
research
searcher

ACEEHRSS
recashes
rechases
searches

ACEEHSST
escheats
sea chest
steaches

ACEEILNR
cinereal
reliance

ACEEILPS
calipees
especial

ACEEIMRR
creamier
rearmice

ACEEINRS
Cairenes
increase
resiance

ACEEINRT
centiare
creatine
increate
iterance

ACEEIRTV
creative
reactive

ACEELNRS
cleaners
cleanser
recleans

ACEELNRU
cerulean
Laurence

ACEELNST
cleanest
latences

ACEELRSS
careless
rescales

ACEELRST
clearest
scelerat
treacles

ACEEMRRS
creamers
re-scream
screamer

ACEENOST
acetones
notecase

ACEENRRT
recanter
recreant

ACEENRST
centares
crenates
reascent
re-enacts
sarcenet

ACEENRTU
enacture
uncreate

ACEERRST
caterers
recaster
recrates
retraces
terraces

ACEERSST
cateress
cerastes

ACEFILOS
fasciole
focalise

ACEFLNOT
conflate
falconet

ACEGHINT
cheating
teaching

ACEGILNN
cleaning
elancing
enlacing

ACEGILNR
clearing
relacing

ACEGILNS
angelics
escaling

ACEGILNT
cleating
eclating
elacting

ACEGIMNR
amercing»

creaming
Germanic

ACEGINNR
enracing
recaning

ACEGINPR
capering
preacing
repacing

ACEGINRS
acresing
creasing
Grecians
searcing

ACEGINRT
arecting
argentic
catering
citrange
creating
reacting

ACEGINSS
caginess
ceasings

ACEGIRST
agrestic
cigarets
ergastic

ACEGORTY
category
grey-coat

ACEHHRTY
hatchery
thearchy

ACEHIKLR
chalkier
hacklier

ACEHILNT
chainlet
ethnical

ACEHILOR
halicore
heroical

ACEHIMPT
empathic
emphatic

ACEHIMST
misteach
tachisme

ACEHINRS
archines
inarches

ACEHINST
asthenic
chanties
teach-ins

ACEHIPRS
aspheric
charpies
seraphic

ACEHIPRT
chapiter
phreatic

ACEHIPST
hepatics
pastiche

ACEHIRST
chariest
Charites
Rhaetics
theriacs

ACEHIRTT
chattier
theatric

ACEHLNST
lanchets
stanchel

ACEHLORT
chelator
chlorate
trochlea

ACEHLOST
cat holes
cholates
eschalot

ACEHLRTU
archlute
trauchle

ACEHNOPR
canephor
chaperon

ACEHNRST
chanters
rechants
snatcher
stancher
tranches

ACEHNSST
chastens
snatches
stanches

ACEHNSTU
nautches
unchaste
uncheats

ACEHORRV
hovercar
overarch

ACEHOSTU
cathouse
soutache

ACEHPRTY
patchery
petchary

ACEHRRST
charrets
charters
Chartres
recharts
starcher

ACEIILNS
salicine
silicane

ACEIILST
ciliates
silicate

ACEILLMR
micellar»

millrace

ACEILMNS
enclaims
melanics
meniscal
mescalin

ACEILMRT
climater
metrical

ACEILMST
climates
clematis

ACEILNNP
pannicle
pinnacle

ACEILNOR
acrolein
caroline
colinear
Cornelia
creolian

ACEILNPT
iceplant
pectinal
planetic

ACEILNRS
carlines
lanciers

ACEILNSS
laciness
sanicles

ACEILORT
erotical
loricate

ACEILPPY
clay pipe
pipeclay

ACEILPRS
calipers
replicas
spiracle

ACEILPRT
particle
prelatic

ACEILPSS
slipcase
specials

ACEILPST
plicates
septical
tieclasp

ACEILRST
altrices
articles
clairest
recitals
sterical

ACEILRSV
calivers
claviers
varicles
visceral

ACEILSST
aseclist
elastics
salicets
scaliest

ACEIMNRS
carmines
cremains

ACEIMNST
amnestic
semantic

ACEIMPRS
parecism
sapremic

ACEIMRST
ceramist
matrices
mistrace
scimetar

ACEINNRS
crannies
narceins

ACEINNST
ancients
canniest
insectan
instance

ACEINOPR
apocrine
caponier
ice apron
procaine

ACEINORT
actioner
anoretic
anticore
ceration
creation
reaction

ACEINORV
Corvinae
veronica

ACEINOST
aconites
canoeist
sonicate

ACEINOTV
conative
invocate

ACEINRSS
arsenics
cerasins
raciness

ACEINRST
canister
ceratins
certains
cisterna
craintes
creatins
nacrites
resciant
scantier

ACEINSST
cineasts
scanties

ACEINSTT
entastic
nictates
tetanics

ACEINSTV
cistvaen
vesicant

ACEIPRST
crispate
paretics
picrates
practise

ACEIRSSU
cuirasse
scauries
uricases

ACEIRSTT
citrates
cristate
scattier

ACEISSTU
sauciest
suitcase

ACEKLMPU
packmule
plumcake

ACEKLRST
racklest
tacklers

ACEKLSST
sacklets
slackest
tackless

ACELLNOT
call note
Lancelot

ACELLOPS
collapse
escallop

ACELLORV
coverall
overcall

ACELMSTU
calumets
muscatel

ACELNSSU
scalenus
unscales

ACELORSS
escolars
lacrosse
solacers

ACELORST
locaters
sectoral

ACELORSY
caloyers
coarsely

ACELOSST
alecosts
coatless
lactoses
scatoles

ACELOSTU
lacteous
locustae
oculates
osculate

ACELPRST
sceptral
spectral

ACELRRSW
crawlers
scrawler

ACEMORRT
cremator
Mercator

ACENNOSS
canoness
sonances

ACENOPST
capstone
opencast

ACENORST
ancestor
cantores
enactors
sortance

ACENORSU
carneous
nacreous

ACENORTU
courante
outrance

ACENOSTT
constate
stonecat

ACENRSTU
caunters
centaurs
Etruscan
recusant
uncrates
untraces

ACENRTUY
centaury
centuary
cyanuret

ACEORSST
coarsest
coasters
recoasts
Socrates

ACEORSTV
overacts
overcast

ACFGINRS
farcings
scarfing

ACGGILNN
clanging
glancing

ACGGINNU
canguing
uncaging

ACGHIMNR
charming
marching

ACGHINNR
charning
ranching

ACGHINNS
chansing
hancings

ACGHINNT
chanting
natching

ACGHINPT
nightcap
patching

ACGHINRS
archings
chagrins
charings
crashing
sarching

ACGHINRT
charting
chatring
ratching

ACGHINST
chasting
chatings
scathing
tachings

ACGIINRT
cairting
granitic

ACGIKLNS
calkings
lackings
slacking

ACGIKNST
stacking
tackings

ACGILLNS
callings
scalling

ACGILNOT
colating
locating

ACGILNPS
clapsing
clasping
placings
scalping
scapling

ACGILNRS
carlings
scarling

ACGILNRU
cingular
crauling

ACGILNSS
classing
scalings

ACGILNST
castling
catlings
sclating

ACGIMNPS
campings
scamping

ACGIMNSY
gymnasic
syngamic

ACGINNST
cantings
scanting
stancing

ACGINOST
agnostic
coasting
coatings
cotingas
scoating

ACGINPRS
carpings
scarping
scraping

ACGINRST
cartings
scarting
tracings

ACGINRSU
acursing
scauring

ACHHNTTU
nuthatch
unthatch

ACHILNOS
lichanos
Nicholas

ACHIMNOR
choirman
harmonic
marchion

ACHIRSTT
chartist
straicht

ACHMNORS
monarchs
nomarchs
Romansch

ACHMNORY
monarchy
nomarchy

ACHOTTUW
outwatch
watchout

ACHPRSTU
pushcart
sharp cut

ACIIMNTY
imitancy
intimacy
minacity

ACIINNOT
inaction
nicotian

ACIIRSST
satirics»

Triassic

ACILNOOT
colation
location

ACILNOSV
Slavonic
Volscian

ACILNSTU
lunatics
sultanic

ACILRTUV
cultivar
curvital

ACIMNORU
conarium
coumarin

ACIMOSST
acosmist
masicots
massicot
somatics

ACIMOSTT
masticot
stomatic

ACINNOST
actinons
canonist
cantions
contains
sanction

ACINORST
anticors
cantoris
carotins
cast iron
castorin
corsaint

ACINOSTT
oscitant
tactions

ACINRTTU
taciturn
urticant

ACINSTTY
sanctity
scantity

ACIOPRST
apricots
piscator

ACIORTTY
atrocity
citatory

ACIRSSTY
sacristy
satyrics

ACKORRST
rock rats
rock star
rock tars
tarrocks

ACLOSSTU
outclass
soul-scat

ACNORSTU
corsaunt
courants

ACORRTUY
carryout
curatory

ADDDEEMN
demanded
maddened

ADDEEEFT
defeated
defedate

ADDEEELN
enleaded
leadened

ADDEEENR
deadener
endeared

ADDEEFIL
defailed
defilade

ADDEEGNR
dangered
deranged
gandered
gardened
grenaded

ADDEEGRR
degrader
regarded
regraded

ADDEEHRT
dearthed
threaded

ADDEEILR
deadlier
derailed

ADDEEILT
delaited
detailed

ADDEEIMN
demained
endiadem
maidened

ADDEEIPR
depaired
diapered

ADDEEKNR
darkened
endarked

ADDEELNR
enlarded
relanded

ADDEEMNR
damneder
demander
mandered
redemand
remanded

ADDEENPR
pandered
repanded

ADDEENRR
darneder»
errander
randered
redarned
reed rand

ADDEENRW
dawnered
redawned
wandered
wardened

ADDEEPRT
departed
petarded
predated

ADDEEPRV
depraved
pervaded

ADDEERRT
redarted
retarded
retraded

ADDEERRW
rewarded
wardered

ADDEESTT
destated
detasted

ADDEGINR
dreading
readding

ADDEHNSU
undashed
unshaded

ADDEILNS
islanded
landside

ADDEIMRS
disarmed
misdread

ADDEINOS
adenoids
adonised
anodised

ADDEINOZ
adonized
anodized

ADDEIORS
roadside
side road

ADDEIPRS
dispread
draipsed

ADDELNOU
duodenal
unloaded

ADDELNRU
laundred
rundaled

ADDELRSW
dawdlers
swaddler
waddlers

ADDENRST
darndest
standerd
standred
stranded

ADDENRTU
draunted
untraded

ADDGILNS
addlings
saddling

ADDGILNW
dawdling
waddling

ADEEELRS
released
resealed

ADEEELRV
laveered
revealed

ADEEENRS
enseared
serenade

ADEEEPRS
rapeseed
repeased

ADEEFHRT
earth-fed
fathered
freathed
re-father

ADEEFLRT
deflater
faltered
flatered
reflated

ADEEFMNR
enframed
freedman

ADEEFNST
fastened
saftened

ADEEFNTT
enfatted
fattened

ADEEFRRY
defrayer
federary

ADEEGIMN
adeeming
ameeding

ADEEGINR
areeding
regained

ADEEGLNR
engraled
enlardge
enlarged
largened

ADEEGMNR
gendarme
mangered

ADEEGMNY
Ganymede
megadyne

ADEEGNNR
endanger
enranged

ADEEGNRR
gardener
garnered

ADEEGNRS
deranges
grandees
grenades
sangered
sangrede

ADEEGNRU
dungaree
underage
under age
ungeared

ADEEGRRT
garreted
gartered
regrated

ADEEGRSS
degasser
dressage

ADEEGRST
agrested
restaged

ADEEHKNR
hankered
harkened

ADEEHLRT
haltered
lathered
threadle

ADEEHLSS
delashes
headless

ADEEHNRT
adherent
neatherd
threaden

ADEEHPRS
ephedras»
reshaped
spheared

ADEEHRRS
adherers
redshare
reshared

ADEEHRRT
dearther
threader

ADEEHRSW
rewashed
washered

ADEEHRTT
hattered
theatred
threated

ADEEILLN
Danielle
leadline

ADEEILMN
endemial
Madeline

ADEEILMR
remailed
remedial

ADEEILNR
enrailed
renailed

ADEEILNT
dateline
date line
entailed
lineated

ADEEILPT
depilate
pileated

ADEEILRR
derailer
rerailed

ADEEILRS
realised
resailed»
sidereal

ADEEILRT
delirate
detailer
elaterid
retailed

ADEEILSS
deiseals
idealess

ADEEILSV
disleave
sea devil

ADEEIMNS
demaines
inseamed

ADEEIMRT
diameter
diametre
mediater
remediat

ADEEINPR
enpaired
pindaree

ADEEINPT
diapente
neaptide

ADEEINRS
arsedine
arsenide
denaries
nearside

ADEEINRT
detainer
retained

ADEEINST
andesite
Stenidae

ADEEIPRR
rapiered
repaired

ADEEIRST
asteired»
readiest
seriated
steadier

ADEEIRTV
evirated
derivate
taviered

ADEEISTV
deviates
sedative

ADEELLMT
malleted
medallet
metalled

ADEELLPR
pedaller
predella

ADEELLPT
palleted
petalled

ADEELLSS
allseeds
leadless

ADEELMNT
lamented
maltened

ADEELMPR
lampered
palmered

ADEELNRT
alterned
antlered
lantered

ADEELNSU
unleased
unsealed

ADEELPRS
pedalers
pleaders
relapsed

ADEELPRT
paltered»
prelated
replated

ADEELPRY
parleyed
replayed

ADEELRST
desalter
resalted
strealed
treadles

ADEELRSY
delayers
reslayed

ADEELSST
dateless
tasseled

ADEEMNNR
mannered
remanned

ADEEMNOR
demeanor
enamored

ADEEMPRT
emparted
tampered

ADEEMPST
empasted
stampede
stepdame

ADEEMRST
mastered
remasted
streamed

ADEEMRSU
Mausered
measured

ADEENOTT
denotate
detonate

ADEENPRX
expander
re-expand

ADEENPTT
patented
pattened

ADEENRRT
erranted
rantered

ADEENRRW
rewarned
wanderer
warrened

ADEENRST
santered
snatered

ADEENRSU
undersea
unerased
unseared

ADEENRTT
attender
nattered
rattened
reattend
tantered
ternated

ADEENRTU
auntered
denature
underate
undereat

ADEENRTV
nervated
taverned
Verdante

ADEENSST
assented
sensated
standees

ADEENSSU
danseuse
Sudanese

ADEENSTU
unseated
unteased

ADEEPPRR
dapperer
prepared

ADEEPRRS
respread
spreader

ADEEPRRT
departer
reparted

ADEEPRRV
depraver
pervader

ADEEPRSS
aspersed
preassed
repassed

ADEEPRST
padtrees
pederast
predates
repasted
trapesed

ADEEPRTU
depurate
epurated

ADEERRRW
redrawer
rereward
rewarder

ADEERRST
arrested
restared
retrades
retreads
serrated
treaders

ADEERSST
asserted
essarted
estrades
sadtrees

ADEERSSV
adverses
asserved

ADEERSTT
asterted
restated
retasted
streated

ADEERSTY
estrayed
restayed

ADEFILSY
dayflies
ladyfies

ADEGHILT
alighted
gilthead

ADEGHINR
adhering
headring

ADEGHINS
headings
sheading

ADEGHLNO
headlong
longhead

ADEGHRTU
daughter
raughted

ADEGIINN
enaiding
indigena

ADEGILLR
gladlier
grillade

ADEGILNP
pedaling
pleading

ADEGILNR
dearling
dragline
ingraled
inlarged
Reginald
relading

ADEGILNS
dealings
leadings
salinged
signaled
sleading

ADEGILRS
draigles
Griselda
slairged

ADEGIMNN
amending
demaning
denaming

ADEGIMNR
dearming
dreaming
margined
midrange
rademing

ADEGINNR
dearning
dreaning

ADEGINNV
advening
envading

ADEGINOR
ingoared
organdie

ADEGINOS
agonised
diagnose

ADEGINRR
drearing
gardiner

ADEGINRT
derating
gradient
ingrated
redating
treading

ADEGINST
gnaisted
sedating»

steading

ADEGLNNU
glandule
ungalled

ADEGLNRS
danglers
glanders

ADEGNNOR
androgen
dragonne

ADEGNRRU
grandeur
unregard

ADEGNRST
dragnets
grandest
stranged

ADEGORTW
Water Dog
water dog
water-dog
waterdog
water god

ADEHIMRS
misheard
semihard

ADEHINPS
deanship
headpins
pinheads

ADEHINSS
inshades
shadines
shandies

ADEHIPRS
parished
raphides

ADEHIRSW
dishware
rawhides

ADEHISST
dashiest»

shadiest

ADEHKNSU
skean dhu
unshaked

ADEHLNSS
handless
handsels

ADEHLNSU
unhalsed
unlashed
unshaled

ADEHLOPS
asphodel
pholades

ADEHMNOS
handsome
hansomed

ADEHMNOT
methadon
thanedom

ADEHNORV
handover
overhand

ADEHNPSU
unhasped
unshaped

ADEHNSSU
sunshade
unsashed
unshades

ADEHOORT
Dorothea
Theodora

ADEHOPST
head post
pot heads
top heads

ADEIILMS
idealism
miladies

ADEIILNT
intailed
liniated

ADEIINOT
ideation
iodinate
taenioid

ADEIINST
adenitis
dainties
naistied

ADEIIPRR
perradii
prairied

ADEIITTV
tidivate
vitiated

ADEILMNR
marlined
remindal

ADEILMPS
impleads
misplead
pelamids

ADEILMSS
maidless
misdeals
misleads

ADEILMST
medalist
misdealt

ADEILNPT
pantiled
plainted

ADEILNRS
islander
lardines

ADEILOPS
episodal
opalised
sepaloid

ADEILORS
darioles
solidare
soredial

ADEILORT
idolater
tailored

ADEILOSS
assoiled
deasoils
isoleads

ADEILOST
diastole
isolated
sodalite
solidate

ADEILOTV
dovetail
violated

ADEILPRS
lip reads
pedrails
predials
spiraled

ADEILPRT
dipteral
tripedal

ADEILRST
dilaters
lardiest
straidle

ADEILRVY
devil ray
variedly

ADEILSTY
diastyle
steadily

ADEILTTU
altitude
latitude

ADEIMNOT
dominate
nematoid

ADEIMNRS
adermins
Amerinds
sirnamed

ADEIMNST
mediants
tidesman

ADEIMPRT
imparted
preadmit

ADEIMRRS
admirers
disarmer
marrieds

ADEIMRSS
misreads
sidearms

ADEIMRST
maistred
mardiest
misrated
readmits

ADEINNOT
anointed
antinode

ADEINORR
inroader
ordainer
reordain

ADEINORT
arointed
deration
ordinate
rationed
Rodentia

ADEINOST
astonied
sedation

ADEINOTT
antidote
tetanoid

ADEINPRU
unpaired»
unrepaid

ADEINPST
depaints
pastined

ADEINQTU
antiqued
quainted

ADEINRRS
drainers
serranid

ADEINRSS
aridness
sardines

ADEINRST
detrains
randiest
rantised
strained
tainders
tan rides

ADEINRSU
denarius
unraised
uranides

ADEINRSV
invaders
sandiver

ADEINRTU
daturine
indurate
ruinated
urinated

ADEINSST
destains
sandiest

ADEINSSW
sea winds
windases

ADEINSTT
daintest
dantiest
instated
sattined

ADEINSTU
audients
sinuated

ADEIOPRS
diaspore
parodies

ADEIPRST
Dispater
rapidest
spirated
traipsed

ADEIPSTT
pistated
stipated

ADEIRSST
asterids
diasters
disaster
disrates

ADEIRSSU
radiuses
sudaries

ADEIRSTT
distater
straited
striated
tardiest
traisted

ADEIRTTT
attrited
titrated

ADEISSST
assisted
disseats

ADEISSTT
distaste
staidest

ADEITTTU
attitude
attuited

ADEJRSTU
adjuster
readjust

ADELLORS
odallers
sollared

ADELLOTT
allotted
totalled

ADELMNOS
lodesman
sandmole

ADELNOPR
Polander
ponderal

ADELNORS
ladrones
solander

ADELNORU
unloader
urodelan

ADELNORV
overland
rondavel

ADELNPRU
pendular
underlap
uplander

ADELNRSU
launders
laundres
lurdanes
rundales
slaunder

ADELNSTU
unlasted
unsalted
unslated

ADELNSTW
wandlest
wetlands

ADELOPRT
portaled
prolated

ADELORST
delators
leotards
lodestar

ADELPRST
plastred
spartled

ADELRSTW
warstled
wrastled

ADEMNOPR
name-drop
pomander

ADEMNORS
madrones
ransomed

ADEMNOTU
amounted
outnamed

ADEMNRRU
underarm
unmarred

ADEMNRSU
duramens
maunders
surnamed

ADENOPRS
operands
padrones
pandores
parsoned

ADENOPRT
patroned
pronated

ADENORST
stroaned
tornades

ADENQRSU
quaderns
quadrens
squander

ADENRRTU
turnerad
untarred

ADENRSSU
asunders
danseurs
Saunders

ADENRSTU
daunters
transude
untreads

ADENRSTY
dry-stane
rent days

ADENSTTU
unstated
untasted

ADENSTUY
unstayed
unsteady

ADEOPRRT
parroted
predator
prorated
teardrop

ADEOPRST
adopters
asported
pastored
readopts

ADEOPSTT
despotat
postdate

ADEORRVW
overdraw
overward

ADEORSST
assorted
torsades

ADEPRSTU
pastured
updaters
upstared

ADERRSSW
stewards
wardress

ADGIILNP
paidling
plaiding

ADGIILNR
drailing
ring-dial

ADGILORY
goliardy
gyroidal

ADGINRSW
drawings
swarding
wardings

ADHILLMN
handmill
millhand

ADIILNTY
daintily
Ladinity

ADIILNUV
diluvian
induvial

ADIIRSTT
distrait
triadist

ADILNORS
nailrods
Rosalind

ADILORTY
adroitly
dilatory
idolatry

ADIMMNOS
monadism
nomadism

ADIMNOST
donatism
saintdom

ADINNOOT
donation»
nodation

ADINNORS
andirons
ironsand

ADINNOTU
in-and-out
nudation

ADINOPST
pintados
satinpod

ADIOPRST
dioptras
parodist
parotids

ADKLOORW
woodlark
workload

ADMNORSW
sandworm
swordman

ADNOQRSU
quadrons
squadron

AEEEGLRT
eglatere
regelate
relegate

AEEEGNRT
generate
renegate
teenager

AEEEGRST
eagerest
etageres
steerage

AEEEHRST
reheates
shea tree

AEEELQSU
sequeale
sequelae

AEEENRTV
enervate»
venerate
veterane
veterean

AEEEPRRT
pear tree
repartee
repeater
re-repeat

AEEERSST
esterase
tesserae

AEEFILRS
filarees
serafile

AEEFILRT
featlier
frailtee

AEEFILST
fealties
fetiales
leafiest

AEEFLMSS
fameless
selfsame

AEEFMNOR
foremean
forename

AEEFNRST
fastener
fenestra
refasten
saftener

AEEGHRRT
gatherer
regather

AEEGILLS
galilees
legalise

AEEGILNS
ensilage
leasinge
lineages

AEEGILNT
Angelite
galenite
gelatine
legatine

AEEGIMRT
emigrate
remigate

AEEGINNT
antigene
gentiane

AEEGINRS
gesneria
renaiges

AEEGINSS
agenesis
assignee

AEEGINTV
gate-vein
negative

AEEGLNST
angelets
Gnetales

AEEGLRSS
eelgrass
gearless
largesse
rageless

AEEGMRST
gamester
gas meter

AEEGNRST
engreats
estrange
grantees
greanest
greatens
negaters
reagents
segreant
sergeant
sternage

AEEGPRRS
asperger»
presager

AEEGRSST
Argestes
restages

AEEHHNST
ensheath
heathens

AEEHHRST
heathers
sheather

AEEHIMNT
hematein
hematine

AEEHIPST
aphetise
hepatise

AEEHIPTZ
aphetize
hepatize

AEEHIRRT
earthier
heartier

AEEHISTT
athetise
hesitate

AEEHLORS
arsehole
earholes

AEEHLRST
halteres
hasteler
leathers
shaltree
tarheels

AEEHMNRS
sharemen
shearmen
sheerman

AEEHNPST
heptanes
phenates
stephane

AEEHNRST
earthens
enhearts
hastener
heartens

AEEHNRTT
haterent
threaten

AEEHNRTW
waterhen
wreathen

AEEHORSS
seahorse
seashore

AEEHPRSS
phearses
reshapes
seraphes
sphaeres
spheares

AEEHPRST
preheats
spreathe
threapes

AEEHRSTT
athester
earthset
theaters
theatres
threates

AEEIKNRT
ankerite
kreatine

AEEILLNT
entaille
tenaille

AEEILMRT
eremital
laimeter
materiel
realtime

AEEILMST
mealiest
metalise

AEEILNPS
alepines
penalise
sepaline

AEEILNPT
petaline
tapeline

AEEILNRT
elaterin
entailer
treenail

AEEILNST
elatines
ensilate
lineates

AEEILNTV
elvanite
ventaile

AEEILPRS
espalier
pearlies
pleasire
sleapier

AEEILRST
ateliers
earliest
leariest
realties
retailes

AEEILRSZ
realizes
sleazier

AEEILRTT
laterite
literate

AEEILRTV
levirate
relative

AEEILRVW
liveware
reviewal

AEEILSTV
elatives»
leaviest
vealiest

AEEIMNST
etamines
matinees
miseaten
seminate

AEEIMRST
emirates
masterie
reamiest
steamier
streamie

AEEIMSST
seamiest
steamies

AEEIMSTT
estimate
etatisme
meatiest
teatimes

AEEINRRT
raintree
retainer

AEEINRST
arsenite
resinate
sin eater
stearine
trainees

AEEINSTT
anisette
tetanies
tetanise

AEEIPRRS
pereiras
re-aspire
repraise

AEEIPRST
parietes
petaries

AEEIRSTT
ariettes
asterite»
iterates
teariest
treaties
treatise

AEEIRSTV
evirates
vesiater

AEEIRSTW
sweatier
taweries
wasterie
weariest

AEEKORST
keratose
kreasote
oak trees

AEEKORTV
overtake
takeover

AEEKRRST
retakers
streaker

AEELLSST
satelles
tessella

AEELMNOS
sea lemon
sea melon

AEELMNSS
lameness
maleness
maneless
nameless

AEELMPRS
empalers
emparles
empearls
resample

AEELMPTT
palmette
template

AEELMSST
mateless»
meatless
tameless
teamless

AEELNRTV
Levanter
relevant

AEELNSSV
enslaves
vaneless

AEELPRRS
pearlers
relapser

AEELPRST
prelates
resplate

AEELPRSU
pleasure
serpulae

AEELRRSV
ravelers
reserval
reversal
slaverer

AEELRSST
salteres
stealers
streales
tearless
tesseral

AEELRSTY
easterly
learyest

AEELSSST
sateless
seatless

AEEMNPRS
prenames
spearmen

AEEMRSST
masseter
masteres
seamster
sea terms»
steamers

AEEMRSSU
measures
reassume

AEENNRSS
ensnares
nearness
rennases

AEENOPRS
peraeons
personae

AEENORST
earstone
resonate

AEENORTV
overneat
renovate

AEENRRSW
answerer
reanswer

AEENRRTT
natterer
rattener

AEENRSST
assenter
earnests
easterns
sarsenet
steaners

AEENRSTT
entreats
ratteens
seat-rent

AEEOPRRT
paterero
perorate

AEEOPRST
operates
protease
soap tree

AEEPRRST
repaster»

repaters
taperers

AEEPRSSS
asperses
esparses
Passeres
preasses

AEEPRSTT
peartest
pretaste

AEEPRSTU
epurates
superate
upas tree

AEERRRST
arrester
rearrest

AEERRSST
asserter
reassert
serrates
terrases

AEERRSSU
erasures
reassure

AEERRSTU
austerer
sauterer
treasure

AEFFIMRR
affirmer
reaffirm

AEFFLSTU
feastful
sufflate

AEFGINST
featings
feasting

AEFGIRTU
figurate
fruitage

AEFHLNOT
halfnote
halftone

AEFIILST
fetialis
filiates

AEFILMNR
inflamer
rifleman

AEFILMNS
flamines
inflames

AEFILRTU
faultier
filature

AEFILSTW
flatwise
flawiest

AEFINRSS
fairness
sanserif

AEFLMORU
formulae
fumarole

AEFLORST
floaters
forestal
forsteal
refloats

AEFMORST
foremast
formates
mortsafe

AEFOPRRT
forepart
raft rope

AEFORSTW
forwaste
software

AEGGILNR
ganglier
lagering»

regaling

AEGGILNT
gelating
gleating
legating
teagling

AEGGINNR
angering
enraging
greaning
renaging

AEGGINNT
agenting
negating

AEGGINRS
gearings
greasing
snaggier

AEGGIOPR
arpeggio
geropiga

AEGHILNR
narghile
nargileh
rehaling

AEGHILNS
healings
leashing
shealing

AEGHILNT
alighten
atheling
leathing

AEGHILRT
litharge
thirlage

AEGHINRS
hearings
hearsing
shearing

AEGHINRT
earthing
hearting»

ingather

AEGHINSV
heavings
sheaving

AEGHNOPT
heptagon
pathogen

AEGHNORV
hangover
overhang

AEGHORST
hostager
shortage

AEGIIMNR
imaginer
migraine

AEGIINNR
arginine
enairing

AEGIKLNS
linkages
snaglike

AEGIKNNR
nakering
rakening

AEGIKNRW
rewaking
wreaking

AEGILLRV
all-giver
villager

AEGILLST
legalist
stillage
tillages

AEGILMMR
aglimmer
lammiger

AEGILMNP
elamping
empaling

AEGILMNR
germinal
maligner
malinger

AEGILMNS
Galenism
mealings
measling

AEGILMNT
ligament
metaling
tegminal

AEGILMRS
gremials
lamigers
regalism

AEGILNNT
gantline
latening

AEGILNNY
enlaying
yeanling

AEGILNOR
geraniol
regional

AEGILNOT
gelation
legation

AEGILNPR
grapline
pearling

AEGILNPS
apelings
elapsing
leapings
pealings
pleasing
spealing

AEGILNQU
equaling
quealing

AEGILNRS
aligners»

arseling
engrails
ingrales
inlarges
learings
nargiles
realigns
sanglier
seal ring
signaler
slangier

AEGILNRT
alerting
altering
integral
rateling
relating
retaling
tanglier
triangle

AEGILNRV
lavering
raveling
revaling

AEGILNRY
layering
relaying
yearling

AEGILNSS
alessing
alesings
gainless
glassine
leasings
salinges
sealings

AEGILNST
Angelist
eastling
Galenist
gelatins
genitals
langites
leasting
lingeats
sleating
stealing
tealings
teasling»

Telingas

AEGILNSV
leavings
sleaving
Svengali
vealings

AEGILNSW
swaleing
swealing
wealings

AEGILOPS
aegilops
spoilage
spoliage

AEGILORS
gasolier
girasole
seraglio

AEGILOST
galiotes
latigoes
otalgies

AEGILRSS
glasiers
glassier

AEGILRST
glariest
regalist

AEGIMNNR
enarming
remaning
renaming

AEGIMNNS
meanings
samening

AEGIMNRR
rearming
remargin

AEGIMNRS
germains
margines
mearings
reamings»
smearing

AEGIMNRT
emigrant
mantiger

AEGIMNST
mangiest
meatings
mintages
misagent
steaming
teamings

AEGIMRST
Gemarist
magister
migrates
ragtimes
sterigma

AEGINNPS
sneaping
speaning

AEGINNRS
aginners
earnings
engrains
enrasing
grannies
snearing

AEGINNRY
renaying
yearning

AEGINNST
antigens
antsigne
gentians
neasting
steaning

AEGINNSU
guanines
sanguine

AEGINORS
organise
origanes

AEGINPRS
pearsing»
preasing
reapings
spearing
spinagre

AEGINPRT
retaping
tapering

AEGINRRV
averring
ingraver

AEGINRSS
assinger
erasings
reassign
searings
seringas

AEGINRST
angriest
angrites
aresting
astringe
erigants
gairtens
ganister
gantries
granites
grantise
Gretians
ingestar
ingrates
ingreats
rangiest
reasting
renigats
sergiant
stearing
straigne
strainge
Tangiers
tearings

AEGINRSV
aversing
ingraves
resaving
vinegars

AEGINRSW
resawing
sewaring»
swearing
wearings

AEGINRSY
resaying
synergia

AEGINRTT
aretting
attering
gnattier
treating

AEGINRTV
averting
grievant
tavering
vintager

AEGINRTW
twangier
watering

AEGINSST
eastings
giantess
gnaistes
seatings
teasings
tsiganes

AEGINSTT
estating
tangiest
teasting

AEGINSTU
sauteing
unitages

AEGIRRTY
argyrite
geriatry

AEGLLOST
galleots
log slate
tollages

AEGLNPRS
grapnels
spangler
sprangle

AEGLNRST
strangle
tanglers
trangles

AEGLOPRY
glory pea
playgoer

AEGLRSTU
gaulters
gestural
tragules

AEGMNRTU
argentum
argument

AEGNORST
estragon
negators
ragstone
stonerag

AEGNRRST
Gartners
granters
regrants
stranger

AEGORRTT
garotter
garrotte

AEHILORT
aerolith
loathier

AEHILPRS
earlship
harelips
plashier

AEHILRSV
lavisher
shrieval

AEHILRTY
aerthily
heartily

AEHILSST
heliasts
shaliest

AEHIMPRS
samphire
seraphim

AEHIMPSS
emphasis
misshape

AEHIMSST
atheisms
mathesis

AEHINNTX
xanthein
xanthine

AEHINPRS
heparins
pharisen
parishen
seraphin

AEHINRSV
enravish
ravenish
vanisher

AEHINSST
anthesis
shanties
sheitans
sthenias

AEHIPPRS
papisher
sapphire

AEHIPPST
epitaphs
happiest
peatship

AEHIPRSS
parishes
sharpies

AEHLNSSU
unlashes
unshales

AEHLORST
hostelar
loathers
ratholes

AEHLPRSS
harpless
plashers
splasher

AEHMNORS
horseman
menorahs
rhamnose
shoreman

AEHNOPST
phaetons
phonates
stanhope
Stephano

AEHNORSS
hoarness
hoarsens
senhoras

AEHOPSST
potashes
spathose
tap shoes
teashops

AEHORSST
asthores
earshots
hoarsest

AEHORSTX
oxhearts
thoraxes

AEHPRSST
shapster
sharpest
sharp-set
sparthes
spathers

AEIILLMR
milliare
ramillie

AEIILMNS
alienism
Milesian

AEIILNST
alienist
intailes
Latinise»
liniates
litanies

AEIILPRT
liparite
Reptilia

AEIIMRST
airtimes
maistrie
maitrise

AEIINRST
inertias
rainiest

AEIINSST
isatines
naisties
sanities
sanitise
teniasis

AEIIRSST
irisates
satirise

AEIKLRST
larkiest
stalkier
starlike

AEIKMNST
mankiest
mistaken

AEILLNSS
ainsells
sensilla

AEILLPST
palliest
pastille

AEILLQSU
quailles
squillae

AEILLRST
literals
restiall

AEILMNNS
linesman»
melanins

AEILMNOS
laminose
mineolas
semolina

AEILMNPW
palm wine
wine palm

AEILMNRS
marlines
minerals
mislearn

AEILMNRT
terminal
tramline

AEILMNSS
islesman
mainless
maslines
mislanes
seminals

AEILMNST
ailments
aliments
manliest
melanist
salt mine
smaltine

AEILMORT
amitrole
rolamite

AEILMPST
implates
palmiest
palmiets
petalism
septimal
tapsimel

AEILMRST
lamister
lamiters
latimers
marliest
marlites
misalter

AEILMSTT
maltiest
metalist
smaltite

AEILMSTY
laytimes
steamily
taleysim

AEILMTTU
mutilate
ultimate

AEILNOPT
antilope
antipole
opentail

AEILNORS
ailerons
alerions
alienors
Rosaline
sonerila

AEILNORT
oriental
relation

AEILNOST
elations
insolate
toenails

AEILNPRT
interlap
triplane

AEILNPSS
painless
spaniels

AEILNPST
panelist
pantiles
plainest
platines

AEILNRSS
arselins
rainless
saliners

AEILNRTT
rattline
trail net

AEILNRTU
auntlier
Lutrinae
retinula
tenurial

AEILNSST
eastlins
elastins
nailsets
salients
saltines
slaintes
staniels

AEILNSTU
alunites
insulate

AEILNTVY
natively
venality

AEILOPRS
pelorias
polarise
rape oils

AEILOPRT
epilator
petiolar
tailrope

AEILORSV
oversail
valorise
varioles

AEILPRRS
reprisal
sparlire

AEILPRST
paistler
paltries
pilaster
plaister
plaiters
replaits
resplait

AEILQRSU
quailers
squailer

AEILQRTU
quartile
requital

AEILRSST
astilers
realists
restials
saltiers
saltires
slaister
slaiters
traisles
traissel
traissle

AEILSSTT
saltiest
slatiest

AEIMMRST
marmites
rammiest

AEIMNOPT
maine top
ptomaine

AEIMNORS
moraines
romaines
Romanies
Romanise

AEIMNOST
amniotes
misatone

AEIMNRSU
aneurism
Sumerian

AEIMNSST
mantises
matiness
Samnites

AEIMORRS
armoires
armories

AEIMORST
amortise
atomiser

AEIMORTZ
amortize
atomizer

AEIMOSST
amitoses
atomises
osmiates
Samiotes

AEIMPRRT
imparter
reimpart

AEIMPRSS
impresas
misparse
sampiers
sampires

AEIMPRST
pastimer
primates

AEIMRSST
asterism
maisters
maistres
mastries
misrates
semitars
smarties

AEIMRSTT
mistreat
teratism

AEIMSSTT
misstate
mistaste
mistates

AEINNORT
anointer
inornate
reanoint

AEINNOST
enations
Estonian»
Etonians
Noetians
sonatine

AEINNOTV
innovate
venation

AEINNSST
ensaints
insanest
sinnates

AEINORSS
erasions
sensoria

AEINORST
arsonite
asterion
notaries
notarise
rosinate
senorita

AEINOSST
assiento
astonies
Ossetian

AEINPPRS
parsenip
parsneip
snappier

AEINPRSS
Persians
prasines
Pressina

AEINPRST
painters
pantries
pertains
pinaster
pine tars
pristane
repaints
spinaret
star pine

AEINPSST
pansiest
ptisanes»
sapients
snapiest

AEINPSTU
petunias
supinate

AEINQRTU
antiquer
quainter

AEINQSTU
antiques
quantise
quinates

AEINRRST
instarre
restrain
retrains
strainer
terrains
trainers
transier
transire

AEINRSST
artiness
asterins
eranists
estrains
rantises
resiants
restains
retsinas
sarients
seriants
snariest
stainers
starnies
stearins
straines

AEINRSSU
anuresis
senarius

AEINRSTT
intraste
intrates
intreats
nitrates
rantiest
straiten»
tainters
tanister
tartines
tertians

AEINSSST
saintess
sestinas

AEINSSTT
antsiest
instates
nastiest
satinets
staniest
Titaness

AEINSTTT
nattiest
sattinet

AEIOPRRT
Pretoria
priorate

AEIORSTU
outraise
sautoire

AEIORSTV
travoise
viatores
votaries

AEIPRSST
pastries
piasters
piastres
raspiest
Tarsipes
tapisser
traipses
trepasis

AEIRRRST
starrier
tarriers

AEIRRSTT
retraits
startier
straiter
tarriest

AEIRSSTT
artistes
rastiest
striates
traistes

AEIRSSTW
waisters
waitress
wastries

AEIRSTTT
rattiest
tartiest
titrates
tristate

AEISSTTV
statives
vastiest

AEKMORTW
teamwork
workmate

AELLNSST
enstalls
tallness

AELLORST
reallots
rostella

AELLORSV
allovers
overalls

AELLORSW
allowers
sallower

AELLORWW
rewallow
wallower

AELLSSST
saltless
tassells

AELMMRST
strammel
trammels

AELMNOPS
neoplasm
pleonasm

AELMNRSU
mensural
numerals

AELMOPRT
prometal
temporal

AELMOPTT
palmetto
pot metal

AELMPRST
stemplar
templars
tramples

AELMPRSY
lampreys
samplery

AELMRSST
lamsters
stramels
tramless

AELMRSTT
maltster
martlets

AELNOPST
lapstone
pleonast
polentas

AELNORSU
aleurons
neurosal

AELNORTT
tetronal
tolerant

AELNORTY
ornately
Tyrolean

AELNPRSU
purslane
supernal

AELNRSTT
slattern
trentals

AELOPPRS
prolapse
propales
sapropel

AELOPRST
petrosal
ploaters
polestar
prolates

AELOPSSU
espousal
sepalous

AELOPSTU
outleaps
petalous

AELORRST
realtors
relators
restoral

AELORSTU
oestrual
rosulate

AELORSTV
levators
oversalt

AELPRSST
partless
pastlers
persalts
plasters
plastres
psalters
spalters
spartels
spartles
staplers

AELPRSSY
parsleys
sparsely
splayers

AELPRSTT
partlets
platters
prattels
prattles
splatter
sprattle

AELPRSTU
aplustre
paulters

AELPRSTY
peytrals
plastery
psaltery

AELRRSTT
rattlers
startler

AELRRSTW
trawlers
warstler
wrastler

AELRSSST
slasters
starless
trassels
tressals

AELRSSTW
wartless
warstels
warstles
wastrels
wrastles

AELRSTTU
lustrate
tutelars

AELRSTUV
vaulters
vestural

AEMNOSTU
notaeums
outnames
seamount

AEMNPSST
enstamps»
passment

AEMNRSTU
menstrua
transmue
transume

AEMNRSTW
strawmen
transmew
trewsman

AEMOPRTW
pomwater
tapeworm

AEMORSST
maestros
sea storm

AEMRSSTT
mattress
smartest
smatters

AENOPRSS
personas
Responsa

AENOPRST
operants
parsonet
patrones
pronates
proteans

AENORSST
assentor
senators
starnose
treasons

AENORSSU
anserous
arsenous

AENPRSTT
patterns
transept
trapnest
trap nets

AENRSSTT
snatters»
stentars
tartness

AENRSSTU
anestrus
saunters

AENSSTTU
nasutest
tautness
unstates

AEOOPRRT
operator
poor rate

AEOPRRST
praetors
prorates
raptores

AEOPRRSV
overpass
Passover

AEOPRSST
espartos
protases
seaports

AEOQRSTU
equators
quaestor

AEORRSST
assertor
assorter
oratress
reassort
roasters

AEORSSTT
stratose
stoaters
toasters

AEORSTTT
attestor
testator

AEORSTTU
outrates
outstare
rout seat»
sea trout
stare out

AEORSTUW
outsware
outswear
outwears

AEPPRRST
pre-parts
strapper
trappers

AEPRRSTU
pasturer
raptures

AEPRSSST
sparsest
trespass

AEQRSSTU
squarest
T squares

AEQRSTTU
quartets
squatter

AFGGILNN
fangling
flanging

AFGIINNR
fraining
infaring

AFGIINRS
fairings
fraising

AFGINRST
fartings
ingrafts
raftings
strafing

AFIINNOS
sainfoin
sinfonia

AFILMNOR
formalin
informal

AFILNORT
flatiron
inflator

AFILNSTU
flutinas
inflatus

AGGGILNR
gargling
raggling

AGGGINNS
gangings
naggings
snagging

AGGIILNS
glaising
silaging

AGGIILNT
ligating
taigling

AGGIILNV
gingival
glaiving

AGGIINNR
graining
inraging

AGGIINRS
agrising
graising

AGGILNNR
gnarling
rangling

AGGILNNS
anglings
glansing
langings
slanging

AGGILNNT
gnatling
tangling

AGGINNOR
groaning
organing

AGGINNST
gantings
gnasting
stanging

AGGINPRS
grapsing
grasping
sparging
spriggan

AGGINRSS
gas rings
grassing
sirgangs

AGGINRSU
arguings
sugaring

AGHIILNS
hailings
hailsing
shailing

AGHIINRS
hairings
shairing

AGHIKNRS
harkings
sharking

AGHILNRS
harlings
ringhals
sharling

AGHILNSS
ashlings
halsings
hassling
lashings
shalings
slangish
slashing

AGHILNSU
haulings
languish

AGHILNSW
hawlings
shawling»
whalings

AGHIMNRS
harmings
marshing

AGHIMNSS
mashings
shamings
smashing

AGHINNST
snathing
tanghins

AGHINPRS
harpings
phrasing
sharping
shraping

AGHINRTW
thrawing
wrathing

AGHINSSW
swashing
washings

AGHINSTW
swathing
thawings

AGIIINRV
Irvingia
Virginia

AGIILNNS
lainings
nailings
snailing

AGIILNOT
intaglio
ligation
taglioni

AGIILNPS
lapising
pailings
palising
plaising

AGIILNRT
ringtail
trailing

AGIILNRV
rivaling
virginal

AGIILNST
laitings
slaiting
stailing
tailings

AGIILNSW
swailing
wailings

AGIINNPR
praining
rapining

AGIINNPS
painings
spaining

AGIINNPT
painting
patining

AGIINNRS
ingrains
inrasing
rainings

AGIINNRT
atrining
training

AGIINNST
sainting
satining
staining
tainings

AGIINNSW
swaining
wainings

AGIINORS
signiora
signoria

AGIINPRS
aspiring
pairings
praising
raipings
spairing

AGIINRST
raitings
stairing

AGIINRTY
Tigrinya
Trigynia

AGIKLNST
stalking
talkings

AGIKNNST
stanking
tangkins
tankings

AGIKNOST
goatskin
stoaking

AGIKNPRS
parkings
sparking

AGIKNRST
kartings
starking
straking

AGILLNPS
pallings
spalling

AGILLNRU
alluring
lingular

AGILLNRY
nargilly
rallying

AGILLNST
langlits
stalling

AGILLNSY
sallying
signally
slangily

AGILLOST
galliots
salligot

AGILMMNS
lammings
malmings
slamming
smalming

AGILMNPS
palmings
sampling

AGILMNSU
Lusignam
maulings
slauming

AGILMNSW
mawlings
slawming

AGILNNPT
pantling
planting

AGILNNST
antlings
slanting
tanlings

AGILNNUY
ungainly
unlaying

AGILNOPS
galoping
sloaping

AGILNOSS
glossina
lassoing

AGILNOST
antilogs
solating

AGILNOTT
alotting
totaling

AGILNPPS
lappings
slapping

AGILNPRS
grapslin
grasplin
parlings
sparling
springal

AGILNPST
platings
spalting
spatling
splating
stapling
taplings

AGILNPSU
slauping
spauling

AGILNPSW
lapwings
slawping

AGILNPTT
pattling
platting

AGILNRST
rastling
ratlings
slarting
starling

AGILNRSW
warlings
warsling

AGILNSTT
sattling
slatting

AGILNSUV
avulsing
valuings

AGIMMNRS
rammings
smarming
wingspan

AGINNRST
rantings
starning
straning
transing

AGIMNNOS
masoning
moanings

AGIMNNRU
manuring
unarming

AGIMNNTU
unmating
untaming

AGIMNORS
maringas
Orangism
organism
roamings

AGIMNOSV
amovings
vamosing

AGIMNPST
stamping
tampings

AGIMNRST
martings
migrants
smarting

AGIMNRSW
swarming
warmings

AGIMNSSU
amusings
assuming

AGINNORT
ignorant
ornating

AGINNPPS
nappings
snapping

AGINNPSW
pawnings
spawning»

AGINNRTU
auntring
naturing

AGINNSTU
saunting
tanguins
unsating

AGINNTTU
attuning
nutating
taunting

AGINORRS
garrison
roarings

AGINORSS
assignor
signoras
soarings

AGINORST
organist
roasting

AGINORTT
rotating
troating

AGINORTY
gyration
organity

AGINOSTT
stoating
tangoist
toasting

AGINPRSS
parsings
pingrass
raspings
sparings
sparsing

AGINPRST
atspring
partings
pratings
sprating
trapings

AGINRRST
starring
tarrings

AGINRSTT
rattings
starting

AGINRSTW
ring taws
strawing
swarting
wrasting

AGINRSTY
stingray
straying

AGMMNOOR
monogram
nomogram

AGORRSST
grossart
rotgrass

AHIMOPRS
aphorism
morphias

AHIPRSST
harpists
tsarship

AHOOPTYZ
zoopathy
Zoophyta

AIILLPRS
sliprail
spirilla

AIILMNOT
limation
miltonia

AIILMRST
mistrial
trialism

AIILMRTY
limitary
military

AIILNPST
alpinist
pintails
tailspin

AIIMNSST
animists
saintism
samnitis

AIIMNSTT
imitants
Titanism

AIIMORTT
imitator
timariot

AIINSTTV
nativist
visitant

AILLORTT
littoral
tortilla

AILMNOPY
Olympian
palimony
Polymnia

AILMOORT
motorail
motorial

AILMORTY
molarity
morality

AILMPSST
palmists
psalmist

AILMRSTU
altruism
ultraism

AILNNOTU
lunation
Ultonian

AILNSSTU
stunsail
unalists

AILOORST
isolator
ostiolar

AILOPRST
strap oil
top rails

AILORSTY
royalist
solitary

AILRSTTU
altruist
titulars
ultraist

AIMNNOTY
antimony
antinomy

AIMNORST
Maronist
Romanist

AIMNRSTT
Tantrism
transmit

AIMOSSTT
atomists
somatist

AINPRSTU
Puritans
Rasputin

AIOPRSST
airstops
prosaist
protasis

AIOPRSTT
patriots
Protista

ALNOOPRT
portolan
pronotal

ALNOPPTT
plant pot
pot plant

ALOPRSTU
postural
pulsator

BBCEILRS
cribbles
scribble

BBEEILPR
pebblier
plebbier

BBEILRST
stibbler
tribbles

BBEIRSTU
stubbier
subtribe

BBGILNRU
burbling
rubbling

BBGINSTU
stubbing
tubbings

BCDEEEHR
breeched
red beech

BCDEEMRU
cumbered
recumbed

BCDEIKRR
brick-red
redbrick

BCEEMRRU
cerebrum
cumberer

BDEEILMO
bemoiled»

emboiled

BDEEILMR
limbered
relimbed

BDEEIRST
bedrites
bestride
bistered

BDEELLOW
bellowed
bowelled

BDEELORT
boltered
rebolted

BDEENRRU
burdener
reburden
reburned

BDEEORST
besorted
bestrode

BDEERTTU
buttered
rebutted

BDEGIINT
betiding
debiting

BDEILRST
bristled
driblets

BDEINOSU
bedouins
unbodies

BDEIORRS
broiders
broidres
disrober

BDELLOOR
bordello
doorbell

BDELRSTU
brustled
burstled

BDENNRUU
unburden
unburned

BDENORSU
bounders
rebounds
suborned

BDGINNOU
bounding
unboding

BEEGINRS
bigeners
breesing

BEEGINST
bee sting
beetings
ting bees

BEEHNORS
bohreens
nose-herb

BEEIJSTU
bejesuit
Jebusite

BEEILNST
stilbene
tensible

BEEINOST
betonies
ebonites

BEEKNOST
betokens
steenbok

BEELLORW
bellower
rebellow

BEELNOSS
boneless
noblesse

BEEMNRRU
numberer
renumber

BEEOORTT
beetroot
boottree

BEERSSUV
subserve
subverse

BEGHINRT
berthing
brighten

BEGILNOW
belowing
boweling
elbowing

BEGILNSS
blessing
glibness

BEGINNOR
enrobing
ringbone

BEHLOOPY
hypobole
lyophobe

BEILQSTU
quiblets
squiblet

BEILRSTU
burliest
subtiler

BEIMRSTU
imbrutes
resubmit
terbiums

BEINOOST
bonitoes
eobionts

BEINORST
bornites
ribstone

BEINRSTU
Burnsite
tribunes
turbines

BELMRSTU
stumbler
tumblers
tumbrels

BELORSTU
boulters
stroubel
strouble
troubels
troubles

BEMORTUW
tube worm
worm tube

BENORSTW
bestrown
brownest

BGGILNNU
blunging
bungling

BGIILNRS
birlings
birsling
brisling

BGILMMNU
bummling
mumbling

BGILNOTT
blotting
bottling

BGILNSTU
bustling
subtling

BGINNORU
bourning
unrobing

BGINOOST
boosting
bootings

BGINRSTU
brusting
bursting
brutings
burtings
sturbing

BKKOOORW
bookwork
workbook

CCEHINOR
corniche
enchoric

CCEINORS
conciser
cornices
croceins

CCEINORT
concerti
necrotic

CCEINOTT
concetti
tectonic

CDDEEIRS
deciders
descried

CDDEEIRT
credited
directed

CDDGILNO
clodding
coddling

CDEEEIRV
deceiver
received

CDEEEJRT
dejecter
rejected

CDEEENRS
censered
deceners
decernes
recensed
screened»

secerned

CDEEENRT
centered
recented

CDEEEPTX
excepted
expected

CDEEERRS
decreers
receders
screeder

CDEEERSS
recessed
seceders

CDEEERST
decreets
decretes
resected
secreted

CDEEFORS
deforces
frescoed

CDEEGINR
creeding
receding

CDEEHINR
enriched
inherced
nichered
richened

CDEEHIPR
ciphered
decipher

CDEEHORT
hectored
rocheted
tochered

CDEEIKLN
lickened
nickeled

CDEEIKLR
deer lick»

re-licked

CDEEILNR
decliner
reclined

CDEEILNS
declines
licensed
silenced

CDEEILNT
cliented
denticle

CDEEINPT
incepted
peincted
penticed

CDEEIPRS
precised
respiced

CDEEIPRT
decrepit
depicter
pre-cited

CDEEIPRU
epicured
pedicure

CDEEIRRS
decriers
descrier

CDEEIRST
decreits
desertic
discreet
discrete

CDEEIRSV
screived
scrieved
serviced

CDEEKLOR
lockered
relocked

CDEEKRTU
Duck Tree»

tree duck
tuckered

CDEELOOR
coolered
recooled

CDEELRSU
recludes
reclused

CDEELRTU
lectured
relucted

CDEENNOU
denounce
enounced

CDEENORS
censored
encoders
necrosed
seconder
seed corn

CDEEORST
corseted
escorted
recosted
sectored

CDEEORTV
coverted
vectored

CDEEOSST
cestodes
cosseted

CDEEPRST
sceptred
spectred

CDEERRSU
recursed
reducers

CDEGINNO
encoding
endocing

CDEGINOS
cognised»

cosigned

CDEGINRS
screding
scringed

CDEGINSU
educings
seducing

CDEGORSU
scourged
scroudge
scrouged

CDEHIMRS
chrismed
smirched

CDEIMOST
Docetism
domestic

CDEINORS
consider
decinors

CDEINORT
centroid
citroned
doctrine

CDEIORRT
creditor
director

CDEIORST
cordites
decorist

CDEIORSV
discover
divorces

CDEIOSTT
cottised
Docetist

CDEIPRST
predicts
scripted

CDEIRSTU
curdiest»

curtsied

CDEKNORU
uncorked
unrocked

CDELOORU
coloured
decolour

CDELORSS
cordless
scolders

CDELRSSU
curdless
scudlers

CDEMNOOW
comedown
downcome

CDEMOSTU
costumed
customed

CDENORST
constred
net cords
scontred

CDENORTU
cornuted
trounced

CDEOPRRU
procured
producer

CDEORSTU
decourts
eductors
seductor

CDGILNOS
codlings
scolding

CDHIIORT
hidrotic
trichoid

CDIIMNOU
conidium»

oncidium

CDIIORSU
Dioscuri
sciuroid

CDIIPTUY
cupidity
pudicity

CDKOOORW
corkwood
rock wood

CEEEHIRR
cheerier
reechier

CEEEILTV
cleveite
elective

CEEEIMRR
mercerie
reermice
remercie
reremice

CEEELRTT
electret
tercelet

CEEENRRT
recenter
recentre

CEEEPRTX
excepter
expecter
reexpect

CEEERRST
erecters
re-erects
secreter

CEEERSST
secretes
sesterce

CEEFHIST
chiefest
fetiches

CEEFINRT
frenetic
infecter
reinfect

CEEFNORR
confrere
renforce

CEEFORST
cost-free
free cost
scot-free

CEEGHINR
cheering
reeching

CEEGINRS
ceringes
creesing
generics

CEEGINRT
erecting
gentrice

CEEGNORT
congreet
co-regent

CEEGNORV
Congreve
converge

CEEHILLN
chenille
Hellenic

CEEHIMRS
Cheremis
chimeres

CEEHINRS
enriches
inherces

CEEHIRST
chestier
heretics

CEEHNRRT
retrench
trencher

CEEHORRT
hectorer
rocheter
torchere

CEEILLNT
clientel
lenticel
lenticle

CEEILNOT
coteline
election

CEEILNRS
licenser
reclines
silencer

CEEILRST
reticles
sclerite
tiercels
triscele

CEEILSTT
telestic
testicle

CEEIMNST
centimes
tenesmic

CEEINNSS
incenses
niceness

CEEINORT
erection
neoteric

CEEINOST
ice stone
seicento

CEEINPRS
crepines
crespine
percines

CEEINPRT
prentice
terpenic

CEEINPST
pectines
pentices

CEEINRST
enticers
rescient
scienter
secretin

CEEINRSU
insecure
sinecure

CEEINRTU
ceinture
enuretic

CEEIORST
coteries
esoteric

CEEIPRST
crepiest
receipts

CEEIRSTU
cerusite
cutesier
eucrites

CEEKLRSS
clerkess
reckless

CEEKORRT
cork tree
rocketer

CEELORSS
coreless
recloses
sclerose

CEELORST
corselet
corslete
costrele
electors
electros
selector

CEELRSSU
cureless»
recluses

CEENORSV
conserve
converse

CEENORVY
conveyer
reconvey

CEENRSST
centress
rescents
scenters

CEEORRST
erectors
secretor

CEEORRSU
recourse
resource

CEEORSTX
coexerts
cortexes

CEFFIORU
coiffeur
coiffure

CEFFLSSU
cuffless
scuffles

CEFIIRRT
ferritic
terrific

CEFIKLOR
firelock
flockier

CEFILMRU
crimeful
merciful

CEFINORS
coinfers
conifers
forensic
forinsec
fornices

CEFINORT
ice front
infector

CEGGILOR
cloggier
cogglier

CEGHINOR
cohering
ochering
ochreing

CEGHINPR
perching
preching

CEGHINST
chesting
etchings
steching

CEGIINPR
piercing
reciping

CEGIINRT
reciting
tiercing

CEGIKNPS
peckings
specking

CEGINORS
cogniser
coreigns
co-resign
cosigner
scoreing

CEGINRSS
cressing
scringes

CEGINRSU
cerusing
recusing
rescuing
securing

CEGINRTU
cutering
eructing

CEGORRSU
scourger
scrouger

CEHIISTT
ethicist
theistic

CEHIKSTT
thickest
thickets
thickset

CEHILNOP
phenolic
pinochle

CEHILORT
chlorite
clothier

CEHIMORT
chromite
trichome

CEHINPRU
punchier
uncipher

CEHINRST
christen
citherns
cithrens
snitcher

CEHINSST
chintses
snitches

CEHIOPRU
euphoric
pouchier

CEHIOPST
postiche
potiches

CEHIORST
orchites
rotchies
theorics

CEHIORTU
couthier»
touchier

CEHIPRST
pitchers
spitcher

CEHIRSTT
chitters
restitch
stitcher
titchers

CEHMORSU
mouchers
smoucher

CEHNNOSU
nonesuch
unchosen

CEIIKLMR
limerick
rice milk

CEIILMNT
limnetic
Milicent

CEIILNOS
isocline
silicone

CEIILOPP
epiploic
epipolic

CEIIMRST
meristic
trisemic

CEIINNOS
coniines
oscinine

CEIINORS
recision
soricine

CEIINRSU
incisure
sciurine

CEIINSTY
cytisine»

syenitic

CEIKKLOR
corklike
rocklike

CEIKLRST
lickster
stickler
strickle
ticklers
trickles

CEIKLSST
slickest
stickles

CEIKNOPR
cork pine
rock pine

CEIKORST
corkiest
corkites
rockiest
Rockites
stockier

CEIKQSTU
quickest
quickset

CEILMOPR
compiler
complier

CEILNOOS
colonies
colonise
eclosion

CEILNORS
incloser
licensor

CEILNOST
lections
telsonic

CEILOPTU
epulotic
poultice

CEILORST
cloister
coistrel
cortiles
costlier

CEILOSST
solecist
solstice

CEILRSTU
curliest
utricles

CEIMMNOU
encomium
meconium

CEIMNORS
cremosin
crimsone
incomers
sermonic

CEIMOPRS
compiers
compires
comprise

CEINOOTZ
entozoic
enzootic

CEINOPRS
conspire
incorpse

CEINORSS
necrosis
sericons

CEINORST
cointers
corniest
corseint
rections

CEINOSSS
cessions
cosiness

CEINOSTT
centoist
stenotic»

tonetics

CEINRSTT
centrist
citterns
cittrens

CEINRTTU
intercut
tincture

CEIOPRSU
precious
rice soup

CEIORSTU
citreous
outcries

CEIORSTV
evictors
vortices

CEIORSTX
excitors
exorcist

CEIPRSTU
crepitus
cuprites
pictures
piecrust

CEIRRSTT
critters
restrict
stricter

CEIRRSTU
crustier
recruits

CEKLORSS
corkless
rockless

CELNOOSS
consoles
coolness

CELORSST
corslets
costrels
crosslet

CELORSTT
clotters
crottels
crottles

CELORSUU
ulcerous
urceolus

CEMORSTU
costumer
customer

CEMPRSTU
crumpets
spectrum

CENORSTU
construe
cornutes
counters
recounts
trounces

CENOSSTU
contuses
countess

CENRSSTU
curtness
encrusts

CEOPRSUU
coupures
cupreous

CEORRSSU
coursers
Cursores
scourers

CEORSSST
crossest
crossets

CFFGINSU
cuffings
scuffing

CGGGINOS
coggings
scogging

CGHIINNS
chinings
chinsing
sinching

CGHIKNOS
chokings
hockings
shocking

CGHINORT
torching
troching

CGHINOSU
chousing
hocusing

CGHINOTU
touching
ungothic

CGIIKLNS
lickings
sickling
slicking

CGIIKNNS
nickings
snicking

CGIIKNRS
rickings
scriking

CGIIKNST
sticking
tickings

CGIKLNOS
lockings
slocking

CGIKMNOS
mockings
smocking

CGIKNNOS
nockings
snocking

CGILLNSU
cullings
sculling

CGILMNSU
clumsing
muscling

CGILMNUU
cingulum
glucinum

CGILNOOR
clooring
coloring

CGILNOSW
cowlings
scowling

CGILNRSU
curlings
scurling

CGIMNNOO
gnomonic
oncoming

CGINNOPU
pouncing
uncoping

CGINNORS
cornings
scorning

CGINOOST
coosting
scooting

CGINORSS
corsings
crossing
scorings
scorsing

CGINORSU
coursing
crousing
scouring
sourcing

CGINOSTW
scowting
stowcing

CGINRSTU
crusting»

ructings

CGINSTTU
cuttings
scutting
tungstic

CHIIORST
historic
orchitis

CHILOTUY
couthily
touchily

CHINOPTY
hypnotic
pythonic
typhonic

CIILOPST
politics
psilotic

CIILORST
clitoris
coistril

CIILOSST
sciolist
solicits

CIIMNOST
mictions
monistic
nomistic

DDDEENRU
dundered
ruddened

DDEEEGNR
dengered
gendered

DDEEENRT
redented
retended
tendered

DDEEERST
deserted
detersed

DDEEFNRU
refunded
underfed

DDEEGINR
dreeding
dreigned
engirded
enridged
ingreded

DDEEGINS
dedeigns
dedignes
deedings
designed
sdeigned

DDEEGLNO
engolded
goldened

DDEEHINR
hindered
rehidden

DDEEIMMR
dimmered
immerded

DDEEINNT
indented
intended

DDEEINRT
dendrite
tindered

DDEEIORV
devoider
devoired

DDEEIPRS
deprised
presided

DDEELMOR
moldered
remolded

DDEELOPR
deplored
poldered

DDEEMRRU
demurred
murdered

DDEENNRU
dunnered
unrended

DDEENOPR
perdendo
pondered

DDEENORS
endorsed
sondered

DDEENORW
drowened
endowred
wondered

DDEENRTU
deturned
entruded
retunded
rudented
tundered

DDEEORTT
detorted
dottered

DDEEORTU
derouted
detoured

DDEERSTU
detrudes
detrused
redusted

DDEGILNU
deluding
indulged
ungilded

DDEGINST
stedding
teddings

DDEGINSW
swindged
weddings

DDEGNORU
grounded
underdog
undergod

DDEILNPS
splendid
spindled

DDEILNSW
dwindles
swindled

DDEILOPS
displode
lopsided

DDEILRST
striddle
tiddlers
triddles

DDEINOSW
disendow
disowned

DDEIRSTU
ruddiest
sturdied

DDELORST
stroddle
strodled
toddlers

DDGIILNN
dindling
niddling

DEEEFINR
fineered
needfire
neifered
redefine

DEEEFRRR
deferrer
referred

DEEEFRRT
ferreted
fertered
referted

DEEEGNRR
genderer
regender

DEEEGRST
deterges
gestered
regested

DEEEILRV
relevied
relieved
reveiled

DEEEINRS
nereides
redenies

DEEEIRRT
reitered
reteired
retiered

DEEELLPR
depeller
repelled

DEEELLRV
develler
revelled

DEEELNSS
lessened
needless
seldseen

DEEELPRT
peltered
repleted

DEEELPST
depletes
spleeted
steepled

DEEELRST
deerlets
streeled

DEEEMNSS
demesnes
seedsmen

DEEENNRT
entender
renneted

DEEENPRT
repented
repetend

DEEENRRR
renderer
re-render

DEEENRRT
rentered
retender
tenderer

DEEENRTT
retented
tentered

DEEENRTV
revented
ventered

DEEENRTX
extender
externed

DEEENSTV
envested
stevened

DEEEPRSS
desperse
speeders

DEEEPRST
depertes
depester
depeters
estreped
pestered

DEEERRST
deterres
deserter

DEEERRSV
deserver
reserved
reversed

DEEERRTV
reverted
verdeter

DEEERSTT
detester
retested
settered
streeted
testered

DEEERSTX
exserted
extersed

DEEFFNOR
offender
reoffend

DEEFIILN
fedelini
lenified

DEEFIIRS
deifiers
edifiers
fireside

DEEFILRT
fertiled
filtered
relifted

DEEFINRS
definers
frenised
frensied
nedfires

DEEFINST
festined
infested

DEEFIRTT
fittered
refitted

DEEFLNOR
enfolder
forelend

DEEFLORW
deflower
flowered»
reflowed

DEEFMORR
deformer
reformed

DEEFNOST
festoned
softened

DEEFOORT
footered
refooted

DEEFORST
deforest
fostered
forested

DEEGGINR
gingered
gredinge
greeding
niggered
renigged

DEEGGLOR
doggerel
loggered

DEEGHINS
dinghees
heedings
sheeding

DEEGILNN
ginneled
needling

DEEGILNO
eloigned
legioned

DEEGILNR
deerling
dereling
derlinge
dreeling
engirdle
ingreled
lingered
reedling

DEEGILNT
deleting
teedling

DEEGIMMR
gimmered
immerged

DEEGIMNR
dreeming
germined
remeding

DEEGINNS
ensigned
indegens
needings

DEEGINPS
deepings
depinges
speeding

DEEGINRS
designer
dreeings
energids
ingredes
redesign
reedings
resigned
re-signed

DEEGINSS
edginess
sdeignes
seedings

DEEGINST
ingested
signeted

DEEGIRST
digester
Erdgeist
estridge
redigest

DEEGLNOR
longered
relonged

DEEHILRS
hirseled»
relished
shielder

DEEHILSV
dishevel
she-devil

DEEHIMRT
hermited
Meredith
mithered

DEEHINRS
denshire
reshined

DEEHIPRS
hesperid
perished
shred pie

DEEHIRSV
shivered
shrieved

DEEHIRTW
red withe
withered

DEEHNORT
dethrone
threnode

DEEHORRS
redhorse
reshored

DEEHORSU
rehoused
rose-hued
shore due

DEEIJNOR
joinered
rejoined

DEEIKLLR
killdeer
rekilled

DEEILLMP
impelled
milleped

DEEILLRT
retilled
tillered
tredille

DEEILLRV
deviller
rivelled

DEEILMOS
melodies
melodise

DEEILMOZ
melodize
modelize

DEEILNOT
deletion
entoiled

DEEILNSS
idleness
linseeds

DEEILNST
dentiles
enlisted
enstiled
lintseed
listened
tensiled
tinseled

DEEILNTT
entitled
inletted
littened

DEEILOPS
despoile
solipede

DEEILOPT
lepidote
petioled

DEEILORT
dolerite
loitered

DEEILRSV
delivers
desilver»
silvered
slivered

DEEILRTT
littered
tiltered

DEEILSST
tideless
til seeds

DEEIMMRS
immersed
simmered

DEEIMNST
dementis
mistened
sediment
tidesmen

DEEIMPRS
demireps
emprised
epiderms
impeders
impresed
premised
simpered

DEEIMRST
demerits
demister
dimeters
mistered

DEEINNRT
indenter
intender
interned
reindent
retinned

DEEINNST
dentines
desinent
intensed
tennised

DEEINORS
indorsee
ordinees

DEEINPRS
enspired
spreined

DEEINPSS
dispense
piedness

DEEINRRT
interred
trendier

DEEINRST
disenter
enditers
indesert
inrested
inserted
resident
sentried
sintered
streined
trendies

DEEINRSV
inversed
venerids

DEEINRTU
retinued
reunited

DEEINSSW
dewiness
wideness

DEEINSTT
dinettes
insetted

DEEINSTV
evidents
invested
stevined

DEEIOPST
deposite
epidotes
poetised

DEEIORSW
doweries
weirdoes

DEEIPRRS
presider
reprised
respired

DEEIPRSS
despiser
disperse
Perseids
presides

DEEIPRST
esprited
pistered
priested
respited

DEEIPRSV
deprives
prevised

DEEIPSST
despites
sidestep

DEEIRRSS
derrises
desirers
dressier
residers

DEEIRRST
destrier
stirreed

DEEIRRTV
diverter
verditer

DEEIRSST
diesters
dress tie
editress
resisted
sistered

DEEIRSSU
diureses
reissued
residues

DEEIRSSV
devisers
disserve»
dissever
diverses

DEEJLORT
joltered
rejolted

DEELLNOR
enrolled
rondelle

DEELLORR
re-rolled
rollered

DEELLORW
rowelled
well-doer

DEELMORS
modelers
morseled
remodels

DEELMPRU
lumpered
replumed

DEELNOSU
ensouled
nouseled

DEELOPRS
deplores
leprosed

DEELORRS
resolder
solderer

DEELORTT
dotterel
toltered

DEELRSTU
lustered
resulted
sultered
tudelers
ulstered

DEELRSTW
lewdster
sweltred»
wrestled

DEEMNOSS
demoness
enmossed

DEEMOORT
odometer
remooted

DEEMRRRU
demurrer
murderer

DEEMRSTU
demurest
mustered

DEENNOST
sonneted
tendones

DEENNSSU
nudeness
unsensed

DEENNTTU
unnetted
untented

DEENOPRR
ponderer
reponder

DEENOPRS
personed
responde
rope's end

DEENORST
ensorted
enstored
erodents
red stone

DEENORSW
endowers
reendows
worsened

DEENOSTT
onsetted
ostented

DEENPRST
pretends
sprented

DEENRRSU
endurers
sunderer
underers

DEENRRTU
entruder
returned

DEENRSSU
end-users
rudeness

DEENRSTU
dentures
entrudes
sederunt
underset
undesert
unrested

DEENRSUV
unserved
unversed

DEENRTTU
enrutted
unretted

DEEOPRRT
portered
reported

DEEOPRST
prestoed
reedstop
reposted

DEEORRST
resorted
re-sorted
restored
rostered

DEEORRTU
rerouted
retoured
routered

DEEORSST
dosseret
oersteds
retossed

DEEORSTT
rosetted
sottered
stotered
tetrodes

DEEORSTY
oystered
storeyed

DEEPRSTU
deputers
pertused

DEERSSST
desserts
stressed

DEFGIINY
deifying
edifying

DEFHIINS
fiendish
finished

DEFILNRU
unrifled
urnfield

DEFINNRU
reinfund
unfriend

DEFINSTU
unfisted
unsifted

DEFLNORU
flounder
unfolder

DEFNRRUU
underfur
unfurred

DEGGIINN
deigning
inedging

DEGGILNS
geldings
ledgings
sledging
sniggled

DEGHILNS
heldings
hindlegs
shelding
shingled

DEGHILST
delights
slighted

DEGHOOSU
doghouse
house dog

DEGIILNT
deliting
diligent

DEGIIMNS
demising
Geminids
Medising

DEGIINNR
dreining
nidering

DEGIINNT
enditing
indigent
teinding

DEGIINRS
desiring
residing
ringside

DEGIINRV
deriving
rediving
virgined

DEGIINST
dietings
dingiest
editings
indigest
steiding

DEGILMNO
gold mine
modeling

DEGILNOS
doglines
glenoids
longside
sidelong

DEGILNSW
swingled
weldings

DEGILNTU
deluting
tudeling

DEGILOST
godliest
goldiest

DEGILRST
glistred
gristled

DEGIMNOS
mendigos
smidgeon

DEGINNPS
pendings
spending

DEGINNRS
rendings
sendring

DEGINNRU
enduring
rudening
undering
unringed

DEGINNST
dentings
stending
tendings

DEGINNSU
enduings
unsigned

DEGINOPS
deposing
disponge
pidgeons

DEGINPRS
spreding
sprindge
springed

DEGINPRU
depuring
perduing

DEGINRSY
synergid
syringed

DEGINSTU
dungiest
undigest

DEGIORST
digestor
stodgier

DEGNOOSS
dog's nose
goodness

DEHILOPS
depolish
polished

DEHINOPS
diphones
siphoned
sphenoid

DEHINORS
hordeins
inshored

DEHNORSU
enshroud
hounders
unhorsed
unshored

DEIILLMT
ill-timed
tidemill

DEIINORS
derision
ironised
ironside
resinoid

DEIINOST
editions
sedition

DEIINRST
disinter
inditers
nitrides

DEIINSST
insisted
tidiness

DEIINSTU
disunite
nudities
unitised
untidies

DEIIPRST
dirt pies
riptides
spirited
tiderips

DEIKLNST
skintled
sklinted

DEILLORS
dolliers
rosilled

DEILMNSS
mildness
mindless

DEILMOST
melodist
modelist
moldiest
old times

DEILNOOS
eidolons
solenoid

DEILNOSU
delusion
insouled
unsoiled

DEILNPRS
prindles
speldrin

DEILNRST
snirtled
tendrils
trindels
trindles

DEILNSSW
swindles
wildness
windless

DEILNSTU
diluents
insulted
unlisted

DEILOPSS
despoils
diploses
solipeds

DEILOPST
pistoled
postiled

DEILOSTU
solitude
toluides

DEILPSTT
spittled
splitted

DEIMNRTU
rudiment
unmitred

DEIMOOST
moodiest
sodomite

DEIMORSS
Messidor
misdoers

DEIMORSU
dimerous
erodiums
soredium

DEINOPRS
disponer
poinders
prisoned

DEINOPRT
dipteron
inported

DEINORSU
dourines
sourdine

DEINORSW
re-indows
windores
windrose

DEINRSSU
insureds
sundries

DEINRSTT
strident
tridents

DEIOPRST
diopters
dioptres
dipteros
peridots
proteids
riposted

DEIOPSST
deposits
possited
sidepost
topsides

DEIORSTU
outrides
outsider
suitored

DEIORSTW
rowdiest
wordiest

DEIPRSTU
disputer
stupider
upristed

DEIRSSST
disserts
distress

DEIRSSTU
diestrus
studiers
sturdies

DELLORSS
drosells
lordless

DELLORST
drollest
strolled

DELMNPUU
pendulum
unplumed

DELMORSU
moulders
remoulds
smoulder

DELMOSTU
modulets
smoulted

DELNOPRS
speldron
splendor

DELNORSU
lounders
noursled
roundels
roundles
unsolder

DELNOSSU
loudness
unlossed

DELNOSUU
undulose
unsouled

DELOPSTU
postlude
stoupled

DEMNOSTU
demounts
mudstone

DENOORTU
tournedo
unrooted

DENOPSTU
outspend
unposted

DENOPSTW
step down
stewpond

DENORSSU
dourness
resounds
sounders

DENORSTU
roundest
tonsured
unsorted
unstored

DENPRSTU
sprunted
uptrends

DEOOPRST
doorstep
strooped
torpedos

DEOPRSTU
postured
proudest
sprouted
strouped

DGGGINRU
drugging
grudging

DGGIILNN
dingling
lindging

DGGIILNR
girdling
ridgling

DGGIINNS
dingings
sindging

DGGILNOS
godlings
goldings
lodgings
slodging

DGGINNSU
nudgings
snudging

DGIINNOR
Girondin
groining
non-rigid

DGIINRST
dirtings
striding

DGILLNOR
drolling
lordling

DGILMNOU
moduling
moulding

DGINNORU
drouning
inground
rounding

DGINNORW
drowning
wondring

DGINNOSU
sounding
undoings

DGINOPRU
drouping
poudring

DGINORSW
drowsing»
swording
wordings

DHIIIOST
histioid
idiotish

DLOOPPUW
pulpwood
wood pulp

DMOOORWW
woodworm
wormwood

DNNORTUW
downturn
turndown

EEEFNRRT
referent
rent free
tree fern

EEEGHINT
eighteen
teheeing

EEEGINRS
energies
energise
reseeing
resignee

EEEGMNRT
emergent
greement

EEEGRRST
greeters
regester
regreets
regretes

EEEHILRW
erewhile
while ere
wire heel

EEEHIRST
etherise
reheites

EEEHRSST
seethers
sheerest
sheeters

EEEILNST
enlistee
selenite

EEEILRST
leeriest
sleetier
steelier

EEEIMRST
eremites
mesterie

EEEINNRT
internee
retinene

EEEINRSS
eeriness
eserines

EEEINRST
estreine
eternise
teensier

EEEIRRST
reestier
retirees
steerier

EEEIRRSV
rerevise
reveries

EEELNOPP
enpeople
penelope

EEELPRSS
peerless
sleepers
speelers

EEELPRST
repletes
resplete

EEELRSST
steelers
treeless

EEEMPRRT
retemper
temperer

EEENPRRT
repenter
re-repent

EEENPRST
preteens
pretense
terpenes

EEENRRST
enterers
reenters
resenter
terreens

EEENRSST
entresse
tenesser

EEENSSTW
sweetens
wee's nest

EEEPRRSV
perverse
preserve

EEERRRSV
reserver
reverers
reverser

EEERRSTV
revester
vesterer

EEERSSTV
Everests
severest
steevers

EEFFRRSU
resuffer
sufferer

EEFGINRR
fingerer
refinger
refringe

EEFHILRS
fleshier
shelfier

EEFHRSST
freshest
freshets

EEFIIRST
feiriest
feistier
ferities
fieriest

EEFILNOS
felonies
olefines

EEFILSST
felsites
selfeist

EEFINRSS
finesser
frenesis
frenises
frensies
rifeness

EEFINRST
ferniest
infester
reinfest

EEFLLORT
foretell
toll-free

EEFLORRW
flowerer
reflower

EEFNORST
enforest
softener

EEFORRST
forester
forstere»
fosterer
reforest

EEGGINNR
greening
reenging
reneging

EEGHINRS
greenish
heerings
neighers
rehinges
sheering

EEGHINST
seething
sheeting

EEGIKLNS
keelings
skeeling
sleeking

EEGIKNRS
kreesing
reekings

EEGILNNV
levening
neveling

EEGILNPS
peelings
sleeping
speeling

EEGILNRS
girleens
ingreles
leerings
reelings
sleering

EEGILNRV
levering
reveling

EEGILNST
engislet
gentiles
leetings
sleeting
steeling

EEGIMNRS
meerings
mereings
reemings
regimens
smeering

EEGIMNRT
metering
regiment

EEGIMNST
meetings
steeming
teemings

EEGINNRS
enginers
ingeners
negrines
serening
sneering

EEGINNRT
entering
eterning

EEGINNRV
enerving
revening

EEGINOPR
perigone
pigeoner

EEGINPRS
speering
spreeing

EEGINPRT
erepting
petering

EEGINPST
speeting
steeping

EEGINPSW
sweeping
weepings

EEGINRRS
reigners
resigner

EEGINRST
gentries
gentrise
ingester
integers
reesting
reetings
reteigns
steering
teerings
treeings

EEGINRSV
everings
reevings
severing
veerings
vinegers
vinegres

EEGINRSW
sewering
sweering

EEGINRTT
tetering
treeting

EEGINRTV
everting
reveting

EEGINRTX
exerting
genetrix

EEGINSTV
steeving
ventiges

EEGIRSST
setigers
tigeress

EEGIRSTT
grisette
tergites

EEGNOORV
engroove
overgone

EEHILRSS
heirless»
relishes

EEHIMRST
erethism
etherism

EEHINPRT
nephrite
prehnite
trephine

EEHINRTW
rewhiten
whitener

EEHIORST
hosterie
isothere
theories
theorise

EEHIPRRS
perisher
spherier

EEHIPRSS
hesperis
perishes

EEHIPRTT
perthite
pith tree
tephrite
threepit

EEHIRRSS
errishes
sherries

EEHIRSTT
etherist
tee shirt

EEHMNORS
horsemen
shoremen

EEHNPRSU
sheep run
unsphere

EEHOPRST
hop trees
sheep rot

EEHPRSST
hepsters
shepster
sperthes

EEIIKLSW
likewise
wiselike

EEIILMNT
ilmenite
melinite

EEIINRSS
resinise
seisiner

EEIINRTT
intertie
retinite

EEIINSTV
invitees
veiniest

EEIKLPST
pikelets
spikelet
steplike

EEILMNRU
lemurine
relumine

EEILMNSU
melusine
selenium
semilune

EEILMSST
smelites
timeless

EEILNNST
entinsel
lenients
sentinel

EEILNPSS
peniless
penisles
pensiles

EEILNPST
penlites
pentiles
plenties

EEILNRST
enlister
listener
reenlist
relisten
silenter

EEILNRSV
liveners
sniveler

EEILNRTT
entitler
inletter

EEILNRTY
entirely
lientery

EEILNSSV
evilness
vileness

EEILORST
literose
oil trees
troelies

EEILORSV
loveries
overlies
relievos
voleries

EEILORVV
overlive
overveil

EEILPRST
epistler
peitrels
peltries
perlites
reptiles
respliet

EEILRRSV
liverers
relivers»
resilver
revilers
silverer

EEILRSST
leisters
liesters
tireless

EEIMMORS
memories
memorise

EEIMMRST
meristem
mimester
mismetre
stemmier

EEIMNOST
monetise
semitone

EEIMNPST
piements
sepiment

EEIMOPRS
promisee
reimpose

EEIMPRRS
premiers
simperer

EEIMPRSS
emprises
impreses
impresse
premises
spiremes

EEIMPRST
emptiers
impester

EEIMRRST
meriters
merriest
miterers
rimester
triremes

EEIMRRTT
remitter
trimeter
trimetre

EEIMRSST
missteer
trisemes

EEIMSSST
messiest
metisses

EEINNRST
innerest
intenser
internes
sternine

EEINNRTT
renitent
tin terne

EEINNRTV
inventer
reinvent

EEINNSTW
entwines
wenniest

EEINOPRS
isoprene
pereions
pioneers

EEINORST
oneriest
serotine

EEINPRSS
enspires
erepsins
ripeness

EEINPRSU
penuries
resupine

EEINPSST
pensiest
pentises
septines

EEINPSTT
psettine
spinette

EEINQRSU
enquires
squireen

EEINRRST
inserter
reinsert
reinters
rentiers
terrines

EEINRRTV
inverter
reinvert

EEINRSST
interess
sentries
trenises

EEINRSTT
insetter
interest
sternite
trientes

EEINRSTU
esurient
retinues
reunites
uterines

EEINRSTV
nerviest
reinvest
servient
sirvente
vintrees

EEINRTTY
entirety
eternity
trey tine

EEINSTTT
nettiest
tentiest

EEIOPPRS
epispore»
poperies

EEIOPRST
poetiser
poetries
poetrise

EEIOPRTZ
poetizer
poetrize

EEIORSST
erotesis
osteries

EEIPRRRS
perriers
repriser
respirer

EEIPRRTT
preterit
prettier

EEIRRSST
resister
serriest
stirrees
tressier

EEIRRSTV
restrive
reverist
riverets
riveters
serviter
verriest

EEIRSSTV
Servites
vestries

EELMNOOS
lonesome
oenomels

EELMRSST
resmelts
smelters
termless

EELNOSSS
noseless
soleness

EELNOSST
noteless
toneless

EELNOSTV
love nest
novelets

EELNSSTU
tuneless
unsteels

EELNSTTU
lunettes
unsettle

EELORTUV
revolute
treulove
truelove

EELPPSTU
septuple
supplete

EELRSSST
restless
slesters
tressels
tressles

EELRSSTY
restyles
strelsey
tyreless

EEMNSSTU
muteness
tenesmus

EEMOPRRS
emperors
premorse

EEMORRTU
mouterer
outremer

EEMORSST
somerset
someters
tree moss

EEMPRRSU
presumer
supremer

EEMPRSST
emprests
sempster

EENNORST
enterons
sonneter
tenoners

EENOPRSS
persones
response

EENOPRST
postrene
protense

EENOPRTT
entrepot
tent rope

EENORSTT
onsetter
setter-on

EENPRSST
pensters
pertness
presents
serpents

EENRSSTT
stenters
sternest
sternets
testerns

EEOPRRTX
exporter
re-export

EEOPRSSS
espresso
opresses

EEOPRSSU
espouser
repousse

EEORRRST
resorter
restorer
retrorse

EEORRSTV
evertors
restrove

EEORRTUV
overture
trouvere

EEORSSST
osseters
retosses

EEPRRSSU
perusers
pressure

EEPRSTTU
setter-up
upsetter

EFGIILNR
fleiring
refiling

EFGIINNR
enfiring
infringe
refining

EFGIINRR
fringier
refiring

EFGILLNO
lifelong
long life

EFGINRRY
ferrying
refrying

EFGINRSU
gunfires
refusing

EFHIORRT
forthier
frothier

EFIIKRRS
friskier
fire risk

EFIILNRT
flintier
infilter

EFIILNTY
felinity
finitely

EFILRSST
riftless
stiflers

EFIMNORR
informer
reinform
reniform

EFIMNORS
ensiform
fermions
fermison

EFIOPRRT
portfire
profiter

EFIORRST
frostier
rotifers

EFLLOSST
self-lost
soft sell

EFNOOSST
eftsoons
festoons

EFORRSST
forsters
fortress

EGGIINNR
greining
griening
ingering
reigning
reinging

EGGIINRT
greiting
grieting
tigering

EGGIINRV
grieving
regiving

EGGILNNT
gentling
glenting

EGGILNNU
engluing
lungeing

EGGILNRS
ginglers
nigglers
slerging
sniggler

EGGINRSS
gressing
sergings
sniggers

EGGLRSTU
gurglets
struggel
struggle

EGHIINST
heisting
nighties
siething
thingies

EGHILNRS
herlings
shingler

EGHILNST
enlights
lightens
slighten

EGHILRST
lighters
relights
slighter

EGHILSTT
lightest
stightle

EGHINRSW
shewring
whingers

EGHIOTUW
outweigh
weigh out

EGHLOOTY
ethology
theology

EGHLORST
glothers
short leg

EGHORSTU
roughest
roughets
toughers

EGIILNNS
enisling
ensiling

EGIILNOR
niger oil
religion
reoiling

EGIILNPS
pleising
sleiping
speiling

EGIILNRS
leirings
resiling
Riesling

EGIILNRT
girtline
retiling
tinglier
tireling

EGIILNRV
livering
reliving
reviling»

riveling

EGIILNST
lignites
lingiest
steiling

EGIIMNRS
Isengrim
misering
remising
semi-ring

EGIIMNRT
meriting
mitering
retiming
ring time

EGIINNPR
preining
repining
ripening

EGIINNRS
reinsing
resining
sirening
sneiring

EGIINNRT
entiring
reniting
retining
tringine

EGIINNST
entising
ginniest
steining

EGIINPRS
espiring
ginipers
peirsing
preising
speiring
spiering

EGIINRST
girniest
igniters
reisting
resiting»

steiring
stiering
stingier
strigine

EGIINRSV
reivings
revising
sivering
visering

EGIINRSW
ringwise
sweiring
swingier
weirings

EGIINRTV
riveting
tivering

EGILLMNS
mellings
smelling

EGILLNST
stelling
tellings

EGILLNSW
swelling
wellings

EGILMNST
meltings
smelting

EGILNNST
nestling
slenting

EGILNORS
leg irons
resoling
solering

EGILNORW
lowering
roweling

EGILNPRS
pinglers
presling
pringles»

sperling
springel
springle

EGILNPST
peltings
pestling

EGILNPSY
spleying
yelpings

EGILNRSS
ringless
singlers
slingers

EGILNRST
glinters
lingster
ringlets
sterling
tinglers
tringles

EGILNRTW
lewtring
weltring

EGILNSSS
glissens
lessings
sessling
signless

EGILNSSU
slueings
ugliness

EGILNSSW
slewings
swingels
swingles
wingless

EGILNSTT
ettlings
glintest
lettings
settling

EGILNSTW
swelting
twingles»

weltings
winglets

EGIMNPRT
tempring
tremping

EGIMNRST
metrings
smerting
streming

EGIMNRSU
remuings
resuming

EGINNORT
ingroten
nitrogen
tenoring

EGINNRST
rentings
ring nets
sterning
strening

EGINNRSU
ensuring
enurings

EGINNRTU
retuning
untinger

EGINNSTT
nettings
stenting
tentings

EGINOPRS
perigons
reposing
spongier

EGINORST
genitors
Negritos
roseting
trigones

EGINORTT
ottering
totering

EGINORTU
outering
outreign

EGINPRRS
respring
sperring
springer

EGINPRSS
presigns
pressing
spersing
spingers
springes

EGINPRST
pestring
presting
springet

EGINPRSU
persuing
perusing
supering

EGINPRTU
erupting
reputing

EGINRRST
grinters
restring
ringster
sterring
stringer
terrings

EGINRSST
restings
stingers
stringes
tressing
trigness

EGINRSTW
strewing
twingers
wresting

EGINRTTU
tiger nut
uttering

EGIORSST
gorsiest
strigose

EGLNORSU
loungers
slounger

EGMNNOOY
monogeny
nomogeny

EGNRRSTU
grunters
restrung

EHIINRST
histrien
inherits

EHILMOST
helotism
homliest

EHILNOST
holstein
neoliths

EHILOPRS
pilhorse
polisher
repolish

EHILOPST
helistop
hoplites
isopleth

EHILRSST
slithers
thrisles
thrissel
thrissle

EHIMORST
isotherm
moithers

EHIMPSTU
humpiest
humpties
tumphies

EHIMRSST
Rhemists
smithers

EHINNRST
thinners
thrinnes

EHINOPST
phoniest
siphonet

EHINORSS
herisons
herisson
inshores

EHINORST
horniest
ornithes

EHINPRSU
punisher
repunish

EHIOPRSS
phoresis
rose hips
sposhier

EHIORSST
hoisters
horsiest
hostries
rehoists
shorties

EHIORSTT
theorist
thorites

EHIPRSST
hipsters
shipster
thripses

EHIRSTTW
whitrets
whitster
whitters

EHLNSSSU
lushness
shunless

EHLOOPST
hopelost
posthole
potholes

EHLRSSTU
hurtless
hustlers
ruthless

EHMSSTUY
mythuses
thymuses

EHNORSSU
onrushes
unhorses

EHNORSTT
northest
thornset

EHNRSSTU
huntress
shunters

EHOOPSTU
housetop
pothouse

EHOPRSST
hotpress
strophes

EIILMSST
elitisms
slimiest

EIILNOSS
elisions
isolines
lionises
oiliness

EIILNRST
nirliest
nitriles

EIILNSTT
intitles
lintiest

EIILOPST
pisolite»
polities
politise

EIIMMNNT
imminent
miniment

EIIMNOSS
emission
simonies

EIIMNRST
interims
minister
ministre
misinter

EIIMPRSS
misprise
pisimers
pismires

EIIMRSTT
meritist
metritis

EIIMSSTT
mistiest
Semitist

EIINORSV
revision
visioner

EIINOSST
inosites
noisiest

EIINPSST
snipiest
spiniest

EIINQTUY
equinity
inequity

EIINRSST
insister
reinsist
sinister
sinistre

EIINRSTV
inviters»
vintries
vitrines

EIIPSSTT
pietists
stipites
tipsiest

EIKLNOOR
inlooker
looker-in
oerlikon

EIKLNPRS
plinkers
prinkles
sprinkle

EIKLNRST
linkster
strinkle
tinklers
trinkles

EIKLNRTW
twinkler
wrinklet

EIKNNORS
einkorns
nonskier

EILLMPSS
misspell
psellism

EILLNSTY
silently
tinselly

EILLQRSU
quillers
squiller

EILLSSST
listless
slitless

EILMNOOS
oinomels
simoleon

EILMNTUY
minutely»
untimely

EILMOPRS
implores
pelorism
sperm oil

EILMOPST
milepost
polemist

EILMPSST
misspelt
simplest

EILNOOST
looniest
oilstone
stone oil

EILNOPRT
Interpol
pointrel
top liner

EILNOSTV
novelist
violents

EILNPRST
splinter
sprintle

EILNPSSU
spinules
splenius

EILNRSTU
insulter
lustrine

EILNSSTT
snittles
tintless

EILOOPST
loopiest
pooliest

EILOORST
oestriol
troolies

EILOPRSS
oil press
spoilers

EILOPRST
pistoler
poitrels

EILOPRSV
overslip
slipover

EILOPSTT
pistolet
plotties
politest

EILORSTU
outliers
touslier

EILOSTUV
love suit
outlives
solutive

EILPPRST
ripplets
stippler
tipplers
tripples

EILPPRSU
periplus
supplier

EILPRSTT
prittles
splitter
sprittle
striplet
triplets

EILPRSTY
priestly
spritely
spritlye

EILQRSTU
quilters
squirtel

EILRSSST
slestirs
slisters
stirless

EILRSSTT
litsters
littress
slitters
sterlits
stilters
strelits
testrils

EILRSSTY
sisterly
styliser

EILRSTTZ
strelitz
streltzi

EIMMOPRU
emporium
pomerium

EIMNOORS
ionomers
moonrise

EIMNOORT
motioner
remotion

EIMNOOST
emotions
mooniest
moonites

EIMNOPST
nepotism
pimentos

EIMNORSS
mersions
minoress

EIMNRSST
entrisms
minsters
trimness

EIMNRSTU
terminus»

unmiters
unmitres

EIMOORST
mooriest
motorise
roomiest

EIMOPRRS
primeros
primrose
promiser

EIMOPRRT
importer
reimport

EIMORRST
mortiers
mortiser
stormier

EIMORSTT
moistest
omitters

EIMORSTW
miswrote
wormiest

EINNORST
intoners
Neronist
ternions

EINNOSTT
tinstone
tontines

EINNRSTU
runniest
sturnine
unsterin

EINOOPRS
poisoner
snoopier
spoonier

EINOORSZ
ozoniser
snoozier

EINOPRSS
poriness
pression
prisones
ropiness
sinopers

EINOPSTT
nepotist
stone pit

EINORRST
introrse
snortier

EINORSST
instores
oestrins
snoriest
tersions

EINORSSU
neurosis
resinous

EINORSTT
snottier
tenorist
tritones

EINORSTU
routines
snoutier

EINOSSST
sonsiest
stenosis

EINPRRST
printers
reprints
sprinter

EINPRSST
spinster
spritens

EINPRSTU
unpriest
unripest

EINQRSTU
quinters
squinter

EIOORSTT
rootiest
tortoise

EIOPRRST
pierrots
sportier

EIOPRSST
periosts
poisters
prosiest
reposits
ripostes
triposes

EIOPRSTT
rispetto
spottier

EIOPRSTV
pivoters
sorptive
sportive

EIOPRSUV
pervious
previous
viperous

EIORRSST
resistor
roisters
sorriest
storiers

EIORRSTV
overstir
servitor

EIORSTUV
virtuose
vitreous
voitures

EIPPRRST
stripper
trippers

EIPPRSTT
strippet
trippets

EIPRSSSU
suspires
susprise

EIQRSTTU
quitters
squitter
triquets

EKOORRVW
overwork
work over

ELLORRST
stroller
trollers

ELMPRSSU
rumpless
slumpers

ELNOSSSW
slowness
snowless

ELOPPRSS
propless
sloppers

ELOPRSTT
plotters
sportlet

ELOPRSTY
prostyle
protyles

ELOPSSST
postless
spotless
stopless

ELORSTUY
elytrous
souterly
urostyle

ELPPSSTU
stupples
supplest

ELRSSSTU
rustless
trussels

EMMNORSU
resummon
summoner

EMMRRRUU
murmurer
remurmur

EMNOOPTY
monotype
Moon type

EMNOORST
mesotron
monteros

EMNOORSU
enormous
nemorous

EMNORSTT
sortment
torments

EMOOPRST
postrome
promotes

ENNOSSTU
neustons
sunstone
unstones

ENOOPSTT
potstone
topstone

ENORRTUV
overturn
turnover

EOOPRRTU
outroper
uprooter

EOOPRSTU
outropes
porteous

EOOPRSTV
overpost
overpots
overtops
stopover

EOPPRSSU
purposes
supposer

EOPRRSST
portress
sporters

EOPRRSTU
posturer
sprouter
troupers

EOQRSSTU
questors
torquess

EORRSSTU
rousters
stourres
trousers

EORRSSTW
strowers
trowsers

EORRSTTU
strouter
tortures
trouters
tutorers

EPPRSSSU
press ups
suppress

FFGILNSU
luffings
sluffing

FFGINSTU
stuffing
tuffings

FGHILNSU
flushing
lungfish

FGIILNRS
frisling
riflings

FGIILNRT
flirting»

trifling

FGIILNST
liftings
stifling

FGIINRST
firsting
fristing

FGILNOSU
flousing
foulings

FGILNOSW
flowings
flowsing
fowlings
wolfings

FGILNOTU
flouting
outfling

FGINORST
fortings
fostring
frosting

FIKLNOSW
wolfkins
wolfskin

GGGIILNN
gingling
niggling

GGGILNOS
loggings
slogging

GGGINSTU
stugging
tuggings

GGIILNNS
gin sling
glinsing
inglings
singling
slinging

GGIILNNT
glinting»

tingling

GGIINNOR
groining
ignoring
ingoring

GGIINNST
stinging
tingings

GGIINNSW
swinging
wingings

GGIINPRS
gripings
grisping

GGILNNSU
lungings
slunging

GGILNOSS
glossing
goslings

GGINOPRS
gropings
gropsing
proggins

GGINORSU
grousing
roguings
rougings

GGINPRSU
purgings
spurging

GHHINSSU
hushings
shushing

GHIIKNRS
hirkings
shirking
shriking

GHIILNRS
hirlings
hirsling
shirling

GHIILNST
hiltings
slithing
tinglish

GHIINNSS
shinings
snishing

GHIINNST
in-things
nithings
snithing

GHIINSSW
swishing
whissing
wishings

GHIINSTT
hittings
shitting
tithings

GHIINSTW
swithing
whisting
whitings

GHIINTTW
thwiting
whitting

GHILNOST
hostling
slothing
tholings

GHILNOSU
housling
shouling

GHILNOTW
night owl
thowling

GHILNRSU
hurlings
rushling
shurling

GHILNSSU
hussling
lushings»

slushing

GHILNSTU
hustling
sunlight
unlights

GHINNORT
northing
thorning
throning

GHINNSTU
huntings
shunting

GHINOOST
hootings
shooting
soothing

GHINORTW
ingrowth
throwing
Worthing

GHINOSTU
shouting
southing

GHINRSTU
hurtings
shurting
ungirths
unrights

GHINSSTU
hustings
unsights

GIIJNOST
jingoist
joisting

GIIKKNNS
kinkings
skinking

GIIKLLNS
killings
skilling

GIIKLNNS
inklings»

linkings
slinking

GIIKNNPS
kingpins
knipsing
pink gins
pinkings
spinking

GIIKNNST
stinking
tinkings

GIIKNNSW
swinking
winkings

GIIKNRST
skirting
striking

GIILLNPS
pillings
spilling

GIILLNST
liltings
stilling
tillings

GIILLNSW
swilling
willings

GIILMNNU
lumining
unliming

GIILMNPS
limpings
simpling

GIILMNRT
mirtling
trimling

GIILMNST
miltings
mistling
smilting

GIILNNPU
lining up»

unpiling

GIILNPPS
lippings
sippling
slipping

GIILNPRS
lirpings
spirling

GIILNRST
slirting
stirling

GIILNSST
listings
sistling
stilings

GIILNSTT
littings
slitting
stilting
tiltings
titlings

GIIMNNTU
minuting
muniting
mutining

GIIMNPRU
impuring
umpiring

GIINNPSU
pinguins
punising

GIINNQSU
quinsing
squining

GIINNRSU
insuring
ruinings
urinings

GIINOPST
positing
sopiting

GIINORST
riotings
roisting
rositing

GIINPRSS
prissing
rispings

GIINPRST
spirting
spriting
striping

GIINQRSU
quirings
risquing
squiring

GIINRRST
stirring
tirrings

GIINSTTW
twisting
wittings

GIKLNNRU
knurling
runkling

GIKNOOPS
pookings
spooking

GILMNPSU
lumpings
plumings
slumping

GILMNRTY
myrtling
trymling

GILNNRSU
nurlings
nursling
snurling

GILNOOPS
loopings
poolings
slooping
soopling»
spooling

GILNOOST
lottings
stooling
toolings

GILNOPSY
posingly
spongily

GILNORSS
rossling
slorings

GILNORST
rostling
slorting
stroling

GILNORSU
lourings
slouring

GILNORTU
routling
trouling

GILNOSTT
lottings
slotting

GILNOSTU
loutings
soluting
tousling
tung oils

GILNPPSU
pulpings
suppling

GILNPRSU
purlings
slurping
spruling
spurling

GILNRSTU
lustring
rustling

GILNRTTU
ruttling»
turtling

GILNSSTU
lustings
singults
tussling

GIMNOORS
morrings
smooring

GIMNOPST
stomping
tompings

GIMNORST
mostring
storming
stroming

GIMNOSSU
mousings
smousing
soumings

GIMNPSTU
stumping
tumpings

GINNOOPS
snooping
spooning

GINNOORS
noorsing
snooring

GINNOOST
snooting
stooning

GINNORST
snorting
stroning

GINNPRSU
prunings
snurping
spurning
unspring

GINNRSTU
snurting
turnings»
unstring

GINOOPRS
roopings
spooring

GINOORST
roosting
rootings

GINOPRST
sporting
stroping

GINOPSST
postings
signpost

GINOPSTT
pottings
spotting

GINOPSTU
poutings
spouting
stouping

GINORSST
sortings
storings
trossing

GINORSTU
outgrins
outrings
rousting
routings
stouring
tourings
trousing

GINORSTW
strowing
trowings
trowsing
worsting

GINORSTY
roysting
storying
stroying

GINORTTU
trouting»
tutoring

GINPRRSU
purrings
spurring

GINPRSTU
spruting
spurting
stupring

GINPRSUU
pursuing
usurping

GINRSSTU
rustings
trussing

GINRSTTU
ruttings
sturting
trusting

GLMNOOOY
monology
nomology

GLOOOPTY
optology
topology

HIMORSTU
humorist
thoriums

HOOOSTTU
outshoot
shoot out

HOORTTUW
outthrow
outworth
throw out

IIILLNOS
Illinois
illision

IIIMMNST
intimism
minimist

IIMNPRST
imprints
misprint

IINNOSTU
inustion
unionist
unitions

ILNOOPSY
snoopily
spoonily

INOOPRST
portions
positron
sorption

IOOPRSTY
isotropy
porosity

IORSTTUY
touristy
yttrious

AAACDNRSS
Cassandra
sandaracs

AAACILNST
Castalian
satanical

AAAELNNTT
antenatal
Atlantean
Tantalean

AAAILNRSU
aularians
Laurasian

AAAILNSST
Alsatians
assailant

AAAIMNORT
amatorian
inamorata

AAAIMNRST
Samaritan
Sarmatian

AAAINOPRS
paranoias
Saponaria

AAAINRSTT
Astrantia
Tatarians

AABBDEORS
Barbadoes
baseboard

AABBEINRT
Barnabite
rabbinate

AABBEIRRS
barbaries
barbarise

AABCDEILL
cable-laid
cebadilla

AABCEELRT
creatable
traceable

AABCEILRT
bacterial
calibrate

AABCEINRS
braincase
carabines

AABCEORST
ascorbate
boatraces

AABCFHKLS
flashback
halfbacks

AABDEFLOR
broadleaf
loafbread

AABDEGINR
bargained
gabardine

AABDEILNR
bird alane
drainable

AABDEORST
adsorbate
teaboards

AABDILORT
broadtail
tailboard

AABEEHRST
sea bather
tabasheer

AABEIKLNS
Balkanise
lake basin

AABEKNRST
bank rates
stank brae

AACCEENRT
cancerate»

reactance

AACCERSTU
carucates
Crustacea

AACCIILST
ascitical
sciatical

AACCILLNO
cloacalin
cloacinal
laconical

AACCIMNOR
carcinoma
macaronic

AACCINOTT
catatonic
toccatina

AACDEEHRS
headraces
scarehead

AACDEEIMT
acetamide
emaciated

AACDEEMRT
camerated
demarcate
macerated
racemated

AACDEILLN
allianced
dalliance

AACDEIMPR
paramedic
preadamic

AACDELSTY
catalysed
staylaced

AACDENNST
adnascent
ascendant

AACDHLNPS
handclaps
handclasp

AACDINORS
Orcadians
Sarcodina

AACEGILLN
angelical
Galenical

AACEGILNS
analgesic
angelicas

AACEGLOTU
catalogue
coagulate

AACEGNRSU
cane sugar
sugar cane

AACEHILPT
caliphate
hepatical

AACEHIRST
catharise
theriacas

AACEILLTV
laticlave
vacillate

AACEILMST
calamites
mica slate

AACEILNNT
cantilena
lancinate

AACEILNRS
arsenical
carnalise

AACEILNRT
lacertian
nectarial

AACEILRST
sectarial»

tailraces

AACEIMRSS
Caesarism
macarises
mesaraics

AACEIMSTT
catamites
masticate

AACEINRST
ascertain
carinates
Cartesian
craniates
sectarian

AACEIPRSS
airspaces
cassaripe

AACEIRSST
Caesarist
staircase

AACELLNOR
lanceolar
olecranal

AACELNNTU
antelucan
cannulate

AACELOTUV
autoclave
vacuolate

AACELPSTU
aspectual
capsulate

AACELSSTY
catalyses
staylaces

AACENRSSU
anacruses
assurance

AACFILNOT
factional
falcation

AACHILNPS
chaplains
ship canal

AACHINOPR
anaphoric
pharaonic

AACHINRST
anarchist
cantharis

AACHIRSST
archaists
catharsis

AACIILMST
ismatical
lamaistic

AACIILRST
racialist
satirical

AACIINNST
actinians
antiscian

AACILNOPT
pactional
placation

AACILNRST
cant rails
carnalist

AACILOPRS
carap oils
prosaical

AACILORTU
auctorial
caliatour

AACILRSTY
rascality
satyrical

AACINNOST
Catonians
santonica

AACINRSST
arcanists»

sacristan

AACLOPRTY
placatory
play actor

AACLPRSUY
capsulary
scapulary

AACORRTTT
attractor
tractator

AADDELMNR
dreamland
raddleman

AADEEHRTW
headwater
waterhead

AADEEPRST
asperated
estrapade
paederast
separated

AADEGINTV
navigated
vaginated

AADEGRSTU
date sugar
graduates

AADEHIPRT
apartheid
hit parade

AADEHLMPS
headlamps
lampshade

AADEILLRT
arillated
lardalite

AADEILPRR
paredrial
perradial

AADEILPST
lapidates»

stapedial

AADEIMNNR
mandarine
meandrian
meandrina

AADEINRST
dentarias
steradian

AADEINRTT
antitrade
attainder

AADEIPRST
aspirated
disparate
parasited

AADEQRSTU
quadrates
squadrate

AADGGLNOR
galdragon
loggarand

AADGINORT
gradation
indagator

AADIINRRT
irradiant
Triandria

AADILNNOT
antinodal
Daltonian

AADILNOTU
adulation
laudation

AADLORTUY
adulatory
laudatory

AADMNORTY
damnatory
mandatory

AADNQRSTU
quadrants»

squadrant

AAEEFLRTW
water flea
waterleaf
water leaf

AAEEIMNTX
examinate
exanimate

AAEEKPRRT
parrakeet
repartake

AAEELMSTT
stalemate
telesmata

AAEFHLLRT
Allfather
earthfall

AAEFHMRTT
aftermath
hamfatter

AAEGGINRR
gregarian
Gregarina

AAEGILNOS
analogies
analogise

AAEGILNPP
appealing
lagniappe

AAEGILNPS
pelagians
Pelasgian

AAEGINNRT
Argentina
tanagrine

AAEGINRSY
asynergia
gainsayer

AAEHINRST
Rhaetians
rhatanies

AAEILLPRT
plate rail
prelatial

AAEILMRST
marestail
mare's tail
materials

AAEILNORT
alienator
rationale

AAEILPRST
parietals
psalteria

AAEIMNSTT
emanatist
staminate

AAELNRSTT
alterants
alternats
translate

AAELRSSTU
assaulter
reassault
saleratus

AAEMNRSSW
manswears
wasserman

AAEOPRRST
sea parrot
separator

AAGHILNRS
ashlaring
Shangri-la

AAGILNOST
analogist
nostalgia

AAIILMPRT
impartial
primatial

AAILLMRTY
maritally
martially

AAILNOPSS
passional
Salopians
sponsalia

AAILNOSTT
saltation
stational

AAILNPRTU
tarpaulin
unpartial

AALLPRSTU
palustral
plaustral

ABBCGILNS
cabblings
scabbling

ABCDENORR
bread corn
corn bread

ABCDENOSU
case-bound
subdeacon

ABCEEGKNR
back green
greenback

ABCEELRSU
rescuable
securable

ABCEILSTU
baculites
bisculate

ABCEINORS
carbonise
escribano

ABCENORST
crab stone
stone crab

ABCIKLLST
blacklist
black tils

ABCILORRU
courbaril
orbicular

ABCNORSTU
obscurant
subcantor

ABDDEENOR
boardened
broadened

ABDDEIORS
broadside
sideboard

ABDEEHINR
haberdine
Hebridean

ABDEEILNR
bandelier
bandileer
breadline

ABDEEINST
besainted
bestained

ABDEELNOR
banderole
bandoleer

ABDEELNST
bandelets
enstabled

ABDEERRST
bestarred
redbreast

ABDEGIIRR
air bridge
brigadier

ABDEGIKNR
bedarking
debarking

ABDEIILST
albitised
sibilated

ABDEIKNRW
break wind
windbreak

ABDEILNOR
bandolier
bird alone

ABDEINOST
bastioned
botanised

ABDELNSTU
Dunstable
unblasted
unstabled

ABDGINORS
adsorbing
boardings
signboard

ABEEERRTV
verberate
vertebrae

ABEEGLOPR
bargepole
porbeagle

ABEEHINRT
hibernate
inbreathe

ABEEIKLST
Bakelites
beastlike
bleakiest

ABEEILNPS
albespine
plebeians

ABEEILRST
beastlier
bleariest
liberates

ABEEILRSV
revisable
verbalise

ABEEILRTV
avertible»
veritable

ABEEIRRSS
brasserie
brassiere

ABEELNSSS
blaseness
sableness

ABEFILOST
boatflies
lifeboats

ABEGIINOR
aborigine
baignoire

ABEGIINRT
ebriating
rebaiting

ABEGINRTT
battering
rebatting

ABEGINSST
basseting
beastings

ABEHILRTY
breathily
heritably

ABEHNORRT
abhorrent
earthborn

ABEHOOSTU
boathouse
houseboat

ABEIILSST
sibilates
stabilise

ABEILNRSU
insurable
sublinear

ABEILRTVY
verbality
veritably

ABEILSTTW
twistable
waistbelt

ABEINOORT
aerobiont
reboation

ABEINPRST
breastpin
stepbairn

ABEINRTTU
tribunate
turbinate

ABEKLORTW
tablework
worktable

ABELNRSTU
subaltern
unstabler

ABGILNQSU
quablings
squabling

ACCDEIILN
Cicindela
Icelandic

ACCDHNPRU
card punch
punch card

ACCEEILNR
arc-en-ciel
cancelier

ACCEENRSU
recusance
securance

ACCEHIMNS
mechanics
mischance

ACCEHIMST
catechism
schematic

ACCEINORT
accretion»
anorectic

ACCEINSTU
encaustic
succinate

ACCELNOVY
concavely
covalency

ACCEORSTU
accoustre
accoutres
coruscate

ACCHLOORT
colcothar
ochlocrat

ACCILNOTU
ciclatoun
noctiluca

ACCMNOORY
monocracy
nomocracy

ACDDEEIMT
decimated
medicated

ACDDEEORT
decorated
redcoated

ACDEEEHRT
recheated
teachered

ACDEEERST
decastere
decreates
desecrate

ACDEEFNTU
fecundate
unfaceted

ACDEEFRRT
redecraft
refracted

ACDEEHRRT
chartered»
recharted
three-card

ACDEEILMN
demilance
enclaimed
endemical

ACDEEILMR
declaimer
reclaimed

ACDEEILNN
celandine
decennial

ACDEEINRT
certained
increated

ACDEEKRST
restacked
stackered

ACDEELLOT
decollate
ocellated

ACDEELNRS
calenders
calendres
encradles
esclandre

ACDEELRST
decretals
scarleted

ACDEENRST
decanters
descanter

ACDEEORST
decorates
recoasted

ACDEFINRT
infarcted
infracted

ACDEGHINR
chagrined
dearching

ACDEGINRT
decarting
redacting

ACDEHNRRU
uncharred
underarch

ACDEHNSTU
staunched
unscathed

ACDEIILMN
adminicle
medicinal

ACDEIILRV
larvicide
veridical

ACDEIIMRT
diametric
matricide

ACDEIINST
actinides
andesitic
diactines
indicates

ACDEILLMY
decimally
medically

ACDEILMNU
unclaimed
undecimal

ACDEIMRST
mistraced
timecards

ACDEINORS
Dinoceras
iron-cased

ACDEINOTU
auctioned
cautioned
education
Noctuidae

ACDEINOTV
advection»

invocated

ACDEINPRT
predicant
tap cinder

ACDEINSTY
asyndetic
cystidean
syndicate

ACDEIPRST
crispated
practised

ACDEIRSTT
cristated
tetracids

ACDEIRTTU
dictature
urticated

ACDENRSTU
encrusted
uncrested

ACDENRTTU
reductant
truncated

ACDEORSTU
ceradotus
croustade
educators

ACDHMOOTW
doomwatch
matchwood

ACDILNORU
rain cloud
uncordial

ACEEGILNR
energical
generical

ACEEGILNT
clientage
genetical

ACEEHILRT
cheralite»
etherical
heretical

ACEEHIMNS
Manichees
mechanise

ACEEHNOPR
canephore
chaperone

ACEEHNSTU
chanteuse
unteaches

ACEEHRRRT
charterer
recharter

ACEEILNPR
percaline
Periclean

ACEEILNRS
reliances
scareline

ACEEILNRT
interlace
lacertine
reclinate

ACEEILPRS
periclase
sale price
specialer

ACEEILRST
cartelise
cerealist

ACEEIMPST
empaestic
space-time

ACEEIMRRS
careerism
cramesier
screamier

ACEEIMRSS
cassimere
racemises

ACEEIMRST
creamiest
ice stream
miscreate
stream ice

ACEEINNRT
ancienter
nectarine

ACEEINRSS
increases
resiances
scenarise

ACEEINRST
centiares
cisternae
creatines
encraties
iterances
nectaries

ACEEIRSTU
cauteries
cauterise

ACEEIRSTV
reactives
viscerate

ACEEISSST
ecstasies
ecstasise

ACEELNNRU
cannelure
uncleaner

ACEELNORT
coeternal
tolerance

ACEELNRSS
cleansers
clearness

ACEELNRTU
calenture
crenulate

ACEELORRT
coral tree
correlate

ACEELPSSS
scapeless
spaceless

ACEELRSST
scelerats
traceless

ACEENNOST
caen stone
Cantonese

ACEENNRST
entrances
renascent

ACEENPTTX
exceptant
expectant

ACEERRSST
creatress
recasters

ACEERRSTT
scatterer
street car

ACEFHMORT
forthcame
homecraft

ACEFINORT
factioner
fornicate
refaction

ACEGHILNS
lachesing
leachings

ACEGHINNR
enarching
enraching
rachening

ACEGHINNS
encashing
enchasing

ACEGHINRS
cashering
reachings
recashing»
rechasing
searching

ACEGHINRT
chatering
rechating

ACEGIKNRS
creakings
recasking
resacking
screaking

ACEGIKNRT
racketing
retacking

ACEGILLNR
cellaring
recalling

ACEGILNNS
cleanings
cleansing
enlacings
enscaling

ACEGILNPR
clapering
replacing

ACEGILNRS
clearings
rescaling

ACEGILNRT
clareting
clatering
treacling

ACEGILNRV
calvering
clavering

ACEGILRTU
curtilage
graticule

ACEGIMNRS
amercings
creamings
Germanics
screaming

ACEGIMNRT
centigram
cremating
mercating

ACEGIMRSS
Graecisms
grass mice

ACEGINNRV
caverning
cravening
encarving

ACEGINORT
coatering
recoating

ACEGINPRS
caperings
escarping

ACEGINRRT
arrecting
recarting
recrating
retracing
terracing

ACEGINRSS
caressing
creasings

ACEGINRST
caterings
creatings
citranges
reactings
recasting

ACEHIKLST
chalkiest
hackliest

ACEHINORT
anchorite
antechoir

ACEHINRRU
hurricane
raunchier

ACEHINRST
chantries»

snatchier

ACEHIRRST
charriest
Reichsrat
starchier

ACEHMORST
chromates
stomacher

ACEHNRSST
chantress
snatchers
stanchers

ACEHNRSTU
chaunters
stauncher

ACEHORRST
carthorse
orchestra

ACEIILNST
Catilines
inelastic
sciential

ACEIILRST
aristical
realistic

ACEIIMNRT
criminate
metrician

ACEIINPRS
periscian
precisian

ACEIINRTT
intricate
triacetin
triactine

ACEILLNOR
collinear
coralline

ACEILMMNO
Commelina
melomanic

ACEILMNRU
melanuric
numerical

ACEILMNSU
masculine
semuncial

ACEILMRTU
climature
tularemic

ACEILMSTU
amuletics
salicetum

ACEILNORS
acroleins
carolines
censorial
creolians

ACEILNORT
clarionet
crotaline

ACEILNOST
coastline
sectional

ACEILNRST
clarinets
larcenist

ACEILORST
loricates
sclerotia
sectorial

ACEILPSSU
Asclepius
capsulise

ACEILRRTU
recruital
reticular

ACEILRSTV
catsilver
verticals

ACEILRTUV
lucrative
revictual»

victualer

ACEIMNORT
cremation
manticore

ACEIMNRST
Encratism
miscreant

ACEIMNRSU
manicures
muscarine

ACEIMOPRS
paroecism
premosaic

ACEIMPRST
impacters
spermatic

ACEIMRSTU
cauterism
Cerastium

ACEINNORT
container
crenation
narcotine

ACEINNOSS
ascension
canonises

ACEINNRSU
insurance
nuisancer

ACEINNRTU
encurtain
runcinate
uncertain

ACEINNSST
cantiness
incessant
instances

ACEINORST
actioners
anticores
castorine
cerations»

certosina
creations
narcotise
ostracine
reactions
tricosane

ACEINOSST
canoeists
cessation

ACEINPRTT
crepitant
pittancer

ACEINRSST
canisters
scenarist

ACEINRSTT
antecrist
interacts

ACEINRSTU
securitan
Teucrians

ACEINSSTT
scantiest
tacitness

ACEIOPRSU
auriscope
parecious

ACEIORSST
ostracise
Socratise

ACEIRSTTU
rusticate
urticates

ACELNOOST
consolate
stone coal

ACELOSTTY
coat-style
octastyle

ACENNOOTT
connotate
Notonecta

ACENOPRRT
copartner
procreant

ACENOPRST
portances
sportance

ACENORSTU
courtesan
nectarous
outrances

ACEOPRSTT
attercops
scarpetto
spectator

ACFINORRY
confrairy
fornicary

ACGHIKLNS
hacklings
shackling

ACGHILNNU
launching
unlaching

ACGHINNST
chantings
snatching
stanching

ACGHINNTU
chaunting
nautching

ACGHINRST
chartings
starching

ACGIINNOT
actioning
incognita

ACGILNNST
cantlings
scantling

ACGILNOST
gnostical
nostalgic

ACGILNRSW
crawlings
scrawling

ACGIMNSTY
gymnastic
nystagmic

ACGINNOOT
cognation
contagion

ACGINNOPY
canopying
poignancy

ACGINNRTU
uncrating
untracing

ACHIINRST
Christian
trichinas

ACHIIRSTT
citharist
trachitis

ACHIMNORS
harmonics
man orchis

ACHIMNOST
macintosh
monachist

ACHIMRSST
chartisms
Christmas

ACHINOPRT
anthropic
rhapontic

ACIIILMST
Islamitic
Italicism

ACIILRSTU
curialist
rusticial

ACIIMNNOS
aniconism»

insomniac

ACIIMNNOT
antimonic
antinomic

ACIINNOST
aniconist
inactions
nicotians
onanistic
Toscanini

ACILLOPTY
optically
topically

ACILLOSTY
callosity
stoically

ACILMNOPT
complaint
compliant

ACILMOPRS
comprisal
proclaims

ACIMNORST
narcotism
romantics

ACIMORSST
acrotisms
ostracism

ACINNORST
constrain
transonic

ACINOORST
consortia
Ostracion

ACINORSST
cast irons
castorins
croissant

ACINORSTT
narcotist
stratonic
tractions

ACINORTTU
curtation
ructation

ACLMNOORU
colourman
monocular

ADDEEEMNR
meandered
reamended

ADDEEENRS
deadeners
serenaded

ADDEEGLNR
enlardged
gladdener
glandered

ADDEEGRRU
redargued
reguarded

ADDEEMNRU
maundered
undreamed

ADDEENOTT
denotated
detonated

ADDEERRSS
addresser
readdress

ADDEGIMNN
demanding
maddening

ADDEHNORU
Roundhead
unhoarded

ADDEIINNR
Indian red
Red Indian

ADDGILNSW
dawdlings
swaddling

ADEEEGLRT
regelated
relegated

ADEEEGNRT
engreated
generated
greatened

ADEEEHNRT
earthened
enhearted
heartened

ADEEEHRST
heartseed
shade tree

ADEEENRTV
enervated
venerated

ADEEEPPRR
paper reed
repapered

ADEEFLORT
deflorate
floreated
refloated

ADEEFMNOR
foremaned
forenamed

ADEEGGRST
raggedest
staggered

ADEEGILNN
enleading
leadening

ADEEGILNR
engrailed
realigned
releading

ADEEGIMRT
emigrated
remigated

ADEEGINNR
endearing»

engrained
grenadine

ADEEGINRR
grenadier
rereading

ADEEGINRT
denigrate
ingreated

ADEEGLNNR
Englander
Greenland

ADEEHIPST
aphetised
hepatised

ADEEHIPTZ
aphetized
hepatized

ADEEHISTT
athetised
hesitated

ADEEHNRTU
unearthed
unhearted

ADEEHRSTW
drawsheet
watershed

ADEEILLNT
entailled
niellated

ADEEILMPR
epidermal
impearled
impleader

ADEEILMRS
misleader
misleared

ADEEILMST
mealtides
metalised

ADEEILNPS
penalised»

spanieled

ADEEILNRT
entrailed
interdeal
tail ender
trenailed

ADEEILPRS
pedaliers
pedlaries

ADEEIMNST
dementias
seminated

ADEEIMRST
diameters
diametres
dreamiest
maistered
mediaters

ADEEIMSTT
estimated
meditates

ADEEINPRT
pertained
repainted

ADEEINPST
diapentes
neaptides
pedantise

ADEEINRSS
arsedines
arsenides
nearsides
readiness

ADEEINRST
dentaries
detainers
estrained
resinated
restained

ADEEINRTT
denitrate
intreated
taintered

ADEEIPRRS
despairer
draperies
re-aspired

ADEEIPRSS
sea spider
spear side

ADEEISSTT
stateside
steadiest

ADEELNPTU
pendulate
unpleated

ADEELNRTU
unaltered
unrelated

ADEELPRST
plastered
spaltered

ADEEMNOPR
open-armed
promenade

ADEEMNORT
emendator
Notre Dame

ADEEMNORU
demeanour
enamoured

ADEENNPRT
partenned
trepanned

ADEENORST
resonated
treasoned

ADEENRSTT
attenders
reattends
snattered

ADEENRSTU
denatures
sauntered
undearest»

undereats

ADEENRTTU
retaunted
untreated

ADEEORRTV
overrated
overtrade

ADEEPPRST
dapperest
prepasted

ADEEPRSTU
depasture
depurates

ADEFNORRW
fordrawen
forwander

ADEGGINNR
dangering
deranging
gandering
gardening
grenading

ADEGGINRR
regarding
regrading

ADEGHINRS
headrings
shreading

ADEGHINRT
dearthing
threading

ADEGHIOPR
eidograph
ideograph

ADEGIILNR
derailing
ingrailed

ADEGIIMNN
demaining
maidening

ADEGIINNR
deraining
ingrained

ADEGIINPR
depairing
diapering
pinigrade

ADEGIKNNR
darkening
endarking

ADEGILNNR
enlarding
relanding

ADEGILNOR
girandole
negroidal
reloading

ADEGILNPS
delapsing
pedalings
pleadings

ADEGILNRT
ratlinged
treadling
triangled

ADEGIMNNR
mandering
remanding

ADEGIMNRS
dreamings
ganderism
midranges
semi-grand

ADEGINNRR
randering
redarning

ADEGINNRW
dawnering
redawning
wandering
wardening

ADEGINORS
dragonise»
grandiose
organdies
organised

ADEGINPRS
preadings
spreading

ADEGINPRT
departing
petarding
predating

ADEGINPRV
depraving
pervading

ADEGINRRT
redarting
retarding
retrading

ADEGINRRW
redrawing
rewarding
wardering

ADEGINRST
adstringe
astringed
dastering
deratings
gradients
straigned
treadings

ADEGINSTT
destating
detasting

ADEGNORSU
dangerous
ganderous

ADEHINORS
rhodanise
Rhodesian

ADEHINRST
interdash
tarnished

ADEHKNOSW
hawk-nosed»
shakedown

ADEIILNRT
deliriant
drain tile

ADEIILNST
disentail
Latinised

ADEIILOPS
apsidiole
episodial

ADEIILQTU
liquidate
qualitied

ADEIIMRST
maistried
maitrised

ADEIIMSSV
admissive
misadvise
misavised

ADEILMNTU
datum line
dentalium

ADEILMSST
dismalest
medalists

ADEILMTTU
mutilated
ultimated

ADEILNOST
delations
insolated

ADEILNRSS
drainless
islanders

ADEILPRSY
displayer
pyralides

ADEIMNORS
Armenoids
masonried»
randomise
Romanised

ADEIMNOST
dominates
misatoned
nematoids
staminode

ADEIMNPRS
panderism
spiderman

ADEIMNRRU
murrained
unmarried

ADEIMORST
amortised
mediators

ADEIMPRST
preadmits
red tapism
spermatid

ADEIMSSTT
misstated
mistasted

ADEINNSTU
inundates
unsainted
unstained

ADEINORRS
inroaders
ordainers
reordains
serranoid

ADEINORST
derations
notarised
ordinates

ADEINOSTT
antidotes
stationed
tetanoids

ADEINRRST
instarred
transired

ADEINRSSV
river sand
sandivers

ADEIORSTT
adroitest
storiated

ADEIRSSTT
distaster
distaters

ADELLOPRT
patrolled
portalled

ADELNRSSU
laundress
slaunders

ADEMNRSTU
transmued
transumed

ADENRRSTU
turnerads
unstarred

ADEOPRRTW
top-drawer
waterdrop

ADEOPRRTY
portrayed
predatory

ADFLORRWY
forwardly
frowardly

ADGIINNOR
inroading
ordaining

ADGIINNOS
adonising
anodising

ADGIINNOZ
adonizing
anodizing

ADGINNRST
ringstand»

stranding

ADIINOSST
soi-disant
stasidion

ADIMNOORT
admonitor
dominator

ADMNORSSW
sandworms
swordsman

AEEFGORST
foregates
forestage
fosterage

AEEFMNORS
forenames
freemason

AEEGILLRS
allergies
galleries

AEEGILMNN
malengine
meningeal

AEEGILNNT
eglantine
inelegant
legantine

AEEGILNRS
algerines
releasing
resealing

AEEGILNRV
laveering
revealing

AEEGILNST
anglesite
galenites
gelatines
teaseling

AEEGILRST
gleariest
religates

AEEGIMNRS
Germanise
reseaming

AEEGIMNRT
germinate
reteaming

AEEGIMNST
geminates
magnesite
magnetise

AEEGINNRS
ensearing
regainers

AEEGINNRT
argentine
tangerine

AEEGINPRT
interpage
pignerate
repeating

AEEGINRST
reseating
stingaree

AEEGINRTT
argentite
integrate

AEEGIRSST
greasiest
stageries

AEEGLNRSS
angerless
largeness
rangeless

AEEGLRSSV
graveless
verglases

AEEGLRSTY
slate grey
steel gray

AEEGNRSST
estranges
greatness»

sangester
sangestre
sergeants

AEEGOPRRT
porterage
reportage

AEEHINPRS
Hesperian
inspheare
seraphine

AEEHINRTW
inwreathe
near-white

AEEHIPRRT
ratheripe
three pair

AEEHIPRSS
apheresis
Pharisees

AEEHIRSTT
athetiser
earthiest
heartiest
hesitater
hetaerist

AEEHLNRST
hesternal
shaltreen

AEEHLPSSS
phaseless
shapeless

AEEHLRSST
hastelers
heartless
shaltrees

AEEHMORST
heartsome
horsemeat

AEEHNRRSS
harnesser
reharness

AEEHPRSST
shepstare
spreathes

AEEHRRSTT
ratherest
shatterer

AEEHRRSTV
harvester
threavers

AEEILLNST
entailles
sea lentil
tenailles

AEEILMNNT
alinement
lineament

AEEILMRST
laimeters
materiels
misrelate
salimeter

AEEILNNTV
Levantine
valentine

AEEILNRTV
entervail
eviternal
intervale

AEEILNSST
ensilates
essential

AEEILPRRV
prevailer
reprieval

AEEILPRST
pearliest
pearlites
prelatise

AEEILRSTV
levirates
relatives
versatile

AEEIMRSST
masteries
smeariest
streamies

AEEIMSSTT
estimates
etatismes
steamiest

AEEINNRTT
entertain
Terentian

AEEINPRSS
parenesis
passerine

AEEINPRST
aperients
pistareen
pistarene
sparteine

AEEINSTTT
enstatite
intestate
satinette

AEEINTTTV
attentive
tentative

AEEIPPRST
appetiser
piperates

AEEIRSSTT
asterites
reastiest
sestertia
treatises

AEEKQRSSU
Quakeress
squeakers

AEELLRSST
tasseller
tessellar

AEELMNOSS
melanoses
sea lemons»

sea melons

AEELMNOST
lemon teas
telemones

AEELMNPSS
ampleness
ensamples

AEELNOPST
antelopes
pleonaste

AEELPRRST
palterers
plasterer
psalterer
replaster

AEELPRRSU
pleasurer
reperusal

AEELPRSTT
saltpeter
saltpetre
steel trap

AEELSSSTT
stateless
tasteless

AEEMNPRTY
pentamery
repayment

AEEMNRSST
mare's nest
steersman

AEEMNSTTT
statement
testament

AEENNPRTT
penetrant
repentant

AEENOPRST
Esperanto
personate

AEENPRSST
apertness
taperness

AEEOPRSTT
operettas
poetaster

AEEORRSTV
overrates
overstare
servatore

AEEPRRSTT
patterers
Pteraster
spatterer

AEERRRSTU
serrature
treasurer

AEFGHINRT
fathering
freathing

AEFGILNRT
faltering
flatering
reflating

AEFGINNST
fastening
saftening

AEFGINNTT
enfatting
fattening

AEFHINORS
fashioner
refashion

AEFHIPRSS
fish spear
spearfish

AEFLLORST
astrofell
forestall
forstalle

AEFLORTWW
water flow»
waterfowl

AEGGHINRT
gathering
night gear

AEGGILNNR
engraling
enlarging
largening

AEGGINRRT
garreting
gartering
regrating

AEGHIKNNR
hankering
harkening

AEGHIKNRS
ringshake
shreaking
shrinkage

AEGHILNRS
ashlering
narghiles
nargilehs
shearling

AEGHILNRT
earthling
haltering
heartling
lathering

AEGHIMNRT
mathering
nightmare

AEGHINNST
hastening
naethings

AEGHINPRS
reshaping
sphearing

AEGHINRRS
garnisher
regarnish
resharing

AEGHINRSS
garnishes
shearings

AEGHINRSW
rewashing
washering

AEGHINRTT
hattering
theatring
threating

AEGIILMNR
regiminal
remailing

AEGIILNNR
enrailing
renailing

AEGIILNNT
entailing
ingenital

AEGIILNRS
nargilies
realising
resailing

AEGIILNTV
genitival
vigilante

AEGIINNST
insignate
sin-eating

AEGIINRST
asteiring
grainiest
granitise

AEGIINRTT
granitite
iterating

AEGIINRTV
evirating
taviering

AEGIKNRST
restaking
retakings»
streaking

AEGIKNSTW
tweakings
twig snake

AEGILLMNT
malleting
metalling

AEGILMNNT
alignment
lamenting
maltening

AEGILMNPR
lampering
palmering

AEGILNNRT
alterning
lantering

AEGILNPRS
espringal
pearlings
relapsing
spanglier

AEGILNPRT
paltering
prelating
replating

AEGILNPRY
parleying
replaying

AEGILNPST
pleatings
splintage

AEGILNRSS
arselings
sangliers
seal rings
signalers

AEGILNRST
alterings
integrals
resalting
strealing
triangles

AEGILNRSY
relayings
reslaying
syringeal
yearlings

AEGILNRTU
granulite
traguline

AEGILNSST
Angelists
eastlings
Galenists
leastings
slangiest
sleatings
stealings
teaslings

AEGILNSSW
swaleings
swealings
wine glass

AEGILRSTU
glauriest
ligatures

AEGILSSST
glassiest
Glassites

AEGIMNNNR
mannering
remanning

AEGIMNNRT
germinant
minargent

AEGIMNPRT
emparting
tampering

AEGIMNRSS
remassing
smearings

AEGIMNRST
emigrants
Germanist
mantigers
mastering»
remasting
streaming

AEGIMNRSU
geraniums
Mausering
measuring

AEGIMNSTT
agistment
magnetist

AEGIMRSTU
mastigure
sugar mite

AEGINNORS
organsine
reasoning

AEGINNPTT
patenting
pattening

AEGINNRRT
erranting
rantering

AEGINNRRW
rewarning
warrening

AEGINNRSS
angriness
ranginess

AEGINNRST
gannister
santering
snatering

AEGINNRTT
integrant
nattering
rattening
tantering

AEGINNRTV
nervating
taverning

AEGINNSST
assenting
sensating»

steanings

AEGINNSTU
unstating
untasting

AEGINOPPR
organ pipe
pipe organ

AEGINOPRT
operating
orange tip
pignorate

AEGINORST
orangeist
orangiest
orangites

AEGINPRSS
aspersing
preassing
repassing
spearings

AEGINPRST
repasting
string pea
taperings
trapesing

AEGINRRST
arresting
astringer
restaring

AEGINRSST
asserting
astringes
essarting
ganisters
ingestars
sangister
sergiants
straignes

AEGINRSTT
asterting
restating
retasting
streating
treatings

AEGINRSTU
gauntries
signature

AEGINRSTV
avertings
grievants
stavering
taverings
vintagers

AEGINRSTW
Wagnerist
wastering
waterings

AEGINRSTY
estraying
restaying

AEGINRTTY
treatying
yattering

AEGLLOSSW
gallowses
Owleglass

AEGLMNORW
angle worm
lawmonger

AEHILORST
aeroliths
horsetail
isotheral

AEHILOSTT
heliostat
loathiest

AEHINNRTU
Hunterian
Ruthenian

AEHINOPST
pantihose
siphonate

AEHINRRSV
revarnish
varnisher

AEHINRSST
sharniest
starshine

AEHIOPRRS
aphoriser
pair-horse

AEIIKLNST
kalinites
saintlike
snail kite

AEIILNOPT
epilation
polianite

AEIILNRST
Listerian
saintlier

AEIILNSST
alienists
Latinises
snailiest

AEIILRSTU
ritualise
uralitise

AEIILRTUZ
ritualize
uralitize

AEIINNRSS
raininess
sirenians

AEIINNRTT
itinerant
nitratine

AEIINOTTV
evitation
novitiate

AEIKNPSST
snake pits
snake spit

AEILLNRTU
ill-nature
tellurian
unliteral

AEILLOPPT
papillote
popliteal

AEILMMNST
immantles
mentalism
Simmental

AEILMNORS
nemoralis
normalise
Orleanism

AEILMNORT
lion tamer
mentorial

AEILMNOSS
loaminess
melanosis
semolinas

AEILMNRSU
lemurians
semilunar
unrealism

AEILMORST
amitroles
mortalise
rolamites

AEILMSTTU
mutilates
stimulate
ultimates

AEILNOPRT
prelation
rantipole

AEILNOPST
antilopes
antipoles
opentails
Platonise
sealpoint

AEILNORSS
sensorial
sonerilas

AEILNORST
orientals
Orleanist
relations

AEILNORTT
natrolite
tentorial

AEILNPRTY
interplay
painterly
party line

AEILNSSST
saltiness
slatiness
stainless

AEILOPRST
epilators
saprolite
tailropes

AEILPRSTT
paltriest
prelatist

AEIMNNOST
mannitose
Mainstone
Minnesota
nominates

AEIMNORRS
Romaniser
rosmarine

AEIMNORSS
masonries
Romanises

AEIMNORST
Maronites
matronise

AEIMNRSTU
antiserum
misaunter
ruminates

AEINNORST
anointers
Nestorian»
rainstone
reanoints
Rosinante

AEINNORTV
innovater
nervation
vernation

AEINNOSST
Estonians
sensation
sonatines

AEINNOTTT
attention
tentation

AEINNRSTT
instanter
transient

AEINNRSTY
tyrannies
tyrannise

AEINOPRSS
aspersion
repassion

AEINOPRST
aspertion
atropines
patronise

AEINORSST
arsonites
assertion
asterions
notarises
rosinates
senoritas

AEINPRRST
terrapins
transpire

AEINPRSST
paintress
pinasters
pristanes
spinarets
spraintes
star pines

AEINRRSST
restrains
strainers
tarriness
transiers
transires

AEINRRSTT
restraint
transiter

AEINRSSTT
resistant
straitens

AEINRSSTU
resustain
sustainer
unsatires

AEINSSTTT
sattinets
tattiness

AEIORSSSU
ossuaries
suasories

AEIPRRSST
sparriest
spiraster

AEIRRSSTT
starriest
traitress

AELLORSWW
reswallow
rewallows
swallower
wallowers

AELNORSTU
outlearns
Solutrean

AELOPRRTY
proletary
pyrolater

AELPRSSST
psaltress
strapless

AELPRSSTU
aplustres
pertussal
supersalt

AEMORSSST
matrosses
sea storms

AENOPRSST
parsonets
patroness
postnares
transpose

AEOPRRSTW
spearwort
straw rope

AEPRRSSTU
pasturers
superstar

AGGIILNNR
ingraling
inlarging

AGGILNNOS
ganglions
sing-along

AGHILMORT
algorithm
logarithm

AGHILNNSU
unlashing
unshaling

AGHILNPSS
plashings
splashing

AGHINNPSU
unhasping
unshaping

AGHINRSTW
swarthing
wrathings

AGHMNOOPR
monograph
nomograph
phonogram

AGHMOOPRT
photogram
tomograph

AGIIILNNT
intailing
liniating

AGIIKNRST
straiking
traikings

AGIILNNPT
pantiling
plainting

AGIILNORS
originals
sailoring
signorial

AGIILNORT
largition
tailoring

AGIILNQSU
quailings
squailing

AGIIMNOST
atomising
sigmation

AGIIMNRST
maistring
misrating

AGIINNORT
arointing
rationing

AGIINNQTU
antiquing
quainting

AGIINNRST
rantising
straining
trainings

AGIINNRTU
ruinating
urinating

AGIINNSTT
instating
taintings

AGIINPRST
piratings
spirating
traipsing

AGIINPSTT
pistating
stipating

AGIINRSTT
attirings
straiting
striating
traisting

AGILLNOSW
allowings
sallowing

AGILLNOTT
allotting
totalling

AGILNNSTU
unlasting
unsalting
unslating

AGILNPRST
plastring
spartling

AGILNPRSY
raspingly
sparingly

AGILNRSTT
rattlings
startling

AGILNRSTW
warstling
wrastling

AGILNRSTY
staringly
strayling

AGIMNNORS
amornings
ransoming

AGIMNNOTU
amounting
outnaming

AGIMNNRSU
manurings
surnaming

AGIMNORST
sigmatron
stroaming

AGIMNPRST
stramping
trampings

AGINNOPRT
patroning
pronating

AGINNORST
ignorants
stroaning

AGINOPRRT
parroting
prorating

AGINOPRST
asporting
pastoring

AGINORSST
assorting
organists
roastings

AGINOSSTT
assotting
stoatings
tangoists
toastings

AGINPPRST
strapping
trappings

AGINPRSTU
pasturing
upstaring

AGINQSTTU
quattings
squatting

AGLMPRSUU
lump sugar
sugar lump
sugarplum

AGMMNOORS
groomsman
monograms

AHINNOPTY
antiphony
Typhonian

AIINNORTU
ruination
urination

AIINORTTT
attrition
titration

AIIOPRSTT
parotitis
topiarist

AILMNORTY
normality
trionymal

AILNOORST
tonsorial
torsional

AILNOPSTU
platinous
pulsation

AILNORSTU
insulator
Solutrian

AILORSUVY
savourily
variously

AINNNOSTU
unisonant
unnations

AINOOPPRT
appointor
apportion

AINOOPRRT
proration
troparion

AINOPRSST
postnaris
sopranist

AINOPRSTU
Proustian
supinator

AIOOPRSUV
apivorous
oviparous

BBEEILPST
pebbliest
plebbiest

BBEGIINRR
bribering
rebribing

BBEINSSTU
snubbiest
tubbiness

BCDEEIRRS
describer
rescribed

BCEEEFHNR
beech fern
free bench

BCEGIMNRU
cumbering
recumbing

BCEKOORRR
cork borer
rock borer

BDDEELORU
bouldered
redoubled

BDDEENORU
boundered»
rebounded

BDEEGHINT
benedight
benighted

BDEEIRRST
bestirred
bestrider

BDEERSSUV
subserved
subversed

BDEHNRSUU
unbrushed
underbush

BEEEGIMNT
bemeeting
beteeming

BEEILLRTU
bulletrie
rubellite

BEELMRRSU
lumberers
slumberer

BEELORSVY
obversely
verbosely

BEFHIRRSU
brush fire
furbisher
refurbish

BEGIILMNO
bemoiling
emboiling

BEGIILMNR
limbering
relimbing

BEGILLNOW
bellowing
bowelling

BEGILNORT
boltering
rebolting

BEGINRTTU
buttering
rebutting

BEHILPRSU
publisher
republish

BENRTTTUU
butternut
nut butter

BGIIMNRSU
imbruings
imbursing

BGILMNSTU
stumbling
tumblings

BGILNRSTU
blurtings
brustling
burstling

CCDEEEHKR
checkered
rechecked

CCDEENORS
conceders
crescendo

CCEENNORT
concenter
concentre
connecter
reconnect

CCEIIIRST
criticise
sericitic

CCHIILORT
chloritic
trochilic

CDDEEINRS
discerned
rescinded

CDEEEINRS
deceniers
residence

CDEEEIRST
decistere
resceited

CDEEEPRST
respected
sceptered

CDEEFIIRT
certified
rectified

CDEEGIILN
ceilinged
diligence

CDEEGINPR
decerping
preceding

CDEEGINRS
recedings
screeding

CDEEGNOST
congested
decongest

CDEEIIMRV
decemviri
vermicide

CDEEILNST
denticles
stenciled

CDEEINRST
cisterned
stridence

CDEEIRSTT
decretist
directest
trisected

CDEEIRTTU
certitude
rectitude

CDEENORST
centrodes
constered

CDEENORSV
conserved
conversed

CDEENORTU
countered
recounted

CDEENRSTU
encrusted
uncrested

CDEEOPRRU
procedure
reproduce

CDEGIINRT
crediting
directing

CDEGINRSY
decryings
descrying

CDEGINSSU
decussing
seducings

CDEHINORT
chondrite
threnodic

CDEIIMRST
miscredit
misdirect

CDEIINORT
cretinoid
direction

CDEIKLNSU
klendusic
unsickled

CDEINNOTU
continued
unnoticed

CDEINOPRS
conspired
incorpsed

CDEINORTU
introduce»
reduction

CEEEHIRST
cheeriest
reechiest

CEEEILRST
electrise
Leicester

CEEEIMRRS
merceries
mercerise
remercies

CEEENNRST
secernent
sentencer

CEEENNSST
senescent
sentences

CEEFIIRRT
certifier
rectifier

CEEFIIRST
certifies
rectifies

CEEFINORR
confrerie
reinforce

CEEGHINPS
cheepings
speeching

CEEGHINRS
cheerings
creeshing
reechings

CEEGHINRW
Greenwich
rechewing

CEEGILNST
electings
selecting

CEEGINNRS
censering»

recensing
screening
secerning

CEEGINNRT
centering
centreing
recenting

CEEGINORS
congeries
recognise

CEEGINPTX
excepting
expecting

CEEGINRST
erectings
gentrices
resecting
secreting

CEEHIKNRT
kitchener
thickener

CEEHISSTT
chestiest
esthetics

CEEHORRST
hectorers
Rochester
rocheters
torcheres

CEEIILNST
insectile
selenitic

CEEIKNQRU
quickener
requicken

CEEIKOPRW
piecework
workpiece

CEEILMRSS
crimeless
merciless

CEEILNOPR
crepoline
pencil ore

CEEILOSSS
isosceles
solecises

CEEINNORS
nine score
recension

CEEINORST
erections
necrotise
neoterics
resection
secretion

CEEINPRST
prentices
prescient
reinspect

CEEIRSSTU
cerusites
cerussite
icteruses

CEELNORSU
counseler
enclosure
recounsel

CEENORRTV
converter
reconvert

CEEORRSST
crosstree
rectoress

CEFHMOORT
forthcome
home croft

CEFIMNORR
confirmer
reconfirm

CEFMOORRT
comforter
recomfort

CEGGILOST
cloggiest
coggliest

CEGHIINNR
enriching
inhercing
nichering
richening

CEGHILOOT
ethologic
theologic

CEGHINOOT
Neo-Gothic
theogonic

CEGHINORS
coshering
ocherings
ochreings

CEGHINORT
hectoring
tochering

CEGIIKLNN
lickening
nickeling

CEGIINNPT
incepting
peincting
penticing

CEGIINPRS
piercings
precising
respicing

CEGIINRSV
screiving
scrieving
servicing

CEGIKLNOR
lockering
relocking

CEGILNOOR
coolering
recooling

CEGILNRSU
reclusing
surcingle

CEGILNRTU
lecturing
relucting

CEGINNORS
censoring
consigner
necrosing
reconsign

CEGINORST
corseting
escorting
recosting
sectoring

CEGINORTV
coverting
vectoring

CEGINPRST
sceptring
spectring

CEHIILNOT
ichnolite
Neolithic

CEHIINPRT
nephritic
phrenitic

CEHIIPRTT
perthitic
tephritic

CEHILNPSU
siphuncle
uncleship

CEHINOPST
Ctesiphon
phonetics

CEHINRSST
christens
snitchers

CEHIORRST
chorister»

rhetorics

CEHIOSTTU
couthiest
touchiest

CEIIMOPST
impeticos
poeticism

CEIIMORST
eroticism
isometric
meroistic

CEIIMOSST
misticoes
semiotics

CEIINORRT
criterion
tricerion

CEIKNORSS
corkiness
rockiness

CEIKOPRRT
rock tripe
rope trick

CEILMOPRY
micropyle
polymeric

CEILNORSU
inclosure
reclusion

CEILNORUV
involucre
volucrine

CEINNORTU
centurion
continuer

CEINOPRST
inceptors
inspector

CEINORSTT
contrites
cornetist

CEIORRSTT
tortrices
trisector

CEIORRSTU
courtiers
scruitore
scrutoire

CEIPRRSTU
picturers
scripture

CEOPRRSSU
percussor
procuress

CFOOORSTW
crowfoots
crow's foot

CGGIINNOS
cognising
cosigning

CGGINORSU
scourging
scrouging

CGHIIMNRS
chrisming
smirching

CGHIINSTT
stitching
titchings

CGHIMNOSU
mouchings
smouching

CGIIKLNST
stickling
ticklings

CGIIMNPRS
crimpings
scrimping

CGIINNOOT
cognition
incognito

CGINNOOTT
cotton gin
cottoning

CGINNORST
constring
scontring

CGINNORTU
cornuting
trouncing

CGINORTUY
congruity
crying out
outcrying

CHIKOPSTW
stock whip
whipstock

CIILNOPTU
punctilio
unpolitic

CIIOPRSTT
proctitis
protistic
tropistic

CIMNOOPTY
monotypic
toponymic

DDEEENORW
endowered
re-endowed

DDEEEPRSS
depressed
despersed

DDEEGHILT
delighted
gilthedde

DDEEGILNR
engirdled
leddering

DDEEILMOZ
melodized
modelized

DDEEINORW
eiderdown
re-indowed

DDEEINRSU
underside
undesired

DDEELMORU
mouldered
remoulded

DDEENOPRS
desponder
responded

DDEENOPRT
portended
protended

DDEENORRU
underdoer
unordered

DDEFGINRU
drug fiend
fuddering

DDEGINNRU
dundering
ruddening

DDEINOSSW
disendows
dowdiness

DDEINRSSU
dissunder
ruddiness

DDGILNPSU
puddlings
spuddling

DEEEENPST
ensteeped
steepened

DEEEFMNRT
deferment
fermented

DEEEGINNR
endeering»
ingenered

DEEEGINRS
energised
Niger seed
reseeding

DEEEILRRV
deliverer
redeliver
relivered

DEEEINRST
eternised
tenderise
teredines

DEEEINRTZ
eternized
tenderize

DEEELOPRV
developer
redevelop

DEEEMORSU
deer mouse
mouse deer

DEEENPRST
presented
serpented

DEEENRSTT
stentered
tenderest
testerned

DEEENRSUV
undeserve
unsevered

DEEEPRRSS
depresser
repressed

DEEEPRRSV
perversed
preserved

DEEEPRSST
depesters
speedster

DEEFGINRR
deferring
refringed

DEEFILRTT
flittered
reflitted

DEEGGINNR
dengering
gendering

DEEGHILNT
enlighted
lightened

DEEGHILRT
delighter
relighted

DEEGHINRT
enrighted
rightened

DEEGHNORU
enroughed
roughened

DEEGIINRT
re-editing
reignited

DEEGILNRS
deerlings
derelings
derlinges
engirdles
reedlings
slingered

DEEGILNST
glistened
legendist

DEEGINNRT
retending
tendering

DEEGINPRS
presigned
spreeding

DEEGINRSS
designers»
ingressed
redesigns

DEEGINRST
deserting
detersing

DEEGNORSS
engrossed
grossened

DEEHIORST
rehoisted
theorised

DEEHIRRTW
wherrited
whirreted

DEEHIRSTW
swithered
whistered

DEEHNORRT
dethroner
northered
rethroned

DEEHNORST
dethrones
shortened
threnodes

DEEIINSST
densities
destinies

DEEILLRST
tredilles
trellised

DEEILLRSV
devillers
ill-versed

DEEILOPRS
despoiler
pelorised

DEEILRSST
slestired
slide rest
slistered

DEEIMMRST
mismetred
mistermed
stimmered

DEEIMNORS
demersion
domineers
domineres
modernise

DEEIMNRTU
undertime
unmerited
unmitered

DEEIMPRRT
permitted
premitted

DEEIMPRST
distemper
imprested

DEEIMRSST
demisters
misdesert

DEEINNRST
dinner set
indenters
intenders
reintends
set dinner

DEEINORST
desertion
detersion

DEEINPRST
president
spritened

DEEINRSST
disenters
dissenter
indeserts
residents
tiredness

DEEINRSTT
snittered
trendiest
tristened

DEEIOPRST
depositer
peridotes
poetrised
poistered
redeposit
reposited

DEEIOPSST
deposites
seposited

DEEIRRSTV
restrived
verditers

DEEIRSTTW
retwisted
switterеd
twistered

DEEKNORST
stonkered
storkened

DEELLMORS
modellers
morselled

DEELLNORS
norselled
rondelles

DEELNPRRU
plunderer
replunder

DEELORRSS
orderless
resolders
solderers

DEELORSTT
dotterels
slottered

DEELPPSTU
septupled
suppleted

DEEMOORST
odometers
osteoderm

DEENNORTU
undernote
undertone

DEENOPRRS
ponderers
reponders
responder

DEENPRSSU
suspender
unpressed

DEENRRSSU
sunderers
undresser

DEENRRSTU
entruders
unredrest

DEENRSSTU
sederunts
undersets
undeserts
untressed

DEEOPRSTT
protested
respotted

DEFGIINNR
friending
infringed
refinding

DEFIIRTVY
devitrify
fervidity

DEFLNORUW
underflow
wonderful

DEGGIILNR
gildering
regilding

DEGGIINNR
dreigning
engirding
ingreding

DEGGIINNS
designing
sdeigning

DEGGILNNO
engolding
goldening

DEGHIILNS
heildings
hieldings
hiledings
shielding

DEGHIINST
insighted
nightside

DEGHILNTU
undelight
unlighted

DEGHINRTU
ungirthed
unrighted

DEGIIIMRS
dirigisme
semirigid

DEGIIIRST
digitiser
dirigiste

DEGIILNRS
gridelins
grisdelin
resliding

DEGIIMMNR
dimmering
immerding

DEGIINNNT
indenting
intending

DEGIINNRW
rewinding
windering

DEGIINNST
destining
indigents»
teindings

DEGIINPRS
deprising
presiding

DEGIINSST
desisting
indigests

DEGILLNOW
dowelling
well-doing

DEGILMNOR
goldminer
moldering
remolding

DEGILNNTU
indulgent
untelding

DEGILNOPR
deploring
poldering

DEGIMNRRU
demurring
murdering

DEGINNORS
endorsing
sondering

DEGINNORW
drowening
wondering

DEGINNRSU
endurings
sundering
undersign

DEGINNRTU
deturning
entruding
retunding

DEGINOPSS
deposings
desposing
disponges
podginess

DEGINORTT
detorting
dottering

DEGINORTU
derouting
detouring

DEGINPSSU
dispunges
pudginess

DEGINRSTU
detrusing
redusting

DEHINOSST
dishonest
hedonists

DEIINRSST
dirtiness
disinters

DEIIORSSS
disseisor
siderosis

DEILLOPST
pistolled
postilled

DEILOSSTU
dissolute
solitudes

DEINORSSW
rowdiness
windroses
wordiness

DEINORSTU
detrusion
roundiest
unstoried

DEINRRSTU
intruders
unstirred

DEINRSTTU
intrusted
untristed

DENOORSTU
tournedos
unroosted

DFGILNNOU
foundling
unfolding

DGHINORTW
downright
rightdown

DGIINNOPS
disponing
poindings

DGIINNORS
Girondins
indorsing

DGILNNORU
roundling
unlording

EEEFHNRRS
freshener
refreshen

EEEGIMNRT
meetinger
remeeting

EEEGIRSTY
geyserite
tigereyes
tiger's-eye

EEEHNRSST
thereness
threeness

EEEILSSTT
sleetiest
steeliest

EEEINRSST
estreines
eternises
sneeriest

EEEINRSTT
reinettes
serinette
teentsier

EEEIPRRTT
pierrette
preterite

EEEIRSSTT
reestiest
steeriest

EEENPRRST
presenter
repenters
represent
re-repents
serpenter

EEENRSSST
entresses
tenessers
terseness

EEEPRRRSV
perverser
preserver

EEFGIINNR
fineering
neifering

EEFGINRRT
ferreting
fertering

EEFHILLRS
fleshlier
shellfire

EEFHILSST
fleshiest
shelfiest

EEFHOORRS
forehorse
foreshore

EEFIIRRSV
verifiers
versifier

EEFINORST
firestone
forestine

EEGGINRST
gee-string»
gestering
greetings
regesting

EEGHILMNT
helmeting
metheglin

EEGHILRST
leighster
leighters
sleighter

EEGHIMOST
egotheism
eightsome

EEGHINRTT
tethering
tightener

EEGIILNRV
inveigler
relieving
reveiling

EEGIINRRT
reitering
reteiring
retiering

EEGILLNRY
leeringly
reelingly

EEGILNPRT
peltering
repleting

EEGILNPST
spleeting
steepling

EEGILNRST
steerling
streeling

EEGILNRTT
lettering
reletting

EEGILNRVY
relevying
veeringly

EEGINNRST
enterings
resenting

EEGINNRTT
retenting
tentering

EEGINNRTU
neutering
untreeing

EEGINNRTV
reventing
ventering

EEGINNSTV
envesting
eventings
stevening

EEGINPRST
estreping
pestering

EEGINRRSV
reserving
reversing

EEGINRSTT
retesting
settering
streeting
teterings
treetings

EEGINRSTV
evertings
revesting

EEGINRSTW
swingtree
tweerings
westering

EEGINRSTX
exertings
exserting
extersing

EEGINRTTV
revetting
vignetter

EEHINOPSU
euphonise
pinehouse

EEHIORRST
rhetorise
theoriser

EEHIORRTZ
rhetorize
theorizer

EEHIORSST
heterosis
hosteries
isotheres
theorises

EEHIPRSST
spheriest
treeships

EEHLNOPTY
polythene
telephony

EEHLORSSS
horseless
shoreless

EEHNORRST
rethrones
shortener

EEHOORSVW
howsoever
whosoever

EEIILRSST
Listerise
sterilise

EEIILRSTZ
Listerize
sterilize

EEIIRSSTT
reistiest
sestertii

EEILMNOST
limestone
milestone

EEILNOPRT
interlope
repletion
terpineol

EEILNOSSS
lionesses
noiseless

EEILOPRST
epistoler
piloteers
pistoleer

EEILPRSUV
prelusive
pulverise
repulsive

EEILRRSSV
resilvers
riverless
silverers

EEIMMRSST
meristems
mesmerist
mimesters
mismetres

EEIMNORSS
emersions
sermonise

EEIMNORST
moistener
neoterism

EEIMNOSST
mestinoes
monetises
semitones

EEIMOPRST
peristome
temporise

EEIMPRRTT
permitter
pretermit

EEIMPRSSS
impresses
premisses

EEIMRRSTT
remitters
trimester
trimestre
trimeters
trimetres

EEINNOPRT
interpone
tin opener

EEINNOPST
penistone
stone pine

EEINNPRST
serpentin
spinneret

EEINNRSST
inertness
tennisers

EEINNRSSV
Inverness
nerviness

EEINOPPST
peptonise
pipestone

EEINORRSV
reversion
versioner

EEINORSTT
neoterist
tenorites

EEINRRSTV
inverters
reinverts
restriven

EEINRSSTT
insetters
interests
resistent
sternites
triteness

EEIORRRST
roisterer
terrorise

EEIPRRSTT
preterist
preterits

EEIRRSSTV
reservist
restrives
reverists
serviters

EELOPRSTY
polyester
proselyte

EEMMNOORT
metronome
monometer
monotreme

EEMOOPRTT
optometer
potometer

EEOPRRSTT
potterers
protester

EEOPRSSTU
pesterous
pestreous
proteuses

EEORRSTVW
overstrew
overwrest

EEORSTTTU
outsetter
setter out
tetterous

EFGHIILRT
firelight
flightier

EFGHINORT
forenight
fothering

EFGHIORST
foresight
grief-shot

EFGIILNRT
fertiling
filtering
relifting

EFGIINNRR
inferring
infringer

EFGIINNST
festining
infesting

EFGIINRST
fringiest
resifting

EFGIINRTT
fittering
refitting

EFGILNORW
flowering
reflowing

EFGINNOST
festoning
softening

EFGINOORT
footering
refooting

EFGINORST
foresting
fostering

EFHIISSTT
fetishist
shiftiest

EFHILORST
rifle shot
short life

EFHINRRSU
furnisher
refurnish

EFHIORSTT
forthiest
fortieths
frothiest

EFIINORRS
fire irons
inferiors

EFIMORRST
fire storm
reformist
restiform

EGGGIINNR
gingering
niggering
renigging

EGGIILNNR
ingreling
lingering

EGGIIMMNR
gimmering
immerging

EGGIINNRS
reignings
resigning
re-signing

EGGIINNST
ingesting
signeting
tingeings

EGGILNNOR
longering
relonging

EGGINOORV
going-over
overgoing

EGHIILNRS
hirelings
hirseling
relishing

EGHIILNRT
girthline
lithering

EGHIILNST
gentilish
sightline

EGHIIMNRT
hermiting
mithering

EGHIINRSV
shivering
shrieving

EGHILNSST
lightness
nightless
slightens

EGHILRSST
rightless
slighters

EGHLNOOPY
nephology
phenology

EGHLNOORS
longshore
sloghorne

EGHNOSSTU
oughtness
toughness

EGIIJNNOR
joinering
rejoining

EGIILLMNR
millering
rimelling

EGIILLNRT
retilling
tillering

EGIILNNST
enlisting
enstiling
listening
tinseling

EGIILNNTT
entitling
inletting
littening

EGIILNORS
niger oils»
religions
resoiling

EGIILNRST
girtlines
listering
tirelings

EGIILNRSV
liverings
relivings
revilings
rivelings
silvering
slivering

EGIILNRTT
littering
tiltering

EGIIMMNRS
immersing
simmering

EGIIMNPRS
emprising
premising
simpering

EGIIMNRSS
griminess
remissing
semi-rings

EGIIMNRST
meritings
mistering
miterings
ring times

EGIINNNRT
interning
retinning

EGIINNPRS
enspiring
repinings
spreining

EGIINNRST
inresting
inserting
streining

EGIINNRTU
retinuing
reuniting

EGIINNSTV
investing
stevining

EGIINPRRS
reprising
respiring
springier

EGIINPRST
pistering
priesting
respiting

EGIINRRST
retirings
stringier

EGIINRSST
reistings
resisting
sistering

EGIINRSTT
resitting
string tie
tie-string

EGIJLNORT
joltering
rejolting

EGILLNORR
re-rolling
rollering

EGILLNORS
Negrillos
sollering

EGILMNOOS
Mongolise
neologism

EGILMNPRU
lumpering
repluming

EGILNNOSU
ensouling»

nouseling

EGILNORST
Lestrigon
ostlering

EGILNORSW
lowerings
rowelings
slowering

EGILNRSTU
lustering
resulting
sultering
ulstering

EGILNRSTW
sweltring
wrestling

EGINNNOST
sonneting
tenonings

EGINNORST
ensorting
enstoring
nitrogens

EGINNOSTT
onsetting
ostenting

EGINNRSTU
insurgent
unresting

EGINOPRRT
portering
reporting

EGINOPRST
prestoing
progestin
reposting

EGINOPRTT
pottering
pottinger
repotting

EGINORRST
ostringer»

resorting
re-sorting
restoring
rostering

EGINORRTU
rerouting
retouring
routering

EGINORSTT
gritstone
sottering
stotering

EGINORSTW
restowing
towerings

EGINRSSST
stressing
tressings

EGINSSSTU
gustiness
gutsiness

EHIINPRST
nephritis
phrenitis

EHILNOOPT
lithopone
phonolite

EHILRSSST
shirtless
thrissels

EHINOPRSW
ownership
ship owner

EHINORSSS
herissons
horsiness

EHIOPRSST
prothesis
sophister
store ship

EHIORSTTU
routhiest»

stouthrie

EHKOORSUW
housework
workhouse

EIILPRSTU
pleuritis
spirituel

EIIMNORSS
missioner
remission

EIIMNPRST
Petrinism
strip mine

EIINNSSTT
insistent
tintiness

EIINRTTUV
nutritive
vetturini

EIKORSTTU
outstrike
strikeout

EILLMNOST
millstone
stone mill

EILLOPRSV
overspill
spillover

EILNOPRSU
prelusion
repulsion

EILNPRSST
printless
splinters
sprintles

EIMMOOPRU
pomoerium
prooemium

EIMNNOSTT
ointments
stonemint

EIMNOORSS
moonrises
roominess

EIMNOPRTU
entropium
importune

EINNOOPRT
entropion
pontonier
prenotion

EINNOORST
ironstone
serotonin

EINNSSTTU
nuttiness
sustinent

EINOOPSST
snoopiest
spooniest

EINOPRSTU
eruptions
pertusion

EINORSSTT
snortiest
tenorists

EINRSSSTU
rustiness
unsisters

EIOOPRRST
posterior
repositor

EMMNORSSU
resummons
summoners
summonser

EMNORSSTT
sortments
sternmost

ENOOPPRST
postponer
pronepots

FGHIINRST
frithings
shrifting

FGIILNRST
firstling
flirtings
triflings

FHLLRTUUY
hurtfully
ruthfully

GGGIILNNS
ginglings
nigglings
sniggling

GGGIINPRS
priggings
sprigging

GGGIINRST
strigging
triggings

GGHIILNST
lightings
slighting

GGILNNPSU
plungings
splunging

GHINNORSU
onrushing
unhorsing

GIIKLNNST
skintling
sklinting
tinklings

GIILNOPST
pistoling
postiling

GIILNPPST
stippling
tipplings

GIILNPRST
spirtling
stripling»

triplings

GIILNPSTT
spittling
splitting

GIIMNNSTU
minutings
mistuning
munitings
mutinings

GIINNORST
ignitrons
instoring

GIINNPRST
printings
sprinting
string pin

GIINOPSST
positings
possiting

GIINPPRST
stripping
trippings

GIINPRSSU
suspiring
uprisings

GILLNORST
strolling
trollings

GILMNOSTU
moultings
smoulting

GINOOPRSS
prognosis
spoorings

GINOPRSST
sportings
Stringops

GINOPRSTU
outspring
posturing
sprouting
troupings

GINOPSSTU
possuting
spoutings

GINORSTTU
strouting
troutings
tutorings

HIIMORSST
historism
histrioms
hit-or-miss

IINORSTTU
introitus
routinist

AAACEINPST
anapaestic
sea captain

AAAILNRSTU
Australian
Saturnalia

AABCILRSTU
arcubalist
ultrabasic

AABEELMNNU
unamenable
unnameable

AABEELMSTT
metastable
stablemate

AABEELRRST
arbalester
arbalestre
arrestable

AABEELRTTW
table water
water table

AABEILRRST
arbalister
breastrail

AACCDELRST
card castle
cat's cradle

AACCEHINRS
cane chairs
saccharine

AACDEGLOTU
catalogued
coagulated

AACDEIORRT
Cortaderia
eradicator

AACEEINPRT
Capernaite
paraenetic

AACEGIMNRT
camerating
macerating

AACEHILMPT
alphametic
emphatical

AACEIINTTV
inactivate
vaticinate

AACEILMNOT
Celtomania
noematical

AACEILNORT
creational
laceration

AACEIMNORT
cameration
maceration
racemation

AACELMPRST
campestral
scrap metal

AACFIILNOR
African oil
California

AACGILNPTY
anaglyptic
play acting

AACGILNSTY
catalysing
staylacing

AACHIMNORS
harmonicas
maraschino

AACHIMNORT
achromatin
machinator

AACIINOTTV
activation
cavitation

AACINORTUY
auctionary
cautionary

AACINPRSTT
pancratist
practisant

AADEEHMRST
headmaster
headstream

AADEEIMNTX
examinated
exanimated

AADEIIMNNT
diamantine
inanimated
maintained

AADELMNPTU
datum plane
paludament

AADIILPRST
lapidarist
triapsidal

AAEEGINRTV
renavigate
vegetarian

AAEGHMNOPR
anemograph
phanerogam

AAEGHOPRRY
aerography
areography

AAEGIMNRRS
margarines
misarrange

AAEGIMRSTT
magistrate
sterigmata

AAEGINPRST
asperating
paste grain
separating

AAEIILMNRS
laminarise
seminarial

AAEIILNNOT
alienation
alineation

AAEILLPRST
plate rails
psalterial

AAEILNORST
alienators
rationales
senatorial

AAEILNORTV
venatorial
Voltairean

AAEINOPRRT
praetorian
reparation

AAELLNPRTY
parentally
paternally

AAGGIINNTV
navigating
vaginating

AAGHILNPST
asphalting
phalangist

AAGIINPRST
aspirating
parasiting

AAGILLMNRY
alarmingly
marginally

AAGINNOSTT
antagonist
stagnation

AAIILMNNOT
antimonial
lamination

AAIILMPRST
partialism
patrialism

AAIINOPRTT
patriation
tritanopia

AAILLNORTY
notarially
rationally

AAILMNRSTU
naturalism
unmartials

AAIMNORTTU
maturation
natatorium

ABCDEIIORT
aborticide
bacterioid

ABCDEIPRRS
crispbread
spider crab

ABCEEHIRST
breachiest
Rechabites

ABDEEHINRT
hibernated
inbreathed

ABDEELNORS
banderoles
bandoleers
endorsable

ABDEGINNOR
boardening
broadening

ABEEHORTTU
outbreathe
thereabout

ABEEILNSUZ
unseizable
unsizeable

ABEELMNRSU
Lebensraum
mensurable

ABEFILLLNU
unfallible
unfillable

ABEGIILNRT
Gilbertian
liberating

ABEGIINNST
besainting
bestaining

ABEGINNRST
banterings
string bean

ABEHNORSST
bassethorn
stonebrash

ABEILMNRTY
liberty man
terminably

ABEKKORSTW
basketwork
work basket

ABELMMNOSU
somnambule
summonable

ABGIIILNST
albitising
sibilating

ABIILNOTTY
bitonality
notability

ABINOOPRST
absorption
probations

ACCDEORSTU
accoustred
coruscated

ACCEEMNRST
marcescent»
scarcement

ACCEENORST
concreates
consecrate

ACCEHINORT
Acherontic
anchoretic

ACCEHNORTT
technocrat
trench coat

ACCEILMOST
cacomistle
cosmetical

ACCEINORST
accretions
cestracion

ACCHIIMSST
mica schist
schismatic

ACDEEEFLNR
fer-de-lance
freelanced

ACDEEHLLST
death cells
satchelled

ACDEEILNRT
credential
interlaced
reclinated

ACDEEILPRY
dice player
icy-pearled

ACDEEIMNRT
endermatic
incremated

ACDEEIMRST
decimaters
medicaster
miscreated

ACDEEINNTU
denunciate»
enunciated

ACDEELNRTU
calentured
crenulated

ACDEELORTU
edulcorate
urceolated

ACDEEOPRRT
deprecator
procreated
tape record

ACDEGIIMNT
decimating
medicating

ACDEIIILST
idealistic
italicised

ACDEIILPST
pesticidal
septicidal

ACDEIIMNOT
decimation
medication

ACDEIMNORS
dormancies
mordancies

ACDEIMORST
decimators
medicastor

ACDEINOORT
carotenoid
coordinate
decoration

ACDEINPRST
discrepant
predicants

ACDEIRSTTU
dictatures
rusticated

ACDELMNOTU
columnated»
documental

ACDGIINOST
dacoitings
diagnostic

ACDIIMNSTY
dynamicist
dynamistic

ACDIINORTY
dictionary
indicatory

ACEEEIRSTV
eviscerate
tea service

ACEEENNPRT
penetrance
repentance

ACEEGHINRT
recheating
reteaching
teachering

ACEEGIORST
categories
categorise

ACEEHHIRST
hatcheries
thearchies

ACEEHIPRST
patcheries
petcharies
preachiest

ACEEIINNRT
creatinine
incinerate

ACEEILMNST
centesimal
lemniscate

ACEEILNRST
centralise
interlaces

ACEEILNRTV
cantilever»
trivalence

ACEEILPPRT
preceptial
tea clipper

ACEEILRTVY
creatively
reactively

ACEEIMPRST
imprecates
spermaceti

ACEEIMRSST
cramesiest
ice streams
miscreates
screamiest

ACEEINNRST
ancienters
nectarines
transience

ACEEINORRT
recreation
re-reaction

ACEEINPPRT
apprentice
pine carpet

ACEENNORTV
contravene
covenanter

ACEENORSTU
nectareous
raconteuse

ACEGHIMNRR
charminger
remarching

ACEGHINNTU
uncheating
unteaching

ACEGIKNRST
restacking
retackings
stackering

ACEHIPRSTU
curateship
pasticheur

ACEHKLNOST
chalkstone
Shackleton
shecklaton

ACEHNRSSTU
chauntress
staunchers

ACEIIIMNST
imitancies
intimacies
minacities

ACEIILPSST
plastecise
specialist

ACEIINOSTV
noviciates
vesication

ACEIINOTTX
excitation
intoxicate

ACEIINPSTT
antiseptic
psittacine

ACEIINSSTT
sanctities
scantities

ACEIIRTTVY
creativity
reactivity

ACEILLORST
corallites
sclerotial

ACEILMNORS
coal miners
sermonical

ACEILNOORT
corelation
co-relation
iconolater»
relocation

ACEILNOPST
neoplastic
pleonastic
point laces

ACEILNOPTU
peculation
unpoetical

ACEILNORTU
inoculater
ulceration

ACEILNOSTU
inoculates
inosculate

ACEILOOSUV
olivaceous
violaceous

ACEILRSTTU
testicular
trisulcate

ACEIMNOPTT
camptonite
pentatomic

ACEINNNOSU
uncanonise
unisonance

ACEINNORTU
enunciator
uncreation

ACEINOPSTT
constipate
costean pit

ACEINORRTT
retraction
triaconter

ACEINORSTU
cautioners
recusation

ACELOOPRRT
coal porter
percolator

ACELOPRSTU
peculators
speculator

ACFGIINNRT
infarcting
infracting

ACFIINNORT
infarction
infraction

ACGHHINTTW
night watch
watch night

ACGIINNOTU
auctioning
cautioning

ACGILMNNOO
cognominal
gnomonical

ACGILORSUY
glycosuria
graciously

ACIINNOSTU
incautions
insouciant

ACIINOPRST
ascription
crispation

ACIINRSTTU
naturistic
unartistic

ACILLNOSTU
clout nails
Collatinus

ACIMNOPRTY
importancy
patronymic
pyromantic

ACINNORSST
constrains
transonics
trans-sonic

ADDEEENRTT
attendered
reattended

ADDEEGHLNO
headlonged
longheaded

ADDENNRSTU
redundants
understand

ADEEENRRSW
newsreader
reanswered

ADEEGIMNNR
meandering
reamending

ADEEGINPRT
interpaged
pignerated

ADEEGINRRT
gradienter
intergrade
retreading

ADEEHILPRS
dealership
leadership

ADEEHNNRTU
unadherent
underneath

ADEEIKNRRT
dreikanter
tea drinker

ADEEILNORT
delineator
relationed

ADEEILNRSU
unrealised
Uredinales

ADEEILPRST
pilastered
plaistered
prelatised
resplaited

ADEEIMNNOT
denominate
emendation

ADEEINRSTT
denitrates
straitened

ADEEINRSTU
denaturise
unreadiest
unsteadier

ADEEMNRSTU
unmastered
unstreamed

ADEGGINRRU
redarguing
reguarding

ADEGIILMNS
misdealing
misleading

ADEGIILNOT
deligation
gadolinite
gelatinoid
intaglioed

ADEGIINNST
destaining
detainings

ADEGIINPRS
despairing
diaperings
pinigrades
spinigrade

ADEGIINRST
granitised
integrands

ADEGILNNRS
relandings
sanderling
slandering

ADEGIMNNRU
maundering
undreaming

ADEGINNOTT
denotating
detonating

ADEGINOORT
derogation
Trogonidae

ADEGINOPRT
pignorated
readopting

ADEGINORRT
denigrator
gradientor

ADEGINPRSS
adpressing
spreadings

ADEHLMNORT
enthraldom
motherland

ADEIILRSTU
ritualised
uralitised

ADEIILRTUZ
ritualized
uralitized

ADEILNOPPT
pedal point
pentaploid

ADEINNOOTT
denotation
detonation

ADFGINORRW
forwarding
frowarding

ADIILNRSTU
diurnalist
industrial

ADIIMNNOOT
admonition
domination

AEEEINRTTV
entreative»
inveterate

AEEELMNNTT
lentamente
tenemental

AEEFGILPRS
persiflage
pilferages

AEEFLLRSSY
fearlessly
self-slayer

AEEGGILNRT
regelating
relegating

AEEGGINNRT
engreating
generating
greatening

AEEGHINNRT
earthening
enhearting
heartening

AEEGHINRRS
rehearings
rehearsing

AEEGILMNRT
remetaling
regimental

AEEGILNORT
regelation
relegation

AEEGILNRST
easterling
generalist

AEEGILNSTV
elevatings
evangelist

AEEGIMNPRT
impregnate
permeating

AEEGIMNRST
germinates»
magnetiser
steamering

AEEGINNORT
generation
renegation

AEEGINNRTV
enervating
venerating

AEEGINRSSV
assevering
vernissage

AEEGLNORTV
graveolent
lovat green

AEEGLOPRSU
grape louse
plague sore

AEEHILMPRT
epithermal
hemipteral

AEEHINRSST
earthiness
heartiness

AEEHMNOPRT
Heptameron
promethean

AEEHMOPRST
atmosphere
metaphores

AEEIILNRTT
retinalite
trilineate

AEEIILRSTV
relativise
revitalise

AEEIILRTVZ
relativize
revitalize

AEEILLMNST
eliminates
enamellist»
Milan steel

AEEILMNSTU
Mustelinae
semilunate

AEEILMRSST
misrelates
salimeters
semestrial

AEEILNPRST
alpestrine
episternal
interlapse
presential

AEEILPRSST
prelatises
psalteries

AEEIMNRSTT
martensite
misentreat
terminates

AEEIMRSSTT
streamiest
tasimeters

AEEINNORTV
enervation
veneration

AEEINRSSTW
earwitness
wateriness

AEEIPRRSTT
praeterist
praeterits

AEEIPRTTUV
reputative
vituperate

AEELMNORTW
lemon water
waterlemon
watermelon

AEELMRSSST
masterless
streamless
matterless
streamlets

AEELMRSSTT
matterless
streamlets

AEELNRSSTT
latterness
least terns

AEEMNORSST
sarmentose
sea monster

AEEMOPRSTW
pomewaters
steam power

AEENSSSTTU
astuteness
tautnesses

AEFGIMNNOR
foremaning
forenaming

AEGGIILNNR
engrailing
realigning

AEGGIIMNRT
emigrating
remigating

AEGHIINPST
aphetising
hepatising

AEGHIINPTZ
aphetizing
hepatizing

AEGHIINSTT
athetising
hesitating

AEGHILNRST
earthlings
halterings
heartlings
latherings
slathering

AEGHINNRTU
nightrauen
unearthing»

unhearting

AEGHINPRRS
rangership
rephrasing
springhare

AEGHINRSTT
shattering
straighten

AEGHINRSTV
harvesting
threavings

AEGHNOPRST
pot hangers
stenograph

AEGIILNNPS
penalising
spanieling

AEGIILNNRT
entrailing
trenailing

AEGIIMNORT
emigrating
remigation

AEGIIMNSTT
enigmatist
estimating

AEGIIMNSTV
negativism
timesaving

AEGIINNPRT
pertaining
repainting

AEGIINNRST
estraining
resinating
restaining
retainings

AEGIINNRTT
intreating
intrigante
taintering

AEGIINRSST
granitises
stingraies

AEGIINRSTT
granitites
instigater
iteratings
treatising

AEGIINRSTV
gainstrive
taiverings

AEGILLNORY
orange lily
regionally

AEGILLNPST
pastelling
stapelling

AEGILLORST
allegorist
legislator

AEGILNORTU
regulation
urogenital

AEGILNPRST
palterings
plastering
spaltering

AEGILNRSTV
starveling
travelings

AEGIMNORSU
gramineous
marigenous

AEGIMNPRST
restamping
tamperings

AEGIMNRSTT
matterings
smattering

AEGINNNPRT
partenning
trepanning

AEGINNORST
Argentinos
treasoning

AEGINNRSTT
astringent
integrants
rattenings
snattering

AEGINNRSTV
servanting
tavernings

AEGINRRSTU
austringer
garnitures

AEHINRSSST
starshines
trashiness

AEHIRSSTTW
swarthiest
sweatshirt

AEHLNOPSTU
house plant
plant house
sulphonate

AEIIILMRST
limitaries
militaries
militarise

AEIILMORST
molarities
moralities

AEIILNOTTV
levitation
tonalitive
velitation

AEIIMNNOST
antimonies
antinomies
Noetianism
semination

AEIINPSSST
antisepsis
inspissate

AEIINRSTTV
revisitant
transitive

AEILMNOPRS
impersonal
prolamines

AEILNOPRST
interposal
prelations
psalterion
rantipoles

AEINRSSSTT
resistants
straitness

AEKMORRSTW
masterwork
workmaster

AEMOPRSSTT
postmaster
sports team
steam ports
team sports

AEMORRSTTW
masterwort
storm water

AFGHHILLST
flashlight
half-lights

AFIILNORTT
filtration
flirtation

AGGHLOOPRY
graphology
logography

AGHINNOSTW
nowanights
Washington

AGHMNOOPRY
gramophony
monography
nomography

AGIILMNTTU
mutilating
ultimating

AGIILNPRSY
aspiringly
praisingly

AGIIMNSSTT
misstating
mistasting

AGIINNRRST
instarring
transiring

AGIMNNRSTU
transmuing
transuming

AHIIILNPPP
Philippian
philippina

AHNOOPSTTY
nostopathy
photonasty

AIILNOOPST
positional
spoliation

BDEFILOOST
fieldboots
soft-boiled

BDEGIINORR
broidering
riding robe

BDEGILNORU
bouldering
redoubling

BDEGINNORU
boundering
rebounding

BDEHNRRSUU
underbrush
undershrub

BEEEIMRRTT
embitterer»

timber tree

BEGILMNRSU
lumberings
slumbering

BEGILNORST
bolstering
bolterings
lobstering

BEGILNRSTU
blustering
butlerings

BEGINRSSUV
subserving
subversing

CCEEGINORT
egocentric
geocentric

CCEILNOSUV
conclusive
vice consul

CCEINNOORT
concertino
concertion

CDEEIINRST
cretinised
indiscreet
indiscrete
iridescent

CDEEIIORRT
cordierite
directoire
directorie

CDEEILRSTY
discreetly
discretely

CDEEINORST
necrotised
recondites

CDEEINRSST
directness
stridences

CDEEIORRSV
discoverer
rediscover

CDEEMOPRSS
compressed
decompress

CDEENORSTU
uncorseted
unescorted

CDEGIINNRS
discerning
rescinding

CDEIIIPSTU
cupidities
pudicities

CDEIILNRTY
cylindrite
indirectly

CDEIIMORTY
iridectomy
mediocrity

CDEIINORST
directions
discretion
soricident

CDEILNOSSU
cloudiness
discounsel

CEEEIPPRTV
perceptive
preceptive

CEEENRSSST
centresses
secretness

CEEGIINRST
genitrices
resceiting

CEEGINNORU
encoignure
neurogenic

CEEGINNRST
centerings
centreings
nigrescent

CEEGINOORT
erotogenic
orogenetic

CEEGINPRST
respecting
sceptering

CEEHINSSTT
stenchiest
tetchiness

CEEILNORST
encloister
relections

CEFGIINRTY
certifying
rectifying

CEGHIINRTT
chittering
retitching

CEGIIKLNNS
nickelings
slickening

CEGIIKNNRS
nickerings
snickering

CEGIKNORST
restocking
stockinger

CEGILNRSTU
clustering
lecturings

CEGINNNOTT
contenting
contingent

CEGINNORST
constering
constringe
conterings

CEGINNORSV
conserving
conversing

CEGINNORTU
countering
recounting

CEHIILMOST
homiletics
Mesolithic

CEHILOPRST
lectorship
splotchier

CEHILORSTY
chrisolyte
chrysolite
chrysotile

CEHINOPSTT
openstitch
pitchstone

CEHIOPRSTT
prosthetic
rope stitch

CEHMOOPRTY
chromotype
cormophyte
ectomorphy

CEIINNOPST
cispontine
inceptions
inspection

CEIINOPRST
isentropic
triniscope

CEIINRSSTU
scrutinies
scrutinise
sinecurist

CEINOPRSSU
croupiness
percussion
supersonic

CEINOPRSTT
cotter pins
introspect

CEOPRRRSUY
percursory
precursory

CFIILMOOSU
fimicolous
music folio

CGIIKLNRST
strickling
tricklings

CGIINNOPRS
conspiring
incorpsing

CHIINORSTU
trichinous
unhistoric

CHIKORSTTW
stitchwork
throwstick

DDEEEINNRT
indentered
reindented

DDEEEINRST
disentered
tenderised

DDEEFINNRU
reinfunded
unfriended

DDEEHNORSU
deerhounds
enshrouded

DDEEILLNRT
tendrilled
trindelled

DDEEIMNORS
endodermis
modernised

DDEEIMNRTU
rudimented»

undertimed

DDEEINORSW
disendower
eiderdowns

DDEENNORTU
undernoted
undertoned

DDEGINNORU
ingrounded
redounding
underdoing

DEEEFINRST
infestered
reinfested

DEEEFLORRW
deflowerer
reflowered

DEEEGINRSS
greediness
niger seeds
reseedings

DEEEILNRST
reenlisted
relistened

DEEEILRRSV
deliverers
redelivers
resilvered

DEEEIMNRST
determines
densimeter

DEEEINRRST
reinserted
residenter
tenderiser

DEEELRRSVY
reservedly
reversedly

DEEENRRSUV
undeserver
unreserved
unreversed

DEEFNORSTU
unforested
unfostered

DEEGINNORW
endowering
re-endowing

DEEGINPRSS
depressing
despersing
spreedings

DEEHINPRSU
repunished
unperished

DEEIILRSST
Listerised
sterilised

DEEIILRSTZ
Listerized
sterilized

DEEIINRSST
insistered
reinsisted

DEEIMNORSS
modernises
sermonised

DEEIMRSSST
misdeserts
mistressed

DEEINRSSTU
unresisted
unsistered

DEGIILMNOZ
melodizing
modelizing

DEGILMNORU
mouldering
remoulding

DEGILNNRUY
enduringly
underlying

DEGINNOPRT
portending
protending

DEGINNRSSU
sunderings
undersigns
undressing

DEGINRSSTU
detrussing
turgidness

EEEGINNPST
ensteeping
steepening

EEEIINRSTT
entireties
eternities

EEEILNSSST
sleetiness
steeliness

EEEIMNNPRT
pre-eminent
repinement

EEEINPRSTV
presentive
vespertine

EEEMNSSSTU
mutenesses
tenesmuses

EEFGILNRSS
fingerless
fringeless

EEGHILOOST
ethologies
theologies
theologise

EEGILLNNSV
nevellings
snevelling

EEGILNRSTT
letterings
resettling

EEGILNRSTW
sweltering
welterings

EEGIMNNOOS
monogenies
nomogenies

EEGINNPRST
presenting
repentings
serpenting

EEGINNRSTT
stentering
testerning

EEGINPRRSV
perversing
preserving

EEHINNORST
enthronise
rhinestone

EEHKNOORTT
heterokont
tenterhook

EEHMOORSVW
howsomever
whomsoever

EEIIINQSTU
equinities
inequities

EEIIMNNPTT
impenitent
pentimenti

EEIIMPRSSV
impressive
permissive

EEIINOPRTT
petitioner
repetition

EEILPRSSST
respitless
stripeless

EEILRSSSST
resistless
sisterless

EEIMNNPSTU
Pennisetum
septennium

EEIMNORSSS
minoresses
sermonises

EEIMOPRRST
spirometer
temporiser

EEIMPRRSSU
impressure
presurmise

EEINNOPSST
penistones
stone pines
stone snipe

EEINPRSSTT
persistent
prettiness

EEIRRSSSTV
reservists
servitress

EELLNOPPRT
prepollent
propellent

EELLRSSSTU
lustreless
resultless

EEOPRRSSTU
streperous
superstore

EFFILNSSTU
fitfulness
snuffliest

EFGIILNRTT
flittering
reflitting

EFIMNORSTU
misfortune
uniformest

EGGGIINNRS
gingerings
sniggering

EGGHIILNNT
enlighting
lightening

EGGHIINNRT
enrighting
rightening

EGGHINNORU
enroughing
roughening

EGGIILNNRS
lingerings
slingering

EGGIINNPRS
presigning
springeing

EGGINNORSS
engrossing
grossening

EGHIILNRST
girthlines
slithering

EGHIINNSTW
swithening
whitenings

EGHIINORST
rehoisting
theorising

EGHIINRRTW
wherriting
whirreting

EGHIINRSTW
swithering
whistering
witherings

EGHILLNOSV
hovellings
shovelling

EGHILOOSTT
ethologist
theologist

EGHINRSTTU
reshutting
shuttering

EGHLMOORTY
mythologer
thermology

EGHLNOOPRY
nephrology
phrenology

EGIILNRSTT
litterings
slittering

EGIIMMNRST
mismetring
misterming
stimmering
timmerings

EGIIMNNRTU
unmeriting
unmitering

EGIIMNPRSS
impressing
simperings

EGIIMNPRST
impresting
springtime

EGIIMNPRTT
permitting
premitting

EGIINNRSTT
snittering
tristening

EGIINOPRST
poetrising
poistering
repositing

EGIINPRSST
persisting
priestings
springiest

EGIINRSSTT
grittiness
resittings
stringiest
string ties
tie-strings

EGIINRSTTW
retwisting
swittering
twistering
witterings

EGIKNNORST
stonkering
storkening

EGILLNNORS
enrollings
norselling

EGILLNORSS
rosselling
sollerings

EGILMNOOOS
monologies
monologise
nomologies

EGILNPPSTU
septupling
suppleting

EGILNRSTWY
strewingly
wrestingly

EGILOOOPST
optologies
topologies

EGIMNNOOST
monogenist
nomogenist

EGINOPRSTT
potterings
pottingers»
protesting
repottings
respotting

EGINORSTTT
stottering
totterings

EGMNNOOOSU
monogenous
nomogenous

EHIOPRSSST
prosthesis
sophisters
store ships

EHLLRSSTUY
hurtlessly
ruthlessly

EHOOPPRTTY
protophyte
tropophyte

EIIMNOPRSS
impression
permission

EIIOOPRSST
isotropies
porosities

EIKNNOSSTT
knottiness
stinkstone

EILNORSSUY
neurolysis
resinously

EILOPRSUVY
perviously
previously
viperously

ELOPPRSTUY
Polypterus
suppletory

FGHIINRSTT
first night
first thing

FGIILLNRTY
flirtingly
triflingly

GGHIINNRTU
ungirthing
unrighting

GHILNOOPST
phlogiston
potholings

GIILLNOPST
pistolling
postilling

GIILNPRSST
slipstring
striplings

GILMNOOOST
monologist
nomologist

GILNPRSUUY
pursuingly
usurpingly

GILOOOPSTT
optologist
topologist

GIMMNNOSSU
summonings
summonsing

HOOPPRRSUY
porphyrous
pyrophorus

ANDAGRAMS

Top word game players make a particular study of high-scoring words of maximum utility for their favourite game. They give all manner of different descriptive titles to their own published compilations, rarely duplicating the same title only because no recognised term exists. As their compilations mirror a typical ploy of a crossword compiler so the writer has coined the word **andagram** to cover all such constructions. An **andagram** is an anagram of a word with the addition of another letter.

Consider the word **cat**. Its anagram is **act**. If one adds the letter H to **cat**, the andagram is **chat**; adding R produces the andagram **cart**; add S and the andagrams are **acts**, **cast**, **cats** and **scat**. Therefore, the andagrams of **cat** in relation to H, R and S are **acts**, **cart**, **cast**, **cats**, **chat** and **scat**.

Top players have discovered that certain words are the basis of a considerable number of andagrams and create lists which relate each letter of the alphabet in turn to a basic word. Their reasoning is very sound. A word with many andagrams is always a word with frequently used letters. That being so, they have a plan for success denied to lesser players.

Take Scrabble® as an example. To be able to play all seven tiles in one 'go' gives a player a bonus of 50 points over and above the basic score for the word. The average family player will consider such a move exceptional and feel a sense of achievement should he or she ever make such a move. Top players would consider only *two* such moves in one game by one player a poor performance – so commonplace is such a move that they set their sights higher! Instead of creating a 7–letter word from their seven tiles, they deliberately set out to achieve an 8–letter word using their own seven tiles plus one already on the board *on a peripheral line* so that they produce a massive score which takes into account the points multiplication factor of two '3 times the word value' squares. In other words, their 8–letter word has its basic score multiplied by 9 together with 50 bonus points. Thus with magical words like **beziques**, **caziques** and **quetzals** they can achieve scores approaching 400 points in *just one move*. This is in sharp contrast with a family player who can account himself as having done well to score 200 points for all of his moves for a whole game!

But words such as those are exceptional and players do not set out to create them on their Scrabble racks. What they *do* set out to create are andagrams.

(Note: In all the examples which follow it is important to appreciate that the words given are those to be found in *Pears Advanced Word-Puzzler's Dictionary*. Many will not be found in *Chambers 20th Century Dictionary* or *The Official Scrabble Players Dictionary*, which are used in various national Scrabble championships. Equally important is the fact that the examples include words with an initial capital letter, which are invalid for many games including Scrabble.)

In building a high-scoring andagram, the player scores in the normal way with various other tiles until he or she has deliberately created the word **stainer** on the rack. Apart from the intrinsic value of that word (see the 30 anagrams at AEINRST [1] of which it happens to be one) it gives direct access to no fewer than 126 different andagrams. The andagrams of **stainer** considered in relation to the letter A are **antisera**, **artesian**, **artisane**, **Asterina**, **Erastian**, **Raetians**, **ratanies**, **resinata** and **seatrain**. Limiting

[1] Also see **atrine** in the *Advanced Dictionary*, which has the potential of raising the total to 31.

further examples to just one word, the andagram of **stainer** with B is **banister**: C, **canister**: D, **strained**: E, **resinate**: F, **fainters**: G, **angriest**: H, **hairnets**: I, **rainiest**: K, **keratins**: L, **entrails**: M, **raiments**: N, **entrains**: O, **arsonite**: P, **pinaster**: R, **restrain**: S, **snariest**: T, **straiten**: U, **urinates** and W, **tinwares**.

To discover all of the andagrams of **stainer** consult the anagram lists. Add the appropriate letter, i.e. stainer + A = AAEINRST, stainer + B = ABEINRST etc, and the 8–letter list will provide most of them. In one or two cases it will be necessary to turn to the 7–letter list where every combination including an S is a plural. In this event still add the letter but ignore the S.

By this deliberate construction of **stainer** the player not only has the pick of 30 different 7–letter words but direct access to the exceptionally high-scoring potential presented by its 126 andagrams. Contrast that with the magical **quetzals**: no anagrams, no andagrams and one could play for weeks and not have those letters available at any one time. The letters which form **stainer** are very *easy* to acquire.

A high total of andagrams is not unique to **stainer**. The 6–letter word, **satine**, for example, is capable of being the basis of 121 different words. Apart from **etesian** (satine + E), **isatine** (satine + I), **intakes** (satine + K), **atonies** (satine + O) and **sextain** (satine + X), all can be found within the anagram lists. The full complement of letters which form andagrams with **satine** is A, B, C, D, E, F, G, H, I, K, L, M, N, O, P, R, S, T, U, V, W, X and Z.

If your ambitions are more inclined towards scoring 7–letter words rather than the 8–letter words of the experts, then there is an even better word than **satine** for use as a basic word. The word to remember is **satire.** If you can deliberately create **satire** amongst your playable letters then it is nigh on impossible not to score a 7–letter word and gain that bonus of 50 extra points. All 132 andagrams of **satire** can be found by direct reference to the anagram lists.

Should you be lucky enough to have the 'blank' tile (a joker which can represent any letter) then save it, *never* waste it: within only a very few 'goes' you cannot help but create the basis of a set of andagrams if you try.[2]

Is **satire** the supreme andagrammable word?

No. Whilst there is not a better basic word for Scrabble, no matter which dictionary you use, it is players of a different game who have the benefit of the superlative in this field.

Pelham, the anagram card game of 6–letter words, has the record-breaker, **aster**. Only one of its andagrams, **ersatz** (aster + Z), doesn't feature in the anagram lists. Pelham's **aster** has no fewer than 270 andagrams!

Finally, for those who are tempted to play 6–letter words in Scrabble for almost worthless scores *never* lay down any of the following: **astern**, **diners**, **genial**, **grains**, **insert**, **regina**, **resaid**, **retail**, **singer**, **slater**, **sortie**, **stride** or **teaser**. All have a much higher than average andagram potential.

2–LETTER WORDS

Forget magical words like caziques and quetzals; andagrams and all the amazing Q words without a U which are found in such numbers in *Pears Advanced Word-Puzzler's*

[2] Also see **POSTAL WORD GAMES** in the *Advanced Dictionary* which gives an example of game play whereby private andagram lists are put to full and effective use during the course of a game.

Dictionary, the most important words of all are the little 2–letter words. Their value cannot be over-stressed. If you know these and your opponent does not, then no matter how brilliant with words he or she may be, you cannot possibly lose in a word game.

These little gems provide the vital link between a word in play and the word you wish to play. Lexicon®, Kan–U–Go®, Word for Word®, Scrabble® or any other crossword-type game you care to mention is dominated by the player who has these at his or her fingertips.[3]

If you saw the Channel 4 programme, *Television Scrabble*, you may recall how often these were used. The better players knew them and won. The poorer players didn't know them and lost. The contestants all knew well in advance that *Chambers 20th Century Dictionary* would be the official reference work, so none could complain of any unfairness. Only when *both* contestants knew all of the 2–letter words did any other factors matter.

Chambers has 92 2–letter words available for play, *The Official Scrabble Players Dictionary* has 86. If the long proposed World Scrabble Championship which will use these two dictionaries finally materializes by 1990, the first likely date, this will give a combined total of 107 super little words (71 being common to both works) assuming that neither adds to the numbers available. The latest edition of *Chambers*, for example, added a further 6 to the ones it featured in earlier editions.

Certainly there is scope for addition and *Pears Advanced Word-Puzzler's Dictionary* provides nigh on 250 for anyone who would be a master of a word game.

If these words are considered in three different groups of 2–letter words, then it is amazingly easy to remember them.

Group one: those which begin with a consonant.
Group two: those which begin with a vowel.
Group three: the oddments – those rare words which consist of two consonants.

Groups one and two each have their own rule. The exceptions are few. Therefore, if you memorize the exceptions to the rule (i.e. the non-words) then every other word is valid for play.

Group one The rule is that every word beginning with a consonant is *always* followed by a vowel or a Y. The exceptions are as follows; JI, JU, JY: QA, QE, QO, QY: VE: XE, XO, XY: YY: ZU, ZY. By knowing these mere 14 exceptions you have committed 112 words to memory. To discover the meanings of such as **ba**, **be**, **bi**, **bo**, **bu**, **by** or **ca**, **ce**, **ci**, **co**, **cu**, **cy**, refer directly to the *Advanced Dictionary*.

Group two The rule is that every word beginning with a vowel is *always* followed by every letter of the alphabet including itself. The exceptions are as follows; AG, AJ, AP, AQ, AV, AZ: EJ, EQ, EV, EZ: IB, II, IJ, IP, IQ, IU, IY, IZ: OG, OJ, OQ, OZ: UB, UC, UD, UE, UF, UI, UJ, UK, UL, UQ, UW, UX, UY.

Not so easy to remember, but, closer examination gives scope for memory. For example, E and O have only 4 exceptions each, of which J, Q and Z are common to both. A has 6 exceptions, but this also includes the same J, Q and Z. I has 8 exceptions,

[3] For two excellent pencil and paper games of this type see **WORD GAMES** in the *Advanced Dictionary*.

again including J, Q and Z. U, unfortunately, has 13 exceptions, yet again including J and Q but, erratically, not a Z. Nevertheless, it is still possible to commit a further 95 words to memory by knowing 35 exceptions.

Groups one and two have provided 207 words from a negative factor of 49 exceptions.

Group three Unlike the other two groups, it is the *real* words, not the non-words, which need to be memorized in this instance.

First, an easily remembered but highly dubious sub-group. Each letter of the alphabet can be considered as a word in its own right describing that particular letter. It may, therefore, take an S as a plural. This fact is recognized by the greatest of the British and American dictionaries, both of which list such 'words' in this plural form. You may disagree, but the writer does not consider them to be 'real' words and he would certainly object to their use in any game he was playing. But, they exist.

The double-consonant words listed in the *Advanced Dictionary* are **dw**, **hm**, **hv**, **hw**, **nw**, **sh**, **st**, **vg**, **vp**, **vs**, **wp**, **wr**, **ws**, **yd**, **yf**, **yk**, **yl**, **yn**, **yr**, **ys**, **yt** and **yw** (plus **ch** and **sq**, which have been specifically listed as examples of words *completely invalid for word play*). Thus, there are 229 2–letter words valid for play (227 for such games as Lexicon and Kan–U–Go which would have to exclude **cy** and **ky** as plurals) but 247 if you accept the dubious sub-group.

2–letter words are frequently encountered in crosswords, where they feature as syllables in cryptic clues of the andagram type. In these instances they are far more likely to refer to **st** not as the word which it truly is, but, as an abbreviation for either street or saint. A typical clue would use the phrase *little saint* to express ST as part of a larger word. Other such crossword ploys are discussed at the CROSSWORD ENGLISH sub-section on page 13.

For a guide to the use of 3–letter words see the special subject **WORD GAMES – BASIC LINKING WORDS**.

WORD FUN

A more lighthearted approach to word games is exemplified by BBC 2's *Call My Bluff*. The *Advanced Dictionary* caters for the addicts of the 'true or false' type of guessing game just as it does for the serious word game player.

Whilst words such as **pomwater** and **Opalina** owe their basic inclusion to being anagrams of other words, many similar candidates for this type of play, such as **Alp-Luachra**, are included purely for their own sake. **Pomwater** is not (as one might suppose) an Australian epithet for English beer and it is a very safe bet that you could devise any number of meanings for **Opalina** far more believable than the true one. As well as glancing at the *Advanced Dictionary*'s definition of **Alp-Luachra**, the word **muggle** is also worth a look in this regard. As the greatest difficulty which faces family groups who enjoy this pastime seems to be the creation of 'false' definitions, the word **philippina** has an extended entry to provide a useful approach to the subject. Equally helpful should be the entry for **archerfish** which carries a footnote on how to disguise an 'obvious' word with an 'unknown' word to accompany a false-sounding, but true, story.

The special subject entries in the *Advanced Dictionary*, those such as **COLLECTIVE**

NOUNS, **DIVINATION** and **MONEYERS WEIGHTS**, are an ideal source of material for a basic 'true or false' game. For example, simply devise a few '-omancy' words to supplement those given at **DIVINATION** and a party game now exists.

Other types of word fun, such as the construction of ANTIGRAMS, DINGBATS and PANGRAMS, are given individual entries in the *Advanced Dictionary*. Classic SPOONERISMS and GOLDWYNISMS are also noted, as are PALINDROMES and PSEUDODROMES.

OTHER WORD PLAY

Traditional pencil and paper word games often become commercial products. Word Mastermind® is one such example and even hangman can now be obtained in a box.

1 *Hangman* One of the arts in 'hanging' a skilful opponent lies in the selection of words of unusual formation – much more difficult to solve than a merely unusual or even previously unknown word.

If your opponent is a sensible player and begins by eliminating the vowels, then a word such as **latchstring** with its six consecutive consonants can be a real 'killer'. Equally frustrating should be **frillless** and you would probably need to prove that **crwths** really does exist by showing its entry in the *Advanced Dictionary*.

Hidden away for your chance discovery are some utterly unbelievable words, such as one with eight O's in succession and, if you would care to use such horrors, how about **Aaaahtamad**, the name of an unidentified town in ancient Palestine?

2 *Postal word games* If hangman is your type of game but you would like a *real* challenge, then you may find that the postal game of CODE BREAKING is perfect for a lonely, wet, miserable afternoon. It is ideal for those who enjoy crosswords, but find themselves restricted for an extended period to some form of lonely confinement. Both the construction of one's own code or the 'cracking' of a code used by a penpal can be very entertaining. The game and technique is discussed in the *Advanced Dictionary* at the entry **POSTAL WORD GAMES**. The subject of codes has its own aspects, covered by the entry **CODES AND CIPHERS**.

3 *Cryptarithmetic* This is strictly a mathematical puzzle but with the appearance of a word puzzle, especially the better ones where the compiler uses real words in a humorous or an apt context. Nevertheless it should appeal to word puzzlers. The following examples are original creations by the writer of this dictionary and have never been previously published.

A typical puzzle looks like this:

```
 TT
 TT+
----
ETC
----
```

and the solver is asked to substitute the only possible digits which could be represented by those letters. Obviously the letter T represents one digit and both E and C represent a different digit each. Simple trial and error reduce the possibilities immediately.

Suppose T represents 1. But, 11 + 11 only equals 22 and a three figure answer is required. This immediately eliminates the possibilities of T representing 2, 3 or 4 as none of these can take the answer into three figures. Could T represent 5? No. 55 + 55 = 110 and the puzzle requires an answer with the digit represented by T repeated in the second position of the addition and this also has to be *different* to the digit of the first position. Conversely, that first digit can only be a 1 as the highest possible combination, 99 + 99, is fewer than 200. From the few remaining possibilities it will be seen that only 99 + 99 matches all requirements so the answer is:

```
 99
 99+
----
198
----
```

The logic is similar to that required for CODE BREAKING, so if you can solve any of the following and also enjoy crosswords you will certainly enjoy 'cracking' a code. The solutions all appear in the *Advanced Dictionary* at the entry for **cryptarithmetic**.

```
             NINE                    FACET
  ££         NINE      WRONG         FACET
  ££+        NINE+     WRONG+        FACET+
 -----      ------    --------      -------
 OOF         HELP      RIGHT         WHOLE
 -----      ------    --------      -------
```

The above, especially the first, are comparatively simple, but a real challenge is presented by this last one. It has a cryptic clue to the vital first stage of solving contained in its intrinsic anagrammatic punning phrase of *draw backward the backward drawback*.

```
  DRAW
 –WARD
 ------
  BACK
 ------
```

given that B + A + C + K = BY and B + Y = K.

4 *Pentery Web* This is one of various other games mentioned in the *Advanced Dictionary*. (No prizes are awarded for discovering the origin of the name!)

WORD GAME RULINGS

Players of word games sometimes find themselves arguing over the merits or otherwise of individual words. Often people confuse the rules of one game with another. Hence, such frequently heard silly comments as, 'You can't use slang in Scrabble!' You can. It is other games which bar slang.

Rather than repeat the general commentary on word rules given in the companion volume, *Pears Word-Puzzler's Dictionary*, individual words (such as **interdeal**) likely to be the subject of controversy are given footnotes and judgments are made *based on known precedents*. Only one word, **decreate**, has proved to be completely outside the scope of known precedent, nevertheless it has a footnote which players may find helpful.

Contentious words are discussed at greater length in the following section.

THE DICTIONARY SECTION

As the *Advanced Dictionary* is, in essence, a supplement to any standard dictionary (i.e. it does not define well known words) it is important to stress from the outset that it will sometimes give a totally different treatment to a word common to both it and a standard dictionary. Whilst this has limited significance for crosswords, it has a major importance with regard to word games which either accept or reject words according to the definition within any particular dictionary.

This is especially true with regard to one particular dictionary where the divergent views are so significant and so numerous that one can only recommend the reader to seek a third opinion where it and the *Advanced Dictionary* are at odds with each other. The differences will be discussed at greater length in the following sub-section which begins by relating different word games to different dictionaries.

DIVERGENT VIEWS

In respect of word play certain dictionaries have special significance. The *Oxford English Dictionary* is not only the greatest of all dictionaries, but neither BBC 2's *Call My Bluff* nor the *In a Spin* feature of BBC 1's *Masterteam* is possible with anything less. It is also used for certain special challenge matches organized by the UK Postal Scrabble Club, though these tend to be private contests between individuals rather than any of the other activities with which it is associated. For its league programmes or international team contests against such as the top Australian players it uses lesser works.

In 1980, *Chambers 20th Century Dictionary* replaced the *Shorter Oxford* as the official reference work for the UK Scrabble® championship. As a repository of words in a single low-cost volume it has no equal and, from a word player's point of view, its method of presenting words in upper or lower case according to the way they occur within a sentence is infinitely preferable to the *Shorter Oxford*'s capitalization of its entries. A speedier confirmation of validity is thus available. In consequence, most Commonwealth countries followed suit including Australia, which is the province of a licensed manufacturer of the game totally independent of those of the UK and the USA.

At the introduction of *Chambers*, the purely local UK rules of its contest barred various words including those defined in *Chambers* as having been used only by Shakespeare, Spenser or Milton together with any other words defined as being obsolete. This purely local rule (there is nothing in the rules of the game itself to invalidate them) was also generally adopted by Commonwealth countries and, in fact, Singapore went a stage further and also declared Scottish and dialect words invalid.

Since that time of virtual Commonwealth unity (Canada excluded, as will be shown below) first gradual and then major differences emerged. South Africa, seeing no reason to bar English words of South African origin, i.e. **aardvark**, amended the ruling in this particular respect with regard to 'foreign' words. Australia and New Zealand also saw no reason to treat their own words as being invalid and they, too, revised their championship rules. Australian players then went a stage further and questioned the wisdom regarding the supposedly 'exclusive' Shakespeare, Spenser and Milton words together with the genuine and not so genuine 'obsolete' words. New Zealand players subsequently followed the lead of the West Indies and had both *Chambers* and the American work, *The Official Scrabble Players Dictionary*, as joint works of reference.

Then came the bombshell: the national organizer of the Scrabble Clubs of Australia announced that, as from the 1st September 1986, *The Official Scrabble Players Dictionary* would replace *Chambers* as the official reference for all words except those of 9 letters and upwards for which *Chambers* would still be retained. The reasons she gave included the facts that, whilst *Chambers* is comprehensive, '*the rules needed to interpret the dictionary are just as comprehensive and as difficult to interpret. Secondly, adjudication at tournaments is not easy using the Chambers. There are many cross-references*[1] *and difficult to read labels and at least two judges are needed to confer on any one adjudication*'. She then went on to praise the American work by saying, '*Word judging with the OSPD is simplicity itself, fast and efficient.*'

Within weeks (on November 25th 1986 to be exact) the UK's equivalent circularized all the British Clubs asking them to vote on accepting the 'exclusive' words of Shakespeare, Spenser and Milton for official UK play and announced that, if accepted, this change would not become effective until '*an Official Scrabble Adjudicators Word Guide for words of up to, probably, eight letters*[2] *(based on Chambers)*' was produced. The circular letter continued, '*Because of the work involved, even starting NOW on such a vast project, the publication could not be ready prior to late 1988/early 1989 ... although 1990 is more likely*'. (The reason given for validating the 'exclusive' words was that '*they are still used in poetry which is read, recited or performed*'.)

The Official Scrabble Players Dictionary is an American work produced specifically for the game of Scrabble. It was originally developed for the North American Scrabble movement of Canada and the USA and gives full recognition of British spelling forms where they differ from the American. Its popularity is such that not only has it made the previously mentioned inroads into the Commonwealth territories but is also used in Indonesia, Japan and Israel and even the UK Postal Scrabble Club has organized play using it as an official work of reference. Whilst it has severe limitations in general usage, it is an excellent work for games players particularly as it gives all verbal inflections, plurals and adjectival comparatives and superlatives so often overlooked by standard dictionaries.

The *Concise Oxford* is used for the Channel 4 television game of Countdown®. The boxed version of the game has no official work.

Collins Minigem Dictionary is used for the children's word game, Dixit®.

From the point of view of Dixit players or potential Countdown competitors on television, *Pears Advanced Word-Puzzler's Dictionary* is useless. The limitations imposed by their official works are such that very few of their words are defined in the *Advanced Dictionary*.

However, the *Advanced Dictionary* has words in common with the *OED*, *Chambers* and the *OSPD* as well as having many which appear in none of these works.

As an example of a divergent view as it affects word game players, consider a word which is so well known that its appearance in the *Advanced Dictionary* might seem to be surprising. This word has *Pears Advanced Word-Puzzler's Dictionary*, the *OSPD*,

[1] The problem is not that of a *given* cross-reference, but how to find a word for which no cross-reference is available. For example, **ablins**. The adjudicator has to know that this will only be listed at the main entry of **able**, where it is included merely because it shares its etymology with **able**.

[2] Which mirrors the style of the *OSPD*.

Collins Minigem and the *Concise Oxford* on one side and *Chambers* and the *OED* on the other. The word is **aardvark**, and the reasons are fully detailed in a footnote which accompanies its definition in the *Advanced Dictionary*.

In most cases, however, the divergent views affect the uncommon words and where *Pears Advanced Word-Puzzler's Dictionary* is at odds with one of the above mentioned dictionaries, the following authorities are consulted.

On questions of periods of word usage, the *Oxford English Dictionary*.

On specifically mentioned localities of dialect words, the *English Dialect Dictionary*.

On currency of American usage, various of their leading authorities such as *Webster*.

On technical matters for a word such as **springhare**, the authorities are specialist works, not dictionaries.

On hyphens: if American words, American dictionaries; if British, various British dictionaries or technical works especially those reflecting current trends.

On nonce words, the *Oxford English Dictionary*.

On rare usage (e.g. a noun as a verb), the *Oxford English Dictionary*.

On the specific question of words solely attributed to Shakespeare, Spenser or Milton, the *Oxford English Dictionary*.

On unusual plural forms, wherever these are specifically noted. This tends to be American dictionaries rather than British as the American works usually pay greater attention to this detail. The divergences in this respect, however, are normally not disagreements but are concerned with inferences drawn by an absence of detail. On plurals of obsolete words, the authority is the *Oxford English Dictionary*.

On obsolete words, this is a particularly vexed question and is discussed separately at the sub-section, **OBSOLETE WORDS**. In this respect it has to be said that, sometimes, the opinion of the *OED* has to be rejected where the writer finds himself in agreement with *Chambers 20th Century Dictionary*, especially when it is supported by such American authorities as *Funk & Wagnalls*. In one or two very rare cases where the *OED* declares a word of comparatively recent usage *for which no possible synonym pertains* to be obsolete and no other dictionary mentions the word, then, as a word of historical relevance, *Pears Advanced Word-Puzzler's Dictionary* is itself the culprit of divergence.

The above authorities are quoted only in respect of divergence as the actual sources of words are many and varied and include technical works, specialist publications, encyclopaedias, atlases and newspapers, with confirming opinions sought from various experts in particular fields as diverse as veterinary medicine and the construction of pianos.

Other than where a divergent view is made the subject of a footnote, no other clue as to the acceptability or otherwise of a particular word for UK championship Scrabble is given. In all cases only the opinion of *Chambers* is valid for that and allied play.

One of the difficulties, of course, when play becomes restricted to a test of knowledge of any one work of reference is not only what it contains but, also, what it fails to include! For example, in *any game* restricted to *Chambers* then, technically, one has to invalidate **millimetre** simply because it is not specifically listed. (The assumption of such as verbal inflections is a different matter.) The writer considers it essential, not only in view of the variety of differences which exist between dictionaries but the considerable numbers of words within each specified category, to highlight these differences with examples in order to dispel any doubts which may arise concerning the quality of research which produced the *Advanced Dictionary*. The categories are as follows:–

1 Many of the words hyphenated in *Chambers* (therefore invalid for word game play) are merely optional forms and the unhyphenated forms can be readily determined elsewhere – even in that same book. A typical case is the word **bladderwrack**. *Chambers* gives this a main entry as **bladder-wrack** and, at this main entry, provides for no optional forms. However, at its entries for **rockweed** and **sea-bottle** it refers to **bladderwrack**. This is not an exceptional example.

The *American* words, **sandhog** and **tarheel**, provide an equally curious case. In contrast to the *American* dictionaries, it hyphenates these words as **sand-hog** and **tar-heel**. It must not be presumed, however, that the excessively numerous hyphenated forms exclusive to *Chambers* all transpose into a single word as many are more commonly written as two separate words.

2 A second divergence from its presentation is shown by a word such as **calliper**. It is mentioned as an adjective and given limited application as a noun but not referred to as a verb. Similarly **semple**, the Scottish form of **simple**. *Chambers* lists it as an adjective but not as a noun, the sense in which Scott, among others, used it.

3 A third divergence is concerned with words such as **diapase**. In the current reference work for the UK Scrabble championship it is labelled in a manner that suggests that only Spenser ever used it. In fact it has a long history of poetic use which, while including Spenser, continues to modern times and is still extant! The word **discounsel** is a more typical example, however, in that it has since become obsolete. But, the curious thing is that whilst the *Oxford English Dictionary* records known users of **discounsel** from Caxton to Donne (see the special subject entry, **WRITERS**, in the *Advanced Dictionary*) it fails to mention Spenser as one who ever used the word!

But, the most remarkable of the Spenser labels in *Chambers* must surely be that for a word given a main entry as **portesse**. Defined as meaning a portable breviary, this Spenser 'exclusive' is then given a further seven variant forms, which makes one wonder why Spenser, having coined the word, couldn't make up his mind how to spell it. Contrast this with the facts presented in the *Oxford English Dictionary*. Under a main heading of **portas**, the *OED* provides considerably more than seven variant forms in this sense as a breviary (other forms apply to other meanings). In a list of writers *from circa 1250 to the present day it does not even mention Spenser*! The form **portesse** (which the *OED* notes as **portess(e)**) is quoted twice, but each time in a plural as **portesses**. The only other likely connection with this spelling form appears with the obsolete nonce verb **portess**, to canonize, which completes its definitive treatment of **portas**.

4 Shakespeare comes in for similar treatment. He appears to have exclusive use of such words as **entame**, **tetter**, **tetterous** and **threnos**, and, with one of the editors of his works, the 'only known' usage of **rother**. All of these 'Shakespeare' words are still extant and **threnos** even has an extant variant form, **threnus**. The editor's word is also still living, though it is now only to be discovered in the dialects of Hereford,

Lancashire, Sussex, Warwick and Worcester. His 'exclusive' use of **germain** is so curious and complicated that this is best considered in context.

5 Milton is the third of three great writers for whom any word designated in *Chambers* as being exclusive to his work is currently deemed invalid for the UK Scrabble championship. **Displode** is a typical Milton 'exclusive'. However, Swift is among the writers of the following century who used it (Swift's 'exclusive' words have never been barred from play) and yet a century later still it appeared in an article published in the *Edinburgh Review* dated November 1812. Certainly it gives the Americans no trouble, as *The Official Scrabble Players Dictionary* accepts it without a qualm. By contrast, a genuine Milton exclusive, **chauntress**, is labelled as extant!

6 The next divergence is concerned with plural forms. For example, *Chambers* considers the word **lasagne** to be a noun plural so obviously incapable of becoming **lasagnes**. Other British experts disagree as do the Americans, hence **lasagnes** is available for play in the North American Scrabble championship. (In the West Indies and New Zealand which, of course, use both reference works simultaneously this must be quite a problem!)

Then there is the noun, **telos**. No plural form is given and it would be logical to assume that 'teloses' is valid for play. However, the plural is **teloi** and so no anagram for **osselet** is available. Scrabble adjudicators though, would have to permit 'teloses' and deny **teloi**. By contrast, the respective entries in the *Advanced Dictionary* and *Chambers* will show agreement on **estovers** but controversy over 'estover'.

7 A seventh divergence ironically occurs in the inflections of the verb **treap**, to argue! This is fully detailed at the entry for that word in the *Advanced Dictionary* as it has significance for other forms.

8 The next divergence concerns nonce words and these are discussed in their own sub-section.

9 A ninth divergence is typified by the entries for **artesian**, **camptonite** and **negro** and concerns initial capital letters. **Artesian**, for example, has two meanings but only one of these is normally given an initial capital letter. *Chambers* allows for no distinction – it capitalizes both.

10 A tenth divergence is typified by **umquhile** which in this case concerns an English word being described as Scottish.

11 This divergence is typified by **aardvark** and concerns the assimilation into English of a word which originated outside the UK.

12 A twelfth and quite rare divergence applies to erroneous forms of words of which **gantline** is a prime example.

13 A very significant and important divergence as it is not concerned with labelling or

form but with the actual meanings of the words themselves! Readers of *Chambers* and the *Advanced Dictionary* might be well advised to seek a third opinion when reading such typical examples as **albacore**, **calamint**, **Daltonian**, **pinguin** and **tarpon**.

14 There is one respect in which it would be illogical to disagree with the view expressed by *Chambers*. **Adnascent**, **alepin**, **aspectual**, **bandelier**, **capsulate**, **falcation**, **haberdine**, **inanimated**, **nodation**, **nudation**, **sortment** and **tractator** are but some of the words in this particular category. The *Oxford English Dictionary* declares them to be obsolete, but *Chambers* has them extant. Thus the mere fact of being extant in *Chambers* means that they are considered available for use and who knows which of these controversial word are circulating in publications as a direct result? Certainly crossword compilers favour its magnificent word power, which readily provides material unavailable elsewhere in a single volume.

But, many of these words are so palpably obsolete that one cannot possibly disagree with the opinion of the *Oxford English Dictionary*. Selecting examples from just one letter of the alphabet produces **caliatour**, **calidity**, **capsulary**, **catsilver**, **cauterism**, **chauntress** and **connotate** among others which *Chambers* lists as being extant.

Chambers is not the only work with which *Pears Advanced Word-Puzzler's Dictionary* finds itself at odds, but none in such variety or such numbers. Readers of *The Official Scrabble Players Dictionary* will find no agreement with their work's definition of a **rhebok** as being a *large* antelope and its acceptance of such as **entastic** and **stonable** is subject to commentary and, as previously mentioned, even the opinion of the *Oxford English Dictionary* has been questioned.

In the various footnotes which accompany these and other divergent views, frequent mention is made to acceptance for Scrabble play. Where the *OSPD* is inferred by such phrasing as 'North American Scrabble championship' this should not be assumed to be a purely American view as the opinion of its dictionary is almost invariably supported by British authorities such as the *Oxford English Dictionary* or *Collins* in these particular controversies as well as by leading American dictionaries intended for international use.

NONCE WORDS

These are words coined purely '*for the nonce*' (for the occasion) and are perfectly valid for word games providing that they are listed in the dictionary previously agreed upon for reference in the event of dispute.

All the great writers have either coined them or used them. For example, Dickens used the word **poor** as a verb and a lesser writer soon copied his example. Dickens copied lesser writers in having **butler** as a verb but, like them, devised his own particular sense. Others who have used nonce words include Austen, Carlyle, Coleridge, Darwin, Disraeli, Jonson, Marlowe, Poe, Shakespeare, Swift and Tennyson.

Some nonce words even appear in dictionaries without being labelled as such. One of the non-Dickensian senses of the nonce verb **butler**, the nonce adjectives **cloacalin**, **cloacinal**, **ismatic**, **ismatical**, **lacerant**, **Scotian** and the nonce noun **ganderism**, are examples which appear in *Chambers 20th Century Dictionary*. All are listed as being standard words!

The Official Scrabble Players Dictionary also carries them (see **coexert**) but unlike *Chambers* it carries no descriptive labels of any type, so leaving the serious reader free to determine for himself or herself the utility of such a listed word in a context other than word play. (Further information is detailed at **nonce** in the *Advanced Dictionary*.)

Within the entry for **antigram** in the *Advanced Dictionary* is the nonce word, 'arch-saint'. Obviously such a word has no legitimacy and is intended purely for fun. All of the antigram examples in that particular entry have either been coined or compiled by the writer, Gyles Brandreth, appearing in his book, *The Joy of Lex* (William Morrow & Co. Inc., New York, 1980) which discusses the fun of words. ('Lex' is itself a nonce word, coined by his wife, to suggest words in general.) In consequence, 'arch-saint' has not a sufficiently serious usage to be considered by this work and certainly does not feature in the anagram lists. A better case could be made for Mrs Brandreth's word, **lex**, especially as the success of the first book produced the sequel, *More Joy of Lex*.

The nonce words which do feature in the anagram lists and are subsequently defined in the *Advanced Dictionary* are, generally speaking, those already noted here and have an additional life by being quoted elsewhere.

The potential for nonce anagrams is huge but, like 'arch-saint', they have all been rejected. For example, research has failed to locate a possible verb, 'resoap' – which is a pity as 'resoaping' has an anagram in **Singapore**. The word **simitar** is a variant form of **scimitar** and that has the adjective **scimitared**. Does 'simitared' exist? The writer cannot discover it, so it is not placed alongside **maistried** and **maitrised** in the lists. 'Unretailed' seems just as sensible but it too failed to surface, therefore, **adulterine** has no listed perfect anagram. 'Restealing' and 'surcoated' could both join other words in the lists, if only they could be found. Apart from any vulgar connotation, 'nutless' would seem equally sensible but this, too, failed to materialize, so leaving **stunsel** without an anagram. 'Reinsulate' would be a perfect anagram, in more senses than one, for **neutralise** if it could only be discovered in print.

Examples such as these can be multiplied over and over again and, for this reason alone, it is so important in word games to agree upon at least one dictionary to be used for reference in the event of dispute. If the word exists and complies with the rules, accept it. If it does not, reject it.

OBSOLETE WORDS

Obsolete words sometimes appear in crosswords, but almost always as an anagram of an answer, very rarely as the answer itself. However, they are of great value in word games.

The *Advanced Dictionary* carries many obsolete words, but it is very important to distinguish between those which have become obsolete in modern times and those which expired before the rules of modern grammar can be safely assumed. In consequence the two labels, *Obs* and *obs*, have been adopted.

1 *Words labelled Obs* These are words which became obsolete *before* AD 1500, the date to accept for all practical word game purposes as being the first year of modern English. Obviously there were 'modern' words before that date, but the truly 'old fashioned' words had expired by that time. Thus any words labelled *Obs* are either Old English (the period up to circa 1150) or Middle English (the period up to 1500).

The grammar of Old English was different and it even had some letters which appear foreign to a modern reader. Middle English is the transitional period during which the modern alphabet and modern grammar were fully established.

Consider the *Obs* verb **theine**. This is a word which expired during the Middle English period yet still retained the Old English letter known as thorn. Thorn looked like this, þ, and was the equivalent of today's *th*. Effectively, therefore, **theine** is a transliteration into modern English of **þeine**. *In this sense only* it exists as a word available for play in a word game and any attempt to suggest that 'theines', 'theined' or 'theining' should be equally valid is nonsense. (**Theining** as a noun happens to exist, but that is not the same as assuming a present participle based solely on the evidence of **theine** as an *Obs* verb. To play the correct *Obs* form of **theining** as a present participle would necessitate one's word game letters having not only a thorn but also a yogh! A yogh was shaped like this, ʒ, and **theining** would have been written **þeiʒnung**.)

Whilst, especially in Scotland, some of these strange letters continued into early modern English times they also ran concurrently with the modern equivalents, thus the modern form can be assumed for all words. The last real usage of an *Obs* letter was the *y* with a dot over it, which appeared in *The Boke of St Albans* in 1486.

Strange letters apart, the grammar of the *Obs* period is even more significant. The *Obs* noun, **ey**, meant egg. The plural was not 'eys' but any of the following: **eyer**, **eiren**, **eyron**, **eyrene** or **eyroun**. An *Obs* spelling of the noun **wound**, an injury, was **wunde** and its usual plural was **wunden** but the 'modern' form of **wundes** was also used. Not that the '-en' plural form is obsolete even today. **Oxen**, for example, the plural of **ox**, or **een** the plural of the Scottish word **ee**, an eye, still retain this 'old fashioned' style. The verbs had inflected forms that are equally strange to the modern reader. The past participle of **trawe** was not 'trawed' but **trawet**. Where, today, we have '-ing', the more common form of the later Middle English period was '-yng'. Some of these strange forms still survive and are shown in the *Advanced Dictionary* where relevant to a particular entry.

Therefore, when using an *Obs* word or an *Obs* spelling form of an extant word, the following rule needs to be adopted for a word game:– *Modern plurals or similar extensions such as verbal inflections or adjectival comparatives and superlatives cannot be applied. The only permitted extensions are those clearly indicated in the agreed work of reference or the conversion of an Obs word into a totally different modern word.* (e.g. turning **ey** into **eye** or **key**.)

2 *Words labelled obs* These are words which have become obsolete in modern times (i.e. *after* 1500). They can be used in any word game and normal modern grammatical rules may be safely assumed. Where this cannot be assumed, as with the *obs* verb **mids**, this is clearly stated.

OVERLOOKED MEANINGS

In many cases the *Advanced Dictionary* will list a word and then, prior to the definition, provide a set of abbreviations such as (*n*) *vb* or even (*adj*/*adv*/*interj*/*pron*/*n*) *obs poet vb*. In the first example, this means that whilst the word is a noun, it is presumed that this is known and understood by the reader. To provide a definition is, therefore, superfluous. But, as the word is also a verb and as this is rather unusual, the word is defined as a verb. In the second example, the brackets indicate that the meanings of the word as an adjective, an adverb, an interjection, a pronoun and a noun are presumed to be known by the reader. But, since the word is also an obsolete modern English poetic verb, as this it has been defined.

Permutations of this type are endless, so the following list of **ABBREVIATIONS USED IN THE ADVANCED DICTIONARY** gives only the meaning of an individual abbreviation. For example, *(collq n/vb) var fm S & dial adj* will not be explained in full as *(colloquial noun and verb not defined) a variant form of the Literary Scottish and northern English dialect adjective*, though the separate parts are explained.

There will even be odd labels such as *(n) n*. For example, with the word **beast**. This signifies that the normal meanings of the word have been ignored, but that an additional meaning or meanings are defined.

Finally, there will be such oddities as typified by the following entry: – '**aprise** *Obs fm obs n* **apprise**, lore'. This means that **apprise** is an obsolete modern English noun which means lore. It has not been independently defined but has been mentioned solely to explain **aprise,** which features in the anagram lists. **Aprise** is an earlier (pre-modern English) spelling form of **apprise**. (The vital differences between *Obs* and *obs* are fully detailed at the sub-section **OBSOLETE WORDS**, page 188.) Such an abbreviation means, therefore, *an Old English or Middle English form of the obsolete modern English noun.*

ABBREVIATIONS USED IN THE ADVANCED DICTIONARY

Before consulting this list the reader is recommended to read the preceding sub-section entitled **OVERLOOKED MEANINGS**. The vital differences between *Obs* and *obs* are fully explained in the sub-section **OBSOLETE WORDS**, and the sub-section **NONCE WORDS** is helpful in giving a better understanding of *nonce n*, *nonce vb* etc. When included with the abbreviations the word *pet* simply means pet, as in pet name.

adj	adjective
adjs	adjectives
adv	adverb
advs	adverbs
Anglo-Ind	Anglo-Indian
Anglo-Ir	Anglo-Irish
approx	approximate, approximately
arch	archaic
Austr	Australian English
Canada	Canadian English
+*cap*	the same word written with an initial capital letter
−*cap*	the same word but written without an initial capital letter
+or −*cap*	the same word, optionally in upper or lower case
cm	centimetres
collq	colloquial
comp	comparative
comps	comparatives
conj	conjunction
dial	dialect (English, unless otherwise specified)
dim	diminutive, diminutive of
erron	erroneous
esp	especially
facet	facetious
fem	feminine
fig	figuratively
fm	form, form of
fms	forms, forms of
Fr	French
Gael	Gaelic
Ger	German
Hebr	Hebrew
her	heraldic
incl	including, includes
indic	indicative
inf	infinitive
infl	inflected, inflection
infls	inflections
interj	interjection
Ir	Irish
Ire	Ireland
It	Italian
L	Latin
lit	literally
masc	masculine
mm	millimetres
modf n	modifying noun (a noun used adjectivally)
n	noun (including substantive phrase)
n of assemb	noun of assemblage (a collective noun)
now dial	formerly standard English, now only extant in a dialect or dialects (*now* designates other such retention in limited use, as *now poet*, *now S* and even *now nonce*)
n pl	noun plural
ns	nouns
n sing	noun singular
NZ	New Zealand English
Obs	obsolete before AD 1500
obs	obsolete after AD 1500
obsol	obsolescent (becoming obsolete)
orig	originally
Ork	Orkney
pa pple	past participle
pa t	past tense
pers n	personal name
pers sing	person singular
phr	phrase
pl	plural
pls	plurals

poet	poetic
poss	possibly
prep	preposition
preps	prepositions
pres	present
pron	pronoun
pr pple	present participle
qv	denoting a cross-reference
rhet	rhetorical
S	Literary Scottish (an independent English)
S & dial	Literary Scottish and a dialect or dialects found in England and elsewhere. Usually, however, in northern England only.
S dial	a dialect of Literary Scottish
S Afr	South African English
Shaks	Shakespeare (essentially nonce)
Shet	Shetland
sing	singular
slg	slang
Sp	Spanish
Spens	Spenser
sup	superlative
sups	superlatives
Swed	Swedish
t	tense
US	American English
US & dial	American English and a dialect or dialects of the British Isles
US dial	a dialect of American English
var fm	a variant form of
var fms	variant forms (of)
vb	verb
vbl infl	verbal inflection
vbs	verbs

A

aa *n* a cooled cindery substance consisting of sand, earth, stones and melted lava *var fm now dial n* **ea** *S adj/vb* (to) owe *obs adv* every, aye, always (+*cap*) *n* any of several small European rivers *incl* two in Latvia both of which empty into the Gulf of Riga

aaber *Ork & Shet adj* eager, anxious

aac *now dial fm n* **oak**

aad *dial fm adj* **old**

aadle *dial vb* to earn, acquire by labour

aag *dial n* a haw, the fruit of the hawthorn

aah *vb* to exclaim in joy or surprise

aak *now dial fm n* **oak**

aal *n* Indian mulberry, an East Indian shrub akin to the madder: the red dye yielded by its roots

aalii *n* a small tropical tree valued for its hard timber

Aalu *var fm n* **Aaru**

aam *n* a former Dutch and German liquid measure (varying from 37 to 41 gallons) *dial n* the chill *dial vb* to fret, grumble: to be peevish: to mock

aan *dial fm adj/vb (*to) **own**

aandorn *dial n* a light meal *dial vb* to work in the later part of the day

Aani *n* the cynocephalus or dog-headed ape of the ancient Egyptian religion

aar *S Afr n* an underground stream *dial interj* used as a word of command to a horse *var fm dial ns* **arr, haar**

aardvark *n* a large, nocturnal, burrowing mammal of South Africa totally unrelated to other creatures. It has very unusual tubed-teeth and diets mainly on termites. (GAME PLAYER'S note: The word comes from the Afrikaans for 'earth pig' and virtually all authorities, other than the dictionary used for the UK Scrabble championship, accept it as being standard English. Whilst the *Oxford English Dictionary* has it listed as a foreign word, later works by the same house (e.g. the *Oxford Illustrated*) clearly show its subsequent acceptance as an English word. Certainly it gives no problems to players in the North American Scrabble championship whose dictionary accepts the word without a qualm. All players of all word games, apart from Scrabble players in the UK championship, may use it. They alone must reject it as 'foreign'. Incidentally, the *Oxford Illustrated* also confirms the updating of aardvark from the old fashioned form of **aard-vark** given in the *Oxford English.*)

aarf *dial adj* timorous, afraid

Aaronic *adj* of or belonging to Aaron, the patriarch of the Hebrew priesthood: pontifical

Aaru *n* in the ancient Egyptian religion, the abode of the blessed dead

Aarvak *n* in Norse mythology, the horse that draws the sun's chariot (also see **Alsvid)**

aas *obs fm n* **as**, the roman coin *Obs fm ns* **ace, aces** (see **as**)

aat *obs fm n* **oat**

aauve *dial vb* to walk blunderingly or stupidly *dial interj* used as word of command to a team of horses

aay *dial adv* yes

ab *dial vb* to hinder: pain: disadvantage *now dial fm n* **abb** (+*cap*) *n* the penultimate lunar month of the Hebrew calendar: in the ancient Egyptian religion, the heart

aba *n* an instrument for measuring latitude and small angular heights: a Syrian cloth made of goat or camel hair: a sleeveless outer garment of such (+*cap*) *n* a Nigerian town N.E. of Port Harcourt

abac *n* nomograph, a graphic representation

of numerical relations *var fm n* **abacus**, a counting frame

abaca *n* a Philippine Islands banana plant: the fibre of this plant used for making rope

abaci *var fm pl* **abacuses**, counting frames (*sing* **abacus**)

abactor *n* one who steals cattle by the herd or other large number at any one act of theft

abada *obs n* a (female) rhinoceros

abatis *n* a defensive arrangement of trees with bent or sharpened branches (*pl* **abatis, abatises**)

abator *n* one who overthrows: a troublesome person: in law, one who illegally takes possession of a freehold

abature *n* a stag's trail through underwood

abawe *dial vb* to daunt, astonish

abb *n* woof or weft in a web

abba *var fm n* **aba** in the senses of a cloth or a garment

abby *Ork & Shet n* the sea gilliflower or thrift, a tufted scapose herb

abdal *n* one of a high degree in the Sufi order of saints (*pl* **abdali**)

abdat *n* an Egyptian measure of length varying between $3\frac{1}{2}$–$4\frac{3}{4}$ inches

Abdera see **Abderite**

Abderite *n* the classical Greek equivalent of a Gothamite, one dwelling in a place noted for its simpletons (The Abdera of Thrace equating to the Gotham of Nottinghamshire)

abetment *n* the action or fact of abetting

abettor *n* one who assists or encourages another *esp* in the committing of a criminal act

abey *vb* to waive

ablate *vb* to remove

ablaut *n* a patterned change in root vowels or verb forms such as r*i*ng, r*a*ng, r*u*ng or s*i*ng, s*a*ng, s*u*ng

able (*adj*) *obs vb* to adapt, prepare, make ready: to vouch for: to endow with strength or power: to empower legally

ablest *sup adj* able

ablet *n* the bleak, a small white freshwater fish

abling *obs n* the act of empowering

ablings *an etymological fm S Ir & dial adv* **ablins**

ablins *S Ir & dial adv* possibly, perhaps

abluent *adj* of medical usage, cleansing *n* a medical cleansing agent

abnet *n* the long scarf of a Jewish priest or officer

Abo *n* Turku, a seaport in S.W. Finland: a negro tribe in the Cameroons (*–cap*) *Austr collq n* an aborigine

abord *arch vb* to accost

aborigen see **aborigines**

aborigin see **aborigines**

aborigines *n pl* the original inhabitants of a country (classically used for those Italian peoples who had possession prior to the arrival of the Romans from Troy or for the Pelasgians who preceded the Hellenes in Greece): the primitive natives of a modern European colonial country *esp* Australia (*sing* **aborigine**, also **aborigen, aborigin**)

aborticide *n* the action of destroying a foetus in the womb: an agent used for this purpose

about (*adv/prep*) *vb* to change the course of a ship *obs vb* to come to a head

abrade *vb* to rub or wear off; to rub away (*lit/fig*)

abreact *vb* to resolve a neurosis by recalling the event which initiated the problem

abret *n* a North African, thin, crisp, wafer of bread

abu *Ir interj* to victory

aburabozu *n* a large fish of the north Pacific akin to the jewfish

abutilon *n* a showy-flowered plant of a genus of the mallow family

aby *arch vb* to atone: to endure *obs vb* to purchase

ac *n* oak (*Obs* except as a syllable in English place names) (*pl* **aec**) *obs conj* but

acarid *n* a mite

acaridan *adj/n* (of) a mite, tick or related (parasitic) arachnid

acarine *adj* of, belonging to or transmitted by mites *n* the Isle of Wight disease, a disease of honeybees caused by infestation by a parasitic mite

acas *Obs adv* by chance

acater *obs n* one who buys provisions

acates *obs n pl* things purchased *esp* foodstuffs required to be bought fresh, such as meat or fish, but excluding items capable of storage such as ale or cakes

acatour *var fm obs n* **acater**

accite *vb* to cite: to summon: to arouse

accloy *arch vb* to drive a nail into a horse's foot i.e. (*fig*) to lame: to block, clog or choke (*lit/fig*): to overfill, burden, oppress: to nauseate: to disgust

accoil *n* welcome *obs vb* to collect

accompt *arch fm n/vb* **account** (the *vb* being more or less *obsol*)

accoustre *obs fm vb* **accoutre**

accoutre *vb* to attire or equip

accretion *n* any gradual increase in size: something added: the growing together of normally separate animal or vegetable parts

accrual *n* the increase in the share of a legacy

accrue *vb* to come as an addition or an increase

accurre *obs vb* to meet

accurse *vb* to curse: to devote to evil or misery

acerb *adj* sour

acerbic *adj* of a sour nature

acerous *adj* like or mixed with chaff: of leaves, needle-like

acetal *n* any of various volatile, colourless compounds having sedative properties which, apart from medicinal use, have value as solvents and in cosmetics

acetamide *n* the amide of acetic acid

acetic *adj* pertaining to vinegar

acetone *n* a colourless, volatile liquid used in the manufacture of various chemicals and also as a solvent for such as paints

acetose *adj* of such as fruit, sour

acetyl *n* the univalent radical of acetic acid (*pl* **acetyls**)

achene *n* any small, brittle, seedlike fruit

acher *n* one who or that which aches

acheri *n* in India, a malevolent ghost of a little girl

Acherontic *adj* of or belonging to the mythical river of the infernal regions, Acheron: dark, gloomy: on the brink of death

achier *comp adj* achy

achkan *n* the traditional long coat of Indians

which has a high collar and is buttoned all the way down to the knees

achromatin *n* biological tissue which, when immersed in colouring matter, does not stain, the opposite of **chromatin**, being stained

aciform *adj* needle-shaped

acker *now dial n* a gentle disturbance on the surface of water *obs n* a flood tide

acloy an earlier and better form of the *arch vb* **accloy**

acmite *n* a soda mineral, the crystals of which are frequently pyramid-shaped

acolyte *n* a follower or attendant

aconite *n* any of a genus of mainly poisonous plants such as monkshood or wolfsbane: the poison of such a plant: the dried root of an aconite sometimes used as a narcotic *poet n* any poison

acosmist *n* one who denies the existence of the universe

acquest *n* an acquisition

acrese *var fm obs vb* **accrease**, to increase (by addition)

acrider *comp adj* acrid

acrogen *n* a plant such as a fern or moss which grows at the apex only

acrolein *n* a colourless, acrid liquid of pungent odour derived from glycerin

acrostic *n* a number of lines, often in verse form, certain letters of which form a name or a saying or some other recognized word or words. A **single acrostic** gives the information in the initial letters of the lines, a **double acrostic** in the initial and final letters, a **triple acrostic** in the initial, middle and final letters.

acroter *n* a pedestal for a statue (*pl* **acroteria, acroters**)

acrotism *n* lack of or weakness of pulsation

acsien *Obs fm vb* **ask**

actinal *adj* of the mouth and its surrounding radiating organs of such a creature as the fanworm

actine *n* an abstract unit of solar radiation

actinian *adj* of or pertaining to a genus of sea anemones of which the best known species is the beadlet anemone *n* one such creature. The beadlet anemone is a common animal of British and European coastal waters generally seen exposed at low tide as a contracted reddish brown mass of stiff jelly just over an inch high. When covered by the sea it expands to a more attractive floral shape.

actinide *n* any of the elements from actinium to lawrencium which have an atomic number of 89 or greater

actinoid *adj* having the form of rays – as a starfish

actinon *n* an isotope of radon, the gaseous radioactive element

actioner *n* one employed in the making of the action element of such as a gun

activation *n* the action of activating

actuator *n* one who puts something into action

acurse *vb* an earlier and better form of **accurse**

acute (*adj*) *obs vb* to sharpen

acuter *comp adj* acute

ad *collq n* an advertisement *n* a heap (*Obs* except as a syllable in English place names) *Obs n* a fire: a blazing pile: a funeral pyre

adad *n* a coarse fibre made from pilewort stems (+*cap*) *pers n* the Assyrian god of storm and thunder

Adamite *n* a descendant of Adam: one who copies the nudity of Adam *esp* as a member of one of various ancient or modern sects

adamsite *n* muscovite, a greenish-black mica

Adaven *n* a community in Nye County, Nevada (note: The spelling is Nevada in reverse)

adda *n* the Egyptian skink, a type of small lizard

addling (*n*) *now dial n* earning

addre *obs fm n* **adder**

addren *Obs pl* adder

addrest *var fm adj* **addressed**

adducer *n* one who brings forward in discussion

ade *n* a (citrus) fruit drink *dial n* a reach in the river Severn: a ditch *dial vb* to cut a ditch or deep gutter across ploughed land

adeem *vb* to cancel a bequest (by a codicil to the original deed)

Adeline *var fm fem pers n* **Adela**, meaning 'noble'

Adeni *n* a citizen of Aden *adj* of Aden

adenitis *n* glandular inflammation

adermin *n* a factor of the vitamin B complex which prevents dermatitis in rats (TRIVIA note: It is now known as either pyridoxin or pyridoxine)

adieu *interj* of parting, (I commend you) to God *n* a blessing on parting (*pl* **adieus, adieux**)

admin *collq n* administration (GAME PLAYER'S note: Though this is a popular short form derived from an abbreviation, nevertheless it is valid for play as it is pronounced as it is spelt – see **antilog**)

adminicle *n* anything which provides support: in law, corroborative evidence

admissive *adj* tending to admit

admonition *n* the action or an act of admonishing

admonitor *n* one who admonishes

adnascent *adj* growing or produced upon something else

Adonai *n* (my) Lord, a Biblical description of God's name which, being sacred, is never mentioned. Jehovah, which some ignorantly assert to be God's name, is a mere 16th century invention which fuses vowels from Adonai to the Hebrew Jhvh (Yahweh), another such Biblical respectful reference to His name.

Adonia *n pl* the festival of mourning for Adonis, the beautiful youth beloved by the Greek goddess Aphrodite

Adonic *n/adj* (of) a type of verse supposedly used during the Adonia

adonise *var fm vb* **adonize**

adonize *vb* to adorn: to dandify

adpress *vb* to lay flat against a surface

Adrian *masc pers n* meaning 'of the Adriatic'

ads *var fm interj* **ods** *obs fm n* **adz** *obs fm vb* **adze**

adsorb *vb* of a solid, to gather a condensed layer on its surface (the opposite of **desorb**)

adsorbate *n* a substance which is being or has been adsorbed

adstringe *obs fm vb* **astringe**

adulatory *adj* of or belonging to one who praises in a servile or hypocritical manner: servilely flattering

adulterine *adj* of, relating to or born of adultery: illegal, illegitimate: spurious (*fig*) *n* an adulterer or adulteress

advection *n* the transference of heat energy in a horizontal stream of air

advene *vb* to add as a (non-essential) part: to reach

adverse (*adj*) *n* an adversary or opponent

advert (*n*) *obs fm vb* **avert**

ady *n* a Malabar unit of length

adz *n* an ax-like tool with the blade set at right angle to the handle and used for slicing away the surface of wood

adze *vb* to cut with an adz *var fm n* **adz**

ae *S adj* one *Obs n* law of nature: law of God: legal custom: marriage *var fm now dial n* **ea**

aea *n* a type of cord made from candletree bark

aeblins *dial fm S Ir & dial adv* **ablins**

aec *Obs pl* oak (see **ac**) *Obs fm adv* **eke**

aedeagus *n* the sexual organ of a male insect

aedile *n* a magistrate in ancient Rome with administrative responsibility for various civic matters such as public buildings, shows and police

aedilis *obs pl* aedile

aegilops *n* a species of oak tree, tallest of those native to Greece: an ulcer in the inner angle of the eye *obs n* the wild oat or other weed of a cornfield (WORD PUZZLER'S superlative note: aegilops is the longest word in the English language to have all of its letters in strict alphabetical order)

aei *Obs fm adj/pron* **any**

ael *obs n* grandfather, forefather

aelph *n* the first letter of the Hebrew alphabet

aen *dial fm adj/vb* **own**

aengel, aengle *Obs fms n* **angel**

aer *obs fm ns/vbs* **air, oar**

aerie *var fm n* **eyrie**, the nest of an eagle *var fm poet adj* **aery**, spiritual or visionary

aeriest *sup adj* aery

aernde *Obs fm n* **errand**

aerobiont *n* an aerobe or organism that requires free oxygen for breathing

aerography *n* meteorology

aerolith *n* a meteorite *esp* one of stone rather than one having metallic traces

aes *n pl* Irish fairies

aestival *adj* of summer

aet *Shet fm n* **oat**

aether *poet fm n* **ether**

aetheric *var fm* (*poet*) *adj* **etheric**

aetites *n* eagle stone, a mythical stone found in the nest of an eagle and supposed to possess magical properties (*pl* **aetites**)

af *dial fm preps* **of, off**

afanc *n* a monster in the folklore of North Wales and variously described as being a beaver or a crocodile

aff *S fm adv/prep* **off**

affret *obs vb* to fret, annoy (*infl* **affretted** etc) *obs n* a furious onset

affy *obs vb* to trust, confide in: to secure by solemn promise: to bind in faith

afield *adv* in or on the field (of battle): at a distance *esp* as far afield, at a great distance

afole *obs vb* to deceive

afreet *var fm n* **afrit**

African oil *n* a type of palm oil yielded by the African oil palm

afrit *n* an evil demon or monster of Muslim mythology

afrite *var fm n* **afrit**

afters *collq n pl* the dessert course

Agave *n* a genus of plants of which the chief

species is the American aloe or century plant (a name which reflects the popular, but erroneous belief that it flowers only once every hundred years). The American aloe has a stately flower stem of up to forty feet in height and the juice of the plant can be tapped for fermenting into a wine (*−cap*) *n* any plant of this genus

agelast *n* one whose disposition is such that he or she seems incapable of laughter

agenesis *n* the absence or imperfect development of any bodily part: sexual impotence (*pl* **ageneses**)

agent (*n*) *S vb* to act as an agent

agential *adj* pertaining to an agent or an agency

agerse *Obs adv* agrass, in the grass

agg *Ork & Shet n* flotsam: a short breach of the sea

agger *n* any artificial elevation: the mound on which the Romans built their camp, created by earth taken from a surrounding defensive ditch

aggress *vb* to (make an) attack

aginner *US n* one who is against change

agister *var fm n* **agistor**

agistment *n* the taking in of livestock at a grazing rate per head: the rate levied, the profit made: the opening of a forest for a specific grazing period: the herbage of a forest, the right to it

agistor *n* one employed in a royal forest to take charge of, and levy a fee for, livestock belonging to others which are grazed in that forest

aglet *n* the metal tag on such as a shoelace

aglimmer *adv* in/into a glimmering state

agment *obs fm n* **augment**, the prefixed vowel which characterizes the past tenses of the verb in the older Indo-European written languages such as Greek and Sanskrit

agminate *adj* arranged in a cluster

agname *n* a name or designation over and above the ordinary forename(s) and surname

agnate *adj* related on the father's side *n* such a relative

agnet *obs fm adj/n* **agnate**

agnise *arch vb* agnize, to recognize, remember, acknowledge, confess

agonic *adj* not forming an angle

agonist *n* a competitor

agrégé *Fr n* one who succeeds in a university competition for a teaching post

agrest *obs adj* rustic *obs n* a countryman

agrested *obs adj* rustic

agrestic *adj* rural

agrise *obs vb* to dread, abhor: to be horrified

ague fit *n* a fit of ague, a violent (malarial) fever

ah *interj* of surprise, joy, pity

ahorse *arch adv* on horseback

ahu *n* the common gazelle of Central Asia: a Polynesian sacred burial place

ai *n* the three-toed sloth, one of a number of curious mammals which not only spend a fair amount of time hanging upside down in a tree but even give birth to their young in this position. Almost useless on the ground, nevertheless they descend to it to bury their dung – thus concealing their presence from predators. *var fm n* **ayu**

aiaiai *n* the roseate spoonbill, a stork-like bird and the only species of spoonbill found in the New World

aiblins *var fm S Ir & dial adv* **ablins**

aidance *n* aid, help

aider *n* one who or that which aids

aidless *poet adj* unassisted, helpless

aig *dial n* sourness *dial adj* eagerness

aiglet *var fm n* **aglet**

aigret *var fm n* **aigrette**, a tuft of feathers worn as a head ornament

aik *S fm n* **oak** *dial n* a rustic dance *S & dial vb* to loiter: to sneak

aiker *var fm now dial n* **acker**

ailante *var fm n* **ailanto**

ailanto *n* a species of tree, the leaves of which are the favoured food of the silkworm

aileron *n* a hinged flap on a trailing edge on an aircraft which is used to provide lateral control

ain *n* the eighteenth letter of the Arabic alphabet *S adj* own *obs pl* eye

aindles *var fm obs S adj* **andless**

ainsell *US n* one self (*pl* **ainsells**) (GAME PLAYER'S note: This word seems to be exclusive to the dictionary used for the North American Scrabble championship. It does not seem to appear in dictionaries of Scottish and northern dialect words where one might suppose it could be found.)

airbath *n* exposure of the body to air (for therapeutic purposes)

air bell *n* a bubble of air

air bends *n* aeroembolism, a disease suffered by airmen who experience too drastic a change in air pressure – the equivalent of caisson disease (the bends) suffered by divers

airt *S n* a compass point, a direction *S vb* to direct or guide

airth *obs fm S n* **airt**

airtime *n* the amount of time allotted to a particular broadcast

ais see **as**

aisled *adj* having an aisle: located in an aisle

aisler *var fm n* **ashlar**

aislet *dial fm n* **haslet**

aister *var fm dial n* **astre**

aistre *var fm dial n* **astre**

ait *n* an eyot *S fm n* **oat**

Aix *n* a genus of freshwater ducks *incl* the Chinese mandarin duck (*–cap*) *obs S fm n/vb* **ax**

ak *n* mudar, either of two Indian shrubs, the root-bark of which is used medicinally *dial fm n* **oak** *var fm obs conj* **ac**

aka *n* any of several species of New Zealand woody vines

ake the better and now *arch fm vb* **ache** (note: **aking** as a noun is *obs* having been superseded by **aching**)

akh *n* in the ancient Egyptian religion, the spirit of a man

ako *n* a Hungarian measure of capacity of slightly less than twelve imperial gallons

al *n/adj* all (*Obs* except as a prefix in such words as almighty, almost, always) *Obs fm n* **awl**

ala *n* pinna (*pl* **alae**)

alabre *obs n* a type of fur, the nature of which is unknown

alaka *n* a Hawaiian shrub which bears large, red, edible fruit

alan *n* a large hunting or baiting dog introduced to Britain in the Middle Ages *obs n* a wolfhound

aland *arch adv* ashore *obs vb* to come ashore

Alastair *var fm masc pers n* **Alexander**, meaning 'defender of men'

Alaster *var fm masc pers n* **Alexander**, meaning 'defender of men'

alastor *n* an evil genius of a house or avenging power which visits the sins of fathers on their sons

alastrim *n* (a resemblance to) a mild attack of smallpox

albacore *n* a smaller species of tunny or tuna fish achieving a mere 70 lbs compared with its close relative the tunny or bluefin which can exceed 1,800 lbs

Albanactus *pers n* one of the sons of Brutus, the founder of Britain, who inherited that part of his father's territories which he named Albany (now Scotland) (see **Brutus** and **Albion**)

albata *n* German silver, a silver-like metallic compound

albedo *n* the sun's light reflected from a planet: whiteness

albeit *conj* although (it be that)

Alberga *fem pers n* meaning 'noble'

albert *n* a type of short watch chain

albespine *arch n* hawthorn

albicore *var fm n* **albacore**

albino *n* a human, animal or plant lacking normal pigmentation (*pl* **albinos**)

Albion *n* the ancient name for the isle of Great Britain. In the legend of Brutus, only a few giants lived here and, in a battle between the invading Trojans and the giants, Gogmagog was the last surviving giant. Gogmagog was then challenged to single combat by the Trojan, Corineus, and, in a wrestling bout, he threw the giant over the cliffs to his death on the rocks below. (See **Brutus** and **Albanactus**)

albite *n* pure sodium-plagioclase, one of a group of feldspars. These minerals have a ratio of sodium to calcium which culminates with anorthite which is pure calcium-plagioclase. The others in this group, in decreasing ratio of sodium to calcium, are oligoclase, andesine, labradorite and bytownite.

albitise *vb* to convert into albite

Alcaic *adj* of or pertaining to the Greek lyric poet Alcaeus (circa 600 BC) or to the kind of verse he invented (in *pl*) *n* Alcaic verses

ald *now dial adj* the original Saxon *fm* of the *adjs* **auld** (*S*), **eld** (*arch*) and **old**, any of which mean having (once) lived or existed (for a long time). The *comps/sups* – **alder, aulder, elder, older/aldest, auldest, eldest, oldest** – more or less relate to the basic *adj* though older and oldest are replacement *fms* for elder and eldest in some of the senses in which they had originally functioned as the *comp/sup* to old *obs n* old age *obs vb* to grow old

aldea *n* a Portuguese (colonial) village or hamlet

aldee *var fm n* **aldea**

aldern *n* the alder tree *adj* of alder

aldest *sup now dial adj* ald

Aldine *adj* of or after the style of the quality printing produced by the celebrated 16th century Venetian printer, Aldus Manutius

aldose *n* a type of sugar

aldress *obs n* the wife of an alderman

aldrin *n* a type of insecticide

aleberry *n* a drink of hot ale, spice, sugar and toast

ale bush *n* an inn sign *obs n* a tavern

alecoast *obs fm n* alecost

alecost *n* the plant, costmary, akin to tansy and formerly used to give an aromatic and bitter flavour to beer

Alecto *pers n* one of the Erinyes or Furies (see **Erinys**)

alectryomancy *n* divination by use of a cock in a circle of grain

aledraper *obsol n* an innkeeper

aleeward *adv* towards the sheltered side (*obs* except as a word used in literature on words)

alegar *n* (vinegar made from) sour ale

aleing *nonce n* the drinking of ale

alepine *n* either of two mixed fabrics, wool and silk or mohair and cotton

alerce *n* an American tree akin to the larch

alerion *her n* an eagle without a beak or feet

alese *obs vb* to release

alesing *obs n* release

aless *obs vb* to lesson, to diminish

aleuron *n* a proteinous substance found in the seeds of plants

alevin see **SALMON**

alewife *n* a female tavern keeper (*pl* **alewives**): a herring-like fish of both the western north Atlantic and North American freshwaters (*pl* **alewife, alewives**)

alexin *n* an unstable, heat-sensitive substance in the blood which, uniting with an anti-serum, gives protection from disease

alf *n* in Norse mythology, an elf

alfilaria *n* filaree or pingrass, a European weed grown for forage in western America

alga *n* any primitive chlorophyll-bearing plant widely distributed in fresh and salt water and on moist land *incl* the pond scums, seaweeds and stoneworts (*pl* **algae, algas**)

algae *pl* alga

algate *now dial adv* everywhere *obs adv* always: in every way: altogether

algates *var fm now dial adv* **algate**

Algerine *n* an Algerian (*—cap*) *n* a pirate

algeses *pl* algesis

algesis *n* sensation of pain (*pl* **algeses**)

algin *n* a gummy compound obtained from seaweed

alginate *n* a salt of alginic acid

algoid *adj* of the nature of alga

algorithm *n* any method of computation *esp* one, such as long division, which involves a series of steps

alicant *n* a type of Spanish wine

alien (*adj/n*) *vb* to alienate: to estrange: to transfer

alienism *n* the position of being a foreigner: the study and treatment of mental disorder

alienist *n* one who treats or studies mental disorders

alienor *n* one, in law, who transfers property

alif *n* the first letter of the Arabic alphabet

alighten *obs vb* to dismount: to relieve: to enlighten

aligner *n* one who aligns

aliment *n* nutriment, food *vb* to sustain, support *S vb* to pension

aline *var fm vb* **align**

alineation *var fm n* **allineation**, the position in a straight line with a given point of two or more (heavenly) bodies

aliner *n* one who lines things up

aliped *adj* having winged feet *n* an animal, such as a bat, having winged feet

aliquant *adj* of or signifying a quantity or number that is not an exact divisor of a given quantity or number (compare with **aliquot**)

aliquot *adj* of or signifying a quantity or number which is an exact divisor of a given quantity or number *n* such a number. For example, the aliquots of 220 are 1, 2, 4, 5, 10, 11, 20, 22, 44, 55 and 110. Similarly, the aliquots of 284 are 1, 2, 4, 71, 142. If the aliquots of 220 are added together, they total 284 and if the aliquots of 284 are added together they total 220. This mathematical coincidence pairs 220 and 284 as *amiable numbers*.

alisma *n* any plant of *Alisma*, the genus of the water plantain

Alister *var fm masc pers n* **Alexander**, meaning 'defender of men'

aliunde *adv/adj* from another source

alives *obs adv* alive

alkali *n* a non-acid chemical compound (*pl* **alkalies, alkalis**)

alkalise *var fm vb* **alkalize**, to convert to an alkali

allegorist *n* one who devises an allegory: one who employs them in his or her writings

Allfather *n* God as the universal father (note: Derived from the Old Norse *Al-fadir*, it was originally used to describe Odin, the supreme god of the Norse myths. By a neat coincidence, the *fm* **Allfather** is the only one used by a writer for God, **All-father** the only *fm* used by a writer for Odin, **All-Father** the only *fm* used by a writer for Jupiter. No overlapping of *fms* exists in literature and even the *obs fm*, **Al-father**, applies only to Odin. This is not an arbitrary rule as is proved by the dictionary used for UK championship Scrabble which has all three classified together as All-father.)

allis *var fm n* **allice**, a species of shad found in the river Severn

allonge *n* an addition for endorsements when all available space has been used on the original document

allover *n* a fabric having a pattern which extends over the whole surface

allseed *n* any of various plants producing a great quantity of seeds *esp* a weed of the flax family

almah *n* an Egyptian dancing girl (*var fms* **alma, alme, almeh**)

almain *n* a leaping dance of German origin (+*cap*) *obs n/adj* German

Almaine *obs n* Germany

Almany *n* Germany

almer *obs n* one who gives or distributes alms

almere *obs n* a place for storage such as a storeroom or a cupboard

Almeric *masc pers n* meaning 'work ruler'

aln *n* a Swedish measure of length of slightly less than two feet (59.4 cm)

alnage *n* the official measurement of cloth in units of ells (see **ell**) and the attestation of value by the affixing of a leadened seal: payment for such an act

alnager *n* the officer who conducted the alnage

aloetic *adj* of aloes: having aloes as a medical ingredient *n* a medicine containing aloes

alongst *now dial prep/adv* along: by the length of

alot *obs fm vb* **allot** (*infl fms* **alotted, alotting**)

alp (*n*) *n* a sleep demon: a bullfinch *Obs n* an elephant

alpeen *n* a heavy staff or club

alpestrine *adj* growing below the alpine level of a mountain

alphametic *n* a popular form of mathematical puzzle probably better known as **cryptarithmetic**, under which heading examples are given

alpine *adj* of any high mountain: growing atop a mountain *n* an alpine plant (+*cap*) *adj* of the Alps

alpinist *n* a specialist alpine mountain climber

Alp-Luachra *Ir n* an Irish parasitic fairy who lives inside a human, eating half of the food consumed by the host, without growing any bigger herself. The worst of these fairies is pregnant – then the host really suffers – and there is only one known cure. He must eat a huge quantity of salt beef without taking a single drink of any description. He then has to lie beside a stream with his mouth open and wait for the fairy to jump out to quench her thirst. The former host is then advised to close his mouth rapidly and run for dear life (*pl* **Alp-Luachra**)

alriche *obs fm S adj* **eldritch**

alsoon *obs adv* immediately

Alster *n* a river in West Germany which joins the Elbe at Hamburg

Alsvid *n* in Norse mythology, the horse that draws the moon's chariot (also see **Aarvak**)

Altair *n* a star in the constellation of Aquila, the Eagle

alterant *adj* altering *n* an alternative

alteres *var fm n pl* **halteres**

altern *adj* alternate *obs vb* to alternate

alternat *n* the diplomatic practice of determining precedence among powers of equal rank by such means as the casting of lots

alterne *n* one of two adjacent but greatly different plant communities

Althing *n* the parliament of Iceland

altre *obs fm vb* **alter**

altrices *n pl* immature birds which are totally dependent upon parental care (*sing* **altrix**)

altruism *n* a selfless attitude governing action – the essential opposite of egoism

altruist *n* one who practises altruism

aludel *n* one of a series of pear-shaped glass or earthenware pots having both ends open and stacked to form an alchemist's vessel, used in the process of changing a solid directly into a gas

alumna *fem fm n* **alumnus**, a former student (*pl* **alumnae**)

alumnus *n* a former pupil (*pl* **alumni**)

alunite *n* alumstone, a white hydrous potassium-aluminium sulphate

alure *obs n* a (covered) walk or passage such as a cloister, gallery, roof of a church or behind a castle's parapets

alured *obs adj* having an alure

alvine *adj* pertaining to (the contents of) the abdomen

Alyssum *n* a genus of yellow or white flowers popular in rock gardens (*– cap*) *n* a species of this genus, such as gold dust: a mass of such plants

am *vbl infl* see **be**

amain *adv* with full force: vehemently: violently *obs vb* to lower (a flag, a topsail)

amarant *var fm n* **amaranth**, a fabled flower which never fades: any species of a genus of flowers which includes love lies bleeding and prince's feather: a purple colour

amate *arch vb* to dismay or dishearten *obs vb* to match or equal

amatorian *adj* of or pertaining to a lover or lovemaking (note: Possibly now *obs* which, if so, is a pity as its apt anagram is **inamorata**)

ambel *obs fm n* **amble**

amber (*n*) *vb* to colour an item amber: to embed in amber: to perfume with ambergris

amberjack *n* any of various species of marine fishes related to the horse mackerels, scads and pompanos

Ambian the former name of **Amiens**, the French city

ambivert *n* one neither an extrovert nor an introvert

ambo *n* a raised platform in some early Christian churches used as a pulpit: in English churches, a reading desk (*pl* **ambos, ambones**)

ame see **be**

ameed *vb* to reward

ameer *var fm n* **amir**, the title of a Muslim prince

amelia *n* a medical condition where one or more limbs is completely absent (+*cap*) *var fm fem pers n* **Emily** (the *fem fm* of **Emile** meaning 'industrious')

amende *Fr n* a penalty

Amen-Ra *pers n* the Egyptian god of the sun, Ra, as the personification of Thebes in glory

ament *n* a catkin

amentia *n* mental deficiency

amerce *vb* to deprive: to punish

amere *var fm obs vb* **amar**, to mar

Amerind *n/adj* the American Indian

amerine *obs adj* bitter or sour tasting

amese *obs vb* to calm: to moderate

Amharic *n* a Semitic language of Ethiopia

amice *n* a linen strip worn on the shoulders by a priest during mass: a cloak: (a cape with) a hood

amide *n* a type of chemical compound from ammonia

Amiens *n* a French city on the river Somme and capital of the Somme department

amildar *n* one, of native stock, who collects revenue in India: extended to cover various other occupations such as that of a manager

amine *n* one of a large class of organic compounds derived from ammonia

amite *var fm obs n* **amit**, a scarf or similar wrap

amitosis *n* the division of biological cells without the formation and splitting of chromosomes (*pl* **amitoses**)

amitrole *n* a herbicide

amlet *obs fm n* **omelet**

amm see **be**

ammeter *n* an instrument for estimating the amperage or force of electrical currents

ammine *n* any of the various complex compounds containing the ammonia molecule

ammocoete *n* a pride or larva of a lamprey

amnestic *adj* pertaining to amnesia: of an agency such as disease, causing loss of memory

amnion *n* the inner of two membranous sacs which envelop the embryo of a bird, reptile or mammal (*pl* **amnia, amnions**)

amniote *n* any of the Amniota, vertebrates *incl* mammals, birds and reptiles, the embryos of which are enclosed in a membranous sac (*pl*, in an individual sense, **amniotes**)

amoret *n* a love-knot: a love song or sonnet *obs n* a lover, sweetheart or paramour: an amorous girl *in pl fm* loving glances

amorist *n* a lover: a seeker of sexual experiences: one who writes on love

amornings *obs adv* in the/of the morning

amortise *var fm vb* **amortize**

amortize *vb* to liquidate a financial liability by periodic payments: to write off (a wasting asset) by transfer to a fund which earns interest during the period of repayment of a long term debt

amove *vb* to remove from a position: to dismiss from office *obs vb* to move the feelings of

amoving *n* removal

amp (*n*) *Ork & Shet n* fear, terror

ampere *n* amp, the metric unit of strength of electrical current

ample (*adj*) *obs vb* to enlarge: to amplify

ampler *comp adj* ample

amrit *n* a sweetened water used in a Sikh initiation ceremony: the ceremony

amrita *n* the drink of the various gods of the Hindus

amt *n* a Danish administrative district (*pl* **amter, amts)**

amuletic *adj* of or pertaining to amulets *obs n* a medicine which owes its properties solely to occult value and not to any intrinsic physical properties (GAME PLAYER'S note: The *adj* is undefined in the dictionary used for the UK Scrabble championship but is given as being extant. The *n* is unmentioned. The meanings given above are those last known to be used in the middle of the 18th century, both of which are considered by other authorities to be equally obsolete.)

an (*indefinite article*) *arch conj* if

Anableps *n* the genus of Central American freshwater toothcarps which appear to have four eyes. Such a toothcarp cruises along the surface of the water with the upper half of its horizontally divided eyes above water (literally 'keeping an eye out' for predators) whilst the lower half searches for food. Having no tear-duct, the fish must constantly duck its head under water to keep the upper half of its eye moist. But its oddness does not end here. As the fish bears live young this involves an act of copulation and, like similar fishes with this reproductive system, the male's organ is a modification of its anal finrays to form a hollow delivery tube. The female's genital opening has a scale on *either* the left or the right side, which restricts entry to only one side. The male's tube, a gonopodium, can only be moved (unlike that of other, similar fishes) to *either* the left or the right side but not both. The result is that a 'right-handed' male can only mate with a 'left-handed' female and a 'left-handed' male can only mate with a 'right-handed' female. (*–cap*) *n* a fish of this genus (also see **four-eyed fish**)

anacrusis *n* an introductory syllable preceding the normal rhythm of a line (*pl* **anacruses**)

anadem *n* a floral headband: a chaplet, a garland

anaepest *n* a metric foot of two short syllables followed by a long syllable (see **metric foot**): a line of verse of such feet

anaglyptic *adj* of or pertaining to embossing or similar forms of low relief

analcime *n* a sodium-aluminium silicate

analcite *n* the mineral, analcime or zeolite

analogise *var fm vb* **analogize**, to use analogy in its sense of logical reasoning: to show the similarities between

analogist *n* one who concerns himself with analogies

analogy *n* a similarity, likeness or resemblance in some respect even where the identities are not common, as the atom and solar system share the same construction of bodies orbiting a central nucleus: in logic, reasoning from known factors that a parallel situation should, other things being equal, produce a similar outcome: in linguistics, the formative process which governs development of word usage by imitating the familiar, as the past tense of the *vb* climb changed from clomb to climbed (*pl* **analogies**)

anapaestic *adj* composed of anaepests *n* verses having such metric feet

anapest *US fm n* **anaepest**

anaphoric *adj* referring to a preceding word or group of words

anatta *n* an orange-red dye produced from the waxy pulp surrounding the seeds of the arnotto tree and used for such as colouring cheese (*var fms incl* **anatto, arnotto)**

anchoress *var fm n* **ancress**

anchoret *n* an anchorite

anchoretic *adj* of or pertaining to an anchoret

anchorite *n* a religious hermit of either sex (a female can also be called an anchoress) *modf n* as **anchorite church**, a church-like cave carved out of the local rock of a bank adjacent to a backwater of the river Trent in south Derbyshire, believed to have been the home of an anchorite. It has a Gothic style entrance and 'window' together with a supporting pillar inside. In a tranquil setting, marred only by a distant view of a power station, it is not promoted as a tourist attraction.

ancienter (*comp adj*) *obs n* an ancestor

ancile *L n* a small oval shield (*pl* **ancilia**): the sacred shield of the Romans said to have dropped from heaven and upon which the safety of the city was held to depend

ancle *var fm n* **ankle**

ancon *n* the elbow: an elbow-like architectural feature (*pl* **ancones**) *modf n* **ancon sheep**, a breed derived from a mutant lamb born in 1791 of which all descendants have the same long body and very short legs of which the front pair are bowed like elbows

ancones *pl* ancon

ancress *n* a female anchorite or religious recluse who lives a completely solitary existence

andagram *n* an anagram of a word plus an additional letter as ANAGRAM + D creates ANDAGRAM. Basically a device of the crossword compiler who cannot produce a perfect anagram so provides a clue where such as EMPIRICAL + D gives LAMPRICIDE. (ANDAGRAM can also be formed by GRANDMA + A or RAMADAN + G though neither of these has the etymological significance of ANAGRAM + D in the sense of *and an anagram around a letter*)

andante *adv/adj* of music, at a moderately slow, even tempo *n* a passage composed in this tempo

andesine *n* one of the plagioclase group of feldspars, a mineral having a 70/30 to 50/50 ratio of sodium to calcium

andesite *n* a type of volcanic rock found in the Andes

andesitic *adj* of the nature of or containing andesite

Andine *adj* of/like the Andes, the great mountain chain of South America

anding *obs n* breath, breathing

andiron *n* a fire dog or iron bar used for supporting a log in a fire

andless *obs S adj* breathless

andolandol *n* a Chinese fly, a tincture of which is used as a blistering agent

androgen *n* any of various hormones that promote development of male sexual characteristics

anearst *dial prep* near, close to

aneast *dial prep* near, close to

aneath *prep* beneath

aneest *var fm dial prep* **aneast**

aneist *var fm dial prep* **aneast**

anele *arch vb* to anoint: to give the sacrament of Extreme Unction

anemic *US fm adj* **anaemic**

anemograph *n* an instrument which records wind speed and direction

anergia *var fm n* **anergy**

anergy *n* lack of energy: inactivity: loss of some or all immunity against a given irritant

anerly *arch S adv* only

anestrus *n* a period of sexual dormancy (*pl* **anestri**)

anetic *adj* of that which is medicinal: soothing

aneurism *var fm n* **aneurysm**, a dilation of an artery due to disease

angary *n* the right, in international law, of a nation in time of war to take possession or destroy such as the ships of a neutral power, accepting that compensation will be made at a future date (*pl* **angaries**)

angele *obs fm n* **angel**

angeled *obs adj* rendered angelic

angelet *n* a cherub

angelic (*adj*) *obs n* a worshipper of angels

Angelin *obs fm n* **Angelina**, a genus of tropical American trees with purple flowers

Angelist *n* one who held heretical views concerning the angels

Angelite *n* an heretical sect which arose in AD 494 and was based in Alexandria

angelot *n* a lute-like musical instrument

angelsite *n* a type of lead sulphate

angelus *n* a short devotional exercise commemorating the mystery of the Incarnation

Angevin *adj* of or pertaining to the French former province of Anjou: relating to the English monarchy from the accession of Henry II in 1154 to either of two dates (*a*) 1204 when John lost Anjou to the French (*b*) 1399 when the last Plantagenet or member of the House of Anjou, Richard II, was murdered *n* a native or inhabitant of Anjou: a member of the House of Anjou

angico *n* a South American tree of the mimosa family (*pl* **angicos**)

angina *n* any disease, such as quinsy or croup, which provokes painful attacks of spasmodic choking: the usual short *fm* of **angina pectoris**, a sudden intense pain in the chest caused by the momentary loss to the heart muscle of a constant supply of blood.

anginal *adj* of angina

anglet *n* a small angle or corner

angle worm *n* any worm used as fishing bait

Anglice *adv* in English (also *−cap*)

anglify *vb* to make English

anglist *n* one greatly versed in the English language, literature and culture

angre *obs fm n/vb* **anger**

angrise *Obs vb* to distress

angrite *n* a type of meteoritic stone

angry (*adj*) *n* an 'angry young man', one who despises the society of his parents' generation: a writer on such a theme *obs vb* to make angry

anguine *adj* of or resembling a snake or serpent (also see **ANIMAL ADJECTIVES**)

Anguis *n* the genus of the blindworm, a legless lizard (*−cap*) *L n* snake

anhinga *n* the snakebird or water turkey (see **darter**)

ani *n* any of three species of tropical American cuckoos, all of which actually build nests and raise their own young. Curiously enough, they choose a similar method of gathering food as does the American cowbird, which acts like a cuckoo in its egg-laying activity, but is totally unrelated. (See **cowbird**)

aniconism *n* the worship of such as a simple pillar or block of stone not fashioned to human form but symbolic of a Greek deity (also see **aniconist**)

aniconist an undefined noun which appears to be exclusive to one particular dictionary and presumably means one who, in ancient Greek times, practised aniconism. Its own definition of aniconism, however, would suggest that the practice is still extant. There are various anagrams.

anicut *n* a dam on a river

anidian *adj* formless, without shape

anigh (*adv/prep*) *obs vb* to approach

anight *arch adv* by or at night

anile *adj* old-womanish *obs fm n* **anil**, the indigo plant: the dye obtained from that plant

anima *n* the soul

anime *n* a resin, originally that of the West Indian locust tree, used for the making of varnish

animist *n* one who believes that animals (and even inanimate objects) possess a soul: one

ANIMAL ADJECTIVES Few of the adjectives which end with the suffix '-ine' give an immediate English reference to the creature in question as most have a basis in Latin or Greek. Some are very limited in application (as nycertine for some species of bat) but many are quite general, such as the well-known canine or feline. Apart from the word musteline, which is used for both members of the weasel family and for the dogfish (a small shark), the adjective in question is used for the named animal and kindred species. Amongst those which refer to well-known creatures are the following:– **agouti** dasyproctine: **American oriole** icturine: **ant** formicine: **ant thrush** pittine: **antelope** antilopine: **armadillo** xenurine: **ass** asinine: **ass** (*little*) aselline: **badger** musteline: **basilisk** basilicine: **bear** ursine: **bird** avine or volucrine: **bird of paradise** paradiseine: **bull** taurine: **bustard** otidine: **cabbage white butterfly** pieridine: **calf** vituline: **camel** cameline: **capuchin monkey** cebine: **carp** cyprine: **cat** feline: **cattle** bovine: **centipede** scolopendrine: **chamois** rupicaprine: **chevrotain** traguline: **civet** viverrine: **cod** gradine: **cotinga** cotingine: **crab** cancrine: **crocodile** crocodiline (*obs*): **crow** corvine: **cuckoo** cuculine: **deer** cervine: **dodo** didine: **dog** canine: **dog fish** musteline: **dolphin** delphinine: **domestic fowl** galline: **dove** columbine: **duck** anatine: **eagle** aquiline: **eared seal** otarine: **elephant** elephantine: **falcon** falconine: **finch** fringilline: **firefly** lampyrine: **fish** piscine: **flycatcher** muscicapine: **flying fox** pteropine: **fox** vulpine: **frog** ranine: **giant herring** elopine: **gibbone** hylobatine: **giraffe** giraffine: **godwit** calidritine: **goat** caprine or hircine: **goose** anserine: **gull** larine: **hare** leporine: **hawk** accipitrine: **hippopotamus** hippopotamine: **horse** equine: **hyena** hyenine: **Indian elk** rusine: **kite** milvine: **lemur** lemurine: **leopard** pardine: **limpet** patelline: **lion** leonine: **lizard** lacertine: **lobster** homarine: **marsupial cat** dasyurine: **mite** acarine: **mole** talpine: **moloch** molochine: **mongoose** herpestrine: **mouse** murine: **musk ox** ovibovine: **night monkey** nyctiphecine: **nathutch** sittine: **oryx** orygine: **osprey** pandionine: **otter** lutrine: **owl** strigine (also, for many species, bubonine): **oyster** ostracine: **parrot** psittacine: **partridge** perdicine: **peacock** pavonine: **perch** percine: **pheasant** phasianine: **pig** porcine or suilline: **pigeon** columbine: **pocket gopher** pseudostomine: **porcupine** hystricine: **quetzal** trogonine: **racoon** procyonine: **rail** ralline: **rattlesnake** crotaline: **reindeer** rangyferine: **rhino** rhinocerontine: **ribbonworm** nemertine: **roebuck** capreoline: **ruff** *sandpiper* calidritine, *pigeon* columbine, *fish* percine: **salamander** salamandrine: **sandpiper** tringine or calidritine (according to species): **seal** phocine: **sea lion** otarine: **sheep** ovine: **shrew** soricine: **slug** limacine: **snake** anguine, colubrine or serpentine: **snipe** scolopacine: **songbird** *in the sense of a perching bird capable of song* oscine, or, *in the sense of any perching bird* passerine (note, passerine also means sparrow-sized and can be used in that sense for birds which are, technically, non-passerine): **spotted** or **axis deer** pseudaxine: **squirrel** sciurine: **stag** elaphine: **starling** sturnine: **swallow** hirundine: **tapir** tapirine: **tern** sternine: **thrush** turdine: **tiger** tigrine: **titmouse** parine: **toucan** pteroglossine: **turbot** psettine: **tyrant flycatcher** taeniopterine: **viper** viperine: **vireo** vireonine: **vulture** vulturine: **wading bird** gralline: **wagtail** motacilline: **walrus** trichechine: **wasp** vespine: **weasel** musteline: **wren** troglodytine: **wild boar** as for **pig** (formerly, now *obs*, aprine): **wolf** lupine: **woodcock** scolopacine: **woodpecker** picine: **worm** lumbricine: **zebra** zebrine.

cont overleaf

Additionally, there are the non-specific *adjs* such as those which refer to any creatures which are **active in the evening** vespertine: **lake dwelling** lacustrine: **marsh dwelling** palustrine: **rock dwelling** rupicoline: **vermin** vermine: **wild** ferine: and **carnivores** of rapine – as *an animal of rapine* or a *beast of rapine*. Apart from the obvious plurality of using any non-specific *adj* with the standard, there are also technical choices such as those for a gull. A typical gull is larine but, as a member of the gull family, it is also laridine. The *adjs* themselves are subject to change as the creatures are often reclassified in different categories so that whilst in one system a particular *adj* is general, under a new system it becomes limited. For example, strigine means owl-like but the latest classification has strigine relevant to only some of the species. This is equally true of the 'non -ine' adjectives and nouns. Thus, some of the creatures mentioned elsewhere under various technical terms will have other and often very different technical terms in the latest scientific classification. However, the words are still extant in general dictionaries and, as such, will feature in crosswords and other non-scientific word usage. In a strictly technical sense such words are obsolete but the *Advanced Dictionary*, in common with other general dictionaries, does not label them *obs*. It is concerned with explaining words in use, not with being a technical manual. The serious student of *any* science should always refer to the appropriate definitive work and treat with suspicion all entries in a general dictionary no matter how respected the work. For example, the two '-ine' *adjs* labelled as *obs* (see **crocodile** and **wild boar**) have never been part of any scientific system and are just general words no longer in use. The remaining '-ine' words are in general use even though the specialist will consider some to be obsolete or valueless. (For a typical change of scientific name see **springhare**.)

Finally, there is even sphinxine for the qualities of the mythical **sphinx**, though this is limited to meaning mysterious or enigmatic – sphinxian being the general *adj*. (Also see **BIRD CLASSIFICATION, COLLECTIVE NOUNS, FISH CLASSIFICATION**.)

who believes that the soul is independent and lives in a spiritual world

anion *n* a negative ion (as opposed to a **cation**)

anise *n* a small plant of the Mediterranean region cultivated for its aromatic seeds which produce the flavour of aniseed

anisette *n* a liqueur flavoured with aniseed

anker *n* a north European measure of wine or spirits which varied in different countries though the Dutch and English shared the same measure of 10 wine gallons ($8\frac{1}{2}$ imperial gallons)

ankerite *n* a mineral resembling dolomite

ankled *adj* having ankles

anklet *n* a ring-shaped leg ornament or fetter

anlage *n* the first rudiment of a biological organ

annalist *n* one who writes annals, year books

anneal *vb* to toughen or temper (*lit/fig*)

annealer *n* one who or that which anneals

annelid *n* a red-blooded worm

annie *var fm obs vb* **anigh**

annual fish *n* any of various fishes which, for climatic reasons, complete their life cycle within a year. Apart from some members of two genera of African fishes, the majority of these are contained in four genera of New World toothcarps which include the beautiful Argentine pearlfishes. An annual fish lives in a pool which only exists for a part of the year. When the dry season is about to commence the eggs are laid in the mud where they survive months of drought until the next rainy season. The metabolic cycle of these fishes is such that, even if kept in an aquarium, the parents still die at the appointed time and, if the eggs are to survive, the tank must be drained to provide a natural 'dry season'.

annuli *pl* annulus, any ring-shaped biological structure

anodic *adj* of an anode, a positively charged electrode

anodise *vb* to coat a metal (such as aluminium) with a protective oxide film

anodize *var fm vb* **anodise**

anodyne *adj* having the power to alleviate pain *n* such a medicament (*lit/fig*)

anoetic *adj* unthinkable

anomic *adj* pertaining to anomie, a condition of hopelessness characterised by a lack of social or moral standards in an individual or a society

anorectic *adj* relating to or suffering from the 'slimmer's disease', anorexia nervosa

anoretic *adj* lacking appetite

anote *var fm obs vb* **annote**, to censure

ansate *adj* having a handle

Anselm *masc pers n* meaning 'divine helmet'

anserous *adj* gooselike: stupid

Anstace *var fm fem pers n* **Anastasia**, meaning 'she who wakes'

Anstice *var fm fem pers n* **Anastasia**, meaning 'she who wakes'

Antares *n* a first magnitude red star in Scorpio

antbear *n* the giant anteater, the largest of the *Myrmecophagidae*: the aardvark

antbird *n* any of 223 species of rather small American perching birds, sometimes called antthrushes though that name is now usually restricted to such genera as *Formicarius* or *Chamaeza* of the antbird family, the *Formicariidae*. Apart from the various antthrush genera, the others combine the prefix ant with such descriptions as catcher, creeper, pitta, shrike, vireo and wren. The designation of ant to the whole family is rather misleading as only a few of these birds, such as the spotted antbird (*Hylophylax naevoides*), has any real association with ants. Equally unhelpful is the fact that the resemblance to such as wrens or thrushes is very slight. None of the family has an exceptionally colourful plumage and their voices are generally harsh and unmusical. They all live in wooded areas.

ant cow see **aphid**

ante (*n*) *vb* to wager: to pay

anteater *n* any species of *Myremecophagidae*, a family of South American mammals *incl* the tamandua and the tamanoir which diet on termites. Despite august opinion to the contrary, the hyphenated *fm*, **ant-eater**, should not be used as a descriptive *name* for such – it should be reserved as a *description of activity* or as a secondary name for any of various unrelated animals *incl* the aardvark, echidna, numbat and pangolin. Modern mainstream opinion favours anteater and ant-eater as stated above, even though ant-eater can be used for all senses. (For the significant difference of anteaters to ant-eaters see **Edentata**.)

antechoir *n* the space in a church in front of the choir

antecrist *Obs fm n* **Antichrist**

antedate *n* an earlier date *vb* to date before the true time: to assign to an earlier date: to cause to occur sooner

ANTELOPES See next page

antelucan *adj* of or pertaining to the hours just before dawn

anter *S vb* to venture, to chance: to saunter *Obs fm n/vb* **adventure**

Anteros *pers n* the nineteenth pope (235–236) and a saint

Anthea *fem pers n* meaning 'lady of flowers'

ANTELOPES Surprisingly, there is no single zoological grouping for these slender, graceful, swift-moving, hollow-horned ruminants. In effect the term is general and covers any member of the family *Bovidae* other than cattle and buffalos, sheep, goats and goat-antelopes. Thus any of the following is an antelope:– addax, beira, blaauwbok, blackbuck, bongo, bushbuck, chiru, dibatag, dikdik, duiker, dzeren, eland, gazelle, gerenuk, goa, grysbok, hartebeest, impala, klipspringer, kudu, nilgai, nyala, oribi, oryx, reedbuck, rhebok, saiga, springbok, steinbok, suni, topi and waterbuck. In addition there are others such as the various bastard hartebeests (of which topi is a subspecies) and those which incorporate antelope into their name. These *incl* dwarf antelope, four-horned antelope, roan antelope, royal antelope and sable antelope. Oddly, the pronghorn antelope is not included in the *Bovidae*. It is the sole surviving member of its own family, *Antilocapridae*.

anthemia *pl* anthemion

anthemion *n* the honeysuckle or palm leaf pattern common to classical Greek decorative art (*pl* **anthemia**)

anther *n* the pollen-bearing part of a plant's stamen

anthesis *n* the time or process of development in a flower: full bloom (*pl* **antheses**)

anthropic *adj* of or belonging to a human being

antiar *n* the Javanese upas tree: a poison obtained from it

antiarch *n* any of various extinct freshwater fishes of rather grotesque, crab-like appearance

Antichrist *n* the Man of Sin, the great opponent of Christ and His kingdom and expected to precede the second advent. In St John's Gospel he is given a numerical identification '*Let him that hath understanding count the number of the beast: for it is the number of a man: and his number is Six hundred threescore and six*'. Various historical people or movements have been suggested on the basis of the numerical value of their names. For example, using the values ascribed in Hebrew to the individual letters of Nero written as Neron Caeser these, added together, total 666. If Greek is used, then the values of the letters of Caligula produce 666. The Roman Empire, if called *Lateinos*, had this same result in Greek
L A T E I N O S
30 + 1 + 300 + 5 + 10 + 50 + 70 + 200 = 666. Others who have been identified in this fashion include Julian the Apostate, the Roman emperor and nephew of Constantine the Great who attempted to reintroduce paganism, Mohammed, Napoleon and the kaiser, William II. At least two of the popes have been included whilst the papacy itself has also fallen suspect, due to the word *mysterium*. Until the time of the Reformation, this word was engraved on the pope's tiara and it, too, can be made to total 666. The existence of the Antichrist or of a number of Antichrists is a major concern of *The Centuries*, the prophetic work of Nostradamus discussed at greater length at **Hister**.

anticor *n* a disease of grazing animals which results in a fist-sized swelling near the heart

anticore *obs fm n* **anticor**

antigen *n* any of such substances as enzymes, proteins or toxins which cause the development of antibodies when injected into an organism

antigene *var fm n* **antigen**

antigram *n* a specialized type of anagram which produces a word or words directly opposed in meaning to the original word. For example, **anarchists** arch-saints: **enormity** more tiny: **filled** ill-fed: **infection** fine tonic: **misfortune** it's more fun: **nastily** saintly: **protectionism** nice to imports: **restful** fluster: **santa** Satan: **violence** nice love. (The reverse of an antigram is simply anagram, but among the most apt are **filaree** leafier (see **alfilaria**): **levirate** relative (see **levirate**): **listerized** sterilized: **Soliman** Osmanli (see **Osmanli**): **star pine** pinaster (see **pinaster**) and the classic, **incomprehensible** problem in

Chinese. One which is either an antigram or an apt anagram (depending upon your political viewpoint) is **alliance** canaille. For a different type of anagram see **andagram**.)

antilate *adj* having a sucking proboscis

antilog *n* the number corresponding to a given logarithm (GAME PLAYER'S note: Whilst being a short *fm* of **antilogarithm** it is, nevertheless, valid for play. Unlike abbreviations which are *pronounced as though written in full* and are invalid for play (e.g. **Dr**, meaning doctor, is not pronounced 'durr' or 'druh' but as 'doctor') antilog is pronounced as it is written.)

antilope *var fm n* **antelope** (*obs* except *+cap* as the genus of the blackbuck)

antimonial *adj* of or pertaining to antimony

antimonic *adj* of or pertaining to antimony

antimony *n* a brittle, bluish-white metallic element

anting *n* the unusual behaviour of birds of the order *Passeriformes* (see **BIRD CLASSIFICATION**) in taking a live ant and rubbing it on the underside of the long flight feathers. The reason is not known nor is an insect the only object of anting, as various items are used. All chosen objects, however, appear to be either aromatic or pungent.

antinodal an undefined adjective which appears to be exclusive to one particular dictionary and presumably means of or pertaining to an antinode in the sense of a point of maximum vibration. (A possible alternative of 'loopy', see **antinode**, can be discounted as a serious definition!) Its anagram is **Daltonian.**

antinode *n* that point of a vibrating medium which lies midway between two points of zero or minimum displacement (i.e. where maximum vibration occurs): a loop

antinomic *adj* of, pertaining to or of the nature of antinomy

antinomy *n* a contradiction between two seemingly valid principles

Antipas *pers n* Herod Antipas or Herod the Tetrarch, the local ruler to whom Pontius Pilate originally turned for judgment in the trial of Jesus Christ. He was a son of Herod the Great, the king who ordered the slaughter of the infant boys at the time of Christ's birth. (Also see **tetrarch**)

antiphony *n* a musical response

antipole *n* the opposite pole

antique (*adj/n*) *vb* to give an antique appearance to

antiquer *n* one who antiques

antiscian *adj* of or pertaining to the Antiscii *n* (also *+cap*) one of the Antiscii

Antiscii *n pl* those who dwell on the same meridian but on opposite sides of the equator. This means that, at noon, their shadows fall in opposite directions (*sing + or −cap,* **antiscian** – contrast with Periscii, see **periscian**)

antisepsis *n* Listerism, the principle of antiseptic surgical treatment by the creation or maintenance of sterile conditions

antiserum *n* a serum containing antibodies (*pl* **antisera, antiserums**)

antisgne *obs fm n* **ensign**

antitrade *n* a wind of the upper atmosphere blowing in the opposite direction from and above a trade wind i.e. in the northern hemisphere, from the S.W., in the southern hemisphere from the N.W.

antlered *adj* having antlers: branched as with antlers

antlia *n* the trunk-like mouth part of an insect which it uses for sucking juices (*pl* **antliae**)

antling *n* a small or young ant

antral *adj* of or pertaining to a cavity

antre *n* a cave

antrum *n* a cavern: a natural cavity *esp* in a bone (*pl* **antra**)

ansty *slg adj* eager, impatient, restless

Anubis *pers n* the ancient Egyptian jackal-headed god of the dead who weighed the soul of each departed person in order to determine the course of his or her afterlife

anuresis *n* inability to urinate (*pl* **anureses**)

anuria *n* the inability to urinate

anurous *var fm adj* **anourous**, of amphibia, tailless

ao *n* the personification of light in Maori legend

aorist *n* a (Greek) tense expressing past time with no implication of continued existence

apaise *obs fm vb* **appease**

apale *obs vb* to make or become pale

apalle *obs fm vb* **appal**

apart (*adv*) *obs vb* to separate: to quit

apatetic *adj* of the marking or coloration of a creature, closely resembling that of another species or of the surroundings

apedom *n* the state of mankind in early evolution

apeling *n* a small or young ape

aperçu *n* a general (intuitive) view: a comprehensive survey (with the mind's eye)

aperient *adj/n* (a) laxative

apern *dial fm n* **apron**

apertness *arch n* openness, frankness

apheresis *n* the (deliberate) suppression of a short or unaccented syllable at the beginning of a word. (Contrast with **aphesis**, a word coined by the original editor of the *Oxford English Dictionary* which, as a consequence, necessitates the inclusion of the word *deliberate* in the above definition to make an essential distinction. Apheresis can still, however, embrace the sense given at aphesis.)

aphesis *n* the gradual and unintentional loss of a short unaccented vowel at the beginning of a word (as in **squire** for **esquire** or **noint** for **anoint**) or a similar loss for a word from either the original or an earlier form of that word (as in **taint** for **attaint** with its earlier spelling forms of **ataynt**, **ataynte**, **ateynte** etc) (also see **apheresis**)

Apheta *n* in astrology, that planet which is deemed, by virtue of its position in a natal chart, to be an individual's planet of birth and thus the life-giving influence. The nature of one's Apheta governs such matters as the start of a career or similar new beginnings in life.

aphetic *adj* of aphesis: of Apheta

aphetise *var fm vb* **aphetize**

aphetize *vb* to shorten by aphesis

aphid *n* any of some 4,000 different species of plant lice, of which about 540 are resident in Britain. Better known as **greenfly**, it is also called an **aphis** but another name, **ant cow**, gives the clue to a remarkable association some of the species have with ants. The common black ant collects the eggs of the aphids, stores them through the winter and, after hatching, carries the nymphs to the most suitable feeding sites where it protects them from predators. The ant will then collect the honeydew produced by the ant cow. All aphids produce honeydew, though it varies with the species and the plant on which it feeds. It is a complex mixture of various substances *incl* sugars, salts, alcohols, amino acids and carbohydrates. It is also eaten by man and is the excrement of the insect. (Also see **parthenogenesis**) (*pl* **aphids, aphides**)

aphides *pl* aphid or aphis (see **aphid**)

aphoriser *var fm n* **aphorizer**, one who utters aphorisms

aphorism *n* a short pithy saying expressing a truth or a principle: a proverb, maxim, precept

apiary *n* a place where bees are kept (*pl* **apiaries**)

apiest *obs S conj* although

apivorous *adj* feeding on bees

aplite *n* a fine-grained rock having affinity with granite

aplustre *n* the ornamentation on the stern of an ancient ship

apocrine *adj* designating those sweat glands which occur throughout the skin of an embryo but which are vestigial in the independent human, only being found in the anogenital region

Apollo *pers n* the Greek god of the sun (*–cap*) *n* a very handsome young man *esp* one with classical features (*pl* **apollos**)

apostil *vb* to annotate *n* a marginal note

apostlebird *n* a highly sociable, fluffy grey Australian bird, so named from the fact that it travels about in a flock of about a dozen birds

apple (*n*) *vb* to bear apples: to gather apples

applejohn *n* a variety of apple which traditionally is supposed to ripen on St John's Day and is said to be best eaten when shrivelled

appres *Obs fm vb* **oppress**

appress *vb* to press close (to a surface/to each other)

appulse *n* a force or motion towards (or against): the arrival of a heavenly body at a specific point

aprine *obs adj* of or pertaining to wild boar (not a former scientific term, see **ANIMAL ADJECTIVES**)

aprise *Obs fm obs n* **apprise**, lore

apsidiole *n* a subsidiary apse or recess

aptest *sup adj* apt

aptote *n* a noun which has no inflected forms

ar *n* the letter R: ploughed land (*Obs* except as a syllable in English place names. Still extant in Welsh, with the meaning 'arable') *var fm dial n/vb* **arr** (also see **be**)

arabin *n* the pure soluble and essential principle of various substances *esp* gum arabic

arabise *var fm vb* **Arabize** or **arabize**, to make like Arabic

Aragon *n* a former independent kingdom within the boundaries of modern Spain

araine *var fm obs vb* **arraign**, to claim, demand or appeal to

araise *obs vb* to elevate, to raise (from the dead)

Aramaic *adj* relating to Aram, a land of Biblical times roughly corresponding to modern Syria *n* any of a group of Semitic languages *incl* that spoken by Christ

araneid *n* a spider

arapaima *n* the largest of the bonytongues and one of the largest freshwater fishes. Found in the Amazon, it is reported to reach fifteen feet in length, though lengths of nine feet have been reliably recorded.

arase *obs vb* to level to the ground: to obliterate

arawana *n* a large, rather primitive freshwater fish closely related to the arapaima

arayse *var fm obs vb* **araise**

arbalester *n* one armed with a crossbow

arbalestre *obs n* a crossbow: the missile used

arbalister *var fm n* **arbalester**

Arbela *pers n* the ancient Assyrian goddess of war

arborist *n* one who studies trees

arbute *n* the strawberry tree, a small tree of the heath family having red berries

arc (*n*) *vb* to form an arc (*infl fms* either **arced** or **arcked** and **arcing** or **arcking**)

Arcadian *adj* of Arcadia, Greece: pastoral: simple, innocent

arcading *n* architectural ornamentation in the form of arcades

arcanist *n* one having knowledge of a secret ceramic process. (This word appears to be exclusive to *Chambers 20th Century Dictionary* whose own definition is given above.)

arcel *obs fm n* **archil**

arcell *obs fm n* **archil**

arc-en-ciel *Fr n* a rainbow

archaist *n* one who studies that which is archaic: a writer who deliberately revives archaic forms (Spenser, for example, was fond of the 'y-' forms of an earlier period (see **y-**) and Scott revived some of the words of Spenser's time (see **WRITERS**)

archerfish *n* any of a number of species of small, southeast Asian freshwater fishes having the ability to shoot down flying insects with droplets of water which they spit with considerable accuracy up to three feet. They were first reported, in 1765, by the governor of a hospital in the then Dutch colony of Java. Unfortunately, the good doctor sent a specimen of a butterflyfish with his report and, as this was known to be a marine fish living where there are no flying insects, no one believed his tale for 137 years! (CALL MY BLUFF player's note: *Toxotes jaculatus* is the best known species of archerfish if you wish to use either word as a 'true' i.e. *Toxotes* is the genus, *jaculatus* is the species. The family is *Toxotidae*. Also see **Pulex** for another example of 'disguise' for a very common word suitable for play.)

archet *obs n* a violin bow

Archie *dim masc pers n* **Archibald** meaning 'truly bold' *slg n* an anti-aircraft gun

archil *n* the name for any one of several species of lichen from which is obtained both a violet dye and litmus, the chemical testing substance: the dye (without differentiation, the various lichens are also known as **orchel, orchil, orchilla, orchilla weed**)

archine *var fm n* **arsheen**

archlet *n* a little arch

archlute *n* a long and large lute used for bass notes

archon *n* in the ancient Greek republic of Athens, the chief magistrate and, eventually, one of nine chief magistrates

arctoid *adj* bearlike

arcubalist *n* a crossbow

ard see **be**

ardeb *n* an Egyptian dry measure the equivalent of 5½ bushels

ardene *Obs fm n* **errand**

are (see **be**) *n* the unit of metric land measure, 100 sq metres

aread *arch vb* to divine the meaning of: to interpret the significance of a dream: to guess or conjecture: to counsel or advise: to decide or adjudge (*var fms* **arede, areed**) *obs n* advice or counsel (*var fm* **arreede**)

arede *var fm arch vb* **aread**

areed *var fm arch vb* **aread**

arende *Obs fm n* **errand**

arent *obs adj* withering *obs fm vb* **arrent**

areography *n* a description of the physical features of the planet Mars

Arepo see **word square**

arest *obs fm n/vb* **arrest**

arête *n* a sharp ridge (on a mountain)

arett *obs vb* to reckon: to impute: to charge or accuse: to allege

arf *var fm now S & dial adj* **argh**

arg *dial vb* to argue

argali *n* the wild rock sheep of Asia

argan *n* an evergreen hardwood tree of Morocco: the oil from its seeds

argent *n/adj* silver *her adj* white

argentic *adj* containing silver in chemical composition

argentine *adj* (made) of silver *n* (imitation) silver

Argentino *n* an Argentine, a native or citizen of Argentina

argentite *n* silver sulphide also known as argyrite or silver glance

argentum *n* silver

Argestes *n* Milton's personification of the northwest wind

argh *now S & dial adj* cowardly, timid, fearful: inert, lazy, slow, reluctant (*S fm* usually **erf**: English *dial fm* usually **arf**)

arghan *n* the fibre of various species of plant *incl* Argave (q.v.) used for the production of pita flax

arginase *n* an enzyme

arginine *n* one of the basic amino acids

Argive *adj* of or pertaining to Argos, the Greek city, and to Argolis, the region of Greece containing Argos: Greek *n* an inhabitant of Argos or Argolis: a Greek

argle *now dial vb* to argue, dispute, wrangle

argon *n* an unreactive, colourless gas (chemical symbol, Ar) used in electric display signs and as a filter for incandescent electric lamps

Argus *pers n* in Greek myth, a man with a hundred eyes which, after his death, the goddess Hera transferred to the tail of the peacock *n* a genus of Asian pheasants of which one species is as large as a turkey (*−cap*) *n* a pheasant of the genus: a person of extreme vigilance: any of various butterflies which have many spots on their wings (*+ or −cap*) *modf n* the sense of many spots, as in **Argus (argus) snake**: the sense of vigilance as in **argus-eyed**

argute *adj* of sounds, shrill: of persons or their attributes, sharp, keen, subtle, quick, shrewd: of plants, sharp-toothed like a serrate leaf

argyle *var fm n* **argyll**

argyll *n* a (silver) vessel, rather like a coffee-pot, designed to keep gravy hot whilst on the table

argyrite *n* argentite

arider *comp adj* arid

ariel *n* a light, elegant species of Arabian gazelle: any of various birds *incl* swallow or petrel (*+cap*) *n* an air spirit

arietta *n* a little aria or musical air

ariette *var fm n* **arietta** (the French *fm* sometimes used for a French arietta)

aright *adv* rightly, properly *obs vb* to make right, to treat properly

aril *n* a partial covering for a seed which develops from the point of attachment of that seed to the parent plant

arillated *adj* having an aril

arimde *see* **arime**

arime *Obs vb* to count (the *infl fms incl* **arimde, arimed, arimen**)

ariole *obs n* a soothsayer

arista *n* a bristlelike appendage on the antennae of some insects (*pl* **aristae, aristas**)

aristate *adj* awned

aristo *collq n* an aristocrat (*pl* **aristos**)

ark *n* a chest, casket or similar container *obs vb* to deposit in an ark

arkite *adj* of Noah's ark *n* an inmate of that ark

arkose *n* a French sandstone containing grains of feldspar and quartz

arles *dial n pl* (*treated as n sing*) money paid on striking a bargain *esp* that given to a person hired for a specific task

arless *var fm dial n pl* **arles**

Armenoid *n* one of the eastern branch of the Alpine race, characterized by a darker skin, a prominent nose and a broad short skull. The Alpine race is one of the main races of white men, generally sallow complexioned, broad headed and short of stature.

armet *n* a type of 15th century helmet.

armite *Obs fm n* **hermit**

armlet *n* a ring-like ornament worn on the upper arm: a branch of a river: a small marine inlet

armoire *n* a cupboard

armories *pl* armory (*US fm n* **armoury**)

armyworm *n* the caterpillar of various species of moths *esp* that of *Leucania unipuncta* which migrate in numbers that reach plague proportions in both North America and Australia, causing enormous damage to crops

arn *see* **be**

arneis *obs fm n* **harness**

arnest *obs fm n* **earnest**, a financial deposit or instalment

arnet *var fm S n* **arnot**

arnit *var fm S n* **arnot**

arnot *S n* a shrimp

Arnica *n* the genus of the plant, mountain tobacco (*– cap*) *n* a tincture used for sprains and bruises obtained from the flowers of that plant

arnotto *n* a small Central American tree, the source of anatta (*pl* **arnottos**) *var fm n* **anatta**

arnut *var fm n* **earthnut**, any of various plants having an edible root or tuber or, like the peanut, an underground pod

aroint *vb* to order away with a curse (also see **roynt**)

aroynt *var fm vb* **aroint**

arpeggio *n* a chord, the notes of which are in rapid succession (*pl* **arpeggios**)

arpen *obs fm n* **arpent**

arpent *n* an old French land measure of *approx* one acre, still extant in the strongly French regions of North America such as Quebec, Canada and Louisiana, USA

arpine *obs fm n* **arpent**

arr *dial n* a scar: a freckle: a grudge: a guilty conscience *dial vb* to scar: to incite: to snarl (as a dog)

arrect *adj* set upright: attentive, alert (*fig*) *obs vb* to set upright: to raise *var fm obs vb* **arett**

arrent *vb* to lease land *esp* forestry at a yearly rent

arrêt *n* a sharp ridge on a mountain: a judgment of a tribunal (– accent) *var fm obs vb* **arett**

arride *vb* to please, gratify *obs vb* to smile (or laugh) at, to scorn

arriero *n* a mule driver

arris *n* a ridge formed by the meeting of two surfaces

arrish *dial fm n* **eddish**

arrowy *adj* of or like arrows

arsadine *var fm n* **arsedine**

arsedine *n* Dutch gold or Mannheim gold, a gold-coloured alloy of copper and zinc

arseling *var fm S adv* **arselings**

arselings *S adv* backwards

arselins *var fm S adv* **arselings**

arsenate *n* a salt of arsenic acid

arsenic (*n*/*vb*) *infl fms* **arsenicked** etc

arsenide *n* an arsenic compound

arsenite *n* a salt of arsenous acid

arsenous *adj* of the nature of or containing arsenic

arsesmart *n* the plant, waterpepper

arsheen *n* either of two measures of length, the Turkish metre or the Russian ell (see **ell**)

arshin *var fm n* **arsheen**

arshine *var fm n* **arsheen**

arsine *n* hydride of arsenic, a poisonous gas

arsle *dial vb* to move backwards: to shuffle

arslet *dial fm n* **haslet**

arsmert *obs fm n* **arsesmart**

arsonite *n* an arsonist, one who commits the crime of arson

arteir *obs fm n* **artery**

artel *n* a workers' guild in the USSR

Artemis *pers n* the Greek goddess of hunting and chastity

arter *obs fm n* **artery**

artesian *adj* of a well sunk into strata which receives water from a higher altitude than that of the top of the well, thus creating a permanent upward flow of water (+*cap*) *adj* of Artois, the old French province where such wells are common

arthropod *n* any member of a great division of the animal kingdom which includes arachnids, centipedes, crustacea, insects, millipedes, tardigrades and any other creatures with segmented bodies and jointed appendages

artic *collq n* an articulated lorry (GAME PLAYER'S note: Even though it is an abbreviated *fm* it is perfectly valid for play because it is pronounced as it is spelt.)

artier (*comp adj*) *obs fm n* **artery**

artiness *n* the quality of being arty

artire *obs fm n* **artery**

artisane *obs fm n* **artisan**

artizan *var fm n* **artisan**

artlet *n* a lesser art

artsman *arch n* one who studies a practical science

art song *n* a song of specific studied composition, as opposed to a folk song

arval *now dial n* a funeral feast *adj* of or pertaining to ploughed land

arx *n* a citadel

as (*adv/conj/pron*) *n* a Norse greater god (*pl* **aesir**): a Roman copper coin of varying value at different periods and which also served as a unit of weight. The coin originally weighed twelve ounces, a pound troy, but was reduced in stages to half an ounce (*pl* **asses**): a ridge of gravel (*pl* **asar**) *obs fm n* **ash**, the residual powder (*pl* **assis**) *Obs fm n* **ass** (*pl* **asse, assen**) *Obs fm n* **ace**, the playing card and the number one in dice (*pl* in dice throwing, plurality was expressed by quantity so that a throw of double one was called **ambes as** (both aces) and still exists in the modern *fm* **ambs ace.** The *var fms* **aas, ais, ase** were also plurals in this fashion though aas was also a plural for as.)

Asansk *n* a town northeast of Krasnoyarsk in west central Siberia

ascarid *n* any species of a genus of worms parasitic on the small intestine (*pl* **ascarids** – also see **ascaris**)

ascaris *var fm n* **ascarid** (*pl* **ascarides**)

ascites *n* abdominal dropsy

ascitic *adj* of, pertaining to or affected with ascites

ascitical *adj* ascitic

Asclepius *pers n* the Greek god of medicine

ascorbate *n* a salt of ascorbic acid

ascription *n* the act of crediting or assigning: a statement crediting something to someone

ase see **as**

aseclist *var fm obs n* **asseclist**

aselline *adj* of or pertaining to a small ass

Asenath *pers n* the wife of Joseph, the Old Testament patriarch

aseptic *adj* not subject to putrefaction *n* such a substance

ash (*n*) *vb* to strew with ashes *dial vb* to beat with an ash stick (i.e. a local *fm* of 'birching')

ashend *obs vb* to ruin: to curse

ashery *n* a place where potash or pearlash is manufactured: an ash pit

ashet *dial n* a platter

ash fly *n* a fly found on an ash tree and favoured by anglers as bait

ashier *comp adj* ashy

ash key *n* the winged seed of the ash tree

ashlar *n* a stone squared for building, facing or paving purposes *vb* to face with ashlar

ashlaring *n* ashlar facing or masonry

ashler *var fm n/vb* **ashlar**

ashlering *var fm n* **ashlaring**

ashling *n* an ash sapling

ashram *n* a place of religious retreat *esp* in India

asiden *dial prep* beside *dial adv* awry

askant *adv* obliquely, sideways

askinge *obs fm n* **asking**

asklent *S fm adv* **aslant**

aslant *adj/adv* on the slant *prep* athwart

aslept *obs adj* overcome with sleep

aspectual *adj* pertaining to aspects

aspen *n* the trembling poplar, a tree which has leaves which quiver in the wind *adj* timorous

asper *n* in Greek grammar, a small sign (ʽ) placed over an initial letter to indicate harsh breathing, thereby creating the sound of our letter H: a small silver Turkish coin, now only a money of account, of which there were 120 to the piastre *obs adj* rough, harsh, savage

asperate *adj* rough *vb* to make rough, rugged or harsh

asperge *vb* to sprinkle *n* the brush used to sprinkle holy water

asperger *var fm n* **asperge**

aspern *obs vb* to despise

asperse *vb* to spread false rumours abroad: to defame

aspersion *n* the act of sprinkling or besprinkling: a shower or spray: unjust insinuations, defamation

aspert *Obs adj* apt, clever

aspertion *obs fm n* **aspersion**

asphalt (*n*) *vb* to cover such as a road surface with this bituminous substance

aspheric *adj* varying slightly from a perfectly spherical shape

asphodel *n* any species of a genus of southern European plants of the lily family with clusters of white or yellow flowers *esp* the white asphodel or king's spear, the leaves of which are eaten by sheep: any of various unrelated plants such as English or bog asphodel, Scotch asphodel and false asphodel native to the USA: the immortal flower of classic legend said to cover the Elysian fields

aspier *obs fm vb* **aspire** *Obs fm n* **espier**

aspirate *vb* to pronounce with a breathing

aspirer *n* one who aspires

asport *vb* to remove feloniously

asprete *Obs fm n* **asperity**, roughness

aspyre *obs fm vb* **aspire**

assart *vb* to create a tract of arable land within a forest by grubbing up trees and shrubs *n* such a tract

assden *var fm n* **arsedine**

asseclist *obs n* a follower

assentor *n* one who, in addition to the proposer and seconder, nominates a candidate in an election (for parliament)

asserve *obs vb* to serve to

asseth *obs n* satisfaction

assethe *obs vb* to satisfy

assett *obs fm dial n* **ashet**

assever *arch vb* to asseverate or affirm solemnly

assiento *n* a treaty (*pl* **assientos**)

assigner *n* one who assigns

assignor *n* one who assigns a right or a property

assoil *arch vb* to absolve from sin: to acquit by sentence of a Scottish court

assot *obs vb* to act like a fool (in love): to become infatuated: to make a fool of (*infl fms* **assotted** etc., with **assote** as a *var fm* **assotted** in the adjectival sense of infatuated)

assott *var fm obs adj* **assote** (see **assot**)

astable *adj* not stable

astare *arch adv* staring or prominent

astart *obs vb* to escape, to avoid: to befall: to happen, to originate

Astarte *pers n* the goddess of sex in Canaanite and related cultures

astatine *n* an unstable chemical element of the halogen series

astead *dial adv* instead

asteed *var fm dial adv* **astead**

asteer *S adv* arising from one's bed

asteir *var fm obs vb* **astir**, to excite physically or emotionally

asteism *n* genteel irony

astel *n* a ceiling board or a ceiling of boards in a mine *dial n* an underground wall *esp* one which dams an underground stream *obs n* a splinter of wood

astely *n* absence of the axial cylinder of vascular tissue in a plant

aster *n* the Michaelmas daisy, a plant having daisy-like flowers the colours of which can be white, blue, purple or pink: a starlike figure *obs n* a star

Astere *Obs fm n* **Easter**

asteria *n* any precious stone cut to exhibit a starlike figure when light is directed upon it

asterid *n* a starfish

asterin *n* a pigment obtained from the flower, China aster, and isolated as crystals of chloride

Asterina *n* the genus of the European cushion star, a five-cornered cushion-shaped starfish

asterion *n* the point behind the mastoidal process of the ear where the paretial, occipital and temporal bones meet *obs n* an unknown herb described as having yellowish flowers like a foxglove, bluish leaves and apparently it grew on walls

asterism *n* a cluster of stars: a group of three asterisks thus ⁂

asterite *n* a gemstone known to the ancients

and described as having in its midst an image of the full moon. It is unknown to modern specialists.

astert *var fm obs vb* **astart**

asthenia *n* lack of bodily strength: general debility: physical weakness

asthenic *adj* of, pertaining to or characterized by asthenia: of or pertaining to an asthenic person or type *n* one who is underdeveloped or physically weak: one of a type characterized by being tall, lean and having light muscular development

asthore *Anglo-Ir n* a term of affection

astiler *obs fm n* **ashlar**

astler *obs fm n* **ashlar**

astone *obs vb* to stun (*lit*/*fig*): to be amazed

astonied, astonies see **astony**

astony *arch vb* to amaze, astonish, paralyze, stun (*infl fms* **astonies, astonied, astonying**)

astrand *adv* stranded

Astrantia *n* a genus of umbelliferous plants with showy bracts

astre *n* a hearth, home *dial n* the back of the chimney

Astrel *n* one of series of rigid amorphous plastics commercially produced from the mid-1970s but no longer manufactured

astrer *n* a peasant householder

astrex *n* a variety of Rex rabbit, a breed of domestic rabbit

astringe *vb* to constrict, compress, bind together

astringer *var fm n* **austringer**

astrion *obs n* the star sapphire

astrogenics *n* the scientific study of astrology. First read to an international conference of scientists, astronomers and mathematicians in London in November 1986, it confirms, in essence, the wisdom of the astrologers but provides a different cause to the effect. Whereas the astrologers speak in terms of planetary influences at the moment of birth, astrogenics is concerned with the effects of the prevailing electro-magnetic fields at the time of conception. It states that the personality of an individual is a description of DNA mutation induced by the intermodulation of the Earth's magnetosphere, which results in the influx of sub-atomic particles from the solar wind, whose origin stems from the differential rotation of the Sun's polar and magnetic field. In simpler terms, it says that the *personality* factors which the astrologers ascribe to the individual star signs bear strict examination when tested on large samplings of people considered from the standpoint of the varying strengths of magnetic shock waves throughout the year. Those whose conception resulted in birth under a particular star sign have personality traits in common. (note: Science, as far as is known, has not considered Chinese astrology in these terms. To the Chinese astrologer the year has a greater significance than the star sign. They relate matters to a 60 year cycle, discussed at greater length at the special subject entry, **CHINESE CALENDAR**. Also see **gematria**, for an even more remarkable scientific examination of ancient wisdom.)

astroid *n* a curve having four cusps and generated by a point on the circumference of a circle which rolls on the inside of another circle

astrut *adv* strutting

astylar *adj* without architectural columns

aswing *adv* swingingly

asyndetic *adj* of or pertaining to asyndeton

asyndeton *n* the omission, in rhetoric, of conjunctions between parts of a sentence

asynergia *var fm n* **asynergy**, lack of co-ordination between those bodily parts, such as muscles, which normally act in concert

at (*prep*) *n* a small Laotian coin: att, a Siamese pewter coin

atabal *n* a Moorish tabour or kettledrum

atabeg *n* a (Turkish) high official (**atabek** *var fm*)

atelier *n* (an artist's or sculptor's) workshop

atelin *var fm dial n* **yetlin**

Atelinae *n* a sub-family of New World monkeys which includes the spider monkeys and the night monkey, the only nocturnal higher primate

athel *obs n* ancestry: one who is noble *obs adj* noble *obs vb* to honour

atheling *n* a prince of the blood royal *obs n* a male of noble or royal blood

Athena *pers n* the Greek goddess of wisdom

Athene *var fm pers n* **Athena**, the goddess

Atherina *n* a genus of small fishes akin to the grey mullet which are sometimes sold as smelt

athestar *Obs vb* to darken

athetise *var fm vb* **athetize**, to render godless: to promote atheism

athetiser *var fm n* **athetizer**, one who renders godless

a'thing *S & dial fm pron* **anything** (GAME PLAYER'S note: Not valid for play by virtue of apostrophe)

athisme *obs fm n* **atheism**

athrob *adj/adv* throbbing

atingle *adj/adv* tingling

Atlantean *adj* pertaining to or having the strength of Atlas

atocia *n* sterility in a female

atomic (*adj*) *obs n* an adherent of a redundant philosophy concerning the atom

atoner *n* one who atones: one who reconciles

atonic *adj* of the nervous system, without tone: of a word, unaccented *n* such a word

atony *n* muscular weakness (*pl* **atonies**)

atopic *adj* of atopy, an inherited hypersensitivity though the allergic reaction need not be the same or even similar to that of the parent

atrap *var fm obs vb* **attrap**, to catch (as) in a trap

atresia *n* the absence of (the function of) a passage in the body

atrial *adj* of atrium

atrine *Obs vb* to touch (*lit/fig*) (TRIVIA note: There appears to be no record of an *infl fm* 'atrines', hence, no opportunity to include it with the superlative combination of anagrams listed at **AEINRST**)

atrium *n* the central hall of a Roman house: the covered portico in front of a church: a large cavity into which the intestine opens (*pl* **atria, atriums**)

atropine *n* a crystalline poisonous substance found in deadly nightshade and the seeds of the thorn apple

Atropos *fem pers n* see **Fates, the**

atslip *Obs vb* to slip away

atspring *obs vb* to spring forth, to originate

att *var fm n* **at** (where indicated)

attainder *n* the consequential loss of all civil rights which formerly accompanied conviction on a capital crime

attar *n* a fragrant oil

attender *n* one who or that which attends: one who gives attention *obs vb* to treat with regard

atter *now S & dial n* pus from a sore or ulcer: poison *dial n* a scab *obs n* snake venom *now S & dial vb* of a sore, to discharge pus *dial vb* to sting *obs vb* to poison

attercop *now dial n* a spider: one who is like a spider in viciousness

attester *n* one who attests, bears witness or vouches for (also see **attestor**)

attestor *n* an attester *esp* in legal usage

attle *n* the rubbish discarded in mining activity *Obs fm now S & dial vb* **ettle**

attorn *vb* to assign or transfer (goods, services, allegiance etc.) to another: of the tenant, to make a legal acknowledgement of the rights of a new landlord: in feudal law, to transfer one's homage and allegiance from one lord to another

attrite *adj* having attrition

attrited *adj* worn down by attrition

attuite *vb* to be aware of by a process intermediate between perception and sensation

au *Obs fm n/vb* **awe**

auctionary *adj* of or pertaining to an auction

auctorial *adj* of or pertaining to an author

audient *adj* listening *n* a listener *esp* one who hears the gospel but is not yet a formal member of the Church

audile *n* one whose mental imagery is mainly concerned with sound

auger *n* a carpenter's tool with a spiral groove for boring holes: an earth-boring tool

aularian *adj* of or belonging to a hall *n* a member of an English university hall

aulder *comp S adj* auld (see **ald**)

auldest *sup S adj* auld (see **ald**)

auning *obs fm n* **awning**

aunter *obs fm n/vb* **adventure**

auntly *adj* of or resembling an aunt *esp* in caring behaviour or attitude (note: Not an especially common word and only recorded in British literature in its basic *fm*. The *Official Scrabble Players Dictionary*, however, provides *comp* **auntlier**, *sup* **auntliest**.)

auntre *obs fm n/vb* **adventure**

aureus *n* a Roman gold coin (*pl* **aurei**)

auricled *adj* having ear-like appendages

auriscope *n* a medical instrument used for examining the ear

aurist *n* a specialist in diseases of the ear

aurochs *n* the extinct wild bison of Europe, of which the last surviving member of the species was killed in Poland in 1627 (*pl* **aurochsen**)

austeer *obs fm adj* **austere**

Austen *dim masc pers n* **Augustine** (derived from **Augustus** meaning 'majestic')

Auster *n* the south wind (*–cap*) *var fm n* **astre**

austerer *comp adj* austere

Austin *dim masc pers n* **Augustine** which, in turn is derived from **Augustus** meaning 'majestic' *var fm modf n* **Augustinian**, in respect of an order of mendicant friars

Austric *adj* of languages which predominate from coastal India to the Pacific and which belong to such language families as Munda, Malayo-Polynesian and Mon-Khymer

austringer *n* a keeper of goshawks

autoclave *n* a type of French stewpan having a steam-tight lid

autre *obs fm n* **altar**

auyt *n* an unknown ingredient of a paste containing crocodile dung which was used in ancient Egypt as a spermicide

avadavat *n* either of two species of Asian weaver finch, the red avadavat or tiger finch and the red waxbill or strawberry finch

avage *n* a payment formerly made by those tenants of the manor of Writtel, Essex, who desired the privilege of feeding their pigs in the manor woods

avahi *n* a nocturnal lemur related to the sifaka

availer *n* one who is helpful

avaling *obs n* descent or descending

averse (*adj*) *obs vb* to turn away

avertible *adj* capable of being prevented

Avesta *n* the holy scriptures of the Zoroastrians

aviette *n* a flying machine driven by manpower

avo *n* a bronze coin of Macao and Timor

avocet *n* any one of four different species of wading bird with webbed feet and a long, slender, curved bill. Related to the stilt and the ibisbill, the various species are of widespread distribution.

avodire *n* an African tree

avoset *var fm n* **avocet**

avulse *vb* to pluck or tear off

aw *n* a type of waterwheel floatboard *dial n* an ear of oats *interj* expressing disgust: sympathy *obs fm n/vb* **awe**

awa *n* the milkfish *S adv/n/interj* away

aweather *adv* a nautical term for towards the windward side

aweel *S interj/conj/adv* well!: well then

aweoweo *n* a species of bigeye which, unlike the others, is found only in comparatively shallow water

awlter *obs fm n* **altar**

awm *dial n* straw *dial vb* to gather straw

awn *n* a bristly growth or beard on barley, oats and certain other grasses *vb* to remove awns from

awner *n* a machine which removes awns from grain

awning *n* the action of the *vb*, awn: a (canvas) rooflike covering: a shelter

awr *var fm dial n* **arr**

awter *obs fm n* **altar**

ax (*n/vb*) *now dial fm vb* **ask**

axes *pl* ax, axe, axis

axil *n* the upper angle between a leaf and the stem from which it grows: that same angle between a branch and a trunk

axillary *adj* pertaining to the armpit: of plants, situated in or growing from the axil

axinomancy *n* divination by the placing of an agate or piece of jet on a red-hot ax to discover the guilty person

axolotl *n* the larva of the mole salamander found only in certain lakes around Mexico City. It is one of nature's curiosities, being able to reproduce at this immature or pre-adult stage and, normally, never develops into an adult. However, if one is placed in (say) a small fish tank and iodine is added to the water it will metamorphose from a creature that looks like an all-white plump fish with tiny legs and large pink gills to the adult form of a dark, mottled, slim, lizard-like creature. (Also see **Proteus** (−*cap*) and **mudpuppy**)

ay *interj* ah! oh! alas *adv* ever, always: continually *Obs fm n* **egg** (*pl* **ayer, ayren**)

ayin *n* the sixteenth letter of the Hebrew alphabet

ayle *obs fm vb* **ail**

Aylmer *masc pers n* possibly meaning 'nobly famous'

ayu *n* a salmon-like fish which the Japanese

traditionally catch with trained cormorants. The birds have rings round their necks to prevent them swallowing the catch and are taken to the fishing grounds in boats, released and allowed to follow their natural instincts. An individual cormorant can catch as many as 50 ayu in a night. (*pl* **ayu**)

aze *Ork & Shet n* a large blazing fire

Azorian *n* a native of the Azores

azyme *var fm n* **azym**, unleavened bread

B

ba *n* the second letter of the Arabic alphabet: the eternal soul in the ancient Egyptian religion *obs vb* to kiss

ba' *S fm n/vb* **ball**, (to form into) a sphere

baa *n* a sheep's cry *Ork & Shet n* a rock exposed at low tide *Ork & Shet var fm dial n* **ball**, a dumpling: the calf of the leg: the sole of the foot: the palm of the hand: a fox's footprint: a nodule: a lump of fuel: a rounded hill: a large shoal of herrings *vb* to bleat (as a sheep) *S vb* to lull to sleep *Ork & Shet var fm dial vb* **ball**, to track the footprints of a fox: to throw at: to beat

Baalist *n* a worshipper of Baal, the chief god of the Phoenicians: one who worships false gods: a term of abuse for one whose religious practice differs

Baalite *n* a Baalist

babarise *var fm vb* **barbarize**, to make barbarous or brutal and uncivilized

babax *n* see **Timaliiae** (*pl* **babaxes**)

babel *obs fm n/vb* **babble**

babiroussa *n* the 'kosher pig', an Indonesian tusked pig which, unlike other swine, chews its cud and has hooves, thereby bringing it within the category of animal which a Jew is permitted to eat. (At the time of writing, 1986, no official decision has been taken on acceptability or otherwise as a farm animal in Israel even though it has been suggested for this function.)

bable *obs fm vb* **babble**

babler *obs fm n* **babbler**

baboosh *var fm n* **babouche**, an oriental slipper

baccare *obs literary interj* back! stand back! (used by writers to indicate a speaker who wishes to impress with what he believes to be Latin but, of course, it isn't)

backet *S n* a shallow wooden trough used for the carrying of such as coal

back green *n* a lawn at the rear

backset *US vb* to plough land for the second time in a year (i.e. to plow in the fall) *obs vb* to attack in the rear *n* an eddy in water

bacterioid *n* an organism shaped like a bacterium

bacterium *n* any of various microscopic, single-celled, rodlike, vegetable organisms found in decaying matter (*pl* **bacteria**)

baculite *n* any fossil of the genus *Baculites* akin to the ammonites and having a long tapering shell

badder *obs comp adj* bad (now replaced by **worse**)

badiner *obs vb* to banter

baetyl *n* a sacred or magical meteoric stone

baggit *S n* a salmon immediately after having spawned (also see **rawner**, **SALMON**)

bagnio *n* a place for the detention of slaves: an Algerian prison: a brothel *obs n* a bathing establishment similar to the modern Turkish bath

baignoir *var fm n* **baignoire**

baignoire *n* a theatre box at stalls level

bail-dock *n* an open-topped but spiked cubicle formerly placed in a corner of London's Old Bailey for the housing of the accused

bailee *n* one to whom goods are bailed

bailsman *n* one who gives bail to another

bair *obs S fm adj* **bare**

Bairam *n* either of two Muslim festivals which last for three or four days

Bairan *obs fm n* **Bairam**

baiter *n* one who baits or worries: a tormentor (*fig*)

baitless *adj* without food or refreshment

Bajocian *adj* of a division of the Middle Jurassic (see **ROCK SYSTEMS AND LIFE FORMS**)

bakemeat *n* pastry, pies

Bakewell pudding *n* the true 'Bakewell tart' and far more tasty than the bland commercial products which use the incorrect name. It originated in Victorian times by accident when the cook, who was making a large jam tart, put the different layers in the wrong sequence, but so successful was the result that they have been produced in Bakewell ever since and are quite a tourist attraction *esp* during the well dressing season (See **well dressing**)

balata *n* gum from the South American bully tree which is used as a rubber substitute

balder *comp adj* bald

bale-dock *var fm n* **bail-dock**

baleen *n* whalebone

baler *n* a machine which makes bales of hay: a scoop, used by sailors, to bale out water

balest *obs fm n* **ballast**

balet *obs n* a small bale

balett *var fm obs n* **balet**

balin *obs n* an unknown herb of great medicinal value

balista *var fm n* **ballista**, an ancient military device in the form of a bow, which fired rocks

ballat *S fm n* **ballad**

balm (*n*) *arch vb* to embalm: to soothe *now dial vb* to smear with a sticky substance *obs vb* to impregnate with balm

balmbe *obs fm arch vb* **balm** (in the sense of embalm) *Obs fm arch vb* **balm** (in the sense of soothe)

balme *obs fm n/arch vb* **balm**

balmer *obs n* he who or that which embalms: a type of coloured cloth

balsamic *adj* of, like or containing balsam: soothing

balter *now dial vb* to tangle *dial vb* to walk in an ox-like fashion *obs vb* to dance clumsily *dial n* a coagulated lump

baluster *n* any of various upright supporting pillars

bananaquit *n* a small grey and yellow bird with a conspicuous white stripe over the eye. It is widespread in tropical America and is probably the commonest bird in the West Indies.

bandar *n* a rhesus monkey

bandelet *n* a small flat moulding surrounding an architectural column

bandelier *var fm n* **bandoleer**

banderole *n* a long narrow flag with a forked end

bandicoot *n* pig rat, the largest species of rat and native to India: a small Australian marsupial *Austr collq vb* to steal root vegetables whilst leaving the stalks and leaves still standing as though no theft had occurred.

bandileer *obs fm n* **bandoleer**

bandiler *obs fm n* **bandoleer**

bandlet *n* a bandelet: a small fillet

bandoleer *n* a military shoulder belt having loops for rounds of ammunition

bandore *n* a lute-like musical instrument

bania *n* (the *var fms*, **banian** and **banyan** apply to all senses) the Indian fig tree: a Hindu trader *esp* one from the province of Gujarat: any Hindu from western India: a loose jacket or gown worn in India: sircar, a broker or financier trading in Bengal *modf n* as **banian day**, **banian hospital** etc denote a vegetarian diet

bankera *n* the stone curlew of Santo Domingo

banshee *n* an Irish death spirit who wails only for members of the old families. Traditionally, she has long streaming hair and wears a grey cloak over a green dress and her eyes are fiery red from continual weeping. If several are seen together it foretells the death of someone very great or very holy: extended to cover other Celtic female portents of death *incl* those of Normandy (see **Melusina**) and the Scottish little-washer-by-the-ford who washes the grave clothes of those about to die. Unlike the Irish banshee, she is an ugly old hag and, generally speaking, the Irish banshees tend to be more beautiful and poetic than those of other Celtic peoples though, in their human aspect, the spirits of Normandy are the most attractive of all.

banter *vb* to speak or tease in a light-hearted fashion *n* repartee

banzai *n* a Japanese battle cry meaning 'forever' and used as a salute to the emperor

Barbadoes *adj* of the Caribbean island of Barbados

Barbary *n* the Mediterranean lands of North Africa (+*or* −*cap*) *n* a black or dun coloured fancy variety of pigeon originally from Barbary, now more commonly known as a barb: a horse of a quality breed from Barbary also known as a barb *obs n* barbarity: heathenism

barbel *n* a large freshwater fish of the carp family: a fleshy organ hanging from the corners of the mouth of fish such as the barbel: a variety of pigeon

barbet *n* a small poodle: any of 78 species of birds mainly resident in tropical countries *obs n* a bristled worm which feeds on aphides: a small beard

barble *n* a membrane under the tongue of a horse or cow: the disease when this membrane is inflamed (*var fm* **barbs**)

Barbus *n* a genus of fishes *incl* the mahseer and similar, but much smaller, freshwater fishes

barca *n* a Venetian barge

bard *n* a poet: a thin slice of bacon covering (white) meat: a protective covering of leather and armour for a warhorse *vb* to armour a warhorse

bardel *obs n* a saddle constructed from a straw-filled sack

bardess *n* a female bard or poetess

barege *n* a light sheer fabric

baret *var fm (arch) n* **barret**

bargee *n* a manager of a barge

bargest *var fm n* **barghest**

barget *obs n* a small barge

barghest *n* a doglike manifestation usually regarded as a portent of death. Most sightings give its appearance as being black, shaggy, fiery-eyed and the size of a calf. It is not a portent of one's own death but, like the Irish banshee, a sign of another's. (*var fms incl* **bargaist, bargest, barghost, barguest**)

barghost *dial fm n* **barghest**, the form used in Belper, Derbyshire, to describe this strange manifestation

barite *n* a mineral

barke *obs fm n/vb* **bark** (in most senses)

barken *S vb* to dry and become a hardened crust

Barnabite *n* a cleric of an order dedicated to St Paul and founded, in 1530, in the church of St Barnabus, Milan

Barnet *n* a borough of Greater London which includes Finchley and Hendon

barney *collq n* an (aggressive) argument

barny *adj* resembling a barn in such as dimensions (*comp* **barnier** *sup* **barniest**)

barony *n* the territory of a baron: a division of an Irish county: any large manorial estate in Scotland

barret *n* a flat cap *esp* the biretta worn by Catholic clergy *obs her n* a small bar

barrow (*n*) *vb* to cart by a barrow

Bartie *dim masc pers n* **Bartholomew**, meaning 'son of Talmai'

Bartle *dim fm masc pers n* **Bartlemy** which, in turn, is a *dim fm* of **Batholomew** meaning 'son of Talmi'

Bartlet *dim masc pers n* **Bartholomew**, meaning 'son of Talmai'

bary *obs vb* to utter the cry of an elephant

baryon *n* a proton, a neutron or any other of the heavier sub-atomic particles

barytes *n* sulphate of barium

basaltic *adj* of basalt, a fine-grained igneous volcanic rock

basbleu *Fr n* a blue stocking or literary lady (*obs English fm* **bas bleu**)

baseboard *US n* a skirting board

basely *adv* in a base manner

basest *sup adj* base

bashaw *n* an arrogant man: an *arch fm* of the Turkish title, pasha

basined *adj* placed in or contained by a basin

basinet *n* a lightweight, skull-shaped, armoured headpiece

basnet *var fm n* **basinet**

basser *obs n* a kisser, one who kisses

basset *n* a short-legged hound bred for hunting badgers: an old game like faro: an outcrop of rock *vb* to play the game basset: to crop out at the surface

bassethorn *n* a tenor clarinet

bassinet *n* a (hooded) wickerwork basket or cradle

bastard wing *n* the 'thumb' of the wing of a bird which, apart from that of a young hoatzin, is covered in feathers

baste *vb* to tack or sew loosely together: to moisten meat during roasting: to apply tar to sheep: to thrash: to beast at card playing

basten *adj* made of bast, a flexible fibre obtained from the inner bark of various trees

baster *n* one who bastes in the various senses of the *vb*: a cudgel: a heavy blow

bastile *var fm n* **bastille**

bastille *n* a (fortified) tower (of a castle): a wooden tower on wheels used by a besieging force: a prison (+*cap*) *n* the prison fortress of Paris destroyed in the Revolution

bastioned *adj* having or defended by a bastion

Basuto *n* the native black African people of Lesotho: their Bantu language (*pl* **Basutos**)

batement *obs n* reduction

bater *n* a hawk which beats its wings impatiently and flutters away from the fist or perch

bathos *n* triteness (*pl* **bathoses**)

bathqol *n* in Hebrew tradition, a divine revelation audibly given to certain Jewish teachers who lived after the era of the Biblical prophets

batlet *n* a modern amended form of **batler**, a word used by Shakespeare and understood to mean a wooden domestic item called a beetle which was used to beat clothes during laundering

batling *dial n* a small stick

battel *vb* to have an account for internal services at a college *now dial adj* of soil, rich and fertile: of pasture, nourishing or fattening for the animals

battue *n* a hunt in which the animals are driven towards the waiting sportsmen: indiscriminate killing

batty *adj* crazy (*comp* **battier** *sup* **battiest)**

bauble (*n*) *obs vb* to trifle

baul *obs fm vb* bawl

bausond *adj* of animals, having a white stripe on the face or white spots against a dark background

bawble *var fm n/obs vb* **bauble**

bawd (*n*) *arch vb* to pander

bawley *n* a small fishing vessel of the Kent and Essex coastal waters

bayle *n* a (simple) barrier *Austr n* a device which restrains a cow's head during milking

baz *dial n* a hit or blow *dial vb* to throw with force: to dash: to thrash

bazique *arch fm n* **bezique**

be (*vb*) *infl fms* note: The *vb* is defective and its conjugation is made up of fragments of three independent *vbs* hence:–
current fms **am, is, are, was, been, were, being**: *arch fms* **art, wast, wert** *now dial fm incl* **bes, bin:** *now dial negative fms incl* **baint, beant:** *now S negative fms incl* **binna:** *compound fms incl* **isn't** (is not) **thou'rt** (thou art, *poet/dial*) **cham** (I am, *dial*): *Obs/obs fms of AM incl* **em, ame, amm, eam, eom, ham:** *Obs/obs negative fms of AM incl* **nam, neom:** *Obs/obs fms of BE both sing* (*now dial*) *and pl incl* **bi, bo, by, bee, ben, beo, bes, bie, bio, bue, byn:** *Obs/obs fms of IS incl* **es, ys, ess, iss, esse, isse:** *Obs/obs negative fms of IS incl* **nis, nys:** *Obs/obs pl fms of IS incl* **sind, sint, synd, synt, sonde, synde:** *Obs/obs fms of ARE incl* **ar, er, arn, ern, ere, aren, arne, aron, arrn:** *Obs/obs fms of WAS incl* **wes, wys, wase, wass, watz, wees, weos:** *Obs/obs negative fms of WAS incl* **nas, nes, neas, nasse:** *Obs/obs fms of BEEN incl* **be, by, ben, beo, bin, byn, ibe, ybe, bene, beon, beyn, buen:** *Obs/obs fms of WERE both sing* (*now dial*) *and pl incl* **war, wer, wor, quar, wair, ware, warn, whar, wher, wore:** *Obs/obs fms of BEING incl* **beand, beyng, bying:** *Obs/obs fms of ART incl* **ard, ert, arrt, eart, hart:** *Obs/obs negative fms of ART incl* **nart, nert, neart:** *Obs/obs fms of WAST incl* **wart, wore:** *Obs/obs negative fms of WAST incl* **nere:** *Obs/obs fms of WERT incl* **werst, werest:** *Obs/obs fms of the compound fms incl* **icham** (CHAM): **nam, neom** (CHAM negative): **artu, ertu** (THOU'RT) *n* the bebization equivalent of **re** *obs fm n* **bee,** the insect (*pl* **been)**

beadle *n* a parish officer with the authority to punish petty offenders: a petty officer of a church or university

beadlet *n* a little bead *modf n* of *Actinia equina* (see **actinian)**

beal *n* a river or valley mouth *now dial n* an eruption of the skin *obs n* a baker's shovel *now dial vb* to suppurate or gather pus

bealing *now dial n* a boil

beamer *n* one who arranges yarn on the beam of a loom

bearcat *n* a small racoonlike carnivore of the southeastern Himalayas better known as the lesser panda but also known as the firefox or the red panda

beast (*n*) *n* an old card game similar to Nap: a forfeit in the card games of beast and ombre *vb* in the game of ombre, to incur a forfeit *obs vb* to treat as a beast (in the normal sense)

beastings *var fm n* **beestings**

beavered *adj* having a beaver, a face-guard attached to a mediaeval armoured helmet

bebization *n* a former system of musical notation which used as syllables the words **la, be, ce, de, me, fe, ge** (also see **bobization**)

becard *n* any species of two genera of cotingine birds *incl* the rose-throated becard which is the only member of this large family of birds (see **cotinga**) found north of Mexico

becharm *vb* to fascinate: to hold by a spell

beck *n* a brook or stream *esp* one with a stony bed or one running through rocky countryside: a large shallow tub such as one used by a dyer: a mute signal by hand or head *vb* to make such a signal

becken *obs fm n/vb* **beckon**

becker *dial n* the sea bream

bedare *obs vb* to defy

bedark *vb* to involve or cover with darkness

bedarken *vb* to cover with darkness (*lit/fig*)

bedash *vb* to dash about: to injure by (the) dashing (of the wind): to cover with dashes of colour

bedeck *vb* to ornament

bedell *arch fm n* **beadle**

bederal *var fm S n* **bedral**

bederk *obs fm vb* **bedark**

bedesman *var fm n* **beadsman**, a man of prayer: one paid to pray for others: one, in Scotland, licensed to beg *var fm arch n* **beadsman**, a petitioner

bedet *obs n* a boy employed to carry the baggage of a horseman or a soldier

bedirt *obs vb* to defile with dirt (*lit/fig*)

bedrail *US n* a board at the side of the bed

bedral *S n* a church officer approximating to the English beadle but usually having additional duties

bedrite *obs S var fm obs vb* **bedirt**

bedrop *vb* to sprinkle with drops (*pa pple* **bedropt** or **bedropped**)

beduck *vb* to immerse completely in water

bedung *vb* to manure: to make foul with dung

bedust *vb* to cover with dust

bedward *adv* towards or in the direction of bed

beech fern *n* a species of fern

beenah *n* a custom in parts of Sri Lanka in which, after marriage, a man goes to live with his wife's relatives and their children belong to her group

beer (*n*) *collq vb* to drink beer

beestings *n* the first milk produced by a cow after giving birth

beet (*n*) *now dial vb* to mend, repair or heal

beeting *obs n* repair, mending

beflum *vb* to make a fool of

beghard *n* a beguin, one of an order of lay monks who copied the way of life of the beguines (lay sisters) by living a monastic life without vows and with the freedom to return to the world as he should choose. Unlike the women, the beghards were soon the subject of scandal and were denounced by the pope and persecuted by the Inquisition: one of various heretical sects such as those of the Albigenses and the Waldenses

begird *vb* to bind (as) with a girdle (*pa t/pa pple* **begirt** or **begirded**)

begild *vb* to cover or overlay with gold leaf

beguin *n* a beghard, the *masc* equivalent of a **beguine**

beguine *n* a woman living as a nun without taking vows and with a personal option to return to ordinary life. Unlike their male counterparts (see **beghard**) the beguines still exist, having been protected by Pope John XXII (1316–1334) when he persecuted the men who copied a similar way of life: a French West Indian dance: the music, in bolero rhythm, for that dance

begum *n* a Muslim title of respect given to a woman whose social status can range from that of a lady to that of a princess

begun (*vbl infl*) *obs fm n* **begum**

behest *n* a command: an earnest request *obs n* a vow or promise *obs vb* to vow or promise

beira *n* a species of dwarf antelope found in Somalia

bejesuit *vb* to subject to or seduce into the theological views held by a Jesuit (of derogatory usage only – also see apt anagram, **Jebusite**)

belabor *US fm vb* **belabour**, to thrash with all one's might: to assail with words

belam *now dial vb* to thrash

belamb *obs fm now dial vb* **belam**

belast *obs adj* burdened

belaud *vb* to praise highly

belay *vb* to secure a rope by a twist around an anchoring point: to besiege: to waylay: to ornament *interj* stop

beldam *n* an aged woman *esp* a loathsome hag and/or a witch *obs n* a grandmother, great-grandmother or an even more remote ancestress (the *fem* equivalent of **belsire**)

beldame *var fm n*/*obs n* **beldam**

belead *obs vb* to lead astray

belgard *obs n* a fair or loving look (WORD PUZZLER'S note: The word is derived from the Italian, *bel guardo*, meaning 'lovely look'. It has only been recorded three times in English, each time in the plural, each time with a different spelling and only between the years 1590 and 1610. The three *fms* are **belgards, belgardes** and **bel-guards**. The *Oxford English Dictionary* records all three *fms* under the single heading of belgard. *Chambers 20th Century Dictionary* gives only belgard, the single *fm*, which it assigns exclusively to Spenser. The *fm* Spenser actually used was belgardes.)

belgarde see **belgard**

Belial *n* the devil

Belinda *fem pers n* derived from **Betlindis,** of which lindis means 'snake'. The meaning of the first part is obscure.

belirt *Obs vb* to cheat, to fool

bell (*n*) *vb* to supply with a bell: to perform a dangerous task (see below, *To bell the cat*): to bellow or roar: of hops, to open and expand to their customary shape *now dial vb* to bubble *obs vb* to swell up (*To bell the cat*, an old saying based on the fable of the mice debating among themselves as to which of them should hang a bell around the neck of the cat so as to warn them of its approach)

bellers *dial var fm n* **bilders**

belomancy *n* divination by arrows – each arrow is labelled with different advice and that which travels furthest is accepted

belord *vb* to address with respect of title i.e. to address as 'my lord'

below (*prep*/*adv*) *obs vb* to humble

belsire *obs n* the *masc* counterpart of **beldam** or **beldame** in the sense of grandfather or ancestor

Beltane *n* an ancient Celtic festival held at the beginning of May when great bonfires were lit on the hills and cattle were driven between two such fires: one of the four historic Scottish quarter days, now replaced by Whit Sunday (see **quarter day**)

beluga *n* the white whale: a species of sturgeon

bemased *obs fm adj* **bemazed**, bewildered

bemeet *obs vb* to meet with

bemete *obs vb* to measure

bemire *vb* to soil or befoul with mire: to sink into a mire (*lit/fig*)

bemoil *obs vb* to bemire

ben *n* a mountain peak: the winged seed of the horseradish tree: that tree *S n esp* of a small dwelling, the parlour or better room (see **but and ben**) *S & dial adv* within (the parlour) *S & dial prep* into (the parlour) *S & dial adj* inner

benedight *arch adj* blessed

benight *vb* to be caught by the darkness of night (before reaching shelter): to involve in moral darkness (*fig*): to blind *arch vb* to hide oneself in the night

benison *n* a blessing

benn *obs fm n* **ben nut**

ben nut *n* the horseradish tree: its seed

benzoxycamphor *n* camphor of which benzoic acid is the hydride (GAME PLAYER'S note: See **quetzal**)

beo see **be**

bepat *arch vb* to pat frequently, to strike

ber *n* jujube, an Indian tree: the fruit of that tree *dial n* force: passion: a rapid whirling motion: turmoil *dial vb* to bustle: to make a whirring noise

Berchta *n* the Teutonic goddess of spinners

bergama *var fm n* **bergamot**, a tapestry of ox and goat hair together with hemp or cotton

berk *slg n* a fool *obs vb* to clot

berne *obs n* a man *Obs n* a hero, a warrior

Bertha *var fm pers n* **Berchta**, the Teutonic goddess of spinners *fem pers n* meaning 'the bright one' (*−cap*) *n* a type of woman's collar

berthe *var fm n* **bertha**

beryllia *n* the oxide of the metallic element, beryllium

bes see **be**

besaile *n* a great-grandfather (*obs* except as a legal term)

besaint *vb* to canonise

beshrew *arch vb* a relic of the *obs vb* to invoke evil upon, retained in such expressions as 'beshrew me' or 'beshrew thee'

besing *vb* to celebrate in song (*infl fms incl* **besang, besung**)

besmear *vb* to cover with a sticky substance *esp* in a sense of making foul

besnow *vb* to cover (as) with snow

besort *obs vb* to match or agree with *obs n* apt company for one's social status

bespat *pa pple arch vb* **bespit**, to befoul with spittle

best *(n/adj) collq vb* to get the better of

bestail *obs fm now S n* **bestial**

bestain *vb* to stain a surface

bestar *vb* to adorn with stars or spangles

bestead *vb* to help or assist *obs vb* to deputise for

bestial (*adj*) *now S n* a farm: a farm animal

bestiary *n* a mediaeval collection of real or imaginary animals put into a moral context (*pl* **bestiaries**)

bestick *vb* to bedeck, adorn (*lit/fig*): to transfix (*pa t/pa pple* **bestuck**)

bestill *vb* to make quiet

Bestla *pers n* one of the evil jotuns or primaeval giants of Scandinavian mythology who ruled the world before the greater gods were created. A goddess, she was the mother of Odin the chief of the greater gods.

bestorm *vb* to storm on all sides

bestraw *obs fm vb* **bestrew**

bestrew *vb* to strew or scatter (*pa pple* **bestrewed, bestrewn, bestrown**)

bestrid *pa t vb* **bestride**

bestrow *var fm vb* **bestrew**, to scatter (*pa t* **bestrowed, bestrown**)

bestud *vb* to adorn (as) with studs

besung *adj* see **besing**

betani *obs fm n* **betony**, a common woodland plant greatly valued in ancient and mediaeval medicine

beteem *vb* to give birth to *obs vb* to grant, permit: to admit the worth of

beth *n* the second letter of the Hebrew alphabet

betoken *vb* to be a sign or omen of: to indicate, to show

betonies *pl* betony (see **betani**)

betoss *vb* to tumble about

betread *vb* to walk upon or tread over (*pa t* **betrod**, *pa pple* **betrodden**)

betrim *vb* to set in order, to dress

betrod *pa t vb* **betread**

Beulah *n* a non-conformist chapel

bezique *n* a card game for two to four players using two to four packs from which cards below the seven have been removed: the combination in one hand of the jack of diamonds and the queen of spades (GAME PLAYER'S note: This word is of especial interest to Scrabble® players – see **quetzal** for full details)

bezoar *n* a stony concentration from the stomach or gall bladder of a ruminant, set as a jewel and esteemed as an antidote to poison: the *Capra hircus*, a species of wild goat and the best source of this stone

bharal *n* the *Pseudois nayaur*, a member of the goat-sheep tribe and better known as the blue sheep. Despite its external appearance, sheep-like grazing habits and sheep-like social activities it is a goat and all attempts to hybridize it with a true sheep have failed. The bharals are native to the higher altitudes of Asia from Kashmir to western Mongolia. Technically, three races *incl* a dwarf Chinese variety have been recognized (*var fms* **burhel, burrel, burrell, burrhel**)

Bharati *adj* of India

bi *var fm n* **by**, a town (*Obs* except as a syllable in English place names) *slg n* a bisexual

Bibler *S n* a country schoolchild whose text-book is the Bible

biblet *Obs n* the meaning is obscure, but it is probably either a book or a collection of books

bibliomancy *n* divination by means of the Bible (see **sortes**)

bickern *n* an anvil having two projecting taper ends: one such end

bie see **be**

bier (*n*) *obs S fm vb* **bear**, to carry

bigener *n* a plant which is a hybrid between two genera

bigeye *n* any of various perch-like fishes of the tropical and subtropical seas. They are bottom-living fishes found, with the exception of the aweoweo, at depths of several hundred feet. The aweoweo is found in water less than six feet deep. They have large eyes and up-turned mouths with most species being bright red in colour. The largest species reach about two feet in length and some species are considered a delicacy in southeast Asia when dried and salted.

biggin *n* a child's hood: a nightcap: a close-fitting (silk) cap worn by a serjeant-at-law: a type of coffee percolator *S n* anything built

bilander *n* a two-masted Dutch merchant vessel used for coastal and canal traffic

bilder *obs n* a horse

bilders *n* the name given by herbalists of historical times to any of various water plants. Still extant in modern *dial* for such as water-cress (*North Ire*), water dropwort (*Cornwall*), cow parsnip (*Devon*) (*pl* **bilders**)

bilge (*n*) *vb* of a ship, to spring a leak

bilgres *Obs n* a plant of some kind *poss* water-cress or water dropwort (see **bilders**)

bilian *n* a timber tree of Borneo which has a natural defence mechanism against ants

biller *US n* one who presents a bill to *obs S n* a ram

billers *dial var fm n* **bilders**

Billingsgate pheasant *n* a bloater or herring partially dried in smoke

bilobed *adj* having two lobes

biltong *n* strips of lean meat (*esp* of such as antelope) dried in the sun

Bimana *n pl* the two-handed animals, an old technical term for mankind

bimensal *adj* occurring once every two months (USAGE note: At least two American dictionaries, *incl* the one used for the North American Scrabble Championship, list it as an extant word in this sense. A similar sense of 'during the space of two months' is the only one recorded in British use and, dated 1676, is considered *obs*. It does not appear in the dictionary used for the UK Scrabble championship.)

bimetal *US n* any object composed of two metals

binary *adj* of two *n* something composed of two parts (*pl* **binaries**)

binate *adj* growing in pairs

bingy *dial adj* of milk, having a sour taste

biocidal *adj* of the destruction of living organisms

biome *n* an ecological community based upon a particular dominant vegetation

biont *n* a living organism

biota *n* the flora and fauna of a region

bipedal *adj* two-footed

bipolar *adj* having two poles

bir *n* a fortified place (*obs* except as a syllable in English place names): the force of the wind: a thrust or violent push: a whirring noise *obs n* a fight or battle *vb* to make a whirring noise (*infl fms* as for the more common *fm*, **birr**) *Obs vb* to belong *var fm dial n/vb* **ber**

birchir *n* any of about ten species of primitive freshwater African fishes capable of living for a while out of water. Once considered to be related to the lungfishes, they have now been reclassified as shown at the entry, **FISH CLASSIFICATION**. (Also see **finlet**)

bird (*n*) *vb* to pursue birds with the aim of capture or killing

bird alane *var fm now poet S adj* **burd alone**

bird alone *var fm now poet S adj* **burd alone**

BIRD CLASSIFICATION See next page

birdie *n* a little bird: in golf, the holing of the ball with one shot fewer than the exact number deemed par or standard for that hole (two shots fewer is called an eagle, three shots fewer is called an albatross) *vb* to score a birdie in golf

bireme *n* an ancient galley having two banks of oars

biretta *n* the black square cap of a Catholic priest, the one worn by a bishop being purple and that of a cardinal, red

birle *now dial vb* to ply with drink

birler *now dial n* one who plies with drink

birretta *var fm n* **biretta**

BIRD CLASSIFICATION The latest system has all the birds in a class called **Aves** (hence the *adj*, **avine**) which is divided into 29 orders, detailed below. The orders are subdivided into families, then genera and, finally, species but with the added complication of occasional sub-orders, sub-families of families and varieties of species. Approximately half of the different species belong to a single order called Passeriformes (*adj* **passerine**) and it is common to refer to the other orders collectively as non-passerine. The orders, with sample species, are as follows:— **Aepyornithiformes** elephant birds (recently extinct): **Anseriformes** ducks, geese, screamers, swans: **Apodiformes** humming birds, swifts: **Coliiformes** mousebirds: **Caprimulgiformes** nightjars, oilbird etc: **Casuariiformes** cassowaries, emu: **Charadriiformes** auks, coursers, gulls, jacanas, plovers, skuas, sandpipers, terns etc: **Ciconiiformes** flamingos, herons, ibises, storks etc: **Coliiformes** mousebirds: **Columbiformes** dodo (recently extinct), pigeons, sandgrouse: **Coraciiformes** bee-eaters, hoopoe, hornbills, kingfishers, rollers etc: **Cuculiformes** cuckoos, turacos: **Dinornithiformes** moas (recently extinct): **Falconiformes** eagles, hawks, vultures etc – the diurnal birds of prey: **Galliformes** curassows, guineafowl, grouse, hoatzin, megapodes, pheasants, turkeys: **Gaviiformes** loons: **Gruiformes** bustards, buttonquail, cranes, rails etc: **Passeriformes** all the familiar perching birds or songbirds and others such as antbirds, lyrebirds, ovenbirds, tyrant flycatchers etc: **Pelecaniformes** cormorants, gannets, pelicans etc: **Piciformes** barbets, honeyguides, toucans, woodpeckers etc: **Podicipediformes** grebes: **Procellariiformes** albatrosses, petrels: **Psittaciformes** parrots: **Rheiformes** rheas: **Sphenisciformes** penguins: **Strigiformes** owls: **Struthioniformes** ostrich: **Tinamiformes** tinamous: **Trogoniformes** trogons (also see **ANIMAL ADJECTIVES, COLLECTIVE NOUNS**)

birsle *S vb* to toast hard *S n* a scorched or toasted surface

birtle *obs n* a summer or sweet apple

bisculate *adj* having two shields

bismar *Ork & Shet n* a type of weighing machine

bison (*n*) whilst the standard *pl* is **bison, bisons** is an acceptable *var fm*

bisson *obs adj* blind

bister *var fm n* **bistre**

bistered *var fm adj* **bistred**

bistre *n* a golden brown pigment made from beechwood soot

bistred *adj* stained (as) with bistre

bitonality *n* the simultaneous use of two musical keys: the effect so produced

bitterling *n* a small, silvery, carp-like European fish which has a remarkable symbiotic breeding relationship with a freshwater mussel. A pair of bitterlings approach a mussel which the female fish gently 'kisses' until it opens its shell. The female then inserts her very long ovipositor (an egg tube, two-thirds of her own length of three inches) directly into the now-open shellfish and releases her eggs. The male fish fertilizes these eggs by releasing his milt over them. In return for this nursery facility, the bitterling carries on her skin the larvae of the mussel which are released at the same time as the fish is laying her eggs. At the appropriate times, the young bitterlings swim free and the young mussels drop off.

bittre *Obs fm n/adv* **bitter**

black ant see **aphid**

blackfish see **SALMON**

black til *n* the plant, ramtil

blader *obs n* one who makes blades: a swordsman *obs fm n/vb* **bladder**

blae *S adj* blackish, blue-black: livid: bleak

blague *n* humbug

blain *n* a fish with an inflatable membrane on its head and known by various names such as **bib, blens, blinds, pout, whiting-pout**: an inflammatory swelling on the skin: a bladder-like growth on the tongue of animals which can eventually choke them *vb* to blister

blaise *S fm n/vb* **blaze** (+*cap*) *masc pers n* possibly meaning 'splay-footed'

blare *vb* to sound a trumpet: to bellow as a calf: to make a continuous roaring sound whilst weeping *n* the sound of the act of blaring: a tar-based preparation used for caulking boats

blase *obs fm n/vb* **blaze**

blaseness *Obs n* brightness

blaser *obs fm n* **blazer**, one who proclaims or publishes

blastema *n* embryonic protoplasm: the formative material of the egg (*pl* **blastemata**)

blastie *n* a dwarf

blasty *adj* gusty (*comp* **blastier** *sup* **blastiest**)

blate *S & dial adj* awkward, backward, bashful, diffident, shamefaced, sheepish *Obs adj* pale or ghastly: without feeling or emotion: curt *vb* to babble or prate

blather *vb* to talk nonsense

blatter *vb* to prattle continuously *S vb* to rush with a clattering sound *S n* the noise of prattle or a similar sound

blead *Obs n* breath *obs S fm vb* **bleed**

bleaky *adj* bleak

blear *adj* dim, watery: blurred *vb* to make (eyes or sight) blurred as with tears: to dupe or trick

blenny *n* any species of usually fairly small, elongated marine or estuarine fishes of fifteen different families classified in the same order as the perches. The species *incl* the **common blenny**, also known as the **shanny** or the **shanny out of water** (the most common British species and according to legend it basks on rocks in the sunshine), the **tompot blenny** or **gattorugine** (the largest British species, growing to a foot in length), the **butterfly blenny** (half the size of the tompot), the **scaleless blenny** (a very common North Atlantic shore fish), the **scaled blenny** or **klipfish** (the female of which gives live birth as the male has modified spines of the anal fin which act as a type of penis), the **gunnel** (the various species of which *incl* an eel-like fish), the **butterfish** (another species of gunnel, see **butterfish**) and the **wolf fish** (the giants among the blennies, normally growing to five feet with the **spotted wolf fish** growing to six feet).

blester *Obs fm n* **blister**

blike *obs vb* to glisten

blindage *n* a temporary military defence against such as splinters or shrapnel, comprising a wooden screen filled with earth

blirre *obs n* a deception *obs vb* to deceive

blitter *dial fm n* **bittern**, the bird

blome *obs fm n/vb* bloom

blood-boltered *obs adj* of hair, matted with blood (GAME PLAYER'S note: As *boltered* has never had an independent existence as a word in its own right, it is not available for play in any game. Equally invalid is *blood-boltered*, as it is hyphenated. Being obsolete is no barrier to use, except for Countdown played on television or the UK Scrabble championship which, unlike many similar tournaments in other countries, has this additional ban.)

blore *arch n* a violent gust of wind *now dial vb* to cry (out): of animals, to utter their cry

blother *var fm S & dial vb* **bluther**

bloure *var fm obs n* **blure**

bloused *adj* wearing a blouse

blowe *obs fm vb* **blow**, to blossom or bloom

blowre *var fm obs n* **blure**

blowse *n* a fat, red-faced, woman

bludder *var fm S & dial vb* **bluther**

bludge *slg vb* to loaf about: to scrounge

bludger *slg n* a loafer or scrounger

blue *(n/adj) vb* to make blue *esp* to heat metal to make it blue

blue blood *n* the colour of the blood of crabs and crayfish: aristocratic blood *(fig)*

bluer *n* one who blues metal

blue rot *n* a fungal blight of coniferous trees

blue sheep *n* a type of goat (see **bharal**)

bluet *n* any of various flowers *incl* the corn bluebottle

blume *obs S fm n/vb* **bloom**

blunge *vb* to mix the basic pottery ingredients (clay, powdered flint etc) with water

blunger *n* one who blunges

blure *obs n* a blister

blurre *obs fm n* **blur**

bluther *S & dial vb* to sob

bo *n* a Japanese Buddhist monk *(pl* **bo**): the bobization equivalent of **doh** or **do** in the tonic sol-fa *(pl* **bos**) *US slg n* a military leader *(pl* **bos**) *interj* to startle (as *saying bo to a goose*) *var fm dial n/vb* **ball** (described at *Ork & Shet var fm* **baa**) *(+cap) n* a town in Sierra Leone

boar *(n) obs vb* of pigs, to copulate

boarde *obs fm n/vb* **board**

boarden *obs vb* to floor with boards

boatage *n* transportation by boat: a charge for same

boatel *n* a boat functioning as a hotel: a waterside hotel specializing in serving owners of boats

boatfly *n* a species of water bug

bobization *n* a former system of musical notation which used as syllables the words **bo, ce, di, ga, lo, ma, ni** (also see **bebization**)

bocland *n* bookland, land taken from the focland (folkland) and granted by boc (a written charter) to the Church or other private owner

bodder *obs fm n/vb* **bother**

boggler *n* one who hesitates, doubts, equivocates

bog iron *n* a brittle, porous type of brown iron ore found in bogs

Bog Latin *see* **Shelta**

boglet *n* a little bog

bog ore see **limonite**

boh *var fm interj/US slg n* **bo**

bohreen *var fm Anglo-Ir n* **boreen**

bolden *now dial vb* to make or be bold *var fm obs S vb* **bowden**

bolder *(comp adj) var fm n* **boulder**, a bulrush

boldne *var fm obs S vb* **bowden**

Boletus *n* a large genus of fungi, both edible and poisonous, with the distinctive feature of the under surface of the pileus being full of pores instead of gills

bolike *n* an (exploding) meteor: a brilliant shooting star

boltered see **blood-boltered** *(esp* games players)

boltering *obs n* the fabric used for sieves (GAME PLAYER'S note: Unlike boltered (see **blood-boltered**) there is no objection to the using of this word, providing that you have agreed to use *obs* words)

bolthead *n* the head of a bolt

bonder *n* a bondstone, a stone larger than neighbouring elements of a wall and usually facing on both sides to give a bonding effect to the structure

bone oil *n* a thick, fetid, blackish oil obtained from the dry distillation of bones

boner *slg n* a glaring and amusing blunder, a howler

bonist *n* one who believes that the world is good

bonita *var fm n* **bonito**

bonito *n* any of various, relatively smaller, tuna-like fishes not necessarily closely related (see **pelamid** and **skipjack**) (*pl* **bonitoes, bonitos**)

bonny (*adj*) *obs n* a mining term for an individual rounded deposit of ore

bonzer *Austr collq adj* very good

boodle *n* the complete crowd or lot – as in the familiar phrase *the whole caboodle* (a *collq fm* of *the whole boodle*): working capital *slg n* a stupid person *var fm n* **buddle,** the corn marigold

booksie *adj* literary to a lesser degree

bool *obs fm n/vb* **bawl**

boor *var fm obs vb* **boar**

boother *dial fm n* **boulder**

bootjack *n* an implement used for removing boots

boottree *n* a footlike object placed in a boot or shoe either to stretch it or to help it keep its shape

boracic *adj* of, pertaining to or composed of the non-metallic element, boron

borane *n* any boron hydride, chemicals efficient as high energy fuel

borate *n* a salt of boric acid

borde *obs slg n* a shilling

bordel *arch n* a brothel *obs n* prostitution

bordello *n* a brothel (*pl* **bordellos**)

borden *obs adj* made of boards *var fm obs vb* **boarden**

bordure *her n* a border *now poet n* a border

boreal *adj* of or pertaining to the north *obs fm n* **beryl**

boreen *Anglo-Ir n* a lane or (*fig*) an opening in a crowd

boride *n* a combination of boron with another element

borne (*adj*) *obs fm n* **bourn**, a stream *Obs fm obs n* **berne**, a man

bornite *n* horseflesh ore or peacock copper, a metallic, reddish-brown, copper-iron sulphide having a purple tarnish

bosdas see **hyrax**

bosh (*slg n*) *slg vb* to talk contemptible nonsense

boshta *Austr collq adj* excellent

boshter *var fm Austr collq adj* **boshta**

bosker *Austr collq adj* excellent

bostangi *n* a guard of a Turkish palace

botanies *pl* botany

botanise *var fm vb* **botanize**, to seek for and collect plants in the interests of study

botanomancy *n* divination by leaves, such as (*a*) writing sentences on leaves, exposing those leaves to the wind and whatever remains gives the answer (*b*) interpreting the crackling noises of leaves cast on a fire or crushed in the hand

botte *obs n* a distinguishing mark or brand daubed on a sheep *obs fm ns* **boat, boot** (in senses other than profit or advantage) *Fr n* a fencing pass or thrust

BOTTLE SIZES the different names for the large wine bottles reflect their relationship to the standard bottle (holding $26\frac{2}{3}$ fluid ounces) as follows:– **magnum** the equivalent of 2 bottles: **jeroboam** 4 bottles: **rehoboam** 6: **methuselah** 8: **salamanazar** 12: **balthazar** 16: **nebuchadnezzar** 20.

boulder *n* a large stone (*var fm* **bowlder** *dial fms incl* **boother, bowder**): the bulrush (*var fm* **bolder**) *vb* of water, to make into large stones (*var fm* **bowlder**)

boule *n* an ancient Greek council or senate: the modern Greek parliament: an imitation precious stone made from synthetic corondum *var fm n* **buhl** *obs fm n* **bowl** (in the sense of a ball, see **boules**) *obs fm vb* **bowl**

boules *Fr n pl* (*construed as sing*) a game similar to bowls except that the balls are usually made of metal and no special attention is given to the playing surface

boulet *n* a horse whose fetlock is bent forward out of natural position

boulle *var fm n* **buhl**

boult *var fm vb* **bolt**, to sift *var fm obs n* **bolt**, a sieve

boulter *n* a long fishing line with many hooks

boun *vb* to get or make ready: to prepare

bounder (*n*) *n* one who marks out limits or boundaries (*lit/fig*) *obs vb* to mark out such limits

bourder *obs n* a jester

bourn *n* a brook *vb* to set a limit to *var fm n* **bourne**

bourne *n* a destination *arch n* a limit *var fm n* **bourn** *var fm obs vb* **burn**, to burnish

bourse *n* a stock exchange (+*cap*) *n* that of Paris

boutade *n* a sudden outburst or outbreak

bouton *n* an enlargement of a nerve fibre

bovid *adj* of or belonging to the *Bovidae*, the family of the cattle, sheep, goats and antelopes (see **ANTELOPES**)

bowat *var fm S n* **bowet**

bowden *obs S vb* to swell

bowder *dial fm n* **boulder**

bowel (*n*) *vb* to remove the bowels of (*infl fms British*, **bowelled** etc: *US*, **boweled** etc)

Bowery, The *n* a street and district in New York City occupying the site of the bowery of Peter Stuyvesant, the last Dutch governor of New Amsterdam (the old name for New York) 1647–1664

bowery *US n* a farm or plantation (*pl* **boweries**)

bowet *S n* a (small) lantern

bowlder *var fm n/vb* **boulder** (as indicated)

bowne *var fm vb* **boun**, to prepare

bowser *n* an early type of petrol pump: a fuel tanker used for such as aircraft or military vehicles *Austr/NZ n* any type of petrol pump *obs n* a treasurer

bowyer *n* an archer: one who makes or sells bows

boxfish *n* any of various species of Indo-Pacific brightly-coloured, poisonous fishes which live among the coral reefs. Also known as a **trunkfish**, a typical individual has its head and body enclosed in a box of bony plates with only the fins, jaws and the end of the tail projecting and free to move. The 'box' can be triangular, rectangular or pentagonal but the underside is always flat. The term, **coffer-fish**, has also been applied – though this seems to be confined to a single report in 1884. However, as one particular dictionary uses that term as its basic name for the various species of *Ostracion* (the genus of the boxfishes), then perhaps the word has a more general usage? It gives trunkfish, but fails to mention boxfish. The term, trunkfish, is the one favoured by various other dictionaries as the basic name.

brabble *n* a discordant babble *arch vb* to quibble *esp* noisily about a mere trifle

brable *obs fm arch vb* **brabble**

braccio *n* an Italian measure of length, *approx* two feet (*pl* **braccia**)

brach *n* a female hound ?*obs n* a term of abuse equivalent to bitch (note: Whilst not specified as *obs* by the *Oxford English Dictionary*, it only records two 17th century quotes, one of 1652 and an earlier one of Ben Jonson's in 1610) *Obs n* a hound, of either sex, which hunts by scent

brache *obs fm n* **brach** (*lit* sense only)

brachet *n* a female hound: a brat

brack *n* a flaw in cloth: the system used in Baltic ports for the sorting of goods *vb* to sort goods by this system

bract *n* a specialized leaf with a single flower or inflorescence in its axil

brade *dial fm n* **bread** *obs fm n/vb* **braid**

Brahmi *n* an ancient alphabet of the Hindus

braide *obs fm vb* **braid** *Shaks adj* deceitful

brail *n* one of a number of small ropes attached to a sail for the purpose of trussing it prior to furling, or for hauling the sail up: a broad belt used to confine a hawk's wings: one of the feathers of a hawk's rump: logs lashed together to form part of a raft *vb* to haul up a sail by means of the brails: to confine the wings of a hawk

braile *obs fm vb* **brail**

braird *n* the first shoots of a crop *vb* to sprout

braize *n* a fish, the sea bream

braless *adj* of a woman, not wearing a bra

brame *vb* to roar or rage *obs n* a bramble bush

brandise *n* a trivet or tripod

brandle *obs vb* to totter: to cause to totter

branke *Obs n* a sword

Branksea *n* an ecclesiastical district in south-east Devonshire

bransel *obs fm n* **bransle**

bransle *n* an old French dance and the music for it

brase *obs fm vb* **braze**, to solder *obs fm vb* **brace**

Brasil *native fm/obs English fm n* **Brazil**

brask *obs vb* obscure, but probably means to scrape or graze

brasse *obs fm n* **brass**

brasserie *n* a small restaurant: a bar which also serves food

brasset *var fm n* **brassard**, a piece of armour for the arm

brassie *n* the number 2 wood, one of the set of golf clubs

brast *dial fm vb* **burst**

brat (*n*) *now dial n* a coarse cloth used as a casual covering for a person or for a sheep

bratte *obs fm n* **brat** *obs fm now dial n* **brat**

brattle *n* any of various sounds such as that of something breaking or that of scampering feet *vb* of a fast flowing mountain stream, to make its customary sound as it passes over a stony bed *S vb* to scamper

bratty *US adj* of or befitting a spoilt child (the equivalent *UK adj* being brattish) (*comp* **brattier** *sup* **brattiest**)

braune *obs fm n/vb* **brawn**

braunite *n* a brownish-black oxide of manganese

brawde *obs vb* to embroider

brawly *S adv* excellently

breachy *dial adj* brackish

bread (*n*) *vb* to cover with bread crumbs: to clean by rubbing with bread: to provide bread

bream *n* any of several freshwater fishes: the sea bream, any of the fishes in two different families (*a*) of spiny-finned fish (*b*) a family akin to the mackerels *vb* to clean the exterior hull of a ship by applying heat to soften the pitch so that barnacles and other accretions can be swept away: of swine, to copulate

breame *obs fm n* **bream**, the fish

breastrail *n* the upper rail of the balcony at the forepart of the quarterdeck

breccia *n* a composite rock made of fragments of the same or various stones cemented together by such as lime

brecham *S n* the collar for a carthorse

breech (*n*) *vb* to clothe (as) with breeches

breese *var fm n* **breeze** in senses other than that of a light wind (of which it is an *obs fm*) *obs fm vb* **bruise**

bret *now dial vb* to crop

brethe *Obs vb* to go to ruin (*pa pple* **brothin**) (note: Whilst this *vb* has been obsolete for some 500 years or more, it is the basis of the existing word, brothel)

Briard *n* a French breed of a large hairy dog

bribering *obs n/adj* thieving

bricke *obs fm n* **brick**

bricken *adj* of brick *obs vb* to hold in one's chin proudly

bricole *n* an historical military engine of war which fired rocks or other missiles by a catapult action: the rebound of the ball from a wall of the court in which real tennis is played: a rebound from the cushion on a billiards table *obs vb* to rebound

bridale see **brideale**

bride (*n*) *vb* to make a married women of

brideale *n* the earlier *fm* of **bride-ale**, an Old English wedding feast, still reflected by the *var fm* **bridale**

bridie *S n* a meat pasty (+*cap*) *dim fem pers n* **Bridget**, a derivative of **Brighid**, meaning 'strength'

brill *n* a turbot-like flatfish *obs vb* to make a vibrating sound as that of the beating of insect wings

brille *obs vb* to shine

brime *obs fm vb* **brim**, of swine, to rut *obs vb* to develop fruit

briming *dial n* the nocturnal glow of the sea

brine (*n*) *vb* to treat with salt water

brisance *n* the shattering effect of high explosives

brise *obs fm n/vb* **bruise**

brisle *now dial fm vb* **bristle**

brisling *n* a Norwegian sprat

brisure *n* a break in the general direction of a fortification *her n* a variation to or an addition to a coat or arms denoting a younger branch

brite *now dial vb* of hops and grain, to shatter when overripe

britle *obs fm adj* **brittle**

broad (*adj/n*) *obs vb* to expand

broadtail *n* fur of a very young Karakul lamb

broadway *n* a broad road

brocked *S adj* piebald

brocket *n* any of four species of small deer of Central and South America: a stag in its second year (the female equivalents, **hearse** or **brocket sister**, both *obs*)

brode *obs fm adj* **broad** *obs fm n/vb* **brood**

brodel *Obs fm n* **brothel**

broder *obs fm vb* **broider**

brodre *obs fm vb* **broider**

broggle *dial vb* to poke a stick into a hole *esp* a baited stick when fishing for eels

broider *vb* to embroider: to ornament with needlework

broidre *obs fm vb* **broider**

broile *obs fm vb* **broil**

brokage *obs n* brokerage

broke (*pa pple*) *vb* to act as an agent or go-between

brokes *n pl* the short staples of wool in a fleece

broll *now dial n* a child *esp* one who is a brat *obs vb* to roar

brome, *n* a grass, rather like oats, cultivated for hay and pasturage

bromide *n* any salt of hydrobromic acid: a dose of sodium or potassium bromide given as a sedative (a legendary ingredient of Naafi tea to keep servicemen celibate by removing desire): a platitude: a boring person

bronde *obs fm n* **brand**

bronstrops *n* a woman who runs a brothel (*obs* except in literature on old or obsolete words)

Bronwen *fem pers n* meaning 'white breasted'

Bronx cheer *Us n* the vulgar derisive sound known in the UK as a 'raspberry'

broom (*n*) *vb* to clean with a broom: to clean, by burning, the sides of a sailing vessel

broomy *adj* abounding in or consisting of the shrub, broom

brose *n* a dish of oatmeal salted and buttered, to which boiling milk and/or water is added *obs fm n/vb* **bruise**

brotel *obs adj* fragile, brittle

brothe *obs adj* passionate, violent, wrathful *obs fm n* **broth**

brotle *var fm obs adj* **brotel**

brouder *obs fm vb* **broider**

brouse *obs fm vb* **browse**

brout *obs fm n* **brut**, a chronicle of British history which begins with the appearance of Brutus, the legendary Trojan leader from whom Britain takes its name (see **Brutus**)

browe *obs fm n* **brow**

browed *adj* having a brow

bru *S n* the interior of a sithien, or mound in which fairies dwell *Ork & Shet n* liquor

bruckle *adj* fragile *now dial vb* to make grimy

Bruger *pers n* he who discovered skatol (see **scatole**)

bruit *arch* (*except US*) *vb* to noise abroad: talk about: make famous *arch* (*except US*) *n* that noised abroad *arch n* noise, clamour

bruke *now dial n* the cricket, the insect akin to the grasshopper and the locust

brule *obs fm vb* **broil**

brumal *adj* pertaining to winter

brumous *adj* foggy, wintry

brune *dial fm adj/vb* **brown** *Obs n* burning

Brunella *n* the genus of selfheal, a low-growing, herbaceous plant having tightly-clustered, violet-blue flowers

brunet *masc fm n/adj* **brunette**

bruse *obs fm n/vb* **bruise**

brush turkey *n* a megapode which, like the mallee fowl, also builds a large incubation mound. In the case of this bird, the male refuses to allow the female near the mound until he is satisfied that the temperature is correct for her to lay her eggs. (See **mallee fowl**)

brusle *var fm obs vb* **brustle**, to bristle

brust *obs n* a bristle *Obs adj* bristled *obs fm vb* **burst**

bruste *var fm obs n* **brust**

brustel *var fm obs vb* **brustle**, to bristle

brustle *obs vb* to make a crackling noise: to bristle

brute (*n*) *obs fm n/vb* **bruit**

brutise *var fm obs vb* **brutize**, to become or act like a brute

Brutus *pers n* the legendary great-grandson of the Trojan hero Aeneas who, after the sack of Troy, established a kingdom in Italy. At the age of 15, Brutus was exiled for the shame of accidentally killing his father and, in Greece, he soon became the leader of the Trojans whom circumstances had forced to live there. Eventually he led them in an epic voyage to the Isle of Albion where they created a great kingdom called Britain after its founder. The Trojans originally landed in Devon and Brutus founded his capital of Troia Nova (London) at the time when Eli was the high priest and judge of Israel. (This legend is a matter of dispute amongst historians. Also see **Albanactus, Albion, Cassandra, Kamber, Locrinus**.): the cousin of the sons of the king of Rome, Tarquin the Proud. Brutus accompanied two of these sons, Titus and Arruns, on a mission to consult the oracle at Delphi. The sons asked an additional question as to who would be the next king of Rome. The reply was, '*He who shall be the first to kiss his mother*'. Titus and Arruns drew lots for the right of the first kiss and agreed to keep the matter secret from their eldest brother, also named Tarquin. Brutus pretended to slip and secretly kissed the earth, mother of all. When Tarquin the Proud was eventually dethroned and Rome declared a republic, Brutus was one of the two consuls who jointly ruled in his stead. (Also see **Lucretia, oracle, Pythia** and **Tarquin**): various other leading Romans *esp* the Brutus concerned with the assassination of Julius Caesar

bry *dial n* the gadfly (*pl* **brees, breese**)

bu *n* a Japanese coin also known as **ichibu** or **itzebu** (*pl* **bu**): a very small Japanese measure of length (3.03 mm), of which there are 10 to the sun (*pl* **bu's**) *Ork n* a manor house (*pl* **bu's**) *obs fm vb* **bow**, to submit or yield to

buat *var fm S n* **bowet**

bubonine *adj* of those owls classified by ear development as belonging to the sub-family *Buboninae* (Also see **strigine**)

bucca *dial n* a spriggan or 'knocker' of a Cornish tin mine, a goblin frequently heard working away at his mining task but only ever seen where a good lode is about to be uncovered. Buccas are believed to be the souls of Jews still being punished for their part in the Crucifixion. (Jews were employed in the 11th and 12th centuries in these mines, but tradition has them back in Roman times. Also see **muryan** and **pisky**.)

bucksaw *n* a type of saw, set in an adjustable H-shaped frame, used with a sawbuck

buddel *obs fm n* **buddle**, the miner's vat

budder *n* that which is in bud

buddle *n* the corn marigold: a shallow vat used for washing ore in Derbyshire lead mines, Cornish tin mines and US silver mines *vb* to wash ore in a buddle

buddler *n* one who uses a buddle for ore

budger *n* one who budges or stirs

bue *see* **be**

bugle (*n*) *vb* to blow a bugle

buglet *n* a little bugle

buhl *n* a complex inlay of such as gold, silver, brass, pewter, ivory and mother of pearl in such as tortoiseshell, forming a panel for furniture: furniture so decorated

Bul *n* Heshwan

bulger *n* a golf club with wooden convex face

bulget *obs S n* a pouch

bullace *n* either of two varieties of wild plum

bullbeggar *n* a supernatural and frightening manifestation associated with a grave in unconsecrated ground which contains or contained two bodies *esp* where these bodies are buried crossways to each other

bulletrie *var fm n* **bully tree**, any of various timber trees

bulter *dial n* a Cornish fishing line, 500 feet long with 60 hooks each 8 feet apart

bummle *var fm n/vb* **bumble**, to do or speak in a clumsy, inefficient fashion

bunder *Anglo-Ind n* a quay or landing stage: a harbour

bungie *slg n* an eraser or rubber

bunia *n* a Hindu merchant

bunt *n* a bag-shaped part of such as a trawling or similar fishing net, the bottom of an eel trap or the middle of a ship's sail where it takes the force of the wind *S & dial n* the tail of a rabbit *now dial n* the puffball *vb* of a sail, to swell in the wind: to butt or hit *dial vb* to sift flour

bunter *n* mottled sandstone *now dial n* a woman who scavenges for a living: a low vulgar woman

buqsha *n* a monetary unit of the Yemen, of which there are 40 to the rial

bur *n* any rough or prickly seedcase or flowerhead: any plant which produces such waste raw silk: a lump: a rough pronunciation of the letter R *vb* to remove burs from (that to which they have become attached): to whisper hoarsely: *var fm dial n/vb* **ber** *Obs vb* to behold

burbel *var fm obs n* **burble**

burble *S dial n* confusion, disorder, muddle, trouble *obs n* a bubble: a pimple *S dial vb* to confuse, muddle *obs vb* to form bubbles

burd alone *now poet S adj* a solitary surviving child

burdash, *n* a fringed sash worn round the waist of men during the reigns of Queen Anne and George I

burde *obs fm n* **board** *Obs fm n* **beard**

burdie *S n* a little bird

burge *obs vb* to bud or sprout

burgee *n* a small (swallow-tailed) pennant

burhel *var fm n* **bharal**

burke *vb* to murder after the fashion of Burke (see below): to murder for the same purpose: to smother (*fig*) (William Burke, an Irish navvy, and his accomplice, William Hare, were secretly employed by the Edinburgh surgeon, Dr Robert Knox, to produce dead bodies for his anatomical research. Having difficulty in stealing fresh corpses, they turned to murder. Aided by their wives, they lured fifteen people to their deaths by smothering. Hare turned King's evidence and, as Burke was led to public execution in Edinburgh in 1829, the crowd shouted '*Burke him . . . don't hang him . . . burke Hare too*'. Of the five involved, only Burke was executed.)

burkha *var fm n* **burqa**

burlace *obs n* a large white grape once cultivated up to the 17th century but no longer in existence

burler *n* one who removes knots or other imperfections from cloth

burlet *obs n* a padded roll of cloth worn by a woman on her head *var fm obs n* **burlace**

burletta *n* comic opera

burne *var fm obs n* **berne**

burnet *n* any of various plants such as the **common burnet** found in meadows or the **salad burnet** found on chalky ground *obs adj* of a dark brown colour *obs n* a (dark brown coloured) cloth of superior quality *modf n* **burnet fly, burnet moth** or **burnet sphinx**, a greenish-black moth with red spots on its wings: **burnet buttons**, burnet flowerheads: **burnet rose**, the Scottish rose

Burnett salmon *n* the rarest of the modern lungfishes, it is found in the Burnett and the Mary rivers of Queensland, Australia where it is a protected species (also see **Ceradotus**)

burnie *S n* a brooklet

Burnsite *n* a devotee of Robert Burns (1759–1796), the Scottish poet

burqa *n* an Arabic loose outergarment which covers the whole body and has veiled eyeholes

burrel *var fm n* **bharel**

burret *obs n* the mollusc, murex

burrie *obs fm adj* **burry**

burry *adj* full of burs: rough or prickly like a bur *dial fm n* **burrow**, as in rabbit burrow

bursae *pl* bursa, a pouch or sac

bursal *adj* of a bursa

bursten *now poet or rhetorical adj* burst

burstle *var fm now dial vb* **bristle**, to scorch *var fm obs vb* **brustle**, to bristle

burt *obs vb* to push or thrust as with horns: to dint or pierce

burte *var fm obs vb* **burt**

burter *obs n* one who dints

bus bar *n* a short bar of such as (uninsulated) copper forming a connection between two or more electrical circuits

bushel *n* an old measure of capacity for dry goods equal to 4 pecks or 8 gallons. The imperial bushel was established in 1826 as the equivalent of 80 lbs of distilled water weighed in the air at 62° Fahrenheit, which produces a capacity of 2218.192 cubic inches. The imperial bushel replaced (among others) the Winchester bushel of 2150.42 cubic inches which also had its equivalent pecks and gallons (see **Winchester measures**): a vessel used to measure a bushel: any large quantity or number *vb* (*mainly fig*) to hide under a bushel (the reference is to the sense of Matt v 15 '*To hide one's light under a bushel*') (note: The saying '*To measure other people's corn by one's own bushel*', means to judge others by one's own standards)

bushet *obs n* a small bush

bussle *now S fm n/vb* **bustle**

but (*prep/adv*) *n* an objection *S n* see **but and ben** *vb* to advance as an objection

but and ben *S n* a small house with only two ground floor rooms. Access is normally made through the but, or kitchen, thence to the ben, or parlour.

butane *n* a colourless, inflammable, gaseous compound found in petroleum or produced synthetically and used mainly in the manufacture of rubber or fuels

butler (*n*) *nonce vb* to take charge of and serve liquor as opposed to food (the sense in which butlering is a *nonce n*): to act as a butler: to be served by a butler (the sense coined by Dickens)

butterfish *n* a gunnel or species of elongated blenny having a slippery, slimy skin. Unusual among fishes, both parents take turns in guarding the eggs which the female compacts into a ball, then conceals in a hole in the rocks.

butyl *n* a hydrocarbon radical

bux *Shet vb* to go: to hurry *var fm n* **buck** (*obs* except as a syllable in English place names)

bwbach *n* a Welsh goblin which differs from similar creatures in that it has an intense dislike of teetotallers and dissenting ministers (*pl* **bwbachod**)

bwca *n* the Welsh brownie, a noseless goblin with a destructive nature

bwg *Welsh n* a ghost

by (*prep/adv*) *n* a town or village (*Obs* except as a syllable in English place names i.e. Derby =(*Obs fm n* deer) + by)

byk *dial n* a bees' nest

byline *n* the printed acknowledgement of a writer's name for such as a newspaper report or a magazine article

byn see **be**

byreman *S n* a cowherd or farmhand who tends cattle (*fem* **byrewoman**)

byrlaw *n* the custom among husbandmen in a rural community of settling local disputes of a legal nature among themselves without the necessity of going to court. The parties to the dispute agree in advance to accept the byrlaw judgment as binding.

byroom *n* a side room

bzzzbzzz *US slg n* gossip

C

ca *S n* a pass or defile between hills: a calf (*pl* **caas**) *n* field (*Obs* except in the *fm* **cae** as a syllable in English place names) *Obs fm S & dial n* **kae**

caa *var fm dial vb* **ka**

caas *pl S n* ca

cabalism *var fm n* **cabbalism**, the science of the cabbala

cabalist *var fm n* **cabbalist**, a student of the cabbala: a mystic

cabbala *n* the oral tradition handed down from Moses and preserved in the *Mishna* of the *Talmud*: secret or esoteric doctrine

cabble *vb* to break up pieces of partially finished iron for an iron-smelting process

cabbler *n* one who breaks up iron into smaller pieces for smelting

Cabecar *n* a Macro-Chibchan language of Costa Rica

cabel *obs fm n* **cable**

caber *n* the trunk of a young (pine) tree used as a heavy pole for tossing by Highland athletes

cabestro *n* a lasso (*pl* **cabestros**) (*var fms incl* the unlisted anagram, **cabresto** (*pl* **cabrestos**))

cabine *obs fm n* **cabin**

cabless *adj* without a cab

cabot see **denerel**

cabresta *var fm n* **cabestro**

cabrie *n* the pronghorn antelope (*var fms* **cabree, cabrit**)

cabriole *adj* of furniture legs, curved *n* a capriole or leap without advancing

cacique *n* a lord or chief of the original native inhabitants (i.e. Red Indian type) in various parts of the Caribbean: a political leader in Spain and Latin America (GAME PLAYER'S note: The *var fm* **cazique** is of especial interest to Scrabble players – see **quetzal** for full details)

cacomistle *n* the ringtailed cat, either of two species (the cacomistle or the rarer Mexican cacomistle) of nocturnal carnivores found in the southern parts of the USA and in Central America. Cat-sized and rather like a slim racoon in appearance, either species is very attractive and can adapt to human company in much the same way as the domestic cat. The cacomistle has long, soft, grey fur with a black and white tail slightly longer than the head and body combined, semi-retractile claws and large round ears. The Mexican cacomistle differs in having a longer tail, pointed ears, naked soles and non-retractile claws. The cacomistles belong to the same family as the racoons, coatis, kinkajous or honey bears and the giant panda.

caddel *obs S fm n/vb* **caudle**

caddle *dial n* trouble: confusion, disorder *dial vb* to trouble: to disturb

Cadell *masc pers n* meaning 'strength in war'

cadene *n* an inferior type of Turkish carpet

cadent *adj* falling (whilst *arch* in the literal sense, it is standard both for rhythm and, in astrology, for the movement of a planet) *obs n* one of the embellishments in old English music

cader *now dial n* a light wooden frame placed over a scythe to make the corn lie more evenly during the harvest: a small wooden frame for a fishing line *Obs n* a cradle

cadi *n* a Muslim civil judge (in a small town or village)

cadrans *n* an instrument used for adjusting the position of a gemstone during cutting

cadre *n* a basic unit or structure: the nucleus of trained professional servicemen around whom expansion is made: a member of a cadre

caen stone *n* a yellowish building stone originally soft but which hardens on exposure

Caesarean *adj* of or pertaining to a Caesar or the Caesars: designating the type of delivery whereby the child is removed from the womb by cutting through the walls of the abdomen, as was the case with Julius Ceasar *n* an adherent of the imperial as opposed to the papal view in a dispute between the two (note: The *var fm* is **Caesarian** but, in the USA, the additional *var fms* are **Cesarean** and **Cesarian**. Further, the *adj* of delivery can be treated as a noun and can be *–cap*)

Caesarism *n* imperialism

caestus *var fm n* **cestus** (as shown)

caesura *n* a pause in the middle of a line of verse (modern prosody): a break between words within a metric foot (classical prosody) (*pl* **caesurae, caesuras**)

cafila *n* a company travelling together whilst crossing a desert

cahow *n* a species of gadfly petrel considered, for more than 250 years, to be extinct until it was rediscovered at the beginning of this century. A small colony of about 80 of these medium-sized seabirds exists on a tropical Atlantic island.

caid *n* an alcade, or magistrate of a Spanish or Portuguese town or city: a cadi

caiman *n* a tropical reptile akin to the alligator

cain hen *n* a hen paid as the cain, or rent payable in the form of rural produce

caique *n* a Levantine sailing vessel: a long, narrow, pointed skiff on the Bosphorus, propelled by two to ten oars

Cairene *adj* of Cairo *n* a citizen of Cairo

cairned *adj* having or surmounted with a cairn or pyramid of rough stones

cairt *S fm n/vb* **cart**

caisson *n* an ammunition chest: an ammunition wagon: a box containing explosives which is buried for use as a landmine: a strong, watertight case used during the laying of foundations for a bridge: a floating gate for a dry dock: an apparatus for lifting a vessel out of water *modf n* of a disease also known as the bends, which affects divers who are too suddenly subject to decreased air pressure

caitive *obs vb* to make captive or subject to

cait sith *n* a black fairy cat of the Scottish Highlands, the size of a huge dog and reputedly a transformed witch (also see **cu sith**)

caking *n* the forming of a cake

cal *n* the Polish equivalent of the inch, but slightly shorter (24 *mm*)

calamine *n* the mineral, zinc carbonate

calamint *n* an odorous perennial herb of the mint family placed within the genus *Satureia,* of which the typical species is *Satureia calamintha*

calamite *n* one of an extinct genus or order of plants commonly found as fossils in coal measures and possibly related to the present day mare's tail: an asparagus green-coloured variety of the mineral, tremolite

calamus *n* any species of a genus of tall palms which are the source of cane or rattan: a herbalist's name for either sweet flag or sweet rush, usually in the *fm* **sweet calamus** (*pl* **calami**)

calander *obs n* a species of Mediterranean lark, slightly larger than a skylark

calandre *var fm obs n* **calander**

Calanus *n* a genus of minute primitive animals which swim in plankton and are important as food for fishes and whales

calcine *vb* to heat in order to effect oxidization, reduction or loss of water

Caldee *obs fm n/adj* **Chaldee**

calender *n* a machine which smooths or glazes by pressing under rollers

calendre *obs fm n* **calender**

calendry *n* a place where a finish is imparted to the surface of such as cloth or paper

calends *n sing/pl* the first day of each Roman month

calenture *adj* fever: zeal, heat, glow (*lit/fig*) *n* a tropical disease suffered by sailors, characterized by delirium so extreme that a sufferer can imagine the sea to be a meadow and wish to take a stroll in it *obs vb* to suffer that disease: to become hot or inflamed

caliatour *n* an unknown timber from which a dye is obtained and its tree grows in a coastal region of India, a stretch of *approx* 450 miles between Point Calimere and the Kistna river, known as the Coromandel or Carnatic coast. A passing reference to this dye wood was made in an issue of the *London Gazette* in 1687 with the spelling, **caleatour**. Some experts suggest it could be sandalwood. All, except as given below, consider the word *obs.* (GAME PLAYER'S note: Participants in the UK Scrabble championship have no problems with the word. The dictionary currently used for their contest not only has the word extant but positively asserts the meaning as 'red-sanders'. The *fm* 'red-sanders' would appear to be exclusive to that book. Writers from Tudor times to the present day – with *fms* varying from **redde sanders** to **red saunders** – have never been known to hyphenate the noun, **red sanders** (red sandalwood))

caliche *n* Chile saltpetre

calico *n* a cotton cloth (*pl* **calicos, calicoes**)

caliditrine *adj* of various birds of the sandpiper family *incl* the smaller, more gregarious sandpipers which make a soft twittering noise (also see **tringa**), the dowitcher, dunlin, godwit, knot, ruff, sanderling and stint

calidity *var fm n* **callidity**, shrewdness *obs n* heat, warmth (GAME PLAYER'S note: UK Scrabble players restricting themselves to the championship rules should have no problems with this word. However, their permitted usage is for the *obs* sense!)

calipee *n* the edible yellowish gelatinous substance of the belly of a turtle

caliper *var fm n/vb* **calliper**

caliphate *n* the rank, dignity, (term of) office or dominion of a caliph

caliver *n* a light musket capable of being fired without the use of a mechanical support and first used in the 16th century *nonce vb* to fire a caliver

calivre *obs fm n* **caliver**

calk *n* a pointed piece on the front of a horseshoe to prevent slipping: a piece of metal projecting from the heel of winter footwear to prevent slipping on icy surfaces *vb* to provide a calk: to copy by colouring the reverse side of the original and then tracing over the original picture to produce a duplicate, rather like a typist's carbon copy, on a fresh sheet

calker *var fm n* **calk**, a pointed piece on a horseshoe *obs n* an astrologer: a conjurer

callbird *n* a bird trained to lure others into a trap

caller (*n*) *S & dial adj* fresh

calliper *n* any of various measuring devices for objects other than round bodies, such as the kind of compasses with hinged bowed legs often called **callipers, pair of callipers** or **calliper compasses**: a metal splint used as a leg support *modf n* used adjectivally in such *fms* as **calliper compasses** or **calliper splint** (see *n* above) *vb* to measure with a calliper

callosity *n* abnormal hardness of the skin

Calluna *n* the genus of heather

callus *n* the new bony tissue which develops when bones are fractured: a thickening of the skin: the soft tissue which forms over a cut in the stem of a plant (*pl* **calluses**)

calm (*adj/n/vb*) *now S n* a mould for casting metal objects

calmant *adj* having a calming effect *n* a medicament with such property

calme *obs fm n/vb* **calm**

calmer *n* one who or that which calms *comp adj* calm

caloyer *n* a Greek monk *esp* of the order of St Basil

calpa *n* a period of 4,320 million years considered as representing a day of Brahma, the chief Hindu god

calque *var fm vb* **calk**, to copy

caltrop *n* a four-spiked iron ball tossed on the ground as a defensive weapon, the spikes being so arranged that one always projected upwards: any of various plants which entangle the feet

calumet *n* the peace pipe of the Red Indians

calver *n* a sexually fertile cow *obs vb* to prepare or cook a freshly caught salmon or trout

calyx *n* the sepals of an individual flower i.e. the outermost series of its leaflike parts: a cup-shaped part or organ of a creature (*pl* **calyces, calyxes**)

camber *n* a slightly arched surface: a timber dock *vb* to create a camber (surface)

cambrel *n* a gambrel as used by a butcher: the gambrel or hock of a horse

camel (*n*) *nonce vb* to ride on a camel

cameral *adj* of or pertaining to a private chamber: relating to the management of (German) state property *dial fm n* **cambrel**

camerate *var fm adj* **camerated** *obs vb* to arch

camerated *adj* of living shells, divided into chambers: arched

cameration *n* the division of such as a shell into chambers

camion *n* a heavy lorry *obs n* a wagon for transporting cannon

camise *n* a loose shirt or gown *esp* the shirt worn by an Arab

camlet *n* any of various exotic fabrics of an eastern origin *incl* one, a mixture of silk and camel's hair and another, linen and the hair of the angora goat

campestral *adj* pertaining to the open countryside: living or growing in fields

camptonite *n* any of various porphyritic rocks of a sodium/calcium series which somewhat resemble basalt (GAME PLAYER'S note: The dictionary currently used for the UK Scrabble championship invalidates the word for play in that contest by listing it *+cap*. Whilst camptonite derives from a proper name, Campton in New Hampshire, USA, this does not mean that the derivation automatically retains the capital letter. Many minerals, all *−cap*, are named after either the person who first discovered or described them or the place of discovery. For example, **ytterium** is named after Ytterby in Sweden and its silicate, **gadolinite**, is named after the mineralogist, Gadolin. Though scientific literature tends to use more specific terms, nevertheless, the *−cap* form is encountered in such. Players of all word games, except UK championship Scrabble, may play camptonite quite freely.)

camrel *dial fm n* **cambrel**

camsho *S adj* crooked

canaille *n* the mob, the vulgar rabble (also see **antigram**)

canal (*n*) *vb* to make or provide a canal

canard *n* a false rumour: a hoax *vb* to spread such rumour: to make the sound of a duck on a musical instrument

Canarese *var fm adj/n* **Kanarase**, (of) a Dravidian people and language of western India

canaster *n* a rush basket used for carrying tobacco: a type of tobacco (also called **knaster**) made from dried leaves coarsely broken

cancelier *vb* of a hawk, to turn on the wing prior to striking: to swerve or digress (*fig*)

cancerate *vb* to be cancerous

cancroid *adj* crab-like: resembling a cancerous growth *n* a skin cancer

canded *obs fm adj* **candied**

candela *n* a unit of luminous intensity

candie *var fm n* **candy**, an Indian weight of approximately 500 lbs avoirdupois

candiru *n* a very tiny and slim catfish which has the unique but greatly feared distinction of being the only vertebrate parasite to feed on man. It normally lives in the gill cavities of large fish where it sticks spines into the host to draw the blood on which it feeds, but, if an unwary bather in that part of the Amazon where it is found should have one enter a bodily orifice, it takes a surgical operation to remove it. The candiru chooses the urinary orifice, so that both men and women need to protect themselves very carefully and the South American Indians who live in the area often obtain condoms solely for the purpose of bathing.

candlefish *n* the largest species of smelt and found in American estuarine rivers. Its skin is so oily that the Red Indians dry it, then burn it in the same way as a candle

canephor *n* a sculptured figure bearing a basket on the head

canephore *var fm n* **canephorus**, a maiden in ancient Greece who carried on her head a basket containing the sacred things used at the feasts of the god Dionysus and the goddesses Athena and Demeter

caner *n* one who creates or repairs cane furniture

cangue *n* the punishment of the cha, whereby a large heavy wooden block is fixed around the neck of a convicted person in China who, though mobile, can no longer use his arms to feed himself and needs to rely upon the charity of others *vb* to undergo such punishment

Canidae *n pl* the canids or members of the dog family

canister (*n*) *vb* to put in a canister

canker *n* an ulceration of the lip: the death and decay of bodily tissue: a disease which causes the horn of a horse's hoof to become spongy: eczema of the lining of the ear of a cat or dog: an ulcer in a bird: an open wound in the trunk of a tree: anything evil that spreads and corrupts: the cankerworm, the larva of either of two moths which destroy North American (fruit) trees *vb* to infect or become infected with canker/as if with canker

cannelure *n* a groove

cannet *her n* a duck without feet or a beak

cannulate *adj* tubular

canoness *n* one of a community of women living under a rule but not subject to a perpetual vow: the wife of a canon (*jocular*)

canonist *n* one versed in canon law

cansel *obs fm vb* **cancel**

cantel *obs fm n* **cantle** *var fm obs vb* **cantle**

canthari *pl* cantharus, a large two-handled drinking vessel

cantharis *n* the famous Spanish fly (*pl* **cantharides**, the medical term for the substance produced from the dried bodies of these blister beetles (see **Spanish fly**))

canthus *n* either corner of the eye where the lids meet (*pl* **canthi**)

canticoy *n* a Red Indian religious dance *vb* to perform such a dance

cantilena *n* the plainsong of old church music: a ballad

cantilever *n* an architectural support which has a length many times its breadth and more than twice its depth: either of two very long projecting arms of a bridge which support the connection that unites them to complete the span *vb* to project such a structural member outward and in balance beyond the base

cantiness *S n* cheerfulness

cantion *obs n* an incantation used in sorcery: (an ecclesiastical) song

cantle *n* an individual portion, segment or section: a thick cut of a foodstuff such as bread, cheese or meat: the raised part of the back of a saddle *dial n* the leg of a young animal *obs S n* the crown of the head *obs vb* to apportion: of cloth, to piece together

cantler *obs n* a rogue

cantling *obs n* a small part or section

canton *n* a political division of Switzerland *her n* a small square device on a shield or escutcheon, usually in the top left hand corner *vb* to quarter, to divide: to quarter, to allocate accommodation to *obs vb* to digress (*fig*)

Cantonese groin *n* a plant known to mediaeval Chinese women of quality as having a sprout which, when soaked in hot water, swelled and hardened into a dildo

cantor *n* the leading singer in the liturgy of a synagogue: the leader of the singing in a church choir

cantore *obs n* a banking house

cantoris *adj* of the north side of the choir where the cantor sits (also see **decani**)

cant rail *n* a timber support for the roof of a railway carriage

cantred *n* a region containing a hundred townships: a hundred

cantus *n* (ecclesiastical-style) melody (*pl* **cantus**)

canves *obs fm n* **canvas**

cany *adj* like, made of or abounding in cane

capel *n* a naturally occurring composite stone of quartz, tourmaline and hornblende found in the lodes of such as tin or copper

capelin *n* a small member of the salmon family found in the North Pacific and which, as part of a huge shoal, swims ashore to lay its eggs on the sand

caperes *obs fm* (*sing/pl*) *n* **caper**

Capernaite *n* one who believes in the theological doctrine of transubstantiation

capet *obs fm vb* **capot**

capitan *n* the chief admiral of the Turkish fleet

capitano *n* a headman (*pl* **capitani, capitanos**)

capitate *adj* having a knob or head

caple *var fm n* **capel** *now dial n* a horse *obs n* a hen

caplin *var fm n* **capelin**

capline *obs fm n* **capelin**

caponier *n* a covered passage across the ditch of a fortified place

capot *n* in the game of piquet, the winning of all the tricks by one player *vb* to win all the tricks (*lit/fig*)

capote *n* a long, shaggy, hooded overcoat worn by men: a gown which reaches the feet worn by women

caprine *adj* goatlike

capstone *n* the top or finishing stone of a structure as one of a set of slabs on the top of a wall

capsular *adj* of, pertaining to or of the nature of a capsule: brief, condensed

capsulary *adj* capsular (*obs* except for participants in the UK Scrabble championship, the current dictionary for which includes it as an extant, undefined *adj*. In the sense of capsular, capsulary was last used in 1656.)

capsulate *adj* having or enclosed within a capsule

capsulise *var fm vb* **capsulize**, to condense

captan *n* a sulphur-based fungicide used in agriculture

car (*n*) *vb* to place or carry in a (motor) car *S adv* left, sinister, awkward, perverse

carab *obs n* an old Celtic, hide-covered, wicker-framed boat capable of crossing the Irish Sea

carabine *var fm n* **carbine**, a light short-barrelled rifle formerly used by the cavalry

caracul *var fm n* **karakul**, the Central Asian breed of sheep which provide the skins of Persian lamb, a dark, glossy, tightly-curled fur used for trimming clothes

caral *obs fm n* **carol**

carap oil *n* an oil expressed from the seeds of a large West African tree and used as a lamp fuel

carbine *n* a cavalry, firearm, shorter than a musket (also see apt anagram of *pl*, **brisance**)

carcinoma *n* cancer: a tree disease (*pl* **carcinomata**)

carder *n* one who cards (combs) wool: a species of wild bee which shreds moss as a lining for its nest *obs n* a card player

CARDINAL HUMOURS According to the physiology and natural philosophy of mediaeval times the ratio of the four qualities – hot, cold, moist, dry – present in any living thing determined which of four internal fluids predominated. Whichever internal or (in the case of man and the animals) bodily fluid held sway over the other three so that fluid determined the basic humour of, for example, the person. The four fluids were black bile, blood, choler and phlegm. Thus a person was one of four basic types:–

choleric choler predominant, so giving rise to a hot, fiery nature of one who could be passionate and/or irascible.

melancholic black bile predominant, so irascible, ill-tempered, sullen, sad, gloomy, dejected.

phlegmatic phlegm predominant, so cold, dull, sluggish, apathetic, cool, calm, self-possessed, even-tempered.

sanguine blood predominant, so hopeful, amorous, courageous, confident of success.

These qualities were also reflected in the complexion so that, for example, one who was sanguine had a ruddy countenance.

careen *vb* to turn (a ship) over on one side for cleaning or repair *obs vb* to clean a wig (*jocular*)

carelin *var fm dial n* **carling**

carème *Fr n* Lent

carer *n* one who cares

caret *n* a mark, ∧, placed just below a line of writing to indicate that something, written elsewhere, is missing

Cariama *n* the seriema

caribe *n* the piraña

Caribes *pl* Carib, one of a Mongoloid race which dominated parts of the Caribbean before the arrival of Columbus and of whom there are very few completely pure survivors

caries *n* tooth decay *pl obs n* cary, a textile fabric

carina *n* a biological term for a keel or keel-like ridge on plants or animals

carinate *adj* of living things, having a keel or central ridge *vb* to furnish with such

carine *obs n* a keel

cariole *n* a smaller, lighter type of cart or carriage

carious *adj* (*esp* of teeth or bones) decayed

cark *arch n* spiritual distress, anxiety *obs n* the burden of responsibility *arch vb* to fret: to labour anxiously

carket *obs n* a valuable ornamental collar

carl *arch n* a countryman: a man of low birth or rude manner *S n* a niggard *modf n* male *now dial vb* to speak in a gruff or snarling manner *dial vb* to roast very lightly (+*cap*) *masc pers n* meaning 'a man'

carle *var fm arch n* **carl**

carlet *n* a comb-maker's three sided file, two sides having teeth and the third side smooth

carlie *S n* a small man

carlin *n* a small silver coin of little value which used to circulate in Naples and Sicily before the time of the unification of Italy *var fm S n* **carline** *var fm dial n* **carling** *obs fm n* **carling**, parched peas

carline *n* a game intermediate between billiards and snooker played with two white balls, two red, one blue and one (called the carline) yellow. The carline scores 6 points in a middle pocket (*var fm* **caroline**) *S n* a witch, an old woman (*var fms incl* **carling, karling**) *var fm n* **carling**, the naval timber *obs fm n* **carling**, parched peas (+*cap*) *n* a genus of thistle-like plants

carling *n* a main support beam for a ship's decking: (usually as **carlings**) parched peas fried in butter, traditionally eaten on the 5th Sunday in Lent known as Carling Sunday *dial n* a beam which supports a hatch *var fm S n* **carline**

carlish *adj* of or pertaining to a carl: churlish, vulgar, coarse

Carlist *n* a supporter of the cause of Don Carlos and his heirs against Isabella II of Spain and her heirs. Don Carlos was the second son of Charles VI (who abdicated in 1808) and Isabella was the daughter of Ferdinand VII (who died 1833). *modf n* of the two wars fought in this cause, 1830–40 and 1872–76

carlot *obs n* a churl, carl or peasant

Carmel *fem pers n* meaning 'vineyard'

Carmela *fem pers n* meaning 'vineyard'

carmine *n* carminic acid, the colouring matter of (the species of insect known as) cochineal: the deep crimson pigment obtained from cochineal in its sense as the dried bodies of those insects: that colour *adj* of that colour

carneous *adj* carnose

carnero *n* the candiru

carnet *n* a licence for the temporary importation of a motor vehicle: a book of tickets or vouchers

carney *var fm dial vb* **carny**

carnose *adj* fleshy

carny *dial vb* to wheedle or coax *slg n* soft, hypocritical speech

caroche *n* a (grand) carriage *obs vb* to travel in such

Carolean *adj* of the period of Charles I or II

Caroline (*fem pers n*) *adj* of or pertaining to any (King) Charles (*–cap*) *var fm n* **carline**, the game

Carolus *n* any of various coins *esp* one of Charles I originally valued at £1

carotenoid *adj* of or pertaining to carotene (carotin)

carotid *adj* relating to (either of) the two great arteries of the neck *n* a carotid artery

carotin *var fm n* **carotene**, any of various deep-yellow or red pigments found in plants

carpe *obs fm n* **carp**, the fish *obs fm vb* **carp**, to find fault unreasonably

carpel *n* the female reproductive organ of a flowering plant

carret *obs fm n* **caret**

Carrie *dim fem pers n* **Carola** (*fem fm masc pers n* **Carolus** which, in turn, is a *var fm* **Charles** meaning 'a man')

carryout *US fm n* **carry-out**, a takeaway food order

carse *S n* low wet land

carte *n* a fencing position which has the foil pointing to the left and slightly raised *S n* a playing card

cartel *n* a commercial combination for the purpose of serving mutual interest: a written challenge: a written agreement concerning the exchange of prisoners *obs vb* to serve with a challenge

cartelise *var fm vb* **cartelize**, to combine into or bring under the control of a business syndicate

Cartesian *adj* pertaining to Descartes (René Descartes (1596–1650) the French mathematician and philosopher famous for his '*I think, therefore I am*') and his subject matter *n* a follower of his mathematics or philosophy

cartle *var fm n* **kartel**

carucate *n* a measure of land determined by the amount which could be tilled in one year by one team of eight oxen harnessed to a plough. This equated to approximately 180 acres of which a third (by annual rotation) would lie fallow whilst the other two-thirds would be put to productive use. Generally speaking, only the land actually under the plough was termed the carucate, the remainder being reckoned with the common pasturage; hence, carucate has an additional general sense of ploughland.

carue *n* an old legal term for ploughland (see **carucate**)

carvel *n* a small (Spanish or Portuguese) ship of the 15th–17th centuries

carven *poet adj* carved

carvene *n* a hydrocarbon found in the oil yielded by the plant, caraway

casco *n* a small Philippine boat used for transporting items from ship to shore (*pl* **cascos**)

casein *n* a milk protein which forms the basis of cheese

caseman *n* a compositor, one who sets up printing type

casern *n* a military barrack *esp* one within a fortified town

caserne *var fm n* **casern**

casher *var fm Ir vb* **cosher**

cashew *n* a tropical American tree, the source of an edible nut and fleshy stalk

casique *obs fm n* **cacique**

Casper *masc pers n* meaning 'horseman'

casque *n* a helmet: any military head covering: in species of birds such as the cassowary or toucan, a helmet-like structure on the upper surface of the beak or on the top of the head

casquet *n* a light, open casque or armoured headgear

cass *now S vb* to annul: to dismiss: to disband

Cassandra *pers n* a daughter of Priam, king of Troy, whose prophecies were fated by Apollo always to be true but never to be believed. For example, she specifically warned against the bringing into Troy of the famous wooden horse apparently left behind by the departing Greeks as a gift to the goddess Athene, despite the Greeks failing in their long siege of this Black Sea city-state. That night the truth of her warning was revealed when the small force of Greeks concealed in the horse slipped out and unlocked the gates to the returned Greek army. Troy was sacked. (For a continuation of the legend see **Brutus** 1, for other prophecies see **Brutus** 2, **Gordian, Hister, oracle**.) *n* anyone, male or female, who utters an unheeded prophecy of disaster

cassaripe *var fm n* **cassareep**, the antiseptic juice of the cassava (see **manioc**)

casser *obs n* one who casses

cassimere *n* a twilled cloth of fine quality used for men's suitings

cassine *obs n* a farmhouse used for military purposes

cassino *n* a card game for two to four players in which players pair cards and attempt to be first to score eleven points with the aid of the 10 of diamonds (two points) or the 2 of spades (one point)

Castalia *n* the name of a spring on Mount Parnassus sacred to the Muses (often used in a *fig* sense)

Castalian *adj* of the Muses or their sacred spring, Castalia

Castalie *var fm n* **Castalia**

caste (*n*) *obs vb* to chasten, chastise

casten *now dial adj* of clothing, cast off

caster *n* a metal founder *var fm n* **castor** (in senses other than association with a beaver)

castor *n* the fur of the beaver: a hat made from such fur: the aromatic secretion of a beaver used in perfumes and medicine: a small swivelling wheel attached to a corner or leg of furniture: a jar with a perforated top used for sprinkling sugar etc

castorin *n* a crystalline substance obtained from the beaver and used in pharmacy and for cosmetics

castorine *obs fm n* **castorin**

catalo *var fm n* **cattalo**, a cross between cattle and bison (or 'buffalo' as it is sometimes called, e.g. Buffalo Bill) (*pl* **catalos, cataloes**)

catalyse *vb* to subject to catalysis

catalysis *n* an alteration in the speed of a chemical reaction by a substance which remains stable (*pl* **catalyses**)

catamite *n* a young boy kept for the purposes of homosexual perversion

catatonic *adj* characterized by a form of insanity which includes epilepsy and catalepsy

cate *n* a choice foodstuff *obs vb* to dress food

catena *n* a closely linked series (*pl* **catenae, catenas**)

cateran *n* a brigand: a Highland freebooter

Cathar *n* one of a sect of mediaeval heretics found in Italy and France (*pl* **Cathari, Cathars**)

catharise *var fm vb* **catharize**, to purify by a ceremony: to make chemically clean

catharsis *n* the cleansing of any bodily passage *esp* the bowels: in the view of Aristotle, the relief of emotion produced by watching tragic drama: in a theory of psychotherapy, the releasing of pent-up emotion or unpleasant memories by reliving them through words, feelings or actions

cat hole *n* either of two holes in the stern of a ship through which a cable or hawser is passed: a deep pool in a river

cathouse *collq n* a brothel

Catiline *n* a conspirator who can be likened to the ancient Roman, Lucius Catiline, in character and activity. Catiline, whose personal crimes included the taking of his daughter's virginity and the murder of his brother, led a conspiracy of disaffected Romans against the current leadership of the nation. This was supported by an external army of 20,000 men. The revolt was defeated by the loyal Romans, led by Cicero in 63 BC.

cation *n* an ion with a positive charge (the opposite of an **anion**)

catling *n* a small cat: a kitten

Catonian *adj* pertaining to either of two classical Romans, Cato the Censor or his descendant, Cato of Utica, hence grave, severe or unbending (as they were) *n* a follower of Cato

catoptromancy *n* divination by use of a mirror

cat's ear *n* either of two different British plants, one of which is also known as mountain everlasting

catsilver *n* mica having a silvery appearance (GAME PLAYER'S note: Variously written as **cat silver, cat-silver** or **catsilver**, most authorities consider it *obs*. The dictionary used for the UK Scrabble championship considers it extant, but invalidates it for that contest by showing only the hyphenated form.)

cat's tail *n* any of several plants *esp* the reed mace

catsup *n* ketchup

cattail *var fm n* **cat's tail**

catte *obs fm n* **cat**, the feline animal

cattie *var fm n* **catty**

catty *n* an Oriental weight varying in different countries but roughly equal to $1\frac{1}{3}$ lbs avoirdupois *adj* of or pertaining to cats: spiteful

Caudata *n pl* the amphibians which, unlike frogs and toads, retain their tails when fully mature i.e. newts, salamanders, the axolotyl etc. (Also known as **Urodela**)

caudate *adj* having a tail (-like appendage): tailed: of any species of Caudata *n* such a species

caudillo *n* the head of state in a Spanish-speaking country

caudle *n* a sweetened, spiced, thin gruel mixed with wine or ale and traditionally served to a woman in childbed and her visitors *vb* to prepare a caudle: to serve a caudle

caudron *obs fm n* **cauldron**

caul *n* a kind of close-fitting cap, often highly ornamented, once worn by women: a membrane covering either the head or the whole body of some newly born children and the tradition is that such children will never drown *obs n* a spider's web: any ornamental network: a sheepfold: a cabbage

cauled *obs adj* sporting a caul (the headdress)

cauler *var fm S & dial adj* **caller**

caules *pl* caulis

caulis *n* the stalk of a plant: one of the four greater supporting stalks in the architecture of the Corinthian capital (*pl* **caules**)

cauller *var fm S & dial adj* **caller**

caulm *var fm now S n* **calm**

caulome *n* a leaf-bearing axis of a plant

caunter *n* a lode which runs crossways to the general direction of that being mined

caurie *obs fm n* **cowrie**

causal *adj* that which is or that being the cause: of a cause or causes *n* an expression of cause or reason

causen *obs infl vb* **cause**, to give excuses for

causey *var fm n* **causeway** vb to pave (*infl fms* **causeyed, causeying**)

caut *obs vb* of a panther, to make its cry

cautel *arch n* a crafty action, a trick: cunning, trickery: a precautionary reservation *obs vb* to devise craftily

cauter *n* a surgical instrument which is heated and used for the burning or destroying of bodily tissue: a caustic drug which achieves the same effect

cauterise *var fm vb* **cauterize**, to apply either type of cauter: to render insensible (*fig*)

cauterism *n* the application of a heated metallic instrument to perform the medical act of cauterization (GAME PLAYER'S note: In the above sense the word was last known to have been used in 1688 and is considered *obs*. The dictionary used for the UK Scrabble championship lists the word as being extant, but provides no definition. Presumably it is aware of some other meaning.)

cautery *n* a cauter in either sense: the action described at cauterism

caveat *n* a (formal) notice or warning

cavel *dial n* a cast lot: the verdict of an oracle: a division or share made by lot *var fm n* **kevel**, a cleat on a ship *obs S n* a low fellow *now dial vb* to cast lots: to apportion

cavie *S n* a hen coop

cavil *vb* to raise empty, trifling objections (*infl fms* British, **cavilled/-lling**: US, **caviled/-ling**)

cavitation *n* the formation of cavities in such as a liquid (i.e. like a whirlpool)

cavitied *adj* having cavities

cavy *n* a small, thickset, South American rodent domesticated as the guinea pig *var fm S n* **cavie**

caw *n* the cry of a crow *vb* of a crow, to utter its cry: of a person, to speak with as much intelligence and beauty of sound as a cry of a crow *var fm n/vb* **coe**, (to give) sheep rot *var fm dial vb* **ka**

cawdel *obs fm n/vb* **caudle**

cawdle *obs fm n/vb* **caudle**

cawler *var fm S & dial adj* **caller**

cawse *obs fm n/vb* **cause**

cayer *obs fm n* **quire**, a small book

Cayuse *n* a member of an almost extinct tribe of Red Indians formerly resident in Oregon (*−cap*) *US n* a Red Indian pony: a horse of little value: a humorous or derogatory term

cazique *var fm n* **cacique** (GAME PLAYER'S note: See **quetzal**)

ce *n* the bebization equivalent of **re**: the bobization equivalent of **mi**: the name of the letter C (note: The alternative name, **cee**, has additional meanings)

ceal *obs fm vb* **ceil**

Ceasarist *n* an imperialist

ceaser *obs n* one who puts an end to

cebadilla *n* the acrid seeds of a Mexican and Central American plant which are a source of a painkiller used for rheumatism and formerly used as a means of destroying intestinal worms: the plant itself (note: **cebadilla** is the original Spanish diminutive of *cebada*, barley, from which the word is derived. The *fms* **cevadilla** and **sabadilla** are used with equal authority as the basic word, with the other two spellings as *var fms*. Which of the three is the preferred spelling is entirely up to the reader.)

cedarn *poet adj* of or pertaining to cedar trees

ceder *n* one who cedes (territory/possession)

cedrat *n* a lemon or citron

cedrate *n* citron, a lemon-like fruit: the citron tree

cedrated *obs adj* anointed with the oil of a cedar tree

cedre *obs n* a cedrat

Cedrela *n* a genus of trees akin to mahogany

cedrine *adj* of or pertaining to cedar

cedula *n* a South American land mortgage bond

cee *n* the letter C: anything in the shape of a C *obs university slg n* a quantity of beer

ceede *obs fm vb* **cede**, to yield or surrender: to concede *obs fm n/vb* **seed**

ceere *obs fm vb* **cere**

ceil *vb* to provide a (plaster) lining for a roof (hence *n*, **ceiling**): to overlay with a valuable or precious metal *obs vb* to wainscot

ceiler *var fm obs n* **celure**

ceili *Ir var fm n* **ceilidh**, an informal gathering to enjoy singing, dancing and story-telling

ceilinged *adj* having a ceiling

ceinture *n* an encircling or girdle

celandine *n* either of two plants having yellow flowers. The **greater celandine**, the thick yellow juice of which the old herbalists believed was good for weak sight or the **lesser celandine**, also known as figwort or pilewort.

celest *obs adj* heavenly

Celsius *pers n* Anders Celsius (1701–1744) the Swedish physicist and astronomer who invented the centigrade thermometer which has the freezing point of water at 0 degrees and the boiling point of water at 100 degrees *adj* of centigrade degrees which now, some two hundred years later, are being promoted as degrees Celsius

celter *obs n* a woollen fabric

Celtomania *n* excessive devotion to or regard for that which is Celtic

celure *obs n* a canopy for such as an altar or a bed

cembra *n* the stonepine tree of Switzerland

cendal *Obs fm n* **sendal**

censer *n* a thurible or vessel for burning incense *obs vb* to burn incense

censual *adj* of or pertaining to a census

cental *n* a weight of 100 lbs avoirdupois

centare *n* a measure of land equal to one square metre

centaury *n* either of the two species of a plant, the medicinal properties of which were said to have been discovered by the centaur, Chiron

center *var fm n/adj/vb* **centre**

centering *n* the bringing of two or more centres into coincidence: the temporary frame upon which such as the arch of a bridge is constructed

centesimal *adj* relating to divisions by one hundred *n* a hundredth part

centiare *var fm n* **centare**

centigram *var fm n* **centigramme**, a weight equal to one hundredth of a gramme (.1543248 of an ounce troy)

cento *n* a work produced from various fragments of the works of other writers (*pl* **centos, centones**)

centoist an undefined noun which appears to be exclusive to one particular dictionary and presumably means one who produces a cento

centrad *adv* towards the middle

centreing *var fm n* **centering**

centress *n* a female leader of a group (in the Fenian movement)

centrist *n* one, *esp* in France, who takes a central political position

centrode *n* a set of points traced out by the successive positions of an instantaneous centre of pure rotation

centroid *n* the centre of mass or gravity

centuary *obs fm n* **centaury**

ceorl *n* in the feudal times, a freeman of the lowest class but superior to the servile classes

cepter *obs fm n* **sceptre**

ceptre *obs fm n* **sceptre**

Ceradotus *n* a genus of extinct lungfishes which formerly included the extant Burnett salmon now given its own genus as *Neoceradotus* (*—cap*) *n* a fossil of this genus

cerain *n* that part of beeswax capable of being sparingly soluble in alcohol (also see **cerasin**)

ceramet *n* a heat-resisting alloy of ceramic particles bonded with a metallic matrix

ceramist *n* one who makes ceramics

cerasin *n* the insoluble portion of the gum exuded by such as the cherry tree (CROSSWORD ADDICT'S note: A *solution* of cerasin is the antigram, cerains!)

cerastes *n* the *Cerastes cerastes*, one of two species of gaudily coloured puff adders also known as horned vipers due to the presence of a hornlike scale over each eye. Both it and *Cerastes cornutus* live in the deserts of the Middle East where they bury themselves in the sand with the head almost completely covered as they lie in wait for such prey as jerboas. The cerastes has a sidewinding means of locomotion after the fashion of the true sidewinder, the American horned rattlesnake, *Crotalus cerastes* (*pl* **cerastes**)

Cerastium *n* the genus of the mouse-ear chickweed

cerata *n pl* large outgrowths usually in rows on the backs of various species of sea slugs which effectively increase the surface area of the body (*sing* **ceras**)

cerate *n* a wax-based stiff ointment

cerated *adj* waxed, covered with wax

ceratin *var fm n* **keratin**

ceration *obs n* in alchemic practice, the act of covering with wax

Cerdic *pers n* the West Saxon chieftain who (circa AD 500) led the tribe which formed the nucleus of the kingdom of Wessex and from whom all but six monarchs of England are directly descended. (The exceptions being the three Skjöldungs (see below) and the first three Normans.) *n/modf n* the English royal house from the first king of England, Egbert (802–839) up to Edward the Confessor (1042–1066) with a break from 1016–1042 whilst the Skjöldungs, or House of Denmark, provided the king. Among the better known of the Cerdic kings were Alfred the Great (871–899) and Ethelred the Unready (979–1016). The best known of the Skjöldungs was Canute (1016–1035). Before Egbert (of Wessex) England consisted of the kingdoms of East Anglia, Essex, Kent, Mercia, Northumbria (a combination of Bernica and Deira), Sussex and Wessex. Canute was the first king of all England.

Cerdon *masc pers n* see **Metro**

cere *n* the waxlike membrane surrounding the nostrils of a bird *vb* to wrap in cerecloth, a waxed cloth used for a corpse

cerealist *n* one who promotes the concept of a diet based on cereals: one who studies cereals

cerebrum *n* the front, larger part of the brain (*pl* **cerebra, cerebrums**) (GAME PLAYER'S note: Participants in the UK Scrabble championship are restricted to cerebrums as this is the only plural which may be presumed from the definition contained in their current reference dictionary. Anyone else in any other circumstances, including competitive Scrabble in the USA, may use either form of plural with complete confidence except for players of the various crossword-type games produced by *Waddingtons*. For reasons best known to the makers, they ban plurals. Thus, neither cerebra nor cerebrums may be played. An exception for cerebrums, however, occurs in their game Kan-U-Go providing the S is already in play as part of an existing word.)

ceresin *n* a type of hard whitish wax

Cereus *n* a large genus of cacti

ceria *n* the oxide of the metallic element cerium (*pl* **cerias**)

cerine *n* a variety of the mineral allanite

cering *n* waxing or covering with wax

ceringe *obs fm n* **cering**

ceriph *var fm n* **serif**, the small line of embellishment added, in some typefaces, to the extremities of a main stroke in a type character

cerite *n* a rare resinous mineral, hydrated silicate of cerium

cerium *n* an iron-coloured metallic element of the rare earth series

cerne *vb* to encircle or surround (an enemy)

cerrial *adj* of or pertaining to the Turkey or evergreen oak

cerris *n* a Levantine species of oak

cersus *n* a tail-like adjunct

certain (*adj/adv/n*) *obs vb* to make certain

certen *obs fm n/adj/adv* **certain**

certes *arch adv* certainly

certie *S n* usually only found in the phrase *by my certie* and having a sense of *by my faith*

certis *obs fm arch adv* **certes**

certitude *n* subjective certainty: unfailing quality

certosina *n* a Renaissance style of elaborate mosaic inlay

cerulean *adj* of the colour of the cloudless sky, hence the shade of blue (poetically) visualized

ceruse *n* white lead: a cosmetic made from it *obs vb* to paint (the face) with that cosmetic

cerusite *var fm n* **cerussite**

cerussite *n* native carbonate of lead

cervine *adj* of or pertaining to deer: of a deep rich tawny colour

cervis *obs dial fm n* **service**

cervise *obs fm n* **service**, the tree with small pear-shaped fruit

Cesarean, cesarean see **Caesarean**

Cesarian, cesarian see **Caesarean**

cess *vb* to assess a tax or levy: to impose such a tax *obs vb* to surrender *n* a tax or levy *now dial n* a peat bog

cesser *n* termination: in law, ceasing to perform legal duties or pay rent for a period of two years

cession *n* the action of ceding or surrendering rights, properties etc. to another

cessor *n* one delinquent in his duty

cesti *pl* cestus, a girdle

cestode *var fm n/adj* **cestoid**

cestoid *adj* ribbonlike *n* a worm of this shape

cestracion *n* the Port Jackson shark (see **horn shark**)

cestui *n* 'that person (who)' used only in phrases (*pl* **cestuis**)

cestus *n* an ancient Roman 'boxing glove' consisting of thongs, often weighted, and wound around the hand and lower arm (*var fm* **caestus**, as in the original Latin) (*pl* **cestus**): the girdle of the Greek goddess, Aphrodite, with the power of awakening love in whoever beheld it: any belt or girdle (*var fm* **caestus**, but this is, strictly, *erron* as cestus in this sense is derived from the Greek, *kestos*, meaning girdle) (*pl* **cesti**)

cesura *var fm n* **caesura,** (*pl* **cesurae, cesuras**)

cesure *obs fm n* **caesura**

cetane *n* hexadecane, a colourless insoluble paraffin hydrocarbon found in petroleum and used as a measure (cetane number) of the ignition quality of diesel fuel

cete *n of assemb* of badgers

cevadilla see **cebadilla**

ch *dial pron* I (GAME PLAYER'S note: ch is an aphetic *fm* of **ich** – one of the earlier *fms* of I – and whilst it may still exist with a few speakers in Shropshire and other southern dialects it will only be in such compound *fms* as **chad** (I had), **cham** (I am), **chud** (I would), **chard** (I heard), **chave** (I have) or **chill** (I will). Whilst ich once existed as an independent word, ch *never has*! Therefore, *its use for play is completely invalid* despite the reports, in various word game magazines, of its being used.)

cha *n* (rolled) tea (for *The punishment of the cha* see **cangue**)

chagrin (*n*) *vb* to embarrass and annoy (*infl fms* **chagrined** or **chagrinned** etc.)

chai *n* the *fem* of **chal**

chainlet *n* a little chain

chaip *var fm obs S vb* **chape** *S fm obs n* **cheap**, a bargain

chaire *obs fm n/vb* **chair**

chal *n* a fellow (*fem* **chai** or **chi**)

Chaldee *adj* of Chaldea, an ancient country mentioned in the Bible and, at Babylon, a centre of occult study *n* Chaldean, an inhabitant of Chaldea: the language of the Chaldees or Chaldeans: a soothsayer

chaldron *n* a dry measure of 4 quarters or 32 bushels: a measure of coal equal to 36 bushels (the more recent usage)

chales *obs fm n* **chalice**

chalkstone *n* a piece of the stone, chalk (compare with **chalkstones**)

chalkstones *n pl* the white concentrations which form around the joints in chronic gout (compare with **chalkstone**)

chalse *obs fm n* **chalice**

cham see **be** (also see **ch**)

chambré *Fr adj* of wine, at room temperature (*–accent*) *obs fm n* **chamber**

chame *var fm now dial n* **chaum**

chamiso *n* a Californian rosaceous shrub (*pl* **chamisos**)

chancre *n* an ulcer of venereal disease

chane *obs fm ns* **chain, khan**

chanse *obs fm n/vb* **chance**

chanter *n* a singer *esp* a chorister: a priest who sings masses in a chantry: that pipe of a set of bagpipes which has the fingerholes: in the *fm* **hedge chanter**, the hedge sparrow *slg n* often in the *fm* **horse chanter**, one who sells horses fraudulently

chanteuse *n* a female night club singer

chantie *var fm n* **shanty**, a (sailor's) song with a chorus

chantress *n* a female singer *Obs n* a female magician

chantry *n* an endowment for the maintenance of a priest or priests with the stipulation that such will sing a daily mass for the soul of the one (and/or others named) who made such a bequest: any part of a church so endowed, as a side chapel, for this same purpose (*pl* **chantries**)

chape *n* the metal plate which covers the tip of a scabbard: the tip of a fox's tail *vb* to tip a scabbard with a chape *obs S vb* to escape

chaper *obs fm n* **japer**

chapiter *n* the capital or head of a pillar

chapka *n* a type of military cap worn by lancer regiments

char *n* any of a number of species of salmon-like fishes *incl* the American **brook trout** and the **Alpine** or **Arctic char**. The Alpine char follows the normal salmon pattern of fresh-water spawning and marine adult life off Greenland. The same fish is found in Britain, but only in completely landlocked lakes: a charred substance *obs n* a chariot *vb* to scorch, to reduce to charcoal by slow burning: to perform domestic or similar cleaning duties

chare *n* an odd job *esp* one in a household *obs n* an action or deed: a return *vb* to perform such (household) tasks *arch vb* to accomplish *obs vb* to return

charet *obs n* a (war) chariot

chariest *sup adj* chary

Charis *n* any of the Greek goddesses (Aglaia, Euphrosyne, Thalia) known as the Graces from their concern with whatever is gracious in life (*pl* **Charites**)

Charites *pl* Charis

chark *n* charcoal: a Russian small liquor glass *vb* to burn to charcoal *now S vb* to make a grating noise with the teeth: to complain continuously

charlet *obs n* a pork custard (the recipe – pork bruised and beaten small, milk, eggs and seasoning boiled to a curd with *chese crustis* as an optional extra)

charm (*n/vb*) *n of assemb* of goldfinches

charme *obs fm n* **charm**, blended singing (of birds)

charminger *comp adj* charming

charne *obs fm n/vb* **churn**

charneco *obs n* a type of sweet Portuguese wine

charnel *n* a mortuary chapel *adj* of or pertaining to such a chapel *obs vb* to hinge

Charon *pers n* in Greek mythology, the ferryman who carried the shades of the dead across the river Styx to Hades

charpie *n* surgical lint produced from shredded linen

charpoy *n* a simple Indian bed of netting stretched between four legs

charret *var fm obs n* **charet**

charta *n* a leaf of papyrus: a charter (*fig*)

charte *obs fm n/vb* **chart**

chartel *obs fm n* **cartel**

Chartism *n* the democratic movement and principles of the Chartists, whose aspirations were embodied in 'The People's Charter' written by Francis Place in 1838. This called for universal manhood suffrage, vote by ballot, equal electoral districts, annual parliament, payment of members, abolition of property qualifications. It was supported by such Christian socialists as Charles Kingsley and was rooted in the working class. Its main period of existence was 1838–1848 after which it slowly expired till, by 1857, it was dead. Apart from an annual parliament, all other demands were met (*–cap*) an undefined noun which appears to be exclusive to the dictionary used for the UK Scrabble championship. This appears to relate to chartist in the sense of one who makes or studies charts of past performances with a view to studying future trends. The word chartist, in this sense, is also given in the dictionary used for the North American Scrabble championship but it does not give the related chartism. Presuming a *pl* of **chartisms** (which would be accepted in the UK contest), this has the anagram, **Christmas**.

Chartres *n* a French town famed for its Gothic cathedral

chaser (*n*) *n* a hunter: a pursuing ship: one who engraves metal: a tool used for cutting the thread of a screw *S n* a ram with only one testicle *obs n* a horse trained for steeplechasing

chaste (*adj*) *obs vb* to discipline: to punish

chate *obs fm vb* **chat**, to talk in a light and informal manner

chater *obs fm n/vb* **chatter**

chates *obs n* the gallows (thieves' cant)

chating *obs nonce n* the first blowing of a hunting horn, thus making **rechating** a subsequent blowing of a horn. Despite this *obs* nonce sense of rechating, the correct *obs* term, however, illogical as it may seem, for a blowing of a hunting horn was rechating – see **recheat**.

chatre *obs fm n/vb* **chatter**

chatta *n* an umbrella

chattle *obs fm n* **chattel**

chaum *now dial n* a cleft or fissure *obs vb* to crack or chap

chaunt *var fm n/vb* **chant**

chaunter *var fm n* **chanter**

chauntress *obs fm n* **chantress** (GAME PLAYER'S note: The dictionary used for the UK Scrabble championship has the word as an extant, but undefined, noun. Milton is the only known writer to have used this particular spelling *fm.*)

chaw *now vulgar n/vb* (to) chew

Cheadle *n* a Staffordshire town formerly associated with coal mining, now a centre of metal manufacture

cheap (*adj/adv*) *obs vb* to trade or bargain *var fm n/vb* **cheep**

cheaper (*comp adj*) *obs n* a buyer

chear *obs fm n* **chair** *obs fm n/vb* **cheer**

cheater *n* a swindler (a systematic swindler being a cheat)

Chebar *n* a river mentioned in the Bible as passing by the village of Tel-abib where Ezekiel lived among the exiles and had his prophetic vision

cheel *obs fm vb* **chill**

cheep *n* a faint shrill sound *vb* to utter a cheep

cheerly *arch adj* blithe, cheerful *arch adv* blithely, cheerfully

cheero *var fm interj* **cheerio**, a friendly farewell

Cheiron *pers n* the wisest of the centaurs, the legendary half-man and half-horse creatures of Greek myth

chela *n* the prehensile claw of a crab or lobster (*pl* **chelae**): a Buddhist novice (*pl* **chelas**)

chelate *adj* having a pincerlike claw: of chelate, the chemical compound *n* a compound, the molecules of which contain a closed ring of atoms *incl* one metal atom *vb* to subject a compound to combination with a metal ion to promote maximum stability for specified uses

chelator *n* one who chelates

cheloid *n* one of the skin diseases

chelp *dial vb* to talk in a manner which annoys or offends the listener

chenar *n* the Oriental plane tree

chenet *Fr n* an iron bar which supports a log or logs on a fire

chenille *n* a type of velvety cord used for trimming and bordering, also for furniture

cheper *var fm obs n* **cheaper**

chepstow *var fm dial n* **shepstare**

cheralite *n* a radioactive mineral

Cheremis *n* a Finnic language of central European USSR

chermar *Obs fm n* **charmer**

cherup *var fm vb* **chirrup**, of birds, to utter their cry

chesil *n* gravel, shingle, pebbles: a small variety of pear

chester *n* a walled city, a Roman encampment (*obs* except as (part of) a geographical name i.e. Chester or Chesterfield) *obs n* one who places a body in a coffin

chete *Obs n* a chamber or cell *obs fm n* **cheat**

chevin *n* the chub, a carp-like fish which, though popular with anglers, is practically inedible, having a taste described as '*like cotton-wool full of needles*'

chevrotain *n* the mouse deer, any of various species of tiny deer-like animals, the smallest of all the cloven-hoofed creatures. Despite their superficial resemblance to deer they are probably more closely related to pigs and camels. (For an even more improbable relationship of superficially different creatures see **hyrax.**)

chewe *obs fm vb* **chew**

chewen *obs fm adj* **chewed**

chewet *obs n* any of various chopped meat or fish dishes mixed with fruit and spices then baked, fried or boiled (in later times, such ingredients for chewet pie): the magpie, extended as a term for anyone who chatters

chewit *var fm obs n* **chewet**, a savoury dish

chi *n* the twenty-second letter of the Greek alphabet *var fm n* **chai** (the *fem* of **chal**)

Chicago typewriter *n* a sub-machine gun

chicle *n* the milky juice of the sapodilla tree used as the basis of chewing gum

chicon *n* the edible shoot of the chicory plant

chiel *obs S fm n* **child**

chier *var fm obs n* **chire**

chigoe *n* a small species of Caribbean flea, the female of which burrows under the skin of the human foot and her hatching eggs cause great distress

chigre *var fm n* **chigoe**

chikor *n* an Indian partridge

childer *now dial n pl* children

chile *var fm ns* **child, chilli**

chimer *n* a bishop's loose upper robe: a long sleeveless tabard: one who chimes bells

chimere *var fm n* **chimer** (in the senses of clothing)

chinar *var fm n* **chenar**

chine *n* a spine or backbone: that part of a pig adjacent the spine: a ridge: a (deep coastal) ravine *obs n* a fissure or crack *dial n pl* the bubbles which rise when an otter dives into water *vb* to cut along the backbone (of a pig/a salmon)

CHINESE CALENDAR The Chinese lunar calendar is the longest chronological record in history. It is based on a 60 year cycle of years reckoned from the 61st year of the reign of the Emperor, Huang Ti, in 2637 BC. Each of these 60 years has an individual name, rooted in Chinese astrology. To appreciate the names it is necessary to understand two basic factors.

The first factor is that, in ancient Chinese belief, all matter is composed of five elements. These are metal, water, wood, fire and earth. An individual element imparts to a year its quality. Thus a year prefixed Metal has the quality of metal; a year prefixed Water, the quality of water i.e. Metal is a 'hard' year, Water a 'fluid' year etc. The second factor is the character of that year. This is represented by the name of an animal. Thus, a year having Tiger as part of its name is a year having a tigerish character; one with Dog in its name is doglike. Therefore, the year of the **Metal Tiger** has both the quality of metal and the character of a tiger; whereas the year of the **Water Tiger** has a different quality, even though it is similar in character.

The animals are those which featured in the legend of the death of Buddha. As he was dying only twelve creatures came to bid him farewell so, to commemorate them, each of a smaller

cont overleaf

cycle of 12 years is named after that animal in the order in which each came to pay its respects. The order is rat, ox, tiger, rabbit, dragon, snake, horse, sheep, monkey, rooster, dog and boar.

As with other lunar calendars, the individual Chinese year is governed by the phases of the moon. This means that not only does it commence on a different day from one year to the next but also, of course, that there are not a fixed number of days to the year. A westerner who wishes to calculate the years should note that the individual Chinese year begins at 11 pm on the night of the first new moon in a period which exactly coincides with the western zodiac sign of Aquarius. In other words, Chinese New Year can begin on any date from 23 January to 19 February.

Ignoring this complication, to determine the Chinese name of any one year involves the application of the following formula.

The cycle commences with Metal and Metal is also part of the name of the second year. Thereafter, it is Water, Water, Wood, Wood, Fire, Fire, Earth, Earth, and back again to Metal. (The reason concerns the Yin and the Yang, but this added factor has been ignored.) To these elements are added the name of the animals in their strict order of visiting Buddha.

The Chinese names, therefore, have both 1900 and 1960 called **Metal Rat**, 1901 and 1961 called **Metal Ox**, 1902 and 1962 both called **Water Tiger**, 1903 and 1963 both called **Water Rabbit** etc.

Whilst these names are no longer used in a general sense, they still exist as important aspects in the casting of an individual's or even a nation's horoscope.

For example, a person born within the period 12 February 1956 to 30 January 1957 is thereafter strongly influenced by the factors of that year, **Fire Monkey**. A nation's horoscope is cast by the year of foundation. With the USA, that is the date of the Declaration of Independence but, for the UK, it is very different and also has a very curious aspect which, to one versed in Chinese horoscopes is very significant even today.

The UK is reborn with each new monarch. Today, we live in the **Land of the Water Dragon**, as that is the name of the year when the Queen ascended the throne. The corresponding influences in recent times have made the Britain of Queen Victoria, the **Land of the Earth Rooster**; of Edward VII, the **Land of the Metal Rat**; of George V, the **Land of the Metal Dog** and George VI, the **Land of the Fire Rat**. But, it is with the late Duke of Windsor, Edward VIII, that the strangeness pertains. The death of his father, George V, was deliberately hastened by his doctor so that it occurred on the 22 January 1936. Had the king survived but a day or so longer, then Edward VIII would have been monarch of the **Land of the Fire Rat** and not, as it transpired, the **Land of the Wood Boar**. To the expert in these matters, the significance of the year of the **Fire Rat** beginning 24 January 1936 would have changed not only the history of that man but also that of his country. The character and quality of a **Wood Boar** specifically states that, despite possessing excellent qualities, such can be dragged down into the mud if too much in the company of unworthy friends. By contrast, the **Fire Rat** never tires of embarking on new campaigns for justice. The Britain of 1939–1945 needed the **Fire Rat**, not the **Wood Boar**. Fortunately, from the 'mud' of the Abdication, a new land was to arise during the year of the **Fire Rat**. Incidentally, the **Land of the Water Dragon** is democratic and liberal-minded, favouring optimum growth and expansion. Less imperious than other Dragons, it can put aside its ego for the good of all. Its wits are as formidable as its strength of will.

chinse *vb* to caulk or seal the seams of a vessel to prevent leakage

chinste *var fm n* **chinch**, a bedbug

chints *var fm n* **chintz** (*pl* **chintses**)

chire *obs n* any of various slender plant growths such as a blade of grass or the stamen of a flower *obs vb* to feast or make merry

chirk *arch vb* to make a noise like the chirping of a bird or the squeak of a mouse *S dial vb* to make a strident, grating noise *US collq adj* lively, cheerful

chirl *S vb* to warble

chirm *n* mingled noise, such as that of a large gathering of birds or children and that of assorted insects on a hot afternoon *vb* of birds, to make their sounds *var fm n of assemb* **charm**

chiromancy *n* palmistry

chirpe *obs fm vb* **chirp**

chirt *now S vb* to squirt

chiru *n* the goat-antelope of Tibet, a creature of uncertain affinity but probably related to sheep

chissel *var fm n* **chisel**, bran or wholemeal

chiter *obs fm vb*/*S & dial vb* **chitter**

chitter *vb* of birds, to twitter *S & dial vb* to shiver

chiven *obs n* the meaning of the word is unknown though it has been given two possible explanations:– (*a*) a noun derived from the *obs adj* **chivie**, meaning fearful or (*b*) a *var fm* of **chevin**, the fish. It appears only in the phrase, *go play the chiven* with a sense of 'dash away quickly' in a context of getting away from danger. The chevin (or chub) is a shy fish which tends to hide in holes so that, effectively, either possible explanation gives a sense of chiven meaning an evader.

chladnite *n* a variety of the mineral enstatite found in meteorites

chlorate *n* a salt of chloric acid

chlorite *n* any of several green hydrous silicates: one of the salts of chlorous acid

cho *n* a Japanese measure of distance equal to 60 ken (119.3 yds or 109.1 m)

choir (*n*) *poet vb* to sing in chorus: to resound as music produced by a choir

cholate *n* a salt of cholic acid

choler *n* anger or ill humour (see **CARDINAL HUMOURS**)

choline *n* a colourless, viscous compound found in many animal and vegetable tissues

chondral *adj* of or pertaining to chondri

chondri *pl* chondrus

chondrite *n* a fossil marine plant found in such as chalk

chondrus *n* carrageen or other cartilaginous red seaweeds of the same genus (*pl* **chondri**)

chone *obs fm now dial n* **chawn**, a gap

chopin *n* an old liquid measure which varied in different countries:– e.g. in France, *approx* half a litre or a Winchester pint; in Scotland, half a Scottish pint or *approx* two pints Imperial *var fm n* **chopine**

chopine *n* a type of shoe having an extremely thick cork sole to exaggerate height, fashionable in Spain and Italy around 1600 and *esp* in Venice where they wore absurdly thick-soled versions. The English confined use to the stage.

choral (*adj*) *n* chorale, a psalm or hymn set to a tune of simple devotional character: any part of a Catholic service sung by the whole choir *vb* to sing in chorus

chorea *n* St Vitus' dance, a nervous disorder (*pl* **choreas**)

choree *n* a trochee, a term in prosody (see **metric foot**)

choreus *var fm n* **choree**

chorine *slg n* a chorus girl

chorist *n* a member of the chorus of an ancient Greek drama

choroid *adj* resembling, *esp* in being vascular, the outer membrane surrounding an embryo

chouse *collq vb* to dupe: to swindle *obs n* a cheat

chouser *n* a cheat

chout *n* an historical Indian protection racket whereby a strong province blackmailed a weaker province into paying a quarter of its revenues in return for freedom from plunder

chowder *n* an American dish based on either fresh fish or clams stewed with such as bacon, onions and biscuit and sometimes *incl* cider or the like

chowre *now dial vb* to grumble

chowse *var fm collq vb* **chouse**

chrism *n* an unguent or ointment of oil and balm used by the Church during the service of the consecration of a person to God in a specific office as in the coronation of a monarch, the enthronement of a bishop or the taking of Holy Orders by a priest: also used in confirmation and baptism *obs vb* to anoint a person with chrism

chrisolyte *Obs fm n* **chrysolite** (in the sense given as *obs n*)

chromate *n* a salt of chromic acid

chromite *n* chrome ironstone or chrome iron ore, the most abundant ore of chromium

chromotype *n* a photographic process using paper sensitized by a salt of chromium: a photograph so produced

chrysolite *n* either the precious or the non-precious forms of olivine *obs n* any of several green-coloured gems *incl* olivine but also such as apatite, topaz, tourmaline and zircon

chrysotile *n* a fibrous, silky variety of the yellowish magnesium silicate, serpentine

chuet *var fm obs n* **chewet**, a magpie

chunder *Austr slg vb* to vomit

church grim *n* unlike the grim (q.v.) the church grim is a guardian spirit of churchyards though it, too, usually assumes the form of a black dog. A portent of death, its duty is to defend souls against witches and the devil. Traditionally, a pure black dog was the first corpse for burial in a new churchyard (the grave is at the north end) and its spirit is charged with the duty of defending the souls of those who follow it to this final earthly resting place. The tradition of the church grim is found in those parts of Britain which had a Viking influence as well as in the Scandinavian countries, where it is known as a *kirkegrim* or *kyrkogrim.*

churpe *obs fm vb* **chirp**

chute *n* a sloping channel used for sliding down specific items such as coal, logs or parcels: a waterfall, a rapid: a (children's) slide in a park or a swimming pool: a parachute *vb* to parachute: to send (logs) down a chute

chypre *n* a perfume from Cyprus

ci *Obs n* a dog (*pl* **cwn**)

cicada *n* a tree-dwelling insect with large transparent wings, the male of which is noted for making a shrill chirping sound

cicala *var fm n* **cicada**

Cicindela *n* a genus of *Cincindelidae*, the family of about 2,000 species of tiger beetles which, *esp* as larvae, are probably the most voracious and ferocious of all insect carnivores

ciclatoun *n* (As a word of understood meaning and normal usage it is *Obs.* As a word of conjectured meaning in normal usage it is both erroneous and *obs.* As a word of historical research it was investigated in the 19th century but, as it has failed to be returned to a normal literary usage, it is technically, *obs.*) The mediaeval writers, *incl* Chaucer, used it (with various spelling *fms*) to mean a cloth of great value with senses ranging from scarlet cloth to cloth of gold. Spenser (using the *fm*, **sheck-laton**, after the manner of Chaucer's **skylatoun**) assumed it to mean a gilded leather and that it was used to embroider Irish jackets. 19th century research produced the *fm* ciclatoun, which combines the first part of the original spelling, **ciclatun** or **ciclatune** with the second part of Chaucer's skylatoun and concluded it was a cloth of gold. The full *Obs* senses are not fully understood; it is possible that the meanings could include a garment of this highly prized material. However, in view of both the Victorian spelling and the one sense which accords with both mediaeval usage and latter day research, it can be defined as '*obs n* a mediaeval cloth of great esteem'.

Cicuta *n* a genus of poisonous plants, of which a British species is water hemlock (*–cap*) *n* a species of this genus

cidaris *n* the royal tiara of ancient Persia

ciel *var fm vb* **ceil**

cieler *obs n* one who fitted wooden panelling

cierge *n* a (large) wax candle

cigaret *US var fm n* **cigarette**

ciliate *adj* having hairlike processes *n* any of about 200 species of parasitic single-celled organisms possessing no mouth. They live in places such as the intestines of earthworms.

cilice *n* haircloth: a garment of this material worn by a penitant

cimar *var fm n* **cymar**, a loose, light dress worn by women as either an under or outer garment in the 17th/18th century: chimer, a loose robe worn by a bishop

cinaper *var fm obs n* **sinoper**

cinch *US n* the type of saddle girth used in Mexico and the southwestern parts of the USA *US vb* to girth tightly

cineast *var fm n* **cineaste**, a film fan or movie goer

cineol *n* a disinfectant obtained from several oils such as those of eucalyptus and wormwood and having an odour of camphor

cinerea *n pl* grey matter, the active part of the ganglia or nerve centres of the body

cinereal *adj* of birds, ash-coloured

cingle *n* a girdle

cingular *n* a wild boar in its fifth year

cingulum *n* girdle or waist in certain applications such as designating a surgical girdle or the girdle of a priest's alb and the zoological usage for any of the series of body bands in the armour of an armadillo or a ring of colour on an earthworm

cinnabar gate *n* a classical Chinese synonym for the vagina

cinoper *var fm obs n* **sinoper**

cinople *Obs fm obs n* **sinople**

cinq *var fm n* **cinque**

cinqfoil *var fm n* **cinquefoil**

cinque *n* the number five as thrown at dice or marked on an individual die *pl* a particular change rung on eleven bells during the course of which five pairs change places

cinquefoil *n* any of various species of plants having compound leaves each consisting of five leaflets: a design of such used for a window or in heraldry

Cinque Ports *n pl* Hastings, Sandwich, Dover, Romney and Hythe, the five ports which, from the 12th century onwards, were granted special privileges in consideration of their providing men and ships for coastal defence. Winchelsea and Rye were subsequently added. To be the Lord Warden of the Cinque Ports is a great honour and among the distinguished holders of the office are King Henry V, the Duke of Wellington, William Pitt, Sir Winston Churchill, Sir Robert Menzies of Australia and H.M. Queen Elizabeth the Queen Mother. (Also see **Pig-iron Bob**)

cintre *n* the centre of an arch

cipers *obs fm n* **cypress**

cipher *n* any Arabic numeral: a nonentity: a design of interweaved personal initials: a continuous sound of a note coming from an organ due to a mechanical defect: see **CODES AND CIPHERS** *vb* to work at mathematics: of an organ, to make that continuous sound: see **CODES AND CIPHERS**

cipres *obs fm n* **cypress**

circar *n* a province of India during the era of Mogul rule: a district under the control of the East India Company by a grant of the Great Mogul *var fm n* **sirkar** or **sircar**, a revenue division of India: the government: a house steward: an accounts clerk

cirque *n* a Roman circus or large arena for such as chariot racing: a cwm or natural amphitheatre *poet n* a circle or ring of any sort

cirrose *adj* of living things, having a tendril or tendrils: of the nature of cirrus clouds

cisers *obs fm n* **scissors**

cispontine *adj* on this side of the bridges

cisted *adj* containing cists, tombs made of stone

cister *obs fm n* **sister**

cistern (*n*) *vb* to install or create a cistern

cisterna *n* a fluid-containing sac (*pl* **cisternae**)

cistron *n* a segment of DNA

cistvaen *n* a cist or kistvaen, a sepulchral chamber excavated in rock or other prehistoric stone-covered tomb

cit *arch n* a citizen below the rank of gentleman but above the lowest classes (*fem* **citess**)

citatory *adj* summoning

citer *n* one who quotes: one who summons

citess *arch n* the *fem* of **cit**

cithara *n* an ancient triangular shaped musical instrument having up to eleven strings

citharist *n* one who plays the cithara

cither *n* a lute-like mediaeval stringed instrument: the zither

cithern *n* a guitar-like musical instrument, common in the 16th/17th centuries, having wire strings and played with a plectrum or a quill

cithren *obs fm n* **cithern**

citola *n* a pear-shaped guitar

citrange *n* a citron and orange hybrid

citrate *n* a salt of citric acid

citrin *n* a constituent of vitamin P found in the citrus fruits

citrine *adj* lemon-coloured *n* that colour

citron *n* the lemon-like fruit of the citron tree: that tree

citroned *obs adj* intoxicated on citron water, a liquor of brandy flavoured with lemon peel

cittern *var fm n* **cithern**

cittren *obs fm n* **cithern**

clabber *Ir & S n* mud *Ir & S vb* to curdle

clade *obs n* a calamity, disaster, plague

clair *dial fm adj* **clear**

Claire *fem pers n* meaning 'bright'

clairt *var fm now S & dial n* **clart**, mud or filth: a dirty person

clamant *adj* clamorous, noisy

clambe *obs pa t vb* **climb**

clame *var fm now dial vb* **cleam**

clamer *obs fm vb* **clamber**

claner *obs fm adj* **cleaner**

clanes *Obs fm adj* **clean**

clape *US n* the flicker or pigeon woodpecker

claper *obs fm n/vb* **clapper** *var fm obs n* **clapper**, a rabbit burrow

clapse *dial fm n/vb* **clasp**

claque *n* an organised group of hired applauders at a theatrical performance: any group, for whatever motive, giving its leader undeserved applause: an opera hat

clare *arch fm adj* **clear** *obs fm n/vb* **clear** (*+cap*) *var fm fem pers n* **Clara**, meaning 'clear' *n* a Poor Clare, a nun of the order founded by St Clare

claret (*n*) *nonce vb* to drink claret

Claribel *dim fem pers n* **Clara**, meaning 'clear'

clarionet *n* a clarinet: one who plays that musical instrument

claro *US n* a type of mild cigar (*pl* **claros, claroes**)

Clarrie *dim masc pers n* **Clarence**, meaning 'renowned' *dim fem pers n* **Clara,** meaning 'clear'

clarte *obs fm n* **clarity**

clary *n* any of various plants *esp* one cultivated as a pot herb *obs vb* to blow a clarion call

claspe *obs fm n/vb* **clasp**

clate *obs n* a wattle-work hurdle designed to take a covering of earth whilst serving as a roof for a temporary structure *obs fm S & dial vb* **claut** *obs fm n* **cleat**

clater *obs fm n/vb* **clatter**

Claude *dim masc pers n* **Claudius**, meaning 'lame'

Claudian *adj* of those Roman emperors of the imperial Claudius family, Tiberius (AD 14–37), Caligula (37–41), Claudius (41–54) and Nero (54–68) or that period of dynastic rule

claused *obs adj* concluded

claut *S & dial n* a grasping hand: a scraping implement such as a hoe or a mud scraper *S & dial vb* to scratch, claw, rake or scrape

clave *obs n* a knotty branch: a form or bench on a ship

claved *her adj* key-shaped

claver *S & dial n* idle chatter: a piece of idle gossip *S & dial vb* to talk idly: to gossip *now dial vb* to climb

claves *pl* clavis

clavier *n* the keyboard of a musical instrument

clavis *n* a key: a key for solving codes or puzzles (*fig*) (*pl* **claves**) (For the literal relationship of a key to a code see the special entry, **CODES AND CIPHERS**)

clay (*n*) *vb* to cover or plaster with clay: to use clay as a filter of liquid in the sugar refining process

clead *dial vb* to clothe (*pa t/pa pple* **cled**)

cleam *now dial vb* to smear or anoint

cleap *obs fm arch vb* **clepe**

cleare *obs fm adj/n* **clear**

cleat *n* a firmly anchored T-shaped piece of wood or metal around which the end of a rope is secured: a wedge: a piece of wood nailed across anything for the purposes of strengthening or securing: one of several pieces attached to the sole of a (climber's) boot for additional grip *vb* to fasten by using a cleat: to strengthen with a cleat

clee *now dial n* a claw: a segment of a hoof: a hoof

cleek *n* a large crook or grapnel used by a fisherman *dial vb* to seize or grasp firmly or eagerly: to snatch

cleer *obs fm n/adj/adv/vb* **clear**

cleet *obs fm n/vb* **cleat**

clematis *n* any of various species of a genus of climbing plants often cultivated for their large colourful flowers

clepe *arch vb* to call by the name of (*pa pple* **yclept**, see **y**-*prefix*)

clere *obs fm n/adj/adv/vb* **clear**

clerke *obs fm n* **clerk**

clerkess *n* a female clerk

clete *obs fm n/vb* **cleat**

cleveite *n* a radioactive variety of pitchblende, rich in uranium oxide and containing helium and yttrium earths

clevis *n* a U-shaped device designed to allow rope to pass through

cley *var fm now dial n* **clee** *obs fm n/vb* **clay**

click beetle *n* the elaterid or skipjack, any of about 7,000 species of dull brown insects which have the ability to spring upwards into the air when placed on their backs. In the performance of this leap they produce a noticeable clicking sound. Their larvae, the wireworm, is a very destructive agricultural pest.

clientage *n* clientele: the relation of a client to a patron

cliented *obs adj* having clients

clientel *var fm n* **clientele**, customers collectively

climater *var fm obs n* **climature**

climature *obs n* climate in the usual sense: climate in the *obs* sense as a region? (note: As climate in the extant sense, the word was in common usage and was last recorded in print in 1806. Shakespeare may have intended 'climatures' (the *pl fm* he used in *Hamlet*) to mean regions. Certainly this is the view of the dictionary used for the UK Scrabble championship, which gives the following definition, '**climature** (*Shak*) a region' but provides no further information.)

clime *n* a region

cline *n* the gradual and progressive change in one particular character of an animal or plant species. For example, over a distance of *approx* 80 miles from the north to the south of the Shetland Isles, a species of moth (*Amathes glareosa*) is almost completely black in the north to, apart from markings, almost completely pale grey in the south. At any point between, the moth is lighter or darker according to distance from either starting point. This is not the same as the **melanism** exhibited by another British moth (*Biston betularia*), the peppered moth. Approximately 100 years ago it was grey; then a mutant black variety appeared. As the grey was indistinguishable from the lichens of the trees, so only the black variety fell easy prey to birds. But, near the big industrial centres, soot in the air killed the lichens and turned the trees black. Here the grey variety was easy prey and the black survived. The result is that, for all practical purposes, the grey variety of the peppered moth can only be found in a natural environment and the black variety in an industrial environment.

clinge *obs fm vb* **cling**

clipe *var fm S vb* **clype**

clive *Obs vb* to climb (*pa pple* **yclive** or **ycliven** (see **y**- *prefix*)) *obs fm vb* **cleave**, to adhere to (+*cap*) *masc pers n* meaning 'a cliff'

cloaca *n* that cavity in birds, reptiles, monotremes and most fishes which is common to the openings of the excretory and sexual systems: a sewer: a water closet: a passage for morbid matter: a sink of filth (*fig*) (*pl* **cloacae**)

cloacal *adj* pertaining to, characterized by or of the nature of a cloaca

cloacalin *nonce adj* cloacal

cloacinal *nonce adj* cloacal

clodde *obs fm n* **clod**

clodder *now dial n* a curdled mass *obs vb* to coagulate

clodly *adv* in a cloddish manner: dully, heavily

cloke *dial n/vb* (to) claw

clone *n* a group of plants, organisms or cells of identical genetic constitution all descended from a common ancestor by artificially induced asexual reproduction: any one individual of that group *vb* to (cause to) produce a clone

clonus *n* a convulsion with alternate contractions and relaxations of the muscles (*pl* **clonuses**)

cloor *dial vb* to claw or scratch

cloose *dial fm n* **clow**, a sluice

cloote *Obs fm n* **clote**

closen *dial pl* close, an enclosure

clote *n* any of several plants such as burweed, butterbur, clivers, coltsfoot, the yellow water lily, but *esp* the burdock: a prickly bur of the burdock

cloter *obs fm vb* **clotter**

Clotho *n* the genus of puff adders *fem pers n* see **Fates, the**

clotter *vb* to coagulate

cloture *n* the closing of a debate in a deliberative body, usually with a sense of such closure before all who wish to speak have done so. For example, in the various legislative chambers of the USA in order to secure a prompt vote or, in the French Assembly, by will of the majority.

clout nail *n* a type of large nail having a flat head

clow *n* a sluice or floodgate (*pl* **clowes**): a type of fork having the prongs bent at right angles for the purpose of scraping dung out of cattle stalls (*pl* **clows**) *vb* to use such a dung fork

clowde *obs fm n* **cloud**

clowes *pl* clow, a floodgate

clowse *var fm n* **closh**, a distemper in the necks of cattle

clud *dial fm n* **cloud**

cludded *dial fm adj* **clouded**

cludder *now dial n* a clutter *dial vb* to heap together *obs vb* to coagulate

clumber *n* a breed of spaniel

clume *dial n* crockery

clumse *now dial adj* stupid, inept, idle, surly *now dial n* one having such negative qualities *obs adj/vb* (to become) numb with cold

clunner *obs n* a monk from the French monastery of Cluny

clupe *obs fm arch vb* **clepe**

clusia *n* one of a number of American climbing plants

clute *var fm S n* **cloot**, a hoof *obs fm vb* **clout**

cly *thieves' cant vb* to steal

clype *S vb* to tell tales *Obs S n* an ugly misshapen fellow

cnidae *pl* cnida, the stinging organ in a jellyfish

co *var fm S n* **cove**, a shed *var fm dial vb* **ka** *obs n* a jackdaw

coacher *n* a coach horse

coact *vb* to act together: to drive forcibly to

coagent *n* a joint agent *adj* acting in concert with

coaita *n* a species of spider monkey

coaler *n* one employed in supplying coal *esp* to steam vessels: a steamship tender

Coalite® *n* a highly reactive smokeless coal

coatee *n* a (military) close-fitting coat with short tails

coater *obs S fm n/vb* **cotter**

coathe *var fm now dial n/vb* **cothe**

coati *n* any of three species of raccoon-like, social, small carnivores found from Oklahoma down to the northern end of South America. Coatis always hold their long tails erect and a band of twenty or more industriously sniffing the ground and leaving no stone unturned makes an amusing sight especially when partially concealed by undergrowth

coatless *adj* not having a coat of arms

Cochin *n* now part of the Indian state of Travancore-Cochin, it was once part of the kingdom of Kerala where Jews and Christians of St Thomas settled in the first century AD: a large, domestic, feathery-legged fowl originally from Cochin China, now part of Vietnam

Cock and Pynot *n* the name of a small Chesterfield inn which is now a museum. In 1688, the Earls of Devonshire and Danby and the heir of the Earl of Holderness met here and planned the revolution which overthrew King James II. The arms of the borough of Chesterfield have the cock and pynot (magpie) as supporters. The Earl of Devonshire was given a Dukedom. (Also see **pie**)

cock of the rock *n* either of two species of cotingine bird *incl* the bizarre **orange cock of the rock**. The males gather at a lek where each selects and fusses over his own very small individual display area. When a dull brown coloured female appears, the males fly to their individual little areas and immediately assume a frozen posture for minutes at a time which is usually followed by a prodigious leap. After she has made her choice and they have mated, the pair have no further association. (*pl* **cocks**

CODES AND CIPHERS A *cipher* substitutes a given symbol (such as a letter) by another and different symbol. A *code* does not necessarily (and in serious usage rarely does) make a simple one-for-one substitution and will render a whole word or even a complete statement into an individual symbol. Examples of a simple cipher (pigpen) and a complex code (the Polybius square) are given below.

1 **Pigpen** The complete pigpen alphabet is produced from geometric figures known as pigpens as each houses an individual character.
First of all the encipherer will draw the pigpens

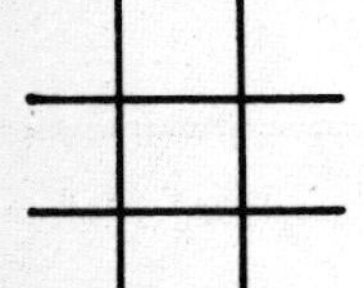
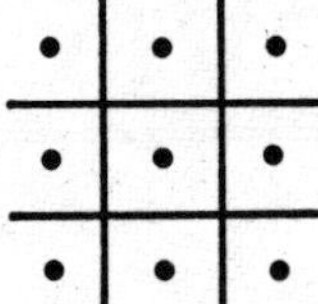

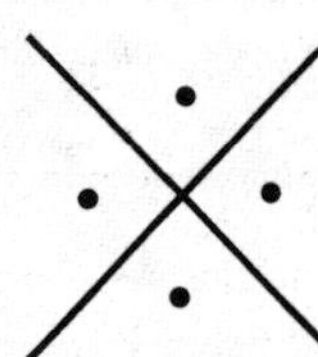

placing dots in the second and fourth. Immediately below these the encipherer will draw the same geometric figures, only this time he or she will include the complete alphabet.

A	B	C
D	E	F
G	H	I

J	K	L
M	N	O
P	Q	R

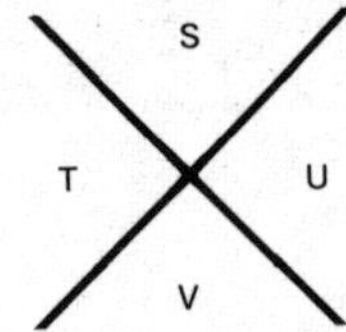

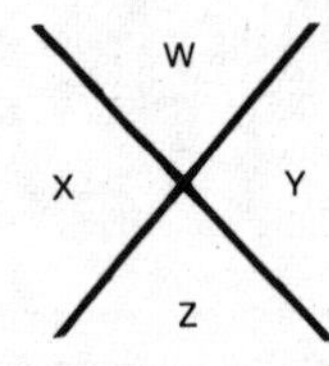

The shape of the individual pigpen will now be used to represent the desired letter as each one is different. For example, the word CAT is written └┘> and the word DOG is written as ⊐[·┐

2 **The Polybius square** In one form or another this ancient Greek device is still used even by the most sophisticated of today's encoding agencies. Basically, it is a simple mathematical cipher converted into a code by the use of a *keyword*. The only secrecy required for a high degree of security lies in the restriction of the knowledge of that *keyword* to those who 'need to know' and, because the *keyword* can be changed as and when required, the system is used by governments.

In this method the individual letters are represented by two-figure numbers produced by direct reference to the Polybius square.

	1	2	3	4	5
1	A	B	C	D	E
2	F	G	H	IJ	K
3	L	M	N	O	P
4	Q	R	S	T	U
5	V	W	X	Y	Z

The word CAT = 13·11·44
The word DOG = 14·34·22
Used as a sophisticated code, two actions are taken. First of all words themselves can mean a complete course of action, thus CAT (13·11·44), DOG (14·34·22), PIG (35·24·22) can be signals for different activities but in order to ensure maximum security, a constantly repeated *keyword* is added. To illustrate the usage, suppose that the original message is FEED THE CAT. Written in simple cipher form it looks like this:–
21·15·15·14 44·23·15 13·11·44
but if the message should be the length of a paragraph it can be deciphered by an 'enemy' easily within an hour. (Note the frequency of the symbol 15 which, in the first word, is almost certainly either EE or OO – a fact confirmed by usage elsewhere in a longer message.)

To convert this simple cipher to a complex code add a *keyword* (say DOG) with the cipher value of DOG (14·32·22) and constantly add it to the original enciphered message, hence:–

plaintext	F	E	E	D	T	H	E	C	A	T
ciphertext	21 ·	15 ·	15 ·	14	44 ·	23 ·	15	13 ·	11 ·	44
keyword	14 ·	34 ·	22 ·	14	34 ·	22 ·	14	34 ·	22 ·	14
codetext	35 ·	49 ·	37 ·	28	78 ·	45 ·	29	47 ·	33 ·	58

No longer does 15 *always* equate to the letter E as, in this example of codetext, the letter E is now disguised as 49, 37 and 29, making codebreaking difficult to impossible. (Also see **syctale** for a very simple but ingenious method of secret writing and **POSTAL WORD GAMES** for further information on the breaking of simple substitution codes.)

of the rock)

cockshy *n* a game of throwing a missile at a cock or other target: a free throw at an object

codder *US n* a person or ship engaged in cod fishing *now dial n* a saddler *dial n* one who gathers peas

codeina *var fm n* **codeine**, the narcotic alkaloid

coder *n* one who codes

CODES AND CIPHERS See opposite

codille *n* in the game of ombre, that game lost which a player challenges to win

codling *n* a variety of elongated and rather tapering apple of which there are several sub-varieties: the tree of such an apple

coe *n* the ovine disease, sheep rot: a small hut built over a mine shaft *vb* to give sheep the coe

coelacanth *n* the famous species of primitive fish thought to have been extinct for millions of years until the discovery of one specimen in 1938. It was considered one of the most exciting finds in the history of zoology. However, the local inhabitants of the Madagascan region were unimpressed – they have a long tradition of salting the coelacanth's flesh for food and using its skin as sandpaper.

coenact *vb* to enact jointly or at the same time (note: The only known British usage, in 1645, mirrors the modern American *fm* of dispensing with a hyphen though the modern British *fm* is more likely to be **co-enact**)

coeval *adj* of the same age *n* a contemporary

coexert defined in the dictionary used for the North American Scrabble championship as '*vb* to exert jointly', it is merely a typical Bishop Ken nonce word which he coined in the early 18th century as co-exert. His coinings include **co-admire, co-adore, co-amiable, co-apostate, co-ardent, co-attend** and continue through an alphabet of words prefixed 'co-' to his 19 letter 'masterpiece', **co-transubstansiated**. The US dictionary gives the *infl fms* **coexerts, coexerted, coexerting**. As that dictionary uses no labels it is impossible to deduce to what extent it takes **coexert** seriously. The only other works to mention that word are the greatest of the British and American dictionaries and both include coexert in the dismissive context of examples of words formed by the prefix 'co-'. As few, if any, of Bishop Ken's words can be found elsewhere, perhaps this one has a merit of sorts.

cogging *n* deceit

coggly *S & dial adj* unsteady

cognate *adj* of the same family *n* in Roman law, a kinsman (*pl* those descended from a common ancestor of either sex): in Scots law, a relative on the mother's side (as opposed to **agnate**, on the father's side)

cognation *n* kinship, relationship not only of people but also of such as languages: in Roman law, relationship from a common ancestor either male or female: in Scottish law, female only

cognise *var fm vb* **cognize**, to take note of: to become aware of

cogniser *var fm n* **cognizer**, one who or that (e.g. the intellect), which notices or observes

cognomen *n* a surname, nickname or self-given epithet *vb* to give a name or nickname to

cognominal *adj* having the same cognomen *obs n* a namesake

coheir *n* a joint heir

cohere *vb* to stick together: to connect or be connected logically

coho *n* one of several species of salmon found in the North Pacific off the Canadian and American coast which, unlike the Atlantic salmon, die after spawning

cohoe *var fm n* **coho**

coiffeur *n* a hairdresser

coiffure *n* a style of hairdressing

coign *n* a short *fm* of **coign of vantage**, an advantageous position for observation or action: a cornerstone: a wedge *var fm vb* **coin**, to provide with a cornerstone *var fm vb* **quoin**, to secure or raise with a wedge (the words **coin, coign, coigne** and **quoin** being interchangeable in some senses)

coigne *var fm n* **coign**

coinfer *US fm vb* **co-infer**, to infer jointly

cointer *US fm vb* **co-inter**, to bury together

coistrel *arch n* one having the duty of tending to the horses of a knight: a knave or other person treated with contempt (GAME PLAYER'S note: Whilst perfectly valid for championship Scrabble in the USA, the word is unavailable for similar UK competition as its reference work considers the sense of a groom to be *obs* and that of a knave to be 'exclusive' to Shakespeare. Scott is among those who used the sense of groom and, apart from the various writers since Shakespeare, it is the sense of knave in which it is accepted as valid for American play. They also accept the *var fm*, **coistril**.)

coistril *var fm arch n* **coistrel**

colate *obs vb* to strain through a strainer *obs adj* strained

colation *n* the action of passing through a strainer

colcothar *n* the pigment, Indian red, formed as a by-product of the distillation of sulphuric acid from ferrous sulphate

cold (*n/adj*) *obs vb* to become cold (*lit/fig*): to chill

colden *vb* to make or become cold

coler *obs fm ns* **collar, choler**

coleus *n* any of various plants akin to the mint cultivated for their attractive foliage (*pl* **coleuses**)

colicky *adj* pertaining to or associated with the acute abdominal pain, colic

colin *n* the Virginia quail

colinear *adj* co-linear, lying in the same straight line

colitis *n* inflammation of the colon

Collatinus *pers n* the man whose wife, Lucretia, was raped by Tarquin, son of the king of Rome (see **Lucretia**)

COLLECTIVE NOUNS See below

collied *arch adj* blackened: grimy

collinear *adj* of three or more points, common to the same straight line

colloid *n* any gluelike or jellylike substance such as gelatin or raw egg white which either fails to diffuse or does so only very slowly through biological membranes, and has components which do not separate as in a true solution

COLLOID SYSTEMS See next page

colonial goose *n* a stuffed roast leg of mutton served on an Australian sheep station

color *var fm (now mainly US) n/vb* **colour**

COLLECTIVE NOUNS Apart from the obvious words such as flock (as a flock of birds or a flock of sheep) and gang, herd, swarm etc., some of the more unusual *incl*:–
ants colony: **apes** shrewdness: **asses** pace: **badgers** cete: **baseball players** nine: **bears** sloth: **bees** grist: **birds** congregation, volery: **bishops** bench: **bitterns** sedge, seige: **boars** sounder: **bucks** brace, leash: **caterpillars** army: **cats** clowder: **cattle** drove: **chickens** peep: **choughs** chattering: **coots** covert: **cranes** herd, sedge, seige: **crows** murder: **curlews** herd: **doves** dule: **ducks** balding, team (in flight): **elk** gang: **ferrets** fesnyng: **fishes** run, school: **foxes** skulk: **geese** gaggle, skein (in flight):**girls** bevy: **gnats** cloud: **goats** tribe, trip: **goldfinches** charm: **grouse** covey (single brood), pack (collectively) (also see **lek** *n/vb*): **hares** down, husk, trip: **hawks** cast: **hens** brood: **herons** sedge, siege: **horses** harras: **hounds** mute: **hyenas** clan: **jellyfish** smack: **kangaroos** troop: **kittens** kindle: **lapwings** deceit: **larks** exaltation: **leopards** leap: **lions** pride: **locusts** plague: **mares** stud: **monkeys** troop: **nightingales** watch: **onions** rope: **owls** parliament: **oxen** drove, team, yoke: **partridges** covey: **peacocks** muster, ostentation: **pheasants** nide, nye: **plovers** congregation, wing: **ponies** string: **porpoises** school: **quails** bevy: **ravens** unkindness: **rhinoceroses** crash: **rooks** building, clamour: **sails** suit: **seals** pod: **sheep** trip (small flock) (also see **hirsel**): **squirrels** dray: **starlings** murmuration: **storks** mustering: **swallows** flight (also see **conglobulate** in a non-serious usage): **swans** bevy, herd: **swine** drift, sounder, trip: **teals** spring: **toads** knot: **trout** hover: **turkeys** rafter: **turtledoves** pitying: **turtles** bale: **whales** gam, pod, school: **wildfowl** trip: **wolves** herd, pack, rout, route: **woodcock** fall (also see **rode** *vb*): **woodpeckers** smack. (Also see **ANIMAL ADJECTIVES, BIRD CLASSIFICATION, FISH CLASSIFICATION**)

COLLOID SYSTEMS A colloid of any combination of two of the three basic states, gas, liquid or solid. GAS in LIQUID = foam (as lather or froth): GAS in SOLID = solid foam (as pumice or rubber): GAS in GAS (not known): LIQUID in SOLID = gel (as glue): LIQUID in LIQUID = emulsion (as blood or milk): LIQUID in GAS = fog (as clouds): SOLID in LIQUID = suspension (as paints): SOLID in GAS = smoke (as iodine vapour): SOLID in SOLID = solid sol (as paper).

colter *var fm n* **coulter**

colourman *n* one who sells colours

columnated *adj* having or supported by columns

colure *n* either of two great circles which intersect each other at right angles at the poles, with one passing through the equinox and the other the solstice

comarb *n* the hereditary head of a division of an Irish tribe: an ecclesiastical successor

comate *n* a friend, companion *adj* pertaining to the nebulous envelope of a comet *obs adj* having long hair, hairy

comber *n* one who or that which combs: a long curling wave of the sea: gaper, a marine perch: a species of wrasse found off the Cornish coast

combre *obs fm vb* **cumber**

comedo *n* a blackhead, black-tipped fatty matter clogging a pore of the skin (*pl* **comedos**)

comity *n* courtesy (*pl* **comities**)

Commelina *n* a genus of tropical plants

compear *S vb* as a party to a cause, to appear in court (extended to include appearance by counsel only)

compeer *n* an equal: a companion

compier *obs fm n* **compeer**

compire *obs fm n* **compeer**

compot *var fm n* **compote**, fruit preserved in syrup

comprisal *n* the action, condition or fact of comprising

comsat. an abbreviation for communications satellite

Comtism *n* the philosophical system of the French philosopher, August Comte (1798–1857) which has mankind seeking the answers to spiritual questions in a development beginning with the theological, moving onto the philosophical and ending with the scientific. At the scientific stage a religion is still needed, so he declared himself the High Priest and drew up a list of historical worthies to be the 'saints' of this new religion. Humanity was the 'god'.

conaria *pl* conarium

conarial *adj* of or pertaining to the conarium

conarium *n* the pineal gland, a body found in the brain – though not part of it – and its purpose is unknown (Descartes (1596–1650), the French mathematician and pioneer of modern philosophy contended that it was the seat of the soul) (*pl* **conaria**)

conative *adj* pertaining to or of the nature of volition and desire: in grammar, denoting endeavour *obs n* endeavour

conatus *n sing/pl* an effort, a striving: an impulse

concavely *adv* with a concave appearance

concent *n* harmony *obs vb* to harmonise: to meet harmoniously

concenter *var fm (esp US) vb* **concentre**

concentre *vb* to direct or bring (as) to a common centre: to come together (as) at a common centre: to focus: to combine

concerti *pl* concerto

concertino *n* a musical composition rather like a concerto but shorter

concertion *obs n* conception is the most likely meaning of this obscure word though some 18th century dictionaries explained it as contrivance

concerto (*n*) *pl* **concerti, concertos**

concetti *pl* concetto

concetto *n* a fanciful, witty or ingenious notion or expression *esp* in a disparaging sense, for which the conventional English term is conceit: the use of such as a quality of literary taste or style (note: Whilst the word is capable of being given a wider usage, it is basically concerned with descriptions of some Italian literature) (*pl* **concetti**)

conciser *comp adj* concise

concreate *vb* to create together

concreation *obs n* the creation of two aspects of a thing or two different things simultaneously

cond *vb* to direct, from a high point on land, fishing boats towards a shoal

conder *n* a land-based signaller who indicates to fishing boats the movement of a shoal

condign *adj* of punishment, appropriate *arch adj* of persons, worthy

condor *n* either of two species of New World vulture, of which the **Andean condor** is the largest flying bird in the world in weight and wingspan measurement. Unlike most raptors, the male of both the **Andean** and the **Californian condor** is larger than the female and can achieve wingspans of $10\frac{1}{2}$ feet and $9\frac{1}{2}$ feet respectively.

coney *var fm n* **cony**

conflate *vb* to fuse: to combine or blend (*esp* two versions of a text) to form one whole

confrairy *obs n* a brotherhood or fraternity, either religious or lay: a guild

confrater *n* a member of a confraternity or brotherhood

confrère *n* a fellow member of such as a learned profession

confrérie *n* a brotherhood (note: This word would appear to be exclusive to the dictionary used for the UK Scrabble championship. An *obs n* **confrairy**, is recorded elsewhere.)

conger *n* an edible marine eel of which, like all eels, the female is considerably larger, attaining a length of up to ten feet: a term of abuse for a man: a cartel of booksellers (now only historical)

congeries *n/n pl* a mass, a heap, an aggregation

congery *erron sing n/n pl* congeries (GAME PLAYER'S note: Valid for play)

conglobulate *vb* to collect in a rounded or compact mass (TRIVIA note: The classical usage is by the great 18th century lexicographer, Dr Johnson, who stated, '*A number of them (swallows) conglobulate together and then all in a heap throw themselves under water*'. This is a reference to the once widely held belief that swallows spent the winter asleep at the bottom of ponds. A contemporary of his once tested the theory by tying dyed threads to the legs of these birds. When, the following spring, the dye had obviously failed to wash out, doubt in the belief began to form. *Chambers 20th Century Dictionary* appears to be unique in carrying the noun, **conglobulation**, which it leaves undefined in a non-hirundine context. Where, however, the word appears in works other than dictionaries, the reference is to Dr Johnson's description of swallows – giving it a sense of a collective noun for a flock of swallows about to plunge into their winter quarters!)

conglobulation see **conglobulate**

congre *obs fm n* **conger**

congreet *Shaks vb* to greet mutually

Congreve *n* either of two items invented by Colonel Sir William Congreve (1772–1828), a lucifer (or matchstick) or a military rocket

conidium *n* an asexual reproductive part of certain fungi (*pl* **conidia** – contrast anagram, **oncidium** and *pl*)

conies *pl* cony or coney

coniine *var fm n* **conine**

conima *n* a fragrant resin obtained from a tropical American tree

conine *n* a violently poisonous oily liquid obtained from hemlock and having a peculiar suffocating odour (*var fms* **coicine, coneine, conia, coniine**)

coning *obs fm n* **cony**, an adult rabbit

conk (*slg n/vb*) *US n* a disease of timber induced by a fungal parasite *var fm dial n/vb* **cank**, (to) chatter

conner *n* one who studies: a conder *arch n* an inspector *esp* as **ale conner** *var fm n* **cunner** *obs S vb* to curry

connotate *vb* to signify in addition: to imply as a consequence (GAME PLAYER'S note: In the first sense the *vb* was last recorded as having been used in 1697. In the second sense, 1660. Both senses, covered by the word **connote**, are considered *obs* by all authorities except the dictionary used for the UK Scrabble championship which has it as an extant *vb* to connote. It does not mention the *obs n* (also 1697), meaning that signified in addition.)

conseil *Fr n* advice, counsel: council (also one of more than 40 different *Obs and obs fms n/vb* **counsel**)

consolate *obs adj* consoled *obs vb* to console (GAME PLAYER'S note: The dictionary used for the UK Scrabble championship credits only Shakespeare with using the *vb* which, in fact, was last used in 1773. It fails to mention the *adj* which was last used in 1818.)

consortia *pl* consortium

constate *vb* to establish

conster *arch fm vb* **construe**

constrain *vb* to compel *esp* by circumstances: to compel to inaction: to confine or restrain as by force

constre *obs fm vb* **construe**

constringe *vb* to constrict: to contract: to become close or dense

contenting *n* satisfaction, contentment

conter *S fm vb* **counter**

contering *S fm n* **countering**

continuum *n* a total that is continuous and uninterrupted: a continuous series no part of which is perceptibly different from an adjacent part i.e. that which has perfect continuity: a basic common character underlying any series however much it may vary in some aspects: in mathematics, a set of numbers or points such that a third number or point may be interpolated between any two (*pl* **continua, continuums**)

conto *n* a Portuguese and Brazilian money of account (*pl* **contos**)

contra *adv/prep* against *n* an argument against

contre *obs fm vb* **counter**

contrite (*adj*) *obs n* a penitent

contuse *vb* to bruise

cony *n* the correct name for the adult rabbit and still used as such in statutes, heraldry and by many country people – the word rabbit being the name for the young of the cony (as leveret is to hare). Originally introduced to Britain in the Middle Ages as a domestic animal bred for its meat and fur, it was confined to a special enclosure called a warren (see **warren**): the fur of the cony: for the Biblical 'cony' see **hyrax**: the West Indian nigger fish *obs n* a term of endearment for a woman (*pl* **conies**)

cooler (*n/comp adj*) *obs fm n/vb* **colour**

coolth *dial n* coldness

coom *n* soot *S n* a coffin lid *obs n* rancid honey *vb* to begrime with soot

coonty *var fm n* **coontie**, a tropical American plant the stems and roots of which yield a starch

coost *S pa t vb* **cast** *obs fm n/vb* **coast**

cooter *var fm slg n* **couter**

coper *n* a dealer (often used in combination as **horse coper, herring coper** etc.): in Derbyshire lead mining, one who directly mines the ore at a cope, or price per ton: a floating grogshop or vessel which carries hard liquor for bartering at sea for the freshly-caught fish

copita *n* a tulip-shaped sherry glass

copula *n* that which joins or binds (*pl* **copulae, copulas**)

copyism *n* a term of contempt for an imitation

Coralie *var fm fem pers ns* **Cora**, meaning 'maiden' or **Coral**, named after the marine substance

coralline *adj* of the nature of, like or resembling coral: red (i.e. the colour of red coral)

corallite *n* a fossil coral

coral tree *n* the red bean tree, a tropical tree having red flowers likened to red coral

coranto *n* the courante (*pl* **corantoes, corantos**)

corban *n* an offering to God in fulfilment of a vow

corbeil *n* a carving in the form of a basket

cordate *adj* heart-shaped

corde *aphetic fm vb* **accord**

corder *n* one who makes or fastens with a cord: an appliance on a sewing machine for stitching cord between folds in cloth

cordierite *n* iolite

coreign *n* a joint reign

corelation *var fm n* **correlation**, a mutual relationship between two or more things: the act of correlation, the state of being correlated

co-relation *n* joint or mutual relation

corella *n* a species of white cockatoo which resides near permanent water and is used by the Australian bushmen as a water guide

corer *n* an instrument for removing the core of a fruit

co-resign a typical Bishop Ken *nonce vb*, see **coexert**

corf *n* a coal miner's tub or trolley (originally a basket): a lobster cage (*pl* **corves**)

corfes *obs fm pl* **corves** (see **corf**)

cork borer *n* an instrument for boring holes in corks to take scientific glass tubes

corkite *n* the mineral beudantite

cork leg *n* an artificial leg

cork oak *n* the tree from which cork is obtained

cork pine *n* the soft pine, a North American pine with a corklike timber

corky *adj* corklike (*comp* **corkier** *sup* **corkiest**)

cormophyte *n* any plant of a 19th century classification system which defined such as having a proper stem

cornage *n* horngeld, a rent for pasturage of feudal times based on the number of horned cattle

corne *obs n* a hornlike musical instrument

cornel *n* the dogwood or other shrub of the same genus

Cornelia *fem pers n* meaning 'regal'

cornet (*n*) *obs vb* to play the musical instrument, a cornet

cornice (*n*) *vb* to fit such an ornamental moulding

corniche *n* a coastal road *esp* one built into the face of a cliff (GAME PLAYER'S note: Not valid for UK championship Scrabble as its dictionary defines the word as French. Other British dictionaries accept it as *of French origin* so, too, do the Americans. Hence valid for play in the USA or for any word game under circumstances other than the above mentioned.)

cornist *n* a horn player

cornit *obs fm n* **cornet**, the musical instrument

cornual *adj* of or pertaining to the grey matter of the spinal cord

cornute *arch vb* to cuckold

cornuto *arch n* a cuckold

corolla *n* the inner floral envelope formed by the petals of a flower

corona *n* essentially the word reflects its Latin meaning of crown as in (*a*) the trumpet of a daffodil, (*b*) a circular chandelier, (*c*) a circular light around the moon (*pl* **coronae, coronas**)

corpes *obs fm n* **corpse**

corpora *pl* corpus

corpse (*n*) *slg vb* to reduce an actor or actress to such a state of laughter that he or she is unable to continue the performance

corpus *n* a body of writings either by a single author or on a specific subject: the main body of something: any special structure in the human body (*pl* **corpora**)

corrade *vb* to erode from the effect of loose solid matter transported by wind or water

corrase *obs vb* to scrape together

corred *var fm obs adj* **corved**

correi *var fm S n* **corrie**

corrie *S n* a semi-circular valley with a stream running through it

corsage *n* the bodice of a woman's dress: a small bunch of flowers pinned to the upper part of that bodice area or to a lapel

corsaint *Obs n* the body of a saint

corsant *var fm Obs n* **corsaint**

corsaunt *var fm Obs n* **corsaint**

corse *poet fm n* **corpse** *now dial vb* to exchange: to barter: to buy (a horse) with the intention of reselling

corseint *var fm Obs n* **corsaint**

corselet *var fm n* **corslet**

corser *n* a jobbing dealer (*obs* except in the combination *fm*, **horse corser**)

corsive *obs adj* corrosive *obs n* a medicament with a corrosive action

corslet *n* a piece of body armour: a (tight-fitting) body garment: the thorax of an insect *vb* to encircle (as) with a corslet

corslete *obs fm n* **corslet**

corsned *n* the historical ordeal of swallowing such as a piece of bread which, if it sticks in the throat, is deemed proof of guilt

Cortaderia *n* a genus of tall South American grasses

corte *obs fm n/vb* **court**

Cortes *n* the parliament of Portugal and of Spain *pers n* Hernando Cortés (1488–1547) the Spanish adventurer who crushed an ancient civilisation in his conquest of Mexico

Cortian *adj* designating various parts of the internal ear as Cortian organ or Cortian membrane etc, after the Italian anatomist Cortian (1729–1813)

cortile *n* an enclosed area or courtyard attached to a building

cortin *n* a substance containing various hormones used for the treatment of such as Addison's disease

coruscate *vb* to flash, glitter, sparkle or otherwise display an intermittent light

corved *obs adj* of freshly-caught herrings, salted prior to drying

corves *pl* corf

corvet *var fm n/vb* **curvet**

corvine *adj* of or pertaining to a raven or crow: akin to a crow: black as a crow (the technical terms *incl Corvus*, the genus of the crow: *Corvinae*, a crow subfamily: *Corvidae*, the crow family)

cory *obs fm vb* **curry**, to comb

Corydon *pers n* applied as a term for a rustic

Corypha *n* a genus of gigantic tropical palms

cosecant *n* the trigonometric function that in a right-angled triangle is the ratio of the hypotenuse to that of the opposite side

coser *var fm obs n* **cosser**

cosher *vb* to pamper *Ir vb* to live with kinfolk at their expense: to feast *collq vb* to chat in a friendly way *var fm adj* **kosher**

cosign *US vb* to sign jointly

cosigner *n* one who signs jointly with another

cosine *n* a trigonometric function of an angle

cosmea *n* cosmos, an American plant akin to the dahlia

cosmetical *adj* relating to cosmetics

cosmist *n* one whose philosophy mirrors Comtism except that where Comte had humanity as 'god' the cosmist has the cosmos. Essentially, an atheist.

coste *obs fm ns/vbs* **coast, cost**

costean *vb* of Cornish tin mining, to drill down to rock in order to ascertain the direction of the lode

costean pit *n* a shallow pit dug to find traces of tin

costrel *now dial n* a wooden keg similar to the pilgrim's bottle *obs n* the pilgrim's bottle, a flask having ears so that it could be suspended from the waist

costrele *obs fm now dial n* **costrel** *var fm obs n* **costrel**

costus *n* an aromatic root of a plant native to Kashmir

coteline *n* a type of muslin

coter *obs n* the tenant of a small cottage

coterie (*n*) *vb* (essentially *nonce*) to associate in a clique or small exclusive group

cothe *now dial n* coe or sheep rot *obs n* general sickness *now dial vb* to transmit rot to sheep

cotinga *n* any of a family of more than 90 different species of mainly brilliantly coloured birds which range in size from that of a sparrow to that of a crow. Apart from one species found in Texas and Arizona, they are residents of Central and tropical South America. The species *incl* attila, becard, bellbird, capuchinbird, cock of the rock, fruitcrow, phia, purpletuft, tityra, umbrellabird as well as many different cotingas. (Also see **becard** and **cock of the rock**)

cotise *her n* a type of inanimate design which appears on a shield where animate supporters are normally placed *her vb* to border the main design with such devices *obs vb* to estimate the worth or dignity of

cottar *n* a mediaeval peasant who occupied a cottage and small piece of land in return for his labour: a similar tenant in today's Scottish Highlands

cotter *n* a simple fastening device, a pin or

bolt, which fits into a hole *dial n* an entertainment: a difficulty or worry (*fig*) *var fm n* **cottar** *vb* to fasten with a cotter: to entangle: to congeal: to crowd together

cotter pin *n* any of various wedges or bolts which fit into a hole to fasten something in place

cottise *var fm her n/vb and obs vb* **cotise**

cotylae *pl* cotyle

cotyle *n* an ancient Greek drinking vessel also used as a measure of capacity: a cuplike cavity within a living body (*pl* **cotylae, cotyles**)

coule *obs fm n* **cowl**

coulter *n* on a ploughshare, the iron blade which makes the vertical cut in the earth whilst the share makes the horizontal slice

coumarin *n* an aromatic crystalline substance obtained from the seeds of such as woodruff, sweet-scented vernal grass, melilot and *esp* the Tonka bean

counseler *obs fm n* **counsellor**

couper *S & dial fm n* **coper**, a trader (also used in combination as **horse couper** etc)

coupure *n* a military ditch or trench

courant *her adj* of an animal, running *n* a newspaper (now only extant in the title of such *esp* in Scotland) *now dial vb* to run or race about *var fm n* **courante**

courante *n* an old French dance in triple time having gliding steps: the music for this *dial n* a run around

courbaril *n* the locust tree of the West Indies: its resin

courie *arch fm n* **cowrie**

courlan *n* the limpkin

courtledge *n* a *var fm* of the now legal term, **curtilage**, but one still in popular (non-legal) usage in the southwest of England

couse *now dial n/vb* (to) chat or gossip

cousse *var fm now dial n/vb* **couse**

couter *slg n* a gold sovereign

couthie *S adj* kindly, pleasant, genial

couthily *S adv* in a couthie manner

couthy *var fm S adj* **couthie**

coutil *n* a type of close-woven canvas used for such as mattresses

covalency *n* the union of two atoms by the sharing of an electron from each as one pair

covenanter *n* one who is party to a mutual agreement and assumes its obligations (+*cap*) *n* a Scottish Presbyterian who signed either of two national covenants, one in 1638 or the other in 1643

covert (*adj/n*) *obs vb* to conceal

covyne *obs fm n* **covin**, a conspiracy

cowbird *n* any of various species of a subfamily of the orioles which follow cattle and harvest the insects disturbed by their associates. Unlike the ani (an American cuckoo) all but one species of these American birds have the cuckoo-like habit of laying their eggs in the nests of other birds

cowier *comp adj* cowy, cow-like

cowle *Anglo-Ind n* a written agreement: an amnesty

cowler *erron fm n* **coolie** (GAME PLAYER'S note: Valid for play)

cowless *nonce n* without cows

cowrie *n* any of various species of a carnivorous marine mollusc having a beautiful, highly polished shell. From early times the shell of the common cowrie of the Indian ocean has been, and still is, used as money.

cowshot *var fm n* **cushat**

coyle *obs fm vb* **coil**

craal *var fm n* **kraal**, a native village in southern Africa

crab stone *n* a calciferous concentration which forms in the stomach of a crustacean prior to its casting off of the existing shell

cradge *n* an embankment to prevent flooding in East Anglia *vb* to create or repair such an embankment of a natural or artificial waterway

crafter *S dial fm n* **crofter**

craim *var fm S n* **crame**

craine *obs fm n* **crane** *obs fm n/vb* **cranny**

crainte *obs n* fear

craise *obs fm vb* **craze**

crake *n* a bird of the coarse grasslands of the northern Palaearctic better known as the corncrake, but also known as the landrail, beancrake or, in Scotland, the craik: its cry, described as sounding like a knife being scraped over the teeth of a comb *dial n* a crow, a raven *vb* of the corncrake, crow or quail, to utter a harsh grating cry (the corresponding *S fm* being **craik**) *now dial vb* to boast or brag

cramble *now dial vb* to crawl, hobble or walk with difficulty *obs vb* of a root or stem, to grow with many twists and turns *dial n* a crooked or twisted branch

crambo *n* a rhyming game (*pl* **crambos, cramboes**)

crame *S n* a market stall *obs n* a pedlar's stock *obs dial n* a (coffin) cramp, a small metal clamp *obs dial vb* to secure with a crame

cramesy *adj/n* crimson

crampe *obs fm n/vb* **cramp**

crampit *var fm n* **crampet**, the chape or metal tip of a scabbard

cranage *n* (dues paid for) the use of a crane for hoisting

cranet *obs n* a piece of armour for the back of a horse's neck *obs dial n* a little red worm

crania *pl* cranium, the skull

craniate *adj* having a skull *n* a creature with a skull

cranse *var fm obs n* **crants**

crants *obs n* a garland, chaplet or wreath which, in earlier times, was worn by a maiden for festivals. The tradition has a long history over many centuries and even as late as Victorian times a church would be decorated with these floral headdresses to honour the funeral of a young maiden.

crape *n* a thin (black) silk fabric *vb* to clothe with crape

crapen *adj* formed of crape

crappie *n* either of two species of sunfish, the **white crappie**, usually found in turbid water or the **black crappie** which prefers clear water. Both are edible and popular American sporting fishes which can reach 21 inches in length. (See **sunfish**)

crare *n* a small coastal trading vessel

crase *obs fm n/vb* **craze**

crases *pl* crasis, a vowel contraction either from two vowels into one long vowel or into a diphthong: temperament

crasse *obs fm n* **cress**

crassie *var fm obs adj* **crassy**, coarse: greasy

craton *n* a comparatively rigid area in the crust of the earth

craul *obs fm n/vb* **crawl**

craule *obs fm n* **crawl**, an enclosure in shallow sea water for such as fish, lobsters or turtles

crawle *var fm obs vb* **crowl**

craye *obs fm n* **crare**

crayer *var fm n* **crare**

crayne *obs fm n* **crane**

creach *var fm n/vb* **creagh**

creagh *n/vb* (to) raid or plunder

creaght *n* an Eastern nomadic herdsman *vb* to herd cattle to a fresh grazing area

creame *obs fm n/vb* **cream**

creant *adj* creative

creaser *n* one who or that (contrivance) which creases

creasy *adj* heavily creased

creatin *var fm n* **creatine**

creatine *n* a nitrogenous compound found in the muscle tissue, brain and blood of all vertebrate animals

creational *adj* of or pertaining to creation

creatress *n* a female creator

credal *var fm adj* **creedal**

crede *obs fm n* **creed** *obs fm vb* **cree**

credent *adj* believing *n* a letter of introduction *esp* one given to a government by an ambassador

credential *adj* recommending credit or confidence *n* a letter of recommendation *esp* one of introduction carried by the envoy of one power to another

cree *vb* to produce a soft pulpy mass (of grain) by soaking or boiling: to become soft and pulpy (*var fms* (*mainly dial*) *incl* **cray, crew, creave, creeve** *obs fms incl* **crey, crede**) *obs vb* to create

creed (*n*) *obs vb* to believe

creedal *adj* credal, of a creed

creel *n* a (large) wickerwork basket of various types such as (*a*) that coupled in a pair across the back of a horse for transporting goods, (*b*) that containing fish and carried on the back, (*c*) an angler's basket: a wickerwork trap for such as lobsters: any of various types of framework of various materials *vb* to put into a creel *S vb* to make a newly-married man perform some ceremony with a creel *esp* to carry one loaded with stones until his bride gives him permission to stop

creem *dial n* a shiver *dial vb* to shiver: to deposit secretly: to squeeze or hug

creen *obs fm vb* **careen**

creeped *arch var fm vbl infl* **crept**

creese *var fm n/vb* **kris**

creesh *S n* grease or fat *S vb* to bribe (i.e. grease the palm)

creeve *var fm vb* **cree**

cremains *US n pl* the ashes of one who has been cremated

creme *n* chrism, a mixture of oil and balm used as an unguent or for anointing *obs vb* to anoint with creme *obs fm S n* **crame** *obs fm n* **cream**

Cremona *n* the town in Lombardy, Italy, famed for its violins and violas *esp* those of Stradivari (*—cap*) *n* an organ reed stop resembling the clarinet in tone (technically an *erron fm* of the German **krummhorn** via a French corruption as **cromorne**. From a grammatical standpoint, krummhorn (and *var fms*) or cromorne (and *var fms*) are acceptable but, from a game player's standpoint, cremona is a perfectly valid word. Also see **krummhorn**.)

cremor *n* a thick juice: a broth

cremosin *obs fm n/adj* **crimson**

crena *n* a notch

crenate *adj* finely scalloped *vb* to mill the edge of a coin

crenation *n* a rounded toothing such as that on the edge of a leaf or shell

crenulate *adj* of such as a leaf or a shell, finely notched

crenulated *adj* crenulate

creolian *adj/n* (of a) creole

creosote *n* an oily liquid having a smoky odour and a burning taste obtained from wood tar and having antiseptic properties: a similar liquid distilled from coal tar *vb* to treat or impregnate with creosote

crêpe (*n*) *vb* to frizz hair with the aid of paper

crepine see **crespine**

crepitant *adj* crackling or rustling

crepitation *n* a crackling noise *esp* that created by the movement of air within the chest of one suffering from pneumonia: the sound of crepitus when other internal gas moves elsewhere: the grating sound of two ends of a broken bone rubbing together

crepitus *n* crepitation: the breaking of wind from the anus

crepoline *var fm n* **crêpeline**, a light, thin, silk-based fabric used for women's dresses

crepon *n* a crape-like fabric made of silk or nylon

crepy *adj* of the nature of crape: crinkly (*comp* **crepier** *sup* **crepiest**)

crese *var fm n/vb* **kris**

cresol *n* an antiseptic produced from coal, beechwood or pinewood

crespine *n* a net of gold thread worn over the hair by women in the 14th and 15th centuries and still extant as the descriptive term for a similar article worn by Italian women as late as the 19th century. The standard *fm* of the word is **crepine**, though this is considered to be *obs*, but which also embraced similar mediaeval nets of such as silver thread or silk lace and had other meanings *incl* a fringe of lace used to decorate furnishings

cress *n* any of various plants of various genera with edible leaves *esp* garden cress and water-cress but *incl* such as the following (all of which are suffixed cress) bitter, cow, dock, French, Indian, lamb's, meadow, mouse-ear, pepper, Peter's, rock, Spanish, swine's, tooth, violet, wild, winter, yellow *var fm* (*arch* or *obs*) *vb* **crease**

cressan *Obs pl* cress

cresse *obs fm n* **cress**

cressed *adj* having cresses

cressen *Obs pl* cress

cresset *n* a metal container of various sorts *obs fm n/vb* **kris**

crestal *adj* pertaining to a crest

creste *obs fm n* **crest**

crete *dial n* a wooden, pronged attachment for a scythe to cause the corn to lay more evenly *obs n* the division between the nostrils: a baby's cot

cretinoid *adj* resembling a cretin

cretism *n* the art of coining or inventing lies

cribble *n* a coarse sieve *vb* to produce a dotted effect in engraving: to sieve (*obs* except for *adj* **cribbled**, sieved)

cribella *pl* cribellum, a spinning organ of certain species of spiders

crike *obs n* the crease in the buttocks

criket *obs n* a small creek

crile *dial n* a dwarf

crime (*n*) *vb* to charge or convict of an infraction of military law

criminate *vb* to charge with crime: to incriminate: to condemn

crimsone *obs fm n/adj* **crimson**

crinal *adj* of or belonging to the hair

crinate *adj* hairy

crinated *var fm adj* **crinate**

crine *n* (a head of) hair *S vb* to shrivel

crinet *obs n* a hair

crinets *n pl* the hairlike feathers which grow near the base of a hawk's beak

cringle *n* a small length of rope containing a metal ring *dial vb* to secure with a cringle

crinite *n* a fossil sea lily

crinose *adj* having long hair: hairy

crious *obs adj* noisy, boisterous

cripes *slg interj* (feigned) surprise/worry

cript *obs fm n* **crypt**

crises *pl* crisis

crisle *obs fm now dial vb* **crizzle**

crispate *adj* having the margin curled or undulated

crispated *adj* crispate

crispation *n* the formation of gentle folds: undulation

crisse *obs fm n* **kris**

crissel *var fm now dial vb* **crizzle** *obs fm n* **gristle**

crista *n* a crest (*pl* **cristas**): part of a cell (*pl* **cristae**)

cristate *adj* having a crest, crested

cristated *var fm adj* **cristate**

criste *obs fm n* **crest**

cristed *obs fm adj* **crested**

crith *n* a unit of weight of gaseous substances based on the weight of a litre of hydrogen at normal pressure and temperature

crizzle *now dial vb* to become rough on the surface: to cause to be so

croape *obs vb* to utter the cry of a raven

Croat *adj* Croatian, of Croatia, a constituent republic of Yugoslavia *n* Croatian, a native of Croatia: the Serbo-Croatian language of Yugoslavia written in the Roman alphabet as opposed to Serbian, the Serbo-Croatian language written in the Cyrillic alphabet: the dialect of Croatia

crocein *n* either of two artificially produced dyes, yellow or bright red

crocine *adj* of or pertaining to the crocus

crock (*n*) *now dial vb* to store in a crock or pot: to smut with soot or grime

Croesus *pers n* the last king of Lydia (560–546 BC) who was so rich and powerful that his name is still used, proverbially, for wealth (i.e. *as rich as Croesus*). Among those drawn to his court were Æsop and Solon and he was overthrown by Cyrus of Persia. (See **oracle**)

croin *S fm n/vb* **croon**

croise *vb* to wear the symbol of the cross in solemnization of a vow *esp* as a crusader against the Saracens (note: Strictly in this sense the word is *obs* but it has been revived and used with a new sense of a noun, meaning a crusade. Whilst the *n pl* **croises**, meaning crusaders, was used for many centuries, the singular *fm* never existed until this revival with a new meaning.)

croiser *obs fm n* **crosier**

croises *n pl* see **croise**

croissant *n* a crescent roll *obs fm n* **crescent**

croker *obs n* a trader in saffron

crone *n* an old (witchlike) woman: an old ewe *obs vb* to separate the old ewes from the rest of the flock

cronel *obs fm n* **coronal**, a coronet: a garland

cronet *obs n* the (three-pointed) head of a spear used in tilting

cronge *obs n* a hilt or handle

croodle *S vb* to make the soft murmuring sound of a dove *dial vb* to cuddle

croop *var fm n/now dial vb* **croup**

crope *var fm obs vb* **croape**, to croak

crore *Anglo-Ind n* one hundred lakhs (ten million rupees)

crose *obs n* the crosier or pastoral staff of a bishop or abbot

crosier *n* a staff surmounted by a crook or cross carried by a bishop or an abbot as a symbol of pastoral office

crosse *n* a lacrosse stick

crossen *Obs infl vb* **cross**

crosset *obs n* a small cross: a plant cutting

crosslet *her n* a small cross *n* an ornamental small cross *modf n* crosslet-shaped *obs n* a crucible

crosstree *n* either of two horizontal timbers which sustain the tops of lower masts on a sailing vessel

croste *Obs fm n* **crust**

crotaline *adj* of or belonging to the rattlesnakes

crotal *n* an Irish pear-shaped bell or rattle used by the early Christian clergy: crotalum, a sort of clapper or rattle used in ancient Greek religious dances *var fm n* **crottle**

crote *var fm obs n* **crot**, a tiny particle

crotels *obs fm n pl* **crottels**

Croton *n* a large genus of tropical plants of the spurge family, many of which have medicinal qualities (*–cap*) *n* a plant of this genus: a florist's term for a plant of a related genus having attractive foliage

crottels *n pl* the excrement of a hare

crottle *n* any of various species of lichens used for the production of a purple dye. One particular crottle, known as cudbear, is a major source of the dye.

croude *obs fm vb* **crowd**

croup *n* a disease of the larynx: the rump of a horse *now dial vb* to make the characteristic sound associated with the disease: of a frog, crane or raven, to utter its cry

croupe *var fm n* **croup**, the rump of a horse

croupiness *n* the condition of having the inflammatory disease, croup

crouse *S & dial adj* vivacious, pert *var fm obs vb* **croose**, to crush

croustade *n* a pastry or other casing in which game is served

croûte *n* a thick slice of fried bread serving as a base on which other foodstuffs are placed

crove *obs fm n* **cruive**

crowde *obs fm n/vb* **crowd** (in most senses)

crowdle *var fm dial vb* **croodle**

crowe *obs fm n/vb* **crow**

crowfoot *n* any of various plants *esp* some or even all species of buttercups but also *incl* such as the wild hyacinth (*pl*, in this sense only, **crowfoots**): a device consisting of small divergent cords passing through a wooden block and used to support an awning: a tool having a claw on its side and used to extract broken rods from a deep bore hole made by a miner: a mark on a drawing to indicate a limit of measurement: a type of embroidery stitch: a form of battery zinc used in a gravity cell: a caltrop in the military sense: a crow's foot in the sense of a wrinkle (*pl*, all other senses, **crowfeet**)

crow's foot *n* a laughter line or wrinkle at the corner of an eye (*pl* **crow's feet**)

crowl *obs vb* of the stomach, to rumble

cru *Ork & Shet n* a pen, yard or enclosure *esp* one for farm animals *Fr n* a vineyard or group of vineyards *Ork & Shet vb* to enclose or pen farm animals

cruces *pl* crux

cruddle *dial fm vb* **curdle**

crude (*adj*) *n* unrefined petroleum

cruells *var fm S n pl* **crewls**, the king's evil or scrofula

cruit *obs fm n* **cruet**

cruive *n* a wickerwork salmon trap used in rivers on the spawning routes *S n* a hovel: a pigsty *Ork n* an enclosed kitchen garden

crume *obs fm vb* **crumb**

crump *n* a hunchback *vb* of horses and pigs, to make their typical chewing noises: of people, to make a similar sound when walking over slightly frozen snow *S & dial adj* of food, crumbly

crunk *now dial vb* to utter a harsh, croaking cry *dial n* such a cry

crunt *S dial n* a blow on the head

cruor *n* coagulated blood

crupe *var fm n* **croup**, a horse's rump

cruse *n* a small earthenware vessel *esp* one used for liquids

cruset *n* a gold or silversmith's crucible

crusie *S n* a small oil lamp

crusta *n* a hard coating: a piece of prepared inlay: an alcoholic drink served in a glass with a sugar coated rim (*pl* **crustae**)

Crustacea *n pl* a very large class of mainly marine animals *incl* such as barnacles, crabs, crayfish, krill, lobsters, prawns, sandhoppers, shrimps, water fleas and woodlice together with a great number of creatures which have no common or popular names. Most, apart from land crabs, woodlice and the parasitic forms (often only recognized as crustaceans by their larvae), can be loosely described as aquatic arthropods breathing by gills or by their general body surface and having two pairs of feelers on their heads.

crustae *pl* crusta, a hard coating

crustal *adj* of, pertaining to or consisting of a crust

cruste *obs fm n* **crust**

crux *n* a cross: the essential point (*pl* **cruces, cruxes**)

crwth *n* an ancient Celtic musical instrument consisting of four strings played by bow and a further two strings which were plucked

cryer *arch fm n* **crier**

cryne *obs fm S n* **crine**

cryogen *n* a substance used for the production of low temperatures: a freezing mixture

cryptarithmetic *n* a mathematical puzzle in which the solver is asked to substitute numerals for letters. The following examples, devised by the writer, illustrate the art of using a humorous or apt statement to make the puzzle e.g. proving that two WRONGS do make a RIGHT or having one's money (OOF) in pounds (£):–

				NINE		3134
££	or	55		NINE	or	3134
££+		55+		NINE+		3134+
OOF		110		HELP		9402

				FACET		16093
WRONG	or	24153		FACET	or	16093
WRONG+		24153+		FACET+		16093+
RIGHT		48306		WHOLE		48279

Whilst the above are fairly simple to solve, the following is much more complex and is really for one with a mathematical bent. It involves the appreciation of the clue contained in the cryptic punning anagram of '*draw backward the backward drawback*'.

```
  DRAW
 -WARD
 ------
  BACK   Given that B+A+C+K=BY
 ------  and that B+Y=K
```

The words DRAW and WARD are anagrams, with either being the other written 'backward'. The 'drawback' is that the solver needs to know two mathematical curiosities before he or she can solve the puzzle. The first curiosity is that the reverse of any combination of two or more digits subtracted from the higher of the resultant two numbers always leaves a multiple of 9. Take a simple example. The digits 2 and 3 are chosen; if the lower (23) is subtracted from the higher (32) this gives the answer 9. Or, say 2 and 4. Subtracting 24 from 42 produces 18. This means that the puzzle answer of BACK must be a multiple of 9. The second mathematical curiosity is that the component digits of any multiple of 9 always add up to another multiple of 9. Thus BY must be a multiple of 9 and, therefore, K has to be 9. Knowing that K is 9 makes the rest of the solution comparatively simple.

```
  4523
 -3254
 ------
  1269   Given that 1+2+6+9=18
 ------  and that 1+8=9
```

(The technique of solving, together with the above set as puzzles without answers, is on page 179)

crypted *adj* vaulted

crystallomancy *n* divination by means of transparent bodies, most notably crystal gazing or scrying but also *incl* polished quartz and precious stones *esp* a beryl

ctenidium *n* a comblike respiratory organ of a mollusc (*pl* **ctenidia**)

ctenoid *adj* of the scales and teeth of certain fishes, resembling a comb

Ctesiphon *adj* designating an arch of an inverted shape hanging freely between two points of support with only gravity as an active force, such as the great ruined arch at Ctesiphon, on the Tigris southeast of Baghdad

cu *n* a fairy dog of great size (also see **cu sith**) *Obs fm n* cow (also see **cy, ky, kine**)

cubit *n* an ancient measure of length which varied from *approx* 18 to 22 inches and was based on the distance between the elbow to the fingertip (as, for example, a foot was the length of a man's foot, and an inch the length of a bent thumb from the knuckle to the tip)

cubomancy *n* divination by dice

cuckold *n* a term of contempt for the husband of an unfaithful wife (he being a cuckoo with his wife visiting another nest) *vb* to make a cuckold of

cucuja *n* the fire beetle, an insect of such luminosity that only a few of them in a bottle provide a night-light powerful enough to use for reading print. In 1520, when a Spanish force was being besieged in Mexico, it mistook the lights of cucujas for an army with matchlock muskets.

cue *n* the letter Q: in the theatre and allied performing arts, a scripted signal to a performer or others associated with the running of a performance to begin a specific course of action (also *fig*): apt humour or disposition: a pigtail or similar arrangement of hair: the tapering rod used in billiards and games developed from it *vb* to twist hair into a pigtail: to use a billiards cue

cueist *n* a skilful billiards or snooker player

cuesta *n* a hill ridge having one face steep and the other side gently sloped

cuffin *thieves' cant n* a man

cuffing *obs fm cant n* **cuffin**

cuirass *n* a piece of (leather) body armour: a piece of armour consisting of a breastplate and backplate still worn by some European cavalry regiments: a woman's close-fitting sleeveless bodice *vb* to protect (as) with a cuirass: to armourplate a ship

cuirasse *obs fm n* **cuirass**

cuisser *var fm S n* **cusser**

cuiter *S vb* to coddle

culch *var fm n* **cultch**

Culdee *n* an anchorite or religious hermit found in the East from the 4th century onwards: one of an Irish and Scottish order which began in the 8th century with men adopting a similar way of life but which order, over the centuries, gradually became the same as any other order of monks

cullery *n* the customary tenure of land or property peculiar to Carlisle

culpe *obs vb* to slice

cultch *n* the basic material, such as stones or old shells, of an oyster bed

culter *now dial fm n* **coulter**

cultivar *n* a cultivated variety of a plant

cumarin *var fm n* **coumarin**

cumber *vb* to hamper, hinder: embarrass: burden

cumberer *n* one who or that which encumbers

cumbre *obs fm vb* **cumber**

cummer *S n* a godmother: a female companion, a gossip: the *fem* equivalent of a fellow

cuneal *adj* wedge-shaped

cunner *n* either of two fishes, the gilthead wrasse or the blue perch *var fm arch n* **conner**

cupel *n* a shallow porous vessel made of bone ash and used in the assaying of gold and silver: a movable hearth of a furnace in which gold or silver is separated from a base metal *vb* to assay in a cupel: to separate from a base metal (*infl fms*:– British, **cupelled**/**-lling**: US, **cupeled**/**-ling**)

cupid *n* a figure similar to the traditional representation of Cupid or his Greek counterpart, Eros *US n* a jam tart

cuple *now dial fm n/vb* **couple**

cupola *n* a dome on a building *esp* a small, pointed or bulbous dome: the ceiling of a dome: a smelting furnace *vb* to furnish with a cupola

cupper *n* one who performs the medical operation of drawing blood by scarifying the skin and applying a cupping glass to that part

cupping glass *n* a surgeon's glass vessel having an open cup-shaped mouth, the air in which is rarefied by heat

cupreous *adj* of, of the nature of, consisting of or containing copper: copper-like, copper coloured

cuprite *n* red oxide of copper

curat *obs fm n* **curate**

curateship *n* the office or position of a curate *nonce n* the personality of a curate

curatory *n* the office of a curator

curdy *adj* full of curds or curd-like coagulations: curd-like: of such as salmon, full of the fatty substance (known as curd) found between the flakes of flesh after boiling (*comp* **curdier** *sup* **curdiest**)

curets *obs fm n* **cuirass**

curialist *n* a member of The Curia or papal court: one who supports its policy or authority

curie *n* a unit of radioactivity measured by the disintegrations per second

curiet *obs fm n* **cuirass**

curiosa *n pl* strange or unusual objects: erotic or pornographic literature

curlet *n* a ringlet or little curl

curpel *var fm S n* **curple**

curple *S n* a strap which passes under the tail of a horse: the rump or posterior

curr *vb* to make a gentle humming sound *n* such a sound

curre *obs n* a chariot

curret *obs fm n* **cuirass**

cursal *adj* of or belonging to a course

cursee *nonce n* one who is cursed

curset *obs fm adj* **curst** or **cursed**

cursive *adj* of or relating to handwriting or a typeface in the style of handwriting *n* a cursive letter or printing type

cursor *n* a sliding part of a measuring instrument: a movable point of light used to pinpoint specific positions on a visual display unit

Cursores *n pl* a now defunct term for the flightless birds (*sing*, never used, **cursor**)

curste *obs fm adj* **curst** or **cursed**

cursus *n* the Latin for **course**, used in English for such as a racecourse or an academic curriculum

curtal *n* anything docked or cut short *esp* a horse with a docked tail: a type of short-barrelled cannon of the 16th/17th centuries: a (short-skirted) whore *adj* short, shortened or docked

curtation *n* the difference between the true and the shortened distance (produced by projection upon a plane of the ecliptic) of two heavenly bodies

curte *obs fm n* **court**

curter *comp adj* curt

curtest *sup adj* curt

curtilage *n* now essentially only a legal term (but see **courtledge**) for the land which comprises the total associated with a residence, i.e. the land covered by the dwelling and any outbuildings together with the garden

curvet *n* in a display such as that of the Spanish Riding School of Austria, a leap by a horse standing on its rear legs *vb* to perform such a leap

curvital *adj* of or pertaining to curvature

cushat *n* the wood pigeon

cu sith *n* a dark-green coloured fairy dog of the Scottish Highlands, the size of a two year old bullock (also see **cait sith**)

cuspate *adj* having a pointed end

cuspid *n* a tooth such as a canine tooth having only one point

cusser *S fm n* **courser**, a stallion

custode *n* a custodian (*pl* **custodi**) *obs n* a vessel used for the preservation of a sacred object (*pl* **custodes**)

custos *n* a custodian

custrel *n* an attendant on a man-at-arms *esp* on a knight

cuter (*comp adj*) *var fm S vb* **cuiter**

cutesy *US adj* self-consciously cute (*comp* **cutesier** *sup* **cutesiest**)

cuth *var fm Ork & Shet n* **cooth**, an immature coalfish

cuthe *obs fm now S & dial vb* **kithe** or **kythe**, to make known (by action)

cutie *n* an attractive girl

cutler *n* a maker of or dealer in knives

cutline *n* a caption *esp* one for an illustration

cutling *n* a small piece cut off something: coarse oatmeal *dial n* the making of cutlery

cutte *var fm n* **cut**, a lot such as one's lot in the drawing of straws

cutter (*n*) *dial vb* to whisper: to coo like a dove: to fondle

cuttle *n* the cuttlefish, a marine mollusc related to the squid and the octopus with two large eyes and a large brain in its well-defined head. It is quite capable of learning, having proved its intelligence in scientific tests. The cuttle has eight arms and two retractile tentacles surrounding its mouth. It has an amazingly rich repertoire of colour changes which it uses both for camouflage and as a courtship display when both the male and female adopt a zebra-like pattern on their bodies. It can also eject a defensive ink, known to artists for many centuries as sepia. During mating, the male transfers his packets of sperm to the female with his fourth left arm. *local n* a pleat in cloth *obs n* a knife *local vb* to fold cloth into pleats (the usage in this sense of *n/vb* being confined to the Yorkshire textile trade, it is not a *dial* term)

cwm *n* a natural ampitheatre caused by glacial erosion *Welsh n* a deep (narrow) valley

cwn *pl obs n* ci

cy *Obs n pl* cows

cyanogen *n* a colourless, intensely poisonous gas having an almondlike odour and burning with a purple flame

cyanosis *n* a livid bluish colour of the skin caused by a disordered circulation of the blood (*pl* **cyanoses**)

cyanotic *adj* pertaining to (the nature of) cyanosis: affected with cyanosis

cyanuret *n* cyanide

cye *var fm Obs n pl* **cy**

cylindrite *n* a compound of antimony, lead, sulphur and tin

cymar *n* a chemise: a chimer (as worn by a bishop)

cypher *var fm n/vb* **cipher**

cypris *n* a species of bivalved barnacle (*pl* **cyprides**)

cystidean *n* an extinct creature rather like a sea urchin

cystoid *adj* of the nature of a cyst *n* a cyst

cytase *n* a digestive enzyme found in the seeds of certain plants

cythe *obs fm n* **scythe**

cytisine *n* a poisonous substance extracted from the ripe seeds of the laburnum

cytoid *adj* cell-like in the biological sense *n* a cell

czar *n* the caesar or emperor of Russia (the *var fms*, **tsar** or **tzar**, also apply to the related words which follow)

czarate *n* the office of czar

czardom *n* the dominion and power of a czar: czarate

czarevitch *n* a son of the czar (the eldest son being the **cesarevitch**)

czarevna *n* a daughter of the czar (the wife of the eldest son being the **cesarevna** – see **czarevitch**)

czarian *adj* czarish

czaric *adj* czarish

czarina *n* the wife of the czar

czarish *adj* of or pertaining to the czar

czarism *n* the system of government which centred on the czar

czarist *n* a supporter of the Imperial Russian system of government headed by the czar

czarlet *n* a petty czar (usually in the *var fm* **tsarlet**)

czarship *n* czarate

D

da *n* ambary, an East Indian fibre plant: **dah** or **dao**, a heavy Burmese knife *dial n* **daa** or **dah**, father *Shet vb* to live: to experience

daa *var fm dial n* **da**

dablet *obs n* a little devil, an imp

dabster *collq n* an expert

dacite *n* a greenstone

dacker *S & dial vb* to saunter: to vacillate: to suffer a relapse in sickness: to potter about *dial vb* to shake to and fro (the *var fms*, **daiker** and **daker**, apply to both the *S & dial vb* and the *dial vb*)

dacoit *n* one of a gang of armed robbers of India and Burma *vb* to plunder as a dacoit

dacre *obs fm n* **dicker**, the number 10

dad (*n*) *n* the fifteenth letter of the Arabic alphabet

daddle *dial n* the hand *dial vb* to toddle like a child: to dawdle: to saunter: to cheat or trick

daedal *adj* skilful

daemon *n* a spirit for good, such as the one who inspired Socrates, but, also *arch fm n* **demon**

daftie *collq n* a silly person

dag *n* a type of heavy pistol: the simple, straight horn of young stag *dial n* a clot of dirty wool at the hindquarters of a sheep: a small projecting stump of a branch: dew, a wet fog, a gentle rain, mist *obs n* an aiglet *now dial vb* to clog with dirt *dial vb* to cut off a sheep's dags: to drizzle: to sprinkle *obs vb* to shoot with a dag: to cut the edge of a garment into long pointed jags

Dagbane *var fm n* **Dagomba**

daggle *vb* to draggle: to walk in a slovenly way *esp* when muddy underfoot: to wet by sprinkling

dago *n* a term of disrespect for one of Latin origin (*pl* **dagoes, dagi** (*humorous*))

Dagomba *n* a language spoken in Ghana (technically, a Gur language of the Western Sudanic sub-group of the Niger-Congo family of languages)

dahl *var fm n* **dhal**

daiblet *S fm obs n* **dablet**

daidle *S n* a pinafore *S & dial vb* to saunter or move in a lazy or slovenly manner

daiker *S vb* to bedeck *var fm S & dial vb* **dacker**

daimen *S adj* rare, occasional

dain *S adj* repellent *now dial adj* repulsive, stinking: haughty, reserved *now dial n* a repulsive smell *obs n* dislike, disdain, distrust *obs vb* to disdain

dainer *comp now dial adj* dain

daint *obs adj* dainty

daker *var fm n* **dicker**, a set of ten *var fm S & dial vb* **dacker**

dal *n* the eighth letter of the Arabic alphabet *var fm n* **dhal**

dalder *obs fm n* **dollar**

dale (*n*) *dial fm n/vb* **dole**

daleir *obs fm n* **dollar**

daler *obs fm n* **dollar**

daleth *n* the fourth letter of the Hebrew alphabet

dalie *obs fm vb* **dally**

dallier *n* one who, without serious regard for the consequences, plays or trifles with anything: one who spends time frivolously: a flirt

daltin see **kerne**

Daltonian *adj* of or pertaining to John Dalton (1766–1844), the English scientist who originated the modern atomic theory, or to that atomic theory (note: It does *not* relate to colour blindness) *n* one who suffers from red-green colour blindness (an affliction suffered by Dalton who was the first to appreciate it as a deficiency)

daltonism *n* red-green colour blindness

daman *see* **hyrax**

damar *var fm n* **dammar**

dambre *obs fm n* **dammar**

Damian *masc pers n* meaning 'one who tames'

Damien *masc pers n* meaning 'one who tames'

dammar *n* a copal or hard resin obtained from various conifer trees for the manufacture of varnish

dammer *var fm n* **dammar**

damned *adj* damnable (*comp* **damneder** *sup* **damnedest**)

damner *n* one who damns

damosel *n* a damsel or young unmarried woman

dander *n* the fermenting of molasses: dandruff *S n* a cinder, a lump of slag: a stroll *US collq & dial n* anger *S & dial vb* to stroll, to wander without purpose

Dandie *var fm masc pers n* **Andrew**

dangeir *obs S fm n* **danger**

danger (*n*) *obs vb* to endanger: to make liable

dangier *obs S fm n* **danger**

danglet *dial n* an icicle

Daniel *n* a wise judge *masc pers n* meaning 'God is judge'

danio *n* any of several species of brightly-coloured perch-like small fishes which swim in shoals in the rivers of Southern India and southeast Asia. Their numbers include one called **zebrafish**, a different species to the American darter of the same name. (*pl* **danios**)

Danite *n* a member of an early Mormon secret society

dank (*adj*) *now dial vb* to damp (*lit/fig*): to drizzle *obs vb* to become damp

danke *obs fm now dial vb* **dank**

danker *comp adj* dank

dannet *dial fm n* **do-nought**

dannot *dial fm n* **do-nought**

danse *obs fm vb* **dance**

danser *obs fm n* **dancer**

danseur *n* a male ballet dancer

danseuse *n* a female (ballet) dancer

dante *n* the South American tapir, a shy ungulate akin to the rhino

Dantean *adj* sublime or austere (after the style of Dante Alighieri, the great classical poet (1265–1321))

danter *obs S fm n* **daunter**

dantie *obs S fm adj* **dainty**

Dantist *n* a scholar of Dante (see **Dantean**)

danton *var fm S vb* **daunton**, to subdue, intimidate, tame, dare

daper *var fm obs n* **dapper**

daple *obs fm vb* **dapple**

dapper (*adj comp*+er *sup*+est) *obs n* a neat tidy fellow

dar *obs fm vb* **dare**

Darazi *n* one of a fanatical, basically Muslim, sect which has Gnostic elements and is found in parts of Syria and the Lebanon (*pl* **Druse, Druz** or **Druze**) (note: The word, Darazi, is the name of one of the 11th century AD founders of this sect and the various *pl fms* are also used as the basic *n sing*)

darbies *slg n pl* handcuffs

Dargin *n* a Dagestan language spoken in parts of the Caucasus region of the USSR

dargle *n* a dell

darices *obs pl* daric, an ancient Persian gold coin

dariole *n* a dish comprising a shell of pastry and filling: a shell of pastry

dark (*adj*/*n*) *arch vb* to cloud, dim or obscure

darkey *n* old-fashioned offensive term for a negro

darkle *vb* of the dark, to grow/render/become/lie in/conceal oneself in

darndest *see* **darned**

darned (*adj*) *corrupt fm* (*mainly US*) *adj* **damned** (*comp* **darneder** *sup* **darndest, darnedest**)

darnel *n* any of several grasses which grow as weeds in European and Asian grain fields

Darrel *masc pers n* meaning 'darling'

darshan *n* in Hindu belief, a blessing which is conferred by seeing or touching a holy person

darte *obs fm n* **dart**

darter *n* one who throws a dart: a person or animal given to darting movement: any of various species of North American freshwater perch-like fish *incl* the **Johnny darter**, the **Eastern sand darter** and the **log perch** or **zebrafish** (not the same as the **danio**, also called zebrafish) *pl* a group of aquatic birds which look like elongated cormorants, the typical species of which is the **anhinga**, also known as the **snakebird** or (USA) the **water turkey**

dartle *vb* to move or dart rapidly

dartre *n* a skin disease such as herpes

Darwen *n* a Lancashire town three miles south of Blackburn

dasel *obs fm n*/*vb* **dazzle**

dasher *n* one who or that which dashes: one who 'cuts a dash': the black velvet hunting cap

dashy *adj* stylish (*comp* **dashier** *sup* **dashiest**)

dasle *obs fm n*/*vb* **dazzle**

dasling *obs fm n* **dazzling**

dassel *obs fm n*/*vb* **dazzle**

dassie see **hyrax**

dastard *n* a mean, despicable coward *esp* one performing malicious acts without putting himself at risk *obs vb* to make a dastard of

daster *obs var fm n* **dastard**

dastur *var fm n* **destour**

dataria *var fm n* **datary**

datary *n* an officer of the papal court concerned with documents directly issued by the pope (*pl* **dataries**)

Datchet *n* a town in Buckinghamshire

date line *n* a short *fm* of International Date Line

dateline *n* a (newspaper) line giving the date *vb* to submit a news item with a time stating the date and place of origin

dative *adj*/*n* in the grammar of English and other advanced Indo-European languages, that case of a noun, pronoun or adjective denoting the indirect object, i.e. that *to* whom or *for* whom the action of the verb is directed: in law (US as well as English), that which may be disposed of at pleasure: in Scottish law, that given by legal authority

datum line *n* the horizontal baseline from which heights or depths are measured

datum plane *n* the horizontal line from which heights and/or depths are measured

daturine *n* a poisonous substance found in the thorn apple or jimson weed

daunder *var fm S & dial n/vb* **dander**, (to) stroll

dauner *var fm S n/vb* **dander**, (to) stroll

daunter *n* one who daunts *obs n* one who breaks horses

dautie *S n* a term of endearment

davit *n* one of a pair of cranelike devices on a ship for the lowering or hoisting of a lifeboat

Davy *n* the miner's safety lamp invented by Sir Humphry Davy

dawner *var fm S & dial vb* **dander**

dawtie *var fm S n* **dautie**

dayfly *n* an ephemerid, an insect which lives for only a few hours in its final, perfect state

dayset *obs n* sunset

dayward *adj/adv* towards the day

de *prep* of: from *n* the bebization equivalent of **mi** *dial n* day

dead (*n/adj*) note: Surprisingly enough the *comp* **deader** and *sup* **deadest** are quite valid

deader *comp adj* dead *slg n* a corpse *obs n* one who or that which deadens

deafer *comp adj* deaf

deafly *adv* in a deaf manner

deame *dial fm n* **dame** *obs fm vb* **deem**

deane *var fm obs n* **dain**

deaner *slg n* a shilling

deanery *n* the office of a dean: his residence: that group of parishes under the authority of a rural dean

deanship *n* the rank or the (tenure of the) office of a dean

dear (*adj/adv/interj/n*) *nonce vb* to address as 'dear' *obs vb* to endear *obs S vb* to make expensive

dearch *obs S fm n/vb* **dwarf**

dearling *obs fm n/adj* **darling**

dearm *obs vb* to disarm

dearn *arch n* secrecy *arch adj* secret *obs fm vb* **darn**

dearth (*n*) *obs vb* to create a scarcity

dearther *obs n* one causing a dearth

deasil *adv* clockwise *n* movement in a clockwise direction as a superstitious practice among Scots, whereby they echo the ancient Celtic belief in the good fortune attendant upon following the apparent course of the sun. Such movement manifests itself as (*a*) a wedding or baptismal procession moving clockwise round a church (*b*) walking in this direction around an ancient rock (*c*) moving clockwise privately, anywhere. (*var fms adv/n incl* **deiseal**, **deasiul**, **deasoil**)

deasiul *var fm adv/n* **deasil**

deasoil *var fm adv/n* **deasil**

deave *S & dial vb* to deafen: to stupefy or worry (with noise)

debarb *obs vb* to remove a beard

debark *vb* to disembark: to strip bark from timber

debile *arch adj* weak, feeble

deblai *n* a supplementary defence of a ditch as a by-product of removing earth to form ramparts

deblet *Obs fm obs n* **dablet**

deboner *US n* one who or that which removes bones

debosh *now S fm vb* **debauch**

debowel *obs vb* to bowel

debtee *n* one to whom the debt is owed

decadi *n* the tenth and final day of the 'week' of the French Revolutionary calendar. Three 'weeks', called decades, constituted a month and decadi was the day of rest, a sort of metric atheistic Sunday. (See **FRENCH REVOLUTIONARY CALENDAR**)

decagram *n* a weight of ten grammes

decaid *Obs S vb* to fail

decal *n* a transfer (of a picture)

decalet *nonce n* a stanza of ten lines

decamp *vb* to break up a (military) camp: to depart suddenly and rapidly

decan *n* the ruler of ten degrees of a zodiacal sign *obs n* a ruler of ten

decanal *adj* of a dean or deanery: decani

decane *n* a paraffin found in coal tar *obs fm n* **decan**

decani *adj* of the south side of the choir where the dean sits (also see **cantoris**)

decarb *var fm collq vb* **decoke**, to decarbonise (a car engine)

decare *n* 1,000 square metres

decart *vb* to remove from a cart *obs S vb* to reject a card

decastere *n* the measure of ten steres (ten cubic metres)

decemvir *n* a ruling body of ten (*pl* **decemviri, decemvirs**)

decener *obs n* one in command of ten troops: the head of or a member of a group of ten householders

decenier *var fm obs n* **decener**

decennial *adj* of or pertaining to a period of ten years *US n* an anniversary of ten years: the celebration of such

deceper *obs vb* to sever, to disunite

decern *vb* to discriminate between: in Scottish law, to judge: to decree

decerne *obs fm vb* **decern**

decerp *obs vb* to extract (*pa pple* **decerpt, decerped**)

decharm *obs vb* to counter the effects of a magic spell

decile *n* the astrological aspect of two planets when distant from each other a tenth part of the zodiac

decimater *var fm n* **decimator**

decimator *n* one who decimates

deciner *var fm obs n* **decener**

decinor *var fm obs n* **decener**

decipher see **CODES AND CIPHERS**

decistere *n* one tenth of a stere

decker *n* one who adorns: a vehicle or ship having a specified number of decks: a gun of a specified deck of a ship (e.g. a lower decker, a gun of the lower deck)

declar *Obs fm vb* **declare**

declinal *adj* bending downward

decoit *var fm n* **dacoit**

decollate *vb* to behead

decolor *var fm vb* **decolour**

decolour *vb* to deprive of colour

decorist *nonce n* one attached to the proprieties prevailing in artistic taste

decount *obs vb* to reckon

decourt *obs vb* to banish from court

decreate *obs implied vb* this word is not known to exist as such, but is implied by the *obs n* **decreator**, one who destroys that which he originally created (GAME PLAYER'S note: The use of this word in any word game has to be a matter of personal judgment. No precedent is known to exist in the rulings of any games, which are used as precedents for other judgments. Detailed word rules arise as a game becomes popular and attracts a following of *serious* players. Though the writer has devised both the pencil and paper word game, **Pentery Web**, and the anagram card game, **Pelham** (see respective entries), he would not wish to pronounce on the validity of words of this type for either game. Instead, should either attract a serious following, he would much prefer to abide by the popular decision, this being the basis of all the detailed word rules.)

decreet *arch S n* a final judgment of a Scottish civil court *obs vb* to decree: to decide

decreit *obs fm arch S n* **decreet**

decret *Obs fm arch S n* **decreet**

decretal *adj* pertaining to a decree *n* a papal decree

decrete *n* a decision given by a Roman emperor on a judicial matter

decretist *n* one versed in papal law

decrial *adj* open disparagement

decrown *vb* to deprive of the crown

decrypt *vb* to decode (see **CODES AND CIPHERS**)

Dectra® *n* a long-range modification of the Decca® Navigator System used by airlines

decurse *obs n* downward course (of time)

decurt *obs vb* to shorten *obs adj* short

decuss *vb* to divide in the form of an X

dedal *var fm obs n* **daedal**, a maze or labyrinth: a skilful fabricator

dedans *n* a screened gallery for spectators of real tennis, the original game which is still played in special courtyards: the spectators

dedeign *obs S vb* to lower

dedigne *obs vb* to disdain

dee *n* the letter D: a D-shaped object *vb* using the pronunciation of the letter D as a euphemism for damn, to damn

deeding *obs n* actual doing

deele *obs fm n/vb* **deal**

deeme *obs fm n* **dime** *obs fm vb* **deem**

deemer *n* one who judges *obs n* a judge in the legal sense

deene *obs fm n* **dean**, the clergyman *Obs fm n* **din**

deep (*n/adj/adv*) *vb* to deepen

deer (*n*) *var fm obs vb* **dere**

deere *obs fm adj* **dear**

deerlet *n* a tiny deer

deer lick *n* a small spring or piece of damp ground impregnated with various salts which deer frequently lick

deerling *obs fm n* **darling**

deer mouse *n* any of various species of North American mice very similar in appearance and behaviour to the various European woodmice (*pl* **deer mice**)

deese *dial n* a place where herrings are dried *dial vb* to dry herrings

deevil *S fm n* **devil**

defail *obs vb* to become weak: to decay: to defeat

defalk *arch vb* to cut or lop off: to deduct or subtract

defarm *obs vb* to take away possession of property

defedate *obs vb* to defile, pollute

defial *n* defiance

defier *n* one who defies or challenges

defilade *vb* to plan and arrange defensive fortifications to provide protection not only from enemy fire but also from the return fire of one's own forces stationed to the rear *n* the act of defilading

deflater *var fm n* **deflator**, one who deflates

deflex *adj* bent downwards

deflorate *vb* to strip a plant of its flowers *Obs vb* to deflower a woman

deflow *obs vb* to flow away (as a bodily fluid flowing away from a puncture of the skin)

deflux *obs n* a flowing down *obs vb* to flow down

defoil *vb* to crush, oppress (the *n* **defoiling** is now *obs*) *var fm vb* **defoul**

deforce *vb* in law, to wrongfully prevent by using violence the legitimate owner from possessing something: to deprive or withhold wrongfully: in Scottish law, to prevent by force an official performing his legitimate duty

deforest *vb* to change, by law, the status of a piece of land from that of forest to ordinary land: to strip of trees

deforme *obs fm arch adj* **deform,** ugly or hideous

defoul *vb* to befoul, defile (the *ns*, **defouler** and **defouling** are both *obs*)

defund *obs vb* to pour down

degasser *n* one who removes gas from

degast *obs n* devastation, ruin

degerm *vb* to remove the germ, or rudiment of a new organism, from such as wheat

degras *n* a fat obtained from a sheepskin

degreed *adj* having an academic degree

degum *vb* to remove the gum from (i.e. to nullify the adhesive quality)

degust *vb* to taste *esp* to appreciate the savour

dehiscence *n* the bursting open of such as a pod at the natural time for seed dispersal

dehorn *vb* to remove the horns from: to prune (a tree)

dehors *prep* in legal usage, not within the scope of *obs n* any fortification beyond the main defensive barrier

dehort *vb* to give earnest advice against

deicer *US fm n* **de-icer**, a mechanical or thermal device for the prevention or removal of ice: a substance used for this purpose

deid *S & dial fm adj/n* **dead** *S & dial fm ns* **death, deed**

deign *vb* to consider that to do a particular thing is fit or worthy of oneself: to condescend *arch vb* to vouchsafe

deigne *obs fm vb* **deign**

deine *obs fm vb* **deign**

Deirdre *var fm fem pers n* **Derdriu**, meaning 'The Raging One'

deiseal *var fm adv/n* **deasil**

deism *n* any of various metaphysical concepts which accept the existence of God but reject divine revelation

deist *n* one who accepts any of the various deisms

dejector *n* one who dejects

dekarch *n* a ruling body of ten

deking *obs vb* to dethrone

delabe *obs vb* to glide down

delace *obs vb* to untie

delaine *n* a light textile fabric used for women's dresses

delait *obs S fm vb* **delate**

delapse *arch vb* to fall or slip, descend, sink (*lit/fig*) *obs n* falling down, descent

delare *Obs fm n* **dealer**

delash *obs S vb* to fire (an arrow)

delate *vb* to accuse, to charge with a crime, to impeach: to inform against, to denounce (*obs S fms incl* **delait, deleat.** Delate has a special connection with Scottish ecclesiastical courts.)

delation *n* an accusation, a denouncement: criminal information: in Roman law, a handing down

delator *n* an informer *esp* one who makes a profession of it

dele *vb* in proof-reading, to instruct the deletion of a letter or word scored in the text and recorded in the margin by the symbol, ₰

deleat *obs S fm vb* **delate**

delenda *n pl* items for deleting

delf *n* an excavation: a drainage canal in the fen district: a quarry (*pl*, in these senses together with the *obs n* given below, **delfs, delves**): **delft** or **Delftware**, a type of glazed earthenware from Delft, Holland (*pl* **delfs, delfts** or **Delftwares**) *obs n* a grave *obs fm vb* **delve**, to dig

Delian *adj* pertaining to the Greek island Delos, the birthplace of Apollo and Artemis, where a classical oracle was consulted

delible *adj* capable of being deleted (*lit/fig*)

delice *obs n* delight, joy, (sensual) pleasure: a dainty

deligation *n* the tying of such as an artery with a ligature

delineator *n* one who sketches or depicts: an implement used for tracing outlines

delirate *obs vb* to become delirious or mad

deliria *pl* delirium

deliriant *adj* having the capacity to produce delirium *n* such a drug

delisk *Ir fm n* **dulse**

delit *obs fm n* **delight**

delite *obs fm n/vb* **delight**

dell (*n*) *obs fm n/vb* **deal**

deloo *n* a savannah-dwelling species of duiker which is found from Ethiopia down to South Africa. It is one of the smallest of these very small antelopes and is also known as the bush or grey duiker. (Also see **duiker**)

deltaic *adj* of, pertaining to, forming a delta

deltan *obs adj* of the Nile delta

delute *obs vb* to daub with moist clay

demaim *obs vb* to maim, mutilate

demain *var fm n* **demesne**

demaine *obs fm vb* **demean**, in the sense of to behave oneself in a specific manner

demane *S fm* (*now obs*) *obs vb* **demean**, to illtreat

demarcate *vb* to mark off or limit

demark *vb* to demarcate, to determine or mark off limits or boundaries *obs vb* demarque, to obliterate

deme *n* one of the districts in which the ten tribes of Attica (classical ancient Greece based on Athens) were divided in the 6th century BC: in modern Greece, a commune *obs fm vb* **deem**

demean *vb* to behave or comport oneself in a specific manner: to lower (oneself) in status, reputation, character or condition *obs vb* to express or exhibit emotion: to manage or employ: to rule or govern: to illtreat

demeanor *US fm n* **demeanour**

dement *arch adj* demented, insane *n* one who is demented or insane *vb* to drive insane

dementi *n* a denial or contradiction (*pl* **dementis**)

dementia *n* mental disorder involving the impairment of coherent thought resulting from an organic or functional breakdown (*pl* **dementias**)

demerse *obs vb* to immerse, submerge

demersion *n* immersion: drowning

demesne *n* the privately used part of a manorial estate as distinct from the complete estate with its tenanted farms etc: an owner-possessed estate not subject to tenancy

demess *obs vb* to reap

Demeter *pers n* the Greek goddess of corn and agriculture

demies *pl* demy

demilance *n* a lance with a short shaft: one armed with such

demirep *n* a woman of dubious character or chastity

demirip *var fm n* **demirep**

demist *vb* to free (the windscreen of a car) from condensation

demit *vb* to lower: to dismiss: to resign

demount *vb* to remove from a mounting, setting or support *nonce vb* to descend *obs vb* to dismount

demot *n* a resident of a deme

demure (*adj*) *obs n* a demure expression *obs vb* to look with an affected modesty: to make demure

demy *n* a size of paper (*a*) printing paper, $17\frac{1}{2} \times 22\frac{1}{2}$ inches (*b*) writing paper, British $15\frac{1}{2} \times 20$ inches, USA 16×21 inches

dename *obs vb* to nominate

denar *n* any of various coins, the Roman denarius; the 16th/17th century Italian denaro; the 16th/17th century Spanish dinero; the Persian and East Indian dinar (an imaginary coin for accounting purposes during the days of the British Raj)

denare *var fm n* **denar**

denarie *var fm obs* n **denary**

denarius see **£ s d** (under **L**)

denary *adj* of ten: decimal *n* a tenth part *obs n* denarius, the Roman penny: (a group of) ten

denature *vb* to change the nature of anything *obs vb* to render unnatural

denaturise *var fm vb* **denaturize**, to alter the nature of something

dendrite *n* any rock or mineral with treelike markings

dendron *n* a branching process of a nerve cell which conducts impulses toward the cell body

dener *slg n* a shilling

denerel *n* the common small unit of dry measure in Guernsey, with three denerels to the cabot and two cabots to the bushel

denger *obs S fm n* **danger**

dengue *n* breakbone fever, an infectious, eruptive disease characterized by excruciating pains in the joints and originating from the bite of a species of mosquito

denies *infl vb* deny

Denise *fem fm masc pers n* **Denis** which, in turn, is a *var fm* of **Dionysus,** the Greek god of wine

denitrate *vb* to remove nitric acid, nitrogen or a nitrogen compound from

denkli *n* an Indian contrivance for raising water to be used for irrigation

dennet *n* a gig-like carriage, fashionable circa 1818–1830

denotate *vb* to denote

denotation *n* the act of denoting: a designation

denotic *adj* of deontology, the science of duty

densate *obs vb* to thicken, condense

dense (*adj*) *nonce vb* to make dense

denshire *vb* to improve land by clearing away the wild vegetation, burning it, and spreading the ashes over the same area (*obs fms incl* **devonshire**)

Densil *masc pers n* the meaning of which is obscure

densimeter *n* an apparatus for measuring specific gravity

dental (*adj*) *n* the letters D, N, T which in various languages, though not strictly English, are dental consonants i.e. the sound is produced by putting the tip of the tongue against the upper teeth: a species of Mediterranean fish: a type of shellfish

Dentalium *n* the genus of the tusk shell (*–cap*) *n* any species of this genus (*pl* **dentalia, dentaliums**)

Dentaria *n* a genus of plants *incl* the toothwort (*–cap*) *n* any plant of this genus

dentary *adj* dental *n* a bone in the jaw of various non-mammalian vertebrates

dente *obs fm n* **dainty**

dentel *var fm n* **dentil**

denter *obs fm n* **denture**, indentation

dentex *n* the largest of the Mediterranean species of sea breams and which occasionally reaches British shores

denticle *n* a small tooth or toothlike projection: a dentil

denties *pl* denty (*obs fm n* **dainty**)

dentil *n* any of the small teeth-like blocks of stone which form decorative moulding in architecture

dentile *n* a small toothlike projection on a seashell

dentin *var fm n* **dentine**

dentine *n* the tissue forming the bulk of a tooth

denunciate *vb* to denounce

deodar *n* a Himalayan cedar tree

depaint *arch vb* to paint: to paint with words

depant *obs fm arch vb* **depaint**

depass *vb* to pass beyond

depasture *vb* of cattle, to graze

depe *obs vb* to immerse

depeach *obs vb* to dispose of: to despatch *obs n* a despatched message

depeller *obs n* one who or that which dispels

deperte *obs fm vb* **depart**

depester *obs vb* to disentangle

depeter *n* plastered work with a finish of dressed stone or with a pebble-dashed effect

depilate *vb* to remove the hair from

depinge *obs vb* to portray

deplace *vb* to displace

depolish *vb* to remove the polish from

depone *vb* to declare upon oath

deposal *n* the act of deposing from office

deposite *arch fm n* **deposit** *obs fm vb* **deposit**

depost *obs n* deposit

depper *obs fm comp* **deeper**

deppest *obs fm sup* **deepest**

deppir *obs fm comp* **deeper**

depraver *n* a corrupter, perverter

depresser *obs fm n* **depressor**

deprise *obs vb* to undervalue

depurate *vb* to (become) free of impurities, to cleanse

depure *obs vb* to cleanse, to purify (*lit/fig*)

depurse *obs S vb* to pay or defray costs or expenses

deputer *n* one who deputes

der *Obs fm n* **deer** (also see **by**)

deraign *vb* old law, to vindicate *esp* by combat *obs n* (a challenge to) a duel or combat

derailer *n* one who or that which derails

derain *obs vb* to rain *obs fm vb* **deraign**

derate *vb* to reduce, in part or in full, a local rate

deration *vb* to cease rationing

Derdre *var fm fem pers n* **Deirdre**, which is derived from **Derdriu**, meaning 'The Raging One'

Derdriu *fem pers n* meaning 'The Raging One'

dere *obs vb* to harm, injure *obs n* harm, injury

dereling *obs fm n* **darling**

derham *var fm n* **dirhem**

derie *obs fm n* **derry** in the meaningless sense (see **derry**)

derivate *adj* derived

deriver *n* one who derives

derling *obs fm n* **darling**

derlinge *obs fm n* **darling**

dermal *adj* pertaining to the derma or true skin

dermatic *adj* pertaining to the skin

dermic *adj* pertaining to or consisting of skin

dermis *n* the derm, derma or corium, the true skin or deep inner layer beneath the epidermis

Dermot *dim masc pers n* **Diarmid,** meaning 'a freeman'

dern *now dial vb* to hide *var fm dial n* **durn** *arch adj* dark, sombre

derner *Obs n* the lintel of a door

dernful *adj* mournful

derob *obs vb* to plunder

derogation *n* the partial repeal of such as a law, treaty or legal right: the taking away of (part of) a person's power or authority: detraction from the reputation of: loss of rank

derout *n* a total and utter defeat *vb* to put (the enemy) completely to flight

derring *pseudo-arch infl vb* **dare** – found only as **derring do** (GAME PLAYER'S note: derring is invalid for play as it has no existence as an independent word. The literal translation of derring do is 'daring to do' and the actual meaning is desperate courage.)

derris *n* a tropical plant, the roots of which yield an insecticide

derry *n* one of the various meaningless words

such as 'nonny' which occur in the refrains of songs though, in this case, the word is extended to mean a ballad

deruet *pa pple Obs vb* **derve**, to trouble or molest

desalt *vb* to remove salt from

desalter *n* one who removes salt from

descanter *n* one who discourses

descrier *n* one who discovers

descry *vb* to cry out (against): to discover by observation (from a distance)

desent *obs fm vb* **dissent**

deserte *obs fm n/adj* **desert** (in all senses of either pronunciation)

desertic *adj* arid and barren

desilver *vb* to remove the silver from

desinent *adj* terminal

desiner *var fm obs n* **decener**

desk (*n*) *obs vb* to supply with a desk or desks: to place (as) in a desk

deslay *Obs fm vb* **delay**

desma *n* one of the spike-like forms of which the skeletal framework of a sponge is constructed: a bandage: a ligament (*pl* **desmas, desmata**)

desman *n* either of two species of aquatic insectivores, the **Russian desman**, the largest member of the mole family and twice the size of the 4″–5″ **Pyrenean desman** (*pl* **desmans**)

desmid *n* any of a family of bright-green freshwater algae

desmine *n* the mineral stilbite

desorb *vb* to release condensation from the surface of a solid (the opposite of **absorb**)

despairer *n* one without hope

desperse *obs fm vb* **disperse**

despite (*prep*) *arch n* contempt, scorn *arch vb* to show contempt for

despoile *obs fm vb* **despoil**

despond *arch n* despondency (often used in the expression **Slough of Despond**, meaning a period or a fit of great depression) *vb* to become depressed *obs vb* to betroth

desponder *n* one who loses heart or resolution

despose *obs vb* to depose

despotat *n* the territory of a despot

dess *S & dial n* a layer or stratum *dial vb* to arrange in layers: to cut in layers

destain *var fm arch vb* **distain**, to stain (*lit/fig*)

destate *obs vb* to divest of grandeur

dester *obs n* the right hand

destert *obs vb* to snort

destil *obs fm vb* **distil**

destin *obs n* destiny

destine *vb* of a supernatural power, to ordain that which will happen

destour *n* a Parsee chief priest

destrer *n* a warhorse

destrier *var fm n* **destrer**

detailer *n* one who relates circumstantially: one who gives details

detane *obs fm n* **dittany**, an aromatic, pink-flowered, Cretan plant once believed to have medicinal properties

detard *obs vb* to delay

detaste *obs vb* to loathe

detein *obs fm vb* **detain**

detent *n* the (spring-loaded) locking piece of a mechanism

deterge *vb* to cleanse *esp* a wound or a sore

deterre *obs vb* to disinter

deterse *obs vb* to clean

detersion *n* the act of (medical) cleansing

detort *vb* to untwist *obs vb* to twist

detrain *vb* to alight or discharge from a train *obs vb* to draw (with a pen or brush)

detrude *vb* to force down (*lit*/*fig*): to expel forcibly (*lit*/*fig*)

detruse *obs S vb* to detrude

detrusion *n* the action of thrusting downward or away (*lit*/*fig*)

detruss *obs vb* to spoil or plunder

dette *obs fm n* **debt**

detter *obs fm n* **debtor**

detur *n* at Harvard University, USA, a prize of a book annually awarded for merit to various students of different academic years

deturn *obs vb* to divert, to turn aside

Deubert *pers n* a proper name for a hare

deuton *obs fm n* **deuteron**, the nucleus of heavy hydrogen

devast *vb* to lay waste

devele *Obs fm n* **devil**

develler *S n* a boxer or pugilist

devest *arch vb* to annul any vested right

devil (*n*/*vb*) *infl fms* British, **devilled**/**-lling:** US, **deviled**/**-ling**

deviller *n* one who tends any of various machines known as a devil such as one in the cotton industry which tears open and cleans fibres prior to spinning: a machine which shakes rags: a literary hack

devil ray *n* any of a family of large ray-like fishes, some species of which grow to enormous size, even reaching 22 feet from tip to tip of the pectoral fins. A surface feeder, it is capable of leaving the water and sailing through the air. It is harmless to man.

devin *obs fm n*/*adj* **divine**

devine *obs fm n*/*vb* **divine**

devling *n* a junior devil

devoider *Obs n* one who expels or drives out

devoir *n* a dutiful act of respect *arch n* one's duty *obs vb* to endeavour

dew (*n*) *vb* to moisten *arch vb* to fall as dew

Dewali *var fm n* **Diwali**

dewan *n* a title used in the Moslem parts of the Indian sub-continent for various offices ranging from prime minister down to the steward of a large establishment but *esp* the financial minister of a state

dewani *n* the office of a dewan (financial minister)

dewater *vb* to remove the water from

dewess *obs n* a goddess

dewier *comp adj* dewy, moist with dew

dewing *n* the depositing of dew: a dampening (as) with dew: a light sprinkling

dewish *obs adj* moist, damp

dewitt *vb* to lynch or kill by mob violence

dewlap *n* a loose fold of skin hanging from beneath the throat of various animals such as dogs and cattle: a similar sight on the throat of an elderly person

dewle *obs fm arch n* **dole**, grief or sorrow

dew-ret *vb* to expose (flax) to the dew to achieve the softening effect alternatively provided by retting (see **ret**)

dew-rot *var fm vb* **dew-ret**

dew-rote *var fm vb* **dew-ret**

dha *n* a measure of area in the East Indies *approx* $\frac{2}{3}$ of an acre

dhal *n* a tropical shrub having edible pealike seeds (also called the **pigeon pea**): the seeds or a purée made from these seeds (also known as **pulse**)

dharna *n* a uniquely Indian method of debt collection by which the collector sits outside the house of the debtor and fasts until satisfaction is made. This form of emotional blackmail is also used to obtain other forms of redress.

dherna *var fm n* **dharna**

dhobi *n* an Indian washerman

dhole *n* the Asiatic wild dog, a fierce dog of great stamina which hunts in packs of up to 40 in number. Whilst a small pack would be no match against a tiger, large packs have been known to attack that great cat losing a dozen of their members in the fight which they win by sheer force of number.

dholl *var fm n* **dhal**

dhoti *n* the loincloth of male Indians

dhow *n* an Arab sailing vessel

dhurrie *n* a type of Indian cotton carpeting used as a general furnishing fabric

di *n* a musical tone between doh and re: the bobization equivalent of **mi**

diactine *adj* of a sponge spicule, having two rays pointed at both ends *n* a spicule with two rays

dialer *var fm n* **dialler**, a surveyor *US fm n* **dialler**, in any other sense

dialing *var fm n* **dialling**

dialler *n* one who uses a dial of some description: one surveying a mine with the aid of a compass

dialog *US fm n/vb* **dialogue** (*infl fms* **dialogged, dialogging**)

dialyse *vb* to separate any gluelike or jellylike substance from another substance where these substances have unequal diffusibility in true solution

dialysis *n* the separation of botanical parts previously or normally joined together: in chemistry, the separating of solutions of mixed substances by using moist membranes (*pl* **dialyses**)

dialytic *adj* pertaining to or of the nature of chemical dialysis

diamantine *adj* of the nature of or consisting of diamond *n* a substance such as crystallized boron used as a steel polishing powder

diametre *obs fm n* **diameter**

diamyl *n* the organic alcohol radical, amyl, in the free state *adj* having two amyl groups

diapase *poet fm n* **diapason**, a burst of harmonious sound: a whole octave: a bass part

diapente *n* in ancient and mediaeval music, the interval of a fifth: in old pharmacy, a medicament having five ingredients

diaper *n* a textile fabric having a basic weave of lines crossing in a diamond formation: that pattern: a towel or napkin having this weave: a baby's nappy of this weave *US n* a baby's nappy of any sort *her n* a pattern on a shield similar to diaper *vb* to cover the surface of anything with the diaper pattern

diarise *var fm vb* **diarize**, to record in a diary

Diasone *n* a proprietary medicament used in the treatment of leprosy

diaspore *n* an aluminium hydroxide of various colours and sometimes translucent

diastema *n* an interval in ancient Greek music: a naturally occurring gap between the teeth of various mammals (*pl* **diastemata**)

diaster *n* a stage in mitosis

diastole *n* the regular expansion or dilation of the heart and of the arteries: a corresponding motion in simple creatures: in Greek and Latin prosody, the lengthening of a naturally short syllable (see **metric foot**)

diastyle *adj* of an architectural construction, having columns about three diameters apart *n* such a building or colonnade

diatom *n* a marine and freshwater plankton of a family of microscopic green algae

diatonic *adj* designating any musical scale of five tones and two semitones

diaxon *adj* of sponge spicules, having two axis-cylinder processes *n* a nerve cell with two extremities

dibber *n* a dibble *US n* an iron dibble used by miners

dibble *n* a gardener's implement, of varying construction and simplicity, used for making holes in the ground *vb* to make such holes: to plant by this method

dibbler *n* one who dibbles: a (mechanical) dibble *var fm now dial n* **doubler**

dibler *S fm now dial n* **doubler**, a large plate

dic *Obs fm ns* **ditch, dike** (see **lich**)

dicentra *n* any of a genus of plants having drooping heart-shaped flowers

dicken *obs n* a water fowl

dickens *collq n* the devil

dicker *n* the number 10 *esp* as half a score, a unit of exchange in various commodities *US n* barter, petty bargaining *US vb* to barter or exchange

dictature *n* dictatorship: a body of dictators

didder *now dial vb* to tremble or shake

diedral *var fm adj* **dihedral**, formed by or having two intersecting planes

dièdre *n* a (cracked) rock angle

diener *var fm slg n* **dener**

diesis *n* in music, the difference in tone between a major and a minor semitone: in printing, the double dagger sign ‡ (*pl* **dieses**)

diester *n* a type of chemical compound

diestrus *n* a period of sexual inactivity (*pl* **diestruses**)

dietist *n* one professing to be an authority on diet

digestor *var fm n* **digester**

diggle *dial vb* to grow thickly together

dighter *now dial n* one who winnows corn

digitiser *var fm n* **digitizer**, one who digitizes

digitize *vb* to use or manipulate the fingers in some fashion

dikdik *n* any of five species of the dwarf antelopes and having a mature height in the range of 12–16 inches. Their natural habitat is a thorn thicket in an African arid zone.

diker *n* one involved in the construction of a dike or ditch

dilate (*vb*) *obs vb* to delay, to defer, to protract *obs fm vb* **delate**

dilater *n* one who or that which dilates: (in the following senses **dilatator** or, less correctly, **dilator** are also used) a muscle or nerve which dilates: a surgical instrument used to dilate an opening

dilator see **dilater**

dildo *n* a substitute for the purpose normally supplied by an erect penis: any of various plants such as a West Indian spiny cactus and the Indian fig tree, also, but in sense only not in name, the Cantonese groin *obs n* a term of contempt for a man of poor vigour

dildoe *var fm n* **dildo**

diluent *adj* diluting *n* a solvent

diluvian *adj* of or pertaining to a flood *esp* that associated with Noah

dimber *thieves' cant adj* pretty

dimble *now dial n* a shady hollow or dell

dimer *n* a compound formed by the process of combining two molecules of the same substance to achieve different properties to that of the original substance

dimeter *n* a verse of either two feet or four feet (see **metric foot**)

dimmen *vb* to grow dim

dimmer (*comp adj/n*) *nonce vb* to appear faintly or indistinctly

dimpler *nonce n* one whose expression of laughter is to make dimples appear in the cheeks

dindge *obs fm n/vb* **dinge** (in the sense of indentation)

dindle *now S & dial vb* to make a sound which causes a vibration: to thrill: to tremble: to tingle *dial n* a tingle

dinero *n* a Peruvian silver coin of which there are ten to the sol (*pl* **dineros**)

dinette *US n* an alcove where meals are served

ding *vb* to make a heavy ringing sound: to speak in a boring and repetitious manner *arch vb* to cover the surface of a brick wall with a thin coat of mortar: to flog or thrash: to surpass (*fig*)

dingbat *n* a small ornamentation used in printing: any small object: one of various names used for a popular word puzzle which has a phrase reduced to a cryptic form. For example, BOCATOTS. This translates as *Puss in Boots* (i.e. boCATots). Another is XES. This expresses a curious facet of nature which is most marked in various marine creatures and the solution to the puzzle is given at **XES**.

dinge *n* an indentation made by a blow *vb* to cause such *dial vb* to make dingy

dingee *var fm n* **dinghy**

dinger *slg n* a humdinger, the best

dingey *var fm n* **dinghy**

dinghee *var fm n* **dinghy**

dinging *n* the action of the *vb* ding and the *arch vb* in the sense of applying mortar

dingle *n* a (well-wooded) deep hollow *vb* to tinkle or ring

dingus *n* a thingamejig, a thingumbob, a what-d'ye-call-it. Anything the name of which the speaker cannot recall.

dink *n* a drop shot in tennis *vb* to play such a shot *S vb* to dress neatly *S & dial adj* neatly or finely dressed

dinnel *var fm now S & dial vb* **dindle**

dinnle *var fm now S & dial vb* **dindle**

Dinoceras *n* a genus of extinct ungulates, an individual of which vaguely resembled a rhinoceros the size of an elephant but having short stumpy legs, three pairs of horns on the head and a comparatively tiny brain

dinte *obs fm n* **dint**, (the mark of) a blow

diopter *n* a type of ancient theodolite or instrument for measuring angles

dioptra *var fm n* **diopter**

dioptre *var fm n* **diopter**

Dioscuri *n pl* the twins Castor and Pollux as sons of Zeus

dioxane *n* a colourless, flammable, toxic

liquid derived from glycol, having a faint, pleasant odour and used as a solvent for resins, oils, waxes and organic compounds

diphone *n* a shorthand sign which represents a double vowel sound having a single pronunciation

diple *n* the sign > used by ancient grammarians in the margins of manuscripts to indicate the start of a new paragraph

diploe *n* the tissue lying between the inner and outer walls of the bones of the skull

diploses *pl* diplosis

diplosis *n* a sexual union of two sets of gamete-like chromosomes (*pl* **diploses**)

dipnet *n* a small fishing net attached to a long pole

dipnoan *n* any species of lungfish

dipole *n* that material system which has a positive and negative charge of equal magnitude such as the proton and electron of a hydrogen atom: a system having two equal but opposite magnetic poles

dipsades *pl* dipsas

dipsas *n* a snake fabled to produce a raging thirst (*pl* **dipsades**) (+*cap*) *n* one of three genera of thirst snakes (see **thirst snake**): a genus of freshwater mussels

dipter *n* dipteran or dipteron, any two-winged insect such as a fly (*pl* **diptera**, **dipterans** or **dipters**)

diptera *pl* dipter, dipteran, dipteron: dipteros

dipteral *adj* of an insect, having two wings: of a building, having two ranges of columns on the pavement

dipteran see **dipter**

dipteron *var fm n* **dipter** (*pl* **diptera, dipterans** or **dipters**) *obs fm n* **dipteros** (*pl* **diptera**)

dipteros *n* a double-winged building (*pl* **diptera**)

Directoire *n* the French Directorate of 1795–1799 (−*cap*) *obs fm adj* **directory** (see **directorie**)

directorie *obs fm adj* **directory**, serving or tending to direct

direst *sup adj* dire

dirge (*n*) *vb* to sing a dirge

dirham *var fm n* **dirhem**

dirhem *n* an oriental unit of weight which varies in different countries but was originally two-thirds of an Attic drachma (44.4 grains, troy): a small silver coin of the same weight

dirigisme *n* state control in the economic and social spheres

dirigiste *adj* of or pertaining to dirigisme

dirken *obs fm vb* **darken**

dirl *S & dial vb* to thrill, to cause to vibrate *S & dial n* a thrill, a vibration

dirt (*n*) *vb* to make dirty

dirten *now dial adj* defiled with dirt or filth

dirt pie *n* a mud pie as a child might make

disbar *vb* to deprive a barrister of his right to practice

discept *vb* to dispute, debate

discounsel *obs vb* to (give) counsel against (GAME PLAYER'S note: The dictionary used for the UK Scrabble championship assigns all known usage to Spenser. Caxton is among those of the century prior to Spenser and Donne among those of the century after Spenser who used the verb. Curiously, the *Oxford English Dictionary* does not include Spenser among those it cites as users. See **WRITERS**)

discrepant *adj* exhibiting difference or lack of harmony: opposite: inconsistent: contrary: discordant

discrete *adj* distinct, separate: discontinuous: composed of distinct parts: denoting opposition

discretely *adv* separately

disendow *vb* to deprive of or remove the endowments of

disendower *n* one who deprives or strips of endowments

disenter *obs vb* to eject *obs fm vb* **disinter**

disert *obs adj* eloquent

disher *n* one who ruins or dishes something *obs n* one who serves food: a maker or seller of dishes

dishorn *vb* to deprive of horns

dishware *US n* tableware

disinter *vb* to exhume

dislade *obs vb* to unload

disleaf *vb* to disleave or remove leaves

disleal *obs adj* disloyal

disleave *vb* to remove leaves from

dismail *arch vb* to divest of mail (armour)

disman *vb* to unman: to deprive of men

dismayl *obs fm arch vb* **dismail** (*infl fms incl* **dismaylled** (Caxton), **dismayld** (Spenser))

disme *obs vb* to divide into tenths (the earlier *fm* **dime** or **dyme** being *Obs*) *var fm n* **dime**, a tithe or tenth part paid as a tax

disnest *vb* to remove (as) from a nest

disparate *adj* essentially different *n* (usually in *pl*) that which is disparate

Dispater *pers n* the Roman god, also known as **Dis**, who equates to **Hades**, the Greek god of the underworld

displode *vb* to discharge with explosive violence: to explode

dispone *S vb* to transfer (property) legally

disponee *S n* one to whom property is conveyed

disponer *S n* one who makes over property

disponge *var fm arch vb* **dispunge**

dispread *arch vb* to spread out or abroad: to extend, expand, open out

dispunge *arch vb* of such as rain, to pour as from a squeezed sponge

disrate *vb* to reduce a sailor to a lower rank

disrest *obs n* disquiet *obs vb* to disturb

disrober *n* one who or that which disrobes (such as the wind stripping off autumn leaves)

disroot *vb* to uproot

disseat *vb* to unseat (*lit/fig*)

disseisor *n* one who dispossesses another of his land

dissert *vb* to discourse

disserve *vb* to serve badly

dissever *vb* to divide (into parts), to disjoin, sever, part etc

dissunder *vb* to sunder, sever

distal *adj* located furthest from the point of origin

distaster *obs n* one who dislikes: one who inspires dislike

distater *n* an ancient Greek gold coin worth two of the staters to which it is related (see **stater**)

dister *var fm obs vb* **disterr**

disterr *obs vb* to exile

distome *n* a fluke, one of a genus of parasitic flatworms

distrait *adj* abstracted: absent-minded

distune *vb* to put out of tune

disuser *obs n* disuse

ditaa *n* a Philippine forest tree of the dogbane family, the timber of which is used for furniture and a quinine substitute is obtained from its bark

dital *n* a thumb-stop on a lute or guitar used to effect a change by one semitone

diter *obs n* a writer: an orator

ditone *n* in music, an interval of two whole tones

diureses *pl* diuresis

diuresis *n* excessive discharge of urine (*pl* **diureses**)

diurnalist *arch n* a journalist

diverse (*adj*) *obs vb* to vary: to diverge (*pa pple* **diversed** *var fm* **diverst**)

diverst *see* **diverse**

diverter *n* one who diverts

divet *var fm n*/*vb* **divot**

divining rod *n* a divining tool of any material which suits the user and which can be metal rather than the traditional hazel of the divining wand (see **divining wand**)

divining wand *n* a two-forked branch of hazel in the shape of the letter Y. The forks are held in the manner of bicycle handlebars with the base of the Y horizontally forward. The dowser advances with his or her concentration on the desired object (usually underground water). Once above that object, the rod moves either up or down. Against all logic, gifted dowsers confound the sceptics by being successful. (For an example of a more esoteric use of a divining wand or rod see **ley**.)

DIVINATION Virtually anything can be used for the purpose of foretelling the future and, apart from such references in the *Advanced Dictionary* to **oracle** (from where other examples can be traced), the following words, each having the suffix '-omancy', relate to this subject:– **alectryomancy**, **axinomancy**, **belomancy**, **bibliomancy**, **botanomancy**, **catoptromancy**, **chiromancy**, **crystallomancy**, **cubomancy**, **empyromancy**, **geomancy**, **gyromancy**, **hydromancy**, **necromancy**, **oneiromancy**, **ophiomancy**, **podomancy**, **psychomancy**, **pyromancy**, **rhabdomancy**, **scyphomancy** and **xylomancy** (Also see **corsned**, **haruspex**, **repele** and **scry**)

divot *n* a slice of turf *esp* that cut for roofing a northern cottage or that accidentally knocked out of the ground by a swing of a golf club: in Scots law, the right of cutting divots from certain land *vb* to cover (a roof) with divots

Diwali *n* the Hindu festival of lamps

diwan *var fm n* **dewan**

djinn *n pl* fire spirits of Muslim mythology possessing great power and capable of assuming various shapes, often as hideous giants of gigantic proportion (*sing* **djinni**)

DNA *abbreviation* deoxyribonucleic acid, any of various acids consisting of complex molecules, present in chromosomes of all plant and animal cells, and carrying the coded instructions for the transmission of hereditary characteristics

do (*vb*) *n* the first note of the tonic sol-fa system of musical notation (*pl* **dos**): a Japanese administrative region

doable *adj* that which can be done

doat *var fm vb* **dote**

doater *var fm n* **doter**

dobber *US n* an angler's fishing float *Austr collq n* an informant *dial n* a child's catapult

doblet *obs fm n* **doublet**

Docetism *n* the heresy of the Docetists

Docetist *n* one of a sect of 2nd century heretics who believed that Christ's body was not truly human but of some insubstantial matter

docken *S & dial adj/n* (of or like) dock, the large-leafed weed traditionally used as an antidote to a nettle sting

documental *adj* of or pertaining to documents

dodder *n* any of various rootless, leafless plants like masses of twining threads which are parasitic on other plants *vb* to move unsteadily: to shake or tremble

dodman *dial n* a snail

dödvand *Swed n* literally 'dead water', meaning the retarding action of underwater waves at the interface between fresh and salt water off the mouths of estuarine rivers. This can be sufficiently strong to stop a sailing ship and is the real cause of the effect long attributed to the remora or shark sucker. (See **remora**)

dogate *n* the office or dignity of a doge, the title of the chief magistrate of either of two historical city republics, Venice or Genoa

dogbane *n* any of various plants believed to be poisonous to dogs

dogeate *var fm n* **dogate**

dogger *n* a former Dutch two-masted sailing vessel: a sandy ironstone of the Lower Oolite period of rock formation: one who dogs the footsteps of someone

doggrel *var fm n/adj/vb* **doggerel**

doghead *n* the hammer of a gun: the head of a nail *obs n* the Aani

doghip *dial n* the rosehip of the dog rose

dog iron *n* an andiron or fire dog

dogline *n* a trace securing a dog to a sledge

dogship *n* the personality of a dog

dog's nose *n* a mixture such as (spiced, hot) ale and gin or (spiced, hot) ale and rum

doh *var fm n* **do** (see **gamut**)

doiled *S adj* stupid, crazy

doler *n* one who doles or dispenses

dolerite *n* a type of coarse, crystalline basalt *US n* any dark, greenish igneous rock not readily identified by a casual examination

doleur *Obs var fm n* **dolour**

dolite *n* a fossil shell of the tun, a gasteropod mollusc

dolium *n* an ancient Roman large earthenware jar or vessel (*pl* **dolia**)

doller *obs fm n* **dollar**

dollier *n* one who uses an implement called a dolly (see **dolly**, *n/vb*)

dolly (*n/adj*) *n* any of various contrivances which bear a vague resemblance to a doll – such as (*a*) the old-fashioned wooden implement consisting of a long handle (the body), a circular base (the skirt) and two short legs, used to twirl clothes in a simple washtub or dolly tub (*b*) a crude type of pile driver used to crush quartz in a gold field *Anglo-Ind n* a basket of fruit brought daily to the master or mistress of the house by the gardener *vb* to wash clothes in a dolly tub: to perform any of various crushing or beating operations (in goldmining, chain-making, smelting etc) using any of various implements called a dolly

dolman *n* a long, Turkish, narrow-sleeved robe open at the front: the uniform jacket of a hussar, worn like a cape: a woman's sleeveless mantle with capelike appendages (*pl* **dolmans**)

dolmen *n* a cromlech or prehistoric stone structure consisting, in its simplest form, of two large upright stones supporting a larger flattish stone (*pl* **dolmens**)

dolomite *n* a brittle mineral which occurs in the form of white to pale pink crystals

dolt (*n*) *vb* to make a fool of: to act the fool

domine *obs n* lord, master: a clergyman *obs vb* to rule

dominere *obs fm vb* **domineer** (note: Only listed in 9-letter anagrams where, ironically, domineres can be made into 'modernise')

don (*n*) *arch vb* to dress

donatism *n* the doctrines or principles of the Donatists

Donatist *n* one of a 4th century schismatic sect of North Africa which began in the year 311 after a dispute as to who should be elected bishop of Carthage

donee *n* one to whom anything is given

doner *obs fm n* **donor**

Donet *n* an introductory book on (Latin) grammar

donnat *dial fm n* **do-nought**

donnerd *S adj* stunned or stupefied

donnert *var fm S adj* **donnerd**

do-nought *n* an idler, a good-for-nothing (*var fms* **do-naught, donnot** *dial fms incl* **dannat, dannet, dannot, donnat, donnet, do-noht, do-nowt**)

donsie *S & dial adj* dim-witted *S & dial n* a dimwit

donsy *var fm S & dial n/adj* **donsie**

doomer *n* a judge

dorbel *obs n* a dunce

dore *obs vb* to glaze foodstuffs

dorea *var fm n* **doria**

doria *n* dorea, a type of Indian striped muslin (+*cap*) *n* Doris, a division of ancient Greece

Dorian *n/adj* (an inhabitant) of Doris or Doria, a division of ancient Greece

Doric (*adj*) *n* the broad, rustic Doric dialect of Greece: an English dialect equally broad and rustic

dories *pl* dory

dorise *vb* to imitate Doric manners: to speak or write in Doric

dorlach *n* a valise

dormancy *n* a dormant or sleepy state

dormie *var fm adj* **dormy**

dormy *adj* in golf, being as many holes ahead of an opponent as there are holes left to play

Dorothea *fem pers n* meaning 'a gift of God' (also see apt anagram **Theodora**)

dorry *obs fm n* **dory**

dorse *n* a young cod *obs vb* of bareknuckle fighting, to put an opponent on his back

dorsel *var fm now dial n* **dossel** *obs fm n* **dossal**

dorser *var fm n* **dosser**

dort *S n* ill humour *S vb* to sulk

dorter *var fm n* **dortour**

dortour *n* a bed chamber or other historical sleeping quarter *esp* in a monastery

dory *n* the John Dory or St Peter's fish, a shining, yellow-coloured, oval-shaped and rather grotesque edible fish of the temperate oceans *US n* a flat-bottomed marine fishing boat *obs n* a dish of food glazed with 'almond milk' *obs adj* of a golden or bright yellow colour: glazed with 'almond milk'

dossal *n* an ornamental (embroidered) altar cloth

dossel *now dial n* a pannier or other carrying contrivance borne by a beast of burden *var fm ns* **dossal, dossil**

dosser *n* a rich hanging or tapestry: a pannier *slg n* one who dosses (or sleeps) in a doss house (a cheap lodging)

dosseret *n* a secondary cap on the top of a classically styled pillar

dossil *n* a plug of such as (impregnated) lint for dressing a wound

dotant *obs n* a dotard

dotel *obs fm n* **dottle**, a fool

doter *n* one who dotes: one of feeble intellect: one with the weakness of old age: one foolishly fond

dotish *arch adj* silly, stupid, childish

dottel *var fm n* **dottle**, a plug of tobacco ash

dotter *n* one who or that which dots *now dial vb* to walk in a doddery fashion: to totter

dotterel *n* a species of lapwing which is very tame in the presence of man *now dial n* a silly person: a tree which has been cut to a pollard *now dial adj* stupid, foolish

dottle *n* the solid plug of tabocco ash which remains after smoking a pipe: an old fool *S adj* silly, foolish

dottrel *var fm n/now dial n/now dial adj* **dotterel**

doty *US & dial adj* stained with decay (*comp* **dotier** *sup* **dotiest**)

doubler (*n*) *now dial n* a platter or large plate

douc *see* **langur**

douce *obs vb* to sweeten

doucet *obs n* a dish of egg and pork, peppered and sweetened with honey: a flute-like wind instrument

doucets *n pl* a deer's testicles

doughe *obs fm n/vb* **dough**

dourer *comp adj* dour

dourine *n* a contagious disease of horses

douser *n* one who drenches something or someone

douset *obs fm n* **doucet**

douste *obs fm n* **dust**

doute *obs fm n/vb* **doubt**

douter *n* one who or that which extinguishes

douty *obs fm adj* **doughty**

dow *var (earlier and better) fm n* **dhow** *now S & dial vb* to have the power to (do something): to thrive, prosper *S & dial vb* to fade *obs vb* to endow

dowcet *var fm obs n* **doucet** (also, as **dowcets,** *obs fm n pl* **doucets**)

dowel *n* a headless pin or peg that joins two adjacent parts through the two halves of a corresponding hole *vb* to fasten in this fashion (*infl fms* British, **dowelled/-lling:** US, **doweled/-ling**)

dowing *obs n* an endowment

dowle *var fm now dial n* **dowl**, down or fluff

downcome *n* a downfall (*lit/fig*): the swooping down of a hawk: a pipe conveying gases from a blast furnace

downe *obs fm n* **down**, first feathers

dowse *vb* to use a divining rod *esp* to search for subterranean water (see **divining wand**) *var fm n/vb* **douse**

dowser *n* one who uses a divining rod *esp* a water diviner

dowset *var fm obs n* **doucet**

dowsets *var fm n pl* **doucets**

dowter *dial fm n* **daughter**

drabbe *obs fm n* **drab**, a slut

drabbet *n* a type of coarse linen fabric

drabble *vb* to become wet and dirty by trailing through mud

drabette *var fm n* **drabbet**

draconic *adj* of (the nature of) a dragon

dragée *n* a sugar-coated medicinal pill: a sweetmeat with a coating of hard sugar icing: a tiny silvered beadlike sweet for decorating a cake: a chocolate drop

draggle *vb* to make wet, limp and dirty *esp* the hem of a garment trailed through muddy conditions *n* the act of draggling

dragle *obs fm vb* **draggle**

dragline *n* a crane-like excavating machine

dragman *n* a man who fishes with a dragnet (*pl* **dragmen**) *obs fm n* **dragoman** (*pl* **dragmans, dragmen**)

dragoman *n* one who interprets *esp* in Arabic (*pl* **dragomans, dragomen**)

dragonise *var fm vb* **dragonize**, to turn into a dragon: to keep guard as a dragon

dragonné *her adj* like the rear of a dragon

dragsman *n* the driver of a horse-drawn coach called a drag: one who drags such as the bed of a river

draie *obs fm n* **drey**, the nest of a squirrel

draigle *S fm vb* **draggle**

drail *obs vb* to trail and drag along (see *US n*) *US n* a combined weight and fishing hook: that hook attached to a line and drailed (see *obs vb*) in the water

draipse *slg vb* to rob with (threat of) violence (a thieves' cant term current among thugs of West Indian origin)

dramme *obs fm n* **dram**

drane *dial fm n* **drone**, the male of the honey bee: a continuous monotonous sound *dial fm vb* **drone**, to give a monotonous sound *obs fm vb* **drone**, to proceed in a sluggish or indolent fashion *obs fm n/vb* **drain**

drant *dial vb* to drone or drawl in speech *dial n* a droning or drawling tone (*var fms n/vb incl* **drate, draunt, drunt**)

drapet *obs n* a cloth, a covering

drapier *obs fm n* **draper**

drappie *S n* a little drop *esp* of liquor

drashel *var fm now dial n* **threshel**, a flail

drate *var fm dial n/vb* **drant**

draunt *var fm dial n/vb* **drant**

drawee *n* the one on whom a bill of exchange is drawn

drawne *obs fm conj* **drawn**

dray (*n*) *vb* to transport on a dray

drayage *n* transportation by dray: the charge levied for such

draye *obs fm n* **dray**

dreame *obs fm n* **dream**

drean *dial fm vb* **drone**, to give a continuous monotonous sound

dreane *obs fm n/vb* **drain**

drearing *obs nonce n* grief (an irregular formation based on drear or dreary, coined by Spenser)

drede *obs fm n/adj/vb* **dread**

dree *arch vb* to endure *arch adj* slow: dreary: tedious

dreed *obs fm n/vb* **dread**

dreel *S vb* to move quickly or hastily *S fm vb* **drill**, to bore or pierce

dreely *now S & dial adv* slowly

dreeme *obs fm n/vb* **dream**

dreen *dial fm n/vb* **drain**

dreep *now dial vb* to drip

dreich *now S & dial adj* tedious, wearisome, dreary *obs fm arch adj* **dree**

dreign *obs fm vb* **drain**

dreikanter *n* an angular pebble, the faces of which have been cut by windblown sand (*pl* **dreikanter, dreikanters**)

drein *obs fm n/vb* **drain**

dreint *var fm obs adj* **drent**

dreip *arch S fm vb* **drip**

dreng *n* a freeholder in mediaeval times whose tenure of land was by a right of service which predated the Norman Conquest

drenkil *var fm Obs vb* **drenkle**

drenkle *Obs vb* to submerge, to drown

drent *obs adj* drenched or drowned

drentse *n* a breed of domesticated sheep akin to the mouflon, the wild mountain sheep of Corsica and Sardinia

drepar *var fm obs n* **dreper**

drepe *obs vb* to kill: to defeat *var fm now dial vb* **dreep**

dreper *obs n* a murderer

dreve *obs vb* to separate

driblet *n* a droplet: a small quantity of anything: a trickle *obs vb* to come in driblets

driche *var fm arch adj* **dree**

driddle *S vb* to move or perform in a feeble fashion

driech *var fm arch adj* **dree**

driest *sup adj* dry

dringe *Obs fm n* **dreng**

dringle *now dial vb* to laze about

drinke *obs fm vb* **drink**

drinkel *var fm Obs vb* **drenkle**

drinkle *var fm Obs vb* **drenkle**

dripe *obs vb* to moisten

dripple *vb* to flow at a gentle but unsluggish pace: to drip

drite *now S vb* to void excrement

droger *var fm n* **drogher**, any of various slow, clumsy, coastal vessels

drogue *n* a device which achieves a dragging or slowing effect such as a parachute at the rear of an aircraft or a floating anchor: a windsock, an open canvas bag which indicates the direction of the wind

droguet *n* a ribbed wollen dress fabric

droich *S n* a dwarf

droile *var fm obs n/vb* **droil**, (to) drudge

drôle *n* a rogue *adj* amusing

droll *adj* amusing *esp* in a quaint or odd manner *n* a jester, buffoon, merry andrew *vb* to jest, to joke

drolly *adv* in a droll manner, quaintly, oddly

drome *collq n* an aerodrome

dromed *obs n* a dromedary, the one-humped camel

dronel *obs n* the male bee

droner *n* a monotonous speaker

dronet *var fm obs n* **dronel**

dronish *adj* like a drone: idle, lazy

droome *obs fm n/vb* **drum**

dropnet *n* a fishing net held in suspension until it can be dropped over a shoal of fish

drosell *var fm obs n* **drossel**

drosen *obs n* dregs

drosera *n* sundew

drossel *obs n* a slut

drosser *n* one of a series of iron frames used as partitions in a glass maker's furnace

drote *obs vb* to stammer or stutter

droter *obs n* a stammerer

droun *obs vb* to roar

droupe *obs fm n/vb* **droop**

drouse *obs fm n/vb* **drowse**

drousen *var fm obs n* **drowsen**

drowen *obs fm vb* **drown**

drowne *obs fm vb* **drown**

drowpe *obs fm vb* **droop**

drowsen *obs n* a pottage of oatmeal mixed with the dregs of beer barrels

drucken *S & dial fm adj* **drunken**

drugge *obs fm n* **drug**, a medicament *obs fm vb* **drug,** to drag

drugget *n* a coarse woollen stuff used for such as floor coverings

druken *var fm S & adj* **drucken**

drumble *now dial n* a layabout *S vb* to make muddy or opaque *now dial vb* to be sluggish, to move sluggishly *obs vb* to sound like a drum

drumfish *n* any of nearly 200 species of mainly marine perch-like fishes *incl* such as the corb, geelbek, meagre, minkfish and totuava. The drumfishes, or croakers, are all capable of making sounds under water.

drunt *var fm dial n/vb* **drant**

drupe *n* a fruit, like a peach or cherry, which has a soft, fleshy covering for a hard seed or nut *Obs fm vb* **droop**

drupel *n* a little drupe

druse *n* a crystal-lined cavity in rock (*pl* **druses**) (+*cap*) see **Darazi**

Drusian *adj* of the Druse (see **Darazi**) *obs n* a Darazi

drwn *obs S fm vb* **drown**

dryad *n* a wood nymph of classical myth: a beautiful maiden who lives in a forest: a tree (*pl* **dryads, dryades**)

dryades *pl* dryad

dry-stane *dial fm adj* **dry-stone**

dry-stone *adj* of such as walls, constructed of local stone and held together without mortar

dso *var fm n* **zho**

dsobo see **zho**

dsobu see **zho**

dsomo see **zho**

du *S fm vb* **do**

dualin *n* a nitro-glycerine based explosive containing fine sawdust and nitre

dualine *var fm n* **dualin**

dubbel *obs fm n/adj/vb* **double**

dubble *obs fm n/adj/vb* **double**

dubbler *obs fm n* **doubler**

duble *obs fm n/adj/vb* **double**

dubler *var fm now dial n* **doubler**, a large plate

ducke *obs fm n* **duck**

ducker *n* one who breeds ducks: any species of bird which dives under water *obs n* a fighting cock which ducks its head

ducket *obs fm n* **ducat**, any of various European gold or silver coins

Duck Tree *n* the name of a particular tree in a village near Bakewell, Derbyshire, of which only the stump now remains. It was given that name in the 18th century when a duck was reported to have flown into the tree and simply disappeared never to be seen again. The name stuck. Then, a hundred years later, the tree was felled and, in the centre of the trunk, was a marking the size and shape of a duck.

ducter *n* a leader

dudder *now dial vb* to shiver or shudder

dudeen *n* a short clay tobacco pipe

dudgen *obs n* trash *obs adj* contemptible

duel (*n*/*vb*) *vbl infl fms* British, **duelled**/**-lling**: US/*arch* British, **dueled**/**-ling**

dueler *var fm* (*now mainly US*) *n* **dueller**

duergar *n* a malicious black dwarf of Northumbrian folklore, solitary in nature and bitterly hostile to man

duetto *n* a musical composition for two performers: the performance of such: the performers of such (*pl* **duetti, duettos**)

duffel *n* a heavy woollen cloth

duffle *var fm n* **duffel**

dufter *n* a business office in the East Indies: a bundle of official papers either bound or unbound (of such an office)

duiker *n* any of a group of small African antelopes of two different genera, ranging in mature height from only a foot tall to less than three feet. Many of the species make delightful pets but, unless they have access to salt, become carnivorous, killing such as chickens and eating their heads and feet. The majority of the species are forest-dwelling and *incl* the West African **banded duiker**, also known as the **zebra antelope**, **Peter's duiker**, which ranges throughout the whole of the African forest region from the Cameroons to the Transvaal, and **Maxwell's duiker** which lives in the forests to the north and west of Peter's duiker. Maxwell's duiker is numbered among those ungulates which indulge in the curious activity known as flehmen but it also uses the more conventional form of pair-bonding, scent-exchange. Special glands on the heads of the duikers enable a mated pair to mark each other with a secretion, that of the Maxwell's being a white liquid whereas the banded duiker has a resinous substance. Peter's, Maxwell's and the banded duiker together with the smallest, the **blue duiker**, constitute four of the *approx* eleven species of the genus, *Cephalophus*. The main species of the other genus, *Sylvicapra*, is the **deloo** which is also known as the **bush** or **grey duiker**. (note: *Chambers* has the following entry, 'a small S. African antelope: a cormorant (*S. Afr*)')

dukery *n* the territory of a duke

dulced *obs fm adj* **dulcet**

dulcet *adj* of a sound, pleasant, soothing, sweet *arch adj* of a smell or taste, sweet *n* an organ stop which produces a dulcet tone

dulciana *n* one of the organ stops

dulcite *n* a saccharine substance obtained from various plants

dulcose *n* the same as **dulcite**

dullen *vb* to dull or make dull

dulosis *n* the enslavement by ants of others of their kind

dulse *n* a bright-red edible species of seaweed

dum *obs fm adj* **dumb**

dumaist *n* a member of a duma or elected council *esp* the Russian parliament between 1906 and 1917

dumble *var fm now dial n* **dimble**

dumose *adj* full of brambles or bushes: of plants, having a development pattern of a compact bushy growth

dumple *vb* to form into a dumpy shape

dunder *n* the dregs of cane juice used to make rum *var fm S n/vb* **dunner**

dundrel *var fm n* **denerel**

dunger *n* any animal which provides dung

dungy *adj* of the nature of or abounding in dung: vile, foul, filthy (*comp* **dungier** *sup* **dungiest**)

dunite *n* a granular igneous rock found in New Zealand

Dunker *n* one of a sect of German–American Baptists who only baptize adults

dunner *S n* (a blow causing) a reverberating sound: a debt collector *S vb* to make a reverberating sound

dunny *n* (an outside) lavatory *obs n* a dunce *adj* dusky brown *dial adj* stupid: dull of hearing or of perception

Dunster *obs n* a type of woollen cloth formerly made in Dunster, Somerset

dunter *n* a spirit which haunts the foundations of old castles in the Border country and makes a constant grinding sound *dial n* the eider duck: a porpoise

duntle *dial vb* to knock

dupion *n* a double cocoon made by two silkworms: silk from such a cocoon

duple *adj* double, twofold *obs vb* to double

duramen *n* the heartwood of a tree

durance *n* forced confinement

durant *n* a strong cloth made of tammy

dure *arch vb* to continue in existence: to harden

duret *obs n* a 17th century dance

durgen *dial n* a dwarf

durian *n* a globular, prickly-coated, foul-smelling but fine tasting fruit of a tropical Asian tree: that tree

during *(prep) n* duration: hardening

durmast *n* a variety of oak tree: its valuable, dark, tough, elastic timber

durn *now dial n* a wooden doorpost: a timber framework in a mine *now US vb* to damn

durse *obs dial vb* of corn, to shed grains

dussel *obs fm n* **dossil**

Dutch nightingale *n* a frog

duyker *var fm n* **duiker**

dw *obs fm S vb* **du**

dwale *n* the plant, deadly nightshade *obs n* a stupefying drink: error, deceit: a heretic, a deceiver

dwarf antelope *n* any of various small gazelles which constitute a group (technically, a tribe) of the smallest living bovid animals. The species *incl* the beira, dikdik, grysbok, klipspringer, oribi, steinbok, suni and the smallest of all, the royal antelope, which falls just short of a foot tall when fully mature. Apart from the beira, the dwarf antelopes live in pairs. Some experts also include the rhebok within this tribe. The rhebok, like the beira, also chooses to live in a small herd. (Also see **chevrotain**, which is unrelated.)

dwele *obs vb* to swoon *Obs vb* to go astray, to be deluded *Obs n* an error, a delusion

dwelte *Obs fm pa pple* **dwelt**

dwilde *Obs n* error, heresy

dwine *arch* (*except S & dial*) *vb* to wither, fade

dwit *n* a very minute unit of weight (see **MONEYERS WEIGHTS**)

dy *obs fm n* **die**, one of a set of gaming dice (*pl* either of the logical plurals, dys or dyce, became obsolete before the singular whilst both dice or dies were in use before, during and after the period that dy was used. Hence; **dice, dies, dyce** or **dys** are suitable *pls*.)

dyb *Shet vb* to indulge in: to work patiently *dial n* a puddle

dyd *Shet n* a meal

dyeline *adj* of a photocopying process, using a compound which decomposes when exposed to light *n* a photocopy so produced

dynamicist *n* one who studies dynamics, the science of matter and motion

dynamistic *adj* of, pertaining to or of the nature of the philosophical theory of dynamism which has it that the phenomenon of the universe is explained in terms of some immanent force

dyne *n* the metric unit of force

dypsas *obs fm n* **dipsas**

dzeren *n* the Mongolian gazelle

dzo *var fm n* **zho**

dzobo see **zho**

dzobu see **zho**

dzomo see **zho**

E

ea *n* water (*obs* except as a syllable in English place names) *now dial n* a river: running water: a Fenland drainage canal (+*cap*) *pers n* the Babylonian god of the waters

eaa *var fm now dial n* **ea**

eager (*adj*) *obs vb* to excite, provoke *var fm n* **eagre**

eagle (*n*) *vb* to score an eagle in golf (see **birdie**)

eaglet *n* a young eagle

eagre *n* an unusually high estuarine tide

ealdre *Obs fm n* **elder**, a person of seniority

eam *see* **be**

ean *obs vb* of a ewe, to bring forth a lamb (also see **eanling, yean, yeanling**)

eangel *Obs fm n* **angel**

eaning *n* the action of bearing a lamb *modf n* as in **eaning time**, the lambing season

eanling *n* a young lamb (as opposed to **yeanling**, a lamb *or* kid)

earcap *arch n* an earflap, one of two coverings for the ears suspended from a cap

eardrop *n* an ornamental pendant suspended from the ear: the flower of the common fuchsia

earer *arch n* a ploughman

earing *n* one of a number of small ropes used in fastening a sail to a yard

earl (*n*) *S vb* to seal a pledge or betrothal by monetary payment

earless *adj* without (external) ears

earlet *n* anything resembling a small ear *obs n* an ear ring

earlship *n* the dignity of an earl

earnest (*adj*/*n*) *obs vb* to use in earnest

earnit *dial fm n* **earthnut**

earstone *n* a hard mass of calcium carbonate and calcium phosphate that forms in the inner ear

earthen (*adj*) *vb* to turn into earth

earthfall *n* a landslide

earth-fed *adj* contented with earthly things

earthling *n* one who is earthy in quality: an earth dweller (see **Terran**) *obs n* a ploughman

earthset *n* the setting of the earth as viewed from the moon

easle *dial n* hot ashes or cinders

eassel *S adv* easterly or eastward

eassil *var fm S adv* **eassel**

east (*n*/*adj*) *vb* to turn, move, veer towards the east

easter *dial n* the back of the fireplace

easterling *n* one, in historical context, who was native to eastern Germany or a Baltic country: a coin or ship of such: one native to the Near East: the smew

eastern (*adj*) *n* one who lives in the East: a member of the Eastern Church

easting *n* the ship's course gained to the eastward: an approach in an easterly direction: of the elements, a shifting eastward to the point of origin: of a heavenly body, reaching the eastern point of its apparent daily route

eastlin *var fm S adj* **eastling**

eastling *S adj* easterly

eastlings *S adv* eastward

eastlins *var fm S adv* **eastlings**

Eastre *pers n* the Teutonic goddess of the dawn whose festival was celebrated at the vernal equinox *obs fm n* **Easter**

eatage *dial n* (the right to) pasturage

eatche *S n* an adz, a type of cutting tool

eathly *obs adj* easy: trifling: of a person or thing, low in worth or estimation *obs adv* easily

eatress *n* the *fem* of eater

eaver *now dial n* rye grass *dial n* a quarter of the heavens: the direction of the wind relative to that quarter

eb *obs fm now dial adj* **ebb**, shallow *obs fm n* **ebb**, the reflux of the tide

ebonist *n* one involved in trading in ebony or similar ornamental woods

ebonite *n* hard rubber

ebriating *adj* intoxicating

ec *Obs fm arch adv* **eke**, also, too, moreover

ecarté *n* a card game: a position in ballet

echidna *n* the spiny ant-eater, an egg-laying marsupial mammal rather like a hedgehog in appearance (*pl* **echidnae, echidnas**) (note: See **anteater** to contrast ant-eater)

echoer *n* one who repeats

echoic *adj* of the nature of an echo

echoist *n* one who repeats like an echo

éclat *n* social distinction, renown: showy brilliance *obs n* notoriety *vb* to become known: to bring into the glare of publicity

eclosion *n* the process of hatching from an egg: the emergence of the adult insect from the pupa

econut *slg n* a derogatory term for one who is 'nutty' about ecology

ectasis *n* the lengthening of a normally short syllable: a disease characterized by a state of dilation (*pl* **ectases**)

ecstasise *var fm vb* **ecstasize**, to go into or fill with a feeling of ecstasy

ectomorphy an undefined noun which appears to be exclusive to the dictionary used for the UK Scrabble championship and, presumably, relates to its definition of an **ectomorph** as being 'a person of light and delicate build'. The adjective, **ectomorphic** (which it also leaves undefined) is used to denote a person having that physical and personality type associated with a body structure as developed from the ectodermal layer of the embryo and characterized by predominance of the nervous system. Such a person differs from an **endomorphic** type (developed from the endodermal layer of the embryo and characterized by predominance of the abdominal system, i.e. plump or fat) or a **mesomorphic** type (developed from the mesodermal layer producing the muscular or athletic person). No clues, however, arise from an investigation of **endomorphy** or **mesomorphy**. Again, it appears to have exclusive, undefined knowledge of these nouns with equally undefined adjectives. The anagrams are **chromotype** and **cormophyte**.

écu *n* a size of paper (see **WATERMARKED PAPER**)

ed *adj* fortunate (*obs* except as a syllable in both Christian names and English place names)

edaphic *adj* pertaining to soil

Eddaic *adj* of Edda, either of two classical works concerning the Scandinavian myths

eddish *n* an aftergrowth of grass (and clover) following a mowing or harvesting: a stubble field *obs n* a park or enclosed cattle pasture (the various *dial fms* – **airish, aish, arish, arrish, errish, ersh, hayrish, herrish** – usually refer to the field itself, with meanings ranging from freshly-harvested to fully overgrown with weeds following an earlier cutting of the crop)

eddyre *Obs fm n* **adder**, the snake

edema *n* oedema, an excessive accumulation of a serious liquid: dropsy (*pl* **edemata, edemas**)

Edenic *adj* of or pertaining to the Biblical Garden of Eden

edental *adj* of the Edentata, those mammals such as the anteaters or sloths which have no front teeth

Edentata *n* an order of mammals consisting of the anteaters (*not* the ant-eaters, see **anteater**), sloths and armadillos. They are among the handful of living mammals whose ancestors were some of the very earliest South American mammals. Edentata means 'without teeth' but only the anteater is completely toothless, both the sloth and the armadillo having some form of primitive molars.

edger *n* one who puts an edge on anything: a type of circular saw

edict (*n*) *obs vb* to decree

edictal *adj* of or pertaining to an edict

edile *var fm n* **aedile**

educe *vb* to extract, elicit (information, solutions etc)

eductor *n* one who or that which educes or brings out

edulcorate *adj* softened, sweetened

ee *S n* eye (*pl* **een**)

eeking *obs fm n* **eking**

eel (*n*) *vb* to fish for eels

eelder *obs fm n* **elder**, a person of seniority

eelet *n* an elver, a young eel

eelgrass *n* a grass-like herb of the pondweed family growing wholly underwater

eel set *n* a net strung across a stream in order to catch eels

eely *adj* eel-like: resembling an eel in movement (*comp* **eelier** *sup* **eeliest**)

een *pl S n* ee

eet *var fm S n* **ett**

ef *dial fm conj* **if** *n* the letter F

eff (*vulg n*/*vb*) *obs fm n* **eft**, a newt (GAME PLAYER'S note: Even the strongest of bad language is perfectly acceptable for play providing it is in the dictionary agreed upon for reference in the event of a dispute. Should, for example, you wish to inflect the vulgar verb this would be accepted without question in

such as the national Scrabble championship. However, if playing at home and you wish to give a polite reply to an opponent's question as to what 'effing' means then the writer suggests 'hunting for newts'. You, however, would have to accept the consequences of your opponent repeating that statement elsewhere!)

eft *n* a newt *arch adv* again, likewise *adj*? (see **eftest**)

eftest *sup adj* 'eft' (Shakespeare's comic character, Dogberry, uses this otherwise unknown superlative in the sense of 'most convenient' (*Much Ado* IV ii 38))

eftsoon *arch adv* again, moreover, likewise: forthwith, immediately

eftsoons *var fm arch adv* **eftsoon**

eg *n* water (*obs* except as a syllable in English place names) *obs fm ns* **egg, edge** *obs fm vb* **egg**, to pelt with (rotten) eggs: to collect (wild bird's) eggs

egally *obs adv* equally, evenly

egesta *n* excreta

eggar *var fm n* **egger**, any of a number of species of moths which, at one stage in their existence, live in an egg-shaped cocoon

eggler *dial n* one who deals in eggs

eggy *adj* abounding with eggs: stained with an egg or eggs

eglantine *n* either of two roselike plants, the sweetbriar or the dog rose: a marble-like stone

eglatere *now poet fm n* **eglantine**, the sweetbriar

egocentric *adj* self-centred

egotheism *n* the identification of self with God

egress *n* an exit: the right to go out: emergence

egret *n* a name given to various herons *esp* those with an all-white plumage

eh *interj* (mild) surprise: inquiry *vb* to say eh

ei *n* water (*Obs* except as a syllable in English place names) *Obs fm adj/pron/adv* **any** *Obs fm adv/interj* **ay**

eident *S adj* diligent, busy

eidograph *n* an instrument for copying a drawing to a different scale

eidolon *n* an image: a phantom

eilder *Obs fm n* **elder**, a person of seniority

einkorn *n* the one-grained wheat, a variety cultivated in central Europe usually bearing only one fertile floret

eiress *var fm obs n* **eriff**

eisel *var fm obs n* **eisell**

eisell *obs n* vinegar

eissel *var fm S adv* **eassel**

Eister *obs S fm n* **Easter**

ek *obs fm adv/vb* **eke**

ekeing *obs fm n* **eking**

eking *n* the action of adding *esp* that of affixing an eke (or tag) to a bell rope

el *n* anything in the shape of the letter L (*pl* **els**): a measure of cloth in Holland (*pl* **ellen**)

elact *obs vb* to suckle

Elaeis *n* the genus of the oil palm

elain *var fm n* **olein**

elamp *obs vb* to shine forth

elance *arch vb* to launch: to throw (a lance or dart)

eland *n* an elk-like antelope of South Africa

elanet *n* the black-winged sparrow hawk

elapid *n* a snake of the family *Elapidae* of which all species (both land and sea) are venomous and include such snakes as the cobras, mambas, kraits and many of the Australian serpents such as the bandy-bandy, tiger snake and taipan

elastin *n* the basic protein constituent of elastic tissue

elater *n* a spiral filament which discharges the spore cases of such plants as horsetail and liverwort: the skipjack beetle: elator, one who or that which elates

elaterid *n* a click beetle

elaterin *n* a poisonous crystalline substance obtained from the squirting cucumber and used for the production of elaterium

elaterium *n* a drastic purgative usually called **English elaterium** to distinguish it from a much weaker product of evaporated elaterin known as **French elaterium**

elatine *var fm n* **elaterin**

elative *adj* capable of producing elation *n* an adjectival *fm* in some languages

elator *var fm n* **elater**, one who or that which elates

elchi *n* an ambassador

eld *arch adj* see **ald** *arch n pl* people of an unspecified historic period *poet n* an old man *now dial n* a person's current age in a general sense *Obs n* fire: a needle *obs vb* to grow old

eldar *obs S fm n* **elder**, a person of seniority

eldere *Obs fm n* **elder**, a person of seniority

eldern *adj* made of elder *now S adj* elderly *arch adj* belonging to earlier times *obs fm n* **elder**, the tree

eldin *dial n* butterbur, a large-leafed plant of wet land: fuel

eldren *obs fm n* **elder**, the tree *obs S fm arch adj/now S adj* **eldern**

eldrich *var fm S adj* **eldritch**

eldritch *S adj* hideous, weird, ghostly

electret *n* a non-conducting, usually rod-shaped, object capable of being strongly charged with positive electricity at one pole and negative electricity at the other

electrise *var fm vb* **electrize**, to electrify

elegise *var fm vb* **elegize**, to write an elegy (upon)

elegist *n* the writer of an elegy

elegit *n* a writ of execution which enables the creditor to obtain possession of the goods and lands of the debtor until satisfaction is made

elegy *n* a lament for the dead

elenge *now dial adj* remote, lonely, dreary

elephant bird *n* an extinct flightless bird of Madagascar which, like the extinct moa of New Zealand, had a height of up to ten feet. Its egg was the equivalent of seven ostrich eggs or 12,000 hummingbird eggs.

elerne *obs fm n* **elder**, the tree

elevens *var fm dial n* **elevener**, a mid-morning snack

elevon *n* a wing flap on a delta wing or tailless aircraft which serves the dual functions of an elevator and an aileron

elfin (*adj*) *n* an elf *S n* a child

elf owl *n* a tiny species of bubonine owl

elfship *nonce n* the personality of an elf

elgins *var fm dial n* **eldin**, butterbur

eliad *obs fm n* **œillade**

Elian *adj* of or like the essays of Charles Lamb (1775–1834) which he penned under the name of Elia *n* an imitator of his style: a devotee of his work

elide *vb* to suppress, abridge *arch vb* to rebut

Elinas *pers n* see **Melusina**

eling *obs fm now dial n* **eyling**

elinge *Obs fm now dial adj* **elenge**

Elisha *masc pers n* meaning 'God is salvation': a Biblical prophet who succeeded Elijah

elision *n* the action of suppressing a letter or syllable in pronunciation, as in 'o'er' for 'over': a suppression of a part

elisor *n* one of two persons appointed under certain circumstances to select a jury

elite (*n*) *obs vb* to choose: to elect

elitra *obs fm pl* **elytra**

ell *n* a unit of length which varied in different countries (English = 45 inches, Scottish = 37.2, Russian = 28.1, Flemish = 27 etc) and was used for the official measure of cloth (see **alnage**) *dial n* a shed built against a dwelling

ellagic *adj* pertaining to gall nuts

eller *dial fm ns* **elder, alder**

elm (*n*) *var fm dial n/vb* **helm**, (to lay) straw (for thatching)

elmy *adj* consisting of or abounding in elms (*comp* **elmier** *sup* **elmiest**)

Elohist *n* the writer (or writers) of those parts of the *Hexateuch* characterized by the use of Elohim rather than Yahweh for the name of God (note: Jehovah is a word of comparatively modern coinage)

eloign *var fm arch vb* **eloin**

eloin *arch vb* to remove *esp* from the jurisdiction of a court or of a sheriff

elrage *obs fm S adj* **eldritch**

elrene *Obs fm n* **elder**, the tree

elrish *obs fm S adj* **eldritch**

elsen *var fm now S & dial n* **elsin**

elsin *now S & dial n* an awl

elson *var fm now S & dial n* **elsin**

Elstra *n* a small town in East Germany *approx* 30 miles due east of Meissen

elt *dial n* a young pig *now dial vb* to knead

eltchi *var fm n* **elchi**

eltrot *dial n* wild parsley

eluant *n* a liquid used for purification or separation by washing

eluate *n* a liquid used for the chemical process of purification or separation by washing

elute *vb* to cleanse

elution *n* washing

elutor *n* a vessel used for chemical purification

elvan *adj* of or pertaining to elves *n* a term for various Cornish igneous rocks such as whinstone or quartz-porphyry

elvanite *var fm n* **elvan**

elver *n* a young eel

elvet *n* a tiny elf

ely *S vb* to disappear gradually from view

elytra *pl* elytron or elytrum

elytral *adj* of or pertaining to a beetle's elytra

elytron *n* one of a pair of thickened forewings which, on a beetle, serve as a protective case for a hindwing: the vagina (*pl* **elytra**)

elytrous *adj* resembling or having the nature of elytra

elytrum *var fm n* **elytron**

em *n* the letter M: a printer's unit of typeface measure

emanate *vb* to issue or proceed from: to emit: to send forth

emanatist *n* one (*esp* a 4th century heretic, an Arian) who believes that Christ was not a man but a manifestation of Divine Power

emanges *Obs fm obs prep* **emonges**

embail *obs vb* to enclose in a ring

embale *vb* to package in bales

embar *vb* to enclose or imprison

embase *arch vb* to lower (*lit/fig*)

embitterer *n* one who or that which embitters

emblase *obs fm vb* **emblaze**, to adorn (with heraldic devices)

emble *obs n* a worm

emboil *obs vb* to cause to rage

embrase *obs vb* to ignite (*lit/fig*)

embrass *Obs fm obs vb* **embrase**

embroid *obs vb* to braid or entwine

embrue *var fm vb* **imbrue**

emburse *obs fm vb* **imburse**

eme *now dial n* uncle *dial n* friend: gossip *obs fm n* **emu**

emeer *var fm n* **emir**, an Islamic ruler

emendator *n* one who corrects

emerit *obs adj* superannuated *obs vb* to obtain by service

emerita *adj* of a woman, retired but retaining an honorary title

emersed *adj* standing out from that in which it has been plunged

emeses *pl* emesis

emesis *n* vomiting (*pl* **emeses**)

emetin *var fm n* **emetine**

emetine *n* a substance obtained from the root of the ipecacuanha plant used as a powerful medicinal vomiting agent

emicant *obs adj* darting, flashing forth

émigré *n* an emigrant *esp* one, such as a royalist during the French Revolution, forced to flee because of the political climate in his native country

emirate *n* the jurisdiction or government of an emir, an Arab prince or governor

emmarble *vb* to sculpture in marble, hence (*fig*) to turn into marble: to inlay or adorn with marble

emmet *arch n* an ant

emonges *obs prep* amongst

emongis *Obs fm obs prep* **emonges**

emoter *n* one who emotes

empaestic *adj* stamped, inlaid (usually in the *fm* **empaestic art**, the art of embossing)

empale *var fm vb* **impale** *obs vb* to make pale

empaler *var fm n* **impaler** (GAME PLAYER'S note: British experts consider the word *obs*, having had a currency in the 16th and 17th centuries. The dictionary used for the North American Scrabble championship (which provides no labels with any word) lists it without comment. It does not appear in the UK equivalent work.)

empare *obs vb* to adorn

emparle *obs fm vb* **imparl**

empaste *obs fm vb* **impaste**

empathic *adj* of or pertaining to empathy

empathy *n* the power of entering into the experience of another person's feelings: the attribution to an inanimate object of one's own feelings

empearl *arch var fm vb* **impearl**

empeople *nonce vb* to establish as the population (a sense originally used by Spenser and treated as extant by various modern dictionaries) *obs vb* to populate (*var fms*, in this sense, **enpeople** or **inpeople**)

emphatical *adj* of speech or writing, stressed forcibly or strongly expressive

empire (*n*) *obs vb* to rule with absolute authority

empirical *adj* relating to or based on experience and observation rather than theory: of or relating to medical quackery

emplane *vb* to (put on) board an aeroplane

empless *obs S vb* to please

emporia *pl* emporium

emporium *n* a trading or marketing centre: a large shop (*pl* **emporia, emporiums**)

emport *obs fm vb* **import**

emprest *var fm obs n* **imprest**

emprise *arch n* an undertaking *obs vb* to undertake

emption *n* the act of buying

empyromancy *n* a very ancient method of divination, the study of the behaviour of certain objects placed on a sacrificial fire. The objects *incl* eggs, flour, incense and even a shoulder-blade.

emulge *vb* to drain out (the contents of bodily organs)

emulsin *n* a neutral substance found in almonds

emulsor *n* an apparatus used for emulsifying

emure *obs fm vb* **immure**, to imprison

en *n* the chief priest of a Babylonian shrine: the letter N, anything having the shape of the letter N: a printer's measure equal to half an em *dial fm prons* **him, her**

enacture *obs n* fulfilment

enaid *obs vb* to aid or assist

enair *obs vb* to give expression to

enamet *var fm dial n* **nammet**

enamor *US fm vb* **enamour**

enapt *vb* to make fit

enarch *var fm vb* **inarch**, to graft

enarm *obs vb* to equip with weaponry: to garnish with bacon: to lard

enarme *n* a strap on a shield or buckler

enarmed *her adj* having the extremities of a beast emphasised with colour

enation *n* an outgrowth from a botanical organ

encarve *obs poet vb* to carve

encase *vb* to enclose in a case

encaustic *n* the ancient process of painting with wax colours and applying heat to fix them permanently: a modern equivalent, such as enamelling *adj* pertaining to either of the above

encave *obs vb* to put in a cellar

enchain *vb* to fetter (*lit/fig*)

encharm *obs vb* to enchant in the magical sense

enchase *vb* from the standpoint of either the stone or the metal, to set a gem in precious metal: to inlay a metal with a precious metal: to engrave or ornament: to enshrine (the relic of a saint) in

enchest *obs vb* to enclose (as) in a chest

enchoric *adj* enchorical or peculiar to a country: native, popular, indigenous

encist *vb* to enclose (as) in a cist or chest

enclaim *obs vb* to bring within the scope of claim

enclasp *vb* to embrace tightly

enclave *n* a portion of a territory detached from the main body and entirely surrounded by foreign territory. For example, until the redrawing of local boundaries in the early 1960s, the town of Dudley was an enclave of Worcestershire within the county of Staffordshire. It is now part of a new county known as West Midlands.

encloister *vb* to confine (*lit/fig*)

encode *vb* to render a message or statement into a form which, if seen by an unwelcome third party, is unintelligible (note: Whilst sometimes used as a synonym for encipher, the differences are quite significant – see **CODES AND CIPHERS)**

encoder *n* one who encodes (see **CODES AND CIPHERS)**

encoignure *n* an (ornamental) piece of furniture designed to fit into a corner

encomium *n* an eulogy (*pl* **encomia, encomiums**)

encora *obs fm n* **encore**

encore (*n*) *vb* to call for an encore

encradle *vb* to lay in a cradle

Encratism *n* the doctrines of a Gnostic sect which was vegetarian, teetotal and celibate. It gradually expired.

encraty *n* self-control *esp* that practised by early Gnostic heretics who abstained from flesh, wine and marriage

encrisp *obs vb* to curl (hair or wool) tightly

encurtain *vb* to surround (as) with a curtain

endarch *adj* of plants, having the first part of the woody tissue on the inner edge

endark *obs vb* to make dark, cast into shade

endart *Shaks vb* to cast with intensity

endeer *obs fm vb* **endear**

endeign *Obs vb* to be indignant

endemial *adj* endemic

endemical *adj* endemic

ender *n* one who or that which ends

endermatic *adj* capable of acting upon or penetrating the skin

enderon *n* the true skin

endiadem *vb* to crown (*fig*)

endite *arch var fm vb* **indite** *obs fm vb* **indict**

enditer *arch fm n* **inditer**

endive *n* either of two species of chicory cultivated for crisp, curling leaves which are used in salad

endlang *S fm adv* **endlong**, on end: continuously

endoce *obs fm obsol vb* **endoss**

endodermis *n* a plant sheath comprising a single layer of cells

endogen *n* a plant which grows, like palm trees, lilies, orchids, grasses, etc, by internal development (see **exogen**)

endors *obs fm n* **endorse**

endoss *obsol vb* to put on the back of (as writing on a document: clothing on one's back)

endower (*n*) *obs vb* to dower (a woman) (*pa t* **endowered, endowred**)

endowred see **endower**

endue *vb* to introduce: to clothe or invest with (that spiritual or that physical)

enduer *obs n* one who invests another or others with such as land

enduro *US n* a long race (*pl* **enduros**)

enema *n* a liquid injected into the rectum for medicinal reasons (*pl* **enemas, enemata**)

energic *adj* vigorous

energical *obs adj* of or pertaining to energy

energid *n* the protoplasm of a cell and the nucleus of that cell considered as a unit

enervate *adj* wanting in strength of character: unmanly, effeminate *vb* to weaken mentally or morally

enerve *obs vb* to enervate, deprive of nerve or energy: to weaken

enfat *obs vb* to flatten

enfile *obs vb* to thread (objects) for the purpose of suspending (them)

enfiled *her adj* having a sword thrust through

enfire *obs vb* to set on fire: to inflame (*lit*/*fig*)

enfoil *vb* an emphatic or poetic *fm* of **foil**

enforest *vb* to convert land into a forest (GAME PLAYER'S note: The last recorded usage was 1662. However, it is not considered *obs* by the dictionary used for the UK Scrabble championship. It is ignored by the dictionary for the North American equivalent.)

engall *obs vb* to affect with gall

engaol *vb* the same as **enjail**, to imprison, though writers from Shakespeare onwards tend to restrict it to a *fig* context. For example, a writer in 1844 used the poetic phrase, '*Engaoled in this unhealthy time*'.

engarb *vb* to clothe

engeal *obs vb* to freeze

engild *vb* to gild: to bathe with golden light (*fig*)

engine (*n*) *vb* to equip with an engine *obs vb* to deceive: to torture

enginer *Shaks fm n* **engineer**

engird *vb* to surround (as) with a girdle

engirt *pa t vb* engird *obs vb* to encircle (with)

engislet *obs her n* a small shield in the centre of and covering an otherwise quartered design of a coat of arms

engist *Obs vb* to arrange the resting places for a journey

englas *Obs fm pl* **angels**

engles *Obs fm pl* **angels**

englot *obs fm arch vb* **englut**

englue *vb* to glue or secure as with glue (*lit*/*fig*): to ensnare (*lit*, as in trapping a bird with birdlime/*fig*)

englut *arch vb* to swallow (up)

engold *obs vb* to plate or cover with gold

engore *vb* to stain with blood

engraff *arch vb* to engraft: to beget

engraft *vb* to graft something on

engrail *vb* to give a (decorative) serrated edge to

engrale *obs fm vb* **engrail**

engram *n* the lasting impression of an experience: the supposed inheritable impression of a stimulus or experience: a memory trace

engreat *var fm obs vb* **ingreat**

en-gree *obs adv* in good part

engrief *Obs S fm obs vb* **engrieve**

engrieve *obs vb* to cause grief: to make grievous

engroove *vb* to form a groove in: to fit into a groove

enheart *obs vb* to encourage: to enclose within the heart

enherd *obs S vb* to express agreement

eniac *n* an early American electronic computer

enigma *n* an obscure or ambiguous statement: a puzzle: a mysterious person or situation (*pl* **enigmas, enigmata**)

enigmata *pl* enigma

enigmatist *n* one who devises enigmas or puzzles *obs n* one who speaks enigmatically

enisle *vb* to place or settle on an isle: to isolate (*fig*)

enlace *vb* to bind with a lace or laces: to enfold or embrace: to entwine or entangle (also *fig*): to cover with a network (*fig*)

enlard *obs vb* to fill with lard or fat

enlardge *obs fm vb* **enlarge**

enlay *var fm n/vb* **inlay**

enlead *obs vb* to fasten or cover with the metal lead

enleve *Obs vb* to raise or represent in relief

enlevé *her adj* raised

enlight *arch vb* to illuminate (*lit/fig*)

enlimn *obs vb* to paint in bright colours

enlistee *US n* one who is enlisted

enlock *vb* to enclose (*lit/fig*)

enmind *obs vb* to remind

enmity *n* ill-will, hostility

enmoss *poet vb* of nature, to cover with moss (GAME PLAYER'S note: The dictionary used for the UK Scrabble championship only lists **enmossed**, the original *fm* as coined and used by Keats)

enmuse *obs vb* to bewilder

ennet *obs vb* to entangle

enodal *adj* without nodes (knots, lumps or swellings)

enorm *adj* in Scottish law, of the damage suffered by a party to a contract being greater than 50% of the whole worth of that contract *arch adj* gigantic: monstrous *obs vb* to make monstrous

enorn *obs vb* to adorn: to adore

enose *obs vb* obscure but probably means to baffle or perplex

enosis *n* the political concept of a united state of Cyprus with Greece

enounce *vb* to state in definite terms: to proclaim

enow *arch adj* the plural of **enough** where the noun is either expressed or implied (essentially restricted to literary Scottish) (note: In the Middle English period from the 13th to 15th centuries, **enough** had such *fms* as **enohw, ynowh** and **inowhe**, even entering modern English as **ynowghe**. Simultaneously an alternative pronunciation, represented by the *fm* **enoff**, was concurrent with **ynowghe** and outlived it by a further two centuries.) *obs fm adv* **enough**

enpair *obs fm n/vb* **impair**

enpeople *var fm obs vb* **empeople**

enpress *Obs vb* to press hard upon: to oppress (GAME PLAYER'S note: Whilst one recorded *infl fm* is the same as would be today's, **enpresses**, a *var fm*, **enprece**, was *infl* as **enprecez**. To illustrate further the error of assuming modern *fms* for an *Obs* word, the *vb* **press** was, at that time, *infl* as **pressen**.)

enrace *obs vb* to implant

enrach *obs vb* to ravish

enrail *obs vb* to enclose (as) with a railing

enrange *obs vb* to arrange

enrapt *adj* in rapture

enrase *obs vb* to erase, obliterate

enravish *vb* to enrapture: to throw into an ecstasy with intense delight

enrib *vb* to put within the ribs

enridged *Shaks adj* formed into ridges

enright *obs vb* to invest with a right or title

enring *poet vb* to encircle

enripe *obs vb* to bring to ripeness

enrive *obs poet vb* to tear

enriven *obs poet adj* torn

enrough *vb* similar to its anagram, **roughen**, to make rough, though far more limited in scope. Basically it is used only for the sea.

enrut *vb* to cause a rutted (road) surface

ensaint *vb* to make a saint of

ensample *arch n* an example: a sound precedent: a practical warning *obs vb* to set forth as, to instruct by or to give an example

ensate *adj* of plants, sword-shaped

enscale *obs vb* to attune

enseal *arch vb* to affix one's personal seal to (a document): to certify by putting a seal or stamp upon: to seal up

enseam *vb* to mark as with a seam *obs vb* to grease: of a hawk or a horse, to build muscle at the expense of fat *obs n* superfluous fat

ensear *obs vb* to dry up

enseat *obs vb* to install

enseem *poet fm vb* **seem**

ensiform *adj* of such as leaves, sword-shaped

ensight *Obs fm n* **insight**

ensign (*n*) *now her vb* to place such as a crown or mitre above the main design

ensilage *n* the preservation, without drying, of green fodder: silage *vb* to preserve such in a silo or pit: to convert into silage

ensilate *vb* to ensilage

ensile *vb* to place (such as grass) in a silo: to convert into silage

ensnarl *now US vb* to entangle *obs vb* to gnash the teeth

ensoap *obs vb* to place in soapy water

ensorte *obs vb* to bewitch

ensoul *vb* to unite with or infuse with a soul

ensphere *vb* to enclose (as) in a sphere: to give a spherical form to (*lit/fig* all senses)

enspire *obs fm vb* **inspire**

enstable *obs vb* to bring to a stable condition

enstage *obs vb* to stage a theatrical production

enstall *obs var fm vb* **install**

enstar *obs fm vb* **instar**

enstatite *n* a variety of the mineral, diallage, which ranges in colour from a greyish or greenish white to olive green or brown

ensteep *obs vb* to immerse

enstile *obs fm arch vb* **enstyle**

enstore *obs vb* to repair

enstyle *arch vb* to style, call

ensuer *n* a follower

entable *vb* to inscribe on a table

entail *n* the settlement of the succession of a landed estate such that a subsequent possessor cannot amend the line of devolution: a predetermined order of succession: a necessary sequence *vb* to make such a settlement: to have as a necessary consequence *obs vb* to carve, to sculpture: to make an incision in: to keep account by a tally of notches

entailer *n* one who entails

entaille *var fm obs vb* **entail** (basically an *Obs fm* but the *infl*, **entailled**, was used as late as 1555)

entame *vb* to tame or subdue *obs vb* to become tame: to make the first cut in, to open such as a discussion (*fig*) *Obs vb* to wound (*lit/fig*) (GAME PLAYER'S note: The dictionary used for the UK Scrabble championship records the *vb* only, but assigns all known usage to Shakespeare. Whilst he certainly used it, so have subsequent writers and it is extant. The *obs* and *Obs vbs* were especially favoured by Caxton.)

entases *pl* entasis

entasia *n* spasmodic contraction of a muscle (*pl* **entasias**)

entasis *n* a very slight swelling at the base of an architectural column (*pl* **entases**)

entask *obs vb* to put a task upon

entastic see **entatic**

entatic *adj* of or pertaining to entasis: of a substance, aphrodisiac (GAME PLAYER'S note: Experts consider the word *obs* and the leading British authority, the *Oxford English Dictionary*, considers **entastic** to be an *erron var fm*. Two different American dictionaries, *incl* the one used for the North American Scrabble championship, accept **entastic** as being the standard *adj* for **entasis**. Neither comments on aphrodisiac properties.)

entellus see **langur**

entender *obs vb* to make tender (*lit/fig*): to weaken

entera *pl* enteron

enteral *adj* of or pertaining to the intestine or its content

enterer *n* one who enters a physical place *obs n* an initiate

enteres *var fm obs n* **entress**

enteric *adj* of or pertaining to the intestines

enteron *n* the alimentary canal (*pl* **entera, enterons**)

entervail *var fm obs n* **intervale**

entest *obs adj* interwoven

enthraldom *n* the condition of being enthralled (*lit/fig*)

enthronise *obs fm arch vb* **enthronize**, to enthrone (*lit/fig*): to exalt (GAME PLAYER'S note: The dictionary used for the UK Scrabble championship considers both *fms* extant and in current standard usage. Also see **inthronize**, a later *fm* than enthronise, but which is not available for that contest.)

entier *obs fm adj/adv/n* **entire**

entine *obs vb* to kindle

entinsel *obs vb* to cause to glitter

entire (*adj/adv/n*) *obs vb* to unite

entise *obs fm vb* **entice**

entitler *n* one who gives a title or name to

entoil *arch vb* to ensnare

entomic *adj* of or pertaining to insects

entopic *adj* situated or occurring in its normal place

entotic *adj* of the interior of the ear

entozoa *pl* entozoan or entozoon

entozoan *var fm n* **entozoon** (*pl* **entozoa, entozoans**)

entozoic *adj* of or pertaining to entozoa: of a disease, caused by such

entozoon *n* any internal parasitic creature (*pl* **entozoa**) (also see **entozoan**)

entrail (*n*) *obs vb* to interlace

entrain *vb* to bring on as a consequence: to board or put aboard a railway train

entral *obs n* entry

entrap *vb* to catch (as) in a trap *obs vb* to supply with trappings

entreative *obs adj* of the nature of an entreaty or earnest request: characterized by such

entrepot *n* a (bonded) warehouse: a port or trading centre through which goods pass without incurring duties

entres *var fm obs n* **entress**

entress *obs n* entry in the varying senses of right or permission, a means or place, initiation

entresse *var fm obs n* **entress**

entrism *var fm n* **entryism**, the practice by a left wing extremist of infiltrating a political or trade union local branch under false colours with a view to eventual control of power

entrist *var fm n* **entryist**, one who practises entryism (see **entrism**)

entropion *n* inversion of the eyelids

entropium *var fm n* **entropion**

entrude *obs fm vb* **intrude**

entruder *obs fm n* **intruder**

enturf *obs vb* to bring to the state of being turf

entwist *vb* to twist round

enunciate *vb* to give a definite expression to: to utter, pronounce or proclaim

enunciator *n* one who or that which enunciates

enure *vb* to take place, to have effect *var fm vb* **inure**

enuresis *n* involuntary urination, bed wetting (*pl* **enureses**)

enuretic an undefined adjective which appears in at least three different dictionaries *incl* those used for the UK and North American Scrabble championships, all of which relate it to **enuresis**. In addition, the UK Scrabble reference work has it as an undefined noun. Its anagram is **ceinture**.

envade *obs fm vb* **invade**

envest *obs fm vb* **invest**

envier *n* one who envies

enwind *vb* to (make into a) coil (*lit*/*fig*)

enwound *pa t vb* **enwind**

enwreathe *vb* to surround (as) with a wreath (*lit*/*fig*)

enzootic *adj* the bovine equivalent of endemic i.e. of a cattle disease, peculiar to a specific situation

eo *Obs fm pron* **you**

eobiont *n* a living organism produced from non-living material

eolith *n* a prehistoric stone tool of the simplest kind

eom see **be**

eonism *n* the addiction of a male transvestite to acting in as complete a female manner as he can

eosin *n* any of various dyes, usually of a reddish colour obtained from coal tar

eosine *var fm n* **eosin**

ep *n* an aspen tree (*obs* except as a syllable in English place names)

epacrid *n* any species of *Epacridae*, a family of

heath-like plants found at the higher altitudes of parts of southern Asia and Australia, the typical genus of which being *Epacris*.

epacris *n* a species of *Epacris* (see **epacrid**)

epact *n* the difference to the nearest day between the lengths of a twelve month solar and lunar year: the age of the moon in days on the first day of the year

eparch *n* the governor of an eparchy or administrative subdivision of Greece: the metropolitan, senior to an archbishop but junior to a patriarch, in charge of an ecclesiastical eparchy

eparchy *n* a Greek province

epe *Obs vb* to cry aloud *var fm obs adj* **yepe**, in the senses of active, nimble, alert, bold, daring (other senses are *Obs* and epe was the last recorded *fm*)

Epeira *n* the genus of the common garden spider (*−cap*) *n* any spider of this genus

ephedra *n* any of a genus of desert shrubs, the source of ephedrine, a substance used in the treatment of asthma

epi *n* a projection of the apex of a roof or spire: a short (coastal) spur of a railway line

epical *adj* of or pertaining to an epic

epicarp *n* the outermost layer of the wall of the ripened ovary of a flower

epicure (*n*) *obs vb* to behave as an epicure with a cultivated taste for the pleasures of eating and drinking

epiderm *n* the skin of a leaf

epidote *n* a yellowish-green to black aluminium calcium silicate, common in many crystalline rocks

epigon *n* one of a generation subsequent to an (illustrious) ancestor

epilate *vb* to pull out or remove hair

epilation *n* the action of removing hair from the body

epilator an undefined noun which appears to be exclusive to one particular dictionary and which presumably means one who and/or that which removes hair (*presumed pl* **epilators**). Anagrams of both the *sing* and *presumed pl* are listed.

epimer *n* either of an isometric pair of compounds (see **isomer**) which differ only in the relative positions of an attached hydrogen and hydroxyl

epinaos *n* a rear vestibule (*pl* **epinaoi**)

epiploic *adj* of or pertaining to the omentum

epipolic *adj* of or pertaining to the surface

epirot *obs n* one who lives inland (as opposed to a coastal dweller)

episod *obs fm n* **episode**

episodal *adj* of the nature of an episode

episodial *adj* episodic

epispore *n* the outer covering of the spore of a fern or a lichen

epistel *Obs fm n* **epistle**

episternal *adj* situated on the breastbone

epistler *n* the writer of an epistle

epistoler *n* one who writes an epistle or letter: one who reads the epistle in the church

epithermal *adj* having energy just above that of thermal energy

epocha *arch fm n* **epoch**, a particular period of time

epode *n* a type of lyric poem having alternate long and short lines: an incantation: a solemn, serious poem

epodic *adj* of the nature of or pertaining to an epode

epopt *n* one initiated into the ancient Eleusinian mysteries, a seer

epsilon *n* the fifth letter of the Greek alphabet

epulis *n* a tumour of the gum (*pl* **epulis**)

epulotic *adj* having the power to form a healing scar *n* a medicament with this quality

epurate *vb* to purify (*lit/fig*)

equale *obs fm adj/n* **equal**

equaled *US fm vbl infl* **equalled**

equaling *US fm vbl infl* **equalling**

equant *adj* of an imaginary circle, the equalizing effect of being an equidistance from a central point. The use is mainly confined to early astronomical theory concerning the movement of heavenly bodies.

equinity *n* the nature or character typical of the horse kind

eqwal *var fm dial n* **hickwall**

er *interj* expressing hesitation

erade *obs vb* to scrape off

erande *obs fm n* **errand**

eranist *n* a meal to which each contributes his or her share: a contribution

erasion *n* (an instance of) the action of erasing

Erasmus *pers n* Desiderius Erasmus (1466–1536) the Dutch humanist whose aim of ecclesiastical reform paved the way for Luther

Erastian *adj* of or pertaining to Erastus and his doctrines *n* an adherent of his doctrines (see **Erastus**)

Erastus *pers n* a 16th century Heidelberg physician who promoted the doctrine that the State was superior to the Church

erbia *n* erbium oxide, one of three earths formerly classified together as yttria

erbium *n* a metallic element of the rare earth series

erc *Ork n* a small quantity

erde *obs vb* to dwell or inhabit

Erdgeist *Ger n* an earth spirit

erding *obs n* a dwelling

erecter *var fm n* **erector**

erimital *adj* of an eremite or hermit

eremite *n* a hermit

eremited *arch adj* of military men, retired

erepsin *n* an enzyme of the small intestine

erept *vb* to carry off

erethism *n* abnormal activity in an organ, tissue or other bodily part

Erewhon *n* nowhere spelt backwards as the name of an imaginary Utopian country in the satirical works *Erewhon* (1872) and *Erewhon Revisited* (1901) by Samuel Butler

erf *S Afr n* a small plot of land (*pl* **erven**) *S fm now dial adj* **argh** *Obs n* cattle

erfkin *Obs n* the bovine animals (i.e. cattle (erf) and their kin)

ergastic *adj* constituting the non-living by-products of a protoplasmic activity

ergat *var fm obs vb* **ergot**

ergate *n* an unfertile female worker ant

ergot *n* a disease of rye and other grasses *obs vb* to argue

eriach *var fm n* **eric**

eric *n* in old Irish law the payment, by the murderer, of compensation to the next of kin of the victim

Erica *fem fm masc pers n* **Eric**, meaning 'ever

king': the genus of heath, a small shrub of barren open country (*–cap*) *n* a plant of this genus

erick *var fm n* **eric**

Eric Lam *pers n* the king of Denmark (1137–1147)

eriff *obs n* a canary more than two years old

erigant *erron fm obs n* **herigaut**

eringo *var fm n* **eryngo**

erinite *n* an emerald green coloured arseniate of copper found in Ireland and Cornwall

Erinys *n* a Fury, any one of three goddesses of vengeance (Alecto, Megaera or Tisiphone) each of whom had snakes intertwined in her hair: an avenging or tormenting spirit: a ferociously angry woman (*pl* **Erinyes**)

eristic *adj* of or pertaining to controversy *n* one who disputes

eristical *adj* eristic (GAME PLAYER'S note: Valid for the UK Scrabble championship as the dictionary it uses for reference considers the word extant. Other authorities, in the view of the fact that the last recorded literary usage was 1673, consider the word *obs.*)

erlish *adj* weird, ghostly

erl king *n* the king of the elves, a goblin who dwells in the Black Forest of Germany (note: The correct translation should be 'alder king')

erme *obs vb* to make miserable, to harass, to vex: to grieve

ermit *obs fm n* **hermit**

ermite *obs fm n* **hermit**

ern *dial fm n/vb* **iron** *dial fm vb* **earn** *obs vb* to flow (also see **be**)

Ernest *var fm masc pers n* **Ernust**

ernit *dial fm n* **earthnut**

Ernust *masc pers n* meaning 'earnestness'

erodent *adj* of a medicine which causes erosion *n* any substance which erodes

Erodium *n* the storksbill genus of the geranium family (*–cap*) *n* any plant of this genus

Eros *n* Cupid or a representation of him as a god of love: an asteroid which comes within 13 million miles of the Earth (*pl* **Erotes**, also (Tennyson) **Eroses**)

erose *adj* of such as a leaf, having the edge marked as though bitten by an animal

Erotes *pl* Eros

erotesis *n* a figure of speech in which the speaker boldly asserts the opposite of what is asked

erotogenic *adj* designating that giving rise to sexual desire

errander *n* one who goes on an errand

errant *adj* wandering in search of adventure: quixotic: straying from accepted standards *n* a knight errant, a knight who wandered in search of adventure *nonce vb* to wander in search of adventure

errish *dial fm n* **eddish**

ersatz *adj* substitute, fake *n* a substitute (*pl* **ersatzes**)

ersh *dial fm n* **eddish**

ert *now S vb* to incite: to irritate: to provoke (also see **be**)

erter *obs n* one who provokes

eruct *vb* to belch

ervil *obs n* bitter vetch, the plant

eryngo *n* the plant, sea holly: the root of the plant coated with sugar and eaten as a delicacy or an aphrodisiac (*pl* **eryngos, eryngoes**)

es *n* the letter S, anything in the shape of the letter S (*pl* **esses**): a Danish unit of weight *Obs n* carrion

escalado *var fm n* **escalade**, the scaling of a defensive wall by ladder (*pl* **escaladoes**)

escale *obs vb* to scale or climb

escarp *n* a fortification provided by a steep bank or wall: a natural formation similar in appearance *vb* to create an escarp

eschalot *n* the shallot, a small onion

eschar *n* a portion of dead tissue

escheat *n* the reversion of land to a superior landowner in the event of the death of the owner intestate without heirs. In the USA, it reverts to the state. In Britain to the Crown though, before 1926, to the Crown or to a local lord of the manor. (note: Technically, in the duchy of Lancaster, it still reverts to the duke and, by one of those delightful British curiosities, the Queen is the duke, not the duchess, of Lancaster): forfeiture of property, real or personal: confiscation *vb* of land, to become an escheat

eschew *vb* to shun, avoid

esclandre *n* notoriety: that which causes it

escolar *n* a large, rough-scaled, highly prized food fish resembling a mackerel found at depths of between 100 and 400 fathoms in the Mediterranean, the Atlantic and the southern seas

escot *obs vb* to pay for the maintenance of

escribano *Sp n* a notary (*pl* **escribanos**)

escroc *Fr n* one who swindles

escrod *n* a broiled codling (also see **scrod**)

escrol *var fm n*/*her n* **escroll**

escroll *n* an escrow *her n* a scroll

escrow *n* a deed held by a third party until a particular condition has been met

escudo *n* the standard monetary unit of (*a*) Portugal (*b*) Chile: an old Spanish silver coin equal to ten reals (*pl* **escudos**)

ese *var fm Obs n* **es**

eserine *n* a white, tasteless, toxic alkaloid obtained from the calabar bean and used medicinally to produce contraction of the pupil of the eye

esile *var fm obs n* **eisell**

esling *dial n* a young salmon spawned in the autumn and yet to go to sea (see **SALMON**)

eslior *obs fm n* **elisor**

eslisor *obs fm n* **elisor**

esloin *obs fm arch vb* **eloin**

espace *Obs n* space

espada *Sp n* a sword(fish): a matador

espalier *n* a latticework on which trees are trained *vb* to train a tree on such

esparse *obs vb* to scatter

esparto *n* Spanish grass, used since ancient times for making of cordage and shoes and now also used for making paper (*pl* **espartos**)

espaut *obs n* millet

Espayne *obs fm n* **Spain**

espeir *var fm Obs n* **espeire**, hope

espial *n* observation

espice *obs n* an aromatic medicament

espier *n* one who watches or observes *obs n* a spy

espiot *obs n* a spear

espire *obs var fm vb* **expire**

esplees *n pl* the products of the land, as hay or corn etc

esplin *S dial n* a young man

espousal *n* adoption or support *arch n* a betrothal ceremony: a marriage

espred *obs adj* spread

espringal *n* a mediaeval military catapult which fired darts

esprit *n* spirit and liveliness

esprite *obs n* mind, spirit

esprited *obs adj* spirited

essart *n* a clearing in a forest *vb* to grub up trees

essel *obs n* a wooden or iron beam

Essene *n* one of a Jewish ascetic sect that flourished in the Holy Land from the 2nd century BC to the 2nd century AD

essign *obs fm vb* assign

essive *n* in the Finnish language (one of the Finno-Ugric languages, completely unlike the Indo-European languages of Western Europe) the name given to one of the fifteen cases of a noun, that which expresses a continuous state of being *adj* of grammar of any language, denoting a state of being

esstat *obs fm n* **estate**

estal *obs n* a place

estale *Obs vb* to hang such as drapery

estall *obs vb* to pay by instalments

estate (*n*) *arch vb* to give an estate or secured position to

ester *n* any of various substances such as oils, natural fats and waxes formed by the reaction of an acid with an alcohol *var fm dial n* **astre**

esterase *n* a type of enzyme

Esther *fem pers n* meaning 'star'

esthetics *var fm n pl* **aesthetics**, the philosophy of taste, the appreciation of beauty in nāture and art

estlar *obs S fm n* **ashlar**

estler *obs S fm n* **ashlar**

estoc *n* a short sword

estop *vb* to stop, bar or hinder: to plug

estovers *n pl* necessaries allowed by law i.e. alimony, maintenance of a convict, that wood deemed essential for such purposes as house or fence repair which a tenant may take from the estate (GAME PLAYER'S note: The dictionary used for the UK Scrabble championship gives a *sing fm*, **estover**, which only appears in other dictionaries as being an Anglo-French *fm* of the Old French *vb* **estovoir**, to be necessary. The dictionary used for the USA championship stays within the mainstream of British and American scholarship and permits only **estovers**.)

estrade *n* a dais or raised platform

estragon *n* the herb, tarragon

estrain *obs vb* to bind tightly

estral *US fm adj* **oestral**

estrange *vb* to alienate: to divert from

estrapade *n* the action of a horse in attempting to rid itself of a rider by such means as bucking: a torture of historic times whereby a person was bound to a rope by hands and feet then drawn to a great height before being dropped

estray *n* in law, a stray animal *arch vb* to stray

estre *obs n* any specified place with no qualification as to size or other limitation. Thus it can be such as a dwelling, an estate, a locality or even a region.

estreat *n* the true extract, copy or note of some original legal document *esp* that given to such as a bailiff for him or her to act upon *vb* to make such an extract for the purpose of prosecution: to enforce that with which the extract is concerned

estreine *var fm dial n* **strene**, a New Year's gift

estrene *var fm dial n* **strene**, a New Year's gift

estrepe *vb* of a tenant, to commit damage to land such as cutting down trees

estrich *n* the trade term for the soft downy feathers of an ostrich *obs n* an ostrich

estridge *var fm obs n* **estrich**

estrin *US n* an oestrogen, any of the female sex hormones

estriol *var fm n* **oestriol**

estrone *US n* an oestrogen, any of the female sex hormones

estrous *US fm n* **oestrus**

estrual *US fm adj* **oestrual**

estrum *US fm n* **oestrum**

estrus *US fm n* **oestrus**

estuar *obs fm n* **estuary**

esurient *adj* hungry (now used in a humorous context) *n* a glutton

et *now dial fm prep* **at** *dial interj* a command to a horse to move forward *obs fm vb* **eat**

eta *n* the seventh letter of the Greek alphabet: a member of the lowest Japanese social class

etacism *n* the pronunciation of eta, the seventh letter of the Greek alphabet, after the manner of Erasmus rather than that of modern Greek (also see **itacism**)

étage *Fr n* a floor or storey

étagère *n* an ornamental stand having shelves

etamin *var fm n* **etamine**

etamine *n* a loosely woven fabric

étape *Fr n* a resting place or other stage in a journey

étatisme *Fr n* rigid control by the state over the individual

eterne *arch adj* eternal *obs vb* to make eternal *Obs n* eternity

etesian *n* an annually recurring wind

ethal *n* a solid transparent fatty substance used in detergents and pharmaceuticals

ethane *n* a colourless, odourless, gaseous compound of the paraffin series: a colourless, odourless hydrocarbon of the methane series

ethene *n* a colourless, flammable, fatty hydrocarbon used in the manufacture of such as polythene and also known as ethylene, heavy carburetted hydrogen or olefiant gas *Obs fm n* **heathen**

etheric *adj* of or pertaining to ether

etherical *adj* (GAME PLAYER'S note: Valid for the UK Scrabble championship with a sense defined in its current reference dictionary as 'ethereal', this same word is considered *obs* by other authorities in the following sense:– of or pertaining to the pre-20th century view of space (called ether) as being a region of air beyond the clouds and extending to the heavens. Discounting 'ethereal' as being relative to ether in this sense (the basic sense) then, presumably, whatever remains is applicable.)

etherise *var fm vb* **etherize**, to convert into the colourless volatile liquid, ether: to render spirit-like

etherism *n* that which occurs within a body due to the administration of the vapour of ether

etherist *n* one who administers ether: one addicted to ether

ethicist *n* an ethician, one who writes or is versed in ethics

ethion *US n* a pesticide

Ethiop *arch n/adj* Ethiopian

ethiops *n* any of various black or dark coloured compounds of metals such as black oxide of iron or black sulphide of mercury

ethnic (*adj*) *obs n* one who is neither a Christian nor a Jew *collq n* (*usually in pl fm*) an immigrant *esp* one maintaining his/her own country's customs and culture

ethologic *adj* ethological or pertaining to the science of human character

ethologist *n* a writer on ethics

ethology *n* the study of animal behaviour (*pl* **ethologies**)

ethyl *n* any petrol which has been treated with an anti-knock substance: a univalent chemical radical of the paraffin series

Etnean *adj* of Mount Etna, the Sicilian volcano

étourdi *Fr adj* thoughtless, foolish (*fem* **étourdie**)

étrier *n* a mountaineer's small rope ladder

Etruscan *n* one of an ancient people in central Italy whose civilization greatly influenced the Romans: the language of the ancient Etruscans *adj* of or relating to the Etruscans, their language, culture and Etruria, their country

ett *S n* habit, custom

ettin *var fm n* **eten**, a giant

ettle *n* purpose: opportunity *dial n* the nettle *now S & dial vb* to purpose: to assign: to aim at (*lit*/*fig*): to guess, to divine

ettler *now dial n* a schemer, one who aspires

ettling *now S & dial n* intention, purpose

eu *obs fm n* **yew** *Obs fm pron* **you**

eucrite *n* a type of coarsely crystalline igneous rock

euouae *n* a Gregorian cadence

euphonise *var fm vb* **euphonize**, to make agreeable in sound

euphroe *n* a wooden block used on a sailing ship to prevent the topsail chafing against the mast by passing attached cords through this block, which is also known as a **uphroe** or **crowfoot deadeye**

eusol *n* an antiseptic solution which contains hypochlorous acid

evader *n* one who evades

Evadne *fem pers n* meaning 'well-tamed'

eve (*n*) *vb* to happen immediately prior to *dial vb* to become moist or damp

evener (*comp adj*) *n* one who or that which evens

event (*n*) *obs vb* to happen as foretold: to expose to (the cooling effect of) the air

Everard *masc pers n* meaning 'brave as a boar'

evereft *Obs adv* ever after

Everest (*geographical n*) *n* the name of a game which is essentially bingo played with three dice. Two or more players each write the numbers 1 to 12 twice on a piece of paper. The dice are thrown by a player who elects to mark off any numbers off either row which correspond with one use of the dots displayed. For example, if the dice show 1, 4 and 5 then the player may eliminate *one* of the ones, *one* of the fours, *one* of the fives or, by adding, he or she may eliminate a one and a nine, or both of the fives, or just one ten, or a six and a four. The first to mark off all of his or her numbers is the winner. *fig n* anything difficult to accomplish

evering *Manx fm n* **evening**

evert *vb* to turn inside out *arch vb* to frustrate: to overthrow (a national power)

evertor *n* a muscle which rotates outwards

evidents *n pl* in Scottish law, title deeds

evil (*n*/*adv*) (*adj*) *comp* **eviler** or **eviller** *sup* **evilest** or **evillest**

evince *vb* to make evident: to prove beyond doubt *arch vb* to overcome

evirate *vb* to castrate: to emasculate (*fig*)

eviscerate *vb* to disembowel

evitate *obs vb* to shun or avoid

evitation *n* the action of avoiding

evite *arch vb* to avoid, shun (+*cap*) *n* a humorous term for a woman wearing very little clothing (i.e. a woman dressed like Eve)

eviternal *adj* eternal with an emphasis on future eternity (GAME PLAYER'S note: Essentially a 17th century word, though it was recorded by Dr Johnson who placed a finite limit upon the implied eternity. Though considered *obs* by other authorities, the dictionary used for the UK Scrabble championship considers it extant.)

evolute *n* a mathematical term for a curve regarded as traced by a point moving under the specific condition of being the centre of curvature of another curve (which is named the **involute**)

ew *n* the fountain-head of a stream (*Obs* except as a syllable in English place names) *dial fm vb* **owe** *Obs fm n* **yew** *Obs fm pron* **you**

ewder *S n* vapour, smoke

ewte *dial vb* to pour in

ex *collq n* one no longer enjoying a particular personal relationship (*pl* **ex's** or **exes**)

examinate *n* one under (legal or scholastic) examination *adj* examined (*obs* except as a revival in a work by Scott) *obs vb* to examine (*pa t* **examinated**)

exanimate *adj* inanimate *obs vb* to dishearten: to kill: to suffocate (note: This essentially early 17th century *vb* was revived in 1878 in a humorous *fig* sense of 'make breathless'.)

exceptant *adj* taking exception *n* one who takes exception *esp* a defendant who objects to the judge or a juror

excitation *n* the action or an instance of exciting

excitor *n* one of the spinal nerves

exempla *pl* exemplum, an example: an anecdote or other tale illustrating a moral

exogen *n* a plant which grows by external deposit rather than by inward development i.e. a typical tree, the age of which is marked by growth rings (the opposite of **endogen**)

exort *obs fm vb* **exhort** *Obs vb* to issue forth

exotic (*adj*) *n* something from another part of the world (*pl* **exotics**)

exquire *obs vb* to search for

exsert *vb* of plants, to thrust forth

extender *n* one who or that which extends

exter *vb* to excavate or remove from the earth

extern *adj* (*mainly poet*) external *n* an outsider: a foreigner

externe *var fm n/adj* **extern** *obs vb* to alienate

exterse *obs vb* to wipe out

extine *n* the outer membrane of a spore or grain of pollen

ey *n* water (*now dial* except as a syllable in English place names) *arch or obsol fm n/interj/adv* **aye** *Obs fm n* **egg** (*pl* **eyer, eiron, eyron, eyrene, eyroun**) *Obs fm vb* **egg** (in the senses given at **eg**)

eyespot *n* the simple organ of vision of the lower animals

eyliad *obs var fm n* **œillade**

eyling *now dial n* a lean-to shed

eyot *n* a small isle in a river

eyster *Obs fm n* **oyster**

ezob *dial n* the herb, hyssop

ezop *var fm dial n* **ezob**

F

fa *n* the twentieth letter of the Arabic alphabet: the fourth musical syllable in the tonic sol-fa system (see **gamut**)

facies *n* a general aspect of such as plant or animal species

facile *adj* easily achieved or performed

facine *var fm n* **fascine**

factioner *obs n* a partisan

facture *n* the action of or the result of making

facula *n* a brighter spot on the face of the sun (*pl* **faculae**)

faddle *now dial vb* to pet or caress

faddler *now dial n* one who faddles

fade in *vb* of such as television, to introduce (sound, picture) in a gradual way

fade-in *n* that faded in (see **fade in**)

fader *now dial fm n* **father**

fady *adj* tending to fade, shading to a paler hue: weak

faerie *arch fm n* **fairy**

fah *var fm n* **fa** (see **gamut**)

faience *n* any glazed earthenware or porcelain

faier *obs fm n/adj* **fair**

failer *n* one who fails *obs fm n* **failure**

fain *adj* glad, well pleased *arch adv* gladly *obs n* gladness, joy *obs vb* to rejoice, to desire, to wish: to pretend kindness: to make glad

fainer *comp adj* **fain**, glad *obs fm n* **feigner**

fainter (*comp adj*) *n* one who faints

fair (*n/adj*) *vb* to make fair: of weather, to become fair

faire *obs fm n* **fair**

fait *obs vb* to act or speak falsely: to deceive: to lead astray

faite *obs vb* to train or tame creatures such as hawks or dogs: to subdue

fakir *n* a Hindu mendicant: a Muslim ascetic

falcate *adj* sickle-shaped

falcation *n* a hook-shaped outgrowth

falconet *n* a species of shrikes: a small field gun in use during the 16th and 17th centuries

falked *obs adj* sickle-shaped: hooked

falset *obs S n* falsehood

faltboat *n* a small collapsible boat of rubberized sailcloth

fand *obs n* a trial *obs vb* to seek: to enquire: to ask: to test: to try: to tempt into evil: to have sexual experience with

fander *obs n* fonder, a flatterer

fangel *var fm obs vb* **fangle**, to trifle *obs fm n* **fangle**, a novelty

fannell *n* a fanon or embroidered band rather like a short stole: a maniple as worn by a priest

fansey *obs fm n/adj* **fancy**

fansie *obs fm adj/n/vb* **fancy**

fansye *obs fm n/adj* **fancy**

fanworm *n* any of various species of marine worms of beauty. It constructs a tube of debris such as sand and bits of shell and, from the upper open end, radiates many feeding spines, giving it the appearance of a highly coloured flower.

faqih *n* a Muslim theologian who specialises in Islamic law (*pl* **fuqaha**)

faqir *var fm n* **fakir**

faradise *var fm vb* **faradize**, to stimulate by means of currents of inductive electricity

farce (*n*) *vb* to spice such as a speech *obs vb* to stuff food: to cram food into *Obs vb* to apply cosmetics

farcing *n* stuffing

farcy *n* a disease (*esp* of horses) rather like glanders

fardel *arch n* a bundle: an emotional or moral burden (*fig*) *obs n* a quarter of anything *obs vb* to make into a bundle

farden *now dial fm n* **farthing**, the pre-decimal British coin worth a quarter of a penny

fardle *var fm arch n/obs vb* **fardel**

fardung *var fm Obs n* **ferding**

farie *obs fm n* **fairy**

farine *obs fm n* **farinha**

faring *n* the action of the *vb* fare: travelling

farinha *n* cassava, mandioc or manihot, a tropical plant the tubers of which are ground into an edible flour

farl *S n* a thin cake of flour or oatmeal *obs S n* a quarter of such *obs vb* to make into a bundle

farle *var fm S n/obs vb* **farl**

farlet *obs fm Sn* **firlot**

farned *var fm obs n* **farnet** or **fernet**, a band, company, train of attendants

farry *obs vb* to shoe a horse

farse *n* an interpolation during a church service whereby the epistle is translated, sentence by sentence, from Latin into the vernacular: any other amplificatory phrase inserted into the liturgical format *vb* to add such explanatory passages

farset *obs n* a casket

fart (*n/vb*) *obs n* a ball of puff pastry (GAME PLAYER'S note: Perfectly acceptable for play in the extant vulgar meaning as both *n* and *vb*)

farte *var fm obs n* **fart**

fasces *n* a bundle of rods encasing an ax which, in ancient Rome, was a symbol of power

fascia (*n*) *pl fms* **fasciae, fascias**

fascial *adj* of fasces: of fascia

fascine *n* a bundle of long sticks used in the construction of such as an embankment

fascio *n* an organised political group (*pl* **fasci**)

fasciole *n* a band of colour

fasset *obs fm ns* **fawcet, facet**

Fastens *n* a short *fm* of **Fastens eve** or **Fastens e'en**, the eve of Fastens Tuesday (Shrove Tuesday)

Fates, the *n pl* any of three groups of three goddesses, Roman, Norse or *esp* Greek. In Greek mythology they determined the life and death of men. Clotho was the goddess who spun the thread of life. Lachesis assigned each mortal his or her destiny. Atropos cut the thread of life. (For the Roman goddesses see **Parca**, for the Norse goddesses see **Norn**.)

fatling *n* a young beast fattened for slaughter

father lasher *n* a bullhead, a shore fish of the eastern Atlantic belonging to the sculpin family

faucal *adj* of the fauces, the upper part of the throat

faulter *n* a culprit, an offender (*obs* except in the *S fms* **fauter** or **fautor**)

faunist *n* one who studies fauna

faunt *obs n* an infant or young child

fautor *n* one who shows favour, a patron

fawter *var fm obs n* **faulter**

fayne *var fm obs vb* **fain**

fe *n* the bebization equivalent of **la** *obs n* livestock (**wild fe**, deer): any moveable property: money *Obs fm n* **fee** *dial vb* to succeed or prosper

feal *arch adj* faithful *dial vb* to hide, conceal

fealty *n* the obligation of loyalty owed to a feudal superior: loyalty

feastful *arch adj* festive

feat (*n*) *arch adj* suitable, proper: neat, elegant *obs vb* to equip, furnish: of a hawk, to wipe its beak after feeding

featly *arch adv* cleverly, deftly: movement with graceful or nimble agility *obs adv* exactly, precisely *arch adj* graceful: of a dress, neat or well fitting

fecial *var fm n/adj* **fetial**

fect *obs var fm vb* **infect**

fecundate *vb* to make fruitful: to impregnate in the sexual sense

fedarie *Shaks n* a confederate, an accomplice

feddan *n* an Egyptian land measure approximating to the acre

feddle *obs n* a pet, a favourite *obs vb* to pamper

fedelini *n pl* the pasta vermicelli, a type of very slender macaroni (*sing* **fedelino**, an individual strand of fedelini)

fedelino see **fedelini**

federary *var fm Shaks n* **fedarie**

feer *n* one who loads coal *S n* a standard from which to judge *obs n* one who pays or receives a fee *vb* to mark out land as it is intended to be ploughed *var fm obs adj* **fere**, fierce or bold

feigner *n* one who simulates, pretends or counterfeits

feirie *S adj* nimble, vigorous

feirst *Obs fm adj/adv/n* **first**

feisty *US adj* full of nervous energy, excitable, touchy (*comp* **feistier**, *sup* **feistiest**)

felinity *n* the quality of being catlike

fellate *vb* to perform fellatio (oral stimulation of the penis) upon

felsite *n* the mineral, feldspar

felter *n* a felt maker or one who works with it *now dial vb* to tangle or mat together

feminal *adj* female, feminine

femora *pl* femur

femur *n* the human thighbone: the corresponding bone in other vertebrates: the third segment of an insect's leg (*pl* **femora, femurs**)

fenestra *n* a small opening or hole in a bone: an opening through a membrane of a plant (*pl* **fenestrae**)

fenitar *obs fm n* **fumitory**

fent *n* an opening in a robe *esp* one at the neck: a remnant of cloth *modf n* as in **fent dealer** or **fent merchant**, remnant *dial n* binding on a woman's dress *obs vb* meaning obscure but possibly to make a slit in

feodal *var fm adj* **feudal**

feodary *var fm n/adj* **feudary**

fer *obs fm arch n* **fere**

feral *adj* funereal, gloomy, of or pertaining to the dead: of an animal, wild or untamed: of a plant, uncultivated *obs n* a wild animal

fer-de-lance *n* the tommygoff, a common, widely distributed venomous snake of the Caribbean and Central American regions

Ferdie *dim masc pers n* **Ferdinand**, meaning 'venturous life'

ferding *Obs n* an army

fere *arch n* a companion or comrade *obs n* companionship *Obs n* ability *now S adj* sound in health *obs vb* to be a companion to: to make a companion of

feret *obs fm n* **ferret**

ferial *n* pertaining to a holiday: of an ordinary day of the week, one which has no special ecclesiastical designation

ferie *obs n* a holiday

ferine *adj* of or pertaining to a wild animal or animals: of a human, having a bestial nature: wild, untamed *n* a wild animal

feringe *Obs adv* suddenly (obsolete by the 12th century, after which it continued as a quasi-adjective in the *fm* **feringes dede**, sudden death, but this also expired before the approximate date of modern English)

ferity *n* brutishness, wildness: ferocity (*pl* **ferities)**

ferkin *obs fm n* **firkin**, a small cask

ferling *n* historically applied to a fourth part of various items such as an acre or a hide and the penny's quartering, the farthing

ferlot *Obs fm S n* **firlot**

fermion *n* one of a group of subatomic particles

fermison *Obs adj* designating the season when it was illegal to kill a male deer *Obs n* a place where deer were kept

ferned *adj* covered in ferns

ferny *adj* of, pertaining to or consisting of fern: overgrown with or abounding in ferns (*comp* **fernier** *sup* **ferniest)**

ferrest *Obs sup adv* far

Ferris *pers n* G W G Ferris the American engineer (1859–96) and inventor of the Ferris wheel, a huge wheel which revolves on a stationary axis and bears swinging observation cars for visitors to such as a fairground or pleasure garden

ferrite *n* any compound which is a derivative of ferric hydroxide: the pure metallic constituent in iron or steel: any of various reddish decomposition products in altered igneous rocks

ferritic *adj* consisting mainly of the pure metallic constituent in iron

ferrous *adj* of or pertaining to iron in the bivalent or divalent state where its combining value is lowest

fers *obs n* the queen in chess *obs fm arch vb* **farce**, to spice (*fig*)

fersie *obs S fm n* **farcy**

ferte *var fm obs n* **fart**

ferter *obs vb* to enshrine

fertile (*adj*) *obs vb* to fertilize

ferula *n* any of a number of species of yellow-flowered herbs of the parsley family, several of which (asafetida, galbanum and sumbrul or muskroot) supply important medicinal products: a rod: a sceptre *esp* that of a Byzantine emperor (*pl* **ferulae, ferulas)**

ferule *n* the plant, giant fennel: a cane or rod used for corporal punishment *vb* to beat with such a rod

fesnyng *n of assemb* of ferrets

festa *It n* a feast, festival, holy day

festal *adj* of or pertaining to a feast *n* a feast

festial *obs n* a festival *obs adj* pertaining to a feast

festin *obs fm n/vb* **festoon**

feston *obs fm vb* **festoon**

festur *Obs fm vb* **fester**

fetial *n* one of an ancient Roman college of priests who performed the rites connected with a declaration of war (*pl* **fetiales, fetials**) *adj* pertaining to the college described above

fetiales *pl* fetial

fetialis *n* a fetial (pl **fetiales**)

fetich *var fm n* **fetish**

fetiche *var fm n* **fetish**

fetor *n* an offensive smell or stench

fette *obs fm n* **feat** *obs fm adj* **fat**

feture *obs fm n* **feature**

feudary *n* a feudal tenant *adj* subject to feudal authority

feuter *obs fm n* **feature**

feutre *Obs fm obs n* **fewter**

feveret *n* a slight fever

fewte *obs fm n* **fealty** *var fm Obs n* **feute**, the tracks of an animal

fewter *obs n* a support on a saddle for a spear or lance *obs vb* to use a fewter

fi *n* a musical tone between **fa** and **so**

fiacre *n* a French hackney carriage

fideal *n* a water demon of the Scottish Highlands which assumes the form of a woman

fierasfer *n* the pearlfish

fiere *var fm arch n* **fere**, a companion

fiery (*adj*) *comp* **fierier** *sup* **fieriest**

figurate *adj* having a definite or characteristic shape: resembling anything of fixed form: of music, florid: designating a series of numbers related to a basic number and from which different series are created by various simple additions *n* any number from such a series *obs vb* to shape: to provide with figures of speech

filaree *var fm n* **alfilaria**

filasse *n* vegetable fibre as a basic ingredient of a manufacturing process

filature *n* the process of forming threads or of reeling raw silk from cocoons: an apparatus which assists in the process: a place where such is done

filet *var fm n* **fillet** (in the senses of a fillet steak: a narrow strip of any material: a piece of ribbon or lace worn as a hair ornament or round the neck)

filiate *vb* to affiliate

filose *adj* having a threadlike termination or appendage

filsen *Obs vb* to aid, support

filsne *Obs vb* to lurk

fimicolous *adj* living in dung

finagle *vb* to wangle: to cheat

fineer *obs vb* to obtain credit on goods by a particular form of commercial blackmail. The purchaser has the goods specially adapted to his own particular and unique fashion, then, when the question of payment arises, demands credit knowing that the trader cannot otherwise dispose of them: to veneer (*lit/fig*)

finesser *n* a schemer

finfoot *n* any of three species of odd, grebe-like birds. Apart from other differences, the **African finfoot** has bright red feet, the **Asiatic finfoot** has bright green feet and the **South American finfoot** has black and yellow striped feet. (*pl* **finfoots**)

finlet *n* a little supplementary fin such as any of the 8 to 15 such appendages found on the back of any species of the birchir. Not displayed during normal swimming, these are only raised when the fish is excited or alarmed.

fingent *adj* having the capacity to mould or fashion

fingerer *n* a thief

finite (*adj/n*) *vb* to make finite: to subject to limitations

finless *adj* without fins

fiqh *n* jurisprudence based on Muslim theology

fique *n* Mauritius hemp, the fibre of the giant lily, a stout tropical American plant

fire ant *n* a species of ant found in Surinam which has a painful bite

fireback *n* the back of a fire: a species of pheasant found in Sumatra

firebrat *n* an insect of the bristletail group found in warm places such as bakeries

firefox *n* the lesser panda (see **bearcat**)

firemouth *n* a species of cichlid fish having a brilliant red colouring for the inside of its mouth. A popular aquarium fish from South America, it belongs to the same genus as the **Jack Dempsey**, the **flag cichlid**, the **banded cichlid** and the bad-tempered **chameleon cichlid**.

Fire Ox *n* the name of the Chinese year for the corresponding period of the western calendar 11 February 1937 to 31 January 1938 (see **CHINESE CALENDAR**)

fire-red *obs adj* red, like fire

firestone *n* soft calcerous sandstone

fire stone *n* any stone which resists the action of fire and is thus chosen for such as the lining of a furnace

fire storm *n* a huge blaze which, by creating its own draught, fans its own flames

firlot *S n* a measure of capacity for grain, *approx* 1½ imperial bushels

first (*adj/adv/n*) *dial vb* to plant using a hoe *obs vb* to propose a motion (i.e. the action before seconding)

firste *obs fm adj/adv/n* **first**

firstling *n* the first of its kind, animate or inanimate

firth *n* a river mouth or other arm of the sea

FISH CLASSIFICATION See next page

fister *n* a punch or blow *obs n* one who breaks wind

fistle *dial fm n* **thistle**

fitché *var fm her adj* **fitchée**

fitchée *her adj* of a cross with a sharpened lower extremity, fixed

fitter (*n/comp adj*) *vb* to break into small pieces (*obs* except as the *now dial n pl* **fitters,** small pieces)

fiz *var fm n/vb* **fizz**

flacon *n* a small stoppered bottle of the type used for perfume or smelling salts

flamen *n* an ancient Roman priest devoted to the service of a particular god (*pl* **flamens, flamines**)

flamines *pl* flamen

flan (*n*) *dial vb* to splay

flâneur *n* one who strolls or saunters about

flaser *n* a streaky, patchy structure developed in igneous rock as a result of dynamic heat and pressure

flask (*n*) *vb* to put in a flask *obs vb* to flap

flate *obs vb* to feel nausea

flated *adj* of consonant sounds, produced by non-vibration of the vocal chords

flater *obs fm n/vb* **flatter**

FISH CLASSIFICATION All fishes are grouped in one of four classes, after which the divisions are complicated by the fact that some of the classifications are exclusive (and bracketed). The descending order of classification is as follows:– class, (subclass), (super-order), order, family, species. The classes are (*a*) **agnatha**, the jawless fishes of which only one order is extant and contains the lampreys and hagfishes (*b*) **placodermi**, extinct armour-plated fishes (*c*) **chondrichthyes**, sharks and rays in one subclass and rabbitfishes in the other (*d*) **pisces**, all other fishes in either eight superorders which contain a total of thirty orders or three subclasses containing fourteen orders of which only five are concerned with living fishes. The whole class comprises some 25,000 differies species. Restricting technical terminology to subclasses and superorders and reducing the excessively long words (all of which are suffixed '-iformes') to letters of the alphabet, a word picture of relationships of Pisces gives, in the first instance, those in the subclasses followed by those in the superorders.

1 Subclasses, **actinopterygii** (*a*) birchirs (*b*) bowfins, garpikes (*c*) sturgeons **sarcopterygii** (*a*) coelocanth (*b*) lungfishes. All other subclasses are concerned with extinct fishes.

2 Superorders, **acanthopterygii** (*a*) squirrelfishes (*b*) boarfishes, John Dories (*c*) dealfishes, oarfish, opah (*d*) pipefishes, sea horses, sticklebacks (*e*) snakeheads (*f*) swamp eels (*g*) bullheads, gurnards, scorpionfishes (*h*) flying gurnards (*i*) sea moths (*j*) perches, perch-like fishes *incl* sandeel (*k*) flatfishes (*l*) boxfishes, filefishes, porcupinefish, pufferfishes, trigger-fishes **atherinomorpha** (*a*) flying fishes, garpikes, guppies, toothcarps **clupeomorpha** (*a*) achovies, herrings, round herrings, shads **elopomorpha** (*a*) giant herrings, tarpons (*b*) eels, gulper eels (*c*) spiny eels **ostariophysi** (*a*) carps, characins, loaches (*b*) catfishes **osteo-glossomorpha** (*a*) African butterflyfish, bonytongues (*b*) elephant-snout fishes **paracan-thopterygii** (*a*) trout perches (*b*) toadfishes (*c*) clingfishes (*d*) angelfishes, frogfishes (*e*) cods **protacanthopterygii** (*a*) salmon and salmon-like fishes (*b*) whalefishes (*c*) beaked salmon, milkfish (*d*) those fishes classified as of the Ctenothrissiformes (also see **ANIMAL ADJECTIVES, COLLECTIVE NOUNS**)

flatty *slg n* one ignorant of the methods of a professional thief (*pl* **flatties**)

flatus *n* the gas which breaks from the anus (*pl* **flatuses**)

flatwise *adv* with the flat side in a stated position, as downward or against another object

flawy *adj* full of defects: gusty (*comp* **flawier** *sup* **flawiest**)

flear *dial fm vb* **fleer** *obs fm n* **fleer**, a jibe

fleat *var fm vb* **fleet**, to float

flèche *n* a spirelet or slender spire *esp* one rising from the intersection of the nave and transept ridges of the roof on some large churches: a point on a backgammon board

flecker *vb* to dapple: to scatter like flakes

fleech *S & dial vb* to flatter, coax or beguile *S n* flattery *dial fm n* **flitch**, a side of bacon

fleer *n* a fugitive: a jibe, a sneer *vb* to jibe, to sneer: to laugh in a coarse manner

flehmen *n* a rather curious activity of various ungulates typified by the action of the male **Maxwell's duiker** (a very small antelope) during the time of his mate's oestrus. Once the female begins to urinate he places his face directly into the spray and, when she has finished, he raises his head, draws back his upper lip and stands perfectly still.

fleir *obs fm vb* **fleer**

flesher *n* a butcher *US n* a saw-toothed knife used in butchery

fletcher *n* one who makes bows and *esp* arrows

fletton *n* a type of mottled yellow and pink coloured brick

flewed *adj* having flews

flews *n pl* the large chaps of such as a bloodhound

flexiloquent *adj* speaking words of double meaning (*obs* except as a verbal curiosity in literature on words)

flier *var fm n* **flyer**

flire *dial fm vb* **fleer**

flirte *obs fm n* **flirt**

flirter *n* a flirt

flite *now dial n* a slanging match between two fliters *now dial vb* to scold

fliter *now dial n* a woman addicted to abusive language

flocky *adj* woolly (*comp* **flockier** *sup* **flockiest**)

flora *n* all the plant life of a given place or time: a descriptive list of such (*pl* **florae, floras**) (+*cap*) *pers n* the Greek goddess of flowers

florae *pl* flora

flore *obs fm n/vb* **floor**

floreat *Latin* may it flourish

floreated *adj* decorated with floral ornament

floret *n* a flowerlet or little flower *esp* one of many which comprise the head of a composite flower

flota *n* a (Spanish) commercial fleet

flotter *S vb* to overflow

flouse *dial vb* to splash

flowe *obs fm vb* **flow**

flowse *dial adj* flowing, flaunting

flowsing *var fm dial adj* **flowse**

flue (*n*) *vb* to expand *now dial adj* shallow: weak, sickly

flunge *obs vb* of a missile, to fling with the object of its effectiveness being in descent (i.e. a portmanteau word, fling + plunge; *pa t* **flundge**, which retains the onomatopoeic sense)

flurn *now dial vb* to sneer (at)

fluter *n* a flautist or flutist, a flute player: one who makes grooves in metal

flutina *n* a type of accordion

fluvial *adj* of, pertaining to, occurring in a river

flux (*n*) *vb* to make or become fluid

flyboat *n* a general term for a canal boat which is faster than the average (i.e. one capable of 4 mph instead of $2\frac{1}{2}$ mph)

fo *dial n* a measure of eight square yards

foamer *n* one who foams

foetor *var fm n* **fetor**

folden *arch adj* folded

folie *obs vb* to mark, with consecutive numbers, the folios of a book *Fr n* madness, insanity

folier *obs n* a leaf of metal serving as a setting for a precious stone

foliose *adj* abounding in leaves, having leaves, leafy

fonder *comp adj* fond *var fm obs n* **fander**

fontlet *n* a little fountain: a little baptismal font

footer (*n*) *dial vb* to idle

foramen *n* a small, naturally-occurring, anatomical hole or opening *esp* one in a bone (*pl* **foramens, foramina**)

foramina *pl* foramen

foray *n*/*vb* (to make) a short raid

forçat *n* one, in France, sentenced to hard labour

fordeal *obs n* advantage *obs S n* the first place, precedence

fordel *var fm obs n* **fordeal**

fordraw *Obs vb* to defer: to tempt (*pa pple* **fordraun, fordrawn, fordrawen**)

fordrawen *pa pple Obs vb* fordraw

foreday *n* the later part of the morning

foregate *n* the front gate *S n* the street

forehorse *n* the leading horse of a team (*obs fms incl* the unlisted anagrams **for-horse, forehors**)

forelay *vb* to embarrass or frustrate *now dial vb* to prearrange: to waylay *obs vb* to lie in ambush for

forelend *arch vb* to grant or resign beforehand

foreman (*n*) *vb* to perform the supervisory office of a foreman (*infl fms incl* **foremaned, foremaning**)

foremean *arch vb* to intend beforehand

forename (*n*) *obs vb* to name or mention beforehand (the *adj*, **forenamed**, is still extant)

forenight *S n* evening *obs n* the previous night

forest (*n*) *vb* to create a forest

forestal *adj* of or pertaining to a forest *obs fm n*/*vb* **forestall**

forestall *n* something situated in front *dial n* the approach to a farmhouse *vb* to anticipate *esp* with a sense of rendering ineffective: to hinder, to obstruct: in historical times, to intercept or buy goods before they reach the market in order to enhance the price (at various times adjudged illegal)

forestine *adj* of or pertaining to forests

foret *obs fm n* **ferret** (in most senses)

foretop *n* a horse's forelock: the top of a foremast *US n* the front seat on the top of a vehicle

forinsec *adj* of feudal service due to the king, foreign (i.e. **forinsec service**, the only sense in which it is used, is that service which the king may require for an overseas activity)

forlay *Obs vb* to lay aside *var fm obs vb* **forelay**

forlend *var fm arch vb* **forelend**

formalin *n* a solution in water of the colourless poisonous gas, formaldehyde, which is used for such purposes as a disinfectant or a preservative for biological specimens

formate *n* a salt of formic acid

formulae *pl* formula (only in scientific or technical use – the standard *pl* being **formulas**)

fornicary *Obs adj* lecherous *Obs n* a fornicator

fornices *pl* fornix

fornix *n* an anatomical part, *esp* of the brain, having the shape of an arch: a vault within a building (*pl* **fornices**)

forpet *var fm S & dial n* **forpit**

forpit *S & dial n* the fourth part of any measure *esp* a peck

forray *obs fm vb* **foray** *Obs fm n* **foray**

forsary *obs n* a galley slave

forsay *obs vb* to renounce, command to exclude, forbid

forset *now dial vb* to entrap

forstalle *obs fm vb* **forestall**

forste *obs fm n* **frost**

forsteal *Obs fm n* **forestall**

forster *obs fm n* **forester**

forstere *obs fm n* **forester**

fort (*n*) *vb* to enclose in a fort: to fortify in a military sense

forthcome *vb* to come forth

forthe *Obs adv* even

forth-nift *obs n* a grand-niece

forthy *S & dial adj* outspoken

fortlet *n* a small fort

forwander *arch vb* to wander until tired and weary

forwaste *obs vb* to waste in such senses as lay waste, exhaust, make weak or be extravagant

fostal *obs fm n* **forestall**

fosten *obs fm n/adj* **fustian**

fosterage *n* the action or responsibility of fostering

fostre *obs fm vb* **foster**

fot *n* the Norwegian foot (31.37 *cm*): the Swedish foot (29.69 *cm*)

fother *n* a (cart) load: a huge quantity of gold or money (i.e. a 'cart load'): a specific quantity of a substance such as 19½ cwts of lead *vb* of marine practice, to cover thickly with oakum: to plug a leak by this method

fouet *S n* the house leek, a plant of the stonecrop family which often grows on roofs *obs n* a whip

foulder *obs vb* to flash or thunder (as turbulent weather or a gun): to crumble

fouldre *obs n* a flash of lightning

foulé *n* a cloth which has been subject to the fulling process *esp* a light woollen dress material with a glossy surface

fouler *n* one who makes foul or filthy

four-eyed fish *n* any of a genus of toothcarps (see **Anableps**) or either of two totally unrelated fishes. The first is a small blenny of the Galapagos Islands with a pair of horizontally divided eyes similar to those of Anableps. The function is unknown and this blenny has the additional oddness of leaving the water to feed on the crustaceans found on wet rocks. The second is a larger marine fish which lives at much greater depths and truly has four eyes. Below the two main eyes are two small eyes with separate retinas which are directed downwards.

foutra *obs fm n* **foutre**, a term of contempt for a person

fowel *obs fm n* **fowl**

fowle *obs fm ns* **fowl, foul** *Obs fm n* **foal**

fowlkin *Obs n* birds collectively: a bird

foxfire *n* the phosphorescent glow produced by certain fungi on decaying timber

foxier *comp adj* foxy

fracted *her adj* having a part displaced as if broken *obs adj* broken

fraenum *n* a connecting fold or membrane which restrains the organ to which it is attached (*pl* **fraena, fraenums**)

fraide *obs adj* of a horse, lame

frail (*adj*) *n* a large or very large fruit basket made of rushes: the quantity of such a fruit as figs contained in a frail

frailtee *Spens fm n* **frailty**

fraine *obs fm now dial vb* **frayne**, to inquire: to ask

fraise *n* a circular pleated collar worn by both men and women during the 16th/17th centuries: a defensive palisade: a tool used for enlarging a circular hole *dial n* commotion *var fm n* **froise**, an omelette *vb* to defend (as) with a fraise (2nd definition)

fraist *obs vb* to try, to test

fraiste *Obs fm obs vb* **fraist**

frale *obs fm n* **frail**, a basket

frase *var fm n/vb* **fraise** *obs fm n/vb* **phrase**

frate *obs fm vb* **fret**

frater *n* a monastic dining hall: a friar: a comrade

fraud (*n*) *obs vb* to cheat or defraud

freal *obs fm n* **frail**, a basket

freat *obs fm vb* **fret**

freath *var fm now dial vb* **frith**

free bench *n* a widow's right to dower out of her husband's estate

freend *S fm n* **friend**

freesed *Obs fm pa pple* **frozen**

free soiler *US n* a freeman: a politician or other person opposed to (the geographical extension of) slavery

freest *sup adj* free

freet *var fm S n* **freit**

freist *Obs fm arch n* **frist**

freit *S n* an omen

freity *adj* superstitious

FRENCH REVOLUTIONARY CALENDAR See next column

frenesi *obs fm n/adj/vb* **frenzy**

FRENCH REVOLUTIONARY CALENDAR A republican nonsense which began with year two already into its first fortnight. Established on 5 Oct. 1793, with year one beginning 22 Sept. 1792, it had a year of twelve months, each of 30 days. There were also five extra days which didn't belong to any month and were tagged on to the end of the year, six extra days in a leap year. The names of the months and the zodiac signs to which they approximately corresponded were Vendemiare (Libra), Brumaire (Scorpio), Frimaire (Sagittarius), Nivose (Capricorn), Pluviose (Aquarius), Ventose (Pisces), Germinal (Aries), Floreal (Taurus), Prairial (Gemini), Messidor (Cancer), Thermidor (Leo) and Fructidor (Virgo). There were three 'weeks', each of ten days, to these months (see **decadi**) and the whole thing was abolished on 31 Dec. 1805. (Also see **Nabonassar**)

frenise *obs fm n/adj/vb* **frenzy**

frensie *obs fm n/adj/vb* **frenzy**

frensied *arch fm adj* **frenzied**

frescade *n* a cool pathway in the shade

fresher (*comp adj*) *n* a fresh breeze *dial n* a young frog *slg n* a freshman

freshet *n* freshwater flowing directly into the sea: a freshwater flood *now poet n* a small freshwater stream *vb* of freshwater, to flood

frette *var fm n* **fret**, an ornamental lacework

frid *n* a supernatural creature of the Scottish Highlands which lives under rocks and devours all milk and crumbs spilt on the ground (*pl* **fridean**)

fridean *pl* frid

Frieda *fem pers n* meaning 'peace'

frillless *adj* without a frill

fringy *adj* resembling a fringe (*comp* **fringier** *sup* **fringiest**)

frisel *obs fm vb* **frizzle**

friska *n* in the csárdás (a Hungarian dance of a slow and a fast movement), the fast movement: the music of that movement

frisle *obs fm vb* **frizzle**

frislet *obs n* a type of small rifle

frist *arch n* a space of time *obs vb* to grant a delay: to give or extend time for repayment

friste *obs fm adj/adv/n* **first** *Obs fm arch n* **frist**

frith *n* peace, security: a woodland area *now dial vb* to fence in (*lit/fig*): to create a hedge of wattle *obs vb* to keep peaceful: to liberate *var fm n* **firth**

frithing *now dial n* material, such as brushwood, suitable for fencing

frogfish *n* any of a group of fishes related to the anglerfishes

Fronde *n* the opposition to Mazarin's administration of France during the minority years of Louis XIV

froste *obs fm n* **frost**

frot *vb* in leather work, to make supple by rubbing

frote *obs fm vb* **frot**

frothe *obs fm n* **froth**

frovere *var fm Obs n* **frover**, comfort

froward *adj* perverse *adv* perversely *obs vb* to make perverse

fruitage *n* fruit collectively: a fruit crop: the bearing of fruit

frump (*n*) *vb* to vex *arch vb* to mock, to taunt

frute *var fm obs n* **froud**, a frog or toad *obs fm n* **fruit**

fu *n* an administrative district in China or Japan (*pl* **fu**)

fudder *n* a tun of wine *arch fm n/vb* **fother** *now dial fm n/vb* **fodder** *S fm obs n* **fouldre**

fuddler *n* a toper

fulder *S fm* (*obs*) *obs n* **fouldre**

fule *S fm n/vb* **fool** *Obs fm n* **fowl**

fulham *n* a loaded die

fulmar *n* any of various birds which, though not related, look like seagulls and *incl* the various petrels and the Cape pigeon. The name itself means 'foul mew' (foul gull), originating from the fact that it has a defensive ploy of spitting an unpleasant stomach oil at an enemy.

fumarole *n* a vent of a volcano from which various hot gases *esp* steam are emitted

fumitory *n* a plant of such rapid growth that it was named in old French *fume terre* (earth smoke) to suggest smoke curling up from the ground. A preparation called **fumitory water** was once used in the treatment of leprosy.

funest *adj* portending evil or death: fatal, deadly

fuqaha *pl* faqih

furcate *adj* fork-shaped *vb* to divide as a fork

furdel *obs vb* to furl, fold

furder *obs fm adj/adv/vb* **further**

furdle *var fm obs vb* **furdel**

furlet *obs fm S n* **firlot**

furole *n* St Elmo's fire, a ball of light sometimes seen on (the higher parts of) a ship during a storm (also see **PATRON SAINTS**) *var fm n* **furfural**, a solvent obtained from the pentose sugars of agricultural waste products

furore *n* an uproar: a sudden widespread enthusiasm: frenzy, rage

fuster *obs n* a saddletree maker

fustian *n* a type of thick, twilled cotton cloth

futon *n* a Japanese floor bed

fy *interj* of disgust

fyz *obs fm n/vb* **fizz**

G

ga *n* the bobization equivalent of **fa** (+*cap*) *n* a language spoken in the Accra plains region of Ghana

gabbler *n* one who chatters in an incoherent fashion

gabion *n* a cylindrical wicker tube which is filled with earth for fortification or engineering purposes

gabler *obs fm n* **gabbler**

gab-line *var fm n* **gob-line**

gad *n* a spear: a sharp metal spike: a steel wedge used in mining: a rope made of the twisted fibres of tough twigs: a measuring rod for land: a division of open pasture in Lincolnshire *dial n* a fishing rod: a stout stick (+*cap*) *arch fm n* **God**, used in exclamations *vb* to wander about with no serious intent: to wander in desire or thought (*fig*): to use a gad in mining *arch vb* of a plant, to spread in an uncontrolled form

gadder *n* an implement for splitting rock: one who gads about

gadge *S vb* to talk idly with a stupid gravity

Gadhel *n* a Goidelic Celt. Specifically, a Celt of Ireland, Scotland or the Isle of Man as opposed to a Brythonic Celt of Wales, Cornwall or Brittany – the difference being the basic language of either grouping.

gadling *n* one of a number of small metal spikes on the knuckles of a gauntlet *obs n* a companion: a vagabond

gadolinite *n* silicate of yttrium which occurs as black crystals

gadroon *n* fluted or oval decoration used in silverwork: an architectural ornament of carved, rounded form

gag-bit *n* a bit used during the process of breaking a horse

gahnite *n* a translucent to opaque oxide of zinc and alumina varying in colour from green to almost black

gaile *obs fm n/vb* **jail**

gailer *obs fm ns* **gaoler, jailer** or **jailor**

gain (*n/vb*) *now dial adj* of roads or directions, very straight (also see *sup* **gainest**): of persons, kindly: of things, useful

gainer *n* one who gains

gainest *sup now dial adj* gain (the most usual *fm* in one of the senses *esp* in the saying, *the gainest way* (the shortest route) or the proverb, *roundabout is sometimes gainest*)

gainless *adj* useless *Obs adj* of no avail

gainly *now dial adj* graceful, comely, well-formed

gainor *obs n* one who cultivated land held under the tenure of socage

gainsayer *n* one who opposes or speaks against

gainst (*poet*) *prep* against (also in the *fm* **'gainst**)

gainstrive *obs vb* to oppose

gair *var fm S adj* **gare**

gairten *S n* a gosling

gaislin *S fm n* **gosling**

Galangalan *n* a mountain in Sorsogon Province, Luzon Island, the Philippines

galdragon *obs Shet n* a witch or sorceress

Galen *pers n* Claudius Galen (AD 131–201), a celebrated Greek physician whose theories held such sway that original investigation was discouraged for more than a thousand years *n* a physician (used in a jocular sense)

galena *n* common lead ore

Galenic *adj* of or pertaining to Galen or a Galenist or a simple vegetable remedy of the type espoused by Galen

Galenical *adj* Galenic

Galenism *n* the medical system of Galen

Galenist *n* one who followed the methods and theories of Galen

galenite *n* galena (+*cap*) *obs n* a Galenist

galeon *obs fm n* **galleon**

galeot *var fm obs n* **galliot**

galer *n* one who granted a gale, or licence to mine: one who collected the gale, or manorial tax on fish

galère *n* an unpleasant situation: an unpleasant group of people

galilee *n* a porch or chapel at the entrance to a church *modf n* for such as **galilee bell, galilee door** etc

galiot *var fm n* **galliot**

galiote *obs fm n* **galliot**

gallate *n* a salt of gallic acid, an acid in crystalline form obtained from such as gall nuts

galleot *var fm n* **galliot**

galley *n* a long, low, single-decked, sea-going vessel of ancient and mediaeval times propelled by oars (and sail): a large rowing boat: the kitchen of a ship: a long tray used by printers for holding composed type: a proof printed from such type (*pl* **galleys**)

Gallice *adv* in French

galliot *n* a Spanish or other Mediterranean small galley powered by oars and sail: a Dutch cargo vessel *obs n* one who rows a galliot (note: Among the *obs fms* are **galyote** (*obs fm n*) and **galeyot** (*var fm obs n*), a pair of anagrams not included in the lists)

gallise *vb* to add sugar and water to inferior, unfermented grape juice to bring it up to standard

galliwasp *n* any of various elongated lizards related to the glass snake and the slowworm

galloglass *n* one of a historic class of Irish fighting men armed with battle axes (Also see **kerne**)

gallowglass *var fm n* **galloglass**

gally *vb* to frighten, scare or startle

galopin *n* an errand boy *obs n* a page: a turnspit

galstre *Obs vb* to make a noise (still extant in various *dial fms* such as **goster** and **gauster**)

galyot *Obs fm obs n* **galliot**

gam *n of assemb* of whales *US n* social intercourse: visit at sea *S n* a tooth, tusk: the mouth *her n* the whole foreleg of a beast *US vb* to indulge in social intercourse *vb* of whales, to associate in a gam

gambado *n* a legging or gaiter: either of a pair of boot-like leathers attached to a saddle serving the dual purpose of a stirrup and a protection for the foot: a prank, a flourish: a spring or bound of a horse (*pl* **gambados, gambadoes**)

gambist *n* a player of the musical instrument, the viola de gamba

gambrel *n* a hooked stick used by butchers to suspend a carcass: the upper part of the hind leg of a horse: a roof which has its slope broken by an obtuse angle, effectively producing an apparent 'upper' roof and 'side' roof

gamete *n* either the female egg cell (ovum) or the male egg cell (sperm) which, when united, form a zygote or fertilized egg

gamin *n* a 'street-wise' urchin

gamine *n* the *fem* of **gamin**, a pert, impish girl

gammer *n* an old woman

gamut *n* the whole range of anything *esp* emotions: the tonic sol-fa or diatonic scale of musical notes which replaced both the bebization and bobization systems. Originally it had the musical syllables **ut, re, mi, fa, so, la, si** based upon a Mediaeval Latin hymn (*Ut* queant laxis *Re*sonare fibris, *Mi*ra gestorum *Fa*muli tuorum, *So*lve polluti *La*bii reatum, *S*ancte *I*ohannes) with **ut** subsequently replaced by **do** or **doh** and **si** replaced by **ti** or **te.**

gamy *adj* plucky (*comp* **gamier** *sup* **gamiest**)

gan *pa t arch vb* gin

gander (*n*) *dial vb* to wander aimlessly: to talk foolishly

ganderism *nonce n* conduct befitting a gander

ganderous *nonce adj* pertaining to a gander

gane *obs vb* to open the mouth in a gape (*var fm incl* **gone, goon**)

ganet *obs fm n* **gannet**

ganglion *n* a cystic tumour on a tendon sheath: a knot on a nerve from which the nerve fibres radiate: a collection of grey matter in the central nervous system: a lymphatic gland: a swelling on some species of fungi (*pl* **ganglia, ganglions**)

gangly *adj* awkardly tall and lanky (*comp* **ganglier** *sup* **gangliest**)

ganister *n* a type of stone found in Yorkshire coal measures which is ground down and mixed with fire clay to make a lining for a furnace

gannister *var fm n* **ganister**

gant *S vb* to yawn or gape

gante *obs fm n* **gannet**

gantline *erron var fm n* **girtline** (GAME PLAYER'S note: Perfectly valid for play, as are all recorded *erron fms* (see **pea** for an example of one such word becoming the standard *fm*). In the case of gantline, both the British dictionary used for the UK Scrabble championship and the American dictionary used for the North American equivalent list it as an independent word of full value. The American work fails to mention girtline whilst the British work defines girtline as a gantline.)

gantry *n* a bridgelike framework for supporting such as a travelling crane or railway signals: a stand for barrels: the display shelving and allied equipment in a licensed bar: the framework attending a large rocket on a launching pad (*pl* **gantries**)

Ganymede *n* a cupbearer: a catamite or boy used by a homosexual: the largest of the satellites of Jupiter

gar *n* either of two different fishes. One has the alternative names of **garfish, gar-pike** or **garr** and is equipped with long powerful jaws. The other, also known as the **alligator-gar**, is a huge fish with a head similar to that of an alligator. *S & dial vb* to make, to cause

Garamond *n* a typeface like that used by the 16th century French printer, Claude Garamond

garble *n* a mixture of base and precious metal *vb* to select the pick of something

gardiner *obs fm n* **gardener**

Gardner *n* a type of 19th century machine gun which has two to five barrels side by side (*−cap*) *obs fm n* **gardener**

gare *vb* to beware: to utter a warning cry of gare *S adj* eager, covetous: miserly *obs n* a javelin or similar weapon: coarse wool from the shanks of a sheep

garet *obs fm n* **garret**

garget *n* an inflammation of the head or throat in cattle, pigs or poultry: an inflammation of the udder of a cow or sheep: a distemper (*lit*/*fig*) *US n* pokeweed, the American or white hellebore

garial *n* an Indian crocodilian having a very long and slender beak-like snout totally unlike that of any other member of the crocodile family. One of the larger reptiles, up to 20 feet in length, it is numbered among the holy animals of the Hindus.

garnel *obs n* an inferior flour: a species of shrimp also called a gernel *obs S n* a granary or barn

garner *n* a granary: a store *vb* to store: to accumulate

garniture *n* furniture: ornament, embellishment: apparel

garote *var fm n/vb* **garrotte**

garotte *var fm n/vb* **garrotte**

garotter *var fm n* **garrotter**, one who garrottes

garrotte *n/vb* (to perform) the Spanish method of execution by strangulation with an iron collar

garten *arch S fm n* **garter**

Gärtner *modf n* of those parts of specifically female anatomy described by the Danish anatomist, Karl F Gärtner, and occurring in such *fms* as **Gärtner's duct, Gärtner's canal**

garvie *S n* a sprat

gasalier *n* a hanging frame for gas jets

gascon *n* a boaster

gaskin *var fm n* **gasket**, a piece of compressible material sandwiched between metal joints to act as a seal: a band of canvas or a piece of line used for binding furled sails on a vessel

gas-lime *n* lime used for purifying coal gas

gasolier *n* a hanging frame having gas burners at the end of each branch

gaspipe *n* a gun of inferior quality (contrast with **gas pipe**, a pipe which conveys gas)

gasser *n* one who operates a gassing machine

gast *S n* a fright *obs fm n* **ghost** *dial adj* barren *obs adj* terrified, afraid *obs vb* to frighten, alarm, scare

gaster *obs vb* to terrify: to destroy

Gaston *masc pers n* meaning 'a Gascon'

gastrea *n* a type of metazoan

gastrin *n* a hormone secreted by the stomach membrane to activate the gastric juices

gate-vein *now fig n* the great abdominal vein

gatter *slg n* beer, liquor

gaudgie *dial n* a fellow

gaulter *n* one who excavates gault, a type of clay

gauntry *var fm n* **gantry**

gauster *var fm dial vb* **goster**

gaybine *n* any of several showy, twining plants

gaz *var fm n* **guz** (*pl* **gaz**)

ge *n* the bebization equivalent of **ti** *var fm slg vb* **gee** (+*cap*) *n* a South American Indian language spoken in the Amazon valley, Brazil

geal *adj* of or pertaining to Earth as a planet *now dial vb* to stiffen as with cold

geant *obs fm n* **giant**

gearless *adj* devoid of gears

gearne *obs fm now S & dial vb* **girn**

gee *interj* a word of command to a horse *S & dial n* a fit of the sulks *slg vb* to behave in a correct manner: to agree

gee-string *var fm n* **G-string**

gelate *US vb* to gel

gelatin *var fm n* **gelatine**

gelatine *n* gelatin

gelatinoid *adj* of, pertaining to or consisting of gelatin: jellylike

gelation *n* making whole or firm *esp* by cooling

gelder *n* one who castrates animals

gelstre *var fm Obs vb* **galstre**

Gemara *n* the second and later portion of the *Talmud* which consists of a commentary on the *Mishna*, or first part

Gemarist *n* one who is concerned with the *Gemara*

gematria *n* a cabbalistic method of interpreting the Hebrew Scriptures by using the techniques of numerology. Whilst this may be scorned as being magical mumbo-jumbo, the latest scientific research using computers has produced the most incredible of complex codes within the original scriptures far beyond the capabilities of mortal man. Whereas the cabbalists concentrated their attention upon interchanging words which have the same numerical value, university researchers have turned their attention to the consideration of every letter which occurs in a particular numbered sequence. In consequence they have produced some amazing facts. For example, in this following passage, '*And the Lord God caused to grow out of the ground every tree that is pleasant to the sight and good for food; and the tree of life in the midst of the garden, and the tree of knowledge of good and evil . . .*' there are, in the original Hebrew, no fewer than 31 of the names of trees which grew in the Biblical Lands. This same code repeated elsewhere in the Bible produces no other trees. Similar amazing coincidences occur throughout the whole text of *Genesis*. (Also see **astrogenics** for another example of scientific examination of ancient wisdom.)

geminate *vb* to double

Geminid *n* one of a swarm of meteors which appears to originate in the constellation of Gemini

gemmy *adj* resembling a gem (*comp* **gemmier** *sup* **gemmiest**)

gemony *n* one of the **gemonies**, the steps on the Aventine Hill down which the ancient Romans had the bodies of executed criminals dragged to the river Tiber *interj* of surprise (also spelt **gemini, jiminy** etc)

gender (*n*) *arch vb* of either parent, to beget

gendre *obs fm arch vb* **gender** *Obs fm n* **gender**

genera *pl* genus

generalist *n* one who devotes himself to general studies, a non-specialist

generic *adj* belonging to a particular genus or class *n* (either rare or nonce) a genus (in *pl fm*) *nonce n* generic questions

generical *adj* generic, general

genesis *n* an origin (*pl* **geneses**)

genet *n* any of six species of small carnivores which look like a cross between a mongoose and a tabby cat. Related to both the mongoose and the civet, they are found from southern France down to South Africa.

genetical *adj* genetic

genetrix *n* a female parent (*pl* **genitrices**) (*masc* **genitor**): one's native country (*fig*)

geneva *n* gin, the spirit distilled from grain and flavoured with juniper berries

genip *n* any of various trees or shrubs *esp* the one bearing the genipap, an orange-like fruit

genital *adj* of the act of production

genitals *n* genitalia, the (external) reproductive organs

genitival *adj* of grammar, belonging to the genitive case

genitor *n* male parent (*fem* **genetrix** or **genitrix**) *obs n* a testicle

genitors *n pl* parents (see **genitor**) *obs n pl* a pair of testicles

genitrices *pl* genetrix or genitrix

genitrix *var fm n* **genetrix** (*pl* **genitrices**)

genome *n* a set of cells each having only one set of chromosomes

gens *n* in ancient Rome, a clan or house having a common ancestor in the male line: in primitive society, a group based on descent in the male line often identified by such as a totem (*pl* **gentes**)

gentes *pl* gens

gentian *n* any of various plants some of which have value as the basis of a tonic

gentiane *obs fm n* **gentian**

gentilish *adj* heathenish *obs adj* of the nature of gentiles

gentle (*adj*) *n* a maggot used as fishing bait *arch n* (usually in *pl*) one of gentle birth *vb* to appease or mollify: to render mild or tractable

gentrice *arch n* noble descent or rank: any of the fine qualities associated with such a person *arch adj* genteel, elegant

gentries *pl* gentry, those of a higher social class

gentrise *obs fm arch n/adj* **gentrice**

gentry *now S adj* neat: pretty: graceful

genus *n* a subdivision of a family of animals or plants, arbitrarily decided on the basis of certain shared characteristics and subject to change (as with all such degrees of classification) by the latest accepted opinion. In the scientific naming of animals, the genus supplies the first or generic name. For example, of the 24 species of **bee-eater** (a bird which eats bees) 21 are considered sufficiently closely related to be classified as belonging to the same genus, that of *Merops*. Thus, the **European bee-eater** and the **carmine bee-eater** (of Africa) are both given scientific names which designate the genus and species, the European bird being called *Merops apiaster* and the African bird *Merops nubicus*. (*pl* **genera, genuses**) (also see **Linnaeus**)

geocentric *adj* having the Earth considered as the centre: viewed as from the centre of the Earth *n* one who adheres to a theory that the Earth is the centre of the universe

geomancy *n* divination by observing the patterns made on a flat surface by a small handful of earth which has been cast into the air: any of various other systems of fortune telling which involve studying earth

geraniol *n* an oily colourless alcohol used in cosmetics and perfumery and found in such plants as the geranium and citronella

Gerard *masc pers n* meaning 'spear hard'

gerbil *n* any of about fifty different species of desert-dwelling rodents akin to the vole and hamster

gerent *n* a leader, a controller *Obs pa pple now S & dial vb* **greet**

geriatry *n* care of the aged, old people's welfare

gering *Obs n* a villain? (the meaning is obscure)

germ (*n*) *vb* to cause to germinate: to bud (*fig*)

GERMAIN/GERMAINE/GERMAN/ GERMANE/GERMEN/GERMIN/GERMINA
See next page

Germanic (*adj*) *n* a Germanic language

Germanist *n* one versed in German literature

germinal *adj* of, belonging to or like a germ or germs: of the nature of a germ: of or in the earliest stage of development (both serious and jocular usage)

germinant *adj* sprouting: of the ground (*fig*)

germon *n* any of various fish *esp* the long-finned tunny

gernal *var fm obs n* **garnel**, a shrimp

gerne *obs fm now S & dial vb* **girn**

geropiga *n* a red-coloured mixture of grape juice, brandy and sugar used to adulterate port

gerret *obs fm n* **garret**

gert *dial fm adj/n* **great**

gerund *n* a verbal noun. In English, a noun formed from a verb and ending in '-ing' denoting an action or state., e.g. (using its anagrams), 'We have a problem in *finding* the dunger,' said the nudger to the durgen.

Gervas *var fm masc pers n* **Gervase**

Gervase *masc pers n* meaning 'spear eagerness'

gesine *obs n* childbed

gesling *dial fm n* **gosling**

gesneria *n* a species of a genus of tropical American plants

gest *n* a story *arch n* bearing, mien *obs vb* to tell a story

gestar *var fm obs n* **gester** *obs fm n* **jester**

gestate *vb* to carry in the womb during the time of pregnancy

gester *obs n* a professional singer of roman-

GERMAIN/GERMAINE/GERMAN/GERMANE/GERMEN/GERMIN/GERMINA – A SERIES OF DIVERGENT VIEWS In various ways these words are related. *Pears Advanced Word-Puzzler's Dictionary* disagrees with the opinions of *Chambers 20th Century Dictionary* concerning this group of words. To appreciate these divergent views it will be necessary to treat them as a group rather than as individual words.

germain *var fm adj/obs n* **german** (GAME PLAYER'S note: Apart from the divergent view concerning german and detailed at the entry for that word, even the spelling *fm* of germain is subject to controversy. The dictionary used for the UK Scrabble championship credits only Shakespeare with ever having used either germain or germaine as a word. It gives Shakespeare this exclusive credit not for german but for a completely different word, **germen**! To understand this complicated word puzzle, first consider Shakespeare's association with both **german** and **germen**. For **german** as an *adj* he used **germane** in a now obsolete sense as akin (*Timon of Athens*) and, in the extant sense, he used **germaine** (*Hamlet*). For **german** as an *obs n* he used the *pl* **germaines** (*Othello*). For **germen**, he used the *pl* **germaines** (*Lear*). Among today's writers who preferred to spell the *adj* **german** as **germain** is no less a scholar than T H Huxley.)

germaine *obs fm adj* **german** *var fm obs n* **german** (note: It was Shakespeare's spelling of the word in this *fm* which inspired the sense of appropriate or relevant. See **german** and **germain**.)

german *adj* appropriate, relevant (in this sense the *var fms* **germane, germain** are more frequently encountered): closely akin (used only as a combining *fm* with one of three exact relationships specified, **brother-german, sister-german, cousin-german**, to distinguish from other usage of such as sister where no common parent is involved) *arch adj* genuine *obs n* a brother or sister by the same father (GAME PLAYER'S note: UK championship Scrabble players will be pleased to discover that their official reference dictionary considers this noun extant. Paradoxically, it considers the usage by such as Darwin to describe a botanical ovary as a **germen** to be *obs*. By contrast, US Scrabble players have no problems with either word and they have the additional meaning for **german** as a noun which follows this note.) *n* the cotillion, an elaborate dance having a series of rounds (*pl* **germans**)

germen *n* a germ or rudiment of an organism (now only *fig*): a botanical ovary (*pl* **germens, germina**) (GAME PLAYER'S note: Also see **german**)

germin *arch vb* to bud *var fm n* **germen** (GAME PLAYER'S note: The dictionary used for the UK Scrabble championship makes no reference to the *vb*)

germina *pl* germen (GAME PLAYER'S note: The dictionary used for the UK Scrabble championship carries no reference to this *pl fm*) ces *obs fm vb* **gesture**

gestor *obs fm n* **jester**

gestural *adj* of or pertaining to gesture: composed of gestures

getron *obs fm n* **gittern**

geyserite *n* sinter

ghain *n* the nineteenth letter of the Arabic alphabet

ghasel *var fm n* **ghazel**, a type of oriental lyric poetry usually of an erotic nature

gherkin *n* a small, immature cucumber used for pickling

ghost word *n* a word arising by error on the part of the scribe which may or may not have a continued existence (see **pailer** for an example of such)

gi *n* a judo or karate costume

gianet *obs n* a type of lance

giant herring *n* whilst, scientifically, this particular popular name is a nonsense it does have the edge on the alternative popular names of **bananafish, bonefish, Cape salmon, springer** or **tenpounder** in that it provides a vague description of its appearance. Technically, such a fish is any species of the *Elops* genus of the *Elopidae* family which, together with the tarpons, forms the order *Elopiformes* of the superorder *Elopomorpha.* This superorder comprises the true eels and their relatives. The order consists of those fishes related to the eels but which resemble 'normal' fishes. (Also see **tarpon**)

giffer *obs fm n* **giver**, one who gives

gigant *obs n/adj* giant

giglet *n* a giddy, fun-loving girl *obs n* a lewd, wanton woman

gigman *n* one of narrow mind for whom 'respectability' is of the greatest concern and measures it by such as ownership of a gig or one-horse open carriage: one who owns or uses a gig

gilden *obs n* a pikeman *obs adj* golden

gilder (*n*) *now dial n* a snare *obs vb* to catch in a snare

gilet *n* a waistcoat-shaped bodice

giller *n* one who guts fish

gilthead *n* a species of sea breams having a golden band running between the eyes: various other fishes with similar or golden-spotted markings such as the bonito, dorado and cunner

gilthedde *obs fm n* **gilthead**

gim *now dial adj* smart, spruce

gimel *n* the third letter of the Hebrew alphabet

gimmer *S & dial n* a ewe after the first shearing and before the second: a term of contempt for a woman *now dial n* a hinge *obs n* a connecting piece of various sorts *obs vb* to provide with a connecting piece

gin *n* the alcoholic spirit also known as **geneva** or **hollands**: a snare, a hoist or any of various other mechanical contrivances: a card game also known as **gin rummy:** an Australian aboriginal woman: a female kangaroo *vb* to trap or ensnare: to use a mechanical gin (*pa t* **ginned**) *arch vb* to begin (*pa t* **gan**)

ginet *var fm n* **jennet**

gineve *obs fm Anglo-Ir n* **gneeve**

ginful *Obs adj* treacherous

gingal *var fm n* **gingall**

gingall *n* a heavy, long-barrelled, hand gun which required mechanical support and was used against the British in India and China in the 19th century.

gingell *var fm n* **jingle**

gingival *adj* of or pertaining to the gums *n* an Arabic speech sound produced by pressing the tongue against a gum

gingle *var fm n/vb* **jingle**

gingler *var fm n* **jingler**

gingran *obs n* a species of stinking toadstool

giniper *obs fm n* **juniper**, the shrub

ginne *obs fm arch vb* **gin**

ginnel *vb* to catch a fish by tickling its gills (*infl fms* **ginneled/-ling**)

ginner *n* one who uses a cotton gin

ginnery *n* a place where cotton is ginned *nonce n* a gin palace

ginnet *obs n* an adz *obs fm n* **jennet**

ginnle *var fm vb* **ginnel**

ginny *adj* of such as a kidney, affected by gin *obs adj* cunning, seductive

gipsen *obs fm n* **gypsy**

gipser *arch n* a pouch on a belt

girandole *n* a branched candlestick *esp* one attached to a wall: a revolving fountain jet: a type of firework

girasol *n* the fire opal, a bluish-white translucent opal which reflects a reddish glow in bright light: any plant of the sunflower family *esp* the Jerusalem artichoke

girasole *var fm n* **girasol**

gird *arch n* a jibe *now dial n* that which functions as a belt, now only such as a hoop of a barrel, a girth of a saddle: a sudden jerk: a spasm of pain *dial n* a burst of laughter *vb* to encircle in various senses but *esp* as a belt round the waist: to wear a sword: to prepare for action (*fig*): to move suddenly or rapidly: to deliver a blow *now dial vb* to jibe or mock (*infl fms* **girt** or **girded**)

girg *var fm S n/obs vb* **jarg**

girkin *var fm n* **gherkin**

girl (*n*) *S vb* to thrill *nonce vb* to man with a girl as that person

girle *obs fm n* **girl**

girleen *Anglo-Ir n* a young girl

girn *S n* a snare with a running noose *now S n* a snarl *now S & dial vb* to snarl: to complain

girne *obs fm now S & dial vb* **girn**

girnel *S n* a granary: a large chest (for storing grain) *obs S vb* to store grain

girnie *dial adj* ill-tempered

girnot *obs S fm n* **gurnard**

giron *var fm her n* **gyron**

Girondin *var fm n* **Girondist**, a member of a moderate republican party of the 1791–1793 French assembly

girse *dial fm n/vb* **grass**

girsle *obs S fm n* **gristle**

girss *S fm n/vb* **grass**

girt *n* a measurement across or around a non-flat surface *now US n* a small girder *now dial n* a saddle girth *vb* to measure the girth (of a tree) with string *dial fm adj* **great**

girthline *var fm n* **girtline**

girtline *n* the first rope used to rig a ship. It passes through a block on the head of a lower mast and is used to hoist up the rigging.

gisarme *n* an historical military weapon consisting of a long pointed blade in line with the shaft

gist (*n*) *now dial vb* to pasture grazing animals at a price per head

gistor *obs n* an agistor: any animal grazing on land for which a grazing fee has been paid

gitano *n* a Spanish gypsy (*pl* **gitanos**)

gitter *n* an optician's diffraction grating

gittern *n* an old type of guitar *obs vb* to play that instrument

giveale *n* a feast, paid for by bequest, and formerly observed in some parishes in Kent

gjetost *n* a hard, dark-brown cheese made from goat's milk

gju *var fm n* **gue**

gladdener *n* one who makes glad

glade (*n*) *obs vb* to create a clearing or glade in a forest

gladen *var fm n* **gladdon**, the iris or fleur-de-lis

glader *var fm obs n* **gladder**, one who makes cheer

gladlier see **gladly**

gladliest see **gladly**

gladly *adv* in a glad manner (note: Though the standard *fms* of a comparative and superlative for an adverb ending '-ly' consist of either the words more or most as *more likely* or *most likely*, the *Official Scrabble Players Dictionary* specifically gives *comp* **gladlier** and *sup* **gladliest**.)

glady *adj* having glades (*comp* **gladier** *sup* **gladiest**)

glair *n* the white of an egg: any similar substance *vb* to smear with such

glairin *n* an organic residue of evaporated mineral water

glaise *S n* a scorch *obs S n* a resounding noise *obs fm vb* glaze

glaive *n* a sword *dial n* a fishing spear *obs n* a lance: a type of halberd: a spear: a prize *esp* the lance set as a finishing post in a race: a soldier armed with a glaive *now dial vb* to fish with a spear

glander *n* an individual swelling in a series of such swellings which afflict a horse (or person) suffering from glanders

glandered *adj* suffering glanders

glanders *n* glander pest, an equine contagious disease characterized by swellings below the horse's jaw and a mucous discharge from its nostrils. Also capable of being communicated to man.

glandes *pl* glans

glandule *n* a small gland

glans *n* a single-celled, non-dehiscing fruit such as an acorn: a glandular structure such as the extremities of the clitoris, *glans clitoris*, or the penis, *glans penis* (*pl* **glandes**)

glanse *obs fm vb* **glance**

glar *S & dial n* mud (*var fms* **glaur, glair, gloar**) *S & dial vb* to make muddy (*var fms* **glaur, glawr**)

glareal *adj* growing on dry, open land

glary *adj* full of glare, glaring: smooth and slippery (*comp* **glarier** *sup* **glariest**)

glase *obs fm vbs* **glace, glaze**

glaser *obs fm n* **glazer**, one who polishes or burnishes: one who applies the glaze to pottery: a wheel used for rough polishing knives

glasier *obs fm n* **glazier**

glasin *obs fm arch adj* **glassen**

glassen *arch adj* glasslike, of glass

glassin *obs fm arch adj* **glassen**

glassine *n* a type of transparent paper

Glassite *n* a member of a religious sect founded by the Rev. John Glass after he had been sacked by the Church of Scotland in 1728. Glassites are also known as Sandemanians after Glass's son-in-law, Robert Sandeman, who continued the movement.

glaster *obs vb* to glitter *obs S vb* to boast

glastyn *n* a Manx water horse which, in its human form, is a handsome young man with dark curly hair, flashing eyes and pointed ears but which can transform itself into a horse. Both as a man and a horse this malevolent spirit is dripping wet.

glathe *Obs fm n* **glad**

glaur *var fm S & dial n/vb* **glar**

glaury *S & dial adj* muddy, miry

glaver *obs vb* to deceive with flattery: to flatter *obs n* loud noise

gleade *obs fm ns* **glede, gleed**

gleane *obs fm vb* **glean**

gleary *dial adj* shiny

gleat *obs fm vb* **gleet**, to discharge a thin pus

glede *n* the kite, a bird of prey

gledge *S vb* to look sideways in a cunning fashion *S n* a sly side glance

glee (*n*) *now S & dial vb* to look asquint *obs vb* to make merry: to delight

gleed *arch n* a live coal *obs n* a fire *pseudo-arch vb* to burn, to glow

gleeman *n* an historical professional musical entertainer such as a singer or a minstrel

gleen *arch n* a gleam of light *obs vb* to gleam

gleit *obs S vb* to glitter or shine

gleman *obs fm n* **gleeman**

glenar *obs fm n* **gleaner**

glene *var fm obs vb* **gleen**

Glenis *var fm fem pers n* **Glynis**

glenoid *adj* socket-shaped *n* a socket

glent *now dial n* a look or glance: a gleam of light: a slip or fall *now dial vb* to shine *obs vb* to move quickly *esp* in an oblique direction *obs adj* glowing

Glenys *var fm fem pers n* **Glynis**

gliadin *n* one of the prolamine proteins, this one occurring in the nitrogenous part of wheat

glibber (*comp adj*) *dial adj* worn smooth *obs vb* to slip

glidder *now dial adj* slippery *now dial vb* to cover with ice *dial n* a loose stone on a slope

glime *dial n* a side glance *dial vb* to look askance

glinse *obs fm vb* **glimpse**

glint (*n*) *obs adj* slippery

glinter *vb* to shine, to gleam

Glires *n pl* a division of mammals which includes the typical rodents

glirine *adj* of Glires

glise *obs vb* to glitter or shine

glisen *Obs fm vb* **glise**

glissen *now dial fm vb* **glisten**

glister *n* brilliance, lustre *arch vb* to sparkle (the correct word for the proverb *All that glisters is not gold* for which *glitters* is often substituted in ignorance)

gliter *obs fm vb* **glitter**

gloater *n* one who gloats

globin *n* a protein of red blood corpuscles

glode *obs n* a glade in a wood where birds are snared

glore *now dial n* excessive wobbly fat on a person *now dial vb* to glare or glower

gloria *n* any of various prayers or hymns which begin with the Latin word *Gloria* (glory): the music to which some are set

glory pea *n* any plant of the Australasian genus of *Clianthus*

glose *var fm n/obs fm vb* **gloze**

gloser *var fm obs n* **glozer**, a writer of glosses: a flatterer

glossan *Anglo-Ir n* the coalfish

Glossina *n* the genus of the tsetse fly (*–cap*) *n* any fly of this genus

glote *obs fm vb* **gloat**

gloter *obs fm n* **gloater**, one who gloats

glother *obs vb* to flatter

glotun *Obs fm n* **glutton**

gloue *obs fm vb* **glow**

gloze *n* a marginal note *vb* to comment

glucinum *n* the metallic element, beryllium

gluder *S var fm obs vb* **glother**, to flatter

gluey *adj* resembling glue: sticky: smeared with glue (*comp* **gluier** *sup* **gluiest**)

glutaeus *n* any of three large muscles which form the buttock, the *glutaeus maximus*, the *glutaeus medius* or the *glutaeus minimus* (*pl* **glutaei**) (note: The *var fm* is **gluteus** (*pl* **glutei**) and the term, *glutaeus maximus*, is sometimes used as a playful synonym for the buttocks)

gluten *n* a protein present in such as wheat: any sticky substance

gluter *Obs fm obs vb* **glother**

gluteus *var fm n* **glutaeus** (*pl* **glutei**)

gluton *Obs fm n* **glutton**

gly *obs fm now S & dial vb* **glee**, to look asquint

glycin *n* a sweet, colourless amino acid obtained from various proteins

glycine *var fm n* **glycin**

glycosuria *n* the presence of glucose in the urine, a symptom of such as *diabetes mellitus* in which the diabetic also suffers emaciation with excessive hunger and thirst

Glynis *fem fm masc pers n* **Glyn**, meaning 'a valley'

gnaist *var fm obs vb* **gnast**

gnaiste *var fm obs vb* **gnast**

gnare *obs vb* to strangle: to snare or entrap *obs n* a trap

gnarl *n* any knotty swelling on a tree: a snarl *vb* to (cause to) knot *obs vb* to snarl

gnarre *var fm obs n/vb* **gnare**

gnast *obs vb* to gnash *obs n* a spark

gnaste *var fm obs vb* **gnast**

gnaster *obs n* one who gnashes his teeth

gnastie *obs fm adj* **nasty**

gnathic *adj* of or pertaining to the jaw

gnatling *n* a little gnat: an insignificant person (*fig*)

gnatte *obs fm n* **gnat**

gnatty *adj* infested with gnats (*comp* **gnattier** *sup* **gnattiest**)

gneeve *Anglo-Ir n* a twelfth part (capable of individual ownership or rental) of a parcel of ploughland

gneiss *n* a granite-like rock having a distinctive laminated structure: any of various metamorphic rocks containing feldspar

Gnetales *n pl* those gymnosperms which differ from conifers in such details as the absence of resin canals and in having a perianth

Gnetum *n* a genus of tropical trees and shrubs which belong to a family of trees which differ from conifers in such respects as having no resin canals

gnide *Obs vb* to bruise or crush (*infl fms incl pa t sing* **gnade** *pa t pl* **gniden**)

gniden see **gnide**

gnidge *S vb* to rub or squeeze

gnomic *adj* of a gnome, in the sense of a pithy saying (also see **gnomish**)

gnomish *adj* of a gnome, in the sense of a sprite, dwarf or goblin (also see **gnomic**)

gnomist *n* a writer of gnomic verses

gnomonic *adj* pertaining to a sundial

gnomonical *adj* pertaining to a sundial

gnoses *pl* gnosis

gnosis *n* a knowledge of that which is mystical or of a secret spiritual nature *esp* the secrets of the (higher-ranking) Gnostics, the early heretics of Christianity (*pl* **gnoses**)

gnostic *adj* having knowledge (+*cap*) *n* a member of one of various sects which arose in the 2nd century using an heretical form of Christianity as a base. They survived until the 5th century though some of their theories and practices influenced later heresies and are still found in some of the modern cults. Essentially, the Gnostics believed in a form of oriental dualism with the existence of two worlds, good and evil. The body was regarded as the enemy of spiritual life.

gnostical *adj* gnostic

go (*vb*) *n* a Japanese liquid and dry measure

goa *n* the Tibetan gazelle

goateed *adj* having a goatee beard

go-away bird *n* either of two species of grey turacos which annoy hunters in Africa by following them and uttering a cry which sounds like '*Go away*' and disperses the game

Gobelin *n* a type of damask used for upholstery (−*cap*) *Obs fm n* **goblin**

gob-line *n* a back rope, a ship's rope leading from the guying rope, known as a martingale, inboard (*var fms* **gob-rope**, **gab-line** (or-**rope**), **gaub-line** (or-**rope**))

godet *obs n* a drinking goblet of inexpensive material such as wood or earthenware

godlet *n* a petty god

godling *n* a minor god of limited power

godship *n* the status or personality of a god *esp* in a jocular sense

Godwin *masc pers n* meaning 'God friend'

goety *arch n* the employment of evil spirits: necromancy

goglet *n* a long-necked vessel made of a porous earthenware so that the contents, water, is kept cool

Gogmagog *masc pers n* the last surviving giant of ancient Albion (See **Albion**)

Goidel *n* a Celt of Irish, Scots or Manx descent and speech (as opposed to a Celt of the Brythonic branch, comprising the Welsh, Cornish and Bretons). Whilst both Manx and Cornish are being revived as living languages, the last true native Cornish speaker died in 1771 and, by 1969, there was only one person left for whom Manx was his first choice tongue. The postal Scrabble magazine, *Onwords*, has reported a game of Scrabble® played in Cornish. (See **POSTAL WORD GAMES**)

Goidelic *adj* of the Celtic people and language of Scotland, Ireland and the Isle of Man as opposed to Brythonic, which describes the Welsh, Cornish and Breton Celts and language

goistre *obs fm n* **goitre**

goiter *US fm n* **goitre**

goitre *n* an enlargement of the thyroid gland better known as **Derbyshire neck** due to the proportionately greater number of sufferers in parts of that county than elsewhere in Britain

golan *obs fm now dial n* **gollan**

golded *obs adj* made or possessed of gold

golder *comp adj* gold (in the sense of golden)

golding *dial n* the marigold: the ladybird *obs n* a gold coin: an apple

Goldwynism *n* a phrase or sentence said to have been uttered by Samuel Goldwyn, though many of his classics probably originated at his MGM publicity department. Examples:– *'If Roosevelt were alive he'd turn over in his grave', 'I'll give you a definite maybe', 'Include me out', 'A verbal contract isn't worth the paper it's written on', 'Anybody who goes to see a psychiatrist ought to have his head examined.'*

goldy *now dial adj* golden *dial n* either of two birds, the goldfinch or the yellowhammer

golf (*n*) *vb* to play golf *obs S vb* of a pig, to grunt

goliard *n* a mediaeval writer of satirical Latin verse who travelled through England, France and Germany giving performances in the style of an educated jester

goliardy *n* the practices of a goliard: the composition of goliardic verse

gollan *now dial n* any of various yellow flowers such as marigold, corn marigold, marsh marigold, globeflower, crowfoot etc

golpe *her n* a purple-coloured roundel

gonadial *adj* of the gonad, an organ which produces sex cells

Gondwanaland *n* the southernmost of two ancient landmasses held to have split and drifted to form South America, Antarctica, Australia, Africa and India (also see **Laurasia**)

gone (*pa pple*) *var fm obs vb* **gane**

gonia *pl* gonion and gonium

gonion *n* the tip of the angle either side of the lower jaw (*pl* **gonia**)

gonium *n* an immature reproductive cell (*pl* **gonia**)

gony *now dial n* a simpleton: the albatross or any of various other birds which are poorly adapted for terrestrial activity (in this sense the usual (non-*dial*) term for the albatross is **gooney bird** or **gooney** (*pl* **goonies**))

goober *US n* the peanut

gooney *var fm now dial n* **gony** (not *dial*, however, in the sense of a bird – see **gony**)

goorde *obs fm n* **gourd**

gooste *obs fm n* **ghost**

goote *obs fm n* **gote**, a watercourse

gor *now dial n* an unfledged bird: a seagull

goramy *n* a large Malayan freshwater fish

gorblin *S n* an unfledged bird

Gordian *adj* of or pertaining to Gordius, the classical king of Gordium in Phrygia who tied the famous, highly intricate, Gordian knot. It enjoined the pole of a chariot with the yoke, and an oracle declared that whoever could untie it would rule Asia. All failed except Alexander the Great who slashed it with his sword – and proved the prophecy true. Hence, extended to any highly complex difficulty or puzzle.

gorget *n* various items of neckware such as a necklace, a collar, armour for the throat or a crescent-shaped badge suspended from a chain round the neck which was worn by officers on duty: a patch of colour on the throat of a bird

gorlin *S n* an unfledged bird: a boy or girl

gorre *var fm now dial n* **gor**, a seagull *obs fm now dial n* **gore**, dirt or filth *obs fm vb* **gore**, of such as a bull, to pierce with its horns

gorsed *adj* of a show jumping fence, topped with gorse

gorsedd *n* an assembly of Welsh bards and druids

gorsey *var fm adj* **gorsy**

gorsse *obs fm n* **gorse**

gorsy *adj* of or pertaining to the plant, gorse: abounding in gorse

Goshen *n* in ancient Egypt, the fertile land

where the Jews lived and where there was light during the plague of darkness

goslet *US n* any of various species of small goose

goslin *var fm n* **gosling**

gosling *n* a young goose

goster *dial vb* to laugh noisily or heartily

gouber *var fm US n* **goober**

gourde *n* an early 19th century dollar which circulated in the French Caribbean colonies and in French Louisiana before it became part of the USA

gousty *S & dial adj* of such as a building, a cave or a ruin, large and empty and dreary as a consequence

grabble *vb* to grope

graben *n* a rift valley, a valley formed by subsidence

grable *obs fm vb* **grabble**

gracile *adj* slender

graddan *S n* toasted or parched grain *S vb* to toast or parch grain in the husk

gradden *var fm S n & vb* **graddan**

gradienter *US n* a surveyor's instrument for determining such as gradients

gradientor *var fm US n* **gradienter**

gradin *n* one of a series of steps or seatings arranged on a slope as in an amphitheatre: a shelf or ledge at the rear of an altar for items not essential to the service

gradine *n* a sculptor's toothed chisel *var fm n* **gradin**

gradino *n* artwork decorating the gradin of a church

gradus *n* a dictionary of Latin prosody intended as an aid to versification (*pl* **graduses**)

Graecism *n* an idiom of the Greek language *esp* when used within another language: (an instance of) Greek style

Gräfin *n* the *fem* of **Graf**, the German equivalent of an earl

graiel *Obs fm n* **grail**, an antiphon

grail *n* the Sangrail: an antiphon or gradual, a psalm sung between the readings from the Epistle and the Gospel: a book of such antiphons: a comb-maker's file *poet n* gravel

graile *obs fm n* **grail** (all meanings other than a file)

Graina *var fm fem pers n* **Graine** meaning 'love'

graine *n* silkworm eggs *obs fm n/vb* **grain** (+*cap*) *fems pers n* meaning 'love'

grainer *n* one who or that which grains (i.e. produces such as grains of salt or sugar): one who paints in imitation of the markings in wood or marble: one who uses a fishing spear which has two or more prongs (or grains)

Grainne *fems pers n* meaning 'love'

grainse *arch n* a fishing spear having two or more grains or prongs (*pl* **grainse** *var fm* **grains**)

grait *obs fm now dial vb* **graith** *obs fm adj* **great**

graith *now S n* clothing: material: apparatus *now dial vb* to prepare, to equip

grainy *adj* granular: in photography, having large grains, hence indistinct (*comp* **grainier** *sup* **grainiest**)

graise *obs fm vb* **graze**, to touch lightly

Grallae *n* in a now defunct classification system of birds, an order which comprised the wading birds (see **BIRD CLASSIFICATION**)

grame *arch n* grief, sorrow: harm *obs n* anger, wrath or ire (*pl* for both *arch n/obs n* **grames** *Obs pl* **gramen**) *obs adj* angry, vexed: grieved, sorrowful: of heat, fierce *obs vb* to be displeased or angry: to anger, grieve or vex

gramen *Obs pl arch n* **grame**

gramineous *adj* of or pertaining to grass: grassy

gramophony *n* gramophone reproduction

grand (*adj/n*) *obs vb* to make greater

grandie *obs fm n* **grandee**

grane *now dial vb* to strangle or choke *obs n* a noose

graner *obs n* a granary

granier *var fm obs n* **graner**

granitic *adj* of, pertaining to or of the nature of granite: containing or composed of granite: of water, flowing through or present in a granitic environment: hard, rigid (*fig*)

granitise *var fm vb* **granitize**, to metamorphose into a granite-like rock: to permeate with granitic material

granitite *n* muscovite granite

grante *Obs fm n/vb* **grant**

grantee *n* one to whom a conveyance or grant is made

Granth *n* the holy book of the Sikhs

grantise *Obs n* permission

granulite *n* a finely granulated crystalline rock consisting of feldspar and quartz intimately mixed and often carrying garnet

grape (*n) n* a small anchor with three or more flukes: grapeshot, small cannonballs linked together to form a collective missile: a size of paper (see **WATERMARKED PAPER**) *obs n* cascabel, the knob at the rear end of a cannon *obs S n* graip, a vulture (in *pl fm*) a diseased growth (on a horse) resembling a bunch of grapes *S & dial fm vb* **grope** *obs vb* to seize and hold (a ship) with a grapnel: to fasten with grappling irons

graped *adj* of a beast, having the mangy tumour, grapes

graper *obs n* that part of lance held in the hand *var fm obs n* **grapper**, a grappling hook

graphology *n* the study of handwriting *esp* as an art or science of determining the character of the writer

grapien *Obs fm vb* **grope**

grapin *Obs fm vb* **grope**

grapline *corrupt var fm n* **grappling**, a grapnel or grappling iron (GAME PLAYER'S note: Valid for play. The fact of being corrupt does not influence matters as corrupt versions can become standard *fms*, as pea is a corruption of pease (see **pea**). The dictionary used for the North American Scrabble championship lists the word without comment. It does not appear in the one used for the UK equivalent.)

grapnel *n* a small anchor with several claws: a hooking implement *vb* to use a grapnel (*pa t* **grapnelled**)

grapse *obs fm n/vb* **grasp**

grapslin *dial n* twilight

grase *obs fm vb* **graze** *obs fm ns* **grace, grass**

graspe *obs fm n* **grasp**

grasplin *var fm dial n* **grapslin**

grass girl *obs n* meaning obscure but probably a young maiden who would grant her immodest favours in a meadow

grass mouse *n* any of various species of little brown mice abundant in South America (*pl* **grass mice**)

graten *obs pa pple now S & dial vb* **greet**

graticule *n* a design to scale made on paper which has a basic grid

gratin *n* a crust baked on food

gratis *adv/adj* free of charge

graupel *n* hail or soft frozen rain

grave (*n/adj*) *vb* to clean the hull of a ship in dry dock: to render a musical note grave: to impress deeply (fig) *arch vb* to engrave: to entomb *now poet vb* to carve (*lit/fig*) *now dial vb* to dig: to excavate

graveolent *adj* rank, fetid

gravet *obs n* a person of grave aspect *obs fm n* **gravy**

gravie *obs fm n* **gravy**

gravitas *n* seriousness, importance

gravure *n* the process of intaglio printing: the engraved plate, copperplate or wooden block of this process: a print taken from it: the fact of being engraved

grawe *obs fm n* **grave** *obs fm vb* **grow**

grawls *see* **SALMON**

grayest *sup adj* gray (*var fm now mainly US*, **grey**)

greane *obs fm n/adj/vb* **green**

greanest *obs fm sup adj* **greenest**

greaten *arch vb* to render great: to enlarge *obs vb* to become pregnant

greave *n* armour for the lower leg *obs n* brushwood, a thicket: a sandy riverside (in *pl fm*) cooked animal fat, cracklings: tallow dregs *obs n pl* branches, twigs *obs fm vb* **grieve**

grece *now dial n* a flight of stairs

Grecian (*adj*) *n* a Greek scholar *arch n* a Greek *slg n* an Irishman

Grecise *var fm vb* **Graecize**, to make or become Greek: to conform to Greek ways: to use the Greek language

grede *obs n* an outcry: noise *obs vb* to cry out: to wail: of the cock, to crow (essentially an *Obs n/vb* though usage by Caxton in 1480 suggests that it would still have been extant after 1500, the arbitary date for an *obs* label)

gredinge *var fm Obs n* **greding**, an outcry, a wailing (see **grede**)

greed (*n*) *vb* to indulge one's greed

Greek fire *n* an incendiary missile in liquid form also known as **wet fire** as it is self-igniting when brought into contact with water. Invented by Callinicus, a Syrian in the employ of the Byzantine emperor Constantine IV (668–685), it is pre-eminently a naval weapon but was also used during seiges, most notably those of the Crusades. (Whilst Greeks had used incendiary missiles in classical times, those were different in having to be ignited before discharge.)

greement *obs n* agreement, accord

green (*n/adj/vb*) *S vb* to desire earnestly

greenback *n* originally the US paper dollar first issued in 1862 which had devices printed in green on the reverse side: any subsequent US paper dollar irrespective of colouring: the golden plover of the USA: the garfish: a book with a green back *slg n* a frog *vb* to bind a book in a green cover (+*cap*) *modf n* as **Greenback party**, a US political party of 1874–1884) which advocated a currency of paper denominations only

greene *obs fm n/adj/vb* **green**

greenfly see **aphid**

greese *var fm now dial n* **grece** *obs fm n/vb* **grass** *Obs fm vb* **grease**

greest *obs fm n* **grist**

greet (*vb*) *now S & dial vb* to lament, to weep, to grieve (*pa t* **grat** *pa pple* **grutten**) *now S n* lamentation

gregarian *adj* of a soldier, having the lowest ranking (i.e. a private)

Gregarina *n* a genus of parasitic protozoans so microscopic as to be able to live in an earthworm's testicle

Gregorian (*adj*) *n* one of a group of 18th century freemasons (−*cap*) *n* a type of wig worn in the 16th and 17th centuries

greige *n* any of various fabrics such as cotton, linen, silk, rayon in the greyish coloured state prior to any form of dyeing, sizing or other processing

grein *var fm S vb* **green**, to desire *obs fm n/adj/vb* **green**

greine *obs fm n/adj/vb* **green**

greisen *n* a rock compounded of quartz and mica

greist *obs fm n* **grist**

greit *var fm now S & dial vb* **greet**, to lament *obs fm n* **grit**

grelot *n* a small metal bell on harness

gremial *adj* intimate: of a friend: resident: of or pertaining to the internal affairs of a society: in full membership: pertaining to the lap or bosom (*obs* except in the *fm* **gremial veil**, a *var fm n* gremial in the sense of apron) *n* a silken apron or cloth placed upon a bishop during certain ceremonies: a resident member of a (university) society of an historical period

grenade (*n*) *vb* to attack with grenades

grenadine *n* a silkly textile used for dresses: a meat dish of various sorts such as veal or poultry glazed with its own juices

grene *obs fm n/adj/vb* **green**

grese *var fm now dial n* **grece** *obs fm vb* **grease**

gressing *obs fm now dial n* **grece**

grete *obs fm n* **grit** *obs fm vb* **greet**

Gretian *obs fm n/adj* **Grecian**

greve *var fm n* **greave**, armour for the lower leg

grey (*n/adj*) *vb* to make, become or grow grey

grey-coat *n* a Cumberland yeoman

gribble *n* a small marine creature rather like a wood louse *now dial n* the blackthorn: a walking stick made of blackthorn

grible *obs fm now dial n* **gribble**

grice *arch n* a (young) pig

gride *vb* to pierce with a weapon: to make a strident noise by scraping a surface (*pa pple* **grided** *obs pa pple* **gride**) *n* a strident or grating sound

gridelin *n* a colour variously described as pale purple, grey-violet or even pale red (also see **sinople** for another example of colour confusion) *adj* of this colour

griece *var fm now dial n* **grece**, a stairway

grief-shot *Shaks adj* pierced with grief

grien *obs fm S vb* **green** *obs fm n/adj/vb* **green**

griest *obs fm n* **grist**

griet *var fm now S n* **greet** *var fm now S & dial vb* **greet** *dial fm n* **grit**

grievant *US n* one who submits a complaint for arbitration

griffe *n* a claw: a zambo

grillade *n* grilled meat: the rubbing of a hot iron over meat in order to brown it *vb* to grill (GAME PLAYER'S note: The last British recorded literary usage in the first sense is 1725, in the second sense 1747 and the *vb* by Goldsmith in 1762. The dictionary used for the UK Scrabble championship accepts the first sense as being extant and makes no mention of either the second sense or the *vb*. The dictionary used for the North American Scrabble championship is the same but, as it uses no labels (see **motioner**), no inference on dates can be drawn. Other authorities consider both the *n* and *vb* *obs*.)

grille (*n*) *vb* to fit with such a grating

grilse *n* see **SALMON**: a child

grim (*adj/adv*) *vb* to make or cause to be fierce *n* a goblin, usually in the form of a black dog, originally allied to Odin but, later, a creature of the devil (also see **church grim**)

grimme *n* the coquetoon, a West African antelope *obs fm adj/adv/vb* **grim**

grinde *obs fm n* **groin**, the bodily part

grindel *Obs adj* fierce: angry *obs fm now dial modf n* **grindle**

grindle *US n* the mud fish *now dial n* a narrow ditch *now dial modf n* as **grindle stone**, a grindstone

grine *obs fm n* **grin**

grinne *obs fm now dial vb* **grin**, to ensnare: to strangle

grint *obs vb* to grind the teeth

grinter *obs S n* one in charge of a granary

gripen *obs adj* of the fist, clenched *Obs pa pple vb* gripe

grisdelin *obs fm n* **gridelin**

grise *obs vb* to shudder with fear: to dread: to terrify

Grisel *pers n* see **Grizel** (*–cap*) *obs fm n/adj* **grizzle** *obs fm n* **gristle**

Griselda *var fm fem pers n* **Griseldis** (see **Grizel**) *n* a proverbial Grizel

Grisell *var fm fem pers n* **Grisel** (see **Grizel**)

grisette *n* a grey, inferior dress fabric: a female shop assistant or other French working girl of the same social status: a species of moth

griskin *n* the lean part of the loin of a pig

grisle *obs n* horror: terror

grisled *var fm adj* **grizzled**

grison *n* either of two species of tropical American, small, weasel-like mammals which are land-based despite having partially webbed feet. Easily tamed, they make engaging pets. Peruvians use them as ferrets are used in Britain to pursue prey in burrows: a species of South American monkey *obs n* a servant in grey livery *obs adj* grey

grisp *obs vb* to grasp, to grope

grisping *obs n* twilight (a similar word, **gropsing**, is *now dial* and the *dial* words, **grapslin** and **grasplin**, also mean twilight)

griss *dial fm n/vb* **grist** *dial fm arch n* **grice** *obs fm n/vb* **grass**

Grissel *var fm fem pers n* **Grisel** (see **Grizel**) (*–cap*) *obs fm n* **gristle**

grissle *obs fm n* **gristle**

grist *n* corn due for grinding

griste *obs fm n* **grist**

gristel *obs fm n* **gristle**

gristle (*n*) *S n* the nose

gristled *obs adj* formed into gristle

grite *S fm n/adj/adv* **great** *obs fm n* **grit**

grive *obs fm vb* **grieve**

Grizel *fem pers n* a later form of **Grisel** which is a diminutive of **Griseldis**, meaning 'grey battle-maid': the proverbial name for a meek, patient wife *vb* to make one's wife a proverbial Grizel

grizle *obs fm n/adj/vb* **grizzle**, in the senses of grey or grey-haired

grizzel *adv* horribly

grizzle (*adj/n*) *vb* to render or become grey (-haired): to grin or laugh mockingly: to fret or sulk, to whimper (the senses in which **grizzling** is both *adj/n*)

Grobian *n* a stupid, slovenly person

grockle *dial n* a tourist

groin (*n*) *now dial n* the snout of a pig *vb* to construct an arch with a groin or curved arris formed by the intersection of two vaults *obs vb* of a buck, to utter its rutting cry

groine *obs fm n* **groin**

groiner *Obs n* a grumbler

grosbeak *n* a hawfinch or any of various finches of several genera which specialize in feeding on large hard fruit

groser *now S & dial n* a gooseberry *var fm now dial n* **grosser**

groset *S n* gooseberry

gropsing *now dial n* twilight

grossart *var fm S n* **groset**

grosse *Obs fm arch vb* **grush**, to crumble

grossen *vb* to render coarse

grosser (*comp adj*) *now dial n* one who has a monopoly of something *obs fm n* **grocer**

grosté *Obs n* grossness

grote *obs vb* to lament

groten *Obs vb* to glut

Grotian *adj* of or pertaining to Grotius, the Latin name of Huig van Groot (1583–1645), the Dutch jurist and founder of international law. He was given life imprisonment for religious reasons, but escaped to Paris where he wrote his classic treatise entitled *De Jure Belli et Pacis*.

grouper *n* any of various large, perch-like marine fishes *incl* one ten foot Australian species which has been known to attack and kill pearl fishermen. Another species has such ability to change colour that it was formerly classified as 24 different species!

groyne *n* a wall or breakwater which extends directly into the sea to act as a retaining agent to prevent the beach being washed away by the action of the tides *vb* to construct a groyne

gruin *var fm now dial n* **groin**

grume *n* a clot of blood *obs fm n/vb* **groom**

grumose *adj* composed of grains

grunte *Obs fm n/vb* **grunt**

gruper *var fm n* **grouper**

gruse *S & dial vb* to crush, press or squeeze

grusle *Obs fm n* **gristle**

grutten *see* **greet**

G-string *n* of the four strings on a violin the one tuned to G is the strongest and so is the one least likely to break during a performance. Hence, the humourous adoption of G-string as the name of a string-suspended garment which provides a striptease artiste with the absolute minimum coverage for the pubic region. (*var fm* **gee-string**, implying a pun on the *US interj* gee!)

gu *var fm n* **gue**

guaiacum *n* the tree, lignum vitae: its hard brownish-green timber: a resin of that tree: a drug from that resin

guanin *n* a white amorphous compound found in the dung of seabirds, fish scales, muscle tissue, various animal organs and the germ cells of plants

guanine *var fm n* **guanin**

guarde *obs fm n* **guard**

guarder *n* a guard

gubbin *n* a mining term for a kind of ironstone

gubbins *n pl* the historical inhabitants of a district near Brent Tor, Dartmoor, said to have been savages or heathens *now collq n sing/pl* rubbish *now collq n sing* a trivial object, a device

guddle *S vb* to fish by hand from a stream *now dial vb* to drink greedily

gue *n* a primitive two-stringed kind of Shetland violin

Gueber *var fm n* **Guebre**

Guebre *n* an (ancient) Persian Zoroastrian or fire-worshipper (also known as a **Parsee** or **Parsi**, **Gheber**, **Ghebre** or **Gueber**)

Guelph *pers n* the historic founder of a European princely family which still exists as the ducal family of Brunswick and the royal house of Windsor *n* in mediaeval Italian politics, one of those who supported the popes against the emperors (the imperial supporters being known as **Ghibellines**)

guerdon *now poet & rhetorical n/vb* (to) reward

guester *n* one who plays the host

guetre *obs n* a gaiter

guidage *n* guidance

guidon *n* a forked flag or pennant

Guignol *n* the chief puppet of the French puppet shows

guiler *obs n* one who beguiles or deceives

guise (*n*) *arch vb* to dress (fantastically)

guiser *n* a mummer, a masked performer in a folk play

gulden *n* a (silver) coin of various European countries

gule *var fm dial vb* **yule**

gulpin *n* simpleton

gundi *n* any of a small family of about half a dozen species of rodents which are not closely related to any other rodents and, in consequence, are placed in their own order. Resembling guinea pigs, gundis are found in the rocky hills of the Sahara and they groom themselves with a comb of stiff bristles on each hindfoot.

gundy *S n* a spiced treacle sweetmeat

gunnies *n* a crevice in a Cornish tin mine from which a lode has been extracted and which crevice is then used as a rough measure of quantity

gunnise *var fm n* **gunnies**

gunnist *n* one who uses a (sporting) gun

gunny *n* a coarse, strong jute fabric used for making sackcloth

gunsel *US slg n* an armed criminal: a young sexual pervert: a callow youth

gunster *obs n* one who clowned with a gun or similar explosive device

gunter *n* any of various devices or mathematical concepts invented by the English mathematician, Edmund Gunter (1581–1625), such as his quadrant, land surveying chain and logarithmic scale

gurge *n* a whirlpool *vb* to swirl

gurglet *n* a tiny whirlpool *var fm a* **goglet**

gurlet *n* a type of pickaxe having one cutting edge and one sharp point

gurnard *n* any of several species of marine, bottom-living fish which grow to a length of between two and three feet and are capable of making noises

gurnet *var fm n* **gurnard**

gurnipper *obs US n* a small, black, New England fly the size of a flea

gusla *n* either of two musical stringed instruments, a Balkan with one string or a Russian with several strings

guslar *n* one who performs on a gusla

guste *obs fm ns* **gust, guest**

guyot *n* a flat-topped mountain under the sea

guz *n* a linear measure of India, Persia etc, the *approx* equivalent of the yard or the metre, but which varies considerably from 14 inches to more than 44 inches in different localities (*pl* **guz**)

gwakin *obs fm n* **guiacum**

gwiniad *var fm a* **gwyniad**, the Bala lake whitefish (see **whitefish**)

gy *obs vb* to control or direct

gymnasic *adj* pertaining to a German or other Continental high school known as a gymnasium

gymnosperm *n* any seed-bearing plant in which the ovules are borne naked on open scales, the conifers and related plants

gyn *obs fm n* **gin**, a mechanical contrivance

gyrant *adj* of a circular or spiral movement

gyroidal *adj* rotary: spiral

gyromancy *n* divination by means of walking in a circle until dizzy and placing significance upon the direction of the resultant fall to the ground

gyron *her n* a triangular design in a quarter of a shield

gyrose *adj* marked with wavy lines: having a folded surface

H

ha *n* though written differently, the sixth and the twenty-sixth letters of the Arabic alphabet: a short form of **ha-ha**, a fence concealed in a ditch to avoid breaking a panoramic view from a (manor) house, yet still keeping the cattle enclosed *interj* of surprise, wonder, joy, suspicion etc *vb* to utter the *interj*

haberdine *n* salted or sun-dried cod

haboob *n* a sandstorm

hackel *obs fm n* **hackle**

hackly *adj* jagged (*comp* **hacklier** *sup* **hackliest**)

hadji *n* a Muslim who has made the pilgrimage to Mecca: also adopted as a title before a name

hadron *n* a baryon, meson or other member of a class of subatomic particles

hadronic *adj* of or pertaining to hadrons

haematin *n* a brownish-black powder containing iron obtained from haemoglobin by treatment with acid

hafter *n* one who makes tool handles *obs n* one who makes empty argument

hagden *n* the greater shearwater, a marine bird allied to the petrels (*var fms incl* **hackbolt, hagbolt, hagdon, hagdown**)

hagdon *var fm n* **hagden**

hagle *obs fm vb* **haggle**

haglet *var fm n* **hacklet**, the kittiwake, a small species of seagull

hag-ride *vb* to be subjected to a very disturbing nightmare either of conscience or of diabolic symbolism – literally to be ridden by a hag (or witch) in one's sleep (*pa pple* **hag-rid, hag-ridden**)

hail (*n*/*vb*) *obs adj* sound, safe: healthy: uncorrupt (*fig*)

haile *obs fm n*/*vb* **hail** (in most senses)

hailse *obs vb* to greet

haine *obs n* hatred: a niggard or miserly wretch

haique *n* an oblong cloth worn by Arabs as a head and body covering

haire *obs n* a coarse, rough cloth: a hair shirt of the type worn by ascetics

hairn *var fm now S n* **harn**, a brain

hairst *S fm n* **harvest**

hairt *S fm n* **heart**

haist *obs S fm n*/*vb* **haste**

hake (*n*) *vb* to fish for hake *S & dial vb* to wander idly: to urge, to pester

halbert *var fm n* **halberd**, the weapon which is a combined battle ax and spear

haler *n* one who hales (hauls)

halest *sup adj* **hale**, healthy

halicore *n* the dugong, a large, totally aquatic herbivorous mammal which lives in the warm Indo-Pacific seas

halide *n* any of the compounds bromide, chloride, flouride or iodide combined with a metal *adj* resembling sea salt

halite *n* rock salt

halitus *n* a vapour

halke *obs n* a hiding place

hallan *S & dial n* a partition wall in a cottage: a draught-excluding screen: an interior porch

haller *obs fm n* **heller**

halloo *n* a cry to urge a chase *vb* to cry dogs onto the chase

halma *n* an event in the ancient Greek pentathlon consisting of a long jump whilst holding weights: hoppity, a game played on a checkerboard of 256 squares with moves similar to those in draughts

halper *obs vb* to stumble

halse *now S & dial n* the neck, the throat *now S vb* to embrace *obs vb* to invoke

halsen *now dial vb* to auger or predict (evil) *obs vb* to call upon a holy or a supernatural force *dial adj* of hazel

halser *var fm n* **hawser**

halteres *n pl* dumb-bells used by gymnasts: balancers or poisers, the rudimentary hindwings of diptera

hamal *var fm n* **hammal**

hamarith *n* a Babylonian prostitute associated with the temple of Ishtar but of lower rank than either an **ishtaritu** or a **qadistu**

hamer *obs fm n/vb* **hammer**

hamfatter *n* a third rate theatrical performer *vb* to perform badly

Hamite *n* a descendant of Ham, a son of Noah: one said to descend from him, i.e. an African, either Arabic or black: a type of hook-shaped fossil shell *adj* (usually **Hamitic**) of the ancient Egyptian language and allied, extant languages

hammal *n* a Turkish or oriental porter: one, in western India, who bears a palanquin

hamose *adj* hooked

hanap *n* an ornate mediaeval drinking goblet

hance *n* an abrupt curved incline on any part of a ship's structure: the arc of smaller radius at the flank of an arch *obs n* a lintel: a curved part of the body *obs vb* to raise or elevate

hande *obs fm n* **hand**

hander *n* one who delivers: a punishing strike delivered to the palm of the hand *modf n* position – as in left hander, back hander etc

handmill *n* a quern or other small mill worked by hand

handsel *n* the first use or test of anything: first taste, first fruits: the first coin received by a trader on any day: a first payment: a New Year's gift *vb* to inaugurate: to be the first to test: to give a handsel on New Year's day

handy (*adj*) *dial n* a small wooden vessel with an upright handle

hanker *n* a (secret) yearning or longing *obs n* one who participates in bull-baiting *vb* to have a longing or craving *now dial vb* to linger or loiter

hansel *var fm n/vb* **handsel**

hansom (*n*) *vb* to travel in this type of cab

hantle *S & dial n* a goodly number

hanuman see **langur**

haptic *adj* pertaining to the sense of touch

haptics *n* the study of data acquired by haptic means

haptor *n* a posterior adhesive organ by which certain flukes, the monogeneans, attach themselves to the host on which they are parasitic

haram *var fm n* **harem**

hard (*adj/adv*) *n* a firm foreshore or jetty *obs n* that which is hard *obs vb* to make hard or harder

harde *obs fm adj/n* **hard**

harden (*vb*) *n* a coarse fabric of flax or hemp

hardset *adj* set so as to be hard: beset by difficulty: determined: of the features, set rigidly

hardy (*adj*) *n* a blacksmith's chisel

hareem *var fm n* **harem**

hareld *n* a species of sea duck

harem *n* that part of a Muslim household reserved exclusively for women: the occupants of such: a Muslim sacred place

harim *var fm n* **harem**

hariot *obs fm n* **heriot**

harke *obs fm vb* **hark**

harl *S & dial vb* to drag: to roughcast *dial vb* to ravel or confuse: to entangle, to twist *n* a fibre of a feather

harle *var fm n* **harl**

harling *S & dial n* the act of trailing from a boat a long line baited with an artificial minnow: pebbledash

harne *obs fm now S n* **harn**, a coarse fabric

harnest *obs fm adj* **harnessed**

harnse *obs fm vb* **harness**

haron *obs fm n* **heron**

harpe *obs fm n/vb* **harp** (in *pl fm*) *obs fm n* **herpes**

harpens *obs fm n pl* **harpings**

harper *n* a harpist: one of various 16th/17th century Irish coins bearing a harp: the Greenland seal or harp seal

harpings *n pl* pieces of timbering used for various purposes connected with wooden sailing vessels

harre *now dial n* that part of a gate which bears the hinge

Harris *n* the southern part of the Isle of Lewis in the Outer Hebrides: any of various small islands

harsell *obs vb* to aggravate, to irritate

harslet *var fm n* **haslet**

harte *obs fm ns* **art, heart**

hartely *obs fm adv* **heartly**

haruspex *n* a Roman official of Etruscan origin who interpreted the will of the gods by inspecting the entrails of previously sacrificed animals. This particular method of divination is exemplified today by the wishbone of a chicken being a token of luck. (*pl* **haruspices**)

haslet *n* a loaf of cooked pig's offal

hassar *n* a remarkable tropical American freshwater fish which both builds a regular nest and is capable of travelling considerable distances over land

haster *dial n* one who or that which hastens

hastler *obs n* one whose kitchen duty is the supervision of meat-roasting: a turnspit

hatel *obs n* anger *obs adj* fierce, bitter, hostile

haterent *S n* hatred

hatress *nonce n* a woman who hates

hatter (*n*) *now S & dial vb* to harass

haulst *obs fm pa t now S vb* **halse**

hault *obs fm vb* **halt**

haunte *obs fm n/vb* **haunt**

haver *n* an owner *S & dial n* foolish talk (usually in *pl fm*) *dial n* oat grass *S & dial vb* to talk nonsense

hawer *n* one who too frequently utters the expression 'haw'

hawle *obs fm vb* **haul** *obs fm n* **hail**, frozen rain

hawler *obs n* the steward of a hall

hawling *var fm obs n* **halling**, tapestry hung on a wall

hawse *n* that part of a ship where the hawse-holes (holes through which anchor ropes pass) are situated: the distance from the bow of an anchored ship to the anchor *obs vb* to raise

hawser *n* a marine (steel) cable used for mooring purposes

hayel *obs fm n* **hail**, frozen rain

hayer *var fm obs n* **haire**

hayle *obs fm n* **hail**, frozen rain

haysel *n* the hay season

he (*pron*) *n* the fifth letter of the Hebrew alphabet

headlong (*adj/adv*) *obs vb* to precipitate: to proceed with blind impetuosity

headpin *n* in the triangular formation of an undisturbed set of tenpins, that bowling pin which is nearest to the bowler. In order to achieve a strike knocking all ten down simultaneously, it is essential to hit this pin with a glancing blow. A direct frontal hit has a tendency to leave two separate sets of pins known as a split. A light glancing blow is likely to leave a solitary set of pins, but excessive force is not necessary. (Also see **tenpin**)

head post *n* either of the posts at the head of a four-poster bed

headrig *S n* the border of a field where the plough turns

headring *n* a South African native palm leaf headdress worn by married men

headwater *adj* designating (as **headwater stream**) one of the headwaters: designating (as **headwater mark**) a line on a weir above which water should not be allowed to rise

headwaters *n pl* those streams which, collectively, form the basis of a river

heape *obs fm n/vb* **heap**

heard (*pa pple*) *obs fm n/vb* **herd** *obs fm adj/n* **hard**

heark *obs fm vb* **hark**

hearn *obs fm n* **hern** or **heron**

hearse (*n*) *vb* to lay a corpse on a bier: to carry in a hearse: to bury with rites and ceremonies

hearst *n* a hind of the second or third year

hearsy *adj* hearse-like

heart (*n*) *vb* to give heart to: to take to heart: in masonry, to fill a cavity with rubble: of cabbage-like plants, to have the central part growing into a tightly compacted ball

heartling *obs n* a term of affection

heartseed *n* balloon vine, a tropical American climbing plant

heartsome *adj* capable of providing cheer: cheerful, merry

heaten *obs vb* to heat

hebona *obs n* a term used by Marlowe, Shakespeare and their contemporaries for a poison

HEBREW CALENDAR See next page

Hecate *pers n* an ancient Greek goddess of Thracian origin. In classical Greek and Roman times, deities were freely adapted from other cultures and the authority ascribed to them varied from time to time. It is the association of Hecate with the infernal regions which makes her the goddess of witches in Shakespeare's *Macbeth* though she has had other, more pleasant, aspects elsewhere.

HEBREW CALENDAR A year based on lunar months adjusted to the solar year by intercalating the month Veadar between Adar and Nisan 7 times in a 19 year cycle. The months, of alternate 30 and 29 days, are Tishri, Heshwan, Kislew, Tebet, Shebat, Adar, (Veadar), Nisan, Iyyar, Siwan, Tammuz, Ab, Elul. The year begins on the first day of Tishri, though, anciently, it began at Nisan.

hectar *var fm n* **hectare**

hectare *n* a metric measure of 100 ares (10,000 square metres or 2.471 acres)

hector *n* a blustering bully *vb* to bully or bluster (*+cap*) *masc pers n* meaning 'defender'

hectorer *n* one who bullies or hectors

hed *var fm Obs n* **hede** *Obs fm n* **heed** *Obs pa pple vb* **hide**, to conceal

hede *Obs n* rank, order *obs fm vb* **heed**

heder *dial n* an unshorn male sheep over the age of eight months (*fem* **sheder**)

Hedera *n* the genus of ivy

hederal *adj* of or pertaining to ivy

hedonist *n* one who regards pleasure as the greatest good

heering *dial fm n* **herring**

heest *obs fm arch n* **hest**

heete *obs fm vb* **heat** *obs fm arch vb* **height**, to make high

heier *obs fm n* **heir**

heild *obs S vb* to cover, to hide: to take shelter

heilding *obs fm arch n* **hilding**

heirdom *n* the state and dignity of an heir: succession by right: (an) inheritance

heire *var fm obs n* **haire** *obs fm n* **heir**

heist *slg vb* to steal *esp* in a particularly clever or spectacular fashion *slg n* an act of theft

heister *slg n* one who heists

heit *obs S fm vb* **hate** *obs S fm n* **heat** *obs S fm adj* **hot**

heive *obs S & dial fm vb* **heave**

hejra *n* Mohammed's flight from Mecca in AD 622 from which date the era of Islam is marked: any flight (*var fms* **hegira, hejira, hijra, hijrah**)

helcoid *adj* resembling an ulcer

held (*vbl infl*) *obs n* grace, favour, kindness: allegiance *var fm obs S vb* **heild**

helding *obs fm arch n* **hilding**

hele *now dial n/vb* (to) cover *var fm now S n* **heal**, sound in mind and limb *Obs vb* to conceal (*infl fms incl 2nd sing* **hilest**)

heliast *n* one of citizens of ancient Athens qualified to sit as a judge

helices *pl* helix

Helicon *n* a Greek mountain range, the legendary home of the Muses (*−cap*) *n* a large, horn-shaped bass tuba

heling *now dial n* a covering: the act of covering

heliostat *n* a 'clockwork mirror', a device which, powered by clockwork, reflects sunlight in a given direction for as long as possible: a *porte lumière* or similar mirror adjusted by hand throughout the relevant period

helistop *n* a helicopter landing place

helix *n* a spiral: the rim of the ear: the garden snail or other mollusc of the same genus (*pl* **helices, helixes**)

hellbender *n* the largest species of salamander in North America which often reaches 18 inches in length at its peculiar semi-adult final stage (see **mudpuppy**)

Hellenic *n/adj* Greek (also see **Pelasgian**)

heller *n* one of various low value German or Austrian coins

helot *n* a (Spartan) serf (see **helotism**)

helotism *n* the Spartan system of serfage which had the helots treated as a permanently inferior class immediately above the slaves but below the free citizen

helter *obs fm n* **halter**

helve *n* a handle of such as an ax, chisel or hammer *vb* to affix a helve to the metal head

helver *var fm n* **helve**

hematein *n* a reddish-brown crystalline substance obtained from the logwood tree of Central America and used as a stain (note: Whilst found in more than one American dictionary, it does not seem to appear in any similar British work even with a likely spelling *fm* of 'haematein'. The technical name of the logwood tree is *Haematoxylon campechianum*. Also see anagram, **hematine**.)

hematine *n* a brownish-black powder derived from haemoglobin treated with acid (note: Whilst found in more than one American dictionary, it does not seem to appear in any similar British work even with the likely spelling *fm* of 'haematine'. **Haematine** is recorded as an *obs adj*, meaning blood red, even though the 17th century writer used the 'American' *fm* of hematine. Also see anagram, **hematein**.)

hemipteral *adj* of or belonging to the *Hemipetera*, an order of insects which includes such as the true bugs, cicadas, crickets and plant lice which, typically, have suctorial mouth parts and four wings, thick at the base and membranous at the exposed end

hengil *obs fm now dial n* **hingle**

henry *n* the unit of inductance (*pl* **henries, henrys**)

henter *obs n* a grasper

hepar *n* any of the reddish-brown coloured compounds of sulphur

heparin *n* a substance found in various animal tissues and, having the power to delay the clotting of blood, used in surgery

hepatic *adj* pertaining to or acting upon the liver: liver-coloured: pertaining to the liverworts *n* a liverwort: a medicine for the liver

hepatical *adj/obs n* hepatic (GAME PLAYER'S note: The dictionary for the UK Scrabble championship lists only the *adj* which it declares extant. Other authorities declare both the *adj* and *n obs*.)

hepatise *var fm vb* **hepatize**

hepatize *vb* to convert into a liver-like substance

hepster *slg n* a hipster

heptad *n* a group, sum or series of seven

heptagon *n* a closed plane figure having seven sides

Heptameron *n* the title of a book containing a collection of stories told in seven days and ascribed to Queen Margaret of Navarre (1492–1549) though probably written in collaboration with writers attached to her court. Illogically, the *+cap* form is extended to any similar work concerning the activities of seven days (the prefix 'hepta-' means seven) even though *−cap* would seem reasonable *esp* where it bears no relationship to the form or contents of Queen Margaret's book.

heptane *n* a colourless, inflammable liquid hydrocarbon of the methane series used in the determination of the octane number of motor fuels and as a solvent

her (*pron*) *obs n* lord, master: man (*pl fms incl* **hereis**)

Heraclid *n* a Spartan aristocrat claiming descent from Heracles, the legendary hero

herden *var fm n* **harden**

herdic *n* a low-slung American (two-wheeled) carriage with a rear entrance and seats at the side

hereis *pl obs n* her

herie *var fm obs vb* **hery**

heriet *Obs fm n* **heriot**

herigaut *obs n* an upper garment worn by either sex in the 13th and 14th centuries (note: 18th century historical reference used the *fm* **herigald**)

heriot *n* the mediaeval equivalent of today's death duty which required such feudal payment as the best live beast of a deceased tenant to the lord of the manor

herison *obs fm n* **herisson**

hérissé *her adj* bristled

herisson *n* a defensive barrier consisting of a revolving beam heavily studded with iron spikes: a spiked wooden horse on which a military offender was once made to sit *obs n* a hedgehog

heritably *adv* by way or right of inheritance

heritor *n* one who inherits: in Scotland, one required to make certain payments for the public good due to ownership of land or property

herk *obs fm vb* **hark**

herling *S dial n* a finnock or young sea trout

herlot *Obs fm n* **harlot**

Hermes *pers n* a son of Zeus and messenger of the gods, god of science, eloquence and cunning, the patron of thieves, travellers and commerce, protector of boundaries and guide of souls on their way to Hades

hermet *obs fm n* **hermit**

hermit (*n*) *vb* to live as a hermit

hernas *obs fm n* **harness**

hernia *n* a rupture or protrusion of an organ through its surrounding wall (*pl* **herniae, hernias**)

hernis *Obs fm n* **harness**

hero shrew see **Soricidae**

herpes *n* any of several inflammatory eruptions on the skin *esp* herpes simplex or cold sore

herriot *obs fm n* **heriot**

herry *S fm vb* **harry**

herse *n* a harrow-like portcullis with defensive iron spikes *obs n* a spiked agricultural harrow which doubled, when laid flat, as part of a defence: a harrow-shaped military formation *her n* a design of a portcullis or a harrow *Obs vb* to glorify (*infl fms incl* **hersid, hersude**)

hersed *obs adj* of a military herse

hersid see **herse**

hert *obs fm n/vb* **heart**

herte *obs fm ns* **hart, heart** *Obs fm n* **hurt**

herth *obs fm ns* **earth, hearth**

hery *obs vb* to praise, honour, worship

Heshwan *n* a Hebrew month (*var fms* **Bul, Hesvan, Marchesvan.** Also see **HEBREW CALENDAR**)

Hesper *poet n* the planet Venus in the sense of the evening star

Hesperian *poet adj* western: of or pertaining to the Hesperides *adj* of or pertaining to the skipper butterflies *n* one dwelling in a western land

Hesperid *n* one of the Hesperides (+ *or* – *cap*) *n* one of the *Hesperidae*, the family of the skipper butterflies

Hesperides *n pl* the daughters of Hesperus who, according to the classic Greek myth, lived in the Isle of the Blest at the far end of the world. With the aid of a dragon, they guarded a tree which bore golden apples and was the property of the goddess, Hera. (*sing* **Hesperid**)

Hesperis *n* a genus of plants *incl* the dame's violet (*–cap*) *n* the night-scented gilly flower

hest *arch n* behest *obs vb* to grant: to wish: to command: to promise

Hester *var fm fem pers n* **Esther**, meaning 'star'

hesternal *adj* of yesterday

Hestia *pers n* the Greek goddess of the hearth

hestre *var fm obs n* **estre**

Hesvan *var fm n* **Heshwan**

het *now US & dial adj* heated *S adj* hot *obs S fm n/vb* **heat** *Obs fm n* **hate**

hetaera *n* a courtesan, concubine or harlot (*pl* **hetaerae, hetaeras**)

hetaeric *adj* of or belonging to hetaerae

hetaerism *n* concubinage as an openly admitted fact of society: a supposed form of communal marriage within a tribe of prehistoric man

hetaerist *n* one who is involved in hetaerism

hetaira *n* hetaera (*pl* **hetairai, hetairas**)

hetairia *n* a club or society

heter *obs adj* rough, fierce, cruel: keen, eager

heterokont *n* any of various yellow-green algae

heterosis *n* cross-fertilization: a figure of speech by which one form of such as a noun is used for another

heth *n* the eighth letter of the Hebrew alphabet

hetire *Obs fm obs adj* **heter**

hetman *n* a Polish military officer in command of a fighting unit when Poland was a dominant power: extended to other nationals who held command under Polish dominion *esp* the officer commanding the Cossacks (*pl* **hetmans**)

hetter *var fm obs adj* **heter**

heugh *S & dial n* a cliff *esp* one by the sea or a river

heurt *obs fm now dial n* **hurt**

hewel *obs fm dial n* **hickwall**

hewer *n* a worker who cuts such as coal, stone or wood *var fm obs n* **huer**, one employed to drive deer for hunting

heyer *var fm obs n* **haire**

heyre *obs fm n* **heir** *Obs fm obs vb* **hery**

hi *interj* to attract attention

hiate *vb* to gape: to cause an opening

hiatus *n* a break in continuity: a break between adjacent vowels in the pronunciation of a word, as in **coop** (meaning a cooperative society shop) contrasted with **coop** (a cage for fowl): a gap: an opening (*pl* **hiatuses**)

hicatee *n* a freshwater tortoise of the Antilles

hickwall *dial n* the green woodpecker

hidder *obs fm dial n* **heder** (*obs fem fm* **shidder**)

hider *n* one who hides (in the various senses of the *vb*)

hidling *var fm S & dial adj* **hidlings** *erron sing S & dial n pl* **hidlings**

hidlings *S & dial adv* secretly *S & dial adj* secret, clandestine *S & dial n pl* hiding places: clandestine activities

hidrotic *adj* of or pertaining to sweat *n* a medical agent producing sweat

hielding *obs fm arch n* **hilding**

hilder *obs fm n* **elder**, the tree

hilding *arch n* a worthless woman

hileding *obs fm arch n* **hilding**

hilest see **hele**

hilt (*n*) *vb* to provide a hilt (or handle) for such as a dagger

hilte *obs fm n* **hilt**

hind (*n*) *obs vb* to hinder

hindgut *n* the posterior end of the alimentary canal

hingel *var fm now dial n* **hingle**

hingle *now dial n* a hinge

hinter *n* one who or that which gives a hint

hipper *n* a salmon in its second year, thus both a parr and a smolt (see **SALMON**) (*+cap) n* the Derbyshire river which joins the Rother at Chesterfield

hippus *n* a disorder of the eye characterized by spasms of alternate contractions and expansions of the iris when exposed to light

hiren *obs n* a harlot

hirking *obs fm n* **irking**

hirling *var fm S dial n* **herling**

hirpes *obs fm n* **herpes**

hirsel *S & dial n* a flock (of sheep or people) *S & dial vb* to form a flock

hirsle *S & dial vb* to slide with a degree of friction *var fm S & dial vb* **hirsel**

hirste *Obs fm n* **hurst**

hirundine *adj* of or pertaining to a swallow (also see **conglobulate**)

hist (*interj*) *now poet vb* to incite: to be silent

Hister *pers n* the conjectural name of Hitler in two of the famous quatrains of *The Centuries*, the classic work of prediction written by Michel de Nostredame (Nostradamus) and published in two parts, the first in 1555 and the second in 1568. Both are rather obscure but neither Hitler nor his astrological advisors doubted the reference to him. Translated from a basic French work into which Nostradamus interwove Latin, Greek, Italian and the Romance dialect of Provençal, the quatrains read as follows:–
'*Beasts wild with hunger will cross the rivers, the greater part of the battlefield will be against Hister. He will drag the leader in a cage of iron, when the child of Germany observes no law.*' '*At a nearby place not far from Venus, the two greatest ones of Asia and Africa will be said to have come from the Rhine and Hister; cries and tears at Malta and the Ligurian coast.*'

One of the difficulties of understanding Nostradamus is not merely the translation (the above are by Erika Cheetham and taken from the Corgi 1978 reprint of her 1973 work) but in interpreting the quatrains in the light of current knowledge. For example, Miss Cheetham interprets the following as being concerned with James II and William III, '*In the North great efforts will be made, across the seas the way will be open. The rule in the island will be re-established, London fearful of the fleet when sighted.*' However, this could just as easily be concerned with the Falklands conflict which occurred subsequent to the publication of her work. Unfortunately, the quatrains are not published in chronological order, thus they are wide open to almost any interpretation.
Hitler is sometimes recognized as being either the first or second Antichrist (for a possible first Antichrist see **Antichrist**) and the various Antichrists are the subject of much of *The Centuries*. Miss Cheetham rather chillingly suggests that when the USA and the USSR become friends the (third) Antichrist will appear in some land other than America or Russia. In the following quatrain the Antichrist is described as *'the man of blood'*:–
'*One day the two great leaders will be friends; their great power will be seen to grow. The new land will be at the height of its power, to the man of blood the number is reported.*'

(For other prophetic pronouncements also see **Brutus, Cassandra, Gordian, oracle**)

histie *var fm obs S adj* **hirstie**, dry or barren

histioid *adj* like or of the nature of (connective) tissue

histone *n* one of a group of simple proteins which yield amino acids

historism *n* a theory that all phenomena of human social relations or conditions are historically determined

histrien *obs erron fm n* **histrion**

histrion *n* an actor (usually derogatory)

hitter (*n*) *var fm obs adj* **heter**, fierce or rough

hiver *n* one who gets bees into a hive (also *fig*)

hm *interj* expressing doubt, perplexity etc

ho *interj* of exultation: surprise *vb* to cry 'ho' *dial vb* to care *obs fm pron* **who** *Obs n* the heel (+*cap*) *n* a minor language of the Munda family of languages and spoken in India

hoan *obs fm n/vb* **hone**

hoare *obs fm n* **whore**

hoarness *obs n* hoariness: a growth of white or grey hairs

hoarsen *vb* to make or become hoarse

hoatzin *n* the stink bird, a very primitive South American species of bird which resembles a smelly, clumsy, underfed and particularly untidy chicken. It constructs a scruffy nest in the lowest branches of a tree just above water for its equally ungainly young. At this stage in their life, the young possess claws on the 'thumb' and 'first finger' of their wings which they use for clambering about *esp* back into the nest, as they have a tendency to fall into the water.

Hobart *var fm masc pers n* **Hubert**, meaning 'mind bright' *n* the capital and chief port of Tasmania, Australia

Hobbism *n* the philosophy of Thomas Hobbes (1588–1679) who favoured strong government and supported the supremacy of the state: a synonym for irreligion

hock (*n/vb*) *vb* to kidnap and bind or otherwise make use of a person for charitable fun purposes during the festival of Hocktide *var fm vb* **hough**

Hockday *n* either **Hock Monday** or **Hock Tuesday** (see **Hocktide**)

hocker *var fm n* **hougher**

Hocking ale *n* a beer specially brewed for Hocktide

Hocktide *n* the second Monday and Tuesday after Easter, the days of great rustic merriment with the serious purpose of raising funds for the parish. The origins are unknown and it may be true that it is to celebrate the expulsion of Viking invaders as it does, to some extent, satirize their rapine activities, especially in the kidnapping which is the main feature of this centuries-old festival. On **Hock Monday**, the men kidnap the women who are bound and held for ransom. On **Hock Tuesday**, the greater festival day, the women kidnap the men who are also bound and held to ransom.

hocus *vb* to trick: to spike alcohol with a drug *n* a drugged drink *arch n* trickery

Hogen *obs adj* Dutch *obs n* a Dutchman (*pl*) the Dutch

hogmane *n* hog mane, the mane of a horse cut very short (note: The *adj* is hyphenated as **hog-maned**) *var fm n* **hogmanay** or **Hogmanay**, the Scottish New Year festival

hoiden *var fm n/vb* **hoyden**

hoine *now dial vb* to whine, to mutter

holde *Obs n* allegiance, fidelity *obs fm n* hold, the action of holding

holet *obs n* a small cave *Obs n* a tent, a tabernacle

holist *n* one who holds the theory that the fundamental principle of the universe is the creation of wholes, complete self-contained systems of mind or matter

holloa *var fm n/interj/vb* **hello**

holpen *arch pa pple vb* to help

Holstein *n* a former Danish duchy now part of northern West Germany: one of a breed of cattle originally developed in the Dutch province of Friesland (*−cap*) the *fm* given in the dictionary used for the North American Scrabble championship in the sense of cattle

home croft *n* a cottage with sufficient land for growing vegetable produce for all home needs but insufficient for a full independent existence as a market gardener

Homerid *n* a Homeric scholar: one of the Homeridae

Homeridae *n pl* a guild of Greek poets centred at Chios who claimed to be descendants of Homer and who recited his works publicly (*sing* **Homerid**)

homiletics *n* the art of preaching: homilies

hondre *Obs fm n* **hundred**

honest (*adj*) *obs vb* to (confer) honour (upon)

honied *var fm adj* **honeyed**

hoodman *n* a hooded man (*obs* except in the *fm* **hoodman-blind**, an alternative name for blindman's buff, which is no longer used by children but is still extant in literary use)

hopelost *obs adj* despairing, desperate *obs n* one who has lost hope

honeydew see **aphid**

hoplite *n* an ancient Greek foot soldier

hop tree *n* the shrubby trefoil, a small North American tree the bitter fruit of which is used as a substitute for hops

Horace *masc pers n* meaning 'punctual'

horde (*n*) *vb* to form or live as a great company (of warriors or animals)

hordein *n* one of the prolamine simple proteins, this one being obtained from barley

Hornie *S n* Satan

horn shark *n* any of a family of primitive fishes with large, blunt heads found in all temperate seas except those of the Mediterranean and Atlantic. The best known species are the **Port Jackson shark** of Australian waters and the **Pacific horn shark** of North American waters. Both reach a length of about four feet and all species lay eggs in curious cases shaped like a headless screw.

horre *obs vb* to detest vehemently

horrent *adj* bristling: shuddering

horsen *obs adj* of or pertaining to horses

horser *n* one who provides horses for a coach

horsetail *n* the tail of a horse: such used as a symbol of military authority by the Turks: any of a genus of plants which bear a fancied resemblance to a horse's tail: any of a family of fossil bivalve molluscs, an individual of which is more usually called a hippurite: the nerves at the end of the spinal cord

horter *obs fm n* **hurter**

hory *now dial adj* dirty, foul, filthy

hosel *obs fm n/vb* **housel**

hostager *obs n* a hostage

hostel (*n*) *now dial vb* to lodge

hostelar *S n* a hostelry

hoster *n* a serving soldier, i.e. one of the host *obs n* an innkeeper

hosterie *obs fm arch n* **hostry**

hostle *var fm now dial vb* **hostel**

hostler *n* a stableman *esp* one at an inn *US n* one in charge of a roundhouse or railway locomotive shed

hostre *obs fm arch n* **hostry**

hostry *arch n* a hostelry or house where lodging is provided

hotel (*n*) *vb* to lodge at an hotel

hotpress *n* a contrivance which uses hot metal plates in the process of imparting a smooth, glossy surface to paper or cloth *vb* to use or produce from such

hough *vb* to hamstring, to disable by cutting the tendons of the ham or hock (for examples see **hougher**)

hougher *n* one of a band of Irish rebels who began their protest activities in 1711 by hough-ing cattle: a minor official of Newcastle upon Tyne who was also known as the **whipper and hougher** as his main duties were the whipping of criminals and hanging of felons, though the houghing was confined to stray pigs wandering through the city's streets. His annual salary, in 1827, was £4.6s.8d.

houle *obs fm ns* **hole, owl** *obs fm vb* **howl**

hoult *obs fm n* **holt**, a (small) wood (on a hill)

hounde *obs fm n* **hound**

housel *n* Holy Communion *vb* to give Holy Communion to

housle *obs fm n/vb* **housel**

hovel (*n*) *vb* to dwell in a hovel: to provide a roof: to bring (a vessel) into harbour, to assist in the unloading of its cargo (*infl fms* British, **hovelled/-lling:** US, **hoveled/-ling)**

hovelling *n* piloting

hower *obs fm n* **hour**

howle *obs var fm n* **owl** *obs fm vb* **howl**

howlet *n* an owl

howre *obs fm ns* **hour, whore** *obs fm pron* **our**

howse *dial fm arch vb* **hoise**, to hoist

howsel *obs fm n/vb* **housel**

howsomever *now dial adv* nevertheless (note: In this sense the *adv* is retained in literature but only in the reported speech of a provincial. Writers *incl* Scott and Thomas Hughes, the author of *Tom Brown's Schooldays.*) *obs adv* in whatever manner (Shakespeare was the last known writer to use it in this sense. Earlier users *incl* Caxton.)

hox *now dial vb* to disable (cattle) by cutting the hamstrings

hoyden *n* a rude, ill-bred (young) woman *esp* one who is noisy and given to merriment *vb* of a (young) woman, to behave in such fashion

hoyne *var fm n/vb* **hone**

Hrimfaxi *n* in Norse mythology, the horse of night (also see **Skinfaxi)**

Hsiang *n* a Chinese dialect of which there are 15 million speakers

hu *n* a Chinese measure of capacity, roughly the equivalent of $13\frac{2}{3}$ gallons *Obs fm n* **hue** *Obs fm adv* **how**

hubert *var fm dial n* **oobit**

huia *n* a New Zealand bird which has been extinct since about 1910. (Man is responsible for this tragedy: the Maoris wore the feathers in their hair; the Europeans had the birds stuffed for museums.) What is so poignant about the loss is that, in order to survive, it was essential for a pair to live together. The male had a strong beak which enabled it to chisel a hole through bark and the female had a long slender beak which enabled her to reach the grubs that formed the basis of their diet.

hulet *obs fm n* **howlet**

Hulsean *adj* of Cambridge divinity lectures founded by John Hulse in the 18th century

Humean *adj* pertaining to the philosophy that '*No amount of testimony can render a miracle possible*' postulated by the Scottish philosopher David Hume (1711–1776)

humidor *n* a humid place or container *esp* one for the storage of cigars

humile *obs adj* humble

Humist *n* an adherent of the sceptical philosophy of David Hume (1711–1776)

humlie *S n* a hornless cow

humpty *Austr n* a (settler's) very small primitive dwelling *adj* hump-backed, humped

humpy *adj* humped, lump-like: full of humps (*comp* **humpier** *sup* **humpiest**)

Hunterian *adj* of or belonging to either of two Scottish surgeons, the brothers Hunter (William 1718–1783, John 1728–1793) and the anatomical research with which they are associated: designating the museum in London housing the anatomical collection created by John or a similar museum in Glasgow founded by William

hurden *var fm n* **harden**

hurle *dial fm n* **harl**

hurlet *n* a stick or club used for striking (a ball)

hurn *now dial fm vb* **run**

hurst *n* a (sandy) hillock: a copse

hurste *Obs fm n* **hurst**

hurt *(n/vb) her n* of a man's coat of arms, a small bilberry-coloured ball (note: On a woman's coat of arms, the same deep blue ball is known as a **tongue mole**) *now dial n* the bilberry, also known as the hurtleberry or wortleberry

hurte *var fm her n* **hurt** *obs fm n/vb/now dial n* **hurt**

hurtel *obs fm vb* **hurtle**

hurter *n* one who or that which causes hurt or injury

hussar *n* a soldier of a light cavalry regiment

hussle *obs fm vb* **hustle**

hussler *var fm n* **hustler**

hust *obs vb* to silence (ironically, the opposite of husting(s))

husting(s) *n* electioneering: formerly, the platform on which parliamentary candidates gave their addresses after nomination: the principal court of the City of London: an assembly of historic times *esp* one summoned by the monarch (note: **husting** is rarely used for other than the historic assembly: **hustings** is treated as both *n sing* and *n pl*)

hutia *n* the hog rat, any of various species of edible, tropical American rodents

hv *Obs fm adv* **how**

hw *Obs fm n* **yew** *Obs fm adv* **how**

hwa *Obs fm pron* **who**

hwo *Obs fm pron* **who**

hwr *obs fm n* **whore**

hwu *Obs fm adv* **how**

hy *dial interj* to attract attention

hyaloid *adj* like glass *n* the thin transparent membrane enveloping the vitreous humour of the eye (also called the **hyaloid membrane**)

hyde *var fm n* **hide**, an old measure of land which varied according to circumstances. It was deemed to be that amount of land sufficient to support a freeman and his family and came to be reckoned by the amount of land which could be ploughed in one year (*approx* 120 acres). *var fm obs vb* **hide**, to measure land by hides

hydrate (*n*) *vb* to combine chemically with water

hydromancy *n* divination by water

hydrous *adj* containing water

hydrozoan *n* any of over 2,700 species of various of the lower marine animals such as the jellyfishes (*pl* **hydrozoa**)

hyetal *adj* pertaining to rain: rainy

hyper *n* one who or that which artificially stimulates (sales)

hypha *n* any of the hyphae or long threadlike 'roots' of a fungus. Amazingly, over 50 species of fungi are capable of using their hyphal threads as traps for eelworms on which they feed. The predatory fungi form, in some species, lasso-like traps or, in other species, sticky networks like a spider's web in which they snare the colourless, transparent, microscopic worms. Equally remarkable is the fact that none of the fungi needs eelworms for survival and only develops these snares if the animals are actually present in the soil. (*pl* **hyphae**)

Hypnos *pers n* the Greek god of sleep

hypobole *n* anticipation of objections

hyraces *pl* hyrax

hyrax *n* a rabbit-sized relative of the elephant, found in Africa and southwest Asia. Superficially like a marmot, there are both tree hyraxes and rock hyraxes. The rock hyrax has many different names *incl* dassie, dassy, Cape daman, rock rabbit and rock cony whilst the tree hyrax is also known as a bosdas. The **Syrian hyrax** is the 'cony' of the Bible and is a species of rock hyrax. The **rock hyrax** uses a communal latrine in its den, thus facilitating the gathering of its excrement which contains an ingredient used in the manufacture of perfume. (*pl* **hyraxes, hyraces**)

hysop *obs fm n* **hyssop**

hyssop *n* an aromatic medicinal herb

I

ia *obs S fm n* **jay** *Obs fm arch adv* **yea**

iaspre *Obs fm n* **jasper**, the precious stone

ibe see **be**

ic *Obs fm pron* **I**

ice apron *n* a structure on the pillar of a bridge to break or ward off ice

ice front *n* the face of a glacier

icelped *obs fm arch pa pple* **yclept**

iceman *n* one who is concerned with ice, such as a dealer in ice

icepan *n* a slab of floating ice

iceplant *n* a southern African low-growing plant with white fleshy leaves which, in the sun, glisten like ice

ice run *n* a track for a toboggan

icespar *n* a variety of potash feldspar, a crystalline silicate of aluminium and potassium

ice stone *n* cryolite or Greenland spar

ice stream *n* a valley glacier with a riverlike form: a stream of ice floes following a particular marine course such as that which sweeps round the southern tip of Greenland at Cape Farewell (contrast with **stream ice**)

ich *obs fm pron* **I** (also see **ch**)

ichnite *n* a fossil footprint

ichnolite *n* an ichnite or fossil of a footprint preserved in stone (apt anagram, **Neolithic**)

ichor *n* the ethereal blood of the (Greek) gods: blood (*fig*): a watery discharge from some wounds and sores

icker *S n* an ear of corn

iconolater *n* one who worships an image

icterus *n* jaundice: a plant disease in which the leaves turn yellow (*pl* **icteruses**) (+*cap*) *n* a genus of troupials also known as the American orioles

ictus *n* metrical stress: the pulse beat

icy-pearled *adj* having sparkling drops of ice

id *n* a term in psychoanalysis for a concealed part of the psyche motivated by instinct independent of a sense of reality, logic and morality: a theoretical element of a chromosome representing the characteristics of an ancestral member of the species *var fm n* **ide**

ide *n* the orfe, a European carp-like fish which is not native to Britain. However, a cultivated form known as either the golden orfe or golden ide is now living freely in a British river. During floods some of these fishes escaped from garden ponds and are now found in the Embe, a tributary of the Thames at Hampton Court.

idealess *adj* devoid of ideas

ideatron *n* the formation of ideas from that not perceptible to the senses

ideagraph *n* a graphic representation of a meaning as distinct from the representation of the sound expressing it, i.e. like any Chinese character or most Egyptian hieroglyphics rather than a word in a language: a symbol as + or −, £ or $

idiotish *adj* idiotic (GAME PLAYER'S note: Last recorded usage 1785. Considered extant by the dictionary used for the UK Scrabble championship. Ignored by the North American equivalent. Deemed *obs* by the *OED*.)

idlesse *poet n* idleness

ido *Obs vb* to do (+*cap*) *n* an international language developed from Esperanto

Idoist *n* one who speaks Ido

idolater *n* a worshipper of idols: one who admires greatly (*fem* **idolatress**)

idolet *obs n* a small idol

idolum *n* a phantom: an idea: a false conception (*pl* **idola**)

idorgan *n* a potential or ideal organism

ie *n* any of various screw-pines, climbing plants having a screw-like arrangement of the leaves: a product of ie, such as a mat used by the Samoans as currency *Obs fm n* **eye** (*pl* **ien** – the *pl fm* was also used in early modern times) *var fm* (*S dial*) *now dial n* **ea**

ieast *obs fm n* **joist**

ieaster *obs fm n* **jester**

ie-ie *var fm n* **ie**, a screw-pine

ieldra *Obs fm n* **elder**, a person of seniority

ien see **ie**

iengle *obs fm vb* **jingle**

iester *obs fm n* **jester**

if (*conj*) *n* a condition: a supposition

ig *Obs fm pron* **I**

igname *obs fm n* **yam**, the starchy tuberous root

ignaro *n* an ignoramus (*pl* **ignaros, ignaroes**)

ignitron *n* a device which starts ionization by conducting electric current through a pool of mercury

ignorant (*adj*) *n* an ignorant person

ignote *obs adj* unknown *obs n* one who is unknown

igrave *Obs fm vb* **grave**, in the *fig/arch/now poet/now dial* senses (*infl fms incl* **igraven, igraved**)

igraven see **igrave**

igripen *Obs pa pple vb* gripe

Iguvine *adj* pertaining to Iguvium or its bronze tablets

Iguvium *n* a former name of Gubbio, central Italy, which has seven tablets of bronze, the chief monument of the ancient language of the region in which it is located

ih *Obs fm pron* **I**

ihram *n* the special clothing worn by Muslim pilgrims as they approach Mecca

ik *Obs fm pron* **I**

il *Obs n* a hedgehog

i-lengd *Obs pa pple obs vb* leng (see **y-** prefix, of which 'i-' is a *var fm*)

ilenge *Obs vb* to get as far as

i-lenged *Obs pa pple obs vb* leng (see **y-** prefix, of which 'i-' is a *var fm*)

Ilex *n* the genus of holly (*– cap*) *n* the holm or evergreen oak (*pl* **ilices, ilexes**)

iliac *adj* of the ilium, a bone in the pelvic region *n* a short form of **iliac artery**, an artery of this part of the body *obs n* a short form of **iliac passion**, not (unfortunately) some type of delight but, as described in 1585, '*the paynes of the small guttes*'

ilices *pl* ilex

illission *n* the act of something hitting or striking against something else

ilmenite *n* an opaque, black titanium-iron oxide

im *Obs fm pron* **him**

imaginer *n* one who imagines

imaret *n* a Turkish inn

imbar *var fm vb* **embar**

imbower *var fm vb* **embower**, to shelter

imbring *var fm obs vb* **inbring**

imbrue *vb* to wet: to soak: to stain (*esp* with blood or slaughter)

imbrute *vb* to make bestial

imburse *vb* to store up

imeint *obs pa pple now dial vb* meng (also see **y-** prefix of which 'i-' prefix is a *var fm*)

imengd *Obs pa pple now dial vb* meng

imengde *Obs pa pple now dial vb* meng (also see **y-** prefix of which 'i-' prefix is a *var fm*)

imenget *Obs pa pple now dial vb* meng (also see **y-** prefix of which 'i-' prefix is a *var fm*)

imitancy *nonce n* the quality or property of imitating: imitativeness (GAME PLAYER'S note: UK championship Scrabble players can have no doubts as to the validity of this word as it is available to them as a standard noun with a meaning of 'the tendency to imitate') *presumed pl* **imitancies**

imitant *n* a counterfeit article

immane *arch adj* huge, vast, enormous: monstrous in character

immanent *adj* inherent, indwelling: remaining within

immantle *vb* to cover (as) with a mantle

immerd *vb* to cover with excrement, dirt, dung or anything unclean

immerge *vb* to immerse (*lit/fig*)

impacter *n* one who makes an impact

impaint *vb* to depict (with paint)

impaler *n* one who or that which impales

imparl *vb* to obtain, in old law, licence to settle a litigation amicably

imparle *obs fm vb* **imparl**

impash *obs S fm vb* **impeach**

impass *obs fm vb* **impeach**

impaste *vb* to encrust (as) with a paste: to form into a paste or crust: to spread or paint thickly

impearl *vb* to adorn (as) with pearls *esp* said of dew or tears: to make pearl-like

impeder *n* one who or that which impedes

impenitent (*adj*) *n* an unrepentant person

impester *obs vb* to entangle, to hobble such as a horse

impeticos *Shaks burlesque vb* a word used by the clown in *Twelfth Night* presumably for

impocket (to pocket) with a punning hint of petticoat hence, presumably, to pocket in one's petticoat

impire *var fm obs vb* **empire**

implate *vb* to cover with (iron) plate: to sheathe

implead *arch vb* to raise a legal action against

impleader *n* an accuser or prosecutor (GAME PLAYER'S note: Considered extant by the dictionary used for the UK Scrabble championship; other authorities consider that, as the last recorded usage was 1770, it is *obs*)

importancy *obs n* the quality of being important: urgency: an important matter (GAME PLAYER'S note: The dictionary used for the UK Scrabble championship lists it as an undefined noun, all usage of which can be ascribed to Shakespeare. Shakespeare only used the word in the first sense, which was still recorded in use in 1693, in the second sense it was last used in 1673 and Southey used it in the third sense in 1803. See **WRITERS**.)

impost (*n*) *vb* of US customs, to classify imported items according to a scale of tariffs

impot *school slg n* an imposition

imprecate *vb* to pray for: to invoke

impresa see **imprese**

imprese *n* a device or emblem: a motto for such: a maxim or proverb (GAME PLAYER'S note: The word **impresa** has the same meanings as **imprese**. The last recorded date for usage of **impresa** is 1653 and **imprese** also expired at a similar date except for a revival by Lamb in the early 19th century in the solitary sense of motto. Both British and American experts agree that imprese and impresa are *obs*. The dictionary used for the North American Scrabble championship lists both imprese and impresa in the sense of emblem but without dated comment. As it carries no labels of any description one can only presume that it agrees with other American dictionaries in considering the words to be obsolete.)

impresed *obs adj* having an imprese

impreso *var fm obs n* **impresa** (see **imprese**)

impresse *var fm obs n* **imprese**

impressure *n* the action of exerting pressure upon: the result of such action

imprest *n* an advance of money *obs n* the act of forcibly taking into armed use or service *obs vb* to lend money: to impress for the army or navy

impure (*adj*) *n* a harlot *obs vb* to defile

impute *vb* to ascribe *esp* evil: to charge: to transfer qualities in a theological sense, i.e. man's guilt to Christ during His crucifixion, Christ's goodness to man by His crucifixion

imputer *n* one who imputes

imshi *slg interj* depart

in (*prep/adj/adv/n*) *vb* to harvest: to gather *now dial vb* to enclose or reclaim economically marginal land

inaction *n* absence of activity: inertness

inactivate *vb* to render inactive

inamed *Obs fm adj* **named**

inamorata *n* a female lover such as a sweetheart or a mistress

inane (*adj*) *n* a void or empty space

inaner *comp adj* inane

inanimated *adj* not having life

inarch *vb* to arch in: enarch, to graft by connecting a growing branch without detaching it from the original stem

inbreak *n* a breaking in, an invasion

inbreathe *vb* to breathe something in (*lit/fig*): to inspire

inbring *obs vb* to bring in (by Scottish legal authority): to introduce

incage *var fm vb* **encage**, to enclose (as) in a cage

incall *obs vb* to invoke

incase *var fm vb* **encase**

incaution *n* want of caution: carelessness, unwariness

incede *vb* to advance or march with a stately pace

incept *vb* to take in, as a cell or organism *obs vb* to begin

inchase *var fm vb* **enchase**

incher *n* used in combination with a number to express relative value where the object can be found in different lengths and is sufficiently well known to remain unnamed

inchest *var fm obs vb* **enchest**

incisure *n* a cut, notch, slit or cleft

inckle *obs fm n* **inkle**

inclasp *var fm vb* **enclasp**

inclose *var fm vb* **enclose** and the legal and statutory *fm* in respect of the inclosing of common or waste land

incloser *var fm n* **encloser**, one who encloses (common land)

inclosure *var fm n* **enclosure** (note: Whilst there was an *obs n* **inclosurer**, one who squatted on enclosed common land, there does not appear to have been an 'enclosurer')

incognita *n* a female incognito

inconie *var fm obs adj* **incony**

incony *obs adj* possibly meaning fine, delicate or pretty (the meaning is obscure but is probably a slang term and was current in late Elizabethan/early Stuart times. Different writers tended to spell it differently. For example, Shakespeare used both **inconie** and **in-conie**, Marlowe **incony**, Jonson **in coney**.)

incorpse *vb* to incorporate (GAME PLAYER'S note: Whilst valid for championship Scrabble in the USA, it has to be rejected for the UK equivalent as its reference work attributes its usage exclusively to Shakespeare. Other authorities treat Shakespeare's use of **incorpsed** as an *adj* and it is certainly extant in the UK in this *fm* with a sense of incorporated. Incorpsed, however, is not given in the UK reference work.)

increate *adj* of divine beings, not created

increated *obs fm adj* increate

incremate a word apparently exclusive to one particular British dictionary which it defines as '*obs vb* to burn: to cremate' and adds the undefined noun, **incremation**. The noun is known to other experts who consider it rare or possibly obsolete and having the meaning of cremation. Presuming the *vb* to be *obs*, not *Obs* (no date of usage is given), then the *infl fm*, **incremated**, has the anagram, **endermatic**. (GAME PLAYER'S note: Whilst **incremate** is safe for play, the *infl fms* on this evidence are dubious)

incudes *pl* incus, one of the bones of the middle ear

indagator *n* one who investigates

indart *var fm Shaks vb* **endart**

indeign *Obs vb* to be angry: to disdain

indenter *n* one who indents

indesert *n* want of merit

indicatory *adj* serving to point out or indicate something: indicative of something

Indian red *n* colcothar

indices *pl* index

indigen *var fm n/obs adj* **indigene**

indigena *var fm n* **indigene** (*pl* **indigenae**)

indigene *n* a native *obs adj* native

indigent (*adj*) *obs n* one who is poor and needy

indigest *adj* crude, shapeless: of a person, immature *n* a shapeless mass *vb* to fail to digest (GAME PLAYER'S note: The last recorded usage of the *adj* in the sense of crude was 1806, in the sense of immature was 1513. Shakespeare is the only person known to have used the *n*. The *vb* was last used in 1882. One leading authority declares all three words obsolete. The reference for the UK Scrabble championship ignores the *vb* and declares both the *adj* and Shakespeare's *n* to be extant. The word is not valid in any sense for the equivalent contest in North America.)

indign *now poet adj* unbecoming, disgraceful *obs vb* to resent

indiscrete *adj* not divided into distinct parts *obs fm adj* indiscreet

indite *vb* to write or compose

inditer *n* an editor, writer or composer

indole *n* a white crystalline substance extracted from such as human excrement and, highly diluted, used in perfumery

indorse *var fm vb* **endorse**

indorsee *var fm n* **endorsee**, one in whose favour transference by endorsement (or, indorsement) is made

indow *obs fm vb* **endow**

indue *var fm vb* **endue**

indurate *vb* to harden

indusia *pl* indusium, a larva case

induvial *adj* of a calyx, remaining to provide a covering for a fruit

indwell *vb* to inhabit (*pa t/pa pple* **indwelt**)

inear *obs fm now dial n* **neer**

inearth *arch vb* to inter

inedge *obs vb* to get in surreptitiously

inegal *obs adj* unequal

ineger *obs vb* to excite

inequity *n* unfairness, partiality (in *pl fm* as **inequities**, an unfair or unjust action or matter)

inertia *n* the tendency of a body to resist change of movement (*pl* **inertiae, inertias**)

infamer *obs n* one who defames or one who brings infamy

infarct *n* a portion of bodily tissue extensively infiltrated with blood or serum *vb* to obstruct a bodily organ or vessel

infarction *n* the morbid condition of bodily tissues wrought by obstruction of the circulation

infare *US & S n* the first feast given by a bride in her new home *obs vb* to enter

infaust *adj* unlucky, ill-omened

infelt *adj* inwardly experienced

infere *obs adv* together, in company

infester *n* one who or that which infests *obs vb* to cause to rankle

infile *var fm obs vb* **enfile**

inflatus *Latin n* a blowing or breathing into

inforce *var fm vb* **enforce**

infract *vb* to break: to violate

ingan *S & dial fm n* **onion**

ingate *n* tedge, an inlet in a mould for the admission of molten metal *dial n* an entrance

ingather *vb* to gather in (the harvest)

ingear *S n* the internal possessions of a household (as opposed to **outgear**)

ingem *vb* to set with gems

ingener *obs vb* to engender *obs fm n* **engineer**

ingenital *adj* inate, inborn

ingénu *Fr n* the *masc fm* of **ingénue**

ingénue *Fr n* a naïve young woman (*masc* **ingénu**)

ingere *obs vb* to presume

ingert *var fm obs vb* **engirt**

ingest *vb* to take food or drink into the body

ingesta *n pl* food and drink (*sing* **ingestus**)

ingestar *obs n* an Italian early 17th century wine bottle: the quantity, somewhat greater than a pint, it contained

ingester *var fm obs n* **ingestar**

ingin *var fm S & dial n* **ingan**

ingird *obs fm vb* **engird**

inglobe *obs fm vb* **englobe**, to make spherical: to enclose (as) in a sphere

inglut *var fm arch vb* **englut**

ingle *n* a fire (in the domestic fireplace) *obs n* a boy used by a man for unnatural sexual practices *obs vb* to fondle or caress (in pleasant as well as unnatural senses)

ingoar *obs fm vb* **engore**

ingore *obs fm vb* **engore**

ingowes *Spens fm n pl* **ingots**

ingrafe *obs fm arch vb* **engraff**

ingraff *var fm arch vb* **engraff**

ingraft *var fm vb* **engraft**

ingraif *obs S fm vb* **engrave**

ingrail *obs fm vb* **engrail**

ingrain *adj* dyed in the fibre: of a type of carpet which has the pattern on both sides (e.g. a Kidderminster carpet as opposed to an Axminster): of such as qualities or habits, firmly fixed *n* a wool or fabric which has been dyed in the fibre *US n* an ingrain carpet *arch fm vb* **engrain**

ingrale *obs fm vb* **engrail**

ingram *now dial adj* ignorant *now dial n* an ignorant person (+*cap*) *masc pers n* meaning 'Ing's raven' (Ing being a Norse hero)

ingrant *obs adj* ignorant

ingrate *n* an ungrateful person *arch adj* ungrateful

ingrave *obs vb* to entomb

ingraver *obs fm n* **engraver**

ingreat *obs vb* to magnify or make great

ingrede *obs vb* to add as a medical ingredient

ingrele *obs fm vb* **engrail**

ingress *n* entering: an entrance: an entrance fee *obs vb* to have sexual intercourse with

ingreve *Obs fm obs vb* **engrieve**

ingross *obs fm vb* **engross**

ingroten *Obs vb* to glut

inground *obs vb* to root (*fig*)

ingrum *obs adj* ignorant

ingulf *var fm vb* **engulf**

inherce *obs fm vb* **enhearse**, to put into a hearse

inhere *vb* to exist: to be vested in

inhume *vb* to bury the dead

inhumer *US n* one who inhumes

inisle *var fm vb* **enisle**

inkbag *var fm n* **inksac**

inkle *n* a type of linen tape *dial vb* to give an inkling of

inksac *n* the pouch in a cuttlefish containing the sepia or camouflaging ink which it releases when making an escape

inlace *var fm vb* **enlace**

inlard *var fm obs vb* **enlard**

inlarge *obs fm vb* **enlarge**

inlead *obs vb* to bring (in)

inletter *obs n* one who gives admittance *obs vb* to inscribe

inlier *n* a stratum completely encased in another (the **outlier**)

inlock *var fm vb* **enlock**

inlooker *n* an inspector

inmated *adj* housed as an inmate

inmeat *n* a rare *sing fm* of **inmeats**

inmeats *n pl* edible entrails

inmest *obs S fm adj/adv/n* **inmost**

inmost *adj* most inward or intimate *adv* most inwardly *n* the inmost part (*lit/fig*)

innate (*adj*) *obs vb* to endow by nature in: to be naturally endowed with

innerest *obs sup* with a sense of innermost

innerve *vb* to supply a bodily part with nerves: to animate (*fig*)

inoculater *obs fm n* **inoculator**

inornate *adj* not ornate: simple

inosculate *vb* to unite

inosite *var fm n* **inositol**

inositol *n* inosite or muscle sugar, an alcohol widely distributed in plant and animal tissue

inparts *n pl* the internal parts of a body

inphase *adj* of electrical currents, being of the same phase

inport *obs fm n/vb* **import**

inqilab *n* a revolution in an Urdu-speaking country, such as Pakistan

inrage *obs fm vb* **enrage**

inrase *var fm obs vb* **enrase**

inrest *obs vb* to place in rest *var fm obs sup* **innerest**

inrode *obs fm n/vb* **inroad**

insanie *obs n* madness (also used for the original 'infamie' of Shakespeare's *Love's Labour's Lost* by one editor and subsequently copied by others)

inscape *n* the essence of such as the nature of a person or a work of art

insculp *vb* to carve or engrave (*pa pple* **insculpt, insculped**)

inseal *obs fm arch vb* **enseal**

inseam *obs fm vb* **enseam**

Insecta *n pl* the insects as a class (*−cap*) *obs pl* insect

insectan *adj* of or belonging to an insect: pertaining to insects

insectile *adj* of, pertaining to or of the nature of an insect: consisting of insects: insect-like (*fig*) *obs n* an insect

inseem *Shaks fm obs vb* **enseam**

inserta *see* **variola inserta**

inset *vb* to insert (GAME PLAYER'S note: The British *pa t* is **inset** with an *Obs fm* as **insetted**. The dictionary for the North American Scrabble championship ignores **inset** (rather surprisingly as it is usually excellent on English *fms* for its Canadian and, now, Australian users) and gives **insetted** as the only extant *pa t*. Presumably this is a modern American *fm*.)

insetted see **inset**

insetter *US n* one who inserts something *obs n* resident

inshade *obs vb* of painting, to shade one colour into another

inshed *vb* to pour in: to infuse (*obs* except as the *n* **inshedding**)

inshore (*adj*) *obs vb* to land or put on shore

insight (*n*) *obs vb* to give sight to

insign *var fm obs adj* **insigne** *obs fm n* **ensign**

insignate *obs vb* to mark: to engrave

insigne *n* a badge, ensign or emblem *esp* one distinguishing a person, office or nation (*pl* **insignia**) *obs adj* noted, distinguished, remarkable

insignia *pl* insigne (note: In the USA insignia is treated as *n* sing, hence *pl* **insignias**)

insister *n* one who insists *obs vb* to admit as or make into a sister

insnare *var fm vb* **ensnare**

insolate *vb* to expose to the sun's rays

insomniac *n* one who suffers from sleeplessness

insouciant *adj* carefree, light-hearted: careless, indifferent, heedless, unmindful (note: The pronunciation is French and some experts consider that it has yet to be fully assimilated into English. However, from a game player's viewpoint it is a valid word.)

insoul *var fm vb* **ensoul**

inspan *n* a yoked team of draught animals *vb* to yoke a team (of horses, mules or oxen etc) to a wagon: to harness a wagon

inspheare *obs fm vb* **insphere** (see **ensphere**)

insphere *var fm vb* **ensphere**

inspissate *vb* to thicken: to become thick

instanter *adv* at once

instar *vb* to adorn (as) with stars

instarre *obs fm vb* **instar**

instate *vb* to install, establish

instigater *obs fm n* **instigator**

instile *var fm obs vb* **instyle**, to call by the name of: to entitle

instop *obs vb* to seal or close up

instore *var fm obs vb* **enstore**

insula *n* a block of ancient Roman buildings: a clot of blood floating in serum (*pl* **insulae**)

insulse *adj* dull, insipid, stupid

insureds a *pl fm n* **insured**, specifically given in the dictionary used for the North American Scrabble championship (note: Other American dictionaries mirror British usage of insured as a noun in both *sing* and *pl* senses, i.e. one who is or those who are covered by an insurance policy)

intagli *pl* intaglio

intaglio *n* that decoratively incised or engraved (in hard material): the process of such: that having this work (*pl* **intagli, intaglios**) *vb* to engrave with a sunken pattern or design

intaile *obs fm vb* **entail**

integer *n* an individual entity or whole unit: any whole number

integral (*adj*) *n* a complete thing

integrand *n* a mathematical term with a sense of to be integrated

integrant *adj* constituent *n* a component

inteir *obs S fm adj/adv/n* **entire**

intender (*n*) *var fm obs vb* **entender**

intensed *obs adj* intensified

intenser *comp adj* intense

intercut *vb* to insert other material into a film during the editing *obs vb* to cut into, to intersect

interdash *vb* to set here and there with dashes or strokes

interdeal *vb* to negotiate mutually *n* mutal dealing (GAME PLAYER'S note: The dictionary used for the UK Scrabble championship declares both the noun and verb archaic and credits Spenser with sole usage of the *var fm n* in an 'old fashioned' spelling as **enterdeale**. Other experts disagree in no uncertain manner. In the first place, they consider the verb to be in normal use, not archaic. Secondly, they consider Spenser to be merely the first to use the form **enterdeale**. Thirdly, they consider the noun to be obsolete. The dates and spelling forms they quote are:– **enterdeale** (Spenser) 1591, **interdeale** 1596, **enterdeal** 1605, **enterdeale** 1612. Whilst accepting the noun should be considered as being **interdeal** in a modern spelling, they have no record of it ever having been used as such. Not that this affects Scrabble players in any way – 'archaic' words are quite valid in the game – and, in any event, any use of the noun is overshadowed by the more versatile verb. It is, however, of consequence to players of the boxed version of the television game, Countdown, if they use the same rules as those of Channel 4. Unlike the rules given in the boxed game, the TV programme specifically bars archaic words.)

intere *obs fm adj/adv/n* **entire**

interess *obs n/vb* (to) interest

intergrade *n* an intermediate grade *vb* to advance or otherwise change by intervening stages

interlap *vb* to rest one upon another

interlapse *n* an intervening space of time

intern *adj* internal *n* an inmate of a residential establishment (either willing or unwilling) *US n* a residential student of a hospital sufficiently advanced to practise a degree of medicine *vb* of people or such as enemy warships, to confine or contain within *US vb* to undergo residential training within a hospital for a medical degree

interne *var fm n/US n/vb/US vb* **intern**

interpage *vb* to insert on intermediate pages

interpone *vb* to interpose one's authority in Scottish law

interposal *n* intervention

intertie *n* a short length of timber used as a horizontal support for two vertical pieces *vb* to tie mutually

intervale *US n* a low tract of land beside a river *obs n* an interval, either of time or of space

inthronize *obs fm arch vb* **enthronize** (note: Apart from a *poet* use of enthronize in 1871, inthronize has the last recorded use of the *vb* in standard literature. This is in connection with a report on the coronation of Queen Victoria in 1838. The last recorded dates for some other *fms* are 1734 for **enthronise** and 1557 for **inthronise**. Also see **enthronise**.)

intier *obs fm adj/adv/n* **entire**

intima *n* the innermost layer of an organ or other bodily part (*pl* **intimae, intimas**)

intime *adj* intimate

intimism *n* an early 20th century genre of French impressionist painting of everyday objects

intine *n* the inner membrane of a grain of pollen

intire *arch fm adj/adv/n* **entire** *var fm obs vb* **entire**

intitle *now US var fm vb* **entitle**

intoed *adj* having the toes turned inward

intort *vb* to twist inward

intraste *Obs vb* to trust in

intrat *obs n* the entrance of a stage character

intrate *obs n* income

intreat *arch fm vb* **entreat**

intres *var fm obs n* **entress**

intrigante *n* a woman who intrigues

introitus *n* the entrance to the vagina

introrse *adj* of the anther of a plant, turned inwards

introspect *vb* to look into or within (the mind, thoughts or feelings)

intrust *var fm vb* **entrust**

intuse *obs n* a bruise

inula *n* a plant once cultivated for the medicinal value of its root

inulase *n* an enzyme produced by the action of certain species of fungi on a starch-like substance which occurs on the underground parts of various plants *incl* the dandelion and the dahlia

inure *vb* to harden or toughen by use, habit or continual exercise: to accustom

inurn *vb* to place the ashes of a cremation in an urn: to entomb

inustion *obs n* branding with fire (*lit*/*fig*): cauterization (GAME PLAYER'S note: Whilst all authorities agree that the word is no longer in use, it should be noted that it was used as a medical term as late as 1834)

inveigh *vb* to speak with violent or invective language against

inveigler *n* one who cajoles, entices or seduces

inventer *var fm n* **inventor**

inverse *adj* inverted *n* an inverted state *vb* to invert

inveterate (*adj*) *arch vb* to implant deeply: to make old: to confirm by age or long continuance: to embitter

invisible ink *n* any substance which is capable of being used as an 'ink' but leaves no visible trace unless treated in some form. The simplest invisible inks are organic liquids such as urine or fruit juices which reveal the message when carefully heated. Chemical 'inks' include iron sulphate which, when painted over with a solution of potassium cyanate, changes into Prussian blue, and copper sulphate which reveals the message in red when treated with ammonia fumes.

invitee *n* one who is invited

invocate *vb* to invoke

involucre *n* that which envelops, used *esp* in various zoological or botanical senses

inwith *now S adv* inwards

inwreathe *var fm vb* **enwreathe**

inyet *obs vb* to infuse (*infl fms incl obs n* **inyetting**, infusion)

io *n* a large Hawaiian hawk and the only raptor indigenous to those islands: a cry of the *interj* io (see below) (*pl* **ios**) *interj* of joy or triumph (used in English only in an ancient Greek or Roman context) (+*cap*) *pers n* the daughter of the Greek river god, Inachus, who was beloved by Zeus but the object of the enmity of his wife, Hera, who turned Io into a heifer: a Maori god *n* the innermost of the four moons of the planet Jupiter (the Roman name for Zeus)

iodate *n* a salt of iodic acid *vb* to treat with iodine

iodide *n* a compound or salt in which iodine is the acid radical: a binary compound of iodine

iodinate *US vb* to treat with iodine

iodiser *n* one who or that which iodises

iodism *n* a morbid condition due to excessive use of iodine or its compounds

iodous *adj* of a compound with a greater proportion of iodine than oxygen

ioduret *obs n* a salt of hydriodic acid, an iodide

iolite *n* a gemstone of a bluish silicate of magnesium, aluminium and iron, also known as cordierite

ionet *obs fm n* **jennet**

ionomer *n* a type of plastic characterized by toughness and a high degree of transparency

iorden *obs fm now dial n* **jordan**

iota *n* the ninth letter of the Greek alphabet: a jot

ipecac *n* a short form of **ipecacuanha**, a Brazilian plant whose root has valuable medicinal qualities: the emetic produced from the root of the ipecacuanha or from other similar plants (GAME PLAYER'S note: **ipecac** is perfectly valid for play as it is an *abbreviated form* NOT an abbreviation – i.e. it is pronounced as it is spelt NOT as it is pronounced when written in full)

ir *obs fm n* **ire** *Obs fm pron* **her**

irade *n* a written edict of the Sultan of Turkey

iratest *sup* irate

ireless *adj* without ire or anger

irenics *n* oecumenical theology

irideal *adj* belonging to the iris family of plants

iridectomy *n* the surgical removal of a portion of the iris

irides *pl* iris (an alternative to **irises**)

irisate *adj* iridescent or displaying a spectrum of colours that shimmer and change *vb* to make iridescent

irised *adj* displaying colours like a rainbow

irk (*n*) *arch vb* of something, to trouble

ironise *vb* to use irony

ironsand *n* sand containing particles of iron ore: the steel filings used in fireworks

Ironside *n* an appellation denoting bravery and specifically used for the English king, Edmund II (1016): an appellation of hardness of heart or character (more usually, **Ironsides**) and specifically used for Cromwell: extended to various others to denote strength of character (either + or −*cap* or + or − the letter S): one of the **Ironsides**, the troops of Cromwell or any other Puritanical military force (−*cap*) *n* as shown above: a ship plated with iron

ironstone *n* iron ore: any stone or mineral containing iron

irradiant *adj* shining brightly (*lit/fig*)

Irving *pers n* either a forename or surname e.g. Henry Irving, Irving Berlin

Irvingia *n* a genus of tropical trees, the seeds of which provide a butter

is see *infl fms vb* **be**

Isabel *var fm fem pers n* **Elizabeth,** meaning 'consecrated to God' (−*cap*) *n/adj* a dull yellow colour

isabella *var fm n/adj* **isabel**

Isadore *fem pers n* meaning 'equal gift'

isatin *n* a crystalline compound with a bitter taste obtained by oxydizing indigo and used as a reagent

isatine *var fm n* **isatin**

isehtne *Obs vb* to reconcile

Isengrim *pers n* the name of the wolf in the classic tale *Reynard the Fox*

isentropic *adj* without change in an index of the degree in which the total energy of a thermodynamic system is uniformly distributed and is thus unavailable for conversion into work

Ishtar *pers n* the Babylonian personification of Astarte, the Canaanite goddess of sex

ishtaritu *n* a prostitute of the temple of Ishtar of lower rank than a **qadistu** but above that of a **hamaritu**

Isidore *masc pers n* meaning 'gift of Isis'

Islamitic *adj* Moslem

island (*n*) *vb* to make (as) into an island: to place as or on an island: to isolate: to set (as) with islands

isleman *n* an island dweller *esp* one in the Hebrides

Isle of Wight disease *n* acarine (disease)

islesman *n* an inhabitant of one of a group of islands (as opposed to an **isleman** or an **islander**, an inhabitant of a solitary island)

islet *n* either an eyot or a small marine isle

isleted *adj* having islets or small isles

ism *n* any faddish or ridiculous theory or doctrine

ismate *nonce vb* to append the suffix '-ism' to form an abstract noun which indicates a particular sense understood by the basic word. For example, the media regularly coin isms using the surnames of politicians, as *Thatcherism* or *Kinnockism*.

ismatic *nonce adj* pertaining to an ism or isms *nonce n* one who belongs to a particular ism

ismatical *nonce adj* ismatic

isocline *n* a rock fold in which the strata have parallel sides

isogone *n* a line on a map or chart used to show characteristics of the Earth's magnetic field

isograph *n* a line on such as a map connecting points which have equal values in relation to a particular specification

isolead *n* a curved line on a chart indicating the track of ballistic missile

isolet *obs n* a little island

isoline *n* an isogram or line drawn on a map or diagram which connects all points having an equal numerical value with respect to a variable factor

isomer *n* either of two compounds which have identical molecular weight and formula but, by differing in the spatial arrangement of their atoms, have different properties

isope *obs fm n* **hyssop**

isopleth *n* a nomogram: a nomograph: an isogram: a meteorological graph showing the variations of a specific climatic element with respect to two coordinates

isoprene *n* a volatile liquid hydrocarbon of a group found chiefly in the essential oils of the conifers

isosceles *adj* of a triangle, having two equal sides

isotheral *adj* designating any line on a map which connects points having the same mean summer temperature

isothere *n* a line on a meteorological chart which connects points having the same average summer temperature

isotherm *n* a line connecting points on the surface of the Earth having the same temperature at a given time or the same mean temperature over a given period

isotron *n* a device for separating isotopes

isotropy *n* the quality of exhibiting equal physical properties or actions (*pl* **isotropies**)

isteed *var fm dial adv* **astead**

isthmus *n* a narrow strip of land connecting two large land areas: extended to various similar connections (*pl* **isthmi, isthmuses**)

istle *n* a Mexican fibre used for such as carpets

it (*pron*) *n* a thing

itacism *n* the opposite of etacism (i.e. modern Greek pronunciation of eta)

Italicism *n* an Italian idiom

iterance *n* repetition

iterant *adj* repeating, echoing

iterate *vb* to say or do again: to repeat

itzebu see **bu**

iudge *obs fm n/vb* **judge**

iunquet *obs fm n* **junket**

iv *dial fm adv/n/prep/vb* **in**

Ivan and Maria *n* a beautiful Russian weed which has purple leaves and yellow flowers, the name being derived from a legend of two young lovers. Forbidden to marry, they died of broken hearts and were reincarnated as this lovely plant.

ivorist *n* a worker in ivory

iw *Obs fm n* **yew**

ix *dial fm n* **ax**

ixtle *var fm n* **istle**

izzard *arch n* the letter Z

J

ja *dial n* a jaw *dial vb* to talk *obs S fm n* **jay**

jaap *var fm S & dial n/vb* **jaup**

jackman *S n* a retainer who wore a jack or defensive doublet quilted with iron

jacquery *arch/obsol anglicized fm Fr n* **Jacquerie**, a revolt by the peasantry

jade stalk *n* a classical Chinese synonym for the penis

jadish *adj* of a horse or a woman, having the nature of a jade i.e. inferior or worthless

jak *var fm n* **jack**, a fruit similar to the breadfruit: the tree on which it grows

jakes *n* a privy *dial n* excrement

jale *obs fm n/vb* **jail**

jalouse *S vb* to suspect

jambul *n* the rose-apple tree, a small tropical tree with edible, sweet-scented fruit and beautiful foliage: any other tree of the same genus, *Eugenia* (*var fms* **jambolan, jambolana, jambool, jambu**)

jap *var fm S & dial n/vb* **jaup**

jardon *obs n* a tumour on a horse's leg

jarg *S n* a creaking noise *obs S vb* of a gate or door, to creak or otherwise be less than perfect in action

jarkman *obs n* an educated beggar capable of forging documents (*pl* **jarkmen**)

jarl *n* an old Norse chieftain

jarless *adj* free from jarring: causing no jarring *n* the wife of a jarl

jarta *Shet n/adj* heart, used as a term of endearment

jarvey *collq n* the driver of a hackney carriage *collq vb* to drive such a vehicle

Jashar *var fm n* **Jasher**

Jasher *n* one of the lost books of the ancient Hebrews twice mentioned in the Bible

jasper *n* an impure, opaque quartz of various colours admitting a high polish and used for ornamentation: a fine hard porcelain (+*cap*) *masc pers n* meaning 'master of the treasure'

jasponyx *obs n* an onyx resembling the precious stone, jasper

jaup *S & dial n/vb* (to) splash

je *obs fm arch adv* **yea**

Jebusite *n* a tribe of Canaanites whom King David dispossessed of Jerusalem: a 17th century nickname for a Jesuit

jeg *n* a template used for verifying various shapes in the manufacture of parts of a gun

jelab *n* a hooded cloak worn in Morocco

jelick *n* a type of bodice worn by a Turkish woman

jennet *n* a small Spanish horse

jeopard *vb* to put in jeopardy

jerbil *var fm n* **gerbil**

jereed *var fm n* **jerid**

jerg *var fm S n* **jarg**

jerid *n* a wooden javelin carried by Turkish, Persian and Arabic horsemen and thrown in sporting contests: such a contest

jerque *vb* of a customs officer, to examine a ship's papers to ensure that all cargo has been duly entered

jerquer *n* one who jerques

jeton *var fm n* **jetton**, a metal token used for such as a counter in gambling at a card table

jetson *arch fm n* **jetsam**, that jettisoned from a ship and washed up on shore (as opposed to **flotsam**, that from a shipwreck)

Jew (*n*) *collq vb* to cheat (note: While normally written +*cap*, it can also be −*cap*, *esp* the *n*, **jewing**, the action of the *vb*)

jewel terrace *n* a classical Chinese synonym for the clitoris

jezail *n* a heavy Afghan musket

jeziah *n* the tax formerly imposed by the Moghul emperors on non-Muslim residents in India

jheel *n* in India, a pool or lagoon similar in nature to an oxbow lake

jhil *var fm n* **jheel**

jhow *n* an evergreen shrub of the genus, *Tamarix*, abundant on Indian marshy land

jihad *n* a war, declared holy by Muslims

jim *n* the fifth letter of the Arabic alphabet *obs fm now dial adj* **gim**

jin *var fm n* **gin**, an Australian aboriginal woman: a female kangaroo *obs var fm n* **gin**, the alcoholic drink

jingal *var fm n* **gingall**

jirble *S vb* to spill whilst pouring: to pour noisily

jird *n* any of about ten species of gerbils which are the most rat-like in appearance, though differing from rats by having a hairy tail

jirg *var fm S n* **jarg**

jo *n* a Japanese measure of distance, roughly $3\frac{1}{3}$ yards (*pl* **jo**) *S n* a beloved one (*pl* **joes**) *obs fm n* **joe**, a Portuguese gold coin

jobo see **zho**

jod *var fm n* **yod**

jodler *var fm n* **yodeller**, one who yodels

jomo see **zho**

jordan *now dial n* a chamber pot: one who commands as much respect as a chamber pot

jow *S & dial n* a knock *S n* the sound of a bell: the dashing of a wave on the shore *S & dial vb* to knock: to ring

juck *vb* of a partridge, to utter its cry

jud *n* a large block of coal

Judaic *adj* pertaining to the Jews

Judica *n* Passion Sunday

juke *var fm vb* **juck**

> **JULIAN CALENDAR** Instituted by Julius Caesar in 46 BC, it was the basic European calendar until the introduction of the slightly more accurate Gregorian calendar in 1582. Britain, however, did not adopt the Gregorian calendar until 1752, which necessitated the removal of eleven days from that year in order to be in line with most of Europe. When people had to experience the unique phenomenon of 2 September 1752 being followed by 14 September 1752, many thought they were being cheated out of eleven days and eleven days' pay and raised an outcry at the time. Russia did not change to the Gregorian calendar until 1918 and refugee groups from the Russian Revolution still continue to use the Julian calendar. This has, for example, the effect that a Ukrainian community in a Yorkshire town celebrated Christmas in early January 1987. (Also see **CHINESE CALENDAR, FRENCH REVOLUTIONARY CALENDAR, HEBREW CALENDAR, Metonic cycle** and **Nabonassar**)

jumbal *n* a ring-shaped thin, crisp, sweet cake

junglefowl *n* any of five species of megapodes classified within three genera. Unlike other mound birds, several breeding pairs may contribute to the construction of the incubation mound. These are members of the species *Megapodius freycinet* which build the largest mound of all, 15 ft high and over 35 ft in diameter. (Also see **mallee fowl**): any of various species of the pheasant family

juzail *var fm n* **jezail**

jynx *n* any species of wrynecks

K

ka *n* in the ancient Egyptian religion, the spiritual self *S n* a jackdaw *dial vb* to call: of a partridge, to utter its cry: to be delirious: to announce: to publish the banns of marriage *now dial vb* found only in such phrases as '*Ka me and I'll ka thee*' which has a sense of '*You scratch my back and I'll scratch yours*'. In other words, mutual help.

kaa *var fm dial vb/now dial vb* **ka**

kaas *var fm n* **kas**

Kabyle *n* a Berber people of Algeria and their language

Kachan *n* the former name of Quang Nam, Vietnam

kae *n* the cry of a jackdaw *S & dial n* a jackdaw

kaesar *obs fm n* **kaiser**

kaf *n* the twenty-second letter of the Arabic alphabet

Kafir the better *fm* of the more usual spelling **Kaffir** and its *var fms* **Kaffer** and **Kaffre** *n* a native of Kafiristan, the land of the Kafirs of the Hindu Kush, a mountainous region mainly in Afghanistan: any member of the Bantu race living in South Africa: any Bantu language spoken in South Africa (*pl*) *n* South African mining shares (*— cap*) *var fm n* **caffre**, an infidel

kaiser *n* the German form of Caesar used as a title for the emperors of Germany (1871–1918)

kakapo *n* the owl parrot of New Zealand, an entirely flightless endangered species of nocturnal polygamous parrot. At night, the males congregate in a lek where they call to the females with loud booming cries. A responding female mates with the individual of her choice. Afterwards, she and the male take no further interest in each other. (*pl* **kakapos**)

kakkak *n* a species of small bittern on the island of Guam

kalamdam *n* a Persian writing case

kalinite *n* native potash alum

kalmia *n* the American laurel, an evergreen shrub

kalpis *n* a water vase

Kamber *pers n* one of the sons of Brutus who, after his death, inherited that part of Britain which he called Kambria (Wales) (see **Brutus**)

kame *obs S fm vb* comb

kamila *n* a fine orange-coloured powder obtained from the hairs on fruit capsules of an East Indian tree of the spurge family and used as either a yellow dye or a worm-killing agent: the tree itself

kaneh *n* a Hebrew measure of length equal to six cubits

kanoon *n* an Eastern dulcimer-like musical instrument, having between 50 and 60 strings played by hand

kantar *n* a weight, nominally 100 Arabic pounds, but which varies considerably in different Mediterranean countries

kantel *var fm obs vb* **cantle** *Obs fm n* **cantle**

kantle *obs fm n* **cantle**

kaper *var fm S n* **caper**, an oatmeal cake buttered and topped with a piece of cheese

kaph *n* the eleventh letter of the Hebrew alphabet

kar *var fm S adv* **car** *obs fm n/vb* **care**

karasse *obs fm n* **cress**

Karenni *modf n* of three Burmese states treated as one unit of the Union of Burma, with the local capital at Loikaw

karite *n* the shea tree, the nuts of which provide shea butter *Obs fm n* **charity**

karl *obs fm now dial vb* **carl**

karling *var fm S n* **carline** (+*cap*) *adj* Carolingian or Carlovingian, pertaining to Charlemagne and his Frankish dynasty

karoo/Karoo *var fms* (*respectively*) *n/adj* **karroo/Karroo**

karroo *n* a dry South African plateau (*pl* **karroos**) (+*cap*) *adj* of a rock system of the Paleozoic and Mesozoic eras

kartel *n* a wooden bed in a South African ox wagon

karting *n* racing with go-carts, car-like vehicles of essential elements only

karung *n* the leather of a wart snake

kas *n* a massive, often highly decorated cupboard of the early Dutch settlers in America

Kassan *n* a town southwest of Samarkand in Uzbekistan

kater *var fm obs n* **cater**, a buyer of provisions

Katrine *dim fem pers n* **Katherine**, meaning 'pure'

kavass *n* a Turkish policeman: an armed servant or courier in Turkey (*var fms* **cavash, cavass, kawass, kaous, kervass**)

kaw *obs fm vb* **caw**

ke *obs fm S & dial n* **kae**

kea *n* a green mountain parrot of New Zealand with a reputation as a killer of sheep

keale *obs fm now dial vb* **keel**, to cool

kealer *obs fm now dial n* **keeler**

keasar *obs fm n* **kaiser**

kebab *n* shish kebab, a meal on a skewer consisting of small cubes of meat interspersed with various vegetables, both cooked and eaten in this form

kebl *arch fm n* **kiblah**

keeler *n* a manager of coal barges in Northumbria *now dial n* any of various types of shallow vessel or tub used for such purposes as cooling liquids or dressing mackerel

kef *var fm n* **kif**

keir *obs S vb* to drive off

keister *US n* the buttocks (*var fm* **kiester**, unlisted anagram)

kelare *obs fm now dial n* **keeler**

kelder *obs n* the womb

kele *obs S fm vb* **kill**

kelpie *n* unlike many other water horses, this spirit of the Scottish Highlands haunts rivers rather than coastal waters. In its human form, it appears as a rough, shaggy man and its most frequent equine manifestation is that of a young horse.

kelson *n* a beam secured to the keel of a vessel as part of the strengthening

kelt see **SALMON**

kelter *n* soundness of health or spirits *dial n* money: rubbish *obs n* an outer garment made of a coarse cloth: that cloth

Keltic *var fm adj* **Celtic**

keltie *var fm S n* **kelty** (*+cap*) *pers n* the surname of the laird whose capacity for drink was legendary and after whom the word was coined

kelty *S n* the complete draining of a glass of liquor and the indication of such by turning it upside down: the imposition of a subsequent glass, filled to the brim, if the current glass is not drained to the satisfaction of other drinkers (Also see **keltie**)

Kendal *n* the town in Westmorland (now part of Cumbria) which produced the historic Kendal green, a type of cloth: dyer's greenweed, the plant from which the green dye used for that cloth was extracted

kenit *var fm obs n* **kennet**, a small hunting dog

kenno *n* a cheese secretly prepared to be eaten by gossips at the birth of a child (also see **nidget**)

ker *n* a (malignant) spirit or soul of one who is dead *var fm S adv* **car**

keratin *n* a highly insoluble compound that forms the essential ingredient of the horny tissue of such as nails or claws

keratose *adj esp* of certain sponges, pertaining to or characterized by horny tissue

Keresan *n* a Red Indian people and language of New Mexico

keri *n* in the Hebrew text of the Bible, a word given in the margin which should be substituted for one retained in the main text for reasons of tradition

kerling *Obs fm S n* **carline**

kermis *n* an annual fair in a Benelux country: an indoor fair in the USA

kermiss *var fm n* **kermis**

kerne *n* of the five classes of followers of an historic Irish warrior chieftain, one of the lower ranking. The classes were **horsemen, galloglasses** (who used a battle ax), **kernes** or **kerns** (sword and shield or bow and arrows), **grooms** and **daltins** (boys): a similarly lightly-armed Irishman in mercenary service: the poorer class of Irish from which such men were recruited

kersis *obs pl* cress

kertel *obs fm n* **kirtle**

kertle *obs fm n* **kirtle**

Keuper *n* the uppermost division of strata in the Triassic system which, in Britain, consists mainly of marls and sandstones

kha *n* the seventh letter of the Arabic alphabet

Khanty *n* an Ugric language (also called Ostyak) of Western Siberia

khilat *n* an Indian robe of honour

ki *n* a Chinese liliaceous plant

kiang *n* the tallest of the three species of Asiatic wild ass (the others being kulan and onager), it is found in Tibet and the Himalayas

kibbutz *n* a collective farm in Israel (*pl* **kibbutzim**)

kiblah *n* the position of the temple at Mecca relative to a Muslim at prayer and, therefore, the direction towards which he or she faces

kidden *obs adj* made of kidskin *obs vb* of a goat, to bring forth young

kidel *var fm n* **kiddle**, a weir or barrier in a river specially constructed so that a fishing net can be placed in an opening

kiester *var fm US slg n* **keister**

kif *n* marijuana or any other similar drug: the euphoric dreamy state produced by smoking such a drug

killdeer *n* a noisy species of North American plover, so named because of its frequently repeated cry of '*kill deer*'

Kilner *n* a proprietary brand of glass jar for the storing and preserving of perishable foodstuffs

kilter *var fm* (*esp US*) *n* **kelter**, good health

kimmer *var fm S n* **cummer**

kind (*n*/*adj*) *obs vb* to beget (only found as a *pa pple* in Spenser): to treat kindly? (the meaning is obscure)

kindle (n/vb) *now dial vb* of an animal, to give birth to (note: The collective noun associated with this sense is still extant in standard English – see **COLLECTIVE NOUNS)**

kindler *n* one who ignites something: one who inflames a passion: that which will readily combust

kine *n pl* cows

king (*n*) *vb* to make (one) a king: to perform the duties of a king

kingbird *n* any of a certain species of a genus of North American tyrant flycatchers

king crab *n* a large, bright red species of stone crab which, like all stone crabs, is not a true crab but related to the hermit crabs: the horseshoe crab, a 'living fossil' which is not a crustacean but a large marine arthropod (i.e. having affinities with such as spiders, scorpions and mites)

kingcup *n* the buttercup

king hit *Austr slg n* a knockout blow

kingle *S n* sandstone: hard rock

king rod *n* a main bolt in a mechanical structure

kink (*n*) *vb* to twist or curl *S & dial vb* to gasp convulsively for breath either from excessive laughter or a medical condition (the *n* **kinking** is the action of either *vb*)

kinone *var fm n* **quinone**

kipe *now dial n* a basket (used as a unit of measure): a basket used as a fishing device *now dial vb* to fish by this method

kirle *obs fm n* **curl**

kirsch *n* a cherry brandy (from the Black Forest region of Germany)

kirset *S n* a former privilege granted to a newly-appointed burgess, that of being exempt from taxes for the first year of office

kirsett *obs fm n* **cresset**

kirtel *obs fm n* **kirtle**

kirtle *n* a garment of various types (*a*) for women, a gown: a skirt: an outer petticoat once worn as a protective garment whilst riding (*b*) for men, a coat: a garment which once functioned as the basic unit of clothing, reaching to the knee or lower: a coating of any type (*fig*) *vb* to cover (as) with a kirtle

kitchener *n* one employed in a (monastery) kitchen: a cooking range

Kitchi Manito *pers n* the Algonquian Red Indian name for the Great Spirit (see **manito**)

kiter *n* one who flies a kite

kithe *now S & dial vb* to make known

kitsch *n* any trashy work in any of the arts

kittle *adj* risky, precarious *now S & dial vb* to give birth to kittens *S & dial vb* to tickle: to puzzle with such as a riddle

kiver *now dial n* a shallow wooden tub *dial fm n/vb* **cover**

kiz *dial conj* because

kleet *var fm n/vb* cleat

klendusic *adj* of plants, naturally able to withstand disease

klipfish *n* the scaled blenny (see **blenny**)

knar *n* a knot in wood *dial n* a stone covered in incrustations formed by insects

knare *arch fm n* **knar**

knared *obs fm adj* **knarred**, knotted or gnarled

knarre *Obs fm n* **knar**

Knaster *Ger n* a type of tobacco (also used in English *–cap*, see **canaster**)

knifer *n* in boot making, one who trims the soles and heels

knipse *obs S vb* to rap or hit sharply

knite *obs fm vb* **knit**

knurl *n* a knob, nodule or similar small projection *dial n* a deformed dwarf *vb* to make small projections such as the milled edge of a coin

ko *n* a Chinese liquid measure (*pl* **ko**) *var fm obs n* **co**

koa *n* a species of acacia tree found in the Sandwich Islands, valued both for its hard timber and its bark which is used in tanning

koi *n* a variety of ornamental carp originally bred in Japan and now kept in special breeding ponds in such countries as the UK, USA, Israel and Singapore. Some are extremely valuable, one 2½ foot long specimen dappled in fiery red, black and silvery-white, imported from Japan to Britain in 1986, is reputed to be worth £70,000. They live to a great age, the oldest on record being a 20 lb female with the personal name of Hanako living in a Japanese pond. Study of her scales (in 1986) has shown that she is 230 years old and is reported to be 'still as sprightly as a minnow'. (*pl* **koi**)

kongoni *n* a subspecies of the common hartebeest

koo *var fm obs n* **co**

koph *n* the nineteenth letter of the Hebrew alphabet

korora *n* the blue penguin

krait *n* one of a number of species of highly venomous snakes of tropical Asia which exist mainly on a diet of other snakes

kraut *slg n* a German

kreasote *var fm n* **creosote**

kreat *obs fm n/vb* **creaght**

kreatine *var fm n* **creatine**

kreese *var fm n/vb* **kris**

kreil *obs fm n* **creel**

krele *obs fm n* **creel**

krempt *n* a heavy rainfall in Ethiopia

krime *obs n* a rather obscure word which probably means frost

kris *n* a Malay dagger with a wavy blade (*pl* **krises**) *vb* to stab or kill with a kris (*var fms n/vb incl* **crease, creese, crese, creeze, kreese, kriss**)

Krishna *pers n* a deified hero of later Hinduism regarded by true Hindus as being an incarnation of one of the greater gods, Vishnu. The various 20th century American cults which combine Buddhism and Hinduism with other cultural traditions claim a much greater antiquity for him and give him solo status as that of the supreme being.

krummhorn *n* an old German cornet-like musical instrument with a curved end: an organ reed stop resembling the clarinet in tone and having an eight foot pitch (*var fms* for the organ stop are **cremona** (*erron*), **cremone** (*obs*), **cremorne** (*erron*), **cromorna, cromorne, crumhorn, krumhorn** – also see **cremona**)

ku *dial n* an eye ulceration *Obs fm ns* **cue, cow** (also see **kine, ky**)

kulan *n* an Asiatic wild ass found in Mongolia

kurbash *var fm n* **kourbash**, an Oriental whip of hippopotamus hide

kurgan *n* a prehistoric tumulus in those Russian lands native to the Tartar peoples

kurl *obs fm vb* **curl**

kursaal *n* a (German) health resort

kurta *n* a collar-less Indian tunic

kuter *var fm S vb* **cuiter**

kvutza *n* a communal and co-operative unit which may combine with others to form a kibbutz (*pl* **kvutzot**) (WORD PUZZLER'S note: This word features in a very rare holoalphabetic sentence or pangram which reads '*Cwm kvutza qoph jynx fled brigs*' which roughly translates as '*The wryneck bird from the communal farming unit known by the Hebrew letter qoph and situated in the valley, escaped from confinement aboard ship.*' For other, less complex, holoalphabetic sentences see **pangram**.)

kwacha *n* the basic unit of currency in both Malawi and Zambia

kwanza *n* the unit of currency in Angola which (Sept. 1986) is officially circa 30 to the $ but, on the black market, is more than 1,500 to the $ (*pl* **kwanza**)

ky *now S & dial n pl* cows

kyanise *var fm vb* **kyanize**, to preserve (wood) from decay by impregnating with a solution of corrosive sublimate

kye *var fm now S & dial n pl* **ky**

kylie n an Australian boomerang

kylin *n* any of various Chinese and Japanese fabulous composite animals which feature on porcelain *esp* the Chinese unicorn which has the body of a deer, the tail of an ox and a single horn

kylix *n* an ancient Greek shallow cup with a tall stem (*pl* **kylikes, kylixes**)

kyu *n* one of the student grades in judo

L

la *interj* lo! see! *n* the sixth musical syllable in the tonic sol-fa system: the bebization equivalent of **doh** or **do** in the tonic sol-fa

laager *n* a defensive encampment (of wagons in a circle): a group of people who band together to defend their shared viewpoint *vb* to form a laager

laater *var fm dial n* **laughter**

lab *now dial n* a blabbermouth or tell-tale *obs vb* to blab

labbe *obs fm now dial n* **lab**

labeler *US fm n* **labeller**, one who labels

labiate *adj* lipped, used for both flowers and bodily orifices: of those plants with such a feature *n* such a plant

labile *adj* unstable

labret *n* an ornament for the lip

labrose *adj* having (large) lips

labrum *n* a lip: a liplike structure (*pl* **labra, labrums**)

Labrus *n* the genus of wrasse

lac *n* an East Indian insect found in uncountable numbers and which exudes a substance which is refined to produce a commercial resin: that resin: the resinous sap of certain trees which is treated in similar fashion: a scarlet dye derived from the resin (also called **lac dye**): the number 100,000: 100,000 rupees: an uncountable number, hence lac as the name of the insect *obs vb* to coat with a varnish of lac (i.e. lacquer a surface) (note: In the senses of number, **lakh** is a *var fm*. In the senses of resin, **laque** and **lacque** are *obs fms*)

laceman *n* a man who manufactures or deals in lace (*fem* **lacewoman**)

lacerant *nonce adj* of a sound, harrowing

lacert *obs n* a lizard: a muscle

lacertian *adj* of or pertaining to lizards *n* a lizard

lacertid *n* any of a family of around 180 species of lizards distinguished by the presence of bony plates on the surface of the skull. The European species *incl* the sand lizard, the green lizard, the common wall lizard and the viviparous lizard. Closely related to the skinks, they lack the very smooth scaling of these relatives.

lacertine *adj* lacertian; of an ornament, consisting of intertwined lacertian figures

lacet *n* a type of braidwork

lache *dial n* a wet ditch, a bog *obs S & dial vb* to loiter: to neglect

laches *n* negligence (in the performance of any legal duty) (*pl* **laches**) *obs adj* lewd, wanton: careless *obs vb* lachesse, to neglect

Lachesis *n* a genus of snakes *incl* the bushmaster *fem pers n* see **Fates, the**

lachter *var fm dial n* **laughter**

lacier *comp adj* lacy

lacken *obs vb* to disparage

lacket *obs n* a lackey

lackey *n* a liveried male servant *esp* one who gives close personal service: a servile follower: one treated as a servant *vb* to act as a lackey (to)

lacmus *n* litmus, a chemical substance turned red by an acid or blue by an alkali

laconical *adj* laconic (TRIVIA note: The dictionary used for the UK Scrabble championship accepts this word as extant. Other authorities consider that, as the last recorded usage of the word was 1698, it is *obs*. The anagrams of laconical (**cloacalin** and **cloacinal**) are both considered to be nonce words, but are also listed as extant standard English in the above dictionary.)

lactase *n* an enzyme of the digestive juices

lacteous *adj* of the nature of, of the colour of, resembling milk: milky

lactose *n* sugar of milk, a saccharine substance in milk

lacuna *n* a space or gap *esp* in a manuscript: an inscription in a manuscript (*pl* **lacunae, lacunas**)

lacunal *adj* of or pertaining to a lacuna

lad (*n*) *obs n* a thong

ladde *obs fm n* **lad**

ladded *obs adj* thonged

ladden *obs pa pple vb* lade

laddery *adj* like a ladder

laddess *nonce n* a girl

lade *n* a mill race: an extension to the width of a cart *vb* to load: to draw water

laden *vb* to load

lader *arch n* one who freights a vessel

Ladin *n* any Rhaeto-Romantic dialect *esp*

that spoken in the Engadine region of Switzerland

Ladinity an undefined noun which appears to be exclusive to one particular dictionary where it is included as a derivative of Ladin. (The suffix '-ity' attached to a noun denotes the state or condition of being.) No plural has been presumed and its anagram is **daintily**.

ladise *obs pl* lady

ladne *obs S fm vb* **laden**

ladren *obs fm S n* **ladrone**

ladrone *S n* a rogue

lady (*n*) *vb* to behave in a ladylike manner *obs vb* to raise to the rank of lady: to make feminine

ladyfy *vb* to make a lady of

ladyism *n* affecting the airs and style of a lady

laesie *obs fm adj* **lazy**

lafter *var fm dial n* **laughter**

lagan *n* a legal term for goods or wreckage on the seabed: such goods marked with a buoy for intended recovery

lagena *n* a bottle with a narrow neck

lagend *arch fm n* **lagen**

lager (*n*) *US var fm n/vb* **laager** *nonce vb* to drink lager

lagger *n* a loiterer: an (ex-)convict *obs vb* to loiter

laggin *S & dial n* the rim beneath the base of a barrel

lagniappe *n* a gratuity or similar gift beyond that strictly essential

lagoon *n* a lake-like stretch of salt or brackish water separated from the sea either by low sandbanks or else contained within an atoll

Lagting *n* the upper chamber of Norway's parliament

laguna *arch n* the Italian *fm* of lagoon used, in English, *esp* for one in the neighbourhood of Venice (*pl* **lagune**)

lagune *var fm n* **lagoon** *pl* laguna

lahar *n* a volcanic or other mud flow

laid (*adj*) *S fm n* **load** (also, but only in *S dial*, extended to the *vb* **load**)

laide *S & dial fm n* **load**

laimeter *var fm S & dial n* **lameter**

lain (*pa pple*) *now S vb* to conceal *obs n* concealment: a stratum

laine *n* a local name for a tract of arable land in the area of the Sussex downs

lainer *n* a lace, lash, strap or thong

laip *obs S fm vb* **lap**, of animals, to sup liquid

lairage *n* the placing of cattle in a lair, a shed or enclosure where they can lie down

laird *S n* the owner of a (large) landed estate *obs S n* a lord

lairdie *n* a petty laird

laire *now dial n* mud, clay or mire

lairge *obs S fm adj/adv/n* large

lairwite *n* a fine paid in mediaeval times for fornication or adultery *esp* with a bondwoman

lairy *dial adj* wet, miry, swampy

laise *obs S fm vb* **lace**, to fasten or tighten with a lace

laisse *n* a string of verses to the same rhyme

lait *now dial vb* to seek, to search for *obs vb* to flash *var fm obs n* **laiting**

laitance *n* a milk-like surface deposit on fresh concrete

laite *obs fm now dial vb* **lait**

laiter *var fm dial n* **laughter**

laith *var fm now dial vb* **lathe** *S & dial fm adj* **loath** or **loth** *obs S & dial fm vb* **loathe**

laithe *var fm now dial vb* **lathe**, to invite *obs S & dial fm adj* **loath** or **loth** *obs S & dial fm vb* **loathe**

laiting *obs n* lightning

laker *n* a general term for a person or thing having an association with a lake, such as a lake-dwelling fish, a boat on a lake, a visitor to the Lake District

lakh *var fm n* **lac** in the senses of 100,000 (rupees), an uncountable number

laky *adj* of or pertaining to a lake: of the colour of blood (*comp* **lakier** *sup* **lakiest**)

laldie *S n* a beating

lam *n* the twenty-third letter of the Arabic alphabet: a type of fishing net *vb* to thrash (now *slg* except in the *dial* sense of thrashing water to chase eels into a net)

Lamaism *n* the form of Buddhism practised in Tibet and Mongolia

lamaistic *adj* of or pertaining to one who follows the teachings and beliefs of a lama

lambaste *var fm vb* **lambast**, to thrash

lamber *n* a ewe in lamb: one who tends such a ewe *now dial n* amber

lambie *S n* a term of endearment for a child or a lamb

lamed *n* the twelfth letter of the Hebrew alphabet

lamen *var fm n* **lamin**

lamer *var fm now dial n* **lamber** *comp adj* lame

lameter *S & dial n* a cripple

lamia *n* a female demon of Greek and Roman mythology who drinks blood (*pl* **lamiae, lamias**)

lamiger *dial n* a cripple

lamin *n* a lucky charm made of metal

lamina *n* a thin plate or layer (*pl* **laminas, laminae**)

laminae *pl* **lamina**

laminar *adj* consisting of or arranged in (thin) layers

laminarise *var fm vb* **laminarize**, to give to a surface that which will produce a streamline flow over it

lamine *obs fm n* **lamin**, a thin plate or layer (of metal): a thin metal charm of an astrological design

laminose *adj* having the form of or consisting of laminae

lamister *var fm US n* **lamster**

lamiter *var fm S & dial n* **lameter**

lammar *var fm dial n* **lamber**

lammiger *var fm dial n* **lamiger**

lamp (*n*) *vb* to provide with lamps: to shine (*lit/fig*) *S vb* to walk with long, fast strides

lampago *her n* the mantiger or manticore (note: The *pl* is unrecorded but, if it mirrors lumbago (**lumbagos**), it has the anagram, **sago palm**, in that *fm*)

lampas *n* an upholstery material of silk and wool

lampe *obs fm n/vb* **lamp**

lamper *US collq n* a woman who held a contract to trim lamps *dial vb* to walk with big strides

lampist *n* one involved in the manufacture of lamps

lamprey *n* any of various species of freshwater and marine, primitive, jawless fishes. Apart from a few North American freshwater species, all in their adult stage use their round suckling mouths as an attachment for a parasitic life on the bodies of other fishes. Those which fail to do this as adults merely breed and die. Eel-like in appearance, a parasitic species rasps a hole in the side of a host fish and sucks out the blood and body fluids. Satiated, the lamprey swims away, leaving the host apparently little harmed except for a wound which continues to bleed due to a chemical in the lamprey's saliva which prevents clotting. The lamprey begins life as a blind wormlike larva known as a **pride** or an **ammocoete**, hatching from an egg to spend several years of a burrowing life filter-feeding. The pride is so unlike the form it will assume after metamorphosis into an adult that it was once classifed as a totally different creature complete with scientific nomenclature. Apart from the Maoris of New Zealand, few now eat the lamprey though it was once considered a great delicacy – King Henry I of England having died from '*a surfeit of lampreys*'.

lampricide *n* a chemical substance used to kill lampreys *esp* in the Great Lakes of North America where they are a considerable pest to more conventional fishes (see **lamprey**)

lamster *US n* a fugitive

lanare *obs fm n* **lanner**

lanaret *obs fm n* **lanneret** (see **lanner**)

lanate *adj* having a woollen surface or covering

lanceolar *adj* resembling the shape of the head of a spear

lancer *n* a (cavalry) soldier armed with a lance *pl* a type of quadrille and the music for this dance

lancet *n* a surgical cutting instrument

lanchet *var fm dial n* **landshard**

lancier *obs fm n* **lancer**

lanciers (GAME PLAYER'S note: The dictionary used for the North American Scrabble championship has the following definition, '*n* a French dance'. The type of quadrille known as **The Lancers** may have some relationship to this dance. The word **lancer** first appeared in its modern *fm* in the 17th century running alongside the *fm* **lancier**, which was used from the 16th to the 18th centuries. The dance, however, has always been known to the British since its introduction in 1836 as **The Lancers**; hence, *US n* a French dance.)

lancinate *vb* to pierce or tear

lande *n* French moorland or wild land

lander *n* one who goes ashore: a worker in a slate quarry concerned with the unloading of slate from the site wagon

landrace *n* a Danish breed of large white pig

landshard *dial n* a strip of unploughed land

lane (*n*) *S fm n/vb* **loan** *obs dial vb* to mark the route of an intended road

laner *obs fm n* **lanner**

lanere *obs fm n* **lanner**

laneret *var fm n* **lanneret** (see **lanner**)

lang *dial fm adj/vb* **long**

lange *obs fm vb* **launch**

langer *obs S & dial adv* long since, before long

langet *dial n* a shackle for an animal: a long narrow strip of (wooded) land *var fm dial n* **landshard** *obs fm n* **languet**

langier *var fm obs S & dial adv* **langer**

langish *S fm adj* **longish**

langit *var fm dial n* **langet**, a shackle

langite *n* a crystalline mineral

langle *now dial n* a rope or thong used as a hobble to prevent an animal straying *now dial vb* to fasten with a langle

langlit *var fm dial n* **langet**, a shackle

langot *dial n* a shoelace *var fm dial n* **langet**, a strip of land

LANGUAGE OF FLOWERS See page 417

langue *n* language as an abstract concept as opposed to everyday speech *obs n* a language

languet *n* a narrow, projecting piece of land: a tongue-shaped part of an implement *obs n* a tongue-shaped ornament

langur *n* any of a family of three genera and two sub-genera of Asian leaf-eating monkeys. The main genus, *Presbytis*, has 20 known species ranging in size from the maroon langur of Borneo (12 lbs adult male weight) to the hanuman, entellus or sacred monkey of India (30 lbs adult male weight). The second genus, *Nasalis*, comprises the pig-tailed monkey and the proboscis monkey, both of which have large noses. The third genus, *Pygathrix*, has two sub-genera, one of which is also called *Pygathrix* whilst the other is called *Rhinopithecus*. The sub-genus, *Pygathrix*, comprises the douc of Indo-China together with two sub-species, neither of which has a common name. The sub-genus, *Rhinopithecus*, comprises various rare, snub-nosed monkeys which live in the wild parts of north Vietnam, China and Tibet.

lanier *obs fm n* **lanner**

lank (*adj*) *n* a lanky person *obs vb* to make or become lank

lanker *comp adj* lank, long and slender

lanket *Manx vb* to hobble a beast *var fm dial n* **langet**, a shackle for an animal

lanner *n* a species of falcon found in Mediterranean countries (male, **laneret** or **lanneret**)

lanneret *n* the male of the lanner

lanret *obs fm n* **lanneret** (see **lanner**)

lanshet *var fm dial n* **landshard**

Lansing *n* the capital of the state of Michigan, USA

lant *n* urine: stale urine used for industrial purposes: a fish, the launce or sandeel *obs vb* to mix urine with another substance, *esp* beer to add strength

lanter *dial n* the card game of lanterloo *Obs fm n* **lantern** *dial vb* to gamble: to be late

lantren *var fm dial vb* **lanter**, to be late *obs fm n* **lantern**

lape *obs fm vb* **leap**

laper *dial n* a limestone bed of a freshwater stream

lapidarist *n* an expert in the nature and kinds of precious stones (GAME PLAYER'S note: Whilst other experts consider the word *obs*, having a last recorded literary usage in 1620, the dictionary currently used for the UK Scrabble championship considers the word extant.)

lapidate *vb* to throw stones at: to stone to death

lapides *pl* lapis

lapis *n* a stone (*pl* **lapides**)

lapise *obs vb* of hounds, to cry or bay when in pursuit of game

lapper *n* one who takes up liquid with the tongue: one who folds linen: one who uses a stone grinding wheel

lappet *n* a flap or fold in a garment: a flap or appendage of any kind *vb* to cover (as) with a lappet

Lappish *adj* of or pertaining to the Lapps or Laplanders *n* the language of the Lapps (technically, a minor language of the Finnic branch of the Finno-Ugric group of the Uralic family of languages)

lapser *n* one who lapses or falls away from

lapstone *n* a stone on a shoemaker's lap for beating leather upon

lapwing *n* any of a genus of plovers *esp* the

green plover, a common European bird also known by various other names, most notably **peewit**, after its cry. Some of the other names *incl* **pewit** (*var fm*): **peewee, peaseweep, pees-weep** (*S fms*): **wype** (*now dial*): **pywipe** (*dial*)

laque *obs fm n* **lac** (in the senses indicated, see **lac**)

larbets *dial n pl* the testicles of a lamb

larboard *n/adj* the port or left side of a ship (*obs* only in practical naval usage, still extant as a curiosity)

larche *obs fm n* **larch**

larchen *adj* consisting of larch

lardalite *n* one of the coarse-grained basaltic rocks

larde *obs fm S n* **laird**

lardet *obs n* a lardon

lardine *n* a cooking fat of lard and seed oil

lardon *n* a piece of bacon used for larding meat

lardy *adj* containing or full of lard: resembling lard: fat (*comp* **lardier** *sup* **lardiest**)

laree *obs fm n* **larin**

larew *obs n* a teacher

large (*adj/n*) *vb* of the wind, to become stronger (a naval term)

largen *poet vb* to grow large or larger: enlarge

largition *n* the imparting of a gift

lariat *n* a lasso

Laridae *n* the gull family of birds (see **laridine**)

laridine *adj* of any gull, noddy, skimmer, skua or tern classified as belonging to the family *Laridae* (see **ANIMAL ADJECTIVES**)

larin *n* a former Persian and Arabic unit of currency in the form of a falcate strip of metal

larine *adj* of certain seagulls classified as belonging to a particular sub-family, the distinguishing factor being that the upper and lower mandibles are of equal length and encased in a single sheath *n* a gull of this sub-family, the *Larinae*

larke *obs fm n* **lark**

larky *collq adj* playful (*comp* **larkier** *sup* **larkiest**)

larm *obs n/vb* (to) alarm

larme *var fm obs n* **larm**, a call to arms

larmier *n* a projecting moulding on a building designed to throw off rain (also called a drip or corona)

larry *var fm n/now dial n/obs n* **lurry** *dial n* confusion, excitement: a dense mass of white fog: a long-handled tool used for making mortar: grout *dial vb* to grout

larva *n* an animal or insect in an immature state markedly different to that which it will eventually assume as an adult. Normally this state includes the inability to reproduce but, for an exception, see **axolotl**: a ghost (*pl* **larvae, larvas**)

larval *adj* of larva

larvicide *n* a substance which kills larvae

lasagne *var fm n* **lasagna**, a form of pasta consisting of wide, flat pieces: a dish of this with such as cheese or meat (*pl* **lasagnes**)

lascar *n* an oriental (*esp* East Indian) sailor: an inferior class of artilleryman

lase *obs fm vb* **lace**

laser *n* a resin known since at least ancient Roman times and obtained from the plant, laserwort: a device which converts light of mixed frequencies into an intensely narrow beam of light of a single frequency

LANGUAGE OF FLOWERS There are two distinctly different messages contained in a floral gift. The first message, according to modern analysts, is as individual as handwriting and can be interpreted as such. The second message is the traditional meaning so beloved of the Victorians.

1 MODERN ANALYSIS Assuming that the giver has made an individual selection to the extent whereby even the wrapping is of his own choice and the delivery is under his direct control, the character is as follows:–
(*a*) APPEARANCE The flowers suggest the giver. Hence, droopy, formal, half dead, miserable, perky, thrusting or upright flowers are the choices of a giver who could be so described. A single offering and the giver is likely to think his gift is unique, a huge bouquet of mixed flowers may suggest mixed emotions. (*b*) COLOUR **red** Passion. **yellow** Youthful, exciting. **white** Idealistic. **blue** Cold. **flecked** Not as perfect as he supposes himself to be. **dyed** False. (*c*) VARIETIES **roses** Love. **carnations** Strong, affectionate feelings. **spring-like flowers** Helpful. (*d*) PLANTS The more they need looking after so the more he needs looking after. (*e*) WRAPPING **unwrapped** Nothing to hide. **see-through cellophane** Either transparent or an exhibitionist. **totally obscured in paper** Somewhat secretive. **with ribbon** A bit of a baby. (*f*) SELF-DELIVERY Suggests that no barriers exist between you.

2 THE TRADITIONAL MEANINGS Each individual flower represents a message such that a complete romance can be told in just three deliveries – **white lilac** Love is dawning, **white phlox** I love you, **white poppy** My affections are dead. A selection of the traditional meanings follows:–
acanthus Undying devotion: **anemone** A parting: **angelica** Inspiration and joy: **aster** Are you deceiving me?: **azalea** Vain regrets, passing fancy: **begonia** Inconstancy in affection: **belladonna** Bad luck: **blackthorn** Love isn't smooth: **buttercup** Spitefulness, mockery: **camellia** Undying love: **campanula** Pride mars your charm: **carnation** (*a*) **pink** You are welcome (*b*) **purple** No feeling for you (*c*) **red** Worldliness will separate (*d*) **white** Your purity inspires (*e*) **double** Let me think: **clover** Any hope for me?: **columbine** Passionate love: **convolvulus** I suspect you flirt: **cornflower** I love your innocence: **daffodil** I mistrust your love: **dahlia** Your promises mean nothing: **dandelion** Jealousy tortures me: **elderflower** Is there hope of further favours?: **fern** Trust and devotion: **forget-me-not** A reminder of love: **fuchsia** Not wanted: **gardenia** I have a secret passion for you: **geranium** (*a*) **pink** You act foolishly (*b*) **red** I have no use for you: **gorse** Thoughts of you: **holly** Be cautious: **hollyhock** In admiration of your beauty: **honeysuckle** Always together: **hyacinth** (*a*) **blue** I suspect deceit (*b*) **white** I wish you well: **hydrangea** You are too cool for me: **jasmine** (*a*) **red** Love leads us astray (*b*) **white** The sweetness of love (*c*) **yellow** Passionately in love: **jonquil** Love drives me mad: **laburnum** I despair of your coldness: **larkspur** my feelings are obvious: **laurel** Love triumphant: **lavender** Steadfast devotion: **lilac** (*a*) **mauve** Do you still have the same feelings? (*b*) **white** Love is dawning: **lily of the valley** Hope of reconciliation: **lobelia** Loving thoughts: **lupin** I need consolation: **marguerite** Is there hope?: **marigold** All is not well: **marjoram** Comfort and sympathy: **mignonette** Modesty, quiet affection: **mint** Passion consumes me: **mistletoe** Nothing shall separate us: **myrtle** I, too, care for you: **narcissus** Selfishness will part us: **nasturtium** You inspire me: **olive branch** Reconciliation: **pansy** Frequent thoughts of you: **parma violet** Will you accept me? **peony** Please forgive: **periwinkle** Happy past memories: **petunia** I am angry (or) Why are you angry?: **phlox** (*a*) **blue** You enchant me (*b*) **white** I love you: **pimpernel** Victory: **poppy** (*a*) **black** Neglect and forgetfulness (*b*) **red** Rest and tranquillity (*c*) **white** My affections are dead: **primula** Joy of youth: **privet** I am wary: **rose** Your beauty enchants (Also see **tea rose, wild rose**): **rosemary** You alone I love: **sage** My deepest respect: **saxifrage** Your indifference wounds: **snowdrop** Promise of happy future: **sunflower** Thoughts only of you: **sweet william** You are perfect: **syringa** Safeguard our friendship: **tea rose** Our love breeds good: **tiger lily** Richness and abundance: **tulip** Your beauty dazzles: **violet** Modest charm: **wild rose** Constancy

lasie *obs fm adj* **lazy**

lask *n* animal diarrhoea: a piece of mackerel used as fishing bait *vb* to sail across the wind

lasket *n* a nautical term for a loop of rope

lasque *n* an inferior diamond

lasset *n* the ermine or stoat in its winter coat

lassoer *n* one who uses a lasso

lastage *n* a levy of various sorts such as that for unloading a (fishing) vessel *obs n* ballast *obs vb* to add ballast

laste *obs fm n* **last**, a shoemaker's or cobbler's model of a foot

laster *n* one who or that which lasts: a boot or shoemaker who fixes the parts of a shoe on a last

late (*adj/adv*) *obs fm n/vb* **let**

lateen *adj* of a type of sail commonly used on the Mediterranean, being triangular in shape it is suspended from a long yard and set obliquely to the mast *n* a boat with such a sail

laten *vb* to become, grow or make late

latence *n* the quality of being latent

later (*comp adj*) *var fm dial n* **laughter**

Lateran *adj* pertaining to the papal cathedral St John Lateran in Rome (*−cap*) *S fm ns* **latrine, lectern**

laterite *n* a red porous clay of tropical regions

latex *n* a whitish, milky fluid produced by many plants, such as that of the rubber tree which is the basis of rubber (*pl* **latices, latexes**)

lathe (*n*) *n* one of five divisions of Kent *now dial n* a barn *now dial vb* to invite

lathen *adj* made from a thin strip or strips of wood

lathi *n* a heavy stick

Latian *adj* of Latium, ancient Rome

latices *pl* latex

laticlave *n* the distinguishing mark of two broad purple bands worn on the edge of the tunic of a senator or other person of high rank in ancient Rome

latigo *US n* a strap used for fastening a saddle (*pl* **latigos, latigoes**)

latimer *obs n* an interpreter

Latinate *adj* imitating Latin style

Latiner *collq n* a Latinist

latish *adj* somewhat late

latria *n* veneration accorded to God

latron *n* a robber *obs S fm n* **latrine**

latten *arch n* any brass-like alloy beaten into thin sheets *dial n* any thin sheet of metal

latter (*adj*) *var fm dial n* **laughter**

latterness *obs n* the condition of being subsequent

laudation *n* the action or an instance of praising

laudatory *adj* eulogistic *obs n* a eulogy

lauder *n* one who praises

laughter (*n*) *dial n* the total number of eggs laid by a hen as a clutch for brooding

launce *n* the sandeel

laund *arch n* a glade

launde *obs fm n* **lawn**, a type of fine linen

laundre *obs fm n/vb* **launder**

launt *obs fm arch n* **laund**

laura *var fm n* **lavra**

Laurasia *n* the northern of two ancient land-masses held to have split and drifted to form North America, Greenland, Europe and N Asia (also see **Gondwanaland**)

Laurasian *adj* of Laurasia

laure *obs n* the laurel or bay tree: a chaplet woven from its leaves

laurel (*n*) *n* a salmon which remains in fresh-water when others return to the sea *vb* to crown or wreathe with laurel leaves

laveer *vb* of a ship, to beat to windward: to tack

laver *n* any edible species of marine algae: the baptismal font: spiritual cleansing (*fig*) *now poet n* a wash basin *her n* a ploughshare *obs vb* to bathe *obs fm vb* **lather**

lavies *pl* lavy, the guillemot

lavisher (*comp adj*) *n* one who lavishes

lavra *n* a collection of individual cells each housing a recluse monk

law (*n*) *vb* to bring or contest a lawsuit: to impose as law: historically, to mutilate the forefeet of a dog to prevent mischievous behaviour

lawer *obs S fm n* **layer**, a stratum *Obs fm obs n* **laure**

lawing *n* in an historical context, the act of cutting off parts of the forefeet of a dog (see **law**) *arch n* litigation *S n* an innkeeper's bill

lawland *S fm n/adj* **lowland**

lawmonger *n* a paltry, cavilling lawyer

lawn (*n*) *vb* to create a lawn

lawnde *var fm arch n* **laund**

lawter *var fm dial n* **laughter**

laxism *n* a convenient view for one who enjoys a sinful life that an opinion, only slightly probable, may be safely followed in moral practice

layter *var fm dial n* **laughter**

laytime *n* the total time allotted for the loading and unloading of cargo

le *var fm n* **li** *obs fm n* **lye**

leach *arch n* a dish of sliced meat, eggs, fruits and spices in aspic *now dial n* a perforated trough used for the production of lye by pouring water over wood ashes *vb* to subject to the filtering action of a liquid *arch vb* to slice

leaden (*adj*) *vb* to make leaden or dull

leadline *n* a weighted line used for measuring depth

leadsman *n* a sailor who uses the lead plum-met for sounding depths

leager *arch fm n* **leaguer**, a cask

leagre *obs fm n* **leaguer**, a cask

leaguer *n* a member of a league: a cask for such as wine or oil: a military camp (of a besieging force): a siege *vb* to besiege

leaker *n* that which leaks

lealty *arch n* loyalty, faithfulness

leam *now S & dial n* a flame: (a gleam of) light: brightness *dial n* a fenland watercourse: a nutshell *now S & dial vb* to gleam *dial vb* to shell a nut

leamer *var fm arch n* **limer**, a bloodhound *dial n* a ripe nut *obs n* that which radiates light

leamon *obs fm n* **lemon**

Leander *masc pers n* meaning 'lion-man'

leaner *n* one who leans or reclines *comp adj* lean

lear *n* the colour of sheep or other grazing animals due to the nature of the soil *arch n* (religious) instruction, learning *arch vb* to teach (**leare, leir, lere** *var fms arch n/vb*) *obs n* a thickened sauce: binding tape for fabric (*var fms incl* **leer, leere, lyer, lyre, lyere**)

leare *var fm arch n/vb* **lear**

lea-rig *n* a fallow field

learing *obs n* the act of binding fabric with tape

learne *obs fm vb* **learn**

leary *var fm adj* **leery**, suspicious (*comp* **learier** *sup* **leariest**) (note: The *obs adj* **leary**, the meaning of which is obscure but was used for good quality short hay, had the *sup* **learyest**)

learyest *sup obs adj* leary

lease (*n/vb*) *now dial n* pasture *now dial vb* of grain, to handpick foreign matter (liable to be seeds of weeds) from that which is due for sowing

leasing (*n*) *arch n* lying, falsehood *now dial n* gleaning *adj* lying, gleaning

leasinge *Obs fm arch n* **leasing**

leasow *now dial n/vb* (to) pasture

least (*adj/adv*) *obs n* a minimum

leasting *obs n* the atom

least tern *n* the most common and widely distributed of the species of little terns. During the breeding season it develops a black cap.

leate *var fm obs n* **laiting**

leath *now dial vb* to soften, to relax

leaver (*n*) *obs fm n/vb* **lever**

leavings *n pl* that which remains (as refuse)

leavy *adj* consisting of (natural or artificial) leaves *var fm* (*now mainly poet*) *adj* **leafy** (*comp* **leavier** *sup* **leaviest**)

leazing *S & dial fm arch n* **leasing**, falsehood

Lebensraum *Ger n* living space, used in English with reference to Hitler's territorial expansionist policies prior to the commencement of the Second World War

lecanora *n* any of a genus of lichens which includes the edible manna lichen

lecker *obs fm n* **liquor**

lection *n* a reading of a text of a particular edition: a portion of a sacred text appointed to be read in church

lector *n* a university lecturer: one who reads the lesson at certain Catholic services: one, in a convent or monastery, appointed to read aloud during a meal

lectorship *n* the post of lector

ledare *obs fm n* **leader**

ledder *obs fm n/vb* **leather** *obs S fm n/vb* **ladder**

leddre *Obs fm n* **ladder**

leear *S n* a liar

leede *obs fm vb* **lead**, to guide *obs fm vb* **lead**, to work with lead, the metal

leeder *Obs fm ns* **leader, leather**

leef *var fm obs vb* **leve**, to allow, grant or permit

leeke *obs fm vbs* **leak, like**

leen *S fm obs vb* **lin** *obs fm vb* **lean**

leeper *obs fm n* **leper**

leepre *obs fm n* **leper**

leer (*n/vb*) *now dial adj* unburdened *dial adj* hungry *obs adj* indirect, sly

leere *obs fm arch vb* **lear**

Leerie *S pers n* a nickname for a lamplighter

leerne *Obs fm vb* **learn**

leery *now dial adj* empty *slg adj* shrewd, suspicious, sly (*comp* **leerier** *sup* **leeriest**)

leese *obs vb* to destroy: to loosen: to set free

leesing *obs n* loss *Obs n* redemption

leet *n* a former court of record which the lords of certain manors were entitled to hold for jurisdiction over petty offences and civil affairs: the district so covered – ranging from a manor to the old division of a county called a hundred *S n* a list of persons eligible for an office *S vb* to nominate (for such a list)

leetor *obs n* a member of a leet or local manorial court

leeve *obs fm n/vb* **leave** (in the conventional senses i.e. excluding meanings based on leaf)

lefties *pl* leftie or lefty, anyone whose political leaning is to the left *esp* towards the extremist element

legalist *n* a stickler for legality: one who believes in a doctrine of justification by works

legantine *var fm* (*erron*) *adj* **legatine**

legate *n* a Papal ambassador: the governor of a province of a former Papal state: the governor of a province in the historic Roman empire *obs n* a legacy *vb* to bequeath

legatine *adj* of, pertaining to or having the authority of a legate

legato *n* a smooth and flowing musical style (*pl* **legatos**)

legator *n* one who makes a bequest by will

legendist *n* one who writes legends

legger *n* one who propels a canal barge through a tunnel by pushing against the sides with his legs

leggins *var fm n pl* **leggings**

legioned *poet adj* arranged in legions

legist *n* one skilled or versed in law

legit *slg adj* legitimate *slg n* legitimate drama *obs n* claim to Benefit of Clergy based upon the ability to read a verse of the Bible

leglan *var fm S n* **leglen**

leglen *S n* a milking pail

leglen girth *S n* the lowest hoop of a milking pail ('*Cast a leglen girth*', have an illegitimate child)

leglin *var fm S n* **leglen**

legman *n* a newspaper reporter

leg man *collq n* one for whom a woman's legs are her most sexually attractive feature

leighster *Obs n* a female liar

leighter *obs fm n* **lighter**, a flat-bottomed barge

leimon *obs fm n* **lemon**

leinten *Obs fm adj* **lenten**

Leipoa *n* a megapode genus containing the single species of the mallee fowl (– *cap*) *n* the mallee fowl

leir *var fm arch n/vb* **lear**

leiring *var fm obs n* **learing**

leister *n* a salmon spear *vb* to fish with a leister

leith *var fm arch n* **lith**, a limb

lek *n* an Albanian unit of currency, the metric division of which is the qintar: a display area used by the males of an individual species of bird such as the black grouse in Britain or the kakapo in New Zealand. All the males in the area congregate at one location where they advertise their suitability for mating, leaving an individual female to make her choice from amongst them. *vb* of birds, to congregate (+ *cap*) *n* the northern branch of the Rhine delta in central Holland

leman *obs fm n* **lemon**

leme *var fm now S & dial n* **leam** *obs fm dial vb* **leam**

Lemnian *adj* of or pertaining to Lemnos

lemniscate *n* a plane which is mathematically produced in the shape of a figure 8

Lemnos *n* a Greek island 40 miles S.W. of the Dardanelles

lemond *obs fm n* **lemon**

lemon tea *n* Russian tea, tea with lemon instead of milk

lempira *n* the monetary unit of Honduras (*pl* **lempiras**)

lemur *n* one of a family of small, fox-faced relatives of the monkeys found only on Madagascar and nearby islands. The majority of species grow to the size of a domestic cat but some only attain the size of a mouse, weighing a mere two ounces when fully adult. (*pl* **lemurs**): the ghost of an ancient Roman (*pl* **lemures**)

lemures see **lemur**

lemurian *adj* of, pertaining to, connected with or characteristic of lemurs (GAME PLAYER'S note: The dictionary used for the UK Scrabble championship lists the word as an undefined *n* and *adj*. Unfortunately it seems to have exclusive knowledge of the noun, but if one presumes a *pl* as **lemurians**, this gives a choice of two anagrams.)

lemurine *adj* of the lemurs *n* any species of the lemurs

lende *obs fm vb* **lend**

lene *obs n* a phonetic term for a (voiceless) stopped consonant *obs adj* of such a consonant (i.e. of B, D, G, K, P and T) *obs fm n/adj/vb* **lean** *obs fm now S vb* **lain**, to conceal

leng *obs vb* to lengthen, prolong, linger, tarry, dwell

lenger *obs fm comp* **longer**

lengest *obs fm adj/adv* **longest**

lenient (*adj*) *obs n* a soothing medicament: anything which soothes

lenify *vb* to mitigate: to soften

lenity *n* mildness: clemency

lennet *obs fm n* **linnet**

lense *obs vb* to make or become lean

lentamente *adv* of music, in slow time

Lented *obs adj* showing signs of having fasted over the period of Lent i.e. gaunt

Lenten, lenten *adj* of or pertaining to Lent: as is appropriate to Lent (note: As a rough guide it tends to be +*cap* for the period of Lent and −*cap* for the quality of Lent (meatless, mournful etc) though either *fm* can be used. See examples below.)

lenten chaps *obs n* a term of contempt for one who is thin-faced

Lenten corn *n* corn sown at Lent

lenten fig *dial n* a raisin *obs n* a dried fig

Lenten grain *n* Lenten corn

lenten kail *S n* a meatless broth

lenten pie *n* a meatless pie

Lenten tide *n* the period of Lent

lentic *adj* of that associated with or inhabiting ponds, swamps etc

lenticel *n* a loose mass of cells concerned with a plant's breathing and part of its corky layer

lenticle *n* a geologist's term for a lens-shaped body

lentil *n* a plant of the pea and bean family having pale blue flowers and broad pods: an edible seed of such *var fm n* **lintel**

lentisc *arch fm n* **lentisk**

lentisk *n* the mastic tree

lentor *n* sluggishness: clamminess

lentran *obs fm adj* **lenten**

Leonid *n* any meteor of a swarm which appears to originate in the constellation Leo: the first name of L I Brezhnev (1906–82), First Secretary of the Soviet Communist Party

lep *dial vb* to ladle

Lepcha *n* a Tibeto-Burman language of Sikkim, an Indian state on the southern slopes of the Himalayas

lepe *now S fm n* **leap**, a (fish) basket *obs fm n/vb* **leap**, (to) jump

leper (*n*) *vb* to infect with leprosy *obs fm now S & dial vb* **lopper**

lepere *obs fm n* **leper**

lepidote *adj* scaly: scurfy

lepir *var fm obs n* **leper**, leprosy

lepra *n* leprosy: a scurfy white matter which exudes from some plants

lepre *var fm obs n* **leper**, leprosy *obs fm n* **leper**

lepress *obs n* a female leper

leprose *adj* having a scurfy appearance *obs fm adj* **leprous**

leprosed *obs adj* made leprous

leprus *Obs fm adj* **leprous**

lere *var fm arch n/vb* **lear**

lering *obs n* learning

lerk *var fm S & dial n/vb* **lirk**

lerm *obs vb* to weep

lern *obs fm vb* **learn**

lernaean *adj* pertaining to the *Lernaea*, parasites which infest the gills of cod *n* such a parasite

Lerne *n* the name of a swamp near Argos, the home of the mythical Hydra killed by Hercules (*– cap*) *obs fm vb* **learn**

lerot *n* the dormouse

lerrie *var fm n* **lurry**

lese *var fm obs vb* **leese** *obs fm arch n/vb* **leach** *obs fm now dial n/vb* **lease**

lesion *n* damage, an injury

leske *var fm now dial n* **lisk** *obs fm n/vb* **lask**

less (*adj/adv/conj/n*) *obs vb* to make or become less

lessun *Obs fm n* **lesson**

lest (*conj*) *obs fm n/adj/vb* **last** *obs fm n/adj/adv* **least**

Lester *masc pers n* derived from the surname meaning 'of Leicester'

Lestrigon *obs n* according to Homer, one of a cannibal people of pre-Roman Italy (note: Though considered *obs* by experts, nevertheless it mirrors the Latin, *Laestrygon*, and Dryden is among the 16th/17th century writers who used it. A rare current *fm* is **Lestrigonian.**)

let (*n/vb*) *S infl fms, pa t* **loot** *pa pple* **litten, looten** or **lutten** *arch vb* to prevent or hinder (*pa pple* **let** or **letted**) *arch n* hindrance or delay *arch adj* hindered

lether *obs fm n* **ladder**

letre *obs fm n* **letter**

letted *pa t arch vb* let, to hinder

lettes *obs fm n* **lettuce**

Lettish *n* Latvian, the Indo-European language of Latvia

leucin *var fm n* **leucine**, a white crystalline amino acid produced during the decomposition of proteins in the pancreas

leucoma *n* a white opaque scar on the cornea of the eye

Levanter *n* one who lives in the Levant: a ship trading there: a strong easterly wind in the

Mediterranean: a welsher or absconder *esp* in connection with a gambling debt

Levantine *adj* of or pertaining to the Levant, that part of the Middle East approximating to Israel, Lebanon and Syria which formerly constituted part of the Ottoman empire *n* one native to that region

levator *n* a muscle having the function of elevating that to which it is attached

levee *n* a reception of visitors held on rising from bed: a morning assembly held by a dignitary: a male-only afternoon assembly held by a British monarch: an embankment alongside a river to prevent flooding *esp* one in the USA: a landing place or quay *esp* in the USA *vb* to construct such an embankment *obs vb* to attend a social levee

leven *var fm arch n/obs vb* **levin**

levere *Obs fm n* **lever**

levers *now dial n* the wild yellow iris

levet *obs n* reveille, a signal given on a musical instrument to arise

levier *n* one who levies (in the various senses of the *vb* levy)

levin *arch n* lightning: a bright flame or light *obs vb* to emit flashes of light

levirate *n* the ancient Hebrew custom, required by Mosaic law, of marriage between a man and his brother's widow when there was no male issue and both brothers lived on the same family estate

levit *var fm obs n* **levet**

Levite *n* a descendant of Levi, the third son of Jacob: an inferior priest of the ancient Hebrews (*–cap*) *slg n* a clergyman

lew *now dial adj* lukewarm, tepid: sheltered *dial adj* pale, weak *now dial n* warmth, heat: shelter *obs S n* a French gold coin once circulated in Scotland (*pl* **leois**) *now dial vb* to make tepid or warm: to shelter *var fm vb* **lue**

lewdster *arch n* one addicted to lewd pleasures

lewte *var fm arch vb* **lout**, to bow or make obeisance (to) *var fm obs n* **lewty**, loyalty *obs fm n/vb* **lute**

lewter *obs fm n* **luter**

lewth *now dial n* warmth, shelter

lewtre *obs fm vb* **loiter**

ley *n* a perfectly straight line, not marked on any map, which connects features of the pre-Roman British civilizations (such as ancient burial mounds, stone circles and churches built on earlier, pagan sites) and which is presumed to have either a magical or cultural significance. Leys are first determined by reference to large-scale Ordnance Survey maps and then walked. There are two main schools of folklore. One believes them to be, in effect, trade routes of which these are the only remaining signs, some thinking them not merely straight paths (as the crow flies) but navigational aids. The other school of thought concentrates on a magical aspect and tests the theories with such aids as divining rods. The more scientific of such researchers contrast the results with a similar walk on a random line. (For divining rod see **dowse**) *var fm n/vb* **lye**

lezzar *var fm* (*dial*) *now dial n* **leasow**

li *n* a Chinese unit of distance approx $\frac{1}{3}$ of a mile: a Chinese unit of weight, 1,000 li to a liang: a Chinese coin (*pl* **li** – also see **lis**)

liana *n* any of the twisted woody climbing plants found in tropical forests

liane *var fm n* **liana**

liang *n* tael, a Chinese unit of weight of approximately $1\frac{1}{3}$ ounces avoirdupois: this weight in silver is a money of account, the value of which varies with the price of silver

liard *n* a former very small French coin worth a quarter of a sou *Canadian n* the North American tree, balsam poplar *var fm now dial adj* **lyard**, grey

liart *S fm now dial adj* **lyard**, grey

Liassic *adj* of Lias, the lowest of the rock series in the Jurassic system

lib (*collq n*) *now dial vb* to castrate

libate *vb* to pour out wine in honour of a god

libber (*collq n*) *now dial n* one who castrates

libbet *now dial n* a fragment

liber *n* bast, the inner bark of a tree categorized as an exogen (i.e. trees other than palm trees)

liberty man *n* a sailor with permission to go ashore

libra *n* the English pound as a unit of weight avoirdupois (16 ozs) or as a unit of weight troy (12 ozs) which, in silver, equated to the English monetary pound (*pl* **librae**): a former gold coin of Peru (*pl* **libras**) (+*cap*) *n* the balance, the seventh sign of the Zodiac

librae *pl* libra (where indicated)

librate *n* a unit of land measured by value at a reckoning of a £1 per unit per year *vb* to oscillate: of such as a bird, to balance itself

lic *Obs fm n* **lich**

lice *pl* louse, a parasitic insect which infests human hair and skin: extended to other parasitic creatures which infest animals, birds, fish and plant life (also see **louses**)

licensor *var fm n* **licenser**, one who grants a licence or otherwise gives permission

lich *n* a (dead) body (*arch* except in the *S & dial fm* **like**, and as a *modf n* for such as:– (*a*) **lich gate**, the roofed gateway to a churchyard where the coffin is set down to await the arrival of the minister (*b*) **lich owl**, an alternative name for the screech owl, based on the traditional belief that it utters its cry near a house where a death is due *pl* **liches, likes** (*S & dial*)) (note: **lich** and **like** mirror **ditch** and **dike** in the transition from the original old English common forms of **lic** and **dic** respectively)

lichanos *n* the string of an ancient Greek musical instrument struck by the forefinger: the note so produced

lichee *var fm n* **litchi**

liches see **lich**

licken *now dial vb* to trust to

lickster *Obs n* a lecherous female

lidder *obs fm arch/now dial adj* **lither**

lidgate *now dial n* a gate erected for the specific purpose of preventing cattle from straying

lidger *obs fm n* **ledger**

lief *adj* willing (*comp* **liefer** or **liever** *sup* **liefest** or **lievest**)

lienal *adj* of or pertaining to the spleen

lientary *n* a type of diarrhoea characterized by the food passing through only partially digested

lierne *n* a branch rib in Gothic vaulting

liester *var fm n* **leister**

liever *var fm comp* **liefer**

lieves *obs pl* life

lievest *var fm sup* **liefest**

life (n) *vb* to give life to

lifer *n* one serving a life sentence

lig *now dial fm vb* **lie**, to be in a recumbent position (*infl fms* **lig** (lie): **ligs** or **liggen** (lies): **lig'd** or **ligged** (lay): **lig'd** (lain): **ligging** (lying))

ligan *var fm n* **lagan**

ligand *n* an atom, molecule, radical or ion forming a complex with a central atom

ligate *vb* to tie up

ligation *n* the act of binding

ligature (*n*) *vb* to bind with such a bandage

liger *n* the cross between a lion and a tigress (also see **tigon** and **litigon**)

ligged see **lig**

liggen see **lig**

ligger *dial n* a simple bridge of planking: in a method of fishing for pike on the Norfolk Broads, that bundle of reeds which is bound together and acts as a float for the baited line *dial vb* to fish by this method

ligget *var fm now dial n* **lidgate**

lighte *obs fm vb* **light**, to lighten: to alight *Obs fm vb* **light**, to shine

lignage *obs fm n* **lineage**

ligne *obs fm n* **line** (in most senses)

lignee *obs n* lineage

lignin *n* an organic substance which is one of the main constituents of woody tissue

lignine *var fm n* **lignin**

lignite *n* brown coal, a sedimentary rock with a woody texture, used as a fuel

lignot *obs fm arch n* **lingot**

lignum *n* wood *Austr n* any species of the shrub, polygonum

ligroin *n* a compound of petroleum used as a solvent

ligula *n* a narrow, tongue-like strip: a cestoid worm of the genus *Ligula* (*pl* **ligulae, ligulas**)

ligule *n* a narrow strip or fillet *obs n* a spoonful

ligure *n* a precious stone of occult tradition

lii *obs fm n* **li**

liliaceous *adj* of or pertaining to a large, widely distributed family of plants (*incl* the lily, bluebell, onion, tulip and many perennial herbs and shrubs) having radially symmetrical flowers and a bulb or bulblike rootstock

lillypilly *n* an Australian tree with fine, hard-grained wood

limace *obs n* a snail: (note: The *pl*, **limaces**, is extant – see **limax**)

limacel *n* the reduced or embedded shell of a slug

limaces *pl* limax

limation *n* the action of using a rasp or file (also *fig*)

limax *n* a common slug or land-based mollusc (*pl* **limaces**)

limbate *adj* of a flower, having a border, *esp* one of a different colour

limen *n* in psychology, the threshold or limit below which a stimulus ceases to be perceived

limer *n* one who uses lime: one who snares with birdlime, a sticky substance smeared on a branch or other place where a bird might perch *arch n* a bloodhound

limete *obs fm n* **limit**

liming (*n*) *obs n* copulation

limitary *adj* of or pertaining to a limit or boundary: serving as such: of a friar, licensed to beg within defined geographical limits *n* such a friar

limites *pl* limes, a (Roman) boundary

limn *vb* to paint (a portrait): to portray or depict (a subject)

Limnaea *n* a genus of water snails *incl* the great pond snail. Water snails are usually hermaphrodites with one acting as a male and the other a female, though self-fertilization is possible. (This is not the same as sex reversal, see **XES**)

limner *arch n* a (portrait) painter: an illuminator of manuscripts

limnetic *adj* living in fresh water

limone *obs fm n* **lemon**

limonite *n* any hydrous semi-oxide of iron which contains *approx* 15% water but, originally, only bog ore (an iron ore found in marshy ground) was called limonite

limper (*comp adj*) *n* one who limps

limpkin *n* a long-legged wading bird which perches in trees, builds its nest on the ground and diets almost exclusively on water snails. Found anywhere from southern Georgia down to Argentina, it is the only species of its family and is classified among the *Gruiformes*. (See **BIRD CLASSIFICATION**)

lin *var fm n* **linn** *obs vb* of the wind, to drop: to cease (from)

linage *n* position (of figures) in line: quantity of printed matter in line: payment according to the number of lines

linchet *dial n* a ridge or strip of land left untilled: a terrace along the face of a chalk down

lindane *n* a powerful insecticide

linden *n* the lime tree, *not* the tree bearing the fruit, lime, but any of a genus of deciduous trees having fragrant yellowish flowers and cultivated both for beauty and timber

lindge *var fm now dial vb* **linge**

lineal *adj* of the nature of an ancestral line: made with lines

lineament *n* a facial feature *obs n* an outline or sketch, a diagram *obs vb* to trace in outline

linear (*adj*) *obs n* a linear equation

lineate *adj* marked with lines *vb* to mark with lines

linecut *n* a type of printing plate

linet *dial fm n* **lint** *obs fm n* **linnet**

line up *vb* to align

line-up *n* people or objects in a line

linga *var fm n* **lingam**

lingam *n* the penis, worshipped by Hindus as a god

lingan *obs fm now dial n* **lingel**, waxed thread

lingeat *var fm obs S n* **linget**

linge *now dial vb* to beat or thrash

lingel *now dial n* waxed thread such as used by a shoemaker: a thong *S vb* to use such thread *now dial vb* to use a thong

linget *obs n* an unidentified yellow bird *obs S n* the seed of flax

lingle *var fm now dial n/vb* **lingel**

lingot *arch n* an ingot: the mould in which it is founded *var fm dial n* **langot**

lingster *var fm now US n* **linguister**

lingua *n* the tongue: a tongue-like part (*pl* **linguae**)

lingual *adj* of or pertaining to the tongue or a tongue-like part: of sounds, formed by the tongue: pertaining to language(s) *n* a lingual sound

linguister *now US n* an interpreter

lingula *n* a little tongue(-like part): any species of *Lingula*, a genus of bivalve molluscs (*pl* **lingulae**)

lingular *adj* of or pertaining to a lingula

lingy *adj* abounding in or covered with heather (*comp* **lingier** *sup* **lingiest**) *dial adj* supple

liniate *obs fm vb* **lineate**

liniel *var fm now dial n* **lingel**

linke *obs fm n/vb* **link**

linkster *var fm now US n* **linguister**

linn *n* a cataract or waterfall: the pool into which such descends: a deep ravine

Linnaean *adj* of Linnaeus and *esp* his bionominal system (see **Linnaeus**)

Linnaeus, Carolus *pers n* the Swedish botanist (1707–1778) who devised the bionominal or two name system of classification though his original, artificial categories have been completely replaced by a system which is concerned with relationships. The French botanist, Antoine de Jussieu (1748–1836), presented the modern system which (see **genus**) is constantly being revised. Linnaeus was ennobled in 1761 and styled himself Carl von Linne. He was the originator of the symbols ♂ and ♀ for male and female.

linnet *n* a small European songbird: also extended to the greenfinch, the green linnet and the siskin, the pine linnet

linsang *n* either of two species of very slender and beautiful viverrine mammals related to the civets, genets and mongooses

linsey *n* a dress material of a coarse inferior wool woven upon a cotton warp

lintel *n* a horizontal block which bears the weights of the material above an opening for such as a door or window *obs fm n* **lentil**

linter *US n* a machine which strips cotton fibres from cotton seed *dial fm n/modf n* **lean-to**

lintie *S n* a linnet

lintle *obs fm n* **lintel**

lintseed *S & dial fm n* **linseed**

linty *adj* resembling, full of or soft like lint (*comp* **lintier** *sup* **lintiest**)

liny *adj* resembling a line (*comp* **linier** *sup* **liniest**)

lionel *her n* a young or small lion of which there must be at least two on a coat of arms which has such an animal (+*cap*) *pers n* meaning 'little lion'

lionet *n* a young lion

lionse *obs vb* of a lioness, to give birth

liparite *n* rhyolite, a highly acidic, variously coloured volcanic rock

lipase *n* an enzyme or protein substance concerned with acting upon fat

lipen *obs fm S vb* **lippen**

liper *obs fm n* **leper**

liplet *n* a little lip(-like appendage)

lippe *obs fm n* **lip** *Obs fm vb* **leap** *Obs fm now dial n* **lipe**, a portion

lippen *S vb* to confide: to entrust

lipper *n* a slight rippling on the surface of the sea: an implement used by glass makers to create a lip on a vessel: a large ladle used by whale fishermen to gather oil from the deck *vb* of the sea, to ripple: to gather whale oil from a deck

lippet *obs n* the lobe of the ear

lippie *S n* a little lip *var fm S n* **lippy**, an old measure of a quarter of a peck

lippre *var fm obs n* **leper**, leprosy

lipse *obs fm vb* **lisp**

liqor *obs fm n* **liquor**

liquate *vb* to make liquid

lique *n* a small swift marine vessel propelled by oars (note: Whilst the authenticity of the word is disputed it is, nevertheless, used to describe historical vessels of this type)

liquer *obs fm n* **liquor**

liquore *obs fm n* **liquor**

liring *var fm obs n* **learing**, binding with tape

lirk *S & dial n* a wrinkle *S & dial vb* to wrinkle

lirp *obs vb* to snap one's fingers

lis GAME PLAYER'S note: Whilst most authorities stipulate that **li** is its own plural, nevertheless the *Official Scrabble Player's Dictionary* specifically gives a plural of **lis**. Lis is equally valid for the UK Scrabble championship as this plural is the logical inference from *Chambers*' definition of li.

lisard *Obs fm n* **lizard**

lish *dial adj* nimble, active

lisk *now dial n* the groin

lispar *obs fm n* **lisper**

lispe *obs fm vb* **lisp**

lisper *n* one who lisps

lissen *dial n* a layer or stratum: a cleft in rock above or below such a layer: a strand of rope

lisste *Obs fm arch vb* **list**, to desire

listable *US adj* capable of being listed

liste *obs fm arch vb* **list**, to desire

listel *n* a small flat band or fillet used in architecture

lister *n* one who enlists in the armed forces *US n* one who lists items: a type of plough *var fm n/vb* **leister** *obs n* a reader (in church)

Listerian *adj* designating the antiseptic surgery as devised by Lister

Listerise *var fm vb* **Listerize**, to treat according to the practices of Baron Joseph Lister (1827–1912) who founded antiseptic surgery

listeth *3rd pers sing pres t vb* list, to please: to have pleasure in: to choose

listre *Obs fm obs n* **lister**

listred *n* a Welsh measure of corn equal to $3\frac{3}{4}$ imperial bushels

lit (*pa pple*) *now dial vb* to colour, dye or stain: to blush *now dial n* a colour

litchi *n* a Chinese tree having round edible fruit: that fruit

lite (*n/adj/adv*) *now dial vb* to delay (the *n* **liting**, delay, is now *obs*)

liter *var fm* (*now mainly US*) *n* **litre**

literal (*adj*) *n* a misprinted letter

literose *adj* affectedly literary

litharge *n* lead monoxide

lithate *n* a salt of lithic acid

lithe (*adj*) *S n* warm shelter *now dial n* a mixture of oatmeal and water used as a thickening for broth *obs vb* to thicken broth *arch vb* to listen: to hear of

lither *comp adj* lithe *arch adj* pliant, supple *now dial adj* lazy, sluggish *obs adj* evil *obs adv* ill: wickedly *obs vb* to hurl (as) from a sling *Obs vb* to act wickedly

lithic *adj* pertaining to lithia, an oxide of the lightest metallic element, lithium

litho *n* a short *fm* of **lithograph**, a print made from a surface which is made ink-receptive rather than the ink-repellent method of a raised surface (*pl* **lithos**)

lithopone *n* a mixture of barium sulphate and zinc sulphide used as an ingredient for such as rubber tyres and lino and also as a white paint

lithp (*humorous*) *var fm vb* **lisp** (*infl fms incl* **lithpth** for lisps)

lithre *var fm Obs vb* **lither**

litigon *n* a cross between a lion and a tigon

litle *obs fm adj/adv/n* **little**

litotes *n sing/pl* a figure of speech in which an assertion is made by the negation of the opposite, such as '*Attila the Hun was no mere tourist*' or '*An invitation to dine with the Borgias was not greeted with great enthusiasm*'

litster *n* a dyer

litten *pseudo-arch adj* lighted (usually in such *fms* as **dim litten, red litten** etc) *S fm pa pple* **let** *now dial n* a churchyard *obs vb* to rely on

littery *adj* of or pertaining to litter: untidy

litting *obs n* the action of dyeing or colouring

little (*adj/adv/n*) *obs vb* to diminish: to belittle: to dwindle

littoral *adj* pertaining to the shore *n* a shore and the land adjacent to it

littre *obs fm n* **litter**

littress *n* a smooth type of paper used for cards

liver (*n*) *now dial vb* to deliver

livere *Obs fm n* **liver**, the bodily organ

liverei *Obs fm n* **livery**

liverer *obs n* livery

liveware *n* all those involved with a particular computer system

livier *n* one who holds a tenement on lease for life

livre *n* an old French coin worth twenty sous and replaced by the franc: a French pound avoirdupois

livyer *n* a native or other permanent resident of Newfoundland, Canada

liza *US n* either of two species of grey mullet, the thin-lipped mullet or the golden mullet

lo (*interj*) *n* the bobization equivalent of **so, soh** or **sol** in the tonic sol-fa: a hill (*Obs* except as a syllable in English place names)

loaden *now dial vb* to load

loafbread *now dial n* bread in a loaf as opposed to bread in any other form

loaminess *n* the nature of loam

loath *var fm adj* **loth**, reluctant, unwilling: repulsive *obs n* dislike, disgust

loathy *arch adj* loathsome

lobate *adj* having lobes

lobated *var fm adj* **lobate**

lobing *n* the forming of a lobe or lobes

lobose *adj* having many lobes: having large lobes

lobstering *n* the catching of lobsters

lobule *n* a small (subdivision of a) lobe

locater *var fm* (*US*) *n* **locator**, one who locates

lochter *var fm dial n* **laughter**

locke *obs fm n/vb* **lock**

locker (*n*) *obs S vb* to curl hair

loco (*collq n/slg n/slg adj*) *US n* any of several plants, also known as **locoweed** or **crazyweed**, of the bean family which grow wild in western and southwestern USA and are poisonous to grazing animals (*pl* **locos, locoes**) *US vb* to poison (livestock) with loco

Locrian *adj* of or pertaining to the Locri, a people who claim the distinction of being the earliest of the Greeks, or of their country, Locris *n* one of the Locri

Locrinus *pers n* one of the sons of Brutus who, after his death, inherited the English part of Britain (see **Brutus**)

locule *var fm n* **loculus**

loculus *n* a small compartment, cavity or chamber in any plant, animal or human: a small recess in an ancient catacomb for an urn (*pl* **loculi**)

locusta *n* a spikelet of grass (*pl* **locustae**)

loder *obs n* the lodestone, a natural magnet

lodesman *n* a pilot

lodestar *n* the Pole Star, essentially in a *fig* sense as the star that guides

lodicula *var fm n* **lodicule**, a small scale in a glass flower (*pl* **lodiculae**)

loeri *var fm n* **lory**

logan *n* a large stone or rock which, by act of nature, is so placed that it can be rocked by quite a gentle touch

loggarand *Obs S adj* straddling

logger (*n*) *now dial adj* heavy, stupid *S & dial vb* to walk in a loose-limbed fashion

logget *n* an old (gambling) game of throwing a missile at a stake in the ground: that missile (also called a **loggerhead**)

loggin *dial n* a bundle *esp* of straw

loging *obs fm n* **lodging**

logion *n* a traditional maxim of a religious teacher *esp* any of the sayings attributed to Jesus but not recorded in any of the Gospels (*pl* **logia, logions**)

logography *n* the use of logotypes or individual printer's characters which consist of syllables or words instead of letters: a method of longhand reporting by which members of a team each write a few successive words

log slate *n* a slate upon which details for the ship's log are temporarily recorded prior to permanent entry

loined *adj* having loins of a specified nature (i.e. **slack loined, loose loined** etc)

loment *n* lomentum, a pod – such as that of the peanut – which narrows between the individual seeds (*pl* of loment, **loments**: of lomentum, **lomenta** or **lomentums**) *obs n* bean meal, used as a cosmetic

lomenta *pl* lomentum (see **loment**)

lomentum see **loment**

longer (*comp adj/n*) *obs vb* to linger

longhead *n* a person with a long skull

longshore *modf n* frequenting, found, employed or existing on the shore *n* a longshoreman, one employed on the shore

longside *obs adj* of garments, long and flowing

loo *n* an old card game of the whist type which, in the five card version, has the jack of clubs (called pam) as the highest individual card and anyone failing to take a trick pays into the kitty (the game was formerly known as **lanterloo**): the sum forfeit to the kitty: a session of the game (see TRIVIA note, below): a woman's velvet mask in vogue during the 17th century *vb* to pay the forfeit in the game of loo (extended to *incl* the paying of other forms of forfeit) *S fm n/vb* **love** *var fm* **lew** (in all senses other than *dial adj*) (TRIVIA note: Horace Walpole (1717–1797), the English writer chiefly remembered for his *Letters*, was a regular player of the game as shown by these quotes from his *Letters*, '*I was commanded to the duke's loo*' and '*Lady Falkener's daughter is to be married to Mr Crewe . . . of our loo*')

loof *S & dial n* the palm of the hand

loon *n* any of various birds *esp* the great northern diver, the great crested grebe and the dabchick or little grebe: an oaf, rogue, idler, lout, simpleton: a strumpet *arch n* a man of low birth or estate *dial n* a strip of ploughed land divided by a water furrow

loone *obs fm n* **loon** (*incl arch n* and *dial n*, for all senses except that of a bird)

loons *n pl* a group of birds which comprise the order known as *Gaviiformes*. The experts, however, cannot agree as to which birds are loons and whether there are three, four or five species of them!

loope *obs fm n* **loop**

loor *dial n* a lull in a storm: a sore in the hoof of a sheep or cow: foot rot *dial vb* to abate or lull *dial interj* of surprise

loore *var fm dial n* **loor**, a sore in a hoof

loper *n* either of the two sliding pieces which project to form the supports for the writing surface of a bureau bookcase: a swivel on which strands are secured prior to their being twisted to form rope

loppe *obs fm vb* **lop**

lopper (*n*) *now S & dial vb* to curdle: to dabble: to besmear

loppet *dial vb* of such as a hare or rabbit, to move with a heavy gait

loquat *n* a Far Eastern tree of the rose family: its small yellow fruit

lorate *adj* strap-like

lorcha *n* a light fast-sailing ship built in China, with a hull of European design but rigged in the fashion of the traditional junk

lordless *adj* without a lord: of a woman, not having a husband

lordling *n* a petty lord

lorel *S fm arch adj/n* **losel**

loricae *pl* lorica, an ancient Roman corselet: a protective covering or shell such as the hard, bony shell of a lobster or the hard external casing of vegetable seeds

loricate *adj* of such as any crocodilian, covered with a natural armour *vb* to cover with a protective coating

loring *obs n* instruction, teaching

loris *n* either of two species of small nocturnal mammals related to the lemurs (*pl* **lorises**)

lorre *var fm obs n* **laure**

lorrie *var fm n* **lurry**

lory *n* any of about 65 species of some of the most vividly coloured parrots and found in Australasia and islands of the central Pacific (*pl* **lories**)

losel *arch adj* worthless *arch n* a good-for-nothing

losh *n* the untanned hide of an elk *obs n* an elk *vb* to fall with a splash

loss (*n*) *obs S vb* to unload

lossel *var fm arch adj/n* **losel**

losset *obs dial n* a large flat wooden dish or tray

lotah *var fm n* **lota**, a small metal pot made in India

lote *arch n* the nettle tree *obs vb* to bathe (the eyes) with a medicated lotion

loter *var fm dial n* **laughter**

lothe *obs fm now dial n* **lewth**

lotter *n* one who holds an allotment of land

Lottie *pet fm fem pers n* **Charlotte** (the *fm* of **Charles** meaning 'a man')

louden *vb* to make, become or grow loud or louder

lough *n* the Irish equivalent of the Scottish **loch**

loun *var fm S & dial adj/adv/n/vb* **lown**

lound *var fm S & dial adj/adv/n/vb* **lown**

lounder *S vb* to beat or thrash *S n* a heavy punch or blow

loup *n* a woman's silk or velvet mask *S n/vb* (to) leap

loupe *n* the small magnifying glass worn in the eye socket by a jeweller or watchmaker *obs fm S vb* **loup**

louper *obs n* an artificial fishing fly

lour *n* a frown, scowl *slg n* money *vb* to convey opinion with a frown or scowl

lourde *Obs fm n* **lord**

loure *n* a type of old slow dance (tune) *obs fm n/vb* **lour**

lourie *n* a turaco

louse see **lice, louses**

louser *n* one who removes lice

louses *infl vb* louse, to remove lice from *infl now dial vb* lous (or louse), to loosen *pl slg n* louse, a contemptible person

lout (*n*) *vb* to bow or stoop

louter *Obs n* a worshipper *var fm dial n* **laughter**

louver *n* a turret designed to allow smoke to escape *US fm n* **louvre** *dial n* a chimney

louvre *n* a set of horizontal parallel slats in such as a door, sloping outwards to throw off rain whilst admitting air *var fm n* **louver** *obs n* a type of slow dance fashionable in the 18th century

lovage *n* a salad plant akin to angelica having greenish-white flowers and aromatic fruits: a liquor made from its seeds and roots: any of various other plants *incl* Scottish lovage

lovebird *n* any of eight or nine species of small African parrots, all of which have an extremely close pair-bonding that includes either mutual preening or, in some species, the male preening the female

lovedrury *n* a love token or keepsake (*obs* except in literature on old or obsolete words)

lovery *obs fm n* **louver**

lovier *dial fm n* **lover**

low (*adj*/*adv*/*n*) *vb* of cattle, to moo *now dial vb* to humble: to flame or glow *obs vb* to permit

lowan *n* the mallee fowl

lowery *adj* of the sky, dull or gloomy

lowing *n* mooing

lowist *Obs fm sup* **lowest**

lown *S & dial adj* calm, quiet, still *S & dial adv* quietly, softly *S & dial n* quiet, calm, shelter *S & dial vb* to shelter, to calm (down)

lowne *var fm n*/*arch n* **loon** (all senses other than that of a bird)

lowpe *var fm S vb* **loup** *obs S fm n* **loop**

lowre *var fm slg n* **lour** *obs fm n*/*vb* **lour**

lowrie *S n* a hypocrite (+*cap*) *S pers n* a proper name for the fox

lowry *US n* an open boxcar on the US railways

lowse *S vb* to unyoke (a team of horses): to redeem (*pa t*/*pa pple* **lowsit**) *dial fm vb* **loose** *dial fm n* **louse** *Obs fm n* **luce**

lowsit *pa t*/*pa pple S vb* lowse

lowter *var fm dial n* **laughter**

lowtre *Obs fm vb* **loiter**

lox *n* loxygen: a kind of smoked salmon

loxygen *n* liquid oxygen

£ s d *Latin abbreviation* **librae, solidi, denarii** or pounds, shillings, pence (the *sing fms* being **libra, solidus, denarius**) (note: Elsewhere, historical coins will often be defined in £ s d rather than £ p. This is to avoid confusion between the exchange rates then current and a grossly distorted picture which would result from an attempt to compare with £ p. For example, today's penny is an almost despised coin whereas, in historic times, it was even worth minting in silver. Ironically, the decimal penny was introduced as a coin worth more than the traditional penny which now, in real terms, is a nonsense. There were 240 old pennies to the pound.)

lu *Ork vb* to listen *var fm dial n* **lew**, a sheltered place

lub *obs S fm vb* **love**

lubbe *var fm* **lub** (*obs S fm vb* **love**)

lubber *n* a big, clumsy (idle) oaf: a lout:

landlubber, a clumsy seaman *vb* to behave as a lubber: to navigate a boat in an unseamanlike fashion

luber *obs fm n* **lubber**

lubra *Austr n* an adult female aborigine

lucarne *n* a skylight

luce *n* the fish, pike *esp* when fully mature

lucern *n* the lynx: its fur *var fm n* **lucerne**

lucerne *n* a clover-like plant cultivated as fodder

Lucina *pers n* the Roman goddess of childbirth *arch n* a midwife

Lucretia *fem pers n* the chaste and devoted wife of Collatinus, whose suicide following rape by Tarquin, the son of Tarquin the Proud, was the spur to the complete overthrow of the monarchy of Rome. Brutus seized this latest example of evil by the Tarquins to lead the successful revolution which established Rome as as republic. (Also see **Brutus** and **Tarquin**)

lucumo *n* the ruler of a lucumony, an Etruscan noble who had both princely and priestly powers (*pl* **lucumas, lucumones**)

ludge *obs S fm n/vb* **lodge**

lue *vb* in mining, to sieve (*infl* **lueing**) *var fm now dial n/adj* **lew** *obs fm now dial vb* **lew**

lufe *var fm S & dial n* **loof** *obs fm n/vb* **love** *obs fm n* **luff**

luff *n* the sailing of a ship close to the wind: the leading edge of a fore-and-aft sail: the broadest part of a ship's bow *vb* to bring the head of a vessel close to (or into) the wind: to sail near the wind

luffer *var fm n* **louvre** *obs fm n* **liver** *Obs fm n* **lover**

lufter *var fm dial n* **laughter**

luge *n* a light sledge *vb* to travel by such a sledge

lugent *adj* weeping

lugsail *n* a type of four-cornered sail

luiten *S fm pa pple* **let**

lumbar *adj* of the lower part of the spine

lumbred *obs fm adj* **lumbered**

lumen *n* the metric unit of luminous flux (*pl* **lumens, lumina**)

lumina *pl* lumen

lumine *vb* to illuminate (a manuscript)

lumpen *adj* pertaining to the lowest urban social group

lumper *n* a labourer involved in loading or unloading: one who lumps things together (see **nonce**) *now dial vb* to stumble or move in a clumsy fashion (*lit/fig*)

lunary *adj* of or pertaining to the moon: monthly, menstrual: lunatic *n* a lunatic: the fern, moorwort

lunate *adj* crescent-shaped

lunated *adj* lunate

lunation *n* a lunar month ($29\frac{1}{2}$ days)

lunder *obs fm n* **lunda**, the puffin

lunette *n* a crescent-shaped ornament: a horseshoe which consists of the front semicircular portion only: a semicircular architectural feature of a dome or a concave ceiling: the circular hole for the neck of one being executed by guillotine: a blinker for a horse: a type of watch-glass which is flattened in the centre: a circular display case in a monstrance for the Host: a defensive fortification having two faces and two flanks: a square flue in a furnace

lunge (*n/vb*) *infl fms incl n/pr pple* **lunging** *var fm pr pple* **lungeing**

lungee *var fm n* **lungi**

lunggi *var fm n* **lungi**

lungi *n* an Indian loincloth

lungie *var fm n* **lungi**

lunist *obs n* one who, by virtue of birth, has the astrological influence of the moon

lunt *vb* to emit smoke: to kindle *S n* smoke: a torch *dial adj* short: surly

luny *var fm adj* **loony**

lupine *adj* having the nature of a wolf *var fm n* lupin, the flower

lurdan *n* a sluggard, vagabond or loafer

lurdane *var fm n* **lurdan**

lurden *var fm n* **lurdan**

lurgan *n* the white ragworm, a common marine worm used as fishing bait

lurne *obs fm vb* **learn**

lurry *n* a (railway) wagon: a bridge over a mine pit (*var fms* **larry, lorrie, lorry, lurrie**) *now dial n* a lesson or set speech *esp* one learned by rote: a hubbub or noisy babble: a confused assembly *obs n* diarrhoea (*var fms now dial n/obs n* **larry, lerry, lorry**) *now dial vb* to carry or drag a difficult object (such as a heavy object or a struggling child): to push or struggle

lusher (*comp adj*) *n* a heavy drinker, a lush

lushings *n pl* abundance

Lusignam see **Melusina**

luster *var fm* (*now US*) *n/vb* **lustre**

lustra *pl* lustrum

lustrate *vb* to purify

lustrine *n* a type of glossy silk fabric

lustrum *n* a period of five years (*pl* **lustra, lustrums**)

lute (*n*) *vb* to perform on the musical instrument, a lute: to coat with lute, a compound of pipe clay and various other substances mixed to produce a filler

lutein *n* a yellow colouring matter in such as the yolk of an egg

luter *n* a lute player

lutine *arch fm n* **lutein**

lutong *n* the banded leaf-monkey or any other species of langurs native to Malaysia

Lutrinae *n pl* the otter sub-family of the *Mustelidae*

lutten see **let**

lutter *Obs adj* pure

ly *n* an Ammanese measure of length *var fm n* **li**, the Chinese unit of distance *obs fm n* **lye**

lychee *var fm n* **litchi**

lychnis *n* any of various plants *esp* those of the genus of the campion and ragged robin (*pl* **lychnides**)

Lycosa *n* the typical genus of the wolf spiders *incl* the true (and deadly) tarantula

lyddite *n* a type of high explosive

lye *n* an alkaline solution of water and the salts of wood ash used as a detergent *vb* to wash with lye (also see **leach** *vb/now dial n*)

lyke *var fm arch n* **lich** *obs fm vbs* **like, lick**

lyophobe *adj* denoting lack of a strong affinity between a gluelike or jellylike substance and the liquid in which it is dispersed

lyrate *adj* lyre-shaped: of a leaf, split in the middle with the upper lobes much larger than the lower

lyrated *adj* lyrate

lysine *n* an important amino acid produced from the decomposition of various proteins

lyster *Obs fm obs n* **lister**

lythe *S n* the pollack, a common fish of the cod family *var fm arch vb* **lithe** *var fm obs vb* **lithe**

M

ma (*childish n*) *n* the bobization equivalent of **la**

maat *obs fm n/vb* **mate**

mabble *obs vb* of dressing, to wrap up

mable *var fm obs vb* **mabble** (+*cap*) *dim fm fem pers n* **Amabel**, meaning 'lovable'

macarise *var fm vb* **macarize**, to declare to be happy or blessed

macaronic *adj* designating a type of comic verse which has latinized vernacular words in a Latin context *n* that resultant language (in *pl fm*) macaronic verses

macer *n* a mace bearer; an official who keeps order in a Scottish court *slg n* a swindler

macerals *n pl* a geologist's term for the individual constituents of the composition of coal

macerate *vb* to soften by steeping in a liquid: to wear away by steeping

maceration *n* (an instance of) the process or action of steeping a solid in a liquid either to soften it or to break down its structure (also see **ret**)

machair *n* land which provides very poor pasturage

machinator *n* one, usually in a bad sense, who intrigues, plots or schemes

macho *adj* ostentatiously masculine *n* a man of this fashion (*pl* **machos**)

machree *Anglo-Ir n* (my) dear

macle *n* a twin crystal (see **macled**): a spot of a deeper hue than the rest of the surrounding mineral: a yellowish-white variety of andalusite, a very hard mineral found in crystal form *var fm n* **mascle**, a metal plate on an historic military tunic

macled *adj* of a twin crystal, not only having identical form of each part of this composite crystal but, if it is assumed that one part could be turned through half a revolution, then the corresponding faces and edges would be seen to be parallel

Mâcon *n* a burgundy from the Mâcon district of France

macrami *var fm n* **macramé**, a type of ornamental work of knotted thread

macula *n* a spot (*pl* **maculae, maculas**)

Madeline *var fm fem pers n* **Magdalen**, meaning 'of Magdala' (a Biblical location, the details of which are unknown)

madras *n* a fine cotton fabric: a large (highly-coloured) headscarf sported by negroes

madrasa *n* a Muslim theological college

madrona *var fm n* **madrono**

madrone *var fm n* **madrono**

madrono *n* an evergreen hardwood tree of western North America bearing yellow berries

madtom *n* any of various species of North American catfishes of the horned pout family. The species *incl* the stonecat, the tadpole madtom and various blind, cave-dwelling species. All madtoms possess a poison gland at the base of the pectoral fin spines, so making these small fishes dangerous to handle.

maenad *n* a Bacchante, a priestess or female follower of Bacchus the Roman god or Dionysus the Greek god, of wine: an uncontrollably furious woman

maestro (*n*) *pl* **maestri, maestros**

Magian *adj* of or pertaining to the Magi, the three wise men who visited the infant Christ (−*cap*) *n* a magus, one skilled in the magic arts to the highest degree (*pl* **magians** or, of magus, **magi**)

magister *n* a master, one entitled to teach in a mediaeval university

magnes *arch n* a magnet

magnesite *n* a granular carbonate of magnesium

magnetiser *var fm n* **magnetizer**, that which imparts magnetism: a hypnotist

magnetist *n* one skilled in magnetism: a hypnotist (i.e. one skilled in animal magnetism in the sense of it being the supposed power used by a hypnotist)

Magyar *n* one of the people of the principal race in Hungary: the Hungarian language (*−cap*) *adj* of a garment which has the sleeves cut as a piece with the rest

Mahican *n* one of either the Mohegan or Mohican tribes of Red Indians, each of whom spoke a different dialect of an Algonquian language and occupied a territory which lay between the Hudson river and Narragansett Bay (see both **Mohegan** and **Mohican**)

mahmal *n* an empty litter sent to Mecca during a pilgrimage

mahoe *n* the New Zealand whitewood tree

mahseer *n* any species of *Barbus*, a genus of huge (up to nine feet in length), freshwater, carp-like fishes found in the rivers of the Himalayan foothills: name also extended to a similar, but much smaller, African species of the same genus

mahsir *var fm n* **mahseer**

maid (*n*) *vb* to perform the actions of a maid, a female domestic servant

maidan *n* an open space in or near a town of India or Persia

maiden (*n*/*adj*) *dial vb* to wash with a maiden, a washerwoman's dolly

maidless *adj* without a maid

maigre *n* a large food fish of the Mediterranean *adj* not consisting of flesh or its juices hence suitable for days of abstinence

mail drag *n* a conveyance for transporting the mail

maile *n* **mail** or **maille**, the names for two different English coins (*a*) the halfpenny (*b*) the **maille noble**, a gold coin of Edward III

mailer *n* a mail boat, a vessel which carries the public mail *US n* one who posts a letter *S n* one who pays rent

maille *var fm n* **maile**

main (*n*/*adj*) *obs vb* to lower a sail *obs fm now S & dial vb* **mean**

Maine *n* the Pinetree state of New England, USA, capital Augusta (*−cap*) *obs vb* to lower a sail on a ship

maine top *obs fm n* **maintop**

mainless *Obs adj* powerless

Mainstone *n* a town in Shropshire

maintop *n* the top of a ship's mainmast

mairt *var fm S n* **mart**, a cow or ox fattened for slaughter

maister *S & dial fm n* **master** *Obs fm n* **mastery**

maistre *obs fm n*/*vb* **master** *Obs fm n* **mastery**

maistri *Obs fm n* **mastery**

maistrie *obs vb* to master *obs fm n* mastery

maitrise *obs vb* to conquer

makebate *n* one who or that which creates strife or discord

malander *n* a skin eruption behind the knee of a horse

malate *n* a salt obtained from an acid found in unripe fruit

male *(adj/n) var fm now dial vb* **mole**, to spot, stain, discolour *obs fm now S n/vb* **mail**, (to pay) tax, rent *obs fm now dial n* **meal**, a sandbank

maleic *adj* of an acid produced by the dry distillation of malic acid (an acid found in unripe fruit)

maleis *obs fm n* **malice**

malengin *obs n* fraud, deceit; evil intent (a word of common usage from the 14th to the 17th centuries with such spelling *fms* as the anagram, **malingen**, and the delightful, **male engine** – which should appeal to any wife not especially sweetly disposed to her spouse or men in general!)

malengine *var fm obs n* **malengin**

malet *n* a portmanteau or small bag *obs fm n* **mallet**, a (wooden) hammer *obs fm vb* **mallet**, to strike with a mallet

maligner *n* one who maligns

maline *n* a delicate net used for veils

Malines *n* a Belgian town on the river Dyle once famous for lace

malinger *vb esp* of members of the armed forces, to feign illness in order to escape a particular duty

Malinke *n* a Mande language of the Western Sudanic sub-group of the Niger–Congo family of languages, spoken in such countries as Senegal and Gambia

malise *obs fm n* **malice**

malison *arch n* a curse *dial n* a plague or torment *obs S vb* to put a curse upon

malist *n* one who holds to the dictum that the world is an evil place

mallee fowl *n* the lowan, a megapode or incubator bird also known as a mound bird due to its method of incubating eggs inside a mound. A breeding pair of these Australian, large, chicken-like birds excavate a pit as deep as four feet and up to fifteen feet in diameter. Over the winter this is filled with vegetation then, after it has been dampened by rain, covered with a two foot thick layer of sandy soil. As the female lays her eggs over a period of several months and the chicks hatch at intervals, so special circumstances prevail. An egg chamber is created in the centre of the mound directly above the heat of the rotting compost and beneath the insulation of the soil. The male constantly attends to the mound throughout the incubation period in order to maintain the temperature of the chamber at 92°F. This he achieves either by allowing heat to escape or by adding additional insulation. Apparently his beak, which he is constantly poking into the mound, has the capacity of acting as a type of thermometer. This situation is unique to the mallee fowl as other megapodes, whilst still building mounds, have a more conventional breeding season.

mallei *pl* **malleus**, the largest of three small bones in the middle ear of mammals

mallet (*n*) *vb* to hammer (*lit/fig*)

mallie *obs adj* dotingly fond to the point of foolishness

malm *n* a soft chalky rock: the loamy soil formed of this when in a crumbled state *vb* to convert clay into artificial malm for making bricks *dial adj* mellow, soft

malshave *n* a caterpillar (*Obs* except in literature on old or obsolete words)

malster *obs fm n* **maltster**

maltase *n* a digestive enzyme that produces grape sugar from a hard crystalline sugar known as maltose

malten *S vb* to malt

malter *now dial n* a maker of malt

maltier *comp adj* malty

maltster *n* one who is employed in the making of malt

manatee *n* the seacow, any of three species of

large, herbivorous mammals found in the estuarine rivers and tropical Atlantic waters from Virginia to the Amazon and across to the coast of West Africa. Despite its ugly face with a pig-like, bristly snout, this sirenian is the origin of some of the mermaid sightings, including that by Christopher Columbus.

manati *var fm n* **manatee**

Manaton *n* a town in Devonshire

mand *n* a species of grass found in India *obs n* a question *obs vb* to send for: to send forth

mander *obs fm vb* **maunder**

mandioc *var fm n* **manioc**

mandora *n* a large type of mandolin, the musical instrument

manège *n* horse management: horse training: the actions of a trained horse: a riding school *vb* to train a horse

maneir *obs fm n* **manner**

maneto *obs fm n* **manito**

mange *n* a contagious disease affecting hairy animals: a dirty, scabby skin condition *obs n* a meal *obs vb* to eat

mangel *n* a small, blae beetle whose larvae attack the mangle wurzle

manger (*n*) *obs vb* to eat

mangold *var fm n* **mangel**

mangy *adj* affected with mange (*comp* **mangier** *sup* **mangiest**)

Manichee *n* one who followed a religion which flourished in the 3rd to the 5th centuries and was a compound of Gnostic, Christian and pagan beliefs adapted to a basis of Persian fire worship

manihoc *var fm n* **manioc**

manil *obs fm n* **manilla**, an arm bracelet used as a medium of exchange by some African tribes

manila *n* a square-cut cigar made in Manila, the Philippines: abaca

manioc *n* any of various tropical plants, the roots of which yield a starch which is the basis of tapioca: the starch (*var fms* **manioca, mandioc, mandioca, mandiocca, manihoc, manihot** – also **cassava**, the widely cultivated variety)

maniple *n* one of the three companies of Roman infantry which, together, formed a cohort. Two of these had 120 men each and the third had 60. Ten such cohorts of 300 men comprised a legion: one of the priestly vestments which, like all such, has a symbolic significance. In this instance it is a short strip of cloth worn over the arm to represent a handkerchief to wipe away the tears of sin *obs n* a handful (*lit/fig*): the hand: a small company of soldiers

manito *n* the term originally used by the Algonquian Red Indians to describe the unfathomable spirit or power behind life and the universe (in this sense the Sioux Indians use the term, wakanda): an aspect of that spiritual power present in any object (*var fms incl* **manitou, manitoo, manitu** – also see **Kitchi Manito**) (*pl* **manitos**)

manitou *var fm n* **manito**

manitu *var fm n* **manito**

manjack *n* a species of large tree found in the West Indies

man jack *n* an individual man (as in the phrases *every man jack* or *no man jack*)

mannering *obs n* instruction in manners *obs fm n* **manuring**

mannitose *n* a fermentable sugar obtained from the manna tree

mannose *n* a sugar obtained by oxidizing an alcohol from various seaweeds

man orchis *n* an orchid, the flowers of which resemble little men

manred *obs n* homage: men available for military service: sexual intercourse

manrent *S n* homage

manse (*n*) *obs vb* to curse

manswear *arch vb* to swear falsely: to perjure oneself (*pa t* **manswore** *pa pple* **mansworn**)

mant *S n* a stammer *S vb* to stammer

mante *var fm obs n* **mantie** *obs fm S vb* **mant**

manteel *obs n* a (military) cloak

mantes *pl* mantis

manticore *n* a fabulous monster having the head of a man, the body of a lion, the quills of a porcupine and the sting of a scorpion *her n* the mantiger, a monster having the horned head of a man and the body of a beast of rapine which, sometimes, has the feet of a dragon

mantid *n* any of the various species of insects called mantis or praying mantis (see **mantis**) all of which are cannibalistic *incl* one species held in reverence by the Asmat tribe of New Guinea who are themselves cannibals

mantie *obs S n* the charge of uttering a falsehood

mantiger *her n* the manticore

mantis *n* a mantid or praying mantis, any of various, mainly tropical, long, narrow, carnivorous insects *incl* the well-known *Mantis religiosa* (see below) of the Mediterranean region (*pl* **mantes, mantises, mantids**)

mantises *pl* mantis

Mantis religiosa *n* possessing a somewhat human face and with its forelegs in an attitude of prayer, this particular mantid is anything but saintly. It holds this posture whilst waiting to pounce on any passing insect and the female of the species is equally lethal to her mate. Once he has mounted her, she bites off and eats his head, leaving the remainder of the body to continue the sexual act stimulated by this supreme 'love-bite'. (Also see **mantid, mantis**)

mantissa *n* the decimal part of a logarithm

mantua *n* a loose gown worn by a woman in the 17th/18th centuries

manty *S fm n* **mantua**

manwise *adv* in a manner characteristic of man

Maoism *n* the theory of communism as espoused by Mao Tse-Tung (1893–1976) the Chinese revolutionary leader which, in essence, is communal effort and self reliance in a revolutionary environment.

Maoist *n* one who follows the precepts of Maoism (also see the apt anagram, **Taoism**)

mapel *obs fm n* **maple**

mapled *adj* having maple trees

mapper *n* a map maker

mapwise *adv* in the manner of a map

marabout *n* a Moslem hermit: a Moslem shrine

maraca *n* a simple percussion instrument consisting of a gourd filled with beans

marah *n* bitterness

maranta *n* any species of the *Maranta* genus of the arrowroot medicinal herb

marasca *n* a small black cherry of Yugoslavia, the basis for the liqueur, maraschino

maraschino *n* a cherry liqueur

marbler *n* one who or that which produces a marbled effect on paper

marc *n* the residue after grapes have been pressed and the resultant liquid drained off: brandy made from this residue

marcel *vb* to create a wave in hair by means of a heated iron and a comb *n* that wave

marcescent *adj* of plant parts, withering but remaining attached *n* a plant having such

Märchen *Ger n* (*sing/pl*) a folk tale

marchese *n* an Italian marquis (*fem* **marchesa**)

marchion *Obs n* the mediaeval Latin equivalent of marquis, used to designate a captain with responsibility in the border territories known as the marches

marchon *S var fm Obs n* **marchion**

Marcus *masc pers n* meaning Mars, the god of war

mardy *dial adj* timid, fearful, cowardly

mare (*n*) *var fm now dial n* **mere**, a marsh or fen *obs fm ns* **marc, mayor** *obs fm vb* **mar** *obs fm adj* **more**

marenga *var fm n* **moringa**

mare's nest *n* a great discovery which proves to be worthless (the equivalent term in Scotland being **skate's nest** and, in Cornwall, **wee's nest**)

mare's tail *n* the marsh plant formerly known as the **female horsetail** (*pl*) the long streaky cirrus clouds which usually precede stormy weather

marestail *adj* of mare's tails, the clouds

margay *n* a South American tiger cat

marge *now poet n* a margin *vb* to edge

margent *arch n* a margin *obs vb* to insert as a marginal note

margine *obs fm n* **margin**

margosa *n* the nim tree or neem tree, a species of *Melia* which grows in East India. A gum is obtained from its trunk, a tonic from its bark and a bitter oil from both the seeds and the fruit.

Marian *adj* of Mary or a supporter or devotee of a Mary of consequence, such as the Virgin Mary or a Queen Mary *var fm fem pers n* **Miriam**, meaning 'bitterness' via the adaptions Marian from Marion from Marie from Maria from Miriam

marid *n* a very powerful djinni (see **djinn**)

marigenous *adj* produced by or in the sea

marine (*n*/adj) *obs vb* to marinate (pickle fish in a sauce of spiced oil, wine and vinegar)

marish *now poet & dial n* a marsh *now poet & dial adj* marshy: of a marsh

Marist *n* a member of a Catholic society devoted to teaching and foreign missionary work

maritage *n* the right possessed by a feudal superior to arrange the marriage of a vassal (in England only the king held this right whereas, in Scotland, various superiors held it by gift from the Scottish monarch): the profit accruing from this source

marite *obs n* a husband

marl *n* a type of clay-based soil containing carbonate of lime and valued as a fertilizer *vb* to fertilize with marl *vb* (*of naval usage*) to secure with a marline *now dial vb* to marvel

marle *dial n* the knot or redbreasted sandpiper *var fm now dial vb*/*naval vb* **marl**

marlet *obs n* the martlet or swift

marley *obs fm adj* **marly**

marlier *comp adj* marly

marline *n* a small naval rope *var fm naval vb* **marl**

marlite *n* 'rotten limestone', a type of marl resistant to the action of the air

marlot *var fm obs n* **marlet**

marly *adj* resembling/composed of/abounding in marl, a limy clay *S & dial adj* spotted or streaked

marm *var fm vb* **ma'am**, to address a woman as ma'am (GAME PLAYER'S note: **marm, marmed** etc are valid for play: **ma'am, ma'amed** etc should be rejected as the words require an apostrophe)

marmite *n* a large metal or earthenware cooking vessel used *esp* for soup

Maro *pers n* Publius Vergilus Maro (70–19 BC), the Roman epic poet known as Virgil. Two different words have arisen from his cognomen, Maro. The first is **Maronian** (*adj* Virgilian, the last recorded usage of which was 1693 and so considered *obs* by all experts other than *Chambers 20th Century Dictionary*). The second is **Maronist** (*obs n* a disciple or student of Virgil, last recorded usage 1599).

marocain *n* a dress material having a finish like morocco leather

maron *obs n* a mountain guide

Maronian *see* **Maro**

Maronist *see* **Maro**

Maronite *n* a Lebanese Christian of a sect originally independent but, since 1216, allied to the Catholic Church

marque *n* a brand: a privateer, a ship licensed with a letter of marque which enables it to conduct acts against the merchant vessels of an enemy power which would otherwise be condemned as piracy

marret *var fm n* **marrot**, a guillemot

married (*adj*) *US collq n* one who is married (*pl* **marrieds**)

marseir *var fm n* **mahseer**

marsh (*n*) *obs fm vb* **mash**

mart *n* a market *S n* a beef ox or cow *dial n* the marten *obs vb* to trade at a market

marte *obs fm n*/ *S n*/ *obs vb* **mart**

martel *n* a hammer *obs vb* to hammer

marten *n* any of a number of cat-sized carnivores of the weasel family *incl* the pine marten, stone marten and the sable

martensite *n* the chief constituent of hardened steel, being iron with a carbon content of 2% or less

marter *obs n* the marten: its fur

Martes *n* the genus of the marten

marthe *obs fm n* **marrow**

martlet *n* the swift: formerly also applied to the swallow and the house martin *her n* an imaginary bird without feet, a symbol of a fourth son *obs n* the marten: its fur

martre *Obs fm obs n* **marter**

mary *obs fm vb* **marry**

marye *obs fm vb* **marry**

mascle *n* one of the lozenge-shaped plates of metal which formed an armoured outer surface of a 13th century military tunic *her n* a lozenge-shaped framing to an heraldic design *obs n* a spot or speck

mascon *n* any of a number of mass concentrations of dense material lying beneath the surface of the moon

mase *obs n* a freckle *obs fm n*/*vb* **mess** *obs fm ns* **maze, mease, mace** (a Malayan gold coin) *var fm obs vb* **mace**, to spice with mace

maseer *var fm n* **mahseer**

maser *n* the microwave equivalent of a laser

mashlam *var fm now dial n* **maslin**

masicot *obs fm n* **massicot**

maslin *now dial n* mixed grain such as wheat and rye: bread made of a mixture of corn: false outward show (*fig*): a type of brass: an object made of such

masline *obs fm now dial n* **maslin**, (an object of) brass

masonry (*n*) *vb* to build or strengthen with masonry

masoolah *n* a type of Indian boat with many oars

Masora *n* a collection of critical notes compiled from the 10th century onwards by Jewish scholars on the traditional information relating to the text of the Hebrew Bible (*var fms* **Masorah, Massora, Massorah, Masoreth)**

masque *n* a dramatic entertainment of the 16th and 17th centuries in which masked performers provided pantomime, dancing, dialogue and music: the words and music for this: a masquerade or masked ball: a masked person

masquer *n* a participant in a masquerade

Massah *n* a place mentioned in the Bible as being a resting point for the Jews on their flight from Egypt

masser *n* a Protestant term of derision for one who celebrates or attends mass: a masseur or masseuse

masseter *n* one of the principal muscles of the jaw

massicot *n* lead monoxide: a lead-based, yellowish pigment

mast (*n*) *vb* to supply a ship with a mast *obs vb* to feed mast (chestnuts etc) to pigs: to eat like a pig

mastere *obs fm n* **mastery**

masterie *obs fm n* **mastery**

masterwort *n* any of several plants *esp* one formerly cultivated as a pot herb and used in medicine

mastic (*n*) *obs vb* to use the resin, mastic, as a varnish

mastich *var fm n* **mastic**, a pale yellow resin exuded by the bark of the lentisk and various other trees

masticot *var fm n* **massicot**

mastigure *n* any of twelve species of agamid lizards which change colour as they get warmer in the sun. All are basically dark but an African species exhibits the greatest colour change, becoming light green-grey with a reddish head and tail at the hottest time of the day. All mastigures are about a foot long at maturity and are found in North Africa and southwest Asia.

mastoid *adj* breastlike, nipplelike: pertaining to or situated near a process of the temporal bone behind the ear *n* that process

mastri *obs fm n* **mastery**

mastrie *Obs fm n* **mastery**

mastry *obs fm n* **mastery**

mastrye *obs fm n* **mastery**

masula *var fm n* **masoolah**

mateco *var fm n* **matico**

matelot *slg n* a sailor

matériel *n* (military) material and equipment

mathe *now S n* a maggot

mather *dial n* stinking camomile *dial vb* of an animal, to turn round before lying down

mathesi *obs fm arch n* **mathesis**

mathesis *arch n* mental discipline: learning or (mathematical) science

matico *n* a Peruvian shrub, the leaves of which have styptic qualities (*pl* **maticos**)

matie *n* a herring considered to be in perfect condition for eating

matin *adj* of the morning: of matins *n* a French watchdog *poet n* an early morning bird song

matiness *collq n* friendliness

matins *n* the first of the seven canonical hours of prayer; a morning prayer service in the Church of England (*pl* **matins**)

matlo *var fm slg n* **matelot** (*pl* **matlos**)

matrices *pl* matrix

matrix *n* that in which something has origin, takes form or is enclosed (*pl* **matrices, matrixes)**

matronise *var fm vb*/*US vb* **matronize**

matronize (*vb*) *US vb* to act as the hostess to

matross *n* an old military rank below that of gunner in artillery

matte *n* an impure and unfinished metallic product containing sulphur, obtained from the smelting of various ores *var fm adj* **matt**, having a dull or lustreless surface *var fm vb* **matt**, to give (a surface) a matt finish

mattering *obs n* the formation of pus: caring

maturation *n* the action or process of ripening

maula *n* the scaup duck, a marine duck of the northern hemisphere

maule *obs vb* of a cat, to miaow

maunde *var fm obs vb* **mand**

maunder *n* incoherent speech (or writing) of an idle nature *obs cant n* a begger *vb* to talk, act or move in a dreamy or foolish fashion *obs cant vb* to beg

maure *var fm obs n* **maur**, an ant

Maurist *n* a French Benedictine monk of a congregation founded by St Maur in 1618 *adj* of that congregation

Mauser *n* the German military rifle which first came into service in 1871 *nonce vb* to shoot with a Mauser

mauther *now dial n* a young girl *var fm dial n* **mather**

mavis *n* the song thrush

maw *n* the stomach of an animal *esp* the fourth stomach of a cow or other ruminant: the gullet of a fish *now dial n* the seagull *dial fm vb* **mow**

mawer *obs fm adj*/*adv*/*now dial n* **more**

mawl *var fm n*/*vb* **maul**

mawpus *slg n* a small coin

mawre *obs fm now dial n* **more**

mayest *obs 2nd pers sing vb* may (still extant in either a humorous or an historical piece of reported speech)

mayster *obs fm ns* **master, mastery**

maystre *obs fm n* **master** *Obs fm n* **mastery**

mbori *n* a disease which affects camels

me (*pron*) *n* the bebization equivalent of **soh** or **so** in the tonic sol-fa *var fm n* **mi** (see **gamut)**

meade *obs fm n* **mead**, the alcoholic drink made from honey *obs S fm now poet & dial n* **mead**, a meadow

meader *dial n* one who mows *obs fm Anglo-Ir n* **madder**, a square wooden drinking vessel

meal (*n*) *vb* to grind into meal: to make a meal: to eat

mealer *n* an implement for rubbing meal into a fine powder

mealon *obs fm n* **melon**

mealtide *n* a meal, the time of a meal: the quantity of milk produced by a cow at a single milking (GAME PLAYER'S note: Whilst other authorities consider the word to be *obs* except in the *S var fm* **meltith**, the dictionary used for the UK Scrabble championship declares it to be *arch*. It invalidates the word for play, however, by giving it a hyphen.)

mean (*adj*/*n*/*vb*) *now S & dial vb* to complain of, to lament: to moan: to pity

meandrian *obs adj* winding, meandering

Meandrina *n* a genus of corals, the surface of which resemble the human brain (*−cap*) *n* a polyp of this genus

meane *var fm now S & dial vb* **mean**, to lament or mourn: to complain

meaned *see* **mean**

meanie *collq n* a small-minded, mean, petty and/or malicious person

mear *var fm arch n/now dial vb* **mere**

mearing *var fm n* **mering**

mease *n* a measure of quantity of herrings, which varies according to local custom but is usually five long hundreds. The long hundred is like the baker's dozen or the printer's ream, being more than the name suggests. The Isle of Man mease, for example, being five long hundreds, each of 123, makes a mease 615 herrings. The Pembrokeshire long hundred of 122 makes a mease of 610 but, by contrast, in North Devon it is four times 155, giving a mease of 612. *obs fm n/vb* **mess**

measle *vb* to infect with or develop measles

meat (*n*) *now dial vb* to supply with food: to eat

meatal *adj* of meatus, an anatomic canal or passage

meated *adj* of animals, well fleshed: of cheese, rich in quality

meath *obs fm n* **mead**, the drink made from honey

meating *obs n* feeding: pasturing

meche *var fm obs n* **miche**, a wedge

meconium *n* the first faeces of a newborn child (*pl* **meconiums**)

medalet *n* a small medal *esp* one of a saint

medalist *US fm n* **medallist**, a designer, maker or collector of medals

medallet *var fm n* **medalet**

Mede *n* one of the people of Media, an ancient country which flourished around 600 BC but which, circa 500 BC, was absorbed by the Persians. It was situated in what is now the N.W. Iranian plateau. The Medes (which to the ancient Greeks also meant Persians) were the great enemies of Greece, thus anything Medic meant either Persian or, if used in connection with a Greek, treacherous. (See **Medise, Medism**)

media *n* the middle layer of a blood or lymph vessel: a middle primary vein of an insect's wing (*pl* **mediae**) *var fm n* **medial** (*pl* **mediae**) *pl* medium (of communication) treated in the USA as *n sing* hence *pl* **medias** (+*cap*) *n* see **Mede**

medial *adj* intermediate: median: pertaining to an average: of a letter or voiced stop consonant occurring within a word *n* media, a medial letter (*pl* **medials, mediae**) (for the use of *medias* see **media**)

median *adj* of, relating to, directed towards or situated in the middle *n* a middle part

mediant *adj* intervening *n* the third note of any musical scale

mediater *obs fm n* **mediator**

Medic *adj* of or pertaining to the Medes (−*cap*) *US fm n* **medick**, any of various clover-like plants having yellow or purple flowers

medicaster *n* a medical charlatan, a quack

medicastor *obs fm n* **medicaster**

medina *n* the ancient native quarter of North African cities

Medise *vb* of an ancient Greek, to dress and behave in the manner of a Mede: to side with the Medes

Medism *n* a word or idiom of the language of the Medes: of an ancient Greek, to show sympathy for the Persian cause (see **Mede**)

medite *obs vb* to meditate

medlar *n* a fruit resembling a small brown apple which is eaten when in a soft, pulpy state: the tree bearing that fruit

medlor *obs fm n* **medlar**

medusa *n* see **sea fir** (*pl* **medusae, medusas**)

(+*cap*) *pers n* one of the three mythological Gorgons, each of whom had snakes for hair and the direct sight of which turned the beholder into stone

medusan *adj* of or pertaining to a jellyfish *n* a jellyfish

meede *var fm obs vb* **meed**, to reward or bribe

meeder *obs n* one who bribes

meer *var fm now dial vb* **mere** (also a *var, arch* or *obs fm* **mere** in most other senses)

meercat *var fm n* **meerkat**, a species of small mongoose native to South Africa and often kept as a household pet to eradicate rats and mice

meerest *obs fm sup* **merest**

meering *obs fm n* **mering**

meese *obs n* a tomtit *obs fm n* **mess** *obs fm S & dial vb* **mese**

meeter *n* one who attends a meeting

meeth *obs var fm n* **mead**, the alcoholic honey drink *var fm Obs n* **methe**

meetinger *n* a Methodist or similar nonconformist

megabar *n* a million bars, where bar is used in the sense of a metric unit of the measure of pressure

megadyne *n* a million dynes

megapode *n* an incubator bird (see **mallee fowl**)

megasse *var fm n* **megass**, the refuse cane after the sugar has been extracted

megilp *n* either of two preparations, one consisting of linseed oil and turpentine used with oil paints, the other a thick, treacly compound used for painting a wood grain *vb* to use either preparation

megrim *n* any of various types of headache *esp* one which is severe and confined to a side of the head: vertigo: a species of North Atlantic flatfish related to the scaldfish and sometimes marketed as **white sole** (the name has been adopted from the Cornish *dial* where it is used for the **scaldfish** or **smooth sole** and **megrin** is a *var fm* in this sense)

megrin see **megrim**

meine *obs fm now S & dial vb* **mean**

Meissen *modf n* for fine porcelain, also known as Dresden, from Meissen, E. Germany

meistri *Obs fm n* **mastery**

meith *S n* a landmark, a boundary *S vb* to mark out a boundary

melanic *adj* having black hair and a dark or black complexion: of animals, suffering melanosis: designating the black pigmentation of melanosis: relating to or resembling melanosis or melanism *US n* one affected with melanism (i.e. the opposite of an albino)

melanin *n* the dark pigment of the body

melanism *n* the abnormal development of dark colouring matter in such as skin or feathers (for a striking example see **cline**)

melanist *US n* one having an abnormally dark pigmentation of the skin

melano *n* an abnormally dark person or animal

melanoses *pl* melanosis

melanosis *n* a disease which produces an abnormal black pigmentation in bodily tissue; black cancer (*pl* **melanoses**)

melanuric *adj* pertaining to or characterized by the pathological condition, melanuria, in which the urine is either black or dark blue

meld *vb* to merge or blend: in some card games, to lay down a set of cards for a points score *n* a set of such cards

melder *S n* the quantity of meal ground at any one time

Melia *n* a genus of trees of the mahogany family (*–cap*) *n* any tree of this genus including the nim and the Spanish cedar

melic *n* any grass of the genus *Melica* *adj* of (Greek) poetry, intended to be sung

Melica *n* a genus of grasses having a slender leaf sheath with a small, pointed extension: a genus of slender perennial herbs

melinite *n* a very high explosive based on pitric acid

meling *Obs n* conversation

Melissa *fem pers n* meaning 'honey'

mellay *n* a confused conflict *obs n* a mixture of colours *obs vb* to dispute

melling *obs n* dealing: meddling *Obs n* copulation

melodist *n* a singer: a composer of melodies

melomania *n* a mania for music

melter *n* a small furnace: a worker at such as the Mint who melts metals: a freestone peach *obs fm n* **milter**

meltet *obs fm now S n* **mealtide**

meltit *arch fm now S n* **mealtide**

meltith *see* **mealtide**

Melusina the name, in classic French folklore, of one of the daughters of King Elinas of Albany (Scotland) by his liaison with a fairy. The fairy, Pressina, was later to curse her daughter with the horrid affliction of, periodically, turning from the waist down into a serpent. The cure was true love and Melusina's wanderings eventually took her to Normandy. Here she met her love, they married and lived together in his castle at Lusignam. But, he broke a vow not to see her on a certain day (the day of affliction) and his horror forced her to flee and her tragic life culminated in her being the banshee of Lusignam. Later his estates became the property of the French royal house and the legend is that she appeared at Lusignam before the death of any King of France. (Also see **melusine**)

melusine *n* a beautiful female water sprite of Normandy folklore which affects a loving and modest nature but will, if sprinkled with holy water, turn into a dragon (also see **Melusina**)

mem *n* the thirteenth letter of the Hebrew alphabet

memento (*n*) *pl* **mementos, mementoes**

Memnon *pers n* an Ethiopian king who fought on the side of the Trojans against the Greeks

memoire *arch fm n* **memoir**

ménage *n* a household

menal *obs fm n* **menial**

mendigo *n* a word which appears to be exclusive to the dictionary used for the North American Scrabble championship which it defines simply as 'a freshwater fish' (*pl* **mendigos**)

meng *now dial vb* to mix or blend

mengel *obs fm vb* **mingle**

mengid *Obs S pa pple now dial vb* meng

mengle *obs fm vb* **mingle**

meningeal *adj* of or pertaining to the meninges (see **meninx**)

meninges *pl* meninx

meninx *n* any of three membranes (the dura mater, the pia mater or the arachnoid) covering the brain and spinal cord (*pl* **meninges**)

meniscal *adj* of the form of a meniscus

meniscus *n* a crescent-shaped body (*pl* **menisci, meniscuses** *obs pl* **meniscusses**)

menorah *n* the seven branched candlestick which is a feature of Jewish religious services

mensal *adj* monthly: of the table: for the table

as (*a*) **mensal bed**, the couch on which Romans reclined whilst feasting (*b*) **mensal land**, land set aside in Ireland and Scotland to provide for the table of the ancient and historic kings (*c*) **mensal church** or **mensal benefice**, revenue from a particular church or benefice to provide for the table of a bishop *n* a mensal church or benefice

mense *now S & dial n* decorum, neatness *now dial vb* to grace: to be a credit to: to do honour to

menstrua *pl* menstruum

menstruum *n* a solvent (*pl* **menstrua, menstruums**)

Mensur *Ger n* a duel as sport between two German students (*pl* **Mensuren**)

mensurable *adj* capable of being measured

mensural *adj* pertaining to measure: of music, characterized by notes which have fixed values

ment *obs fm arch vb* **mint**, to intend, to venture

mentalism *n* idealism in the sense of being the opposite of materialism: the process of mental action

mentigo *obs n* an outbreak of scabs on the mouth of a sheep (no recorded *pl*)

mentor *n* a wise or trusted counsellor

mentorial *adj* containing advice

mentum *n* the chin: the central part of the underlip of an insect (*pl* **menta**)

menuet *obs fm n* **minuet**

mercal *n* an Indian measure of weight equal to 24 lbs avoirdupois *Ork & Shet n* a plough shoe, the piece of timber supporting the ploughshare

mercate *obs fm n/vb* **market**

Mercator, Gerhardus *pers n* the Flemish geographer (1512–1594) who pioneered the making of accurate navigational maps

merce *obs aphetic fm vb* **amerce**

mercerie *obs fm n* **mercery**

mercerise *var fm vb* **mercerize**, to treat cotton to a chemical process prior to dyeing which results in a silklike finish

mercery *n* the goods sold by a mercer or dealer in textiles (*pl* (rare) **merceries**)

Mercia *n* the great Saxon kingdom of central England, the most famous monarch of which was Offa (757–796) who had a dyke constructed as a boundary between his kingdom and the Welsh, whom he defeated in battle in 779. Mercia was itself defeated by Egbert of Wessex (see **Cerdic**) in his creation of England and the northeastern part was later lost to the Vikings and only finally reunited as an English administrative unit when Canute was king. It ceased to exist as an administrative entity when William the Conqueror created his own feudal organization.

mere *n* a lake or pond: a Maori war club: a trinket of such shape *arch n* a boundary, a landmark: in Derbyshire, a measure (32 yards) of land containing lead ore (also see **stowce**) *now dial n* a marsh or fen *obs n* a mother: a mermaid or merman: (an arm of) the sea *adj* having nothing greater than the designation implies: executed by none other than the one or those specified *obs adj* pure: unmixed: renowned, famous, noble: beautiful *now dial vb* to mark out land by boundaries (note: The *n* mering is still standard English – see **mering**) *obs vb* to purify

Meredith *masc/fem pers n* meaning 'sea protector'

mereing *var fm n* **mering**

mereit *obs S fm n* **merit**

merell *var fm n* **meril** (see **nine men's morris**)

mergin *obs fm n* **margin**

meri *obs fm adj* **merry**

meril *n* a counter in a two-person rustic game called by various names but probably best known as nine men's morris (see **nine men's morris**)

mering *n* the fixing of boundaries: a boundary, a landmark (note: The *vb* mere is now *dial*)

merino *n* a Spanish breed of sheep: a fine dress fabric *orig* of this wool: a fine cotton and woollen yarn: products of this (*pl* **merinos**) *adj* of the sheep, its wool, or merino fabric

merion *obs n* midday

merise *n* a type of small black cherry

merism *n* the repetition of biological parts

merist *n* a divider

meristem *n* the developing cellular tissue of the younger parts of a plant

meristic *adj* pertaining to merism

merite *obs fm n* **merit**

meriter *obs n* one who or that which has merit

meritist *obs n* one who believes in the merit of good works

merl *obs fm vb* **marl**

merle *n* the blackbird (+*cap*) *fem pers n* meaning 'blackbird'

merlin *n* a species of European falcon (*arch n* the female of that species, the male being a **jack merlin**)

merling *obs n* the whiting *obs fm n* **merlin**

Mermis *n* the genus of the thunderworm, a slender, threadlike nematode which begins life as an internal parasite of a grasshopper, later spending adult life in the earth. Its name is derived from the fact that, during thunderstorms, it climbs plants and especially favours rose bushes.

meroistic *adj* producing imperfect ova alongside the perfect

Merops *n* of the three genera of birds called bee-eaters, 21 of the 24 species are placed in this genus

merrit *obs fm n* **merit**

merse *S n a* marsh or similar wetland *var fm obs vb* **merce**

mersion *n* the act of dipping, as in Baptism

mertil *obs fm n* **myrtle**

mertle *obs fm n* **myrtle**

mesail *n* the type of visor made for an armet

mesally *adv* mesially

mesaraic *adj* of or pertaining to the mesentery *n* one of the mesaraic veins

mesarch *adj* of plants, having the xylem or woody tissue formed in two stages

mescal *n* an intoxicating spirit made from aloes: a globe-shaped cactus of Mexico and southwestern USA, the small rounded nodules of which are chewed by certain Red Indians for their hallucinogenic effects

mescalin *n* a narcotic which induces powerful colour hallucinations and is obtained from the tops of a spineless cactus native to the border region of USA/Mexico

mese *n* the middle string of an ancient Greek seven-stringed lyre: the note it produced *now dial n* moss *S & dial vb* to appease: to settle (a dispute): to calm

meseems *arch vb* it seems to me (*var fm* **meseemeth** *pa t* **meseemed**)

mesentery *n* the double layer of a serous sac that is attached to the abdominal cavity and supports most of the small intestine (*pl* **mesenteries**)

mesher *obs fm n* **masher**

mesial *adj* pertaining to, situated in or directed to the median plane or middle line of a body

mesially *adv* in a mesial position or direction

mesian *adj* mesial

mesite *n* any of three species of flightless bird akin to the rail and found only in Madagascar

mesmerist *n* a hypnotist

mesne *adj* of a lord, holding an estate of a greater lord: of persons, acting in an intermediate capacity: of time, at a point between two specific dates *obs n* a mesne lord

Mesolithic *adj* belonging to the transitional period of Stone Age culture between food gathering and a settled agriculture

mesonic *adj* of a meson, a short-lived subatomic particle

mesotron *n* a meson (see **mesonic**)

Mesrop *pers n* St Mesrop the Teacher (circa 345–439) devised the Armenian alphabet and translated the New Testament and the Book of Proverbs into Armenian

messan *S n* a lapdog: a despised person

messen *obs fm S n* **messan**

messer *n* one who supplies meat to ships

messet *dial n* a lapdog

Messidor *n* harvest, the tenth month of the French Revolutionary calendar roughly corresponding to Cancer in the zodiac calendar

Messie *Obs fm n* **Messiah**

messin *arch fm S n* **messan**

messire *n* the equivalent of sir, formerly used as a mode of address for a Frenchman

mess tin *n* an all-purpose, military, individual catering utensil designed to serve in the field such purposes as those of saucepan, plate, cup etc

meste *obs fm n* **mustee**

mestee *var fm n* **mustee**

mester *dial fm n* **mister**

mesterie *Obs fm n* **mastery**

mesti *obs fm n* **mustee**

mestino *US n* a person of mixed ancestry (*pl* **mestinos, mestinoes**)

metage *n* the official weighing of various items such as grain, malt, apples and coal: the charge made for such weighing

metaled *US fm adj* **metalled**

metaling *US fm vbl infl* **metalling**

metalise *var fm vb* **metalize**, to treat with metal

metalist *var fm* (*esp US*) *n* **metallist**, one who works in metals: one who advocates a metal currency (contrast with **Greenback**)

metamer *n* a compound which shares the same composition and molecular weight as another but which has different chemical properties

metaphore *obs fm n* **metaphor**

metastable *adj* of such as atoms, gasses and liquids, in a state of unstable equilibrium

metel *n* the hairy thornapple

meteles *var fm Obs n* **metels**

metelis *var fm Obs n* **metels**

metels *Obs n* a dream

meter (*n*) *US fm n/vb* **metre**

methadone *n* a narcotic similar to morphine

methe *Obs n* respect, kindness: modesty *Obs adj* gentle *Obs vb* to have mercy upon *obs var fm n* **mead**, the alcoholic honey drink

metheglin *n* a spiced or medicated mead originally produced in Wales

methel *obs fm n* **metel**

métier *n* one's calling or profession: one's strong point or speciality

métis *n* a Canadian who is half French and half Red Indian (the *sing* is *masc* with a *fem* **métisse**, but the *pl* for both is **métisses**)

métisse *fem fm n* **métis** (*pl* **métisses**)

met man *n* a weather forecaster

metol *n* a sulphur-based salt used as a photographic negative developer

Metonic *adj* pertaining to Meton, the 5th century BC Athenian astronomer, or *esp* to the cycle of phases of the moon he was the first to observe (see **Metonic cycle**, below)

Metonic cycle *n* a cycle of nineteen years of the old Julian calendar in which the moon returns to approximately the same position relative to the sun, thus the phases of the moon occur at the same dates in the corresponding Julian year of each cycle. Since 1582, when the Gregorian calendar replaced the Julian, the reckoning has to be by the synodic month and this now means that the phases of the moon recur on the same day of the month of a cycle of 235 synodic months.

metrer *obs n* a versifier

metric foot *n* in prosody, or the study of the manner of verse construction, a metric foot is a number of syllables grouped together as a unit, as though that unit represented the tapping of one's foot to the rhythm of the verse. Each unit contains one syllable of main stress but the number of syllables within a unit varies and different names are given to the different types of metric foot. For example, **dactyl verse** has a metric foot consisting of one long syllable followed by two short syllables; **trochee verse** has a long followed by a short syllable; **spondee verse** consists of two long syllables.

metrician *n* a student of or a specialist in poetic metre

metrics *n* the science of measurement: the art that deals with (Latin and Greek) versification metre

metring *obs n* versification

metritis *n* inflammation of the uterus

metro *n* an underground railway *esp* that of Paris (+*cap*) *fems pers n* a character in a short Greek comedy of the 3rd century BC who, wishing to borrow her girl friend's olisbos, discovers that she has lent it to another girl friend who, unfortunately, has lent it to another. The friend, Coritto, recommends a cobbler called Cerdon but Metro, who knows two such men of that name is too embarrassed to visit either. (The humour is in the frustration – see **olisbos**.)

metronome *n* an instrument which produces a constant ticking sound to mark the time for a musician. The number of ticks to the minute is regulated by means of a weight which is adjusted on a reversed pendulum.

mettel *obs fm n* **metal**

mettle *n* courage, spirit: character

meuse *var fm n* **mews**, a stable converted into a dwelling *now dial n* muset (in all extant senses) *now dial vb* to escape through a muset

mewl *vb* of an infant, to whimper: of a cat, to miaow

mho *n* the unit of electrical conductance of a body with the resistance of one ohm (now replaced, in the latest metric system, by siemens)

mi *n* the third note of the tonic sol-fa system of musical notation (see **gamut**)

miasmal *adj* containing germs

Miastor *n* a genus of gall midges which, like the neotentic salamanders, remain at and reproduce at the larval stage. However, unlike salamanders but like aphids, reproduction is by parthenogenesis for several generations until a normal adult male and female generation arises. (See **neoteny, parthenogenesis**)

mica schist *n* a slaty rock of mica and quartz

micate *vb* to supply with mica, a mineral used as an insulator and as a substitute for glass

micella *n* a theoretical unit of living matter (*pl* **micellae**)

micellar *adj* of or pertaining to micella

miche *now dial vb* to skulk: to play truant *obs n* a wedge used for a ship's cannon *Obs n* a loaf of bread

micher *now dial n* a truant

micron *n* the one millionth part of a metre (*pl* **micra, microns**)

micropyle *n* the orifice through which pollen penetrates the female aspect

miction *obs n* the act of urinating

midden *n* a dunghill: a pile of rubbish (note: Usage is now mainly *dial* except as a *modf n* (examples below) or in the old proverb, *'A cock may crow on its own midden'*)

midden creel *n* a basket for carrying manure

midden mavis *arch n* a ragpicker

midden pit *n* a pit for manure

middenstead *n* the place where a midden is sited

middes *var fm now S n/obs vb* **mids**

middler *n* the worker who performs the second of three operations in the preparation of flax

midhour *n* the middle time: an intervening hour

midler *obs fm n* **middler** *obs comp adj* middle

midrange *n* the middle of a range

Midrash *n* one of a number of Jewish commentaries on the Old Testament which date between the 4th and 12th centuries AD and used allegorical interpretation (*pl* **Midrashim** or **Midrashoth**)

mids *now S n* the middle (part): a compromise *obs vb* to take the middle view of (WORD PUZZLER'S note: Whilst usage was in comparatively modern times, the *infl fms* cannot be presumed standard, e.g. in a work, published in 1693, the *3rd pers sing pr tense* is **midseth**)

midseth *obs vbl infl* see **mids**

mignote *obs n* a woman of loose morals

mihrab *n* an object in a mosque which marks the direction towards Mecca

miken *obs n* a herb used in salad

mikron *var fm n* **micron**

milady *n* the spoken form of 'my lady' used as a description of one for whom such an address would be made

Milan *modf n* for a type of steel made in the Italian city of Milan and formerly used for swords and armour (*−cap*) *obs n* the kite, a bird of prey

milden *vb* to make or become mild or milder

milder (*comp adj*) *dial vb* to crumble away (*lit/fig*)

Mildred *fem pers n* meaning 'mild power'

Milesian *adj* of or pertaining to Miletus, an ancient port of western Asia Minor, or to its inhabitants: of or pertaining to Milesius or his people, the legendary original Celts of Ireland (see **Milesius**) *n* an inhabitant of Miletus: a son or a subject of Milesius: an Irishman (*jocular*)

Milesius *pers n* a figure of Irish myth, also known as Miledh, whose activities mirror those of Brutus, the legendary founder of Britain. He journeyed from Asia Minor, via Spain, to Ireland where he and his people settled with him as the first Celtic king.

milge *obs vb* to dig round about

miling *obs n* a stripe

military (*adj/n*) *obs n* a military officer (*pl* **militaries**)

milkfish *n* of its various alternative names (awa, bandeng, bangos and salmon herring), the last of these best describes this six foot marine fish, as it is herring-like in appearance and salmon-like in lifestyle

Millen *obs fm n* **Milan**

milleped *var fm n* **millipede**, any of over 8,000 different species of slow-moving, armoured arthropods which adopt a different defence to the other well-known, multi-legged 'creepy-crawlies', the centipedes. Millipedes freeze or curl themselves up and rely on their armour and stink glands. Centipedes run away 'As fast as their little legs and legs and . . '

millering *n* the trade or work of a miller

milliare *n* a thousandth part of an are

millrace *n* the channel for, and the water which, turns a millwheel

milne *obs fm n* **mill**

milner *dial fm n* **miller** *obs fm n* **milliner**

milrea *obs fm n* **milreis** (*pl* **milreas**)

milreis *n* either of two coins, a Portuguese gold coin worth 4s $5\frac{1}{4}$d or a Brazilian silver coin worth 2s 3d (see **£sd** – under **L**) (note: The *var fm* is **milree** and only one of the earlier spelling forms had a letter S in the singular. The *obs fms incl* **milrea, milrey, millreye, milleray** and **milreise**.)

milrey *obs fm n* **milreis** (*pl* **milreys**)

milsey *S n* a milk strainer

milsie *obs fm S n* **milsey**

milt *n* the testes of a fish: the seminal fluid from such *vb* of a male fish, to release milt over freshly laid roe

milte *obs fm n* **milt**

milter *n* any adult male fish

milting *obs n* the classical description is one of 1587 which reads, '*The milting of Oxe, Cow or other beast is called of husbandmen when he will sodaine lie down if ye shall neuer so little, being at plough or cart*'. If one ignores today's sense of milting, it presumably means the sudden dropping to the ground of a draught animal (as though exhausted).

miltonia *n* any of various species of tropical American orchids having brightly coloured flowers

milz *var fm Obs n* **milce**, mercy

mim *n* the twenty-fourth letter of the Arabic alphabet

mimester *n* a mimic

mimosa *n* the sensitive plant, the leaves of which move as though the plant was annoyed or irritated by being touched

min *obs adj* less (only used in conjunction with more as **mair or min** (more or less)) *obs vb* to mention

minacity *n* the disposition to use threats: denunciation

minargent *n* a white-coloured alloy of copper, nickel, tungsten and aluminium

Mindel *adj/n* (of) the second of four glacial epochs which succeeded each other during the period of prehistory known as the Pleistocene

mineloa *n* an orange-like citrus fruit developed from a tangerine and grapefruit hybrid

Minerva *pers n* the Roman goddess of wisdom, corresponding to the Greek Athena

ming *dial n* a mixture *obs vb* to remind: to remember *var fm now dial vb* **meng**

mingde *obs pa pple now dial vb* meng

minge *vb* to urinate (*obs* except as the *vulgar n* for a woman's privy parts) *var fm now dial vb* **meng**

mingel *obs var fm vb* **mingle**

mingent *obs adj* of urination, incontinent

mingler *n* one who mingles

miniate *vb* to colour with vermillion

miniment *obs fm n* **muniment**

minimism *n* whilst the word can be broadly defined as the tendency to minimize the implications of accepted dogma, it is essentially concerned with papal infallibility. Effectively it means that, by appreciating the absolute minimum of subject matter on which considered papal judgment is deemed infallible, a theologian has the greatest possible liberty in taking a contrary view to that of a pope, even one in council *nonce n* absorption in minute details

minimist an undefined noun which appears to be exclusive to one particular dictionary and presumably means one who advocates or adheres to the theological view of minimism as used by Newman, rather than the nonce use of Coleridge. Its anagram is **intimism**.

ministre *Obs fm n* **minster**

minla *see* **Timaliiae**

Minoan *adj* of prehistoric Crete and its culture *n* a Cretan of that period

minoress *n* a Poor Clare, a nun of the second order of St Francis

minot *n* a former French dry measure which generally equated to three French bushels (39.36 litres) but varied according to product, region and historic period

minster *n* a monastery church or one of monastic origin: extended to a church of great importance *esp* a cathedral

minstre *Obs fm vb* **minister** *Obs fm n* **minster**

mintage *n* the process of minting (coins): coins or other products of minting: the fee paid for minting a coin: an impression stamped on a coin

minte *obs fm n/vb* **mint**

minuet (*n*) *vb* to dance a slow, stately minuet

minute (*n*) *vb* to ascertain a minute of time: to draft a document: to record a minute or memorandum

minuter *comp adj* minute

miqra *n* the Hebrew text of the Bible: a liturgical reading from it

Mirabel *fem pers n* meaning 'wonderful'

mirable *obs adj* wonderful *obs n* that which is wonderful

miret *dial n* the common tern, a species of birds akin to the gull

mirke *obs fm now dial vb* **mirk**, to darken or obscure

mirled *S adj* speckled

mirtel *obs fm n* **myrtle**

mirthe *var fm obs vb* **mirth**, to rejoice: to gladden *obs fm n* **mirth**

mirtle *now dial fm n/vb* **myrtle**

miry *adj* swampy (*comp* **mirier** *sup* **miriest**)

misadvise *vb* to advise incorrectly *obs vb* to take wrong advice

misagent *US n* a bad agent

misalter *vb* to alter wrongly

misate *see* **miseat**

misatone *US vb* to atone wrongly

misaunter *now dial n* misadventure

misavise *obs fm vb* **misadvise** (also, Chaucer used the spelling **misavyse** *Obs fm obs vb* **misadvise**)

miscel *obs fm n* **missel**

misdesert *arch n* the condition of being undeserving

misdiet *obs n* wrong diet *obsol vb* to diet improperly

misdo *vb* to do evil, wrong, harm or injury to: to do work improperly (*pa t* **misdid** *pa pple* **misdone**)

misdoer *n* a wrong or evil-doer, an offender

misdread *obs n* dread of evil *obs vb* to be in dread

misease *arch n sing/pl* trouble, misery, distress

miseat *US vb* to eat improperly (*infl fms* as the *vb* eat – **misate, miseaten** etc)

misentreat *vb* to ill-treat or ill-use (GAME PLAYER'S note: Designated extant by the dictionary used for the UK Scrabble championship. Other experts, however, consider that, as the last recorded literary usage was 1583, it is *obs.*)

miser (*n*) *vb* to hoard: to extract earth by the use of a miser (see **mizer**)

misère *n* in solo whist, a bid to take no tricks despite the attempts of the other three players to force such a happening (**misère ouvert** *n* a similar but more difficult bid as, this time, the player exposes his or her hand after the first card has been led (also called **open misère**))

misgo *now dial vb* to go astray (*lit/fig*) (*infl fms* the same as the *vb* to go, i.e. *pa pple* **misgone** *pa t* **miswent**)

Mishna *n* the first part of the *Talmud*, a summary of all rabbinical scholarship prior to the great rabbi, Juda (born AD 150), in the form of his decisions and traditions: a paragraph from this work (*pl* **Mishnayoth**) (also see **Gemara**)

misinter *vb* to inter improperly

misken *S & dial vb* to misunderstand: to be ignorant of

mislane *obs fm now dial n* **maslin** (in senses other than brass)

misleader *n* one who or that which misleads

misleared *S & dial adj* ill-bred

mislearn *vb* to learn incorrectly

mismake *vb* to make badly (*pa pple* **mismade**)

mismean *obs vb* to misinterpret: to intend wrongly

mismetre *vb* to spoil the metre of (a poem)

misname *vb* to name wrongly

mison *obs fm n* **mizen**

misparse *vb* to parse incorrectly

misplead *vb* to plead wrongly

misprise *var fm vb* **misprize**, to scorn: to fail to appreciate the qualities of

misrate *vb* to estimate incorrectly

misread *vb* to read incorrectly

misrelate *vb* to relate incorrectly

missal *n* a book containing the basic service of the Mass, the different prayers and other varying parts which accord to the complete year e.g. the different forms for such as Easter, Christmas etc

missaw *see* **missee**

missee *vb* to misinterpret that which is under observation (*infl fms* **misseen, missaw, misseeing**)

misseen see **missee**

missel *n* a short *fm* of **missel thrush** or **mistle thrush** *obs n* mistletoe

missen *obs fm n* **mizen** or **mizzen**

missend *vb* to make an error in sending (*pa t* **missent**)

missent *pa t vb* missend

misser *obs n* a term of contempt for a Catholic priest during the period of the persecution of Catholics

misset *vb* to misplace *S vb* to upset *obs fm dial n* **messet**

missioner *n* a missionary

missle *obs fm n* **missel**

misson *obs fm n* **mizen**

misstate *vb* to state incorrectly

missteer *vb* to steer incorrectly

mistaste *obs vb* to spoil the taste of: to have no taste for

mistate *obs fm vb* **misstate**

miste *obs fm n* **mist** *Obs vb* to take mixtum, a light breakfast in a monastery

misteach *vb* to teach badly or wrongly

mistel *Obs fm n* **missel**

mistell (*vb*) *pa t/pa pple* **mistold**

misten *obs vb* to cloud another's perception

mister (*n*) *vb* to address as Mr *obs vb* to require: to have need of: to be necessary

misters *obs fm n* **mistress**

mistery *var fm n* **mystery** in the sense of one's trade or profession, *arch* or *obs* in other senses

mistico *n* a Mediterranean, two-sailed coasting vessel (*pl* **misticoes**)

mistide *Obs n* a mishap *Obs vb* to suffer misfortune

mistle *var fm dial vb* **mizzle**, to rain gently *obs fm n* **missel**

mistrace *vb* to trace wrongly

mistral *n* a cold, dry, violent northwest wind of southern France: a type of worsted dress fabric

mistre *obs fm n* **mister** *var fm obs vb* **mister**

mistres *obs fm n* mistress

mistress (*n*) *vb* to provide with a mistress: to become the mistress of (an art): to dominate as a mistress

mistrie *obs fm n* mystery in all senses

misween *obs vb* to have a wrong opinion: to misjudge

miter *var fm* (*mainly US*) *n/vb* **mitre**

miterer *US n* one who or that which produces the right-angled joints in woodworking known as mitres (*US*, miters)

mither *dial vb* to worry, to bother, to confuse, to perplex

Mithra *pers n* the Persian god of fire and one of the many local gods adopted by the Romans who called him Mithras and extended his worship throughout their empire. He is either an independent god or, possibly, the fire aspect of Mazdha, the great Persian god of light and creation whose worship is still continued by latter-day Zoroastrians in Iran and India. By chance, during relatively recent excavation work in London, an ancient Roman temple to Mithras (Mithra) was discovered.

Mithras *see* **Mithra**

mitoses *pl* mitosis

mitosis *n* the series of changes in indirect cell division before final division into two fully mature daughter cells (*pl* **mitoses**)

mitral *adj* of, pertaining to or resembling a mitre *n* a valve of the heart having such a shape

mittle *S vb* to hurt or injure

mitty *dial n* the storm petrel

mity *adj* infested with mites (*comp* **mitier** *sup* **mitiest**)

mizen *n* mizzen, a sail on the mizen mast or mizzenmast of a ship

mizer *var fm n* **miser**, an extremely long cylindrical tube used for boring long tubular holes in the earth

mlechchha *n* one who does not practise Hinduism

mna *n* an ancient coin and unit of weight in Greece and Greek-speaking countries of the eastern Mediterranean

mnam *Obs n* mna

mnemon *n* a name for a supposed unit of memory

mo *n* a Japanese unit of weight (ten mo = one fun)

moate *obs fm ns* **moat, mote**

moater *var fm n* **moter**

Möbius strip *n* a mathematical curiosity which is fun for the non-mathematician. A single long strip of paper (the length and width are immaterial) is given a twist of 180° and the ends are joined together. The centre of this 'twisted loop' is now marked with a long continuous line until that line meets itself. The first surprise is that this line is on 'both sides', but the second surprise comes when you cut the whole length of that line. What you will have proved, if you try it, is that it is a one-sided surface, not a two-sided surface, of a normal loop.

moble *now dial vb* to muffle or wrap up

mocha *n* one of several species of moths, basically brown in colour but with variegated grey markings *dial n* a cat with intermingled black and brown colouring (+*cap*) *n* a fine quality coffee originally from Mocha on the Red Sea

modder *dial vb* to mutter *var fm now dial n* **mauther** (*obs* except as a *modf n* for a calf as **modder calf**, a young calf)

model (*n*/*vb*) *infl fms* British, **modelled/-lling**: US, **modeled/-ling**

modeler *US fm n* **modeller**

modelist *n* one who makes models

modelize *obs vb* to construct to the specifications shown by a model: to model: to give a particular shape to: to organize: to symbolize

modena *n* a rich purple or crimson colour

modiste *n* a milliner, a dressmaker

modius *n* an ancient Roman measure of capacity for corn (*approx* a peck): a liquid and dry measure of the Middle Ages (*approx* a bushel – for bushel and peck see **bushel**): a conical headdress sometimes worn by such classical deities as Jupiter, Pluto and Demeter (*pl* **modii**)

modren *Obs n pl* mothers

module (*n*) *obs vb* to sing: to mould or shape

modulet *obs n* a small model

moduli *pl* modulus

modulus *n* a term used in mathematics for various numerical properties such as a whole number which can be divided exactly into the difference between two other whole numbers (e.g. 5 is the only modulus of 13 and 38 (38 – 13 = 25 and 25 can only be divided by 5) whereas 2, 4, 5 and 10 are all moduli of 13 and 33) (*pl* **moduli, moduluses**)

Mohegan *n* a Mahican who formerly dwelt with his tribe near the rivers of lower Connecticut (see **Mahican**)

Mohican *n* a Mahican who formerly dwelt with his tribe at the Hudson river section of their territory (see **Mahican**)

moider *var fm dial vb* **mither** *obs fm n* **moidore**

moidore *n* a Portuguese gold coin worth *approx* 27 shillings, which circulated in Britain during the early part of the 18th century: that value

moil *arch n* toil, drudgery *dial n* turmoil, confusion: mud, mire: a hornless cow *obs n* a very sweet variety of apple: cider from that apple *dial adj* hornless *arch vb* to moisten: to toil *now dial vb* of a pig or badger, to root up

moile *var fm arch n*/*obs n* **moil** *var fm dial n* **moil** (all senses other than cow) *obs fm arch vb*/*now dial vb* **moil**

moiler *n* one who toils or labours

moire *n* silk or other material having a watery appearance *vb* to give a watery appearance to

moist (*adj/n*) *now dial vb* to moisten

moiste *obs fm n/now dial vb* **moist**

moister *comp adj* moist

moite *obs fm n* **moiety**, one of two (equal) parts: the better half (i.e. wife)

moither *var fm dial vb* **mither**

mol *n* the gram-molecule, that weight of a substance expressed in grams numerically equal to its molecular weight

molarity *n* the concentration of a solution expressed in mols

molder *now US fm n/vb* **moulder**

moldy *US fm adj* **mouldy** (*comp* **moldier** *sup* **moldiest**)

molen *obs fm n* **mullein**, any of various species of herbaceous plants having woolly leaves and yellow flowers

moler *n* a mole-catcher

molerat *n* any of various rodents which adapt to the way of life of the totally unrelated mole. Unlike moles – insectivores who burrow with their feet – the various molerats are vegetarians and normally tunnel with their teeth.

molies *pl* moly

moline *her adj* of or resembling the curved and expanded extremities of the spindle of the upper millstone of a corn mill *her n* a short *fm* of **cross moline**, a cross having a horizontal bar which resembles an upper millstone spindle

molla *var fm n* **mullah** (see **mollah**)

mollah *var fm n* **mullah**, a Muslim teacher or preacher (also see apt anagram, **ollahm**)

Moloch *n* the Phoenician chief god as known to the Canaanites and to whom children were sacrificed as burnt offerings (*–cap*) *n* the 'thorny devil' of the Australian desert regions, a harmless but extremely ugly, thorned, ant-eating lizard

moly *n* in Greek myth, a fabulous herb with white flowers and black roots that has power against sorcery: various plants which might be that moly *esp* a species of wild garlic (*pl* **molies**)

momente *obs fm n* **moment**

monacid *adj* of an acid, having one hydroxal group that can replace the hydrogen (also see *n* **triacid**)

monad *n* the number one: a single-celled organism such as a flagellate of the genus *Monas*: a metaphysical concept of the indivisibility of a spirit, thus any spirit: any indestructible unit: an atom, ion or radical with a valency (or property relative to an atom of hydrogen) of one (*pl* **monads, monades**)

monades *pl* monad

monadic *adj* composed of units

monadism *n* the theory of the monadic nature of matter: a philosophical concept devised by Gottfried Wilhelm Leibnitz (1646–1716), a German philosopher and mathematician, concerning monads: any other such concept related to atomic theory

monal *n* the monaul or Himalayan pheasant, the male of which is the most brilliantly coloured of all the many different species of pheasants

Monarda *n* a genus of North American aromatic herbs, one species of which yields both an oil and camphor (*–cap*) *n* a plant of this genus

moner *n* a conjectured simplest possible animal life-form (*pl* **monera**) *obs fm n* **manner**

monera *pl* moner or moneron

moneron *var fm n* **moner** (*pl* **monera**)

Moneta *pers n* the supreme Roman goddess Juno in a relatively minor personification as the goddess of finances

monetise *var fm vb* **monetize**, to put into circulation as money

moneto *var fm n* **manito** (*pl* **monetos**)

MONEYERS WEIGHTS At the Mint, the Company of Moneyers (abolished in 1837) recognized a system of very minute weights which were subdivisions of the grain (troy), the lowest weight legally recognized. The moneyers weights were 24 blanks to the perit, 20 perits to the dwit, 24 dwits to the mite, 20 mites to the grain. The grain, which is still used for precious metals and gemstones, continues in the troy system as follows: – 24 grains to the pennyweight, 20 pennyweights to the troy ounce, 12 troy ounces to the troy pound. (By contrast there are 7,000 grains to the pound avoirdupois.)

monger *n* a dealer or trader, now mainly used as the second element of such as cheesemonger or fishmonger etc

monial *arch n* a mullion or vertical bar dividing glass in a window *obs n* a nun

Monica *fem pers n* meaning 'unique'

monier *var fm n* **moneyer**, one who mints or coins money

monism *n* the philosophical concept that, in the ultimate, only one being exists

monist *n* one who believes in the existence of a solitary supreme force (i.e. God but no Satan or Satan but no God)

monistic *adj* of or pertaining to monism

monit *obs n* a remainder

monocracy *n* government by one

monocular *adj* of, pertaining to or having only one eye *n* a one-eyed person

monogenist *n* one who maintains the theory that mankind originated from a single pair

monogenous *adj* asexual

monogeny *n* the theory that mankind is descended from a single ancestral pair: asexual reproduction: direct development of an ovum into an organism resembling the parent

monogram *n* a design of two or more letters interwoven as one symbol i.e. ♇, the combination of P and L used to represent the planet Pluto in both astrology and astronomy: a single character in writing or a mark representing a word

monography *n* a monograph on a scientific subject other than natural history for which the term is now considered to be *obs*

monologise *var fm vb* **monologize**, to talk in monologue

monologist *n* one who talks in monologues

monology *n* the habit of talking in monologue

monometer *n* a line of verse comprising one metric foot: a poem of such lines

monotreme *n* one of an order of primitive egg-laying mammals which comprises two families, the echidnas and the platypuses

monotype *n* a sole species which is the only member of its genus and family and even, like the hoatzin, of its own sub-order. Whilst the hoatzin is included in the order *Galliformes* (see **BIRD CLASSIFICATION**), some authorities would have it in its own order: a print taken from a metal plate on which the illustration has been directly painted, hence only one copy is possible

monotypic *adj* having or containing only one type (i.e. such as a genus having only one species)

monstre *adj* gigantic, huge *obs n* a monstrance *obs fm n* **monster**

montaria *n* a Brazilian canoe cut from a single log

monte *n* a card game: a small forest in a Spanish-American country

montem *n* an old festival (last celebrated in 1844) by scholars at Eton who wore fancy dress in a walk through the streets

montero *n* a Spanish huntsman's round cap having flaps for drawing over the ears (*pl* **monteros**)

montre *n* an organ stop, the pipes of which form part of the case: the visible pipes of an organ

monture *n* a mounting or setting as that for a diamond

moocher *now dial n* a truant: one who gathers blackberries *now slg n* an idler

mood (*n*) *obs vb* to brood (in the reflective sense)

mooder *obs fm n* **mother**

moonite *n* one who dwells on the moon (an extant word coined in 1762)

moonset *n* the nocturnal equivalent of sunset

Moon type *n* a system of embossed lettering for the blind devised by a Dr Moon

moony *adj* relating to the moon: moon-shaped: illuminated by the moon: stupidly dreamy (*comp* **moonier** *sup* **mooniest**)

moore *obs fm adj/adv/now dial n* **more** *obs fm n/vb* **moor**

moory *n* a type of Indian cloth *adj* of or pertaining to a moor or heath, abounding in heath: marshy (*comp* **moorier** *sup* **mooriest**)

mooter *n* one who initiates a question

moper *n* one who mopes

morainal *adj* of or pertaining to a moraine

moraine *n* a ridge of mainly surface material such as earth and stones carried by a glacier and deposited at its edge

moraled *var fm adj* **moralled**, having morals

morat *n* a mulberry-flavoured honey drink

morate *n* a salt of moric acid (a variety of tannic acid)

morbus *L n* a disease (used as a combining form with another Latin term which specifies the actual type)

mordancy *n* sarcastic force

more (*adj/adv*) *now dial n* the root of a plant: the stump of a tree *now dial vb* to take root: to uproot

moreish *collq adj* that makes for more of the same

morel *n* the plant, black nightshade: other species of nightshade: morello cherry: a type of edible fungus: a dark-coloured horse

moren *obs fm ns* **morn, mourn, murrain**

morendo *adj/adv* of music, fading away

morfer *n* the lesser puffin, a species of auk

morgay *n* the bounce or lesser spotted dog-fish, a small shark marketed, in Britain, as rock salmon (also see apt anagram, **goramy**)

morgen *n* a Dutch and American measure of land (*approx* two acres): a mermaid in Breton folklore *Obs fm n* **morn**

morice *obs fm n/vb* **morris**

moriche *n* a South American palm, the fruit of which is known as either the moriche apple or the moriche nut

moringa *n* the horseradish tree which is the source of both ben nuts and an edible pod-like capsule. Oil of ben nut is a watchmaker's lubricant.

morish *var fm adj* **moreish**

morkin *n* a farm animal which dies from a cause other than slaughter

mormaer *n* the high steward of a province of ancient Scotland, a rank immediately below that of king (also see **toisech**)

mormaor *var fm n* **mormaer**

mornay *n* a cheese-flavoured cream sauce

morne *n* the blunted head of a tilting lance: a small round hill *adj* dismal *obs fm ns* **morn, mourn**

morned *her adj* of a spear, having a blunt head

morris *n* see **nine men's morris**: see **morris dance**: the troupe performing that dance (*var fm* of above **morrice** *obs fms* of above *incl* **morice**): a fish named after a Mr Morris which was believed to be a new species but turned out to be the aborted young of a conger eel *vb* to dance (a particular measure)

morris dance *n* though the word 'morris' is derived from an earlier spelling of 'Moorish' (i.e. Arabic) the dance itself is a British folk celebration. Traditionally, the dancers represent the characters in the Robin Hood legends.

morse *n* a highly decorated and valuable fastening for a cope: the walrus (+*cap*) *vb* the sending of a message by Morse code

morsel (*n*/*vb*) *infl fms* British, **morselled**/**-lling**: US **morseled**/**-ling**

morsse *obs fm n* **morse**, the walrus

mort *n* see **SALMON**: a harlot: lard: the note sounded on a horn at the kill of a deer *arch n* the death or kill of such *dial n* the skin of a sheep which has died a natural death: a great quantity *obs vb* to put to death

mortalise *var fm vb* **mortalize**, to make or become mortal

morte *obs fm n*/*arch n*/*dial n* **mort** (in all senses other than lard or quantity)

morter *obs fm n*/*vb* **mortar**

mortier *n* an ornamental velvet cap formerly worn by high officials in France

mortise *n* a slot made to receive a tenon *vb* to cut a mortise: to join together by a mortise and tenon (also, in this sense, to tenon)

mortiser *n* a woodworking machine for cutting mortises: one who tends such

mortre *obs fm n* **mortar**, a vessel

mortsafe *n* a heavy grating used to cover a corpse to prevent rising from the dead

morunga *obs fm n* **moringa**

Mosaism *n* the laws and ceremonies as defined by Moses: adherence to such

moser *var fm obs n* **mosser**

mossel *Obs fm n* **morsel**

mosser *n* one who cuts peat: a collector of moss *obs n* one employed in covering a roof with moss

moster *var fm obs vb* **moisture**, to moisten or make damp *obs fm n*/*vb* **muster**

mostre *obs fm n*/*vb* **muster**

moter *n* one who removes motes (imperfections) from wool

moth (*n*) *vb* to hunt for moths

mothy *adj* full of moths (*comp* **mothier** *sup* **mothiest**)

motioner *obs n* a proposer, an instigator (GAME PLAYER'S note: The dictionary used for the North American Scrabble championship lists the word without dated comment. As it does not employ labels of any description (*arch, dial, nonce, slg*, etc) so one presumes that it agrees with the last recorded British usage of 1665, but accepts the soundness of using *obs* words for word games (other examples pertain). The dictionary, incidentally, is produced by a leading American lexographic publishing house specifically for Scrabble. The word does not appear in the general dictionary used for the UK Scrabble championship.)

motmot *n* any of eight species of medium-sized, bright green or turquoise-coloured insectivorous birds akin to the kingfisher and found in Central and South America

motorial *adj* causing, conveying, imparting motion

motser *Austr n* a large sum of money (from gambling)

motza *var fm Austr n* **motser**

mouch *now dial vb* to eat greedily (the *obs n* **mouching** is presumed to mean eating greedily)

moucher *var fm now slg n/now dial n* **moocher**

moul *obs n* a mould or shaped cavity used for the giving of a specific shape to the cooled solid form of a liquid: a mould or woolly growth which develops on damp organic matter *now dial vb* to grow mouldy *obs vb* to mould or shape

moule *var fm obs n* **moul**, the mouldy growth *var fm obs vb* **moul** *obs fm now dial vb* **moul**

moure *var fm obs ns* **more**, a mulberry tree, **maur**, an ant

mouse (*n*) *vb* of a cat or owl, to hunt for mice: of a person, to prowl after the fashion of a mousing cat

mousebird *n* any of six species of finch-sized African songbirds with a tufted crest and a long, slender tail

mouse deer *n* any species of chevrotains

mousel *obs fm n/vb* **muzzle**

mousle *arch vb* to pull about in a rough manner

moutan *n* a tree peony

mouter *S fm n* **multure**

mouterer *S fm n* **multurer**, one who pays a toll for the grinding of his corn at a mill

mowle *var fm obs n/vb* **moul** *obs fm now dial vb* **moul**

mowsle *var fm arch vb* **mousle**

moyle *n* a large wedge used in quarrying: a type of drill used in quarrying *var fm dial n/adj* **moil,** hornless (cow) *obs fm n/vb* **moil** (in all other senses)

mu *n* the twelfth letter of the Greek alphabet: such used as a symbol for micron (GAME PLAYER'S note: The local rules of the UK Scrabble championship bar this and all similar words which describe a letter of any language unless, like **zed**, another meaning pertains. By contrast, the Americans, Australians, Canadians etc reject this exclusion and play both mu and its *pl* mus. Other than for the UK Scrabble contest, it is perfectly valid for all word games. So, too, is any similar word.)

mudge *S vb* to budge *dial vb* to damage

mudpuppy *n* any of four species of salamanders which retain their larval gills in adult life but which, unlike the axolotl, cannot be induced to metamorphose into complete adults. Mudpuppies look like eels with tiny legs and are found in North America. Their only near relative is the degenerate olm of Yugoslavia. (Also see **axolotl, Proteus** (*– cap*))

mudstone *n* a grey shale which readily decomposes into mud

Muffet *pers n* the real Miss Muffet who, in the nursery rhyme, sat on a tuffet was Patience Muffet, the daughter of a 16th century doctor. It is hardly surprising that she was scared by the spider, as her father used to prescribe them for swallowing as pills! (*– cap*) *dial n* the whitethroat, a species of insectivorous warbler

muggle *obs n* an ideal word for a party game as it has one, two or possibly even three different meanings and nobody knows what any of them are. In a 17th century drinking contest for 'the muggle' the first drinker drinks one pint, the second two pints, etc. Ten years earlier (in 1607) part of a poem read, '*Oh the parting of us twain, hath caused me mighty pain, and I shall never be married until I see my muggle again*'. The third possibility is that it is alleged to be a Kentish word for a tail (**muggling** being an *obs* word for a tailed man) – scholars dissociate the Kentish tail from the other meaning or meanings of muggle, which is a pity as it spoils a possible meaning of the poem.

Mujahed *n* an Afghan Islamic freedom fighter of any group which, since 1979, has been contesting the Russian invasion (*pl* **Mujahedin**)

mule (*n*) *var fm vb* **mewl**

mu-meson *n* a subatomic particle with a weak interaction

mumpoker *dial n* an Isle of Wight mischievous, solitary fairy which delights in frightening humans

muniment *n* a charter, title deed or other document preserved as evidence of the rights or privileges of those to whom it pertains: anything serving as a defence

munite *vb* to fortify

munster *Obs fm n* **minster**, a church (+*cap*) *n* a province in Eire: a port on the Dortmund–Ems canal, West Germany

munter *obs S n* a watch (the timepiece)

muntjac *n* any of various species of Asian deer which, unlike many ungulates, have the scent-marking gland on their feet (see **tear pit**)

muqaddam *n* in India, a leading minor official or local headman of some description

muraena *n* a name applied by the ancient Romans to any edible eel and now confined to the moray eel

murdre *Obs fm n/vb* **murder**

mure *vb* to wall in: to wall up

murein *n* a type of polymer or complex chemical compound

murena *var fm n* **muraena**

murex *n* any of various species of carnivorous molluscs *incl* Venus comb and dye murex, the Mediterranean rock shell known since ancient Phoenician times as the source of Royal Tyrian purple, a rich red-purple dye subsequently used for the robes of the Roman emperors (*pl* **murices, murexes**)

murices *pl* murex

murine *adj* resembling a mouse: of the mouse family *n* a member of that family (also see **ANIMAL ADJECTIVES**)

murn *now dial fm vb* **mourn**

Murngin *n* one of the aboriginal languages spoken in the northern part of Australia

murr *now dial vb* to make a harsh sound

murrain *n* a disease of sheep or cattle

murrained *adj* suffering from murrain

muryan *dial n* a Cornish fairy which is the soul of a dead heathen, too good for Hell and not good enough for Heaven. Like the various Celtic water horses (see **Water Horse**) it, too, has the power of shape-shifting but, with each manifestation as a different creature, it gradually diminishes in size until it is the size of an ant and eventually disappears out of the world altogether. (Also see **bucca** and **pisky**): an ant, another Cornish meaning of the word but allied in the sense that, in Cornwall, it is considered unlucky to kill an ant

muscal *n* any species of moss

muscarine *n* a poison found in certain fungi

muscatel *n* a rich sweet wine made from muscat grapes: the (dried) grape of the muscat vine *obs n* a variety of pear

muset *now dial n* a gap (in a hedge) through which hunted animals (*esp* hares) escape: a loophole (*lit/fig*): the agility and skill of a hare in evading capture (also see *now dial vb* **meuse**) *obs n* a shrew, the rodent

musett *obs fm now dial n* **muset**

musha *Ir interj* of surprise

musher *n* the driver of a dog-sled team in Alaska and the Canadian Arctic

musk deer *n* any of three species of deer, the buck of which scent-marks territory with musk, a brownish, waxlike substance valued as an ingredient in perfume. The gland which produces musk is located near the abdomen. (Also see **tear pit**)

musmon *n* the moufflon, the wild sheep of southern Europe

musmone *obs fm n* **musmon**

musrole *var fm obs n* **musrol**, the noseband of a bridle

mussit *var fm now dial n* **muset**

must (*vb*) *adj* of the state of sexual frenzy to which the male of the elephant and the camel are periodically subject *n* new wine: mouldiness *dial n* apple juice used for cider: pear juice used for perry *now dial vb* to become mouldy (*infl fms* **musted/-ing**) *Anglo-Ind vb* of an elephant, to develop a state of sexual frenzy (*infl fms* **musted/-ing**)

mustee *n* the offspring of a union between a white and a quadroon

Mustelidae *n pl* the weasel family, comprising badgers, ferret, grisons, martens, minks, otters, polecats, ratel, skunks, stoat or ermine, tayra, weasel (or weasels, if the least weasel is accepted as a different species), wolverine and zorilla (note: The sub-families *Lutrinae* and *Mustelinae* have their own *adjs*, lutrine and musteline respectively, though musteline is also extended to any member of the family. To add to the confusion, musteline also applies to the dogfish – see **ANIMAL ADJECTIVES**.)

Mustelinae *n pl* the weasel and marten subfamily of the *Mustelidae*

mustre *obs fm vb* **muster**

musti *obs fm n* **mustee**

mutagen *n* a substance that produces biological mutations

mutant *n* that living form which has arisen due to a process of mutation *adj* of, undergoing or the result of mutation

mu'ter *obs fm n* **multure** (GAME PLAYER'S note: Not valid for play due to apostrophe)

muteness *n* the state of being mute

mutest *sup adj* mute

mutine *adj* of a woman, unsubmissive *obs n/vb* (to) rebel

mutism *n* the condition of being mute or completely incapable of producing speech: the process of checking the fermentation of wine

muumuu *n* a type of loose dress worn in Hawaii

mwami *n* the native ruler of the former country Ruanda-Urundi, Africa

mwile *var fm now dial vb* **moil** *dial fm arch vb* **moil**

my (*possessive adj/interj*) *obs fm n* **mi**

mygale *n* the shrew-mouse: the bird spider

myleon *n* the spinal cord

myogen *n* a water-soluble protein found in muscle

myosin *n* a substance present in muscular tissue which coagulates after death

myosote *n* the forget-me-not

myotic *adj* of myosis, excessive contraction of the pupil of the eye

myrebane *var fm n* **mirbane**, a substance having an aroma like that of bitter almonds and used in perfumery

myringa *n* the eardrum

myrtel *obs fm n* **myrtle**

myrtle *n* any of various evergreen shrubs *esp* a southern European species having white or pink flowers, shiny leaves and aromatic blue berries *now dial vb* to waste away, crumble

mysteri *obs fm n* **mystery** in all senses

mythe *obs fm n* **myth**

mythologer *n* a mythologist, a writer of myths or one versed in them

mythus *n* a myth (*pl* **mythuses**)

N

na *S adv* no: not

naa *dial fm adj/adv* **no**

naam *n* the distraint of personal goods and chattels *vb* to distrain

Nabonassar *pers n* a king of ancient Babylon, from whose accession the Babylonians began their calendar at midday Wednesday 26 February 747 BC. Presumably the French Revolutionary Calendar was modelled, in part, on this early chronological record as it, too, had a year of twelve months, each of thirty days, with an additional five days. However, as the Babylonians made no adjustment for leap years, the Julian calendar was an essential replacement within the Roman Empire. This failure to adjust meant that the Babylonian year fell one day earlier every four years than the more accurate Julian year. In time this would have made 1,461 Babylonian years equal to 1,460 Julian years.

nache *arch n* the rump *esp* that of an ox or cow

nacre *n* a smooth, shining, irridescent substance, more popularly known as **mother-of-pearl**, which forms the inner layer of certain shells such as those of pearl oysters, abalones and mussels: the shellfish which yields mother-of-pearl

nacred *adj* having the hues of mother-of-pearl

nacreous *adj* consisting of or resembling nacre: displaying the hues of nacre

nacrite *n* a pearly-scaled mineral usually found in mica slate

nadder *obs fm n* **adder**

naddre *obs fm n* **adder**

naething *S fm n/adv* **nothing**

nagari *n* the group of alphabets which includes devanagari, the official script for Hindi

naggin *var fm n* **noggin**

nagor *n* a West African antelope

naides *pl* nais

naïf *see* **naïve**

naile *obs fm n/vb* **nail**

nailer *n* a maker of nails

nailrod *n* a strip of iron from which nails are cut: that particular metal *Austr/NZ n* a stick of coarse dark tobacco

nailset *n* a steel rod used for driving a nail into something

nailsick *adj* of a boat, leaking at its nail holes

nainsel *S n* own self

Naire *obs fm n* **Nair**, a member of the noble and military caste of the Malabar region of India

nais *n* a river nymph of Greek myth: a freshwater worm akin to the earthworm (*pl* **naides**)

naist *dial vb* to tease: to remind someone of a disagreeable task

naisty *var fm now dial vb* **nasty**

nait *obs vb* to use (extant in the *dial fm* **nate**): to refuse

naite *var fm obs vb* **nait**, to use

naïve *adj* simple, natural, artless, ingenuous (**naïve** (*fem*) and **naïf** (*masc*) are treated as neutral *var fms* of each other though a literal 'rough' diamond was formerly known as a **naïf stone** and never referred to as a 'naïve stone') *US n* one who is naïve

naker *n* a kettledrum *obs vb* to beat upon a naker

nallah *n* a river, stream or watercourse: a riverbed, a ravine (*var fms* **nulla, nullah**)

nam *var fm n* **naam** *var fm Obs n* **mnam** (see **mna**) *Obs pa t vb* nim

namechild *n* a child named after oneself

nameson *n* a male namechild

nammet *dial n* a snack (*var fms incl* **enamet, neemit** and **nummet**)

nape (*n*) *obs vb* to hit on the back of the neck, hence **naping** *obs n* the action of the *vb*

napery *S n* (table) linen

napet *obs n* a napkin

napier *n* one in charge of the Royal table linen

nappe *n* a fold in rock in which the axial plane is horizontal or sub-horizontal *obs fm n/vb* **nap**

nar *now dial adj* near (*comp* **narer, narrer** or **narder** *sup* **narest, narrest**) *now S & dial adv* near, nigh

narceia *var fm n* **narceine**

narcein *var fm n* **narceine**

narceine *n* a bitter, crystalline derivative of opium

narcotine *n* a bitter derivative of opium having medicinal properties

narcotise *var fm vb* **narcotize**, to adminster a narcotic to: to deaden or dull

narcotism *n* the state of stupor or insensibility produced by the use of narcotics

narcotist *n* a drug addict

nard *n* a plant from the East which was the source of the ancient aromatic ointment, nard or spikenard (now generally reckoned to be the root of *Nardostachys Jatamansi* of northern India): that ointment: matgrass or marram grass, the species which is commonly found on sand dunes *vb* to anoint with nard

narder *comp now dial adj* nar

narel *obs n* a nostril

narest *sup now dial adj* nar

narghile *n* a hookah, a Turkish smoking device in which the tobacco is placed in a (coconut) receptacle and the smoke is then breathed through water

nargile *var fm n* **narghile**

nargileh *var fm n* **narghile**

nargilly *var fm n* **narghile**

nargily *var fm n* **narghile**

narine *adj* of the nostrils

narr *now dial vb* of a dog, to snarl or growl

narre *obs fm now dial vb* **narr** *obs fm now dial adj* **nar**

narrest *sup now dial adj* nar

nas see **be**

Nasalis *n* the genus of the proboscis monkey and the pig-tailed monkey (see **langur**)

nasalise *var fm vb* **nasalize**, to speak through the nose: to render nasal in pronunciation or sound

nasard *n* an organ stop

nascent *adj* in the act of birth: starting to develop or grow

naselin *Ork adj* well-matched

nash *slg vb* to go away

nasion *n* the point where the nasal bones meet the skull

Naskhi *n* Arabic flowing handwriting

Nassak *n* the name of a famous diamond

Nasser, Gamal Abdel *pers n* (1918–70) the second president of Egypt and the only president of the short-lived United Arab Republic, a federation of Egypt, Syria and Yemen

nastaliq *n/adj* (of) an Arabic script, developed in the 15th century, used mainly for Persian poetical writings and in Urdu and Malay manuscripts

naster *dial vb* to befoul: to render nasty

nastic *adj* of plant movements, governed by internal cellular pressure superior to the direction of the external stimulus

nastier *comp adj* nasty

nasty (*adj*) *collq n* an offensive person, film or object *now dial vb* to make unpleasant: to commit a nuisance

nasute *n* a soldier termite with beaked mandibles *adj* beaked: keen-scented *obs adj* sagacious, wise (*comp* **nasuter** *presumed sup* **nasutest**)

nat *n* a Burmese spirit or demon *now dial n* a mat *dial n* a straw mattress

natal (*adj*) *obs n* a birthday feast

Natalie *fem pers n* meaning 'birth'

natatorium *US n* a swimming pool

natch *var fm n* **nautch** *now dial n* a notch *now dial vb* to cut notches in

nater *dial fm n* **nature**

nateur *obs S fm n* **nature**

nathe *now dial n* the hub of a wheel

nather *obs S fm conj* **neither**

nativism *n* prejudice *esp* in US politics in favour of natives against strangers: the philosophical doctrine that space is an innate idea: the theory that articulate sounds are associated with certain ideas

nativist *n* one who supports nativism in either the US political or the philosophical senses

natle *var fm dial vb* **nattle**

natre *obs fm n* **natron**

natrolite *n* needlestone, a white or colourless hydrous silicate of aluminium and sodium occurring in prismatic needlelike crystals

natron *n* a brittle, vitreous alkaline substance usually found as a salt in various African lakes

natter *dial vb* to grumble, to nag *collq vb* to chatter

nattery *adj* peevish

nattier *comp adj* natty

nattle *dial vb* to make a light rattling or tapping noise: to nibble

natur *obs S fm n* **nature**

naturistic *adj* pertaining to or connected with nature

naunt *arch fm n* **aunt**

naupe *obs fm n* **nape**

nautch *n* an East Indian dancing girl: an exhibition of dancing by such girls *vb* to dance as a nautch: to dance in a nautch

nautic *var fm adj* **nautical**, pertaining to naval matters

nautics *n sing* naval science

navarin *n* a lamb or mutton stew with such root vegetables as turnip

navier *var fm obs n* **navire**

navire *obs n* a ship, shipping

naw *dial fm vb* **know** *dial fm n/adv* **no**

nawder *obs fm now dial conj* **nauther**, neither

nawpe *obs fm n* **nape** *var fm obs vb* **nape**

nayle *obs fm n/vb* **nail**

nayless *obs adj* accepting no refusal

ne *arch adv/conj* not *dial fm adj* **no** *Obs n* a nephew *Obs S vb* to deny

nea *S & dial fm adj/adv* **no**

neager *var fm now S & dial n* **neger** *dial fm n* **niggard**

neal *now dial vb* to fire (earthenware): to soften or toughen glass or metal by a process of heating and slow cooling: to burn (*fig*)

neanic *adj* pertaining to the adolescent period of an individual

neap *n/adj* (of) a tide which has the lowest high-level mark and which occurs shortly after the first and third quarters of the moon: of the time (**neap season**) of such a tide *vb* of a tide in neap season, to become lower: to reach its highest point during that season

neapil *obs fm n* **nipple**

neaple *obs fm n* **nipple**

neaptide *n* a tide of minimum amplitude

near ygo *obs adv* recently

neast *obs fm n/vb* **nest**

neat (*adj/adv*) *arch n* a domestic bovine animal but, more usually, meaning the *pl* cattle *obsol vb* to make neat (in the adjectival sense): to receive a net value of

neaten *vb* to make neat

neatherd *n* a cowherd (*fem* **neatherdess**)

neavil *var fm S & dial vb* **nevel**

neaving *obs n* yeast (still extant in the *dial fms* **newin, newing**)

nebeck *var fm n* **nebk**

nebk *n* a shrub common to Israel and the one which provided Christ's Crown of Thorns

nebris *n* a fawnskin worn by Bacchus and his worshippers

nebula *n* a cloud-like interstellar mass (*pl* **nebulae, nebulas**)

necromancy *n* magic, enchantment: the raising of the spirits of the dead in order to divine the future

necrose *vb* to become gangrenous

necrosis *n* the death of living tissue (*pl* **necroses**)

necrotic *adj* in a state of or displaying necrosis

necrotise *var fm vb* **necrotize**, to affect with or undergo necrosis

nectared *adj* having nectar: deliciously sweet or fragrant (*lit/fig*)

nectareous *adj* of the nature of, consisting of or similar to nectar

nectarial *adj* of the nature of a nectary

nectarous *adj* resembling nectar

nectary *n* that organ of a flower which produces honey

necter *obs fm n* **nectar**

neddy *n* a donkey

nedfire *obs fm n* **needfire**

needer *n* one who needs

needfire *n* fire obtained from dry wood by friction (once credited with a magical power to cure cattle diseases)

neeger *var fm now S & dial n* **neger** *dial fm n* **niggard**

neele *obs fm n/vb* **needle**

neemit *var fm dial n* **nammet**

neep *n* a turnip *obs fm vb* **neap**

neer *now dial n* a kidney *obs fm adj* **near**

neere *obs fm adj/vb* **near**

neese *var fm now S & dial n/vb* **neeze**

neeze *now S & dial vb* to sneeze

nefast *adj* nefarious, wicked

negard *obs fm n* **niggard**

negate *vb* to nullify: to contradict

negater *var fm n* **negator**

negativism *n* any doctrine characterized by denial

negator *n* one who denies *esp* one who is a member of a sect of Russian anarchists

neger *now S & dial n* a negro

Negrillo *n* one of a race of pygmy negroes of central and southern Africa: a little negro (*pl* **Negrillos**)

negrine *adj* resembling that of negroes *obs n* a negress

Negrito *n* one of a pygmy negroid race native to the Indo-Pacific islands

negro (*n*) GAME PLAYER'S note: The word is optionally written + or −*cap*, but the dictionary used for the UK Scrabble championship only gives the +*cap* version, thus invalidating the word for play. Players in Australia, Canada, New Zealand, the West Indies and the USA have no such problem with their dictionary – except where they use both books! (*pl* **negroes**)

neice (*n*) *obs fm adj* **nice**

neider *Obs fm adj/adv* **neither**

neifer *var fm S & dial vb* **niffer**

neigher *n* a horse *S n* a loud laugh *S vb* to laugh loudly

neil *obs fm now dial vb* **neal** *Obs fm n* **nail**

neip *S fm n* **neep** *obs fm n/vb* **neap**

neipce *obs fm n* **niece**

neire *var fm now dial n* **neer** *obs S fm adj/vb* **near**

neis *var fm obs vb* **nese**

neise *obs fm n* **niece**

neive *var fm arch n* **nieve**

neiver *var fm S & dial vb* **niffer**

nelies *n* a winter pear (*pl* **nelies**)

nematic *adj* of a liquid crystal, in a phase in which the atoms or molecules are arranged in parallel lines

nematoid *n/adj* (of) a threadlike worm

nemeses *pl* nemesis

Nemesia *n* a South African genus of brightly-coloured garden flowers of the figwort family (−*cap*) *n* a plant of this genus

nemesis *n* retribution (*pl* **nemeses**) (+*cap*) *pers n* the Greek goddess of retribution

nemoral *adj* of, pertaining to, frequenting or living in woodland

nemoralis *n* the brown-lipped snail, a species of land snail which attempts to stimulate its partner with a 'love dart' rather than perform the snail dance. If accurately fired, this flexible calcified dart sets things in motion.

nemorous *adj* woody, shaded by trees

neolith *n* a Stone Age implement

Neolithic *adj* of or belonging to the later Stone Age

neologism *n* a new word or expression: the practice of using such: change, *esp* towards the rational, in religion

neoplasm *n* a tumour

neoplastic *adj* pertaining to or of the nature of a neoplasm

neotentic *adj* of neoteny

neoteny *n* the retention, by certain salamanders, of larval characteristics at sexual maturity. The larval aspects retained are external gills, gill-slits and tail fins. Of these aquatic amphibians, only the Mexican axolotl can be artificially induced to metamorphose if iodine is added to water in which it swims. It then changes dramatically from a pale creature which looks like a fish with little legs into a much slimmer, dark animal resembling a lizard. The term has been extended to include various invertebrates which also reach sexual maturity during the larval stage. (See **Miastor**)

neoteric *adj* modern, recent *n* a modern writer (*pl*) the study of modern things

neoterism *n* the use of new words or phrases

neoterist *n* one who uses a new word or phrase

nep *now dial n* catmint *US n* a small knot on cotton fibres *US vb* to form such knots during the manufacturing process

Nepali *n* an Indic language of Nepal

neper *n* a unit for expressing the ratio of two currents or two voltages

Nephila *n* a genus of spiders which spin huge, strong, orb webs. In Fiji, fishermen place a female of this genus on a large bamboo hoop and, when the webster has finished her task, they use the almost invisible net for fishing. The thick golden threads of the largest species of *Nephila* can be woven into silken garments but attempts to produce the silk on a commercial basis have so far failed. The spiders keep eating each other!

nephology *n* the study of the clouds

nephric *adj* of, pertaining to or connected with an excretory organ or kidney

nephrite *n* one of the two species of the mineral, jade (the other being jadeite) and formerly worn as an amulet to guard against kidney disorders (*nephros* being the Greek for kidney): the mineral, jade

nephritic *adj* of ailments, originating in the kidneys *obs n* a medicine for a kidney complaint

nephritis *n* inflammation of the kidneys

nephrology *n* the study of the kidneys and the diseases which affect them

nepit *n* a unit of information in computer jargon

nepotic *adj* of or inclined to nepotism

nepotist *n* one who practises nepotism, the giving of preferential treatment to relatives aspiring to office

nereid *n* a sea nymph of Greek myth: a sea centipede (*pl* **nereids, nereides**)

Nergal *pers n* the Assyrian god of the chase

nerita *n* a species of sea snail (*pl* **neritae, neritas**)

neritae *pl* nerita

nerite *var fm n* **nerita**

neritic *adj* belonging to the shallow waters near land

Nerium *n* the genus of oleander, an evergreen shrub

Neronist *n* one whose depravities are the same as those of Nero

nerrast *obs fm sup* **narrest**

nerrest *obs sup now dial adj* nar

nerte *obs n* the plant, myrtle

nerval *adj* of, relating to or affecting the nerves *obs n* a veterinary ointment made from pig's fat

nervate *adj* of leaves, having veins *obs vb* to give nerve or strength to

nervation *n* venation in the botanical sense: the action of the nerves

nervine *adj* having a medicinal effect upon a nervous disorder *n* a nerve tonic

nes *see* **be**

nese *now S n* the nose *obs vb* of an animal, to scent

nesh *now dial adj* unable to endure cold conditions: tender, delicate, weak *now dial vb* to turn faint-hearted

Nesiot *n* an Indonesian

ness *n* a headland or cape *obs vb* of the sea, to form such a headland

nessel *dial n* a short line of twisted twine fastened to a hook and used for fishing for smaller fish

nesset *obs n* a very obscure word conjectured to mean a nest or personal retreat

nestage *n* nests: nesting

nester *n* a bird building a nest: a nesting bird

nestler *n* a bird of a nest, either the mother or young: a child

Nestor *n* a Homeric hero famed for age and wisdom (+ or −*cap*) *n* a (wise) old man

Nestorian *adj* pertaining to or connected with Nestorius, patriarch of Constantinople (428–431) or his opinion that the divinity and humanity of Christ were not united as one individual personality: of later years of life when age and wisdom combine (a rare *poet* reference to Nestor, the Homeric hero famed for these qualities) *n* a follower of the heresy of Nestorius

nete *obs fm adj* **neat**

net fish *n* any fish caught by a net as opposed to other means of capture: a species of starfish with long, curling filaments on its rays

netter *n* one who makes or uses a net

netty *adj* netlike *obs adj* neat, natty

neu *obs fm adj* **new**

neume *n* in plainsong, one of the symbols in a system of notation originally used to indicate the direction of the melody which later included the pitch and accents (*in pl fm*) *n* this system

neural *adj* of or pertaining to the nerves or nervous system: of or pertaining to the side of the body containing the axis of the main nervous system – in man, and all vertebrates, the back

neuritis *n* inflammation of a nerve (*pl* **neuritides, neuritises**)

neurogenic *adj* stimulated by the nervous system

neurolysis *n* the breaking down or destruction of nerve tissue: relief, by stretching, of nerve tension: nervous exhaustion through overstimulation

neuroma *n* a swelling on a nerve (*pl* **neuromas, neuromata**)

neuron *n* the basic cellular unit of the nervous system

neurosal *adj* arising from a nervous disorder

neuston *n* an aggregate of minute organisms found on the surface of water (*pl* **neustons**)

neutre *obs fm adj/n* **neuter**

nevel *S & dial vb* to punch with the fist (*infl fms* **nevelled** etc) *S n* a punch

neveling *Obs adv* face downwards

nevil *var fm S & dial vb* **nevel**

New Holland vulture *obs n* a turkey (an erroneous early designation, unlike the ironically intended **Dutch nightingale**)

new-old *adj* renewed: simultaneously old and new

nexter *obs adj* next

ngaio *n* a New Zealand whitewood tree

Ngotongota *n* a town on the western shore of Lake Malawi

ni *n* the bobization equivalent of **ti** or **te** in the tonic sol-fa *dial fm n of assemb* **nye** *Obs fm arch adv/conj* **ne**

nicher *n* a neigh: a neighing kind of laugh *S vb* to neigh: to laugh in a neighing fashion

nickel (*n/vb*) *infl fms* British nickelled etc: US, **nickled** etc

nicotian *adj* of or pertaining to tobacco *n* one who smokes

nictate *vb* to wink

nid *n* a pheasant's nest: a pheasant's brood *n of assemb* of pheasants

nidder *var fm now S & dial vb* **nither**

niddle *S vb* to move rapidly

nide *n of assemb* of pheasants *vb* of pheasants, to nest

nidering *var fm n/adj* **niddering**, a coward or cowardly

nidge *vb* to quiver *S vb* to rough trim (stone)

nidget *n* a hoe *arch n* a fool *vb* to hoe *dial vb* of a man, to assist a woman in labour *esp* by going for the midwife and the gossips in the middle of the night (also see **kenno**)

niegre *dial fm n* **niggard**

niellated *adj* with niello inlay

nielli *pl* niello

niello *n* (ornamental work of an engraving filled with a) black composition of copper, lead, silver and sulphur alloys (*pl* **nielli, niellos**)

niepce *obs fm n* **niece**

niere *var fm now dial n* **neer**

nies *obs S fm adj* **nice**

niese *obs fm n* **niece**

nieve *arch n* the fist

niffer *S n* an exchange *S & dial vb* to exchange: to bargain, to haggle

nift *obs n* a niece

nifty (*adj*) *US n* something that is stylish or pleasing (*pl* **nifties**)

nig *dial n* a piece *obs n* a miserly person *obs vb* to be miserly

nigard *obs fm n* **niggard**

nigarde *obs fm n* **niggard**

nigel *obs n* the plant fennel: its seed

niger *obs fm n* **negro**

niger oil *n* an oil obtained from the black seeds of an East African plant

Niger seed *n* the plant, ramtil (note: For a peculiarity of **niger seeds**, see **ramtil**)

niggard *n* a miser

nigger (*n*) *US vb* to exhaust land by tilling without fertilization

niggery *n* an administrative division in the former Dutch East Indies *adj* of, belonging to, or characteristic of, negroes

night monkey *n* the only nocturnal higher primate and found in South America

night raven *now poet n* a nocturnal bird of ill-omen. It is probably a nightjar or some species of owl but is, and always has been, treated as being a distinct and separate bird. (TRIVIA note: By contrast to *Chambers 20th Century Dictionary* which attributes sole usage to Shakespeare, the *Oxford English Dictionary* in a list of writers from circa AD 725 to the present includes such as Spenser, Milton and Shelley but does not mention Shakespeare)

nightside *n* the dark, gloomy mysterious aspect of a thing

night trader *obs n* a prostitute

nightrauen *obs fm now poet n* **night raven**

nigrescent *adj* blackish: growing black

nilgai *n* a species of large antelope found in India, the male of which is a slaty-grey colour and the female brownish

nilgau *var fm n* **nilgai**

nilghau *var fm n* **nilgai**

Nilot *n* one who dwells in the Upper Nile region

Nilote *var fm n* **Nilot**

nim *n* a very ancient game, probably of Chinese origin, commonly played in public houses with fifteen matchsticks in rows of three, five and seven matches. Two players compete in attempting to force the other to pick up the last of the fifteen matches by taking alternate turns to pick up as many or as few matches from *one row only* as he or she deems strategic: neem or margosa, a species of *Melia* which yields a bitter oil *arch vb* to steal (standard *infl fms*, though **num** is an *obs fm* and **nam** is an *Obs fm* of **nimmed**. Other *Obs fms incl* **nimest**, *pres indic 2nd sing.*)

nimest *Obs vbl infl* see **nim**

nimp *obs vb* to bite or nibble

nine men's morris
n an ancient game played either on a board or, in country districts, marked on the ground. Two players attempt to eliminate their opponent's nine counters, called merils, originally placed, one at a time, at any corner or intersection of the playing area shown in the diagram.

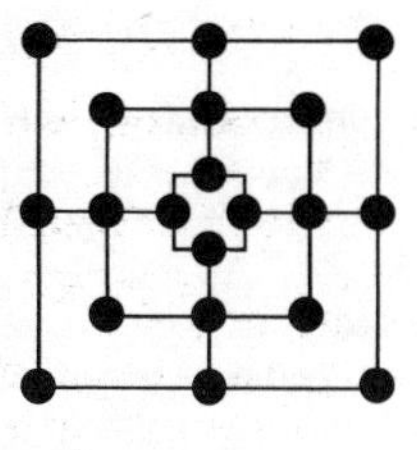

Once all eighteen counters have been placed, the players take alternate moves in an attempt to get three of their own merils in one straight line. When a line of three merils has been achieved this enables the successful player to remove one of his opponent's pieces. A move can be in any direction but only to an adjacent corner or intersection. The game ends when one player is either completely boxed so that he cannot move or has only two merils left in play. The game is also known as **marls, marrels, merells, merels, merils, miracles, morals, morris** or **ninepenny morris**. It is also known as **fivepenny morris** if only five merils are used from the outset by each player.

Ningal *pers n* the wife of Sin, the Babylonian god of the moon

niobic *adj* of niobium, a metallic element formerly known as columbium

nipa *n* a species of palm tree, the fruit of which is used for wine *obs n* that wine

nipar *obs fm n* **nipa**

nipe *obs vb* to nip

niper *obs n* one who nips *obs fm n* **nipa**

niplet *obs n* a small nipple

nipter *n* the ecclesiastical ceremony of washing the feet

nirl *S n* a crumb: a lump *S vb* to shrink or shrivel

nirles *S n* a skin rash

nirlie *S adj* knotty: stunted

nirvana *n* in Buddhist philosophy, the sublimation of all carnal desires and passions and the attainment of perfect beatitude

nis *n* a friendly goblin of Scandinavian folklore which frequents barns and stables (*pl* **nisses**) *obs vbl infl* is not (see *vb* **be**)

nise *obs fm adj* **nice**

nisei *n* a 2nd generation Japanese-American

nisket *obs n* the orifice of a whale's uterus

nist *dial fm adj* **nice**

nitchie *US n* a term of abuse

niter *now US fm n* **nitre**

niterie *collq n* a night club

nither *now S & dial vb* to humble

nitrate (*n*) *vb* to use nitric acid for some purpose

nitratine *n* sodium nitrate in its unrefined state

nitre *n* a crystalline white salt known as saltpeter, saltpetre or potassium nitrate: sodium nitrate

nitride *n* a nitrogen based compound

nitrile *n* any of a group of compounds derived from cyanide which yield ammonia during a particular chemical process

nitrite *n* a salt of nitrous acid

nitroso *adj* containing the univalent radical, nitrosyl

nitter *n* an insect which is a pest to a horse

nittle *obs fm n* **knittle**, the drawstring of a bag

nivel *obs n* a long iron bar at the centre of a mould used by gunners

niveous *adj* white, snowy

nizam *n* a Turkish soldier: the princely title for the former ruler of Hyderabad, India

njave *n* a very large, tropical African tree

no (*adv*/*adj*) *n* the Japanese religious dance drama

noble (*n*/*adj*) *obs vb* to ennoble, make noble

nocent *adj* harmful: guilty *n* a guilty person

nock *n* either of the notches cut into the ends of an archer's bow to hold the string (originally such a notch cut into a horn tip): a notched horn butt-end of an arrow: that notch *vb* to provide a nock for a bow or arrow

noctiluca *n* a marine protozoan visible to the naked eye. It is highly luminescent and, as it often occurs in enormous numbers on the surface of water, it is responsible for the 'phosphorescence' of the sea at night and the reddish tint it may have in the day. (*pl* **noctilucae**)

Noctua *n* the genus of the owlet moth

noctuid *n* any of a large family of nocturnal moths

Noctuidae *n pl* the owlet moths

nodated *adj* knotted

nodation *n* knottiness

nodden *obs adj* compact

nodder *n* one who nods in the various senses of the *vb*

node (*n*) *obs vb* to form a knot

nodose *adj* knotty or knotted

noematical *obs adj* originating or existing in the mind (GAME PLAYER'S note: The dictionary used for the UK Scrabble championship has **noematical** and **noematically** as extant but undefined adjective and adverb respectively. The *adj* defined above was last recorded in use in 1688 and an *adv* meaning intellectually is equally *obs*, having been last used in 1672.)

noesis *n* the facility of appreciating self-evident knowledge: pure intellectual comprehension

Noetian *n* one who accepted Noetianism *adj* of, pertaining to or relating to Noetus or his followers

Noetianism *n* the heresy of Noetus, a presbyter of a church in Asia Minor who, circa AD 230, professed that the Godhead comprised only God the Father

noetic *adj* of or relating to the mind

noh *var fm n* **no**

noint *aphetic fm vb* **anoint** (see **aphesis**)

noiser *obs n* a slanderer

nomade *var fm n* **nomad**

nomadism *n* the practice, state or fact of having a nomadic lifestyle

nomarch *n* the governor of either a modern Greek nomarchy or an ancient Egyptian administrative territory called a nome (*pl* **nomarchs**)

nomarchy *n* a modern Greek province (*pl* **nomarchies**)

nomism *n* the belief that moral conduct consists in the observance of (religious) law

nomistic *adj* based upon law

nomocracy *n* government based on a code of laws

nomogenist *n* one who maintains that life is a totally natural phenomenon without any miraculous intervention

nomogenous *adj* produced by or resulting from the laws of nature

nomogeny *n* the theory of the origin of life as a natural rather than a miraculous process

nomogram *n* a nomograph or isopleth, a graph consisting of three lines graduated for different variables so that a straight line intersecting all three gives the relative values of the variables (both **nomograph** and **isopleth** also have other meanings)

nomograph *n* nomogram: any graphic representation of numerical relations

nomography *n* a description of laws: the art of drawing them: the expression of law in a written form

nomologist *n* one versed in the science of law

nomology *n* that which deals with conformity of actions to rules: the science of law

nonce *n* once – used either in the expression **for the nonce** (see below) or to describe a word coined by a writer, often very eminent, for a particular occasion but which word has not become part of normal usage. Nonce words are usually a form of literary shorthand – such as nouns used as verbs – but they can sometimes take the form of such creations as **unhousehold-name, uncome-at-able** or even Ben Jonson's **un-in-one-breath-utterable**. By contrast, other nonce words become accepted standard English, as Darwin's **lumper**. In referring to those who classify species as being either **lumpers** (too ready to lump different species together) or **splitters** (too ready to separate on even the slightest of differences) he gave a lead which others followed. **for the nonce**, for the time being: for the occasion (GAME PLAYER's note: Nonce words are acceptable for play providing they appear in the dictionary you have agreed upon as your arbitration medium. Words of your own coinage (using the prefixes of (say) 're-' or 'un-') are highly dubious no matter how reasonable they may sound.)

nonest *obs fm n* **nonce**

nonesuch *n* one who or that which is unrivalled: the flower, the scarlet lychnis

nonet *n* piece of music for nine instruments or nine voices

nonett *obs n* a titmouse

nonetti *pl* nonetto

nonetto *n* a nonet (*pl* **nonetti, nonettos**)

nonskier *US fm n* **non-skier**, one who does not ski

nooking *n* an inglenook

noorse *dial fm n/vb* **nurse**

nooser *n* one who uses a noosed rope (to catch elephants)

noote *obs fm n* **note**

nooze *obs fm n/vb* **noose**

norce *obs fm n* **nurse** (in senses other than that of the shark)

noria *n* a water-raising device consisting of buckets attached to a wheel in an endless chain

norice *var fm obs n* **nourice**

norie *n* the puffin (note: The *S fm*, **Tammie norie**, reflects the ancient tradition of adding a personal name to a bird such as **Jenny wren, Maggie pie** (now magpie), **Jack daw** (now jackdaw), **Robin redbreast** (now robin, originally redbreast) etc, **Tammie** being a *S fm pers n* **Tommy**)

norise *var fm obs n* **nourice**

norite *n* a variety of the coarse crystalline igneous rock called gabbro

norma *n* a rule: a standard: a (mason's) square for measuring right angles (*pl* **normae**) (+*cap*) *n* the Rule, a small southern constellation situated between Scorpio and Lupus (+*cap*) *fem pers n* meaning 'a pattern'

normae *pl* norma

Norn *n* in Norse mythology, one of three Fates of time:- **Verdante**, who controlled time present; **Urd**, time past; **Skuld**, time future

norreis *var fm obs n* **nourice** (+*cap*) *Obs n pl* Norwegians

norse *obs fm n* **nurse** (all senses except that of the shark)

norsel *n* a short length of cord fastened to a net *vb* to attach such cord

norsse *obs fm n* **nurse** (all senses except that of the shark)

nort *var fm obs vb* **nurt**

north (*n/adj/adv*) *vb* of the wind, to begin to blow from the north or to turn towards the north: to navigate towards the north of

northe *obs fm n/adj/adv* **north**

northen *obs adj* northern

norther *n* a northerly wind *vb* of the wind, to veer or shift northward *obs adj* the more north of two (oddly, **northest** is still extant)

northest *adj* the most northerly (note: Of the four cardinal compass points, the *adjs* **norther, souther, easter** are *obs* but **wester** is Scottish and extant. Only **northest** has ever appeared to exist among the superlative descriptions.)

nose-herb *obs n* a herb cultivated or gathered for its aroma

nose rag *slg n* a handkerchief

noset *n* the magical toadstone

nossel *obs fm n* **norsel**

nostoc *n* any of a genus of freshwater algae which form greenish masses on such as damp earth

nostopathy *n* an acute or even morbid fear of returning to a familiar scene such as home

nostos *Greek n* a poem of a return (journey to) home

nosy (*adj*) *n* one who pries

notaeum *n* the surface of a bird's back

notarial *adj* of, belonging to, drawn up by or executed by a notary: characteristic of notaries

notarise *var fm vb* **notarize,** to attest to

notary *n* notary public, an officer (usually a solicitor) authorised to administer oaths, certify deeds etc *arch n* a clerk or secretary

noter *n* one who takes or writes notes

nother *now dial adj/adv/conj* neither (note: **a nother** is a *now dial fm* of **an other**)

notise *obs fm vb* **notice**

Notoneca *n* a genus of aquatic bugs resembling the waterboatmen in appearance but, unlike them, are vicious predators and swim on their backs. The word was originally used (still +*cap*) to describe an individual bug but, in the 17th and 18th centuries, was treated as being a *n pl* with a *sing* of **Notonectum**. It is also still used in this original, non-technical, sense to mean an individual.

notour *S adj* notorious

noule *obs fm now dial n* **noll**, the crown of the head

nourice *obs n/vb* (to) nurse

noursle *obs fm vb* **nuzzle**

nous *n* intellect *slg vb* to understand

nousel *var fm vb* **nuzzle** (note: The *infl fms* of **nousled** and **nouseling** are both current American and have a long tradition in British literature, though today's British usage would incline towards **nouselled** and **nouselling**)

novalia *n pl* waste land recently brought under cultivation

novelet *var fm n* **novelette** in the sense of a short novel (i.e *not* in the musical sense)

noviciate *n* the probationary period of a religious novice: the state or time of being any type of novice (*lit/fig*)

novitiate *var fm n* **noviciate**

now (*adv/adj/conj/n*) *nonce vb* used in the sense of contrast in consideration of factors pertaining to a question, as '*The theologian would now it and then it when choosing between this or that*' *Obs S vb* to beat or hit

nowanights *adv* now-a-nights, the nocturnal equivalent of nowadays

Nowel *n* Christmas

Nowell *n* Christmas

nowle *var fm now dial n* **noll**, the crown of the head

nowsel *obs fm vb* **nuzzle**, to nurse

nth *adj* pertaining to an indefinitely large ordinal number, as in the phrase **to the nth degree**

nu *n* the thirteenth letter of the Greek alphabet *Obs fm adj* **new** *Obs fm adj/adv/conj/n* **now**

nubia *n* a soft, fleecy wrap worn about the head and shoulders by women at the turn of the 19th/20th centuries

nuchal *adj* of or pertaining to the nape of the neck

nuclei *pl* nucleus

nucleus *n* an essential core (*pl* **nuclei, nucleuses**)

nuclide *n* any species of nucleus

nucule *n* a nutlet

nudation *n* the act of making nude or bare

nudgel *obs vb* to squeeze

nudger *n* one who or that which nudges

nudie *collq n* a film with a high percentage of scenes of nudity

nudities *pl* nudity (note: The *pl fm* usually refers to nude figures with the privy parts concealed – i.e. a man with a fig leaf – whereas the original meaning was of such parts specifically exposed)

nuisancer *n* one who causes a nuisance

nulled *var fm adj* **knurled**

num *obs pa pple vb* nim

numbat *n* the banded ant-eater, a pouchless marsupial which dwells in the fallen, hollow limbs of wandoo trees in southwestern Australia. The adult achieves the size of a rat and numbats are related to the marsupial cat. (Also see **anteater**)

nummet *var fm dial n* **nammet**

nun (*n*) *n* the fourteenth letter of the Hebrew alphabet: the twenty-fifth letter of the Arabic alphabet

nunlet *n* any of three species of small South American puffbirds which, like all such, remain utterly motionless whilst waiting for insect prey

nurice *var fm obs n* **nourice**

nurl *var fm n/vb* **knurl**

nurser *n* one who or that which nurses or encourages

nursle *vb* to nuzzle: to cherish

nursling *n* that, such as an infant, being nursed

nurt *obs vb* of a horned animal, to butt

nutarian *n* one who considers nuts to be the finest possible food

nutate *vb* to droop: to nod

nuthatch *n* any of a family of small, dumpy, insectivorous birds closely related to the tits

nutlet *n* a little nut

nv *Obs fm adj/adv/conj* **now**

nvreis *obs S fm vb* **nourish**

nw *Obs fm adv/adj/conj* **now**

nwe *Obs fm adj* **new**

nwreis *S fm* (*obs*) *obs n* **nourice** *obs S fm vb* **nourish**

ny *obs fm n of assemb* **nye** *Obs fm arch adv/conj* **ne**

nye *n of assemb* of pheasants

nys see **be**

nystagmic *adj* of the nature of nystagmus

nystagmus *n* a condition to which miners are prone, which consists of a spasmodic movement of the eyes, either rotary or from side to side

oa *S dial fm pron* **I**

oaker *obs fm n* **ochre**

oar (*n*) *vb* to row

oarlaps *n* a rabbit with ears which stick out sideways like oars

oast (*n*) *obs fm n/vb* **host**

oat (*n*) *US vb* to feed oats to a horse

oaten *adj* of the plant, oat: made of oat stems, composed of oatmeal *n* a musical pipe made from the stem of an oat plant

oater *dial fm n* **otter**

ob *n* a familiar, attendant upon a Hebrew witch *obs n* a wizard, sorcerer *dial fm n* **abb**

obdurate *adj* hard-hearted: impervious to persuasion

obdure *arch adj* obdurate *vb* to strengthen (*lit/fig*)

obeisant *adj* deferential, obsequious *obs n* a subordinate

obeism *n* belief in the West African and Caribbean heathen religions based on the witchcraft and knowledge of poisons possessed by the obi-man or obi-woman

obelion *n* the point on the sagittal suture between the parietal formina of the skull

obelus *n* a sign (– or ÷) used in ancient documents to indicate suspect or spurious words and passages: an obelisk, a dagger sign (†) used in modern printing and with the meaning designated by the author or editor (*pl* **obeli**)

obi *n* a Japanese broad sash worn with a kimono: West African and Caribbean witchcraft

oblast *n* a (Russian) province or district

oblate *n* a layman residing in a monastery: an exchequer roll containing a list of debts *adj* of a spheroid, flattened at the poles *obs vb* to offer

obligant *n* one, in Scottish law, who puts himself under an obligation to pay or to perform a duty

obscurant *adj/n* (of) one who obscures *esp* one opposed to popular enlightenment or freedom of thought

obsess *vb* of an evil spirit, to harass or assail

the human victim: of a fixed idea, to haunt the thinker

obsign *vb* to seal (a document): to ratify by sealing

obtest *vb* (in the name of something sacred or for the sake of something sacred) to call to witness, to charge

oc *Obs fm obs conj* **ac**

ocarina *n* an egg-shaped wind instrument which produces an almost pure tone

Oceanid *n* in Greek mythology, a nymph of the ocean (*pl* **Oceanids, Oceanides**) (*–cap*) *n* any marine mollusc

ocellar *adj* of the simple eyes of such as an insect

ocelli *pl* ocellus

ocellus *n* the simple eye, consisting mainly of light-sensitive cells, of an insect and certain other invertebrates: an eyelike spot of colour (*pl* **ocelli**)

ocelot *n* the painted leopard, a medium-sized American member of the cat family found from Texas down to Brazil: its fur

oche *n* the mark behind which the dart player stands when taking aim at the board *obs vb* to lop off (derived from an *Obs vb* to cut a notch in)

ocher *var fm n/vb* **ochre**

ochlocrat *n* one who favours mob rule

ochre *n* ocher, a class of native earths which consist of varying proportions of hydrated oxide of iron to clay and are the basis of pigments ranging in colour from light yellow to a deep, rich orange-brown *vb* to colour with ochre/ocher (*infl fms* **ochred, ochered: ochring, ochreing, ochering**) hence, **ochring** (etc) *n* the action of the *vb*

ochrea *common but erron var fm n* **ocrea**, a pair of stipules (*pl* **ochreae**)

ochroid *adj* pale-yellowish

ocker *Austr slg n* an uncultured oaf *obs vb* to lend money at a rate of interest

ocrea *n* a thin sheath around the slender spine of a moss: a legging-shaped sheath formed of a pair of stipules about the stem of a plant – in this sense the common but *erron var fm* is **ochrea** (*pl* **ocreae**: or the *var fm*, **ochreae**)

ocreated *obs adj* wearing leggings

octastyle *adj* of a building, having eight columns *n* such a building

octuple *vb* to increase eightfold

ocular (*adj*) *n* the eyepiece of such as a telescope

oculate *adj* having eyelike spots *obs vb* to eye, to behold

oculist *n* a medical or surgical eye specialist

od *n* a supposed magnetic force which creates the effect of hypnotism *var fm interj* **Od** (*+cap*) *interj* a minced form of the word God used with, or as a prefix for, exclamatory words and phrases many of which are now *obs* though some survive as *arch* or *dial* expressions. Examples:– **Odrabbit it, od-rat it** or **od rot it** (extant in the *fm* **Oh drat it!**) **od's blood, od's body, oddzooks, Odsbodikins, Odd's life, od's my life, od's my little life** etc.

odaller *var fm n* **udaller**

odd-man *n* one who has the casting vote: an umpire (in this sense the *S fm* is **oddsman**)

oddsman *S n* an umpire (*fem* **oddswoman**)

odeon *var fm n* **odeum** (*pl* **odea, odeons**)

odeum *n* a building (*esp* in ancient Greece or Rome) for musical entertainment (*pl* **odea, odeums**)

odium *n* hatred: blame: offensiveness (*pl* **odiums**)

odometer *var fm n* **hodometer**, a device for

measuring distance by the technique of recording the revolutions made by a wheel over the desired length

odorant *adj* emitting a (pleasant) smell

odslife *interj* see **od** (+*cap*)

oe *n* a small island: a whirlwind in the Atlantic off the Faroe Islands *var fm S n* **oy** *obs vb* to decorate with spangles (*pa pple* **oed**)

oecist *n* the founder of a (ancient Greek) colony

œillade *n* an amorous glance of the eye: an ogle

oenomel *n* a drink of wine and honey: anything which combines sweetness with strength

oerlikon *n* a Swiss anti-aircraft gun

oersted *n* a metric unit of magnetic field strength

oestral *adj* of oestrus

oestre *Obs fm n* **oyster**

oestrin *n* estrin

oestriol *n* an oestrogen found in the urine of pregnant women

oestrual *adj* of oestrus

oestrum *n* oestrus

oestrus *n* sexual heat *esp* in female mammals: a stimulus, a passion: a gadfly, a botfly

œuvre *n* a work of art

of (*prep*) *obs fm adv/adj/prep/n* **off**

ogress *n* a female ogre *her n* a black circular spot rather like a cannonball

oh *interj* of such as pain, terror, shame *n* such a cry *vb* to utter such a cry

ohm *n* the unit of electrical resistance

oi *interj* to attract attention

oilnut *n* any of various seeds which yield oil such as those of the castor oil plant, the butternut, the buffalo nut or elk nut and the oil palm: the plant or tree of that seed

oilseed *n* seed capable of producing oil

oilstone *n* a smooth and fine-grained whetstone (a stone used for imparting an edge to a tool), the surface of which is covered in oil

oil tree *n* any tree from which an oil is obtained

oinomel *var fm n* **oenomel**

oister *obs fm n* **oyster**

oistre *obs fm n* **oyster**

ok *Obs fm obs conj* **ac** *Obs fm n* **oak** *Obs fm adv* **eke**

ol *n* a hydroxyl group which has the oxygen atom bonded to two metal atoms

olders *obs n pl* predecessors

oldie *collq n* that which is old and extant such as a person, a song, a film etc

oldster *n* a senior midshipman: an elderly person

olea *pl* oleum

olecranal *adj* pertaining to the olecranon, the bony prominence of the elbow

olefin *var fm n* **olefine**

olefine *n* any of a group of open-chain, unsaturated, hydrocarbon compounds having a double bond

olein *n* the chief constituent of fatty oils (*pl*) a group of constituents having similar properties to olein

Olenus *n* a genus of a type of fossil arthropod, one of a division of lower animals

oleum *n* a mixture of acids better known as **fuming sulphuric acid** (*pl* **olea, oleums**)

olisbos *n* an ancient Greek dildo of padded leather

olivaceous *adj* of the colour of an unripe olive, dark green with a tinge of yellow: of an olive, dark green

olived *adj* having olive trees or olive branches

oliver *n* a tilt hammer, a drop hammer worked mechanically for the production of nails

olivet *n* an olive-shaped button: an oval mock-pearl *obs n* an olive grove

olivine *n* the green garnet, a precious stone of a pale yellowish-green colour being a transparent to translucent magnesium iron silicate found in lava and in meteorites: a dark bottle-green variety not considered precious (both varieties are also known as **chrysolite**)

ollahm *n* among the ancient Irish, the equivalent of a professor at a modern university (also see apt anagram, **mollah**)

olm *n* a species of salamander which never develops beyond the larval stage (see **Proteus** (*−cap*))

om *n* a type of mantra or passage taken from a Hindu religious work and uttered as an incantation

omber *arch var fm/US var fm n* **ombre**

ombre *n* a three-person card game played without the eights, nines and tens in the pack

omenta *pl* omentum

omental *adj* of or pertaining to the omentum

omentum *n* a free fold of the serous membrane which encloses the viscera in the abdominal and pelvic cavities. The small omentum passes from the stomach to the liver, the great omentum from the stomach to the transverse colon. (*pl* **omenta, omentums**)

omicron *n* the fifteenth letter of the Greek alphabet

omlahs *erron fm n pl* **omlah**, the staff of a civil court in Northern India (GAME PLAYER'S note: Erroneous forms given as such in the dictionary you use for arbitration, are valid for play as they reflect a reasonably general usage. In some cases (e.g. pea) the erroneous form has become the standard.)

on (*prep/adj/adv/n*) *interj* forward!

onager *n* the shortest of the three species of Asiatic wild ass (the others being **kiang** and **kulan**), it is found in Iran, Afghanistan and western India (*pl* **onagers, onagri**)

Onagra *n* the genus of the evening primrose, a technical term now replaced by **Oenothera**

onagri *pl* onager

onanism *n* masturbation: coitus interruptus

onanist *n* one who practises onanism

onanistic *adj* relating to onanism

oncer *slg n* a one pound note

oncidium *n* the butterfly plant or other species of the same genus of orchids (*pl* **oncidiums** – contrast anagram, **conidium** and *pl*)

oncost *n* an overhead or standard fixed cost

onding *S n* an on-ding or persistent heavy fall of rain or snow

oneiromancy *n* divination by dreams

onery *var fm US dial adj* **ornery** (*comp* **onerier** *sup* **oneriest**)

onestep *n* a dance of American origin in quick march time *vb* to dance the onestep

oniric *var fm adj* **oneric**, pertaining to dreams

Oniscus *n* a genus of woodlice

onrese *Obs vb* to make an assault

onsair *obs fm adj* **unsore**

onset (*n*) *obs vb* to attack

onsetter *arch n* an assailant

onstead *S & dial n pl* those buildings other than the living quarters which are part of a farm

ontend *Obs vb* to inflame (*lit/fig*)

oo *S n* wool *S pron* we

oobit *dial n* the woolly bear or hairy caterpillar of the tiger moth: a term of contempt for a person

oocyte *n* an immature ovum

oof *slg n* money

oogeny *n* the production or development of an ovum

ool *var fm dial vb* **yule**

oolite *n* one of a series of fossiliferous rocks consisting of carbonate of lime around a nucleus of a grain of sand

oon *dial fm n* **oven** *var fm now dial vb* **oven**, to bake in an oven

oostre *obs fm arch n* **hostry**

op *n* an operation: optical art (GAME PLAYER'S note: Perfectly valid for play *even where the rules prohibit abbreviations* as, technically, this is a 'short form' not an abbreviation. The essential difference lies in pronunciation as, for example, **Mr** is still pronounced 'mister' or **Dr** as 'doctor' whereas **op** is pronounced 'op'. Thus **Mr** and **Dr** are *invalid* for play whereas **op** and **ad** are *valid* for play.)

opaled *adj* made colourful like an opal

Opalina *n* a genus of protozoans or single-celled animals which live in the rectums of British frogs

opalise *var fm vb* **opalize**, to display colours like an opal: to make iridescent like an opal

opensteek *S fm n* **openstitch**

openstitch *n* a type of openwork stitching

opentail *n* an unchaste woman (*obs* except in *slg* usage with varying shades of meaning)

operand *n* a mathematical function or quantity to be operated upon

operant *adj* that in operation, operative or which operates *n* one who or that which operates

ophiomancy *n* divination by the observation of a snake or snakes

Ophism *n* the creed of the Ophites

ophite *n* any of various metamorphic, usually green-coloured, rocks having a snakelike marking (+*cap*) *n* one of a Gnostic sect which gave special reverence to the snake as a symbol of divine wisdom

opine *vb* to hold or state as an opinion

opiner *n* one who holds or expresses an opinion

oppugn *vb* to oppose *esp* in speech or writing

opress *obs fm vb* **oppress**

optime *n* one placed in the second or third division of the Mathematical Tripos at Cambridge as a senior or junior optime, below a wrangler. These are former honours gradings.

optologist *n* one versed in optology

optology *n* the science of testing the eyes by lenses

optometer *n* any of various instruments for testing vision

Opuntia *n* the genus of the prickly pear or Indian fig (−*cap*) *n* any plant of this genus or its fruit

opuscle *n* a small (literary or musical) work

or (*conj/arch adv*) *her n* a gold or yellow tincture *arch fm adv/prep/conj* **ere** *obs fm pron* **our**

orach *n* a plant of the goosefoot family sometimes used as a substitute for spinach

orache *var fm n* **orach**

oracle *n* classically, the answer of a Greek or Roman deity (speaking through one who is inspired) to an enquiry concerning the future: the god or goddess making that answer: the human speaker (usually a priest or *esp* a priestess): the place where such may be obtained (most notably, the shrine of Apollo at Delphi and that of Zeus at Dodona): extended to any person whose utterances are regarded as profoundly wise and authoritative (note: Oracles are often highly ambiguous and it takes an expert to interpret them correctly. Two classical examples will show why:– Croesus consulted the Delphic oracle respecting a war. The answer was, '*When Croesus crosses the river Halys he will overthrow the strength of an empire*'. Croesus believed this to mean he would win. But, it was his own empire which lost. On a different occasion the Delphic oracle gave an answer which included the phrase, '*safety promised in a wooden wall*,' which the Greek leader, Themistocles, correctly interpreted as meaning ships and so won a decisive victory over the Persians by the use of the navy he founded. For other examples of prophetic statements see **Brutus, Cassandra, Gordian** and **Hister**. An example of a miraculous event taken as a portent of greatness is given at **Servian**. For additional detail see both **Pythia** and **sibyl**. Related material can be found at **CHINESE CALENDAR, DIVINATION, Oscines** and **sortes**.)

orage *n* an organ stop which gives the sound of a storm *obs n* a storm

orale *n* a papal ceremonial veil

orang *n* the orang-utan, a manlike large ape of the forests of Borneo and Sumatra with strong arms and shaggy, reddish-brown hair

orangeist *var fm n* **orangist**, a supporter of the Dutch royal house of Orange

orange lily *n* a flower native to Austria, being a garden lily with large orange flowers

orange tip *n* a species of butterfly having wings with orange tips

Orangism *n* the principle of Protestant supremacy in Ulster

orangite see **thorite**

orang-utan see **orang**

orangutang *var fm n* **orang-utan** (see **orang**)

orant *n* a Jewish and early Christian position for prayer whereby the supplicant's arms are fully extended horizontally in the form of a cross

orarian *adj* coastal *n* one who dwells at the coast

orate *vb* to deliver a formal speech

oratress *n* a female public speaker

oratrix *n* an oratress (*pl* **oratrices**)

orb (*n*) *n* a blank window-like panel in a pre-18th century building, not to be confused with those true windows which were subsequently bricked-up to avoid paying window tax *vb* to form into, or enclose in, an orb (in the globular or circular sense)

orbicular *adj* spherical, globular: circular: having a ringlike form *n* a muscle of circular form

orbing *obs n* the making of an orb or blank panel

orbital (*adj*) *n* a subdivision of a nuclear shell

orblet *n* a small orb

Orcadian *adj* of Orkney *n* a native or an inhabitant of Orkney

orcein *n* a purple dye obtained from orcine

orchel *var fm n* **archil**

orchis *n* any of several species of (British) orchids (*pl* **orchids, orchises**)

orchites *pl* orchitis

orchitis *n* inflammation of the testicle (*pl* **orchites**)

orcine *var fm n* **orcinol**, a weak acid obtained from various species of lichen

ord *Obs n* a point (of a weapon): a spear

ordinary (*adj*) *n* one who, by right, has ecclesiastical jurisdiction, such as an archbishop in a province or a bishop in a diocese: one of the five judges of the Scottish Court of

Session: a meal at a fixed charge: that which is of the common run, mass or course *US n* a tavern *her n* a figure of simple or geometric form and convention in character *obs n* a stage prompter

ordinate *adj* of markings on insects, arranged in a row: regular *n* a mathematical term variously applied to points, distances and lines *vb* to place side by side in series: to order, regulate, control, govern: to institute, establish

ordinee *n* one (newly) ordained

ordines *pl* ordo

ordo *n* either of two ecclesiastical books, one giving directions for services according to the calendar, the other a book of rubrics for administering the sacraments (*pl* **ordines, ordos**)

ordure *n* excrement

oread *n* a mythical Greek mountain nymph (*pl* **oreads, oreades**)

oreide *n* one of a small number of alloys of differing compositions which produce a brass of a golden brilliancy used mainly for imitation jewellery

orell *obs n* a stone used for marking

organdie *n* fine muslin

organise *var fm vb* **organize**

organity *n* an organized whole *obs n* the condition of being organic

organsine *obs fm n* **organzine**, the strongest type of silk thread formed of several strands twisted together in a direction directly opposite to that of the individual strands

organum *n* a counterpoint or primitive harmony in mediaeval music

orgeat *n* a drink now made from almonds, sugar and orange blossom but which, originally, was a barley drink

orgiast *n* a participant in an orgy

orgone *obs fm n* **organ**

orgue *n* either of two historic defensive arrangements:– (*a*) a portcullis-like effect achieved by a series of long, thick stakes of wood which functioned in unison (*b*) a linking together of a number of weapons, such as muskets, so that one operator could fire them individually or collectively

oribi *n* one of the dwarf antelopes and found in tall grassland in many different parts of Africa

oriel *n* a bay window *esp* one of an upper storey supported by brackets

orifex *obs erron fm n* **orifice** (used by Shakespeare and Marlowe among others)

origan *n* the plant wild marjoram

origane *var fm n* **origan**

origen *obs fm n* **oryx**

origes *obs pl* oryx

orignal *Canadian n* a moose

oriole *n* any of a family of slender-bodied, usually thrush-sized, woodland songbirds, many of which are brightly coloured. The true orioles occur only in the Old World, but the name is also extended to some species of American troupials which bear a superficial resemblance to them. The family is comprised of orioles, Madagascan tylas and Australasian figbirds. Combined with black as a secondary colour, the males are mostly yellow, red, maroon or green whilst both the females and the young are duller and usually olive green. Both the male and female golden oriole are yellow, the male being a brilliant yellow with black wings and tail and the female duller and less dramatically marked. (+*cap*) *fem pers n* possibly meaning 'window'

Orleanism *n* the political principles of those who supported the princes of the house of Orleans, which provided the last king of France, Louis Philippe (1830–1848) and who are still claimants for the throne

Orleanist *n* one who supported Orleanism

ornate (*adj*) *obs vb* to ornament or embellish

ornell *Obs n* a type of white stone used for building purposes

ornery *US dial adj* mean, low, common: unruly, stubborn (*comp* **ornerier** *sup* **orneriest**)

ornis *n* the birds of a given region (*pl* **ornithes**)

ornithes *pl* ornis

orogenetic *adj* characterized by development along straight lines

oronge *Obs fm n/adj* **orange**

orp *S vb* to fret

orpent *obs fm n* **orpine**

Orpheus *pers n* a mythical musician of Thrace credited with the power to enchant animals, trees and rocks by the sound of his lyre and who was supposed to have knowledge of ancient mysteries

Orphism *n* the alleged mysteries of Orpheus

orpin *var fm n* **orpine**

orpine *n* livelong, a common British medicinal herb

orping *S n* fretting

orrest *Obs n* a battle

orris *n* any iris with a scented root

orsade *var fm n* **arsedine**

orsden *var fm n* **arsedine**

orval *obs n* clary, a plant with pale blue flowers

ory *adj* of or like ore, metallic *dial adj* seaweedy

oryx *n* any of a number of species of medium to large-sized antelope

os *n* a geological ridge (*pl* **osar** or **osars**): an orifice (*pl* **ora**) *L n* a bone (*pl* **ossa**)

Osbert *masc pers n* meaning 'divinely bright'

oscheal *adj* of or pertaining to the scrotum

oscine *adj* of the Oscines, the songbirds

Oscines *n pl* either of two groups of birds. One is those whose calls were studied by the ancient Roman augurs (fortune tellers) as portents for good or ill. Some of these – such as magpies, owls and ravens – are still part of superstitious folklore. The augurs also paid particular attention to the eagle as it was interpreted as representing either the emperor or Rome itself. The other group is the technical classification of those birds listed as being of the sub-order *Oscines* of the order *Passeriformes*. In this sense, the classification concerns 40 different families of birds of which one family alone comprises over 1,300 species. In simple terms it represents the songbirds.

oscinine *adj* oscine

oscitant *adj* drowsy, dull, indolent

oscula *pl* osculum

oscular *adj* of or pertaining to any of the following – the mouth, kissing, the pit-like sucker on the head of a tapeworm

osculate *adj* having oscula

oscule *n* a small mouth(-like aperture)

osculum *n* a kiss: a mouth of a sponge (*pl* **oscula**)

osier *n* any of various willow trees having branches and twigs sufficiently flexible for the making of such as a basket: such a branch or twig: any of the North American dogwood trees *esp* the red osier

osiered *adj* having osiers

Osmanli *adj* of or belonging to the dynasty founded by Osman I (AD 1288–1326) which created and ruled the Ottoman Empire until the large remnant was declared the republic of Turkey in 1924. It reached its greatest extent under Soliman the Magnificent (1520–1566) whose dominions included Syria and Egypt to the south and, in the north, most of Hungary. *n* an Ottoman, in the senses of either a member of the family or a Turk subject to the ruler

osmate *var fm n* **osmiate**

osmiate *n* a salt of osmic acid

osmund *n* a high quality iron formerly imported from the Baltic countries and used for such as arrowheads: any of the various species of the plants better known as the **flowering fern** but also known as **osmund royal, royal fern** or **king fern** and formerly known as **osmund the waterman** or **St Christopher's herb** (+*cap*) *masc pers n* meaning 'divinely bright'

oss *now dial vb* to recommend

ossein *n* a soft protein substance of the bone tissue

osseine *var fm n* **ossein**

osselet *n* a little bone as used in gambling games: a hard substance which grows on the inside of a horse's knee: a cuttlebone

osseter *n* a species of sturgeon

Ossetian *n* an Iranian language of the Caucasus Mountains region of the USSR

ossuary *n* any place or receptacle for the bones of the dead

osteal *adj* of or pertaining to bone

ostein *var fm n* **ossein**

ostent *n* a sign or portent: a manifestation: a (vainglorious) display *vb* to make a show of: to show off

osteoderm *n* a dermal bony plate

osteoma *n* a tumour of bone or of cartilage (*pl* **osteomas, osteomata)**

oster *obs fm n* **oyster**

osteria *n* an inn or hostelry in an Italian speaking country

ostery *obs fm arch n* **hostry**

ostiolar *adj* of or pertaining to an ostiole

ostiole *n* a small orifice in a plant or animal

ostler *n* a stableman or groom *esp* one at an inn

ostlering *n* the occupation of an ostler

Ostmen *n* the Norse invaders of Ireland and Iceland

ostraca *pl* ostracon

Ostracion *n* the genus of the boxfishes or trunkfishes (see **boxfish)**

ostracod *n* any of a class of minute crustacea with bivalve shells

ostracon *n* in ancient Greece, one of the fragments of earthenware on which people recorded their vote in a trial for which the punishment was ostracism (*pl* **ostraca)**

Ostrea *n* the genus of oysters

ostreal *adj* of or pertaining to oysters

ostrey *obs fm arch n* **hostry**

ostrie *obs fm arch n* **hostry**

ostringer *var fm n* **austringer**

ostrye *obs fm arch n* **hostry**

Ostyak *n* one who speaks Khanty, an Ugric language of the Finno-Ugric sub-group of the Uralic family of languages, spoken in Western Siberia: Khanty

ot *dial n* an urchin

otalgy *var fm n* **otalgia**, earache

otarid *n* an eared seal

otary *n* a sealion or other seal with external ears (*pl* **otaries)**

Othniel *pers n* the first judge of Biblical Israel

Otidae *n* the family of the bustards, 22 species of birds of various genera

ottar *var fm n* **attar**

otter (*n*) *vb* to hunt the otter: to fish in freshwater using more than one hook

ottre *obs fm n* **otter**

ou *S interj* of concession *Obs fm pron* **you** *Obs fm adv* **how**

oubit *var fm dial n* **oobit**

ouert *var fm obs n* **overt**

oughtness *n* moral obligation

oundy *adj* wavy

ousel *var fm n* **ouzel**

ouster *n* the act of legal eviction

outbar *vb* to bring into the open a barrier

outbreathe *now poet vb* to breathe out *obs vb* to die

outbreed *vb* to surpass or excel in the act of breeding

outer (*n*) *nonce vb* to make external

outfling *vb* to fling out

outgear *S n* the external possessions of a household (as opposed to **ingear**)

outgrin *US vb* to surpass in grinning

outhire *vb* to give out as if on hire

outlead *obs vb* to lead out

outlearn *vb* to exceed in learning: to go beyond the study of

outler *S & dial n* an animal which remains outdoors both at night and during the winter

outlier *n* one sleeping away from home: one sleeping in the open air: an outsider: an animal which sleeps beyond a specific and otherwise normal limitation as a house pet outside the house or a deer beyond the owner's estate: an outlying portion of anything

outman *vb* to outnumber or exceed in number of men: to excel in manliness *obs n* one who is out, in senses such as dwelling beyond a boundary or one whose work is in the open air

outname *vb* to exceed in the quality for which the named person is famous or infamous. The classic example occurs in Hamlet's speech to the players where he says,'... *it out-herods Herod*'. Shakespeare's formula has been copied by others and extended to include religious groups (*out-mormon Mormons*) and even complete peoples. The name is treated as a verb, so that such as **out-heroded** or **out-heroding** are used if suitable. Alexander, Brutus, Darwin, Milton, Nero, Quixote and Trollope are just some of the names employed in this fashion. The name is not necessarily repeated, e.g. *he might out-boniface an humble moderator* and the use of upper or lower case is optional. Sometimes the suffix '-ise' is added, as **out-Germanise** or **out-Calvinise** with this treated as a verb. The verb, to outname, is concerned with this process and used where the formula is understood, e.g. *I could outname a dozen such (characters)* or *Shakespeare originated the formula of outnaming*.

outraise *vb* to surpass in raising

outrance *n* excess: the utmost extremity (normally now used in English only as part of a French phrase, as *à outrance, à tout outrance*) (*pl* **outrances**)

outrate *nonce vb* to exceed in rating

outré *adj* beyond the bounds of that considered proper *obs n* an extravagant or fantastic thing

outred *vb* to surpass in redness *obs S vb* to clear of debt or other liabilities

outreign *vb* to reign longer than or beyond the time of

outremer *n* the region beyond the sea

outring *n* an outer ring or circumference *S n* an outwick or shot in curling which impels another stone nearer the tee *US vb* to ring louder than (*infl fms* as *vb* ring, i.e. **outrang, outrung**)

outroop *obs n* an auction (compare with **roup, rouper, rouping wife**)

outrooper *obs n* an auctioneer (compare with **rouper**): a former title for the common crier of the City of London

outrope *var fm obs n* **outroop**

outroper *var fm obs n* **outrooper**

outsetter *obs n* one who lived outside a particular territory as that of a parish *obs S n* one who set forth

outswear *vb* to outdo or surpass in swearing (*infl fms incl* **outswore** or **outsware, outsworn**)

outtake *n* a passage outwards *obs vb* to extract, to deliver: to except (*pa pple* **outaken, outtaken, outane, outtane**)

outtop *vb* to surmount

outworth *Shaks vb* to exceed in worth

ouzel *n* the blackbird: the ring ouzel, a kindred species but which differs by having a pale crescent on the breast: the dipper or water ouzel, a bird with dark plumage which feeds in fast flowing streams in which it either walks or swims

ov *Obs fm pers pron* **you**

ovate *adj* egg-shaped *n* the third Eisteddfodic grade, the others being bard and druid *vb* to make egg-shaped: to greet with applause

overarch *n* an overhead arch *vb* to form an arch over

overgo *vb* to exceed *now dial vb* to surmount, to cross (over): to overcome, to overpower: to overflow: to pass by (*vb/now dial vb pa t* **overwent** *pa pple* **overgone**)

overgod *n* a chief or senior god

overlie *vb* to lie upon or above: to smother by lying upon

overlive *vb* of anything, to survive beyond a specified or anticipated time, date, event etc

overly *adj* excessively

overply *vb* to exhaust by too much exercise

overpost *vb* to get over such as the ground quickly and easily

overpot *vb* to plant in too large a pot

overtop *adj* overhead *vb* to rise over (*lit/fig*)

overred *obs vb* to colour red (used *fig* by Shakespeare and Scott to suggest a bold red-faced opposite of cowardly whiteness) (GAME PLAYER'S note: Another Shakespeare 'exclusive' of the dictionary used for the UK Scrabble Championship which had it mentioned Scott would, according to the current rules of that contest, have made the word valid for play)

oversail *n* the projection of anything over its base *vb* to sail across: to cross in a sailing ship *dial vb* to lay such as bricks so that they have an overhanging pattern: to provide a roof for a passage between houses

oversalt *vb* to salt in excess

overset *vb* to overcome mentally or physically: to upset, overturn *n* the setting up of more type than the size of the paper to be printed upon can accept

overt (*adj*) *obs n* the open *Obs n* an opening

overveil *vb* (usually *poet*) to veil over

overward *n* the upper of two geographical wards (the other being the **nether ward**) *obs adv/prep* across

oviparous *adj* producing eggs as opposed to live young

ow *interj* of pain *var fm S interj* **ou** *obs fm vb* **owe** *Obs fm pers pron* **you**

owche *var fm n* **ouch**, a brooch: the socket of a precious stone

Owenism *n* the theory or system of communistic cooperation advocated by Robert Owen (1771–1858)

Owenist *n* a supporter of Owenism

owerby *S adv* a little way over

owl (*n*) *vb* to prowl in the dark: to smuggle wool or sheep *out* of England (a practice which began during the reign of Charles II when the export of wool and sheep was banned. The main smuggling areas were Kent and Sussex.)

Owleglass *var fm n* **Owlglass**

owler *n* one who engaged in the illegal practice of owling (see **owl**): a vessel used in owling *dial n* the alder tree

owlery *n* an abode of owls

owlet *n* a young owl

Owlglass *n* a roguish jester (the English version of *Eulenspiegel*, a German mischievous clown of mediaeval times)

owling *n* the practice of smuggling out as described at **owl** *vb*, above

ownder *dial n* the evening

owr *obs fm pron* **our**

owt *obs fm adv/adj/n/vb* **out**

owter *var fm obs n* **outer**, one who minted counterfeit coins

ox (*n* (*pl* **oxen**)) *dial vb* to fret: to seek: to walk noisily *var fm now dial vb* **hox**

oxbow lake *n* a residual stretch of water created by a river's change of course

oxster *obs fm n* **oxter**

oxter *n* the armpit

oy *S n* a grandchild *var fm vb* **hoy**, to urge on with cries of '(h)oy'

oyster (*n*) *vb* to fish for oysters

oystre *Obs fm n* **oyster**

oz *abbreviation* for **ounce** (GAME PLAYER'S note: *Not* valid for play – see **op**) (+*cap*) *collq adj/n* (of) Australia

ozoniser *var fm n* **ozonizer**, an apparatus for turning oxygen into ozone

P

pa *n* a Maori fortified village (*pl* **pas**)

paa *var fm Obs n* **po**

pac *n* a type of Red Indian moccasin having a large sole turned over and sewed onto the upper: a half-boot worn by lumberjacks in winter

paca *n* the spotted cavy or waterhare, a large South American rodent

pacable *adj* capable of being pacified

pacation *n* pacification

Pace *S & dial n* Easter (compare with **Pasch**)

pachak *n* an aromatic root from Kashmir

paction *n* a bargain, an agreement *S vb* to make such

pactional *adj* of, pertaining to or of the nature of a pact

padang *n* a playing field

padde *obs fm n* **pad**, a footpath

padder *n* a robber: one who pads *obs S vb* to tread

padella *n* a shallow dish for oil or fat which, with the addition of a wick, is used for illumination

padfoot *dial n* a barghest: a footpad

padle *S n* paddle or paidle, the lumpfish or lumpsucker, a clumsy sea fish: paidle, a hoe or hoe-shaped scraper *S vb* paidle, to hoe the ground

pad nag *n* an easy-going horse *vb* to ride at an easy pace

padrero *var fm n* **pederero**, a type of old gun which fired a variety of missiles such as stones or pieces of metal (*pl* **padreros**)

padrone *n* the master, in an Italian or Italian-American context *esp* in the catering trade: historically applied to the master of a Mediterranean trading vessel, to the leader of a group of street musicians or to the adult running a gang of child beggars (*pl* **padrones, padroni**)

padroni *pl* padrone

padtré *var fm n* **padtree**

padtree *n* a wooden or metal frame which gives rigidity and shape to a harness pad

paederast *n* a homosexual who practises his perversions on a boy

paella *n* a saffron-flavoured chicken stew

paeon *n* a metric foot of four syllables, any three of which are short and one is long (see **metric foot**)

paerl *Shet fm n* **pearl**

paginal *adj* of or pertaining to a page or pages of paper

pai *var fm n* **pie**, the Indian coin

paidle *var fm S n/vb* **padle**

pail (*n*) *dial vb* to beat or thrash

paile *var fm dial n* **pale**, a rail

pailer *erron fm obs n* **pailet** (TRIVIA note: Though pailet ceased to be a *fm* of **pallet** in the 17th century, a misprint as 'pailer' in a 1634 edition of a book was revived in 1881 as being a genuine *var fm* of pallet. This '*var fm*' has since appeared as such in subsequent dictionaries. Hence, the misprint is extant, the correct *fm* obsolete!)

pailet *obs fm n* **pallet**, a straw bed (also see **pailer**)

paine *obs fm n/vb* **pain** *obs fm n* **pane**

painen *obs fm arch n* **paynim**, a pagan or heathen: a Muslim

painterly *adj* artistic *adv* artistically

paintress *n* a female artist

painty *adj* having been coloured with too much paint

pairer *obs n* one who injures or weakens something

pair-horse *adj* as in **pair-horse harness** or **pair-horse chariot**, designating two horses paired together

pairt *obs S fm adj/n* **pert**

paistler *var fm obs n* **pastler**

paiter *dial fm n/vb* **patter**

palanquin *n* a light litter or box borne on poles carried on men's shoulders

paleis *obs fm n* **palace**

palen *vb* to make or cause to be pale

paler *comp adj* pale *obs n* one who put up a paling or fence: an officer in a park who ensured that fences were maintained in a good state

palet *n* palea, a small leaf-like part of a plant

palice *obs fm n* **palace**

paliest *sup adj* paly, somewhat pale

palimony *n* alimony sought by one who has lived 'in sin' with another

palindrome *n* a word, phrase or sentence which reads the same when written in reverse order. Examples:- *redivider* (the longest known palindromic word in everyday English), *saippuakauppias* (a Finnish word meaning 'soap seller', the longest known in any language), and the classic sentences:– *Sums are not set as a test on Erasmus. Madam, I'm Adam. A man, a plan, a canal – Panama.* Napoleon's, *Able was I ere I saw Elba.* (Also see **pseudodrome**)

palise *var fm obs n/vb* **palis**, (to enclose with) a palisade or fence of stakes *obs fm n* **palace**

palki *n* a palanquin or form of individual transportation comprising a canopied seat carried on poles borne on the shoulders of four men

pallae *pl* palla, a mantle worn by the women of ancient Rome

palleted *adj* carried on a pallet or pallets

palling *n* the losing of such as freshness, flavour or interest

pally *collq adj* companionable, marked by close friendship (*comp* **pallier** *sup* **palliest**) *var fm her adj* **paly**

Palmae *n* the family of the various palm trees and shrubs

palmary *adj* pre-eminent

palmated *adj* handshaped

palmer *n* one who returns from a pilgrimage to the Holy Land and possesses a souvenir palm leaf: an itinerant monk: a wood louse: a destructive hairy caterpillar: a hairy, caterpillar-like, artificial fly used by a fisherman: one adept at concealing an item in his hand *S & dial vb* to wander idly from place to place

palmette *n* a carved or painted ornament in ancient art resembling the palm leaf: an appendage on the head of certain gasteropod molluscs (GAME PLAYER'S note: It may appear to those who restrict themselves to the UK championship Scrabble words that this word is French. It isn't. It is *from* the French.)

palmetto *n* any of various palms *esp* the cabbage palm of the southern United States (*pl* **palmettos, palmettoes**)

palmier (*comp adj*) *obs n* a palm tree

palmies *pl S n* palmy

palmiet *n* a South African riverside plant of the rush family

palm wine *n* wine made from the sap of any of various palm trees

palmy *adj* marked by prosperity (*comp* **palmier** *sup* **palmiest**): of or pertaining to a palm or palms: palmlike *S n* the punishment of being caned on the palm of the hand (*pl* **palmies**)

palmyra *n* a species of tall palm tree of the Indian sub-continent, the wood of which is used as timber, the leaves for matting and the sap for a sugar and a wine; the outer pulp is either roasted or made into a jelly and the nuts, roots, shoots and seedlings are also edible

palolo *n* a silver coin of Pope Paul V (1605–1621) (*pl* **paoli**)

palp *n* palpus, either of a pair of sense organs attached to the mouthpart of an insect or a crustacean (*pl* **palps, palpi**) *vb* to touch, feel: flatter, cajole

palsy *n* paralysis *vb* to paralyse

palter *vb* to equivocate, to play fast and loose with, to trick *dial vb* to pilfer a shipwreck

palterer *n* one who palters

paludament *n* a military cloak worn by an ancient Roman general: a royal cloak: a herald's coat

palustral *adj* pertaining to or dwelling in marshes

paly *adj* (somewhat) pale (*comp* **palier** *sup* **paliest**) *her adj* having an even number of vertical stripes of alternate colours

pam *n* the jack of clubs in the game of loo or lanterloo (see **loo**)

panatel *obs n* a light dish of bread boiled to a pulp and flavoured with such ingredients as sugar, currants and nutmeg

panchax *n* any of various small, egg-laying, freshwater toothcarps of Africa and southeast Asia (*pl* **panchaxes**)

pancratist *n* one who competed in an ancient Greek sport which combined both boxing and wrestling

panderess *n* a woman who procures women for lewd practices

panderism *n* the trade or occupation of a pimp

Pandion *n* the genus of the osprey *pers n* the father of two daughters who, in a classic fable, were turned into birds (see **Philomel** and **Progne**)

pandit *var fm n* **pundit**

pandore *var fm n* **pandora**, a banjo

pane (*n*) *vb* to fit a pane (either glass to a window or fabric to fabric)

panelist *US fm n* **panellist**, one who sits on a panel

paner *obs fm n* **pannier**, a large basket

pangamic *adj* of pangamy, random mating

pangolin *n* the scaly ant-eater, any of seven species of Asian mammals which have a protective coat of scales not unlike roof tiles in appearance (also see **anteater**)

pangram *n* a sentence which includes every letter in the alphabet at least once. Most typists know *The quick brown fox jumps over a lazy dog* but shorter ones *incl:– Pack my box with five dozen liquor jugs. The five boxing wizards jump quickly. Quick wafting zephyrs vex bold Jim* and the classic, *Cwm, fjord-bank glyphs vext quiz*. This gem, which uses each letter only once, roughly translates as 'Carved figures on the bank of a fjord in a rounded valley irritated an eccentric person'. (Also see **kvutza**)

panick *var fm n* **panic**, a type of grass which includes several species of millet

panicle *n* a loose compound flower cluster having branches of different lengths

panier *var fm n* **pannier**, a large basket

panisc *n* a godlet attendant on Pan

pannicle *var fm n* **panicle** *obs n* an animal or plant membrane

panse *S & dial vb* to dress a wound

pansie *obs fm n* **pansy**

pansy (*n*) *slg n* an effeminate male: a male homosexual *slg adj* effeminate, prissy, homosexual (*comp* **pansier** *sup* **pansiest**)

pantein *var fm n* **pantine**

pantel *obs fm now dial n* **pantle**

panter *n* one who controls the supply of bread in a large establishment *now dial n* a (fowling) net, trap or snare *slg n* the heart *obs fm n* **painter**

pantile *n* a roofing tile which is curved in cross-section

pantiled *adj* covered with pantiles

pantiling *n* the action of covering a roof with pantiles: pantiles collectively

pantine *n* a fashionable 18th century toy of a jointed cardboard human figure which (like a marionette) was operated by wire or thread

pantle *now dial n* a bird snare made out of horsehair *now dial vb* to pant

pantler *n* a panter, one having charge of bread

paper reed *n* the plant, papyrus

papillote *n* greased paper used in cooking: frilled paper used to decorate cooked meat

papisher *now dial n* a papist

papule *n* a pimple (*pl* **papulae, papules)**

paq *var fm n* **paca**

par *n* equality of worth *dial n* an animal enclosure *vb* to equate in worth *now dial vb* parr, to enclose or confine animals *var fm n* **parr** *var fm dial n* **parre**

paraenetic *adj* of, pertaining to or of the nature of exhortation, advice or counsel: advisory

parafle *S n* ostentatious display

parament *obs n* an ornament, a decoration: a robe of state

parasite *(n) vb* to infest as a parasite: to behave as a parasite

parboil *vb* to boil partially

Parca *n* a Fate, one of the three Roman goddesses **Nona, Decuma** or **Morta** (*pl* **Parcae)**

Parcae *pl* Parca

parded *adj* spotted like a leopard

pardie *arch interj/adv* perdie, verily, indeed

pardine *adj* of or pertaining to the leopard

Pareas *n* a genus of thirst snakes (see **thirst snake**)

parecious *var fm adj* **paroecious,** having the male and female organs growing side by side as in certain of the more primitive plants

parecism *US var fm n* **paroecism**

paredri *pl* paredrus

paredrial *obs n* a familiar or advisor from the spiritual world acting jointly with the living person in making assessments

paredrus *obs n* a paredrial (*pl* **paredri)**

parenesis *var fm n* **paraenesis**, advice or counsel, an encouraging composition

parer *n* one who or that which pares

pareses *pl* paresis

paresis *n* partial loss of the ability to move (*pl* **pareses)**

paretic *adj* of or pertaining to paresis *n* one suffering paresis

parge *vb* to plaster a surface

pargie *obs fm US n* **porgie**

pariah *n* one of a very extensive low caste in Southern India: a social outcast (*fig*): a yellow vagabond dog which scavenges in the urban areas of the East

Parian *adj* of Paros, a Greek island *n* a native of Paros: a marble-like porcelain

paries *n* a biological or zoological internal wall or boundary not only of a living nature but also extended to include such as a cell in a honeycomb or in a wasp's nest (*pl* **parietes)**

parietal *adj* of a wall or walls: belonging to or connected with a biological wall or cavity *esp* to a pair of bones which forms part of the side and top of the skull *n* either of such bones

parietes *pl* paries

parine *adj* of titmice

paris *n* herb paris or truelove, a plant of moist woodland bearing a single greenish flower above four large ovate leaves in the shape of a cross (*pl* **parises)**

parishe *obs fm n* **parish**

parished *adj* having parishes

parishen *S dial n* a parish *obs n* a parishioner

parison *n* in rhetoric, an even balance of the component parts of a sentence (*pl* **parisa**): the mass of molten glass extracted from the furnace in a glassworks (*pl* **parisons)**

paritor *obs n* the summoning officer of an ecclesiastical court (an aphetic *fm* of **apparitor**

used by many writers from Tudor times to Scott in the 19th century) (GAME PLAYER'S note: A Shakespeare 'exclusive' of the dictionary used for the UK Scrabble championship which, had it mentioned Scott, would have made the word valid for play under the local rules of that contest)

parka *n* an Eskimo-style (weatherproofed) hooded outergarment

parkee *var fm n* **parka**

parle *arch n* speech, talk, conversation: a conference *esp* one conducted under terms of a truce *arch vb* to speak, to talk in conference: to hold a parley: to treat with

parley *n* speech, conversation: debate *S & dial n* a gingerbread cake *S dial n* a truce in various activities *vb* to speak (in a foreign tongue): to discuss terms of a treaty *US vb* to have an accumulator bet on racehorses

parling *n* speaking: a conference

parnel *now dial n* the mistress of a priest: a harlot

parodic *adj* of the nature of a parody

parodist *n* the writer of a parody

paroecism *n* of certain plants, the condition of having male and female reproductive organs growing side by side

parol *n* an oral statement (now extant only in the legal phrase **by parol**, by word of mouth) *adj* expressed orally (now extant only in such legal phrases as **parol evidence**, verbal evidence)

parotic *adj* situated in the proximity of the ear

parotid *adj* near the ear *n* a salivary gland in front of the ear

parotis *n* the largest of the three salivary glands in man (*pl* **parotides**)

parotitis *n* mumps

parpen *n* a stone which has a face on both sides of a wall

parpend *var fm n* **parpen**

parpent *var fm n* **parpen**

parr *n* see **SALMON**: a coalfish less than one year old *var fm dial n* **parre** *var fm now dial vb* **par**

parre *dial n* a leveret

parret *obs fm n* **parrot**

parroty *adj* like or of the nature of a parrot

parsable *adj* capable of being parsed

parse *vb* to describe grammatically by giving the form, function etc of each component part (of a sentence)

parsec *n* parallax-second, a unit (about nineteen billion miles) for the measurement of star distances

parsed *dial adj* married

Parsee *n* a Persian Zoroastrian or fire worshipper (*–cap*) *var fm obs n* **persue**

parsel *obs fm n* **parcel**

parsenip *obs fm n* **parsnip**

parser *n* a grammarian: a book on the subject of **parse**

Parsi *var fm n* **Parsee**

parsie *var fm obs n* **persue**

parsneip *obs fm n* **parsnip**

parsnep *var fm n* **parsnip**

parsonet *n* a freshly-appointed parson: a child of a parson

partan *S & dial n* the common crab: the shore crab: a crabby person

parte *obs fm n/vb* **part**

parteis *Obs pl* **party**

parten *var fm S & dial n* **partan** *obs vb* to share

parter *n* one who or that which parts

parthenogenesis *n* virgin birth, typified by the aphid which hatches from the winter egg as a wingless female. Several generations of such wingless females arise during the course of the warmer months until the final generation which consists of wingless females and, for the only time, males (which are winged). After mating, the female produces winter-resistant eggs.

parti *Fr n* one who, in English, would rate the description 'eligible bachelor': the female equivalent of same: a group of people

partialism *n* any theory which does not take account of all the relevant factors

partim *Latin adv* in part

partin *var fm S & dial n* **partan**

partise *Obs pl* party

partite *adj* divided into parts

partlet *n* a woman's collar, ruff or other neckwear as worn in historical times (+*cap*) *n* the proper name for a hen, usually in the *fm* **Dame Partlet** (also see **redbreast**)

parton *var fm S & dial n* **partan**

parture *obs n* departure: offspring, fruit

parulis *n* a gumboil

parvise *erron var fm n* **parvis**, the enclosed court in front of a building *esp* an ecclesiastical one

pascal *n* a unit of pressure in the metric system

Pasch *arch n* Easter: Passover (**Pasch eve, Pasch morn** etc refer to the Christian Easter not the Jewish Passover)

Pasche *obs fm arch n* **Pasch**

pasear *US slg n/vb* (to take) a walk

pashim *n* the fine underfleece of the goats of Northern India

pashm *var fm n* **pashim**

pashmina *var fm n* **pashim**

Pashto *adj/n* (of) a language of the Indo-Iranian family of languages spoken by Afghans

pasment *obs fm n* **passement**

pasnep *obs fm n* **parsnip**

pasper *dial n* samphire

passade *n* a turn or movement of a horse backwards and forwards over the same ground

passado *obs n* a fencing thrust made simultaneously with a forward step (*pl* **passados, passadoes**)

passement *n* a decorative trimming of such as gold or silver lace: a similar trimming of such as silk braid *vb* to edge or otherwise adorn with passement

passen *poet (pseudo-arch) vb* to pass

Passeres *n pl* a now obsolete term for a grouping of birds which included within this classification more than half of all the known species

passerine *adj/n* see both **BIRD CLASSIFICATION** (introductory comments) and **ANIMAL ADJECTIVES** (entry for **songbird**)

passim *Latin adv* here and there: throughout

passional *adj* of or pertaining to passion or the passions

passman *n* a university student who reads for, and takes, a pass degree

passment *var fm n* **passement**

paste grain *n* a sheepskin with a better grain which has been produced by applying a paste to the back

pastelling *n* the production of a picture in pastel

paster *n* one who pastes *US n* a gummed label

pastern *n* that part of a horse's foot between the fetlock and the hoof: the corresponding part in other four-legged animals: the human ankle *vb* to fetter

Pasteur *pers n* the great French chemist (1822–1895)

pastiche *n* a jumble: a composition in any of the arts made up of bits of other works

pasticheur *n* one who makes pastiches

pastier *comp adj* pasty

pastill *obs fm n* **pastil** or **pastille**

pastimer *obs n* one given to sport or pastimes

pastine *Obs n* land prepared for planting *Obs vb* to plant in such land (*pa t* **pastined**)

pastis *n* an absinthe-like alcoholic drink

pastler *obs n* a pastry cook

pastre *North Ire n* the pastern of a horse

pastree *obs fm n* **pastry**

pasturer *n* a herdsman

Patarin *n* one of an 11th century movement based in Milan which was opposed to the marriage of priests: a term used, from the 12th century onwards, for a member of any of various heretical groups

Patarine *var fm n* **Patarin**

patchery *n* the action of patching or mending in a rough and ready fashion: anything made of bits and pieces *obs n* knavery

patel *n* an Indian village headman (*pl* **patels**): the patella or kneecap (*pl* **patellae**)

patella *n* the kneecap (*pl* **patellae, patellas**)

paten *n* a (communion) plate: a metal disc

pater *n* the paternoster or the Lord's Prayer *schoolboy slg n* father *obs n* a monk or priest

patera *n* a round flat dish *esp* one used in ancient Roman sacrificial rites: any round flat architectural ornamentation such as a rosette (*pl* **paterae**)

paterero *var fm n* **pedrero**

path (*n*) *obs vb* to take a path (*lit/fig*)

pathe *obs fm n/var fm obs vb* **path**

pathed *adj* having a path

pathic *adj* passive

pathogen *n* a micro-organism or any other agent that can produce disease

patin *obs fm ns* **paten, patten**

patina *n* a sheen acquired from handling or polishing: a surface film which develops on various substances: a communion plate (*pl* **patinae, patinas**)

patine *vb* to cover with a patina

patined *adj* set like inlaid dishes

patle *var fm dial vb* **pattle**

patlet *obs n* an object of apparel such as a neckerchief

patness *n* aptness

patois *n* a local (illiterate) dialect (*pl* **patois**)

patrial *adj* of or belonging to one's native country: of a word which is nationally or locally descriptive, as **Derbeian** is descriptive of a native of the city of Derby *n* a patrial word

patrialism an undefined noun which appears to be exclusive to the dictionary currently used for the UK Scrabble championship. The prefix 'patri-', meaning father, is sometimes used for words of recent coinage to imply male dominance in a primitive society. The suffix '-ism' has various meanings *incl* 'an abnormal condition resulting from an excess of', though the balance of probability suggests that it is 'the system of'. Its anagram is **partialism**.

patriation *n* the transferring of the responsibility for the Canadian constitution from the UK parliament to the Canadian parliament

patrico *slg n* a hedge priest, an illiterate or ill-educated priest of inferior status (*pl* **patricoes**)

PATRON SAINTS See below

patrone *obs n* the galley which carried the second in command of a squadron of galleys *obs fm n* **patroon**

patronymic *adj* of a personal or a family name: derived from the name of an ancestor *esp* by the addition of prefix or suffix indicating

PATRON SAINTS Traditionally, individual saints are deemed to have special concern for a grouping of some description and/or for a particular problem. For example, the 7th century Irish hermit, St Fiacre, is considered to be the patron saint of taxi drivers, one of the patron saints of gardeners and he is also invoked by sufferers of haemorrhoids in search of a cure. A saint with much wider responsibilities is the popular St Nicholas (Santa Claus), concerned with children, virgins, Russia, Greece, bakers, pawnbrokers and travellers. A short selection follows.

1 PROBLEMS:– **desperate straits** Jude: **epilepsy** Vitus: **eye diseases** Lucy: **haemorrhoids** Fiacre: **mental disorders** Dympna: **physical diseases** Rock: **pressing emergency** Expeditus: **throat infections** Blaise: **toothache** Apollonia: **troublesome husbands** Wilgefortis.

2 OCCUPATIONS or OTHER CATEGORIES OF PEOPLE:– **accountants and bankers** Matthew: **actors** Genesius: **airmen** Our Lady of Loretto, Joseph Cupertino, Thérèse of Lisieux: **architects** Barbara, Thomas: **artists** Luke: **athletes** Sebastian: **authors** Frances de Sales: **bakers** Elizabeth of Hungary, Nicholas: **barbers** Cosmas, Damian, Louis: **bell founders** Agatha: **blacksmiths** Dunstan: **booksellers** John of God: **brewers** Augustine of Hippo, Luke, Nicholas of Myra: **bricklayers** Stephen: **carpenters** Joseph: **children** Nicholas: **comedians** Vitus: **cooks** Lawrence, Martha: **cripples** Giles: **dentists** Apollonia: **doctors** Cosmas, Damian, Luke, Pantaleon, Raphael: **editors** John Bosco: **engineers** Ferdinand III: **farmers** George, Isidore: **firemen** Florian: **florists** Dorothea, Thérèse: **funeral directors** Dysmas, Joseph of Arimathea: **gardeners** Adelard, Dorothea, Fiacre, Phocas, Tryphon: **goldsmiths** Anastasius, Dunstan: **grave diggers** Anthony: **grocers** Michael: **hired workers** Notburga: **housewives** Anne: **hunters** Hubert: **innkeepers** Amand: **jewellers** Eloi: **journalists** Frances de Sales: **Knights of Malta** John the Almsgiver: **lawyers** Genesius, Ivo, Sir Thomas More: **Lebanese Maronite Christians** Maro: **librarians** Jerome: **maidservants** Zita: **midwives** Peter Nolasco: **miners** Barbara: **motorcyclists** Our Lady of Grace: **motorists** Christopher, Frances of Rome: **musicians** Cecilia, Dunstan, Gregory the Great: **natural sciences (students of)** Albert the Great: **nurses** Agatha, Alexius, Camillus of Lellis, John of God, Raphael: **paratroopers** Michael: **parish priests** John Vianney (the Curé d'Ars): **poets** Cecilia, David: **policemen** Michael: **postal and other communications workers** Gabriel: **printers** Augustine of Hippo, John of God: **sailors** Brendan the Voyager, Christopher, Cuthbert, Erasmus (Elmo), Eulalia, Peter Gonzales, Phocas: **scholars** Bridget: **scientists** Albert: **scouts** George: **sculptors** Claude: **secretaries** Cassian, Genesius: **Serbs** Sava: **shoemakers** Crispin, Crispinianus: **sick (the)** Camillus, John of God: **soldiers** Adrian, George, Ignatius, Joan of Arc, Martin, Sebastian: **students** Catherine, Thomas Aquinas: **tailors** Homobonus: **tax collectors** Matthew: **taxi drivers** Fiacre: **teachers** Catherine, Gregory the Great, John Baptist de la Salle: **travellers** Anthony of Padua, Christopher, Nicholas, Raphael: **virgins** Nicholas: **wine growers** Vincent: **workers** Joseph: **yachtsmen** Adjutor.

3 COUNTRIES and CITIES The list is far too long to cover, but the European countries include:– **Belgium** Joseph: **Czechoslovakia** John of Nepomuk, Procopius, Wenceslas: **Denmark** Asgar, Canute: **England** George: **France** Our Lady of the Assumption, Joan of Arc, Thérèse: **Germany** Boniface, Michael: **Greece** Andrew, Nicholas: **Holland** Willibrord: **Hungary** Our Lady, Stephen: **Ireland** Patrick: **Italy** Catherine of Sienna, Francis of Assissi: **Norway** Olaf: **Poland** Our Lady of Czestochowa, Casimir, Stanislaus: **Portugal** The Immaculate Conception, Anthony of Padua, Francis Borgia, George, Vincent: **Russia** Andrew, Nicholas, Thérèse of Lisieux: **Scotland** Andrew, Columba: **Spain** James, Teresa: **Sweden** Bridget, Eric: **Wales** David.

descent (e.g. Mac or Mc, son of) *n* a family name, an ancestral name

patroon *n* the master of a ship or boat: the possessor of a landed estate and certain manorial rights granted by the government of the colonial territory of New Netherland. Whilst both the territory and its capital, New Amsterdam, became British in 1664 (New Amsterdam then becoming New York) the manorial rights, *incl* that of a manorial court, continued until approximately 1850.

patte *n* on a coat the front edges of which do not overlap, a short strap attached to one edge and having a buttonhole for securing it to the other edge

pattel *var fm obs n* **patel**, a (frying) pan

patten *n* a Chinese thick-soled wooden shoe: a chopin or thick-soled shoe formerly worn by women to increase their height: a wooden sole strapped to any shoe for use in muddy conditions: a similar device for the hoof of a horse: a base or foundation for a wall or an architectural column *vb* to walk on pattens

patter (*n*/*vb*) *Austr vb* to eat

patterer *n* one who patters: one who mechanically repeats prayers

pattle *S & dial n* a long-handled, spade-like tool used mainly as a mud scraper *obs S vb* to scrape with a tool of various sorts *dial vb* to caress

patulin *n* a drug obtained from a mould fungus

paul *obs fm vb* **pall** *obs fm n*/*vb* **pawl**

paulter *var fm dial vb* **palter**

paune *obs fm n*/*vb* **pawn**

pautre *obs n* a beam

pavie *S n* bodily dexterity: a trick

pavier *arch fm n* **paviour**, a paving stone: one who lays paving stones

pavis *n* a very large personal shield which was employed during static circumstances such as a siege or a sustained archery attack *vb* to defend with a pavis

pavise *var fm n*/*vb* **pavis**

paviser *n* a soldier bearing a pavis

pawen *var fm obs n* **pawn**, a covered walk *esp* one with market stalls

pawl *n* a lever with a catch for engaging in the teeth of a bar or wheel *vb* to stop or secure by means of a pawl

pawmie *var fm S n* **palmy**

pawne *obs fm n*/*vb* **pawn**

pawse *obs fm n*/*vb* **pause**

paye *obs fm n* **pie**, a pastry

payne *obs fm ns* **pain, pane** *Obs fm obs n* **pain**, bread

pe *n* the seventeenth letter of the Hebrew alphabet: a Portuguese and Brazilian measure of length *var fm obs n* **pee** (*pl* **peys**)

pea (*n*) note: The true singular for this word is **pease**. Its correct plural is either **peasen** or **peason**, though **peases** is an acceptable modern form. The change occurred by the error of assuming that pease was a plural and, therefore, the singular had to be pea. The basic word, pease, is still extant though as an archaic word or within various dialects. The plural as peasen tends to be the archaic plural, with the plural as peason now only dialect. (Also see **gantline** and **pailer** for examples of similar erroneous forms which, due to dictionary errors, have either overtaken the correct form or appear likely so to do.)

peace (*n*) *arch vb* to be or become silent

peach (*n*) *vb* to give incriminating evidence against

peacher (*n*) an accuser or informer

peachick *n* the chick of the peafowl

pea crab *n* a species of crab of which the male remains the size of a pea whilst the female grows much larger. Both sexes choose to live inside other creatures, such as molluscs or sea cucumbers, though the female eventually grows too large to escape. This the male puts to good advantage when he nips in for a captive mating.

peai *n* a witch doctor in Guyana and adjacent lands in South America *vb* to practise as such: to be treated by such (*infl fms incl* **peaied, peaiing**)

pea iron *n* limonite, an ore of iron in the form of little round nodules

pealer *now dial n* one who makes a (legal) appeal

peanie *S n* a turkey hen

pear (*n*) *now dial vb* to appear

peare *obs fm now dial vb* pear

pearl (*n*) *vb* to make pearly in colour: to reduce such as barley into a pearl-like shape

pearl ash *n* crude potassium carbonate

pearlfish *n* any of various elongated marine fishes related to the cod and also known as cucumberfishes due to their habit of living inside the animal known as the sea cucumber with only their head showing through the anus of the host (note: The pearlfish is not the only pest of the sea cucumber – it also suffers from crabs – see **pea crab**): any of various toothcarps known as Argentine pearlfish (see **annual fish**)

pearlin *var fm S & dial n* **pearling**, a trimming for the edge of a garment

pearling *n* fishing for pearls: a pearl-like grain or pellet: a coating of such *S & dial n* a lace or silk trimming for the edge of a garment

pearlite *var fm n* **perlite**

pearlstone *n* perlite

pearse *obs fm vb* **pierce**

pearst *obs fm vbl infl* **pierced**

peart *adj* lively, brisk, sprightly: clever, intelligent (*comp* **pearter** *sup* **peartest**) *dial fm adj/n* **pert** *var fm obs vb* **pert**, to perk

pearte *obs fm adj/n* **pert**

peartly *now dial fm adv* **pertly**

pease *n* the pea: the pea plant (*pl* **peases** *arch pl* **peasen** *now dial pl* **peason** – see **pea**) *obs vb* to make peace (between): to pacify

peasen *arch pl* pease (see **pea**)

peason *now dial pl* pease (see **pea**)

peat (n) *arch n* a later spelling of **peate** revived by Scott and others in the senses of a defamatory term for a woman or a term of abuse for a man *esp* for a lawyer favoured by a judge without regard to the justice of his cause. The *obs* senses of this word (for which Shakespeare used the *fm* **peate** and Jonson the *fm* **peat**) are a term of endearment for a woman or a pet name for an animal.

peate see **peat**

peatship *obs n* the personality of a peat in the senses of the *arch n* (GAME PLAYER'S note: Scott is the last known writer to have used this term – a 17th century writer having used the spelling **petship** – and, for Scrabble players in the UK championship, this is accounted acceptable for valid play. He used it in *Redgauntlet* in 1824.)

peche *obs fm vb* **peach**

pecher *obs fm n* **peacher**

Pecora *n pl* cattle and other grazing animals, apart from camels and mouse deer, which chew their cud

pecten *n* a comblike anatomical structure: the part covered by the pubic hair (*pl* **pectens, pectines**) (GAME PLAYER'S note: Only **pectines** is available for UK championship Scrabble as that is the only *pl fm* given in its reference work. In the corresponding North American championship both *fms* are permitted as their dictionary gives the generally accepted *fms* on both sides of the Atlantic.)

pectin *n* any of various compounds in such as apples or lemons and which forms the basis of fruit jellies

pectinal *adj* of or resembling a comb: belonging to the pubes (in this sense probably now *obs* except as the origin of the *slg n* **pecker**, meaning penis, with the obvious pun as cock!) *n* (in *pl fm*) flatfish

pectines *pl* pecten

peculation *n* embezzlement by an official of that which belongs to the public

peculator *n* one who commits an act of peculation

ped *arch n* a spade or shovel *dial n* a pannier or hamper

pedaler *var fm n* **pedaller**

pedalier *n* a pedal keyboard for a piano

pedaling *var fm n* **pedalling**

pedaller *n* one who pedals

pedalo *n* a boat operated by pedal (*pl* **pedalos, pedaloes**)

pedal point *n* a musical note sustained in one part through a succession of harmonies

pedant *n* one who flaunts his knowledge

pedantise *var fm vb* **pedantize**, to speak, write or behave pedantically

pedder *now S & dial n* a pedlar

peder *obs fm now S & dial n* **pedder**

pedera *obs n* the opal

pederast *var fm n* **paederast**

pedesis *n* the irregular movement of microscopic particles

pedicel *n* a small stalk: a peduncle

pedicle *n* a minute, stalk-like support of such as a seed (also see **pedicel** and **peduncle**)

pedlary *n* the occupation or the goods of a pedlar (*pl* **pedlaries**)

pedler *var fm n* **pedlar**

pednan *dial n pl* small pieces of turf

pedrail *n* a tractor having footlike appendages on its wheels

pedrero *n* a small naval gun which, in former times, fired stones, pieces of metal or any other suitable loose material (there are quite a number of *var fms* such as **paterero** and **pederero** and the *pl fms* are either '-os' or '-oes' in most, if not all, cases)

peduncle *n* the stalk of a flower or fruit: the main stalk of a cluster of flowers: a stalk(-like) process, either natural or morbid, in a creature

pee (*slg n/vb*) *n* the letter P: that portion of ore common to intersecting veins *obs n* a type of coarse woollen cloth: a garment of this material, usually a coat of some description (note: Of the *var fms* **P, pe, pea** and **py**, pea is still extant as a *modf n* in the *fms* **pea coat** or **pea jacket**, a coarse woollen coat or jacket worn by a sailor) *obs fm n* **pie**, the magpie *dial vb* to squint

peen *n* the thin or sharp end of the head of a hammer *now dial vb* to hammer

peert *dial fm adj/n* **pert**

peever *n* the object thrown in the game of hopscotch

peinct *obs S fm n/vb* **paint**

peir *obs S fm now dial vb* **pear**, to appear

peirse *obs fm vb* **parse**

peirt *obs fm adj/n* **pert**

peirte *obs fm adj/n* **pert**

peise *now dial n* a weight *esp* any object used as the standard by which the weights of similar objects are judged *now dial vb* to estimate weight by handling

peitrel *n* a (richly ornamented) piece of breast armour for a horse, often retained as a decorative item *obs vb* to place such on a horse (also see **peytral**)

pekin *n* a silken material

Pelagian *adj* of or pertaining to Pelagius, a 5th century British monk who conceived a heresy based on the rejection of the concept of original sin, or his heresy *n* a follower of his heresy (*–cap*) *adj* of or belonging to the open sea *n* an inhabitant of the open sea

pelamid *n* the Atlantic bonito, a tuna-like fish which can attain a length of three feet and its high quality white meat is canned in the USA (also see **skipjack**)

Pelasgian *n* one of the Pelasgi or Pelasgians, an ancient race of the eastern Mediterranean and believed to have occupied Lemnos prior to the coming of the Hellenes or classical Greeks. (This possibility is strengthened by the Greek myths, which lay great emphasis on the overthrow of earlier gods by the later generation led by Zeus.) *adj* Pelasgic

Pelasgic *adj* of, pertaining to or characteristic of the Pelasgians

pele *arch fm n* **peel**, a fortified building *S fm vb* **peel**, to pillage *obs fm ns* **peal, peel, pell** (in some senses only) *obs fm vb* **peal** (all senses except the *dial* of cooling)

pelfish *obs adj* rubbishy

PELHAM A card game in which players amass sets of 6-letter words. At the culmination of the 'rummy-like' stage, each player in turn reveals his or her words, doing so one at a time. As will be seen in the 6-letter anagram listing, the potential for anagrams is enormous. Consequently, the player scores points for every other word he or she can devise (within a time limit) from any particular word. However, once a player has made a complete declaration for any one set, that points value can be captured by an opponent who successfully creates another anagram. The rules are simple and any number of players from two to six can be accommodated. (note: At the time of writing, both the name of the game and its rules are copyright © Peter Newby 1986 but it is anticipated that the game will be commercially available at a time which coincides with the publication of *Pears Advanced Word-Puzzler's Dictionary*. At such time the name, **Pelham**, will be a registered trade mark of the manufacturer.)

pelham *n* of the various types of bridle-bit used to restrain horses, the **curb** is the most severe, the **snaffle** the least severe and the **pelham** midway between them

pelite *n* a sedimentary rock composed of clay, quartz particles and glacier meal (rock crushed to a powder by the action of glaciation): other rock of a similar nature

pelitic *adj* composed of fine sediment

peller *obs fm now dial n* **pealer**

pellit *obs fm n* **pellet**

peloid *n* any natural substance used for a poultice

peloria *n* symmetry of structure in plants where such structure is normally unsymmetrical

pelorise *obs fm vb* **pelorize**, to change by developing peloria

pelorism *n* abnormal regularity in a flower which is normally irregular in structure

Pelorous Jack *n* a famous dolphin which frequented the Pelorous Sound near Wellington, New Zealand, where it swam near the bows of ships. As museums and fishermen wanted to capture this animal, it was protected by an Order-in-Council and, for 24 years, was a popular welcoming sight for all who sailed.

pelorus *n* a type of navigational compass

pelota *n* a competitive game of Basque origin, similar in form to squash or fives, with the ball caught and thrown with force from a basket-like device

pelow *obs fm n* **pillow**

peltast *n* an ancient Greek foot soldier armed with a short spear and the light shield known as a pelta

peltate *adj* of a leaf, shield-shaped

pelter *n* one who or that which pelts or strikes *obs n* a person of little consequence *vb* to continue pelting or striking: of rain, to patter

peltier *Obs n* a furrier

peltre *obs fm n* **peltry**

peltrie *obs fm n* **peltry**

peltries see **peltry**

peltry *n* animal pelts (*pl* **peltries**, different types of peltry) *obs S n* rubbish, trash *S adj* worthless

penates *n pl* household gods, the deities of Roman mythology who were the guardians of the house or of the state

pencel *n* a small flag or streamer *obs n* a lady's token carried by a knight (on his lance)

pencil ore *n* graphite occurring as an aggregate with a rounded surface resembling a bunch of grapes

pendel *obs fm now dial n* **pendle**

pendis *obs fm n* **penthouse**

pendle *n* any upper stratum or strata of non-commercial material in a quarry *now dial n* a pendulum

pendular *adj* of, pertaining to or resembling a pendulum

pendulate *vb* to swing like a pendulum (*lit/fig*)

penede *obs fm n* **penide**

Penelope *fem pers n* meaning 'weaver' (– *cap*) *n* the widgeon

penetrance *n* the frequency, expressed as a percentage, with which a gene displays an effect *obs n* penetration

penguin (*n*) for a ludicrous divergent view see **pinguin**

penial *adj* of the male sex organ

penide *n* a stick of barley sugar used as a cold remedy

penie *obs fm n* **penny** (*pl fms incl* **penies, pens**, the rather curious **penis** being of earlier date and *Obs*)

penile *adj* of or pertaining to the penis *obs n* a peninsula

peniless *obs fm adj* **penniless**

penisle *var fm obs n* **penile**

penistone *n* a type of coarse woollen cloth formerly made at Penistone, Yorkshire (+ *cap*) *modf n* **Penistone flags**, sandstone paving stones from Penistone

penlite *US n* a small flashlight

pennate *adj* pinnate: having the form or appearance of a feather: winged: very swift (*fig*)

Pennisetum *n* a genus of grasses which includes the pearl millet

penquin *var fm n* **pinguin**

pensal *Obs fm n* **pencel**

pensil *var fm n* **pencel**

pensile *adj* hanging (down): suspended *arch fm n* **pencel**

penster *n* a literary hack

pensy *now S & dial adj* pensive: neat: self-conceited: fretful: peevish: fastidious

pentad *n* (a group of) five: a period of five years

pentadic *adj* having five digits

pentail *n* the pen-tailed tree shrew, a very rare species of these small squirrel-like mammals which, unlike others, is nocturnal

pentamery *n* the condition of a plant or animal in having five parts or organs (e.g. a starfish)

pentane *n* any of the paraffins of the pentacarbon series

pentaploid *adj* fivefold

pentas *dial fm n* **penthouse**, the shed beside a smithy

Pentateuch *n* the first five books of the Bible

pentatomic *adj* of a molecule, containing five replaceable hydrogen atoms

penter *obs fm n* **painter**

Pentery Web *n* an anagram guessing game rather like hangman except that the competitor is attempting to discover a pair of anagrams with the fewest number of letters revealed as possible. It is played for points, with a maximum of 10 points available for each game. The smallest pair of words is two 6-letter words in which an identical letter is revealed in each word to begin with. Thus, if the chosen pair of anagrams is **strain** and **trains** the competitor is faced with something like the first diagram and now has to decide if he or she is prepared to forfeit score for additional letters. As the same letter is added to both words the points available diminish.

. . . A . .
. . A . . .

The taskmaster adds a second letter of his or her own choice once the competitor has either made an incorrect guess or simply 'passed'. 8 points (the number of uncovered dots or points) is now the possible score.

. . . A I .
. . A I . .

Still no success and another letter is added to both words. Only 6 points can now be won.

S . . A I .
. . A I . S

So it continues until the final 2 points are available. With a pair of 7-letter words, 2 letters are given at the start. With a pair of 8-letter words, 3 letters are given etc. Players usually begin with a pair of fairly ordinary words but soon progress to pairs such as **touristy/yttrious** as expertise develops. (note: Devised by Peter Newby who retains the copyright for any commercial exploitation.)

penthouse (*n*) *vb* to construct a penthouse: to cover as with a penthouse: to cause to project

pentice *arch fm n/vb* penthouse

pentile *erron fm n* **pantile** (*orig* noted by Dr Johnson and subsequently copied as a genuine *var fm* by other lexicographers)

pentimenti *pl* pentimento

pentimento *n* something which has been painted out of a picture but subsequently becomes visible (*pl* **pentimenti**)

pentis *now dial fm n* **penthouse**, the shed beside a smithy

pentise *var fm n* **penthouse**

pentose *n* any of various simple sugars having five carbon atoms in the molecule

penye *Obs fm n* **penny** (*pl fms incl* **penyes**)

pepe *obs fm vb* **peep** *obs fm arch vb* **peep**, to speak in a weak, shrill tone

peplos *n* an ancient Greek woman's shawl: one woven annually for the statue of Athene at Athens

peplus *var fm n* **peplos**

peptonise *var fm vb* **peptonize**, to subject food to artificial predigestion as a nursing aid

peraeon *var fm n* **perion**

perai *var fm n* **piraña**

percale *n* a closely woven non-glossy cotton fabric

percaline *n* a type of glossy French cloth

percase *now dial adv* by chance

perce *obs fm vb* **pierce**

percept *n* that perceived

percine *adj* belonging to the family of the perch *n* such a fish

percuss *vb* to tap gently a part of the body for the purpose of medical diagnosis

percussor *n* one who or that which hits *esp* a small hammer used by a doctor to test reflexes

perdendo *adj/adv* of music, dying away

perdie *var fm arch interj/adv* **pardie**

perdu *adj* hidden, concealed (*esp* in ambush)

n a soldier who is assigned to a dangerous static position (*pl* **perdus**) *obs vb* to lie or place in ambush

perdue *obs fm n/adj* **perdu** *var fm obs vb* **perdu**

perdure *vb* to endure

pere *obs fm S & dial vb* **peer**, to pour

pereia *pl* pereion

pereion *n* the limb-bearing thorax of a crustacean (*pl* **pereia**)

pereira *n* a Brazilian tree, the bark of which has medicinal properties: that bark

perial *dial adj* fine, superior *dial fm n* **prial**

perianth *n* the combined calyx and corolla of a flower when so alike as to be indistinguishable

periapt *n* an amulet or other charm worn personally

periclase *n* a mineral consisting mainly of magnesia but also having a small quantity of protoxide of iron

Periclean *adj* of or pertaining to the statesman, general and orator, Pericles (circa 495–429 BC) who raised Athens to its greatest prosperity and architectural beauty, and to the age represented by his period in history

peridot *n* olivine, a variety of chrysolite, a green-coloured gem

peridote *var fm n* **peridot**

perie *var fm obs n* **perry**, a pear tree

perigon *n* one exact revolution considered as an angle of 360° (180° being a **hemiperigon**)

perigone *n* a perianth: a male perianth or leafy covering of the male organs of mosses

peril (*n/vb*) *infl fms* British, **perilled/-lling**: US, **periled/-ling**

periost *var fm n* **periosteum**, a tough membrane covering the surface of bones

periot *var fm n* **perit**

periplus *n* circumnavigation: an account of a voyage around such as a coastline: a manoeuvre of ancient Greek naval warfare to enable their lighter craft to avoid a direct collision with heavier vessels

perique *n* a dark, strongly-flavoured Louisiana tobacco which is the usual type chosen for a roll of tobacco called a carotte (TRIVIA note: The origin of the word is obscure, with a British dictionary suggesting it is the nickname of a grower and an American dictionary suggesting it is a Creole pronunciation of the *slg* word prick due to the phallic shape of a carotte)

periscian *adj/n* (of or pertaining to) one who lives within either polar circle and, therefore, during a polar summer day of 24 hours constant daylight, has a personal shadow which makes a complete circle around him or her in that day (also *+cap*) (*pl* **periscians, Periscii** – contrast with **antiscian, Antiscii**)

peristoma *var fm n* **peristome** (*pl* **peristomata**)

peristome *n* a fringe of small, delicate teeth around the mouth of a capsule of a moss: the space between the mouth and the tentacles of a sea anemone: the margin of the mouth of a univalve mollusc: the border of the mouth of various insects

perit *n* a very minute unit of weight (see **MONEYERS WEIGHTS**)

perkin *n* a poor quality perry (pear cider) *var fm n* **parkin**, gingerbread

perl *obs fm n/vb* **pearl**

perle *n* a pellet

perlite *n* an acid, volcanic, glassy rock divided into small spherical bodies due to the stress of contraction on cooling

perlous *obs fm adj* **perilous** *obs fm arch adj* **parlous**

permain *obs vb* to remain

Permian *adj* of, denoting or formed in the approximately 25 million years which comprised this particular period of the history of the Earth (see **ROCK SYSTEMS AND LIFE FORMS**)

Pernis *n* the genus of the honey buzzard

peron *obs fm n* **perron**

perona *var fm n* **perone**

perone *n* the fibula or outer of the two bones of the lower leg

perorate *vb* to deliver a lengthy speech *esp* in a formal manner: to conclude a speech or sum up

peroun *Obs fm n* **perron**

perpal *S n* a partition

perradial *adj* pertaining to the primary rays of a hyrdrozoan

perradii *pl* parradius, any one of the primary radii of various free-swimming marine organisms

perre *var fm obs n* **perrie**

perrie *obs n* jewellery *obs fm n* **perry**

perrier *obs n* a military device which fired stones: a small type of ship's cannon

perron *n* a large block of stone, often stepped, used as the base of a market cross or as a platform for a similar monument

perry *n* a type of cider made from pears *obs n* the (wild) pear tree *var fm obs n* **perrie**

persalt *n* a salt formed by the combination of a negative radical with a metal at a high state of oxidation

perse *arch n/adj* a purplish blue-black colour (+*cap*) *obs n* a Persian

perseic *adj* of or pertaining to perseity

Perseid *n* any meteor, in a shower of meteors, which approaches from the direction of the constellation Perseus

Perseis *Obs pl obs n* Perse

perseity *n* an independent existence

persel *obs S fm n* **parsley**

Perseus *pers n* the fabled Greek hero who slew the Gorgon, Medusa, and rescued Andromeda from a sea monster *n* a constellation in the northern sky

Persic *adj* Persian *n* the Persian language

persico *n* a cordial flavoured with the kernels of apricots and peaches

persie *obs fm n* **parsee**

persiflage *n* light banter: frivolous treatment of a subject

persil *Obs fm n* **parsley**

Persism *n* a Persian idiom

persle *Obs fm n* **parsley**

person (*n*) *obs vb* to represent a person in writing: to symbolize

persona *n* a character in a play or novel (*pl* **personae**): the conscious and artificial personality which, in Jungian psychology, masks one's true thoughts and feelings (*pl* **personae, personas**)

personae *pl* persona

persone *obs fm ns* **person, parson**

persue *obs n* the trail of blood left by a wounded animal *obs fm vb* **pursue**

pert (*adj*) *n* one who is pert or lively *obs vb* to perk (raise briskly): to behave in a pert fashion

perte *obs fm adj/n* **pert**

perthite *n* a type of reddish feldspar first discovered at Perth, Ontario, in 1832

perthitic *adj* pertaining to, resembling or containing perthite

pertuse *adj* having holes or hollow dots

pertused *var fm adj* **pertuse**

pertusion *n* the action of stabbing or otherwise causing a puncture: a hole so produced (GAME PLAYER'S note: The above senses are *obs*. The former was last recorded in 1735, the latter in 1657. The dictionary used for the UK Scrabble championship has pertusion as an extant but undefined noun, presumably having a meaning similar to either of the above.)

pertussal *adj* of or pertaining to whooping cough

peruke *n* a periwig, a type of wig fashionable with men of the 17th and 18th centuries *vb* to supply or provide such a wig

pervader *n* one who or that which pervades

perverse *(adj) obs vb* to pervert

perverser *obs n* a perverter

Pesach *n* Passover, the Hebrew festival

pesade *n* a dressage manoeuvre in which the horse remains stationary whilst raising its front legs

pesan *obs fm n* **pisane**

pesant *obs n* weight, a weight *obs fm n* **peasant** *obs dial n* a stern, hard-hearted miser

pesante *adj* of music, heavy or weighty

pesaunt *var fm obs n* **pesant**

pese *var fm now dial vb* **peise** *var fm obs n* **pece**, a (wine) cup *obs fm n/vb* **piece** *obs fm n* **pease** *Obs fm n* **peace**

peseta *n* the standard monetary unit of Spain: a silver coin equivalent to 100 centesimos

Peshito *n/adj* (of) the *Syriac Vulgate*, a version of the Bible in the ancient Syriac tongue

pesil *obs fm n* **pizzle**

pess *now dial n* a hassock or cushion for kneeling on (in church) *obs fm n* **pease** *var fm obs vb* **pease** *(+cap) obs fm S & dial n* **Pace** *obs fm arch n* **Pasch**

pesse *obs fm n/vb* **piece** *var fm obs vb* **pease** *(+cap) obs fm arch n* **Pasch**

pessel *obs fm n* **pestle**

pessen *obs fm arch n pl* **peasen**

peste *vb* to invoke a plague or other dreadful calamity upon

pestel *obs fm n* **pestle**

pesterous *adj* troublesome, cumbersome

pesticidal *adj* pertaining to a pesticide

pestle *n* the club-shaped instrument used for grinding substances in a bowl called a mortar *vb* to use a pestle in this manner

pestre *obs fm n/vb* **pester**

pestreous *obs fm n* **pesterous**

petaled *var fm adj* **petalled**

petaline *adj* pertaining to, resembling, situated on or in the form of a petal: consisting of petals

petalism *n* a practice in ancient Syracuse by which the name of a person banished for a period of five years was written on an olive leaf

petalled *adj* having petals

petalous *adj* having petals

petar *obs fm n* **petard**

petara *n* a box or basket for clothes taken on a journey

petard *n* an explosive device, encased in a chamber resembling a woman's breast, suspended from a framework placed against the door or wall it was intended to breach and the charge being lit at the 'nipple' point of the chamber: a later development of this early engine of war with the explosive in a box and lit by a fuse: a small paper bomb which imitated the sound of musket fire *vb* to fire off a petard *obs vb* to blow open with a petard

petary *n* a peat bog

petchary *n* one of the kingbirds

peter *vb* to diminish gradually and then disappear (*infl* with *adv* out) *var fm n* **petre**

pether *var fm now S & dial n* **pedder**

petiolar *adj* of, pertaining to or of the nature of a botanical petiole

petiole *n* the stalk of a leaf: a slender, stalk-like animal part such as the abdomen and thorax of an ant or the eye stalk of a crab

petioled *adj* having a petiole

petit *obs n* a younger schoolboy: a variety of domestic pigeon

petre *n* nitre

petrel *n* both a specific and a general name for many different species of marine birds as (*a*) petrel, any of various species of small web-footed birds which, by fluttering close to the water's surface, appear to be walking on water (hence, petrel from St Peter) (*b*) any of the various species of diving petrels, gadfly petrels or storm petrels (*c*) any of the various fulmars, prions or shearwaters

Petrina *fem fm masc pers n* **Peter**, meaning 'rock'

Petrine *adj* of or pertaining to the apostle Peter

Petrinism *n* the doctrine attributed to St Peter

Petrist *n* a follower of Peter the Lombard, a 12th century scholar

petrol (*n*) *vb* to supply with petrol

petrosal *adj* designating the densest and hardest portion of the temporal bone and of parts belonging to or connected with it *n* the petrosal portion of this compound bone of the ear considered, *esp* in birds and reptiles, as a separate entity

petrous *adj* of the nature of rock: hard (as rock): pertaining to or near the hard part of the temporal bone

peyne *obs fm n* **pain**

peyote *n* the cactus mescal

peytral *var fm n* **peitrel** (a 19th century revival of an *Obs fm*, treated by the dictionary used for the North American Scrabble championship as being the standard *fm*)

Phaeton *pers n* the son of the Greek sun god, Helios, and Clymene, who came to grief when he drove the chariot of the sun *n* a genus of the three species of tropicbirds, large white seabirds related to the pelicans, but unlike them in appearance (−*cap*) *n* a type of four-wheeled, light, open carriage

phairse *obs S n* a farce in the historical sense of a short (comic) entertainment performed in the interval between the long acts of a traditional mystery play

phalanger *n* any of a family of Australasian herbivorous mammals better known as possums, due to their superficial resemblance to the opossums of the Americas. The most common species is the brush possum, which is a grey or black arboreal fox-faced creature about the size of a domestic cat. It has a long, prehensile tail which is bushy on the top but hairless beneath. Introduced into New Zealand in 1837 it soon became a pest but still exists there despite eradication attempts.

phalangist *n* a phalanger

phanerogam *n* any flowering plant

pharaonic *adj* of or pertaining to, of the nature or character of a pharaoh

phare *n* a lighthouse *obs n* the navigable water adjacent to a phare (+*cap*) *n* the Straits of Messina

pharise *obs fm n* **pharisee**

pharisen *Obs pl* pharisee

pharynx *n* that cavity adjacent to the mouth and the nasal passages which functions in both the digestive and breathing activities (*pl* **pharynges, pharynxes**)

phaseless *adj* of unchanging aspect

phasic *adj* of a phase

phasmid *n* any of various insects which resemble vegetation

phatic *adj* communication of feeling by touch

phaune *obs erron fm vb* **fawn**, to seek favour by servile demeanour

phear *var fm arch n* **fere**, a friend or companion: a spouse

phearse *var fm obs n* **fers**

pheer *obs fm arch n* **fere**

pheirs *var fm obs S n* **phairse**

phenate *n* any of the salts of phenic acid

phene *n* an old name for benzene

phenol *n* carbolic acid

phenolic *adj* of, pertaining to, derived from or containing phenol

phenology *n* the study of natural phenomena in relation to time of recurrence (i.e. such as first flowering or the arrival and departure of migratory birds)

phere *obs fm arch n* **fere** *var fm obs n* **fere**

phi *n* the twenty-first letter of the Greek alphabet

Philippian *n* one native to Philippi in Macedonia

philippina *n* a nutty game played at American dinner parties. Everyone eats nuts except any which are discovered to contain a double kernel. These are saved to the last when a finder offers one to a member of the opposite sex. Both now eat a kernel and nothing else happens. The word itself has various *fms*, **philopoena, phillipins, philopena, phillipine, fillipeen** or **philopoene**, and presumably it matters that one remembers which word was used at which party because, the next time the couple meet, the first who shouts 'Philippina!' or 'Philopoena' or . . . is entitled to a gift from the other. (CALL MY BLUFF PLAYER'S note: This definition is so absurd that it might be more fun to use it a few times as a 'false' answer for some other words before using it as a 'true'. Additionally, or alternatively, the fact that it has a number of different spelling forms means that each spelling form can also be used as a 'true' definition, thus causing the opposing team to wonder just when it will stop proving true. An additional fact, if you wish to use this approach, is that the game is believed to be German in origin. The word (or words, if you give the usage away too soon) is an Anglicization of *vielliebchen*, a diminutive of *viellieb* meaning 'much loved'. The anagram, **Philippian**, might be worth considering in a 'run' of using the *var fms*.)

Philomel *fem pers n* the sister of Progne who was turned into a nightingale: the personal name now given to the nightingale (also see **Progne** and **redbreast**)

Phineas *masc pers n* possibly meaning 'whitehouse'

phleam *obs fm n* **fleam**, a lancet

phlogiston *n* the supposed principle of inflammability, a substance formerly believed to be present in anything capable of combustion

phoca *n* a seal, the marine mammal (*pl* **phocae, phocas**)

phocine *adj* relating to seals, the marine mammals: seal-like

pholades *pl* pholas

pholas *n* a piddock, any species of *Pholas*, a genus of bivalve molluscs which burrow into soft rock (*pl* **pholades**)

phonate *vb* to produce vocal sound

phoneme *n* one of a group of speech sounds that serve to distinguish one word from another in any given language

phonic *adj* of (vocal) sound: voiced

phonogram *n* a graphic character representing a sound such as a word or a syllable: a tracing produced by an apparatus which records articulated sounds: a type of telegram via a message from a telephone

phonolite *n* clinkstone, any of various volcanic rocks which have a ringing sound when struck

phoresis *n* the passage of ions through a membrane by means of an electric current

phoresy *n* an association between two creatures, usually of different species, in which one is either temporarily or permanently attached to the other. For example, the female warble fly cements her eggs to the abdomen of a female mosquito which she catches specially for this purpose. The larvae of the famous Spanish fly attach themselves to bumblebees and then release themselves in the bee colony to feed on pollen, honey and bee larvae. Other examples are given at **pearlfish** and **remora**.

photogram *n* a photograph

photonasty *n* the response, by an organism, to the stimulus of changed intensity of light irrespective of direction

phpht *var fm interj* **pht**

phraseman *n* one who makes telling phrases

phrase monger *n* one who makes or repeats trite phrases

phraser *n* a phraseman: a phrase monger (for difference, see above)

phreatic *adj* pertaining to (the potential of) underground water supply

phrenic *adj* of, pertaining to or affecting the diaphragm *n* a remedy for a mental disease (*pl*) *n* psychology

phrenitic *adj* subject to fits of delirium or madness

phrenitis *n* brain fever

phrenology *n* a would-be science which some doctors took quite seriously, giving it an equally fanciful alternative name of **comparative psychology**. Essentially it purported to give a character analysis by the interpretation of lumps or other formations of the skull. The ancient Egyptians had far greater success with 'mole reading' i.e. a mole on the face is lucky, one on or near the genitals indicates sexual prowess, adjacent to the belly button indicates fruitfulness etc.

pht *interj* expressing mild annoyance

phyton *n* a propagation unit of a plant i.e. the smallest part of any detachment from any part of the parent plant which is capable of development as a separate and individual plant

pi *n* the sixteenth letter of the Greek alphabet: in mathematics, that letter used to express the ratio of the circumference of a circle to its diameter (3.142): a pious person *var fm n/vb* **pie** (in the senses given at **pie** *pr pple* **pying**)

pianet *n* the magpie (see **pie**): a chatterbox

piannet *n* the magpie (see **pie**): a chatterbox

Pianola® *n* a type of mechanical piano which plays music from a perforated roll

Piast *pers n* a 9th century Polish peasant of great renown and, from whom, the historic Polish kings were descended *n* a Polish nobleman *esp* of ducal status, such as any of the rulers of Silesia until 1675

piaster *var fm n* **piastre**

piastre *n* any of several coins such as the Spanish piece of eight: the dollar of various Spanish-American countries: a Turkish coin worth one hundredth of a Turkish pound

picador *n* the mounted bullfighter who begins proceedings by piercing the bull with a lance

picamar *n* an extremely bitter, transparent, thick oil obtained in the distillation of tar

picene *n* a hydrocarbon obtained from tar

picot *n* a small loop of twisted thread in an ornamental edging: in embroidery, a raised knot *vb* to stitch or embroider picots

picoté *adj* having picots *her adj* speckled

picrate *n* a salt of picric acid used as the basis of a high explosive

picturer *n* a painter

piddle *vb* to trifle, to dally: to toy with one's food: of a bird, to poke about for food *dial n* the kite, a bird of prey

pidgeon *var fm n* **pidgin**

pidgin *n* a language based on two or more often very diverse languages which essentially distorts both (or all) to a jargon for communication e.g. **Motu** is a compound of native Papuan tongues and English. **Police Motu** is a simpler form which the police use. Either of these can also be described as a pidgin English.

pie *n* a sweet or savoury food in a pastry (*var fm* **pye** *obs fms* **py, paye**): the original name for the magpie which now (like jackdaw – Jack the daw) has either of its personal names added, the main form being **magpie** (Margaret or Maggie), the less common being such as **pianet** or the historic **pynot** (see **Cock and Pynot**) with the name Ann (Anne or Annette) as a suffix – the pie, Ann (*obs fms* **pee, py, pye**): the set of rules of the pre-Reformation Church concerning which services are used when a clash of celebration occurs due to the changes in date of Easter (*var fm* **pye**): printer's type all muddled together (*var fms* **pi, pye** *obs fm* **py**): a former Indian coin, the twelfth part of an anna (*var fms* **pai, pi**) *vb* to store (potatoes) in a covered pit to protect against frost (*infl fms incl pr pple* **pyeing** *n* **pying** for both **pie** and *var fm* **pye**): to mix or jumble (printing type) (*pr pple* **pying** *var fms* **pi, pye**)

piecen *vb* to join *esp* broken threads in spinning

piedness *n* the quality of being coloured as a magpie (black and white) or white blotched with any other colour

pielet *n* a little pie

piement *var fm obs n* **piment**

piend *n* the edge formed at the meeting of two surfaces

pienet *n* either of two birds, the oyster catcher – also known as a sea pie – or the magpie (see **pie**)

pierrette *n* a female member of a troupe of pierrots

pierst *obs fm adj* **pierced**

piert *dial fm adj/n* **pert** *var fm obs vb* **pert**, to behave pertly

pierte *obs fm adj/n* **pert**

pieta *n* a representation of the Virgin Mary mourning over the body of Christ

pietist *n* one who cultivates piety (+*cap*) *n* a follower of the German Protestant theologian P J Spener (1635–1705) (*q.v.*) *adj* (characteristic) of a pietist or Pietist

pigeoner *n* a swindler

Pig-iron Bob *pers n* an affectionate nickname for the great Australian prime minister, Sir Robert Menzies, whose periods of office covered the years 1934–41 and 1949–1966 and who succeeded Sir Winston Churchill as Lord Warden of the Cinque Ports in 1965 (see **Cinque Ports**)

pignerate *var fm vb* **pignorate**

pignorate *adj* pledged, pawned *vb* to pledge, pawn

pigpen (*n*) *n* an ancient form of cipher consisting of geometric symbols, traditionally used by stonemasons to mark their work (see **CODES AND CIPHERS** for full description)

pigsney *arch n* a term of endearment to a woman

pigsnie *var fm arch n* **pigsney**

pigsny *var fm arch n* **pigsney**

pike (*n*) *vb* to supply or use a (military) pike *now collq vb* to die *dial vb* to stack such as hay into pyramidical stacks called pikes

piker *S n* an instrument for cleaning a hole *dial n* a wanderer such as a tramp or a gypsy *obs n* a soldier armed with a pike

pilaster *n* a rectangular column or pillar *esp* one set into a wall: a rectangular or square-shaped support

pilastered *adj* having or supported by a pilaster

pileate *adj* of fungi, having a pileus: of birds, having a crest

pileated *adj* pileate

piler *n* one who heaps: one who hoards

pileus *n* an ancient Greek or Roman brimless, felt cap: the cap of a fungus (*pl* **pilei**)

pilhorse *Shaks fm n* **thill-horse**

pillau *var fm n* **pilau**, an Eastern rice dish, highly spiced and usually containing meat

piller *now dial n* one who peels: an implement used for peeling: a plant which exhausts the soil

pillet *obs fm n* **pellet**

pilling *n* blackballing *now dial n* peeling

pilose *adj* hairy

pilotee *n* one who is piloted

piloteer *obs n* a marine pilot

pilous *adj* hairy

pilser *obs n* a moth which singes itself in the flame of a candle

pilula *var fm n* **pilule**, a little pill

piment *obs n* wine sweetened with honey and spiced

pimento *n* a spice from the dried aromatic berries of the Jamaica pepper tree : that tree: its timber (*pl* **pimentos**)

pinaster *n* a species of pine also known as the cluster pine or star pine

pindaree *var fm n* **pindari**

pindari *n* one of a body of mounted marauders who gave mercenary service to various local princes in the earlier years of British India but were finally crushed in 1817

pinder *n* a manorial official with the duty of impounding stray animals

pindust *n* metallic dust produced during pin manufacture

pineal *adj* shaped like a pine cone

pine carpet *n* a moth, the larvae of which feed on pine trees

pinehouse *n* a hothouse within which pine-apples are grown

piner *n* one who or that which pines: in Tasmania, one who cuts pine trees *now dial n* a labourer *esp* one who cuts peat

pineta *pl* pinetum

pine tar *n* a dark viscous tar obtained during the destructive distillation of pine timber and valued as a skin medication

pinetum *n* a plantation of pine trees (*pl* **pineta, pinetums**)

ping *n* the sound of such as a bullet *vb* to make such an abrupt ringing sound *now dial vb* to prick: to urge

pinge *var fm n/vb* **ping**

pingle *S n* a struggle: a long-handled metal cooking pot *now dial n* a paddock *dial vb* to struggle

pingler *now dial n* one who trifles or dallies

pingrass *n* alfilaria

pinguin *n* a West Indian plant akin to the pineapple (*var fms* **penguin, penquin**) *obs erron fm n* **penguin**, the flightless bird (CROSSWORD SOLVER'S note: *Chambers 20th Century Dictionary* does not consider pinguin to be either obsolete or erroneous in use as a variant form of penguin. Further, it considers that this 18th century spelling form applies to penguin in the 20th century slang senses of a 'training aeroplane that cannot fly' and 'a member of the Women's Royal Air Force'!)

pinigrade *n* any of various starfishes which move by means of their fins (contrast with **spinigrade**)

pinite *n* a white, very sweet, crystalline substance obtained from the resin of the sugar pine: an aluminium silicate occuring in various crystalline forms

pinke *obs fm n* **pink**, the flower

pinker (*comp adj*) *n* one who cuts out such as borders for a woman's dress *dial vb* to squint

pinleg *S n* an artificial leg

pinna *n* a single leaflet of a feather-shaped leaf composed of such leaflets: any botanical or zoological expansion such as a leaflet or a wing, fin or feather: the (broad upper part of the) external ear: ala, any winglike anatomical process (*pl* **pinnae, pinnas** (*now US*))

pinnae *pl* pinna

pinnate *adj* having winglike parts: of a plant, having the shape or arrangement of a feather

pinner *n* one who uses a pin: a woman's coif or close-fitting cap having two long flaps to the breast and fashionable in the 17th and 18th centuries *dial n* a pinafore

pinnet *n* a pennant or streamer

pinochle *n* an American card game rather like bezique

pinocle *n* a dish of ground parched Indian corn mixed with milk: extended to similar seeds: a mixture of vanilla and aromatic substances added to chocolate

pinole *n* a dish of the California/Mexico border region consisting of parched corn flour and the sweet flour of mesquit beans sugared and spiced: a vanilla-based mixture used for flavouring chocolate

pinor *obs fm now dial* n **piner**

pinsal *obs fm S n* **pinsell** (see **pencel**, of which it is a *var fm*)

pinse *obs vb* to torture

pinsell *S fm n* **pencel**

pinsers *obs fm n pl* **pincers**

pinta *n* a contagious tropical skin disease occasioning a loss of skin pigmentation: an informal word promoted by the Milk Marketing Board for a pint of milk, presumably unaware of its other meaning

pintado *n* the Spanish mackerel, a large, spotted member of the mackerel family of fishes found in tropical Atlantic waters (*pl* **pintados**)

pintail *n* any of various birds the tail of which is unusually pointed, as two species of ducks and two species of grouse: a woman (*ironic*)

pintel *obs fm n* **pintle**

pintle *n* a pin or bolt which serves as a spindle in such as a hinge: the penis (*now vulgar*)

pinto *adj* piebald *n* a piebald horse (*pl* **pintoes, pintos**)

pintre *obs fm n* pine tree

pinule *obs var fm n* **pinnule**, either of the two sights on an instrument such as a quadrant

piny *adj* of or pertaining to pine trees: suggestive of or covered in pines (*comp* **pinier** *sup* **piniest**) *now dial var fm n* **peony** (*pl* **pinies**)

piolet *n* a climber's ice ax

pion *var fm n* **pi**, the Greek letter *obs vb* to dig or excavate *obs fm n* **peon**

pioner *obs fm n* **pioneer**

piot *n* the magpie (also see **pie**)

pioted *adj* piebald

pipage *n* the conveying of a liquid or gas by pipeline: the laying of pipes for this purpose: such pipes collectively

piperate *n* a salt of piperic acid (an acid produced from boiling piperine with potash) *obs adj* peppery, pungent

piperine *adj* peppery *n* an alkaloid of pepper, normally crystalline, which can be melted to a pale yellow, limpid oil

pipestone *n* catlinite, a hard red clay used by Red Indians for their tobacco pipes

pipet *obs fm n* **pipit**, the bird

pir *obs fm S dial n* **pirr**

piraña *n* the ferocious small fish of South American rivers which hunts in shoals and can strip a horse to the bone within a matter of minutes (also known as **caribe** *var fms* **perai**, **pirai**, **piranha**, **piraya**)

pirat *obs fm n* **pirate**

piraya *var fm n* **piraña**

pire *now dial vb* to look intently at with narrowed eyes

pirl *S n* a twist or curl *arch S & dial vb* to twist, wind or spin: to curl

pirnie *S adj* having multi-coloured stripes *S n* a nightcap with such a decorative form

pirr *n* the tern, a seabird *S dial n* a breeze *S vb* of the wind, to blow as a breeze

pisane *n* a piece of armour for the neck and upper part of the chest

piscator *n* an angler (*fem* **piscatrix**)

pisimer *obs fm now dial n* **pismire**

pisky *dial n* a Cornish fairy which is the soul of an unbaptised child and most frequently manifests itself at twilight in the shape of a little white moth (also see **bucca** and **muryan**)

pisle *obs fm n* **pizzle**

pismire *now dial n* an ant: one worthy of scorn

pistareen *adj* petty, paltry *n* a small silver coin which circulated in those tropical parts of North America and the West Indies which had a strong Spanish influence

pistarene *obs fm adj/n* **pistareen**

pistate *obs vb* to bake

piste *n* a beaten track, such as that made by horses or that in snow

pistel *var fm obs n* **pistle**

pister *dial vb* to whisper

pistle *var fm dial n* **pistol**, a term of contempt for a disorderly person *obs n* a written communication

pistler *obs n* one who reads the epistle in church

pistol *(n) vb* to shoot with a pistol (*infl fms* **pistoled/pistolled** etc)

pistole *n* any of various coins including a Spanish gold piece of circa 1600 then worth between 16/6d and 18/-, the Louis d'or of Louis XIII issued in 1640 and the Scottish twelve pound piece of William III worth an English pound (see **£ s d** – under **L**)

pistoleer *n* one who uses or is armed with a pistol

pistoler *obs n* one who makes pistols

pistolet *n* any of various historic gold coins worth the equivalent of six English shillings of the appropriate period: a small firearm

pitchstone *n* an acid volcanic glass with a resinous lustre

pitchy *adj* of or like pitch, the distilled shning black residue of tar (*comp* **pitchier**, *sup* **pitchiest**)

pitta *n* the jewel thrush, any of a number of species of beautifully coloured, ground living birds which live in the tropical parts of Asia and Australasia: a type of slightly leavened bread in the form of a hollow flat cake

pitel *obs fm dial vb* **pittle**

pith tree *n* a tropical African tree having soft, pith-like wood

pitless *adj* of a theatre, having no pit

piton *n* an iron spike with an attached ring for rope, used by mountaineers

pitsaw *n* a long two-handled saw used in a sawpit for cutting logs

pittancer *n* one in a religious house who, historically, had the duty of accounting for the monies which were provided for additional allowances of such as food or wine. These allowances, called pittances, came in the form of pious bequests from layfolk.

pitte *obs fm n* **pit**

pittel *n* a bird of prey, probably the marsh harrier (*Obs* except in the *dial fms* **piddle**, a kite: **pickle**, a marsh harrier)

pitter *n* a small stream *US n* one who or a device which removes stones from fruit *vb* to make a gentle running or tapping sound

pittle *now dial vb* to piddle

pivoter *n* one who makes or fits pivots: a golfer who turns his body during the action of driving

pizzle *n* a bull's penis used as a flogging instrument

pjolls *Shet n pl* old working clothes

placit *n* an opinion: a judgment: a decree

placita *pl* placitum, a decision of a court or an assembly

placoid *adj* of the scales of a fish, plate-shaped *n* any of various fish, such as sharks or rays

plain *(adj/adv/n) arch vb* to lament

plainant *n* one, in law, who complains

plaint (*n*) *obs vb* to complain

plaise *dial fm n/vb* **please**

plaist *obs S fm vb* **place**

plaister *now S fm n/vb* **plaster**

plaite *obs fm ns* **plat, plate**

plaiter *n* one who or that which plaits

planer *n* one who planes or levels: a planing machine: a cushioning block of wood which a printer interposes between the blow of a mallet and raised type

planetic *adj* of astrological usage, erratic, erring or extravagant (also see note following **planetical**)

planetical *adj* of or pertaining to the planets: of astrological usage, wandering, roving, vagrant (GAME PLAYER'S note: Whilst both **planetic** and **planetical** are *obs* in all given senses, nevertheless UK Scrabble players can safely use them in championship play as they appear in their dictionary as being extant words. Unfortunately, however, no definitions are supplied.)

planta *n* the sole of the foot

plantain *n* any of various annual or perennial herbs of the temperate regions *esp* the great plantain which has broad, flat leaves spread close to the ground and a slender spike of small greenish flowers: a large tropical plant with green-skinned, edible, banana-like fruit

plantan *var fm n* **plantane**

plasce *Obs fm n* **place**

plasher *n* a sapling with which a hedge is interlaced: one who produces an interlaced hedge

plashing *n* a section of interweaved hedge: noisy plunging *adj* designating that splashing or making a sound like it

plashy *adj* wet and sloppy: marshy, swampy: of a watery consistency: growing in wet places: designating that which splashes (where applicable, as marshy) (*comp* **plashier** *sup* **plashiest**)

plasit *obs S fm vb* **place**

plasma *n* the liquid part of blood, milk and lymph: a translucent type of quartz: glycerite of starch

plasse *Obs fm n* **place**

plaste *obs S fm vb* **place**

plastery *adj* of the nature of plaster: like plaster

plastre *obs fm n/vb* **plaster**

platan *var fm n* **platane**

platane *n* the oriental plane tree

platen *n* a flat plate in a printing press which presses the paper against the type: the roller in a typewriter which performs a similar function

plater *n* one who or that which plates: an inferior racehorse

plate rail *n* a flat rail which has a flange

platine *n* one of a number of flat lead weights (*approx* 6 in × 3 in) suspended on strings which formed part of an early industrial weaving machine

plating *n* the action of the *vb* **plate** in various senses such as the coating of a metal surface with a (more) precious metal, the making of metal plates for spades and shovels, the shoeing of a horse with special racing shoes called plates and plate racing: the result of any of these or other actions covered by the *vb*

platinous *adj* designating any compound of the metal, platinum, which exists in a lower degree of valency

Platonise *var fm vb* **Platonize**, to render Platonic

platy *adj* split into thin, flat pieces (*comp* **platier** *sup* **platiest**)

platypi *pl* platypus

platypus *n* one of a family of primitive, web-footed, duck-billed, egg-laying mammals which is so unusual that, when the first complete skin arrived at the British Museum from Australia in 1799, the assistant keeper of natural history thought it was a fake and tried to prise off its beak with scissors (*pl* **platypi, platypuses**)

plaustral *adj* pertaining to a cart

plaw *dial fm n/vb* **play**

plea (*n*) *S & dial vb* to plead

pleach *vb* to entwine or plait: to form a hedge of intertwined branches of small trees or brushwood

pleader (*n*) *obs n* pleading

pleasir *Obs fm n* **pleasure**

pleasire *obs fm n* **pleasure**

pleasurer *n* a pleasure seeker

pleb *n* a commoner of ancient Rome *collq n* a person of low, vulgar taste

plebby *collq adj* of or pertaining to a pleb (in the *collq* sense)

plectre *var fm n* **plectrum**

plectrum *n* any small item used for plucking the strings of a musical instrument (*pl* **plectra, plectrums**) (*var fms* **plectron, plectre** *pls* **plectra, plectrons, plectres**)

plede *obs fm n/vb* **plead**

pleen *obs fm arch vb* **plain**

pleet *obs fm vb* **plead**

pleete *obs fm vb* **plead**

Pleiad *n* any of the seven daughters of Atlas and Pleione, all of whom were changed into stars (*pl* **Pleiads, Pleiades**) (+ or −*cap*) *n* the *sing fm* used for a group of seven distinguished people

plein *dial fm n/vb* **plain**

pleise *obs S fm n/vb* **please**

plene *obs adj* complete *obs fm arch vb* **plain**

plenist *n* one who believes that there is no such thing as a vacuum

plenties *pl* plenty

plenum *n* fullness, as in an assembly of people where everyone is present or, in physics, a space which is completely filled with matter (*pl* **plena, plenums**)

pleonasm *n* the use of needless words: an instance of this, as in *a tiny little kitten*: a redundant word or phrase: a superabundance of parts

pleonast *n* one who uses pleonasm *var fm n* **pleonaste**

pleonaste *n* ceylonite, a variety of spinel

pleonastic *adj* using more words than necessary

plese *obs fm vb* **please**

pleser *obs fm n* **pleasure**

plessor *var fm n* **plexor** *obs S fm n* **pleasure**

plete *obs fm vb* **pleat**

pleter *obs fm n* **pleader**

pletere *Obs fm obs n* **pleader**

pleugh *S fm n* **plough**

pleura *n* one of the two serous membranes which line the thorax and envelope the lung in mammals (*pl* **pleurae, pleuras**)

pleuritis *n* the disease pleurisy

plexor *n* a small hammer or other implement (*incl* fingers) used by a doctor to test reflexes or sound a chest

pley *obs n* a river bank *obs fm n/vb* **play** *obs fm n/S & dial vb* **plea**

pleyer *obs fm n* **player**

plicae *pl* plica, a disease-induced condition of hair making it matted and filthy: Polish plait, a similar condition produced from simple neglect: a fold (of the skin)

plicate *adj* folded *vb* to fold

plide *obs fm vb* **plead**

plider *obs fm n* **pleader**

plier *n* one who plies (*pl*) *n* pincers

plinker *US n* one who shoots at random targets

plise *obs fm vb* **please**

plissé *Fr adj* of a fabric, chemically treated to produce a gathered effect

plite *obs fm n/vb* **plight**

ploat *S & dial vb* to remove the outer covering of a bird or animal: to fleece (*fig*)

ploater *obs n* a plucker

plodde *Obs fm now dial n* **plud**, a puddle

plore *obs vb* to weep or wail

plotie *var fm S n* **plotty**

plottie *var fm S n* **plotty**

plotty *S n* a hot spicy drink of diluted wine or spirit

plouter *S vb* to dabble or splash about in anything wet or dirty

plovery *adj* abounding in plovers

plow *var fm (now mainly US) n/vb* **plough**

plowe *obs fm n/vb* **plow** or **plough**

plower *n* a ploughman

plowre *Obs fm obs vb* **plore**

plowter *var fm S vb* **plouter**

ploy (*n*) *vb* to move (military forces) from line into column (i.e. the reverse of **deploy**)

ploye *var fm obs n* **ploy**, a fold in cloth

plumbic *adj* of or pertaining to lead

plume (*n*) *vb* to provide or cover with plumes

plumer *Obs n* a dealer in feathers

plumose *adj* full of feathers: feathery

plusage *n* an extra amount

plutei *pl* pluteus

pluteus *n* the larva of such echinoids as the sea urchin or such ophiuroids as the brittlestar which breed sexually – some of either of these marine groups reproduce by division, with each half of the animal growing a replacement half (*pl* **plutei**)

pluton *n* a mass of solidified rock below the surface of the earth

plyer *arch fm n* **plier**

po (*slg n*) *Obs n* a peacock (TRIVIA note: The saying, '*as proud as a po*', really did exist in those days)

poachy *adj* swampy

poadler *var fm S & dial n* **podler**

poar *obs fm vb* **pore**

pochay *collq fm n* **post-chaise**, a type of horse-drawn carriage capable of carrying up to four passengers

podalic *adj* of or pertaining to the feet

poddle *var fm S n* **podley**

podel *obs fm n/vb* **puddle**

podite *n* the single leg of such as a crustacean

podium *n* a pedestal: a raised platform surrounding the arena of an ancient amphitheatre: a continuous bench round a room: an animal's hindfoot: a plant footstalk (*pl* **podia**, **podiums**)

podle *var fm S n* **podley** *obs fm n/vb* **puddle**

podler *S & dial n* the fry of the coalfish: the true pollack

podley *S n* an earlier and still extant *fm* of **podler**

podomancy *n* divination by inspection of the foot

poeste *obs fm now arch S n* **poustie**

poetaster *n* a petty poet or writer of trashy verse

poetise *var fm vb* **poetize**, to render poetic

poiet *obs fm n* **poet**

poilu *Fr n* the French equivalent of the British Tommy or the American G.I.

poind *S vb* to distrain: to impound

poinder *S n* an official who has the authority to distrain (a debtor's) goods: one who has the charge of woods and hedges and the power to impound straying cattle (compare with **pinder**)

poiner *var fm now dial n* **piner**

pointe *Fr n* in ballet, (the position of) standing on the extreme tip of the toe *obs fm n* **point**

pointel *n* a writing or engraving instrument

point lace *n* needlepoint, lace made with a buttonhole stitch

pointrel *n* the pointed extremity of a leaf

poister *obs vb* to fetter, entangle

poite *obs fm n* **poet**

poitrel *n* a piece of breast armour for a horse

Polander *obs n* a Pole

polar (*adj*) *n* in geometry, a curve having a relationship to both a fixed point (called the pole) and to another curve in a manner specified

polarise *var fm vb* **polarize**

polder *n* a piece of low-lying land reclaimed from the sea (originally, any of the individual tracts which, piecemeal, transformed the Zuider Zee into the territory, in Holland, now called Ijsselmeer) *now dial n* a pollard tree *vb* to create a polder or tract of reclaimed land

pole (*n*) *vb* to provide with or use a pole

polemic *adj* of or involving controversy *n* an argument *esp* one concerning belief or doctrine: one engaged in such an argument or controversy

polemist *n* one who engages in controversy

polenta *n* a type of (Italian) porridge that includes sweet chestnuts

poler *n* one whose work involves the use of a pole, such as one who sets up hop poles or a boatman who uses a pole for propelling purposes: a draught animal harnessed alongside a pole *obs n* a pole used for stirring

Poless *n* a female Pole

poleyn *n* armour for the knee

polianite *n* manganese dioxide occurring as grey metallic crystals (CROSSWORD SOLVER'S note: A typical 'about' word favoured by the cryptic compiler, as '*polite* about *Ian*' or '*polite* about *ani*', depending upon which letter *i* is chosen for *polite*. In a particularly difficult crossword the clue might begin '*Polite about a cuckoo* ...' (see **ani**). For further examples of this technique see CROSSWORD ENGLISH in the **INDICATORY SECTION**.)

Police Motu see **pidgin**

polie *obs fm n* **pulley**

polite (*adj*) *obs vb* to polish or refine

polities *pl* polity

politise *var fm vb* **politize** in the sense of to deal in politics (the other senses being *obs* or, in the case of 'to make into citizens', the '-ize' *fm* is the only one recorded in use)

polity *n* civil order: civil government: any particular form of political organization or government (*pl* **polities**)

pollard *n* a base foreign coin used as a penny until declared illegal in 1299: flour containing the finest bran: an animal of the horned kind which either has no horns or (like a deer) has shed them: a tree which has had its upper parts removed to produce a fresh growth of young branches *vb* to cut a tree in this fashion *adj* bald (*fig*)

poller *n* a voter: one who prunes trees

pollet *obs n* an epaulet

poloist *n* a polo player

poltis *obs fm n* **poultice**

poltre *obs fm n* **poultry**

polymeric *adj* of, pertaining to or manifesting polymerism: having identical chemical composition but different molecular weight and properties

polymerism *n* the condition of one substance having an identical percentage composition to another substance but a different molecular weight

Polymnia *var fm pers n* **Polyhymnia**, the Muse of sacred song

polyp *n* either of two very different types of marine animal life, one of which produces a like creature while the other exists in the same form only every alternate generation (see **sea fir** for an example of this natural curiosity) (*pl* **polypi, polyps**)

Polypterus *n* the genus of the birchirs

polyse *obs fm n* **police**

pomade *n* a perfumed grease applied to hair to give it a smooth, shiny appearance

pomander *n* a perforated container housing a ball of perfumes: the contents

pomeria *pl* pomerium

pomerium *US fm n* **pomoerium** (*pl* **pomeria**)

pomewater *now dial n* a large juicy apple having a sour taste *obs n* a variety of large, juicy, sweet-tasting apples: the applejohn

pomoerium *n* an open space around a town (*pl* **pomoeria**: also see **prooemium**, the anagram of pomoerium)

pomwater *var fm obs n* **pomewater**

poncer *obs fm n* **pouncer**

ponderal *adj* of or pertaining to weight: ascertained by weight

pondre *obs vb* to lay eggs

pongid *adj* of the *Pongidae* *n* any individual primate of this family

Pongidae *n* a family of primates which consists of three genera:- the gibbons (genus *Hylobates*), the orang-utans (genus *Pongo*), the chimpanzees and gorillas (genus *Pan*)

poniard *n* a dagger

pons *n* an anatomical connecting part (*pl* **pontes**)

pontes *pl* pons

pontie *var fm n* **punty**

pontile *adj* of or pertaining to a band of nerve fibres in the brain

pontonier *var fm n* **pontoneer**, one in charge of (the construction of) a pontoon bridge or bridges

poodler *var fm S & dial n* **podler**

poofter *slg n* a male homosexual

pook *n* a heap *esp* one of harvested produce not exceeding five feet in height and which has been gathered for carting: a narrow cone-shaped stack of corn up to ten feet in height, left to dry out prior to taking to the main storage place *vb* to form either of such (and **pooking** is the *n* for either action) *S vb* to pluck (*lit/fig*)

poole *obs fm n* **pool**, a small stretch of water

pooler *var fm obs n* **poler**

poor (*adj/n*) *obs vb* to impoverish *nonce vb* to call (a person) 'poor'

poort *Obs or obs fm n* **port** (in most senses)

Pooter *n* a conventional and unimaginative petit bourgeois

poperin *var fm n* **poppering**, a variety of pear

popery *n* a term of hostility towards that which is exclusively or essentially Catholic

popet *obs fm n* **poppet**

popish *adj* Catholic (used in a hostile sense)

popler *obs fm n* **poplar**

poplet *obs n* a female favourite

popliteal *adj* pertaining to, situated in or connected with the hollow at the back of the knee

por *obs fm now dial vb* **poor**

porbeagle *n* either of two species of large sharks related to the Great white shark immortalized in the book and film *Jaws*. Both grow to about twelve feet in length, one living in the temperate Atlantic waters and the other in similar Pacific waters.

porcine *adj* of pigs: swinish

pore (*n/vb*) *now dial var fm adj* **poor**

poreing *obs fm n* **poring**

poret *obs fm now dial n* **porret**

porge *vb* of the Jewish method of ritual slaughter, to further the koshering process by removing certain parts of an animal's carcass

porger *n* one who porges

porgy *US n* any of various sea fishes *esp* the sea bream

poriness *obs n* the condition of being porous

porism *n* one of a class of ancient (Greek) geometrical propositions intermediate between a problem and a theorem

porite *n* any of various species of coral

porosity *n* the fact of being porous (*pl* **porosities**)

porphyrous *poet adj* purple

porr *now dial vb* to thrust or poke (the fire) *dial vb* to kick (whilst wearing heavy boots or clogs)

porre *obs fm now dial vb* **porr**

porret *now dial n* a leek: an onion

porser *Obs fm n* **purser**

porta *n* the portal vein, a vein connected to the liver (*pl* **portae, portas**)

portae *pl* porta

portage *n* an act of carrying: the cost of the route taken *vb* to convey goods *esp* by water

portaled *var fm adj* portalled

portalled *adj* having a portal

portance *arch n* bearing, demeanour

portas *n* a mediaeval breviary or book of psalms, prayer etc for the different days of a church year: in old Scottish law, a roll of offenders' names

porte *n* the Turkish government *obs fm n/vb* **port**

porteous *var fm n* **portas**

porter (*n*) *vb* to carry as or by means of a porter

porterage *n* the work of a porter: transportation of items, the fee paid for this

portes *var fm n* **portas**

portess *var fm n* **portas** *obs nonce vb* to canonize

portfire *n* a missile fuse

portlet *n* a small port: a creek

portolan *var fm n* **portolano**, a naval guide book illustrated with charts and giving such as sailing directions

portous *var fm n* **portas**

portress *n* a female porter or doorkeeper *esp* one in a nunnery *obs n* the gate of a fortification

Portuguese man-of-war *n* in appearance a single large jellyfish, but in fact it is a hydrozoan or complete colony of simple animals including parents and offspring. The individual animals serve specific functions on behalf of the colony. Some catch food, some digest it, some act as light sensors, some are sex organs and some take the form of long thin tentacles which can be as much as 55 yards in length. This colony not only stays together as a unit but it can alter its shape to form a sail and, using the wind, travel the oceans.

posada *n* a Spanish(-American) inn

poseuse *n* a female poseur

posit *vb* to situate, to place: to postulate *dial fm n/vb* **posset**

posite *obs fm vb* **posit**

positon *var fm n* **positron**

positron *n* the positive equivalent of an electron, a particle of an atom which carries a negative charge

posnet *arch n* a small three-legged cooking vessel complete with a handle

posnit *obs fm arch n* **posnet**

poss *now dial vb* to knock

possest *var fm adj* possessed

posset *n* a milk-based hot drink containing such as ale or wine with additional sugar and spices *dial n* the milk thrown up by a baby *vb* to make a posset *dial vb* of a baby, to bring up its milk

possett *dial fm n/vb* **posset**

possie *Austr collq n* a position

possit *dial fm n/vb* **posset**

possnet *obs fm arch n* **posnet**

possut *dial fm n/vb* **posset**

POSTAL WORD GAMES See next page

postee *Obs fm now arch S n* **poustie**

posteen *n* an Afghan long (sheepskin) great-coat

postel *obs n* a gatepost *obs fm n* **postil** *var fm n* **postle**

postiche *adj* counterfeit: designating an inappropriate ornament subsequently added to a finished work of sculpture or architecture *n* a counterfeit substitute

postie *S & Austr collq n* a postman *obs fm now arch S n* **poustie**

postil *n* a marginal note of a text *obs vb* to write such a comment (*infl fms* earlier, **postiled** etc: later, **postilled** etc)

postin *var fm n* **posteen**

postle *obs n* an apostle *obs fm n* **postil**

postless *nonce adj* without a postal service

postlude *n* a concluding part of various pieces of music

postnares *n pl* the openings of the nasal chamber into the pharynx (*sing* **postnaris**)

postnaris *sing* postnares

postrem *obs fm n* **postern**

postrene *obs fm n* **postern**

postrome *obs fm n* **postern**

postron *obs fm n* **postern**

postural *adj* relating or pertaining to posture

posye *obs fm n* **posy**, a bunch of flowers

potager *obs fm now dial n* **pottinger**

pot ale *n* grain distillery refuse

potamic *adj* of or pertaining to rivers

Potamon *n* a genus of river crabs which includes an edible species of classical fame. The *Potamon edulis* was the crab which, according to the Babylonians and accepted by all other contemporary civilizations, was transmuted to the skies as the constellation Cancer. Pliny the Elder (AD 23–79), the Roman naturalist, recommended a drink of a decoction of the ashes of *Potamon edulis* in ass's milk as an antidote for all poisons.

potassa *n* potassium monoxide

pote *now dial vb* to push, poke or kick (the *n* **poting** either the action of the *vb* or a *modf n* as **poting stick**, a stick used for stirring clothes being washed)

poteen *n* illicit Irish whiskey

potel *Obs fm n* **pottle** (*pl* **potels**)

potell *obs fm n* **pottle**

poter *n* one who drinks alcohol (also see apt anagram, **toper**)

pot hanger *obs n* a device for hanging such as a kettle over a fire: a rack with hooks for suspending pots (WORD PUZZLER'S note: *Chambers 20th Century Dictionary* considers the word extant despite the fact that the last recorded literary usage was in the late 17th century)

pot head *collq n* a fool

pother *n* an atmosphere of smoke or dust: a turmoil, an uproar: a din: trouble, sorrow *vb* to confuse, perplex: to worry

pothouse *n* a tavern

POSTAL WORD GAMES Essentially there are two different games played by post: Scrabble® which is played one move per delivery of the mail or Code Breaking in which the whole challenge arrives in one letter. The Postal Scrabble Club organizes leagues, private individual contests and even international team matches using one or more dictionaries according to the degree of difficulty desired. Most of the top UK players belong to this nationwide club as it accords them the opportunity to practise the game by consulting their own *aide-mémoires* such as private andagram lists. It also caters for players of lesser ability and would match two beginners in a game limited to a single dictionary. It is essential to belong to the PSC in order to play Scrabble by post because an independent third party, who draws the game tiles and adjudicates on words used, is needed to control the match. Obviously such as andagram lists are not permitted in normal face-to-face games but, in postal play, a single move is given far more consideration than normally pertains. (Also see **Goidel**.)

Code Breaking is completely different and only two people are needed. One who devises a code and one who breaks it. Addicts devise codes for each other and honestly note the time it takes to solve the other's message. On average it equates to the time normally taken for solving a crossword. The challenge is played to certain strict rules.

1 One or two paragraphs of standard English text are selected and written down in a code *completely unknown* to the player being challenged. *No clues whatsoever are provided.* There is no indication as to which book was used for the encoded passage and no hint as to even one letter of the actual code.

2 The coded message is written in a form which mirrors the exact arrangement of the passage as if written in normal English.

3 Each letter of the alphabet is given a different symbol and that same symbol is used every time for that letter. For example, in pigpen code (see **CODES AND CIPHERS**) a square always represents the letter E. Thus if the pigpen code was being used, then *every* time an E appeared in the encoded passage it would be represented by a square. Written in pigpen, the nursery rhyme of Jack and Jill begins:–

·┘ ┘ └ ⊔·   ┘ ⊡]   ·┘ ┌ └· └·   V̇ □ ⊡ >   < ┐·   > ⊓ □   ⊓ ┌ └· └·

4 To solve the puzzle, the player first takes a blank piece of paper and copies the format of the encoded message by placing dots in *exactly the same positions* as the mystery symbols i.e.

. . . .

It is vital to mirror that *exact* placing. Then the solver studies the message for its inevitable 'giveaways'. For example, in the pigpen message the symbol └· appears four times, each time as a double letter. Making the logical assumption that it is a double consonant means that the symbol preceeding it must be a vowel. As, both times, └· └· is preceeded by ┌ and as ┌ can only be A, E, I, O or U if the basic assumption is correct, does ┌ appear in any word likely to be either 'and' or 'the'? No, it does not. So, it cannot be A or E and must, therefore, be I, O or U. Now it should be checked against likely possibilities for 'it', 'if', 'on', 'to', 'up'. Eventually a letter is known for certain. Once it is known, it *must* be entered on the blank piece of paper directly above *each* dot which represents *every* one of the spaces to which the corresponding symbol relates. Finding the first letter is the hardest part of all; thereafter it becomes progressively easier until, eventually, the last dozen or so letters are mere child's play.

Providing that at least a full paragraph is encoded, then any symbols of any sort can be used and the complete message decoded in comfortable and pleasurable crossword time. Whilst code breaker's clubs and societies exist in the USA none, as far as is known, exist in the UK. The game as explained above is that played privately in Britain. The details concerning American challenges are not known to the writer.

potiche *n* a type of Oriental vase narrowing at the neck

potin *n* an alloy of tin, copper, lead and zinc used by the ancient Gauls for their coins: an alloy of lead and copper formerly used for making pots (often called **pot metal**)

potman *n* one employed to serve ale *dial n* one who sells earthenware

pot metal *n* cast iron as used for pots: an alloy of copper and lead used for larger pots: a type of glass which is coloured throughout whilst still in the molten state

potometer *n* an instrument which measures the amount of water absorbed by a growing plant

Potoooooooo *pers n* given to an 18th century racehorse and pronounced *potatoes* (pot + 8 o's)

potstone *n* a granular variety of soapstone

pottel *obs fm n* pottle

pottingar *obs S n* an apothecary (GAME PLAYER'S note: As defined in the dictionary used for the UK Scrabble championship the word is valid for play)

pottinger *n* one, in historical times, who cooked pottage *now dial n* any vessel in which liquid food such as soup is served

pottle *n* the liquid or dry measure of half a gallon: a vessel of this capacity: a small wicker basket

pouchy *adj* having pouches: of the nature of a pouch: baggy, pouchlike (*comp* **pouchier** *sup* **pouchiest**)

pouder *obs fm n/vb* **powder**

poudre *obs fm n/vb* **powder**

poule *n* one of the movements in a quadrille *obs fm vb* **poll**, to lop

poulet *n* a love letter *esp* one folded in the shape of a chicken's wing

poulter *arch n* a poulterer, one who deals in poultry

pouret *var fm now dial n* **porret**

pouse *obs vb* the meaning is obscure but is probably to trap fish brought into estuarine rivers with the tide. (In Stuart times an ordinance was enacted against those who poused on the Thames using pousing nets.) *var fm n* **pouze** *dial fm n* **pulse**, edible seeds *S & dial fm vb* **push**

poussin *n* a chicken intended for eating rather than for egg-laying or breeding

pouste *var fm now arch S n* **poustie**

poustie *now arch S n* power, might, authority

poute *obs fm n/vb* **pout**

pouter (*n*) *S vb* to poke (about)

pouze *n* the refuse from the production of cider

powle *obs fm n* **pole**, either compass point, North or South *obs fm n* **poll**, the head *obs fm vb* **poll**, to lop

powlter *obs fm arch n* **poulter**

powre *obs fm n/vb* **pore**

powte *obs fm vb* **pout**

powter *var fm S vb* **pouter**

practisant a word clearly defined in the dictionary used for the UK Scrabble championship as an extant noun meaning an agent or fellow in conspiracy. However, other authorities only know of this word through a single mention in Shakespeare's *Henry VI Part III* and are not sure exactly what it means. They consider that it may mean a conspirator or one who uses a stratagem. Either way, they label the word *obs*.

prade *dial n* talk, chat

praent *obs dial adj* saucy

praeses *var fm n* **preses** (*pl* **praeses**)

praeterist *var fm n* **preterist**

praeterit *var fm adj/n* **preterite**

praetor *n* a consul as leader of the army of the ancient Roman republic: one of the magistrates of ancient Rome in subsequent imperial times: one holding high civic office in modern times

praetorian *adj* of, belonging to or pertaining to a praetor: of or belonging to the bodyguard of the Roman emperor

prage *obs n* a spear-like weapon

prain *obs fm vb* **preen**

Prairial *n* the ninth month of the French Revolutionary calendar

prairied *adj* having or characterized by prairies

praite *obs fm vb* **prate**

praline *n* an almond-based sweet confection

prane *obs fm n* **prawn**

prangle *Obs vb* to pinch

pranse *arch fm vb* **prance**

prase *n* a variety of leek-green coloured translucent quartz *obs fm n/vb* **praise**

prasine *adj* leek-like: of the colour leek-green *n* a green mineral

prasne *obs fm n* **prasine**

prate *vb* to speak in a continuous, boring fashion about matters of little or no consequence *n* such talk

prater *n* one who prates

pratie *Anglo-Ir n* potato

pratle *obs fm vb* **prattle**

prattel *obs fm vb* **prattle**

prawe *var fm n* **proa**

prawle *Shaks fm n* **brawl** (as would be spoken by a Welshman)

prawne *obs fm n* **prawn**

prayes *obs fm vb* **praise**

praying mantis see **mantid, mantis, Mantis religiosa**

prayne *Obs fm n* **prawn**

prayse *obs fm n* **praise**

preace *obs fm n* **press**, a crown *obs fm vb* **press**, to exert pressure

preachy *adj* inclined to preach

pread *var fm obs n/vb* **prede**

preadamic *adj* existing before Adam

preadmit *vb* to admit beforehand

preak *obs S fm n/vb* **prick**

preal *dial fm n* **prial**

prease *dial fm vb* **press** *obs fm n* **press** *obs fm n/vb* **praise**

preasse *obs fm n/vb* **press**

preast *var fm obs n* **prest** *obs fm n* **priest**

precept *n* a rule for (moral) action or conduct: a maxim

preceptial *adj* instructive

preceptive *adj* mandatory: instructive

preces *n pl* short petitions in the form of a verse by the celebrant or minister and a response by the congregation

preche *obs fm vb* **preach**

precisian *n* one, *esp* a Puritan, who is rigidly precise in religious observance: one who is equally punctilious in the observance of any other set of rules

prede *obs n/vb* (to) plunder

predella *n* the platform on which an altar is placed: an altar step

predial *adj* pertaining to, consisting of (farm) land *n* a slave attached to the land

predicant *adj* characterized by preaching *n* a preacher

predy *obs vb* to make ready

preem *n* a comb used by weavers to loosen the yarn *vb* to use a preen

preen *vb* of birds, to trim their feathers: of people, to dress carefully: to exhibit pride *now S & dial vb* to secure with a pin *now S & dial n* a (decorative) pin: something of little value (*fig*) *dial n* the bar-tailed godwit, a wading bird

preent *Obs fm n/vb* **print**

preest *obs fm n* **priest**

preeve *obs fm n* **proof**

prehnite *n* a silicate of calcium and aluminium similar to zeolite

preik *obs fm vb* **prick**

prein *var fm now S & dial n/vb* **preen**

preise *obs fm vb* **praise**

preist *obs fm n* **priest**

prelate (*n*) *obs vb* to perform the office of a prelate: to exalt: to affect an air of dignity

prelatial *adj* of or pertaining to a prelate or to his office, position or dignity

prelatic *adj* of, pertaining to, of the nature of or like a prelate: in a hostile sense, governed by or attached to prelates

prelation *n* preferment: preference

prelatise *var fm vb* **prelatize**, to make episcopal: to bring under an episcopal government

prelatist *n* a term of abuse for an episcopalian

prelaty *obs n* the office of a prelate

prelect *vb* to (deliver a) lecture

prelial *obs adj* of or pertaining to battles

prelim *slg n* a preliminary examination

prelusion *n* (the performance of) a prelude

prelusive *adj* serving as a prelude

preme *obs fm n* **preem**

premise (*n*) *vb* to state or set forth

premiss *var fm n* **premise**

premit *obs vb* to send forth

premorse *adj* of a plant part, terminating abruptly as though broken off

premosaic *adj* before the time of Moses

prename *n* a forename

prene *obs fm vb* **preen**

prenotion *n* a premonition: a preconceived idea

prent *now S fm n/vb* **print**

prente *obs fm n* **print**

pre-part *n* the previous or preceeding part

prepollent *adj* predominating, prevailing

presage *n* an omen, sign or portent *vb* to portent, to foreshadow: to predict

presager *n* one who or that which portends

prescient *adj* having foresight

prese *obs fm vb* **praise** *obs fm n* **press**, a crowd

presential *adj* of or pertaining to presence

presentive *adj* the opposite of symbolic *n* such a word

preses *n* praeses, one who presides (*pl* **preses, praeses**)

preset *vb* to set beforehand

presign *arch vb* to give an advanced indication of

presle *obs n* the plant, shavegrass or rough horsetail *obs vb* of such as fletchers, to polish woodwork with shavegrass

presse *obs n* a clingstone peach

pressen see **enpress**

Pressina *pers n* see **Melusina**

pression *n* pressure

prest *obs n* a loan: enlistment money paid to one undertaking naval or military service *obs vb* to lend, advance or borrow money: to pay enlistment money

preste *obs fm n/vb* **priest**

Prestel® *n* the British Telecom viewdata system

presto (*adj/adv/n*) *vb* to conjure

presurmise *obs vb* to surmise in advance (an inference from a usage, in 1664, of **presurmised**)

preteen *US n* a child less than the age of thirteen though essentially having teenage aspirations

pretense *var fm (essentially US) n/vb* **pretence**

preterist *n* one whose chief interest is the past

preterit *var fm adj/n* **preterite**

preterite *adj* of or pertaining to bygone time *n* one who is not destined for heavenly salvation: the past tense

pretermit *vb* to omit: to miss: to overlook intentionally

pretor *var fm n* **praetor**

previse *vb* to foresee, to forecast: to inform beforehand

prewse *Obs fm obs n* **pruce**

prial *n* a pair royal, three playing cards each of the same denomination: three dice each showing the same number

pride (*n*, also see **lamprey**) *vb* to fill with pride

pridian *adj* of or pertaining to the previous day

prient *Obs fm n* **print**

priente *obs fm n* **print**

prier *n* one who pries

priest *(n) vb* to ordain to the priesthood: to function as a priest

priesting *n* ordination to the priesthood: functioning as a priest

prieve *obs var fm vb* **prove**

prigging *slg n* pilfering

prike *obs fm n* **prick**

prile *dial fm n* **prial**

primage *n* any of various marine percentage payments now mainly historical such as that formerly paid to the master and crew on the safe delivery of the cargo (also dubbed **hat money**): the percentage of water lost from a boiler in the form of steam

primal *adj* first, original, chief, fundamental, most important

primatial *adj* of or pertaining to a primate (churchman or ape): superiority

primero *n* an old gambling card game which was very fashionable in England from about 1530 to 1640 (*pl* **primeros**)

primeur *Fr n* anything new or early

primo *adj* first (*fem fm* **prima**) *n* in music, the first part of such as a duet (*pl* **primi, primos**)

primsie *S adj* demure, formal, precise, prim

primus *adj* first *n* the presiding bishop of the Scottish Episcopalian Church who has certain, mainly ceremonial, additional dignity (*pl* **primuses**)

prindle *var fm obs dial n* **pringle**

prine *var fm now S & dial n/vb* **preen** *obs n* ilex

pringle *vb* to experience a prickly tingling feeling *obs dial n* a silver coin described by one late 17th century writer as being Scottish, about the size of a penny and having two x's on it

prinkle *S vb* to experience the sensation of 'pins and needles': to twinkle

printe *obs fm n/vb* **print**

prion *n* whale bird, a small seabird and one of the most common of the southern hemisphere petrels

priorate *n* the (term of) office of a prior: the dignity of a prior in either the ecclesiastical sense or of the chief magistrate (prior) of the former republic of Florence: a priory: the inmates of such

priore *obs fm n* **priory**

prisage *n* an ancient duty on wine abolished in 1809

priser *obs fm n/arch n* **prizer**

prison (*n*) *vb* to imprison (now usually *S/poet/rhetorical*)

prisone *obs fm n* **prison**

priss *obs fm n* **price** *obs fm vb* **prize** (in senses other than capture or taking by force)

prist *obs fm n/vb* **priest**

pristane *n* a chemical compound

priste *obs fm n* **priest**

prittle see **prittle-prattle**

prittle-prattle *n* idle chater *obs vb* to chatter idly (GAMES PLAYER'S note: Whilst **prattle** exists as an independent word and is perfectly valid for play, the first element, **prittle**, does not. Hence **prittle** cannot be used for a word game.)

prizer *n* one who esteems something highly *arch n* a prize figher

proa *n* a Malayan sailing boat which has an outrigger or small canoe attached in parallel to give greater stability (*var fms* **prahu, praw, prawe**)

proat *dial vb* to prod or poke

procaine *n* a white crystalline compound which, in its hydrochloride form, is used as a local anaesthetic

proctal *adj* of or pertaining to the anus

proctitis *n* inflammation of the anus

proem *n* a preface

proette *US n* a female professional sports player

profet *obs fm n* **profit**

progestin *n* any substance which promotes gestational activity after the fertilization of the ovum

proggins *slg n* a proctor at Oxford or Cambridge

Progne *fem pers n* the name of the daughter of Pandion who, in a classic fable, was turned into a swallow: the personal name now given to a swallow (also see **Philomel** and **redbreast**) *n* a genus of American swallows which includes the purple martin

prognosis *n* a (medical) forecast (*pl* **prognoses**)

progue *var fm n* **prog**, any simple piercing implement

proign *obs fm obsol vb* **prune**, of a bird, to preen

proigne *Obs fm n* **Progne**, in the sense of the personal name of a swallow (Chaucer tended to treat it as being a species of bird rather than a personal name)

proine *obs vb* to prime

proker *dial n* a poker

prolamine *n* any of various simple proteins which are insoluble in pure water or absolute alcohol

prolapse *n* a slipping from its correct position of an internal organ *vb* of an organ, to slip out of position

prolate (*adj*) *obs vb* to lengthen in utterance

prole *obs fm vb* **prowl**

proles *n pl* progeny, offspring

proletary *adj*/*n* proletarian

prolle *obs fm vb* prowl

prometal *n* a kind of cast iron highly resistant to heat

promethean *adj* of, pertaining to or resembling any of the facets of the life of the mythical Prometheus *n* one likened to him

Prometheus *pers n* a demigod of the Greek myths and sometimes said to be the creator of mankind. He stole fire from Olympus and taught men how to use it and also instructed them in other arts. For this he was punished by Zeus and chained to a rock in the Caucasus where his liver was daily preyed upon by a vulture until Heracles rescued him.

pronaos *n* the vestibule of an ancient Greek temple (*pl* **pronaoi**)

pronate *adj* bent into a prone position *vb* to render prone

prone (*adj*) *n* an ecclesiastical homily *obs vb* to read out

pronephew *obs n* a great-grandson

pronepot *obs S n* a pronephew

proniece *obs n* a grand-niece (but see **pronephew)**

pronota *pl* pronotum, a hard outer plate of an insect

pronotal *adj* of or pertaining to the pronotum

pronotum *n* the central ridge of the upper surface of the first of three divisions of the thorax of an insect (*pl* **pronata**)

pronto *adv* at once

proole *obs fm vb* **prowl**

prooemium *n* a proem (note: No *pl* recorded, hence no listed anagrams for the likely *pl*, **prooemia**, with **pomoeria** – see **pomoerium**)

prootic *adj* in front of the ear *n* the prootic bone

propale *arch vb* to publish

proper (*adj*) *n* an ecclesiastical office, such as a psalm, which is appropriate for a certain occasion or time of year *obs vb* to appropriate, to take possession of

propine *arch vb* to offer *esp* drink *arch S n* a gift

prorate *vb* to distribute on a proportional basis

proration *n* the act or an instance of a pro rata division

prore *now poet n* the prow of a ship

prosaical *adj* unpoetic, unromantic (basically now *obsol* with **prosaic** as the preferred term)

prosaist *n* one who writes prose: one who is unpoetic

proselyte (*n*) *vb* to cause the change of holding one particular opinion to that of another *esp* to convert from one religious faith to another

proser *n* a writer of prose: one who writes or talks in a dull, tiresome fashion

proset *obs nonce n* a small, insignificant piece of prose

prosist *n* a writer of prose

prosit *interj* good health, used as a drinking toast

prosne *obs fm n* **prone**

prosse *var fm obs n* **pruce**

prosthesis *n* see **prothesis** (4th definition)

prosthetic *adj* pertaining to or of the nature of prosthesis

prostyle *n* a portico in front of a Greek temple

prosy *adj* dull, tedious, wearisome (*comp* **prosier** *sup* **prosiest**)

protases *pl* protasis

protasis *n* the introductory part of (ancient) classical drama: the introductory clause of a conditional sentence: a proposition, a maxim (*pl* **protases**)

prote *var fm dial vb* **proat**

Protea *n* a genus of mainly S. African shrubby trees bearing cone-like flowers (*–cap*) *n* a shrub or small tree of this genus (*pl* **proteas**)

protean *adj* changing, varying *n* an actor playing multiple roles

protease *n* an enzyme that digests proteins

proteid *n* a protein: a species of neotentic salamander (see **neoteny**)

protense *obs n* duration

proter *dial n* a poker

Proteus *pers n* a Greek sea god who assumed different shapes to avoid having to tell the future (*–cap*) *n* the olm, a blind elongated salamander which lives in deep subterranean caves in Yugoslavia and, like the mole salamander of Mexico (see **axolotl**), remains in a permanent larval stage: an amoeba: a group of bacteria: an inconstant person or thing

prothesis *n* a service of the Greek Church concerned with the preliminaries to Holy Communion: the table on which the elements of Communion are placed: the part of the church where the service is held: the etymologically better *fm* of **prosthesis**, the addition of a letter or syllable at the beginning of a word

protist *n* any organism of the *Protista* which includes bacteria, protozoans and fungi regarded as distinct from plants and animals

Protista *n pl* organisms having isolated cells and which constitute borderline cases between plants and animals

protistic *adj* of the Protista

proton *n* a stable, positively-charged particle of an atom, the number of which found in any atomic nucleus equates to the atomic number of the respective element

protophyte *n* the vegetable equivalent of a protozoan or protozoon, in being any species of the simplest type of plant life

protyl *var fm n* **protyle**

protyle *n* one of various names for a hypothetic basic material from which all the elements in the universe are supposedly derived (note: The *pl* **protyles** is given in the dictionary used for the North American Scrabble championship. However, if there is more than one protyle surely it would cease to be what it is supposed to be?)

proule *obs fm vb* **prowl**

Proustian *adj* pertaining to the French novelist, Marcel Proust (1871–1922) *n* an admirer of his work

prowde *obs fm adj* **proud**

prowe *obs fm n* **prow**

prowes *obs fm n* **prowess**

prowest *sup arch adj* prow, valiant

prowle *obs fm vb* **prowl**

prowse *obs fm n* **prowess**

prowte *obs fm adj* **proud**

pruce *obs n* Prussia (usually written without an initial capital letter and frequently used as a *modf n* with the sense of Prussian)

pruche *var fm obs n* **pruce**

pruder *Obs fm comp* **prouder**

prudest *Obs fm sup* **proudest**

prunel *obs n* the herb, selfheal

prunt *n* a piece of overlaid ornamental glass on such as a glass vase: the tool used for such work

prunted *adj* having prunts

pryer *var fm n* **prier**

prysone *obs fm n* **prison**

psalme *obs fm n* **psalm**

psalmist *n* the author of a psalm (**The Psalmist** being the *fm* always used for King David): a member of one of various historical minor orders which provided choristers

Psalter *n* the *Book of Psalms* (*—cap*) *n* a book of psalms

psalterer *Obs n* one who played the psaltery

psalteria *pl* psalterium

psalterial *adj* pertaining to the psalterium

psalterion *now poet n* the psaltery

psalterium *n* the manyplies or omasum, the third stomach of a ruminant (*pl* **psalteria**)

psaltery *n* a dulcimer-like mediaeval stringed instrument played by plucking the strings (*pl* **psalteries**)

psaltress *n* a female psaltery player

psauter *Obs fm n* **psalter**

psealm *Obs fm n* **psalm**

psellism *n* any defect of enunciation such as stammering or lisping

psettine *adj* of such flatfish as the turbot and brill *n* a turbot or related flatfish

Pseudis *n* the genus of the paradoxical frog, a South American frog having a tadpole more than three times the length of the parent

pseudodrome *n* a type of palindrome in which the words of a sentence read the same when written in the reverse order. Examples:– *Bores are people that say that people are bores. You can cage a swallow, can't you, but you can't swallow a cage, can you? Women understand men; few men understand women. Girl, bathing on Bikini, eyeing boy, finds boy eyeing bikini on bathing girl.*

psi *n* the twenty-third and penultimate letter of the Greek alphabet

psilosis *n* the loss of hair: a tropical disease marked by anaemia, emaciation and gastrointestinal disturbances (*pl* **psiloses**)

psilotic *adj* of or pertaining to psilosis

psittacine *adj* of or belonging to a parrot or its family: parrotlike *n* a parrot

psychomancy *n* occult communication with a spirit *obs n* divination by communication with the dead

ptarmic *adj* causing to sneeze *n* that which causes such

Pteraster *n* a genus of an American cushion star, a five-cornered, cushion-shaped starfish

ptere *n* a winglike part of an animal

pteria *pl* pterion

pterin *n* any of various pigments which occur in the wings of butterflies

pterion *n* the region of the skull where various bones meet in the shape of an H (*pl* **pteria**)

Pteris *n* a genus of ferns *incl* bracken

pterlya *n* that part of the skin of a bird which has the contour feathers (*pl* **pterlyae**)

pterna *n* the sole of a bird's foot

ptisan *n* a medicinal drink made from barley *vb* to give ptisan to

ptisane *arch fm n* **ptisan**

ptisen *obs fm n* **ptisan**

ptomaine *n* any of various substances of putrefying animal or vegetable matter, some of which are poisonous

ptoses *pl* ptosis

ptosis *n* the permanent drooping of the upper eyelid due to the paralysis of the elevator muscle (*pl* **ptoses**)

ptyalin *n* the active ferment substance of saliva which converts insoluble starch into soluble sugar

pu *n* a Chinese measure of distance of *approx* three miles: an ancient Chinese coin (*pl* **pu**)

pucelle *n* a slovenly woman

puck (*n*) *now dial vb* to hit

puddel *obs fm n/vb* **puddle**

puddle (*n*) *vb* to make a puddle or mixture of wet clay and sand which is used as a lining for such as a pond: to mess about in a puddle of water

pudent *adj* modest

pudicity *n* modesty, chastity

puer *var fm vb* **pure**, to treat (hides) with dog dung

puisne *adj* junior: more recent *n* a short *fm* of **puisne judge**, a judge of the High Court inferior to the Lord Chancellor, the Lord Chief Justice of England, the Lord Chief Justice of Common Pleas, the Master of the Rolls and the Lord Chief Baron

puja *n* worship (by Hindus)

pulce *obs fm n/vb* **pulse**

pule *vb* to cry, to whimper: to talk in a whining fashion *n* a whine

puler *n* a whining weakly person

Pulex *n* the genus of the human flea, which is equally at home on a badger or a pig. Only the human flea is suitable for a flea circus and the most prized of these are imported from Russia. In return for performing such acts as towing a carriage up to 240 times its own weight, the individual flea is cossetted in its own personal box and allowed to feed, morning and evening, on its trainer's hand

pulie *obs fm n* **pulley**

pulpiter *n* a preacher

pulsator *n* one who or that which beats or throbs: a machine which separates diamonds from the earth *obs n* the deathwatch beetle

pulter *obs fm arch n* **poulter**

pultes *obs fm n* **poultice** (*pl* **pultes**)

pultess *dial fm n* **poultice**

pulton *n* an Indian infantry regiment

pultre *obs fm n* **poultry**

pumelo *n* a grapefruit: a shaddock (*pl* **pumelos**)

punchy *adj* squat, stumpy, short and stout, thickset: vigorous, powerful: of the nature of the mixed beverage, punch *collq adj* dazed or punch drunk (*comp* **punchier** *sup* **punchiest**)

punctilio *n* a minute detail, a scruple (*pl* **punctilios**)

punder *dial fm vb* **ponder** *var fm S n* **poinder**

pundet *arch fm n* **pundit**

pundit *n* one learned in Indian scholarship: an authority on a subject *esp* one who considers himself or herself such

pundler *obs var fm S n* **poinder**

pundre *var fm obs n* **pounder**, a former English balance and weight *obs fm vb* **ponder**

punge *obs vb* to pierce: to sting

punger *now dial n* the large edible crab

pungled *dial adj* financially embarrassed: of fruit or grain, shrivelled

punier *comp adj* puny

punise *obs S fm vb* **punish**

punler *var fm obs S n* **pundler** (see **poinder**, of which it is an *obs var fm*)

punnet *n* a small light basket for such as fruit

punse *dial fm vb* **pounce**, to poke or thrust

punty *n* an iron rod used by a glassmaker

pupate *vb* of an insect larva, to experience the immobile non-feeding stage of development as a pupa where it changes from being a grub to being a mature adult insect

pur *var fm now dial vb* **porr** *dial fm interj* **purr** *obsol fm n/vb* **purr**, the feline sound *var fm obs n* **purre**

purdah *n* a curtain or screen *esp* one concealing women from visitors to the general quarters: the material of such a screen: the state of seclusion created (for the women) (*lit/fig*)

purée (*n*) *vb* to make a purée of

purger *n* one who or that which purges (*lit/fig*)

purim *n* (often + *cap*) the Jewish festival of Lots which honours the deliverance from an historic plot of massacre, as described in the *Book of Esther*

purine *n* a white crystalline substance which, when oxidized, become uric acid (*pl*) *n* the group of its derivatives which includes caffeine

purism *n* exaggerated correctness *esp* of style or language

purl *n* gold or silver thread: any of the small loops which form an edging to such as lace: a similar appearance to the edge of a leaf: in knitting, an inversion of stitches to produce a ribbed effect: dog's nose, a mixture of hot beer and gin *S n* dried cow dung (used as fuel) *collq n* a heavy fall *dial n* the tern *vb* to embroider with gold or silver thread: to knit as described above *dial vb* of a cat, to purr

purle *arch fm n* **purl**, a thread *obs fm n* **purl** (most other senses)

purler *n* a spectacular fall *Austr n* something excellent

purpel *Obs fm n/adj* **purple**

purply *adj* somewhat purple (note: No *comp* or *sup*)

purr (feline *n/vb*) *n* an extinct breed of wild pigs once found in the Isle of Man *interj* a call to pigs

purre *n* the bird, the dunlin, in its winter plumage *obs n* an inferior cider or perry made from the residual fruit after the juice has been extracted *var fm n* **pirr**

purrel *obs fm n* **purrell**, a transverse stripe of different colours woven at the beginning and end of a piece of cloth to comply with a law dating back to Elizabethan times which was instituted to prevent fraudulent shortening

purser *n* a ship's officer in charge of accounts

purset *obs n* a small purse

pursie *S n* a purse

purslane *n* a succulent herb used in salads and as a pickling ingredient

pusel *obs fm vb* **puzzle**

Pushto *var fm adj/n* **Pashto**

Pushtoo *var fm n* **Pashto**

pusle *obs fm n/vb* **puzzle**

pussel *obs fm n* **pucelle**, a slovenly woman *obs fm vb* **puzzle**

pussle *obs fm vb* **puzzle**

pussy (*n*) *adj* full of pus

pustel *obs fm n* **pustule**

pustle *obs fm n* **pustule**

pustule *n* a pimple which contains pus

puteal *n* a cylindrical ring of stone surrounding the mouth of an ancient Roman well

puteli *n* a flat-bottomed vessel of the Ganges

putlock *var fm n* **putlog**, one of the short horizontal timbers of a scaffolding

putor *obs n* a stench

puzzel *obs fm n* **pucelle**

py *obs fm n* **pie** (in the senses given at **pie**) *var fm obs n* **pee**

pya *n* a Burmese copper coin

pyanit *var fm n* **piannet**

pye *var fm n/vb* **pie** (in the senses given at **pie**) *var fm obs n* **pee**

pyeing *pr pple* see **pie**

pying *n* see **pie**

pyle *n* a pore of the body *dial fm n* **peel**, a (baker's) shovel *obs fm n/vb* **pile** *obs fm n* **pillow**

pynot *n* the magpie (see both **pie** and **Cock and Pynot**)

pyoner *obs fm n* **pioneer**

pyoses *pl* pyosis

pyosis *n* the formation of pus (*pl* **pyoses**)

pyr *obs fm interj* **purr**

pyralid *n* one of various moths *incl* a species which is a vineyard pest

pyralides *pl* pyralis

pyralis *n* a pyralid (*pl* **pyralides**) *obs n* a fabulous fly which was generated by and could live in fire (*pl* **pyralides**)

pyre *n* (the site for) a pile of wood for a (funeral) fire *var fm now dial vb* **pire**

pyrene *n* a fruit stone: a hydrocarbon obtained from coal

pyrite *n* a cubic crystalline form of iron sulphide used mainly in the manufacture of sulphuric acid (also called **pyrites** or **iron pyrites**)

pyrogen *n* a substance causing fever or heat

pyrolater *n* a fire worshipper

pyromancy *n* divination by fire or the shapes observed in fire

pyromantic *adj* pertaining to or practising pyromancy

pyrope *n* the fire garnet, a gem of a deep red colour

pyrophorus *n* any substance capable of spontaneous combustion when exposed to the air (*pl* **pyrophori**)

pysse *obs fm n/vb* **piece**

Pythia *n* either of the two priestesses of the shrine of Apollo on Mount Parnassus, Delphi, Greece who, in a state of frenzy, spoke the oracles. To achieve this state she inhaled sulphurous vapours which issued from a hole in the ground over which she sat on a three-legged stool. Oracles, delivered in verse, were only available in the spring: a genus of gasteropod molluscs

Pythian *adj* of or pertaining to Delphi or the Pythias (the ancient games held near Delphi) *n* a native of Delphi: a Pythia

Pythic *adj* an alternative to Pythian: of the nature of a Pythian priestess when she delivers her oracle hence, in general usage, ecstatic

pythonic *adj* of or pertaining to divination: prophetic: of, pertaining to or resembling a (mythical) python

Q

Q Apart from the words listed below which start with Q plus a consonant or a different vowel from the usual U, there are a number of other words which feature the letter Q without a letter U immediately following it, as follows:– **bathqol, buqsha, burqa, cinq, cinqfoil, eqwal, faqih, faqir, fiqh, fuqaha, inqilab, liqor, miqra, muqaddam, nastaliq, paq, sambuq, shoq, sqadwe, sqvare, sqwate, sqwere, sqwier, sqwoil, sqwug, suq, taluq, taluqdar, taluqdari, tariqat, umqwhile, wymqwhyle** and **zindiq**. (Also listed, but invalid for word game play, are **seq, seqq, sq** and **sqq**. Unlisted words *incl* for instance, the names of the Arab countries, **Iraq** and **Qatar**, and such a person as an **Iraqi**.)

Apart from the obvious value of combatting the frustration of having a Q but no U in a crossword-type game, many of these words are ideal for other forms of word play. For example, **qwaste** has the anagram **sqwate** and could be chosen for Pentery Web played at an advanced level; it also provides a double high score in Pelham. **Qweysye** is a particularly devilish choice for hangman and **qwetyll** might well be considered for a guessing game of the Call My Bluff variety. **Qwyet, qwyle, qwyne** and **qwyte** would form an especially nasty group of words in a paragraph given to a code breaker whilst any one of them should prove wickedly frustrating in the game of Words. Finally, the word **qwa** has been specifically annotated for a particularly valuable technique in the playing of word games of the crossword-type.

qabab *var fm n* **kebab**

qabbala *var fm n* **cabbala**

qabbalah *var fm n* **cabbala**

qadhi *var fm n* **cadi**

qadi *var fm n* **cadi**

qadistu *n* a Babylonian sacred prostitute of the temple of Ishtar (also see **hamaritu** and **ishtaritu**)

qaf *n* the twenty-first letter of the Arabic alphabet: a mountain range (+*cap*) *n* a mythological mountain range made of emerald

qaid *var fm n* **caid** (in the sense of **cadi**)

qalamdam *var fm n* **kalamdam**

qanat *n* a pipe or underground tunnel used for irrigation water

qaneh *n* an ancient Hebrew measure of length of six cubits ($10\frac{1}{4}$ feet or 3.13 metres) (*pl* **qaneh**)

qanon *var fm n* **kanoon**

qantar *var fm n* **kantar**

qanum *var fm n* **kanoon**

Qaraqalpaq *n/adj* (of) a Turkic people of Central Asia

qasab *n* an ancient measure of length in such as Assyria, Chaldea and Persia of $12\frac{1}{2}$ feet (3.84 metres) (*pl* **qasab**)

qasaba *n* an ancient Arabian measure of area of *approx* eighteen square yards (*pl* **qasaba**)

qasida *n* a satiric poem of various related oriental cultures

qat *n* an Ethiopian bush which yields a narcotic

qazi *var fm n* **cadi**

qcepo *n* a type of skin infection

qere *var fm n* **keri**

qeri *var fm n* **keri**

qhat *Obs fm pron/adj/adv/conj/n* **what**

qhete *Obs S & dial fm n* **wheat**

qhom *Obs fm pron* **whom**

qi *n* in Chinese philosophy, the physical life-force

qibla *var fm n* **kiblah**

qiblah *var fm n* **kiblah**

qindah *var fm n* **qintar**

qintar *n* an Albanian coin equal to one hundredth of a lek

qirk *obs fm n* **quirk**

qiviut *n* the wool of the undercoat of the musk ox

qoph *var fm n* **koph**

qre *var fm n* **keri**

qri *var fm n* **keri**

qu *obs n* half a farthing *obs fm n* **cue**, in the senses of the letter Q: the signal to an actor: apt humour

qua *adv* in the capacity of *obs S fm pron* **who**

quaa *var fm S n* **quaw**

quabling *obs n* a gudgeon, a small carp-like fish

quack (*n*/*vb*) note: The *vb* is also extended to the noise made by a frog – though not very often!

quackle *vb* of a duck, to quack *now dial vb* to choke

quader *obs vb* of mathematics, to square

quadern *var fm obs n* **quadran**

quadle *obs var fm vb* **coddle**, to boil gently

quadral *adj* by four, divided into four parts

quadran *obs n* a square (note: The *var fms*, **quadern** and **quadren**, only appear in the anagram lists at **ADENQRSU)**

quadrant *n* a quarter section of a circle

quadrat *n* an area selected for ecological study: a printer's small block used for making a space

quadrate *n* a cube-like object: one of a pair of upper jaw bones of amphibians, birds, fishes and reptiles

quadren *var fm obs n* **quadran**

quadron *n* a square

quaestor *n* originally one of two magistrates of ancient Rome who inquired into and punished capital crimes: in later ancient Roman times any of various officials concerned with financial affairs: in mediaeval times, a public prosecutor in certain criminal cases

quag *n* a marshy place

quage *obs fm n* **quag**

quagga *n* a now extinct member of the horse family, the front half of which looked like an ass and the rear half a zebra. Formally abundant in South Africa, the last wild quagga was killed by 1860 and the last surviving zoo specimen died in Amsterdam in 1883.

quail (*vb*) *n* one of a species from either of two distinct groups of game birds. The New World group includes the California quail and the Virginia quail. The Virginia quail is also known as the colin or the bobwhite – its call sounds like 'bob white'. Of the many Old World species one of the most interesting is the painted quail. This sparrow-sized bird was kept in their voluminous sleeves by the Chinese mandarins who used it to keep their hands warm. *dial n* the small spotted waterhen: the corncrake *obs n* a courtesan

quailer *n* one who or that which quails

quaille *obs fm vb* **quail**

quaint (*adj*) *now dial vb* to acquaint *obs vb* to beautify (note: The *adj* had *Obs* or *obs fms* which are decidedly quaint *incl* **coinite, koynt, qwent** and **whaint**. One of the many early *fms* which might be worthy of revival is **qwaint**, for it not only looks and sounds quaint but is suggestive of that which is ancient.)

quair *obs fm n* **quire**

quale *n* the quality of a thing (*pl* **qualia**) *obs n* death, destruction (also used as a *modf n* as **quale house**, a house of torture) *obs fm n/vb* **quail** *Obs fm n* **whale**

qualitied *adj* having the quality or qualities suggested by the noun to which it refers

quall *obs fm n* **whale**

qualm (*n*) *vb* to make sick

quam *Obs S fm pron* **whom**

quame *var fm obs vb* **queme**, to please *obs fm n* **qualm**

quane *obs fm n* **quean**

quank *n* the moo of a gnu (a *vb* to quank does not appear to be recorded)

quannet *n* a comblike file used by a comb maker

quant *n* a flat-capped punting pole for use against a base of soft mud

quante *obs fm adj* **quaint** *Obs fm n* **quant**

quantise *var fm vb* **quantize**

quantize *vb* to express (an energy relationship) in accordance with the theory that energy is manifested by the emission from radiating bodies of discreet particles and is not a smoothly flowing continuum.

quap *obs vb* to beat: quiver *obs n* a fish, described as being 'poison to man and man to him'

quar see **be**

quare *N Ir fm adj/adv* **queer** *obs vb* to square *obs fm n* **quire** *Obs S fm adv/conj* **where**

quark *vb* of such as frogs or various birds, to utter a harsh cry or croak

quarl *n* a large curved fire brick: the jellyfish *obs vb* to curdle

quarle *var fm n* **quarl**, a brick

quarn *obs fm n* **quern**

quart (*n*) *obs n* health *obs adj* healthy

quarte *n* the fourth of eight attacking positions in fencing, this one having the fingernails uppermost and the blade at arm's length: a sequence of four in various card games

quarter day *n* any of four days in the year when certain payments fall due. In the British Isles, apart from Scotland, these are Lady Day, Midsummer Day, Michaelmas and Christmas. In Scotland these are now Candlemas, Whit Sunday. Lammas and Martinmas but were, originally, Candlemas, Beltane, Lammas and Hallowmas.

quarterland *n* a division of land in the Isle of Man varying from 120 to 140 acres

quarterman *n* a shipwright foreman

quartern *n* a quarter of various measures for such as bread, flax and malt: a quarter of a sheet of paper *now dial n* a quarter of anything *Obs n* a prison

quartful *n* the full capacity of a quart pot (*pl* **quartsful**) *obs adj* healthy, prosperous, safe

quartile *adj* of astrology, designating an aspect between planets (in astrology this term also includes the sun and the moon) when their longitudes differ by 90° and which is signified on a horoscope by the symbol of a small square: relating to or connected with such an aspect: of statistics, denoting 25% of the observed cases in a study on frequency distribution: of or pertaining to such *n* a quartile aspect

quartine *n* crotonylene, a hydrocarbon having a liquid state below 15°C

quartzine *adj* quartzy

quartzoid *n* a crystal having the form of a double six-sided pyramid

quartzy *adj* of the nature of or resembling the mineral, quartz

Quashie *pers n* a name, common in the various Kwa languages of West Africa, for a child born on a Sunday (*–cap*) *n* any negro

quat *now dial vb* to extinguish: to squash: to sate: of an animal, to crouch down in hiding

quate *var fm Obs n* **whate**

quater *obs fm n* **quatre** (as used in English)

quatern *n* a set of four lottery numbers

quatre *n* the French word for the number 4, used in English for the number 4 in dice and formerly anglicized as **cater**

quave *obs vb* to tremble *obs n* a tremble

quaw *S n* a bog, a quagmire

quawk *dial vb* of a rook, to utter its cry

que *dial n* the shoe of an ox *dial vb* to shoe an ox

queal *now dial vb* to extinguish

quean *n* a harlot *S n* a pleasant young lass

quear *obs fm n* **quire**

quease *obs vb* to squeeze

queasom *now dial vb* to choke or stifle: to be choked or smothered

queazen *obs fm now dial vb* **queasom**

queazie *obs fm adj* **queasy**

quebas *obs n* an unknown (card?) game played with or in the company of 'gaming madams'

queck *obs vb* of ducks, to quack

qued *obs adj* evil *obs n* evil: an evil person: the Devil

queek *vb* of an owl, to utter its cry

queel *var fm now dial vb* **queal**

queening *n* a variety of apple

queenite *n* a partisan of a queen

queenlet *n* a petty queen

queer (*adj*) *collq n* a male homosexual *slg vb* to swindle

queest *n* the wood pigeon

queeze *var fm n* **queest**

queint *var fm obs vb* **quent**

queir *obs fm adj* **queer**

queist *var fm n* **queest**

quele *Obs vb* to die *obs S fm n* **wheel**

quelea *n* a species of weaverbird and one of the most numerous in the world. Other than during the breeding season (when the male takes on brighter colouring and the female's beak becomes bright yellow) it looks rather like a red-beaked sparrow. Unfortunately they are a pest when a flock, numbering millions, descends upon ripening wheat or other similar crop of an African farmer.

quelt *obs fm n* **kilt**

queme *obs vb* to please

quene *obs fm ns* **coin, queen**

quent *obs vb* to quench

quer *obs fm adj* **queer**

quercin *n* a neutral crystalline substance obtained from oakbark

quercine *adj* of or pertaining to the oak: made of oak

quercite *n* a sweet crystalline alcohol obtained from acorns

quere *obs vb* to inquire *obs fm n* **quire**, paper

querent *n* one who asks or inquires *esp* one seeking the advice of an astrologer *adj* complaining

querist *n* a questioner or interrogator

querl *US n* a curl

quern *n* a small handmill for grinding such as pepper

quesal *var fm n* **quetzal**

quest *(n/vb) S fm n* **queest** *now dial n* an inquest *obs vb* to crush

queste *obs fm n* **quest**

quester *n* one who quests

questor *var fm n* **quaestor** (in all senses in the USA: in the mediaeval sense in the UK, otherwise *obs*) *n* one who quests

quethe *vb* to speak, say, tell, declare: to bequeath (*obs* except in the *pa t* **quoth**)

quething *obs n* **bequeathing**

quetzal *n* a large bird of the dense mountain forests of Central America, the male of which has a dazzlingly beautiful plumage of shimmering iridescent green with a crimson and white belly. It has been adopted as the national symbol of Guatemala: the Guatemalan dollar (GAME PLAYER'S note: As the 8-letter word, **quetzals**, this once held the official world record for the highest single move ever achieved in a genuine game of Scrabble®. To emulate such a move it is essential to possess the letters Q, S and Z together with four of the remaining five letters. The fifth letter has, by lucky chance, to be already in play on the board and, in order to make a phenomenally high score, be positioned in the correct square on the outermost line of the board. The remaining letters are then set down so that the Q and the S coincide with the triple-word squares, with the Z on the double-letter square. Such a move scores a minimum of 20 points for Z, plus one point each for U, E, T, A, L, S and 10 points for the Q, all multiplied by 3, then multiplied by 3 again, plus 50 points for using all seven tiles i.e. 374 points (or fewer if a blank is used). The record has since been beaten by the word **caziques** which, with **beziques**, is one of the three most highly prized words in the game. The ultimate, of course, lies in playing a 15-letter word along the complete length of the outermost line with all three triple word squares available. This has never yet been achieved in a known genuine game though it has been contrived with the blockbuster word **benzoxycamphors** and, for a time, featured in the *Guinness Book of Records* until it amended its rules to consider only those scores achieved in actual, witnessed play.)

quey *S & dial n* a heifer

quezal *var fm n* **quetzal**

quhaup *S dial n* an evil goblin with a nose like a pair of tongs

quhy *obs S fm adv* **why**

qui *Obs fm S & dial n* **quey** *Obs fm adv* **why**

quib *obs n* a quibble: a jibe *obs vb* to jibe (at)

quibbe *var fm obs n* **quib**

quiblet *now US n* a quibble

quickhatch *n* the wolverene

quickset *n* a cutting, *esp* of whitethorn or other shrubs, set in the ground to develop as part of a hedge *adj* of a hedge, formed of such cuttings: of a beard, rough and/or bristling *obs vb* to plant such a hedge

quickwood *n* (usually *modf n*) quickset

quide *Obs n* a saying, a statement: a will or bequest

quier *obs fm n* **quire**, paper

quiest *obs fm n* **queest**

quietant *n* anything which soothes or makes quiet

quiff *n* a lock of hair brushed up above the forehead

quile *var fm vb* **coil**, to put hay in haycocks or small cone-shaped piles which are left in the field to dry

quiler *var fm dial n/modf n* **quoiler**

quill (*n*) *vb* to flute or crimp such as the edge of lace: to plait in quill-like form: to wind thread on a quill (a bobbin)

quiller *obs n* a fledgling bird

quilter *n* one who or a machine which makes quilting

quinate *n* a salt of quinic acid *adj* of a leaf, comprised of five leaflets

quince *n* a pear-shaped, golden-coloured fruit used as the basis of jellies, marmalades etc: the tree bearing that fruit

quine *S fm n* **quean**, a harlot *var fm S n* **quean**

quinet *var fm dial n* **quinnet**, an iron wedge

quink *Ork n* the golden-eye duck

quinnat *n* either of two species of salmon native to the North American Pacific coastal area, the king salmon or the Chinook salmon

quinone *n* either of two crystalline compounds obtained from benzene *esp* a golden yellow compound with a pungent aroma: various other derivatives of benzene

quinse *obs vb* to cut

quinsy *n* tonsillitis or a similar throat infection

quint *n* a sequence of five consecutive playing cards of the same suit *esp* the **quint major**, the ace, king, queen, jack and ten and the **quint minor**, the jack, ten, nine, eight and seven

quinta *n* a (Spanish or Portuguese) country house

quintan *adj* of a fever which has recurring symptoms every fourth day (fifth day on an inclusive basis) *n* such a fever

quinte *n* the fifth of the eight thrusts recognized in the sport of fencing

quinter *S fm n/adj* **twinter**

quinze *n* a card game in which the object is to score exactly fifteen points

quinzell *var fm obs n* **quinsell**, a horse rein

quinzie *obs fm n* **quinsy**

quire *n* the twentieth part of a ream of sheets of paper, thus a set of 24 sheets (see **ream**): four sheets of paper folded to form sixteen pages: a set of sheets necessary to form a book *vb* to arrange sheets in quires *var fm n/poet vb* **choir** (the sense in which **quiring** is a *n*, meaning the action of the *vb*)

quirk (*n*) *dial n* a twist, a bend *vb* to use quirks or verbal tricks *dial vb* to grunt, groan: to grumble

quirl *vb* to curl *var fm US n* **querl**

quirm *Shet vb* to disappear quickly and mysteriously

quirt *n* a Spanish-American riding whip *vb* to strike with such

quisle *vb* to behave as a Quisling and collaborate with the enemy *obs fm vb* **whistle**

quist *n* the wood pigeon *obs fm now dial vb* **whist**

quiste *Obs fm n* **queest**

quister *Obs fm n* **whitster**

quite (*adv*) *obs fm vb* **quit**

quitter (*n*) *obs S vb* to twitter

quixotize *vb* to act in an absurdly generous and extravagantly chivalrous manner (GAME PLAYER'S note: In Scrabble®, to score the maximum value from this 9-letter word it needs to be played in those corners opposite to the ones discussed at the entry for **quetzal**. As such it will score a minimum of 428 points and break the world record currently held with the word **caziques**. However, it needs to be stressed that quixotize does not appear in either of the two basic dictionaries currently used for official championships in the English language.)

quo *Obs fm pron* **who**

quoiler *dial n* (in *pl*) the breech harness of a carthorse *modf n* of such a harness

quoin *n* an external angle of a wall or building: a cornerstone: a wedge *vb* to secure or raise with a wedge

quoist *n* the wood pigeon

quoit (*n*) *vb* to play the game of quoits

quokka *n* the short-tailed scrub wallaby (GAME PLAYER'S note: Whilst only a poor Scrabble® player would waste a blank tile to supplement the lack of a second K to play the word in its singular form, a top player would certainly do so as a very high-scoring 7-letter plural, **quokkas**. But, as a 'word-game word', it has excellent potential for hangman.)

quoll *n* a small carnivorous marsupial cat of Tasmania and eastern Australia

quonet *var fm n* **quannet**

quop *now dial vb* to palpitate, to throb

quore *obs fm n* **core**

quorse *Obs n* a corpse

quot *dial adj* cloyed

quotal *obs adj* capable of division into equal parts

quoth see **quethe**

quow *Obs fm adv* **how**

quoy *var fm S & dial n* **quey**

quoyle *obs fm arch n* **coil**, a turmoil

quoz *obsol n* a queer person

quy *obs fm S & dial n* **quey** *Obs fm adv* **why**

qvare *obs fm n* **quire**

qvarte *Obs fm n* **quart**

qvavyn *Obs fm obs vb* **quave**

qvayr *Obs fm n* **quire**, paper

qvene *Obs fm n* **queen**

qveyse *Obs fm obs vb* **quease**

qvyk *Obs fm arch vb* **quick**, to quicken

qvylle *Obs fm n* **quill**

qvylte *Obs fm n* **quilt**

qwa *Obs fm pron* **who** (GAME PLAYER'S note: In the crossword-type word games, poor players tend to see words only in a single plane. Such a player faced with qwa as the only word in play would be likely to make one of two moves – either incorporate the Q, the W or the A in another word or extend qwa to such as **qwate**. The better player having that same T and E available would devise a word including the T so that a supplementary score for the word **qwat** is the by-product of a totally different word on a tangential line, thus obtaining a score for two words instead of one. This still leaves the potential of either **qwate** or **qwats** as a similar link in a subsequent move. If **qwate** is then chosen, **sqwate** becomes available as yet a further link. Similarly, another such sequence of links is provided by qwa to **qwal** to **eqwal** to **eqwals**. Naturally, the same is true of many different words but few have the same facility for maintaining the high-scoring value of this useful little word. Just as significant is the fact that qwa can itself have been produced from an earlier playing of the 2-letter word, **wa**. Though **wy** to **qwy** to **qwyk** to **qwykn** has a higher scoring value, the opportunity for such a series of linking moves is much rarer than any series based on qwa due to the frequency of letter distribution.)

qwaelke *Obs fm n* **whelk**, a pimple

qwaint *Obs fm adj* **quaint**

qwaire *obs fm n* **quire**, a set of 24 sheets of paper

qwal *Obs S fm n* **whale**

qwappe *Obs fm obs vb* **quap**

qwar *Obs S & dial fm adv/conj* **where**

qware *Obs S & dial fm adv/conj* **where**

qwarfor *obs S fm adv* **wherefore**

QUOTABLE DEFINITIONS Probably the most famous dictionary definition is that by Dr Johnson in his *Dictionary of the English Language*, published in 1755, in which he describes a patron as being, 'Commonly a wretch who supports with insolence, and is paid with flattery'. However, some delightful definitions exist in works which are not intended to be taken quite so seriously. *The Devil's Dictionary*, for example, provides such gems as:–

'**absurdity** *n* a statement of belief manifestly inconsistent with one's own opinion'

'**alone** *adj* in bad company'

'**barometer** *n* an ingenious instrument which indicates what kind of weather we are having'

'**bore** *n a person who talks when you wish him to listen'*

'**clairvoyant** *n* a person, commonly a woman, who has the power of seeing that which is invisible to her patron – namely, that he is a blockhead'

'**congratulation** *n* the civility of envy'

'**déjeuner** *n* the breakfast of an American who has been in Paris. Variously pronounced.'

'**diplomacy** *n* the patriotic art of lying for one's country'

'**egotist** *n* a person of low taste, more interested in himself than in me'

'**future** *n* that period of time in which our affairs prosper, our friends are true, and our happiness is assured'

'**lawyer** *n* one skilled in circumvention of the law'

'**male** *n* a member of the unconsidered, or negligible sex. The male of the human race is commonly known (to the female) as Mere Man. The genus has two varieties: good providers and bad providers.'

'**opportunity** *n* a favourable occasion for grasping a disappointment'

'**overwork** *n* a dangerous disorder affecting high public functionaries who want to go fishing'

'**positive** *adj* mistaken at the top of one's voice'

'**price** *n* value, plus a reasonable sum for the wear and tear of conscience in demanding it'

'**telephone** *n* an invention of the devil which abrogates some of the advantages of making a disagreeable person keep his distance'.

Other non-serious dictionaries tend to place too great an emphasis on puns but they can still produce such as:–

'**acorn** *n* an oak in a nutshell'

'**auctioneer** *n* a man who looks forbidding'

'**caterpillar** *n* an upholstered worm'

'**dentist** *n* someone who looks down in the mouth'

'**goblet** *n* a small turkey'

'**kindred** *n* a fear of relatives coming'

'**nail** *n* a long, round object with a flat head which you aim at before you hit your thumb'

'**pillow** *n* headquarters'

'**racetrack** *n* the only place where windows clean people'

'**raisin** *n* a worried grape'

'**snoring** *n* sheet music'.

Finally, a classic which appears in *Chambers 20th Century Dictionary*: '**middle-aged** *adj* between youth and old age, variously reckoned to suit the reckoner'.

qwarte *Obs fm obs n/adj* **quart**

qwarter *Obs fm n* **quarter** (*pl* **qwarters**)

qwarterage *Obs fm n* **quarterage**, a quarterly payment such as a tax

qwartful *Obs fm obs adj* **quartful**

qwartter *obs fm n* **quarter**

qwash *Obs fm vb* **quash** (*infl fms incl* **qwaste**)

qwaste see **qwash**

qwat *dial vb* to squash flat

qwate *var fm Obs n* **whate** (GAME PLAY-

ER'S note: Whilst one cannot assume that 'qwates' is the plural – it being an *Obs* word – nevertheless an equally suitable link is available with **sqwate**)

qway *obs fm n* **whey**

qwech *Obs fm adj/pron* **which**

qwed *Obs fm obs n* **qued**, in the sense of the Devil

qwede *var fm Obs n* **quide**, a will or bequest

qwedyr *Obs fm S & dial vb* **whither**, to rush: to tremble: to strike violently

qweer *obs fm n* **choir**

qwel *Obs fm adj/pron* **which**

qwele *obs S fm n* **wheel**

qwell *Obs S fm n* **wheel**

qweme *Obs fm obs vb* **queme**

qwene *obs fm n* **queen**

qwent *obs pa pple vb* **quench**

qwer *Obs S & dial fm adv/conj* **where**

qwere *obs fm n* **choir**

qwerf *Obs fm n* **wharf**

qwerk *var fm dial n* **quirk**

qwerle *Obs fm n* **whirl**

qwern *obs fm n* **quern**

qwert *Obs fm obs n/adj* **quart**

qwerte *Obs fm obs n/adj* **quart**

qwest *obs fm n* **quest**

qwesye *Obs fm adj* **queasy**

qwet *Obs S & dial fm n* **wheat**

qwete *Obs fm vb* **whet** *Obs S & dial fm n* **wheat**

qwetyll *Obs fm now dial n* **whittle**, a (large) knife (CALL MY BLUFF additional detail note: Whilst the modern spelling is **whittle** and describes such as a carving knife, qwetyll is the earliest recorded *fm* of the word and a 14th century writer noted its use for the scraping of bark from timber)

qweysye *Obs fm adj* **queasy**

qwha *obs S fm pron* **who**

qwhar *Obs S & dial fm adv/conj* **where**

qwhare *Obs S & dial fm adv/conj* **where**

qwharefore *Obs S fm adv* **wherefore**

qwharte *Obs fm n* **quart**

qwheet *Obs S & dial fm n* **wheat** (note: Unlisted anagram, **qwhete**)

qwhele *obs S & dial fm n* **wheel**

qwhene *Obs fm n* **queen**

qwher *Obs S & dial fm adv/conj* **where**

qwhete *Obs S & dial fm n* **wheat** (note: Unlisted anagram, **qwheet**)

qwhil *obs S fm n* **while**

qwhit *Obs S fm adj* **white**

qwhois *obs S fm pron* **whose**

qwhoise *obs S fm pron* **whose**

qwhom *Obs fm pron* **whom**

qwhos *Obs S fm pron* **whose**

qwhy *obs fm S & dial n* **quey** *Obs S fm adv* **why**

qwhyet *Obs fm adj* **white** (note: Unlisted anagram, **qwhyte**)

qwhyl *obs S fm n* **while**

qwhyt *Obs fm adj* **white**

qwhyte *Obs fm adj* **white** (note: Unlisted anagram, **qwhyet**)

qwi *Obs fm adv* **why**

qwikn *Obs fm vb* **quicken**

qwil *Obs fm n* **quill** *Obs S fm n* **while**

qwile *Obs S fm n* **while**

qwill *Obs S fm n* **while**

qwince *Obs fm n* **quince**

qwine *dial n* money: a corner

qwirk *var fm dial n* **quirk**

qwo *Obs fm pron* **who**

qwom *Obs fm pron* **whom**

qwop *dial vb* to throb with pain

qworle *Obs fm pron* **whorl**

qwose *Obs S fm pron* **whose**

qwot *var fm dial vb* **qwat**

qwy *Obs fm S & dial n* **quey** *Obs fm adv* **why**

qwye *obs fm S & dial n* **quey**

qwyet *Obs S & dial fm n* **wheat**

qwyght *Obs fm adj* **white**

qwyk *obs fm adj/adv/n* **quick** *Obs fm arch vb* **quick**, to quicken

qwyken *Obs fm vb* **quicken**

qwykkesand *Obs fm n* **quicksand**

qwykn *Obs fm vb* **quicken**

qwyl *obs fm n* **wheel** *obs S fm n* **while**

qwyle *Obs S fm n* **while**

qwylte *Obs fm n* **quilt**

qwyne *Obs fm obs S & dial adv* **whyne**, whence (note: The last recorded *fm* was **quhyn**)

qwynse *Obs fm n* **quinsy**

qwyt *obs fm adj* **white**

qwyte *obs fm adj* **white** *Obs S & dial fm n* **wheat**

qwyuer *Obs fm now dial adj* **quiver**, nimble: rapid

qwyver *obs fm n* **quiver**

R

ra *n* the tenth letter of the Arabic alphabet *obs S n* a sailyard, a spar on the mast of a vessel from which a sail is suspended (*+cap*) *pers n* the supreme Egyptian god, god of the sun

raa *obs fm n* **roe**, the deer

rab *n* a crutch-shaped wooden beater used in the mixing of mortar *vb* to use a rab

rabato *var fm n* **rebato** (*pl* **rabatos, rabatoes**)

rabatte *vb* of geometry, to rotate into coincidence with another plane

rabbet *n* a channel, groove or slot cut to receive an edge (*var fm* **ravet**): a spring-pole: a ledge *vb* to channel: to join together by the use of a rabbet

rabbinate *n* the dignity or the (term of) office of a rabbi: rabbis collectively

rabble (*n*) *vb* of a mob, to attack: to use a rabble (an iron bar used for stirring molten metal) *now dial vb* to gabble: to work in a rushed and careless fashion

rabies *n* hydrophobia, canine madness

rable *obs fm vb* **rabble**, to attack *obs fm now dial vb* **rabble**

racemate *n* a salt of racemic acid

racemated *adj* containing racemic acid

racemation *n* the gathering of grapes: that gathered or that remaining to be gathered: a cluster of animate or inanimate objects (GAME PLAYER'S note: The last recorded usages of the word in the above senses are 1685, 1660 and 1654 respectively and most experts consider the word *obs*. The dictionary used for the UK Scrabble championship considers the word extant in all senses.)

raceme *n* an irregular arrangement of flowers in the direction of the apex of a solitary main stalk of a plant: a similar arrangement of spore cases

racemed *adj* having racemes

racemic *adj* derived from grapes

racemise *var fm vb* **racemize**, to remove the optically active property of a compound

rache *arch n* a dog which hunts by scent *now dial n* a white blaze on a horse's face *obs vb* to pull off

Rachel *fem pers n* meaning 'a ewe'

rachen *var fm obs vb* **reche**

rachis *n* the spinal column: the shaft of a feather: a receme (*pl* **rachides, rachises**)

racier *comp adj* racy

rackan *now dial n* a means (such as a chain) by which a cooking pot is suspended over a fire *obs n* a fetter

rackel *obs fm S adj/now S & dial adj* **rackle**

rackle *S adj* vigorous in old age *now S & dial adj* hasty, rash, headstrong: rough in action

rackles *S fm (obs) obs vb* **reckless** (*pa t* **racklest**)

raconteuse *n* a female raconteur

racoon *n* an American, small, nocturnal carnivore akin to bears and having a celebrated bushy tail of black and white bands: the fur of the animal

rad *now S adj* afraid, alarmed *now dial adj* quick, hasty, prompt, eager, elated

radder *comp adj* rad

raddle *n* ruddle or red ochre *now US & dial n* a slender rod or wattle interwoven between the uprights of fencing: a section of fencing or other work similarly constructed *vb* to paint or mark with red ochre: of a woman, to apply red cosmetics far too liberally *dial vb* to beat or thrash

raddleman *n* one who deals in red ochre *obs n* a nickname for England's smallest county, Rutland (now, sadly, a mere adjunct of Leicestershire. RUTLAND PARTISAN'S note: Its apt anagram is **dreamland**.)

rade *var fm S & dial vb* **rede**, to put in order *var fm now dial n* **rathe** *obs fm vb* **raid** *obs fm S & dial vb* **redd**, to clear

rademe *obs S fm vb* **redeem**

radiale *n* a radiating segment of a sea lily: a wrist bone (*pl* **radialia**)

radian *n* a unit of circular measure taken from an angle based at the centre of the circle

Radiata *n pl* the lowest order of animal life in a now obsolete classification system

radicant *adj* rooting from the stem

radicel *n* a little root

radices *pl* radix

radicle *n* the embryonic primary root of a plant

radix *n* any number which is the base of a number system, as 10 is the base of the decimal system: the source or origin (*pl* **radices, radixes**)

radling *var fm dial n* **raddling**, a slender rod or raddle used for fencing: a stick of wood: the crookedness or bowing-in of a wall

radome *n* a protective covering for radar antenna made from a material which does not interfere with transmission signals

rae *var fm obs S n* **ra** *obs fm n* **roe**, the deer

raesin *dial fm n* **reason**

Raetian *var fm n/adj* **Rhaetian**

raf *arch fm n* **raff** (*+cap*) *vulg n* the Royal Air Force, not used by airmen with a pride in their service

rafe *obs fm n/vb* **rave** *var fm obs S vb* **rave**, to take away by force

raff *n* a low worthless person: foreign timber *now dial n* rubbish *now dial vb* to huddle together

raffia *n* a species of palm tree: the soft fibre from its leaves used as a gardening string

rafle *obs fm vb* **raffle**, to indent or serrate: to crumple

raft (*n*) *vb* to use a raft in various ways, such as to travel by

rafte *obs fm n* **raft**

raft rope *n* a rope used for towing blubber

rageles *var fm obs adj* **rageless**

rageless *obs adj* without rage

ragge *obs fm n/vb* **rag** (in most senses)

raggee *var fm n* **ragi**, a type of millet

raggle *S n* a groove in stone *US n* a strip (of fur): a rag *vb* to cut a groove in stone

ragler *obs n* the constable of a commot, or historical Welsh district

raglet *n* a small rag, a scrap

ragman (*n*) *obs n* a sealed document: a roll, a catalogue: a lottery played for fun whereby the player chose one of a number of strings at the end of which was a roll containing a verse descriptive of the player's character *obs S n* a rigmarole

ragmen *(pl) S fm (obs) obs n* **ragman**

ragment *S fm (obs) obs n* **ragman**

ragstone *n* a large roofing slate *now dial n* a piece of hard, rough stone

ragtag *n* the rabble

rag tree *n* a tree upon which rags are hung as a superstitious observance (also, **rag bush** where a bush is used)

ragulé *var fm her adj* **raguly**

raguled *her adj* having a jagged edge

raguly *her adj* in the pattern of a battlement set obliquely

ragweed *n* any of several plants also known as ragwort

raif *obs S fm vb* **rave**

raigner *var fm obs n* **reigner**

raik *n* a journey *obs n* the territory of an animal *esp* the grazing area to which a cow limits herself *obs vb* to stroll or wander

raike *var fm obs vb* **raik**

raile *var fm obs n* **rail**, a woman's neckerchief

railer *n* a reviler: a maker, supplier or fitter of rails

raim *var fm S & dial vb* **rame**

rainer *n* a rain-maker

raines *obs n* a type of fine linen made in Brittany

rainstone *n* any stone used in a rain making ceremony

raintree *n* either of two trees. One is found in South America, the branches of which house a multitude of cicadas, very noisy insects that shower a constant rain of their waste liquid. The other is in North America and its flowers develop a rather unpleasant odour just before rain.

raipe *S & dial fm n/vb* **rope** *obs S fm n/vb* **reap**

rair *S & dial fm n/vb* **roar** *obs S fm adj* **rare**

raird *var fm now S & dial n/vb* **rerde**

rait *var fm vb* **ret**, to soak or rot

raiter *obs fm n* **reiter**

raith *S n* one of four quarters of a year

raiting *obs fm n* **retting**

raken *obs fm vb* **reckon**

raket *var fm obs vb* **racket,** to strike (as) with a racket: to bandy about

rale *n* the sound from a diseased lung *S dial fm adj* **real**

Ramadan *n* the ninth month of the Muslim calendar, the time of the annual fast of 30 days: the fast

ramate *adj* having branches

ramb *obs fm vb* **ram**

ramcat *n* a male cat

rame *n* a branch of a tree *S n* a cry *now dial n* a skeletal framework: a human skeleton: dried stalks *S & dial vb* to cry aloud: to scream: to make a continuous sound (*var fms vb* **raim, ream, rhame**)

Ramean *adj* of Ramism, a system of logic expounded by Peter Ramus (1515–1572)

ramee *var fm n* **ramie**

rumekin *n* a mixture of eggs and cheese baked in a small mould: a dish for such

Rameses *pers n* the name of twelve of the pharaohs of Egypt, most notably Rameses II (1292–1225 BC) who constructed many temples and may be the pharaoh who oppressed the Israelites

ramie *n* a Chinese and East Indian plant of the nettle family also known as **rhea** or **China grass**: its fibre, used for various purposes *incl* cloth and banknote paper: a garment of this cloth

ramillie *modf n* designating a wig, the long tail of which is tied with a bow at the top as well as a bow at the bottom (also *+cap*) *n* a ramille wig (also *+cap*) (GAME PLAYER's note: Of the two *fms*, + or *−cap*, it is the *−cap* which is slightly more common on either side of the Atlantic. The dictionary for the North American Scrabble championship recognizes this fact, so the word is valid for play in the USA and Canada. But, in the dictionary for the UK Scrabble championship, only the *+cap* version is noted, hence it is invalid for the UK championship.)

ramish *obs fm now dial adj* **rammish**, having a highly disagreeable smell or taste

Ramist *n* a follower of an anti-Aristotelian system of logic expounded by Ramus (Pierre de la Ramée, 1515–1572)

rammel *now dial n* rubbish *dial n* a hard infertile soil *obs vb* to crumble

rammy *adj* characteristic of or resembling a tup or ram (*comp* **rammier** *sup* **rammiest**)

ramon *var fm n* **ramoon**

ramoon *n* a cattle fodder of the leaves and top young branches of a species of West Indian and Central American tree

ramose *adj* branched

ramous *adj* of a ramus or branch (of a nerve)

ramsden *dial fm n* **ramson**

Ramses *var fm pers n* **Rameses**

ramson *n* the bulbous root of a species of broad-leafed garlic used as a relish (*dial fms incl* **ramsen, ramsden, ransom**)

ramtil *n* an annual herb, also known as **Niger seed** or **black til**, cultivated in Ethiopia and India for its seeds which produce a sweet tasting oil. The seeds are known as **ramtil seeds** or **niger seeds**. (note: The peculiarity of **Niger seed** and **niger seeds** is simply that these happen to be the most commonly encountered forms. There does not appear to be a rule governing this convenient convention.)

rance *n* a liver-coloured marble with veins and

spots of blue and white: a prop or support *vb* to prop or support

rancel *Ork & Shet vb* to pursue enquiries into crime of a petty nature: to search for stolen property

rancho *n* a hut, or group of huts, for workers on a ranch: a stock farm: a ranch (*pl* **ranchos**)

rand *n* the monetary unit of South Africa: a strip of various items such as fish, iron or of leather used to form part of the heel of a shoe *now dial n* other such strips, such as meat or land *dial n* a strip of cloth *dial vb* to canvass *obs vb* to cut into strips: to rant or rave *obs S vb* to melt tallow

randem *n/adj/adv* three horses harnessed singly, one in front of the other

rander *S vb* to talk idly

randie *var fm S & dial n* **randy**

Randle *dim masc pers n* **Randolf** meaning 'house wolf' (*—cap*) *S & dial modf n* as in **randle perch** or **randle tree**, an iron bar across a chimney from which pots and pans are suspended

random (*adj*) *n* a building stone of irregular size: a haphazard course *obs S n* a straight course

randy *S adj* having a rude, aggressive manner *collq & dial adj* wanton, lustful, sexually eager *dial adj* boisterous, disorderly, unruly *S & dial n* an aggressive beggar: randie, a loud mouthed (aggressive) woman *dial n* a noisy revel *dial vb* to revel *obs vb* to canvass

ranee *var fm n* **rani**

ranet *obs n* a deer net

rangaranga *n* the local name in the Caroline Islands for parsley fern growing in the cracks of walls

rangeless *adj* having no limit

rangership *n* the office of a forest or park ranger

rangier *comp adj* rangy, tall and slender

rangle *obs n* grit fed to hawks as a digestive aid *obs vb* to rove, wander, stray

rani *n* the *fem* of **rajah** (an Indian prince or a Malayan chief)

Ranidae *n pl* the order comprising the true frogs

ranine *adj* of the upper tip of the tongue: frog-like

ranish *var fm now dial adj* **renish**

ranite *n* a variety of zeolite, a hydrous silicate usually found in the cavities of igneous rock

ranke *obs fm n/adj/vb* **rank**

ranker (*n*) *comp adj* rank

Rankine *adj* pertaining to an absolute scale of temperature, the units of which are expressed in degrees Fahrenheit

rankish *obs adj* somewhat rank

rannel *var fm Ir & dial vb* **rantle**

rannle *var fm Ir & dial vb* **rantle**

ranny *now dial n* the shrew: the field mouse

ranse *var fm n/vb* **rance**, (to) prop or support

ransel *var fm Ork & Shet vb* **rancel**

ransom (*n/vb*) *dial fm n* **ramson**

ranter *n* one (*esp* a preacher) who declaims in an extravagant, high-flown manner: a Primitive Methodist *S n* a lively singer *vb* to darn or mend

rantipole *adj* wild, disorderly *n* a wild, ill-behaved person *dial n* the wild carrot *vb* to behave in a rude or noisy fashion

rantise *var fm obs vb* **rantize**, to sprinkle

rantle *Ir and dial vb* to punish (a boy) by pulling his hair or ears *var fm S & dial modf n* **randle**

ranty *S & dial adj* wild, excited, riotous *North Ire n* the rowan tree

rape oil *n* a thick oil obtained from rapeseed and used as an ingredient of such as soap

rapeseed *n* the seed of the plant, rape

raphe *n* a seamlike ridge between two halves of a part or organ (*pl* **raphae, raphes)**

raphia *var fm n* **raffia**

raphides *pl* raphis

raphis *n* a minute needle-like crystal found in the cells of many different plants (*pl* **raphides)** (*var fms* **raphide**, **rhaphide** *respective pls* **raphides, rhaphides)**

rapider *comp adj* rapid

rapiered *adj* having a rapier: sharp-pointed

rapine *n* plunder, pillage *obs vb* to plunder (also see **ANIMAL ADJECTIVES)**

rapines *n pl* acts of robbery or pillage

raping *now dial n* the small particles produced by the act of rasping or scraping (wood)

rapparee *n* an Irish pikeman or irregular soldier of the late 17th century: subsequently, an Irish outlaw or freebooter

rappel *n* a drum roll calling soldiers to arms *obs vb* to recall (a hawk)

Rappite *n* a follower of an American religious sect founded by Johann Georg Rapp (1757–1847)

rapt (*adj*) *n* a trance, extasy *obs vb* to remove by force: to enrapture

rapte *obs fm n* **rapt**

rapter *obs n* one who ravishes

raptor *n* a bird of prey (see **raptores)** *arch n* a ravisher *obs n* a plunderer or robber

raptores *L pl* raptor (+*cap*) *n* formerly used to describe an order of birds of prey *incl* eagles, hawks, vultures, owls etc but now abandoned in favour of more specialized terminology which has the owls in their own order called *Strigiformes* and the other raptors in an order called *Falconiformes*

rare earth element *n* any of the series of metallic elements which have the atomic numbers 57 to 71 inclusive, are closely similar in chemical properties and very difficult to separate. Some are very rare.

rash (*adj/adv/n*) *S vb* to rush hastily *obs vb* to cut: to erase: to drag *dial adj* dry

rashen *S fm adj* **rushen**

rask *obs vb* to yawn

rasper *n* one who or that which scrapes: in hunting, a high, difficult fence likely to scrape the horse

raspes *var fm obs n* **raspis**, the fruit

raspies *var fm obs n* **raspis**, the fruit

raspis *obs n* a 15th/16th century wine made from berries: the raspberry bush (*pl* **raspises** =raspberries)

raspise *var fm obs n* **raspis**, the wine

raspy *adj* rough (*comp* **raspier** *sup* **raspiest)**

rassle *obs fm n/vb* **wrestle**

rastel *obs n* a portcullis

raster *n* a complete set of horizontal lines traced by an electronic beam on a television screen

rastle *now dial fm n/vb* **wrestle**

raston *Obs n* a cheese tart

rasty *dial fm adj* **reasty**

rasure *n* an act of erasure: obliteration

ratable *var fm adj* **rateable**

ratan *var fm n* **rattan**

ratany *var fm n* **rhatany** (*pl* **ratanies**)

ratch *now dial vb* to exaggerate, to lie *var fm arch n/now dial n* **rache**

ratche *obs fm now dial vb* **ratch**

rateably *adv* proportionately

ratel *n* a powerful badger-like mustelid which gets its alternative name of honey badger from an amazing association with the indicator, a species of honeyguide bird. The bird guides the ratel, by a series of call notes, to a bee nest which the mammal rips open and both the bird and animal feed on the combs and larva. An omnivore – its diet includes snakes – it is a fearless fighter and is reported as being a match even for a pack of dogs. It is native to Africa and tropical Asia. *obs n* the spleen

rateling *Obs fm n* **rattling**

rath *n* the home and small (circular) fort of a chief of an ancient British tribe: a hill fort

rathe *poet & dial adj* quick: eager: earnest: early *poet & dial adv* quickly, rapidly, soon *now dial n* a cart rail *obs n* advice, help *obs vb* to counsel, advise

rathed *adj* enclosed within an earthen wall (see **rath**)

rathel *obs fm vb* **raddle**, to interweave

ratherest *adv* most of all, most particularly (*now dial* except in the phrase *rather of the ratherest*, just a touch too much or, conversely, just a touch too little)

ratheripe (note: The word is a combination of the *poet & dial adj* rathe + ripe and can also be written as two words or a hyphenated word. In consequence, the *var fms* are **rathripe, rath ripe, rath-ripe**) *now poet adj* of such as fruits, ripening early *now dial adj* precocious (*fig*) *arch or poet n* an early fruit or vegetable

rathest *arch adj* earliest

ratine *var fm n* **ratteen**

Ratitae *n* the ratites, the following flightless birds:– cassowary, emu, kiwi, ostrich, rhea, together with the extinct species of moa and elephant bird (see **ratites, elephant bird**)

ratite *adj* of the ratites

ratites *n pl* a general term denoting those birds (listed under **Ratitae**) which share the characteristic of a flat, unkeeled, breastbone which prevents the development of flight muscles

ratle *obs fm n* **rattle**

ratlin *n* one of the ropes lashed between a ship's rigging, effectively like a rung on a ladder *obs vb* to furnish such a rope

ratline *var fm n/obs vb* **ratlin**

ratling *n* a small rat *var fm n/obs vb* **ratlin**

ratoon *n* a new shoot arising from the root of a cropped sugar cane *vb esp* of sugar cane, to send up fresh shoots after having been cropped

rat pit *n* a pit in which rats are kept to be worried by dogs

ratsbane *n* any of several poisonous plants: white arsenic or any other rat poison

rattan *n* one of several climbing plants with a very long thin stem: a cane of rattan

ratteen *n* a thick twilled woollen cloth: a piece of such

rattel *obs fm n/vb* **rattle**

ratten *vb* to harass *esp* as a form of trade union policy

rattener *n* one who rattens

rattening *n* the (Sheffield) practice of minor industrial sabotage as a policy of enforcing compliance with the rules of a trade union

rattline *var fm n* **ratlin**

ratton *now S & dial n* a rat

rattoon *var fm n/vb* **ratoon**

Ratuma *n* the former name of Rouen, the French city where Joan of Arc was burned at the stake

raty *dial adj* of weather, cold, wet or stormy

raucle *var fm S adj* **rackle**

raught *obs vb* to snatch at

raun *var fm S & dial n* **rawn**

raunchy *slg adj* slovenly: dirty: lecherous: smutty (*comp* **raunchier** *sup* **raunchiest**)

rauned *var fm S & dial adj* **rawned**

raveled *US fm vb infl* **ravelled**

raveler *US fm n* **raveller**, one who ravels

raveling *US fm vbl infl* **ravelling**

ravenish *Obs adj* blackish

ravet *var fm n* **rabbet**, a groove

ravine (*n*) *vb* to hollow out

ravisht *obs fm adj* **ravished**

rawhead *n* a nursery figure of wickedness usually partnered by an equally frightening character, **bloody-bones** (both usually +*cap*)

rawn *S & dial n* (the roe of) a female fish

rawned *S adj* of a female salmon, full of roe

rawner *S n* a rawned salmon (also see **baggit**, **SALMON**)

rawp *var fm S & dial vb* **roup**

rax *S, Ir & dial vb* to stretch (the legs)

ray (*n*) *vb* to radiate *now dial vb* to array *var fm dial vb* **ree**

rayle *obs fm vb* **rail**, to scoff *obs fm arch vb* **rail**, to flow

rayless *adj* devoid of, not illuminated by, any ray of light

raylet *n* a small ray (of light)

rayne *obs fm vb* **reign**

rayse *obs fm vb* **raise**

re *n* the second note of the tonic sol-fa system of musical notation (see **gamut**) *obs fm n* **roe**, the deer

reactance *n* the opposition to the flow of alternating current by the capacitance or inductance of an electrical circuit. Its unit of measure is the ohm

reactive (*adj*) *n* a chemical reagent

readd *vb* to add again

readies *slg n pl* cash

ready (*adj*) *adv* only the *comp* **readier** and *sup* **readiest** are extant, with senses of more readily or the most readily *n* the position of a firearm when the bearer is ready to aim or fire *S & dial vb* to cook *now dial vb* to prepare *slg vb* to retard the progress of a racehorse in one race to obtain better odds in a subsequent race

reagent *n* a chemical which produces a reaction in another substance (for examples see **invisible ink**)

reagin *n* a type of antibody

realest *sup adj* real

realia *n pl* objects or items used as teaching aids to illustrate the actual real life aspects of that being discussed theoretically

realme *obs fm n* **realm**

realte *var fm obs n* **realty** *obs fm n* **realty**

real tennis see **tennis**

realter *US fm vb* **re-alter**

realtie *obs fm n* **realty** *var fm obs n* **realty**

realtime *adj* of a computer system, having the facility of processing data as it is generated

realtor *US n* the American equivalent of a British estate agent of high professional standing. Specifically, a realty broker affiliated in membership to the National Association of Real Estate Boards.

realty *n* property or estate *obs n* reality: sincerity, honesty: a right: royalty: royal estate *obs S n* a kingdom or realm

ream *n* a quantity of paper which, like a baker's dozen (13), varies to suit the recipient. Strictly it is 20 quires (480 sheets) but a printer's ream is $21\frac{1}{2}$ quires to allow for wastage. *now dial n* cream: a scum on any liquid *obs n* great sorrow vb to widen a hole *S vb* to froth or foam: to skim *now dial vb* to stretch (oneself): to tear open *obs vb* to rush *var fm S & dial vb* **rame**

reame *obs fm n* **realm**

reamy *adj* creamy, frothy: made with cream

rear *(adj/adv/n/vb) now dial adj* slightly or imperfectly cooked

rearmice *pl* rearmouse

rearmouse *n* the flying mammal, a bat (*var fm* **reremouse** *dial fm* **reermouse** *pl* **rearmice, reremice, reermice**)

rearward (*adj/adv*) *arch n* the reserve troops or ships stationed behind the main fighting force

reascent *n* the act of reascending

rease *obs fm vb* **raise**

re-aspire *vb* to aspire again

reassign *vb* to assign anew

reast *var fm now dial vb* **reest** *obs fm vb* **rest**

reasty *now dial adj* rancid

reata *n* a lasso

reate *n* a species of water crowfoot

reattend *vb* to attend again: to return attention to

reave *arch vb* to plunder or pillage (*pa pple* **reaved** or **reft**) *now dial vb* to tear, to cleave (*pa pple* **reft**)

reaver *n* a marauder, plunderer, robber

rebail *obs vb* to hand over again

rebait *vb* to bait (a fishhook) again

rebald *obs fm adj/n* **rebel**

rebat *obs S n* a collar *obs fm vb* **rebate**

rebato *n* a stiff, wide, lace-edged collar fashionable with either sex at the turn of the 16th century (*pl* **rebatos, rebatoes**)

rebeat *obs vb* to repel an attack

rebeck *n* a mediaeval, fiddle-like, three-stringed instrument played with a bow

rebell *obs fm n/adj/vb* **rebel**

reboant *adj* re-echoing loudly

reboation *n* a rebellowing echo (GAME PLAYER'S note: Given as an extant but undefined noun in the dictionary used for the UK Scrabble championship, the sense detailed above is that recorded by Dr Johnson. Other experts consider it *obs.*)

rebolt *vb* to bolt (a door) again: to perform the second of two actions in the process of splitting timber into lathes whereby the first begins the action by creating the splits and the second uses wedges to complete the task

reboot *obs S fm vb* **rebut**

rebute *S & dial n* refusal, denial, rejection

recal *arch fm n/vb* **recall**

recane *vb* to replace damaged or missing cane in furniture

recap *vb* to provide (a cartridge) with a new cap *collq vb* to recapitulate

recaption *n* the re-arrest of one who has escaped: the retaking, by peaceful means, of one's property or family from one having wrongful possession: a writ for this purpose

recart *vb* to cart off or back again

recash *vb* to make repayments

recaster *n* one who refashions, remodels or otherwise recasts

recense *vb* to review or revise

recension *n* a survey or review: a revision of a text

recent (*adj*) *obs fm vb* **resent**

recept *n* a compound idea *obs n* a receipt *obs vb* to harbour

Rechab *pers n* a reformed prostitute mentioned in the Bible as the mother of Jonadab the tent-dweller who abstained from wine (see **Rechabite** below)

Rechabite *n* a descendent of Jonadab (see **Rechab** above): a tent-dweller: a total abstainer: a member of an order so named

rechase *now dial vb* to drive back farm animals from one pasture to another *obs vb* to chase a deer back into a forest

rechate *var fm arch n*/*obs vb* **recheat**

reche *obs vb* to tear or rend

recheat *arch n* the blowing of the horn at the beginning or at the end of a stag hunt *obs vb* to blow either call

rechid *Obs fm vbl infl* **reached**

rechild *vb* to become (as) a child again

recision *n* the act of pruning

reck *vb* to (take) care (of) *now poet n* care

reckan *var fm now dial n* **rackan**

reckle *obs S n* a chain

reckless *(adj) obs vb* to neglect (*pa t* **recklest** or (*var fm*) **racklest**)

reclad *infl vb* reclothe, to clothe again: to provide clothing again

reclear *vb* to make or become clear again

reclinate *adj* of such as stems or leaves, bending downwards

reclinated *adj* reclinate

reclude *obs vb* to open such as a gate: to shut up/out/off from

recluse *(adj/n) obs vb* to seclude

reclusion *n* the state of being a (religious) recluse: imprisonment *esp* solitary confinement

recoast *vb* to (sail by the) coast again

recoin *vb* to pass coins again through the minting process

recomb *vb* to comb (in a *fig* sense) again

recond *obs vb* to set apart

recondite (*adj*) *obs vb* to conceal

recool *S var fm obs vb* **recule**, to recoil

recrate *vb* to repack items in a crate

recray *obs vb* to surrender in a cowardly fashion

recreant *now poet adj* cowardly, craven, faint-hearted: false *now poet n* a coward, a deserter

recrew *obs n* a body of military reinforcements *obs vb* to reinforce

recruital *n* recuperation

rect *obs aphetic fm vb* **erect**

rectal *adj* of or belonging to the rectum

rection *n* the government of one word by another: the relation which one word in a sentence has to another depending on it

rectitude *n* virtue, righteousness: correctness of such as nature or procedure

rectoress *collq n* the wife of a rector *obs n* a female ruler

rectus *n* a straight muscle (*pl* **recti**)

recull *obs fm vb* **recoil**

recumb *obs vb* to recline

recure *obs n* recovery of health *obs vb* to restore to health: to redress a wrong

recurse *obs vb* to recur

recusance *n* refusal to obey lawful authority *esp* failure to attend the services of the Church of England during the period 1570–1791. Aimed primarily at Catholics (the last English Catholic to be fined for non-attendance paid the penalty in 1782), it also included others, such as Quakers. In 1667, for example, the fine was £1 for a month's absence, with conviction as a Papist resulting in the loss of two-thirds of one's estate. By contrast, a Quaker whose house had been used for worship in 1671 was fined £20 and those attending 5 shillings each.

recusant *adj* refusing to submit to authority *n* any person who so refuses *esp* a Catholic (in 16th to 18th century England) who did not attend the services of the Church of England

recusation *n* an objection to a particular judge on the basis of his/her having a known or likely bias for or against a party to an action

recuse *vb* to reject or renounce: to object to (a judge) on grounds of prejudice

redact *vb* to prepare material for publication

redan *n* a defensive fortification in the shape of the letter V

red ant *n* a common British species of ant: also any of various other reddish-coloured ants such as the hill or horse ant and the American house ant

redargue *now S vb* to disprove by argument: to disprove such as an argument or statement (since 1700 only used in Scottish law in this sense)

redarn *vb* to darn (clothes) again

redart *vb* to dart (a thing) back in return

red ash *n* either of two Australian trees *incl* the silky oak: a North American ash tree *US n* coal which produces a red-coloured ash

redawn *vb* to dawn again

redback *n* an Australian small venomous spider, the female of which is marked with a red stripe

redbait *US vb* to denounce as a communist

red bass *n* the red drumfish

red bat *n* a common American bat

red bay *n* an American tree of the laurel family

redbeak *n* a South African species of mousebird

red beech *n* either of two species of tree, one American, the other Australian

redbill *n* any of three different Australian birds *incl* the swamp hen

redbone *US n* a white person with a distant ancestor who was either Red Indian or negro (GAME PLAYER'S note: The dictionary used for the North American Scrabble championship carries an apparently exclusive definition as a hunting dog)

redbreast *n* the original and still correct appellation for the bird more commonly known as the robin (note: The reverse is a popular misconception. For example, the children's TV quiz programme *Connections* added to its not infrequent errors the question,

'*What is the nickname of the robin*?' But, Robin is the traditional *personal* name of the redbreast. Many birds had and still have such personal names of which Jenny the wren is the best known. There is also Jenny the owl, Jack the daw (now called jackdaw), Maggie the pie (now magpie), Dame Partlet the hen, Philomel the nightingale and Progne the swallow among others. Curiously, Mavis the song thrush is not the same. The word mavis (a song thrush) developed independently as a description for the bird and the feminine personal name arose from that. Now it is often treated as being the bird's personal name. (Also see **pie** for the various combinations with Ann.) The Breton legend of how the robin obtained its colouring is especially charming. Originally a dull-coloured bird, though just as brave as it is now, it once attempted to pull a thorn from the crown of the crucified Christ. It was spashed with His blood and, ever since, its descendants have carried that mark. What makes this legend believable is the fact that the cock robin does not assume this colour as a mere mating display but uses it as a sign of warning. Should an intruder invade its territory, the bird immediately faces it and erects the red feathers on its breast and throat – the intruder usually flees.

redbud *n* the Judas tree, any of a genus of early-flowering trees which have great numbers of reddish-purple flowers (note: The alternative name is from a tradition that this was the tree on which Judas hanged himself)

red bug *US n* any of several harvest ticks: the cotton stainer

redcap *n* the goldfinch: a malignant goblin found in a number of Scottish castles who can only be overcome by the sight of a cross *slg n* a military policeman

red char *n* the case char, a species of salmon-like fish, in its spawning colour

redcoated *adj* wearing a red coat: coated with red

red cock *n* the grouse, a British game bird: a euphemism for arson

red cod *n* any of various species of cod having a reddish tinge

redcowl *var fm n* **redcap**

red cusk *n* a Californian codlike fish

redd *n* a trough which the salmon excavate in order to house their eggs and which they subsequently cover over

reddle *n/vb* (to paint or mark with) red ochre

reddy *adj* reddish (*obs comp fms incl* **redier**)

rede *arch n/vb* (to give) advice or counsel *now dial vb* to put in order *dial vb* to remove fat from the entrails of slaughtered animals

redeck *vb* to adorn again: to supply with a new deck

redecraft *arch n* logic

redefine *vb* to define again: to define anew

red elm *n* the American slippery elm tree

red els *n* a species of South African tree rather like the red birch

redented *obs adj* formed like the teeth of a saw (compare with **sierra**)

red eten *S n* a monster: a morose, grumpy person

redface *n* a species of lovebirds, the mature male having a red face, the female an orange face, whilst the immature birds have yellow faces

redfin *n* any of various species of fish *incl* the shiner surfpercher (see **surfpercher**)

red fire *n* a pyrotechnic effect achieved by a mixture of nitrate of strontia, calomel, chlorate of potash and sulphate of copper: that mixture in its correct proportions

redfish *n* any of three different fishes, the Norway haddock, the redhorse, the salmon at a particular stage in its life cycle (see **SALMON**)

red fog *n* a sea haze containing sand or similar dust

red gum *n* a skin rash to which children are susceptible: a type of rust on grain: a type of resin exuded from the bark of various (semi-) tropical trees: any of various Australian species of eucalyptus tree which yield such a resin: the timber of such a tree

red hat *n* a cardinal

redhorse *n* any of various large N. American freshwater fishes related to the carps, the males of which have red fins in the breeding season

redhot *n* a metal which is red-hot

redia *n* the larval stage of the trematode flatworm (*pl* **rediae, redias**)

rediae *pl* redia

redial *vb* to dial a telephone number again

redie *obs fm adj/adv* **ready**

redimar *obs S fm n* **redeemer**

redive *vb* to dive again

red lane *collq n* the throat

redleg *n* a term of contempt for a poor white resident of a Caribbean island

red man *n* a term loosely applied to the North American Indians: an old alchemic substance: the red soldierfish or squirrelfish, a marine fish whose courting noises are so loud they can be heard by a person in a nearby boat

red metal *n* any alloy of copper

redoom *vb* to doom again

redoubt *n* the final defensive fortification to which retreat can be made: any isolated fortified stronghold: in Germany, a public hall used for gambling and entertainment: a masked ball or other entertainment held in such a hall *vb* to dread or fear

redout *n* a condition which has blood driven to the head *arch fm n* **redoubt** *obs fm vb* **redoubt** *her adj* of a cross, having the appearance of a fortification (redoubt)

redowa *n* a Czech dance: music for it

red owl *n* a small American owl

redpoll *n* any of various birds with red markings on the head such as the male of the linnet in its mating plumage: one of a breed of red-coloured, hornless cattle

red rot *n* the sundew, an insectivorous bog plant

red rust *n* a fungus which attacks grain

red scale *n* a species of scale insects which infest orange trees

redsear *adj* of metal, malleable when cold but brittle when heated *obs vb* of cooling metal, to break under the blow of a hammer

redshare *var fm adj* **redshort**

redshort *adj* brittle when red hot

red silver *n* silver ore which has a reddish streak in it

red sole *n* the little sole, a species of flatfish

red stone *n* ruddle

red tapism *n* the system of adhering strictly to official routine without deviation from a purely mechanical approach

redtop *US n* any of certain grasses valued for hay and pasturage *esp* herd's grass: a variety of turnip

reductant *n* a reducing agent

reduit *n* an inner stronghold of a fortification

reduite *obs fm n* **reduit**

redundant (*adj*) *obs n* a redundant chord: something redundant (*lit/fig*)

redust *vb* to dust again

red withe *n* a tropical American vine

ree *n* the female of the **ruff**, a species of sandpiper *S n* a walled enclosure for farm animals: a coal merchant's yard *obs n* a watercourse *dial vb* to sift grain

reech *var fm n/vb* **reek**, (to) smoke

reechy *now dial adj* smoky, grimy, squalid

reed (*n*) *vb* to supply with reeds: to thatch with reeds

reede *obs fm vb* **read** *obs fm arch n/vb* **rede** *obs fm adj* **red**

reeden *adj* reed-like: made of reed

reeder *n* a thatcher: a frame of thatch used as a movable rain-cover

reediemadeasy *S n* reading-made-easy, a child's first reading book!

reed rand *dial n* a Norfolk term for a thicket of reeds on a river or on marshy ground

reeding *n* the milled edge of a coin

reedit *US fm vb* **re-edit**

reedstop *n* a set of reed pipes controlled by a single organ stop

reef (*n*) *vb* to reduce the amount of a ship's sail exposed to the wind

reeke *obs fm vb* **reek**

reem *n* a Biblical animal identified as the wild ox *var fm obs vb* **reme**, to lament

reemit *US fm vb* **re-emit**

re-emit *vb* to reissue such as banknotes

reenact *US fm vb* **re-enact**

re-endow *vb* to endow again (note: The less common unhyphenated *fm* is mainly found in the USA)

reenge *dial fm vb* **rinse**

reenter *US fm vb* **re-enter** *obs n* re-entry

reep *obs fm n/vb* **reap**

reermice see **rearmouse**

reese *now dial vb* to become rancid *obs vb* to burn

reest *now dial vb* to become rancid *S & dial vb* of herrings, bacon etc, to cure or dry by smoke: of horses, to stop suddenly and refuse to continue

reesty *var fm adj* **reasty**

reet *dial fm adj/adv/n/vb/interj* **right** *dial fm n/vb* **root** *dial fm n/vb* **wright** (the sense in which **reeting** is a *n*)

reeve *n* an old English official of high rank (shire reeve = sheriff): an overseer in a coal mine: the president of a Canadian town council: the female of the **ruff** *now dial n* a string of onions *vb* to pass (a rope) through a hole *now dial vb* to sift corn (the sense in which **reeving** is a *n*) *dial vb* to wind or unwind

reever *n* a vessel which collects the crushed apples from a cider mill

reexpect *obs vb* to re-expect or expect again (note: In common with today's American *fms*, this rare *vb* had no hyphen for a *vb* beginning with an E, prefixed 're-')

refaction *obs n* recompense

re-father *nonce vb* to make one again a father

refeel *vb* to feel again

refel *obs vb* to refute or disprove an opinion or argument: to cast doubt upon: to reject or refuse

refell *var fm obs vb* **refel**

referent *adj* referring *n* a word which refers to another: one who is consulted

referse *obs vb* to cram

refert *obs adj* stuffed, filled

referted *var fm obs adj* **refert**

refet *var fm obs n/vb* **refete**

refete *obs n* food *obs vb* to feed

refil *arch fm vb* **refill**

refile *vb* to file again

refind *vb* to find again

refinger *vb* to finger again

refire *vb* to fire again

reflate *vb* to inflate again: to be inflated again

reflirt *obs vb* to toss back again

reflit *dial vb* to change residence (yet) again

refreid *Obs vb* to cool or chill: to become cold (*pa pple* **refreid**) (**refreiding** *obs n* cooling)

refringe *obs vb* to refract light (*lit/fig*): to infringe a liberty

refry *vb* to fry again

refutal *n* the action of refuting or disproving (a charge)

regal (*adj*) *n* a small portable organ having sufficiently few keys that, whilst one hand played the music, the other hand operated the bellows *now dial n* a groove

regale *n* the historic right of French kings to the revenue from vacant bishoprics and abbacies: other rights and privileges of royalty (*pl* **regalia**): a choice feast or banquet: a delicacy (*pl* **regales**) *vb* to delight: to give unusual pleasure to: to feast: to entertain royally or sumptuously

regalia *n pl* royal rights and privileges (*sing* **regale**): the insignia of royalty such as the crown, orb and sceptre: Masonic insignia *n sing* a large choice cigar (*pl* **regalias**)

regalian *adj* pertaining to a sovereign: regal

regalism *n* royal supremacy in ecclesiastical matters

regalist *n* one who supports the concept of the sovereign being supreme in ecclesiastical matters

regaurd *obs fm n* **regard**

regeal *obs vb* to melt

regelate *vb* to freeze together again

regelation *n* the fusion of two pieces of ice

regender *obs vb* to beget again: to create afresh

regest *obs n* a register *obs vb* to register

regester *obs n* a registrar

reggae *n* a West Indian type of rock music

régie *Fr n* the system of French government monopoly in a commodity such as tobacco: the particular department concerned: the commodity sold

regimen *n* a prevailing system: a government: a particular course of diet or exercise

regiminal *adj* of, pertaining to or of the nature of a medical regimen

regina *n* a (reigning) queen

reginal *adj* of a queen, queen-like: taking the side of a queen

regius *adj* royal, used for certain professorships in England which were founded by a monarch or, in Scotland, where the appointment is by the Crown

reglet *n* a flat, narrow, architectural moulding: a thin, narrow strip used in printing to create a space between lines

regmata *pl* regma, a dry fruit having three or more cells which open when ripe

regnal *adj* of a sovereign or his or her reign: designating a year of reign calculated from the date of accession

regnee *Obs n* a realm

regrate *vb* to produce a clean face for old stone by chiselling away the weathered surface: the historical practice of buying at one market to sell the same products at another *obs vb* to reward: to grate upon (the eye) *obs S vb* to lament *obs n* oppression: a request *obs S n* sorrow, regret

regreen *obs vb* to make green again

regrete *obs fm n/vb* **regret**

reguard *obs vb* to guard doubly

regula *n* a decorative architectural band or fillet (*pl* **regulae**)

regulae *pl* regula

rehale *obs vb* to drag back

rehear *vb* to hear (judicially) again

reheate *var fm obs vb* **rehete**, in the unpleasant senses of attacking or rebuking

reheite *var fm obs vb* **rehete**, in the unpleasant senses of attacking or rebuking

rehete *obs vb* to cheer or comfort: to entertain: to attack: to rebuke

rehinge *vb* to hinge again

Reichsrat *n* the upper house of the parliament of the former Austrian Empire: a deliberative council of the 1919–1933 Weimar Republic (Germany)

reifar *obs S fm n* **reaver**

reigne *obs fm n/vb* **reign**

reigner *obs n* one who reigns

reik *S fm vb* **reach**

reill *obs fm n* **reel**, a spool: a dance *obs S fm n* **reel**, a whirl

rein arm *var fm n* **rein hand**

reindent *obs vb* to supply false teeth

re-indow *obs fm vb* **re-endow**

reine *obs fm n* **rein** *Obs fm n* **reign** *Obs fm vb* **rain**

reinette *var fm n* **rennet**, a variety of apple

reinfund *obs vb* to pour or flow in again (GAME PLAYER'S note: Swift is the only known writer to have used this verb. He did so in 1704, hyphenating it as **re-infund**. The unhyphenated form would appear to be an editorial amendment favoured by the *Oxford English Dictionary*. *Chambers 20th Century Dictionary*, by contrast, credits Swift with the unhyphenated version and thus validates the word for play in the UK Scrabble championship as the addition of the label '(Swift)' overrides, under the local rules of that contest, the fact of its being obsolete.)

reinge *dial fm vb* **rinse**

rein hand *n* in the act of driving horses, the hand holding the rein as opposed to the hand holding the whip (note: Unlike **whip hand**, rein hand has no additional *fig* sense)

reinse *obs fm vb* **rinse**

reinser *obs fm n* **rinser**

reinter *vb* to inter again

reiot *ob fm n* **ryot**, an Indian peasant

reird *var fm now S & dial n/vb* **rerde**

reise *obs n* a journey, raid or foray *obs vb* to travel, to raid

reist *var fm now dial vb/S & dial vb* **reest**

reisty *var fm now dial adj* **reasty**

reite *obs n* seaweed

reiter *n* a German cavalryman of the 16th and 17th centuries *obs vb* to reiterate

reive *S fm arch vb* **reave** *var fm now dial vb* **reave**

reiver *var fm n* **reaver**

rejerk *obs vb* to jerk back

rekeles *Obs fm obs n* **rekels**

rekels *obs n* incense

rekles *obs fm adj* **reckless**

relace (*vb*) *obs fm n* **release**

relade *vb* to lade again

relaid *pa t vb* relay, to lay again – contrasted with **relayed** (*pa t vb* relay, to transmit by relay)

reland *vb* to land (cargo/passengers) again

relank *obs vb* to become lank again

relasch *obs adj* careless

relat *obs fm n* **relate**, either of two related objects of thought considered in logic *var fm obs n* **relate**, a relation or kin

relate (*vb*) *obs n* a relative

relation (*n*) *vb* to form relations

relativise *var fm vb* **relativize**

relativize *vb* to make or become relative

relator *n* a narrator: an informer

relay (*n*) *vb* in the sense of to lay again the *pa pple* is **relaid**: in the sense of using a relay the *pa pple* is **relayed**

re-lay *n* an oyster which has been transferred from one bed to another

relaying *n* the action of the *vb* in the sense of to lay again

rele *obs fm n* **reel**, a spool *obs fm vb* **reel**, to whirl

relead *vb* to treat again with the metal lead

relection *n* a dissertation on a subject, specifically applied to any of various divisions of a theological work by Franciscus de Victoria

releef *var fm obs n* **relief**, the remainder *obs fm n* **relief** (*pl* **releves, relevis** or **relevys**)

releke *Obs fm n* **relic**

releves *obs pl* relief

relevis *obs pl* relief

relevy *obs vb* to set up again

relide see **rely** *obs vb*

relievo *n* an artwork in relief (*pl* **relievi, relievos**)

religate *vb* to bind together: to compel *esp* by circumstances: to restrain as by force

relimb *vb* to supply with a new limb

reliver *obs vb* to restore

relong *obs vb* to postpone: to extend

relove *obs vb* to return love

reluct *vb* to struggle or strive

relume *vb* to relight or rekindle (*lit/fig*)

relumine *vb* to relight or rekindle: to make bright again

rely (*vb*) *obs vb* to gather (people) together, to assemble: to rally: to be devoted to: to adhere to (a cause) (*infl fms* the same as for the extant senses, though Spenser had **relide** for the *pa pple* **relied**)

rem *Shet n* an oar

remaid *obs fm now arch S n/vb* **remeid** (see **remede**)

remail *US vb* to repost mail

reman *vb* to make manly again: to man (a weapon) again: to resupply with men

remane *obs fm vb* **remain** *obs S fm n* **remain**

remanié *n* a relic of an older rock discovered in a later deposit

remargin *vb* to provide a fresh margin to the leaf of a book

remass *vb* to mass together again

remast *vb* to fit a ship with a new mast

remblai *n* any material used to fill a cavity resulting from the excavation of coal: earth as used for the construction of a simple military fortification

reme *Obs n* an oar *obs vb* to lament, to weep: to depart from

remead *now S fm n/vb* **remedy**

remede *now arch S n/vb* **remeid**, (to) remedy: (to) redress

remediat see **remediate**

remediate *vb* to mediate again *Shaks adj* remedial (this being the spelling *fm* of the first folio, the quarto spelling being **remediat**)

remeet *vb* to meet again

remeid *var fm now arch S n/vb* **remede**

remend *vb* to mend again

rement *obs fm n* **raiment**

remercie *var fm obs n* **remercy**

remercy *obs vb* to thank *obs n* thanks

remetal *vb* to coat again with metal (*infl fms* British, **remetalled/-lling**: US, **remetaled/-ling**)

remex *n* one of the large primary or secondary feathers of a bird's wing (*pl* **remiges**)

remiform *adj* oar-shaped (TRIVIA note: One 19th century lexicographer, knowing that **remus** is Latin for oar, gave what he believed to be the correct meaning for a word in a rival dictionary. Unfortunately he had misread the word – it was **reniform**, kidney-shaped!)

remigate *vb* to row (a boat)

remigation *n* the action of rowing

remiges *pl* remex

remindal *n* the act of reminding

remise *n* a coach house: a carriage, of a better quality than a hackney, which was once available for hire: a second fencing thrust during the same lunge in which the first failed to strike: an individual stake in the kitty of a card game *obs n* a property transfer *vb* to surrender or release (a right or property): to make a remise in fencing

remiss (*adj*) *vb* to make over such as property to another

Remist *obs fm n* **Rhemist**

remlin *dial fm n/adj* **remnant**

remling *dial fm n/adj* **remnant**

remold *now US fm vb* **remould** *US n* (the British *fm* being **remould**) a tyre which has had a fresh tread added

remoot *vb* to raise a matter for discussion again

remora *n* the shark sucker, a remarkable fish possessing a large oval suction disc on the top of its head which it uses to attach itself to such as the belly of a shark and from which host it can detach itself at will. It even uses the hull of a ship in a similar fashion, a fact known to the ancients which they gave as the explanation for the phenomenon of a sailing ship suddenly and inexplicably stopping dead. (For the actual reason see **dödvand**.) This belief continued to the Middle Ages and the remora's 'magical properties of arrest' caused the fish to be caught for use as the basis of certain potions. These potions were used to delay a legal action, arrest age in greying matrons and slow down the course of love. Today, in different parts of the world, a more sensible use is made of the remora. Once one has been caught, a line is tied to its tail and it is released back into the sea. After a while, both it and the fish or turtle to which it has attached itself are hauled back to the fisherman's boat. (For other examples of free transportation see **phoresy**.)

remote (*n/adj*) *obs vb* to remove

remotion *n* remoteness: removal

remue *obs vb* to remove

remuing *obs n* removal

renage *dial fm vb* **renegue**

renaige *dial fm vb* **renegue**

renail *vb* to nail again

renal *adj* of or pertaining to the kidneys *n* a renal artery

Renald *obs pers n* for the fox, an alternative to **Reynard**

renascent *adj* born-again *n* one who contributes to a renaissance

renat *obs fm n* **rennet**, the apple

renate *obs vb* to be born again: to form again

renay *obs n* a renegade *obs vb* to renounce one's spiritual or temporal allegiance (*infl* **renayed** or **renied**)

rend *vb* to tear forcibly apart: to tear one's clothing (as a sign of grief or rage): of a noise or cry, to disturb the silence (*infl* **rent** or **rended**)

rendles *now dial n* rennet

rendre *obs fm n/vb* **render**

rendy *obs n* surrender (*pl* **rendies**)

renegate *now dial adj/n* (of) a renegade or (of) a deserter

renegation *n* the action of renouncing

renege *var fm n/vb* **renegue**

reneger *var fm n* **reneguer**, one who renegues

renegue *vb* to fail to keep a promise or commitment: to revoke at card playing *arch vb* to denounce, deny, abandon *dial vb* to jilt (*var fms* for all *vbs*, all senses, **renege** or **renig** *infl fms incl* **renegued, reneguing; reneged, reneging; renigged, renigging**)

renels *obs fm now dial n* **rendles**

renet *obs fm n* **rennet**, that which curdles milk

reney *var fm obs vb* **renay**

renforce *obs vb* to reinforce

renga *n* a form of Japanese verse with different poets penning succeeding verses

renied *var fm obs pa pple* **renayed**

reniform *adj* kidney-shaped

renig *var fm vb* **renegue**

renigat *obs S fm now dial n* **renegate**, a deserter

renin *n* a protein substance secreted by a kidney or blood vessel suffering from a localized deficiency of blood

renish *now dial adj* strange, uncouth

renisht *obs fm now dial adj* **renish**

renite *obs vb* to resist

renitent *adj* offering resistance to any influence or force

rennase *n* the enzyme chymosin or rennin, present in rennet

rennet *n* an agent for curdling milk in the cheese-making process either obtained from the stomach of a slaughtered animal or made from lady's bedstraw or any of various other plants which achieve this effect: a variety of dessert apple of French origin *obs vb* to curdle milk with rennet (*infl fms* either **renneted** or **rennetted** etc)

rennit *obs fm n* **rennet**

rense *obs fm vb* **rinse**

rental (*n*) *S vb* to rent (out) land

rente *n* annual income

renter (*n*) *obs vb* to sew cloth in a manner which disguises the seam

rentier *n* one having an income from investments

renvoi *n* the expulsion by a government of an alien (*pl* **renvois**)

reny *var fm obs vb* **renay**

reoil *vb* to oil again

rep *n* the *masc* equivalent of a **demirep**: a worthless item: a textile fabric with a corded surface

repace *vb* to pace again: to pace back

repale *vb* to provide with a new paling

repand *adj* of a leaf, having an undulating or wavy edge

repanded *obs fm adj* **repand**

repare *obs fm n/vb* **repair** *obs fm n* **reaper**

repart *obs vb* to distribute: to say in reply

repassion *obs n* a counter effect

repast *n* food and drink: a meal: mealtime *vb* to feast

repaste *vb* to paste (a surface) again *Obs fm n* **repast**

repaster *obs n* one who dined (at the Inns of Court)

repater *obs S vb* to feed

repe *obs fm vb* **reap**

repeak *obs fm vb* **repique**, to score a repique or 30 points against an opponent in the game of piquet

repease *obs vb* to appease

repele *obs n* an additional wager in an ancient gambling game using five small objects which are tossed and caught in various ways. It is now only played by children and known by such names as dibs, five stones, hucklebones, knucklebones, jacks, snobs etc but was originally a Roman method of divination. *obs fm n/vb* **repeal**

repend *obs vb* to repay

repet *obs fm S n* **rippet**

repete *obs fm vb* **repeat**

repetend *n* a digit of an indeterminable decimal fraction or a musical note or a word or phrase which recurs

repine *vb* to fret, murmur, complain, grumble

repinement *n* discontent

repiner *n* one who grumbles

repique *n* in the card game of piquet, a score of 30 points obtained before play which entitles the player to begin his or her score at 90 points *vb* to score a repique

repise *var fm obs n* **raspis**, the wine

repises *var fm obs n* **raspis**, the wine

repit *obs fm S n* **rippet**

replait *obs S vb* to adjourn (also see **resplait**): to remand

reple *obs fm n* **ripple**, a comb-like implement used for the removal of seeds from flax (also see **riple**)

replete (*adj*) *vb* to replenish

replow *obs fm vb* **replough**, to plough again

replum *n* the central part of the fruit of such as an orchid (*pl* **repla**)

replumb *obs vb* to unsolder

replume *vb* to arrange anew

repoin *obs vb* to regret or repent

repone *S vb* to restore to a particular legal status: to restore (a church minister) to his office

reportage *n* news, gossip

reposal *n* the act of reposing such as trust or confidence

reposit *vb* to store

repositor *n* a surgical replacing instrument

repost *var fm n/vb* **riposte**

repot *vb* to plant seedlings or young plants in a fresh pot

repoussé *adj* of metal work, raised in relief by being beaten from behind or within *n* such work: the action of performing such

repped *adj* having a corded surface

repraise *Obs vb* meaning obscure but possibly to regard with disfavour

repray *vb* to pray again

reprieval *n* a reprieve

reprise (*n*) *arch vb* to resume: to compensate

repriser *obs n* one receiving a reprise

repro *n/adj* a short *fm* of **reproduction (furniture)** (*pl* **repros**)

reptant *adj* creeping, crawling

repugn *vb* to resist: to object

repung *obs fm vb* **repugn**

repure *vb* to repurify

reputative *adj* regarded as such

requital *n* recompense, reward

rerail *vb* to replace (a railway engine) on the rails

re-rate *vb* to recalculate a (local) rate

rerde *now S & dial n/vb* (to make) any kind of noise or din (*var fms incl* **raird, reird**)

rerdose *Obs fm n* **reredos**

reredos *n* an ornamental screen at the rear of an altar

reremice *see* **rearmouse**

rereward *var fm arch n* **rearward**

resada *n* a pale green colour

resalt *vb* to salt again

resarce *obs vb* to mend

resaw (*vb*) *infl fms incl* **resawn, resawed**

resawing *n* the action of sawing again

resay *vb* to say again: to say in reply

resbon *obs n* a cheesecake

rescale *vb* to plan or form on a different scale

rescant *var fm arch n* **resiant**

rescat *obs n* ransome

resceit *obs fm n/vb* **receipt**

rescent *obs fm vb* **resent**

resciant *obs fm arch n* **resiant**

rescient *obs fm arch n* **resiant**

rescribe *vb* to rewrite

reseam *vb* to seam (a garment) again

reseau *n* a mesh background for such as lacework: a network of fine lines etched on a glass plate used in astronomical photography to provide a reference grid (*pl* **reseaus, reseaux**)

resect *vb* in surgery, to cut or pare off

resection *n* the surgical operation of the cutting away of bone

resee *vb* to see again

reserval *n* reservation

reset (*vb*) *S vb* to receive stolen goods, to harbour one wanted by the police

resh *n* the twentieth letter of the Hebrew alphabet

reshore *obs vb* to return to the shore of

resiance *arch n* an abode, residence

resiant *arch n* a resident

residenter *US & S n* an inhabitant

resigne *Obs fm n* **raisin**

resile *vb* to retract: to recoil: to draw back (from)

resin (*n*) *vb* to treat with resin

Resinat® *n* any of various preparations of polyaminemethylene resin

resinata *n* Greek white wine with a resinous flavour

resinate *vb* to infuse or impregnate with resin

resine *obs fm n* **resin** *obs fm vb* **resign**

resiner *n* a resin gatherer

resing *vb* to sing again *obs n* an attack

resinise *var fm vb* **resinize**, to treat with resin

resinoid *adj* resembling resin *n* a substance having a (partial) resinous nature: any of various synthetic resins having the property of assuming a fixed shape after being moulded under heat

resister *n* one who or that which resists

resite *vb* to site elsewhere

resitting *n* a second sitting

reslant *vb* to change the bias or emphasis

reslay *vb* to slay again

reslide *vb* to slide back (*pa t* **reslid**)

resoil *vb* to make dirty again

resonate *vb* to produce resonance

resorb *vb* to absorb again

resorp *obs fm (poss erron) vb* **resorb**

respas *var fm obs n* **raspis**, the fruit

respice *var fm obs n* **raspis**, the wine

respire *vb* to breathe (again (*fig*))

respirer *n* one who respires

respis *var fm obs n* **raspis**, the fruit

respit *obs fm n/vb* **respite**

respitless *adj* without relief

resplait *obs S vb* to adjourn: to defer consideration or payment *obs S n* adjournment

resplate *var fm obs S vbs* **replait, resplait**

resplete *var fm obs S vb* **resplait**

respliet *var fm obs S n* **resplait**

responde *modf n* of Scottish law, designating a book, the **responde book**, in which are recorded certain duties paid by heirs *obs n* an entry in the responde book: the duties specified at that entry (GAME PLAYER'S note: If you agree to use obsolete words then responde is valid. On the other hand, if you stick strictly to extant words then responde now exists solely as part of responde book. In this event you cannot use it, as responde now has no independent existence as a word in its own right.)

Responsa *n pl* a collection of written decisions by leading rabbis on various matters within their jurisdiction (*sing* **responsum**, one such written decision)

resport *Obs n* regard

respot *vb* to return to play a previously potted snooker ball

resque *obs fm n* **risk**

restable *obs vb* to re-establish

restage *vb* to stage again

restain *vb* to stain afresh

restall *obs n* a burial plot

restand *vb* to stand again (for office)

restant *adj* persistent

restare *obs var fm vb* **restore**

restay *obs vb* to restrain

reste *obs fm n/vb* **rest**

restem *vb* to stem again

restial *obs dial n* a fee for burial within the church *incl* the charge for tolling the bell

restiall *var fm obs n* **restall**

restiform *adj* cordlike

restle *var fm S n* **ristle**

restles *dial n pl* the stakes to which cattle are fastened in stalls

restoral *n* the act of restoration or restitution

restow *vb* to stow again

restren *Obs fm vb* **restrain**

restrike *n* a fresh impression on a coin

restrive *vb* to strive anew (*infl fms* as *vb* strive, i.e. **restrove, restriven**)

restud *vb* to re-ornament with studs

resty *now dial adj* restive *obs adj* stale, rancid: inactive, lazy

resuit *vb* to clothe again

resupine *adj* lying on the back

reswarm *vb* to swarm again

reswear *vb* to swear again

reswill *vb* to swill again

ret *vb* to soak (*esp* flax) in water in order to soften (also see **maceration**): to rot *obs vb* to accuse

retack *vb* to tack again, in either the sailing or sewing senses

retaile *obs fm n/vb* **retail**

retale *obs fm n/vb* **retail**

retama *n* a class of shrubby plants *incl* Spanish broom

retape *vb* to record again on magnetic tape

reteach *vb* to teach again

reteign *obs fm vb* **retain**

retein *obs fm vb* **retain**

reteir *obs S fm n/vb* **retire**

retend *obs vb* to return

retene *n* a colourless crystalline compound obtained from resinous (*esp* fossil) pine wood

retent *n* that retained *obs adj* reserved, restrained *obs vb* to cause to ring or echo with sound

rethel *obs fm n* **rotl**

rethor *obs fm n* **rhetor**

retial *adj* of rete, a network (of nerves or blood vessels)

reticle *n* a reference grid attached to such as a telescope

reticular *adj* netlike

retier *obs fm vb* **retire**

retill *vb* to till again

retime *vb* to time (an activity) again

retina *n* the light-sensitive membrane of the eye (*pl* **retinae, retinas)**

retinae *pl* retina

retinal *adj* of or pertaining to the retina

retinalite *n* a variety of the mineral, serpentine, having a resinous lustre

retine *obs S fm vb* **retain**

retinene *n* a yellow pigment of the retina

retinite *n* a resin obtained from brown coal: pitchstone, a vitreous rock resembling hardened pitch

retinue (*n*) *vb* to supply with a body of retainers: to accompany as such

retinula *n* a cell acting as a retina in the eye of an arthropod (*pl* **retinulae, retinulas**)

retiree *n* one who retires from work

retitch *dial fm vb* **retouch**

retrait *obs adj* reserved *obs n* a place of retreat: a military retreat or withdrawal: a portrait *obs vb* to retreat

retrate *var fm obs n* **retrait**, a portrait *var fm obs vb* **retrait**

retree *n* damaged or defective paper

retret *obs n* reconsideration of a subject matter

retro *n* a short *fm* of **retrorocket**, a small auxiliary rocket engine on a larger rocket or spacecraft which has the function of producing a thrust in the reverse direction (*pl* **retros**)

retrorse *adj* turned backwards

retruse *obs adj* hidden, secret

retruss *obs vb* to load or burden again

retsina *n* a resin-flavoured Greek wine

retter *n* one who rets such as flax

retting *n* the preparation of such as flax for soaking (see **ret**)

retund *vb* to weaken or diminish the effect of: to repress: to blunt: to force back

retuse *adj* of plant leaves, having a rounded tip in which there is a slight notch or indentation

reume *obs fm n* **rheum**

reut *dial fm n/vb* **root**

revale *obs vb* to lower

reve *arch fm n* **reeve**, the high official *obs fm arch vb* **reave**

reveil *var fm n* **reveille** *obs vb* to reveal, disclose

reveir *obs S fm n* **river**

revel (*n/vb*) *infl fms* British, **revelled/-lling**: US, **reveled/-ling**

revele *arch fm n* **reveal**, a side window *obs fm vb* **reveal**

revene *obs vb* to return

revent *vb* to provide (a firearm) with a new vent

reverer *n* one who reveres or admires

reverist *n* a dreamer

revers *n* a lapel or other part of a garment which is turned back (*pl* **revers**)

reversi *n* either of two adult games which originated in Victorian times, one played on a chessboard, the other with cards. The board game uses 64 pieces, white on one side and black on the other. Each player has half the number with one electing to play with white uppermost, the other black. The pieces are added to the board one at a time with the object of trapping one or more of the opponent's counters between two of one's own. This achieved, the counters are reversed, so becoming the colour of the player effecting a trap. The game ends when all the pieces are the same colour. A game of skill, it is now marketed under the brand name of *Othello*. The card game is basically the bid of misère in solo whist played as the complete game.

revery *var fm n/vb* **reverie**

revest *vb* to reinvest: to vest (something) again in a person

revester *obs n* a church vestry *obs vb* to dress

revet *vb* to face (*esp* a fortification) with masonry

revete *vb* to face a (fortification) wall or embankment with material such as sods or stone

revie *obs vb* of gambling in card games, to raise the stake (rather like the system of modern poker) hence, **revying** *obs n* the act of venturing a larger stake

reviewal *n* the act of reviewing or revising: a review (of a book), a revision

reville *Obs fm vb* **revile**

revin *obs S fm n* **raven,** the bird

revince *obs vb* to refute or disprove

revisal *n* a revision: a re-examination

revisitant *adj* returning to a particular place

revolute *vb* to revolt *obs vb* to revolve

rew *now dial n* a hedgerow *obs S n* a street *obs vb* to mark with stripes

rewalt *obs vb* to overturn

rewarn *vb* to warn again

rewden *obs dial adj* made of combed straw

rewend *vb* to wend again

rewet *obs n* the lock of an old gun such as a harquebuss *vb* to make wet again

rewill *obs fm n* **rule**

rewish *obs adj* of the pigeon, vehement in copulation

re-wish *vb* to wish again

rewl *obs fm n/vb* **rule**

rhabdomancy *n* divination by the use of a divining wand

rhabdus *n* the stalk of various fungi

Rhaetia *n* an ancient Roman Alpine province

Rhaetian *adj* Rhaeto-Romantic, of those dialects of the Romance family spoken in Switzerland and northern Italy *n* such a dialect

Rhaetic *adj/n* (of or pertaining to) a group of rock strata representing the upper division of the Triassic system in Britain and western Europe *var fm n* **Rhaeto-Romantic**

Rhaeto-Romantic *n/adj* (of) a group of Romance dialects of Switzerland and Italy

rhame *var fm S & dial vb* **rame** *var fm S n/now dial n* **rame**

rhamnose *n* a sugar found in plants

rhapontic *n* rhubarb

rhatany *n* either of two shrubby South American plants of the pea family (*pl* **rhatanies**)

rhe *var fm obs n* **ree**

rhebok *n* the *Pelea capreolus*, a species of antelope which ranges from 28–32 inches in height when fully mature. Found at altitudes above 4,000 ft in South Africa and Botswana, it has unusual rabbit-like fur and behaves like a mountain goat. In the rutting season, the males are not merely aggressive towards each other but also attack sheep or goats. Some experts classify it with the dwarf antelopes, others as a relative of the reedbuck. (*pl* **rhebok, rheboks**)

rhein *var fm dial n* **rhine**

Rhemist *n* one, based at the Roman Catholic English college at Rheims, who translated into English an edition of the New Testament which was published in 1582

rhenium *n* a heavy metallic element of the manganese group

rhesis *n* a set speech

rhesus *n* a species of macaque, a medium-sized monkey common in many parts of Asia

Rhetian *var fm n/adj* **Rhaetian**

rhetor *n* an orator: a teacher of rhetoric

rhetorise *var fm vb* **rhetorize**

rhetorize *vb* to use rhetorical language

rheum *n* any watery discharge from such as the nose, eyes or mouth: any species of *Rheum* (+*cap*) *n* the genus of rhubarb *obs vb* to discharge rheum

rhime *arch fm n/vb* **rhyme**

rhine *dial n* a large open ditch

rho *n* the seventeenth letter of the Greek alphabet

rhodanic *adj* thiocyanic

rhodanise *var fm vb* **rhodanize**, to electroplate with the metallic element, rhodium

rhodic *adj* of, pertaining to or derived from rhodium

rhodium *n* a whitish-grey metallic element of the platinum group, the salts of which are often rose-coloured

rhone *S n* a rooftop guttering or rainwater pipe

rhyton *n* an ancient Greek wine cup having only a small drinking hole and *esp* one in the form of the head of such as a lion or a sphinx (*pl* **rhyta**)

ri *n* a Japanese measure of distance and of depth

Rialto *n* a district and island of Venice (−*cap*) *n* a marketplace (*pl* **rialtos**)

riante *var fm adj* **riant**, smiling or mirthful

riata *var fm n* **reata**

ribaud *obs fm n/adj* **ribald**

ribble *vb* to plough and leave fallow

ribbonworm *n* any of nearly 600 species of mainly marine, elongated, soft-bodied invertebrates ranging from a mere two inches in length to the 60 yards of the bootlace worm

riblet *n* a little rib

ribston *n* a ribston pippin *modf n* designating a choice variety of winter apple, the **ribston pippin**, first grown in England at Ribston Park, Yorkshire, having been introduced from Normandy in 1707

ribstone *var fm n/modf n* **ribston**

rice milk *n* a dish of rice served in boiled milk optionally *incl* other ingredients

ricer *n* a kitchen utensil having perforations through which such vegetables as potatoes are passed to make them into tiny pieces rather like grains of rice

ricey *adj* of or pertaining to rice: rice-like (*var fm* **ricy**)

rich *(adj/n) obs vb* to enrich: to become rich

richen *vb* to make or become richer: to make more intense

richt *S fm n/adj/adv* **right**

rick *n* a stack of hay, corn or peas: a sprain *esp* one in the back or neck *obs n* a ridge *dial fm n* **reek**, smoke *vb* to stack hay etc: to sprain: in coursing, to cause the hare to make an almost complete change of course

ricker *n* a naval spar made from the stem of a young tree

ricket *var fm n* **rickets**

rickets *n* a disease (of children) caused by a deficiency of vitamin D which is characterized by softness of the bones

rickle *S & dial n* a loose heap or pile: a ramshackle object *dial n* a clatter *S & dial vb* to make a heap *dial vb* to clatter

ric-rac *n* rick-rack, a braid with a zigzag decorative form

rictal *adj* of or pertaining to a rictus

rictus *n* the expanse of the open mouth: a gaping: a fissure or cleft

ridable *var fm adj* **rideable**, capable of being ridden (through/over)

riddel *var fm arch n* **ridel**

rideable *adj* capable of being ridden

ridel *arch n* (an altar) curtain

rident *adj* radiantly cheerful

ridered *adj* having a surmounting object

ridgel *now dial n* an animal with only one testicle or one having been imperfectly castrated

ridger *n* a subsoiler, an implement which creates furrows in soil during the seeding process *dial n* a backband, a strap or chain which passes over the back of a horse and is part of the attachment of a cart

ridgling *var fm now dial n* **ridgel**

ridless *dial fm n* **riddle**, a puzzle

riegne *obs fm n* **reign**

riend *obs fm n* **rind**, the peel of various fruit

Riesling *n* a German dry white wine

rieve *S fm arch vb* **reave**

riever *var fm n* **reaver**

rifel *obs fm vb* **rifle** (in senses other than forming grooves)

rifeness *n* the condition of being rife

rifest *sup adj* rife

riff *now dial n* the itch or mange *obs vb* to break up (land)

riffe *var fm obs vb* **riff** *obs fm now dial n* **riff**

riftless *adj* having no rift(s)

riggle *var fm now dial n* **riggal**, a groove in stone or wood *var fm n/vb* **wriggle**

righten *vb* to put or set right

riglet *var fm n* **reglet**

riglin *S n* a ridgel

rigling *var fm S n* **riglin**

rigne *obs S fm vb* **reign**

Rigveda *n* the oldest collection of hymns and verses in Hindu sacred literature, said to date back to 2000 BC

rike *Obs vb* to reign *S fm vb* **reach**

rikels *Obs fm obs n* **rekels**

riking *S fm n* **reaching**

rillet *n* a little brook

rim (*n*) *vb* to add a rim *US vb* to slash the sides (of a fish) to give a fatter appearance *now dial n* the peritoneum, the sac that lines the walls of the abdominal cavity (the usual *fm* is **rim of the belly** or **rim of the womb** though it is often shortened to rim)

rimate *adj* chink-like

rimel *vb* to prepare an existing hole for a fresh rivet *obs n* a fissure or crack

rimester *n* a versifier or poet of little account

rimlet *dial fm n/adj* **remnant**

rimme *obs fm n/now dial n* **rim**

rimose *adj* (*esp* of plants) full of fissures and cracks

rimple *vb* to wrinkle *now dial n* a wrinkle: a ripple on water

rimy *dial fm adj* **reamy**

rince *dial fm n/vb* **rinse**

rinche *obs fm vb* **rinse**

rind (*n*) *vb* to remove the rind or bark from *S & dial vb* to melt

rinde *obs fm n* **rind**, the peel of various fruit

rindge *obs fm dial n* **ringe**

rindles *obs fm now dial n* **rendles**

riner *n* a propelled object which touches its target, as a ball touching the jack in bowls or a quoit the peg

ringbit *n* a horse's bit with rings at the ends

ringbone *n* a bony growth on the foot of a horse

ring-dial *n* a portable sundial

ringe *dial n* a heap of anything laid in a long row *S fm n/vb* **rinse**

ringel *obs fm now dial n* **ringle**

ringen *var fm obs vb* **ringle**

ringent *adj* gaping

ringgit *n* the Malaysian unit of currency

ringhals *n* an unusual species of cobra found only in South Africa and Zimbabwe. It not only spits its venom but, unique for a cobra, bears live young.

ringle *S n* a ringing tone *now dial n* a metal ring *esp* that for a pig's nose *now dial vb* to cut a complete ring of bark off a tree either to stunt or kill: to jingle *obs vb* to wrestle

ringshake *n* a defect in timber, having separation along the annual rings

ringstand *n* a stand with ringlike clamps used for chemical vessels

ringster *US n* a member of a political ring

ringtail *n* either of two birds, the female of the hen harrier or a golden eagle before its third year: any of approximately fifteen different species of phalangers or possums, Australian herbivorous marsupials also known as ringtail possums *adj* of possums, having a tail with ringlike markings. Other creatures are described as being ring-tail (as dove or eagle), ringtailed (as lemurs) ringtailed or ring-tailed (as the cacomistle, a catlike carnivore related to the racoons and known as the ringtailed or ring-tailed cat).

ring taw *n* a game played with marbles

ring time *nonce n* (*Shaks*) the time for the giving or exchanging of rings

ringwise *adj* of a boxer or wrestler, experienced

rink (*n*) *vb* to skate on a rink

rinkle *obs var fm n* **wrinkle**

rinnet *obs var fm n* **rennet**

rinser *n* one who rinses

riot (*n/vb*) *obs adj* wanton, licentious

riote *obs fm n* **riot**

riotest *sup obs adj* riot

ripare *obs n* defence or shelter

riparial *adj* of, pertaining to or situated upon the banks of a river: of animals, frequenting or living upon the margins of fresh water

ripe (*n/adj*) *vb* to grow, become or make ripe: to grope: to cleanse: to plough

ripeck *var fm n* **ryepeck**, an iron-tipped pole driven into a riverbed as a mooring for a punt or a marker for watersport

ripel *obs fm vb* **ripple** (as given at **riple**, below)

riper (*comp adj*) *n* a ripener *dial n* a metal prod used for cleaning holes *obs n* one of the tools of a fletcher's trade (the others being a baldock, a nocksaw, a rasp, a share and a thwitting knife – and nobody really knows what they were either)

ripest *sup adj* ripe

riple *obs fm vb* **ripple**, to remove seeds from flax with a comb-like implement (also see **reple**)

rippet *S n* uproar, noisy dispute

ripplet *n* a little ripple

riptide *n* a tide rip or (*US*) tiderip

rishew *Obs n* a rissole

risme *obs fm n* **rime** (rhyme)

rismme *obs fm now dial n* **rim**

risp *n* a type of antique door knocker consisting of a ring which is rasped against a serrated bar *S & dial n* a rasp *S n* swordgrass, a species of sedge *now dial n* a bush: a branch, a stem *now S vb* to rasp or file: to make a harsh grating sound

rispetto *n* (music for) a type of Italian folk song (*pl* **rispetti**)

rispings *S n pl* filings or risped particles

risque *arch fm n/vb* **risk**

risqué *adj* audaciously bordering on indecency

Rissian *adj* of Riss, a stage in Alpine glaciation

rist *vb* to engrave *now dial n* a rise, in land or in price

ristle *S n* a type of plough with a sickle-shaped blade, formerly used in the Hebrides

risus *n* a laugh or grin

rit *now S & dial vb* to tear, to scratch: to cut

rithe *now dial n* a little brook

ritte *obs fm now S & dial vb* **rit**

ritter *n* a (knightly) warrior on horseback

rivage *now poet n* an estuarine river bank: a landing place: the coast

rive *vb* to tear, lacerate, pull asunder

rivel *vb* to become, or cause to be, wrinkled or shrivelled *obs vb* to become entangled (*infl fm (both vbs)* **rivelled/-lling**: also see **riveling**, below)

rivele *Obs fm vb* **rivel**

riveling *n* a shoe made of raw hide *obs n* one who wore such, e.g. a Scot: a brook or stream

river (*n*) *vb* to wash sheep or a fleece of wool in a river (a statute of Henry VIII made it illegal to wind wool which had not been rivered or washed)

rivere *Obs fm n* **river**

riveret *n* a riverlet or small river: a small blood vessel

rivet (*n/vb*) *infl fms* either **riveted** or **rivetted** etc

riveter *n* one who or a machine which rivets (also spelt **rivetter**)

ro *obs n* rest, repose *obs S vb* to take repose *obs fm n* **roe**, the deer

roach *n* a small European fish of the carp family: any of various American fishes similar in appearance *US vb* to trim a horse's mane so that the hair stands upright

road (*n*) *vb* to clear of weeds: of a dog, to track by scent *US vb* to travel by road

roader *n* a road sweeper: a dog which pursues by scenting: a ship at anchor

roadie *slg n* one who assists with the transportation of the equipment of such as a pop group

roale *var fm obs vb* **roll**, to enter (a name) upon a roll or register

roaming *n* a wandering journey

roap *obs fm n/vb* **rope**

roary *S adj* noisy or garish *obs n* a noisy person

roat *obs fm vb* **rote**, to repeat from memory

roate *obs fm n* **rote**, mechanical memory or repetition of facts without regard to meaning

rober *n* a maker or robes: one having charge of robes

roble *n* any of various trees, *incl* the Californian weeping oak *obs fm n* **rouble** *erron fm vb* **rumble**

roblet *obs n* a night goblin who leads people astray in the dark *obs vb* to be led astray by a roblet

roc *n* a mythical gigantic bird of Eastern legend

roche *vb* to recrystallize after previous dissolution *obs vb* to form crystals: to make as hard as a rock: to tear asunder *now dial n* a rock or cliff *Obs n* some unknown type of wine

Rochester *n* a city in New York: a town in Minnesota

rochet *n* a linen vestment worn by a bishop or an abbot: a smock-like outer garment *now dial n* the fish, red gurnard

rocheted *adj* wearing a rochet

rocheter *obs n* one, *esp* a prelate, who wears a rochet

rockat *obs fm n* **rocket**

rock borer *n* a species of bivalve mollusc

rocke *obs fm ns* **rock, rook**

rocketer *n* any swiftly moving game bird

Rockite *n* one of an early 19th century Irish rebel movement

rock mouse *n* a South African rodent also known as a rock rat

rock oak *n* the rock chestnut oak, a tree of rocky terrain

rock pine *n* an Australian tree

rock rat *n* the rock mouse

rock shell *n* any of various marine molluscs which feed on other molluscs *esp* on bivalves which they attack either by forcing their shells apart or by drilling a hole. The species *incl* dog whelk, sting winkle, Venus comb and other murices (see **murex**).

ROCK SYSTEMS AND LIFE FORMS See next page

rock tar *n* petroleum

rock tripe *n* any of various edible Arctic lichens

rock wood *n* a compact type of asbestos

rocquet *now dial n* an outer garment such as a smock *obs n* a small Caribbean lizard

rod (*n*) *US vb* to install a lightning conductor

rodde *obs fm n/vb* **rod**

rodden *adj* made of rods *S n* a berry of the rowan tree

rode (*pa t*) *US n* a (boat anchor) rope *obs n* a measure of length for a dyke (*prob* ten feet) *vb* to clear (a dyke or other watercourse) of weeds: of wildfowl, to fly towards land in the evening: of woodcock, to perform a regular evening flight during the breeding season

Rodentia *n pl* the rodents

roding *n* an anchor rope

rodless *adj* having no (fishing) rod

rodman *n* an angler

rodsman *var fm n* **rodman**

rodster *n* an angler

roemer *n* a large drinking glass

rog *now dial vb* to shake

roge *obs n* a pyre *obs fm n/vb* **rogue**

roger *n* a ram *obs n* a goose: one who pretended to be a poor university scholar in order to gain some advantage

roggel *var fm now dial n* **riggald**, a ridgel

roggle *now dial vb* to (cause to) shake

rogue (*n*) *vb* to behave as a rogue

roil *n* a stirring up (*lit*/*fig*) *obs n* an inferior horse: a fat clumsy woman *vb* to salt (fish) *now US & dial vb* to render muddy by stirring up: to vex or irritate: to create disorder (*fig*) *now dial vb* to romp or frolic *esp* in a rough manner

roiler *US n* an apparatus used in salting fish *obs n* an idler

roin *obs n* a scab *obs vb* to clip or curtail: to growl

roiner *obs n* one who or that (such as a lion) which growls

roist *vb* to roister

roister *n* a hound following a false trail *arch n* a swaggering or noisy reveller (now usually **roisterer**) *dial n* a romp *vb* to behave as a roisterer

roisterer *n* a noisy and/or swaggering reveller

roite *obs fm n* **root**

rolamite *n* a mechanical device which is almost frictionless

Roland *masc pers n* meaning 'land fame'

roler *obs fm n* **roller** (all senses other than that of a bird)

ROCK SYSTEMS AND LIFE FORMS

(For the chronological sequence read from bottom to top)

Rock System	Life Forms
Caenozoic era	(*2% of the age of Earth*)
Quaternary	rise of Man
Upper Tertiary	modern animals and plants
Lower Tertiary	development of modern mammals, insects and plants
Mesozoic era	(*8% of the age of Earth*)
Upper Cretaceous	primitive mammals: last dinosaurs
Lower Cretaceous	rise of flowering plants
Jurassic	first birds: first mammals: diversification of reptiles: coniferous trees
Triassic	rise of dinosaurs: bony fishes
Palaeozoic era	(*20% of the age of Earth*)
Permian	rise of reptiles: modern insects
Carboniferous	first reptiles: primitive insects: primitive conifers
Devonian	first amphibians: first land snails: primitive land plants
Silurian	scorpions: lungfishes: first traces of land life
Ordovician	first fishes
Cambrian	first marine invertebrates
Pre-Palaeozoic eras	(*70% of the age of Earth*)
Pre-Cambrian	first signs of life: algae

(note: The rock systems of the Caenozoic era are subdivided into epochs, each with its own name. In chronological order these are: – *Tertiary*: Palaeocene, Eocene, Oligocene, Miocene, Pliocene. *Quaternary*: Pleistocene, Holocene. Taken together, they represent a period of 65 million years. Similarly, other names are given to subdivisions within other geological eras.)

rolle *obs fm vb* **roll**

romaine *n* a variety of lettuce

romal *n* a silk or cotton square sometimes used as a headdress: the scarf with which Indian Thugs used to strangle their victims

Romanes *n* the pure form of the Indic language of the gypsies

Romanian *adj* belonging to the gypsies

Romanic *adj* of languages, based on Latin

Romanise *var fm vb* **Romanize**, to make Roman or Roman Catholic

Romaniser *var fm n* **Romanizer**, one who favours the Catholic Church or its rites: one who advocates the principles of Roman law

Romanist *n* a Roman Catholic: one versed in Roman law: a student of Roman antiquities: a student of Romance languages *adj* of the Catholic Church

ROMAN NUMERALS Apart from **I**, **V**, **X**, **L**, **C**, **D**, **M** which are still in use today, there were, in mediaeval times, others. The complete alphabet of Roman numerals is as follows:– **A** 50 or 500: **B** 300: **C** 100: **D** 500: **E** 250: **F** 40: **G** 400: **H** 200: **I** 1: **K** 250: **L** 50: **M** 1,000: **N** 90 or 900: **O** 11: **P** 400: **Q** 500: **R** 80: **S** 7 or 70: **T** 160: **V** 5: **X** 10: **Y** 150: **Z** 2,000. The addition of a stroke above a letter gave it a multiplying factor of 1,000 as **C̄** 100,000. This is also true of **A** taken as 50, **S** taken as 70 and applied to both values of **N**. The exception is **B**. **B̄** 3,000. This curious exception raises the intriguing possibility of a mediaeval error being repeated by two of today's respected works of reference, from which this alphabet has been compiled. Was **B** also 3, or should **B̄** really mean 300,000? *Pears Advanced Word-Puzzler's Dictionary* will be pleased to hear from any reader who can provide a reason for this inconsistency.

Romansch *n* one of the official languages of Switzerland, the Rhaeto-Romantic dialect of northern Italy

rome *obs fm vb* **roam**

romel *var fm n* **romal**

Romeo *n* a young male lover (*pl* **Romeos**)

Romish *adj* Catholic (used in a hostile sense)

Romist *arch n* a Catholic

rompish *adj* inclined to romp

rond *dial n* an East Anglian *fm* of **rand**, a margin, in the specific sense of a reed-covered marshy strip lying between the natural river-bank and a defensive embankment *obs fm n/adj/vb* **round**

rondache *n* a buckler

rondavel *n* a (grass-roofed) round hut of the type common to South Africa: a more sophisticated building in the same style

ronde *n* a typescript which resembles handwriting *obs fm n/adj/vb* **round**

rondel *n* a circular object of any sort: a circle: a type of short poem of fourteen lines on two rhymes

rondelle *n* a circular part

ronder *obs fm comp* **rounder**

rondle *var fm n* **rondelle** *var fm Ir & dial vb* **rantle**

rondure *n* a round or circular object: a circle

roneo *vb* to produce duplicate copies on a Roneo® machine

ronnet *S fm now dial n* **runnet**

ronte *obs fm n* **runt**

roo *obs fm n* **roe**, the deer

rood (*n*) *vb* to spawn

roodge *vb* to move with effort

rooge *dial fm vb* **roodge**

rool *vb* to ruffle or rumple clothing

roome *obs fm now dial n* **room**, dandruff *obs var fm n* **rhomb** (+*cap*) *obs fm n* **Rome**

roop *n* hoarseness *vb* to make a hoarse sound

rooping *var fm S & dial n* **rouping**

rooste *obs fm n/vb* **roast**

roote *obs fm n/vb* **root** *obs fm n* **rote**, a mechanical device *Obs fm vb* **rot**

rooter *n* one who uproots something: a pig

rootle *vb* to root or grub (up)

rootlet *n* a secondary root

rooty *adj* consisting of or abounding in roots *var fm dial adj* **rowty,** coarse or rough *slg n* bread

roove *vb* in mining, to knock against the roof *S vb* to rivet

ropeing *obs fm n* **roping**

roper *n* a maker or user of rope: a jockey who intentionally loses a race: one who entices others to enter a gambling house

ropier *comp adj* ropy

roque *n* an American modified form of the game croquet *obs fm n* **roc**

roquet *n* the action of one croquet player's ball hitting that of another *vb* to make such a hit

rorter *Austr n* a spiv

rory *var fm S adj* **roary** *obs adj* dewy

Rosabel *fem pers n* meaning 'pretty rose'

rosace *n* a roselike ornament or design: rose window, a circular window *esp* one filled with tracery suggestive of a rose

Rosalind *fem pers n* meaning 'fair as a rose', though 'horse serpent' is the sense which the Goths had for its earliest recorded form, Roslindis

rosarian *n* a specialist rose grower

rosat *obs fm n/adj* **russet**

roscid *adj* dewy

roseal *adj* roselike *arch adj* roseate, having the colour of a rose

roseat *obs fm adj* **roseate**

roseate *adj* rose-coloured: rosy (*lit/fig*) *vb* to render rosy

rose-cut *adj* cut in a nearly hemispherical form

rose drop *n* a lozenge flavoured with rose essence and coloured with cochineal: a pink blotch on the face

rosel *obs n* a reed

roselet *n* a little rose: the sandsmelt

rosella *n* the Australian rose parakeet *var fm n* **roselle**

roselle *n* a rose-coloured species of dock also known as Indian or red sorrel, the calyxes of which are used for flavouring sweet foods and drinks whilst the stem provides the fibre called gayal

rosen *obs adj* rose-coloured, rosy: of roses *obs fm n* **rosin**

rosene *var fm obs adj* **rosen**

roseola *n* German measles: the rash of rose-coloured spots characteristic of measles and similar diseases

roser *obs n* a rose bush

roset *S n* rosin *S vb* to treat (a violin bow) with rosin

Rosetta *pet fm fem pers n* **Rose**, meaning the flower of that name

rosety *S adj* resinous

rosier (*comp adj*) *now poet n* a rose bush

rosil *dial fm n* **rosin** or **resin** *dial vb* to apply rosil to the strings of an instrument

rosin *n* resin in a solid, amber-coloured state, obtained from the residue of a distillation of oil of turpentine from crude turpentine *vb* to treat with rosin

Rosinante *n* a pathetic horse similar to the sorry nag of that name which carried Don Quixote

rosinate *n* a salt of any acid occurring in a natural resin

rosine *obs n* a rose

rosing *n* the act of reddening with a suitable chemical agent

rosist *n* a rose grower

rosit *var fm S n/vb* **roset**

rosmarine *obs n* the plant, rosemary: sea dew: the walrus (GAME PLAYER'S note: In the sense of rosemary, this is yet another of the UK Scrabble dictionary's Spenser 'exclusives'. In fact, it was first recorded in this sense in AD 1000, first spelt in this way in 1390 and continued in popular usage until at least 1742. In the other senses, sea dew is exclusive to Jonson and walrus exclusive to Spenser.)

ross *n* the scaly outer bark of trees *US vb* to remove that bark

rossal *dial vb* to disturb, to stir up, to shake, to wrestle

rossel *var fm dial vb* **rossal**

rossen *obs fm n* **rosin**

rosser *US n* a rossing machine (see **ross**)

rosset *Obs fm n/adj* **russet**

rossle *var fm dial vb* **rossal**

rossy *adj* rubbishy

rost *var fm n* **roost**, a swift tidal current between the Orkney and Shetland Isles *obs fm n/vb* **roast** *obs fm n/vb* **rust**

roste *obs fm n/vb* **roast** *obs fm vbs* **roost, rust**

rostel *n* a root of a seed

rostella *pl* rostellum

rostellum *n* a small beaklike structure on the pistil of an orchid: the hooked, knoblike head of a tapeworm (*pl* **rostella**)

rostle *var fm dial vb* **rossal**

rostra *pl* rostrum

rostrum *n* a beaklike process or part: a platform for public speaking (*pl* **rostra, rostrums**)

rosula *n* a leaf rosette

rosulate *adj* in a rosette

rotan *var fm n* **rotang**

rotang *n* a species of rattan palm tree

rotas *see* **word square**

rotche *n* the little auk

rotchie *var fm n* **rotche**

rotel *obs fm now dial vb* **rottle**

rotgrass *n* any plant (such as butterwort, pennywort or soft grass) reputed to cause sheep rot

rother *now dial n* a domestic bovine animal (*pl* **cattle, neat** or **oxen**) (+*cap*) *n* the river which runs through Chesterfield and Rotherham

rotifer *n* a wheel animacule or minute, aquatic, multicellular invertebrate which is almost invariably female. Rotifers living in a puddle, for example, continue to reproduce females for several generations until that puddle starts drying out. Some then produce smaller eggs which hatch as males. Other females, fertilized by these males, then lay eggs which have the capacity to remain dormant in the dried mud until the rain recreates conditions for a new female-only environment.

rotl *n* an Eastern unit of weight which varies,

according to locality, between one and five pounds

rotnes *var fm Obs n* **rotness**

rotness *Obs n* rottenness

rottan *var fm S & dial n* **ratton**, a rat

rotte *obs fm n* **rot**

rottel *obs fm now dial vb* **rottle**

rottle *now dial vb* to rattle *Obs n* the spleen

rotula *n* the kneecap: the point of the elbow: one of five pieces which form the skeleton of the chewing apparatus in a sea urchin (*pl* **rotulae**)

rouet *var fm dial n* **rowet**

roughet *dial n* a stretch of wasteland: a field overgrown with such as bracken: coarse dried grass for use as winter fodder

roulade *n* a quick succession of musical notes

roule *obs fm ns/vbs* **roll, rule**

rounce *n* the handle of a winch

roundel *n* a small circular object: the small round shield used in the 14th century: a round decorative medallion: a circular window: a bead moulding: a number of people or things forming a circle: a roundelay or round dance: a form of rondeau consisting of three stanzas each of three lines with a refrain after the first and third: a round plate of armour used to protect the armpit *S n* a round turret *now dial n* a circle *var fm her n* **roundle** *esp* for those of the RAF

roundle *n* a ring or circle: a round object: the rung of a ladder *her n* a coloured circular design, such as either of those used by the RAF as distinguishing marks on aircraft, one roundle being red, white and blue and the other, red and blue *obs n* a sphere or globe: a rundlet

roundling *obs n* a variety of apple

roundy *now dial adj* of a round shape

roup *n* a disease in poultry *S & dial n* an auction *S & dial vb* to sell by auction: to cry, shout or roar

roupe *obs fm n* **roup** *Obs fm S & dial vb* **roup**

rouper *S n* an auctioneer: one who shouts or roars

rouping wife *S & dial n* a woman who buys at an auction for the purposes of re-selling

rousant *her adj* of a bird, rising as if taking flight

roust *now S n* a voice, shout, roar *S vb* to shout or bellow *US & dial vb* to rout out

rouster *US n* a roustabout or waterfront labourer

rousti *Obs fm adj* **rusty**

rousty *arch S fm adj* **rusty**

router (*n*) *vb* to use a router (a type of plane) for cutting and hollowing out in the construction of a moulding *var fm n* **rowter**

routhie *var fm S adj* **routhy**, abundant or plentiful

routinist *n* one governed by self-imposed routine

routle *dial fm vb* **rootle**

rout seat *n* one of the cane top benches specially hired for a rout – a large fashionable gathering in the 18th and 19th centuries – or for any other social purpose

routte *obs fm n* **route**

rowel *n* the small spiked wheel at the tip of a spur *vb* to prick (a horse) with a rowel (*infl fms* British, **rowelled/-ling**: US, **roweled/-ing**)

rowen *n* the second crop (of hay) of a season

rowet *dial n* coarse grass

rowle *obs fm ns* **rowel, role** *obs fm n/vb* **roll**

rowlet *obs fm n* **roulette**

Rowley, Old *pers n* one of the nicknames of Charles II

rowse *var fm arch n* **rouse**, a drinking session

rowste *Obs fm now S n* **roust**, a shout

rowte *var fm S & dial vb* **rout**, of cattle, to bellow *obs fm now dial vb* **rout**, to snore *obs fm n* **rout**

rowter *n* one who snores *var fm obs n* **router**, a bully or robber

royle *obs fm n/vb* **roil**

royne *S n* a strip of cloth *var fm obs vb* **roin**, to curtail

roynt *dial vb* to order to stand aside or give way (possibly linked to the *vb* **aroint** which was first known in *Macbeth* and has since been adopted by other writers, notably the Brownings)

royst *var fm vb* **roist**

royster *var fm vb/arch n* **roister**

rozet *var fm S n/vb* **roset**

rta *n* in Vedic tradition, the cosmic-moral principle of order which establishes righteousness

ru *Obs fm vb* **rue**, to repent

rubato *adv/adj/n* of music, (in) distorted rhythm (*pl* **rubati, rubatos**)

rubbel *obs fm ns* **rubble, rouble**

rubbet *pa t S vb* rub, to rob

rubble (*n*) *now dial vb* to poke about amongst rubbish

rubel *obs fm n* **rouble**

rubella *n* German measles

rubellan *n* a red-coloured variety of ferromanganese mica occurring in small hexagonal forms

rubellite *n* a red (transparent) variety of tourmaline used as a gem

rubine *obs n* a ruby (colour)

ruble *var fm n* **rouble** *obs fm now dial vb* **rubble**

ruby (*n*) *adj* of the colour ruby (*comp* **rubier** *sup* **rubiest**) *vb* to make ruby-coloured (a glowing purple-tinged red)

ruc *var fm n* **roc**

ruck *n* a crease or wrinkle: a ridge: a heap of any combustible material *S & dial n* a haystack *dial n* a heap *vb* to crease or wrinkle, to become creased or wrinkled *dial vb* to stack *obs vb* to belch

rucke *obs fm n/vb* **ruck**

ruckle *n* a small fold or ridge (as in a blanket or the like): the death rattle *S & dial n* a pile or heap *vb* to form into small folds: to make the death rattle in the throat: to crouch *now dial vb* to pile up

ruct *obs vb* to belch

ructation *obs n* belching

ructer *obs n* one who belches

rud *arch n* redness *now dial n* the marigold *dial n* frogspawn *now dial vb* to mark sheep with red ochre

rudden *obs vb* to become red

ruddle *n* a red-coloured ochre used *esp* for marking sheep *vb* to mark sheep with ruddle

ruden *vb* to make rude (i.e. simple)

rudent *arch adj* rudented

rudented *arch adj* of pillars, having the decorative feature of slim convex lines (the opposite of **fluting**)

rudge *dial fm vb* **roodge** *dial fm n* **ridge**

rudget *dial n* a backband (see **ridger**)

rudiment (*n*) *vb* to initiate

rueth *obs fm arch n* **ruth**

ruff *n* the type of starched linen neckwear fashionable with either sex during the reigns of Elizabeth and James I: a collar of hair or feathers around the neck of certain animals or birds: a male sandpiper, a bird which has such a collar during the breeding season (the female being called a **ree** or **reeve**): a variety of domestic pigeon: a small freshwater fish of the perch family: the act of trumping with a card of a different suit to that led *vb* to trump a card when unable to follow suit: to work beaver felt into a hat *S vb* to beat upon a drum (**ruffing** *n* the action of the *vb* in any of the above senses)

ruffe *var fm n* **ruff**, the small freshwater fish of the perch family *var fm obs n* **ruff**, excitement *obs fm n/vb* **ruff** in most senses *obs S fm n* **roof** *obs fm adj* **rough**

ruffet *var fm dial n* **roughet**

rug (*n*) *S & dial vb* to pull with force or violence

rugate *adj* of animals, wrinkled

ruge *obs n* a fold or wrinkle *obs vb* to wrinkle (skin)

rugge *obs fm S & dial vb* **rug**, to tug forcefully *obs fm n* **rug**, a coverlet *obs fm n* **ridge**

ruggle *obs n* a plaything

rugine *obs n* a surgeon's scraping instrument *obs vb* to use such an instrument

rugose *adj* wrinkled

ruinate *adj* ruined *vb* to ruin

ruing *var fm n* **rueing**, repentance

ruit *S fm vb* **root**

ruite *obs fm n* **root**

ruly *adj* orderly *obs adj* pitiful *obs adv* pitifully

rumbo *n* rum punch (*pl* **rumbos**)

rumen *n* the first stomach of a ruminant (*pl* **rumens, rumina**)

ruminate *vb* to meditate: to chew the cud (*lit/fig*)

rump-fed *Shaks adj* meaning obscure, but likely polite interpretations could be either fed on rump (steak) or sufficiently well-fed that the rump is well-rounded (it was used in conjunction with a term of reproach for a woman)

rumple *n* a crease *S & dial n* a tail *vb* to crease

rumpy *n* a Manx cat

runcinate *adj* of leaves, having edges like the teeth of a saw

runcinated *adj* runcinate

rundale *n* land jointly owned and parcelled off into individual strips

rundaled *adj* land divided according to the system of rundale

rundel *dial fm n* **rundle** *var fm now dial n* **rundle**, an enclosure *obs fm now dial n* **rundle**, a brook

rundle *n* a wooden roller: a rung of a ladder *now dial n* a circular enclosure or field: a small stream or brook

rundled *adj* rounded

rundlet *n* a secondary umbel or subordinate flowering mass *dial n* a small circle

runk *obs vb* to whisper

runkle *S n* a crease or wrinkle *S vb* to crease or wrinkle

runlet *n* a little stream or brook: a cask or barrel of varying size: the quantity contained

runned *obs adj* congealed

runnet *now dial n* any of the various plants used as rennet, the curdling agent *obs n* a stream or brook

runrig *S n* rundale

runt (*n*) *dial vb* to grow old: to grub up tree roots: to hum or whistle

rusalka *n* a Russian water nymph

ruscus *n* any of a genus of small European evergreen shrubs

ruse (*n*) *now dial vb* of seeds, to drop from the pod when ripe

rushet *obs fm n/adj* **russet**

rushle *obs fm vb* **rustle**

rusine *adj* of the rusa deer *incl* the Indian elk (also known by various other names *incl* sambur and sambar), the various sambar species and the various rusa species all of which are native to southern Asia

russat *obs fm n/adj* **russet**

russet *n* a coarse homespun woollen cloth: a reddish-brown colour: a variety of dessert apple of a yellowish reddy-brown colour: a species of moth (*pl*) *obs n* a garment of russet cloth *adj* of a reddish-brown colour *vb* to make or become russet in colour

russhe *obs fm vb* **rush**, to gather (or strew with) the plant rush

rustable *adj* capable of being attacked by rust

rusten *Obs fm vb* **rust**

rusticate *vb* to retire to the country: to countrify: to send away (from a university) for a specified period as a punishment

rusticial *pseudo-arch fm adj* **rustical** (a *fm* used by Scott in *The Monastery*)

rustie *obs fm adj* **rusty** *var fm obs vb* **rusty**

rustre *her n* a lozenge-shaped design with a hole in the centre

rustred *her adj* having rustres

rusty (*adj*) *obs vb* to render or become rusty

rustye *obs fm adj* **rusty**

rute *dial vb* of a child, to cry fiercely

ruter *obs fm n* **rutter**

ruth *arch n* compassion, pity

ruthe *Obs vb* to awaken *obs fm arch n* **ruth**

Ruthenian *adj/n* (of or pertaining to) a Ruthene, Russniak or Little Russian, one of a race found in the south of Russia and in Austria: their language: their Church

ruther *var fm now dial n* **ridder**, a sieve *S & dial fm n* **rudder**

rutile *n* an ore of titanium

Rutland *n* once England's smallest county and now, sadly, part of the county of Leicester since the days of the ill-fated Heath administration: a type of superior leather used for book binding (also see **raddleman**)

rutsel *obs vb* to slide

rutte *obs fm n* **rut**

rutter *n* a (German) cavalryman of the 16th/17th centuries

ruttle *now dial n* a rattle in the throat *now dial vb* to rattle: to make a rattling noise (in the throat)

ry *obs fm n* **rye**, the plant *Obs fm obs n* **rye**, a disease of hawks

rye (*n*) *var fm dial vb* **ree**

ryewolf *n* an evil creature which haunts fields of rye in Germany

rynt *obs fm vb* **aroint**

S

sa *n* the fourth letter of the Arabic alphabet

sabadilla see **cebadilla**

sabella *n* any species of fanworms

saber *US fm n/vb* **sabre**

Sabian *n* an adherent of a religion considered tolerable by the authority of the Koran

Sabina *fem pers n* meaning 'a Sabine' (*—cap*) *var fm n* **savin**

sable (*n*) *poet vb* to clothe in black

sableness *n* blackness

sabre (*n*) *vb* to cut, strike or wound with this type of sword

saccos *n* a type of alb worn by a bishop of the Greek Orthodox Church

saceret *obs fm n* **sakeret**

sachem *n* a Red Indian hereditary chief: any chief *esp* one of the leaders of the Tammany Society in New York, a political society devoted to the Democratic Party and notorious for its corrupt influence in the city politics during the 19th century

sacheted an undefined adjective which appears to be exclusive to one particular American dictionary where it is included after a definition of the noun, **sachet**

sackbut *n* an old type of musical instrument rather like a trumpet with a trombone slide: a Biblical stringed instrument

sacket *now dial n* a bag *dial n* a term of abuse

sacklet *n* a small sack

sacque *n* a sham-French spelling of **sack**, a woman's loose fitting, waistless dress

sacral *adj* of or pertaining to rites of a sacred nature

sacre *arch fm n* **saker**, the bird *obs fm n* **saker**, the gun *obs n* a religious service (*pl* rites of worship) *obs vb* to consecrate: to wed: to dedicate

sacred prostitution *n* an ancient practice most notable in that of the worship of Ishtar (see **qadistu, Ishtar** etc) and currently employed as a recruiting device for one or two of the more bizarre cults which have proliferated in recent years

sacret *obs fm n* **sakeret**

sacring *n* consecration: the ordination and consecration of a bishop or a monarch *modf n* as in **sacring bell**, a bell rung during the consecration of the host in a Catholic church

sacrist *n* one who has charge of the contents of a church: a sexton

sacristan *n* a sacrist or official having charge of the sacred objects in a church: a sacristine or nun having the same charge in a convent *arch n* the sexton of a parish church

sacristine *see* **sacristan**

sacristy *n* that part of a church in which such as the sacred utensils and vestments are stored

sacrum *n* the large wedge-shaped bone in the lower part of the back (*pl* **sacra**)

sad (*adj*) *n* the fourteenth letter of the Arabic alphabet

sade *n* the eighteenth letter of the Hebrew alphabet

sadiron *n* a heavy flat iron

sadtree *n* the night jasmine of India, a tree which, during the day, loses its brightness

saeter *n* a Norwegian upland meadow used for summer pasture: a hut on such a meadow

safari (*n*) *vb* to go on such a hunting expedition

safire *obs fm n* **sapphire**

safrol *var fm n* **safrole**

safrole *n* sassafras oil, an ingredient of neuralgic medicaments, perfumes, soaps and insecticides

saften *S fm vb* **soften**

saftener *S fm n* **softener**

safter *S fm adj* **softer**

sagene *n* a fishing net

saggar *n* a clay box used in pottery baking (the TV programme *What's my line?* twice featured a contestant whose occupation was that of a *saggar maker's bottom knocker*)

sagger *var fm n* **saggar**

sagoin *n* any of three species of South American marmosets: extended to include the related tamarin and various other monkeys

saguin *var fm n* **sagoin**

sagy *adj* flavoured with sage (*comp* **sagier** *sup* **sagiest**)

saibling *n* the fish, char

saidest *arch fm 2nd pers sing vb* say

Saigon *n* the former capital of South Vietnam, now called Ho Chi-minh City in the unified communist country of Vietnam: the river on which it stands

saile *obs fm n/vb* **sail**

sailer *n* a sailing vessel *obs n* a sailor

sailoring *n* the work of a sailor

sain *arch vb* to make the sign of the cross

sainfoin *n* a cloverlike herb of the bean family which has variegated flowers and is cultivated for foliage

saint (*n*) *arch vb* to canonise

saintdom *n* the status of a saint: saints collectively

sainte *Fr n* the *fem* of **saint**

saintess *n* an unattractive English equivalent of the French **sainte**, a female saint

saintism *n* the principles or the practice of a Puritan who declares himself and his fellow believers to be saints (*obs* except, perhaps, in a sense of sanctimoniousness)

sair *S fm n/vb* **savour** *S fm vb* **serve** *S fm adj* **sore**

Saite *n/adj* (an inhabitant) of Sais, an ancient city of Lower Egypt

saithe *S n* a mature coalfish

sakaret *obs fm n* **sakeret**

sake (*n*) *an aphetic fm vb* **forsake**

saker *n* a lanner or species of falcon (the male of which is a sakeret): a type of small cannon used on sailing ships

sakeret *n* a male saker

sakret *obs fm n* **sakeret**

salade *var fm n* **sallet**

salariat *n* those paid by salary considered as a class

sale (*n/adj*) *vb* to sell

salep *n* dried tubers of any of various orchids used as a food or a drug

saler *obs fm n* **sailer** *var fm obs n* **sailer**

saleratus *n* baking soda

Salesian *adj* of St Francis de Sales (1567–1622) the French bishop and writer: of the Order of the Visitation which he jointly founded with St Jane Frances de Chantal, the widow of a French baron *n* a nun of that order

salet *var fm n* **sallet** *dial fm n* **salad**

salewd *pa t obs vb* salew (see **salue**)

salfer *S fm obs n* **salfay**, the reward paid for the restoration of lost property

Salian *adj* of or pertaining to the Salii, priests of Mars in ancient Rome whose method of worship included dancing: of a tribe of Franks who inhabited a region in what is now Holland and to whom the ancestors of the Merovingian royal house of France belonged *n* one of the Salii, of whom there were twelve: a Salian Frank

salicet *n* an organ stop with the tone of a willow pipe

saliceta *pl* salicetum

salicetum *n* a thicket of willows (*pl* **saliceta, salicetums**)

salicine *n* a substance obtained from the bark of willow and poplar trees and used in the treatment of rheumatism

salient *adj* of objects, prominent: of animals, leaping: of water, jetting: of qualities, conspicuous *poet adj* of the pulse, beating *n* a prominent aspect of a fortification

saligot *n* the water chestnut

salimeter *n* a device used to measure salinity

salina *n* a salt lagoon, lake, pond, well, spring or marsh: a salt works, either natural or artificial

saline *adj* of or pertaining to any salt *n* a salt

saliner *obs n* a salt maker

salinge *dial vb* to dig about the surface of the ground: to investigate (*fig*)

salivate *vb* to secrete saliva *esp* in excess: to cause (an animal by the administration of mercury) to produce saliva

sallet *n* an often ornately engraved 15th century helmet with a neckguard

salligot *obs fm n* **saligot**

salmi *n* a highly seasoned game stew (*pl* **salmis**)

SALMON See next column

salmonet *n* a samlet or young salmon (see SALMON)

Salopian *adj* of Shropshire *n* an inhabitant of Shropshire

salse *n* a mud volcano

saltation *n* a leap: a dance: an abrupt movement (*fig*)

salte *obs fm n/vb* **salt**

saltee *slg n* a penny

SALMON Apart from the various *S & dial* names, the standard terms to describe this fish by its age are as follows:– **alevin**, newly-hatched with a yolk sac hanging beneath like a huge distended stomach: **samlet, salmonet** or **fingerling**, a young salmon now resembling a normal fish: **parr**, a juvenile approximately five inches long and marked with dark bands: **smolt**, aged from about eighteen months to two years, now silvery-coloured without dark bands and ready to migrate: **grilse** or **grawls**, some two feet in length and, having spent a year or so at sea, returning to the home river to spawn for the first time: **kelt, blackfish** or **redfish**, one which has spawned is now exhausted and returning to sea. (At this stage in their life cycles, Pacific salmon in North American rivers now die.) There are various other terms used for salmon such as **mort**, a salmon in its third year, thus covering part of the **grilse** and **kelt** stages (**samlet** is also a fluid term extending into the **parr** stage); **lax** is an exceptionally fluid term, originally meaning any salmon, later it was restricted to an overgrown salmon (the plural of the word in that sense being **lacks** or **lackes**). At this 17th century period of usage it became *obs*. It has since been revived with a sense of Norwegian salmon. (Also see **baggit, esling, hipper, laurel, rawner, shedder, skirling**.)

salter *n* a maker of or dealer in salt: one employed at a salt works: one who salts foodstuffs: one who salts bodies during the embalming process *dial n* a vessel in which meat is salted *obs n* an ax used to rough plane bricks

saltere *obs fm n* **psalter**

saltern *n* a place where salt is produced by a process of evaporation, either within a building where salt water is boiled or on open land where artificial pools of sea water evaporate naturally

saltier (*comp adj*) *var fm her n* **saltire**

saltine *US n* a salted wafer biscuit

saltire *her n* a St Andrew's cross ordinary (see **ordinary**)

salty *adv* with the taste or smell of salt

saltpan *n* a natural or artificial pond from which salt is obtained by the evaporation of (sea) water: a vessel serving a similar function

saltpeter *now US fm n* **saltpetre**

saltpetre *n* potassium nitrate

Salt Sea *n* a Biblical term for the Dead Sea

saltus *n* in logic, a leap to a conclusion

salue *obs n* salew, a salutation *obs vb* salew or salwe, to salute (*infl fms incl* **salewd, salewed, saluyd**)

salve *n* anything that heals or soothes *vb* to apply a salve: to soothe, comfort, appease

salver *n* a tray *var fm n* **salvor**

Salvia *n* the genus of sage (*– cap*) *n* a plant of this genus

salvor *n* one who salvages

salwe *var fm obs vb* **salue** *Obs fm n* **sallow**, the tree

samber *var fm n* **sambur**

samble *var fm obs n* **semble**

sambook *n* a type of small, two-masted, sailing vessel of Arabian coastal waters

sambre *var fm n* **sambur**

sambuq *var fm n* **sambook**

sambur *n* the Indian elk

samek *n* the fifteenth letter of the Hebrew alphabet

samen *obs vb* to examine

Samian *adj* of Samos, a Greek island *n* a native of Samos

samiel *n* the simoon, a suffocating sand wind of the African and Asian deserts

Samiot *var fm n* **Samiote**

Samiote *n* a native of the Greek island of Samos

samisem *n* a Japanese three-stringed musical instrument not unlike an elongated ukulele

samite *n* a rich silk material of the Middle Ages *obs n* a garment or furnishing of such

samlet *n* a young salmon older than an alevin and extending into the period when it is known as a parr (see **SALMON**)

Samnite *adj/n* (of) a language of an ancient Sabine people of central Italy: (of) one such person: of such people

samnitis *Spens n* an unknown poisonous plant (in his *Faerie Queene* he links it with cicuta (hemlock) as the poison given to Socrates)

Samoyed *n* one of a Mongolian people of Siberia *adj* of such and their language

sampan *n* any small Chinese boat

samphire *n* any of various plants *esp* that which grows on coastal rocks and has edible fleshy divided leaves and clusters of small white flowers

sampier *obs fm n* **samphire**

sampire *obs fm n* **samphire**

samplery *n* the making of embroidered samplers: such a sampler

samshu *n* a Chinese spirit distilled from rice

Sancha *var fm fem pers n* **Sanchia**, meaning 'saintly'

sancti *var fm obs n* **santy** (*pl* **sonties**)

Sanctus *n* the 'angelic hymn': the music to which it is sung

sand (*n*) *obs n* that which is sent: a dispensation or ordinance (from God): the action of sending (for): one (or more) sent on an errand: an ambassador (also called a **sandman**, in which sense the word is still extant in nursery lore) *vb* to run aground on a sandbank: to cover with sand: to mix sand with another substance

sandarac *n* a pale yellow aromatic resin used in lacquer and as an incense, yielded by the North African sandarac tree

Sandawe *n* a Khosian language of Tanzania

sand dart *n* a species of British moth

sandeel *n* a small, silvery fish related to the perch which spends much of its time buried in the sand hidden from such predators as cod and halibut. Eel-like in appearance it is not connected with the true eels, in contrast to the giant herring which is. Oddly, a better name would be sandfish, but that is the name of a lizard. (To compare the relationships of eels, herrings and perches see **FISH CLASSIFICATION** – also see **sandfish**)

sandel *var fm S dial vb* **sandle** *Obs fm n* **sendal**

sander *n* one who or that which is involved in the usage of sand: a worker whose task is to sandpaper the solec of shoes: the zander or pike perch, a pike-like true perch widely distributed across central Europe and which feeds mainly on other fish

sanderling *n* one of the calidritine sandpipers, a small wading bird which spends the summer close to the North Pole

sanders *n* sandalwood

sandfish *n* any of eight species of skinks, a type of lizard which spends much of its time 'swimming' in sand as it burrows through, looking for insects

sandhi *n* a circumstance whereby a word undergoes assimilative change from its absolute form under the influence of neighbouring words, e.g. rather than say, '*My lady, the cat has had kittens*' the more likely spoken form is, '*Milady, the cat's had kittens*'

sandhog *US n* one who works under air pressure as in tunnel-building or inside a sunken caisson

sandier *comp adj* sandy

sandiver *n* a saline matter which occurs on the surface of glass after vitrification

sandle *S dial vb* to wade *S dial n* the smelt

sandmole *n* a South African species of molerat

sandre *obs n* a type of striped silk

sane (*adj*) *obs vb* to heal

sangar *n* a stone breastwork *vb* to provide such

sangaree *n* a diluted and spiced wine served as a cold drink in tropical climates

sangered *var fm obs dial n* **sangrede**

sangester *Obs fm n* **songster**

sangestre *Obs fm n* **songster**

sangister *obs fm n* **songster**

sangle *obs fm n* **cingle**

sangler *var fm obs n* **sanglier**

sanglier *her n* a wild boar *obs n* a fully mature wild boar: a boar separated from the rest of the group (for a choice of names for that group see **COLLECTIVE NOUNS**)

Sangrail *n* the Holy Grail, the chalice or cup used by Christ at the Last Supper and, traditionally, preserved by Joseph of Arimathaea who added to it some of the blood from the Crucifixion. He was supposed to have brought it with him to England where it disappeared and became the subject of quest *esp* in the Arthurian legends. In a 12th century French account, the Holy Grail takes the form of a dish on which the Last Supper was served.

sangre *var fm n* **sangaree**

Sangreal *var fm n* **Sangrail**

sangred *var fm obs dial n* **sangrede**

sangrede *obs dial n* a service for the dead

sangria *n* a Spanish drink of sweetened, spiced and diluted wine

sanguine (*adj*) *n* a red crayon: a drawing in red *obs vb* to stain with blood: to paint red (also see **CARDINAL HUMOURS**)

sanicle *n* any of various umbelliferous plants such as the wood sanicle, the white snakeroot (or American sanicle), the black snakeroot, Lady's mantle (or great sanicle (*obs*)) and butterwort (or Yorkshire sanicle (*obs*))

sanies *n* a greenish, blood-tinged fluid discharged from ulcers

sanious *adj* of the nature of sanies: containing sanies

sanitate *vb* to make sanitary

sanke *obs vb* to assemble

sannup *n* the husband of a Red Indian squaw

sanserif *n* any typeface which has no embellishment in the form of small lines or serifs at the extremities of the main strokes

santal *n* sandalwood

santalin *n* the colouring matter of red sandalwood

santer *now dial fm vb* **saunter**

santie *var fm obs n* **santy** (*pl* **sonties**)

santir *n* an Oriental dulcimer

santon *n* a Muslim hermit: a Hindu ascetic

santonica *n* Levant wormseed, the dried flowerheads of a species of Asian plant used to combat intestinal worms

santour *var fm n* **santir**

santre *var fm now dial vb* **santer**

santred *obs fm vbl infl* **sauntered**

santrel *obs n* a little saint

santur *var fm n* **santir**

santy *obs n* a word (presumed to mean sanctity) used in an oath of affirmation (*pl* **sonties**)

São Tomé *n* the capital (population 30,000 in 1985) of a former Portuguese West African colony, now an independent island republic known as São Tomé and Principe

sapele *n* any of various West African trees yielding a mahogany-like timber: that timber

sapient *adj* wise *n* a wise man

Saponaria *n* the genus of the soapwort

sapota *n* the mammee apple, the fruit of a Central American tree

sapremic *US fm adj* **sapraemic**, of, pertaining to or suffering **sapraemia**, septic poisoning

saprine *n* a non-poisonous ptomaine formed in the decomposition of substances associated with the bowels

saprolite *n* any naturally situated decomposed rock

sapropel *n* slimy (organic) sediment laid down in water

sap rot *n* dry rot

sar *n* a sea bream of the genus *Sargus*

sarangi *n* an Indian fiddle-like musical instrument

sarcen *var fm n* **sarsen**

sarcenet *var fm n* **sarsenet**

sarche *obs fm vb* **search**

Sarcodina *n pl* a class of the Protozoa

sard *n* a golden yellow coloured cornelian, a beautiful mineral composed of silica *obs vb* to have sexual intercourse

sardel *var fm n* **sardelle**, a small fish akin to the sardine

sardine *n* a small fish of the herring family: a Biblical precious stone

Sargus *n* a genus of sea bream (*–cap*) *n* a fish of this genus

sarient *obs fm n* **sergeant**

sark *S & dial n* any outer or undergarment of the upper part of the body worn next to the skin *S & dial vb* to wear such a garment

Sarmatian *adj* of or belonging to Sarmatia, an ancient region which covered territory now occupied by Poles and Russians *n* one of the nomadic peoples formerly dwelling in Sarmatia

sarment *n* a twig: a sarmentum *obs n* a tree cutting

sarmenta *pl* sarmentum

sarmentose *adj* of such as the stem of a plant, long and weak

sarmentum *n* the runner of a plant (*pl* **sarmenta**)

sarney *var fm slg n* **sarnie**

sarnie *slg fm n* **sandwich**

sarong *n* a Malayan unisex skirt-like garment

sarpe *obs n* a hooked tool used for pruning: a neckband of gold or silver

sarsden *var fm n* **sarsen**

sarsen *n* an eroded block of sandstone or quartzite which, from a distance, looks like a grazing sheep, hence the alternative name, grey wether

sarsenet *n* a very fine tissue of thin silk often used for linings: a dress of this material

sarsnet *var fm n* **sarsenet**

sarten *Obs fm adj/adv/n* **certain**

sartor *n* a tailor

sashay *vb* to flounce

sasine *n* the act, in Scottish law, of giving legal possession of feudal property: the instrument granting such possession

sass *US vb* to talk impudently to

sassle *dial adj* sleepy, drowsy

saster *S n* a type of meat and tripe pudding

sateen *n* a satin-like cotton or woollen fabric

satelles *n* a planetary satellite (*pl* **satellites**)

sater *obs fm n* **Psalter**, a book of psalms

Sathan *obs fm pers n* **Satan**, the devil

satiable *adj* capable of being satiated

satin (*n*) *vb* to give (wallpaper) a satin-like surface

satiné *n* a kind of satinwood

satinpod *n* the garden plant, satinflower or honesty

satirics *n pl* satiric writings

satirise *var fm vb* **satirize**

satle *dial fm vb* **settle** in the senses of determining a quarrel or sitting down *obs fm vb* **settle** in other senses

sator *see* **word square**

satori *n* in Zen Buddhism, sudden enlightenment

satrap *n* a governor of an ancient Persian province: a tyrant: any powerful and ostentatiously rich local governor

sattel *dial fm vb* **settle**, in the sense of sitting down

sattin *obs fm n* **satin**

sattined *obs fm adj* **satined**

sattinet *obs fm n* **satinette** or **satinet**

sattle *dial fm vb* **settle**

sattler *dial n* that which determines a quarrel or brings a person to silence

Saturnalia *n* the Roman festival of Saturn held in the middle of December which was a time of general merriment even for the slaves: a period of unrestrained revelry (*lit/fig*)

Saturnia *n* a genus of large moths

satyra *n* a female satyr

satyral *her n* a creature with the body of a lion, the tail and horns of an antelope and the face of an old man

satyric *adj* pertaining to satyrs, a class of woodland gods or demons which were part-human and part-beast: pertaining to a type of classic Greek drama in which the chorus dressed as satyrs *obs n* such a drama

sauger *n* a small American pike perch, a pike-like fish of the perch family

saule *obs vb* to satisfy (with food)

saulge *obs fm n* **sage**, the aromatic herb

sault *US n* a waterfall

saulter *Obs fm n* **psalter**

saumer *var fm n* **sambur**

Saunders *var fm masc pers n* **Alexander**, meaning 'defender of men'

saunt *S fm n/vb* **saint**

saurel *n* a fish found in most of the oceans of the world and variously called cavalla, horse mackerel, jack, pompano, scad or skipjack. The young of the common saurel have an unusual method of survival – they take shelter in the bell of the sombrero jellyfish.

saurian *adj* of or pertaining to a lizard: formerly of lizards, crocodiles and dinosaurs *n* such a creature

saute *var fm obs n* **salt**, sexual desire *var fm obs n/vb* **sault**, (to) assault

sauté *vb* to fry quickly in a little fat (*infl fms* **sautéed, sautéing** or **sautéeing**) *n* a dish of food so cooked

sauteer *Obs fm n* **psalter**

sauter *Obs fm n* **psalter**

sautere *Obs fm n* **psalter**

sauterer *var fm Obs n* **psalterer**

sautoire *var fm her n* **saltire**

sautre *Obs fm n* **psalter**

savate *n* a style of boxing popular in the East in which kicking is an integral part

savin *n* a shrubby evergreen bush or small tree of the cypress family the young shoots of which are the source of a medicinal oil: those shoots: any of various other trees *incl* the dwarf juniper, the sea wormwood and the red cedar (USA)

savine *var fm n* **savin**

sawarry *var fm n* **sowarry**

sawbuck *n* a type of sawing frame which holds timber fairly rigid between the two V-shapes of the top half of a frame comprising two X-shapes joined by a bar or bars

sawder *collq n* flattery *collq vb* to flatter

sawer *n* one who saws (wood) *obs fm n* **sewer**, one who sews

sawgate *n* a hole specially cut to allow the use of a fretsaw

sawgeat *Obs n* a ball of pork

sawger *obs n* a bed or plot of sage

sawlter *Obs fm n* **psalter**

sawney *adj* foolish *n* an accident in which all the threads are broken simultaneously on a cotton mule *vb* to wheedle: to act the fool

sawpit *n* an excavation in which one man stands to use one end of a pitsaw whilst his fellow worker stands on a raised platform using the other end

sawter *Obs fm n* **psalter**

sawtere *Obs fm n* **psalter**

sawtre *Obs fm n* **psaltery**

sawtrer *var fm Obs n* **psalterer**

sawtyr *Obs fm n* **psalter**

sawyer *n* one who saws timber: a species of beetle, the larvae of which live inside and bore through wood *US n* a felled tree which is floated downstream on a river

sax (*collq n*) *n* a pointed hammer for trimming slates *Ork & Shet vb* to scare with a pointed instrument

sayler *obs fm n* **sailer** *var fm obs n* **sailer**

scabble *vb* to rough-dress stone

scabbler *n* one who rough-dresses stone: a hammer used in such work

scabine *obs n* an official in a French or Belgian town approximating to an English alderman

scable *arch fm vb* **scabble**

scade *obs fm arch n* **scathe**

scafe *var fm n* **scaife**

scaife *n* a cutting wheel attached to a plough

scaith *S fm vb/arch n* **scathe**

scalar *adj* ladder-like *n* a mathematical quantity possessing only magnitude, not direction

scalder (*n*) *dial vb* to scald

scale insect *n* any member of two families of insects which are a serious pest to plant life in the tropical regions. In either family the male is minute and two-winged whereas the female is large, wingless, legless and covered with a shell. This is either very hard or very large and waxy but, in either case, serves as a protective device for the eggs which she lays in prodigious numbers before dying. One particular species of scale insect is believed to be a possible explanation of the Biblical manna. This species infests tamarisk trees, living on the protein in the juices and excreting the bulk of a carbohydrate-rich fluid which, on contact with the dry air, solidifies into a white mass which is edible either raw or cooked.

scalene *adj* of a triangle, having no two sides equal *n* such a triangle

scalenus *n* any of several muscles of the neck (*pl* **scaleni**)

scaler *n* one who or that which removes scales (from a fish): one who climbs: one who measures logs: one who uses a scale in survey work

scalet *obs n* a wagon or carriage jack mainly used for taking the strain whilst a wheel was extricated from mud

scaleworm *n* one of the various marine creatures which, like the pearlfish and the pea crab, uses the sea cucumber as a home. Not all scaleworms are wormlike nor do all live inside another animal. (See **sea mouse**)

scall *now S & dial n* a scaly or scabby condition *esp* of the scalp

scalled *adj* scabby

scalling *obs adj* producing scall

scally *obs adj* scabby

scalpe *obs fm n* **scalp**

scalter *var fm Obs n* **shaltree**

scaltre *var fm Obs n* **shaltree**

scaly *adj* resembling or covered in scales: peeling off in flakes (*comp* **scalier** *sup* **scaliest**)

scamble *S & dial n* a bench *vb* to remove piecemeal *now dial vb* to scatter items into a crowd to be jostled for: to muddle through: to walk in a very ungainly fashion: to scrape together or collect in a haphazard manner

scamel *Shaks n* a bird of some kind, possibly the kestrel or the bar-tailed godwit or even a seagull

scantel *var fm obs vb* **scantle**

scanter *comp adj* scant

scanties *n pl* women's very brief knickers

scantity *n* scarceness

scantle *n* a small portion: a slater's measuring gauge: a small, irregular-shaped piece of roofing slate *obs vb* to limit or restrict

scape *n* a long flower stalk: the stem of a feather: a scenic view: a nickname for the snipe *arch n* an escape *vb* to escape *interj* an imitation of the cry of the snipe

scapel *n* a botanical term for the neck formed between the seed leaf and the root at the time of germination

scapeless *adj* inevitable

scaper *obs fm n* **shaper**

scaple *obs fm vb* **scapple**, to rough-work the face of a block of stone

scapose *adj* having a scape, or a long naked stem like a dandelion: or a stemlike part such as the shaft of a feather or an insect antenna

scapular *adj* of the scapula or shoulder blade

scapulary *adj* of or pertaining to the scapula

scapus *n* the shaft of a feather (*pl* **scapi**)

scarab *n* the species of dung beetle held sacred by the ancient Egyptians: a beetle-shaped gem *obs n* an abusive term applied to a man

scarcement *S & dial n* a flat ledge projecting from such as a rock face

scarehead *n* a sensational headline in a newspaper *vb* to produce such

scareline *n* a scarehead

scarer *n* one who or that which scares

scarey *var fm adj* **scary**

scarf (*n*) *vb* to cover (as) with a scarf: to bevel or flatten the edges of metal prior to welding: to make an incision in the blubber of a whale

scarle *obs n* a scarecrow

scarlet (*n/adj*) *obs vb* to colour scarlet

scarp *her n* a half-width design of the most simple and common kind running in the opposite direction to normal, as a sign of bastardy *var fm n/vb* **escarp**

scarpe *var fm her n* **scarp** *obs fm n/vb* **scarp** (a *var fm n/vb* **escarp**)

scarpetto *n* a boot or shoe with a hemp sole (*pl* **scapetti**)

scarre *obs fm ns/vbs* **scar, scare**

scart *S n* the cormorant: a scratch *S vb* to scratch

scarth *dial n* a cliff *obs n* an abortion: a monster: an hermaphrodite: a fragment

scarum the second element of the *adj* **harum-scarum**, reckless or daring (GAME PLAYER'S note: As this element has no independent existence as a word in its own right, it should be treated as invalid for play)

Scarus *n* the genus of the parrotfish, a brightly-coloured fish with teeth fusing to form a type of beak. The species vary in colouring and they range in size from two to twelve feet in length, but all feed on coral. (*−cap*) *n* an individual parrotfish (*pl* **scari**)

scate *arch fm n* **skate**, a fish *obs fm n/vb* **skate**, (to move by means of) an ice skate

scater *obs fm n* **skater**

scathe *vb* to injure or destroy by fire: to sear with invective or satire (*fig*) *arch vb* to injure or damage *arch n* injury, damage: that which injures or damages

scatole *var fm n* **skatol**, an aromatic substance of human excrement discovered by a Mr Bruger (of whom not much else is known)

scaud *S fm vb* **scauld**

scaup *n* maula, a marine duck also known as the scaup pochard

scauper *n* an engraver's tool used for hollowing out the bottom of a sunken design

scaur *n* a cliff, the ridge of a hill *obs S fm vb* **scare**

scaurie *Ork & Shet n* a young seagull

scawed *obs adj* spotted

scear *var fm n* **sear**, that part of a gunlock with notches to hold the firing position at half or full cock

sceat *n* an old English coin approximating to the pre-decimal penny (*pl* **sceattas**)

sceatt *var fm n* **sceat**

scede *obs n* a manuscript of papyrus, the ancient, classical writing material

scelerat *arch n* a villain

scenarise *var fm vb* **scenarize**, to make a scenario of

scenarist *n* a writer of motion picture scenarios

scenical *adj* of or belonging to the stage: theatrical in style (*fig* and usually in a bad sense)

scepter *now US fm n/vb* **sceptre**

sceptral *adj* pertaining to a sceptre

sceptre (*n*) *vb* to supply with a sceptre, the ornamental wand of royal authority: of a monarch, to touch with a sceptre as a sign of approval

scerne *obs vb* to discover

schate *obs fm n* **skate**

schema *n* a generalised diagram or plan (*pl* **schemata**)

schide *obs fm now dial n* **shide**

schine *obs n* the mastic tree, an evergreen shrub

schismatic *adj* of, pertaining to, of the nature of or guilty of a schism *n* one who promotes a breach of (external) unity with the Church: one who subsequently joins such a schism

schive *Obs fm n* **shive**, a slice of bread

schlep *slg vb* to pull or drag

schout *n* an administrative official in Holland or a Dutch colony

schtik *var fm n* **shtik**

schuit *n* a Dutch flat-bottomed riverboat

sciard *n/adj* (of) any of various minute, dark-coloured flies

sciatic *adj* of, belonging to or affecting the hip *n* a short *fm* of **sciatic nerve**, the longest nerve in the body which extends from the thigh to the calf of the leg

sciatical *adj* of or pertaining to the nature of sciatica, the form of neuralgia which affects the sciatic nerve: affected with sciatica

scient *adj* having knowledge or skill *arch n* a scientist

scienter *adv* knowingly

sciential *adj* of or pertaining to knowledge: endowed with such

scilla *n* any of the various plants of the squill genus of the lily family

scimetar *var fm n* **scimitar**

scintle *var fm vb* **skintle**

sciolist *n* one with a conceited pretence to knowledge which, at best, he or she can only display at a superficial level

Scirpus *n* the club rush genus of the sedge family of plants

scite *obs n* a decree or statute *obs fm vb* **cite**

scitie *obs S fm n* **city**

sciurine *adj* of or pertaining to a squirrel or closely related rodent *n* one such animal

sciuroid *adj* of or pertaining to the squirrel family: like the tail of a squirrel

sciver *var fm n* **skiver**, a skewer

sclate *S fm n/vb* **slate**

Sclave *obs fm n/adj* **Slav**

sclaer *Obs fm n* **slayer**

sclera *n* the white fibrous outer coat of an eyeball (*pl* **sclerae, scleras**)

sclerae *pl* sclera

scleral *adj* of or pertaining to the sclera

sclere *n* a skeletal element

sclerite *n* one of the hard skeletal plates of such as a cockroach

sclerose *vb* to affect with the morbid condition of sclerosis: to harden

sclerotia *pl* sclerotium

sclerotial *adj* of or pertaining to a sclerotium

sclerotium *n* a compacted mass of hardened hyphae (see **hypha**) and reserve food material found in certain higher fungi which, when mature, detaches and remains dormant until a favourable opportunity for growth. At that time it sends out either hyphae or spore fruits: a waxy mass of protoplasm in slime moulds (*pl* **sclerotia**)

scoat *obs fm now dial vb* **scote**

scog *S & dial vb* to shelter

Scogan *n* a buffoon

scolopacine *adj* of the snipe and woodcock, birds of the sandpiper family (also see **caliditrine** and **tringa**)

scomber *n* a mackerel (*pl* **scombers, scombri**) (+*cap*) *n* one of the genera of the mackerels

scombre *obs fm n* **scomber** *Obs fm now dial vb* **scumber**

sconner *arch fm S & dial n* **scunner** *obs fm S & dial vb* **scunner**

scontre *obs vb* to encounter

scoot *S n* a gush of water *US & S vb* to slip *S vb* to eject or squirt *collq vb* to dash away

scopate *adj* tufted

scoper *obs fm n* **scupper**

scopula *n* a small tuft of hairs (*pl* **scopulae, scopulas**)

scordato *adj* of music, put out of tune

scoreing *obs fm n* **scoring**, a marked line

scorie *var fm Ork & Shet n* **scaurie**

scorne *obs fm vb* **scorn**

scorper *n* a tool for hollowing-out: a jeweller's tool for enlarging the settings of precious stones

scorse *now dial vb* to barter, exchange

scorser *obs n* one who scorses or barters

scorte *var fm obs vb* **short**, to grow short

scotart *obs n* the hare

scote *dial n* a dragstaff, an ironshod pole attached to the axle of the rear wheels and dragged behind a cart but which acts as a brake in the event of that cart attempting to roll backwards *now dial vb* to place a chock of some description (such as a stone or a piece of wood) against the wheel of a cart to prevent it rolling forward

scoter *n* a species of marine duck

Scotia *poet n* Scotland

Scotian *obs nonce adj* of or belonging to Scotland (SCOTTISH CURIOSITY note: The dictionary used for the UK Scrabble championship (which, incidentally, happens to be Scottish) considers it to be both extant and, though rare, standard. All other experts know of only one *nonce* literary usage, in 1803.)

Scotism *n* the metaphysical system of John Duns Scotus (circa 1265–1308) which is in direct conflict with that of Thomas Aquinas. Scotus' system is reflected by the Franciscans, that of Aquinas by the Dominicans.

scouder *obs fm S n/vb* **scowder**

scoule *obs fm n/vb* **scowl**

scouper *S n* one who, or a creature which, bounds and leaps

scourie *var fm Ork & Shet n* **scaurie**

scourse *obs fm now dial vb* **scorse**

scouse *dial n* a stew made of leftovers (*+cap*) *n* a Liverpudlian: the Liverpool dialect *adj* of or from Liverpool

scouter *n* an adult worker in the Boy Scout movement *obs n* a spy or military scout

scouth *S n* opportunity: abundance

scowder *S n* scorching *Anglo-Ir n* a type of oat cake *S vb* to scorch

scower *arch* or *obs fm vb* **scour** *obs S fm n* **score**

scowle *obs fm n/vb* **scowl**

scowre *obs fm vb* **scour**

scowrie *var fm Ork & Shet n* **scaurie**

scowt *obs fm n/vb* **scout** (in most senses)

scowte *obs fm n* **scout** (in most senses)

scrabble *vb* to scribble: to write or depict something in a scrawling manner: to scratch or scrape: to scramble on hands or feet *n* a scrabbled work of writing or drawing (*+cap*) ®*n* the classic crossword-style word game invented in the USA in the early 1930s but which was not accepted by a manufacturer until 1949. It is now produced by three manufacturers each of whom has strictly defined, geographical sole rights of production. Whilst there is a world championship for French-speaking players, attempts to produce one for the English speakers have, so far, failed to materialize even though the subject has been under discussion for a number of years. Recognized world records for English speakers exist and one of these is mentioned at the entry for **quetzal**.

SCRABBLE® ADJUDICATION See below

SCRABBLE® ADJUDICATION On 13 April 1987 the *Daily Mirror* published a small article entitled 'Ten Words You Are Not Allowed In Scrabble'. It listed those ten ordinary, everyday words together with its reasons for declaring them to be invalid. However, the *Daily Mirror* made a slight error – nine out of its selection of ten words *are* allowed in Scrabble!

It is reasonable to suppose that the writer of the article had knowledge of the rules of the UK Scrabble championship and used *Chambers 20th Century Dictionary* (the internal evidence of that article permits no other interpretation), so how can such a catalogue of errors have arisen? First, the words and the judgement of the *Mirror*:– **aardvark**, foreign; **castanet**, but you can use **castanets**; **mini**, an abbreviation; **dieter**, classed as Shakespearean; **pizza**, foreign; **tsarina**, not listed; **pasta**, foreign; **moaner**, not listed; **coleslaw**, only with hyphen; **dodgems**, needs capital letter.

For a start, both **moaner** and **tsarina** *are* listed in *Chambers*. These are found under the main entry headings of **moan** and **tsar** respectively. It would seem that the writer of that article, having failed to discover separate, individual entries for **moaner** and **tsarina**, assumed that they did not exist in that major work. **Mini** is *not* an abbreviation. *Chambers* gives a choice of its being either a short form of **mini-skirt** or **mini-car** or a colloquial adjective with a *sense* of

Cont overleaf

miniature. Perfectly valid for play. **Dieter**. *Chambers* gives two meanings for this word only *one* of which it assigns to Shakespeare. In the cases of **pizza** and **pasta**, the label [*It.*], which is given *after* the definitions of the words, signifies their etymology. They are *not* foreign. What the *Mirror*'s writer has done here is to confuse *Chambers'* labelling system for differentiating between words of foreign origin and foreign words.

The reasons given in the *Mirror* article for disallowing **aardvark, castanet** and **coleslaw** are correct *but* only in respect of *Chambers* and the UK championship. They are *not* correct as far as the game itself is concerned. *The Official Scrabble Players Dictionary* accepts all three of them and the *Advanced Dictionary* fully agrees with its verdict. The *Daily Mirror* was, however, correct in its judgment on **Dodgems**.

Basic errors such as these are one of the reasons why the serious UK Scrabble movement attends courses on word adjudication conducted by the editor of *Chambers Dictionary*. But, even these are not foolproof.

The March 1987 issue of the Scrabble enthusiasts' magazine, *Onwords*, challenged no fewer than 11 of the 55 adjudication verdicts of the editor of *Chambers*; a ratio of 1 in 5 where a word is likely to prove contentious. Three simple examples should suffice.

1 **abies**. *Invalid*, said *Chambers*, which is sensible as the *vb* **aby** is inflected as **abought, abying, abys**. *Valid*, said *Onwords*, quoting *Chambers*' own definition: '**Abies** *n* the genus of the true firs: (without *cap.*) a tree of the genus'.

2 **maguses**. *Valid*, said *Chambers*. *Invalid*, said *Onwords*, the only plural of **magus** is **magi** which is clearly given in *Chambers*. (It is also the only plural shown in every other dictionary apart from the *Oxford English*, which additionally supplies the *Obs* form, **magy**.)

3 **uns**. *Valid*, said *Chambers*. *Invalid*, said *Onwords*, pronouns do not take plurals.

The magazine article concluded with some sensible advice on adjudication which is worth repeating.

'Always check for a word in its logical alphabetical position first.
Always read the entire entry carefully, twice if necessary.
Be wary of misreading definitions that span more than one line.
Look for the positions of commas, colons and full stops.
If you can't find the word then check at likely "root" entries or variant spellings that it might be given under.
If the entry is dubious allow the benefit of the doubt to give greater consistency.'

No such problems arise with the American work, *The Official Scrabble Players Dictionary*. It supplies all verbal inflections, plurals and adverbial and adjectival comparatives and superlatives where applicable. The rule is simple. If the word is listed, you can use it. If the word is not listed, you cannot. The only drawback is that its word power is inferior to *Chambers*.

SCRABBLE® AS PLAYED IN FRANCE The foreign language Scrabble sets can be very different to the English. Naturally the Russian and the Arabic versions are bound to be completely different, but even the French, Dutch and German sets are different to ours due to differences in frequency of letter usage. Even so, the basic game is the same.

The French, however, play all of their major championships to a completely different version of the game known as **duplicate**. **Duplicate** is very popular and is sometimes played, in English, in the British Scrabble Clubs. It is an ideal game for a large group of people so, for the sake of convenient illustration, imagine the game played in a full classroom.

Each student has a Scrabble set. The letter tiles are removed and displayed face uppermost so that every letter can be seen. The teacher also has a Scrabble set but his or her tiles remain in the bag. The teacher now draws the first seven tiles at random. Suppose that the letters A, C, H, Q, T, Y and Z are drawn. The students select those same letters and now attempt to make the highest score each can create. At the expiry of no more than two minutes the students record their own individual scores. The *highest* individual score is now determined. Scores for such as CAT (10 points), HAT (12 points), CHAT or HAY (18 points each) are easily beaten by YACHT which can score 26, 28 or 34 points according to where it is positioned relative to either 'double-letter' square on the central line containing the 'starting' square. If the highest score obtained happened to be YACHT for 28 points then the teacher copies this *exact* placement directly onto his or her own Scrabble board. *Without amending their scores*, the students remove their various CAT's, HAT's, CHAT's and HAY's from their own boards replacing these with YACHT *exactly as scored* (i.e. if the 34 points position has now been discovered it *cannot* be used). The Q and the Z remain on the rack.

The teacher now draws five replacement tiles and play continues as before (note: As Scrabble® is a proprietary game it is a breach of copyright to produce a large scale Scrabble board for convenient demonstration. Any group leader who would wish to do so must first approach the licensed manufacturer.)

scrabe *S & dial n* the Manx shearwater, an oceanic bird which skims the water surface pursuing fish

scrae *var fm* (*erron*) *n* **scree**

scrapen *obs pa ppl vb* scrape

scrapie *n* a virus which causes acute itching in sheep

scraul *obs fm now dial vb* **scrawl**

scraule *obs fm now dial vb* **scrawl**

scrawl (*n*/*vb*) *now dial vb* to crawl

scrawle *obs fm now dial vb* **scrawl**

scraye *var fm n* **scray**, the common tern

screak *n* a shrill cry *vb* to utter a shrill cry – hence, **screaking** *n* the uttering of a screak

screamy *collq adj* inclined to scream: various *fig* senses such as of colour or of temperament

screde *obs vb* to clothe, array

scree *n* a steep slope of loose material, mainly stones, on a mountain side: the material of such a slope

screed (*n*) *now dial vb* to tear: to make the sound of tearing

screeder *n* one who lays a finishing surface of mortar to a floor or wall

screeve *S n* a begging letter *now dial vb* to ooze *dial vb* of a horse, to have the legs split apart when running on ice *slg vb* to create the work of a pavement artist

screigh *var fm S n*/*vb* **skreigh**

screive *var fm now dial vb* **screeve**

screme *Obs fm vb* **scream**

screpe *Obs vb* to scratch (out)

screte *obs adj* supple

scried *pa pple vb* scry

scrier *obs fm n* **scryer**

scries see **scry**

scrieve *var fm S n*/*slg vb* **screeve**

scrike *now dial n*/*vb* (to utter) a shrill, harsh cry

scriker *now dial n* one who scrikes

scrine *obs n* a box containing a relic of a saint

scringe *n* a foot seine (see **seine**) *dial vb* to fish with a foot seine *now dial vb* to flinch, cower: hunch the shoulders from the effects of cold

scripe *obs fm n* **scrip**, a small satchel

scrive *vb* using a pointed instrument to mark (wood or metal) with the outline of intended cutting or shaping *n* a tool for this purpose *Obs n* a noise

scrod *US n* a (cooked) cod of less than 3 lbs *US vb* to break into small pieces prior to cooking

scrode *var fm US n* **scrod**

scrofula *n* tuberculosis *esp* of the lymphatic glands. It is also known as the king's evil as, traditionally, it can be cured by the touch of an annointed king (the coronation of a monarch being a religious ceremony of great significance). The first British monarch to apply the touch was the saint, Edward the Confessor (1042–1066) and the last who attempted it was Queen Anne (1702–1714) who touched Dr Johnson, in 1712, but failed to cure him. The tradition had existed in France long before the time of Edward the Confessor

scrone *obs S fm n* **scorn**

scroop *n* a harsh, strident noise

scrotal *adj* of or pertaining to the scrotum

scroudge *var fm n/vb* **scrouge**

scrouge *n/vb* (to) crowd (ironically, the American dictionaries tend to regard the word as British *dial* whereas British dictionaries tend to regard it as an American noun meaning a difficult task, with the above senses as *collq*)

scrouger *US n* something large

scrowe *obs fm n* **scrow**, a strip of leather used for making glue

scruitore *var fm n* **scrutoire**

scrump *dial vb* to steal apples from an orchard or garden

scrunt *S n* a tree stump

scrutoire *n* a writing desk

scry *vb* to see images of a clairvoyant nature in such as a crystal ball or a bowl of clear water (*infl fms* **scries, scried, scrying**)

scryer *n* one who scries (see **scry**)

scryne *var fm obs n* **scrine**

scuddle *now dial vb* to run away *obs S vb* to perform menial kitchen duties

scudler *var fm Shet n* **skudler**, the leader of a festive group wearing disguises: one who conducts a festival *obs S n* a scullion

sculpe *var fm obs vb* **sculp**, to carve or engrave

sculpin *n* any of various small, spiny, worthless fishes *US adj* worthless

scumber *now dial n* fox dung *dial n* dirt, filth *now dial vb* of a fox, to dung

scumer *obs fm now dial vb* **scumber**

scummer *n* a shallow ladle used for removing scum off a liquid *obs n* one who gathers scum: a pirate *obs vb* to scoop up: to make a piratical raid *obs fm vb* **scumber**

scunner *S & dial n* a strong disgust *S & dial vb* to disgust or sicken

scurling *var fm S & dial n* **skirling** (see **skirle**)

scut *n* a short, erect tail as that of a rabbit or a deer *obs vb* to cut short

scutal *adj* of or pertaining to a shield

scutate *adj* of animals, covered with large flat scales: of botanical features, buckler shaped

scutter *n* a noisy rush *collq & dial vb* to rush about *obs vb* to suffer diarrhoea

Scylla *n* the mythical six-headed monster who sat on a rock in the sea opposite to the underwater lair of Charybdis, an equally dangerous monster, whose swallowing of seawater created a whirlpool. The phrase, *between Scylla and Charybdis*, (between dangerous rocks and treacherous currents) is a proverbial expression for a choice between evil or disaster.

scyphi *pl* scyphus

scyphomancy *n* divination using a cup

scyphus *n* a large, Greek, stemless drinking vessel: a cup-shaped botanical structure (*pl* **scyphi**)

scytale *n* the Spartan method of secret writing consisting of two identical wooden batons and a long narrow strip of parchment. Both the sender and the receiver of a message possess one of these batons. The parchment is wound around the sender's baton so that the edges touch, there is no space between the folds and the entire surface is covered. The message is then recorded in a series of horizontal bands around the baton so that when the spiralling parchment is unwound the letters have no connection and appear to be all broken up. Only the receiver's baton can be used for deciphering as it is the only one with identical dimensions. (For more sophisticated secret transmissions see **CODES AND CIPHERS**.): such a baton (*pl* **scytalae**): the parchment used

scytalae *see* **scytale** (2nd definition)

sdaine *var fm obs vb* **sdeign**

'sdeath *arch interj* an abbreviated form of the expression, *God's death*, used as an oath of affirmation (GAME PLAYER'S note: Unlike accents, apostrophes invalidate words for games play)

sdeign *obs vb* to disdain

sdeigne *var fm obs vb* **sdeign**

sdein *var fm obs vb* **sdeign**

se *n* a Japanese measure of area

sea-born *adj* (of mythological beings) originating in the sea (GAME PLAYERS see **sea-card** below)

sea-card *n* a compass card *obs n* a sea chart (GAME PLAYER'S note: Hyphenated, therefore not valid for play)

sea cat *n* any catfish capable of a marine existence: a weeverfish, a marine, bottom-living, poisonous fish related to red mullet

sea cucumber *n* any of 900 different species of marine animals which vaguely resemble a plump, slimy sausage with sprigs of parsley at one end (the mouth part) and a hole at the other (also see **pearlfish, pea crab** and **scale-worm**)

sea devil *n* a devil supposed to dwell in the sea: any of various ugly marine creatures *esp* the toadfish, frogfish and octopus: the devil ray

seadog *n* a fogbow, a sort of fog rainbow

sea dog *n* an old sailor: a pirate or privateer: a dogfish: the common seal *dial n* a rough wave in an estuary *her n* a dog, similar in appearance to the extinct breed of talbot, with a scaly skin, fins, webbed feet and a tail like a beaver's

sea fir *n* a marine animal which, remarkably, only exists every alternate generation. As a sea fir it looks like a tiny tree and it produces, asexually, a small bud of tissue on the end of each branch. Each bud eventually floats free as either a male or female medusa and this generation of mobile animals reproduces in a sexual fashion. The fertilized seed of the medusa generation then anchors itself to a suitable substratum – such as a frond of a large oarweed – and there develops into the plant-like sea fir. The common jellyfish, among other lower creatures, also exists only every other generation – being the offspring of a polyp called scyphistoma and, in turn, the parent of this plant-like animal.

sea fire *n* phosphorescence at sea

seafowl *n* any seabird

sea fret *n* a sea fog

seagirt *adj* (almost) completely surrounded by the sea

seake *obs fm vb* **seek**

sea king *n* a Norse piratical leader: a god of the sea

sealant *n* that which effectively plugs a leak

sealch *Ork & Shet n* a seal, the marine mammal

seale *obs fm n/vb* **seal**

sea lemon *n* a marine invertebrate closely related to the sea slug

sea lentil *n* gulfweed, a large, olive brown seaweed which occurs in huge 'meadows' in parts of the tropical Atlantic

sealer *n* one engaged in the trade of killing seals for their fur: a ship involved in such trade: one who affixes a (wax) seal to a document *obs n* an inspector of weights and measures

sealgh *var fm Ork & Shet n* **sealch**

sealpoint *n* a variety of Siamese cat having on its points, or extremities, the seal brown colour normally associated with its close relative, the Burmese cat

seal ring *n* a signet ring

sea-mat *n* hornwrack, a common seaweed-like colony of animals very low in the evolutionary scale (GAME PLAYERS see **sea-card**)

seame *obs S fm vb* **seem**

sea melon *n* a species of sea cucumber

seamer *n* a seaming machine

sea moth *n* a little fish of the Indo-Pacific waters so peculiar that it not only comprises its own family but even has an order to itself. It has a tiny mouth underneath an elongated snout and large, winglike pectoral fins, but is incapable of using them to stimulate any form of flight.

seamount *n* an undersea mountain of or greater than 3,000 ft

sea mouse *n* a fat, furry scaleworm which lives, for the most part, buried in coastal sand or mud (*pl* **sea mice**)

seamster *n* a tailor, a seamstress

Seamus *var fm pers n* **James**, meaning 'a heel'

sean *var fm n/vb* **seine** (+*cap*) *var fm masc pers n* **John**, meaning 'God is gracious'

sea orm *n* a supposed sea creature which lives off the Norwegian coast and was described by Pontopiddan in his *Natural History of Norway* (also see **Stronsay monster**)

sea owl *n* the henfish or lumpsucker, a bulky, ungainly, marine fish of British and European coastal waters which can attain a length of two feet. The female lays a mass of eggs in a loose ball which the male zealously guards and has been known to suffer great injury in their defence. Not eaten in Britain, it is a smoked delicacy on the continent.

seap *US & dial var fm vb* **seep**, to ooze, drip or percolate, with the additional sense, to soak

sea pansy *n* a species of sea pen

sea parrot *n* the puffin

sea pen *n* a colony of polyps living on a central axis, the total effect of which gives an appearance of a quill pen. The whole unit, like the Portuguese man-of-war, functions as a single marine animal. (See **Portuguese man-of-war)**

seapt *obs fm n* **sept**, a clan

sear *vb* to burn, to scorch (*lit/fig*): using a hot iron, to brand or to cauterize: to (cause to) wither: to destroy feeling (*fig*) *poet adj* dried up

searat *n* a pirate

searce *arch n* a riddle, sieve or strainer *arch vb* to sieve (also *fig*)

searer *comp adj* sear

searest *sup adj* sear

sea risk *n* any insurable marine hazard

sea robin *n* the noisiest species of gurnard

sea slug *n* any of various exquisitely coloured marine gasteropods which, unlike the land slugs, are among the most beautiful of the invertebrates. It is an hermaphrodite and mutual cross-fertilization is the rule. The typical sea slug, like the sea lemon, feeds on sponges though others prefer to eat other plant-like animals such as the sea anemone and the sea fir. (Also see **cerata**)

sea squirt *n* one of various species of marine creatures which resemble neither fishes nor plants but look like leather bottles. Despite its lifeless appearance it is included in the same major group of the animal kingdom as Man himself. It is a possible ancestor of the vertebrates, a fact which has given rise to the delightful thought that, '*Man was once a leather bottle*.'

sea star *n* starfish, a star-shaped marine animal akin to the sea urchin, sea lily and sea cucumber

seasure *obs fm n* **seizure**

sea tang *n* any of various types of brown seaweed

sea term *n* any word of specific maritime usage

seatl *obs fm n* **settle**

seaton *obs fm n* **seton**

seatrain *US n* a ship equipped to carry railway rolling stock

seat-rent *n* the amount paid for reserved personal seating in a church (GAME PLAYERS see **sea-card**)

seaver *obs fm vb* **sever**

sea wasp *n* any of various jellyfishes which have a boxlike shape and can deliver some form of sting. One particular Australian species is not only one of the most deadly creatures living, but its 30 foot tentacles are practically invisible. Its poison, even when diluted 10,000 times, can kill laboratory animals within seconds.

sea wolf *n* a wolf fish, one of the comparatively gigantic species of blennies (see **blenny**): a pirate, a pirate ship *obs n* a fabulous four-footed beast of rapine which lived both in the sea and on land, dieting mainly on fish

seaworm *n* any wormlike marine creature

Sebat *var fm n* **Shebat**

secant *adj* of one geometric line or surface to another, cutting or intersecting *n* a trigonometric function of an angle

secede *vb* to make a formal withdrawal from membership of such as a political party, religious body or federation

seceder *n* one who secedes (+*cap*) *n* a member of the Secession Church

secern *vb* to separate in thought: to discriminate

secernent *adj* designating that which secretes *n* a secreting organ

seckel *n* a pear

seckle *var fm n* **seckel**

seconde *n* the second of the eight parries in sword fencing

secreta *n* something kept hidden (*pl* **secretae**) *n pl* secreted matter, such as dung

secreter (*comp adj*) *obs n* one who conceals himself

secretin *n* a hormone which stimulates the pancreas

secretness *n* a secrecy: that which is secret (GAME PLAYER'S note: The dictionary used for the UK Scrabble championship lists the word as an undefined but extant noun. In the first sense the last recorded usage was 1654, in the second sense 1623. Other experts consider the word *obs* in both senses.)

secretor *n* one who or that which secretes

sectarial *adj* pertaining to or distinctive of a sect

sectoral *adj* pertaining to a sector

sectorial *adj* of or pertaining to a sector: of premolar teeth, having a cutting function

secund *adj* of plants, having parts on, or turned to, the same side

securance *n* assurance, security

securitan *obs n* one who is characterized by a sense of freedom from fear

sedarim *pl* seder

sedater *comp adj* sedate

sede *obs fm n/vb* **seed**

sedelip *Obs fm n* **seedlip**

sedent *adj* sitting

seder *n* a Jewish ceremonial dinner (*pl* **seders, sedarim)**

sederunt *S n* the sitting of a judicial body *esp* an ecclesiastical assembly: a sitting for a discussion: the persons present at either of such *modf n* as **sederunt book** the book of record

sedge *(n) dial vb* of oats, to suffer sedging

sedging *n* a disease of oats characterized by a swelling of the stem near the ground

sedile *n* see *pl* **sedilia**

sedilia *n pl* a series of (three) seats, often very ornate, placed on the south side of the choir for use by the clergy (*sing* **sedile**, either one of these seats separately considered or a single seat serving a similar purpose)

sedlep *Obs fm n* **seedlip**

seductor *obs n* one who misleads, a seducer

seed-lac *n* the resin lac, crushed into small pieces and washed clean of colouring matter (GAME PLAYERS see **sea-card)**

seedlip *n* the basket of seeds carried by one sowing by hand

seedman *obs n* an ironic term for a Catholic clergyman who, during the persecution of the 16th and 17th centuries, was educated at a French seminary (the pun being related to semen): a seedsman, one who sells seeds (*pl* **seedmen)**

seed oil *n* oil from seeds

seedsman *n* one who sells seeds

seeer *n* one who sees in a simple sense as opposed to a **seer**, one with psychic gifts

seeing *n* the action of the *vb* see: sight, vision

seel *vb* to stitch together the eyelids of a hawk *esp* during the period of falconry training: to hoodwink (*fig*) *obs vb* of a horse, to grow white hairs above the eyes: of a ship, to lurch suddenly to one side (during a storm)

seele *obs n* a canopy: a sudden lurching of a ship (also see **seel**) *obs fm vb* **ceil**

seeling *n* the action of the *vb* **seel** in senses other than growing hair

seely *now dial adj* happy, blissful, fortunate: pious, holy, good: innocent, harmless: deserving of pity: insignificant, trifling, feeble: frail, worn out: foolish, simple

seemer *n* one who makes a pretence or show

seene *var fm obs n* **sene**, a synod

seenle *var fm S adv* **sendle**

seering *var fm n* **cering**

seether *Obs n* one whose task is to boil something *nonce n* a kettle

seggar *var fm n* **saggar**

segno *n* a sign which marks the beginning and the end of a musical repetition (*pl* **segni, segnos)**

segreant *her adj* of a griffin with raised wings

seicento *n* the 17th century in reference to Italian arts

seiger *obs fm n* **sieger**

seile *obs fm vbs* **ceil, sail, seel**

seindle *var fm S adv* **sendle**

seine *n* one of various marine fishing nets the open ends of which are drawn together to enclose the catch. The different types are (*a*) the **great** or **deepwater seine**, the largest of the seines (*b*) the **tuck net** or **tuck seine**, a smaller net used inside the great seine (*c*) the **foot** or **ground seine**, a small net used close to the shore *vb* to fish with a seine

seinel *var fm S adv* **sendle**

seiner *n* a fisherman who uses either the great or the foot seine

seing *var fm obs n* **sene**, a synod

seinle *var fm S adv* **sendle**

seip *US & dial var fm vb* **seep** (see **seap**)

seipter *Obs fm n* **sceptre**

seise *vb* to seize in the legal sense of to put in possession

seisen *obs fm n* **seisin**

seiser *obs n* seizure

seisin *n* freehold possession *obs vb* to seize

seisiner *Obs S n* one in lawful possession (of land)

seism *n* an earthquake

seismal *adj* relating to or caused by earthquakes

seisor *var fm obs n* **seiser**

seldseen *obs adj* seldom seen

sele *now dial n* happiness: favourable time *obs adj* good *obs fm vb* **ceil**

Selene *pers n* the Greek goddess of the moon

selenic *adj* of the moon: of the non-metallic element, selenium

selenite *n* a stone known to the ancients and having some magical properties: sulphate of lime in crystalline form: a salt of selenious acid: a moonite or, as explained by the coiner in 1645, a 'lunary man' (other writers preferred it to moonite and, even as late as 1864, had these 'lunary men' living in hillocks on the moon)

selenitic *adj* of or pertaining to the moon

selenium *n* a grey, crystalline, non-metallic element of the sulphur group (symbol Se)

selfeist *obs fm n* **selfist**

selfer *Obs fm n/adj* **silver**

selfist *n* a self-centred or selfish person

self-lost *adj* lost through one's own actions (GAME PLAYERS see **sea-card**)

selha *n* a Hebrew scriptural word with the sense of 'pause'

Selima *fem fm masc pers n* **Solomon**, meaning 'peaceable'

Selina *fem pers n* meaning 'heavenly'

selly *obs adj* strange, marvellous *obs adv* strangely, marvellously *obs n* strangeness: that which is strange or marvellous

selvas *n pl* tracts of wet forest in the Amazon basin (*sing* (rare) **selva**)

selver *Obs fm n/adj* **silver**

sely *obs fm now dial adj* **seely**

semantic *adj* of or pertaining to meaning: of or pertaining to semantics *n pl* (as *n sing*) the study of speech forms etc

semantra *pl* semantron

semantron *n* a percussion bar struck in Greek churches and in mosques (*pl* **semantra**)

sematic *adj* of the conspicuous colouring of

various creatures, acting as a warning of danger (i.e. certain brightly coloured creatures are poisonous if eaten, and others are capable of delivering a poison without endangering themselves)

semble *vb* used in legal pronouncements with a sense of 'it seems' *obs vb* to assemble: to resemble *obs adj* like or similar *obs n* assembly

seme *obs fm n/vb* **seam** *obs fm vb* **seem** *var fm Obs vb* **seem**, to reconcile: to confirm

semée *her n* a repetition of a small figure, such as the fleur-de-lys, over the whole design

sememe *n* a unit of meaning

semen *n* the germinating fluid of a male (*pl* **semens, semina**)

semese *adj* half-eaten

semestrial *adj* half-yearly

semie *var fm collq n* **semi**, a semi-detached house

semi-grand *n* a word exclusive to one particular dictionary which defines it as 'a square piano with a curtailed keyboard'. The writer consulted two of the country's leading piano makers, neither of whom knew the term, and could only suggest that it is a synonym for a **square grand**, the earliest of the grand pianos. If so, it would be Victorian (GAME PLAYERS see **sea-card**)

semilunar *adj* half-moon shaped *n* an object of such shape

semilunate *adj* half-moon shaped

semilune *n* any half-moon shaped object

semina *pl* semen

seminal (*adj*) *obs n* a seed (*lit/fig*): a duct conveying semen

seminarial *adj* of or pertaining to a seminary

seminate *vb* to sow: to propagate

semination *n* the production of seed: the natural dispersion of such: the process of sowing (*lit/fig*)

semiotics *n* the theory of sign systems in language

semiped *n* a metric half foot (see **metric foot**)

semi-ring *n* a half ring (GAME PLAYERS see **sea-card**)

semitar *obs fm n* **scimitar**

Semite *n* one who speaks a Semitic language such as Arabic or Hebrew: a descendant of Shem, the Biblical character after whom the group of languages is named

Semitist *n* a Semitic scholar

semlar *var fm obs n* **somler**

semper *Latin adv* always

semple *S fm adj/n* **simple**

sempre *adv* in music, always or throughout

sempster *var fm n* **seamster**

semuncial *adj* of or belonging to half an ounce

senarius *n* (Greek or Latin) verse of six metrical feet (*pl* **senarii**)

senary *adj* pertaining to the number 6

sendal *n* a thin, rich, silken material: a fine linen: a garment made from sendal

sendet *obs pa t vb* send

sendle *S adv* seldom (*var fm incl* **seindle, sindle, seenle, seinel, seinle**)

sendre *obs vb* to putrify

sene *obs n* a synod: senna *Obs n* vision: a senate *obs S fm arch vb* **sain**

Seneca *n* a member of a Red Indian tribe of New York State: the language of that tribe

senega *n* an American milkwort: its dried root, supposedly good for snakebite

senescent *adj* growing old, elderly

sengle *obs fm n* **cingle**

Senhora *n* the Portuguese style of address for a married woman (*–cap*) *n* a Portuguese or Brazilian married woman

senie *var fm obs n* **sene**, senna

senile (*adj*) *n* one who is senile

sennet *n* the barracuda, a fierce marine fish one species of which (the great barracuda) achieves a length of up to eight feet *var fm n* **sennit** (see **sinnet**)

sennit *n* sinnet

senoper *var fm obs n* **sinoper**

senopia *n* an improvement of near vision (*pl* **senopias**)

señor *n* the Spanish equivalent of Mr when placed before a name, or of sir as a mode of address: a Spaniard (*pl* **señors, señores**)

señora *n* the *fem* equivalent of señor

señorita *n* an unmarried Spanish woman or girl

sensate *adj* perceived by the senses *vb* to perceive by sense

senser *obs fm n* **censer**

sensile *adj* capable of perception

sensilla *pl* sensillum

sensillum *n* a simple sense organ of an insect (*pl* **sensilla**)

sensism *n* the doctrine that all knowledge is derived from the senses

sensor *n* anything capable of detecting a stimulus and producing a response *obs fm ns* **censer, censor**

sensoria *pl* sensorium

sensorial *adj* of or relating to the senses or the power of sensation

sensorium *n* the nervous system: the complete sensory apparatus of an organism (*pl* **sensoria**)

sent (*pa pple*) *arch fm n/vb* **scent**

sentencer *n* one who sentences

senting *obs fm n* **scenting**

sentre *Obs her n* an obscure word defined, in 1486, as '*a stakar of tentis*' in the army (a tent stake?)

sepad *ghost vb* to suppose (see **ghost word**)

sepal *n* one of the individual leaves of the outer covering of a flower

sepaline *adj* of or belonging to a sepal

sepaloid *adj* of the nature of a sepal, resembling a sepal

sepalous a word which appears in three different dictionaries as an adjective, though none supplies a definition. (As a suffix, '**-sepalous**' is used to mean having sepals of a specified type and number.) Its anagram is **espousal**.

separator *n* one who or that which separates

sephen *n* a species of stingray common to the Red Sea

sepiment *n* a hedge

sepiost *var fm n* **sepiostaire**, cuttlebone, the internal shell of the cuttlefish

seposit *obs vb* to set aside or apart

sepses *pl* sepsis

sepsis *n* invasion by bacteria (*pl* **sepses**)

septa *pl* septum

septal *adj* pertaining to a sept or clan: of a partition

septar *obs fm n* **sceptre**

septaria *pl* septarium, a nodule of limestone or ironstone formerly used for cement

septate *adj* partitioned

septennium *n* a period of seven years (*pl* **septennia**)

septer *obs fm n* **sceptre**

septic *(adj) n* an agent producing sepsis

septical *adj* septic

septicidal *adj* designating a form of dehiscence whereby the pod splits through its natural partitions

septier *n* an old French measure of capacity for corn, approximating to four bushels

septile *adj* pertaining to a septum

septimal *adj* of a numerical system, based on the number 7

septime *n* one of the parries in the sport of fencing

septine *n* a poisonous substance produced during an organic disorder

septir *Obs fm n* **sceptre**

septor *obs fm n* **sceptre**

septour *obs fm n* **sceptre**

septre *obs fm n* **sceptre**

septum *n* a partition (*pl* **septa**)

septuple *adj* sevenfold: having seven musical beats to the bar *n* the seventh multiple *vb* to multiply by seven

seq *abbreviated fm of Latin* **sequens**, it follows (*pl* **seqq**, the following) (GAME PLAYER'S note: Both **seq** and its *var fm* **sq**, together with their respective plurals **seqq** and **sqq**, are invalid for play)

seqq *see* **seq**

sequar *var fm Obs n* **siquare**, a moment of time

sequeale *obs fm n* **sequel**

sequela *n* a morbid condition resulting from a previous disease: a consequence (*pl* **sequelae**)

sequin *n* a gold coin of the former Venetian republic: a Turkish gold coin: a (gold) coin-shaped ornament or small spangle for such as a dress *vb* to ornament with such spangles (hence, *adj* **sequinned**)

sérac *n* a tower of ice on a glacier

serafile *n* one of or the complete body of officers or men detailed to ride in the rear rank of a squadron when in line

seragli *obs pl* seraglio

seraglio *n* the harem of a Muslim house or palace: the inmates of that harem: the palace of a sultan *esp* that at Istanbul (*pl* **seraglios** *obs pl* **seragli**)

serail *n* seraglio

seral *adj* of a plant community in a stage of succession: of millstone grit formation in coal measures *n* such millstone grit

serang *n* a lascar boatswain or captain

serape *n* a Spanish-American shawl or plaid: a Mexican riding blanket

seraph *n* an angel or being of the highest order, seen in Isaiah's vision hovering above the throne of God (*pl* **seraphim**): a fossil shell (*pl* **seraphs**): a former gold coin of Turkey (*pl* **seraphs** *obs pl* **seraphes**)

seraphim *pl* seraph *n* a Swedish order of chivalry: a fossil crustacean with feather-like markings on its shell: a type of moth, the wings of which are so shaped as to give it an appearance of having six wings (*pl* **seraphims**)

seraphin *n* any of various coins *esp* a silver coin formerly current in India *obs fm n pl* **seraphim**

seraphine *n* a type of coarse-toned early harmonium *obs fm n* **seraphin**

Serapic *adj* of or pertaining to Serapis

Serapis *pers n* the monotheistic god worshipped by the pharaoh, Ptolemy I, who rejected the traditional gods of Egypt

serce *obs fm arch n/vb* **searce** *obs S fm vb* **search**

serd *var fm obs vb* **sard**

serdab *n* a secret room in a pyramid: an underground chamber

sere *var fm n/vb* **cere** *var fm vb* **sear**

serein *n* a fine rain falling after sunset

Serena *fem pers n* meaning 'calm'

serenata *n* a (symphonic) serenade

serene *(adj) n* serenity, tranquility *vb* to make serene

serest *sup adj* sere, withered or dry

serf *(n) obs fm vb* **serve**

serfish *adj* like a serf in the sense of being servile

sergiant *obs fm n* **sergeant**

serging *US n* a process of applying a finish to the raw edges of fabric

seriant *obs fm n* **sergeant**

seriate *adj* forming a series *vb* to put into a series

sericin *n* silk glue, the gelatinous constituent of silk

sericitic *adj* containing or having the character of the fibrous variety of common mica, seritice

sericon *n* one of ten different names (the other names no longer extant) given by alchemists to a substance which, they believed, assisted in the transmutation of base metal into gold (note: It is reasonable to ignore any definition of the word which gives an explanation – even a conjectured explanation – of that substance. If the mediaeval alchemists had one particular chemical in mind they would be bound, by the very nature of the subject, to be utterly secretive about it. Most definitions are based on the 'etymology' of that surviving word which is *only one of ten different names*. If the word *does* contain any clue it is probably cryptic and, if it is as simple as an anagram, which language would it be in?)

seriema *n* either of two species of South American birds resembling small brown cranes. Poor of flight, the adults are treated as game by the South American Indians who also capture the young, which they rear among their chickens. These captive birds warn the domestic fowl of predators long before they would otherwise be aware of them. The diet of the seriema includes snakes.

serif *n* in typefaces such as used by a printer, that small decorative line at the extremity of a main stroke of a letter

seriff *var fm n* **serif**

serine *n* an amino acid

serinette *n* a bird organ, a small barrel organ used for teaching birds to sing

seringa *n* any of various plants *esp* a species of shrub popular in gardens

serion *Obs fm n* **surgeon**

seriph *var fm ns* **serif, shereef**

serment *obs n* an oath *obs fm n* **sermon**

sermonic *adj* (usually in a deprecatory sense) of the form or nature of a sermon

sermonical *adj* sermon-like

sermonics *n pl* sermonizing

seron *n* a package of exotic items wrapped in the hide of an animal

serone *arch fm n* **seron**

seroon *var fm n* **seron**

serosa *n* a thin membrane lining certain bodily cavities (*pl* **serosae, serosas**)

serosal *adj* of or pertaining to serosae

serotine *adj* late in development (*lit/fig*) *n* a species of small European bat which flies late in the evening: any late flowering plant

serotonin *n* a crystalline protein found in many plants and animals and in the serum of clotted human blood

serou *var fm n* **serow**

serous *adj* of or resembling serum

serow *n* a medium-sized, Asiatic goat-antelope with long, mule-like ears

serpe *var fm obs n* **sarpe**, a neckband

serpenter *obs n* a snake-like trail

serpentin *n* a long, coloured, paper ribbon thrown into the air as a celebration

serpigo *n* ringworm or a similar skin disease (*pl* **serpigines, serpigoes**)

serpula *n* the wormshell, a marine annelid (*pl* **serpulae**)

serpulae *pl* serpula

serra *n* a saw: a saw-like range of mountains (*pl* **serrae, serras**)

serrae *pl* serra

serran *n* the black sea-bass or other fish of the genus *Serranus* or the family *Serranidea*

serranid *n* a grouper

serranoid *adj/n* (of) a grouper

serrate *vb* to make saw-toothed

serrature *n* serration or indentation like that of a saw

serreli *Obs fm obs adj* **sirly**

serry *vb* to (cause to) press lines of military personnel closely together *dial fm adj* **sorry**

sertain *Obs fm adj/n* **certain**

sertan *Obs fm adj/adv/n* **certain**

serte *obs n* the service owed to a lord by a servant

serten *obs fm n/adj/adv* **certain**

serval *n* an unusually long-legged and large eared member of the cat family found in sub-Saharan Africa

servant (*n*) *obs vb* to provide with a servant: to put (oneself) in subjection to

servat *dial fm arch n* **servet**

servatore *obs fm n* **servitor**

serven *Obs fm vb* **serve**

servet *arch fm n* **serviette** *obs fm n* **sherbet**

servewe *obs fm arch n/vb* **surview**

Servian *adj* of Servius Tullius, a little boy who, according to Livy, was lying asleep when his head was suddenly and inexplicably encased in flames. Tarquin, the king of ancient Rome, and his queen were rushed to the spot and the queen refused permission for anyone to douse the fire. When the boy awoke he was completely unharmed by the experience and was adopted by Tarquin, eventually succeeding him as king to have a glorious reign which lasted 44 years. *var fm adj/n* **Serbian**

servient *adj* subordinate

servit *dial fm arch n* **servet**

Servite *n* a friar or nun of the order of the Servants of the blessed Virgin Mary, founded at Florence in 1233 *adj* of or pertaining to this order

serviter *S n* a table napkin *obs fm n* **servitor**

servitor *n* one to whom James I assigned land in Ulster for military service: a lover: a manservant

servitress *n* a female servant

sesame *n* an East Indian plant widely cultivated for its seeds which produce gingili or sweet oil: a magic password

sese *var fm obs vb* **cess** *obs fm vbs* **cease, seize**

seseli *n* any of several umbelliferous plants

sess *obs vb* to assess for taxation: to tax

sessile *adj* stalkless

sessle *dial vb* to fidget

sesster *obs fm n* **sester**

sester *n* a former dry measure equal to eight bushels: a former liquid measure for alcohol

sesterce *n* an old Roman coin of varying value, originally the equivalent of $2\frac{1}{2}$ asses, later 4 asses (see **as**): a quarter of a denarius (see **£ s d** – under **L**)

sestertia *pl* sestertium, the sum of a thousand sesterces

sestertii *pl* sestertius, a sesterce

sestet *n* in prosody, the last six lines of a sonnet: in music, a group of six performers (vocal or instrumental): music specially written for such a group

sestina *n* a poem of six six-line stanzas introduced by a triplet and also known as a **sestine** or **sextine**

sestine *var fm n* **sestina**

seston *n* a species of plankton

sete *Obs S n* a group of wildfowl hunters (*pl* **setis**) *Obs adj* suitable *obs fm vb* **set**

sether *var fm Obs n* **seether**

Sethic *adj* of (the lineage of) Seth, the third son of Adam and Eve

setier *var fm n* **septier**

setiger *n* any bristly worm

setine *obs n* a wine made near Rome

setler *obs fm n* **settler**

setline *n* any of various strong fishing lines suspended between such as buoys and having shorter, baited lines attached

setness *n* the fact of being set

seton *n* a surgeon's thread which is used when it is necessary to seal a cavity in such a manner that it prevents healing up *vb* to apply such a thread

sette *var fm obs n* **settee**, a type of Mediterranean sailing ship having a long pointed prow *obs fm n* **set** *Obs fm n* **seat**

settel *Obs fm n* **settle**

setter *(n) dial vb* to perform an act of primitive immunization of doubtful efficacy by inserting a piece of foreign matter (such as the plant, setterwort) under the skin of an animal. The theory is that settering encourages the production of antibodies and the usual part of a cow chosen for this operation is its dewlap.

settlor *n* one, in law, who makes a settlement of property

setuale *obs fm n* **setwall**

setwall *n* the medicinal herb, valerian

sevener *n* one sentenced to seven years imprisonment: a score of seven runs from one hit at cricket (e.g. by such means as three actually run plus four from overthrows. The highest known score for a single hit in first class cricket is ten runs, which has been achieved twice.)

severer (*comp adj*) *n* one who severs

sevile *obs fm adj* **civil**

Sèvres *adj* of porcelain, made at Sèvres near Paris *n* such porcelain

sewar *obs fm n/vb* **sewer** (all senses other than one who sews)

sewarry *obs fm n* **sowarry**

sewel *var fm n* **shewel**

sewer *n* an (underground) drain: one who sews: an attendant at a meal or banquet concerned with such as seating and table arrangements and the tasting of food. The office of sewer to the Royal Household had expired by the 15th century though it continued for a while longer as a ceremonial office at a coronation. *vb* to furnish a system of (underground) drains *obs vb* to act as a sewer to the table *obs S fm n/vb* **sever**

sewrte *Obs fm n* **surety**

sewster *now S n* a seamstress

sewter *obs fm n* **suitor**

sextain *n* a stanza of six lines

sextan *n* a recurrent malarial fever

sextans *n* a Roman bronze coin worth a sixth of an as *obs n* a sixth part of an acre (+*cap*) *Austr n* a constellation, the sextant

sextar *n* an ancient Roman liquid measure

sexters *obs pl* sesterce

sextine *n* a sestina

sh *interj* command to silence

shaar *var fm obs n* **share**, the groin or pubic region *Obs fm n* **share**, a ploughshare

shackel *obs fm n* **shackle**

Shackleton *pers n* Sir Ernest Henry, (1874–1914) the Antarctic explorer

shadder *vb* to break up the larger pieces of lead ore

shaddock *n* a large, pear-shaped citrus fruit, the smaller and more globular variety of which is the grapefruit: the tree on which it grows (both the shaddock and grapefruit are also known as **pompelmoose, pomelo** or **pumelo**)

shader *n* one who or that which shades

shade tree *n* any tree planted for the specific purpose of providing shade

shadine *n* the fish, menhaden, preserved in oil (a trade term after the style of sardine)

shaglet *nonce n* a young shag or cormorant

shail *dial n* a crooked, shuffling or awkward manner of walking or moving *obs n* a scarecrow *now dial vb* to stumble: to walk or move in an awkward or shuffling manner

shaire *obs fm vb* **share**

shairn *var fm dial n* **sharn**, cow dung

Shaitan *pers n* Satan (−*cap*) *n* an evil spirit: a person of wickedness: a dust storm in India

Shaiva *n* a devotee of Shiva, a Hindu god of destruction and reproduction

shakey *var fm adj* **shaky**

shakle *now dial fm n* **shackle** *obs fm vb* **shackle**

shale (*n*) *now dial vb* to remove the shell or pod from (a nut or beans)

shaler *obs n* one who shells nuts

shalke *var fm obs poet n* **shalk**, a man

shalom *Hebr n* peace, a salutation used by Jews and sometimes used by a gentile as a gesture of goodwill towards a Jew

shalot *var fm n* **shallot**, an onionlike bulb with a mild garlic flavour *var fm n* **eschalot** or **shallot**, a small onion

shaltre *var fm Obs n* **shaltree**

shaltree *Obs n* a pole used on old ships presumably for such purposes as pushing the vessel away from the quayside (*pl* **shaltreen**)

shaltreen *pl Obs n* shaltree

shaly *adj* composed of or resembling shale (*comp* **shalier** *sup* **shaliest**)

shama *n* a type of Indian millet: a species of Indian songbird

shamal *n* the north(west) wind

shamer *n* one who or that which shames

shamus *US slg n* a gumshoe or private detective (*pl* **shamuses**) (+*cap*) *masc pers n* an Irish *fm* of **James**, meaning 'a heel'

shane *S fm (obs) obs vb* **sane**

shanker *n* one employed in making or finishing a (button, pin or nail) shank *S n* a stocking knitter: one who sinks shafts

shanny out of water see **blenny**

shapster *dial only var fm now dial n* **shepster**

shard *n* a fragment *esp* of broken earthenware: the hard outer coating of various beetles: a gap in a hedge *S n* a remnant *now dial n* a patch of cow dung *dial n* a notch in the blade of a tool *vb* to break into fragments: of a tree, to shed bark in flakes

sharde *obs fm now dial n* **shard**

share (*n*/*vb*) *obs n* the pubic region, hence the **sharewort** or **codwort** (both *obs*), a plant of such shape and identified as being *Pallensis spinosa*

shareman *n* a fisherman employed on a basis of a share of the profits from a catch *obs fm n* **shearman**

sharen *var fm S & dial n* **sharn**

sharling *obs fm n* **shearling**

sharn *S & dial n* cattle dung

sharne *obs fm S & dial n* **sharn**

sharnie *var fm dial n* **sharny**

sharny *dial adj* covered with dung *dial n* one who cleans out a cowshed

Sharon *fem pers n* derived from a Hebrew place name

sharp (*adj*/*adv*/*n*) *vb* to swindle or obtain by swindling *now dial vb* to sharpen

sharpe *obs fm now dial n* **shrape** *obs fm n*/*adj* **sharp**

sharpie *US n* a long, sharp, flat-bottomed sailing boat originally used for inshore fishing for such as oysters (GAME PLAYER'S note: The dictionary used for the North American Scrabble championship carries what appears to be an exclusive definition, '*a very alert person*'. The sense of a boat is found in both British and American dictionaries.)

sharp-set *adj* very hungry: eager, keen: keen for sexual gratification

'sharte *obs fm interj* **'sheart**

shaster *n* Hindu holy writing

shault *var fm S dial n* **shalt**, a pony *obs fm now dial n* **sholt**, a dog

shaw *arch n* a thicket or small wood *S n* the stalk and leaves of potatoes or turnips, treated as a single assembly of such: an individual item of such waste vegetation (*pl*, in either sense, **shaws**) *obs n* a hedge *S vb* to remove the shaws of vegetables *obs vb* to construct a hedge for a field

shawl (*n*) *vb* to cover with a shawl

shawle *var fm dial n* **shaul**, a wooden tub

shaya *n* an Indian plant, the root of which is the source of a red dye (*var fms* **chay, chaya**)

shayre *obs fm vb* **share**

she (*pron*) *var fm n*/*vb* **ski**

sheading *n* an administrative district of the Isle of Man

sheal *var fm now dial vbs* **sheel**, to shell: **shill**, to curdle *var fm S & dial n* **shiel**, a hut or similar small building

shea nut *n* the fruit of shea or buttertree

shearing (*n*) *var fm n* **shearling**

shearling *n* a sheep after its first shearing

shearman *n* one who shears metal: one who, in historical times, sheared woollen cloth

shearn *var fm S & dial n* **sharn**

'sheart *interj* meaning God's heart and used as an oath (GAME PLAYER'S note: This word should be rejected for play as it requires an apostrophe)

sheat *dial n* a pig less than one year old

sheather *n* one who makes sheathes: one who or that which sheaths

shea tree *n* the buttertree

Shebat *n* the fifth month of the Hebrew lunar calendar which occurs in parts of January and February

shecklaton see **ciclatoun**

shedder *n* one who or that which sheds: a female salmon or trout after spawning: a crab during the period of casting its shell

sheder *dial n* an unshorn female sheep over the age of eight months (*masc* **heder**)

sheed *dial fm n* **shed** in the senses, a ridge of high ground: the top of the head: a parting made in the wool of a sheep for the application of a medicament *obs fm vb* **shed**, to place in a shed

sheen (*n*) *now S & dial vb* to shine: to give a sheen to

sheep rot *n* butterwort or Yorkshire sanicle, a common weed: liver rot in sheep supposedly caused by eating butterwort

sheerman *obs fm n* **shearman**

sheeten *obs adj* consisting of a sheet

sheeter *n* a machine which forms wool into sheets of uniform thickness

sheire *obs fm n* **shire**

sheitan *var fm n* **shaitan**, a person of evil

sheld *dial adj* piebald *obs fm vb* **shield**

Sheldru see **Shelta**

shelfy *adj* abounding in sandbanks: having terraces *dial adj* full of slaty rock

Sheila *var fm fem pers n* **Celia**, meaning 'heavenly' (*—cap*) *Austr n* a young woman

sheller *n* one who or a machine which shells peas or shellfish

Shelta *n* a cryptic jargon based on Gaelic and Irish words which are often disguised by the alteration of initial consonants so that only fellow Irish tinkers can understand it (known by various other names such as **Bog Latin, Sheldru, Shelter, Tinker's Cant** and **Auld Thing**)

shelty *n* a Sheltland pony

shepstare *dial n* the starling

shepster *now dial n* a dressmaker *var fm dial n* **shepstare**

sherd *var fm n* **shard** (other than the beetle covering) *var fm vb/S n/dial n* **shard**

shereef *n* a descendant of the prophet Mohammed, through his daughter Fatima: a Muslim title for people of varying degrees of high rank, such as the sovereign of Morocco or the chief magistrate of Mecca (*var fms incl* **sherif, sharife, shareef, seriph** *pl fms incl* **shorfa**)

shereefa *n* a wife of a shereef

sheria *var fm n* **sheriat**

sheriat *n* the Islamic religious law as held sacred by the Turks

sherie *obs fm n* **sherry**

sherif *var fm n* **shereef** (*pl* **shorfa, sherifs**)

Sherpa *n* one of a Tibetan people living on the southern slopes of the Himalayas in Nepal and noted for their agility as mountaineers

sherpe *Obs n* a small bag such as that carried by a pilgrim or a shepherd

sherte *obs fm n* **shirt**

shete *obs fm n* **sheet**, a ship's rope *obs fm vb* **shut** *Obs fm vb* **shoot**

sheter *obs fm n* **shooter**

shettle *var fm obs adj* **shittle** *obs fm n* **shuttle** (in senses other than a floodgate)

sheugh *S & dial n* a furrow, a ditch or similar linear excavation *S & dial vb* to furrow or dig such as a ditch: to store plants under earth

shew *var fm n/vb* **show**

shewel *n* a scarecrow

shewer *arch fm n* **shower**, one who exhibits *obs fm n* **shower**, rain *obs fm n* **sewer**, one who sews: one who superintends a meal

shewre *obs fm n/vb* **shower**, (to) rain

shicker *n* alcohol (derived from **shiker**, the Yiddish for intoxicated)

shidder *obs fm dial n* **sheder** (*obs masc fm* **hidder**)

shide *now dial n* a piece of wood: as a measure, half a cubic foot of timber *obs vb* to cleave

shider *obs vb* to splinter

shier *var fm n* **shyer**, one who throws

shiere *Obs fm adj* **sheer**

shiest *var fm sup* **shyest**

Shiism *n* the sect of the Shiites

Shiite *n* a member of a Muslim sect which recognises Ali (the son-in-law of Mohammed) as his successor

shikar *n* blood sport: game *vb* to hunt animals for sport

shikra *n* a small Indian hawk used in falconry

shin (*n*) *n* the thirteenth letter of the Arabic alphabet: the twenty-first letter of the Hebrew alphabet (also called **sin**)

shiness *obs n* light, brightness *var fm n* **shyness**

shingler *n* one who applies a coating of pebble dash (to the exterior wall of a house): one who or a machine which expels impurities from iron during the smelting process

shinlog *n* the temporary wall (of bricks bonded together with mud) which closes the mouth of a brickmaking kiln *vb* to build a shinlog

Shinto *n* the primitive native religion of Japan centred (until 1945) upon the emperor but consisting in the main of ancestor worship and the power of rustic deities

shiplap *n* an arrangement of such as boards which gives an overlapping of an edge when assembled

shippo *n* an enamelled objet d'art of Japanese origin

shipster *var fm dial n* **shepstare**

shirke *var fm obs n* **shirk**, a disreputable, parasitic person *obs fm vb* **shirk**

shirl *now dial adj/adv* shrill (*comp* **shirler** *sup* **shirllest**) *now dial vb* to trim with shears *dial vb* to slide *obs n* a shrill cry

shirle *obs fm now dial adj/adv* **shirl**

shirra *S fm n* **sheriff**

shirte *obs fm n* **shirt**

shirtee *US n* a shirt front

shit *(now vulgar n/vb) dial fm n* **sheet**

shite *(now vulgar n/vb) obs fm n* **sheet**

shittle *dial fm n* **shuttle**, a floodgate *obs adj* fickle, flighty: of things, unstable

shoder *n* an envelope of skins in which gold is given its initial beating during the gold-beating process *obs fm vb* **shudder**

shofar *n* a trumpet made from the horn of a ram, originally used to rally Jewish troops to battle and now used in religious ceremonies (*pl* **shofars, shofroth**)

shole *dial fm n/vb* **shovel**

sholve *dial fm n/vb* **shovel**

shome *obs n* a decorative item for a horse *obs vb* to bedeck a horse with a shome

shoq *n* an East Indian tree, the pods of which, when infested with insects, yield a tanning extract

shoran *n* a short-range radar system used for navigation purposes

shore due *S n* a fee paid for using a harbour

shoren *obs fm adj* **shorn**

shorer *n* a prop or other supporting item

shorfa *pl* shereef

short *(n/adj/adv) vb* to shortchange: to short-circuit, to cause or develop a path of low resistance through which an excessive electrical current may flow

shorte *obs fm n/adj/adv* **short** *obs fm n* **shirt**

shorty *collq n* a short person or garment

shough *n* a shaggy kind of lapdog, said to have originated in Iceland where the possession of such a dog would now be illegal, as the only dogs permitted are those which herd livestock

shoule *obs fm ns* **shoal**, a sandbank or other shallow part, **shovel** *obs fm adj* **shoal**, shallow *obs fm now dial vb* **shoal**, to divide into groups

shoult *var fm now dial n* **sholt**, a dog

shovel *(n/vb) infl fms* British, **shovelled/-lling**: US, **shoveled/-ling**

showel *obs fm n* **shovel**

showle *obs fm n* **shovel** *obs fm adj* **shoal**, shallow

showre *obs fm n/vb* **shower**, (to) rain

shraep *obs fm now dial n* **shrape**

shrape *now dial n* bait laid for birds: the place where such bait is laid *obs vb* to scratch or scrape

shreading *n* a timber strip, also known as a **furring** or **shreeding**, used by builders for the raising of a surface for lathing or boarding

shreak *obs fm n/vb* **shriek**

shred pie *n* mince pie

shreik *obs fm n/vb* **shriek**

shrewe *obs fm n* **shrew**

shrieval *adj* of or belonging to a sheriff

shrieve *pseudo arch fm vb* **shrive** (*pa t/pa pple* **shrieved**)

shrife *Obs fm vb* **shrive**

shrift *n* confession to a priest *vb* of a priest, to hear a confession

shrike *(n) now dial vb* of birds, to utter their cry

shrine *(n) vb* to enclose (relics) in a shrine

shrive *vb* to hear the confession of (*pa t* **shrove** or **shrived** *pa pple* **shriven** or **shrived**)

shroudy *adj* giving shelter

shrove *now dial vb* to indulge in the various merrymaking activities of Shrovetide

shrowe *obs fm n* **shrew**

shtetel *n* a Jewish village (*pl* **shtetlach**)

shtick *var fm n* **shtik**

shtik *n* a familiar line of patter or routine associated with a particular person

shunless *adj* that which cannot be avoided (GAME PLAYER'S note: This word is 'exclusive' to Shakespeare according to the dictionary used for the UK Scrabble championship. However, the word is extant and was used, for example, in a publication dated 1897.)

shurl *obs fm dial vb/now dial vb* **shirl**

shurt *obs vb* to pass the time (in an idle amusement)

shute *n* a weft *dial n* a natural or artificial watercourse of various types *obs fm vb* **shoot**

shy cock *n* a cock difficult to capture *obs n* a coward: one who evades the bailiff

shyrpe *var fm Obs n* **sherpe**

si *n* the original seventh musical syllable of the tonic sol-fa (see **gamut**) *Gaelic n pl* fairies

sialic *adj* of or relating to saliva

siamang *n* a species of large, black-haired ape of southeast Asia

siamese *vb* to join such as pipes in a way suggestive of Siamese twins

sibilate *vb* to hiss

sibyl *n* a prophetess of classical times *esp* the sibyl of Cumae who offered nine books of oracular pronouncements to Tarquin, king of Rome. He rejected the offer, so she burned three and offered him six for the same price. He still refused, so she burned three more and, eventually, he bought the remaining three for the price originally asked for all nine. These sibylline books were highly prized long after the Tarquins were expelled and Rome was a republic. When, in 83 BC, these books were destroyed by fire, together with the temple in which they were housed, a fresh set was made from copies held in other parts of the empire. Later, in 12 BC, Augustus ordered that they should be retained at the temple of Apollo. The sibylline books were consulted by the senate in times of emergency or disaster. It is believed they were destroyed circa AD 405: any female prophetess or woman fortune teller

sicker (*comp/adj*) *S & dial adj* secure, safe *arch vb* to secure

sickled *adj* provided with or cut by a sickle

sickler *n* a reaper

sickling *n* a sick or delicate person: the action of cutting with a sickle

siddle *dial n* a slope *dial vb* to slope

sidearm *US adj* thrown with a sideways sweep of the arm

sidearms *n pl* weapons, such as swords or bayonets, worn at the side

sideman *US n* a member of a jazz band

sidepost *n* a doorpost or similar

sideral *adj* of or pertaining to the stars: starry: (malign) influence from the stars (also see **sidereal**)

sidereal *adj* of or pertaining to the stars: star-like: of time or of planetary or lunar motion, measured by reference to a star or stars (also see **sideral**)

siderosis *n* a lung disease arising from the inhaling of metal particles

sieger *n* a besieger, one who lays siege to

siemens *n* in the latest metric system, the official replacement for the mho

sienna *n* a natural clay of a browny orange-yellow colour used as a pigment: that colour

sierra *n* a Spanish or (Spanish-)American mountain range, the peaks of which suggest the appearance of the teeth of a saw

sierran *adj* of a sierra: of the flora of a sierra

siesta *n* an afternoon nap

sieth *obs fm now dial vb* **sithe**, to sieve

siever *n* a maker of sieves

sifaka *n* either of two species of lemurs, both of which have colourful markings, are diurnal, completely arboreal and found only in Madagascar

sightline *n* the direct line from the eye to the object of focus

sigma *n* the eighteenth letter of the Greek alphabet, corresponding to the English S: a mathematical symbol to indicate that the sum is to be taken of the sequence following: a symbol for 200

sigmate *adj* shaped like a sigma or the English equivalent *vb* to add a sigma or letter S to a word

sigmation *n* the adding of the letter S to a word

sigmatron *n* a machine which generates very high-energy X-rays

signal (*n/adj/vb*) *infl fms* British, **signalled/-lling**: US, **signaled/-ling**

signaler *US fm n* **signaller**

signary *n* a signatary or signatory, one whose signature is attached to a document

signat *obs fm S vb* **signet**

signet (*n*) *S vb* to sign with a signet

signeur *obs var fm n* **senior**

signior *var fm n* **signor**

signiora *obs fm n* **signora**

signor *n* treated as an English word in lower case to describe an Italian gentleman (*pl* **signori, signors**)

signore *var fm (Anglicized) n* **signor**

signoria *n* the governing body of an historical city-state which has now been incorporated into Italy

signorial *adj* pertaining to lordship, dominion, rule

sike *S & dial n* a small stream *esp* one dry in summer *now dial n/vb* (to) sigh

silage *n* any fodder crop harvested whilst green and kept succulent by partial fermentation in a pit or (cylindrical) tower *vb* to preserve the crop by this means

silane *var fm n* **silicane**

silen *n* the silenus (*pl* **silens**) (+*cap*) *n* a Silenus (*pl* **Sileni**)

silene *n* catchfly or limewort, any of a genus of plants having a sticky stalk and variously coloured, showy flowers

silent (*adj*) *n* a device on a clock which prevents the sound of a chime or an alarm being made

silenus *n* the liontailed monkey, a species of macaque of the Western Ghats, India: an optional *fm* of **Silenus** (*n*) below (*pl* **sileni**) (+*cap*) *pers n* in Greek myth, the foster-father of Dionysus and chief of the satyrs *n* a satyr or minor god of the woodlands (*pl* **Sileni**)

Silesia *n* now a geographical region of Central Europe split between Czechoslovakia, East Germany and Poland, though it has been an independent state. For example, the Piasts (Polish rulers) signed a pact with Prussia which gave them uninterrupted control between 1537 and 1675. It was then seized as a Bohemian fief of the Holy Roman Empire. In 1740, Frederick the Great of Prussia took it as part of his dominions. In 1920 came the first partition and 1945, the second. (+ or −*cap*) *n* a type of fine linen or cotton fabric: a variety of lettuce

silicane *n* a compound of silicon and hydrogen

silicate *n* a salt of salitic acid, all of which salts form a large part of the earth's crust

silked *adj* covered in silk

siller *S fm n/adj/vb* **silver** *var fm obs n* **silour**

silo (*n*) *vb* to put or keep in a silo or grain store (*infl fms incl* **silos, siloed**)

silour *obs n* a canopy of ceiling

silva *n* the trees of a region (*pl* **silvae, silvas**) *erron fm n* **selva** (see **selvas**)

silvae *pl* silva

silvan *adj* of woods, woodland

silver (*n/adj*) *vb* to plate with silver

sim *n* a religious or quiet man *obs n* a crafty person *dial fm vb* **seem**

simagre *obs n* an affected air

simarre *var fm n* **cymar**

Simeon *masc pers n* meaning 'obedient'

simitar *var fm n* **scimitar**, the Turkish and Persian broad-bladed, curved sword

Simmental *n* a breed of Swiss cattle

simmon *S n* a rope of straw or heath *now dial n/vb* (to) cement

simnel *n* a type of rich currant cake: formerly, a type of bread of the finest flour, first boiled, then baked *modf n* of mid-Lent Sunday (Mothering Sunday) when a simnel is traditionally baked

simoleon *US slg n* a dollar

simon *obs fm now dial n/vb* **simmon** *obs slg n* a sixpence (+*cap*) *masc pers n* meaning 'snub-nosed'

simony *n* traffic in sacred things: trading in ecclesiastical preferment

simpel *Obs fm adj* **simple**

simple (*adj*) *n* a person of humble birth: one easily duped: a simple word: a medicine with a single constituent: a simple quantity: a single ingredient *arch n* a medicinal herb *arch vb* to search for or gather such herbs (also see **simples**, below)

simples *now dial n pl* foolish behaviour (note: The *n*, **simple**, in respect of a person is more common in the *pl fm*)

sin (*n/vb*) *n* the twelfth letter of the Arabic alphabet: the twenty-first letter of the Hebrew alphabet (also called **shin**)

sinch *var fm US n/vb* **cinch**

sind *n* a draught of liquid *S & dial vb* to rinse

sindel *obs fm S adv* **sendle**

sinder *S fm adj/adv/vb* **sunder**

sindge *obs fm vb* **singe**

sindle *var fm S adv* **sendle**

sindre *S fm adj/adv/vb* **sunder**

sine (*n*) *var fm S & dial vb* **sind**, to rinse

sin eater *n* one hired as a form of personal scapegoat. He or she takes upon him/herself the sins of the recently deceased person by eating a meal beside the body.

sin-eating *n* the practice of a sin eater

sinecurist *n* one having or desiring a sinecure

sinfonia *n* a symphony (orchestra): in early operas, the overture

singel *Obs fm n* **shingle**

singler *n* one who thins out plants *vars fm obs n* **sanglier** *obs adj* singular

singult *arch n* a sob

sinistre *obs fm adj* **sinister**

sinkage *n* the act of sinking: that which is sinking or has sunk

sinnate *arch fm n* **sinnet**

sinnet *n* a flat cord, braided from three separate strands

sinoper *obs n* the colour red: a red earth used as a pigment

sinople *obs n* the colour green: also, oddly, the colour red as it was used in the same senses as **sinoper** (also see **gridelin** for an extant colour confusion) *obs adj* of a green colour

sinque *obs fm n* **cinque**

sin rent *n* a payment made to a clergyman for forgiveness of sins

sinter *n* silica deposited by hot springs *vb* to heat a mixture of powdered metals

sinuate *adj* of a margin, winding in and out: tortuous, sinuous: wavy: of a leaf, having a recess or rounded curve between two projecting lobes

sinuated *adj* sinuous, winding: sinuate as for a leaf

sinue *obs fm n/vb* **sinew**

sinward *adv* in the direction of sin

siphac *obs n* the peritoneum, the double membrane or sac which lines the cavity of the abdomen

siphonate *adj/n* (of) a mollusc having a siphon

siphonet *n* the tube from which an aphis excretes honeydew (see **aphid**)

siphuncle *n* a small tube connecting the shell chambers in such as a cuttlefish

sippet *n* a crouton or small piece of fried bread served in soup: a small piece of anything: a fragment *vb* to cut into small pieces

sipple *vb* to drink liquor slowly

sir (*n*) *vb* to address a person as 'sir'

sirdar *n* a military chief of an Indian or other Eastern army: also, once used as a title for the British commander-in-chief of the Egyptian army

sire (*n*) *vb* to father

siren (*n*) *vb* to entice: to make a signal with a siren

sirene *var fm n* **siren**, the small acoustical instrument

sirenian *n* any of a class of aquatic mammals *incl* the sea cows, dugongs and manatees known, collectively, as the Sirenia *adj* pertaining to or having the characteristics of any of the Sirenia

sirenic *adj* melodious, charming, alluring: sweet-voiced

sirgang *n* the Chinese roller, a species of long-tailed, crested, jay-like bird, pale green in colour when freshly moulted, but later changing to blue

Sirian *adj* of Sirius, the dog star and the brightest star in the heavens: of any other star which produces the same spectrum as Sirius *n* a star with that spectrum

sirly *obs adj* haughty, imperious (GAME PLAYER'S note: The *adj* **surly** is an amended spelling *fm* of sirly and originally carried the same meaning. If there were *comps/sups* of both sirly and its *var fm* **serly**, these are not recorded and it must be a matter of your own judgement whether you allow them or not. They are not shown in the anagram lists.)

sirname *var fm n/vb* **surname**

sirrah *n* sir, used to emphasize anger or contempt

sirree *US & dial n* sir or sirrah

sirvent *n* a (satirical) poem composed and performed by a troubadour in the Middle Ages (also see **tenson**)

sirvente *var fm n* **sirvent**

sist *n* in Scots law, a stay of some proceeding *S vb* to suspend, *esp* a judicial proceeding

sistle *vb* to produce a kind of hissing noise

sistra *pl* sistrum

sistre *obs n* a sistrum, a musical instrument consisting of tubes suspended inside an oval frame and shaken like a rattle, originally used by the ancient Egyptians in their worship of Isis

sistrum *n* an ancient Egyptian percussion instrument used in worship of Isis (*pl* **sistra, sistrums**)

sitar *n* a guitar-like plucked string instrument used by Indians

sithe *n* a chive (usually in *pl fm*) *S & dial n* a sieve *now dial n* a sigh *obs n* (good fortune on) a journey: the course of one's life: misfortune, trouble *now dial vb* to sieve: to sigh

sithen *arch conj* seeing that

sithien *S n* a mound in which fairies share a communal, non-family lifestyle

sithre *Obs adv* subsequently

sitient *adj* thirsting, desiring

sitrep *collq n* a report on the current military situation

sittar *var fm n* **sitar**

sittine *adj* of or pertaining to the nuthatch *n* any bird of the sub-family *Sittinae* which includes the true nuthatches in the genus *Sitta*

siver *obs vb* to simmer

six ale *n* a mixture of the best and the cheapest ale (originally, a pint which is half at a rate of 4d per pint and half at a rate of 8d, working out at 6d – i.e. $2\frac{1}{2}$p)

ska *n* a type of reggae, or music of West Indian origin

skaapsteker *n* any of several South African venomous snakes

skale *dial n* a hut or shed *obs fm n/vb* **scale** (in most senses)

skealt *obs n* a tale: a rumour

skean dhu *var fm n* **skene dhu**, the small dagger worn in the stocking of a Scot in Highland dress

skee *var fm n/vb* **ski**

skeeling *dial n* an outhouse with a sloping roof against the side of a building *Ork modf n* as **skeeling goose**, the sheldrake

skeely *var fm S & dial adj* **skilly**

skeily *var fm S & dial adj* **skilly**

skelder *arch vb* to beg *esp* in the guise of an ex-serviceman: to swindle

skelet *now dial n* a skeleton

skelte *var fm obs n* **skealt**

skelter *vb* to hurry or scurry

skeptic *var fm n/adj* **sceptic**

skerl *var fm obs n* **scarle** *obs fm S & dial vb* **skirl** (see **skirle**)

skerry *adj* shaly *S fm adj* scary *n* shaly earth or stone *Ork n* a reef

skier (*n*) *var fm n* **skyr**

skill (*n*) *arch vb* to make a difference, to matter

skilly *n* skilligalee, a thin, watery, oatmeal-based gruel formerly served to convicts and inmates of workhouses *S & dial adj* skilful or skilled

Skinfaxi *n* in Norse mythology, the horse of day (also see **Hrimfaxi**)

skink *n* any of a family of more than 600 species of lizards found on every continent except Antarctica and ranging in length from barely three inches to the two feet of the giant skink of the Solomon Islands. Half of the species lay eggs, the other half giving birth to live young. Some of the Australian species are so attractive that they are adopted as house-hold pets. One American species proves the exception to the rule of reptiles ignoring their eggs or young from the moment of delivery – it not only cares for its eggs, but tends the young after hatching: the last person to arrive for breakfast who, in consequence, performs some domestic chore *S n* liquor: beef soup *obs n* ham: the skunk *arch vb* to serve liquor

skinlet *n* a membrane

skintle *vb* of the drying process in brick-making, to separate and reset half-dried bricks at right angles to each other to complete the process *n* a brick set diagonally into a wall

skipjack *n* the oceanic bonito, a tuna-like fish having bluish bands running horizontally along the lower part of the body and famed for its speed. It can swim at 25 mph when chasing flying fishes, often leaping out of the water in pursuit: any species of click beetle: a toy constructed from the merrythought of a fowl and designed to skip automatically: a merrythought or wishbone, the forked bone between the neck and breast of a bird *arch n* a conceited fop

skire *S adv* altogether *var fm dial vb* **skirr**

skirl *vb* of a bird or insect, to fly with a sweeping motion *S & dial vb* to scream or shriek: to produce the shrill sound of a bagpipe *S & dial n* a shrill cry or scream: a shrill sound *esp* that of a bagpipe (this latter sense has now become standard English usually as part of the phrase *the skirl of the pipes*)

skirle *obs fm S & dial n/vb* **skirl**, (to create) a shrill sound

skirme *var fm Obs vb* **skirm**, to fight with a sword

skirr *vb* to flee: to move rapidly *dial vb* of a partridge, to make a whirring sound with its wings when taking flight: to skim a stone on the surface of water: to slide swiftly: to jerk: to graze

skirret *n* a species of water parsnip: its edible tuber: extended to various other, similar, plants: a wooden T-shaped marking tool, one of the symbols of a master mason in freemasonry

skirte *obs fm n/vb* **skirt**

skiver *n* a skewer: a thin type of sumach-tanned leather used for such as book covers and hat linings: one who splits leather: a tool used for such work *vb* to fasten with a skewer: to pare leather *US vb* of birds, to scatter widely at the sound of gunshot

sklate *S fm n* **slate**, a roofing tile

skleir *Obs n* a veil

sklint *var fm now dial vb* **slent**, to tear, rent, split or cleave

skolion *n* an ancient Greek drinking song (*pl* **skolia**)

skreen *var fm n/vb* **screen**

skreich *var fm S n/vb* **skreigh**

skreigh *S n/vb* (to) screech (*var fms incl* the unlisted anagram, **skriegh**)

skrene *obs fm n* **screen**

skriech *var fm S n/vb* **skreigh**

skrine *obs fm n* **screen**

skryer *var fm n* **scryer**

Skuld *pers n* see **Norn**

skulpin *var fm n* **sculpin**

skute *var fm vb* **scoot**

skyr *n* an Icelandic dish of sour curd

slabbe *obs fm n* **slab**

slabber *n* saliva *S n* mud *vb* to salivate *esp* in a disagreeable way *S vb* to work in a sloppy fashion

slacker *(comp adj) n* an idler or shirker

slade *n* a dell or valley: a forest glade: a strip of marshy land: the sole of a plough *now dial n* a sledge *dial vb* to use a sledge: to slide

slaer *obs fm n* **slayer**

slag (*n*) *vb* to convert into or become cinders

slagger *now dial vb* to walk slowly or lamely

slahter *Obs fm n* **slaughter**

slaide *obs fm n* **slade**, a valley

slaie *var fm n* **sley** *obs fm vb* **sley**

slàinte *Gael interj* good health

slaire *var fm Obs n* **skleir**

slairg *var fm S vb* **slerg**

slaister *S & dial n* a filthy mess or substance *S & dial vb* to eat or work in a wet, slobbering manner: to plaster in this fashion

slait *var fm dial n* **sleight** *obs fm S & dial vb* **slate**

slaiter *obs fm n* **slater**

slaken *obs vb* to assuage: to grow slack

slaker *n* a sluice: one who slakes

slalom *n* a race against the clock which tests ability as well as speed, as (*a*) on a downhill ski run with a zigzag track (*b*) a (white water) obstacle course for a canoe *vb* to move in a zigzag course

slammer *n* a violent gust of wind: one who slams (doors)

slangier *comp adj* slangy

slangish *adj* of or like slang

slanter *comp adj* slant

slape *dial adj* slippery, smooth, cunning: of ale, strong and sweet *dial fm vb* **sleep** *dial n* a flag-shaped slate

slapen *dial vb* to render slippery

slaper *var fm dial n* **sleeper**, a dormouse

slappet *n* a fragment or splinter of ore *vb* to cause such fragments (in mining)

slare *dial vb* to walk with a noisy sliding action

slart *dial vb* to sprinkle with water

slaster *var fm S & dial n/vb* **slaister**

slate (*n/vb*) *S & dial vb* of dogs, to use them to attack, bait or drive

slater *n* one who lays slates *obs n* a spaniel which forced game birds to fly so that they could be attacked by a hawk

slatey *obs fm adj* slaty

slathe see **slithe**

slather *vb* to slip or slide *n* a large quantity (usually in *pl fm*)

slatier *comp adj* slaty

slatre *Obs fm obs vb* **slatter**, to split, to shiver (*pa t* **slatred**)

slatte *obs fm n* **slat**, a long narrow strip of wood

slatter *vb* to clatter *obs vb* to make a slit in clothing: to split, to shiver *now dial n* a slater *obs n* a woodlouse

slattern *n* a slovenly female

slaty *adj* of or resembling slate (*comp* **slatier** *sup* **slatiest**)

slaum *var fm S & dial n/vb* **sloom**

slaunder *obs fm n/vb* **slander**

slaunt *S fm n* **slant**

slaup *var fm S & dial n/vb* **slorp**

slaven *obs adj* split

slaver *n* dribbling saliva: nonsense: a slave ship, trader or owner *vb* to let saliva dribble: to fawn

slaverer *n* one who dribbles saliva: a servile flatterer

slaw *US n* a salad with a sliced cabbage base *now dial fm adj/adv/n/vb* **slow**

slawm *var fm S & dial n/vb* **sloom**

slawp *var fm S & dial n/vb* **slorp**

slay (*vb*) *var fm vb* **sley**

slead *now dial n* a sled or sledge *obs vb* to travel by sled or sledge

sleaper *obs fm n* **sleeper**

sleapie *obs fm adj* **sleepy**

slear *obs fm n* **slayer**

sleat *now dial vb* to incite (a dog)

sleating *n* hunting: instigation (*fig*)

sleave *now dial vb* to separate (silk) into fine fibres *dial vb* to cleave, split or rend

slede *obs fm now dial n* **slead**

sledger *n* one who uses a sledge

sleech *n* alluvial mud *dial vb* to dip or take up water

sleechy *adj* slimy, muddy

sleed *var fm now dial n* **slead**

sleekit *S adj* smooth: cunning, sly

sleepe *obs fm n/vb* **sleep**

sleepry *S fm adj* **sleepy**

sleer *dial vb* to sneer

sleere *obs fm n* slayer

sleety *adj* resembling sleet (*comp* **sleetier** *sup* **sleetiest**)

sleeve (*n/vb*) *var fm now dial vb* **sleave**

sleever *n* a former Welsh measure of capacity *approx* thirteen fluid ounces

sleight *n* skill: adroitness: dexterity *esp* that used in the skilful manipulation of cards by a conjuror *now dial n* a special knack *dial n* a (sheep) pasture *obs n* trickery *now dial vb* to cheat

sleighter *obs n* slaughter *obs fm n* **slighter**, one who slights

sleip *obs S fm n/vb* **sleep** (*pa t* **sleipet**)

sleipe *obs S fm n/vb* **sleep** (*pa t* **sleipet**)

sleipet *pa t* sleip or sleipe

sleitch *S fm n* **sleech**

sleive *obs S fm n* **sleeve**

slent *now dial n* a slope *obs n* a splash *now dial vb* to slip: to turn aside: to tear, rend, split or cleave *obs vb* to throw

slepar *Obs fm n* **sleeper**

slepare *Obs fm n* **sleeper**

sleped *obs fm pa t* **slept**

sleper *obs fm n* **sleeper**

slepere *Obs fm n* **sleeper**

slerg *S vb* to befoul with saliva

slester *var fm S & dial vb* **slaister**

slestir *var fm S & dial n/vb* **slaister**

slew *n* a turn, a twist *US & Canada n* any of various stretches of still water such as a pond, a small lake, a marshy pool or a backwater *vb* to swing round without shifting basic position: to intoxicate

slewse *obs fm n* **sluice**

slewth *var fm n/vb* **sleuth**

sley *n* a weaver's instrument for separating the threads of a warp and compacting the weft *vb* to set a warp

slicker (*comp adj*) *n* a tool used for scraping *US n* an oilskin raincoat

slidden *adj* of that having slipped

slidder *now dial vb* to slip: to make slippery *dial n* a steep slope *obs adj* slippery *obs adv* in an unstable manner

slidre *Obs fm now dial vb* **slidder**

slide rest *n* an apparatus for carrying the cutting tool for such as a lathe

sliest *var fm sup* **slyest**

slifter *now dial n* a crack: a crevice

slighten *obs vb* to treat with indifference or disrespect

slike *S & dial n* mud, slime *dial fm vb* **slake**, to quench a thirst *Obs vb* to slide

slime (*n*) *vb* to smear with slime: to move in a slimy fashion

slinge *dial vb* to idle, to slink

slinger (*n*) *obs S vb* to swing

slinke *obs fm n/vb* **slink**

slinked *dial fm pa pple* **slunk**

slinker *n* an animal which moves in a sneaky fashion: a cow or other (farm) animal which casts prematurely

slint *var fm now dial vb* **slent**, to tear, rend, split or cleave

slinte *Obs fm now dial vb* **slent**

slipcase *n* a protective box for a book

slipe *now US & dial n* a long, narrow strip *S & dial n* a sledge *obs n* a permanently slippery surface clay *now dial vb* to strip *Obs vb* to polish

slippet *n* a fall of sand in a mining operation *obs n* a strip

slippie *obs fm adj* **slippy**

sliprail *Austr n* a gate in the form of a moveable rail: the associated gateway

slipstring *now dial n* one who deserves to be hanged, a rogue

slirt *US vb* to jerk lightly *dial vb* to squirt water

slister *var fm S & dial n/vb* **slaister**

slit (*n/adj/vb*) *infl fms incl* **slitted** (*var fm pa t* **slit**) **slitten** (*S & dial fm pa t* **slit**)

slite *vb* to slit or split: to wear out (*pa t* **slited**) *S vb* to sharpen (*pa t* **slait** or **slate**) *now dial n* wear and tear

slithe *Obs vb* to slip or slide (*pa t* **slathe**)

slitless *adj* of a spectroscope, not possessing a slit for the admission of light

slitten see **slit**

slitter (*n*) *now dial vb* to slip or slide

slive *now dial n* a slice *now dial vb* to split, divide (*pa pple* **slived, sliven** or **sloven**): to dress hastily (*pa pple* **slived**)

sliven *pa pple now dial vb* slive

sliver *n* a splinter *now dial n* a protective outer garment such as an overall *vb* to cut or split

slivery *n pl* small, straight shoots of ash cut into hoops

sloam *var fm n/S & dial n/vb* **sloom**

sloap *obs fm n/vb* **slope**

slock *S vb* to extinguish *now dial vb* to entice (away)

slocke *obs fm now dial vb* **slock**

slocken *S vb* to extinguish (*lit/fig*): to soak: to quench (the thirst)

slockin *var fm S vb* **slocken**

slodge *dial vb* to walk in a slovenly fashion

slodger *dial n* one who lives in the Fen district

sloghorne *obs fm n* **slogan**

sloid *var fm n* **sloyd**, a system of training in elementary woodwork

sloke *var fm S vb/now dial vb* **slock**

sloken *var fm S vb* **slocken**

slome *var fm S & dial n/vb* **sloom**, (to) doze or slumber

sloom *n* a blackish type of clay found near coal measures (*var fms incl* **sloam, slum, slumb**) *S & dial n/vb* (to) slumber or doze (*var fms incl* **slaum, slawm, sloam**) *S vb* of soft, heavy grass or grain, to lay flat (so as to decay)

sloop (*n*) *vb* to haul timber on a sloop, a type of simple drag used in lumbering

sloope *obs fm n* **sloop**, a sailing vessel

sloper *US n* one who lives on the Pacific slope of the USA

slopper *n* one who deals in loose-fitting outer garments

slopy *adj* sloping

slore *now dial var fm n/vb* **slur**

slorie *obs fm now dial vb* **slurry**

slorp *S & dial vb* to eat or drink in a noisy fashion: to wash in a noisy, sloppy manner *S & dial n* a sloven or uncouth person (*var fms n/vb incl* **slaup, slawp**)

slort *var fm dial vb* **slart**

slote *n* a theatrical trapdoor: a bar or crossbar such as used to strengthen the underside of a cart or a chair

sloted *adj* having a slote or slotes

sloth (*n*) *vb* to be or become lazy

slothe *obs n* a muddy or miry place

slotter (*n*) *S vb* to make slovenly *now dial vb* to make foul or dirty

slounge *S & dial vb* to idle in a sloppy fashion

slounger *S & dial n* one who slounges

slour *slg vb* to lock, secure or fasten

slouse *dial vb* to wash with a great quantity of water

slouze *var fm dial vb* **slouse**

sloven *n* one untidy in appearance and dress *adj* slovenly (also see **slive** *vb*) *US adj* uncultivated *vb* to treat in a slovenly manner

Slovene *n/adj* (of) a Slav resident in Yugoslavia

slower (*comp adj/n*) *vb* of a railway train, to slow down (as it approaches a station)

slub *n* mire, ooze: a lump on a thread *vb* of such as wool or cotton, to draw out and twist after carding, to prepare it for spinning *dial vb* to cover with mud

slubber *n* a slubbing machine: one who works such (see *vb* **slub**) *dial n* mud, ooze, slime *vb* to stain, smear (*lit/fig*): to obscure: to skim over in a hurried, sloppy fashion: to eat in a rather disgusting way

sludge (*n*) *vb* to create this liquid mud: to use it for such purposes as filling cracks in an embankment: to clear away unwanted sludge

sludger *n* a device for removing sludge from a bore hole or for boring in quicksand

slue *var fm n/US & Canada n/vb* **slew**

slueing *var fm n* **slewing**

sluff *dial fm n/vb* **slough**, (to cast off) unwanted skin

sluffer *obs vb* to eat noisily and greedily

slumper *vb* to flounder

slunge *var fm S & dial vb* **slounge**

slunger *var fm S & dial n* **slounger**

slurrie *obs fm now dial vb* **slurry**

slurry *now dial vb* to soil or dirty

slush (*n*) *vb* essentially to splash in various senses such as, to wash with a copious supply of water: to soil with mud: to grease the timber of a sailing vessel: to apply a mixture of white lead and lime to certain machinery: of pigs, to eat in a noisy and greedy fashion

slute *obs S fm n/vb* **slut**

sly (*adj/adv/n*) *US & S vb* to slink or move in a sly fashion

smaert *Obs fm adj* **smart**

smaik *arch S n* a rascal

smake *obs vb* to recognize by scent or smell: to give out an odour: to (have a) taste *obs fm arch S n* **smaik** *obs fm n* **smack**, a taste

smalm *var fm vb* **smarm**

smaltine *n* smaltite

smaltite *n* a crystalline cobalt arsenide also known as smaltine

smalto *n* a piece of coloured glass or enamel for use in mosaic work (*pl* **smalti, smaltos**)

smarm *vb* to fawn ingratiatingly: to smear, daub or plaster

smarte *obs fm n/vb* **smart** *Obs fm adv* **smart**

smartie *var fm n* **smarty**

smarty *n* one who attempts to be smart or witty

smeart *Obs fm adj* **smart**

smeath *n* a name applied to various ducks – smew, widgeon, pochard, scaup and pintail

smeech *now dial n* vapour *esp* that which is dense and thick: smoke *now dial vb* to create vapour or smoke: to perfume

smeer *obs fm vb* **smear**

smeeth *now dial adj* smooth *now dial vb* to make smooth *dial n* a level space

smelite *n* kaolinite, a highly purified form of kaolin

smeller *n* one who uses the sense of smell: one who stinks: a tactile organ such as a whisker of a cat *slg n* the nose: one who pries *obs slg n* a garden

smelt *n* any of various species of small fishes related to the salmon. They live in large shoals in coastal and estuarine waters and their flesh has the odour of a cucumber. The species *incl* the candlefish. *vb* to melt in order to separate metal from ore

smere *obs fm n/vb* **smeer**

smerlin *obs n* the loach

smert *now dial fm n/adj/adv/vb* **smart**

smerte *obs fm n* **smart** *Obs fm adj/adv/vb* **smart**

smethe *obs fm now dial adj/vb* **smeeth**

smetin *Obs fm pa pple* **smitten**

smew *n* a small species of merganser, a marine duck

smiche *var fm now dial n* **smitch**, grime or dirt: thick smoke

smidgeon *var fm collq n* **smidgin**

smidgin *collq n* a tiny amount

smilax *n* an African plant of the asparagus family with bright green leaves, often used in floral decoration (*pl* **smilaxes**)

smilet *n* a little smile

smilt *obs vb* to turn a pulp of corn into a thick cream

smirke *obs fm n* **smirk**

smirtle *S n/vb* (to) smirk

smite (*n/vb*) *infl fms pa t* **smote** (*var fms* **smit** (*poet*), **smited** (*rare*)) *pa pple* **smitten**

smiten *Obs fm pa pple* **smitten**

smith (*n*) *vb* to work as a smith: to forge: to fashion

smither *n* a smith

smithers *var fm n pl* **smithereens**, small fragments

smithery *n* the trade, occupation or art of a smith: smithcraft (TRIVIA note: This word contains no fewer than seventeen different pronouns as follows:– **he, her, hers, him, his, I, it, its, me, my, she, their, theirs, them, they, thy** and **ye**. Also see **TRIVIA CHALLENGE** and **Wordsworth.)**

smittel *obs fm S & dial adj* **smittle**

smittle *S & dial adj* of diseaes, contagious

smocker *n* one who makes smocks *obs n* a lady's man

smolder *now US fm n/vb* **smoulder**

smolet *obs S n* a word of very uncertain meaning known only from the sentence, '*Quhen the smy on me smyrkis with his smake smolet*'. This translates as, '*When the rascal/ fish on my smyrkis(?) with his taste/ smell/ rascal smolet(?)*'. It occurs in a book entitled *Twa Mariit Wemen*, which has had little success since 1508.

smolt *see* **SALMON**

smoor *S n* a suffocating atmosphere *S & dial vb* to smother (*lit/fig*)

smore *now S n* smoke *now S & dial vb* to suffocate, to smother: to choke: to smoulder

smoucher *n* one who kisses

smould *obs n* the sandeel

smoult *dial vb* of juvenile salmon, to pass into the smolt stage (see **SALMON**)

smouse *S Afr n* an itinerant trader *S Afr vb* to trade as a pedlar

smouser *var fm S Afr n* **smouse**

smouth *obs fm adj* **smooth**

smoyle *obs fm vb* **smile**

smur *S & dial n/vb* (to) drizzle

smy *n* sea dace *obs S n* a rascal

smyrkis *see* **smolet**

smythe *Obs var fm vb* **smite**

smytrie *S n* a collection of small individuals or things

snackle *vb* to secure

snade *dial n* a piece of mackerel used as bait *obs fm now S & dial vb* **sned**, to prune a tree

snaggy *adj* snaglike: having snags: knotty (*comp* **snaggier** *sup* **snaggiest**) *S & dial adj* ill-tempered, peevish

snaice *var fm now dial n* **snaste**

snail (*n*) *vb* to walk or move very slowly

snail dance *n* the rather slow courtship procedure of various species of land snails (also see **nemoralis**)

snaile *obs fm n* **snail**

snail kite *n* a small, tropical American species of kite which has developed a unique method of feeding on snails. It takes one to its perch and waits for the mollusc to emerge from the shell, then grasps it behind the head and waits for the muscles to relax. Once this happens, it flicks the shell clear of the snail and has its meal.

snaily *adj* snail-like: infested with snails: covered with the slime of snails *Austr adj* curled after the manner of a snail shell: having horns curled in this manner *Austr n* a bullock with curled horns

snaipe *Obs fm now dial vb* **snape**

snaist *var fm now dial n* **snaste**

snake spit *dial var fm n* **cuckoo spit**

snakish *adj* snake-like (also see **ANIMAL ADJECTIVES**)

snape *vb* to taper *now dial vb* to stunt the growth of a plant: to rebuke, to snub *dial vb* to be miserly with food *obs vb* to harm or damage

snaper *obs n* of uncertain meaning, but possibly a twinge

snappe *obs fm n/vb* **snap**

snapy *now dial adj* marshy, boggy, wet (land only)

snar *now dial n* a stump *obs vb* of dogs, to snarl

snarer *n* one who sets snares or traps

snarle *obs fm n/vb* **snarl**

snarpe *var fm Obs adj* **snarp**, keen

snarrel *dial fm n* **snarl**, a tangle *var fm now dial n* **snarl**, a snare

snary *adj* of the nature of a snare: resembling a snare: ensnaring

snash *S n* abuse *S vb* to use abusive language

snaste *now dial n* (the burning or burnt part of) the wick of a candle *obs vb* to snuff a candle

snatchy *adj* irregular: spasmodic (*comp* **snatchier** *sup* **snatchiest**)

snater *obs vb* to stumble

snath *US & dial n* the shaft of a scythe

snathe *dial vb* to prune (a tree)

snatter *obs vb* to chatter

snaw *S & dial fm n/vb* **snow**

snayle *obs fm vb* **snail**

snead *n* the curved shaft of a scythe

sneap *arch n/vb* (to) snub, rebuke

snear *obs fm n/vb* **sneer**

sneath *var fm US & dial n* **snath**

sneathe *var fm US & dial n* **snath**

sneep *obs fm arch vb* **sneap**

sneery *adj* of one with a scornful character

sneesh *S & dial n* (a pinch of) snuff

sneeshing *S Ir & dial n* (a pinch of) snuff (also used as a *modf n*, hence **sneeshing box** etc)

sneest *var fm now dial n* **snaste**

sneeste *var fm now dial n* **snaste**

sneever *var fm dial adj* **snever**

sneir *obs S vb* to sail

sneish *var fm S & dial n* **sneesh**

snerl *var fm dial vb* **snurl**

snevel *obs fm vb* **snivel**

snever *dial adj* narrow, slender

snibble *n* a bar used for scotching tram wheels on an inclined track in a mine *vb* to scotch

snick up *now dial n* a sneezing fit *obs n* a hangman's rope *now dial vb* the basic form is usually **go snick up** (meaning *go and hang yourself*) with the word snick taking the *infl fm* **snicked up** etc

sniddle *dial n* coarse grass

snider *(comp adj)* (+*cap*) *n* a breech-loading rifle invented in the early part of the 19th century

snidge *now dial n* a greedy person

snifle *dial fm vb* **sniffle**

snig *n* a young eel *obs n* an avaricious person *obs vb* to indulge in avarice

sniggle *n* either of two devices used in sniggling, a baited hook or a needle: a snigger *dial n* an eel *vb* to fish for eels by the sniggling method: to snigger *dial vb* to wriggle

sniggler *n* one who uses the technique of sniggling: one who sniggers: one who doesn't play fair and square

sniggling *n* a method of fishing for eels by which they are drawn from the holes in which they habitually lurk. The fisherman uses either a baited hook or a needle thrust into the hole.

snight *obs fm now dial n* **snite**

snipey *var fm adj* **snipy**

snipie *S fm adj* **snipy**

snipy *adj* suggestive of the long, pointed bill of a snipe (used mainly for animal and human facial features as the *S adj* **snipie-nebbit**, having a nose like a snipe's bill): snipe-like: frequented by snipe

snirl *var fm dial vb* **snurl**

snirtle *S & dial vb* to snigger or laugh in a repressed manner

snish *var fm S & dial n* **sneesh**

snishing *var fm S Ir & dial n* **sneeshing**

snitcher *slg n* an informer

snitchers *S n pl* (strings used in place of) handcuffs

snite *now dial n* the snipe, a bird akin to the woodcock *now S & dial vb* to wipe the nose: to snuff a candle

snitel *obs n* a candlesnuffer (*pl* a pair of candlesnuffers)

sniter *n* one who (constantly) wipes his or her nose

sniters *n pl* a pair of candlesnuffers

snithe *now dial vb* to cut *var fm US & dial n* **snath** *obs fm now dial vb* **sny**

snitle *obs fm now dial n* **snittle**

snitter *now dial vb* of snow, to fall

snittle *now dial n* a slip knot

snive *var fm now dial vb* **sny**

sniveler *US fm n* **sniveller**

snock *dial n* a knock or blow *dial vb* to snort contemptuously

snod *S adj* smooth, tidy, trim *S vb* to trim (*pa t/pa pple* **snodded, snoddit**)

snoire *obs S fm n* **snore**

snool *vb* to snub: to submit tamely *S & dial n* an abject wretch: a mean-spirited person

snoopily an undefined adverb which appears to be exclusive to one particular American dictionary where it is given as a derivative of the *US collq adj* **snoopy**. Its anagram is **spoonily**.

snoopy *adj* sneaky *US collq adj* given to snooping (*comp* **snoopier** *sup* **snoopiest**)

snoore *obs fm vb* **snore**

snoose *var fm n* **snooze**

snoot *vb* to regard with contempt

snoozy *adj* drowsy (*comp* **snoozier** *sup* **snooziest**)

snorle *obs vb* meaning obscure but *poss* a combination of **snarl** and **snort**

snorter (*n*) *dial n* the wheatear

snortle *now dial vb* to snort

snorty *adj* given to snoring or snorting *collq adj* captious, bad-tempered *adv* snortingly

snory *adj* tending to snore: drowsy, sleepy

snoter *obs adj* learned, skilful, wise

Snotra *pers n* the Norse goddess of sagacity

snotte *obs fm n* **snot**

snotter *n* a short rope having an eye and used as part of the rigging on a yardarm *S & dial n* nasal mucus: something insignificant *S & dial vb* to snivel: to snuffle

snouty *adj* having a prominent snout: resembling a snout (*comp* **snoutier** *sup* **snoutiest**)

snowre *obs vb* to scowl or frown

snubby *adj* knotty: inclined to snub: short, stumpy: blunt (*comp* **snubbier** *sup* **snubbiest**)

snudge *now dial n* a miser *obs cant n* one who conceals himself in a building until the opportunity for robbery arises *now dial vb* to walk in a meditative fashion: to nestle

snule *var fm S & dial n* **snool**

snurl *dial vb* to disturb: to turn the nose up in disgust

snurp *vb* to become wrinkled

snurt *now S & dial vb* to snort

snurter *now S & dial n* one who snores

snuzzle *now dial vb* to poke about with the nose in such senses as a pig routing, a dog sniffing or a child snuggling

sny *now dial vb* to abound or swarm: to be infested

so (*adv/conj/interj*) *n* the fifth note of the tonic sol-fa system of musical notation (see **gamut**)

soaker *n* one who soaks: a heavy drinker: a sheet of roofing lead: drenching rain

soal *obs fm vb* **sole**

soapberry *n* any of various mainly tropical American trees, the fruit of which contains the substance, saponin, which foams when shaken and has detergent properties: the fruit of such a tree (*pl* **soapberries**)

soap tree *n* any soapberry tree

sobole *n* a creeping underground stem from which fresh roots and buds develop (*pl* **soboles**, which is also the Latin *sing* and the usual technical *fm*)

soc *n* the legal right to hold local jurisdiction

socage *n* the tenure of land by service other than that as a knight errant

socman *n* one who has tenure by socage

Socratic *adj* of Socrates (470–399 BC), the Greek philosopher and intellectual leader and of his methods etc *n* one who follows his teaching

Socratise *var fm vb* **Socratize**, to philosophize in the Socratic manner

sodain *obs fm adj/adv/arch n* **sudden**

sodaine *obs fm adj/adv/arch n* **sudden**

sodalite *n* a vitreous, translucent silicate of sodium and aluminium *incl* some chlorine

sodden (*adj*) *obs n* boiled meat

sodder *dial fm n/vb* **soldier**

soddy *adj* abounding in sods: composed or consisting of sods *US n* a house built of sods (the equivalent British term being **sod house**)

sodger *S & dial fm n/vb* **soldier**

sodlet *obs n* one of a number of iron bars which held glass in place in a window

Sodomite *n* an inhabitant of Sodom, the city which, with Gomorrah, was destroyed by God for its decadence (*–cap*) *n* a homosexual

softne *Obs fm vb* **soften**

soga *US n* a rope of (esparto) grass *US vb* to use such a rope

soger *S & dial fm n* **soldier**

soh *var fm n* **so** (or **sol**) the musical syllable (see **gamut**)

soi-disant *adj* self-styled, would-be

soigné *adj* elegant (the *fem fm* is **soignée**)

soiler see **free soiler**

soilure *n* a stain or blemish: soiling or staining

soir *obs S fm vb* **soar**

sol *n* either of two coins, one Peruvian, the other French, of which there were twenty to the livre (originally the French pound, later the *approx* equivalent of the franc): the fifth note of the tonic sol-fa (also called **so** or **soh**)

solacer *n* one who gives solace

soland *var fm n* **solan**, the gannet, a bird related to the pelican

solander *n* a box in the form of a book

solano *n* in Spain, a hot southeast wind (*pl* **solanos**)

solar (*adj*) *var fm n/vb* **sollar**

solate *vb* to change to a fluid colloid system (see **colloid, COLLOID SYSTEMS**)

soldan *n* a sovereign or ruler of a Moslem country

solde *n* (a soldier's) pay *obs n* a small coin

sole (*n/adj*) *vb* to provide an undersurface for an item of footwear *obs vb* to become foul or dirty

solecise *var fm vb* **solecize**, to use or make use of solecisms or irregularities of speech or diction

solecist *n* one who uses solecisms, violations of the rules of grammar or syntax

solein *obs adj* single or solitary *Obs n* a single portion: a solitary person

solen *n* the razorfish or shrimpfish, any of a family of curious, small marine fishes. A typical razorfish resembles a knifeblade – it is extremely slim and normally swims upright though it is equally adept at swimming on its head. *obs adj* solemn

soleness *n* the condition of being alone or apart

soler *n* one who soles shoes *obs n* a throne *var fm n/vb* **sollar**

solera *n* a (double butt size) wine cask: a well-matured blend of sherry

soleret *n* a small upper room *var fm n* **solleret**

soleus *n* a muscle of the calf of the leg

solidare *Shaks n* a coin mentioned in *Timon of Athens* (probably associated with a solidus – see **£ s d**, under **L**)

solidate *vb* to consolidate

solide *obs n* in the weighing of medicinal powders by the usage of coins as weights, that weight equal to the Roman gold coin, the solidus *obs fm n/adj* **solid**

solider *comp adj* solid

solidus *n* one of various historical coins *esp* a gold coin of the Eastern Roman Empire, worth 25 Roman denarii, or a silver coin of such as the early Norman kings, worth 12 denarii (see **£sd** – under **L**): the sloping line drawn to separate shillings from pence, as 14/6d ($72\frac{1}{2}$p): a curve used to illustrate the temperatures at which alloys become solid (*pl* **solidi**)

Soliman *pers n* either of two rulers of the Ottoman Empire, Soliman the Magnificent (1520–1566) or Soliman II (1687–1691) (also see **Osmanli** which, incidentally, is an extremely apt anagram)

soliped *n* an animal with an uncloven hoof *adj* solid-hoofed

solipede *var fm n/adj* **soliped**

solive *n* a joist or beam other than one which bears the greatest strain

sollar *n* a loft or attic: a room in a church steeple: a mining platform, *esp* one for supporting a ladder: a raised flooring designed to admit the free flow of air *vb* to install such flooring

solle *obs fm n* **soul**

soller *var fm n/vb* **sollar**

sollere *var fm n/vb* **sollar**

solleret *n* an armoured shoe worn by a knight in the 14th and 15th centuries

solute *n* that which is dissolved in a solution *adj* dissolved *obs vb* to solve: to explain

solutive *adj* loosening: laxative: soluble *obs n* a laxative: a solvent

Solutrean *var fm adj* **Solutrian**

Solutrian *adj* of, belonging to or characterized by the leaf-shaped flint implements found in a French cave used by prehistoric man: of that same period

somatic *adj* of, pertaining to or affecting the body of an organism: of or affecting parts of the body (in *pl fm*) *n* the study of properties of bodies

somatist *adj* with the exception of the germ cells, of or pertaining to any organism *n* a materialist

somber *US fm adj* sombre

somerset *n/vb* (to) somersault *modf n* designating a type of saddle padded in front of the knee and behind the thigh

someter *obs fm arch n* **sumpter**

somite *n* one of the distinct segments of the body of such as an insect

somitic *adj* of or pertaining to, having the form or nature of a somite

somlar *var fm obs n* **somler**

somler *obs n* a butler

somlier *var fm obs n* **somler**

somnambule *n* a somnambulist or sleep walker

somnial *adj* of or relating to dreams

sompter *obs fm arch n* **sumpter**

somter *obs fm arch n* **sumpter**

sonance *n* sound

sonancy *n* the character or quality of being sonant

sonant *n* a voiced sound *adj* voiced

sonatine *n* a type of short sonata

sonde *n* any of various devices which give information about high altitude weather and atmospheric conditions *obs fm n/vb* **sand**

sondeli *n* the musk shrew, a species of the *crocidurinae* sub-family of the *Soricidae* (see **Soricidae**)

sonder *obs fm vb* **sunder**

sondre *obs fm vb* **sunder**

soneri *n* a cloth of gold

Sonerila *n* a genus of eastern plants (*−cap*) *n* a plant of this genus

songe *obs fm n* **song**

songlet *n* a little song

songster *n* a singer: a poet

sonica *n* a card which has an immediate effect on play in the game of basset *adv* promptly

sonicate *vb* to disrupt with sound waves

Soninke *n* a Mande language of the Western Sudanic sub-group of the Niger-Congo family of languages, spoken in Mali and Mauritania

sonneter *var fm n* **sonneteer**, a composer of sonnets

Sonnite *var fm n* **Sunnite**, an orthodox Moslem

sonsie *var fm adj* **sonsy**

sonsy *adj* lucky, fortunate: comely (*comp* **sonsier** *sup* **sonsiest**)

sontag *n* a woman's knitted cape, secured at the waist

sonties *pl obs ns* **santy, sancit, santie** (see **santy**)

soodle *dial vb* to stroll or saunter

sool *var fm now dial vb* **sowl**

soonde *var fm obs n* **sand**, an envoy or messenger

soople *var fm S & dial n* **supple** *S & dial fm adj/vb* **supple**

soor *dial fm adj* **sore**

sope *now dial n* a small quantity of drink *var fm obs S vb* **sowp**, to tire or weary

sopel *obs fm vb* **supple**

sophister *n* one who makes use of specious argument

sopient *adj* having a dulling effect *n* a soporific medicine

sopite *vb* to lull to sleep: to make drowsy: to put an end to

sopper *n* one who dips something into liquid

soppet *n* a little sop

sopranist *n* one who sings soprano

soprano (*n*) *pl* **soprani, sopranos**

sora *n* a common species of North American rail, a bird which inhabits dense waterside vegetation

sorage *arch n* the first year of a hawk

sorb *n* any of three trees (*a*) the **service tree**, a European tree cultivated in Britain with round to pear-shaped fruit, edible when overripe; also, the fruit of that tree (*b*) the **service tree, rowan** or **mountain ash**, a tree of supposed magical properties (*c*) the **wild service tree** *vb* to absorb: to adsorb

sorbable an undefined adjective which appears to be exclusive to one particular American dictionary which relates it to the *vb* **sorb**. It has the American anagram, **belabors**.

sorbate *n* a salt formed by the union of sorbic acid with a base

sorbent *n/adj* (of) a substance that absorbs or adsorbs

sorbet *n* sherbet: sweetened and flavoured iced water

sordes *n sing/pl* dirt, filth

sordet *var fm obs n* **sourdet**

sordine *n* a mute or damper for a musical instrument (*pl* **sordines, sordini**) *adj* muffled, subdued

sordino *var fm n* **sordine** (*pl* **sordini**)

soredia *pl* soredium

soredial *adj* pertaining to or of the nature of a soredium

soredium *n* a cell in lichens (*pl* **soredia**)

soree *var fm n* **sora**

sorehon *n* in Ireland, free accommodation which a tenant or freeholder had to provide if required by his lord

sorel *var fm n* **sorrel**, (a horse of) a bright chestnut colour

soreld *var fm obs adj* **sorrelled**

sorell *var fm n* **sorrel**, (a horse of) a bright chestnut colour

sorelt *var fm obs adj* **sorrelled**

soren *obs fm n* **sorren**

sorest *sup adj* sore

sorgien *Obs fm n* **surgeon**

Soricidae *n pl* the family of the shrews – small, mouselike mammals with a long association with witchcraft. Whilst they form an important part of the diet of owls, cats (which play with and eat mice and voles) will play with shrews, but never eat them. The family is divided into three sub-families, the *Soricinae* (which includes the most common and widespread species), the *Crocidurinae* (which includes the world's smallest mammal, the **Etruscan shrew**) and the *Scutisorcinae* (the two species of **hero shrews**, which have a spinal column so strong that they can survive a man standing on them).

soricident *adj* having teeth like a shrew

soricine *adj* of the *Soricinae* sub-family of the *Soricidae* (see **Soricidae**): of the shrew, shrew-like *n* a shrew of the *Soricinae*

soriest *Obs fm sup* **sorriest**

soring *obs adj* of a hawk, having the red plumage of its first year (the modern equivalent being **red hawk**)

sorites *n* a series of propositions which overlap so that a conclusion is drawn from the subject of the first and the predicate of the last. For example:– *Black Beauty is a horse. A horse is a quadruped. A quadruped is an animal. Therefore, Black Beauty is an animal.* However, *Fred is a guinea pig. A guinea pig is a pet. A pet can please any woman. Therefore, Fred can please any woman.* It is also known as 'a pile of faggots'. (*pl* **sorites**)

sorn *S vb* to sponge upon others for food and lodging

sorner *S n* one who takes advantage of the good nature of others

soroche *n* mountain sickness

sorption *n* any process by which one substance takes up and holds the molecules of another

sorptive an undefined adjective which appears to be exclusive to one particular American dictionary, where it is listed as relating to **sorption**. Its anagrams are **sportive** and **pivoters**.

sorré *obs n* a dish of chopped eel (or gurnard) spiced and coloured with saffron and ginger (*obs var fms incl* **sorry**)

sorrel *n* any of a number of species of sour-tasting, small, perennial herbs of the genus *Rumex, esp* the common or wild sorrel: extended to include such as wood sorrel (genus *Oxalis*) and the hibiscus roselle: a drink made from the edible leaves of wild sorrel: a (horse of a) bright chestnut colour: a buck in its third year *adj* of a reddish brown or bright chestnut colour

sorrelled *obs adj* of a horse, having a bright chestnut colour

sorren *S & Ir n* the obligation upon vassals to provide hospitality for a chief and his gallowglasses: a monetary payment in lieu

sorry (*adj*/*interj*) *obs vb* to grieve: to provide for *var fm obs n* **sorré**, a dish of spiced eel

sortance *obs n* agreement, correspondence, suitableness

sortes *n pl* divination by the completely haphazard selection of passages from a book. Virgil's *Aeneid* was the ancient favourite, now it is usually the Bible which is chosen for this purpose.

sortment *n* classification: an assortment

sory *obs n* any type of vitriol: an ore yielding vitriol

Sotadic *n* a coarsely abusive satire after the style of the ancient Greek, Sotades *adj* of such satire

sotter *S & dial vb* of a thick substance, to make a soft sound when being boiled

soudre *obs vb* to arise *obs n* a source

sough *n* a natural, gentle, soothing sound as that of wind or water: a sigh: a rumour: a channel or drain for (rain) water: a drain in a mine *S n* a canting style of preaching *vb* to make a rushing or murmuring sound: to speak in a whining tone: to sigh: to die: to (make a) drain

soul (*n*) *vb* to go souling (see **souler**)

soular *adj* of or pertaining to the soul

souldan *obs fm n* **soldan**

soule *obs fm n* **soul** *var fm Obs n* **saulee**, a satisfying meal

souler *n* one of a group of singers (usually children) who, on All Souls Eve (1 November) or All Souls Day (2 November), go round collecting cakes or money from neighbours after the fashion of carol singers

soulet *obs adj* having the quality of soul – found only in the rather curious *n* **soulet limb** or **sowlet limb**, the head

soul-scat *var fm n* **soul-scot**

soul-scot *n* a payment to a church on behalf of a recently deceased member of that parish

soum *S n* the amount of pasturage needed to graze one cow (a variable factor dependent upon the quality of the grazing): that unit of pasturage extended to cover the grazing of sheep (approximately three sheep to the cow) *S vb* to estimate the soum (for the purpose of letting at a price per head of grazing animal)

soumer *obs n* a baggage horse

soup (*n*) *vb* to provide with soup

soupe *obs fm n* **soup**

souper *n* an Irish protestant clergyman who proselytizes with the aid of free soup: a convert by this method

souple *n* a type of silk fabric *var fm S & dial n* **supple** *S & dial fm adj* **supple**

source (*n*) *obs vb* to rise: of a raptor, to take to the air after seizing its prey: to submerge

sourdet *obs n* a mute inserted into the mouth of a trumpet

sourdine *adj* subdued (*lit/fig*) *n* a muted trumpet

souren *dial vb* to become sour

souser *dial n* a thorough soaking

sout *obs vb* to repair shoes

soutache *n* a narrow braid

soutane *n* a cassock

souter *now S & dial n* a shoemaker or cobbler

souterly *adj* resembling a souter *esp* one who is common or vulgar: appropriate to, or characteristic of, a souter (GAME PLAYER'S note: The above senses were well known to writers in Tudor and early Stuart times, with the last literary reference being in a book about the Isle of Man published in 1626. Whilst other authorities declare the word to be *obs*, nevertheless it appears as an extant but undefined *adj* in the dictionary used for the UK Scrabble championship. In the North American equivalent they accept **souter** but ignore **souterly**.)

south (*adv/adj/prep/n*) *vb* to veer, move or turn towards the south: of the wind, to blow (more) from the south: of a heavenly body, to cross the meridian of a place

souther *n* a south wind *vb* of the wind, to veer or shift southward *obs adj* the more south of two (also see **northest**)

Southey *pers n* Robert (1774–1843) the poet laureate whose best work is considered to be his prose. He wrote histories of Brazil and the Peninsula War and biographies of Nelson and Wesley, among others.

sowarry *n* a mounted attendant accompanying a person of high rank: a cavalcade of such attendants

sowl *now dial n* any foodstuff eaten with bread *now dial vb* to seize (a pig) by the ears *obs vb* to serve as a relish *now dial fm n/vb* **soul**

sowlet *var fm obs adj* **soulet**

sownde *var fm obs n* **sand**, a messenger *obs fm n/adj/adv/vb* **sound**

sowpel *S fm vb* **supple**

sowple *obs fm vb* **supple**

sowre *obs fm n/vb* **sour**

sowse *var fm n/vb* **souse**, in the sense of pickled food or to pickle food *obs fm n/vb* **souse**, in all other senses

sowter *var fm now S & dial n* **souter**

spaad *obs n* a powdered form of such as talc or gypsum used to make the moulds for metal casting

spache *Obs fm n* **speech**

spaddle *obs n* a little spade

spader *n* one who or that which digs with a spade(-like implement)

spadger *slg n* a sparrow

spae *vb* (*orig S*) to prophesy

spaen *obs fm n* **spawn**

spaer *n* one who tells fortunes

spaewife *S n* a female fortune-teller: a witch

spahee *var fm n* **spahi**, a horseman in the cavalry of the old, feudally organized, Turkish army: an Algerian cavalryman in the French army

spaid *obs fm ns* **spade, spayd**

spaier *Obs fm obs n* **spare**, a slit in a garment

Spaigne *obs fm n* **Spain**

spaile *var fm S & dial n* **spale**

spain *var fm S & dial vb* **spane**

spair *obs fm n* **spear** *obs S fm vb* **spare**

spairge *S fm n/vb* **sparge**

spalde *Obs fm S & dial n* **spauld**

spale *S & dial n* a thin strip of wood *dial vb* to penalize (a Cornish miner) for a breach of the rules *var fm now dial vb* **spele**

spalling *n* the action of such as breaking ore into small pieces or dressing stone

spalme *obs fm n* **psalm**

spalt *vb* to splinter

spalter *S & dial vb* to split or chip, to splinter *obs fm n* **psalter**

spancel *n* a rope fetter for such as a cow *esp* during milking

spane *n* a wood chip *S & dial vb* of lambs and babies, to wean: of corn, to begin to take root (*var fms vb incl* **spaan, spain, spean**)

spangler *n* one who or that which spangles *obs n* one bedecked with spangles

spangly *adj* bedecked with spangles (*comp* **spanglier** *sup* **spangliest**)

spaniel (*n/adj*) *vb* to act like a spaniel i.e. to fawn upon or follow submissively

Spanish fly *n* a species of blister beetle which, when dried, is the most famous of all substances claimed to have aphrodisiac properties. Medicinally, it is used externally either to counter irritation or as a vesicant. Internally it is used to stimulate the genito-urinary organs. (See **cantharis**)

sparer *n* a thrifty or miserly person: that which aids in saving: one who refrains from causing injury or damage *comp adj* spare

sparest *sup adj* spare

sparge *vb* to plaster: to besprinkle *n* a spray of warm water sprinkled over malt during the brewing process

sparger *n* a brewing appliance which sprinkles water

sparid *n* any species of sea bream or allied fish

Sparidae *n pl* the family of the sea bream

sparke *obs fm n/vb* **spark** *Spens n* a weapon, *poss* a battle ax

sparling *now S n* the smelt *US n* an immature herring *obs n* a term of endearment: the sprat

sparlire *Obs n* the calf of the leg

sparple *obs vb* to scatter

sparret *obs n* a small spar or bar

sparrowfart *dial n* daybreak

sparry *adj* of the nature of, consisting of or abounding in the crystalline mineral, spar: of land, rich in spar: resembling such as the lustre of spar

sparse (*adj*) *obs vb* to spread (a rumour or doctrine): to scatter

sparser *comp adj* sparse

spart *n* esparto, any of various Southern European and North African grasses used to make ropes, mats etc *S & dial n* a coarse, rushy grass: a dwarf rush

sparte *obs fm S & dial n* **spart**

sparteine *n* a medicinal substance obtained from the plant, broom

spartel *obs fm obs vb* **spartle** *obs fm now dial n* **spartle**

sparthe *n* a long-handled, broad-bladed (Irish) battle ax typically favoured by a gallowglass: one who used such a weapon *esp* a gallowglass

spartle *S vb* to move in a sprawling way *obs vb* to scatter *now dial n* a spatula

sparty *S & dial adj* abounding in rushes

sparwe *Obs fm n* **sparrow**

spase *obs fm n/vb* **space**

spate *n* a flood

spatel *Obs fm now dial n/obs vb* **spattle**

spatell *Obs fm now dial n* **spattle**

spathe *n* a leaflike organ of several members of the lily family

spathed *adj* having a spathe

spather *obs n* a spatula

spathic *adj* of the nature of spar (the mineral)

spathose *adj* of the nature of, resembling, abounding in or consisting of spar: having a foliated texture: sparry

spatill *Obs fm now dial n* **spattle**

spatle *obs fm n/now dial n/vb* **spattle** *var fm obs vb* **spattle**

spattee *n* a protective item of legwear which is a combined spat and puttee

spatter (*n*) *vb* to scatter or disperse in fragments: to spit: to walk in some splashy substance

spatterer *n* one who spatters

spattle *n* a spatula *now dial n* spittle *dial n* a spade *vb* to sprinkle *obs vb* to spit

spatula *n* a simple implement with a broad, flat blade used for mixing or spreading

spatule *n* a spatula: the broad, rounded end part of the tail feathers in some birds

spaul *var fm S & dial n* **spauld** *obs vb* of a horse, to be injured in the shoulder

spauld *S & dial n* the shoulder (of man or beast)

spaulde *Obs fm S & dial n* **spauld**

spaune *obs fm n/vb* **spawn**

spawde *var fm obs n* **spaad** *Obs fm S & dial n* **spauld**

spawne *obs fm n/vb* **spawn**

spawner *n* a female fish at spawning time (the male being a **milter**): one who or that which spawns in various senses *obs n* a woman viewed as a potential childbearer

spayd *arch n* a male deer in its third year

spayer *obs n* a sluice *obs fm arch n* **spayd** *obs fm vb* **spare**

Spayne *obs fm n* **Spain**

spayre *var fm obs n* **spare**, a slit in a (woman's) gown *var fm obs n* **spayer**

speach *obs fm n* **speech**

speal *var fm S & dial vb* **speel** *var fm S & dial n* **spale**

speale *var fm obs vb* **spele**

spealer *var fm* **speler** (*obs fm n* **speller**)

spean *now dial n* a (cow's) nipple *dial n* a bar of a gate: a prong of a fork *var fm S & dial vb* **spane**

spearfish *n* any of various unrelated fishes having a fancied resemblance to a spear, such as the quillback sucker (a freshwater fish related to the carp) or the sailfish of the tropical and sub-tropical oceans

spear side *n* the male line of descent

spearwort *n* any of several species of plants *incl* ratsbane, favoured, in historical times, by beggars who used it to raise blisters on themselves in order to elicit sympathy

speary *adj* spear-like: slender *obs adj* of grass, hard and stiff

speat *var fm n* **spate**

specialer *comp adj* special

specie *n* coined money as opposed to paper money or bullion

species *n* of animals, a subdivision of a genus in which the various members are capable of interbreeding: of plants, a similar relationship: any group of animals or plants which are closely related though not necessarily possessing that facility of union (see **genus**): a kind, sort or variety: the bread or wine of Holy Communion (*pl* **species**)

specter *now US fm n* **spectre**

spectra *pl* spectrum (**spectrums** is also an acceptable *pl*)

spectre (*n*) *vb* to fill with phantoms

spectrum *n* a colour display through a prism (*pl* **spectra, spectrums**)

specula *pl* speculum

speculum *n* a mirror or reflective (metal) surface used for scientific purposes: any of various surgical instruments which dilate bodily orifices during an examination of such: a lustrous mark on the wings of various birds (*pl* **specula, speculums**)

speder *obs fm n* **speeder**

speeder *n* one who travels fast: that which regulates speed *arch n* one who helps

speedo *collq n* a car's speedometer (*pl* **speedos**)

speel *S n* the act of climbing *now dial n* a strip of wood or metal *var fm S & dial n* **spale** *S & dial vb* to climb

speeler *S n* one of a pair of spiked irons attached to shoes to assist in the climbing of trees or poles *Austr n* a fast horse *obs S n* a performer *esp* an acrobatic one *var fm Austr slg n* **spieler**

speer *n* (sea) spray *S n* an enquiry *now dial n* a domestic anti-draught screen *obs n* a prong of a deer's horn *S vb* to enquire *US & dial vb* to peer

speet *arch var fm n/vb* **spit**, (to cook on) a slender rod *dial fm n* **spit**, the depth in the earth of the length of the blade of a spade

speid *obs S fm vb* **speed** *obs fm arch n* **speed**, success or good fortune

speil *var fm S & dial vb* **speel**

speir *var fm S vb* **speer** *obs n* hope

speire *obs fm S vb* **speer**

speiss *n* a mixture of the arsenides of certain metals (such as copper or iron) which concentrate in the smelting process of such ores

speit *obs fm n* **spit**

speitt *obs fm n* **spit**

spelaean *adj* cave-dwelling

spelair *var fm obs S n* **speeler**

spelare *Obs fm obs S n* **speeler**

spelder *S vb* to stretch oneself *dial vb* to spell words *obs n* a splinter

speldin *var fm S n* **speldring**

speldrin *var fm S n* **speldring**

speldring *S n* a small fish which has been split and sun-dried

speldron *var fm S n* **speldring**

spele *now dial vb* to deputize for, to represent: to use sparingly *obs vb* to signify *var fm now dial n* **speel**

spelean *var fm adj* **spelaean**

speler *obs fm n* **speller**, an authority on spelling *obs fm arch n* **speller**, any of the horns on the top of a deer's antlers

spelter *n* zinc: a zinc-based alloy or solder *vb* to solder with spelter

speltre *arch fm n* **spelter**

spend (*vb*) *vb* to break ground whilst mining *S vb* to spring, leap or bound *now dial vb* to brace up the collar of a draught horse's harness *obs vb* to grasp (also see **spended**) *S n* a leap or bound

spended *pa t/pa pple* whilst this is an *obs fm* of **spent** in the standard meaning of the *vb*, it may have currency with regard to other meanings of to spend e.g. the *obs vb* **spend** (in which the *now dial vb* **spend** is etymologically rooted) had the *infl* **spendyd**

spene *obs vb* to spend: to use *var fm now dial n* **spean**

Spener *pers n* Philipp Jakob Spener who, in Frankfurt circa 1670, founded the Pietist movement in the Lutheran Church which concerned itself with religious education and the deepening of piety

spense *now dial n* an out of pocket expense: (pocket) money

Spenser *pers n* Edmund (1552–1599), '*the poet's poet*'. Though born in London and educated at Cambridge, he spent the greater part of his later years in Ireland where he wrote his classic, *The Faerie Queene*. (*– cap*) *Obs fm obs n* **spencer**, a butler

spere *obs fm n* **spear** (in most senses) *obs fm now dial n* **speer** *obs fm n* **sphere**

sperel *Obs n* a fastening device

sperit *var fm n* **spirit**

sperite *var fm n* **spirit**

sperling *var fm now S n* **sparling**

spermaceti *n* a fatty substance obtained from the sperm whale and other whales for medicinal uses and for candle fat

spermatic *adj* consisting, conveying, producing or full of sperm: productive *n* (in *pl* only) the vessels which convey sperm

spermatid *n* an immature sperm cell

spern *var fm n/vb* **spurn**, (to) prop or support

sperr *obs fm arch vb* **spar**, to fasten

sperre *obs fm n/vb* **spar**, (to fasten with) a rod or pole *Obs fm ns* **sphere, spur**

sperse *arch vb* to scatter: to drive (or take) different directions

sperst *obs fm adj* **spersed**, scattered

spert *obs n* a basket

Spertan *obs fm n/adj* **Spartan**

sperte *var fm obs n* **spert**

sperthe *var fm n* **sparthe**

spertle *obs fm now dial vb* **spirtle**

sperwe *Obs fm n* **sparrow**

spete *obs vb* to spit

spew (*vb*) *vb* of bees, to swarm for the fourth time in one season

spewer *n* one who spews

spey *arch fm vb* **spay**, to sterilize

Speyne *obs fm n* **Spain**

sphaer *obs fm n* **sphere**

sphaere *obs fm n* **sphere**

sphear *obs fm n/vb* **sphere**

spheare *obs fm n* **sphere**

sphene *n* a variously coloured, lustrous mineral of calcium and titanium in crystalline form (also called titanite)

sphenoid *adj* wedge-shaped: designating a compound bone of irregular form situated at the base of the skull, the sphenoid bone *n* that bone: a wedge-shaped crystal with four faces each of which cuts all three axes (i.e. each axis)

sphere (*n*) *vb* to enclose (as) in a sphere: to make into a sphere

spheric (*adj*) *n* (usually *pl*) the mathematical study of the sphere

sphery *adj* resembling a sphere (*comp* **spherier** *sup* **spheriest**)

spicate *adj* of flowers, spiked

spicule *n* a minute, needle-like body or process

spide *obs fm n* **speed** *obs fm arch n* **speed**, success or good fortune

spiece *var fm obs n* **spece**, a spice: a part: a variety of something

spiel *S n* a curling match *var fm S n/S & dial vb* **speel**

spieler *n* one with a glib tongue *esp* one delivering sales patter (originally *US slg* now spreading into general use) *Austr slg n* a gambler: a card sharp

spier *n* an espier: a spy *var fm S vb* **speer**

spiere *obs fm n* **spire** *obs fm S & dial n* **spire**, a sapling

spiet *obs fm n* **spite**

spignel *n* the plant baldmoney or meum, the aromatic root of which was formerly dried and ground, then used in medicine or as a cooking spice

spiker *n* one who renders a gun unserviceable: one who hammers in a spike *obs fm n* **speaker**

spilde *obs fm pa pple* **spilt** or **spilled**

spile *n* a spigot *vb* to stop up a hole with a spigot

spille *obs fm vb* **spill** *Obs fm n* **spill**

spillen *Obs infl* (*inf*) *vb* spill

spilte *obs fm pa pple* **spilt**

spilter *obs n* a splinter or fragment

spilth *n* anything spilt: excess

spinage *var fm n* **spinach**, the common vegetable

spinagre *Obs n* a plant mentioned in mediaeval texts but unidentified by modern research

spinal (*adj*) *arch fm n* **spinel**

spinar *n* a galactic body which spins rapidly

spinaret *var fm n* **spinneret**

spinate *adj* spined, possessing a spine

spindel *obs fm n/vb* **spindle**

spine (*n*) *vb* to hit in the spine *obs vb* to grow spine-like

spinee *obs n* a dish flavoured with the flowers of the hawthorn

spinel *n* a ruby-like precious stone

spinet *n* an old type of keyboard musical instrument rather like a harpsichord *arch n* a thicket

spinette *var fm n* **spinet**, the musical instrument

spiney *obs n* the shoot of a plant (*pl* **spinies**) *var fm adj* **spiny**

spinger *obs n* a musical note which immediately follows another without any pause

spinie *obs fm adj* **spiny**

spinigrade *n* any of various starfishes which move by means of their spines (contrast with **pinigrade**)

spink (*n*) *vb* of such as a young blackbird, to utter its cry

spinke *obs fm now dial n* **spink**, the chaffinch

spinked *dial adj* of cattle, speckled

spinneret *n* the organ used by such as spiders and silkworms to discharge their thread

spinnet *var fm n* **spinet**

spinode *n* a cusp

spinone *n* a rare Italian breed of dog in the gundog class

spinous *adj* full of spines or thorns: thornlike

spinule *n* a small, needle-like growth which supports the tissue of such as a sponge

spiny *adj* bearing or covered with thorns (*comp* **spinier** *sup* **spiniest**) *var fm obs n* **spiney**

spiracle *n* a respiratory aperture of various sorts such as the blowhole of a whale; a small, paired, rudimentary gill slit in a skate, ray or related fish; and any of several paired apertures in an insect

spiraea *n* one of a number of species of rosaceous plants or shrubs of which only dropwort and meadowsweet are truly native to the UK

spiraled *US fm adj* **spiralled**

spirant (*adj*) *n* a consonant with a sound capable of extension

spiraster *n* a sponge spicule with radiating spines

spirated *adj* spirally twisted

spire (*n*) *vb* to rise in a spire-shaped form: to curl or twist *esp* in an upward direction *arch vb* of seeds, to develop shoots *now dial vb* of plants, to stalk *esp* at the expense of lateral growth *obs vb* to breathe

spirea *var fm n* **spiraea**

spireme *n* any of a number of filaments which appear during a stage in the division of a cell: that particular stage

spirilla *pl* spirillum

spirillum *n* any of a group of bacteria *esp* the species having a spiral structure found in the blood during a relapsing fever (*pl* **spirilla**)

spirituel *adj* of a highly refined (and quick witted) nature (*fem* **spirituelle**)

spirling *now S n* the smelt

spirometer *n* an instrument used for measuring lung capacity

spirtle *n* a sprinkle *now dial vb* to sprinkle

spiset *infl Obs vb* spise, to despise

spital *arch n* a hospital

spitcher *slg adj* done for

spitel *var fm obs n* **spittle** *Obs fm now dial n* **spittle** *Obs fm vb* **spittle**

spitle *var fm obs n* **spittle**

spitte *obs fm n* **spit**

spittel *var fm obs n* **spittle**

spitter (*n*) *now dial n* a spade: one who uses such *obs n* a young deer

spittle *n* saliva *now dial n* a (small) spade: a hoe *obs n* a lazar house or hospital for those either of a low class or suffering a particularly foul disease *vb* to spit

splate *var fm vb* **splat**, to split open (*obs* except as an *arch* 'correct' usage for splitting open a pike for cooking) *var fm obs vb* **splat**, of a horse, to strain its shoulder

splayer *n* a device used in the production of moulded tiles in order to effect a cylindrical shape

spleen (*n*) *vb* to feel deep anger: to remove the spleen from (the carcase of an animal)

spleet *now dial n* a small strip of willow *obs vb* to fit such a strip to a beehive *S vb* to split

splendor *var fm* (*now US*) *n* **splendour**

splene *obs fm n/vb* **spleen**

splenia *pl* splenium

splenic *adj* of, pertaining to or connected with the spleen

splenium *n* a compress or bandage (*pl* **splenia**)

splenius *n* a broad muscle at the upper part of the back of the neck (*pl* **splenii**)

spleter *obs n* a splinter

spley *dial fm vb* **splay**

spline *n* a slat: a device which permits longitudinal movement of a wheel attached to a shaft *dial n* a measure of $10\frac{1}{2}$ feet *vb* to attach the mechnical device

splintage *n* the using of surgical splints

splite *obs n* a narrow opening

splitted *obs fm adj* **split**

splore *S n* a revel: a commotion *S vb* to revel or riot

splotchy *adj* covered with stains (*comp* **splotchier** *sup* **splotchiest**)

splunge *US & dial vb* to plunge

splurge *n/vb* (to make) an ostentatious display

spode *n* a medicinal powder obtained from various substances *incl* bone ash: a fine porcelain containing bone ash made at the Stoke-on-Trent works founded by Josiah Spode (1754–1827)

spoilage *n* the action of spoiling: the fact of being or that which is spoilt

spoile *obs fm n* **spoil**

spodium *n* any of various fine powders obtained by calcination

spole *dial fm n/vb* **spool**

spoliage *n* spoliation in the senses indicated

spoliation *n* an act of or the action of despoiling or plundering: seizure by violent means: the condition of being despoiled (in the above senses, **spoliage** has the same meaning): an ecclesiastical writ brought by an incumbent claiming that another has false title to his benefice: the action of destroying or otherwise tampering with a document so as to void its value as evidence

spond *obs vb* to bind by a promise

spondee see **metric foot**

spondie *obs fm n* **spondee**

sponsalia *n* marriage

spool (*n*) *vb* to wind such as thread on a spool

spooler *n* one who winds thread onto spools

spoonerism *n* the transposition of the initial consonants or consonant clusters of a pair of words so as to form some ludicrous combination. It is named after the Rev. W A Spooner (1844–1930) who accidentally coined them. Among his classics, during his period as Warden of New College, Oxford (1903–1924), are:– '*We all know what it is to have a half-warmed fish within us*' (for '... *half-formed wish*'). '*You have tasted a whole worm.*' '*I have just received a blushing crow.*' '*You have hissed all my mystery lectures.*' '*Yes, indeed, the Lord is a shoving leopard.*' '*You will leave by the town drain.*' '*Is the bean dizzy?*'

spoony *adj* foolish, silly: overly sentimental (*comp* **spoonier** *sup* **spooniest**)

spoor *n* the trace or track left on the ground by a moving animate or inanimate object *vb* to trace an animal by following its spoor: to follow a spoor

sporal *adj* relating to or consisting of spores

spore *n* a reproductive body of some of the lowest forms of animal life and of many plants which can, according to the parent stock, be either sexual or asexual *vb* to produce, carry or release spores *now dial fm n/vb* **spur**

spoorn *obs n* a malicious ghost or phantom

sporge *obs fm n/now dial vb* **spurge**

sporles *Obs fm adj* **spurless**

sporne *var fm obs n* **spoorn** *obs fm vb* **spurn**

sporre *obs fm n/vb* **spur**, (to prick with) a device attached to a horse rider's heel

sportance *n* sport, sportive play

sporte *obs fm n/vb* **sport**

sportlet *Obs n* a small basket

sporule *n* a small pore

sposhy *US adj* slushy

spotel *obs fm now dial n* **spattle**

spotle *obs fm now dial n* **spattle**

spotte *obs fm n/vb* **spot**

spottle *vb* to cover as with spots or blotches *obs fm now dial n* **spattle**

spoune *obs fm n/vb* **spoon**

spourge *var fm obs vb* **spurge**

spouse (*n*) *arch vb* to give a woman in marriage

spoute *obs fm n/vb* **spout**

spowle *obs fm n* **spool**

spowte *obs fm n* **spout**

spowter *obs fm n* **spouter**

spoyle *obs fm ns* **spoil, spool**

spraid *var fm dial adj* **sprayed**

spraint *rarely used sing fm n pl* **spraints**

spraintes *obs fm n pl* **spraints**

spraints *n pl* otter dung

sprait *var fm S n* **spret**

sprangle *now US & dial vb* to struggle, to sprawl: of a plant, to spread out in branches *US n* a branching rootlet: a sprawl

sprat (*n*) *vb* to fish for sprats

sprate *obs fm n/vb* **sprat**

sprattle *S n/vb* (to) struggle

sprayed *dial adj* of skin, roughened or made sore by exposure to cold (*var fms incl* **spry, spraid**)

spreat *var fm S & dial n* **spret**

spreathe *var fm vb* **spray**, to chap or make the skin rough (the usage is mainly *dial* and most commonly encountered as a *pa pple*)

sprede *obs fm n/vb* **spread**

spreder *obs fm n* **spreader**

spree (*n*) *vb* to participate in merrymaking

spreed *dial fm vb* **spread**

spreet *var fm n* **sprit**, a (punting) pole

sprein *obs fm n/vb* **sprain**

spreit *obs fm n* **spirit**

sprent *now S & dial vb* to spring or leap: to sprinkle *S & dial n* a leap: a lock spring: a fastening of such as a chest or trunk: a snare

spret *S & dial n* coarse, reedy, rush-like grass

sprete *obs fm n* **sprit**, a (punting) pole

sprewse *obs fm adj* **spruce**

spriest *var fm sup* **spryest**

spriggan *dial n* a bucca or Cornish mine goblin (see **bucca**)

sprigging *n* a needlework design of sprigs

sprindge *obs fm n* **springe**

springal *n* a bouncy young man *obs fm n* **springle**, a snare

springe *n* a (bird) snare *adj* agile *vb* to (set a) trap *now dial vb* to sprinkle water

springel *obs n* a holy water sprinkler

springet *obs n* a young shoot of a plant (*lit/fig*)

springhare *n* a large, very bizarre, nocturnal burrowing rodent of southern Africa. The mature length is about 15 inches, which is doubled by an equally long bushy tail. It has long hindlegs and especially long hindfeet, short front legs and disproportionately short front feet which have long, curved claws. The quaint head has long ears, large bulging eyes, prominent whiskers and a deep muzzle with large, protruding, orange teeth. Also known as the **springhaas** or **Cape jumping hare**, it is the sole member of its family, the *Pedetidae*. Whilst vaguely resembling the much smaller jerboa, which occupies the same ecological niche in northern Africa, it is *not* related. (WORD PUZZLER'S note: The word springhare is the basic popular term given in the specialist work used as the source material for the above. This same work gives it the alternative popular name of Cape jumping hare, the scientific name of *Pedetes capensis* but carries no reference to springhaas. The *Oxford English Dictionary* has springhaas as the basic English term, Cape jumping hare as the alternative name but *Pedetes caffer* as the scientific name. It carries no mention of springhare. (It should be noted that the last international conference on the scientific naming of animals occurred many years after the *OED* published its definition of springhaas in its *Supplement*.) *Chambers 20th Century Dictionary* is very different. It has jumping-hare as the basic term; as an English alternative name it has spring-hare; as 'foreign', spring-haas; it gives no scientific name and, finally, has the creature 'akin' to the jerboa.)

springle *n* a snare: a thatching rod *arch vb* to sprinkle *Obs vb* to sparkle

sprintle *Obs n* a twig or shoot (*pl* **sprintles**)

sprit *n* a (punting) pole: a shoot or sprout of a plant *S n* a rush or rushlike plant *now dial vb* to sprout: to germinate

sprite (*n*) *obs vb* to inspire with courage

spritely *adj/adv* now *obs* and replaced by **sprightly**

spriten *obs vb* to enliven

spritlye *earlier fm obs adj/adv* **spritely**

sprittle *now dial vb* to scrape or dig up with an implement

sproat *n* a type of fish hook specifically designed for salmon and trout

sproket *arch fm n* **sprocket**, a toothlike projection which engages with the links of a chain

sproot *obs fm n* **sprout**

sprote *now dial n* a splinter: a twig

sproute *obs fm n/vb* **sprout**

sprowt *obs fm vb* **sprout**

sprowte *obs fm n/vb* **sprout**

spruit *S Afr n* a small watercourse which usually disappears during the dry season *obs fm vb* **sprout**

sprule *S & dial fm vb* **sprawl**

sprunt *adj* smart, spruce *now dial vb* to dart or run

sprute *obs fm vb* **sprout**

spry (*adj/adv*) *vb* to smarten up: to bustle about *dial n* a flat broom of birch twigs

spuddle *now dial vb* to work feebly

spule *S n* a shoulder

spuller *obs fm n* **spooler**

spune *S fm n* **spoon** (and *vb* only in the sense of using a spune)

spunge *obs fm n/vb* **sponge**

spure *obs fm S vb* **speer**

spurge *n* any of various species of plants having an acrid, milky juice with medicinal value *now dial vb* of the fermenting process of such as ale or wine, to cast impure material *obs n/vb* (to) sprout

spurgel *Obs n* a water cistern

spurger *obs n* a purgative

spuriae *n pl* the feathers of the bastard wing, those three, four or five feathers (dependent upon species) which grow from the equivalent of a thumb on the wing of a bird

spurl *S vb* to sprawl

spurling *var fm now S n* **sparling**

spurne *obs* (*Spens*) *vb* to spur *obs fm n/vb* **spurn**

spurre *obs fm n/vb* **spur** *obs fm S vb* **speer**

spurtel *var fm S & dial n* **spurtle**

spurtle *vb* to besprinkle: to spurt: to sputter *S & dial n* a porridge stirring stick: a sword

spute *now dial vb* to dispute *Obs vb* to spit

spy *adj* nimble (*comp* **sprier** or **spryer** *sup* **spriest** or **spryest**)

spyler *n* a scoop used by a cheese taster

sq see **seq**

sqadwe *var fm obs adj* **scawed**

sqq see **seq**

squable *obs fm vb* **squabble**

squader *obs n* a small military company

squadrant *obs n* a military or naval squadron

squadrat *obs S fm adj* **squadrate**

squadrate *adj* square-shaped

squage *obs vb* to make dirty

squail *dial n* a skittle *vb* to throw a squailer *dial vb* to pelt with sticks

squailer *n* a weighted stick for throwing at such as fruit high in a tree or small game

squair *obs fm n* **square** *obs S fm adj* **square**

squake *obs fm n/vb* **squeak**

squale *var fm dial vb* **squail**

squame *n* a scale as a natural part of the covering of a fish or reptile *obs n* a scale as an unhealthy part of a human

squark *vb* of birds, to utter a squawking cry

squate *Obs fm n* **squat** (now *dial* except in the sense of the act of squatting)

squean *obs vb* to squint

squear *obs fm adj* **square**

squeck *obs vb* a disease of poultry

squeek *obs fm n/vb* **squeak**

squeel *arch fm n/vb* **squeal**

squeil *obs S fm vb* **squeal**

squeke *obs fm vb* **squeek**

squele *obs fm vb* **squeal**

squelt *var fm dial n* **squilt**

squene *var fm obs vb* **squean**

squere *obs fm n* **square**

squibbe *obs fm n* **squib**, the firework

squiblet *n* a little squib

squier *obs fm ns* **square, squire**

squiff *var fm collq adj* **squiffy**, tipsy *obs n* a small light boat

squill *n* the sea onion or related plant: the bulb of that plant

squilla *n* the mantis shrimp (*pl* **squillae, squillas**)

squillae *pl* squilla

squiller *obs n* a servant in charge of the scullery

squilt *dial n* a pimple

squince *obs n* quinsy

squine *dial vb* to squint *Obs fm n* **swine**

squink *Ir vb* to squint

squiny *var fm vb* **squinny**, to squint

squireen *n* a petty squire

squiret *n* a petty squire

squirk *n* a squeaking sound: a partly suppressed laugh

squirte *obs fm n/vb* **squirt**

squirtel *obs n* a syringe

squirting cucumber *n* the wild cucumber, the seeds of which are expelled with considerable force

squitter *now dial n* diarrhoea *now dial vb* to void such

squog *dial n* a squirrel

squoyle *var fm n* **squailer**

sqvare *obs fm vb* **square**

sqwate *Obs fm adj* **squat**

sqwere *obs S fm n* **squire**

sqwier *obs fm n* **square** *Obs fm n/vb* **squire**

sqwoil *var fm dial vb* **squail**

sqwug *var fm dial n* **squog**

st *interj* to attract attention

stabel *obs fm n/vb* **stable**

stabile (*adj*) *n* a stationary abstract sculpture

stablet *obs n* a small stable or similar animal housing

staccato *adj* of musical notes, short, clipped and separate: of speech etc, characterized by such sound *adv* in a staccato manner *n* a staccato manner, performance or passage (*pl* **staccatos**)

stacket *obs S n* a defensive wall of stakes *obs S vb* to build such a defence (*infl* **stacketed** etc)

stacte *n* the finest liquid myrrh, a Hebrew fragrant spice

stade *n* stadium, an ancient measure of length equal to an eighth of a mile: an arena for sport

staen *dial fm n* **stone**

stafe *obs fm n* **staff**

stag (*n*) *vb* to inform: to turn informer *S & dial vb* to walk with long strides *dial vb* to take off the top of a hedge and not remove the clippings

stagery *n* theatrical items or contrivances: exhibition on the stage

stagier *comp adj* stagy, having a theatrical quality

staid (*adj*) *S fm n* **stade**

staider *comp adj* staid

staier *obs fm n* **stair**

stail *S var fm n/vb* **stale**

staile *var fm now dial n* **stale**

staine *obs fm ns/vbs* **stain, stone**

stainer *n* one employed to stain wood

staint *obs fm now S n* **stent**

stair (*n*) *obs vb* to ascend

staire *obs fm n* **stair**

stairer *obs n* a guardian of a stairway

staith *var fm n* **staithe**

staithe *n* a (coal) wharf: a landing stage: an embankment *dial vb* to construct a staithe

stale *adj* not fresh *obs adj* of malt liquor, mead or wine, old and strong *n* a bird used as a decoy to ensnare other birds, either its own species or a bird of prey: a stuffed bird serving the same purpose: horse or cattle urine *now dial n* a rung of a ladder: a stave of a rack in a stable: a long slender handle: a stalk or stem: the stem of an arrow or spear (also see *now dial n* **steal)** *obs n* a thief's accomplice who acts as a decoy: an ambush: one whose love and devotion is derided by a rival for that affection *vb* to render stale in the adjectival sense: to render (ale) old and strong: of horses and cattle, to urinate *obs vb* to decoy: to put rungs in a ladder *var fm now dial n/vb* **steal**

staler *comp adj* stale

stalke *obs fm n/vb* **stalk**

stalky *adj* of the nature of a stalk or stalks: long and slender like a stalk: consisting of or abounding in stalks (*comp* **stalkier** *sup* **stalkiest)**

stamen *n* the pollen-bearing male organ of a flower (*pl* **stamens, stamina)**

stamin *n* a coarse worsted cloth: a garment *esp* an undergarment woven from this material for an ascetic

stamina *n* endurance (*pl* **staminas)** *n pl* stamens: germinal elements

staminate *adj* having or producing stamens

stamine *var fm obs n* **stamin**

staminode *n* a sterile stamen

stammel *n* a coarse woollen cloth: an undergarment of this, worn by ascetics

stampee *n* a counterfeit coin also known as a black dog which circulated in the West Indies during piratical times and could be purchased at a rate of three shillings a gross

stan *dial fm n/vb* **stand** *obs fm n/vb* **stone** *obs fm dial n* **stend**, a butcher's stick

stanch *n* that which stops external bleeding: a dam in a river: an offensive vapour in an underground working *vb* to stop the flow (of blood): to relieve pain *arch vb* to quench a fire *obs vb* to put an end to anything unpleasant *var fm adj* **staunch**

stanchel *now S n* a prop *S & dial n* a kestrel

stancher *n* one who or that which stanches

stande *obs fm n/vb* **stand**

standee *US n* one compelled to stand

standen *obs pa pple vb* stand (now, **stood)**

stander *n* one who stands

standerd *obs fm n* **standard**

standred *obs fm n* **standard**

stane *S fm n/vb* **stone** *obs fm n/vb* **stain**

staner *Obs fm n* **stoner**, one who throws stones

stang *vb* to sting *dial vb* to throb with pain: to spear eels *now S & dial n* a sting: the pipefish: the lesser weeverfish: an eel spear: the tongue of a Jew's harp *dial n* a pole or stake *obs n* a measure of land equal to a rood, or quarter of an acre, in England; or an acre in Wales

stange *obs fm dial n/vb* **stang** *obs fm now S & dial n* **stank**

stanhope *n* a type of light, open carriage having either two wheels (the earlier models) or four (WORD PUZZLER'S note: Also see **phaeton** which, in *pl*, is an apt anagram)

stanie *obs S fm adj* **stony**

staniel *n* the kestrel: a useless person (i.e. one like a kestrel which is useless for falconry)

stanier *comp obs S adj* stanie

stank (*vbl infl*) *n* a weir or floodgate *now S & dial n* a pond or pool: a ditch or dyke in which the flow of water is very sluggish *now S & dial modf n* see examples below *obs adj* weary, faint *vb* to strengthen the banks of a stream *obs vb* to surround with a moat

stank brae *S n* the edge of a stank

stanke *obs fm now S & dial n* **stank** *var fm obs adj* **stank**

stank hen *S & dial n* the moorhen

stank meadow *S & dial n* a meadow containing a stank

stannic *adj* of, pertaining to or containing tin, *esp* that tin of a higher valence

stanze *obs fm n* **stanza**

stape *dial fm n* **staple**, the small, U-shaped, metal fastening device *Obs fm n* **step** (*pl* **stapen, stapes**)

stapedial *adj* pertaining to stapes in the anatomical sense

stapel *obs fm n/vb* **staple**

stapella *n* any plant of the genus of the carrion flower

stapen see **stape**

stapes *n* a stirrup: the stirrup-shaped innermost of three bones of the ear: a bandage used for the ankle

stapple *var fm S & dial n* **stopple**

staragen *obs fm n* **tarragon**

starche *obs fm n/vb* **starch**

starets *var fm n* **staretz**, a holy man in Russia

stark (*adj/adv*) *arch vb* to make stiff

starke *obs n* the redstart, a common European singing bird with a red tail which it darts rapidly from side to side

starken *vb* to make stark or inflexible

starle *obs n* a starling *var fm obs n* **strale**

star man *n* an astrologer

starn *now S & dial n* a star *S & dial n* a single grain

starne *var fm now S & dial n/S & dial n* **starn**

starnel *dial n* the starling

starnie *S n* a little star

starnose *n* the star-nosed mole, a unique North American species of mole which is a very good swimmer and often seeks aquatic food. It has a radiate arrangement of 22 fleshy processes around its snout tip, covered with tiny sense organs of touch, hence the name. (GAME PLAYER'S note: Another typical example of a word valid for championship Scrabble® play in the USA but denied to UK players due to a hyphen. The most commonly encountered descriptive names for the *Condylura cristata* are starnose or star-nosed mole.)

star pine *n* the pinaster (of which it is also an anagram)

starty *dial adj* apt to startle, nervous

starveling *adj* ill-fed, hungry *n* a person or animal that is such

starven *now dial adj* starved

stasidion *n* a stall in a Greek church

stasis *n* an arrest (of growth, bleeding etc)

statable *adj* capable of being stated

stater *n* an alternative name for various ancient coins such as the Persian gold daric and the Roman silver tetradrachm, as well as being a standard coin of issue for various Greek city-states: an ancient unit of weight: one who states

statical *adj* of or pertaining to forces in equilibrium

Statice *n* the sea lavender genus of herbaceous perennial plants (*—cap*) *n* the plant, thrift or sea pink

stational *adj* of or pertaining to a station

stative *adj* of Roman antiquities, stationary or fixed: of Hebrew grammar, denoting a verb expressing a state or condition *n* such a Hebrew verb

stator *n* the stationary part of a machine or device having a rotary action

staunch (*adj*) *var fm n/vb* **stanch**, to stop the flow of

stauncher (*comp adj*) *obs S n* stanchion

staver *US & dial n* an active, energetic person *S & dial n* a rung of a ladder *dial n* a bar in a hayrick: a stake *S vb* to wander about in a restless or aimless fashion

staw *S & dial fm n/vb* **stall** (in all conventional senses)

stawle *obs fm n* **stall**

staylace *n* a lace or cord which tightens a woman's stays *vb* to use such

steach *obs fm dial n* **stitch**, a narrow strip of land

stead (*n*) *vb* to stand in stead

steading *S & dial n* the outbuildings of a farm: a farmhouse and its outbuildings

steal (*vb*) *vb* of a hen, to nest in a concealed place *US vb* of a ewe, to lamb out of season *now dial vb* to furnish a tool with a steal or handle *dial vb* to catch (wildfowl) *now dial n* the stalk or stem of a plant, leaf, flower or fruit: the handle of a tool or utensil *esp* that of a rake or broom: the stem of a tobacco pipe *obs n* an upright side of a ladder: the shank of a candlestick

steale *var fm now dial n/vb* **steal**, (to furnish with) a handle

stealer *n* a thief *var fm n* **steeler**

stealings *n pl* gains made by theft

stealt *S pa t vb* steal, to take by theft

steamie *S n* a public laundry

stean *n* a jar, pitcher, pot or urn *var fm vb* **steen** *dial fm n/vb* **stone**

steane *dial fm n* **stean** *obs fm vb* **stain** *obs fm n/vb* **stone** *Obs fm vb* **steen**

steaner *dial n* the one who lays the second and inner rows of sheaves

steaning *dial n* (the process of making) a stone lining for a well

steap *obs fm vb* **steep**

stear *obs fm arch n* **stare**, the starling *obs fm n* **steer**, a young ox *obs fm vb* **steer**, to guide *obs fm n/vb* **stir**

steare *obs fm vb* **steer**

stearic *adj* containing or derived from stearin

stearin *n* fat in solid form

stearine *var fm n* **stearin** *adj* made of stearin

stech *S & dial vb* to gorge to the limit of capacity

stedding *obs fm S & dial n* **steading**

steden *obs fm S & dial n* **steading**

steding *obs fm S & dial n* **steading**

steeld *Shaks fm pa pple arch vb* stell

steele *obs fm n/vb* **steel**

steeler *n* one of the planks at either end of a continuous line of planking which forms part of the side of a wooden sailing ship

steelie *US n* a steel marble used for playing marbles

steely *adj* resembling steel (*comp* **steelier** *sup* **steeliest**)

steem *dial vb* to obtain credit *obs vb* to estimate *obs n* estimation or value

steeme *var fm obs n* **steem**

steen *vb* to line a well with stone *var fm n* **stean**

steenbok *var fm n* **steinbok**, one of the dwarf antelopes

steene *obs fm n* **stean**

steepen *vb* to make or become steep or steeper

steeper (*comp adj*) *n* one who infuses: that in which something is infused *dial n* a central branch of a hedge

steeple (*n*) *vb* to place or imprison in a steeple: to rise like a steeple

steerie *var fm S adj/n* **steery**

steerling *n* a young steer *obs fm n* **starling**, a protective outwork on a bridge

steery *S adj* busy *S n* a commotion

steeve *vb* to stow cargo *now S & dial adj* firm, unyielding

steever *n* a Jewish stiver or penny (pre-modern Israel)

steiar *obs fm n* **stair**

steiding *obs fm S & dial n* **steading**

steil *var fm now dial n* **steal**, a handle *obs fm n* **steel** *obs S fm vb* **steal**

stein (*n*) *var fm vb* **steen**

steing *obs fm S & dial n* **sting**, a pole

steip *obs S fm n* **steep**

steir *obs S fm vb* **steer**, to guide the course of a vessel *S fm* (*obs*) *obs n* **steer**, a rudder: a helmsman

steire *obs S fm vb* **stir**

steirk *obs fm n* **stirk**

stela *var fm n* **stele** (*pl* **stelae, stelai**)

stelae *pl* **stela** or **stele**

stelai *pl* **stela** or **stele**

stelar *adj* pertaining to a stele

stele *n* stela, a decoratively inscribed, upright stone slab or column: a surface area on a rock or building to which an inscription has been added: ornamentation of the ridge of a Greek temple (*pl* **stalae, stelai, steles**): vascular tissue in the central portion of a plant's stem (*pl* **steles**) *dial var fm n* **stile**, a stepped section of a fence *obs fm now dial n/vb* **steal** *obs fm n/vb* **steel**

stell *S & dial n* a pool, either natural or artificial, in a river suitable for the laying of a net, which is drawn when salmon are in position (in 1783 an action was brought against the corporation of Carlisle for having such a stell in the river Eden) *S n* a shelter, either natural or artificial, for grazing animals *dial n* a ditch *S Afr n* a wild animal trap *vb* to stare fixedly *arch vb* to portray *S vb* to station or place military personnel or equipment in position

stella *n* a natural star-shaped object such as a projection on a type of coral or any of a number of crystals (*pl* **stellae**): a former coin of the USA (*pl* **stellas**) (+*cap*) *fem pers n* meaning 'star'

steme *obs vb* to esteem *obs fm vb* **steam**

stemlet *n* a little stem

stemme *obs vb* to encircle

stemmer *n* a tree of sorts, resulting from the pruning of all but the strongest of the shoots put out by the stump of a tree which has been cut down: one who strips tobacco leaf: in mining, a metal bar which is used to ram clay into shot holes to make them watertight

stemmy *adj* stemlike: having, containing or abounding in stems (*comp* **stemmier** *sup* **stemmiest**)

stemner *var fm n* **stemmer**, the tree from a shoot

stempel *var fm n* **stemple**

stemplar *var fm n* **stemple**

stemple *n* one of a series of pegs driven into a rock face to act as a climbing aid

stencil (*n/vb*) *infl fms* British, **stencilled/-lling**: US, **stenciled/-ling**

stend *S n* a leap (*lit/fig*) *dial n* a stick used by a butcher to hold a carcass open *S vb* to leap

Stenidae *n* the family of the long-beaked dolphins

Stenkil *pers n* the king of Sweden (1060–1066)

stenn *var fm S vb* **stend**

stenograph *n* a character in shorthand: a keyboard machine which types shorthand *vb* to record in shorthand

stenosis *n* the narrowing of a bodily passage, duct or canal (*pl* **stenoses**)

stenotic *adj* relating to or resulting from stenosis

stensil *obs fm n* **stencil**

stent *n* rubble from tin mining *now S n* the value of an assessment of property for a taxation purpose *S n* a stake holding a fishing net in position in a river *S vb* to set a fabric such as a curtain in position *obs S vb* to assess for taxation purposes *S adj* assessed, taxed *obs S adj* taut, extended

stentar *obs S fm n* **stenter**

stente *Obs fm now S n* **stent**

stenter *n* the wooden frame better known as a tenter *vb* to impart an elastic finish to thin cotton fabrics

stenth *Obs fm now S n* **stent**

stentor (*n*) *S n* one who assessed taxes

steore *Obs fm n* **steer**, a young ox *Obs fm obs n* **steer**, a rudder

steorm *Obs fm n* **storm**

stepbairn *S n* a stepchild *obs S vb* to treat as such *Obs n* an orphan

stepbarn *var fm Obs n* **stepbairn**

stepdame *arch n* a stepmother

stepe *obs fm n/adj/adv/vb* **steep**

stephane *n* an ancient Greek coronet or diadem worn by military commanders and depicted as being worn by the goddess Hera

stepil *obs fm n* **steeple**

steple *obs fm n* **steeple**

steradian *n* a unit of measurement for solid angles expressed in a geometric formula

sterap *obs fm n* **stirrup**

stere *n* a cubic metre *obs vb* to burn or perfume with incense *var fm n* **stire**

steric *adj* relating to the space between atoms in a molecule

sterical *adj* steric

sterie *Obs fm vb* **stir**

sterigma *n* the stalk or filament of a fungal spore (*pl* **sterigmata**)

sterigmata *pl* sterigma

steril *arch fm n* **sterile** *obs n* a former measure of corn used in Sardinia and Sicily

sterit *Obs S pa t vb* steer

sterke *obs fm n* **stirk** *obs fm adj* **stark**

sterlet *n* a Russian small species of sturgeon

sterlit *var fm n* **sterlet**

sterner (*comp adj*) *obs n* a ship's pilot

sternet *obs n* an unknown species of bird which cries *'t' Ely, t' Ely'* (unfortunately, the early 17th century writer gave no further details other than it was 'loftie')

sternine *adj* of a tern, a seabird of the gull family

sternite *n* a segment of the underpart of such as an insect

sternmost *adj* nearest the rear: last in a line of ships

sterol *n* any of various waxy, insoluble substances such as the natural steroid alcohol, cholesterol

sterre *obs fm vbs* **steer, stir** *obs fm n* **star**

stert *obs fm n/vb* **start**

sterter *obs fm n* **starter**

sterum *n* the breastbone (*pl* **sterna, sterums**)

steure *Obs S fm vb* **stir**

steven *now dial n* a loud voice: an outcry: a din *obs n* a (set or appointed) time, a citation or summons *obs S n* either extremity of a sailing vessel *slg n* money *now dial vb* to make a noise *obs vb* to summon: to direct the course of (a ship)

stevene *var fm obs n* **steven** *obs fm now dial n* **steven**

stever *var fm n* **steever** (the Jewish stiver) *obs fm n* **stiver**

stevin *obs fm now dial n* **steven** *var fm obs n* **steven**, a time *var fm obs vb* **steven**, to direct the course of

stewer *n* one who stews

stewin *obs fm now dial n* **steven** *var fm obs n* **steven**, a time *var fm obs S n* **steven**

stewpond *var fm n* **stew**, in the sense of a pond in which fish are kept until taken for the table

steyne *var fm vb* **steen** *var fm n* **stean**

steynte *obs fm now S n* **stent**

steyr *obs fm n* **steer**, a young ox *obs S fm obs n* **steer**, a rudder

steyre *Obs S fm vb* **stir**

sthenia *n* excessive energy (*pl* **sthenias**)

sthenic *adj* of a medical condition, marked by excessive nervous energy

sthere *obs fm n* **steer**, a young ox

sti *Obs fm n* **sty**

stibble *S fm n/vb* **stubble**

stibbler *S n* a remover of stubble, either a man who cuts it down or a horse which eats it *obs S n* a probationary minister

stibler *var fm obs S n* **stibbler**

stiddie *var fm n/vb* **stithy**

stiel *obs fm n* **style**

stiep *obs fm n/vb* **steep**

stier *obs S fm vb* **stir**

stiera *Obs fm obs n* **steer**, a helmsman

stiere *obs S fm vb* **stir** *obs fm n* **steer**, a young ox *Obs fm vb* **steer** *Obs fm obs n* **steer**, a rudder

stieve *var fm now S & dial adj* **steeve**

stigean *obs fm adj* **Stigian**

stightle *Obs vb* of its many and varied senses, that of to strive, contend or fight was the last recorded (its period of use was circa 1350–1470)

stern (*adj/adv/n*) *vb* to propel a vessel hindpart first: to place astern: to dock the tail of a dog

sterna *pl* sternum

sternage *Shaks n* the collective sterns of a fleet

sternal *adj* of, pertaining to or connected with the breastbone *n* a sternal bone

stilbene *n* a crystalline hydrocarbon used in the making of dyestuffs

stile (*n*) *obs fm vb* **style**

stilet *var fm n* **stylet**

stillage *n* an industrial stool or stand *esp* within the brewing industry *dial vb* to place (a barrel of ale) on such

stille *var fm obs vb* **still**, to trickle in droplet form

stilter *n* one who walks on stilts: any wading bird with long, stilt-like legs

stime *var fm S n/vb* **styme** *var fm obs vb* **steem**

stimmer *vb* to move about in a confused manner

stine *var fm now dial n* **styan**, a sty

stingaree *n* either of two species of the largest of the stingrays, the *Dasyatis brevicaudata*, first sighted by Captain Cook in Australasian waters, or the *Dasyatis centroura* of the western North Atlantic. Not, however, used for other species of the *Dasyatis* genus – except as given below – or for any other of the stingrays. *US & Austr n* any stingray (the original usage which has now been generally adopted for the two species mentioned above)

stinge *obs fm n* **sting**

stinged *adj* having a sting (*lit/fig*) *obs adj* stung

stinger *n* a brandy and crême de menthe cocktail: one who or that which stings *S & dial n* a thatcher

stingle *Obs n* sting, delightfully described, in 1422, as, '*The bee is a passing wrathful beast and full of fight and for vengence they lowereth their stingle in the wound, but the king of bees is without a stingle*'

stingo *n* strong malt liquor (*pl* **stingos**)

stingraies *obs pl* stingray

stingray *n* any of a family of about 90 species of ray-like fishes with a venomous sting at the base of a whip-like tail, ranging in size from less than one foot across the disc of the body to the six to seven feet of the two **stingaree** species. Most stingrays are marine but some freshwater species exist in South American rivers. Closely related to the stingrays are the **butterfly fishes** which have shorter tails but not all of the species possess venom. Usually placed in a separate family, the largest of these exceeds twelve feet across the pectoral wings. The **round stingrays** are more distantly related, have stubby tails and all are venomous.

stinke *obs fm n/vb* **stink**

stinkstone *n* any of various limestones which give out an unpleasant odour when scratched or broken

stinte *var fm obs S vb* **stent**

stinter *n* one who or that which stints

stiora *Obs fm obs n* **steer**, a helmsman

stipa *n* feather grass, a grass with a feather-like awn

stipate *adj* crowded *obs vb* to have a crowd in personal attendance

stipe *n* the stalk of a mushroom or similar fungus (*pl* **stipes**) (note: Stipes is also a *var fm* of **stipe** with its own *pl* **stipites**)

stipel *n* either of a pair of tiny leaflets at the base of a larger leaflet on a plant

stiper *now dial n* a prop

stipes *var fm n* **stipe** (*pl* **stipites**)

stipites *pl* stipes (see **stipe**)

stiple *obs fm n* **steeple**

stipre *Obs fm now dial n* **stiper**

stipule *n* a paired (leafy) appendage at the base of a leaf

stire *n* a type of cider apple: the cider from such apples *obs fm vbs* **steer, stir**

stirk *n* a young bullock or heifer

stirke *obs fm n* **stirk**

stirling *S fm n* **starling**

stirpe *obs fm n* **stirp** (see **stirps**)

stirpes *pl* stirps, stirpe

stirps *n* a branch of a family (*pl* **stirpes**) (note: **stirp** *var fm n* **stirps**, with *pl* **stirps**)

stirre *obs fm vb* **stir**

stirree *obs dial vb* to give a light ploughing, at right angles to the normal line of ploughing, to fallow land

stithy *n* an anvil: a forge *vb* to forge

stive *n* (flour) dust *vb* to pack tightly *esp* in the hold of a ship: to stifle, to suffocate

stiver *n* any of various coins *incl* a Dutch five cent piece *dial vb* of hair, to stand erect

stoak *vb* to block the passage of water on board a ship

stoat (*n*) *vb* to sew only part way through a cloth to achieve an invisible stitch

stoater *n* a heavy gambling wager

stoccata *n* a thrust in fencing (*pl* **stoccatas**)

stockinger *n* one who operates a stocking handloom

stoep *S Afr n* a verandah

stofne *Obs vb* to found

stogie *US n* a type of cheap cigar

stoile *obs fm n* **stole**, a long robe

stoit *S & dial vb* to stumble: of a fish, to leap above the surface of the water

stoiter *S & dial n/vb* (to) stumble

stole (*n/vbl infl*) *vb* to provide a stole or embroidered strip of linen for an altar: to develop (as the strawberry plant) a stolon or shoot capable of development as an independent plant

stomacher *n* a woman's ornamental chest covering worn under the bodice

stomatic *adj* of a medicine, apt for diseases of the mouth *n* such a medicine

stonable an undefined adjective which appears in two different American dictionaries, one of which gives a *var fm* of **stoneable**, whilst the other provides a clue to the meaning which is curious to say the least. The clue is that it follows a definition of the *vb* **stone**, defined as 'to pelt with stones'. Thus the *adj* would seem to mean 'capable of being pelted with stones'. But, isn't every material object capable of being 'pelted with stones'? The dictionary in question specializes in giving a single, terse definition and it may be that the *adj* really refers to some other sense of the *vb* such as paving with stone, or giving a stone to a falcon as a purgative, turning into stone or, less likely, castrating. Its anagram is **notables**. (Also see **unstone**)

stonebrash *n* a subsoil of loose broken rock

stonecat *n* a larger (eight inches) species of madtom, being twice the size of the tadpole madtom

stone coal *n* anthracite or other hard coal

stone crab *n* any of various decapod crustaceans which, though bearing a superficial resemblance to spider crabs, are not true crabs and are classified in the same sub-order as the hermit crabs, the robber crab and the squat lobsters

stonemint *n* a perennial American herb of the mint family with lilac blossoms and also known as dittany

stonen *now dial adj* made of stone

stone oil *n* rock oil or petroleum

stone pine *n* either of two pine trees native to southern Europe

stonerag *var fm n* **stoneraw**, a species of lichen which produces a dye of a dirty orange colour used for stockings, nightcaps and the dresses of some moorland fairies

stonern *now dial adj* made of stone (probably now *obs*)

stonery *n* a rockery

stone snipe *n* any of various birds *incl* the stone curlew

stonied *obs adj* stupefied: stony

stonker *slg vb* to kill or destroy

stonne *obs fm n/vb* **stone** *obs fm vb* **stun**

stooden *S pa pple vb* stand

stool (*n*) *vb* to defecate: of a plant, to throw out new shoots *US vb* to entice wildfowl by means of a decoy bird (e.g. a stool pigeon)

stoon *obs fm n* **stone**

stoone *obs fm n/vb* **stone**

stope *vb* to excavate in layers *n* a layered or step-like working in an excavation

stopel *Obs n* a footprint *obs fm S & dial n* **stopple**

stoper *n* one who excavates ore

stopine *obs n* a piece of medicated cloth

stople *obs fm n/S & dial n* **stopple**

stopple *n* a stopper or plug *S & dial n* the stem of a tobacco pipe *vb* to plug with a stopple

stopsel *obs n* a flaming missile

storax *n* a fragrant resin with commercial and pharmaceutical uses: the tree, styrax, from which it is obtained (*pl* **storaxes**)

storem *Obs fm n* **storm**

storge *n* natural affection – as that of a parent for a child

storiated *adj* having elaborate ornamental decorations

storie *obs fm n* **storey**

storier *dial n* a liar *nonce n* a story teller *obs n* an historian

storke *obs fm n* **stork**

storken *S & dial vb* to become sturdy: to congeal

storme *obs fm n* storm

stormer *n* one who rages: one who takes by storm

stormi *Obs fm adj* **stormy**

stormie *obs fm adj* **stormy**

storre *obs fm vb* **stir** *Obs fm n* **star**

storye *obs fm n* **storey**

storyer *var fm obs n* **storier**

stoter *var fm S & dial vb* **stotter** *obs slg vb* to hit hard

stotre *var fm S & dial vb* **stotter**

stotter *S & dial vb* to stagger or stumble

stoule *obs fm n* **stool**

stoup (*n*) *obs fm n/vb* **stoop**

stoupe *var fm n* **stoup**, a vessel for holy water

stouple *obs n* a cotton wick soaked in a composition of gum, spirits, water and gun-powder used for firing such as a cannon *obs fm n/vb* **stubble**

stour *arch n* a battle *now S & dial n* a storm: tumult, uproar *adj* strong, sturdy, stiff, stub-born, harsh, rough *S & dial vb* of a substance, to rise in a cloud of dust: of snow, to drive

stoure *var fm now dial n/obs vb* **stower** *var fm adj/now S & dial n* **stour**

stourre *obs fm ns* **stour, stower**

stoury *S & dial adj* **dusty**

stoute *obs fm adj/adv* **stout** *Obs fm now dial n* **stout**, a gadfly

stouten *vb* to make or become stout

stouthrie *now S n* theft: stolen goods

stover (*n*) *now dial n* stubble

stovies *S n pl* stewed potatoes with onion and small pieces of meat

stowable *adj* capable of being stowed

stowce *n* a type of windlass for lifting ore from a leadmine: in Derbyshire, a model of such an apparatus set into the ground to comply with an old law that the presence of an owner's stowce secures his right of possession *vb* in Derbyshire, to mark (a mere of) land with such a type of stowce

stowe *obs interj* calling a hawk to one's wrist *obs fm n/vb* **stow**

stower *n* one who stows *now dial n* a stake or pole: a rung of a ladder *obs vb* to fence with stakes

stowle *obs fm n* **stool**

stownde *obs fm n* **stound**, a shock or sharp pain

stowre *var fm arch n/now S & dial n* **stour**

stowse *var fm n/vb* **stowce**

stowte *obs fm adj/adv* **stout** *obs fm now dial n* **stout**, a gadfly

strack *obs fm n* **strake**, part of an iron rim

strae *S fm n* **straw**

strafe *vb* to rake the enemy with rapid gunfire from an aircraft

strage *obs n* slaughter

stragel *obs fm vb* **straggle**

stragle *obs fm vb* **straggle**

straicht *S fm adj/adv* **straight**

straidle *dial fm vb* **straddle** (also see **striddle**)

straigne *obs fm vb* **strain**

straik *S n* a piece of wood coated with an abrasive used for sharpening a scythe (*pl* **straiks**) *S fm n* **stroke** (*pl* **strax**) *S vb* to level (corn) as a measure of quantity

strail *obs n* a blanket

straine *obs fm n/vb* **strain**

strainge *obs fm adj* **strange**

straint *n* application of pressure

strait (*adj/n*) *obs vb* to narrow, confine or restrict

straiten *vb* to embarrass or distress *esp* financially: to limit or confine *arch vb* to make or become narrow

straitness *n* the quality of being strait in such senses as narrowness, tightness or having difficulty in breathing

strake *n* part of the iron rim of a cartwheel: a strip of iron on the left side of a plough: a plank used as a unit of vertical measure for the side of a ship: a stripe of a different colour to the rest of the surface: a whisp of straw: the length of a stride: a box or pit in which ore is washed *vb* to wash ore in a strake *now dial vb* to move or go *obs vb* to make a call on a hunting horn: to smear or grease lightly: to mark with a streak *var fm S n/vb* **straik**

strale *dial n* a two year old sheep *obs n* the pupil of the eye

stramel *var fm now dial n* **strammel**

strammel *now dial n* a gaunt, ill-favoured person or creature (in 18th century literature it served as a convenient rhyme for **camel**)

stramp *S vb* to stamp the foot (on something)

strane *obs fm vb* **strain** (in almost all senses)

strang *S & dial fm adj* **strong** *obs fm adj* **strange** *obs fm n* **strand**, a single thread

strange (*adj*) *obs vb* to banish: to alienate: to wonder

strape *obs fm n* **strap**

strap oil *slg n* a flogging

strapper *n* a tall and robust person: one who grooms horses: a temporary worker *dial n* a cow which yields little milk

strase *obs pl* straw

straser *var fm obs modf n* **strosser** (*pl*) *var fm obs n* **strossers** (trousers)

strata *pl* stratum, a layer of material (*var fm* **stratums**)

strate *obs fm n* **street**

stratonic *adj* of an army

stratose *adj* of botanical usage, arranged in layers

stravaig *S & dial vb* to wander about aimlessly

strave *obs pa t vb* strive

strawe *obs fm n* **straw**

strawen *arch adj* made of straw

strawer *n* one in the street who offers for sale a straw and with it gives a 'free' sheet (libellous, pornographic etc) which, otherwise, he dare not sell

strawman *n* the figure of a man, made of straw *US n* a man of no backbone (*fig*)

strawne *obs fm arch adj* **strawen**

strax see **straik**

strayle *var fm obs n* **strail**

strayling *n* a stray person, creature or thing

strea *dial fm n* **straw**

stread *obs n* the 'beat' of a constable

streal *var fm vb* **streel** *dial n* an arrow

streale *now dial n* an arrow

stream ice *n* a continuous ridge of ice which follows the line of the current and is formed by pieces of ice which have drifted into this position (contrast with **ice stream**, 2nd definition)

streamie *S poet n* a little stream

streap *var fm S n* **stripe**, a stream

streape *obs fm S n* **stripe**, a stream

streat *obs n* an extract or copy *esp* of a legal document *obs vb* to extract or copy

stree *now dial fm n* **straw**

streek *now S & dial vb* to stretch one's limbs: to lay out a corpse

streel *vb* to trail in water or on the ground: to stroll aimlessly

streem *obs fm n* **stream**

streeme *obs fm n* **stream**

streen *obs fm n* **strain**

street (*n*) *vb* to create a street or streets

streete *Obs aphetic fm n* **estreat**

streetlet *n* a little (narrow) street

streety *adj* characteristic of the streets

streik *obs fm now S & dial vb* **streek**

streim *Obs fm n* **stream**

strein *obs fm vb* **strain** *obs fm n* **strain** (in senses other than progeny)

streing *Obs fm n* **string**

streke *obs fm now S & dial vb* **streek** *obs fm vb* **strike**

Strela *n* the name of a river in Czechoslovakia which rises near the German border and flows north of Pilsen to Prague: the name of a town in the USSR

strelits see **strelitz**

strelitz n a Russian infantryman of a body raised by Ivan the Terrible (1533–1584) and abolished by Peter the Great in 1682 (*pl* **strelitzes, streltzi**) (note: The *sing* and *pl* have frequently been confused, *esp* as the *sing* had a *var fm* of **strelits**. *obs pl fms incl* **strelsies, strelsey, strelitzi**)

strelsey see **strelitz**

streltzi see **strelitz**

streme *obs fm n/vb* **stream**

strene *now dial vb* of dogs, to copulate *dial n* a New Year's gift; a shoot of a tree

strener *obs fm n* **strainer**

strep *collq fm n* **streptococcus**, any of various species of bacteria which cause such diseases as scarlet fever or pneumonia (*pl* **streps** for **streptococci**) (GAME PLAYER'S note: This is another example of an abbreviated form being valid for play on the basis of pronunciation)

streperous *adj* noisy, harsh in tone (GAME PLAYER'S note: Both the *adj* and its related *adv*, **streperously**, are considered extant by the dictionary used for the UK Scrabble championship. The *adj* was in fairly common use till 1688 then, in 1822, an obscure writer not only made use of it but also placed on record the only known usage of the *adv*. Other experts consider both to be *obs*.)

strete *obs aphetic fm n* **estreat**

stretta *var fm n* **stretto** (*pl* **strettas, strette**)

strette *pl* stretta (see **stretto**)

stretti *pl* stretto

stretto *n* a concluding musical passage played at a faster tempo: a counterpoint or overlapping of two musical themes in a fugue (*pl* **stretti, strettos**)

strewe *obs fm vb* **strew**

strewer *n* one who strews

stria *n* a fine furrow, usually one of a series in parallel (*pl* **striae**)

striae *pl* stria

strich *obs n* the screech owl

strickle *n* a piece of wood used to brush away grain surplus to the measure: a mechanical grinder: any piece of wood cut to a special shape and used to impart a contour to a bed of foundry sand *vb* to use a strickle in a foundry

striddle *now dial vb* to straddle: to stride *S n* a stride (WORD PUZZLER'S note: *Chambers 20th Century Dictionary* records only the *vb* and considers it to be extant standard English in the sense of 'to straddle'. It makes no mention of the second sense which was used by both Burns and Scott. The last recorded literary usage of the sense 'to straddle' was circa 1640 – nearly 200 years prior to Scott's death. (For a similar curiosity see **stroddle**.)

stridence *n* the fact of being strident, harsh in tone

strie *obs fm now dial vb* **stray**, to scatter

striek *obs fm now S & dial vb* **streek**

strig *n* a stalk *esp* of a leaf, flower or fruit *vb* to remove such from gathered fruit

striga *n* a bristle: a fine, thread-like line (*pl* **strigae**)

strigae *pl* striga

striges *n pl* the channels of a fluted column (*sing* **strix**, implied by the *pl*, but unused)

strigine *adj* of those owls classified by ear development as belonging to the sub-family *Striginae*: of any owl, irrespective of classification: owl-like

Strigops *n* the genus of the kakapo

strigose *adj* streaked: covered with stiff hairs

striked *obs pa t vb* strike (now **struck**)

strime *Obs fm n* **stream**

strind *obs n* generation, lineage: an inherited quality

strine *dial n* a long straggling branch (+*cap*) *n* humorous Australian-English (as opposed to individual English words of Australian origin) whereby the pronunciation of such as *glorious home* is written as *Gloria Soame*

stringe *dial vb* to be too exacting *obs fm n* **string**

Stringops *var fm n* **Strigops**

string pea *US n* a pea with edible pods

string pin *n* any of the pins which secure a musical string of a piano at the non-tuning end

strinkle *vb* to scatter, sprinkle or strew *arch vb* to sprinkle a person with holy water

stripey *var fm adj* **stripy**

striplet *n* a small strip

strippe *obs fm n/vb* **strip**

strippet *obs n* a little brook

Strix *n* a genus of owls which includes the wood owls and the tawny owl (−*cap*) *n* the unused *sing fm* of **striges**

stroam *now dial vb* strome, to walk with long strides

stroan *S vb* to urinate

stroap *obs fm now dial n* **stroup**

strobe *n* a high-intensity flashing light of the sort used in a discotheque: the apparatus which produces this effect

strobila *n* bodily segmentation in which each segment contains a complete and largely independent set of organs, though some co-operation between segments does occur. This is exhibited by such as larval jellyfish, which can bud off to form independent creatures, and by tapeworms, where it may be merely a device to overcome a diffusion problem in a long creature lacking a circulatory system. (*pl* **strobilae**)

stroble *Obs fm obs vb* **strouble**

stroddle *now dial vb* to straddle (WORD PUZZLER'S note: *Chambers* gives the definition, 'strodle, stroddle (*obs* or *dial*). Same as straddle'. **Stroddle** is *now dial* and **strodle** is a 17th century form of **stroddle** last used by Bunyan in 1678. As players in the UK Scrabble championship restrict themselves to *Chambers* but, though accepting *dial* words, bar *obs* words, they will break their own local rules by accepting **strodle**! When the Australians used *Chambers* for their contest, they very neatly sidestepped many of these curiosities by the sensible acceptance of both *obs* and *dial* words as labelled in that dictionary.) *dial n* anything small or worthless (*var fm* **sthroddle**)

strodle *obs fm now dial vb* **stroddle**

strogel *Obs fm vb* **struggle**

strogle *obs fm vb* **struggle**

stroie *Obs fm arch vb* **stroy**

strole *obsol fm n* **stroll** *obs fm vb* **stroll**

stroma *n* the tissue which forms the framework of an organ or cell of a living creature: a structure in fungi containing the organs of fructification (*pl* **stromata**)

strome *var fm now dial vb* **stroam** *obs S fm n* **storm**

strone *S n* the last hill of a ridge of hills *obs n* one in Westmorland having a duty to assist with the hunting of deer *var fm S vb* **stroan**

Stronsay monster *n* a creature, the decayed remains of which were cast up on an Orkney island in 1808. The Scottish naturalist, Patrick Neill, described this species which was completely new to science. It was 55 feet long, had a long neck and tail, a small head and three pairs of limbs. An admirer of Pontopiddan, the Norwegian who is famed for writing about the sea orm (a creature which no-one else has been able to identify), Neill proudly named the monster *Halsydrus pontopiddani* after his hero and despatched some specimens of the bones and other bodily parts to fellow experts. Unfortunately, Neill had discovered the rotten carcase of a huge basking shark! (For another scientific mare's nest see **morris**, for a third error of this type see **New Holland vulture** and a fourth is given at **lamprey**.)

stroop *var fm now dial n* **stroup**

strooped *var fm now dial adj* **strouped**

strope *obs vb* to strip such as leaves from a branch

strophe *n* a verse sung by the chorus in an ancient Greek play whilst moving from left to right (the verse of right to left being an **antistrophe**): the first of two alternating metrical systems in a poem: a stanza (*pl* **strophae, strophes**)

strosser *obs modf n* trouser

stroubel *Obs fm obs vb* **strouble**

strouble *obs vb* to disturb: to make cloudy

stroule *obs fm n* **stroll**

stroup *now dial n* the throat: a spout of such as a kettle

stroupe *obs fm now dial n* **stroup**

strouped *now dial adj* having a spout

strouse *obs n* knee breeches

strout *arch fm vb* **strut**, to walk with an affected air

strouter *obs fm n* **strutter**

strow *arch fm n/vb* **strew**

strowen *obs fm arch adj* **strawen**

strower *n* one who scatters things

strowle *obs fm n/vb* **stroll**

strowp *obs fm now dial n* **stroup**

strowpe *obs fm now dial n* **stroup**

stroy *arch vb* to destroy

stroye *obs fm arch vb* **stroy**

strude *erron n* a stock of mares (GAME PLAYER'S note: Valid for play)

strudel *n* a filling of such as fruit or cheese enveloped in a very thin pastry

struggel *obs fm vb* **struggle**

strugle *obs fm n/vb* **struggle**

struma *n* the disease, scrofula, better known as the King's Evil (*pl* **strumae, strumas** (*obs* except USA))

strumae *pl* struma

strume *obs n* a tumour or a goitre

strund *obs fm n* **strand**, a gutter or channel *Obs fm obs n* **strind**

stubber *n* one who stubs

studden *S pa t/pa pple vb* stand

studding sail *n* a sail used in fair winds in front of any of the principal sails and normally pronounced as **stunsel** (an alternative *fm*)

stuer *var fm obs n* **sture**

stufer *obs fm n* **stiver**

stuffet *obs S n* meaning obscure but could be one who is employed in a stable, or some mild term of abuse for a person

stug *S n* a stab or thrust *obs n* a pig trough *S vb* to stab or pierce

stugger *var fm obs n* **stug**, a pig trough

stuiver *var fm n* **stiver**

stumb *obs fm vb* **stum**, to renew such as wine by mixing with must to bring about a new fermentation

stumer *slg n* a sham such as a forged cheque or a counterfeit coin

stumor *var fm slg n* **stumer**

stunsail *n* a studding sail

stunsel *n* a studding sail

stupe *n* a medicated dressing used for such as a wound *vb* to prepare a dressing with a suitable medicament

stupider *comp adj* stupid

stupple *obs n* a row of stepping stones

stupre *obs n/vb* (to) rape

sturb *obs vb* to disturb, upset

sturbe *Obs fm obs vb* **sturb**

sturdie *obs fm n/adj* **sturdy**

sturdied *adj* of sheep or cattle, afflicted with turnsick

sture *Shet n* a penny *obs n* a surgeon *Obs fm vbs* **steer, stir**

sturer *obs fm n* **stirrer**

sturie *Obs fm vb* **stir**

sturine *n* a ptomaine obtained from the fertilizing element of the male sturgeon

sturme *Obs vb* to storm

sturnine *adj* resembling a starling

Sturnus *n* the genus of the starling

sturre *obs fm vb* **stir** *Obs fm n* **star**

sturt *n* contention *obs n* a sudden impulse *now S vb* to be startled *obs vb* to start suddenly *obs S adj* turbulent

sturte *obs fm n* **sturt**

stuver *obs fm n* **stiver**

sty (*n*) *vb* to house swine in a sty

Stygian *adj* pertaining to the river Styx, the river of Hades, over which the shades of the dead were ferried by Charon and by which the gods swore their most solemn oaths: hellish: of an oath, supremely binding (note: Styx is also the name of an underground river in Derbyshire, which surfaces from a huge cavern in Castleton which once contained a hamlet.)

stylate *adj* of plants, having a persistent style: of creatures, having a stylet

styler *n* one who styles in the various senses of the *vb*

stylet *n* a surgeon's slender probe: a piercing part of an insect's jaws: a writing instrument: a bristle-like part

styliser *var fm n* **stylizer**, one who makes (something) conform to a particular style

stylite *n* an ascetic who lived on top of a pillar, of whom the most famous was St Simeon or Simeon Stylites. St Simeon (circa AD 521–597) was a monk who spent the last 45 years of his life squatting atop a stone pillar on the Hill of Wonders near Antioch, Syria. This mode of religious life was practised from the time of Simeon to about the 12th century.

styme *S & dial n* the least part: a glimmer of light: a moment of time: a glance *S & dial vb* to squint

styre *var fm n* **stire** *obs fm vbs* **steer, stir** *obs S fm obs n* **steer**, a rudder

styrene *n* a colourless, oily, volatile liquid used in making synthetic plastics and rubbers

styrre *obs fm vb* **stir**

styver *obs fm n* **stiver**

su *dial fm pron* **she**

suable *adj* capable of being sued

suasible *adj* capable of being persuaded

suasion *n* the act of urging

suasory *adj* persuasive *n* used as a term to describe any work by Seneca, the Roman philosopher (circa 4 BC – AD 65)

subarid *adj* almost arid

subcantor *n* a subordinate cantor

subdane *obs S fm adj/adv/arch n* **sudden**

subedar *var fm n* **subahdar**, the governor of a province of the Mogul empire: an Indian army captain

suberin *n* a waxlike cellular tissue of cork

subimago *n* the penultimate stage in the life of a mayfly, that immediately prior to its one day of life as an adult (*pl* **subimagines, subimagos**)

subito *adv* in music, suddenly

sublinear *adj* placed below a line of writing: of such as leaves, nearly linear

subman *n* a creature or person immediately either side of the fabled 'missing link', thus, either the most manlike animal or the lowest kind of man

suborn *vb* to cause another to commit an unlawful act *esp* to bribe another to commit perjury

subrent *US n* rent from a sub-tenant

subserve *vb* to be subservient to: to be instrumental in serving the purpose of another

subtack *n* in Scots law, a lease granted by a leaseholder (as opposed to the **tack** which the leaseholder has from the owner)

subtile *adj* subtle (*comp* **subtiler** *sup* **subtilest**)

subtle (*adj*) *obs vb* to argue with subtlety: to reduce (note: Strictly the *vb* should be labelled *Obs* but a usage in 1624, which is either *fig* or *nonce*, does suggest that it may have continued into modern English times)

subverse *vb* to upset, subvert

succade *n* fruit preserved in sugar

succinate *n* a salt of succinic acid (an acid obtained from amber and formerly known as spirit of amber)

sucket *obs n* fruit preserved in sugar: a term of endearment

sucrase *n* invertase, an enzyme of certain plants and the intestines of animals which is capable of splitting sucrose and related sugars into glucose and fructose

sucre *n* a silver coin of Ecuador, equating to the florin

sucrier *Fr n* a (porcelain) sugar bowl

sucrose *n* any sugar with the properties of cane sugar

sudamen *sing* sudamina

sudamina *n pl* minute, whitish pustules which appear on the skin, caused by copious sweating during certain fevers (*sing* **sudamen**)

sudaries *pl* sudary

sudarium *n* a cloth for removing facial sweat *esp* that used by St Veronica which was miraculously imprinted by the features of Christ when she wiped His face during His climb to the Crucifixion (*pl* **sudaria**)

sudary *var fm n* **sudarium** (*pl* **sudaries**)

sudate *vb* to sweat

suddent *dial fm adj/adv/arch n* **sudden**

sudder *Anglo-Ind adj* of bureaucrats, chief

suede (*n*) *vb* to give leather a suede appearance

sueing *obs fm n* **sewin**, the bull trout

suerte *obs fm n* **surety**

sufflate *obs vb* to inflate (*lit/fig*)

sugger *obs vb* to suggest

Suidae *n pl* swine

suiden *obs S fm adj/adv/arch n* **sudden**

suidian *adj* pertaining to swine

suitor (*n*) *vb* to woo: to be a suitor to

sulcal *adj* grooved or furrowed

sulcate *adj* grooved *obs vb* to cleave the surface of the sea as though ploughed (by the wind or a ship)

sullage *n* filth *esp* that carried or deposited by water

sulp *obs vb* to pollute

sulphonate *n* a salt of sulphonic acid *vb* to convert into such by the action of sulphuric acid

sultanic *adj* of, belonging to or characteristic of a sultan: despotic, tyrannical

sulter *obs n* a period of sultry weather *obs vb* to swelter

sultre *var fm obs n* **sulter**

sumach *n* any of the small trees or shrubs of the genus *Rhus*, the dried leaves and shoots of which are made into a preparation which has commercial uses: that preparation used as a dyeing agent in the tanning industry and, medically, as an astringent: other plants such as bog myrtle, once called wild sumach (also see **tanbark**) *vb* sumac, to dye or tan with sumach

sumatra *n* a violent storm in the Straits of Malacca blowing from the direction of Sumatra

Sumerian *adj* of the language of a non-Semitic people in ancient Babylonia *n* such a person: that language

summist *n* a writer of a summa or treatise giving a complete summary

sumpter *arch n* a beast of burden

sumpy *dial adj* marshy, boggy

sumtar *obs fm arch n* **sumpter**

sumter *obs fm arch n* **sumpter**

sun bear *n* the smallest member of the bear family and native to the Malay peninsula. Omnivorous – its diet is mainly fruit and insects – it can often be an amusing pet in its younger years but later turns aggressive.

sun-beat *adj* describing that upon which the sun beats

sunbow *n* a rainbow-like arc formed by the sun shining through a mist

sundari *var fm n* **sundri**, either of two Indian trees, the looking glass tree or one, abundant in the Ganges delta, which yields a hard timber

sun deck *n* the upper deck of a ship

sunder (*adj/adv*) *now rhetorical/poet vb* to separate or part one from another

sunderer *n* one who separates or parts something

sundew *n* an insectivorous plant of marshy places

sundog *n* a false sun: a small rainbow

sundrie *var fm n* **sundri**, either of two trees of the same genus one of which is better known as the looking glass tree *obs fm adj* **sundry**

sunfish *n* any of a family of North American, perch-like, freshwater fishes *incl* the black basses, bluegills and crappies. Other than the Sacramento perch, all are native to the eastern rivers and streams though many have been introduced to the western part of the USA. The spotted sunfish is reputed to linger beside a half-submerged log waiting for a frog or an insect to settle, and then to charge the log to knock its prey into the water: any of various unrelated fishes which have a globular form, a brilliant appearance or bask in the sun. *US collq vb* to behave like a sunfish in a bucking action

sungod *n* any of various gods of the sun (an aspect of most early religions) from the standpoint of being an example of such, as opposed to an individual sun god

sun pan *n* a pan used in evaporating processes such as the production of salt from brine

sun rose *n* any of a genus of plants, the flowers of which expand in the sun

sunstone *n* amber: any of several reddish or yellow varieties of feldspar

supering *n* the action of performing as a super (a supernumerary or extra) in such as a crowd scene on the stage: the placing of a super hive (a removable upper compartment) on top of a beehive

supernal *adj* that above or on high: upper, lofty: of high rank or dignity: supremely great: existing in the heavens: pertaining to a higher state of existence in the afterlife *arch adj* celestial, heavenly *n* supernatural being

supersalt *n* any acid salt

supinate *vb* to move the hand so that the palm is uppermost or facing outward: to move the leg outwards

supinator *n* either of two muscles in the forearm or foreleg

supine *adj* lying on the back: inactive, negligent, listless *n* of Latin grammar, a type of verbal noun

suple *var fm S & dial n* **supple** *S & dial fm vb* **supple** *obs S fm adj* **supple**

supple *(adj) vb* to make such as leather pliant *S & dial n* a cudgel

supplete *obs vb* to supplement

suppletory *adj* supplementary *obs n* a supplement

suq *n* a local market in various Arabic countries

surah *var fm n* **sura**, a section of the Koran

surat *n* coarse (uncoloured) Indian cotton

surbase *n* a cornice

surbate *obs vb* to make (an animal or person) footsore (by excessive walking)

surbed *obs vb* to set sideways, as stone in a wall or coal on a fire (*infls* **surbedded/-dding**)

surbet *var fm obs pa pple* **surbated**

surcingle *n* a (large) girth for a pack animal

surd *vb* to deaden the sound of

surdine *obs fm n* **sordine**

sure *(adj/adv) now dial vb* to assure

Sûreté *Fr n* the French criminal investigation department

surete *obs fm n* **surety**

surety *(n) arch n* sure knowledge

surfpercher *n* any of a family of mainly marine, perch-like fish which give live birth. The best known species is the shiner or shiner surfpercher common in the region of San Francisco, the young of which are not only well-developed at birth but the males are sexually mature. The only freshwater species of this family is the tule perch.

surgent *adj* surging (*lit/fig*) *obs n* an insurgent

surger *obs n* a surgeon

surgien *obs fm n* surgeon

Surinam *n* an independent (since 1975) state in South America formerly known as Dutch Guiana

surlier *comp adj* surly

surples *obs fm n* **surplice** *Obs fm n* **surplus**

surtey *Obs fm n* **surety**

surtie *obs fm n* **surety**

surtye *obs fm n* **surety**

surview *arch n* a view *esp* one in the mind's eye: consideration, contemplation *arch vb* to behold

suspire *vb* to sigh (mainly *poet & fig*) *obs n* a sigh

susprise *obs vb* to surprise

suster *obs fm n* **sister**

sustinent *adj* sustaining

suter *dial n* a wooden plug used for plug draining, a system of draining clay land whereby channels are kept open by means of suters *obs fm n* **suitor**

sutler *n* a pedlar (*esp* one who follows a travelling army) of such as foodstuffs to soldiers

sutra *n* in Hinduism, grammatical aphorisms in Sanskrit literature which require additional commentary: in Buddhism, the sermons of Buddha and other relevant doctrinal matter

suttee *n* ritual suicide of an Indian widow who throws herself onto the funeral pyre of her husband: such a woman

suttler *var fm n* **sutler**

swabble *dial vb* to wobble: to make a noise like that of moving water

swadder *obs cant n* a (thieving) pedlar

swail *var fm US, S & dial n* **swale**, a hollow *var fm dial n* **swale**, a shady place *var fm now dial vb* **sweal**

swain *n/vb* (to play the) lover

swaining *n* love making

swaleing *var fm n* **swealing**

swale *US, S & dial n* a hollow, low place: a marshy depression in a tract of land *dial n* timber such as a lath or plank: shade, a shady place: the cool, the cold *dial adj* cool, chill *dial vb* to move or sway from side to side *var fm dial n/now dial vb* **sweal**

swaling *dial n/adj* swaying *var fm n/adj* **swealing**

swallet *n* an underground stream *esp* one which breaks through into mining operations: a short *fm* of **swallet hole**, the hole through which a stream disappears underground

swalte see **swelt**

swami *n* a form of address or title for a Hindu religious teacher: a Hindu idol

sware *arch pa t vb* **swear** *obs n* an oath: a reply *Obs vb* to answer *obs S fm vb* **square**

swarme *obs fm n/vb* **swarm**

swarmer *n* one of any creature which swarms: a skep or beehive adapted for swarming *obs n* a type of firework

swarne *obs pa pple vb* swear

swart *arch adj* black, dusky: malignant *obs vb* to make (a complexion) dark

swarth *now dial n* grassland *dial n* a wraith or spiritual manifestation of a dying person *adj* dusky, black *vb* to darken *now dial vb* to cover with turf

swarve *dial vb* to be silted up

swash *adv/interj/n* the sound of a crash *esp* of water *n* (wet) filth: the action of water striking something: a waterlogged condition of land: swagger *now S n* a swaggerer *S n* a drum *adj* inclined obliquely to the axis: of the capital letters of a typeface, having flourished strokes which decorate the spaces between the letters *dial adj* soft *vb* to dash violently (about): to splash

swasher *n* a swashbuckler: a boastful bully *S n* a show-off: a drummer

swather *n* one employed by an embalmer to wash the body and to wrap it in a shroud: a device attached to the front of a mowing machine for the purpose of raising uncut, fallen grain

swaver *dial vb* to stagger

swayne *obs fm n* **swain**

sweal *dial n* a blaze, a flame *now dial vb* to burn: to set fire to: to singe: of a candle, to melt *Ir vb* to roast whole and unskinned *var fm S vb* **sweel**

swealing *adj* burning, blazing: of a candle flame, guttering *n* burning, singeing (note: Still in general usage even though the *vb*, **sweal**, is *now dial*)

sweard *obs fm n* **sward**

sweel *S vb* to swathe or swaddle

sweer *S & dial adj* indolent, slothful: reluctant (*var fms incl* **sweered, sweert, sweir, sweirt)**

sweered *var fm S & dial adj* **sweer**

sweering *obs n* sloth, negligence

sweert *var fm S & dial adj* **sweer**

sweir *S fm vb* **swear**

sweirt *var fm S & dial adj* **sweer**

sweit *obs S fm vb* **sweat**

swelde *obs fm adj* **swelled**

swele *var fm now dial vb* **sweal** *obs fm vb* **squeal**

swelt *now dial vb* to overheat, scorch, broil: to exert oneself to the utmost: to die, to perish: to swoon, to faint (*pa pple* **swelted** *var fms pa pple* **sweltit, swilted** *obs fms pa t incl* **swalte)**

swelte *obs fm now dial vb* **swelt**

sweltit see **swelt**

sweltre *obs fm n/vb* **swelter**

swepir *Obs fm now dial adj* **swipper**

swerde *obs fm ns* **sward, sword**

Swerga *var fm n* **Swarga**, the Hindu paradise

swicket *var fm pa pple now S dial vb* **swike**

swidder *var fm S & dial vb* **swither**

swike *now S dial n* a deceiver: deceit *now S dial vb* to deceive (*pa pple* **swiked, swicket**)

swinden *obs adj* enfeebled

swindge *now poet fm vb* **swinge** *obs fm now dial n* **swinge**

swinge *now dial n* a leash which couples hounds together *dial n* a blow or hit *vb* to beat, flog or whip *now US & dial vb* to singe, scorch

swingel *var fm n/vb* **swingle**

swingle *n* a wooden implement used for beating and cleaning flax or hemp: a flail-like weapon *vb* to use the implement *dial vb* to dangle

swingtree *n* a swingletree or crossbar to which the traces of a draught animal are fastened, in order to give freedom of movement to its shoulders when pulling such as a plough or a cart

swingy *adj* marked by swinging (*comp* **swingier** *sup* **swingiest**)

swink *arch n/vb* (to) labour or toil

swiper *n* a heavy drinker: one who hits: that hit

swipper *now dial adj* quick, nimble

swire *n* a hollow near the summit of a hill

swithe *now dial vb* to burn, singe: to smart (*obs pa pple* **swithen** – also see **swithen)**

swithen *now dial vb* to be singed *obs pa pple* singed

swither *S & dial n* a flurry, a fluster: doubt, uncertainty *S & dial vb* to falter: to hesitate *dial vb* to burn

switter *dial vb* to splash about in water (like a duck)

swivel (*n/vb*) *infl fms* British, **swivelled/-lling**: US, **swiveled/-ling**

swivle *obs fm n* **swivel**

swone *obs fm vb* **swoon**

sword (*n*) *vb* to arm with a sword: to use a sword

sworde *obs fm ns* **sward, sword**

sworder *n* one who uses a sword: a gladiator: a cut-throat

sworen *Obs fm adj* **sworn**

swyper *Obs fm now dial adj* **swipper**

sy *dial fm n* **scythe**

syenite *n* a crystalline, granitic rock composed mainly of feldspar

syenitic *adj* of, pertaining to, composed of, allied with or having the nature of syenite

synapse *n* the junction or interlacing between two nerve cells

syndet *n* synthetic detergent

syneper *var fm obs n* **sinoper**

synergia *var fm n* **synergy**

synergid *n* either of two cells in the embryo sac of a plant, regarded as associated with the guiding of the pollen tube

synergy *n* united action: correlation of action between bodily organs

syngamic *adj* of syngamy

syngamy *n* the fusion of male and female gametes in fertilization

syngle *obs fm n* **cingle**

synodic *adj* relating to or involving a conjunction or two successive conjunctions of the same heavenly body

synoper *var fm obs n* **sinoper**

synople *var fm obs n* **sinople**

synopre *var fm obs n* **sinoper**

sype *var fm S & dial vb* **sipe**, of liquid, to drip, to soak

syphon *var fm n/vb* **siphon**

syringa *n* any of various ornamental shrubs of the genus of the mock orange (*pl* **syringas**)

syringeal *adj* of or pertaining to the syrinx or vocal organ of a bird

syrtes *pl* syrtis

syrtis *n* a quicksand (*pl* **syrtes**)

systole *n* the rhythmical contraction of the heart or other organs or organisms

sythe *var fm n/vb* **scythe** *var fm obs n* **sithe**

sybarite *n* (also +*cap*) a devotee of luxury and the sensual vices *adj* luxurious, sensual

T

ta *n* though written differently, the third and the sixteenth letters of the Arabic alphabet: an Annamese unit of weight: an infantile *fm* of the expression 'Thank you' *dial fm prep* **to** *Obs fm n* **toe** (*pl* **tan, taan**)

tabard *n* a knight's short surcoat emblazoned with his armorial bearings worn over armour: a similar garment still worn as the official dress of a herald

tabaret *n* an upholstery fabric of alternate satin and watered silk stripes

tabasheer *n* bamboo salt, a translucent fluid of the jointed cavities of bamboo which, after extraction, thickens and eventually hardens into a white or bluish-white substance, greatly valued in the Middle East for its medicinal properties

tabber *arch fm n* **tabor**

tabel *obs fm n* **table**

taber *now US var fm n/vb* **tabor**

taberde *Obs fm n* **tabard**

tabert *obs fm n* **tabard**

tabinet *n* a poplin-like fabric

tableau (*n*) *pl fms* British & US, **tableaux**: also, US, **tableaus**

tabler *n* one who pays for meals at another's table *obs n* the game of backgammon: the backgammon board: a backgammon player: a chess board: a money changer

tabor *n* a type of small drum often used to accompany a pipe: the drummer of that instrument *vb* to play the tabor

taboret *now US var fm n* **tabret**

taborin *n* a drum of historical times, narrower but longer than a tabor, which the instrumentalist played with one stick as an accompaniment to his own flute playing *var fm now US n* **taborine**

taborine *now US n* a tambourine *US n* a side drum: a taborin

tabour *var fm n/vb* **tabor**

tabouret *var fm n* **tabret**

tabret *n* a small tabor or drum

tabula *n* an ancient writing tablet: a body of laws inscribed on such a tablet: an altar frontal: a flattened construction (*pl* **tabulae**)

tabulae *pl* tabula

tache *n* a shallow pan *arch n* any contrivance which holds two parts together *now dial n* a distinctive mark *obs n* a fault or vice: a blemish *now dial vb* to fasten, fix or secure: to arrest *obs vb* to dry (tea) in a shallow pan: to attack

tachism *var fm n* **tachisme**

tachisme *n* abstract painting in clotted layers

tachist *adj* of the art of this school of painting (see **tachisme**) *n* one who produces work of this nature

tacke *obs fm n* **tack**

tacket *now S & dial n* a hobnail

tackless *adj* made without or having no tacks

tacle *obs fm n/vb* **tackle**

taction *n* the action of touching

tae *S fm n* **toe**

tael *n* liang

taenia *n* a ribbon: a long narrow ribbon used as a ligature in surgery: a tapeworm (*pl* **taeniae, taenias**)

taenioid *adj* of tapeworms, ribbonlike

taest *obs fm n* **taste**

tagena *var fm n* **tanghin**

tagetes *n sing/pl* any species of a genus of Central American plants which have yellow or orange flowers

taglioni *n* an early 19th century overcoat named after a family of ballet dancers

tagrag *n* a low or despicable person: a ragged appendage *var fm n* **ragtag** *adj* consisting of or dressed in rags

tahina *n* a paste of crushed sesame seeds

tahsil *n* a subdivision of a district originally designated by the Mogul emperors of India, retained by the British, and now still used as a unit of administration for revenue collection

taiche *obs fm now dial n* **tache**

taigle *S vb* to entangle: to hinder: to retard: to embarrass: to linger: to trudge

tailer *n* any fish which, in natural activity, exposes its tail above the surface of the water

taille *n* cut, shape, form: a French tax formerly levied upon the unprivileged classes

tailrace *n* that part of a millrace below the waterwheel

tain *n* thin tinplate: tinfoil used for mirrors *obs vb* to obtain, prevail

tainder *obs n* the removal of all civil rights and capabilities *incl* all property, possessions and even sexual relationships from one convicted of outlawry or treason

taing *var fm dial n* **tang,** a sharp point *dial fm n* **tang**

taining *obs n* a device for catching river fish

tainter *obs fm n/vb* **tenter**

taipan *n* the largest and deadliest of the Australasian snakes, a slender elapid which can attain a length of eleven feet

tair *obs S fm vb* **tear**, to pull apart

taira *var fm n* **tayra**

taisch *n* a manifestation of the body or the voice of one about to die

taise *var fm obs vb* **teise**, to take aim *var fm obs n* **teise**, a fathom

taisel *S fm n* **tassel**

taith *var fm S & dial n/vb* **tath** or **tathe**

taiver *var fm S n/vb* **taver**

taivering *var fm S n* **tavering**

takel *obs fm n/vb* **tackle**

taken (*vbl infl*) *obs fm n* **token**

takle *obs fm n/vb* **tackle**

talage *var fm obs n* **tallage**

talar *n* a long robe which reaches the ankles

talbot *n* a now extinct breed of hound, white with a broad mouth and large ears (see *her n* **sea dog**) (+*cap*) *masc pers n* meaning 'faggot cutter'

talc (*n*) *vb* the application of talc (a hydrated silicate of magnesium) to a surface (GAME PLAYER'S note: Correctly inflected, the verb takes the letter K (**talcked, talcking**) but **talced** and **talcing** are popular *var fms* and given as such, without comment, in the American *Official Scrabble Players Dictionary*. From a game player's viewpoint the non-K versions, though erroneous, are quite valid for play.)

talced *erron fm adj/vbl infl* **talcked** (see **talc**)

talcing *erron fm vbl infl* **talcking** (see **talc**)

talcose *adj* abounding in or mainly talc

talcous *adj* of the nature of, abounding in or consisting largely of talc

tale (*n*) *vb* to count up: to deal out by number *obs vb* to discourse, talk or gossip: to shout

taler *n sing/pl* any of various large silver coins issued by different German states from the 15th century onwards: a dollar *obs S n* condition, state

taleysim see **tallith**

taling *n* the telling of tales: talking, gossiping

taliped *adj* club-footed *n* a club-footed person

talipes *n* club-footedness: the natural twisted disposition of the foot of a sloth

talke *obs fm n/vb* **talk**

talkier *comp adj* talky, given to verbosity

tallage *n* a tax, *esp* that levied by the Norman and early Angevin kings upon the towns *obs n* the sense of taste *vb* to tax

tallet *dial n* a loft over such as a cowshed or a stable

tallier *n* one who tallies

tallith *n* a Jewish prayer shawl (*pl* **taleysim, tallaisim, tallithes, tallithim, tallitoth**)

talm *now dial vb* to tire: to become exhausted: to faint *now dial n* exhaustion

Talmud *n* the body of Jewish civil and religious law – other than that of the *Pentateuch* – consisting of the *Mishna* and the *Gemara*

talpe *obs n* the mole, the small insectivore

Talpidae *n pl* the family of the moles

talpine *adj* pertaining to the mole (the animal)

taluq *n* a subdivision, comprising a number of villages, of a revenue district in east India: an Indian hereditary estate somewhat similar to a British manorial landholding

taluqdar *n* the officer who collects the revenue of a taluq (subdivision): the owner of a taluq (hereditary estate)

taluqdari *n* the office of a taluqdar, the revenue collector

talus *n* the ankle bone (*pl* **tali**): a slope formed by an accumulation of rock debris (*pl* **taluses**)

tamale *erron fm n* **tamal**, a Mexican dish of highly-seasoned, crushed maize with meat (*pl*, of tamal, **tamales**)

tamandua *n* a species of anteater which, fox-sized, falls midway between the **giant anteater** and the tiny **silky anteater**. Whilst the giant anteater is terrestrial and the silky anteater arboreal, the tamandua is equally at home on the ground or in trees.

tamanoir *n* the giant anteater

tamanu a tree of the East Indies which is a source of gum resin

tamari *n* a Japanese sauce made of salted soya beans

tamarin *n* a member of the marmoset family of monkeys of which there are various species and subspecies, such as the brown-headed tamarin, red-bellied tamarin, white-footed tamarin, pied tamarin, cottontop tamarin and moustached tamarin

Tamarix *n* the genus of the evergreen shrub, tamarisk

tamboura *n* a guitar-like, eastern instrument

tamein *n* a sari-like, draped garment worn by a Burmese woman

tameless *adj* untamed, untameable

Tamil *adj/n* (of) a Dravidian language and person who speaks it, native to the adjacent parts of India and Sri Lanka (Ceylon)

tamin *n* highly-glazed, thin, woollen stuff *obs n* stamin

tamine *var fm n* **tamin**

tamis *n* a cloth sieve or strainer

tamise *n* any of various thin, woollen fabrics *obs fm n* **tamis**

tammel *obs n* a (black-coloured) cloth or garment of such

tamp *vb* to pack (with clay) a bore hole prior to firing a charge: to ram earth or clay into anything

Tampico *n* a Mexican seaport on the river Panuco, nine miles from the Gulf of Mexico

tampion *n* a wooden plug for the muzzle of a gun *vb* to plug

tampon *n* a medical or sanitary plug *vb* to plug with a tampon

tanager *n* any of about 200 species of small, colourful birds which range in size from that of a tit to that of a finch and are found throughout the warmer climates of the Americas. The most colourful of all species belong to the genus *Tangara*, the prime member of which is the paradise tanager. It is velvety black on the upper parts, the crown and sides of the face are green, the lower back is scarlet, the rump yellow and the underparts are mostly turquoise.

tanagrine *adj* of, pertaining to or belonging to the genus *Tangara* (see **tanager**) (note: Not included amongst the **ANIMAL ADJECTIVES**)

tanaiste *n* the deputy prime minister of Eire

tanbark *n* the bark of the oak (or certain other trees), one of the sources of tannin (a class of yellowish compounds – or, in pure form, colourless), used for such purposes as a tanning agent, a medical astringent and as a corrosive fluid (tannic acid). Tannin is also obtained from gall nuts or sumach. (Also see **sumach**)

Tancred *masc pers n* meaning 'graceful speech'

tandle *n* a (festive) bonfire

tang (*n*) *vb* to affect with an unpleasant taste: to make a ringing or clanging sound

tanga *n* any of a number of small coins of varying values which circulated in India, Tibet, Turkestan and Persia

Tangatanga *n* a name for a trinity of ancient Peruvian divinities, Mamakotcha, Pachama and Virakotcha

tange *obs fm ns* **tanga, tang**

tangel *obs fm vb* **tangle**

tangelo *n* a hybrid fruit from a cross between a tangerine and a pomelo (*pl* **tangelos**)

tanghin *n* a poison obtained from the kernels of the purple coloured fruit of a Madagascan shrub, formerly used in witchcraft practices for testing the guilt of a suspect: that shrub

tangi *n* a Maori funeral lament

tangie *n* a water horse, of the type only found in the Goidelic Celtic parts of the British Isles, which haunts stretches of water in Orkney and Shetland. In its human form it is an old man, and, as a horse, it has a shaggy coat. Both as a man and a horse it is covered in seaweed.

tangier *comp adj* tangy

tangina *var fm n* **tanghin**

tangkin *var fm n* **tanghin**

tangly *adj* tangled (*comp* **tanglier** *sup* **tangliest**)

tangoist *n* an exponent of the dance, the tango

tangram *n* the classical Chinese perpetual challenge to artistic ingenuity whose Western devotees have included such diverse characters as Napoleon and Edgar Allan Poe. The diagram is of a square which comprises the seven pieces, or tans, which are the only shapes used to construct literally hundreds of different forms. Any number of animals can be produced from these shapes, every numeral is possible and so too is the complete alphabet. Western innovators have added all manner of modern gadgetry such as microscopes, sports cars and television sets to the repertoire of the natural items so beloved by the Chinese for centuries. All are possible by arranging these seven shapes without adding, duplicating, mutilating or doubling up and covering any other part in any way.

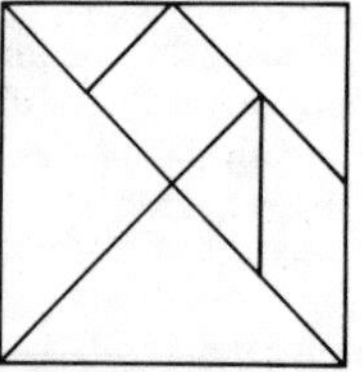

tanguin *obs fm n* **tanghin**

tania *n* a farinaceous tuber akin to the eddoe and cultivated as food in Brazil and the West Indies

tanier *var fm n* **tania**

tanist *n* the elected heir to a Celtic chief

tanister *obs var fm n* **tanist**

tanka *n* a type of Japanese five-line poem: the people of Canton who dwell on boats

tanke *obs fm n* **tank**

tankle *n* a sound less acute than a tinkle *vb* to make such a sound

tanling *n* a person with dark or tanned skin

tannage *n* the art or skill of tanning: the resultant product

tannic *adj* of, relating to, containing or produced from tan or tannin (see **tanbark**)

tannier *var fm n* **tania**

tanny *obs fm n/adj* **tawny**

tan ooze *var fm n* **tanpickle**

tan ouse *var fm n* **tanpickle**

tanpickle *n* the tanning liquid, based on oak, used in a tanning vat (*var fms incl* **tan liquor, tan ooze, tan ouse**)

tanquen *var fm n* **tanghin**

tanrec *var fm n* **tenrec**

tan ride *n* a riding track laid with spent bark

tansie *obs fm n* **tansy**

tansy *n* a perennial herb with a strong aromatic scent and a bitter taste: extended to other plants such as wild tansy (also known as cleavers, goosegrass or silverweed), goose tansy (also known as dog's tansy, ragwort or yarrow), Cape tansy, maudlin tansy, shrubby tansy and white tansy *arch n* an omelette or pudding flavoured with tansy *dial n* a festive gathering on Shrove Tuesday

tant *dial vb* to rage: to argue in a capricious manner: to idle *var fm now dial adj* **taunt**, saucy or pert

Tantalean *adj* of or pertaining to Tantalus, the mythical king doomed to a punishment of being eternally tantalized: tantalizing

tantalic *adj* of or derived from tantalum, the metallic element (+*cap*) *adj* tantalizing

tantara *n* a fanfare of trumpets

tanter *dial vb* to quarrel, argue, dispute

Tantra *n* a Hindu or Buddhist writing concerning a facet of religious teaching

Tantrism *n* the doctrines enshrined in the Tantras

Taoism *n* one of the three great traditional religions of China, alongside Buddhism and Confucianism. It combines magic and the worship of many gods within a philosophical framework set down in the *Tao Te Ching* and other extremely ancient works. (Also see the apt anagram, **Maoist**.)

tap cinder *n* the slag resulting from the process of making malleable iron

tapeline *n* a tape for measuring distances

taperer *n* one who carries a taper

taperness *n* a tapering shape

tapet *n* a projection on a machine which transmits motion by a tapping action

tapeti *n* the South American forest rabbit and the source of myxomatosis, the disease fatal to all other species of rabbits but which merely produces local tumours in the tapeti

tapir *n* any of four species of an inoffensive, long-snouted, plump, thick-skinned relative of the rhino. One species, the natural enemy of which is the tiger, lives in southeast Asia; the remainder are found in Central and South America.

tapiser *Obs fm n* **tapisser**

tapisser *n* a weaver of tapestry

tapist *n* one who adheres strictly to the bureaucratic regulations or red tape

taplash *n* very weak or stale beer

taplin *obs n* one of the bars of iron which support a pan of brine over the fire in a saltworks

tapling *var fm obs n* **taplin**

taplings *n pl* the strong double leathers fastened to the ends of each piece of a flail, the hand-held implement used for threshing grain

tapnet *n* a basket used for the export of figs: a measure of quantity of figs

tapple *var fm vb* **topple** (extant only in the phrase, **tapple up tail**, to turn somersaults)

tapre *obs fm n/adj* **taper**

tapser *obs fm n* **tapisser**

tapsimel *obs n* a medicinal plaster of herbs and honey

tapsman *S n* the leader of some group or unit

tapster *n* a man who serves ale in a bar or tavern *obs n* a woman who serves ale

tapstrie *obs fm n* **tapestry**

tar acne *n* an inflammatory skin disease caused by rubbing with tar

taramasalata *n* a Greek dish consisting of a paste made from the roe of either grey mullet or smoked cod, mixed to a creamy consistency with olive oil and garlic (HANGMAN PLAYER'S note: The only vowel is the letter A, of which there are six and these occur as every alternate letter)

tarand *obs n* a reindeer

Tarasco *n* a North American Indian language spoken in Mexico

tarbet *S n* a narrow, low-lying isthmus

tarcel see **tercel**

tarche *Obs fm arch n* **targe**

tarde *obs vb* to retard, delay

tardle *dial n* a tangled mess, a tangle

tardy (*adj*) *obs vb* to delay, retard

tare *n* any of various species of vetch: the seed of these plants: a Biblical weed (*poss* darnel) which grows among wheat: hence, a seed of wickedness: in chemistry, an empty vessel used as a counterweight: the weight of a container or the wrapping in which goods are packed: a deduction from gross weight to make allowance for such packaging: the weight of an unladen vehicle *vb* to weigh in order to calculate the tare

targe *arch n* a light shield borne by an archer *obs n* the privy seal of kings Edward I, II and III which bore a shield as its device: delay *obs vb* to shield: to delay *S vb* to cross-examine: to keep in strict order: to reprimand, to chastise physically

tarheel *US n* the nickname of the state of North Carolina: a resident of that state

tariqat *n* in the Sufi belief, the way of spiritual development via the stages of meditation, nearness to God, love, fear, hope, longing, intimacy, tranquillity, contemplation, certainty

tarle *S dial vb* to work in a lazy or sluggish fashion: to labour under the strain of illness (*infl fms incl pa t* **tarlet)** *S dial n* a weak person or animal

tarlet see **tarle**

tarlies *obs S fm n* **trellis**

tarmac *US n* an asphalt road *n* an aerodrome runway

tarnal *US adj* damned

tarne *var fm obs n* **therne**

taroc *var fm n* **tarot** (*pl* **tarocks, tarocchi**)

tarock *obs fm n* **taroc** (see **tarot**)

tarot *n* taroc, a set of playing cards with non-standard suits and additional cards, illustrated with unusual characters, used *esp* in fortune telling

tarpan *n* an extinct wild horse of southern European Russia approximately the size of a mule

Tarpeian *adj* denoting a rock face, the **Tarpeian Rock**, on the Capitoline Hill at Rome from the top of which persons convicted of treason were thrown to their death

tarpon *n* either of two fishes of two different families of an order of fishes (*Elopiformes*) which, together with the eels and gulper eels (order *Anguilliformes*) and the spiny eels (order *Notacanthiformes*), constitute the superorder *Elopomorpha* of the bony fishes. The tarpon of the Indo-Pacific waters (*Megalops cyprinoides*) grows to a length of three feet and the tarpon of the Atlantic waters (*Tarpon atlanticus*) grows to a length of ten feet. In other words, of the two different fishes *related to the eels*, the one found in the Indian and Pacific oceans belongs to the genus *Megalops*, and is comparatively small. (Also see **giant herring**.) By contrast, the dictionary used as the ultimate authority for the UK Scrabble championship carries the following definition:– 'a gigantic fish (*Megalops*) akin to the herring, angled for on the Florida and Gulf coasts'. Herrings belong to a completely different order (*Clupeiformes*) of a totally different superorder (*Clupeomorpha*).

Tarquin *pers n* either of two kings of ancient Rome, one known as **Tarquin** and the other as **Tarquin the Proud**. Tarquin was the fifth king in a line of elected monarchs which began with Romulus, the founder of Rome. Tarquin the Proud was the seventh and last king whose overthrow was sparked off by his son (also named Tarquin) committing an act of rape. After his overthrow, Rome became a republic until Augustus became the first of the emperors. (Also see **Brutus, Lucretia** and **Servian**)

tarragon *n* an aromatic plant of the wormwood family, the leaves of which are used as seasoning: those leaves

tarres *obs fm n* **terrace**

tarress *obs fm n* **terrace**

tarrier *n* one who tarries or delays

tarrock *n* a name locally applied to various seabirds such as the Arctic tern, the kittiwake, the common guillemot and the young common gull

tarsal *adj* relating to the ankle (tarsus) *n* see **tercel**

tarse *var fm n* **tarsus**, the posterior part of the foot *var fm obs n* **tars**, a rich and costly fabric from the Orient *obs n* the penis

tar-seal *vb* to seal a (road) surface with tarmac

tarsel see **tercel**

tarsia *n* a type of decorative inlay in wood

tarsier *n* any of three species of rat-sized, nocturnal, large-eyed mammals akin to the lemurs and distantly related to the monkeys

Tarsipes *n* a long-snouted Australian marsupial also known as the honey mouse

Tarsius *n* the genus of the tarsiers

tarsus *n* the group of seven bones which, in man, comprises the ankle: the corresponding part in other mammals and in amphibians and reptiles: a plate of connective tissue in the eyelid: the shank of a bird's leg: the five-jointed foot of an insect (*pl* **tarsi**) (*+cap*) *n* a Turkish port on the Mediterranean, the birthplace of St Paul

tartana *n* a small, Spanish covered wagon: tartan or tartane, a flat-bottomed, Mediterranean fishing boat with a lateen sail

Tartarian *adj/n* Tartar *adj* infernal

tarter *comp adj* tart

tartest *sup adj* tart

tartine *n* a tartlet, bread and jam: any simple item of common character

tartlet *n* a little tart

tarweed *n* any of various, heavily scented, American flowering plants

tash *S fm now dial vb* **tache**, to fasten *var fm now dial n* **tache**, a distinctive mark

tasimeter *n* an apparatus for measuring minute changes in such as temperature or moisture

tasker *n* a taskmaster *dial n* one paid by the task *obs n* one who assesses a price or rate

tasler *obs fm n* **teaseler**, one who raises a smooth nap on cloth: the implement used: a horse comb

taslet *arch S n* see **tasset**

tasque *obs fm n* **task**

tassar *var fm n* **tusser**

tassel *n* a pendant ornament of a tuft of threads: anything resembling a tassel – such as the inflorescence of the plant, maize *vb* to furnish or adorn with a tassel or tassels: to flower or bloom like maize (*infl fms* British, **tasselled/-lling:** US **tasseled/-ling**) *var fm n* **torsel** (also see **tercel**)

tassell see **tercel**

tasseller *n* one who wears a tasselled cap

tasses *var fm n* **tassets** (see **tasset**)

tasset *n* an individual plate of metal which overlaps a series of others to form an armoured kilt called a tassets or tasses or, in Scotland, a taslets

tassie *S n* a small cup

tastable *adj* capable of being tasted

tastle *obs fm n* **tassel**

tatami *n* a Japanese floor covering made from rice stalks

Tatar *var fm n* **Tartar**, one of the warlike people of Central Asia, first known to the west as part of the horde of Genghis Khan

tater *vulg n* a potato

tath *S & dial n* the dung of grazing animals such as cattle or sheep *S & dial vb* to manure land by grazing farm animals upon it

tathe *var fm S & dial n/vb* **tath**

tatle *obs fm n* **tattle**, gossip

tatler *arch fm n* **tattler**

tattler *n* one who chatters, a gossip: a species of sandpiper

tau *n* the nineteenth letter of the Greek alphabet: a cross in the shape of the letter T also known as St Anthony's cross

taune *var fm obs vb* **tawne**

taupe *n/adj* (of) a greyish-brown colour

tauric *adj* of a bull

taurine *adj* of or pertaining to a bull *n* a neutral substance found in animal bile

tauten *vb* to make or become taut

tav *n* the twenty-first and last letter of the Hebrew alphabet

tavel *var fm obs n* **tavell**, a bobbin for silk (extant in the modern French *fm* **tavelle**) *Obs n* a dicing game: the playing die: the board on which it was played *Obs vb* to dice

taver *S n* a shred *S vb* to wander aimlessly: to talk idly or foolishly

tavering *S n* wandering

tavern (*n*) *vb* to frequent taverns

tawer *var fm n* **whittawer**, a saddler or harness maker

tawery *n* a leather manufactory which dyes hides with alum (*pl* **taweries**)

tawn *obs vb* to bronze *obs n* a tan

tawne *obs vb* taune, to exhibit or show *obs S vb* to tame or soften

tawnier *comp adj* tawny

taws *n* a leather strap divided at the end, the traditional instrument of corporal punishment in Scottish schools

tawse *vb* to punish with the taws *var fm n* **taws**

tawtie *S adj* matted, tangled

taxer *n* one who levies a tax

taxor *var fm n* **taxer**

tayra *n* a large, arboreal, omnivorous member of the weasel family found throughout the Americas from Mexico to Paraguay. Natives claim that a particular well-developed part of the male tayra's anatomy has aphrodisiac qualities.

tayse *var fm obs n/vb* **teise**

te *var fm n* **ti**, the musical note (see **gamut**)

tea (*n*) *collq vb* to entertain with or at tea

teaberry *n* the plant, wintergreen

teaboard *n* a (wooden) tea tray

teabowl *n* a teacup without a handle such as that used for a delicate China tea

teacher (*n*) *obs vb* to tutor

teachie *obs fm adj* **tetchy**

teade *var fm obs n* **tede**, a torch made from a resinous piece of pine

tea dish *arch n* a teacup

teagle *dial n* a mechanical hoist: a vicious, illegal bird trap using a baited fish hook and line *dial vb* to use a teagle (either type)

teale *dial fm n/vb* **tale**

tealer *obs fm n* **tiller**, one who tills land

tealing *dial fm n* **taling**

teamer *n* one who drives a team

teamless *adj* without a team

teanal *var fm now dial n* **teanel**

teanel *now dial n* a basket

teared *pa t vb* tear, to cry

tearily *adv* in a tearful manner

tearless *adj* void of tears: without sorrow

tear pit *n* a gland near the eye of many species of deer which contains a waxy secretion used for scent-marking a territory. (For examples of such a gland located elsewhere on the body of a deer see **muntjac** and **musk deer**. For a different use of such scent by an ungulate see **duiker**.)

teary *adj* tearful (*comp* **tearier** *sup* **teariest**)

teasel *n* a prickly-leaved and prickly-flowered herb: the dried flowerhead of fuller's teasel used for teasing cloth to raise a nap on its surface: a tool for the same purpose *vb* to raise a nap on cloth (*infl fms* **teaseled/-ling** (also *n*))

teasle *var fm n/vb* **teasel**

teasling *var fm n* **teaseling**

teast *now dial fm vb* **taste** *obs fm n* **taste**

teater *US & dial var fm n* **teeter**

teather *obs fm n* **tether**

teatre *obs fm n* **theatre**

teaware *US n* a tea service

tebbad *n* a sandstorm

teche *obs fm vb* **teach**

techier *arch fm comp* **tetchier**

techtonics *n pl* (functioning as *sing*) the study of (building) construction: the study of the processes by which the earth has its present surface appearance

tected *obs adj* covered

tectonic *adj* pertaining to a building: of such as landforms, resulting from internal pressures and movements: of structural deformation, resulting from similar pressures within the earth's crust

ted *vb* to spread out such as new mown hay for drying: to give a serrated edge to a tool

teddar *obs fm n* **tether**

tedder *n* one who teds *now dial fm n/vb* **tether**

teddir *obs fm n* **tether**

teddy (*n*) *US n* a woman's undergarment which is a combined chemise and pair of knickers (*pl* **teddies**)

tede *obs n* a torch of resinous pine *obs fm vb* **ted**, to spread out hay

teder *obs fm n* **tether**

tedesco *adj/n* (of) the German influence on some aspects of Italian art (note: The *adj* has the *var fm* **tedesque**. The *n* has the *pl* **tedeschi** but it also has a *fem fm* **tedesca**, with a *fem pl* **tedesche**.)

tedge *n* an ingate or aperture in a mould used in founding

tedure *obs fm n* **tether**

teeder *obs fm n* **tether**

teedle *S vb* to hum a tune

teel *dial vb* to set up on end: to lean an object against a wall: to prop up: to pile up: to set a trap *dial fm vb* **till**, to cultivate

teeme *obs fm vb* **team**

teemer *n* one who or an animal which gives birth: one who empties or unloads

teeming *n* fruitfulness: the act of pouring moulten steel into an ingot

teen *arch n* pains taken over something *now S n* anger, wrath, ill-will, malice *now dial vb* to vex, irritate, annoy: to injure *dial vb* to construct a hedge or fence

teend *var fm now dial vb* **tind**

teene *var fm arch n/now S n* **teen** *obs fm now dial vb* **teen**

teener *n* a teenager *dial n* one who makes or repairs a raddle fence

teenish *adj* youthful

teensy *var (facet) fm adj* **teeny**

teentsy *adj* tiny (usually with a facetious slant *comp* **teentsier** *sup* **teentsiest**)

teer *vb* to cover with clay or plaster

teery *dial adj* smeary, sticky

teest *n* a small anvil fitted into a socket *obs fm n* **test**

teeter *n* a seesaw (*US & dial var fm* **teater**) *vb* to seesaw: to sway on the edge of something (*US & dial var fms* **teater, teter**)

tegir *obs S fm n* **tiger**

tegmen *n* a covering: either of the leathery forewings of the cockroach or related insect: the inner covering of a seed (*pl* **tegmina**)

tegmina *pl* tegmen

tegminal *adj* covering, protecting

tegular *adj* of or pertaining to tiles

tehee *interj* expressing a titter *n/vb* (to) titter, giggle

teil *n* the linden tree *obs S fm vb* **till,** to cultivate

teind *S & dial n/vb* (to pay) a tithe

teir *obs S fm vb* **tear**, to pull apart or rip

teise *obs n* a fathom (*var fms incl* **taise, tayse, tese**) *obs vb* to bend a bow, to take aim with an arrow (*var fms incl* **taise, tayse, tese**): to drive (a hunted beast), to chase, to urge on (*var fms incl* **tayse, tease, teese**) *obs fm vb* **tease**

teiser *obs n* one who rouses game for hunting

telamon *n* a column in the shape of a figure of a man (*pl* **telamones**)

telamones *pl* telamon

telar *adj* of or pertaining to a web *obs fm n* **tiller**

telare *obs S fm n* **tiller**, one who tills land

telary *adv* in the manner of a web *adj* web-spinning

tele-ad *n* a newspaper advertisement secured from selling via the telephone

teledu *n* the stinking badger of Java and Sumatra

telega *n* a four-wheeled Russian cart of simple construction

teleman *S fm (obs) obs n* **tillman**

telephony *n* communication by telephone

teler *obs n* a seller of cloth

teleran *n* an air navigation system

teleses *pl* telesis

telesis *n* planned progress (*pl* **teleses**)

telesm *n* a talisman, *esp* one deposited under foundations as a charm

telesma *obs fm n* **telesm** (a Greek *fm* in vogue during the 17th century, hence *pl* **telesmata**)

telesmata *pl* telesma (*obs fm n* **telesm**)

telesme *obs fm n* **telesm**

telestic *adj* relating to the (ancient Greek) sacred mysteries: mystical

Telinga *n* a Gentoo, a Telugu-speaking person of southeast India: Telugu, one of the Dravidian languages

telisme *obs fm n* **telesm**

tellar *var fm n* **tiller**, a young tree

tellurian *adj* earthly, terrestrial *n* an inhabitant of the Earth

Tellus *pers n* the Roman earth goddess

telos *n* the ultimate objective or end (*pl* **teloi**)

telson *n* the sting of a scorpion or other final segment of a similar creature

telsonic an undefined adjective which appears in at least two American dictionaries and presumably means of or pertaining to a telson

Telugu *n/adj* (of) a Dravidian language of southeast India: a native speaker of the language (*pl* **Telugus**)

telwe *obs vb* to thwite

temenos *n* that land adjacent to a temple considered part of the sacred site

Temmes *obs fm n* **Thames**, the river

template *var* (*pseudo-etymological*) *fm n* **templet** in all senses other than a small temple. (note: The original source word is unknown but the more likely of two possibilities is the French word **templet**, a weaver's stretcher, which, in English, is either **temple** or **templet**. The other possibility is the Latin word **templum**, a beam. **Plate** has no association with the word's origin.)

temple (*n*) *vb* to enshrine: to enclose (as) in a temple: to honour with a temple: to construct a temple (to or for)

templet *n* a horizontal timber in a wall for taking stress: a gauge or pattern used in moulding: a shape, the outline of which is drawn or etched upon that to be cut: a pattern in the form of a strip containing holes indicating the positions for drilling: a temple or contrivance for keeping cloth stretched on a loom (also see note following entry for **template**): a small or miniature temple

temporiser *var fm n* **temporizer**, a time server, one who temporizes

tempra *var fm n* **tempera**, the method of painting which, by the addition of a glutinous substance such as egg yolk, gives water colours an effect more like oil colours

tempre *obs fm vb* **temper**

temse *now dial n* a sieve *now dial vb* to sieve

temser *var fm now dial n* **temse**

tenables *var fm obs n* **tenebres** (a corruption which expired earlier than the correct *fm*)

tenace *n* in a hand of bridge or whist, the possession of two non-consecutive, high cards in one suit where such cards have a value of one immediately above and one immediately below a 'missing' court card i.e. having only the ace and queen or only the king and jack

tenail *var fm n* **tenaille**

tenaille *n* a small low part of fortifications between bastions

tenasm *obs fm n* **tenesmus**

tenasme *obs fm n* **tenesmus**

tence *obs fm n/adj/vb* **tense**

tender hooks see **tenter**

tendle *now dial n* dried twigs or any other suitable kindling

tendon *n* a sinew

tendones *obs pl* tendon

tendre *n* a tender feeling or regard *obs fm n/vb* **tender**

tendril *n* a slender (usually spiralling) appendage of a plant which attaches itself to something else as a support for that plant. Unlike a twining stem it does not bear leaves: a ringlet or curl of hair *nonce vb* to curl like a tendril (*infl fms* as for the *adj* **tendrilled/tendriled** meaning curly)

tendron *n* the bud of a plant

tene *var fm now dial vb* **tind**

tenet see **word square**

tenebrae *n pl* the office of matins and lauds, sung during the Wednesday, Thursday and Friday of Holy Week, at which the candles lit at the beginning of the service are gradually extinguished one by one to commemorate the darkness of the crucifixion

tenebre *obs adj* of tenebrae, as **tenebre candle** or **Tenebre Wednesday**

tenebres *obs n pl* darkness: tenebrae (note: The *n pl* only became *obs* in the last century whereas the *sing* expired together with the *adj*, **tenebre**, in the 16th century)

tenemental *adj* of, pertaining to or of the nature of a tenement

tenesmic *adj* of, pertaining to or of the nature of tenesmus

tenesmus *n* the condition of having an urgent desire to urinate but being unable to relieve that pressure by passing water (*pl* **tenesmuses**)

tenesser *var fm obs n* **tenniser**

tenet *n* a doctrine, dogma or principle

teneur *obs fm n* **tenor**

tenia *var fm n* **taenia** (*pl* **teniae, tenias**)

teniasis *var fm n* **taeniasis**, infestation with tapeworm

tenice *obs fm n* **tennis**

tenioid *var fm adj* **taenioid**

tenise *obs fm n* **tennis**

tenné *her n/adj* the colour bright chestnut

tennel *var fm now dial n* **tendle**

tennil *var fm now dial n* **teanel**

tennis (*n*) *obs vb* to play the game of royal or real tennis (the original form which was, and still is, played in a special courtyard)

tenniser *obs n* a real tennis player (i.e. not a lawn tennis player but one who played the Tudor game of real or royal tennis, which is still extant but requires a special court)

tennle *var fm now dial n* **tendle**

tenon *n* a projection (at the end of a piece of wood) designed to slot into a corresponding mortise cut in another piece *vb* to cut a tenon (on a piece of wood): to join (wood) with a mortise and tenon (a *var fm vb* **mortise**)

tenoner *n* a machine which cuts tenons

tenor (*n*) *vb* to sing tenor: to join together in the manner of a tenon and mortise

tenorist *n* one who sings tenor or who plays the tenor violin

tenorite *n* black copper ore found in the lava at Mount Vesuvius

tenour *now US var fm n* **tenor** *obs fm n* **tenure**

tenpin *adj* of tenpins, the form of bowling at skittles which originated in the USA to circumvent its laws against the imported traditional European game of ninepins. The diamond-shaped formation of ninepins became triangular in tenpins, thus ensuring that a correctly delivered ball could still knock all of the pins down (see **headpin**). Both ninepins and bowls are very ancient and may owe their common ancestry to an Egyptian rain-making ceremony where a rolling ball was used to imitate the sound of thunder. In the centre of the

Derbyshire town of Chesterfield there is a bowling green which has been in continuous use for hundreds of years and is the oldest in Britain.

tenrec *n* any one of a number of different species of insectivores akin to the moles and shrews, though many resemble hedgehogs. There are six different types: 1 **common tenrec**, rabbit-sized and like a hedgehog in appearance and activity. 2 **striped tenrec**, rat-sized, hedgehog-like. 3 **hedgehog tenrec**, mouse-sized and the only type capable of rolling itself into a ball. 4 **rice tenrec**, the size of a large mouse with soft fur and mole-like in activity. 5 **long-tailed tenrec**, nearly twenty different species all of which have soft fur and are mole-like in activity. 6 **water tenrec**, rat-sized with soft fur and otter-like in activity.

tenser (*comp adj*) *n* one, not a citizen or freeman, of a borough who paid a rate for permission to live and trade in that town or city

tensible *adj* capable of being stretched

tensil *obs fm adj* **tensile**

tensile *adj* of or related to tension

tensiled *adj* made tensile

tenson *n* a competition between rival troubadours before a court of love in which each sang or recited a sirvent specially written for the occasion

tensor *n* a muscle that stretches or tightens a part: in mathematics, a vector quantity which requires reference to more than three components for a full description

tentation *n* working by 'trial and error'

tente *obs fm n* **tent**

tenter *n* a wooden frame on which cloth is stretched for drying during part of the manufacturing process (note: The '*tender*' *hooks* of common usage (*incl* the national press) are really the **tenterhooks** of this frame): one who dwells in a tent *dial n* a minder or watchman: a watchdog *vb* to stretch cloth on a tenter

tenterhook see **tenter**

tentor *obs fm n* **tenter**

tentorial *adj* of or pertaining to the outer membrane of the brain

tenty *S adj* watchful, attentive, cautious, observant

tenue *n* bearing: manner of dress

tenues *pl* tenuis

tenuis *n* a voiceless sound in various languages, in English the sound of the letters k, p, t (*pl* **tenues**)

tenurial *adj* of, pertaining to or of the nature of land tenure

tenuto *adj/adv* of music, held or sustained *n* a note held or sustained (*pl* **tenuti**, **tenutos**)

tepal *n* a petal

tephrite *n* any of various volcanic rocks akin to the basalts

tephritic *adj* pertaining to or containing tephrite

tequila *n* a Mexican alcoholic liquor made from the plant, maguey

terai *n* a type of wide brimmed, ventilated hat for use in tropical climates

terand *obs S fm n* **tyrant**

terane *Obs S fm n* **tyrant**

terant *Obs fm n* **tyrant**

teraph *n* an image used in ancient Hebrew religious divination (*pl* **teraphim**)

teratism *n* love of the marvellous or of the prodigious: a biological monstrosity *esp* a malformed human or animal foetus

terbia *n* an oxide of the metallic element terbium

terbium *n* one of the rare metallic elements (*pl* **terbiums**)

terce *n* in Scots law, unless otherwise provided for, a pension for a widow of one third of her late husband's estate, subject to the marriage having lasted at least for a year and a day or her having his living child

tercel *n* any male hawk *esp* the male peregrine falcon (also known as a **tercel gentle**) or the male goshawk (also called **tercel jerkin**). The *var fm* is **tiercel** and **tercelet** also has the same meaning. (GAME PLAYER'S note: The dictionary used for the UK Scrabble championship also gives **tarsel** and **tassel** as *var fms* which other experts consider to be, at best *arch* but, more probably, *obs*. The other *var fms* it gives, **tarcel, tarsal** and **tassell**, are considered by other experts to be unequivocally *obs*.)

tercelet *n* a tercel

tercio *n* a (Spanish) infantry regiment (*pl* **tercios**)

tere *obs S & dial adj* difficult, tedious *obs fm vb* teer *Obs fm vbs* **tar, tear** (to rend)

terebra *n* a modified ovipositor of certain insects which is both a drilling organ as well as the tube throegh which the female lays her eggs

teredines *pl* teredo

teredo *n* the ship worm, a marine pest which bores into submerged timbers: any other mollusc of the same genus: any plant disease caused by an insect's boring (*pl* **teredos, teredines**)

terefa *adj* not kosher

terefah *var fm adj* **terefa**

terek *n* a species of sandpipers which has a long upturned bill and ranges from Finland down to the mouth of the river Terek on the Caspian Sea

Terentian *adj* pertaining to or in the style of Terence (circa 184–159 BC), a former slave from Arabic North Africa who rose to be a great dramatic poet of ancient Rome (the apt anagram is **entertain**)

terete *adj* cylindrical and slightly tapering in form and having a round cross-section

tergal *adj* dorsal, of the back

tergite *n* one of the backplates of such as a centipede

termer *n* one who used to visit London (usually for amusement or intrigue) during the period of a legal term

termes *n* the white ant (*pl* **termites**)

terminably *adv* in the way of being limitable, not perpetual or of being terminated

termly *adj* periodical *adv* periodically

termor *n* one who holds property for a fixed tenure

tern *n* the sea swallow, any of about 43 species of birds of the sub-family of the gulls, *Sterninae*: a set of three: a three-masted schooner (*pl*) *obs n* a double three in dice throwing *Obs vb* of dice throwing, to throw terns (the *vb* is slightly obscure and may mean simply throwing a three)

ternal *adj* of three, threefold or triple

ternate *adj* produced or arranged in threes, *esp* of a leaf comprising three leaflets or of plants with groups of three members

ternated *obs adj* of three leaves on a common stalk

terne *n* an alloy mainly of lead and tin *vb* to coat with this alloy *obs S adj* gloomy: fierce

terned *var fm obs S adj* **terne**

terning *Obs n* the action of the *Obs vb* **tern**

ternion *n* a set of three

terp *n* an artificial mound or hillock created as a foundation for a (prehistoric) village, usually where the region is subject to flooding (*pl* **terpen**)

terpen *pl* terp

terpene *n* any of various hydrocarbons obtained from the volatile oils of plants, *esp* the conifers

terpenic an undefined adjective which appears to be exclusive to one particular American dictionary which has it related to the noun, **terpene.** Its anagram is **prentice**.

terpin *n* water-based compound of oil or turpentine

terpine *var fm n* **terpin**

terpineol *n* a colourless oil used in pharmacy and having an odour of hyacinths or white lilac

terra *L n* earth – used, in English, as a *modf n* to form names such as **terra alba** (pipe clay), **terra cariosa** (tripoli or rottenstone), **terra nobilis** (a diamond (*obs*)) (*pl* **terrae**)

terrae *pl* terra

Terran *n* in science fiction, a term for an inhabitant of the planet Earth. Unlike earthling (a term generally used to imply a status inferior to that of an alien being), a Terran tends to be the equal or superior of other life forms.

terras *var fm n* **trass**, a rock composed of earth, fine volcanic fragments and dust, used as a hydraulic cement (*pl* **terrases**)

terre *obs n* land (in *pl fm*) lands and/or possessions *obs vb* to throw to the ground

terreen *obs fm n* **tureen**

terren *obs fm adj* **terrene**

terrene *adj* belonging to the earth or the Earth: earthy: earthly

terret *n* a harness or leash ring

terrie *obs n* a trodden path

terrien *obs adj* earthly, worldly, territorial

terrine *n* (an earthenware) dish for a casserole: a casserole

terring *S n* provocation

territ *var fm n* **terret**

tersal *obs fm n* **tercel**

terse (*adj*) *var fm obs n* **tarse**, the penis

tersion *n* wiping

terter *var fm obs n* **tertre**

tertia *n* one of three divisions of a large military force, usually one of three regiments

tertian *adj* of a fever, occurring every other day *n* such a fever

tertre *obs n* a hillock or little hill

tese *var fm obs n/vb* **teise** (where indicated)

Teshub *pers n* the Hittite equivalent of Adad, the Assyrian god of storm and thunder

tesla *n* the unit of magnetic flux density

tessar *obs fm n* **tusser**

tessel *obs fm n* **tessella**

tessella *n* a small tessera: a medicated lozenge (*pl* **tessellae, tessellas**)

tessellar *adj* of the nature of tessellae

tessera *n* an individual piece of a mosaic: a token: a password (*pl* **tesserae**)

tesserae *pl* tessera

tesseral *adj* of, pertaining to, composed of tesserae

tesson *n* a fragment, such as marble or brick, used for mosaic work

tessur *obs fm n* **tusser**

tessy *dial adj* angry

testa *n* the outer shell of a seed (*pl* **testae**)

testae *pl* testa

testator *n* one who makes a will, used *esp* of one now deceased *obs n* a witness

teste *n* the final clause in a royal writ *obs n* the head

testee *n* one who is tested *obs n* a witness

testered *adj* having a tester or canopy

testern *arch n* a sixpence *Shaks nonce vb* to tip with a sixpence

testes *pl* testis

testicular *adj* of, pertaining to, containing, having the nature or function of testes: shaped like a testicle

testis *n* a testicle, either of the two male reproductive glands (*pl* **testes**)

teston *n* any of various silver coins *incl* the shillings of Henry VII, Henry VIII and Edward VI: a Scottish coin of Mary Stuart: foreign coins of a similar historical period such as a French coin of Louis XII, a Portuguese coin of Manoel I and an Italian ducal coin

testril *n* a sixpence

testudo *n* a tortoise (now only used +*cap* as the genus): a tumour resembling the shell of a tortoise: an historical engine of siege warfare in which the attackers concealed themselves under a large protective canopy like that of the shell of a tortoise: a similar defensive arrangement, with a body of troops holding shields over their heads to guard against missiles fired at ground level (*pl* **testudines, testudos**)

tetanic *adj* of or pertaining to the disease tetanus or lockjaw *n* a medical remedy which, during the course of application, causes convulsions

tetanise *var fm vb* **tetanize**, to produce the disease tetanus in or tetanic spasms in

tetanoid *adj* of the nature of or resembling the disease tetanus *n* an attack or spasm of tetanus

tetanus *n* lockjaw

tetany *n* a condition characterized by painful muscular spasms: tetanus (*pl* **tetanies**)

tetel *obs fm n/vb* **title**

teter *US & dial fm n/vb* **teeter**

teth *n* the ninth letter of the Hebrew alphabet

tetra *n* one of a number of fairly small, highly coloured, freshwater fish which adapt well to living in an aquarium containing slightly acid, peaty water and rejoice in such names as neon tetra, cardinal tetra, flame tetra, rosy tetra etc

tetracid *adj* designating a base capable of combining with four molecules of a monobasic acid to form a salt *n* a base having four replaceable hydroxal radicals

tetrad *n* a group of four as one collective unit

tetradic *adj* having four digits

tetrarch *n* one of four joint rulers (of an ancient Greek state): a dynast of a region or area subordinate to a larger territory directly under the control of the Roman Empire, a title revived from the original Greek usage to cover such local rule as that of the Biblical lands after the death of Herod the Great. By order of Augustus, the Biblical kingdom was divided into four and two of Herod's sons, Antipas and Philip, were each given a quarter to rule over with the title of tetrarch. The other two quarters were given to another of Herod's sons, Archelaus, who was granted the more important title of ethnarch. (Also see **Antipas**)

tetrode *n* a type of sponge spicule (the firm portion of a sponge) which has four equal rays in the same plane

tetronal *n* a highly toxic sedative drug

tetrous *adj* foul, offensive

tetter *n* any of various skin eruptions such as ringworm *Shaks vb* to affect with such

tetterous *adj* of the nature of, causing or proceeding from a tetter

Teucrian *n/adj* Trojan

Teuton *n* a German

tew *US & dial n* an excited or worried state *S & dial n* a pair of pincers for drawing hot iron from a forge *obs n* fishing tackle *now US & dial vb* to bustle about *now dial vb* to treat (material such as leather) to a manipulative or beating process (the *n* **tewing** is applicable to both bustling and treating material) *obs vb* to drag, pull, tug

tewart *var fm n* **tuart**

tewel *now dial n* the anus of a horse

tewer *var fm n* **twyer**

tewhit *dial n* a lapwing

thaine *obs fm n* **thane**

thairm *S n* catgut

thaler *n* a taler, a silver coin first issued in Bohemia in 1518 and the prototype of the thalers of Germany, Austria and Switzerland and the dollar of the USA

thana *n* an Indian police station *obs n* a fortified military post in India (*var fms n/obs n* **tana, tanna, tannah, thanna, thannah**) (WORD PUZZLER'S note: **tannah/thanna** are examples of unlisted anagrams as they are *var fms* of each other; such *var fms* are only listed where they are also anagrams of a totally different word.)

thane *n* a warrior companion of a Saxon king: one above the status of ordinary freeman but below a peer: the chief of a Scottish clan: a Scottish baron: one of the old nobility in the service of a Scottish king

thanedom *n* the domain of a Scottish thane

thaness *n* the wife of a thane

tharfe *obs fm now S dial adj* **tharf** or **thar**, to be under some form of obligation

thawer *n* a mining apparatus for thawing frozen ground

thearchy *n* government by God or by a god or gods (*pl* **thearchies**)

theater *var fm* (*now mainly US*) *n* **theatre**

theatre (*n*) *vb* to go to the theatre

theatric *adj* theatrical *n* (in *pl fm*) theatricals

Thebes *n* a city of ancient Egypt on the banks of the Nile, the site of which is now partly occupied by the villages of Karnak and Luxor

theca *n* a protective anatomical or botanical covering (*pl* **thecae**)

thecal *adj* of a theca

thecate *adj* having a theca

Thecla *n* the genus of hairstreak butterflies

theic *n* one who drinks too much tea or suffers ill-health as a consequence of such

theine *n* caffeine (originally thought to be an alkaloid exclusive to tea) *Obs vb* to minister to

theism *n* belief in one God but, unlike deism, not denying revelation: an illness caused by excessive tea drinking

theist *n* one who adheres to a belief in theism (1st definition)

theistic *adj* of or pertaining to theism or a theist

themer *n* one who originates a theme

Themis *pers n* the Greek goddess of law and justice

thenar *n* the palm of the hand: the sole of the foot

Theobald *masc pers n* meaning 'folk bold'

Theodora *fem fm masc pers n* **Theodore**, meaning 'God's gift' (also see apt anagram **Dorothea**)

theogonic *adj* of or pertaining to theogony, the study of the genealogy of heathen gods

theologic *adj* of or belonging to theology

theorb *obs fm n* **theorbo**

theorbo *n* a double-necked, large lute with two sets of tuning pegs – the lower tunes the melody strings, the upper the bass (*pl* **theorbos**)

theoric *arch n* a theory *adj* of a fund for the provision of public spectacles and religious functions in ancient Athens: pertaining to such activities in ancient Greece generally

theoriser *var fm n* **theorizer**

theorizer *n* one who theorizes

Theras *n* an ancient Canaanitic city captured by Joshua which later became the capital of the Northern Kingdom

thereness *n* existence in a specified place (usually contrasted with **hereness**)

Theresa *var fm fem pers n* **Teresa**, meaning 'reaper'

theriac *arch n* an antidote to poisonous bites or stings *esp* that of a snake

theriaca *var fm arch n* **theriac**

therle *Obs fm now dial vb* **thirl**

therme *obs fm arch n* **therm**, a public bath *obs fm now dial n* **tharm**, an intestine

thermology *n* the science of heat

therne *obs n* a young woman

theses *pl* thesis

thesis *n* a (formal) proposition: a formal treatise on a particular subject *esp* for a university degree (*pl* **theses**)

thestel *Obs fm n* **thistle**

thew *n* custom: trait: quality (*pl* **thews, thewes**)

thewes *pl* thew

thible *var fm S & dial n* **thivel**

thick (*adj/adv*) *n* the thick part of an object *arch vb* to make or become thick

thighe *obs fm n* **thigh**

thill-horse *n* the wheeler or shaft-horse in a team of horses

thime *obs fm n* **thyme**

thingal *nonce adj* pertaining to things

thinge *obs fm n* **thing**

thinger *n* one whose motivation for action is basic and concrete rather than intellectual, i.e. the doer, not the thinker

thiocyanic *adj* pertaining to or designating a particular colourless acid with a pungent odour and which is soluble in water

thiol *n* any of a class of sulphur compounds analogous to alcohol

thirl *S n* the duty of tenants in thirlage *now dial n* a hole or aperture *S adj* bound in thirlage *S vb* to bind in thirlage to *now dial vb* to perforate

thirlage *n* in Scottish law, the obligation on tenants to grind their corn at a particular mill or pay a duty in lieu (the mill being that owned, or formerly owned, by the original landlord of the whole estate): also, various other local obligations, such as restriction to a particular smithy

thirle *obs fm S n/now dial vb* **thirl**

thirse *obs fm n* **thurse**

thirst snake *n* any of various small, inoffensive, nocturnal snakes in three different genera. Those of the genus *Dipsas* diet exclusively on snails, those of *Sibon* eat slugs and those of *Pareas* eat both. The term, thirst snake, is merely a reference to the mythical dipsas. (See **dipsas**)

thissel *obs fm n* **thistle**

thistel *obs fm n* **thistle**

thistle (*n*) *vb* to clear of thistles

thivel *S & dial n* a (porridge) stirring stick

thole *n* a pin or peg *arch vb* to suffer or endure (without complaint) *dial vb* to be patient

tholus *n* a dome (*pl* **tholi**)

thonder *S fm adj/adv* **yonder** *obs fm n/vb* **thunder**

thondre *obs fm n/vb* **thunder**

thoner *Obs fm n/vb* **thunder**

thoracic *adj* of, pertaining to or contained in the thorax

thorax *n* that part of the body encased by the ribs: the middle region of an insect's body, the corresponding part in other arthropods (*pl* **thoraces, thoraxes**)

thorite *n* a crystalline yellow to black thorium silicate, the yellow to orange range also known as orangite: an explosive invented by a Dr Tuttle of Tacoma, Washington, USA

thorium *n* a grey, radioactive element found only in small quantities in certain rare minerals (*pl* **thoriums**)

thorle *Obs fm now dial vb* **thirl**

thorn (*n*) *vb* to make thorny: to vex

thorne *obs fm n* **thorn**

thornen *now dial adj* of thorns: thorny

thornset *adj* set or beset with thorns

thorpe *arch n* a hamlet or village

thoul *obs fm n* **thole**

thowel *var fm n/arch vb* **thole**

thowle *obs fm n/arch vb* **thole**

thrafe *obs S fm n* **thrave**

thraip see **threap**

thrang *S & dial fm n* **throng** *dial fm vb* **throng**

thraped see **threap**

thrave *n* a measure of harvested produce which varies according to the locality but generally equals 24 sheaves (of corn)

thraw *vb* to turn, twist or contort *S & dial adj* twisted

threaden *arch adj* composed or made of (linen) thread

threadle *vb* to thread

thready *adj* thread-like (*comp* **threadier** *sup* **threadiest**)

threap *now S & dial vb* to rebuke: to argue: to haggle: to assert obstinately (note: *Incl* the *var fm*, **threep**, this produces a choice for the *pa t/pa ppl* of **threaped, thraped, threeped** or **threepit**, with **threaped** by far the most common *fm*. **Threepit** is a typical revival by Scott, in 1816, of the mediaeval style of the *pa t* but one which ignored the fact that the 'th-' was then represented by the single character, thorn (þ). The *vb* had various spelling *fms* during the period between the replacing of thorn by 'th-' and the simultaneous replacing of '-it' by '-ed' for the *pa t* and Scott's revival of '-it' in 1816. These *obs fms incl* **thraip, threape, threip, threpe**, and **threppe**. This is of significance to games players not only concerned with *obs fms* but with modern usage too. For the *pa t/pa pple*, the dictionary used for the UK Scrabble championship permits only **threapit** (a *fm* not recorded in other reference works) and **threepit**. The dictionary used for the North American equivalent permits only **threaped** or **threeped**. Neither mentions **thraped**, nor any of the various *obs fms* given above.)

threape see **threap**

threapit see **threap**

threate *obs fm arch vb* **threat**, to threaten (*pa t* **threated**)

threave *var fm n* **thrave**

threaver *n* a reaper paid on a basis of amount harvested

three-card *adj* of the 'Find the Lady' confidence trick which apparently uses three cards, one of which is a Queen. The dupe is shown three cards and asked to wager on the position of the Queen after the cards have been shuffled in such a way which suggests he knows where that card is. The dupe *always* loses as the Queen has been palmed in the so-called 'three-card trick' and an ordinary card substituted.

threeness *n* three as a basis e.g. the essence of the Trinity

threep *var fm S & dial vb* **threap**

threepit see **threap**

threip *see* **threap**

threne *n* a song of mourning or lamentation *vb* to compose or sing a threne

threnode *n* a dirge or lament for the dead

threnodic *adj* mournful

threnos *n* a threne (also written in the Latin *fm* **threnus**)

threnus see **threnos**

threpe see **threap**

thridace *n* thickened lettuce juice

thrile *Obs adj* threefold or triple

thrin *adj* threefold or triple (in *pl*) *dial n* triplets

thrine *obs fm adj* **thrin**

thrinne *var fm adj* **thrin**

thrinnes *var fm n pl* **thrins**, triplets

thrip *dial vb* to make a slight jerking movement *erron 'sing' fm n* **thrips**

thrips *n* any of various minute, four-winged insects (*pl* **thripses**)

thrisle *arch fm n* **thistle**

thrissel *S fm n/vb* **thistle**

thrissle *arch fm n* **thistle**

thrope *dial fm arch n* **thorpe**

throwstick *n* any stick used as a missile, from a simple club to a primitive type of boomerang not as sophisticated as those produced by some natives: a piece of wood used to facilitate the ejection of a harpoon

thruble *Obs fm n/vb* **trouble**

thrusse *Obs fm n* **thurse**

thulia *n* an oxide of the metallic element, thulium (*pl* **thulias**)

thurse *n* like the troll of Scandinavian myth, this too was a huge ogre or giant but is now a mere hobgoblin

thursse *Obs fm n* **thurse**

thwite *now dial vb* to whittle, pare or shave

thyme (*n*) *vb* to cover or scent with the herb, thyme

thymus *n* a glandular organ of unknown function situated near the base of the neck in vertebrates. In man and other mammals it is most prominent in the young and is the neck sweetbread of calves and lambs. (*pl* **thymi, thymuses**)

thyrse *var fm n* **thyrus** (*pl* **thyrses**)

thyrsi *pl* thyrsus

thyrsus *n* a wand wreathed in ivy or vine and crowned with a pinecone, carried by Dionysus or Bacchus or their followers: a type of dense flower cluster such as that of the grape, in which the middle branches are longer than the outside branches (*pl* **thyrsii**) (*var fm* **thyrse** (*pl* **thyrses**))

ti *n* a small Pacific liliaceous tree: the seventh note of the tonic sol-fa system of musical notation (see **gamut**)

Tiamat *pers n* the primeval goddess of the Babylonians

tiara (*n*) *vb* to adorn (as) with a tiara

tib *n* the ace of trumps in the old game of gleek *obs n* a young woman: a whore *var fm schoolboy slg vb* **tibble**

tibble *schoolboy slg vb* of residential confinement, to slip out of bounds in a secretive manner

Tibert *n* a traditional proper name for a cat (*–cap*) *arch n* a cat

tice *n* in cricket and croquet, an enticing opportunity deliberately presented by the opponent but from which he or she hopes to gain *now dial vb* to entice

tidder *obs vb* to fondle: to engender (offspring)

tiddy *n* in the card game of gleek, the four of trumps *dial adj* tiny

tidemill *n* a mill driven by tidal water

tide rip *n* a disturbance of the sea caused by opposing currents; a tidal wave (GAME PLAYER'S note: The standard American *fm* is **tiderip**, which validates the word for play where American spellings are accepted)

tidesman *n* one whose work is conditional on the tide *obs n* a tide waiter, a customs officer of former times whose work arrived with the tide

tidivate *var fm slg vb* **titivate**, to smarten up

tieclasp *US fm n* **tie clasp**, a tie clip

tierce *n* the name of the third (*a*), or the name of a third (*b*), or the name of three (*c*), in certain specific usages as:– (*a*) in the historical division of the day into hours of set prayer, that canonical hour which ends at 9 am: the prayers set for that hour: of the positions in fencing, the third of eight parries (*b*) an old measure of capacity (for wine) equal to a third of a pipe, a measure which varied in different countries, but the English tierce was generally 42 gallons: a cask of such capacity (*c*) a sequence of three playing cards *her adj* divided into three

tierced *anglicized fm her adj* **tierce**

tiercel *var fm n* **tercel**

tierer *n* one who arranges anything in tiers

Tiernan *masc pers n* meaning 'kingly'

tie-string *n* a string specifically for tying – such as that on a woman's bonnet

tietac *n* a tie clip

tieth *obs fm adj/n* **tithe**

tifle *var fm vb* **tiffle**, to entangle

tigel *n* the primitive stem which bears the first leaves of a sprouting seed

tiger (*n*) *nonce vb* to behave as a tiger

tigeress *arch fm n* **tigress**

tigereye *var fm n* **tiger's-eye**

tiger nut *n* the earth almond or rush nut, a bean-sized West African tuber eaten raw or cooked and having medicinal properties

tiger's-eye *n* a semi-precious golden brown gemstone

tiglon *var fm n* **tigon**

tigon *n* the cross between a tiger and a lioness (as opposed to a **liger**) (also see **litigon**)

tigre *obs fm n* **tiger**

tigrine *adj* of a tiger

Tigrinya *n* a Semitic language of Ethiopia

til *n* either of two plants, the sesamum, which has seeds from which an oil is expressed, or the black til, a tree of the Canary Isles, the timber of which has a fetid odour

tilde *n* the distinguishing mark used in Spanish for such as señor to indicate a change in the pronunciation of the letter N

tile hat *S n* a top hat

tiler *n* one who lays tiles *var fm n* **tyler**

tillage *n* ploughed land: land under crops as opposed to pasturage: those crops: cultivation: the condition of being cultivated: culture of the mind or spirit (*fig*)

tille *obs fm vb* **till**, to cultivate land

tiller (*n*) *vb* to produce side shoots from the root or base of the stem of such as corn

tillet *n* a type of coarse cloth *obs n* the linden tree

tillman *obs n* one who tills the soil

til seed *n* the seed of sesamum (see **til**)

tilsent *obs fm n* **tinsel**

tilter (*n*) *dial vb* to sway

Timaliiae *n pl* the babblers, some 250 or so species of birds unusually classified within tribes, technical groupings between genera and sub-family. The tribes have technical names suffixed '-ni', such as *Timaliini* which groups the genus of the tree babblers with the genus of the tit babblers. The genera and species *incl* Arabian babbler, babaxes, chatterers, common babbler, Iraq babbler, jungle babbler, laughing thrushes, minlas, scimitar babblers, shrike babblers, song babblers (a complete tribe which includes the laughing thrushes and the Pekin robin), tit babblers, tree babblers, wren babblers and yuhinas. The ground babblers (species *incl* the quail thrushes and rail babblers) and the rockfowl or bald crows are variously included within the sub-family of the *Timaliiae* or given independent groupings of their own. All of these birds belong to the same family as the thrush.

Timaliini *n pl* a tribe of babblers (see **Timaliiae**)

timar *n* a fief held by military service in the Ottoman empire (see **Osmanli**)

timariot *n* one holding a timar

timbale *n* the membrane of such as a cicada by which that insect produces its chirping noises: a savoury dish cooked in a cup-shaped mould

timmer *now dial fm n/vb* **timber**

timor *n* fear

timpani *pl* timpano

timpano *n* a kettledrum (*pl* **timpani**)

timse *var fm now dial n* **temse**

timser *var fm now dial n* **temser**

tinamou *n* any of some 50 species of guineafowl-like, mainly South American, birds with a pheasant-like plumage and distantly related to the ostriches. Classified as a family of nine genera, the species include Bonaparte's tinamou, the male of which has up to three mates all laying in the same nest. (*pl* **tinamous**)

tinchel *S n* an ever decreasing circle of hunters bunching together a herd of deer

tind *now dial vb* to set fire to

tindal *n* a lascar petty officer

tinder *n* any readily combustible material *esp* partially charred linen or corkwood fungus which will ignite, without explosion, on contact with a spark

tindered *adj* burnt to tinder

tindle *dial n* a small outdoor fire

tineid *n* a clothes moth or any other species of its family, the *Tinaeidae*

tinesm *obs fm n* **tenesmus**

ting (*n*) *vb* to make the sound of a bell: to ting bees, to induce swarming bees to settle by making such a sound

ting bees see **ting**

tingeing *US var fm n/adj* **tinging**

tingent *adj* designating that colouring

tinger *n* one who or that which tinges *obs n* one of two gangs of workmen engaged in the unloading, by tipping, of a cart. The untingers unfastened the cart and tipped the load; the tingers then righted the cart and resecured it to the draught animal(s).

tingler *n* that causing a tingling sensation

tinier *comp adj* tiny

tink *vb* to make a bell-like sound of a very short resonance *n* such a sound

tinke *obs fm vb* **tink**

tinne *var fm now dial vb* **tind**, to kindle *obs fm n/vb* **tin**

tinner *n* one who works with tin at any stage from its mining to its usage in manufacture

tinnet *now dial n* brushwood used for fencing

tinnie *var fm S n* **tinny**

tinny (*adj*) *S n* a small tin mug

tinsel (*adj/n/vb*) *infl fms* British, **tinselled/-lling:** US, **tinseled/-ling**

tinsey *n* tinsel

tinstone *n* cassiterite, a brown to black tin dioxide, the most important tin ore

tinte *obs fm n* **tent**, a deep red Spanish wine with a low alcohol content

tinter *n* an artist who specializes in tinting

tin terne *var fm n* **terne plate**, an inferior type of tinplate

tipcat *n* an old rustic game of the rounders or baseball type where, instead of a ball, the player strikes a small piece of wood pointed at both ends and known as a 'cat'. The batsman first hits the cat lightly into the air, then strikes it as hard as he can.

tipet *obs fm n* **tippet**, a cape or short cloak

tiple *obs fm vb* **tipple**

tipler *obs fm n* **tippler**, a drinker

tiplet *n* a very small tip or point

tippe *obs fm n* **tip**

tippel *obs fm vb* **tipple**

tipula *n* the daddy-long-legs or other fly of its genus

tiran *obs fm n* **tyrant**

tirand *obs S fm n* **tyrant**

tirane *obs fm n* **tyrant**

tiranne *obs fm n* **tyrant**

tirasse *n* a draw net used for catching such as partridges: an organ foot pedal

tirdel *obs fm now dial n* **treddle**

tireling *n* a tired person or animal

tirer *n* one who dresses

tirl *vb* to turn (over) *S & dial vb* to strip, to uncover *S vb* to pluck a string

tirle *obs fm vb* **tirl**

tiro *n* a novice or beginner (*var fm* **tyro** *pl fms* **tiros**, **tiroes**, **tyros**, **tyroes**, **tyrones**) (note: The *var fm* **tyrone** is *obs* even though the *pl* is extant)

tiroes *pl* tiro

tirr *S & dial vb* to uncover, to strip *esp* of roofing materials: to undress: to remove the surface layers of soils and clays prior to quarrying (in this sense **tirring** is a *n*, meaning the action of the *vb*)

tisane *var fm n* **ptisan**

tische *obs S fm n* **tissue**

tissed *obs adj* woven (used in a rather attractive manner as **of gold tissed** or **of linen tissed** *not* 'tissed gold' or 'tissed linen')

tissue (*n*) *vb* to weave with gold or silver threads

tist *obs S fm now dial vb* **tice**

tiste *obs fm now dial vb* **tice**

Titan *n* in Greek mythology, one of the earlier giant gods overthrown by Zeus (*–cap*) *n* anything gigantic: a man of great intellect but lacking the highest inspiration

Titanism *n* defiance of or rebellion against constituted authority (in the specific case of the Titans of Greek myth, it is revolt against the order of the universe): similarly applied to opposing social convention: the character of a Titan: Titanic power

titcher *dial fm n* **toucher**

titching *dial fm n* **touching**

titer *US fm n* **titre**

titfer *collq n* a hat

tithe *adj* tenth *n* a tenth part of annual produce paid as a levy to support the priesthood – originally that of the ancient Hebrews, subsequently that of the Christians *vb* to pay such a levy: to impose such a levy

tither *n* one who pays or receives a tithe *now S & dial fm n* **tether**

titler *n* a conical loaf of sugar *obs n* one who claims a title

titless *collq adj* flat-chested

titling *n* the giving of a name or title *now S & dial n* the hedge sparrow

titrate *vb* to determine the amount of a particular constituent present in a mixture by the process known as titration

titration *n* volumetric analysis, the determination of the ratio of a mixture by comparison with a solution of known ratio. A known reagent is added until a point is reached at which reaction occurs or ceases.

titre *n* the fineness of gold or silver

ti tree *n* see **ti**

tittler *now dial n* a gossip

titular (*adj*) *n* one who has a title of some sort

tiver *dial n* red ochre *dial vb* to mark sheep with red ochre

tlac *n* a small copper coin of 19th century Mexico

Tlingit *n* a Red Indian language and people of Alaska

tmeses *pl* tmesis

tmesis *n* the separation of the elements of a compound word by an intervening word or words, or the rearrangement in this manner of the words of a phrase, e.g. *a young bride and beautiful* instead of *a beautiful young bride* (*pl* **tmeses**)

to (*prep*) *n* a Chinese measure of distance: a Japanese liquid measure

toad (*n*) *vb* to behave as a sycophant or servile flatterer

toader *n* a sycophant, parasite

toadfish *n* any of a family of sluggish, heavily-built fishes found in all tropical seas and distantly related to the anglerfishes. One genus, found in the Pacific coastal waters of Panama, has poisonous spines which, though not lethal to man, can inflict severe pain. Many toadfishes make grunting noises.

toadlet *n* a very small amphibian, such as the corroboree toadlet which lives in moist areas of up to 4,000 ft in the Australian Alps. Unlike other frogs and toads which move by jumping, the corroboree toadlet walks clumsily on the tips of its toes: any small or young toad

toadstone *n* a legendary precious stone found in the head of a toad. It has the power to cure snakebite and both changes colour and becomes warm in the presence of venom. To test the genuineness of such a stone, it is placed near a toad, which will immediately swallow it; the only way of extracting it without killing the toad is to place the creature on a red rag or cloth where it will disgorge it: a Derbyshire lead mining term for a type of igneous rock marked like the skin of a toad

to bell the cat see **bell**

Tobias *masc pers n* meaning 'God is good'

toccata *n* a rapid keyboard composition usually in a rhythmically free style (*pl* **toccatae, toccatas**)

toccatina *n* a short toccata or musical composition in rapid style

tocher *S & dial n/vb* (to supply with) a dowry

tocke *obs fm n* **toque**

tocsin *n* an alarm: an alarm bell

todder *now dial n* frogspawn

todies *pl* tody

tody *n* any of five species of small, insectivorous Caribbean birds akin to the kingfisher and the motmot (*pl* **todies**)

toe dance *n* a dance performed on tiptoes

toenail (*n*) *vb* of carpentry, to join by driving in a nail at an oblique angle

toe rag *slg n* one who is beneath contempt

tofore *obs prep/adv/conj* before

togaed *adj* clad in a toga: peaceful, at peace

toggel *obs fm n/vb* **toggle**

togger *slg n* one of the boats used in the torpids

toile *n* a dress material of silk and linen

toise *n* a linear measure of 6 French feet (*approx* $6\frac{3}{5}$ English feet or 1.949 metres) compared to a **teise** which was 6 English feet or a fathom *vb* to measure with the eye

toisech *n* a noble of the third rank in ancient Celtic Scotland, immediately below king and mormaer (or mormaor) and the equivalent of a chief of a clan (*pl* **toisechs**)

tokay *n* a species of gecko, a type of lizard, found in Malaysia (*+cap*) *n* a sweetish, heavy, Hungarian wine with an aromatic flavour: the grape from which it is derived

tole *now US & dial vb* to attract, entice or decoy *esp* fish or wildfowl *now dial n* a clump of trees

toler *var fm n* **toller**, a (canine) decoy

tolfre *Obs fm adj* **toll-free**

toling *US n* the usage of scattered bait to attract fish to a particular spot

tollage *n* a toll: the payment of such

tolle *obs fm now US & dial vb* **tole**

toller *n* one who collects tolls or payments: one who tolls a bell: a decoy *esp* a small dog trained for the capture of ducks

tolman see **tolmen**

tolmen *obs n* an ancient stone monument of a type found in Cornwall and Brittany consisting of a huge stone supported by two other rocks which admit free passage between them (originally *n sing* with *pl* **tolmens**, subsequently *pl* of new singular **tolman**)

tolsel *n* the ancient name for a guildhall, still retained in some English and Irish towns

tolser *obs fm n* **tolsel**

tolsey *var fm n* **tolsel**

tolter *S & dial adj* unstable *dial vb* to move unsteadily

toluic *adj* of toluene, a colourless liquid used as a solvent

toluide *n* one of a series of compounds obtained from the hydrocarbon, toluene, which is a product of the distillation of coal tar

tombac *n* one of two alloys of copper, either with zinc or with arsenic

tomograph *n* a machine which produces X-ray photographs

tomping *obs fm n/vb* **tampion**

tompot *n* the tompot blenny, the largest British species of blenny

tonalitive *adj* of or pertaining to musical tonality

toname *n* an additional name or description applied as a distinguishing epithet for a person *vb* to give a toname to

toneme *n* a phoneme which differs from another only in the respect of tone

tonemic *adj* of the toneme aspect of compared phonemes

toner *n* one who or that which tones

tonetic *adj* of or relating to linguistic tones

tonetics *n pl* the study of linguistic tones

tonga *n* a light, two-wheeled Indian cart: a drug extracted from the root of a Fijian plant and used as a remedy for toothache: a narcotic drink brewed by Peruvian Indians

tonger *US n* one who gathers oysters with oyster-tongs

tonic sol-fa see **gamut**

tonish *adj* fashionable, stylish

tonne *n* the metric ton and (ironically) *obs fm n* **ton**

tonner *n* a ship or boat of a named number of tons, such as a **fifty tonner** or a **sixty tonner**

tonse *now dial vb* to dress up *obs vb* to cut the hair of

tonsile *obs adj* that (capable of being) clipped

tonsorial *adj* of or pertaining to a barber or his craft

tontine *n* a fund from which each subscriber receives an annuity which increases as the number of participants is diminished by death, until the last survivor enjoys the whole income: a share in such: a card game played on the tontine concept

tony *US adj* stylish *obs n* a simpleton (*pl* **tonys, tonies**) *obs vb* to make a tony of: to fool, cheat or swindle

tooler *n* one who impresses the ornamental designs on the cover of a book: a stonemason's broad chisel

toorie *S n* a small heap: a bobble on a bonnet

toothcarp *n* any small, essentially freshwater fish of a group of families within the super-order *Atheriniformes* (see **FISH CLASSIFICATION**) which includes both egg-laying fishes and those which bear live young. The most remarkable toothcarps are separately discussed at the entries, **Anableps** and **annual fish.**

tootler *n* a writer of twaddle

topee *var fm n* **topi**, a pith helmet

toper *n* a heavy drinker of alcohol (also see apt anagram, **poter**)

top head *n* a channel drilled in the upper part of a thick seam of coal to release any gas

top hole *var fm n* **top head** *collq n* first rate

tophus *n* a soft, porous, stony substance deposited by calcareous springs

topiarist *n* one skilled in landscape gardening

topinel *obs n* a rope for hoisting or supporting the boom on a sailing ship

topman *n* one employed at the higher or highest point, such as the upper man in a sawpit or a sailor at the highest point of a ship *obs slg n* a hangman

topnet *obs fm n* **tapnet**

topologist *n* one versed in geographical topology

topology *n* the scientific study of a locality: the relation of the presenting part of the foetus to the pelvic canal: quantative geometry

toponymic *adj* pertaining to toponymy, the study of the place names of a district

toppe *obs fm n/vb* **top**

top rail *n* the upper rail of a piece of framing

topsman *S n* a foreman

topstone *n* the top stone (*lit/fig*)

toque *n* a small, close-fitting, brimless hat worn by women: the tall, conical hat formerly worn by the doges of Venice: a black velvet cap worn by either sex before the restoration of the French monarchy: the bonnet monkey, a species of macaque

tor *n* a rocky peak, a hill

toran *n* a gateway considered sacred by the Buddhists: a suspended garland of flowers

torbel *Obs fm n/vb* **trouble**

torble *Obs fm n/vb* **trouble**

torcas *Obs fm n* **turquoise**, the gemstone

torch (*n*) *vb* to supply with or light a torch: to apply mortar to the inside joints of slating laid on laths

torchère *n* a tall, ornamental candlestick or lampstand

torero *n* a Spanish-style bullfighter on foot (*pl* **toreros**)

torkes *var fm obs vb* **turkess**

tormen see **tormina**

tormina *n pl* the gripes, acute pain in the bowels (unused *sing* **tormen**)

tornade *poet n* a tornado

tornal *adj* of or pertaining to a tornus

tornus *n* the anal or inner angle of an insect's wing (*pl* **torni**)

toroid *adj* shaped like an anchor ring *n* a coil of that shape

torpid (*adj*) *n* one of the torpids or races rowed at Oxford with eight-oared, clinker-built boats

torpide *obs fm adj* **torpid**

torple *now dial vb* of an animal, to die

torque *n* a metal ornament such as a collar or bracelet worn by the ancient British

torques *n* a ringlike marking around the neck of various birds and animals *var fm n* **torque** *obs adj* twisted, bent

torquess *var fm obs adj* **torques**

torre *obs fm n* **tor**

torret *n* a ring used to attach something to a chain

torsade *n* a twisted cord or ribbon used for ornamentation

torse *n* a surface, in geometry, capable of development: the torso *her n* the twisted wreath used to join the crest to the helmet

torsed *her adj* having a torse

torsel *n* a templet in a brick wall supporting the end of a beam

torsion *n* a twist: (the strain produced by) a twisting

torsional *adj* of, pertaining to, caused by or resulting from twisting

torte *n* a rich sweet (Austrian) pastry (*pl* **torten, tortes**) *obs n* a round (bread) cake *obs fm n* **tort**

tortel *Obs fm n* **turtle**

torten *pl* torte

tortile *adj* twisted, coiled

tortilla *n* a type of thin, round, Mexican bread cake, eaten hot

tortive *adj* twisting, twisted

tortle *Obs fm n* **turtle**

tortlet *obs her n* a small cake of bread

tortrices *pl* tortrix

tortrix *n* either of two very different creatures, a coral snake (see general comment towards the end of **ANIMAL ADJECTIVES**) or a leaf-roller moth (*pl* **tortrices**)

torula *n* a small, rounded swelling: a micro-organism of such as yeast (*pl* **torulae, torulas**)

Toscanini *pers n* the Italian conductor (1867–1957) famed not only for his ability but also for his remarkable musical memory

tose *var fm now dial vb* **toze** *obs fm vb* **toze**

toser *var fm obs n* **tozer**

tosh (*slg n*) *S vb* to tidy or trim

tosher *n* a small fishing vessel *slg n* a thief who steals the copper protective covering from the hull of a vessel berthed in the Thames

tosing *obs fm now dial n* **tozing**, the act of combing wool

tossel *dial fm n* **tassle**

tossen *obs infl vb* toss

tossily *adv* pertly

tossy *adj* haughty, pert, scornful

total (*n/vb*) *infl fms* British, **totalled/-lling:** US, **totaled/-ling**

toter *US collq n* one who carries something *obs fm vb* **totter**

tother *now dial pron/adj* the other of two

totre *obs fm n* **totter**

tou *obs fm n/vb* **tow** (in most senses)

tougher (*comp adj*) *obs fm S & dial n/vb* **tocher**

toule *obs fm now US & dial vb* **toll**, to attract, entice: to decoy

toupé *obs fm n* **toupee**, a small hairpiece

toupet *n* a toupee or small hairpiece

tourbel *Obs fm n/vb* **trouble**

tourel *Obs fm n* **tourelle**, a turret

touret *Obs fm n* **torret**

tournedo *obs fm n* **tornado**

tournedos *n* a small fillet of beef served with a garnish (*pl* **tournedos**)

touse *vb* to drag or push about: of a dog, to worry *dial n* a commotion: horseplay

touser *n* one who tussles or rummages

tousle *S n* a rough romp with a woman *vb* to handle (a woman) in a rough, indelicate manner: to dishevel (hair or clothing)

tously *adj* dishevelled

toute *obs n* the buttocks *var fm obs n* **tot**, a fool *obs fm n* **tout**

touter *n* one who touts for custom: one who spies on racehorses during training

towage *n* the action of towing or being towed: the charge for such

towle *obs fm n* **tool**

towler *obs fm n* **toller**, a toll collector

townie *var fm collq n* **towny**, one who lives in a town on a native or permanent basis

towpe *obs fm n* **tup**, a ram

towre *obs fm n/vb* **tower**

towret *obs fm n* **turret**

towse *var fm vb* **touse**

towsel *var fm vb* **tousle**

towser *var fm n* **touser**

towte *var fm obs n* **toute**

toyer *n* a trifler

toysome *obs adj* playful, (amorously) sportive

toze *vb* of tin mining, to sieve tin ore from ore by a washing process *now dial vb* to comb wool

tozer *n* one who washes the newly-mined tin *obs n* one who cards or combs wool

T-plate *n* a T-shaped metal plate

trabea *n* a toga having horizontal purple stripes and worn by men of the highest rank in ancient Rome (*pl* **trabeae**)

tracheid *n* a long, tubelike, closed cell in xylem

trachitis *n* inflammation of the windpipe

trachle *S n* an exhausting effort: drudgery *S vb* to bedraggle, dishevel: to exhaust by strenuous activity: to drudge

tract (*n*) *obs vb* to negotiate

tractator *n* one who writes tracts e.g. Cardinal Newman, who wrote *A Tract for the Times*, published by the Oxford Movement of the mid-19th century *obs n* one who writes a treatise

traduce *vb* to speak badly or maliciously of

traget *S fm* (*obs*) *obs n* **treget**

tragic (*adj*) *n* a tragic actor or poet

tragule *n* a small, hornless, deer-like quadruped of India and Java

traguline *adj* of or pertaining to the chevrotain

traik *S n* a plague: a disaster: mischief: an annoying person: the flesh of sheep which has died as opposed to that from a slaughtered animal *S vb* to decline in health: to wander or go idly about

traiking *S n* strolling, wandering

trail net *n* a net which is trailed or dragged for fish, a literal dragnet

traine *obs fm n/vb* **train**

trainel *obs n* a dragnet of various sorts used for catching fish or birds *obs vb* to use such for catching birds

traipse *vb* to trudge, to walk with a heavy tread or in a tired fashion (*var fms* **trapes, trape** (*now dial*)) *var fm n* **trapes**

traisle *obs S fm n* **trestle**

traison *obs S fm n* **treason**

traissel *var fm obs S vb* **traissle**

traissle *obs S vb* to trample

traist *obs S & dial adj* trusty, trustworthy *obs S & dial n* trust *obs S & dial vb* to trust

traiste *var fm obs S & dial n* **traist** *Obs fm obs S & dial adj/vb* **traist**

trait *n* a characteristic

traitress *n* a female traitor: treachery personified as a woman

trake *obs fm S n/vb* **traik**

trale *obs fm n/vb* **trail**

traleis *obs S fm n* **trellis**

trame *var fm n* **tram**, silk thread used for the weft of the finest silk products

tramel *obs fm n* **trammel**

trammel *n* a long, narrow fishing net: anything which confines (*lit/fig*) *vb* to use the fishing net: to entangle or hinder (*fig*) *infl fms* **trammeled/-lled** etc

trampe *var fm obs n* **tramp**, the temper of steel *var fm obs S vb* **tramp**, to soak

trampel *Obs fm vb* **trample**

tranche *n* a slice, a portion

trane *var fm obs n* **train**, treachery, guile or deceit *obs fm vb* **train**, to instruct

trangam *n* a toy, a trinket or any little gadget despised by the one who speaks of it

trangle *her n* a bar

trankum *n* a trinket

trannie *slg fm n* **transistor radio**

transe *var fm S n* **trance**, a passage or alley *obs fm n/vb* **trance**

transience *n* the quality of having a short existence: that which has such

transier *var fm obs vb* **transire**

transire *n* a customs warrant which permits the passage of goods *obs vb* to pass across

transiter *n* a recording micrometer, an apparatus attached to the end of a telescope used in an observatory

transmue *var fm arch vb* **transmew**

transonic *adj* of or pertaining to conditions at or near the speed of sound

transonics *n* the study of speed from the subsonic to the supersonic

trans-sonic *n* a pedantic *fm* of **transonics**

transude *vb* to ooze out

transume *vb* to make an official copy of a document (*obs* except in an historical context)

trapan *var fm n/vb* **trepan**

trape *now dial vb* to walk in a heavy, clomping fashion

traper *obs fm n* **trapper**, a trapping (such as a cloth) for covering a horse

trapes *n* a slattern *var fm vb* **traipse**

trapnest *US vb* to determine the productivity of hens with a type of nest

trappean *adj* pertaining to, consisting of or of the nature of trap rock

trap rock *n* a dark, fine-grained igneous rock

trapse *arch fm n* **trapes**

trash (*n*) *US vb* to free from trash

trass *n* a naturally compounded substance of volcanic pumice and surface materials reduced to powder for use as a hydraulic cement

traste *Obs fm obs S & dial adj* **traist**

trattle *n* an individual, small, rounded dropping of such as a rabbit, hare or sheep *obs n* idle talk *obs vb* to chatter, gossip, talk idly

trauchle *var fm S n/vb* **trachle**

traul *obs fm n* **trawl**, a strong, bag-like fishing net dragged along the seabed by a fishing boat

trauma (*n*) *pl fms* **traumas, traumata**

trave *now dial n* a wooden beam: a travis at a blacksmith's forge *dial n* two shocks of corn

traveling *var fm n* **travelling**, journeying

travis *n* an enclosure at a blacksmith's forge for the stabling of a restive horse: a wooden partition in a stable

travish *dial fm vb* **traverse**

travois *n* a drag devised by the Red Indians which consists of a framework suspended between two poles and pulled along the ground by a horse (*pl* **travois, travoises**)

travoise *var fm n* **travois**

trawe *obs fm vb* **throw**, to cast or hurl *Obs fm obs n* **throw**, a space of time *Obs fm arch vb* **trow**, to trust (*Obs pa pple* **trawet**)

trawet see **trawe**

trayle *obs fm n/vb* **trail**

trayste *Obs fm obs S & dial n/adj/vb* **traist**

treacle (*n*) *vb* to spread (as) with treacle (*lit/fig*)

treand *obs fm n/vb* **trend**

treddle *now dial n* a pellet of goat's or sheep's dung (*pl* **treddles** – also see **treddling**)

treddling *dial n* a mass of treddles

tredille *var fm n* **tredrille**, a type of three-handed whist played with 30 cards

tree (*n*) *vb* to take a treelike form: to plant with trees: to climb or take refuge in a tree: to stretch or shape on a boot tree or a saddle tree – hence, **treeing** *n* the action of the *vb* in this sense

tree duck *n* any of various ducks which perch in a tree

treenail *n* a pin of hard wood which functions as a nail *vb* to secure with such

treeship *n* existence as a tree

treet *now dial n* in the rating of bran by quality, that of the second of three grades – with **sharp** the best and **chizzel** the worst *obs fm n* **treat**

treete *obs fm vb* **treat**

trefoil *n* a clover: any of various plants having leaves or flowers with three lobes: a set of three, closely united (*fig*) *adj* three leaved

tregat *var fm obs n* **treget**

treget *obs n* trickery: deceit: the art of a juggler *obs vb* to perform the art of juggling

treine *obs fm now dial adj* **treen**, wooden

treison *Obs fm n* **treason**

treist *Obs fm obs S & dial adj* **traist**

trele *obs fm n/vb* **trail**

trelies *obs S fm n* **trellis**

trelis *obs fm n* **trellis**

trelys *obs fm n* **trellis**

tremal *Obs S fm n/vb* **tremble**

tremel *Obs fm n/vb* **tremble**

tremie *n* a combined hopper and movable tube used for depositing concrete under water

tremis *n* a gold coin of the later Roman Empire

tremle *Obs fm n/vb* **tremble**

tremp *obs vb* to mix

trempe *var fm obs n* **tramp**, temper or iron

tremulate *vb* (to cause) to tremble or vibrate: to quiver

tremyl *Obs fm n/vb* **tremble**

trenail *var fm n/vb* **treenail**

trende *Obs adj* of obscure meaning but possibly 'rounded'

trenise *n* the fourth movement of a quadrille

trenle *Obs fm n/vb* **tremble**

trental *n* a set of 30 requiem masses sung on specific dates for the repose of a soul: the payment for such

trepan *vb* to remove part of the skull

trepas *Obs fm n* **trespass** (*pl* **trepasis)**

trepasis *pl* trepas

trephine *n* a surgeon's cylindrical saw *vb* to use such

trepid *adj* trembling, fearful

tresle *obs fm n* **trestle**

tressel *var fm n* **trestle**

tressle *var fm n* **trestle**

tressy *adj* having or resembling tresses

trestle (*n*) *vb* to place upon a trestle

treulove *obs fm n* **truelove**

treves *obs n* a truce

trevis *var fm n* **travis**

treviss *var fm n* **traverse**, a stall

trew *Obs S vb* to protect by a truce (*infl fms incl* **trewis, trewit)** *S fm arch vb* **trow** *obs fm n* **truce** *obs fm adj* **true** *Obs fm n* **tree**

trewis see **trew**

trewit see **trew**

trewsman *n* one who wears (tartan) trews

trey tine *n* the third spike of a deer's horn

triable *adj* that capable of being tried

triacetin *n* a colourless liquid with a very high boiling point (258/259° centigrade) found in the seeds of the spindle tree

triacid *n* an acid containing three hydroxal groups of atoms, each group functioning as an atom

triaconter *n* an ancient Greek vessel having 30 oars

triactine *adj* of a sponge spicule, having three rays

triad *n* any group of three: in Welsh literature, a form of composition having subjects or statements in groups of three (+*cap*) *n* a Chinese secret society founded during the reign of the emperor Yung Cheng (1723–1736), ostensibly as an anti-Manchu dynasty organization. It is still extant in any city such as Hong Kong or London which has a large Chinese population, though it has now degenerated into a series of criminal brotherhoods rather like the Mafia of the Italians.

triadic *adj* of, pertaining to or consisting of a triad

triadist *n* one who composes Welsh triads

triage *n* the action of sorting into different grades or qualities: the third grade of coffee beans, those which are broken

trialism *n* the concept of man as a union of body, soul and spirit: a union of three nations

Triandria *n pl* in a now obsolete classification system (that of Linnaeus), those plants having hermaphrodite flowers with three stamens

triapsidal *adj* having three apses

Triassic see **ROCK SYSTEMS AND LIFE FORMS**

tribade *n* a female homosexual

tribble *n* a wired frame used for drying paper *dial fm adj* **treble**

trible *obs n/vb* (to bring about) tribulation

triblet *n* a goldsmith's tool used for making rings

tribunate *n* the office or dignity of a tribune: government by tribunes: a body of legislators established by the French Revolutionary government

trice *n* an instant *vb* to pull (up) with a rope

tricerion *n* a three-branched candlestick as found in a Greek church

trichina *n* any of a genus of minute parasitic worms (*pl* **trichinae, trichinas**)

trichinous *adj* of a human or an animal, infested with the minute parasitic worms, trichinae: of the nature of or suffering the disease, trichinosis: caused by such

trichoid *adj* hairlike

trichome *n* a hair, bristle, prickle, scale or any other surface appendage or epidermal outgrowth of a plant: one of the threads of filamentous algae

tricke *obs fm n* **trick**

tricosane *n* a hydrocarbon of the paraffin series

tridacna *n* any species of a genus of giant clams of the Indian Ocean, the largest known bivalves, which can achieve lengths of $4\frac{1}{2}$ feet

triddle *var fm now dial n* **treddle** *dial vb* to trickle slowly

tridel *obs fm now dial n* **treddle**

triel *obs fm n* **trial**

triene *n* a type of chemical compound

triennially *adv* every three years: once every three years (TRIVIA note: Every alternate letter forms a completely different word. The odd-numbered letters form **tinily**, the even-numbered letters form **renal**.)

triens *n* either of two ancient Roman coins, an early copper coin worth one third of an as or a later gold coin worth one third of an aureus (*pl* **trientes**)

trientes *pl* triens

triflet *nonce n* a small literary work

triger *obs n* the chigoe, a tropical flea, the female of which burrows into the skin of various animals *incl* man

trigging *n* the action of wedging a wheel

trigle *obs S fm vb* **trickle**

trigness *n* neatness

trigon *n* a three-sided figure such as a triangle

trigone *n* a triangular area at the base of the bladder

Trigynia *n* in the Linnaean classification of plants, an order comprising those plants with three pistils

trike (*n*) *Obs vb* to fall in a flowing manner *obs fm n* **trick**

triles *obs fm n* **trellis**

trilineate *adj* of creatures, marked with three stripes or lines

trille *obs fm arch vb* **trill**, to cause to rotate or revolve

trimer *n* a compound (such as benzene from acetylene) formed by three molecules of another substance

trimester *n* a period or term of three months

trimestre *obs adj* of a three month period

trimeter *n* a verse of three measures or feet (see **metric foot**) *adj* of a verse, having such

trimetre *obs fm n/adj* **trimeter**

trimle *dial fm n/vb* **tremble**

trimme *obs fm n/adj/vb* **trim**

trimsie *obs adj* artfully trimmed in a tricksy fashion

trinal *adj* of three

trind *dial fm vb* **trend**

trindel *obs fm now dial n/vb* **trindle** (*Obs infl fms incl* **trindeld**)

trindle *n* either of a pair of simple clamps used during the bookbinding process *now dial n* a wheel *now dial vb* to wheel or roll (*S fms now dial n/vb incl* **trintle** and the unlisted anagrams **trinnel, trinnle**)

trine *adj* threefold, triple *n* a group of three: in astrology, the aspect of two planets when 120° apart *vb* in astrology, of a planet, to take a trine aspect *obs vb* to go, march *Obs vb* to touch

tring *n* a sandpiper

tringa *n* any tringine wading bird. This includes nine species of sandpipers (basically the larger, less gregarious sandpipers which make loud ringing noises – also see **caliditrine**), the curlew, greenshank, redshank, tattler and terek (+*cap*) *n* the genus of these birds

tringine *adj* of any tringa

tringle *n* a curtain rod or similar long, slender rod *var fm vb* **trinkle**, to trickle

triniscope *n* a cathode ray tube for colour television

triode *n/adj* (a valve) with three electrodes

triole *n* a group of three musical notes played in the same time as two

triolet *n* a stanza of eight lines constructed on two rhymes running *a*b*aaa*b*a*b, with the first line repeated as the fourth and seventh and the second as the eighth

triones *n pl* the seven principal stars of Charles's wain or Ursa Major

trionymal *adj* consisting of three technical descriptive terms, the variety (or subspecies), the species and the genus

tripe (*n*) *obs n* an imitation velvet

triped *obs adj* of velvet, having the appearance of the foodstuff, tripe

tripedal *adj* three-footed

tripet *var fm now dial n* **trippet** *var fm Obs n* **trippet**

tripos *n* the list of candidates who have gained an honours degree in mathematics

triposes *pl* tripos

tripot *erron fm n* **try-pot**

trippe *obs fm n of assemb* **trip** (for the various applications see **COLLECTIVE NOUNS**) *obs fm n* **tripe**

trippet *n* a mechanical device designed to strike at regular intervals *now dial n* a trivet or three-legged stand for such as a kettle *dial n* tipcat, the cat of tipcat *obs n* an act of tripping up *Obs n* an evil or malicious scheme

tripple *S Afr n* a horse's gait between a fast walk and a slow trot *S Afr vb* of a horse, to move at that pace *now dial vb* to move lightly, to skip

tripsis *n* massage

tripus *obs n* a (cooking) vessel with three legs

triquet *obs n* a set of verses in a triangular shape: a triangle *obs adj* triangular

trireme *n* an ancient Greek or Roman galley with three ranks of oars *adj* having three ranks of oars

triscele *var fm n* **triskelion**

trise *obs fm vb* **trice**

trisected *adj* of a leaf, divided into three lobes almost, but not quite, to the point of being three separate leaflets

trisector *n* one who or that which divides into three equal parts

triseme *n* a metric foot of three short syllables

trisemic *adj* containing, consisting of or equivalent to three short syllables

trishaw *n* a type of three-wheeled, pedal-powered, rickshaw which has the driver seated behind the passengers

triskelion *n* the figure of three legs which is the symbol of the Isle of Man (*pl* **triskelia**) (*var fms* **triscele, triskele**)

trismus *n* lockjaw

trisome *n* an organism having one chromosome in addition to the usual diploid number

tristate *adj* pertaining to an area comprised of three different states

triste *arch adj* sad, melancholy *var fm obs vb* **trist**, to trust

tristen *obs vb* to trist

trisula *n* the trident used as a symbol of the Hindu god, Siva, and as a symbol of Buddhism

trisulcate *adj* marked with three grooves

tritanopia *n* the inability to distinguish the colour blue

trite (*adj*) *n* the third string of a tetrachord, an ancient Greek four-stringed musical instrument

triter *comp adj* trite

tritest *sup adj* trite

triton *n* a newt: a species of gasteropod mollusc

tritone *n* a musical interval of three whole tones

trittle *obs n* a trattle

triune *adj* of any three in one deity *n* a trinity

trivalence *n* the quality of having the combining power of three atoms of hydrogen or other univalent element

trive *obs nonce vb* to contrive

trivess *S dial fm n* **travis**

TRIVIA CHALLENGE Many word buffs enjoy a solitary investigation and, for them, *Pears Advanced Word-Puzzler's Dictionary* offers a unique feature. Words such as **aegilops**, **smithery**, **triennially**, **uncomplimentary** and **zoosporous** have unusual features worthy of recording as footnotes to their individual entries and readers are invited to submit their superlatives for like words. The best of these will be included in future editions. The author will gladly acknowledge an individual reader's contribution and be pleased to send a copy of the first printing of the book containing such an addition directly to the contributor. The field is wide open and the only stipulation is that the word must appear in an English dictionary which the reader is asked to name. Of particular value are words which relate to the pencil and paper game, **Crossword** (see **WORD GAMES**), in terms of length and flexibility. For example, the letter S in the basic word, CROSSWORD, can be developed by single letter additions from S to AS to HAS to HAST to HASTE to HASTEN to HASTENS to CHASTENS or HASTE to CHASTE to CHASTEN to CHASTENS. Equally useful will be other, better, words based on S or the best words available for the remaining letters C, R, O, W and D. As the game may use any basic long word, every letter of the alphabet is a potential starting point for this aspect of Trivia Challenge. (Also see **APPENDIX – READERS' PAGES**)

troade *obs fm now dial n* **trod**

troan *var fm S & dial n* **tron**

troat *vb* of a buck at rutting time, to bellow

trobel *obs fm n/vb* **trouble**

trobil *obs fm n/vb* **trouble**

troble *obs fm n/vb* **trouble**

trocar *n* a surgical perforator

trochaic *adj* of or pertaining to trochee verse formation (see **metric foot**) *n* a trochaic verse

troche *n* a medicinal lozenge: a cluster of three or more points at the summit of a deer's horn *obs vb* of a deer, to develop such a troche

trochilic *adj* of or pertaining to rotary motion *n* the study of such (also in the *fm* **trochilics**)

trochlea *n* an anatomical grooved, pulleylike surface (*pl* **trochleae**)

trod (*pa pple*) *now dial n* a footpath or other trodden track: the tread of a wheel *obs n* a footprint

trode *obs fm now dial n* **trod**

troelie *n* the bussu palm

trogon *n* any of 34 species of brightly coloured birds found in tropical forests. Stout, large-headed birds with distinctive long, broad tails, they range in size from that of a thrush to that of a dove. They belong to the family, *Trogonidae*, which includes the famous quetzal.

Trogonidae see **trogon**

troke *now dial vb* to fall: to deceive

trole *obs fm n/vb* **troll**

troll *n* routine: a type of song in which the individual parts are sung in succession: a method of fishing (see *vb*): in Norse mythology, a supernatural being originally described as a giant but, in later myth, a subterranean dwarf *modf n* as **troll wife**, **troll garden** etc, the reference is to a mythological relationship *vb* to sing a round song: to fish by trailing a moving line behind a boat or, *esp* for pike, by baiting a hook with a small fish and spinning it in the water to imitate the live action of that fish: to move, sing or speak nimbly: to roll, to spin: to pass an object round the assembled company

trolle *var fm n* **troll**, a Norse mythological being *Obs fm vb* **troll**

troller *n* one who sings a round song: a fisherman who trolls

trome *var fm obs n/vb* **trume**

trompe *n* an apparatus which produces a blast of air for a furnace *var fm obs vb* **trump**, to deceive *obs fm n* **trump**

tron *S & dial n* a (public) weighing machine

trona *n* the mineral, hydrous sodium carbonate, as found in its natural state

trone *var fm S & dial n* **tron**

troner *S & dial n* the official in charge of the tron

tronne *obs fm S & dial n* **tron**

troolie *n* the bussu palm tree

troope *obs fm ns* **troop, trope**

troose *var fm S n* **trews**, trousers

troparion *n* a short Greek hymn (*pl* **troparia**)

trope *n* the figurative use of a word: a figure of speech: a verse of embellishment in part of a sung Mass: a short cadence interpolated in a Gregorian melody: a sceptical argument in Greek philosophy: in geometry, a plane touching a given surface in a stated way

tropel *obs n* a small military company

troper *n* a book containing tropes or ecclesiastical verses for the Mass

trophe *obs fm n* **trophy**

trophee *obs fm n* **trophy**

tropine *n* an alkaloid constituent of atropine

tropism *n* the turning of an organism towards some special stimulus such as light

tropist *n* one who explains the Bible in terms of its metaphors

tropistic *adj* pertaining to tropism

trople *var fm obs n* **tropel**

tropophyte *n* any plant which adapts to a climate which is alternately moist and dry

troppe *obs fm n* **troop**

troque *obs n* the hoop used in quoits

trosse *obs fm n/vb* **truss**

trosser *obs fm modf n* **trouser** (*pl*) *obs fm n* **trousers** (note: unlisted anagram, **strosser**)

trote *obs fm n/vb* **trot**

trotlet *nonce n* a little trot

trottle *var fm n* **trattle**

troubel *obs fm n/vb* **trouble**

troule *obs fm vb* **troll**

troup *obs fm n/vb* **troop**

trouse *n* knee-breeches *now dial n* brushwood *obs vb* to cut brushwood

trouser *n* one of the legs of a pair of trousers *modf n* of trousers

trout (*n*) *obs fm vb* **troat**

troute *obs fm n* **trout**

trouter *n* one who fishes for trout

trove (*n*) *obs S & dial fm n* **turf**

trouvère *n* one of the various epic poets of northern France whose work was created during the period of the 11th to the 14th centuries

trow *n* a name for various British boats as:– (*a*) a double canoe used in the north and in Scotland when spearing salmon by torchlight (*b*) a flat-bottomed herring barge on the south coast (*c*) a large, flat-bottomed sailing barge formerly on the Severn *Ork n* a troll, the creature of Norse myth *arch vb* to trust or believe

trowe *obs S fm arch vb* **trow**

trowel (*n/vb*) *infl fms* British, **trowelled/-lling**: US, **troweled/-ling**

trower *Obs n* a believer

trowet *obs fm n* **trout**

trowp *obs fm n* **troop**

trowpe *obs fm n/vb* **troop**

trowple *var fm obs n* **tropel**

trowse *obs fm vb* **truss**

trowsers *obsol fm n pl* **trousers**

trowte *obs fm n* **trout**

troy *n* the standard system of weights for gemstones, precious metals and, formerly, for bread (for further details see **MONEYERS WEIGHTS**) (*pl* **troys**)

Troyan *obs fm n/adj* **Trojan**

troye *obs fm n* **troy**

troyne *obs fm S & dial n* **tron**

truble *obs n* a small fishing net for a pond *obs fm n/vb* **trouble**

truce (*n*) *vb* to make a temporary peace

trucial *adj* of a truce

trudgen *n* a type of double overarm breast-stroke swimming action

true (*adj/adv/n*) *vb* to make (a piece of mechanism) accurate or correct: to adjust, level, place, position, shape etc accurately (note: Both **trueing** and **truing** are acceptable *infl fms*, but **truing** is the preferred *fm* as a *n*)

truel *obs fm n* **trowel**

truelove *n* a true love or sweetheart: the Herb Paris, a plant of the lily family having an arrangement of four leaves surrounding the flower, suggestive of a lover's knot *obs n* the four-leaved clover

trug *n* an old measure for wheat equal to two-thirds of a Winchester bushel (used locally only – see **Winchester measure**): a shallow wooden tray or basket of various sorts *now dial n* a whore *obs fm vb* **trudge**

trugge *obs fm now dial n* **trug**, a whore

truism *n* a self-evident truth

truke *var fm now dial vb* **troke**

trule *obs S n* an old game played with balls *obs fm n* **trowel**

trull *arch n* a prostitute (*pl* **trulls**): a terrestrial fairy-devil (*pl* **trulli**)

trume *obs n* a body of people *obs vb* to assemble such a body

trumpe *var fm obs vb* **trump**, to deceive *obs fm n* **trump**

trunkfish see **boxfish**

trusel *obs fm n* **trestle**

trussel *obs n* a bundle or package: a device for making impressions on a coin *obs fm n* **trestle**

trussle *obs fm n* **trestle**

trusten *now dial vb* to trust

trw *obs fm adj* **true**

trwmp *Obs S fm obs vb* **trump**, to deceive *Obs S fm n* **trump**, a trumpet

tryel *obs S fm n* **trial**

trymle *obs fm n/vb* **tremble**

try-pot *n* a pot used in the testing of oil extracted from blubber

Tsabian *var fm n* Sabian

tsaine *n* the banteng, a species of wild ox of southeast Asia

tsar (etc) see **czar**

tsatlee *n* a superior kind of white raw silk

tserin *var fm n* **dzeren**

tsetse *n* any of various bloodsucking African flies which transmit parasites and cause such diseases as sleeping sickness in man and nagana in grazing animals

tsigane *var fm n* **tzigany**

tsine *n* the banteng, a species of wild ox of southeast Asia

tsotsi *n* a young, black, South African hooligan

tsunami *n* a very high, swiftly moving, wave of the sea (of Japanese waters)

tu *n* a Chinese measure of distance equal to 250 li *var fm S & dial n* **tew**

Tuareg *n* one of the nomadic Arabs of the Sahara: another name for Tamashek, the Berber language of the Tuaregs

tuart *n* an Australian eucalyptus tree with very hard timber

tuatera *var fm n* **tuatara**, a lizard-like living fossil found only on several small islands off the New Zealand coast. The only remaining species of an order of reptiles even older than the dinosaurs, it is very strictly protected by the New Zealand government.

tubate *adj* having the form of a tube: of or pertaining to a tube or tubing

tubber *n* one who makes tubs

tubble *var fm n* **tubbal**, a mining tool rather like an adz

tuber *n* a fleshy root or underground stem which, like the potato, has a more or less rounded form: a diseased swelling, an enlargement of a gland (*pl* **tubers**, also see **tuberes**)

tuberes *pl obs n* **tuber**, an apple (tree)

tube worm *n* any worm which constructs a tube in which to dwell

tucet *obs n* a scrap of meat

tucke *obs fm n/vb* **tuck** *obs fm n* **toque**

tucker *n* a frill of lace worn round the neck (essentially now only extant in the phrase, **best bib and tucker**) *now dial n* a fuller *Austr slg n* victuals *collq vb* to tire, to weary

Tucson *n* a city in Arizona, USA, on the Santa Cruz River

tudel *vb* to perform badly on a musical instrument (*infl fms* **tudeled, tudeling**)

tudeler *n* a poor instrumentalist or singer

tudle *interj* an imitation of the sound of such as a flute

tue *var fm n/vb* **tew** (all senses other than the *obs n*) *var fm n* **tui**

tuell *obs fm now dial n* **tewel**

tuf *var fm n* **tuff**

tuff *n* any light, porous, cellular rock *obs vb* to make an explosive sound with the breath *obs fm adj* **tough**

tuffet *n* a hillock or mound: presumed to mean a footstool in the nursery rhyme though it could equally be a hillock (also see **Muffet** for the strange truth behind the nursery rhyme and an ironic *dial* meaning of the word)

tuffing *n* the tufts of wool woven into the end of a bell rope

tui *n* the parson bird, a New Zealand bird with dark plumage and a white collar

tularemia *n* rabbit fever, a disease of rodents, *esp* rabbits, capable of being transmitted to man via insects and causing an undulent fever

tularemic an undefined adjective which appears to be exclusive to one particular dictionary and presumably means of or pertaining to **tularemia**. Its anagram is **climature**.

tulchan *S n* a calf's skin used as a ploy for inducing a cow to give freely of her milk: a derisive epithet for those Scottish bishops appointed immediately after the Reformation

Tulipa *n* the genus of the tulip

tulle *n* a type of fine silk net used for such as women's garments

tumbrel *n* a mediaeval instrument of punishment which 16th century writers identified with the cucking stool: a dung cart or other cart which tips back to empty: any of the carts which conveyed victims to the guillotine during the French Revolution (*var fm* **tumbril**)

tumor *var fm n* **tumour**

tump *n* a heap of anything: an anthill, a molehill: a hillock: a clump of trees, a clump of grass *esp* one forming a dry spot in a bog *vb* to store roots in a heap: to make a mound around the root of a tree (the senses in which **tumping** is a *n* as the action of the *vb*) *US vb* to haul by means of a strap tied around a person's head (originally a practice of some Red Indian tribes and copied by early settlers)

tumphy *S n* an oaf: coaly fireclay

tumpy *dial adj* hillocky

tunable *adj* tuneful, musical: in tune: capable of being tuned: harmonious (*fig*)

tunder *now dial fm n* **tinder** *Obs n* a funnel

tundered *now dial fm adj* **tindered**

tundra *n* a level, treeless expanse of Arctic land

tung oil *n* oil obtained from the seeds of the Chinese varnish tree

tungstic *adj* pertaining to or formed from tungsten

tunicle *n* a three-quarter length outer vestment worn by a subdeacon at the celebration of communion *obs n* a small tunic (*lit*/*fig*) (GAME PLAYER'S note: The last recorded usage in the *lit* sense was 1656, in the *fig* sense 1744. The dictionary used for the UK Scrabble championship omits the *fig* sense and has the *lit* sense extant.)

tunne *obs fm n*/*vb* **tun**, (to store in) a cask *obs fm n* **ton**

tunnel (*n*/*vb*) *infl fms* British, **tunnelled/-lling**: now mainly US, **tunneled/-ling**

tunner *now dial n* a funnel

tunster *obs S n* presumed to mean the official who supervised or certified the quantity of liquor in a tun

tupelo *n* any of various species of a genus of American hardwood trees which grow in swampland

tur *n* the Caucasian ibex, either of two species of wild goats

turacin *n* a crimson pigment found in the wing feathers of various species of birds

turaco *n* any of a family of twenty species of often highly-coloured, fruit-eating African birds, placed in the same order (*Cuculiformes*) as the cuckoos. Also known as plantain-eaters or louries, the family includes the two species of go-away birds. (*pl* **turacos**)

Turanian *adj*/*n* (of) a language native to the nomadic peoples of Asia which is neither Iranian nor Semitic (note: No longer used as a scientific term)

turb *n* a crowd: a clump of trees

turbel *obs fm n*/*vb* **trouble**

turbinal *adj* top-like, top-shaped: scroll-like *n* a scroll-like bone of the nose

turbinate *adj* resembling the conical shape of a spinning top *n* a shell of such shape

turble *obs fm n*/*vb* **trouble**

turbo *n* any gasteropod mollusc having an inverted, cone-shaped shell (*pl* **turbines**) *collq n* a turbine engine (*pl* **turbos**)

turcas *obs S fm n* **turquoise**, the gemstone

turcase *var fm obs vb* **turkess**

turdine *adj* of the thrush

tureen *n* a large, deep, covered serving dish for such as soup

turet *obs fm ns* **torret, turret**

turfe *obs fm n* **turf**

turfel *obs adj* of a hat, having a cock

turfen *adj* covered with or made of turf: turfy

turfer *obs n* one who had the right to dig turf (or peat) on a particular piece of land for use as fuel

turfite *n* a racing man or frequenter of racecourses

turgent *adj* swollen, distended: bumptious

turkeis *obs fm n* **turquoise**, the gemstone

turkes *obs fm n* **turquoise**, the gemstone

turkess *obs vb* to alter for the worse, to distort, to pervert: to change (not necessarily for the worse) (+*cap*) *nonce n* a female turk: (+ **the**) the consort of the sultan of Turkey

turkies *obs fm n* **turquoise**, the gemstone

turkise *arch fm n* **turquoise**, the gemstone *var fm obs vb* **turkess**

Turkish Van *n* the Van cat of Turkey, a breed of domestic cat, white with auburn patches, which is especially fond of swimming

Turkman *var fm n* **Turkoman**

Turkoman *n* a nomadic pastoral member of the Turkish race living beyond the borders of Turkey in what was once part of the Ottoman Empire, embracing a region of the USSR, Afghanistan and Iran, on the east of the Caspian Sea: the Turkish language of such a person (also see **Osmanli**)

turle *obs fm vb* **tirl**

turnerad *n* one of a small order of tropical herbs and undershrubs with blue or yellowish axillary flowers

turnsick *n* a brain disease of sheep and cattle which causes them to turn round and round in circles

turple *var fm now dial vb* **torple**

turr *now dial vb* of or as a ram, to butt or push down with the head

turre *obs fm now dial vb* **turr**

turret *n* a small or subordinate tower *vb* to construct such *var fm n* **torret**

turves *var fm pl* **turfs**

tusche *n* a substance used in silk screen printing and lithography as a protective coating

tusk (*n*) *vb* of an animal, to use its tusks: to project like a tusk or tusks (*fig*)

tuskar *Ork & Shet n* a peat spade

tusk shell *n* any of various molluscs intermediate in many respects between snails and bivalves. The marine creature lives in a small shell, shaped rather like an elephant's tusk, which is open at both ends. Most of the shell is buried vertically in the sand with only the narrow end projecting into the sea. It draws in water for oxygen at this exposed end, the mouth being fed by tentacles which project into the sand at the larger end.

tussal *adj* of or pertaining to a cough

tussar *obs fm n* **tusser**

tusseh *var fm n* **tusser**

tussel *arch fm n/vb* **tussle**

tusser *n* a coarse brown silk: the silkworm which produces it: a dress of the material

tussore *var fm n* **tusser**

tussre *obs fm n* **tusser**

tussy *obs n* a posy of flowers or leaves: an ornament in this form (*pl* **tussies**)

tut *n* piecework or work paid for by the piece *vb* to perform such work

tutee *n* one who is tutored

tutelar *adj* of supernatural power *n* one having such

tutman *n* one who does piecework

tutorer *n* a tutor

tutress *n* a female tutor

tutsan *n* parkleaves, any of a small number of plants once considered to have healing properties

twaite *var fm n* **twait**, a species of the marine fish, shad

twangy *adj* twanging (*comp* **twangier** *sup* **twangiest**)

tweel *S fm n* **twill**

tweer *var fm arch vb* **twire** *var fm n* **twyer**

tweir *var fm n* **twyer**

twig snake *n* a species of vine snake which, apart from the head, resembles a branch covered in lichen

twile *obs fm n* **twill**

twiner *n* one who or a machine which twines: a twining plant

twinger *n* one who or that which twinges

twingle *now dial vb* to twist, to wriggle

twinter *adj* of two winters: two years old *n* a two year old farm animal

twire *arch vb* to look covertly: to peep *var fm n* **twyer**

twisle *obs S fm dial vb* **twistle**

twissle *var fm dial vb* **twistle**

twister (*n*) *now dial vb* to meander

twistle *S n* a twist *dial vb* to twist

twite *n* a species of linnet *dial fm vb* **twit**, to blame or find fault with

twoer *n* anything with a value of two

twyer *n* an air nozzle of a blast furnace

ty *obs fm n* **tie**

tye *n* a large common or similar expanse of pasture: a box or trough which collects the refuse from the washing of ore in Cornish tin mining *vb* to separate by using a tye

tyle *vb* to protect a masonic lodge from intrusion: to bind to secrecy: to keep secrecy

tyler *n* one (often a janitor) whose duty is to maintain security at a masonic lodge

tylet *var fm obs n* **tillet**

tylose *n* a growth within woody tissue

tyloses *pl* tylosis

tylosis *n* an inflammatory disease of the eyelids: a disease of the mouth characterized by white spots (*pl* **tyloses**)

tynde *obs fm now dial vb* **tind**, to kindle

Typhon *pers n* a hundred-headed monster of Greek myth, the father of the winds which, though buried under Mt Etna, still breathes fire

Typhonian *adj* pertaining to or connected with Typhon

typhonic *adj* having the character of an extremely violent wind

typy *adj* characterized by conformity to the group (*comp* **typier** *sup* **typiest**)

tyranne *obs fm n/vb* (to play the) **tyrant**

tyrant flycatcher *n* any of over 300 species of small, non-singing, perching birds found throughout the New World. The species *incl* the kingbird or bee martin, pewee and phoebe.

tyrante *obs fm n* **tyrant**

tyre (*n*) *vb* to supply or fit with a tyre

tyrle *obs fm vb/S vb* **tirl**

tyroes *pl* tiro

tyrone *obs fm n* **tiro** (note: The *pl fm*, **tyrones**, is still extant)

tzar (etc) see **czar**

tzigany *n* an Hungarian gypsy

U

ua *Obs fm adj/adv/n/interj* **woe**

uakari *n* either of two species of agile, shaggy-haired South American monkeys

udal *n* the form of freehold tenancy peculiar to Orkney and Shetland

udaller *n* a tenant holding land by udal right

ug *now dial vb* to dread, fear: to affect with horror or loathing

Ugrian *n/adj* (of) the languages of Hungary and parts of Russia which form a branch of the Finno-Ugric sub-group of the Uralic family of languages: (of) the Magyars, Ostyaks, Voguls and other peoples who speak one of these languages

uh *interj* the representation of an inarticulate sound

uhlan *n* a Polish or other Slavonic cavalryman armed with a lance: a lancer in the former imperial army of Germany

ulema *n* a professional Muslim theologian: the body of such exponents

ulicon *n* the candlefish

ullage *n* the amount of liquor by which a cask or bottle falls short of being completely full *vb* to estimate that amount

ulmin *n* a substance exuded by the inner bark of such trees as the elm: a brown pigment produced either from rotting timber or from the application of certain chemicals to sugar

ulnare *n* a bone of the wrist, on the ulnar side of the proximal row of carpal bones (*pl* **ulnaria**)

ulnaria *pl* ulnare

ulster *n* a long loose overcoat made from a rough cloth

ulstered *adj* wearing an ulster

ultimate (*adj/n*) *vb* to complete: to result finally

ultion *n* vengeance

Ultonian *adj* of or belonging to Ulster *n* one of or from Ulster

ultra (*adj*) *n* an extremist

ultrabasic *adj* of the composition of rocks, extremely basic

ultraism *n* the principles of one holding any extremist viewpoint: the holding of such: an instance of such

ultraist *n* an extremist

um *interj* expressing hesitation in speech

umbel *n* a floral cluster comprising individual flowers on stalks of equal length, the youngest of which are in the centre

umbelliferous *adj* of or belonging to the plant family which includes carrot, fennel, parsley and parsnip and which typically have hollow stems, divided or compound leaves and flowers in umbels

umbra *n* a region of complete shadow: the darker central part of a sunspot: a ghost: an uninvited guest appearing with one who was invited (*pl* **umbrae, umbras**)

umbral *adj* of an umbra

umbrated *her adj* faintly traced

umbrel *obs n* a helmet visor

umbrous *adj* shady, shadowed

umlaut *n* the two dots placed over a vowel in German to indicate a modification in sound

umpirer *obs n* an umpire

umquhile *arch adv* formerly *arch adj* former, late: of persons, dead (GAME PLAYER'S note: John Ruskin (1819–1900) is one of the English-born writers noted by the *Oxford English Dictionary* as having used this word. Frances Trollope (1780–1863) is noted by the *OED* as being an English-born writer who used the *var fm*, **umwhile**. However, *Chambers 20th Century Dictionary* considers **umwhile** to be the basic *fm* (standard not *arch*) and **umquhile** to be a Scottish *fm*. (This effectively invalidates **umquhile** for play in an official Scrabble® contest in Singapore.))

umqwhile *Obs S fm arch adv/adj* **umquhile**

umwhile *var fm arch adv/adj* **umquhile**

un *dial fm prons* **one, him**

unact *obs vb* to undo, to reverse the act

unadherent *adj* incapable of providing adherence

unalist *n* one who holds one benefice

unarm *vb* to disarm

unbare *vb* to lay bare, expose to view

unbear *vb* to free from the tether

unbeast *vb* to remove the nature of a beast from *obs S & dial n* a monster

unbed *vb* to remove from a bed

unbias *vb* to remove bias from

unbody *vb* to remove from a body *obs vb* to become a spirit

unboot *vb* to take off (one's own) boots

unbow *obs vb* to straighten

unbred *adj* ill-bred

uncanonise *vb* to remove from the calendar of saints: to reject from the canon of Scripture

uncase *vb* to remove from a case: to free from a casing: to undress: to uncover (*fig*) *obs vb* to skin an animal

uncast *adj* not cast or thrown: not moulded by casting: not calculated: not marred by a squint in the eye *vb* to change the throw of the die (*fig*)

uncate *adj* hooked

uncheat *vb* to reverse the effect of cheating

uncial *adj* divided into twelve equal parts: of or pertaining to an inch or an ounce: of letters, having large rounded forms *n* an uncial letter: an uncial style of writing: a manuscript written in uncials

uncipher *obs vb* to decipher (see **CODES AND CIPHERS**)

uncleaner *comp adj* unclean

unclere *obs fm adj* **unclear**

uncleship *n* the state of being or the relationship of an uncle

uncolt *Shaks vb* to deprive of a horse (a typical Shakespearian pun using the *obs vb* **colt**, to cheat. Falstaff asks Hal why he has been colted and is given the reply that he has not been colted but uncolted.)

uncomplimentary (*adj*) TRIVIA note: The longest of three English words which contain all five vowels, once only and in reverse alphabetical order (the other two words being **subcontinental** and **unnoticeably**). By contrast, **abstemious** and **facetious** are examples of words in which the vowels are in alphabetical order. (See **TRIVIA CHALLENGE**)

uncope *vb* to remove the cope or top layer of clay

uncore *vb* to remove the core: to reveal the core (*fig* for the truth)

uncost *n* lack of cost *obs n* evil nature

uncrate *vb* to remove from a crate

uncreate *vb* to unmake

uncreation *n* the act of uncreating

undared *adj* cowardly

undate *var fm adj* **undated**

undear *adj* not regarded with affection

undelight *n* lack of delight

under (*adv/adj/prep*) (in *pl fm*) *n* underclothes *now dial n* an undervalue *obs vb* to depress

underage *n* a shortage

underarch *vb* to support as an arch

underate see **undereat**

undere *obs fm prep* **under**

undereat *vb* to eat less than sufficient (*infl fms* as *vb* **eat**, e.g. **underate, undereaten**)

underer *obs n* an inferior

underf *adj* irresolute, weak

undergod *n* a lesser god

underlap *vb* to extend beneath and beyond the edge of

undern *now dial n* the afternoon: an afternoon meal

underntide *arch n* undern

underntime *arch n* undern

underset *vb* to prop up or otherwise support from beneath (*lit/fig*) *n* the lower of two veins of ore: an undercurrent in the sea

undertimed *adj* of a photograph, not given sufficient exposure

undesert *n* unworthiness

undeserve *vb* to fail to deserve

undig *vb* to exhume

undigest *obs adj* undigested (*lit/fig*)

undight *S adj* unwinnowed *arch adj* not adorned *obs vb* to unfasten

undine *n* a mythical water nymph

undipt *obs or poet fm adj* **undipped**, not dipped in a liquid: not baptized

undose *adj* having undulating depressions which gradually merge together

undreaming *adj* not dreaming

undrest *arch fm adj* **undressed**

undry *vb* to lose dryness

undulose *adj* (characterized by an) undulating (motion)

uneath *arch adj* troublesome, distressing *arch adv* with difficulty

uneaths *obs adv* uneath

unedge *vb* to blunt

unerased *adj* not erased

unfaceted *adj* not developed by having facets, essentially basic or simple

unfallible *obs adj* infallible

unfast *adj* insecure *obs dial fm vb* **unfasten**

unfeed *adj* not in receipt of a fee, unpaid

unfest *obs vb* to untie

unfist *vb* to unhand

unfolder *n* one who or that which unfolds

unfret *obs vb* to untie: to make smooth

unfriend *n* an enemy: one who is not a Quaker *vb* to cease being a friend

unfriended *adj* friendless

ungain *adj* unpleasant: awkward: incompetent: indirect

ungalled *adj* not made painful by an abrasive action (*lit/fig*)

ungelt *var fm adj* **ungelded**, not castrated

ungilt (*adj*) *obs vb* to remove the gold from

ungird *vb* to free from that which binds round the middle (e.g. a person's girdle or such as the leather straps of a pack animal or the saddle of a horse)

ungirt *adj* not wearing a girdle *obs vb* to remove a girdle

unglee *Obs n* sadness

ungod *vb* to deny God His omnipotence and even His existence: to undeify any god

ungored *adj* not pierced *obs adj* not wounded

ungothic *nonce adj* not gothic

ungual *adj* of or having a claw

ungula *n* a hoof (*pl* **ungulae**)

unhale *var fm now dial vb* **unhele**

unhalsed *S adj* not greeted

unhap *obs vb* to bring misfortune

unhasp *vb* to unfasten: to disclose (*fig*)

unhaspe *obs fm vb* **unhasp**

unhat *vb* to remove one's hat as a sign of respect

unheal *var fm now dial vb* **unhele**

unhele *now dial vb* to discover: to reveal

unherd *vb* to remove from a herd

unhoard *vb* to remove from a hoard

unhose *vb* to remove hose or leggings

Uniat *n* a member of an eastern European and Asian Christian community which, though coming under papal supremacy, retains its own customs and practices *incl* liturgy and a married clergy. Once, all Christian clergy had the option of marriage – Adrian II, for example, the 106th pope who reigned from 867 to 872, was the last married pope – but the option was abolished to ensure that only the truly dedicated were attracted to priesthood. The only other married priests directly under papal authority are one or two former Lutheran ministers who have since become Catholic priests.

Uniate *var fm n* **Uniat**

unideal *adj* having or following no ideal

uniliteral *adj* having flowers on one side of the peduncle

Unioner *US n* one who sided with the Union during the American Civil War

uniped *adj* one-footed, one-legged *n* such a person or creature

unipod *n* a one-legged mechanical support

unisonance *n* identity of sounds

unisonant *adj* of the same sound or pitch

unitage *US n* amount in units *obs n* the action of uniting

uniter *n* one who or that which unites

unition *n* the action of uniting. Now confined to abstract concepts whereas, up to the mid-18th century, it was also used of physical union.

unitise *var fm vb* **unitize**, to form into a unit

unlach *obs S fm n/vb* **unlaw** *var fm obs S vb* **unlaw**

unlade *vb* to unload

unlaid (*adj*) *S n* a blanket of untarred wool

unlast *vb* to fail to last (*obs* except the *adj* **unlasting**)

unlated *obs S adj* undisciplined

unlaw *n* illegal action *obs n* an evil custom *obs S n* a fine or penalty *vb* to annul a law *obs vb* to pay a fine *obs S vb* to fine

unlay *vb* to untwist such as a rope into several strands

unlead *vb* to remove the metal lead from

unleased *adj* not held on lease: not having a lease

unleast *obs var fm adv* **unless**

unlight (*adj*) *now dial vb* to dismount

unlighted *adj* not lighted

unlime *vb* to remove lime from (dressed hides)

unlive *vb* to annul past life or experiences

unlord *vb* to deprive of the rank of lord

unlossed *obs S adj* of such as cargo, not unloaded

unmail *vb* to break the links of chain mail

unmartial *obs vb* to remove the martial aspect from

unmate *vb* to effect a change in one part so that it no longer corresponds to the other(s)

unmeet *adj* unfitting, unsuitable

unmired *adj* not subject to mire

unmiter *US fm vb* **unmitre**

unmitre *vb* to depose from the rank of bishop

unnation *vb* to deprive of the status of nation

unnest *vb* to remove from the nest (*lit/fig*)

unnoted *adj* characterized by a lack of musical notes: not observed: undistinguished

unorder *vb* to countermand

unowed *obs fm adj* **unowned**

unpale *vb* to remove palings

unpartial *adj* not inclined to favour: unrestricted *obs adj* impartial

unpent *adj* not confined

unpile *vb* to remove from or to demolish a heap

unplume *vb* to strip of plumes (*lit/fig*)

unprest *obs adj* not ready: unwilling

unpriest *vb* to remove from the function of being a priest: to remove priests from

unquiet (*adj*) *n* disquiet, disturbance *vb* to disturb the quiet of

unquite *obs adj* unredeemed

unread (*adj*) *rhet vb* to be obliterated from memory or from understanding

unrealism *n* the condition of being unreal

unredrest *arch fm adj* **unredressed**

unreeve *vb* to remove (a rope) from a hole

unregard *obs vb* to disregard

unrended *obs fm adj* **unrent**

unrent *adj* not torn

unrest (*adj/n*) *obs vb* to disturb (note: Both **unrested** (*adj*) and **unresting** (*adj*) are still extant)

unretted *adj* of flax, not having been subjected to retting (see **ret**)

unrich *adj* not rich

unrig *vb* to remove (a ship's) rigging

unright (*adj*) *obs vb* to wrong *Obs vb* to deprive of rights

unrimed *var fm adj* **unrhymed**

unrocked *adj* not disturbed by a motion of rocking

unroot *vb* to uproot (*lit/fig*)

unrope *vb* to free by unfastening a rope

unsated *adj* not satisfied

unsating *adj* not satisfying

unsatire *vb* the negative *fm* of **satirize** (essentially *nonce*)

unscale *vb* to remove the scales from such as fish: to climb down

unscore *vb* to remove

unseared *adj* not withered: not made hard

unseat *vb* to dislodge from a seat (of office)

unseem *Obs adj* unseemly

unseen (*adj*) *n* an unprepared passage for translation into English

unsent *adj* not sent (for)

unset (*adj*) *vb* to undo the setting of: to put out of position

unshade *vb* to remove the shade from

unshaked *obs var fm adj* **unshaken**

unshale *vb* to strip the husk from: to disclose or reveal (*fig*)

unshoe *vb* to remove a shoe or shoes from (*infl* **unshoed** (*adj*) **unshoeing** (*n*))

unshored *adj* without a shore

unsick *adj* well

unsickled *poet adj* not yet harvested

unsister *vb* to deprive of the status of sister

unsmote *adj* unsmitten, not touched by (emotion)

unsoft *obs adj* hard *obs adv* severely

unsolder *vb* to remove the soldering (*lit/fig*)

unsore *adj* not sore

unsouled *adj* not having or deprived of a soul

unspan *vb* to unyoke (*lit/fig*)

unspeak *vb* to retract

unsped *adj* not accomplished

unsphere *vb* to remove a heavenly body from its sphere (*lit/fig*)

unspied *adj* not having been seen

unspring *vb* to release by pressing a spring

unstabler *comp adj* unstable

unstate *vb* of a person, to deprive of rank or estate: of a nation, to deprive of statehood

unstayed *adj* without stays: unhindered, unimpeded: unsupported *obs adj* unstable

unsteel *vb* to deprive of the *fig* steel of nerve or character

unsterin *Obs fm obs adj* **unstern**

unstern *obs adj* severe

unstone *vb* to change from a stony state: to castrate (note: Ironically, the *vb* **stone** once meant to castrate)

unstop *vb* to free from being closed

unstore *vb* to remove from storage

unt *var fm obs vb* **unct,** to annoint

untame *adj* wild *vb* to influence with a cause or passion which overrides an essential tameness

untasting *adj* failing to taste

unteach *vb* to reverse the effect of teaching

unteam *vb* to unyoke

unteased *adj* not teased by

unteld *obs vb* to remove tents and tentage

unthatch *vb* to remove the thatch from

untidy (*adj*) *vb* to make untidy

untile *vb* to remove laid tiles

untime *obs n* unsuitable time

untimed *adj* not regulated to time

untinger *obs n* see **tinger**

untire *vb* to rest

untone *vb* to deprive of tone

untop *vb* to remove the top from

untrace *vb* to free a horse of its traces

untread *vb* to retrace one's steps (*lit/fig*)

untree *obs vb* to cut down trees

untride *Shaks fm adj* **untried**

untrist *obs n* distrust *obs adj* unfaithful, unbelieving

untristed *adj* unhoped for

unwist *arch adj* strange

unwit *obs vb* to deprive of wit(s)

uo *Obs fm n* **foe**

up (*adj/adv/n/prep/interj*) *vb* to drive and capture such as swans to brand with the owner's mark

upas *n* a fabulous tree in Java, so venomous that it was credited with killing all animal and vegetable life within a radius of fifteen miles: a deadly power (*fig*): a genuine Javanese tree, the poison from which was formerly used to tip arrowheads: that poison

upas tree *n* either the real or fabled upas

upcast *n* material excavated: a throw in an upward direction: (a geological fault caused by) an upward dislocation of a stratum: an accident *S & dial n* a reproach *S n* an upset *vb* to throw or toss up *S & dial vb* to allege as a fault *obs vb* to utter loudly *obs S vb* to force open

upclose *vb* to close up

updater *US n* one who brings up to date

upher *var fm n* **ufer**, a long fir pole of between 20 and 40 feet

uphroe *var fm n* **euphroe**

uplead *vb* to lead up

uplean *Spens vb* to recline (on one's elbow)

upleap *n* an upward leap: a geological fault caused by a subterranean upward movement *vb* to leap up

up-line *n* the railway line leading to a major city, *esp* a capital city (as opposed to the **down-line** which leads from such a centre)

upraise *vb* to raise (*lit/fig*) *US n* a shaft which is dug from the bottom upwards (not impossible as it is begun from a side shaft)

uprate *vb* to upgrade

uprest *var fm n* **uprist**

uprisal *n* an uprising

uprise *n* dawn: origination: the beginning of an ascent: an ascent to higher status *vb* to rise (from bed/to one's feet/to a higher level/from the dead): of the sun, to rise (*infl fms* **uprose, uprisen** (*adj*), **uprises, uprising** (*n*))

uprist *n* an uprising from a place (bed) or a state (dead) *vb* to rise up

upsend *vb* to discharge upwards

upspear *vb* of grass, to grow spear-like

upstare *vb* to gaze upwards

uptear *vb* to uproot, to tear out

upwell *vb* to well up (see **upwelling**)

upwelling *n* the rising to the surface of an ocean of nutrient-enriched water

ur *interj* expressing hesitation in speech *now dial fm pron* **our**

uracil *n* a substance in the bodily acid, ribonucleic acid

uraemia *n* a poisoning of the blood by products which are normally discharged in urine

uraeus *n* the snake symbol on the headdress of an Egyptian god or king (*pl* **uraei, uraeuses**)

Uralian *adj* of, pertaining to or dwelling in the proximity of the Ural Mountains of the USSR

Uralic *n* one of the two major families (or groups) of languages spoken in Europe including Finnish, Hungarian and many of the languages of the USSR. Most other European languages, including such diverse tongues as Polish, Yiddish, French, German, English, Gaelic and Greek, are classified as belonging to the Indo-European family via the different sub-groups, branches and sub-branches to which they are assigned.

uralite *n* any crystalline mineral of the pyroxene group altered to any variously coloured, hydrous silicates such as hornblende

uralitise *var fm vb* **uralitize**

uralitize *vb* to turn into uralite

urangutang *var fm n* **orang-utan** (see **orang**)

Urania *pers n* the muse of astronomy: Aphrodite

uranide *n* uranium or other element falling within the category of the actinide series of fifteen radioactive elements having the atomic numbers ranging from 89 to 103

uranism *n* one of the practices of male homosexuals

uranite *n* an ore or mineral mainly composed of uranium

uranous *adj* of, pertaining to or typical of uranium

uranyl *n* a fundamental constituent of many compounds of uranium

urate *n* a salt of uric acid, a white acid found in small quantities in human urine

urbane *adj* refined and elegant

urceolated *adj* urn-shaped

urceolus *n* any cup-shaped botanical organ

Urd *pers n* see **Norn**

Uredinales *n pl* the rust fungi

uredo *n* any of various skin diseases: a rust fungus which attacks plants (*pl* **uredos**)

ureide *n* any of several nitrogenous compounds

uremic *var fm adj* **uraemic**, of uraemia

ureses *pl* uresis

uresis *n* the action of passing urine (*pl* **ureses**)

ureter *n* a urinary duct

urethan *n* ethyl carbonate, a white crystalline compound, used as an anaesthetic

uretic *adj* of or relating to urine

urger *n* one who urges, incites or instigates

uricase *n* an enzyme of the liver and kidneys

urine (*n*) *vb* to micturate or pass water

urite *n* an abdominal segment

urnet *var fm now dial n* **runnet**

urnfield *n* a late Bronze Age cemetery containing urns of human ashes

Urodela *n pl* the Caudata, amphibia which retain their tails in adult life

urodelan *adj/n* (of) any species of Urodela

urogenital *adj* pertaining or belonging to that bodily region once known as the share *n* an organ of that region (usually only in *pl fm*)

urostyle *n* the rear, unsegmented portion of the spine of certain fishes and amphibians

urring *obs adj* orange-coloured, as in the description **urring tayne** (orange tawny)

ursine *adj* of or pertaining to the bear: bear-like

urtica *n* a nettle

urticant *adj* adapted for stinging: producing a sensation of itching

urticate *vb* to sting: to nettle

us (*pron*) GAME PLAYER'S note: us in royal, papal or editorial usage is singular, hence available for play in those games which specifically bar plural forms

usager *n* one of the clergymen who belonged to the nonjuror element within the Anglican and Scottish Episcopalian Churches who took a particular viewpoint on a theological dispute concerning certain services called the usages

usance *n* usage, a firmly established and generally accepted practice or procedure *esp* in relation to the time permitted for the redemption of foreign bills of exchange

usidge *obs fm n* **usage**

ut *n* the original first musical syllable of the tonic sol-fa (see **gamut**) *dial fm prep* **at**

uterine (*adj*) *obs n* a medicament for the womb and allied organs (*pl*) children of the same mother

uterus (*n*) *pl fms* **uteri, uteruses**

utricle *n* a botanical bottle-shaped part or bladder-like body: an animal or vegetable sac: an anatomical cul-de-sac

uu *Obs fm n* **yew**

uv *Obs fm n* **yew**

uz *dial fm pron* **us** (GAME PLAYER'S note: Invalid for games which bar plurals as hardly the form likely in royal, papal or editorial circles – see **us**)

V

va *Italian n* a musical term meaning 'it proceeds' *Obs fm n/adj* **woe** *Obs S fm n* **way**

vacuolate *adj* of such as the stem of a plant, modified or altered by having a cavity usually containing some fluid

vager *obs S fm ns* **vauger**, a wanderer, **wager**, a soldier

vagile *adj* free to move about

vaginate *adj* enclosed in a vagina or sheath *obs vb* to sheathe

vaginated *var fm adj* **vaginate**

vailer *obs n* one who humbles

vain (*adj*) *obs vb* to frustrate

vainer *comp adj* vain

vair *n* a fur obtained from a variety of the European red squirrel which has a grey back and a white belly

vairé *adj* having vair *her adj* variegated

vaise *dial fm vb* **feeze**, to frighten

vait *obs S fm vb* **wait**

vakass *n* an Armenian white linen vestment

valence *n* the property possessed by such as an element of combining with or replacing other elements in a definite and constant proportion

Valerie *fem fm masc pers n* **Valerius**, meaning 'strong'

valeta *var fm n* **veleta**

valine *n* one of the amino acids

valise *n* a travelling bag for clothes and toiletries

vallar *adj* of a crown or garland awarded by the ancient Romans to the first soldier to mount the enemy's rampart

valonia *n* a substance used in the tanning and dyeing industries obtained from the acorn cups and acorns of a species of Mediterranean oak tree

valorise *var fm vb* **valorize**, of a government, to establish and maintain a particular price

valse *n/vb* (to) waltz

valter *obs S fm n* **water**

valure *obs n* worthiness: importance *obs vb* to estimate the worth of

vamose *US collq vb* vamoose, to depart

vamper *n* one who improvises music (on the piano): one who patches things up *slg n* one who picks a fight (in a tavern) with a person of obvious substance so that, in the ensuing brawl, he can be discreetly robbed by others *obs n* a stocking

Van cat see **Turkish Van**

vance *var fm obs vb* **vaunce**, to advance

vanel *obs n* a vanilla pod

vaneless *adj* not having a vane

vant *dial fm n* **font**, a (stone) bowl containing baptismal water *obs fm vb* **vaunt** *obs S fm vb* **want**

vardy *now dial n* judgment, opinion, verdict

varges *dial fm n* **verjuice**

vargis *dial fm n* **verjuice**

varices *pl* varix

varicle *obs n* a varicose swelling

variedly *adv* diversely

varier *n* a dissenter from *obs n* a prevaricator

variola inserta *n* a medical term for smallpox acquired by inoculation

variole *n* a small anatomical depression: a variolite or dense crystalline variety of basalt

varix *n* a varicose vein (*pl* **varices**)

varlet *n* a rogue or rascal: in an historical context, one attending an important military officer such as a knight *arch n* a menial

varletess *n* a female varlet

varry *var fm now dial n* **fare**, a litter of pigs *dial fm adv* **very** *obs fm vb* **vary**

varsal *collq adj* universal

vasquine *S n* a petticoat (*obs* in common usage but revived by such as Scott for literary effect)

vassail *n* vessel (a *fm* used by Scott)

vast (*adj/n*) *Obs vb* to lay waste *obs S fm n/adj/vb* **waste**

vaster *comp adj* vast

vastre *Obs fm adv* **fast**, in the sense of firmly fixed

vasty *adj* vast, immense *obs adj* slimy

vaticide *n* the killing of a prophet: such a killer

vaticinate *vb* to predict: to speak as a seer

vav *n* the sixth letter of the Hebrew alphabet

vealy *adj* like veal: immature or imperfectly developed (*fig*) (*comp* **vealier** *sup* **vealiest**)

veinous *adj* full of, consisting of, traversed by veins: having prominent veins

velaria *pl* velarium, a large awning which covered a part of a Roman amphitheatre

velaric *adj* of or pertaining to a velar sound

venada *n* the pudu, a species of small deer native to Chile

Ve *pers n* a Norse god, brother of Odin (*– cap*) *obs S fm pron* **we** (players of Waddington word games see **we**)

veal (*n*) *S n* a tank or water barrel used in mining *vb* to rear calves for meat

veale *var fm obs n* **vele**, a veil or covering

vealer *US n* a calf intended for veal

vealing *n* procuring the meat of a calf *S n* the act of getting water out of mines by the use of veals

vear *obs fm n/vb* **veer**

veare *obs fm vb* **veer**

vease *dial n* impetus: a run before a leap *var fm now dial vb* **feeze**, to impel: to frighten

vector *n* an insect or other organism as a carrier of disease or infection: in mathematics, a variable quantity which has magnitude and direction: the course of an aircraft or missile *vb* to direct (from the ground) an aircraft

vedalia *n* a species of Australian ladybird exported to other countries to control insect pests

vedder *obs S fm ns* **weather, wether**

Vedist *n* a student of the Vedas, the holy books of the Hindus

veerer *n* an instrument which whirls things: an old mining term for a banksman or overseer of work above ground

veile *obs fm n* **veil**

veine *obs fm n* **vein**

veiner *n* a wood carver's V-shaped tool used for such as the carving of veins in leaves: one who makes veins in artificial flowers

veiny *adj* of or pertaining to veins: having prominent veins: full of veins (*comp* **veinier** *sup* **veiniest**)

velar *adj* of the phonetic sound formed with the back of the tongue touching the soft palate *n* a velar sound

velate *adj* having a velum or sail-like membrane

velated *adj* velate *obs adj* covered over, veiled or hidden

veleta *n* a sequence dance (tune) in slow waltz time

velitation *n* a skirmish, either of arms or of words

velites *n pl* ancient Roman foot soldiers

velouet *obs fm n* **velvet**

velour *n* a soft pad used for such as brushing a hat: any of various furnishing fabrics having a velvet-like finish

velouté *n* a white sauce made from stock

velvet ant *n* any of a family of wasps of desert and semi-desert regions, the adult females of which are wingless and run over the ground like ants but by no means in such large numbers. They have hairy bodies and legs and exhibit such colorations as a bright red thorax separating a white marked, mainly black head and rear half. All are exceptionally vicious, those in captivity giving an impression of being the most bad-tempered of all insects, humming loudly and menacingly when disturbed and stinging at the slightest provocation.

velwet *obs fm n* **velvet**

venal (*adj*) *obs fm S, Ir & dial n* **vennel**

venation *n* the arrangement of veins in a leaf or in the wings of an insect: either of such collectively: the act of hunting wild animals

venatorial *adj* connected with or given to hunting

vendace *n* either of two species of whitefish, the Lochmaben vendace of lochs in Dumfriesshire Scotland and the Cumberland vendace of Derwentwater and Bassenthwaite in the English Lake District (see **whitefish**)

vendee *n* a person who purchases (real property)

vender *n* one who advocates a particular point of view: a vendor

vendis *var fm n* **vendace**

vendise *var fm n* **vendace**

vendue *US & West Indies n* an auction

venerid *n* any species of *Veneridae*, a family of marine bivalve molluscs which includes the Venus shells, carpet shells and the American piddock

Venetia *fem pers n* meaning 'blessed'

venial *adj* easily forgiven *obs n* a venial offence

venire *n* a shortened form of **venire facias**, a writ of former times to a sheriff requiring him to provide a jury

Venise *fem pers n poss* meaning 'Venus'

vennel *S, Ir & dial n* an alley: an open sewer

ventage *n* one of a series of holes in a wind instrument: a small opening (GAME PLAYER'S note: In the musical sense, the word was coined by Shakespeare with the quarto spelling of **ventage** and the folio spelling of **ventige**. Both *fms* were used, for either sense, up to and *incl* the 19th century though **ventage** appears to be the only spelling in current usage. The labelling in the dictionary used for the UK Scrabble championship is ambiguous. It ascribes either **ventige** or both *fms* exclusively to Shakespeare in both senses. The second sense of **ventage** was in fact first used by John Webster in his play, *The Duchess of Malfi*, in 1623 (seven years after Shakespeare's death) and it was not until 1726 that a writer used the *var fm*, **ventige**, for Webster's sense of a small opening.)

ventail *n* either the lower movable part of the front of the helmet apart from the vizor (the earlier meaning) or that part *incl* the vizor (the current meaning)

ventaile *var fm n* **ventail**

vente *obs fm n* **vent**

venter *n* either (or any) of two (or more) wives each of whom bear a child sired by the same man: the womb: one who gives vent to (an objectionable) doctrine *dial fm n* **venture** *obs fm vb* **venture**

ventige *var fm n* **ventage**

ventose *adj* windy *obs n* a type of cupping glass or medical instrument which extracts blood by a vacuum process (*var fms incl* the unlisted anagrams **vantose**, **ventosa**) *obs vb* to bleed a patient with the aid of a cupping glass

ventre *obs fm ns* **venter**, mother or womb: **vintry** *obs fm vb* **venture**

venturi *n* a wasp-waisted tube used in measuring the flow rate of fluids

venued *obs fm adj* **vinewed**

verbality *n* the fact of being merely words *esp* without real substance (used of crank theories)

verberate *vb* to beat or strike

Verdante *pers n* one of the Norns or three Fates of time (see **Norn**)

verdet *n* a species of fungus which grows on maize: an acetate of copper

verdeter *var fm n* **verditer**

verdit *now dial fm n* **verdict**

verditer *n* one of three different colours, green, turquoise or *esp* light blue, obtained by adding chalk to a solution of nitrate of copper and used as a water colour

vere *obs n* the season of spring *Obs vb* to raise upwards *obs fm n/vb* **veer**

Verein *Ger n* an association of people in such as a club

verges *obs fm n* **verjuice**

vergis *obs fm n* **verjuice**

verglas *n* a fine coating of ice on rock (*pl* **verglases**)

veridical *adj* truthful

verier *comp adj* very

veriest *sup adj* very

verism *n* the style advocated by a verist

verist *n* one who believes in the representation of absolute veracity in art and literature

veritable *adj* genuine: possessing all the distinctive qualities desired

veritably *adv* genuinely

veritas *n* truth (*pl* **veritates**)

verite *obs S fm n* **verity**

verity *n* truth: a fact: a true statement: the quality of being true, correct or real (*pl* **verities**)

verjuice *n* the acidic juice of unripe fruit

vermian *adj* characteristic of worms: wormlike

vermicide *n* an (intestinal) worm-killing agent

vermis *n* the wormlike process of the little or hinder brain

vernal *adj* of the season spring

vernation *n* prefoliation, the arrangement or formation of leaves or fronds in the bud

vernissage *n* varnishing day, the day or one of a number of days prior to the opening of an art exhibition when an artist may apply a varnish or retouch his or her own artwork which is already hanging on display

veronica *n* the various speedwells or other plants of a genus of plants with small blue, pink or white flowers: a pass, in bullfighting, whereby the matador slowly swings the cape away from the charging bull

verrey *var fm adj/her adj* **vairé**

verrie *var fm obs n* **verry**

verriest *obs S fm comp* **veriest**

verruga *n* Peruvian wart, a disease characterized by skin tumours

verry *obs her adj* having two or more colours *obs n* the two-tone colour of vair *obs fm adj/adv/n* **very**

versal *obsol collq adj* universal *obs n* a metric or poetic version of something

versant *adj* conversant *n* (the area of) the slope of a mountain (chain)

verse (*n/vb*) *obs fm n* **verst** (*pl* **versse**)

verser *n* a writer of verses *slg n* one of a gang of swindlers

verset *n* a short piece of verse

versin *n* the versed sine, a trigonometric function of one minus the cosine

versine *n* a mathematical term for one minus the cosine

versioner *n* a translator or any other person who produces a version

versse *pl* verse (*obs fm n* **verst**)

verst *n* a Russian measure of distance *approx* $\frac{2}{3}$ of an English mile

verste *obs fm n* **verst**

versute *adj* cunning, crafty

vert *her n* the colour green *n* the right to cut green trees or shrubs in a wood or forest: arboreal green vegetation capable of providing cover for deer: a convert or pervert *vb* to turn or twist out of normal position: to become a convert or pervert

vertical (*adj*) *n* a vertical angle, circle, line or plane *slg n* of gardening terminology, a plant living on an upright rock

vertue *arch S fm n* **virtue**

vertuse *obs S fm n* **virtuous**

vesiater *obs S n* an inspector

vesica *n* a bladder (*pl* **vesicae**)

vesicant *n* that employed to raise blisters *adj* causing or effective in producing blisters

vesication *n* a blister: the formation, development or a group of such

vespertine *adj* of, pertaining to or belonging to the evening: of a heavenly body, setting at or just after sunset (also see **ANIMAL ADJECTIVES** – after **zebra**) *obs n* evensong

vespine *adj* of or pertaining to wasps: wasp-like

vessail *n* vessel (a *fm* revived by Scott)

vessel (*n*/*vb*) *infl fms* British, **vesselled/-lling**: US, **vesseled/-ling**

vessil *Obs fm n* **vessel**

vestal *adj* of or pertaining to Vesta, the Roman goddess of fire and the hearth: of the virgin priestesses who had charge of the sacred fire in her temple at Rome: of fire: of chastity and virginity *n* a vestal virgin: a virgin: a nun

vestee *n* one invested with such as a right or property

vester *n* an investor *dial fm n* **vesture**

vesterer *Obs n* one having charge of vestments

vestral *adj* of or pertaining to a vestry

vestry *n* a room in which vestments are kept (*pl* **vestries**)

vestur *obs fm n* **vesture**

vestural *adj* of or pertaining to clothing

vesture *n* a garment or vestment: everything, other than trees, which grows upon land

veterane *obs fm n*/*adj* **veteran**

veterean *obs fm n*/*adj* **veteran**

vetoer *n* one who applies a veto

vetturini *pl* vetturino

vetturino *n* one, in Italy, who has a four-wheeled carriage and horses for hire: the driver of such (*pl* **vetturini**)

vew *dial fm n* **yew** (northern dialects) *dial fm adj* **few** (southern dialects)

vg *obs fm now dial vb* **ug**

vi *var fm Obs n* **vie**, a short biography of a saint

vialful *n* the amount that a vial can hold

viator *n* a traveller, a wayfarer (*pl* **viators, viatores**)

viatores *pl* viator

victualer *var fm n* **victualler**, a purveyor of victuals

videnda *pl* videndum

videndum *n* a thing worth seeing (*pl* **videnda**)

vieu *obs fm n*/*vb* **view**

vigner *var fm Obs n* **viner**

vignet *var fm obs n* **vinet**

vignetter *n* a camera lens masking device for producing such as a head and shoulders portrait with the remainder shading off into the background

viker *obs fm n* **vicar**

vile (*adj*/*n*) *obs vb* to degrade

vilens *Obs fm obs adj* **villains,** villainous

vilet *obs fm n* violet

villose *adj* covered with a hairlike process, such as the pile of velvet

vinasse *n* a residual product containing potassium salts, obtained either from beets after the sugar has been extracted or from pressed grapes

vineat *var fm obs n* **vinet**

vinegaroon *n* a large whipscorpion of the southern USA and Mexico. When attacked, it flexes its tail over its head and releases a fine spray of acetic acid which has an odour characteristic of vinegar.

vineger *obs fm n* **vinegar**

vinegre *obs fm n* **vinegar**

viner *n* a wine grower *US n* an implement which gathers pea pods *Obs n* a vineyard

vine rod *n* the vine wood staff of a Roman centurion

vine snake *n* any of various African snakes which prey especially upon chameleons and, though venomous, have a bite which is rarely fatal to man

vinet *obs n* a design of vine leaves and branches

vinew *vb* to make or become mouldy

vinewed *adj* mouldy *obs adj* moulded

viniet *var fm obs n* **vinet**

vinite *var fm obs n* **vinet**

vintager *n* one employed to gather grapes

vinter *obs n* a vintner

vintree *obs fm n* **vintry**

vintry *n* a wine vault, store or shop (*pl* **vintries**)

viny *adj* covered with vines (*comp* **vinier** *sup* **viniest**)

violaceous *adj* purplish blue

viole *obs vb* to violate *obs fm ns* **vial, viol**

violent (*adj*) *obs n* a violent passion or person *obs vb* to constrain

violer *n* one who plays the viol

violet (*n/adj*) *vb* to colour violet: to gather violets

violine *n* a medicinal substance used to produce vomiting and found in the common violet: a violet blue colour

Vipera *n* the genus of the adder or viper

viperal *n* a medicament of former times obtained from the viper and used in the treatment of 'the great pox'

vipered *obs adj* of or pertaining to a viper

virent *adj* green

vireo *n* any of more than twenty species of small brown or grey perching birds having a white or yellow underside and widely distributed in North and Central America. The vireonine family of birds also includes the various greenlet species of South America. (*pl* **vireos**)

viretot *n* dash, rush

virga *n* wisps of water or ice drifting from a cloud and evaporating before reaching the ground (*pl* **virga, virgas**)

virgal *adj* made of twigs

virgate *n* an ancient English measure of land which had considerable variation but approximated to 30 acres: a linear measure equal to a rod, pole or perch

virge *obs fm ns* **verge, virgate**

virgin (*n*) *vb* to remain a virgin: to speak of a virgin (note: Still extant, though modern usage is rare)

virose *adj* poisonous

visa (*n*) *vb* to endorse a passport with a visa (*infl* **visaed** or **viséed**)

viscera *n pl* the internal organs of the trunk

visceral *adj* of or affecting the viscera: pertaining to the viscera of animals used in divination: instinctive rather than intellectual

viscerate *vb* to disembowel (*lit/fig*)

viséed *var fm pa pple* **visaed**

visitant *adj* visiting: having the character of a visitor *n* a (supernatural) visitor

vista *n* an extended linear view or prospect either *lit*, such as that seen through an avenue of trees or *fig*, a mental vision far into the past or future: an avenue of trees or other physical passage: that, such as the trees, which forms the passage *vb* to create or see in a vista (*infl fms* **vista'd, vistaed**)

vistal *adj* of a vista

vitals *n pl* the interior organs essential for life (*sing*) *n* in palmistry, the vital line

vitiable *adj* that capable of being vitiated

vitiate *vb* to render faulty: to impair: to make corrupt: to deprave, pervert: to make invalid

vitness *obs S fm n/vb* **witness**

vitrage *modf n* of a cloth or net, suitable for covering a window (usually in the *fm* **vitrage net**) *n* such a type of thin curtain

vitrail *n* stained glass

vitrain *n* a glassy constituent of bright coal

vitre *obs n* glass

vitreous *adj* (made) of, resembling or containing glass

Vitrina *n* the genus of the glass snails, thin-shelled land molluscs intermediate between slugs and true snails

vitrine *n* a glass showcase for such as objets d'art

vitular *adj* vituline

vituline *adj* of or belonging to a calf or calves: resembling that of a calf

vituperate *vb* to blame: assail with abuse: revile: to use abusive language

vizy *S n* the target: a gunsight: a glimpse *S vb* to look at carefully: to take aim (with a gun)

vlaie see **vlei**

vlei *S Afr n* a shallow pool: a stretch of low-lying land covered by water in the rainy season (*var fms* **vley**, **vlie**, **vly**) *US n* a swamp (*var fm* **vlaie**)

vo *nonce n* a size of book e.g. **octavo** and **post-octavo** are examples of a **vo**; **duodecimo** and **sixteenmo** are examples of a **mo** (*pl* **vos**)

voicer *n* one skilled in giving an organ pipe its voice or tone

voider *n* any receptacle into which something is emptied

voile *n* a thin cotton or woollen material used for such as blouses or dresses

voiture *n* a vehicle such as a carriage

vol *var fm n* **vole**, the winning of card tricks

volable *Shaks adj* quick-witted

volage *adj* fickle: flighty

volatic *adj* that creature capable of flight *n* a winged creature

vole (*n*) *vb* to win the vole, a term used for all of the card tricks available in certain card games such as ombre or quadrille

volery *n of assemb* of birds *n* an aviary: a place for aircraft repair

Volscian *n* one of an ancient warlike Italic people finally subdued by the Romans in the 4th century BC: their language *adj* of, pertaining or belonging to the Volscians

voltaic *adj* of, pertaining to, caused by or connected with electricity generated by chemical action

Voltairean *adj* of, belonging to, holding similar opinions to or expressing them in the style of the French philosopher and writer, François Marie Arouet Voltaire (1694–1778) *n* a follower (in the style) of the critical and mocking scepticism of Voltaire

volucrine *adj* of, pertaining to or arising from birds (also see **ANIMAL ADJECTIVES**)

vortex *n* an eddy or whirlpool: a similar rotary action around an axis of any matter having that capacity and extended, in a *fig* sense, to human affairs (*pl* **vortices**, **vortexes**)

vortices *pl* vortex

vostre *Obs fm vb* **foster**

votary *n* one bound by religious vows (*pl* **votaries**)

voteen *Ir n* a very devout religious person

vp *obs fm adv* **up**

vreter *obs fm n* **ureter**

vrine *obs fm n/vb* **urine**

vs *obs fm pron* **us**

vsance *obs fm n* **usance**

vult *obs S n* face, countenance: facial expression *esp* a cheerful one

vy *obs fm vb* **vie**

W

wa *n* a Siamese measure of length *S & dial fm adj/adv/interj/n* **woe** *Obs fm pron* **who** (GAME PLAYER'S note: Whilst wa has such obvious single-letter extensions as **wad** or **wag**, the value of this type of play is more fully discussed at **qwa**, the less obvious extension) (+*cap*) *n* a minor language spoken in the China/Burma border region

Wabash *n* a tributary of the river Ohio which forms part of the boundary between Indiana and Illinois

wabble *var fm n/vb* **wobble**

wabbler *var fm n* **wobbler**, one who wobbles in gait or opinion: a thing which wobbles

wabler *obs fm n* **wabbler**

wabster *S fm n* **webster**, a male weaver

wach *obs fm n* **watch**, a timepiece: a vigil *obs fm vbs* **wash, watch** (to keep a vigil)

wadder *now dial n* one who stacks the crop in wads or bundles *obs n* one engaged in the land surveying process of determining the wad or line of direction

waddie *var fm n/vb* **waddy**

waddy *n* an Australian aborigine's war club: a walking stick: a cowboy *vb* to strike, beat or kill with a waddy

wadset *n* in Scottish law, the conveyance of land in settlement of a debt with the reserved power of recovery if and when the debt is paid *S vb* to pawn, to mortgage (*infl fms* **wadset** or **wadsetted, wadsetting**)

wadsett *var fm n* **wadset**

wae *S adj* sorrowful *now dial fm n* **woe**

waesome *S adj* pitiful, woeful

wafter (*n*) *obs vb* to arrange ships in a convoy

Wagnerist *n* a cult follower of the works of the German composer, Richard Wagner (1813–1883): one who copies his style of musical drama

wah *n* the red bearcat or panda, a Himalayan racoon-like animal about the size of a large domestic cat

waid *S fm vb* **wade**

wain *n* a large farm cart *obs vb* to transport by wain

waining *obs n* the turning point in ploughing

waister *n* a sailor stationed in the waist or middle part of the upper deck of a ship

waitte *obs fm n* **wait** *obs S fm vb* **wait**

wale *n* a weal or mark on flesh caused by a blow: a raised line in fabric: a horizontal timber which connects and strengthens vertical timbers: a horizontal band of a woven basket *S & dial n* a choice: that which is choice *vb* to mark flesh with a wale or weal: to add a timber wale: to interweave a wale in the making of a basket *S & dial vb* to choose

waler *n* an Australian horse exported to India

walet *obs fm n* **wallet**

waling *n* a timber wale: the act of making a basket wale *S & dial n* the act of choosing

waller *n* one who builds walls: a worker in a salt works concerned with the boiling process: a tree planted adjacent to and affixed to a wall

wallless *adj* without a wall

walse *var fm n/vb* **waltz**

walte *var fm obs S n* **vult**

Walter *masc pers n* meaning 'folk ruler' (*–cap*) *obs S fm n* **water**

wampus *US n* a heavy outer jacket

wan (*adj*) *poet vb* to grow pale (*infl fms* **wanned, wanning** (also *n*))

wand (*n*) *S & dial vb* to interweave (wattle): to beat with a stick

wandle *S & dial adj* of a thing, flexible: of a person, lithe or agile *dial vb* to walk with a weary tread *obs S vb* to recoil or give way

wane *n* a bevelled edge of a board sawn from a log: the decrease as given with the *vb* below: the decrease of the moon's illuminated visible surface: the period of such decrease *vb* to diminish in size, brilliance, magnitude, power, intensity, importance, prosperity etc

wanger *obs n* a pillow

waning *n* the action of the *vb*: of the moon, the periodical decrease in apparent size: the second half of the lunar month

wanter (*n*) *dial n* one who seeks a marriage partner: a mole catcher

wany *adj* waning in some parts (*comp* **wanier** *sup* **waniest**)

wapper *now dial vb* to blink the eyes

war (*n*) *vb* to make war upon

warble *vb* of people or birds, to sing sweetly: to celebrate in song or verse *S vb* to play the quicker measures of bagpipe music *poet vb* of wind or water, to make melody in movement *obs vb* to vibrate or quiver *n* of people or birds, an act of singing: a small hard tumour on a horse caused by the saddle: worble, a tumour or swelling on such as cattle or deer caused by the larva of a gadfly eating its way to the surface: the gadfly or its parasitic larva

wardin *obs n* a landlady, a hostess

warling *obs n* one who is despised or disliked

warme *obs fm adj/vb* **warm**

warne *obs fm vb* **warn**

warpe *obs fm n* **warp**

warple *dial n* a bridle track or similar non-public highway *S vb* to entangle

warppe *obs fm vb* **wrap**

warray *obs vb* to make war (upon)

warren *n* historically, a piece of land specially enclosed for the breeding of game fowl, rabbits (see **cony**) and hares: the inhabitants of such a warren: a series of interconnected rabbit burrows: extended to include the stops, or single burrow bolt holes: a densely populated dwelling or dwellings *esp* where there are residential cellars: a maze of narrow passages *obs n* a brothel *obs fm vb* **warn**

warrey *var fm obs vb* **warray**

warse *var fm obs n* **wrase**

warsle *S & dial n* a struggle: a wrestling match *S & dial vb* to struggle: to wrestle

warstel *obs fm S & dial n/vb* **warsle**

warstle *now US var fm S & dial n/vb* **warsle**

warstler *S & dial n* a wrestler (see **wrastler**)

wart (*n*) *nonce vb* to develop a wart

warth *now dial n* a river meadow: a stretch of land fringing the sea *var fm now dial n* **wath**, a ford

wartle *obs n* a little wart: a hard lump in molten metal

wartlet *n* a proposed name for certain sea anemones

wart snake *n* either of two species of harmless aquatic snakes, the file snake or the elephant's trunk snake, both of which have a unique skin which feels like sandpaper and is used for such as shoes and handbags

warve *arch fm n* **wharve**, the coil of a spindle

wary (*adj*) *obs vb* to (put a) curse (upon) *Obs n* an outlaw

washel *obs n* a bath

washen *arch adj* washed

wasp (*n*) *nonce vb* to sting as a wasp does

wasper *var fm S n* **wawsper**, a fishing spear

wassail *arch n* like 'good health' or 'cheers', a salutation prior to drinking, the reply being, 'drink hail': the spiced ale traditonally served on Christmas Eve and Twelfth Night: a riotous festival *vb* to celebrate in this fashion: to toast, in spiced ale, the living things of the land such as cattle and fruit trees (a Christmas Eve custom)

wassal *n* seaweed used as manure

wassel *var fm ns* **wassal, wassail** *obs fm vb* **wassail** *var fm S adv* **wessel**

wasser *var fm obs n* **wasserman**

wasserman *obs n* a fabled sea monster partly in the shape of a man with the power to destroy ships

wastel (*n*) in an historical context, bread of the finest flour

waster (*n*) *S vb* to use extravagantly

wasterie *var fm S & dial n* **wastry**

wastle *Obs fm n* **wastel**

wastrie *var fm S & dial n* **wastry**

wastry *S & dial n* wastefulness

Water Dog *n* the Chinese years which, this century, have approximated to 1922 and 1982 (see **CHINESE CALENDAR**) (–cap) *n* any dog bred or trained for the water: the water rat: the otter

water-dog *n* a sailor: a good swimmer: a small dark cloud indicative of rain

waterdog *n* a mudpuppy: a hellbender

waterhead *n* the source of a stream: the land surrounding that source

Water Horse *n* the name of the Chinese year for the corresponding period of the western calendar 15 February 1942 to 4 February 1943 (see **CHINESE CALENDAR**) (*–cap*) *n* a type of spirit which haunts stretches of water in the Goidelic parts of the British Isles and which can assume both human and equine forms (for examples see **glastyn, kelpie, tangie**)

waterleaf *n* an unsized paper which absorbs liquids too freely to be used for such purposes as writing paper

water leaf *n* any of a genus of delicate North American woodland herbs having white or blue flowers: (usually hyphenated) an architectural representation of the leaf of a non-specific aquatic plant: (also usually hyphenated) waterleaf

waterlemon *n* a species of passion flower: its edible fruit

WATERMARKED PAPER In ascending order of size, the following are the names of traditional British watermarked papers:– *bell, pot, écu, crown, shell, grape, large grape, jesus, great eagle, great world.*

watershed *n* an imaginary line on high ground which separates two different water systems, so that rain falling on one side eventually reaches one river and that on the other side a different river: the complete area drained by a particular river system (TRIVIAL EXAMPLE: Two drops of rain, falling fractions of an inch apart on a Derbyshire hill overlooking Chesterfield, could take totally different paths. One could flow south, via local streams to the river Amber, and from there to the Derwent, the Trent and finally the Humber. The other could flow north via local streams to the river Hipper, and from there to the Rother, the Don, the Yorkshire Ouse and finally the Humber. They have fallen either side of a watershed *as a line*, in *different* watersheds viewed as, say, those of the Rother and the Derwent river systems but the *same* watershed viewed as that of the Humber river system.)

water table *n* the level below which the ground is saturated with water: a moulding or other projection on a wall, designed to throw off rainwater

wathe *var fm obs n* **waith**, hunting or fishing

wather *obs fm n* **weather** *obs fm conj* **whether**

watle *var fm obs Ork & Shet n* **wattle**, a tax which replaced the historic obligation upon land owners in Orkney and Shetland to provide entertainment for one having judicial responsibilities *obs fm vb* **wattle**, to construct such as a fence with branches and twigs

watter *dial fm n* **water**

wavier *comp adj* wavy

waw *n* the twenty-seventh and penultimate letter of the Arabic alphabet

wayboard *n* a thin stratum sandwiched between thick strata

wayer *obs fm collective sing n* **ware**, goods or commodites

wayne *obs fm adj* **vain** *obs fm vb* **wean** *obs fm n* **wain** *Obs fm n* **vein**

wayre *obs S fm collective sing n* **ware**, goods or commodities

we (*pron*) GAME PLAYER'S note: Some word games, usually those made by Waddington, bar plurals but we is *sing* in royal, papal or editorial usage, hence valid for play

weade *obs fm vb* **weed**

weal *n* happiness, prosperity, welfare: a blemish produced by a blow *vb* to mark the flesh with such a blow

weald *n* open or forested countryside

weard *obs S fm n* **weird**

weared *arch pa pple vb* wear, to turn a sailing vessel with the head away from the wind

wearings *n pl* ornamental lace

weasand *n* the windpipe

weasle *arch fm n* **weasel**

weath *var fm obs n* **waith**, cloth

webstar *Obs fm n* **webster**

webster *n* a weaver (note: As a specific designation of one whose occupation is that of a weaver it applies to a female for the period circa 1100 to circa 1500. For a male it is the period circa 1350 to circa 1850 (later still in the *S fm* **wabster**). Apart from historical reference to either period, it is no longer used as an occupational description. Other usage of the word in a modern context is purely stylistic *esp* where the sex of the weaver is indeterminate.)

wedand *S fm obs adj* **weding**

wedden *Obs fm vb* **wed**

WEDDING ANNIVERSARIES The traditional names, which also designate the nature of a suitable gift, are **First** cotton: **Second** paper: **Third** leather: **Fourth** flower or fruit: **Fifth** wooden: **Sixth** iron: **Seventh** woollen: **Eighth** bronze: **Ninth** copper or pottery: **Tenth** tin: **Eleventh** steel: **Twelfth** silk: **Thirteenth** lace: **Fourteenth** ivory: **Fifteenth** crystal: **Twentieth** china **Twenty-fifth** silver: **Thirtieth** pearl: **Thirty-fifth** coral: **Fortieth** ruby: **Forty-fifth** sapphire: **Fiftieth** golden: (**Sixtieth** or) **Seventy-fifth** diamond. (The sixtieth is sometimes accounted as diamond, due to Queen Victoria's 'Diamond Jubilee' being held to celebrate her sixty years on the throne.)

wede *obs vb* to go mad: to go wild with anger or desire

weder *obs fm n* **wether**, a male sheep

weding *obs adj* raging or raving

wedset *obs fm n/S vb* **wadset**

weeest *sup adj* wee

wee's nest see **mare's nest**

weever *n* either of two species of marine, bottom-living, poisonous fishes related to the red mullets, stargazers and jawfishes. Both the lesser and greater weevers have poison glands at the base of the dorsal fin though only the lesser has an additional gland at the base of the spine. The lesser weever grows to a length of about six inches, the greater weever to about twenty inches. Both are found in British coastal waters. They bury themselves in the sand with only their heads with upward-looking eyes and the black poisonous dorsal fin visible.

wefte *obs fm n* **weft**

wefty *adj* of the nature of a weft: webby, cobwebby

weiner *var fm US n* **wiener**

weir (*n*) *vb* to construct a weir *S & dial fm n/vb* **wire**

weird (*adj*) *n* fate, destiny: magical power, enchantment: a prediction: a witch, wizard, soothsayer: a supernatural event: a predestined event (+*cap, pl*) the Fates of Greek myth

weirdo *n* one whose eccentricity *esp* in dress is not especially engaging (*pl* **weirdos**)

welde *obs fm n/vb* **wield**

weldor *var fm n* **welder**

welfed *obs fm phr* **well fed**

welkin *n* the sky, the firmament: the upper atmosphere

wellar *var fm obs n* **weller**

well dressing *n* an old Derbyshire custom (celebrated in different villages at different times during the summer) whereby the local wells are honoured. Specially constructed, large, shallow wooden trays are filled with soft mud and into the mud is pressed a mosaic of flower petals and other natural objects to produce pictures, often of considerable artistic merit, and usually of a biblical nature. These trays are then placed upright behind each local well or spring where they remain for a number of days.

weller *obs n* a metal founder

welm *dial fm vb* **whelm**, to bury or cover completely

Welshe *obs fm n* **Welsh**

weltre *obs fm vb* **welter**

welvet *obs fm n* **velvet**

wen *n* an excrescence or tumour of various sorts as a sebaceous cyst under the skin *esp* of the head, a goitre or Derbyshire neck, or a tumour on a horse: the Old and Middle English runic letter equivalent to the modern **W**

Wend *n* one of a Slavic people who live in the northern part of East Germany

Wendic *adj* of or pertaining to the Wends *n* the language of the Wends

wendigo *var fm n* **windigo** (*pl* **wendigos**)

wenny *adj* of the nature of a wen: afflicted with wens: similar to a wen (*comp* **wennier** *sup* **wenniest**)

wer see **be**

werde *obs fm ns* **weird, word, world**

werdle *Obs fm n* **world**

were (*vbl infl*) *now S vb* to defend

wereld *Obs fm n* **world**

werlde *obs fm n* **world**

werr *obs fm vb* **wear**, of a ship, to turn away from the wind (the opposite of **tack**)

werrest *Obs fm adj/n* **worst**

werret *dial n* a wart

werse *obs S fm n/vb* **verse**

werste *obs fm n* **verst**

wese *obs fm S vb* **vizy**

wessel *S adv* westward (*var fms incl* **wassel, wastle, wessil, westle**)

west (*adv/adj/n*) *vb* to move towards the west

wester *adj* western *vb* of a heavenly body, to travel westward in its course: of the wind, to shift to the west

westle *var fm S adv* **wessel**

westlin *S adj* western, westerly

westlins *S adv* westward

wete *var fm arch vb* **weet**, to know (of) something *Obs n* liquid

wet fire *n* Greek fire

wetish *var fm adj* **wettish**

wet rot *n* a dark brown decayed state of timber: any of the fungi which cause it

wevil *obs fm n* **weevil**

wex *dial fm n* **wax**

wg *obs S fm now dial vb* **ug**

whakaphoane *NZ n* the Maori insult of showing bare buttocks

whale (*n*) *vb* to participate in whale-fishing: to beat or thrash

whare *NZ n* a Maori hut or dwelling

whate *Obs n* divination: destiny, fortune

whe *dial fm pron* **who**

wheal *n* a flat (circular) hard lump on the skin: a mine in Cornwall *obs n* a pimple *obs vb* to suppurate or gather pus

wheat (*n*) *vb* to grow wheat

wheatear *n* a species of chat, a migrant bird of the thrush family capable of making the journey from Greenland to Africa

wheest *S fm now dial vb* **whist**

whenas *arch conj* in as much as

where (*adv/conj*) *obs fm n* **choir**

wherret *now dial n/vb* (to give) a sharp blow

wherrit *dial vb* to tease, pester *var fm now dial n/vb* **wherret**

whinge *S & dial n* a whine *S & dial vb* to whine

whinger *Austr, S & dial n* one who whines *n* a short sword of the type favoured by Scots in historical times *vb* to stab with such

whipscorpion *n* any of nearly 300 species of terrestrial arachnids usually divided into the whipscorpions proper (creatures which resemble small scorpions) and the tailless whipscorpions. The courtship is an elaborate affair and can, in some cases, last for several days, with the male trying to stimulate his partner by stroking her with his front legs until she is prepared to 'sit' on his little packet of sperm which he deposits on the ground when he thinks she is in a receptive state.

whipstock *n* the handle of a whip

whirret *var fm now dial n/vb* **wherret**

whiss *vb* to hiss: to whistle

whist (*n*) *arch vb* to become silent: to hold one's peace *now dial vb* to command to silence

whiste *obs pa t vb* wit, to know

whister *now dial vb* to whisper

whit (*n*) *vb* to make a shrill, abrupt sound

white (*n/adj*) *vb* to make, become or cover with white

whitefish *n* any of various silvery, salmon-like species of fish found in freshwater of the colder parts of the northern hemisphere and related to various marine fish. The lake-based species – such as the vendace of England and Scotland, the gwyniad of Wales, the pollan of Ireland and the cisco or lake herring of the USA – are believed to be marine fish trapped in lakes at the end of the last Ice Age: a term also used for any commercially important edible marine fish – such as cod or plaice – not necessarily related to the freshwater whitefish

whitewood *n* any of various trees which yield a light-coloured timber *incl* the basswood, cottonwood, tuliptree, wild cinnamon: that timber

whitner *obs fm n* **whitener**

whitret *S & dial n* a weasel

whitster *n* a whitesmith

whitte *obs fm n/adj* **white** *obs fm ns* **whit, wit**

whitter *S n* a chatterbox: a draught of liquor *S vb* to chatter *esp* peevishly: to flutter

whole (*adj/adv*) *n* see **holist** *obs vb* to heal or cure, to make whole

wi *Obs n* a battle, conflict *Obs interj* expressive of regret or anxiety *Obs fm adv* **why**

widder *dial n* a widow

widdle *S & dial n* commotion, bustle or strife *obs S vb* to invoke a curse upon: to beguile or lead astray

widgen *obs fm n* **widgeon**

widgeon *n* the *Anatini penelope*, a migratory surface-feeding duck akin to the teal: name also applied to various ducks of different species *obs n* a fool or simpleton *obs vb* to fool or make a 'widgeon' of

wiener *US n* a frankfurter

wigan *n* a type of stout calico

wigen *obs fm n* **widgeon**

wigeon *var fm n* **widgeon**

wiking *obs fm n* **viking**

wild (*adj/n*) *vb* of a plant or animal, to grow/run/become wild

wild fe see **fe**

willer *n* one who desires (now mainly in combination, such as **ill-willer**): one who exercises his will: one who influences another by will power

willest *2nd pers pres indic vb* will

willet *n* a species of North American snipe

wilne *obs vb* to desire

wiltes *Obs pl* wile, a crafty trick

wimpler *n* a wimple maker: a lock of wavy hair

Winchester measure *n* any of the standard liquid and dry measures of England from AD 972 until their eventual replacement by the imperial system. These were based on those deposited at the ancient Anglo-Saxon capital of England, the city of Winchester. Locally there were various systems, all gradually extinguished over a period of many years. For example, the Winchester bushel and the Scottish ell were both abolished in 1826 but the complete range of imperial measures was not made mandatory until 1878. The Winchester pint was slightly smaller than the imperial pint but both were dwarfed by the mighty Scottish pint which was *approx* three times bigger than the imperial. By contrast, the Winchester pint was much bigger than the Guernsey pint.

windage *n* in such as shooting, an allowance made for the effect of the wind

windas *obs n* an instrument for bending a crossbow

wind egg *n* a soft-shelled or otherwise imperfect egg

windell *obs fm S/now dial n* **windle**

winder (*n*) *now dial vb* to wither

windigo *n* in the mythology of the Chippewa Red Indians, a tribe of cannibals of an island in Hudson Bay: an evil demon in the mythology of various Algonquian Red Indian tribes (*pl* **windigos**)

windle *n* an appliance for winding thread or yarn *S n* a bundle (of straw) *now dial n* a basket: a measure of corn, *approx* 3 bushels *vb* to wind (thread) *now dial vb* to whirl: to meander: to wither: to dwindle

windore *now dial n* a window

windrose *n* any of three poppies, the common wild poppy, bastard wild poppy or the violet horned poppy

wine palm *n* any palm tree the sap of which can be fermented into palm wine

winer *n* one who sells or drinks wine

winge *Austr fm S & dial n/vb* **whinge**

winglet *n* a little wing: the false or bastard wing, a feathered process on the terminal joint of a bird's wing: a small appendage at the base of the wing or wing sheath of various insects and beetles: a small mechanical projection

winse *obs fm vb* **wince**

winser *obs fm n* **wincer**, one who kicks or strikes

winsey *var fm n* **wincey**, a type of cloth

wire heel *n* a defect of the feet of horses or cattle

wireworm *see* **click beetle**

wiselike *S & dial adj* reasonable: becoming, seemly *S & dial adv* fittingly, becomingly

wiseman *n* the earlier *fm* of **wise man** as used for a scholar *esp* one skilled in the magic arts

wisent *n* the zubr

wisk *obs fm n/vb* **whisk**

wisser *Obs n* a leader

wist *pseudo-arch vb* to know

wistle *obs fm vb* **whistle**

witer *S & dial n* one who blames or imputes guilt

withe *n* a binding of such as a flexible strip of willow: a pliant bough: a Jamaican creeping plant, the stalks of which are used for making baskets *now US & dial vb* to bind with a withe

witnes *obs fm n* **witness**

witter *S & dial n* a mark or sign of some kind: a small hole in the ice towards which curling stones are aimed: the barb of such as an arrow or fish hook *Obs adj* wise, knowing: clear, certain *vb* to inform, instruct (*obs* except as the *S & dial n* **wittering**, information)

wivel *obs fm n* **weevil**

wlonk *obs n* something fair or beautiful *Obs adj* rich, splendid (*sup* **wlonkest**, the *comp* is not recorded)

wlt *var fm obs S n* **vult**

wmqwhyle *Obs fm arch adv/adj* **umquhile**

wo *interj* calling a horse to stop: calling a hawk to return *arch fm interj/adv/n* **woe** *obs fm pron* **who**

woader *n* one who cultivates woad, the plant dyer's weed: one who uses the blue dye obtained from its leaves

wodden *obs fm adj* **wooden**

wodder *obs S fm n* **weather**

wodset *obs fm n/vb* **wadset**

wolfe *obs fm ns* **wolf, woof**

wolfkin *n* a young wolf

womby *adj* hollow (*comp* **wombier** *sup* **wombiest**)

womera *n* a stick used as a missile (in Australia)

wonde *obs vb* to hesitate, to avoid, to shrink from

wondred *var fm obs adj* **wondered**, marvellous or wonderful

wondring *obs fm n/adj* **wondering**

wone *var fm now S & dial vb* **won**, to dwell or stay

woning *arch n* the act of dwelling: a dwelling *Obs n* lamentation

wood-end *n* an old shipbuilding term for the end of a plank which fits into a groove

wood pigeon *n* also known as the **ring dove** or, scientifically, as *Columba palumbus*, this bird has a variety of other names (mainly *dial*) such as **cowshot, cowscot, cowshut, cushat, cushie, queece, queest, quice, quist, queist** and **quoice**

woonde *obs fm vb* **wind**, to turn or coil

wor see **be**

worble *var fm n* **warble**, a gadfly induced tumour: the gadfly, the larva of the gadfly *obs S vb* to wriggle or writhe

wordage *n* words collectively: verbiage or excessive wordiness

worde *var fm obs vb* **worth**, to treat with honour *obs fm ns* **word, world** *var fm Obs n* **ord**

worder *n* one who puts something into words

WORD GAMES See below

WORD GAMES – BASIC LINKING WORDS See page 734

WORD GAMES – VERBAL PLAY See page 738

WORD GAMES Apart from the commercially produced games, there are a number of other equally entertaining adult games. They require nothing more than pencil and paper. Of these, both **Code Breaking** and **Pentery Web** are described under **POSTAL WORD GAMES** and **Pentery Web** respectively and **Hangman** is sufficiently well known not to require explanation. Among the remainder, the three best games are **Words**, **French Crosswords** and **Crossword**.

1 **Words** This is an old game known by various names. At its simplest level, one person attempts to guess a 5–letter word chosen by another. However, it is far more entertaining if both players attempt to guess each other's 5–letter word in a simultaneous challenge.

For simplicity of illustration, the following description has Jack attempting to guess a word chosen by Jill. Both players have paper and pencil and both conceal from each other what is written. The description commences with Jill and shows what she writes down, then concerns itself with a continued action by Jack with the emphasis on his technique of play.

(a) Jill chooses the word, (say) **table**. She writes this down on top of her sheet of paper. She gives no clues as to the meaning.
(b) Jack makes a completely random guess at that word. Suppose that he accidently chooses its anagram, **bleat**.
(c) Jill writes this word *directly underneath her own word* as follows:–

T A B L E
B L E A T

Even though both words contain exactly the same letters, *none coincide in position*. Jill says 'Nil'.
(d) Jack guesses again. This time he selects **eager**.
(e) Jill now writes this new word *directly under the last word* thus:–

T A B L E
B L E A T
E A G E R

As the A of **eager** directly corresponds with the A of **table**, she says 'One'. *She provides no other information.*

(f) Jack's paper looks like this:–

· · · · ·

~~B~~ ~~L~~ ~~E~~ ~~A~~ ~~T~~ 0

E A G E R 1

The most sensible ploy available to Jack is to select a new word which *merely changes one letter of* **eager**. The reasons are as follows. Anything else is liable to cause him confusion, no matter what answer Jill gives. But, by changing only one letter, Jill can only give one of three replies and whichever reply she gives will prove helpful.

If she says 'Nil', Jack has found the letter. It *has* to be the one which he *removed* from **eager**. If she says 'One', he knows that he has not found the letter and merely eliminates another letter. If she says 'Two', he has not only found a completely new letter by accident, but *he must still seek that original letter.* Jill cannot make any other reply. If she does, she has made a mistake and Jack must insist that she checks her list. (This, of course, is the reason why Jill *must* write down the words as well.) Jack, therefore, chooses the word **rager**.

(g) Jill replies 'One'. Jack's paper looks like this:–

· · · · ·

~~B~~ ~~L~~ ~~E~~ ~~A~~ ~~T~~ 0

~~E~~ A G E R 1

~~R~~ A G E R 1

(h) Subsequent single letter changes of **rager** to **raged**, **raged** to **raved** and **raved** to **roved** have Jack's paper looking like this:–

· A · · ·

~~B~~ ~~L~~ ~~E~~ ~~A~~ ~~T~~ 0

~~E~~ Ⓐ ~~G~~ ~~E~~ ~~R~~ 1

~~R~~ Ⓐ ~~G~~ ~~E~~ ~~R~~ 1

~~R~~ Ⓐ ~~G~~ ~~E~~ ~~D~~ 1

~~R~~ Ⓐ ~~V~~ ~~E~~ ~~D~~ 1

~~R~~ ~~O~~ ~~V~~ ~~E~~ ~~D~~ 0

Having found the letter **A** by this process of elimination, he now chooses a totally unrelated 5–letter word, which, though it may contain that **A**, has *none* of the letters he has already eliminated.

Within fewer than a dozen further guesses, he should now guess Jill's word *no matter how obscure it may be.*

WORD RULES:–

There are no restrictions as to which words may be used for guessing, except that mere combinations of five letters which are meaningless are invalid. The restrictions as to the categories of words which are the *objects* of guessing is entirely up to the players concerned.

Once expertise has been established, players soon progress from 'easy' words to the 'horrors' such as **crwth** or any of the **Q** words without a **U**. Even so, these should still be discovered within fewer than 20 guesses.

Advanced level players often have three-way or even four-way contests attempting to see who can be the first to discover the other players' words. In these cases, wider sheets of paper are needed in order to record all of the replies from all the players to all of the words.

In such an advanced level contest, Jack would make his first guess at Jill's word, then at Joe's word. Jill would question Joe and Jack. Joe would question Jack and Jill. Assuming

Cont overleaf

that Jack has the word **zyxst**, as his choice, his minimum column headings would be:–

me	*Jill*	*Joe*
Z Y X S T	. . . . .	. . . . .

The clever use of such a 'guessing word' as **eerie** followed by **queen** immediately establishes that the commonest letter, **E**, is not present in Jack's word. Other equally 'vowel-heavy' words used in guessing soon establish that Jack has either a **W** or a **Y** functioning as a vowel and he can still be beaten despite the fact of choosing **zyxst**.

2 **French Crosswords** Two players each draw their own simple 5 × 5 grid. They now take turns at calling out random letters which must be placed in each person's grid but in any square he or she wishes. There are no restrictions as to which letters are chosen and letters may be duplicated. For example, in the sample completed game below, four **E**'s were chosen and only one of these happened to be placed in the corresponding squares of both grids.

After the grids have been filled, scores are made on the following basis. Only the longest word in each vertical or horizontal column counts and a bonus of an extra point is given for a 5–letter word. Thus a 5–letter word scores 6 points, a 4–letter word scores 4 points, a 3–letter word scores 3 points and a 2–letter word, 2 points. The player with the higher total wins.

PLAYER 1

					score
E	A	G	L	E	6
G	D	R	U	N	3 (run)
Y	D	A	T	T	3 (att)
P	A	C	T	E	4 (pact)
T	X	E	L	R	3 (xel)
3* (gyp)	6	6	2 (ut)	6	

*EGYPT is invalid, a proper noun

total 42

PLAYER 2

					score
C	R	Y	P	T	6
L	A	T	L	R	3 (lat)
E	G	G	A	E	3 (egg)
A	D	T	D	E	2 (ad)
N	U	T	E	X	3 (nut)
6	3 (rag)	2 (yt)	4 (lade)	4 (tree)	

total 36

The word rules are entirely up to you, but it is recommended that you use the same as those given for **Crossword**, below.

3 **Crossword** A single grid is drawn. For the purpose of illustration, only the basic game is described and this has a typical grid of 9 × 9. The word, **crossword**, is now inserted on any horizontal or vertical line. Whilst more than two may play, it is ideal for two.

The object of the game is to score points on a basis of one point for each letter used in each valid word created. Players take turns in adding *only* one letter of their own choice to create a valid word. Hence, a 2–letter word scores 2 points, a 3–letter word scores 3 points, but if two 2–letter words are created simultaneously then 4 points are given on a basis of 2 points for each 2–letter word. 5 points are scored if a 3–letter and a 2–letter word are created simultaneously. Obviously only the little words are possible at the beginning but it soon builds up to the much bigger words. There is considerable scope for tactics and, unless one player makes an invalid play, it is an exciting contest with the scores remaining fairly close throughout.

The player who goes first can only create a 2–letter word; the player who goes second has a choice of three different moves. He or she can create a fresh 2–letter word, extend the existing 2–letter word into a 3–letter word or create two simultaneous 2–letter words by placing his or her letter adjacent to that of the first player. The options available to the first player for his or her second move obviously depend upon the situation now prevailing.

Play continues in this fashion until neither player can possibly add any further letters. Should a player make an error, then the offending letter is removed either with a rubber or typewriter correction fluid. In this event, the player not only forfeits his or her turn but also loses *all* of the score he or she has accumulated to date. The word rules are given below and a reasonable time limit should be imposed for each move. At the expiry of a reasonable period of time, play passes to the opponent without loss of score.

The following example of a completed game is one which the author lost to his fellow wordsmith, Tom Wright, the *Derbyshire Times* word-search compiler, by the narrow margin of 91 points to 94 points. A standard dictionary supplemented by access to the words of the *Advanced Dictionary* was available in the event of dispute. Disputes arose, but no loss of score was incurred. Both players were fully aware of the complete range of 2–letter words in the *Advanced Dictionary* and used them liberally.

H			D	A	B	S		
E	S		A		U	T	S	
	W	A	R	P	S		H	
	I	D	E	A		Z		E
C	R	O	S	S	W	O	R	D
O	E	S		S	Y		O	I
X			B	E	E		E	T
Y	E	X	E	S		E	S	S
	U		T		T	E		

Tom has suggested that a bonus score should be available for a 7–letter word, to compensate for loss of all points at a late stage in the game. Perhaps (say) 50 points for a 7–letter word, 60 points for an 8–letter word and 70 points for a 9–letter word. Readers' comments would be welcome on this subject and a consensus view will prevail in future editions of *Pears Advanced Word-Puzzler's Dictionary*.

Whilst a 9 × 9 square is ideal for a fairly quick game and any other 9–letter word may be chosen instead of **crossword**, there are no limits as to the size of the grid. It is essential, however, that the original word extends the whole length of any one horizontal or vertical line.

Cont overleaf

WORD RULES:–

(a) Any standard dictionary supplemented by *Pears Advanced Word-Puzzler's Dictionary* is to be used in the event of dispute.

(b) The guide to word validity is that given in *Pears Advanced Word-Puzzler's Dictionary* as shown by examples of individual words likely to be the subject of dispute together with any other general comments.

(c) Essentially, this invalidates any word which requires an initial capital letter for *all* its meanings, foreign words, hyphenated words and abbreviations.

(d) All other words including American and other non-UK English, literary Scottish, slang, dialects of a language rooted in English, obscenities, plurals, reasonably inferred inflected forms (even though such are rarely given in most dictionaries), obsolete and nonce words are acceptable provided they appear in either the basic standard dictionary or *Pears Advanced Word-Puzzler's Dictionary.*

(Players will find that the following special subject entry, **WORD GAMES – BASIC LINKING WORDS**, very helpful and the sub-section, **2–LETTER WORDS**, provides a mnemonic for success. See page 176.)

This is an original invention by the author, Peter Newby, who retains all copyright for all commercial exploitation. The date of copyright being the date of publication of *Pears Advanced Word-Puzzler's Dictionary.*

WORD GAMES – BASIC LINKING WORDS Restricting examples to those found in just one dictionary (in this case, *Chambers 20th Century Dictionary*), it is amazing just how many 3–letter words can be created from a 2–letter word by the simple addition of another letter. Such 'extended' words are of immense value in the various crossword-type games. (See **Crossword** above and **qwa** for practical illustrations.)

The central column consists of 2–letter words. To convert any of these 2–letter words into a 3–letter word, simply add one letter from either side. For example, **ad**. This is a genuine word valid for play. If the B is selected from the *left-hand side*, this converts **ad** into **bad**. The C converts **ad** into **cad**, the D into **dad** etc. If the D is selected from the *right-hand side* this converts **ad** into **add**. Similarly, the O converts **ad** into **ado** and the S converts **ad** into **ads**.

b c d f g h l m p r s w	AD	d o s
g h k m n s t v w	AE	
b d f h l p y	AH	a s
s t	AI	a d l m n r s t
b c d g h j l m n p r t y	AM	p
b c d f g m n p r t v w	AN	a d e n t y
d e f g h k l m p r t v w	AS	h k p s
b c e f g h k l m o p r s t v w	AT	e
c d f h j k l m p r s t w y	AW	e l n s
l p r s t w z	AX	e
b c d f g h j k l m n p r s w	AY	e s u
	BE	d e g l n t y z
	BO	a b d g h o p r s t w x y
a	BY	e s
	DA	b d g h k l m n p s w y

a u	DO	c d e g h n o p r s t w
k l p s t y z	EA	r s t u
b c d f g j l n p r s t v w	EE	l n
r	EH	s
b c e g m s t z	EL	d f k l m s t
g h r w	EM	s u
b d e f g h k m p r s t w y	EN	d e s
h p	ER	a e g k r s
h l m o r t y	ES	s
h k s v y	EX	
	FA	b d g h n r s t w y
	FY	s
	GI	b e f g n o p s t
a e	GO	b d e o s t v y
	GU	b e m n p r s t y
a c	HA	d e g h j m p s t w y
s t	HE	m n p r s t w x y
c g	HI	c d e m n p s t
m o p w z	HO	a b d e g p s t w y
a b d f g h k l m n r t	ID	e s
g k	IF	s
a b d f g h k l p r s t w y	IN	k n s
b g	IO	n
a b h l m n s t w	IS	h m
a b c d f g h k l n p r s t w	IT	a s
	JO	b e g t w y
s	KA	e s t w y
s	KY	e
a	LA	b c d g h m p r s t w x y
	LI	b d e g n p s t
	LO	b g o p r s t w x y
	MA	c d e g k m n p r s t w y
	ME	l n s t u w
	MI	d l m r s x
	MO	a b d e g o p r u w
	MY	s
a m	NA	b e g m n p y
	NO	b d g h r t w y
b c f g h j k l m n r s y	OB	i s
b c d g h m n p r s t	OD	d e s
d f g h j m r t v w	OE	s
o	OF	f t
b d f n o p s	OH	m o s
p	OI	k l s

Cont overleaf

c d e i o s t w y	ON	e s
b c d g l m t w z	OO	f h n p r s
b c d f h l m o p s t w	OP	e s t
b c d f l m n o t	OR	b c e s t
f m s y	OU	k p r s t
b c d h j k l m n p r s t v w y	OW	e l n s
b c f l p s v	OX	
b c f g h j l n s t	OY	e s
s	PA	d h l m n p r s t w x y
	PI	a c e g n p t x
	PO	a d h i m p s t w x z
a e i o u	RE	d e f h m n p s t v
a i	SH	e y
	SI	b c m n p r s t x
d	SO	b c d g h l n p s t u v w x y
	ST	s y
e i	TA	b e g i j k m n p r s t u w x
a	TE	a d e f g l n s w
	TI	c d e g l n p s t
	TO	d e g m n o p r t w y
b d f h j l m p r t v y	UG	h s
b c f g h l m r s t	UM	s
b d f g m n p r s t	UN	i
c g h o p s t y	UP	s
b c f g l n o p	UR	d e n s
b g o p s y	US	e
b c g h j n o p r t	UT	s
a e o	WE	b d e m n t y
t	WO	e g k n o p s t w
a b d e k l n o p r s t w	YE	a n p s t w x
	YO	b n s u w
a	YU	g k p s
d	ZO	a o s

For the word games, **Crossword, French Crosswords** and **Word for Word®** all of these 2–letter and 3–letter words may be used quite freely. For the word games, **Kan-U-Go®** and **Lexicon®** the 2–letter word, **ky**, has to be rejected (it is a plural); similarly most of the 3–letter extensions using the letter S must not be used. This is not automatic, e.g. the word, **as**, plus S becomes **ass**. It should be noted that **een** is the plural of **ee** and should be deleted from this table by players of either of those games.

Whilst players of **Scrabble®** in the UK, New Zealand, South Africa and the West Indies may use all these words without restriction, championship players in Singapore will need to delete such as **ee** and **een** because, being Scottish words, this renders them invalid under their local rules. Likewise, championship players in Australia, Canada and the USA will need to delete all the words not found in *The Official Scrabble Players Dictionary*. This includes the following 2–letter words: **ea, ee, fy, gi, gu, io, ky, mo, ob, oi, oo, ou, po, st, te, ug, um, ur, yo, yu** and **zo**, together with any given plurals for those words.

Finally, players of the children's game, **Dixit®**, must reject the vast majority of these words as they do not appear in their reference work, *Collins Minigem Dictionary*.

Obviously, there are far more 2–letter and 3–letter words than shown here. *The Official Scrabble Players Dictionary*, for example, lists **aa, ar, ba, bi, de, ef, et, mu, nu, om, os, pe, xi, xu** and **ya**. Whilst some of these are also found in *Chambers*, complicated local rules render them invalid for championship **Scrabble** play in the UK, Singapore and South Africa but not in New Zealand or the West Indies.

A mnemonic for the great number of 2–letter words valid for word game play and listed in the *Advanced Dictionary* is given in the sub-section, **2–LETTER WORDS**, on page 176.

Extending consideration to the remaining 3–letter words of *Chambers*, it will be found that all but 10 of its words valid for word play are capable of being brought into use by the 2–letter words of *Pears Advanced Word-Puzzler's Dictionary*. The ten exceptions are **apt, ave, eve, fry, gju, jib, jiz, jud, nth** and **uds**. Therefore, any of the following words is capable of being produced from at least one 2–letter word. (**Aba**, for example, can be based upon either **ab** or **ba**, neither of which appears in *Chambers*.)

aba	baa	cub	eik	gag	ivy	let	oaf	pyx	sar	uva
abb	bag	cud	eke	gal	jab	leu	oak	qua	sec	vac
ace	bap	cue	euk	gap	jag	lev	oar	rag	seg	veg
act	bar	deb	ewk	gar	jak	lew	oca	raj	sei	vet
aft	bib	dew	ewt	gau	jap	ley	och	rap	set	via
aga	big	dey	fed	ged	jar	lez	oke	ria	sew	vie
age	biz	dib	feu	geo	jet	lud	old	rib	sey	vim
ake	bra	die	few	get	jig	lux	olm	rig	sez	vol
alb	bub	dig	fey	gey	keb	luz	ope	rim	ski	wag
ale	bud	dim	fez	gnu	ked	mud	opt	rip	sly	wap
all	buy	dip	fib	gym	kef	mux	ova	roc	spy	war
alp	cab	div	fie	gyp	keg	neb	pec	rok	sub	why
als	cap	dry	fig	hub	kep	ned	ped	rom	sud	wig
alt	car	dub	fir	hue	ket	nef	peg	rot	sue	wry
ape	cep	dud	fix	huh	key	nep	pep	rub	suk	wud
arc	cig	due	fiz	hyp	kip	net	pet	ruc	suq	yak
ark	cly	duo	flu	ice	koa	new	pew	rud	thy	yap
arm	cog	dux	fly	ich	kos	nib	ply	rue	try	yep
art	col	ebb	fog	icy	led	nil	pro	sab	tub	yip
ary	cos	ecu	fop	ilk	leg	nim	pry	sac	tui	zap
auf	cot	eff	fub	ill	lei	nip	pub	sag	twa	zed
auk	coz	eft	fud	imp	lek	nix	pud	sal	tyg	zip
ava	cry	egg	gab	irk	lep	nub	puy	sap	ule	zuz

The really keen word player can produce even more 3–letter words by consulting the *Advanced Dictionary*. **Aa**, for example, can become **aac, aad, aag, aah, aak, aal, aam, aan, aar, aas, aat** and **aay** as well as such as **caa** and **daa** , none of which is listed above.

When using these tables it should be noted that *Chambers 20th Century Dictionary* has a word power far greater than most single volume dictionaries and, unless your basic dictionary or the *Advanced Dictionary* actually defines any of these words, such extensions as plurals cannot be presumed. Players of games which bar slang or plurals must take extra care.

WORD GAMES – VERBAL PLAY Radio and television have adapted some of the best traditional games of this type, thus giving *20 Questions, Call My Bluff* and *Give Us A Clue.* Television once attempted to duplicate the classic game of *Proverbs*, but presented it in such a silly format with performers who were so inept that it failed to survive a small pilot series. The game, however, is really great fun and the readers who play it will enjoy it far more than any viewer who suffered the version on television.

1 **Proverbs** Essentially a party game but, in any group, there will always be tacit recognition of the players deemed to be experts, those who are average and the 'Oh-dear-how-can-we-fit-so-and-so-into-a-game-of-word-play' people. Fortunately, it is one of the few word games in which all can compete equally providing a little tact is used. The description assumes such a mixture, that it is an equal mix of males and females and a copy of a dictionary of proverbs has been obtained for the party. It is a contest of men versus women with each team attempting to guess the proverb selected by the other. For simplicity's sake assume that there are four men, four women, that both teams have an expert and both teams have a 'so-and-so'. Both teams choose a leader and (say) the women have the first choice of proverb. That being so, the men leave the room.

A proverb is chosen. Suppose it is **Too many cooks spoil the broth**. As will be seen shortly, words such as **cooks** and **broth** will prove to be tricky. These are best handled by an expert or a better than average player. Words such as **many** and **spoil** are about average and words such as **too** and **the** are perfect for the poorer than average and the 'so-and-so'. The best leader is not necessarily the expert but the one with a natural understanding of people, and often that can be the 'so-and-so'. The leader assigns each player one word of the chosen proverb and then gives two players an additional word each. Thus the player sitting in chair no. 1 has the word **too**, the player in chair no. 2 has **many**, chair 3 **cooks** and chair 4 **spoil**. Chair 1 is given the additional word **the** and chair 2 has the additional word **broth**.

The men return. Their 'so-and-so' has already been primed on how to cope, as will be seen shortly. Man no. 1 asks the woman sitting in chair no. 1 any question he wishes. She makes a reasonable reply *ensuring that it contains her first word,* **too**, somewhere. His task is to frame a question which will highlight a contrived insertion of the designated word. Her task is to disguise that word as well as she can. In the case of a word like **too** this is comparatively easy. Man no. 2 asks the woman sitting in chair no. 2 any question he wishes and gives her a task of average difficulty in disguising her use of **many** in the reply. As is now obvious, both **cooks** and **broth** are the 'giveaway' words so these should be handled by the best women. The 'so-and-so' man, who will even have difficulty in thinking of a question to pose, has been told in advance that there is no objection to anyone asking the same question of another player. Thus he repeats the question of a wittier colleague in order to avoid the embarrassment of watching him think in slow motion.

Once the complete proverb has been given, the men have to name it; otherwise they are forced to leave the room whilst the women make a fresh selection. This continues until such time as the men can take over. Alternatively, the teams can take turns. However, if the first choice is made and the men lose the first game then they can be consigned to washing the pots whilst the women take their time choosing the next proverb! The more proverbs the men fail to guess, the more pots are dealt with in the interims.

2 **Word Guessing Games**

(a) Open the dictionary and select an unusual word. Challenge the opponent to guess its meaning. Award points on a basis of maximum points for guessing it completely with fewer points given as more clues to that meaning are made.

(b) Alternatively, name the word, give your own definition and challenge the opponent on a true or false basis.

Essentially this is a simplified form of **Who, What or Where?** which is typical of the verbal word play which requires advanced planning to be effective. Placing the emphasis on the unbelievable but true, a series of facts relating to a particular subject is given. The more obscure data gradually give way to the better known or more likely facts.

Sample question: *Which country had the following monarchs? The first of whom was Gorm the Old.* If no guesses are made or a wrong answer is given then the remainder are named, one at a time, *Harald Bluetooth, Eric the Evergood, Eric Plough-penny, Nils, Svein Forkbeard, Valdemar the Victorious, Knut the Good, Eric Klipping, Frederick I, II, III* etc to *IX* and *Christian I, II, III* etc to *X*.

As a team game, an upper limit of (say) 12 facts is available and points are awarded on a decreasing basis of 12 down to 1 according to the number of facts given. A team is permitted only one guess for each fact given. As an individual competition, anyone may guess at any time but is permitted one guess only and is eliminated from the contest on giving a wrong answer. The answer, incidently, to the above question is Denmark, though Norway with *Halfdan the Black, Erik Bloodaxe, Olaf the Quiet, Magnus Barelegs* and *Harald Greyskin* would have been just as suitable and it is not only the Scandanavian countries which provide the oddly named monarchs. Portugal has had its *Alfonso the Fat, Maria the Mad* and *Pedro the Severe* whilst the Holy Roman Empire has a multitude of oddly named people such as *Charles the Fat* or *Henry the Fowler,* to name but two. By placing the emphasis on such peculiar facts as these, it ensures a game of fun rather than a serious test of general knowledge. Any questions may be asked so long as the researchers can provide a sufficiency of ludicrous details which enable either form of the game to be played. (See entries for **SALMON** and **wood pigeon** for suitable examples.)

(c) A one-off word game which requires no research is **Dreams**. One person volunteers to guess the details of a dream which one member of the party has revealed to everyone else. The volunteer asks any questions about it which he or she wishes so long as the answer can be a 'Yes' or a 'No'. Everyone else choruses yesses and noes and appears to have full knowledge of even the most bizarre details until it finally dawns upon the questioner that every question ending with a consonant gets a 'Yes' and a vowel a 'No'.

wordies *S fm pl* **worthies**

wordle *var fm n* **wortle**

word square *n* a very ancient practice as shown by this Latin example which has been found carved or scratched on stone at Roman sites as far apart as Cirencester, Pompeii and Dura-Europos in Mesopotamia.

R O T A S
O P E R A
T E N E T
A R E P O
S A T O R

Apart from the fact that it reads the same in all directions, many suppose that it has an esoteric significance. Taken at face value **Arepo** is a personal name and the whole square translates as '*The sower, Arepo, controls the wheels with care.*' However, of the various anagrammatic reasons advanced for this concept, the classic is the fact that the constituent letters can be reformed in the shape of a cross centred on the solitary N to produce PATERNOSTER (Our Father) in both directions together with a detached A and O (Alpha and Omega, a synonym for God) at the extremities of this cross. (For similar esoteric word detection see **gematria**.)

The writer's own contribution to this genre has six different words, each an anagram of the other five and also capable of being read in any direction.

T E A
A T E
E A T

The larger squares are much more difficult to produce but among the classics are:

P R E P A R E
R E M O D E L
E M U L A T E
P O L E M I C
A D A M A N T
R E T I N U E
E L E C T E D

```
O R A N G U T A N G
R A N G A R A N G A
A N D O L A N D O L
N G O T A N G O T A
G A L A N G A L A N
U R A N G U T A N G
T A N G A T A N G A
A N D O L A N D O L
N G O T A N G O T A
G A L A N G A L A N
```

The meanings of the various unusual words will be found on the appropriate pages.

Wordsworth (*pers n*) *n* a word game for a group or a classroom which requires advance planning. It can be played in various ways but the essence of the challenge is the same. (note: It can also be played on a one-to-one basis by two players who can produce words and definitions sufficiently quickly not to require advance planning.)

Prior to play, the organizer chooses a word (say) **beard**. From this he or she constructs as many words as considered reasonable e.g. **bad, bar, bard, bare, bear, dab** and **drab**. The contestants try to discover the basic word by being given clues to the other words. In this example, the contestants are told they are attempting to discover a 5-letter word of which the first, third and fifth letters mean '*That which is not good*', or the first, third and fourth letters mean '*Something found in a tavern*'. Clues of this nature continue until the word is discovered.

worl *obs vb* to whirl

worm tube *n* that in which a tube worm dwells

wormwood *n* any of a genus of European herbs *esp* the species also known as absinthe and noted for its bitter taste. Its leaves are used in the making of a medicinal tonic, for destroying intestinal worms and in the making of vermouth and absinthe. They were formerly used as a flavouring for ale and to protect clothes and bedding from moths and fleas: that which embitters or makes bitter (*fig*) *modf n* of various species of moths, as the **wormwood pug** or the **wormwood eyelet**

worn (*adj*) *obs vb* to waste away

worple *var fm dial n* **warple**

worre *obs fm n/vb* **war**

worse (*adj/adv/n*) *now nonce vb* to make or become worse

worser *adj/adv* worse *vb* to make worse

worsest *dial sup* worse

worsse *obs fm adj* **worse** *Obs fm adv* **worse**

worst (*adj/adv/n*) *vb* to defeat

worste *Obs fm adv* **worst**

wort *n* a plant *esp* a herb used as food or medicine, *arch* except in combination as cole*wort*, liver*wort*, navel*wort* etc): the sweet infusion of malt which, after fermentation, becomes beer *obs S n* the snout of a pig *obs S vb* of a pig, to root or dig up with its snout (also see **wroot**)

worte *obs fm n* **wort**, that which after fermentation becomes beer

wortle *n* an implement used for drawing out such as wire or lead piping

wose *obs fm n/vb* **ooze**

wounde *obs fm vb* **wound**

wp *obs S fm adv* **up**

wr *Obs fm pron* **our**

wrabble *obs vb* to wriggle

wrane *obs S & dial fm n* **wren**

wrape *obs erron fm vb* **rape**, to delight

wraple *obs fm S vb* **warple**

wrappe *obs fm vb* **wrap**

wrase *obs n* a band or wreath of cloth placed upon the head of a woman as cushioning when carrying a heavy object

wrasse *n* a perch-like, often highly coloured marine fish of which there are many species *incl* the goldsinny, rock cock, ballan wrasse, saddle wrasse, cuckoo wrasse, rainbowfish, hogfish, and harlequin tuskfish. When resting, tropical wrasses often bury themselves in the sand for safety and one species, the Hawaiian rainbow wrasse, emulates its relative, the parrotfish, by secreting a mucous canopy around itself. Many species feed on the parasites found on larger fish.

wraste *obs fm vb* **wrest**

wrastle *now US, S & dial var fm n/vb* **wrestle**

wrastler *S & dial fm n* **wrestler** (also see **warstler**)

wrath *(n/adj) obs vb* to rage

wrathe *obs fm n* **wrath** *obs pa t vb* writhe

wray *obs vb* to accuse, to inform against: to betray: to disclose: to exhibit: to void excrement

wreathen *adj* wreathed in the senses of twining or twisted, intertwined but not in the senses of garlanded, contorted (used of such as columns) or wrinkled (of a facial expression)

wren tit *n* a titmouse-like American bird with the general habits of a wren and closely related to the babblers. Some experts include it with the babblers whilst others have it in a family of its own, which conveniently keeps all the babblers in the Old World. (Also see **Timaliiae**)

wrester *n* one who wrests in such senses as wrenching, twisting, straining, perverting or distorting

wrimple *obs vb* to pucker the face: to wrinkle *obs n* a fold or wrinkle

wrine *obs vb* to squeal like a pig

wringe *var fm obs n* **wrench**, a trick or cunning device

wrinklet *n* a little wrinkle

WRITERS See below

writhen *adj* contorted

writher *(n) obs n* one who perverts

wroken *arch pa pple vb* wreak

wroot *obs vb* of a pig, to dig up with its snout: *obs n* the snout of a pig *Obs vb* of worms or men, to turn over the soil (also see **wort**)

wrosse *obs var fm adj* **worse**

wrote *(vbl infl) var fm obs vb* **wroot**

wryneck *n* any of various small birds of the woodpecker family rather like ordinary perching birds in appearance

WRITERS Concerning periods of word usage, certain authors, poets, dramatists, men of letters and the historic printer and publisher, William Caxton, are mentioned in the *Advanced Dictionary* in the various footnotes relating to divergent views. In chronological order they are:

'*Obs* period' **Chaucer** ?1340–1400: **Caxton** 1422–1491
'*obs* period' to the present day **Spenser** 1552–1599: **Marlowe** 1564–1593: **Shakespeare** 1564–1616: **Donne** 1572–1631: **Jonson** 1573–1637: **Webster** ?1580–?1634: **Milton** 1608–1674: **Bunyan** 1628–1688: **Dryden** 1631–1700: **Swift** 1667–1745: **Dr Johnson** 1709–1784: **Goldsmith** 1728–1774: **Burns** 1759–1796: **Scott** 1771–1832: **Southey** 1774–1843: **Lamb** 1775–1834: **Shelley** 1792–1822: **Browning**, Elizabeth Barrett 1806–1861: **Darwin** 1809–1882: **Browning**, Robert 1812–1889: **Hughes**, Thomas 1822–1896: **Huxley**, T H 1825–1895.

Additionally, the entry for the word, **coexert**, mentions a certain Bishop Ken whose literary efforts fall somewhat short of this distinguished assembly. His contribution to literature is restricted to numerous nonce words, all prefixed 'co-'. These appeared in his writings of 1721. Where other writers are mentioned, the date of writing has no significance in this context.

ws *obs S fm pron* **us**

wsz *obs S fm pron* **us**

wu *Obs fm adv* **how** (+*cap*) *n* a Chinese dialect of the Yangtse valley (50 million speakers)

wunde *Obs fm n* **wound**, an injury (*pl* **wunden, wundes**)

wy *var fm S & dial n* **quey** *var fm obs S n* **wye** *obs fm n* **way** *Obs fm adv* **why**

wye *n* a Y-shaped object of various sorts *var fm S & dial n* **quey** *obs S n* a warrior: a man of noble stature

wyper *var fm n* **wiper**, a cam or other mechanical part which, periodically, causes a change of movement *obs fm n* **wiper**, other senses

X

xa *obs fm n* **shah**, the title of the former emperors of Persia (Iran)

xal *Obs fm vb* **shall**

xanthein *n* the soluble yellow colouring matter of flowers (compare with **xanthine**)

xanthine *n* the insoluble yellow colouring matter of flowers (compare with **xanthein**)

xebec *n* a small Mediterranean sailing vessel

xel *Obs fm vb* **shall**

xeme *n* a fork-tailed gull of the genus *Xema*

xenia *n* the supposed influence of foreign pollen upon that pollinated *pl* xenium, a present or offering

xenial *adj* of or pertaining to hospitality

xenium *n* a present given to a guest or stranger: an offering such as that made by subjects of a prince as he passes through their estates (*pl* **xenia**)

xenon *n* a heavy inert gas

Xenopus *n* the genus of the clawed frog, often called the pregnancy frog as it was once extensively used by doctors to test pregnancy in women

xerasia *n* a disease of hair manifest in excessive dryness

xeriff *var fm n* **shereef**

xeroma *n* abnormal dryness of a bodily part due to failure of fluid secretion

xerosis *n* xeroma (*pl* **xeroses**)

xerotic *adj* suffering xerosis: of bodily tissues, abnormally dry

XES An example of a dingbat which translates as 'sex reversal' – a rather curious natural phenomenon. Various creatures change sex. The European flat oyster changes sex several times. In cooler waters it usually changes sex once a year but, in the Mediterranean, it will change several times in one year. A particular species of shrimp begins life as a male but later becomes a female. A species of fish found in the China Sea swims in a small group of one male and several females but, if the male is removed, one of the females changes sex and takes over the leadership of the group. The female common frog can be induced to change sex if kept at a permanent temperature of 80°F (27°C). (note: Dingbats®, apart from being a popular newspaper feature, is now available as a commercial game.)

xi *n* the fourteenth letter of the Greek alphabet

xiph *obs n* a swordfish

xu *n* a monetary unit of Vietnam (*pl* **xu**)

xylem *n* wood as a tissue of the body of the higher plants – its functions *incl* conducting water and mineral salts from the roots to all other parts

xylogen *n* xylem

xylomancy *n* divination by the use of twigs

xyrid *n* a sedge-like herb of the genus *Xyris*

xyst *var fm n* **xystus**

xysta *pl* xystum

xyster *n* a surgeon's scraping instrument

xysti *pl* xystus

xyston *n* (the polished shaft of) an ancient Greek spear

xystum *var fm n* **xystus** (*pl* **xysta**)

xystus *n* an ancient Greek covered portico used for athletic contests: an ancient Roman open walkway planted with trees (*pl* **xysti**)

Y

y- *prefix* except for a word such as **yttrium** (a rare earth metal named after Ytterby in Sweden where it was discovered) words which begin with a y followed by a consonant are normally Old or Middle English and *Obs*. Some (such as **ybrent** and **ydight**) continued as *arch fms*, gradually expiring by the 18th century. Only two or three (such as **yclept** and **yclad**) are still extant. Finally, there are the psuedo-archaic words (such as **yravish**) which were coined in early modern English times. The prefix was, originally, a preposition having the sense of 'with, together' but eventually ceased to have any real meaning and was as old fashioned to readers in the days of Queen Elizabeth I as 'Ye olde tea shoppe' is to us today.

ya *n* the twenty-eighth and final letter of the Arabic alphabet *interj* of disgust, contempt, defiance, derision

yables *dial adv* perhaps

yacker *Austr n* hard work

yadder *var fm dial n/vb* **yedder**

yaff *S & dial vb* of a dog, to bark or yelp: of a person, to prattle: to nag

yai *dial fm arch adv* **yea**

yakker *var fm Austr n* **yakka**, hard work

yamen *n* the official residence of a Chinese mandarin

yankie *S n* a rude clamorous woman

Yapese *n* a Micronesian language of Yap Island in the Pacific

yapness *S & dial n* hunger

yard (*n*) *US & colonial vb* to enclose farm animals in a yard: to store such as wood in a yard *Manx vb* of a coroner, to summon a servant for hiring

yardage *n* storage at a yard: the charge levied for such: the cutting of coal at a price fixed per yard: the number of yards so cut

yarde *obs fm n* **yard**

yarely *arch adv* skilfully: promptly

yaren *obs fm n* **yarn**

yark *var fm now S & dial n/vb* **yerk**

yarne *obs fm n* **yarn**

yarrow *n* milfoil or nosebleed, a strongly-scented common herb of wasteland and road-side sometimes used, medicinally, as a tonic

yarta *var fm Shet n/adj* **jarta**

yaspen *obs fm dial n* **yepsen**

yatter *S vb* tiresome, persistent chatter *S vb* to chatter in this fashion

ybe see **be**

yblent *arch adj* blended

yborn *obs adj* born: borne

ybound *obs pa pple vb* bind

ybrent *obs adj* burnt

ych *obs fm pron* **I** (also see **ch**)

yclad *arch adj* clothed

yclept *pa pple arch vb* clepe, to call: to name (the only part still extant and used in a mildly humorous context; used adjectivally it means called, named, styled)

yd *obs n* corn land (still extant in Welsh for corn)

ydant *obs fm S adj* **eident**

ydight *obs adj* prepared

ye *arch pron* you, in the sense of both the person addressed and others. Essentially it is the *pl* of **thou** as:– **thou** (*pl* **ye**), **thee** (*pl* **you**), **thine** (*pl* **yours**), **thy** (*pl* **your**) *arch demonstrative adj* the *obs fm n* **eye** (*pl* **yen**)

yea *arch adv* yes *dial interj* a command to a horse to come forward towards one

yeables *obs S dial adv* perhaps

yean *arch vb* of a ewe or a she-goat, to bring forth young *obs n* an eanling or yeanling

yeanling *arch n* a young lamb or kid (also *fig*)

yeard *obs S fm n* **yard**

yeaspen *obs fm dial n* **yepsen**

yeblins *dial adv* perhaps

yedder *dial n* an osier or pliant twig *dial vb* to interweave with such

yek *dial fm n* **oak**

yelder *obs fm n* **elder**, the tree

yelm *now dial n* a bundle of straw laid out for thatching *dial vb* to select the straw for thatching

yepe see **epe**

yepsen *dial n* the hands cupped together in the form of a bowl: as much as can be held in this fashion

yepsintle *var fm dial n* **yepsen**

yerk *now S & dial n* a kick: a twitch: (the sound of) a blow or strike *now S & dial vb* to whip or strike: to stitch or bind tightly: to jerk: of animals, to spring suddenly

yespen *Obs fm dial n* **yepsen**

yester *poet adj* of yesterday *obs n* yesterday

yestern *arch adj* of yesterday *arch adv* yesterday

yeter *obs n* a founder or caster of metal

yetlin *dial n* cast iron

yetter *var fm obs n* **yeter**

yevall *obs fm n* **giveale**

yex *now dial n* a hiccup *now S & dial vb* to hiccup: to belch

yexer *now S & dial n* one who yexes

yf *obs fm conj* **if**

yft *Obs fm n* **gift**

Yggdrasil *n* in Norse myth, the great ash tree, the roots and branches of which extend throughout the universe

ygo *obs adv* ago

yhi *dial fm arch adv* **yea**

yi *dial fm arch adv* **yea**

yibble *var fm dial vb* **yivel**

yih *dial fm arch adv* **yea**

yivel *dial vb* to make a crooked furrow in ploughing (*infl fms incl* **yiveling**)

yk *Obs fm pron* **I**

yl *obs n* an isle

ylaste *var fm Obs vb* **ylast**, to perform: to endure

ylem *n* the prime substance from which, in some theories, the elements have developed

ylike *obs adj* like: similar *obs adv* likewise: equally *obs vb* to please *Obs n* an equal

ylp *Obs n* an elephant

ymeint *obs pa pple now dial vb* meng

ymone *Obs n* sexual intercourse

ymp *obs fm n* **imp**

ympet *Obs n* impetus

yn *n* a place (*obs* except as a syllable in English place names) *obs fm n* **inn** *obs adj* with young: in lamb *Obs fm prep* **in**

ynambu *n* a large species of tinamou, a bird which resembles a guinea fowl with a pheasant's plumage but is related to the ostrich

yo *interj* of incitement to effort

yod *n* the tenth letter of the Hebrew alphabet

yodler *var fm n* **yodeller**, one who yodels

yogh *n* the Middle English letter, ȝ, which represented various sounds *esp* y and hh and is replaced in modern English by y as in lay, w as in law and gh as in daughter and enough (see **enow**)

yote *dial vb* to pour: to soak: to cast metal

yoter *obs n* one who casts metal

youthe *obs fm n* **youth**

yplasde *obs S pa pple vb* place

yr *obs fm n* **ire** *Obs fm pron* **her**

yravish *obs pseudo-arch fm vb* **ravish**

yrk *Obs fm arch vb* **irk**

ys *adj* low lying (*Obs* except in the modernised form of 'is' as a syllable in English place names though, in Welsh place names, ys is extant with the sense of 'below') *obs fm pron* **his** (also see *vb* **be**)

ysope *obs fm n* **hyssop**

yt *obs fm pron* **it**

yttria *n* the oxide of yttrium

yttrious *adj* pertaining to or containing yttria

yttrium see **y-**

yu *n* precious jade *obs fm pron* **you**

yuehchukene *n* a substance derived from a Chinese shrub of the citrus family used in the treatment of snake bites and the basis of a 'week after' contraceptive pill currently (January 1987) undergoing scientific testing

yuhina see **Timaliiae**

yule (*n*) *dial vb* to celebrate Christmas (the *var dial fms n* (hence *vb*) **yule** are many and varied *incl* such diverse *fms* as **gule, hule, jiul, ool** and **yool**)

yvi *Obs fm n* **ivy**

yw *Obs fm pron* **you**

ywroht *Obs fm arch adj* **ywrought**

ywroken *arch adj* punished, avenged

ywrought *arch adj* worked, made

yzard *obs fm arch n* **izzard**

Z

za *n* though written differently, the eleventh and the seventeenth letters of the Arabic alphabet: a musical term for B-flat in Tartini's system of solmization

zab *slg n* the penis

Zabian *var fm* **Sabian**

zabra *n* a small sailing vessel used in historical times by the Spanish and Portuguese

zabre *obs fm n* **zabra**

zad *now dial n* the letter Z *dial adj* exact

zaffre *n* an impure oxide of cobalt used as a blue colouring matter for such as pottery (note: The *var fm* is the unlisted anagram, **zaffer**)

zährte *n* a migratory bream-like fish found in the Baltic, North and Black Seas which, like the salmon, breeds in freshwater. Landlocked populations also exist in rivers and lakes.

zal *n* the ninth letter of the Arabic alphabet

zam *dial adj* half-hearted *obs dial n* sweat

zambo *n* the offspring of a Negro and a Red Indian

zambra *n* a Spanish dance

zander *n* a species of pike-perch (see **sander**)

zante *n* the wood of the sumach or European smoke tree, a tree which in flower has a smoke-like appearance

Zappit *n* the andagram puzzle game. The taskmaster selects an anagram combination to which he or she adds any suitable letter which produces an andagram. For example, the 6-letter combination DEGNRU with the addition of the letter A provides **enguard** or with an O has a choice of words including **undergo** or with a U provides **unurged**. The andagram (say) **enguard** is then named. The definitions of the anagrams of DEGNRU (**dunger, durgen, gerund** and **nudger**) are given without naming the words themselves. The contestant now has to decide which letter of **enguard** is surplus to requirement.

1 Any animal which provides manure

2 A dwarf

3 A verbal noun

4 One who pokes gently with the elbow

1					
2					
3					
4					

What is that surplus letter?

(Devised by Peter Newby especially for the promotional launch of *Pears Advanced Word-Puzzler's Dictionary*.)

zaptieh *n* a Turkish policeman

zarf *n* a (metal) cup-shaped holder for a coffee cup

zariba *n* in the Sudan, a thorn hedge or other defensive fencing to keep wild animals away from a camp (*var fms incl* **sariba, seriba, zareba, zareeba, zariba, zereba** and **zeriba**) *vb* to construct or form such: to enclose within such (*var fm* **zereba**)

zawn *dial n* a cave

zax *var fm n* **sax**

zay *dial fm vb* **say**

zayin *n* the seventh letter of the Hebrew alphabet

ze *Obs fm demonstrative adj* **the**

zea *n* that part of maize or Indian corn which receives the pollen and was formerly used for medicinal purposes

zeal (*n*) *obs vb* to inspire or act with zeal

zeatin *n* a chemical compound found in maize

zebrafish *n* darter: danio

zebrae *obs pl* zebra

zebu *n* a humped species of domestic ox, common in Asia

zechin *obs fm n* **zecchin**

zed *n* the letter Z: a metal bar of such shape

zee *now US n* the letter Z

zel *n* a type of oriental cymbal, a pair of metal discs which are struck together to produce a ringing tone *dial fm pron/adj* **self**

zele *var fm obs vb* **zeal** *obs fm n* **zeal**

zemstvo *n* a Russian local administrative council created, in 1864, by the czar

zendik *n* from the Islamic standpoint, a heretic *esp* one who performs fire-worshipping magic practices

zenzizenzizenzic *n* in mathematics, the square of a square of a square (*obs* except as a verbal curiosity in literature on words)

zeolite *n* a hydrous silicate of aluminium and sodium, various forms of which are used as water softeners

zep *Obs fm n* **sap**

zequin *obs fm n* **sequin**

zeriba see **zariba**

zet *dial fm vb* **set**

zeta *n* the sixth letter of the Greek alphabet, the equivalent of Z in English: a small room or closet of various kinds

zew *dial vb* of tin mining in Cornwall, to work alongside the lode before it is broken down

zex *dial fm n* **sax** *dial n* a knife

zfoot *var fm obs interj* **sfoot** or **'sfoot**, God's foot

zhe *dial fm pers pron* **she**

zho *n* a hybrid beast of burden from a cross between a yak and Ladakhi cow of Kashmir. The result is an animal smaller than the pure yak and capable of withstanding higher temperatures. They are usually piebald and often hornless, the male being known as a **zhobo** or **zhobu**, the female a **zhomo** (note: For the *var fms* of **zho (zo, dzo, dso)** the suffixes '**-bo**' or '**-bu**' indicate a male and the suffix '**-mo**' indicates a female. Whilst there are also the *var fms* **jobo** or **jomo**, the inferred basic *fm* of 'jo' does not exist.

zhobo see **zho**

zhobu see **zho**

zhomo *see* **zho**

zi *dial* for 'as I' *Obs fm demonstrative adj* **the**

zid *dial n* the extreme end of a fishing line

zij *n* the Persian astronomical tables, revised by Omar Khayyam

zik *Obs fm adj/n* **sick** (note: Not the *comp* but an independent *adj*, **sicker**, had the corresponding *Obs fm* **zikere**)

zil *dial fm pron/adj* **self**

zimb *n* an Ethiopian insect akin to the tsetse fly and harmful to cattle

zinc (*n*) *vb* to coat with zinc (*pr pple* **zincing** *pa pple* **zinced, zincked** or **zinked**)

zincite *n* red oxide of zinc

zindiq *var fm n* **zendik**

zingel *n* a perch-like fish of the river Danube

zinked see **zinc**

zix *Obs fm adj/n* **six**

zizel *n* the ground squirrel

zo *var fm n* **zho**

zobo see **zho**

zobu see **zho**

zod *var fm now dial n* **zad**

zog *dial n* a bad-smelling fungus

zomo *see* **zho**

Zonaria *n pl* a category of a now defunct animal classification system which had carnivores and some ungulates grouped together on the basis of certain common characteristics of parts of the females' internal generative organs

zoonosis *n* a disease, such as hydrophobia, capable of being transferred from an animal to man (*pl* **zoonoses**) (WORD PUZZLER'S note: The relevant British *adj* is **zoonitic** whilst the American is **zoonotic**)

zoopathy *n* animal pathology

Zoophyta *n pl* a now defunct technical term which denoted a group comprising the plant-like animals e.g. the sponges and sea anemones etc.

zoospore *n* a spore in certain algae, fungi and protozoa having the power of spontaneous movement

zoosporous *adj* producing, of the nature of or affected by zoospores (TRIVIA note: This is one of the longest words to be composed solely of letters of the second half of the alphabet, N to Z. Various other 10–letter words are known to exist, but a longer one has yet to be discovered. By contrast, the longest known word comprising letters of the first half of the alphabet is *Hamamelidaceae*, the technical name for a family of shrubs and trees. See **TRIVIA CHALLENGE**.)

zoster *n* an ancient Greek belt or girdle worn by men: shingles *obs n* a species of seaweed *Obs fm n* **sister**

zubr *n* the European wild ox which is still extant: also (*erron*) the aurochs, the extinct wild bison of Europe

zul *dial fm pron/adj* **self**

zule *her n* the castle in chess as a bearing or device on an heraldic shield

zurf *var fm n* **zarf**

zy *Obs fm demonstrative adj* **the**.

zyga *pl* zygon

zygal *adj* of or having an anatomical zygon

zygon *n* the central connecting part of an H-shaped fissure of the brain: a bench for the rowers of an ancient Greek trireme (*pl* **zyga**)

zymase *n* an enzyme found in yeast which causes fermentation by breaking down carbohydrates into alcohol and carbon dioxide

zymin *n* an extract of the pancreas used medicinally

zyxst *Obs fm adj* **sixth**

Zyzzogeton *n* a genus of large South American leaf hoppers, leaping insects which feed on the juices of plants

APPENDIX – READERS' PAGES

Future editions will print here a reader's contribution to the **TRIVIA CHALLENGE** discussed on page 699. Meanwhile, the author offers a superlative of his own, the world's smallest crossword, which he devised especially for a book on word play published in the USA in 1982 by William Morrow & Company Inc. of New York.

1	ACROSS	1. A time of deranged pride encompassing nothing.
	DOWN	1. A marriage portion from a small Dutch coin I leave.

A clue to the essential approach to this puzzle is provided by this previously unpublished teaser, which can justly claim to be the world's second smallest crossword. Unlike the smallest, it is a simple crossword, not cryptic.

1	ACROSS	1. A species of nymphaline butterfly.
	DOWN	1. The bacillus which causes cholera.

The solutions are given at the bottom of the following page.

PELHAM At the time of going to press, only a few sets of a specially printed 'Test Play' edition of the game exist. One such is in the possession of the author. In a game with one of his favourite word game opponents, Miss Julie Titchener, he considered himself to have done well in producing eighteen anagrams from a word he had played as a basic trick. In so doing he quoted many of the obscure words given at the anagram listing, **AELRST**. For these nineteen words he scored 114 points. Julie, smiling sweetly, pointed out that he had not mentioned the word, **alters**, so she not only scored 6 points for that word but also captured his 114 points as well. Her final score for the complete game was 232 points which she has now claimed as a world record.

When the game becomes commercially available, this page will happily detail any reader's score which knocks the smile off her face!

AUTHOR'S POSTSCRIPT The following two words have been left to the last to provide you with an apt word-puzzle.

chimera *n* a fabulous creature of Greek myth variously described as having the head of a lion, the body of a goat and the tail of a serpent or of having three heads, those of a lion, a goat and a serpent: any grotesque monster comprising the parts of different creatures: a fearful phantasm (*fig*): an unreal creature of the imagination (*fig*): an incongruous union (*fig*) (POSTSCRIPT note: The spelling of this word in 1613 was the same as it is today, either **chimera** or, as the Latin from Greek, **chimaera**)

mariche *n* a Cambodian creature described in all seriousness as having the face of a maiden and the tail of a scorpion (POSTSCRIPT note: The history of this word is that an Essex vicar, Samuel Purchas, mentioned the existence of mariches together with lions, tigers and ounces (not necessarily snow leopards) in the forests of southeast Asia in his book, *Purchas his Pilgrimage, or Relations of the World and Religions observed in all Ages and Places discovered from the Creation unto this present*, first published in 1613. His authority for this statement was an Italian work of 1605. However, Purchas is considered 'neither a faithful editor nor a judicious compiler'. Could, therefore, we find ourselves the victims of a literary hoax? After all, **mariche** is the perfect anagram of **chimera**.)

SOLUTIONS The world's smallest crossword. The meaning of the clue for 1 across is **period**, being an andagram of **pride** plus 0 or nothing. A period is also a full stop. The meaning of the clue for 1 down is **dot**, which is derived from the removal of the letter I from **doit**. A doit is a small Dutch coin worth about half a farthing. As a dot or a full stop is the smallest possible symbol which can be written, that provides the miniature superlative in this field. In the case of the second smallest crossword, the answer to both clues is the word, **comma**. Thus its symbol provides the solution.